Principles of Accounting

ABOUT THE AUTHORS*

Eric G. Flamholtz is Professor of Accounting Information Systems and Human Resource Management at the Graduate School of Management, UCLA. He received his Ph.D. degree from the University of Michigan, where he served on the staff of the Institute for Social Research. His doctoral dissertation was co-winner of the McKinsey Foundation for Management Research Dissertation Award. He has served on the faculties at Columbia University and the University of Michigan, has been a Faculty Fellow at Price Waterhouse & Company, and has been an Assistant Project Director in the Accounting Research Division of the American Institute of CPAs. At UCLA, he has served as Director of the Accounting Information Systems Research Program. He is the author of more than fifty articles and chapters on a variety of accounting and management topics and has published a book entitled *Human Resource Accounting.* He has conducted research projects for the National Science Foundation, The National Association of Accountants, and the U.S. Office of Naval Research. He has also served as a member of the editorial board for *The Accounting Review* and *Accounting, Organizations and Society.* He has extensive experience as a consultant to firms ranging from entrepreneurships to members of Fortune's 500.

Diana Troik Flamholtz is Associate Professor of Accounting in the College of Business, Loyola Marymount University, Los Angeles. She received her Ph.D. from the University of Michigan and did postdoctoral work in accounting at the Graduate School of Management, UCLA. Dr. Flamholtz has done writing and research in accounting history, with publications in *The Accounting Historians Journal* and *Accounting, Organizations and Society.* She has presented papers at the regional and national meetings of the American Accounting Association and The Institute of Management Science and serves on the editorial board of *The Accounting Historians Journal.* Dr. Flamholtz is co-author of a monograph published by Touche Ross & Company entitled "Organizational Control Systems—A Practical Tool for Emerging Companies" and has written and presented papers on accounting in The People's Republic of China. She has had a variety of consulting experiences, including cost behavior analysis, the development of contribution margin statements, and the conversion of accounting systems from manual to computerized systems.

Michael A. Diamond is Associate Dean, School of Accounting, University of Southern California. He is a CPA and received his B.A. degree at the University of California, Berkeley, and his M.S. and Ph.D. degrees from the University of California, Los Angeles. Professor Diamond's research interests relate to the use of accounting information especially by those managers in emerging companies. He is actively involved in international accounting research and has served in several capacities with the International Section of the American Accounting Association. His articles have appeared in the *Journal of Accountancy* and the *Harvard Business Review.* Professor Diamond has taught at California State University, Los Angeles, and has been a visiting professor at the University of California, Berkeley, the University of Southern California, and the University of California, Los Angeles. He has had extensive experience teaching introductory financial accounting students and has been recognized for excellence in teaching at several universities. He has taught in executive education programs for a number of Big Eight accounting firms.

*Also by Flamholtz, Diamond, and Flamholtz is *Financial Accounting,* Macmillan Publishing Co., copyright © 1986.

Principles of Accounting

Eric G. Flamholtz
University of California, Los Angeles

Diana Troik Flamholtz
Loyola Marymount University

Michael A. Diamond
University of Southern California

Macmillan Publishing Company
New York
Collier Macmillan Publishers
London

About the Cover: The graphic on the front cover is adapted from
the annual report of Macmillan, Inc., for the calendar year 1985.
It shows the changes in Earnings per Share, Operating Income,
and Sales of Products and Services from 1982 through 1985. The
relevant data are filled in on the back cover of the text.

Copyright © 1987, Macmillan Publishing Company,
a division of Macmillan, Inc.

Printed in the United States of America

Macmillan Publishing Company
866 Third Avenue, New York, New York 10022

Collier Macmillan Canada, Inc.

Library of Congress Cataloging in Publication Data

Flamholtz, Eric G.
  Principles of accounting.

  Includes index.
  1. Accounting. I. Flamholtz, Diana Troik.
II. Diamond, Michael A. III. Title.
HF5635.F5645 1987   657   86-31086
ISBN 0-02-338210-4

Printing: 234567   Year: 7890123

ISBN 0-02-338210-4

Preface

Principles of Accounting is designed to be used in a comprehensive first-year accounting course that covers two semesters or three quarters. It presumes that the student has had no previous exposure to accounting.

This book, like its companion, *Financial Accounting,* is based on two premises. First, knowledge of accounting is important for all members of today's complex economy, whether they are in industry, government, or professional accountancy. With this in mind, this book is written to meet the needs of the general student as well as the needs of those who are prospective accounting majors. Second, accounting is an interesting subject, and we believe that the time spent learning its concepts and practices can be enjoyable. As a result, this book is presented in a highly readable and conversational style that will appeal to those students who enter principles of accounting with a measure of trepidation.

Designing and writing this textbook, we were well aware that it must meet the needs of a wide range of students with varying interests and goals. Potential accounting majors must have a solid foundation in accounting concepts and practices that will enable them to complete successfully their major requirements. Other business as well as nonbusiness majors must be introduced to accounting concepts and practices in such a way that they can apply this knowledge to their various careers. To meet the needs of this diverse group, we have chosen the goal that all students should be able to read, understand, and reasonably interpret financial statements contained in annual reports of major companies after completing their study of this text.

The authors believe that accounting is an interesting as well as an essential topic. To complete successfully their first accounting courses, students spend many hours reading the text and preparing class materials. We have gone to considerable lengths to make this process interesting and enjoyable. We have included quotes from business journals such as *Forbes* and the *Wall Street Journal,* as well as many excerpts from actual financial statements and annual reports, to add realism and to spark student interest. The financial statements of Safeway Stores, Incorporated, are used as an integrating force throughout the text. In addition, to further motivate study, we demonstrate whenever possible the usefulness of specific accounting techniques.

This book has several features that aid student learning and understanding. Such features include (1) balance between concepts and practice, (2) emphasis on the use of accounting information in decision making, (3) contemporary theory and practice, (4) organizational flexibility, and (5) a complete and integrated learning package.

v

Balance between Theory and Practice

Writing this textbook, we carefully planned a blend of concepts and practice that meets the needs of all its users. The purposes and uses of accounting are introduced in Chapter 1 before students are exposed to the mechanics of the accounting cycle. Details of this cycle are then explained, first for a service firm and then for a merchandising firm, in Chapters 2 through 5. In Chapter 6, attention is turned back to more complex financial statements, and the actual financial statements of Safeway Stores, Incorporated, are first introduced. Throughout the accounting cycle chapters, the ongoing example of Lisa Bowman's Law Firm is used to illustrate relevant accounting concepts and procedures. Finally, Chapter 14 contains an in-depth discussion of accounting concepts and theory.

The remaining chapters are designed to reflect the proper balance between concepts and practice. For example, in Chapter 12, "Property, Plant, and Equipment," the concepts behind these topics are explained fully before the various depreciation methods are illustrated completely. In Chapter 20, "The Statement of Changes in Financial Position," the uses and purposes of this statement are explained completely before the student is led carefully through an example illustrating its preparation. Other chapters are designed in a similar manner.

Emphasis on the Use of Accounting Information in Decision Making

In this text we consistently approach accounting as an information system that provides useful financial data. This concept of accounting emphasizes its purpose: providing information for decisions rather than solely for its measurement procedures in recording, classifying, and summarizing financial information.

This emphasis on decision making is reflected in many of the features incorporated in the text and is especially evident in Chapters 22–28, which discuss a variety of managerial and cost accounting issues. These chapters focus on how managers use accounting for planning, decision making, and control. A unique introductory chapter provides a framework on the nature of management and uses of accounting in the management process.

At the end of each financial accounting chapter, we have added a section entitled "Understanding Financial Statements," in addition to a wide variety of other assignment material. At the end of each of the first 21 chapters we have included a "Financial Decision Case" section, and at the end of Chapters 22–28, a "Decision Case" section. In these problems and cases, students are placed in the roles of decision makers and are asked to analyze and interpret financial statements and quantitative data.

Management's role in the selection of accounting principles and in the preparation of the firm's financial statements is emphasized throughout the text. For example, the chapters that cover inventory methods, depreciation methods, leases, and purchase versus pooling all discuss the various effects that different methods can have on a firm's financial statements—and the choice that management then faces among these different approaches.

Principles of Accounting is contemporary in all respects. Where appropriate, current official pronouncements of authoritative accounting bodies are referenced. Problem material reflects our current economic environment with emphasis on service and technology companies. Where appropriate, reference is made to current economic events such as mergers of major companies, the decline in oil prices and the subsequent disinflation that took place in 1986, and the buyout of Safeway Stores.

The treatment of four particular topics—taxation, computers, accounting for changing prices, and international accounting—reflects the current nature of the text. Appendix B contains an up-to-date discussion of the recently enacted Tax Reform Act. In addition, the effects of taxes on a firm's financial statements are discussed in the various chapters in which the relevant accounting principle is discussed. For example, the effects of income taxes are discussed in the chapter on inventories (Chapter 11) and in the chapter on property, plant, and equipment (Chapter 12).

Throughout this book, we recognize the expanding role that computers play in accounting. Chapter 7, "Internal Control, Accounting Systems, and the Role of Computers," first provides an overview of manual accounting systems and then focuses on computerized accounting systems. Special attention is given to the impact of microcomputers. Topics such as computer hardware configurations are deemphasized, whereas contemporary issues such as software packages and internal control are stressed. Furthermore, one of the supplements to the text, *Sentinel*, is the most flexible and useful accounting computer supplement available today.

Chapter 14 contains clear, concise, and up-to-date coverage of accounting for changing prices. This coverage of inflation accounting reflects the latest changes made by the Financial Accounting Standards Board in Statement No. 82 and in the exposure draft issued in late 1986, and is at a level appropriate for a principles of accounting text. The effects of changing prices are treated as an isolated subject but are also discussed in other parts of the book, such as the chapter on inventories (Chapter 11) and the chapter on property, plant, and equipment (Chapter 12).

The second part of Chapter 21 discusses international accounting. The particular topics covered include accounting for foreign currency transactions, the translation of foreign currency statements, and harmonization of accounting standards. Coverage of these topics helps schools to meet current standards of the American Assembly of Collegiate Schools of Business, which relate to the coverage of international topics. Again, this topic is covered with the full understanding of both its complex nature and the fact that this is a principles of accounting text.

Organizational Flexibility

Principles of Accounting is written with the understanding that accounting instructors have various teaching styles and different approaches to the subject. In addition, even over a short period of time, the makeup of individual classes changes, and a text must have the flexibility to meet these changes.

The 28 chapters in this book can be divided easily into six parts. Parts I and II present an in-depth discussion of the accounting cycle. Part I, THE BASIC ACCOUNTING MODEL, consists of Chapters 1–4. These chapters cover in detail the accounting cycle for a service company, using a sole proprietorship, Lisa Bowman's Law Firm, as the unifying example. Part II, EXTENSIONS OF THE BASIC ACCOUNTING MODEL, consists of chapters 5–7 and covers such issues as accounting for a merchandising firm (Chapter 5); an introduction to more complex financial statements (Chapter 6); and internal control, special journals, and computers (Chapter 7). The last two chapters can be omitted or covered in part without interrupting the flow of the text. However, as noted, Chapter 7 is quite useful as a contemporary discussion of software packages and the role of microcomputers in accounting.

The next three parts of the book contain a comprehensive discussion of the various "financial" accounting concepts and practices that both accounting and nonaccounting majors should know. Part III, MEASURING AND REPORTING ASSETS AND LIABILITIES, consists of Chapters 8–14. Short-term assets and liabilities are covered first (Chapters 8–10), followed by inventories (Chapter 11), and then property, plant, and equipment, natural resources, and intangible assets (Chapters 12 and 13). This section ends with Chapter 14, which discusses accounting concepts and accounting for changing prices. Depending on the amount of time available, this last chapter could be omitted with no loss of continuity.

Part IV, MEASURING AND REPORTING OWNERS' EQUITY AND SPECIAL PROBLEMS OF CORPORATIONS, consists of Chapters 15–19. Chapter 15 introduces students to the special problems of partnerships; Chapters 16 and 17 provide an in-depth discussion of corporate organization and operations. Chapters 18 and 19 introduce students to two topics generally associated with corporations: accounting for long-term liabilities and investments in bonds (Chapter 18) and investments in corporate securities (Chapter 19). The chapter on bonds is written in a manner such that students need not be familiar with present-value concepts. Furthermore, this chapter contains a discussion of both the straight-line interest and the effective-interest methods. However, the section on the effective-interest method is self-contained and can be omitted.

Part V, ANALYSIS OF ACCOUNTING INFORMATION, completes the discussion of financial accounting concepts. This part contains two chapters—Chapter 20, "The Statement of Changes in Financial Position," and Chapter 21, "Interpreting Financial Statement Data and Accounting Issues Related to Multinational Enterprises." The FASB is expected to issue a statement calling for the preparation of a Statement of Cash Flows. When issued, Chapter 20 will be revised appropriately.

Part VI, ACCOUNTING INFORMATION FOR PLANNING, CONTROL, COSTING, AND DECISION MAKING, consists of the final seven chapters of the book (Chapters 22–28). The first section of Chapter 22 provides a framework for all of the managerial accounting chapters through discussion of the nature of management and the role of accounting information in the management process. The chapter also covers responsibility accounting, introduces basic cost terminology, and includes the statement of cost of goods manufactured. Chapter 23 presents cost behavior and cost-volume-profit analysis, while Chapter 24 deals with nonroutine short-term decisions. Chapters 25 and 26 relate to the planning process. Chapter 25 covers annual planning in the form of the master budget, while Chapter 26 covers long-term planning—capital budgeting. Chapter 27 turns to product costing, covering both job-order and process costing, and Chapter 28 introduces standard costing and variance analysis. For those instructors who prefer to cover product costing earlier in the course, Chapters 27 and 28 can be easily introduced after Chapter 22.

The book contains four appendices. Appendix A contains an in-depth discussion of concepts related to the time value of money. Appendix B has an up-to-date review of individual and corporate taxes as amended by the Tax Reform Act of 1986. Appendix C contains the financial information package from the 1985 annual report of Safeway Stores, Incorporated, as well as the financial statements of N. V. Philips, a large multinational firm headquartered in The Netherlands. Finally, a complete glossary in alphabetical order is found in Appendix D.

A Complete and Integrated Learning Package

This text and the complete student's and instructor's support packages have been designed as an integrated unit.

Pedagogical Features

The authors have gone to great lengths to design a pedagogically sound textbook. Each of the chapters contains a set of learning objectives at the beginning and a summary of these objectives at the end. Each concludes with the following end-of-chapter material: a list of Key Terms, Self-Review Problem or Problems, Questions, Exercises, Problems, Understanding Financial Statement Problems, and Financial Decision Cases. Beginning with Chapter 7, Using the Computer Problems are introduced.

Learning Objectives

Each chapter is preceded by a concise set of learning objectives. These objectives clearly indicate to students what they should be able to accomplish after studying the chapter. Then each of these objectives is summarized in paragraph form at the end of the chapter.

Key Terms and Glossary

At the end of each chapter is a list of key terms. Key terms are highlighted in **boldface** where they are defined in the chapter. At the end of the book in Appendix D is a complete glossary of these key terms, arranged alphabetically for easy reference.

Self-Review Problems

At the end of each chapter is at least one and in many cases two or three self-review problems that emphasize key points in the chapter. These problems are followed by detailed solutions that allow students to compare their solutions with the correct solution. Many review problems contain notes that anticipate student questions or problem areas.

End-of-Chapter Assignment Materials

The text contains a varied set of end-of-chapter assignment materials. *Questions* relate to the major concepts and key terms introduced in the chapter. *Exercises* relate to single concepts and provide the student with practice in applying these concepts. Exercises, as well as Questions, are arranged in the same order in which the material is introduced in the chapter.

Exercises are followed by *Problem Sets A and B*. These end-of-chapter Problems are more complex and usually cover several related topics. They are generally arranged in the order the topics are presented in the chapter. The content of both sets of Problems is quite similar.

As noted, each chapter also contains an *Understanding Financial Statements Problem* (financial chapters only), *Financial Decision Case* or *Decision Case*, and, beginning with Chapter 7, *Using the Computer Problems*. Understanding Financial Statements Problems are based on actual financial statements of major corporations. Students are asked to interpret these statements and apply subjects learned in the chapter to realistic situations. In the Decision Cases, students are asked to analyze and interpret financial data and address business decisions based on these data. Using the Computer Problems present straightforward exercises specially designed to be worked on any available spreadsheet. These problems introduce students to the number of accounting calculations and problems that are readily adaptable to the power of spreadsheet programs.

The Student Support Package

The student support package contains a "Study Guide," "Working Papers," two "Manual Practice Sets," and two versions of the "Computerized Accounting Simulation."

The Study Guide

Prepared by Lawrence Klein of Bentley College, the two-volume *Study Guide* is designed for maximum flexibility. Volume I covers Chapters 1–15, and Volume II covers Chapters 14–28. Both volumes of the *Study Guide* provide an extensive chapter-by-chapter summary and review. Each chapter in the guide provides a list of learning objectives; summarizes and reviews, in outline form, the major topics in the text chapter; and lists key terms in the chapter. These items are followed by a series of short-answer and multiple-choice questions students can use to test their knowledge of the concepts and procedures. Finally, there is a selection of exercises for each chapter. Answers to and complete explanations of all of these questions and exercises are provided for the student.

Working Papers

Prepared by Mark S. Bettner, the *Working Papers* are in two volumes. Volume I contains working papers for Problem Set A; Volume II contains working papers for Problem Set B. The working papers are designed to reduce the amount of nonproductive pencil work required of the student.

The Practice Sets

Prepared by Antoine Jabbour of California Polytechnic University, Pomona, both practice sets are set up to provide a complete review of the accounting concepts and procedures. The first *Practice Set*, "Glitter Jewelers," can be completed after Chapter 7 and illustrates accounting for a business organized as a sole proprietorship. The second *Practice Set*, "Weston Corporation," can be completed after Chapter 19 and is designed to illustrate accounting for a business organized as a corporation.

Sentinel: A Computerized Accounting Information System Simulation

Prepared by Earl J. Weiss and Donald L. Raun of California State University, Northridge, this unique microcomputer supplement comes in two versions. The short version consists of eight modules and carries students through the accounting cycle and merchandising transactions. This version corresponds to Chapters 1–6 in the text and assumes the business is designed as a sole proprietorship. Students are required to analyze transactions, enter items into the microcomputer general ledger accounting system, and output financial statements.

The comprehensive version contains 13 modules and takes the student through all 21 financial chapters of the book, including material on corporations. Both versions are designed to enable instructors either to use the program throughout the entire course as an ongoing supplement or to assign a traditional accounting cycle practice set. In addition, in the comprehensive version, students may use "What-If" questions to see the effect of various changes on the outputs of the accounting system. Included in both versions are a student disk and workbook, an instructor's disk, and an instructor's manual.

The Instructor's Support Package

The instructor's support package includes the *Solutions Manual, Instructor's Manual, Test Bank, Achievement Tests* (A and B versions), *Transparencies,* and a *Checklist of Key Figures.*

Solutions Manual

The two-volume *Solutions Manual* contains detailed solutions to all questions, exercises, problems, and other end-of-chapter materials. For maximum flexibility, Volume I contains Chapters 1–15 and Volume II contains Chapters 14–28. Complete solutions, including all intermediate calculations, are provided (and have been completely reviewed) by the authors. Solutions were class-tested at the authors' schools, and the exercises and problems were solved independently by various Beta Alpha Psi students and by the firm of Peat, Marwick, Mitchell & Co.

The *Solutions Manual,* as well as the *Instructor's Manual,* includes sample course outlines and a chapter-by-chapter guide to questions, exercises, and problems. Also provided is a more detailed description of the problems, including an estimate of the level of difficulty and the time needed for completion.

Instructor's Manual

The *Instructor's Manual* has been designed as a useful teaching aid and resource guide for the instructor. It contains a matrix of end-of-chapter material by learning objectives for each chapter in the text. Included in the matrix are all the questions, exercises, and problems. In addition, each problem is described fully with an estimate of its level of difficulty and the time needed for completion.

Following the overview of the end-of-chapter materials is an outline of the chapter for use by the instructor, organized by learning goals. In addition to these outlines, additional examples of key computations and illustrations have been developed. These examples follow the same format as the text.

Test Bank

Prepared by Mark S. Bettner, the two-volume *Test Bank* contains 10 true-false, 15 fill-in, and 25 multiple-choice questions per chapter (over 1,400 items in all). In addition, 16 exercises per chapter (448 total) are included. These exercises can be used as classroom examples, for testing, or for assignment material. Detailed solutions of all computational problems are provided for instructors. The objective questions are available to adopters on Macmillan's computerized testing system, *Microtest*, or on IBM, Apple, or TRS-80 formats.

Achievement Tests

Prepared by Mark S. Bettner, both the A and B versions contain 12 preprinted achievement tests (each covering 2–3 chapters) plus 2 comprehensive final exams (1 for Chapters 1–15 and 1 for Chapters 14–28).

Transparencies

Acetate transparencies for problems are in oversized type for easy readability and are available from the publisher to adopters of the text.

Checklist of Key Figures

For the instructor, a list of key figures for appropriate exercises and problems is available in quantity from the publisher.

Acknowledgments

This text would not have been completed successfully without the help of many of our colleagues and friends. Although it is impossible to list all who have made a contribution, we would like to acknowledge those who have provided so much help and insight.

We would like to acknowledge the help of Peat, Marwick, Mitchell & Co., New York, and in particular Bill Hannon, Mark Fitzpatrick, Carolyn Ottaviano, and Benjamin Turner, for their review of the complete text and *Solutions Manual*. Upon completion of the review and revision process, the following opinion was issued:

 **PEAT MARWICK**

Peat, Marwick, Mitchell & Co.
Certified Public Accountants
345 Park Avenue
New York. NY 10154
212-758-9700

Macmillan Publishing Company
College Division
866 Third Avenue
New York, New York   10022

We have examined the accompanying text, <u>Principles of Accounting,</u> including its Solutions Manual to determine the accuracy of the material presented as well as its consistency and appropriateness of references to authoritative literature. Our examination was made in accordance with standards established by the American Institute of Certified Public Accountants and, accordingly, included such procedures as we considered necessary in the circumstances.

In our opinion, <u>Principles of Accounting</u>, including its Solutions Manual, referred to above presents material which is mathematically accurate and in conformity with generally accepted accounting principles.

Peat, Marwick, Mitchell & Co.

PEAT, MARWICK, MITCHELL & CO.

December 3, 1986

In addition, we would like to cite the following companies, the financial statements of which are referenced and discussed at various points throughout the text:

Adam-Mills Corporation
Anheuser-Busch Companies, Inc.
Baxter Travenol Laboratories
Braniff International Corporation
Bristol-Meyers Company
Caesar's World
Carter Hawley Hale Stores, Inc.
General Electric Company
Hershey Foods Corporation
J. C. Penney
Kellogg Company
Lockheed Corporation
Lucky Stores, Inc.
Macmillan, Inc.
Optical Coating Laboratory, Inc.
Pacific Gas and Electric Company
Pacific Lighting Corporation
Priam Corporation
Princeville Development Corporation
Safeway Stores, Inc.
Sears, Roebuck and Co.
Stop and Shop Companies, Inc.
Stride Rite Corporation
Sunshine Mining Company
Times Mirror Company
Transco Exploration Partners, Ltd.
Triad Systems Corporation
Walt Disney Productions, Inc.

We would like to thank the many individuals who provided support during the writing of this text. Special mention goes to Mahmoud Nourayi, Raj Iyengar, Dennis Murphy, Henry Lee, Heidi Liu, and Carol Brittan who provided help in many ways; and to Mark Bettner, who, in addition to working on many of the supplements, provided a detailed critique of the entire manuscript. Both Earl Weiss and Don Raun of California State University, Northridge, were valuable contributors to this text. A special word of thanks goes to Art Weiss for preparing the computer artwork in the text and in *Sentinel*. We would like to thank Gordon Klein for his help on the tax appendix. We would also like to thank the following Beta Alpha Psi chapters for their help in testing many of the exercises and problems found in this text, as well as in its companion volume, *Financial Accounting:*

California State University, Los Angeles, Beta Lambda Chapter
Faculty Advisor: Michael Davidson
Florida State University, Beta Rho Chapter
Faculty Advisor: Homer Black
Northern Illinois University, Gamma Pi Chapter
Faculty Advisor: Cindy Johnson

Oregon State University, Epsilon Chapter
Faculty Advisor: Bob Shirley

Syracuse University, Xi Chapter
Faculty Advisor: Leon Hanouille

University of Iowa, Alpha Psi Chapter
Faculty Advisor: Val Lembke

We have benefited from the detailed and constructive reviews from many individuals, including:

Gerald Ashley	Grossmont College
Harry Baggett	Diablo Valley College
Paul Bohrer	University of North Colorado
Eugene Braun	Northern Virginia Community College
Anthony A. Cioffi	Lorain City Community College
Ellen D. Cook	The University of Southwestern Louisiana
B. Michael Doran	Iowa State University
Shirley Glass	Macomb Community College
Maxwell Godwin	Southwest Texas State University
Raymond Greene	Texas Tech University
Vincent D. R. Guide	Clemson University
George Ihorn	El Paso Community College
Elise G. Jancura	Cleveland State University
Robert Johnson	Jefferson College
Michael Layne	Nassau Community College
R. William Magers	Tarant County Junior College
Trini Melcher	California State University–Fullerton
Douglas R. Pfister	Lansing Community College
Bert Scott	University of Montana
William L. Staats	Hudson Valley Community College
Gil Zuckerman	North Carolina State University

Many individuals at Macmillan contributed mightily to the production of the text, including Nancy Forsyth, Andrea Goodman, Aliza Greenblatt, Gwen Larson, Holly Reid McLaughlin, Bob Pirrung, Katherine Speyer, Harold Stancil, and Andy Zutis. We also want to thank Carla Lakatta of Lubbock, Texas, and Madeline Lewis for their extraordinary efforts on the *Solutions Manual* and other supplements. Sheree Bykofsky, Ellen Falk, Yvonne Freund, and Deborah Harrington deserve special thanks for their copyediting, proofreading, and other work on the book.

We also wish to express our thanks to several individuals who have been supportive both personally and professionally, including John W. Buckley, Paul Kircher, Jack McDonough, Bruce Miller, and Dean Clay LaForce, all of the Graduate School of Management, UCLA; Richard Williamson and John Wholihan of the College of Business Administration, Loyola Marymount University; and Dean Doyle Z. Williams of the School of Accounting, University of Southern California. Finally, this book would never have been written without the support, encouragement, and prodding of Chip Price and Kate Aker. Many thanks!

Notwithstanding the assistance of all of these individuals, we are solely responsible for the final product. Any suggestions for improvement would be greatly appreciated.

E. G. F.

D. T. F.

M. A. D.

Contents

The Basic Accounting Model   1

1   Accounting: Its Nature and Functions   3

Learning Objectives   3

The Nature and Functions of Accounting   4
The Record-keeping Function   4
Classifying and Summarizing Transactions   4
Accounting and Decision Making   5

Accounting and the Forms of Business Enterprises   5
Sole Proprietorships   6
Partnerships   6
Corporations   6

The Primary Users of Accounting Information   7
Present and Potential Investors and Creditors   7
Governmental Agencies   8
The General Public   8
Company Management   8
Other Users   8

Accountants—The Providers of Accounting Information   8
Public Accounting   9
Private Accounting   10
Governmental Accounting   10

The Setting of Accounting Standards   10
The American Institute of Certified Public Accountants   11
The Financial Accounting Standards Board   11
The Securities and Exchange Commission   12
The Governmental Accounting Standards Board   12

The Major Financial Statements and Their Elements   13
The Balance Sheet   13

Summary of Learning Objectives   16

Key Terms   18

Problem for Your Review   18

Questions   19

Exercises   19

Understanding Financial Statements   21

Financial Decision Case   22

2   *Accounting as an Information System*   23

Learning Objectives   23

The Accounting Information System   23
Lisa Bowman's Law Firm   24
Data Input into the Accounting System   25
Recognizing Transactions   26

Effects of Transactions on the Accounting Equation   27

The Components of the Accounting System   31
The Journal   31
The Ledger   32
Asset Accounts   32
Liability Accounts   34
Owner's Equity   34
Revenues and Expenses   34

The Recording Process   35
Recording Transactions in a Ledger Account   36
The Bowman Law Firm Example   38
Analysis of Transactions   39
The Use of Ledger Accounts in Practice   42
Recording Transactions in the Journal   43

The Trial Balance   48
Errors in the Trial Balance   49

Summary of Learning Objectives   49

Key Terms   51

Problem for Your Review   51

Questions   53

Exercises   54

Problem Set A   58

Problem Set B   63

Understanding Financial Statements   68

Financial Decision Case   69

3   *Measuring and Recording Income Statement Transactions*   71

Learning Objectives   71

The Measurement of Income   71

The Income Statement   72
Revenues   73
Expenses   73
The Relationship between Receipts and Expenditures and
  Revenues and Expenses   74
Gains and Losses   74
Net Income   75
Withdrawals by the Owner   75

Important Concepts in Determining Income   76
The Time Period Assumption   76
The Matching Convention   76
The Accrual versus the Cash Basis of Accounting   76

Recording Income Statement Transactions   78
Debit and Credit Rules   79
Journal Entries   80
Transactions for Lisa Bowman's Law Firm   81

Financial Statement Preparation   88
The Bowman Law Firm Financial Statements   88

Summary of Learning Objectives   90

Key Terms   92

Problems for Your Review   92

Questions   97

Exercises   98

Problem Set A   101

Problem Set B   104

Understanding Financial Statements   108

Financial Decision Case   109

4   Completing the Accounting Cycle   111

Learning Objectives   111

Adjusting Entries   111
Expenditures Made in One Period that Affect
Subsequent Periods   112
Receipts Received in One Period that Affect Subsequent Periods   118
Expenditures to Be Made or Receipts to Be Received in
  Subsequent Periods   119
Other Items Requiring Adjusting Entries   123
Lisa Bowman's Law Firm   123

Completion of the Accounting Cycle   126
Posting Entries to the General Ledger   126
The Adjusted Trial Balance   131
Preparing the Financial Statements   131

Closing Entries   133
Post-Closing Trial Balance   137

A Worksheet—A Useful Tool   138
Preparing a Worksheet   138
Limitations of the Worksheet   145

Summary of Learning Objectives   145

Appendix: The Preparation and Uses of Reversing Entries   146

Key Terms   149

Problem for Your Review   149

Questions   153

Exercises   154

Problem Set A   159

Problem Set B   166

Understanding Financial Statements   173

Financial Decision Case   174

II

Extensions of the Basic Accounting Model   175

5   *Recording Sales and Purchases of Inventory for a Merchandising Firm   177*

Learning Objectives   177

Income Statements for a Merchandising Firm   178

Accounting for Sales   178
Trade and Quantity Discounts   179
Sales Discounts   180
Credit Card Sales   182
Sales Returns and Allowances   183

Accounting for Inventory Purchases   184
Perpetual Inventory System   184
Periodic Inventory Systems   186
Issues Involved in Recording Purchases   188
Taking a Physical Inventory   190
Sales, Purchases, and Cost of Goods Sold Summarized   192

Worksheet Techniques for a Periodic Inventory System   192
The Unadjusted Trial Balance, Adjustments, and the Adjusted Trial
  Balance Columns   192
The Income Statement Columns   194
The Balance Sheet Columns   195
Financial Statements for Jacob's Pet Supplies   195
Closing Entries   196

Summary of Learning Objectives　197

Key Terms　199

Problem for Your Review　199

Questions　200

Exercises　201

Problem Set A　204

Problem Set B　208

Understanding Financial Statements　212

Financial Decision Case　212

6　*Financial Statements—The Outputs of the System*　*213*

Learning Objectives　213

General Purpose Financial Statements　214
Objectives of Financial Reporting　214
Classified Financial Statements　215

Classified Balance Sheets　215
Assets　216
Liabilities　218

Owner's Equity　219
Sole Proprietorships　219
Partnerships　219
Stockholders' Equity　220

The Uses and Limitations of Classified Balance Sheets　221
Measuring Liquidity　221
Long-term Measures of Financial Strength　222
Limitations of the Balance Sheet　223

Classified Income Statements　224
The Single-Step Statement　225
The Multistep Statement　225

The Uses and Limitations of Classified Income Statements　227
Measuring Profitability　227
Return on Investment　228
Limitations of the Income Statement　229
Other Financial Statements　229

**The Financial Statements and Annual Report of
Safeway Stores, Inc.**　230
Reporting Requirements of Publicly Held Corporations　230
The Consolidated Balance Sheet　230
The Consolidated Statements of Income　233
The Statement of Stockholders' Equity　234
The Statement of Changes in Financial Position　236

**Other Elements of an Annual Report of a
Publicly Held Company**　236

Footnotes to the Financial Statements   237
The Auditor's Report   237
Other Aspects of the Annual Report   238

Summary of Learning Objectives   238

Key Terms   240

Problems for Your Review   240

Questions   244

Exercises   245

Problem Set A   249

Problem Set B   253

Understanding Financial Statements   256

Financial Decision Case   259

7   *Internal Control, Accounting Systems, and the*
    Role of Computers   263

Learning Objectives   263

Basic Principles of Internal Control   264
Necessity of Internal Controls   265
Attributes of a Strong Internal Control System   265
Limitations to Internal Control Systems   266

Accounting Systems Components   266
The Need for Subsidiary Ledgers   266
Specialized Journals   269
The General Journal   277
Internal Control and Special Journals   278

The Use of Computers in Accounting   278
Computerized versus Manual Accounting Systems   278
Data-processing Services   279
Microcomputers   280
Financial Analysis Program   281
Communications and Word Processing   282
The Use of Computers in Public Accounting   282

Summary of Learning Objectives   283

Key Terms   284

Problem for Your Review   284

Questions   285

Exercises   286

Problem Set A   289

Problem Set B   296

Using the Computer   302

Understanding Financial Statements   303

Financial Decision Case   303

III

Measuring and Reporting Assets and Liabilities   305

8   *The Control and Accounting for Cash Transactions*   307

Learning Objectives   307

Management Control over Cash   308
Internal Control over Cash   308
Cash Receipts   310
Cash Disbursements   315

Bank Checking Transactions   320
The Checking Account   320
The Bank Reconciliation   322

Petty Cash   327
Creating a Petty Cash Fund   327
Making Disbursements from the Fund   327
Replenishing the Fund   327

The Voucher System   328
The Voucher   328
The Voucher Register   330
The Check Register   332
Schedule of Unpaid Vouchers   333
A Voucher System—A Summary   333

Summary of Learning Objectives   334

Key Terms   335

Problem for Your Review   336

Questions   337

Exercises   338

Problem Set A   340

Problem Set B   345

Using the Computer   349

Understanding Financial Statements   349

Financial Decision Case   349

9   *Accounting for Short-term Monetary Assets*   351

Learning Objectives   351

Short-term Investments   352
Accounting for Short-term Investments   352
Valuation of Short-term Investments   352
Application of the Lower-of-Cost-or-Market Rule   353

Accounting for Receivables   353
Credit Sales   353
Credit Policies   354
Uncollectible Accounts   354
Management Control and Analysis of Receivables   364

Notes Receivable   365
Elements of Promissory Notes   366
Accounting for Notes Receivable   367
Using Receivables to Generate Cash   369
Classification of Receivables   371

Summary of Learning Objectives   371

Key Terms   373

Problems for Your Review   373

Questions   375

Exercises   375

Problem Set A   378

Problem Set B   381

Using the Computer   384

Understanding Financial Statements   385

Financial Decision Case   385

10 *Accounting for Current Liabilities and Payrolls*   *387*

Learning Objectives   387

Definition and Recognition of Liabilities   387
Classification of Liabilities   387
Measurement and Valuation of Current Liabilities   387

Types of Current Liabilities   389
Liabilities That Are Definitely Determinable   389
Liabilities That Represent Collections for Third Parties or
Are Conditioned on Operation   393
Contingent Liabilities   394
Balance Sheet Presentation of Current Liabilities   396

Accounting for Payrolls   396
Determining Employee Compensation   397
Recording Liabilities for Employee Payroll Withholdings   398
Recording the Payment of Wages   400
Determining the Employer's Payroll Tax Expense   402
The Payment of Payroll and Payroll Taxes   404
Internal Control for Payrolls   405

Summary of Learning Objectives   406

Key Terms   406

Problems for Your Review   407

Questions   408

Exercises   409

Problem Set A   410

Problem Set B   413

Using the Computer   416

Understanding Financial Statements   416

Financial Decision Case   417

11   Accounting for Inventories   419

Learning Objectives   419

Inventories and Income Determination   419
Measuring Ending Inventories and Income   420
Determining the Cost of Ending Inventories   423

Methods of Assigning Prices to the Ending Inventory   424
Applying Different Cost Flow Assumptions   424
Comparing the Methods   428
How Current Cost Can Alleviate the Problem   430
Selecting an Inventory Cost Method   431

Inventory Valuation—Lower of Cost or Market   432
The Theory of Lower of Cost or Market   432
The Application of Lower of Cost or Market   432

Estimating Ending Inventories   433
The Gross Margin Method   433
The Retail Inventory Method   434

Using Inventory Data for Decision Making   435

Summary of Learning Objectives   436

Appendix: Cost Methods and the Perpetual Inventory System   437
FIFO Perpetual   438
LIFO Perpetual   440
Average Cost Perpetual   440

Key Terms   442

Problems for Your Review   442

Questions   444

Exercises   445

Problem Set A   449

Problem Set B   452

Using the Computer   456

Understanding Financial Statements   456

Financial Decision Case   457

12   Property, Plant, and Equipment   459

Learning Objectives   459

Noncurrent, Nonmonetary Assets   459
Bundles of Future Services Not Held for Resale   460
Long-term Nature of the Assets   460
Allocation of Benefits for Accounting Periods   460
Major Accounting Issues Associated with Noncurrent,
    Nonmonetary Assets   461

Capital versus Revenue Expenditure   461

Measuring and Recording the Acquisition Cost of Property, Plant,
and Equipment   462
Cash Acquisitions   463
Other Methods of Acquiring Property, Plant, and Equipment   463

The Accounting Concept of Depreciation   465
The Nature of Depreciation   465
What Causes Depreciation?   467
Recording Period Depreciation   467

Methods of Computing Periodic Depreciation   468
Factors in Computing Depreciation   468
Methods of Computing Depreciation   469
Comparison of Various Depreciation Methods   474
Other Problems Related to Depreciation   477

Summary of Learning Objectives   479

Key Terms   481

Problems for Your Review   481

Questions   482

Exercises   483

Problem Set A   486

Problem Set B   488

Using the Computer   490

Understanding Financial Statements   491

Financial Decision Case   491

**13   Property, Plant, and Equipment (Continued),
        Natural Resources, and Intangible Assets   493**

Learning Objectives   493

Accounting for Subsequent Expenditures   **493**
Revenue Expenditures   493
Capital Expenditures Subsequent to Purchase   494

Disposal of Property, Plant, or Equipment   **495**
Retirement of Discarded Plant Assets   495
Sale of Plant Assets   496
Trade-in of Plant Assets   497

Management Control for Plant and Equipment   **499**

Natural Resources   **500**
Establishing a Depletion Basis—Successful Efforts
   versus Full Cost   502

Intangible Assets   **502**
Accounting Problems Related to Intangible Assets   503
Accounting for Specific Intangible Assets   505

Summary of Learning Objectives   **508**

Key Terms   **509**

Problems for Your Review   **509**

Questions   **511**

Exercises   **512**

Problem Set A   **514**

Problem Set B   **518**

Using the Computer   **521**

Understanding Financial Statements   **522**

Financial Decision Case   **523**

*14   Accounting Concepts and Accounting for
     Changing Prices*   *525*

Learning Objectives   **525**

Development of Accounting Concepts and Standards   **525**

The Conceptual Framework Project   **526**

Accounting Concepts and Conventions   **526**
Basic Assumptions about the Accounting Environment   526
Qualitative Characteristics of Financial Information   529
Generally Accepted Conventions   533

Accounting for Changing Prices   **536**
Different Types of Changing Prices   537
Problems with Financial Statements Not Adjusted for
   Price Changes   538
FASB Statements 33 and 82   540

The Theory behind Constant Dollar Accounting   **542**

Interpreting Purchasing Power Gains and Losses   545

Current Cost Financial Statements   546
The Theory behind Current Cost Financial Statements   546
Preparing Current Cost Statements   547
Interpreting Current Cost Statements   548

Current Cost/Constant Dollar Statements   548

Accounting for Inflation—A Summary   549

Summary of Learning Objectives   549

Key Terms   550

Problems for Your Review   550

Questions   552

Exercises   553

Problem Set A   556

Problem Set B   561

Using the Computer   565

Understanding Financial Statements   565

Financial Decision Case   567

IV

Measuring and Reporting Owners' Equity and Special Problems Related to Corporations   569

15 *Accounting for Partnerships   571*

Learning Objectives   571

Partnership—The Main Concepts   571
Features of a Partnership   572
Advantages and Disadvantages of Partnerships   573

Accounting Issues Related to Partnership Operations   574
Accounting for the Formation of a Partnership   574
Subsequent Investments and Withdrawals   574
Recording Profits and Closing Entries   575
Distribution of Partnership Profits   576

The Dissolution of a Partnership   583
Admission of a New Partner   583
Withdrawal of a Partner   586
Death of a Partner   587

The Liquidation of a Partnership   588

Summary of Learning Objectives   591

Key Terms   592

Problem for Your Review   593

Questions   595

Exercises   596

Problem Set A   599

Problem Set B   603

Using the Computer   607

Understanding Financial Statements   607

Financial Decision Case   608

16   *Corporate Organization and Capital*
Stock Transactions   *609*

Learning Objectives   609

Characteristics of a Corporation   610
Advantages of a Corporation   610
Disadvantages of Corporations   611

The Formation and Organization of a Corporation   612
Forming a Corporation   612
Organization Costs   613
Organizing the Corporation   613

Types of Capital Stock   615
Common Stock   615
Preferred Stock   616

The Components of Stockholders' Equity   618
Contributed Capital   619
Retained Earnings   621
Treasury Stock   621
Debit Items in Stockholders' Equity   621

Accounting for the Issuance of Stock   621
Stock Issued for Cash   621
Stock Issued for Noncash Assets   623
Donated Capital   624
Conversion of Preferred Stock to Common   625

Use of Stock Information   626
Market Value   626
Book Value per Share   627

Maintaining Internal Control over Stock Records   628

Summary of Learning Objectives   629

Key Terms   630

Problem for Your Review   630

Questions   632

Exercises   632

Problem Set A   635

Problem Set B   637

Using the Computer   640

Understanding Financial Statements   640

Financial Decision Case   641

17   *Stockholders' Equity—Retained Earnings and Dividends*   *643*

Learning Objectives   643

Corporate Income Statements   644
Income from Continuing Operations   646
Discontinued Operations   647
Extraordinary Items   648
Types of Accounting Changes   649

Earnings per Share   652
Calculating EPS—The Basics   652
Calculating EPS for More Complex Capital Structures   654
Presenting EPS on Corporate Income Statements   656
Uses and Limitations of EPS Data   657

Dividends   658
Cash Dividends   658
Noncash Dividends   660
Stock Dividends   660

Stock Splits   662

Prior Period Adjustments, Appropriations, and Treasury Stock   664
Prior Period Adjustments   664
Appropriation of Retained Earnings   666
Treasury Stock   667

Retirement of Capital Stock   669

Statement of Stockholders' Equity   670

Summary of Learning Objectives   671

Appendix: Accounting for Corporate Income Taxes   673
Sources of Differences between Accounting and
   Taxable Income   673
The Need for Income Tax Allocation   674
Journal Entries to Record Income Tax Expense   676
The Controversy Surrounding Interperiod Income
   Tax Allocation   677

Key Terms   677

Problem for Your Review   678

Questions   679

Exercises   680

Problem Set A   684

Problem Set B   689

Using the Computer   694

Understanding Financial Statements   696

Financial Decision Case   696

18   *Accounting for Long-term Liabilities and Investments in Bonds*   698

Learning Objectives   698

Bonds   700
Features of Bonds   700
Types of Bonds   701
Bond Prices   702

Issuers' (Borrowers') Accounting for Bonds   705
Bonds Issued at Par or Face Value   705
Bonds Issued at Other Than Face Value   707
Other Issues Related to Bonds Payable   717
Accounting for the Retirement of Bonds   719

Investor's (Lender's) Accounting for Bonds   721
Accounting for the Acquisition of Bonds   721
Amortizing the Discount or Premium   722
Sale of Bonds prior to Maturity   723

Other Forms of Long-term Debt   724
Notes Payable   724
Mortgages Payable   724
Leases   725

Summary of Learning Objectives   727

Key Terms   729

Problem for Your Review   729

Questions   731

Exercises   732

Problem Set A   734

Problem Set B   737

Using the Computer   739

Understanding Financial Statements   740

Financial Decision Case   741

19 Investment in Corporate Equity Securities   743

Learning Objectives   743

Accounting for Current Marketable Securities   **744**
Accounting for Current Equity Securities   745
Accounting for Current Debt Securities   750
Financial Statement Presentation of
   Current Marketable Securities   752

Long-term Investments   **753**
No Significant Influence or Control   754
Ownership Interest between 20 and 50 Percent   755
Ownership Interest above 50 Percent   757
Preparing Consolidated Financial Statements   758
Pooling-of-Interests versus the Purchase Method   765

Summary of Learning Objectives   **769**

Key Terms   **770**

Problems for Your Review   **770**

Questions   **772**

Exercises   **773**

Problem Set A   **777**

Problem Set B   **781**

Using the Computer   **785**

Understanding Financial Statements   **786**

Financial Decision Case   **787**

V

Analysis of Accounting Information   789

20 The Statement of Changes in Financial Position   791

Learning Objectives   791

**The Purpose of a Statement of Changes in
Financial Position**   **792**
Financial Resources Defined   793
Causes of Changes in Financial Position   793

**Statement of Changes in Financial Position—Working
Capital Basis**   **794**
Transactions That Affect Working Capital   795
Transactions That Do Not Affect Working Capital   796

**Preparing a Statement of Changes in Financial Position—
Working Capital Basis**   **798**
Determining Working Capital from Operations   799
Using a Worksheet to Prepare a Statement of Changes in
   Financial Position   800

Determining the Net Change in Working Capital   801
Setting Up the Worksheet   801
Analyzing the Changes in Various Noncurrent Accounts   803
Completing the Worksheet and Preparing the Statement   809
The Worksheet Approach—A Summary   809

The Statement of Changes in Financial Position—Cash Basis   811
Preparing the Cash Flow Statement   811
Determining Cash Flows from Operations   812
A Cash Flow Statement for BMI Computers   816
Using a Worksheet to Prepare a Cash-based Statement
    of Changes   818

The Statement of Changes in Financial Position—A Summary   820

Summary of Learning Objectives   820

Key Terms   821

Problem for Your Review   821

Questions   825

Exercises   826

Problem Set A   831

Problem Set B   836

Using the Computer   841

Understanding Financial Statements   841

Financial Decision Case   841

21 *Interpreting Financial Statement Data and Accounting for
    Multinational Enterprises   844*

Learning Objectives   844

The Purposes of Financial Statement Analysis   846
Present and Potential Investors and Creditors   846
Management   846

Sources of Financial Information   847
Published Reports   847
External Sources   848

The Techniques of Financial Analysis   849
Horizontal and Trend Analysis   849
Vertical Analysis   852
Ratio Analysis   855

Common Financial Ratios   855
Common and Preferred Stockholders   855
Long-term Creditors   862
Short-term Creditors   863
Ratio Analysis—A Summary   866

Contents   **xxxiii**

Limitations of Financial Statement Analysis   866
Differences in Generally Accepted Accounting Principles   866
The Industry a Firm Is In   868

Accounting Problems Related to Multinational Corporations   868
Exchange Rates   870
Accounting for Foreign Currency Transactions   870
Foreign Currency Translation   872
International Accounting Standards   874

Summary of Learning Objectives   875

Key Terms   877

Problems for Your Review   877

Questions   881

Exercises   881

Problem Set A   887

Problem Set B   894

Using the Computer   899

Understanding Financial Statements   899

Financial Decision Case   900

VI

Accounting Information for Planning, Control, Costing, and Decision Making   *903*

22   *Accounting Information for Management and Cost Terms and Concepts*   *905*

Learning Objectives   905

The Nature of Management   906
Elements of Management Process   906

The Role of Accounting in Management Planning   906
The Nature of Management Planning   906
Accounting's Role in Strategic Planning   906
Accounting's Role in Operational Planning   907
Accounting's Role in Budgetary Planning   907
Accounting's Role in Contingency Planning   907

The Role of Accounting in Management Decision Making   907
Types of Management Decisions   908
Accounting's Role in Decision Making   908

The Role of Accounting in Management Control   911
The Organizational Control System   911
Characteristics of Managerial Accounting   913

Responsibility Accounting   **914**
Cost Centers   914
Revenue Centers   914
Profit Centers   915
Investment Centers   915

Costs for Different Purposes   **917**
Cost Objectives   918
Direct and Indirect Costs   918

Manufacturing Costs   **918**
Direct Materials   919
Direct Labor   919
Factory Overhead   919
Nonmanufacturing Costs   919

Effect of Manufacturing on Financial Statements   **920**
Balance Sheet   920
Income Statement   920

Product Costs and Period Costs   **922**
Product Costs   922
Period Costs   923

Summary of Learning Objectives   **925**

Key Terms   **928**

Problem for Your Review   **928**

Questions   **930**

Exercises   **930**

Problem Set A   **933**

Problem Set B   **936**

Using the Computer   **939**

Decision Case   **940**

23   *Cost Behavior and Cost-Volume-Profit Analysis*   *941*

Learning Objectives   **941**

Cost Behavior   **942**
Variable Costs   942
Fixed Costs   943
Mixed Costs   945

Cost-Volume-Profit Analysis   **946**
Cost-Volume-Profit Formula   946
Break-even Point   947
Profit Planning   948
Contribution Margin   949
Contribution Margin Income Statements   950
Contribution Margin Ratio   951

Changing Variables and Profit Planning   953
Multiproduct C-V-P Analysis   955
C-V-P Analysis and Microcomputers   957
C-V-P Analysis and Income Taxes   957
Assumptions Underlying C-V-P Analysis   959

Summary of Learning Objectives   960

Key Terms   961

Problems for Your Review   961

Questions   963

Exercises   964

Problem Set A   966

Problem Set B   968

Using the Computer   971

Decision Case   971

24 Accounting Information for Short-term Decisions   973

Learning Objectives   973

Information for Decision Making   974
Differential Costs and Revenues   974
Sunk Costs   974
Opportunity Costs   975
Steps in Problem Solving   975

Short-term Decisions   978
Make-or-Buy Decisions   978
Special Orders   980
Adding and Dropping Product Lines and Departments   982
Accounting for Joint Product Costs   984
Sell or Process Further Decision   988
Use of Scarce Resources   990

Summary of Learning Objectives   991

Key Terms   993

Problems for Your Review   993

Questions   995

Exercises   996

Problem Set A   998

Problem Set B   1001

Using the Computer   1004

Decision Case   1004

25 *Accounting Information for Long-term Decisions: Capital Budgeting* 1007

Learning Objectives 1007

What Is Capital Budgeting? 1008
Capital Budgeting Situations 1008

How to Use Present Value Concepts in Capital Budgeting 1009
Return on Investment 1009
The Time Value of Money 1009
The Present Value of Cash Flows 1010
Cash Inflows 1011
Cash Outflows 1012

Discounted Cash Flow Methods 1012
The Cost of Capital 1013
The Net-Present-Value Method 1013
Internal-Rate-of-Return Method 1016

Ranking Decisions 1019
Ranking and the Internal-Rate-of-Return Method 1020
Ranking and the Net-Present-Value Method 1020

Other Capital Budgeting Methods 1021
The Payback Method 1021
Accounting-Rate-of-Return Method 1022

Summary of Learning Objectives 1023

Key Terms 1025

Problems for Your Review 1025

Questions 1027

Exercises 1027

Problem Set A 1029

Problem Set B 1031

Using the Computer 1032

Decision Case 1033

26 *Budgeting for Planning and Control* 1035

Learning Objectives 1035

Budgeting and the Planning Process 1036
The Role of Budgeting 1036

The Budgeting Process 1037

The Motivational Aspects of Budgeting 1038
Behavioral Concepts Relevant to Budgeting 1038
The Level of Budget Difficulty 1039
Centralization or Decentralization of the Budgeting Process 1039
Behavioral Issues When Budgets Are Not Achieved 1040

The Master Budget   1040
Sales Budget   1044
Production Budget   1044
Direct Material Usage and Purchases Budget   1046
Direct Labor Budget   1047
Factory Overhead Budget   1047
Ending Inventory Budget   1048
Cost of Goods Sold Budget   1048
Selling and Administrative Expense Budget   1049
Cash Budget   1050
Budgeted Income Statement   1052
Budgeted Balance Sheet   1052
Flexible Budgeting   1053
Computers and Budgeting   1055

Summary of Learning Objectives   1055

Key Terms   1058

Problem for Your Review   1058

Questions   1063

Exercises   1064

Problem Set A   1067

Problem Set B   1071

Using the Computer   1075

Decision Problem   1075

27 *Accounting Information for Control of Cost Centers:
Job Order and Process Costing   1077*

Learning Objectives   1077

The Nature of Cost Accounting Systems   1078

Flow of Costs in a Manufacturing System   1079

Types of Costing Systems   1080
Job Order Costing   1080
Process Costing   1080

Job Order Costing   1080
Accounting for Materials   1081
Accounting for Labor   1084
Accounting for Actual Factory Overhead   1085
Applying Factory Overhead Using a Predetermined Rate   1086
Cost of Finished Units of Product   1089
Cost of Goods Sold   1089

Process Costing   1091
Steps in Process Costing   1091

Process Costing with Two Departments   1096
Mixing Department   1096
Cost Production Report   1098

Bottling Department   1100

Process Costing—Two Materials   1102
Equivalent Units   1103
Cost per Unit   1105
Calculate Total Cost of Units Produced   1105

Summary of Learning Objectives   1106

Key Terms   1108

Problems for Your Review   1108

Questions   1111

Exercises   1111

Problem Set A   1114

Problem Set B   1118

Using the Computer   1122

Decision Problem   1122

28 *Accounting Information for Control: Standard Costing   1125*

Learning Objectives   1125

What Are Standard Costs?   1125
Standard Costs and Control   1126

Types of Standards   1126

Setting Standards   1127
Materials Standards   1127
Labor Standards   1127
Overhead Standards   1128
Revision of Standards   1128

Preparation of Direct Materials Variances   1128
Direct Materials Price Variance   1129
Direct Materials Quantity Variance   1130

Preparation of Direct Labor Variances   1131
Direct Labor Rate Variance   1132
Direct Labor Efficiency Variance   1132

Analyzing Factory Overhead Costs   1133
Cost Behavior and Flexible Budgets   1134

Preparing Factory Overhead Variances   1134
Calculating Monthly Overhead Variances   1136
Overhead Spending Variance   1137
Overhead Efficiency Variance   1138
Overhead Volume Variance   1139
Over- and Underapplied Overhead   1141
Summary of Variances   1141

Variance Investigation   1141

Advantages and Disadvantages of Standard Cost Systems   1144

Summary of Learning Objectives   1144

Key Terms   1147

Problem for Your Review   1147

Questions   1149

Exercises   1149

Problem Set A   1152

Problem Set B   1155

Using the Computer   1157

Decision Case   1158

Appendixes

A   *Appendix: Time Value of Money Concepts*   *A1*

Interest and the Time Value of Money   A2
Simple versus Compound Interest   A2
The Future Value of a Single Amount   A4
The Present Value of a Single Amount   A6
The Future Value of an Annuity   A9
The Present Value of an Annuity   A11
Accounting Applications of the Time Value of Money   A13

Key Terms   A15

Problem for Your Review   A15

Questions   A16

Exercises   A17

B   *Appendix: An Introduction to Income Taxes*   *B1*

The New Tax System   B1

Introduction to Individual Taxation   B1
Gross Income   B2
Deductions for Adjusted Gross Income   B2
Itemized Deductions   B3
The Standard Deduction   B4
Exemptions   B4
Taxable Income   B5
Tax Credits   B6
Tax Return Filing   B6
Tax Payments   B6

Introduction to Corporate Taxation   B6
Dividends-Received Deduction   B6

Taxable Income   B7
Calculating Taxes Owed   B7

Key Terms   B7

Problem for Your Review   B8

Questions   B9

Exercises   B9

C *Appendix: Illustrative Financial Statements*   *C1*

Excerpts from Safeway Stores, Inc. Annual Report   C1

Excerpts from the Philips Group Annual Report   C19

D *Appendix: Glossary of Key Terms*   *D1*

Index   *I1*

I

The Basic Accounting Model

Accounting: Its Nature and Functions

1

LEARNING OBJECTIVES

After reading this chapter you should be able to:
1. Define accounting and discuss its functions.
2. Explain how accounting is used in various forms of business enterprises.
3. List the primary users of accounting information.
4. Discuss the work of accountants.
5. Explain which groups are involved in setting accounting standards.
6. List the major financial statements and describe the balance sheet and its elements.
7. State the accounting equation.

Early forms of accounting were practiced in ancient societies such as Babylonia and Assyria. Then, as now, accounting not only helped individuals manage their businesses, it also served a broader social function by facilitating the development of commerce. Today, accounting plays a central role in our day-to-day economic activities. Whether you decide to become a stockbroker, a production manager, or an advertising account executive, you will use accounting data. Even if you decide not to enter a business field, knowledge of accounting will help you manage your everyday affairs and aid you in understanding today's economy. For example, understanding the breakup of AT&T requires a basic knowledge of accounting. Indeed, accounting is the language of business, and fluency in that language is needed in today's world. The purpose of this chapter is to introduce you to that language and to the nature and functions of accounting.

The Nature and Functions of Accounting

The nature of accounting is, in part, a function of a specific country's economic, political, and social systems. It is a creation much like language and law and is used as a tool in understanding economic events. Because accounting has been created for economic purposes, it evolves when necessary to adapt to changes in its environment. For example, the modern accounting method, which has its roots in the fourteenth century, has had to adapt to deal with the relatively new phenomenon of multinational firms, such as IBM and ITT. Thus, accounting, despite its use of numbers, is not like mathematics. It does not consist of a system of numbers that, once proven, does not change; rather, it is fluid and changes over time according to economic needs.

Accounting can be defined as a system of providing "quantitative information, primarily financial in nature, about economic entities that is intended to be useful in making economic decisions."[1] Its primary functions are to record, classify, and summarize in a significant manner and in monetary terms, transactions that are of a financial character. This information is then used by groups such as the firm's managers and external parties to make a variety of decisions about an entity. The **accounting system** is the set of principles, methods, and procedures that is used to record, classify, and summarize the financial information to be distributed to its users.

The Record-Keeping Function

All organizations that engage in economic activities need a method of keeping track of their transactions. **Transactions** are business events of a particular enterprise, measured in money and recorded in its financial records. Except in the smallest enterprises, failure to record sales and services or the purchase of goods or services systematically would lead to confusion. In order to be recorded in the accounting records, the transaction must be of a type that can be measured in money.

Classifying and Summarizing Transactions

In order to summarize transactions meaningfully, they must first be classified into similar categories. That is, we aggregate all of a firm's sales during a certain period in order to determine its total sales. Likewise, the accountant aggregates all of the transactions affecting cash in order to determine the amount of cash on hand at any point in time, as well as to analyze how the cash was obtained and used.

Large firms enter into hundreds of thousands or even millions of transactions each year. In order for decision makers to use these data meaningfully, they must be summarized in accounting reports that are presented in useful formats. These reports are called *financial statements* and are the primary way in which financial information about a particular enterprise is communicated to users. **Financial statements** are concise reports that summarize specific transactions for a particular period of time. They show the financial position of the firm as well as the results of its operations.

---

[1]American Institute of Certified Public Accountants, Accounting Principles Board, Statement No. 4, *Basic Concepts and Accounting Principles Underlying Financial Statements of Business Enterprises* (New York: AICPA, 1970), par. 9.

CHAPTER 1

Accounting and Decision Making

The main purpose of accounting is to provide users with information about various entities so that they may make more informed decisions. Accounting is applicable to governmental and not-for-profit organizations such as museums, zoos, and churches as well as to business enterprises. This book's primary concern is the role of accounting within business enterprises.

EXHIBIT 1–1
The Preparation and Dissemination
of Accounting Information

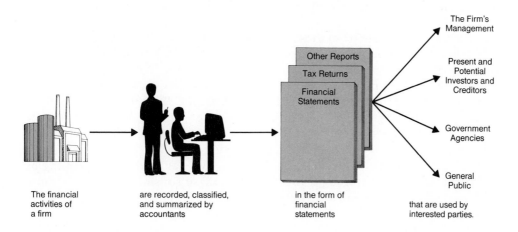

| The financial activities of a firm | are recorded, classified, and summarized by accountants | in the form of financial statements | that are used by interested parties. |

Exhibit 1–1 illustrates the relationships on which we will focus in this book. Central to our discussions are the financial activities of the business enterprise. The primary users of financial information are present and potential investors and creditors, the firm's managers, governmental agencies such as the Internal Revenue Service, and the general public. Accountants prepare accounting information according to certain standards set by their profession. This helps ensure that the information will be useful to those in a decision-making capacity. This information is generally provided to these users in the form of financial statements. On the following pages we discuss these relationships by focusing on:

1. The forms of business organizations.
2. The primary users of financial information.
3. Accountants, the providers of this information.
4. The setting of accounting standards.
5. Financial statements, the primary means of communicating financial information about entities to interested parties.

Accounting and the Forms of Business Enterprises

The three major types of business organizations are (1) the sole proprietorship, (2) the partnership, and (3) the corporation. Good accounting practices are necessary to each form of enterprise.

Sole Proprietorships

A **sole proprietorship** is a business entity in which one person is the owner. The business may employ few or many people, but there is only one owner, who realizes either the profits or losses. A major advantage of a sole proprietorship is that a business may begin under this form of organization with little cost and legal work. Although sole proprietorships often are relatively small businesses, some of today's great businesses began as individually owned enterprises. For example, companies such as the Ford Motor Company, Levi Strauss and Co., and McDonald's originally were founded and owned by one individual.

In accounting theory and practice, a business and its owner are different business entities. **A business entity** is a distinct economic unit whose transactions are kept separate from those of its owners. As a result, the business has an existence independent of its owner's. The scope of accounting for the sole proprietorship is limited to the transactions of the business and does not include the owner's personal transactions. Despite this accounting treatment, under the law a sole proprietorship and its owner are not independent entities. This means that the sole proprietor is legally responsible for the debts or obligations of the business. This accounting distinction between the business and its owner points out that accounting is more concerned with the economic facts of an event than with its legal form. We start our study of accounting by looking at sole proprietorships. In later chapters we consider how the accounting concepts and principles we have discussed are applied to partnerships and corporations.

Partnerships

A **partnership** is a business entity that is owned by two or more individuals. Like a sole proprietorship, a partnership may employ few or many people. Some partnerships, such as the large international CPA firms, have hundreds or even thousands of partners. There are different types of partnership agreements. Individuals may be equal partners or have unequal interests in the partnership's profits and losses. There are silent partners, who contribute funds to the enterprise but do not engage actively in the business, and active partners, who run the business. In addition, corporations can become partners in joint ventures. For example, some of the large oil corporations such as ARCO have formed joint ventures in order to share the costs and risks of oil exploration in such areas as the North Sea and Alaska. The General Motors–Toyota venture to produce small cars in California is a partnership between two of the world's largest corporations.

From an accounting perspective, a partnership is an accounting entity distinct from its owners. As with a sole proprietorship, the partners and the partnership are one legal entity.

Corporations

A **corporation** is a business entity that is viewed legally as separate and distinct from its owners, who are termed *stockholders*. Ownership in a corporation is designated by stock certificates. Ownership of stock is equivalent to ownership of a proportionate share of the corporation. State laws govern the sale or transfer of corporate stock from one person to another.

In contrast to a sole proprietorship or a partnership, a corporation is a separate legal as well as accounting entity. As a result, the owners of the corporation have **limited liability,** which means that they are not legally responsible, as individuals, for the debts incurred by the corporation. However, the amount that they have invested in the corporation is available to satisfy corporate debts.

This limited liability feature of corporations enables them to obtain funds from many owners who merely want to invest for the opportunity of increasing the value of their stock. These owners may not wish to participate actively in the operations of the enterprise. Therefore, corporations, especially large ones, usually have a separation of ownership and management.

Many large U.S. corporations are **publicly owned,** which means that the corporation's stock is bought and sold by the public, often on exchanges such as the New York or American Stock Exchange. Through these exchanges individuals can easily buy or sell shares of stock of corporations. As a result, large publicly held corporations have hundreds of thousands and, in some cases, over a million shareholders. However, not all corporations are publicly held; most are owned by families, a few shareholders, or a single individual, and the stock in these closely held corporations is not traded publicly.

The role of accounting in corporations is important, especially because there is often a separation between ownership and management. Owners require financial reports to appraise the performance of management, and to decide whether to retain, sell, or add to their investment in the corporation. Accounting issues related to corporations are discussed in Chapters 16 through 19.

The Primary Users of Accounting Information

The primary users of accounting information can be divided into two major categories—external and internal users. Major external users are present and potential investors and creditors, governmental agencies, and the general public. The firm's management represents the primary internal user of accounting information.

Present and Potential Investors and Creditors

Present and potential investors use financial statements and other information about an enterprise to make decisions about increasing, decreasing, or maintaining their investment in an entity. These same financial statements are used by creditors when they evaluate whether or not the firm can repay its debts or obligations. For example, a bank will analyze a company's financial statements to determine the risks of making a new loan or to extend a current loan to it. In summary, one of the primary objectives of financial reporting has been stated as:

> Financial reporting should provide information that is useful to present and potential investors and creditors and others in making rational investment, credit, and similar decisions. The information should be comprehensible to those who have a reasonable understanding of business and economic activities and are willing to study the information with reasonable diligence.[2]

[2]Financial Accounting Standards Board, Concepts Statement No. 1, *Objectives of Financial Reporting by Business Enterprises* (Stamford, Conn.: November 1978), par. 34.

Governmental Agencies

Governmental agencies are another major user of financial information about a firm. For example, the Internal Revenue Service uses some of the same information contained in financial statements to help determine the amount of taxes due to the government. Other federal agencies such as the Interstate Commerce Commission and the Securities and Exchange Commission use the firm's financial statements in their regulatory processes. State agencies, such as public utility commissions, also use financial statements and other accounting information in setting utility rates.

Governmental agencies can and do require particular accounting information that meets their individual needs. In many circumstances this information is based on the same accounting principles that govern financial statements presented to investors and creditors. However, it does not necessarily have to be the same, and in some cases there are significant differences.

The General Public

Many of us, whether investors, creditors, or just citizens, are interested in the activities of business entities. The pursuits of large corporations affect individuals throughout the world. For example, IBM's decision regarding whether to manufacture computer components in the United States or abroad affects the employment and income of U.S. residents and residents of other countries. In order to evaluate the actions of IBM and other firms, the public often relies on the same financial information that is summarized in financial statements. Thus society uses a vast quantity of financial information in assessing its economic well-being.

Company Management

Company management is the primary internal user of a firm's financial information. Management's task is to plan and control operations in order to generate a profit. Planning involves deciding on the organization's objectives and on the means to obtain them. Control refers to the process of ensuring that the company's operations are successful at achieving these organizational objectives. **Management accounting** is the system and procedures used to provide information to management for planning and controlling the business. As a result, it is primarily directed at providing information to internal users of financial data and can be tailored to meet their individual needs. The study of management accounting is the subject of the second part of this book.

Other Users

There also are other users of accounting information. For example, labor unions use financial statements to assess a company's ability to increase wage payments to employees. In addition, in deciding whether to join a firm, potential employees may use financial information in evaluating the long-range prospects of the firm.

Accountants—The Providers of Accounting Information

Accountants are qualified through education and experience to perform accounting services. Professional accountants may work in public accounting, private accounting, or governmental accounting. In the course of an accountant's career, he or she may work in all three of these areas.

Public Accounting

Public accounting is the field of accounting that provides a variety of accounting services to individuals and firms for a fee. Professional accountants who work in public accounting firms are usually **certified public accountants (CPAs)** and work in firms called CPA firms. CPAs are licensed by individual states to practice accounting after having met a number of requirements. All states require that individuals pass the uniform CPA examination developed and administered by the **American Institute of Certified Public Accountants,** the professional organization of CPAs. In addition, states have varying requirements regarding education and experience for licensing a person as a CPA. In California, for example, besides passing the uniform examination an accountant must have a bachelor's degree and a minimum of two years of qualified experience in order to become a CPA.

Certified public accounting firms range in size from one-person firms to large, multinational firms. The large firms have offices in the principal cities in the United States and throughout the world. These large firms are organized as partnerships, and some have over 2,000 partners. Whether a firm is large or small, its primary work usually includes auditing and accounting services, tax preparation and planning, and formal and informal management advisement.

Auditing and Accounting Services

Auditing is one of the main functions of a CPA firm. An **audit** is an examination of a firm's financial statements by a CPA. Publicly held corporations are required by the securities laws to have their financial statements audited. Even if not required by law, many firms have their financial statements audited to satisfy the firm's banks and/or its owners that its financial statements have been reviewed by an objective outside party. The auditor evaluates the firm's accounting system, tests to see that economic transactions have been properly recorded, and gathers external evidence from outsiders as to whether all the economic events have been recorded. After this examination, the auditor issues a report, called an **opinion,** on his or her findings regarding the financial statements. In this report the auditor expresses a professional opinion as to the fairness of the financial statements. External users of financial statements can rely on this opinion because the CPA must be independent of the firm he or she is auditing.

Many businesses, especially smaller ones, may not need or desire to have their financial statements audited. However, they often need some review of their records or help in preparing their financial statements. As a result CPA firms also provide accounting services, called **reviews and compilations.** These services are not audits but do provide firms with a review of their financial statements or help in their preparation.

Tax Preparation and Planning

Tax preparation and planning is another function of a public accountant. Tax factors are important to any major financial decision, and so CPAs are often asked for advice about the possible tax consequences of a particular decision. Further, the same CPA is often asked to prepare the firm's income tax return. Almost all CPA firms derive a portion of their fees from their tax practice.

Management Advisory Services

The accountant is more and more often being called upon to provide informal and formal business advisory services. In fact, a recent study noted that the accountant was named the primary business advisor to executives of smaller companies.[3] In order to better serve their clients, many firms have established management advisory service departments in addition to their audit and tax departments. Individuals who provide management services do not necessarily have to be CPAs or even accountants. They are often individuals with broad business education and backgrounds.

Private Accounting

Private accounting is the practice of accounting in a single firm such as McDonald's or General Motors. Accountants who work for individual firms may or may not be CPAs. These individuals are employed in a variety of capacities. For example, the chief accounting officer for a private enterprise is typically known as the controller, and the head financial officer is often called the treasurer. Individuals working in accounting departments of businesses perform a variety of tasks, such as cost accounting, budgetary planning and control, internal auditing, taxation, and financial reporting.

A number of certificate programs have been developed to provide professional recognition to those who work in private accounting. For example, the Institute of Management Accounting now offers a program that allows accountants to earn a Certificate in Management Accounting (CMA). Although this is not a license to practice given by a state as the CPA license is, it does show that the accountant has met certain experience and knowledge requirements.

Governmental Accounting

The management of governmental affairs requires the use of accounting for record keeping, planning, and controlling operations, and the practice of accounting as it relates to government organizations is called **governmental accounting.** Some governmental accountants work for agencies such as the Internal Revenue Service, the Federal Aviation Administration, and the Interstate Commerce Commission. All of these agencies, as well as others, require accountants to help them perform their functions. In addition, individual states, counties, cities, school districts, and other governmental bodies all employ accountants for a variety of functions.

The Setting of Accounting Standards

The concepts and standards underlying accounting for financial reporting purposes are called **generally accepted accounting principles,** often referred to as GAAP. These principles represent the most current consensus about how accounting information should be recorded, what information should be disclosed, how it should be disclosed, and which financial statements should be prepared. Generally accepted accounting principles range from broad assumptions about the economic environment to specific methods of accounting for certain events. These principles help ensure the integrity and credibility of

[3]Jerry Arnold et al., "Meeting the Needs of Private Companies: Executive Summary of Findings" (New York: Peat, Marwick, Mitchell & Co., 1983).

financial information reported to external users. Thus, generally accepted principles provide a common financial language to enable informed users to read and interpret financial statements.

The development of GAAP is a complex process involving a mixture of theory, governmental regulation, and conventions derived from actual practice. It is impossible to specify one source of GAAP or one book that codifies all of the accounting principles. However, some of the major groups involved in the standards-setting process include the American Institute of Certified Public Accountants (AICPA), the Financial Accounting Standards Board (FASB), the Securities and Exchange Commission (SEC), and the American Accounting Association (AAA).

The American Institute of Certified Public Accountants

The AICPA was organized around the beginning of the century and is the professional organization of CPAs. During its more than 80-year history, this organization has had a direct impact on the setting of accounting standards. In the past, the AICPA formed several committees to develop accounting standards. The most important was the Accounting Principles Board (APB).

The APB was established by the AICPA to develop accounting principles and methods. The APB formally issued 31 Opinions (that outline accounting methods for specific matters) before it went out of existence in 1973. These Opinions carry the authority of the AICPA; the burden of justifying any departure from the Board's Opinions has to be assumed by those adopting other practices.

Although the APB went out of existence in 1973, the AICPA continues to play an active role in the accounting standards-setting process. Several AICPA committees provide input to the FASB as well as set accounting guidelines for unique financial reporting problems facing specific industries. Further, auditing guidelines and standards continue to be set by the AICPA.

The Financial Accounting Standards Board

The APB was criticized by many individuals both inside and outside the accounting profession because of its part-time nature and the board's perceived lack of independence from the accounting profession for which it was setting standards. In response to this criticism the **Financial Accounting Standards Board** was created in 1973 as an organization independent of the AICPA. The primary purpose of the FASB is to develop accounting standards. The Opinions issued by the APB, however, remain in force today unless they have been superseded by Statements issued by the FASB.

The FASB consists of seven full-time members who are independent of other responsibilities. Each member's salary exceeds $150,000 per year. Its members are drawn from the CPA community as well as accountants and other individuals in private industry and academia. The FASB has a full-time accounting research and administration staff and also appoints outside task forces to study various accounting issues. The FASB issues Statements of Financial Accounting Standards, Interpretations of these Statements, and concepts Statements. The FASB Statements relate to specific accounting issues, such as accounting for land sales. The concepts Statements are broader in nature and deal with general issues. Through 1986, it issued 88 Statements and 6 concepts Statements.

As we will see next, the SEC has the legal authority from Congress to set accounting standards for publicly held corporations. However, it has generally allowed the private sector to retain primary control over the standards-setting process, with the FASB currently filling that role. As a result, the Statements issued by the FASB and the earlier Opinions issued by the APB are a major portion of generally accepted accounting principles, especially as they relate to specific methods of accounting for certain events.

The Securities and Exchange Commission

The **Securities and Exchange Commission** was established by Congress during the Great Depression that followed the stock market crash of 1929. The securities laws of 1933 and 1934 gave the SEC its power to establish accounting principles governing the form and content of financial statements of companies issuing securities for sale to the public. Because most large U.S. corporations are publicly held, they are required to satisfy SEC accounting standards. These standards are issued through Regulation S-X, which stipulates the form and content of the financial statements issued by publicly held corporations, and Financial Reporting Releases, which cover various accounting issues as they develop.

Because of its power to set accounting standards for publicly held corporations, the SEC's impact on the setting of accounting standards can be considerable. However, the SEC has explicitly recognized the FASB as the primary standards setter for all business entities. For many years, therefore, the SEC promulgated principles for publicly held companies that reflected the existing standards developed by the private sector of the accounting profession, the APB and the FASB. More recently, however, the SEC has moved in its own direction. For example, it issued several pronouncements that were at variance with those of the public accounting profession. These controversial issues, such as accounting for oil and gas, stirred much debate. In these cases, the accounting profession usually had to conform its rules to those of the SEC. Although relatively rare, controversies such as these show that accounting rules are sometimes as much the result of political factors as of good accounting theory.

The Governmental Accounting Standards Board

In 1984 the Financial Accounting Foundation (the group that selects FASB members, funds their activities, and provides general oversight of the Board) created the **Governmental Accounting Standards Board (GASB).** The purpose of the GASB is to establish and improve financial accounting standards for state and local governments. In most respects, the GASB is structured like the FASB. Although this book is primarily concerned with the standards issued by the FASB, GASB standards are important in the study of governmental accounting.

In sum, when we speak of generally accepted accounting principles we mean concepts, opinions, standards, and regulations from various sources. The SEC plays an important role in setting these principles, as do the private standards setters in the accounting profession. As we noted, it is impossible to find these principles in a single book, nor are they represented by laws of the U.S. Congress. These principles represent a consensus at a particular point in time. But accounting principles are not set in this way in all countries. For example, in many European countries, such as France and Germany, the government is the primary standards setter, and so accounting rules tend to be more uniform.

Financial statements are one of the primary means by which economic information about a firm is communicated to interested users. The four major financial statements are: the balance sheet, the income statement, the statement of owner's equity (in a corporation this statement is called the retained earnings statement), and the statement of changes in financial position. These statements summarize the many inputs in the accounting system in a form that is useful to decision makers. Financial statements communicate to external users, as well as to management, information concerning the firm's position, its profitability, and significant changes in its resources and obligations. This chapter introduces the balance sheet and its elements; the other financial statements are discussed in detail in later chapters.

The Balance Sheet

A **balance sheet** presents the financial position of a firm at a particular point in time. Often called a statement of financial position, it shows the financial resources the firm owns or controls and the obligations it has incurred. One of its primary purposes is to help users assess the financial strength of a firm. A balance sheet is prepared at least yearly and, in many cases monthly and/or quarterly.

   The balance sheet for the Carson Company is presented below. At the top of all financial statements is a heading that identifies the name of the entity, the title of the statement, and the period of time the statement covers or the date of the statement. The balance sheet is dated as of a certain date. The body of the balance sheet contains three major categories or elements: assets, liabilities, and owner's equity. By convention assets are listed first, followed by liabilities, and then owner's equity. In this particular example, the assets are listed on the left and the liabilities and owner's equity on the right. In other cases the balance sheet may be vertical with the liabilities and owner's equity listed under the assets.

The Carson Company
Balance Sheet
December 31, 1987

Assets		Liabilities and Owner's Equity	
Cash	$ 40,000	Liabilities	
Accounts receivable	75,000	Accounts payable	$ 96,000
Inventories	155,000	Notes payable	40,000
Supplies	30,000	Other payables	79,000
Land	130,000	Total liabilities	215,000
Plant and equipment	115,000	Owner's equity	
		B. Carson, Capital	330,000
		Total liabilities and	
Total assets	$545,000	owner's equity	$545,000

The **assets** represent the resources of the firm. The **liabilities** of the firm represent its obligations or the claims of its creditors. **Owner's equity** is a general term used to specify the owner's residual interest for sole proprietorships, partnerships, and corporations. Because the Carson Company is a sole proprietorship its owner's equity is specified as B. Carson, Capital and represents B. Carson's ownership in the company.

The Accounting Equation

The total assets of the enterprise equal its liabilities and owners' equity. These relationships can be expressed through the basic **accounting equation:**

$$\text{Assets} = \text{Liabilities} + \text{Owners' Equity}$$

The balance sheet or statement of financial position is a detailed version of the accounting equation, listing the various assets, liabilities, and owners' equity at a particular point in time.

The two sides of the accounting equation must always be equal because they are two views of the same accounting entity. The left-hand side of the equation shows the economic resources controlled by a business, and the right-hand side shows the claims against these resources. Another way to view this equality is that the firm's assets must have sources, and the right-hand side of the equation shows where those resources came from. Using the above data from the Carson Company, we can state the accounting equation as follows:

$$\text{Assets} = \text{Liabilities} + \text{Owner's Equity}$$
$$\$545,000 = \$215,000 + \$330,000$$

In this case the company has assets totaling $545,000. The creditors have claims against those assets of $215,000, and Carson's residual interest is $330,000.

Sometimes the accounting equation is also stated in the following form, which emphasizes that the owner's claims are secondary to those of the creditors:

$$\text{Assets} - \text{Liabilities} = \text{Owner's Equity}$$
$$\$545,000 - \$215,000 = \$330,000$$

Assets

Assets are the firm's economic resources. An asset must have a cost and provide the firm with future economic benefits. They are formally defined by the FASB as "probable future economic benefits obtained or controlled by a particular entity as a result of past transactions or events."[4] This means that in order for an item to be considered an asset, it must (1) result from a past transaction, (2) have a historical cost, (3) provide future economic benefits, and (4) be owned or controlled by the enterprise. It is important to understand that from an accounting perspective, a firm need not legally own an item for it to be considered the firm's asset. All that is necessary is control. For example, in many states, if a firm purchases an automobile and finances that purchase through a bank loan, the bank will retain ownership of the automobile until

[4]Financial Accounting Standards Board, Concepts Statement No. 6, *Elements of Financial Statements* (Stamford, Conn.: FASB, December 1985), par. 25.

the loan is paid off. However, the automobile is considered an asset of the firm because the firm has control over its use.

A business may have several different types of assets. Some assets have physical substance and include items such as cash, inventory, property, plant, and equipment. Other assets have no physical substance and represent legal claims and/or rights. They include such items as receivables and patents. Receivables are claims to future cash, and patents are the exclusive right granted by the federal government to make a product or to use a process. Assets are generally listed on the balance sheet in the order of their liquidity, which is the ease in which the item can be turned into cash. As a result, cash and items that can be turned into cash are listed first. The items such as supplies and equipment that are used in the operations of the business are listed next.

Liabilities

Liabilities are the economic obligations of the enterprise. They comprise primarily the money or services that the accounting entity owes to its creditors. The FASB formally defines liabilities as the "probable future sacrifices of economic benefits arising from present obligations of a particular entity to transfer assets or provide services to other entities in the future as a result of past transactions or events."[5] Liabilities are often sources of assets to a firm. For example, all businesses frequently buy goods on credit rather than paying cash, and this creates the liability called accounts payable. In addition, businesses often borrow money from banks and other lenders for various purposes, such as purchasing land, new machinery and equipment, or additional merchandise. These debts are notes payable, which are formal written promises to repay the lender at a certain time in the future. Notes payable may be short term (less than a year) or long term, and unlike accounts payable, they require the payment of interest to the lender. Other liabilities result from incurring services that are yet to be paid in cash, such as wages earned by employees who have not been paid. Liabilities are generally grouped on the balance sheet according to their due dates. That is, liabilities due within the coming year are listed before liabilities due after a year.

Owner's Equity

The owner's equity in a business enterprise is "the residual interest in the assets of an entity that remains after deducting its liabilities."[6] This definition emphasizes that creditors legally have first claim on the assets of a business, so the owner's equity is equal to assets minus liabilities. The term **net assets** is often used to refer to owner's equity because it also equals assets minus liabilities. For example, the owner's equity of the Carson Company (its net assets) is $330,000 ($545,000 less $215,000).

Owner's equity is increased when the owner of the business invests assets in the firm. As we will see, owner's equity is also increased by the profitable operations of the firm. This is because the firm's profitable operations add to its net assets.

Owner's equity is decreased when the firm distributes cash or other assets to its owner. Essentially, the firm is returning to its owner part of the investment that was made in the company or is distributing the assets earned

---

[5]Ibid., par. 35.

[6]Ibid., par. 49.

through profitable operations. Owner's equity can also be decreased by unprofitable operations, because a net loss decreases the firm's net assets.

Concepts and Conventions Related to the Balance Sheet

There are a number of important concepts and conventions related to the balance sheet. Included are the historical cost convention, objectivity, and the going-concern assumption.

The Historical Cost Convention. Under the **historical cost convention,** assets and liabilities are initially recorded in the accounting system at their original or historical cost and are not adjusted for subsequent increases in value. For accounting purposes, an asset's historical cost is the amount given in consideration at the time of its acquisition. If cash is given as consideration at the time of purchase, the asset will be recorded at the amount of cash paid. If an asset other than cash is given in exchange, the asset received will be recorded at its cash-equivalent price. Liabilities are also recorded in accordance with the historical cost convention. When the liability is incurred, it is recorded at the current market value of the resources received at the time.

In preparing subsequent balance sheets, the assets and liabilities usually continue to be shown at their historical cost. For example, the Carson Company purchased land for possible future use as a building site, paying $130,000 for the property. When the land was acquired, it was recorded at its cost of $130,000. Currently the land might have a market value of $300,000. The current balance sheet, however, will continue to show the land at $130,000, its historical cost, until it is sold. The main reasons for this are the objectivity of that original cost and the going-concern assumption.

Objectivity. Historical cost is **objective** and is not subject to different interpretations, thus meeting the characteristic of being reliable and verifiable. Owners, real estate brokers, or tax collectors each might appraise the market value of the Carson Company's land quite differently. We do not know the actual value of the land until it is sold. Thus, external users can best rely on the financial statements if assets and liabilities are recorded at the objective measure of historical cost.

The Going-Concern Assumption. Another reason for using historical cost when recording and valuing assets and liabilities is the going-concern assumption. The **going-concern assumption** means that unless we have evidence to the contrary, we assume that a particular firm will continue to operate indefinitely. This does not mean we assume that a firm will always be profitable, but only that it will continue to operate. To illustrate, when a firm purchases assets such as plant and equipment, it does so with the intent of using those assets to produce income. Those assets are used in the production and operating cycle of the business, and they are not usually held for the purpose of resale. Furthermore, we assume that the firm will be in existence long enough to use the assets and subsequently derive benefits from them.

Summary of Learning Objectives

1. The nature and function of accounting. Accounting is a system of recording, classifying, and summarizing financial information about economic entities that is meant to be useful in making economic decisions. Accounting is a tool created for economic use, and it changes according to the economic needs of society.

2. *The relationship between accounting and different forms of business enterprises.* Accounting is used by sole proprietorships, partnerships, and corporations. In all three forms of enterprises the transactions of the business are kept separate from those of its owners. In a partnership, the accounting system must keep track of the partners' investments. In a corporation, whose stockholders are its owners, there is frequently a separation of ownership and management, and accounting reports inform the stockholders about the management's performance.

3. *The primary users of accounting information.* The users of accounting information can be divided into two categories, external and internal users. The major external users are present and potential investors and creditors, governmental agencies, and the general public. The primary internal user of accounting information is the firm's management.

4. *Accountants—the providers of accounting information.* Public accountants offer their services to the public for a fee and generally do auditing and accounting work, tax preparation and planning, and some management advisory services. Private accountants are employed by a single firm and perform such activities as cost accounting, budgetary planning and control, internal auditing, and financial reporting. Governmental accountants perform various accounting services for federal, state, and local governmental units and agencies.

5. *The setting of accounting standards.* The development of accounting concepts and standards is a complex process involving government and the accounting profession. The Securities and Exchange Commission has the legal authority from Congress to determine accounting standards, but it has basically accepted the standards determined by the accounting profession, sometimes modifying them or calling for different types of information. The Financial Accounting Standards Board is the organization created by the accounting profession to develop the concepts and standards that constitute generally accepted accounting principles (GAAP).

6. *Financial statements and the elements of the balance sheet.* Financial statements represent the major product of the accounting system. The four primary financial statements are the balance sheet, income statement, statement of owner's equity, and the statement of changes in financial position. The balance sheet presents the financial position of a firm at a particular point in time. The primary elements of the balance sheet are assets, liabilities, and owner's equity. Assets represent the firm's resources; liabilities represent its obligations to outsiders; owner's equity is the residual interest of the owner.

7. *The accounting equation.* The total assets of the enterprise equal its liabilities and owner's equity. These relationships can be expressed through the basic accounting equation:

$$\text{Assets} = \text{Liabilities} + \text{Owner's Equity}$$

The balance sheet is a detailed version of this equation.

Problem for Your Review

At the beginning of 1987, Patti Edwards decided to open a real estate firm called Real Properties. At the end of the firm's first year of operations, Patti's accountant prepared the following balance sheet:

Real Properties
Balance Sheet
December 31, 1987

Assets		Liabilities and Owner's Equity	
Cash	$ 2,500	Liabilities	
Accounts receivable	3,100	Accounts payable	$ 5,500
Office equipment	1,500	Other payables	1,000
Building	25,000	Total liabilities	6,500
		Owner's equity	
		P. Edwards, Capital	25,600
Total assets	$32,100	Total liabilities and	
		owner's equity	$32,100

After reviewing the balance sheet Patti had a number of questions including the following:
1. What does this statement tell me?
2. Why does the total of the assets equal the total liabilities and owner's equity?
3. I do not understand why the building is shown at $25,000. That's what I purchased it for, but today it must be worth at least $32,000.

Required:

Answer Patti's questions so she can better understand what her accountant has done.

Solution

1. The balance sheet shows the financial position of the firm at a particular point in time. It is an expansion of the accounting equation. It tells you what the firm owns and what it owes to whom. The balance sheet is just one of the four statements prepared by firms. In order to see the entire picture all the statements must be examined. For example, net income is shown on the income statement.

2. The left side of the accounting equation shows the economic resources controlled by the firm. The right side shows the claims against these resources. Another way to state this relationship is to say that the firm's assets have many sources, and the right side of the equation shows where those resources came from.

3. Assets are shown on the balance sheet at their acquisition or historical costs, not at their current values. This is because historical costs are more objective and verifiable than current values.

Questions

1. In broad terms, what is accounting?

2. What purposes does accounting serve in (a) a business enterprise and (b) society?

3. What are the similarities and differences among accounting, law, and mathematics? Explain.

4. In what ways do you think accounting would differ for business organizations and for the government?

5. In what ways do you think accounting differs for external and internal users?

6. Identify four outside groups that would be interested in a company's financial statements, and indicate their particular interest.

7. What are the characteristics of the corporate form of organization that would account for its popularity?

8. Is accounting more important in a corporation or in an individual proprietorship or partnership? Explain.

9. Describe in your own words the manner in which accounting standards are set in the United States. How do you think accounting standards would be set in a country with a centralized socialistic government?

10. Describe the role and function of each of the following groups:
    a. The Securities and Exchange Commission.
    b. The Financial Accounting Standards Board.
    c. The American Institute of CPAs.

11. Financial statements are described as the major product of the accounting information system. Explain this statement and state the four principal financial statements.

12. The main elements of a balance sheet are assets, liabilities, and owner's equity. Define and provide at least two examples of each.

13. Name two groups with claims on a firm's assets. Which has the primary claim? Why?

14. List two forms of the basic accounting equation. Why do assets equal liabilities plus owner's equity?

15. If a transaction causes total liabilities to increase but does not affect owner's equity, what change is to be expected in total assets?

16. Assuming that you never took an accounting course, and you were asked to prepare a statement listing your assets and liabilities, would you do so at their historical cost or their current value? Why?

17. Describe the historical cost convention and explain its use in accounting.

18. Describe the going-concern assumption. What relevance does it have to the way accountants record assets?

19. A company purchased land 10 years ago for $200,000. The land has just been appraised at $350,000. When do accountants recognize the fact that the land has increased in value?

Exercises

1. Users of Financial Statements. You are currently being interviewed for the position of manager of financial reporting for a large corporation. You have been asked to explain to the chief financial officer, your potential boss, why each of the following individuals or groups might be interested in the firm's financial statements:

    a. The current owners of the firm.

    b. The creditors of the firm.

    c. The management of the firm.

    d. The prospective stockholders of the firm.

    e. The Internal Revenue Service.

    f. The Securities and Exchange Commission.

    g. The AFL/CIO, the firm's major labor union.

2. Careers in Accounting. You have been asked to lecture on accounting careers to a group of prospective accounting students. Describe to them the types of work available in:

    a. CPA firms.

    b. Private industry.

    c. Government.

3. Accounting Entities. Below are statements concerning sole proprietorships, partnerships, and corporations. Indicate whether each statement is true or false, and if the statement is false, provide an explanation for your answer.

    a. If there are two or more owners of a business, it must be organized as a partnership.

    b. In a sole proprietorship, the owner and the business are one legal entity.

    c. The sole proprietorship and its owner represent the same accounting entity.

    d. Any two individuals, by oral agreement, can form a corporation.

    e. The owners of a corporation are not legally responsible for the individual debts incurred by the corporation.

    f. In a partnership, the partners and the partnership are one legal entity.

    g. All partners in a partnership must share the profits and losses equally.

    h. Ownership in a corporation is evidenced by a share of stock.

4. Recognizing Accounts. Classify the following accounts as assets, liabilities, or owner's equity. If you do not think an item would be recognized as any of the above, so state, and explain.

a. Cash.	h. Office supplies.
b. Notes payable.	i. Interest payable.
c. Office equipment.	j. Prepaid rent.
d. L. Bean, Capital.	k. Notes receivable.
e. Accounts payable.	l. Land.
f. Accounts receivable.	m. A trademark such as
g. A firm's good management.	McDonald's golden arches.

5. The Accounting Equation. Answer each of the following independent questions:

    a. The New Company's assets equal $52,000 and its owner's equity totals $22,500. What is the amount of its liabilities?

    b. The liabilities of the Old Company are $25,200 and its owner's equity is $15,800. What is the amount of its assets?

    c. The Rose Company has total assets of $75,000 and total liabilities of $34,500. What is the amount of its owner's equity?

    d. The Barney Company started July with assets of $150,000 and liabilities of $90,000. During the month of July owner's equity increased by $24,000 and liabilities decreased by $10,000. What is the amount of its total assets at the end of July?

6. Preparing a Balance Sheet. The following data are available for Pam's Peanut Shop as of August 31, 1987:

Cash	$3,000	Accounts receivable	$2,000
Accounts payable	4,500	Supplies	3,500
P. Pam, Capital	?	Notes payable	2,000
Office equipment	8,000	Land	15,000
		Wages payable	1,000

Required:

Prepare a balance sheet for the company as of August 31, 1987, using the format shown in the chapter. Show figures for total assets, total liabilities, and owner's equity.

7. Preparing a Balance Sheet. The following data are available for Jose's Supply Store as of June 30, 1987:

a. The purchase cost of all equipment owned by the store was $20,000. When making the purchase, a note for $18,000 was given to the supplier. An additional payment of $2,000 has subsequently been made on the note.

b. Several years ago the company purchased a plot of land for $100,000 cash, to be used for future store expansion. Although the land has yet to be used, the company still owns it. Recently it has been appraised at $140,000.

c. Supplies on hand cost $15,000.

d. The firm owes various suppliers $12,000.

e. F. Jose's capital account amounts to $120,000.

f. Various individuals owe the firm $2,500.

g. The firm has inventory for resale of $10,000.

h. The firm has some cash in a checking account but is unable to determine the amount. All other items are given to you.

Required:

Prepare a balance sheet for Jose's Supply Store as of June 30, 1987, using the format shown in the chapter.

8. Accounting Concepts. State whether each of the following statements is true or false; if false, explain your answer.

a. In order for an item to be considered an asset of an enterprise, the enterprise must have legal title to it.

b. The historical cost convention requires that when an asset is acquired it is recorded at its historical cost. However, when subsequent balance sheets are prepared, the asset is adjusted to reflect its current value.

c. One of the main reasons for employing the historical cost convention is that historical cost is objective.

d. The Almost Corporation has had several terrible years and has decided to sell all of its assets and go out of business within the next few months. If a balance sheet is prepared immediately after this decision is made, but before liquidation, the firm's assets should be listed at their historical cost.

Understanding Financial Statements

The following accounts, in random order, have been taken from the balance sheet of Hershey Foods Corporation (in thousands):

Property, plant, and equipment	$539,914
Accounts payable	110,582
Income taxes payable	85,165
Cash and short-term investments	17,820
Inventories	178,585
Owners' equity	532,495
Prepaid assets	13,411
Notes payable (due within 12 months)	19,579
Notes payable (due after 12 months)	140,250
Investments and other assets	73,212
Accounts receivable	65,129

Required:

a. Prepare a balance sheet for Hershey Foods at December 31.

b. Describe what each account represents.

c. Evaluate, as well as you can at this early point in your studies, the financial position of Hershey Foods Corporation.

Financial Decision Case

One of your friends is the sole owner of a small company that makes banners. Although the firm has been relatively successful, it had experienced little growth the last few years. However, the company was contacted recently by an Olympic organizing committee to be the official banner supplier to the Olympics. As a result, the firm is planning a great deal of expansion and is in need of funds for the expansion.

Your friend has always prepared his own financial statements. However, in negotiating a bank loan the loan officer insisted that the statements be audited by a CPA. Because your friend was unfamiliar with the accounting profession, he asked you the following questions:

a. What is a CPA, and what functions are provided by CPA firms?

b. The loan officer mentioned an audit. What is an audit and why would the banker want my financial statements audited?

c. The loan officer mentioned that my financial statements should be prepared in accordance with generally accepted accounting principles. What does she mean, where can I go to find these generally accepted accounting principles, and who sets these principles?

Required:

Write a brief memo responding to your friend's questions.

Accounting as an Information System

2

LEARNING OBJECTIVES

After reading this chapter you should be able to:
1. Explain why accounting functions as an information system.
2. Describe the characteristics of information admitted to the accounting system.
3. Explain the effects of transactions on the accounting equation.
4. Detail the components of the accounting system.
5. Record balance sheet transactions in the journal and ledger.
6. Prepare a trial balance and describe its uses and limitations.

This chapter begins our discussion of the accounting system, which is the set of methods and procedures used to record, classify, and summarize the financial information that is distributed to interested users. In the first part of the chapter we discuss which economic events are recorded in the accounting system. In the second part we start a discussion of the standard accounting procedures that are used to record, classify, and summarize the information recorded in the accounting system.

The Accounting Information System

Accounting is a system designed to provide financial information about economic entities. Any system, including accounting, may be viewed as comprising three parts: (1) inputs, (2) a transformation process, and (3) outputs. The inputs are the system's raw materials, and the transformation processes convert these inputs into the intended outputs.

The following diagram illustrates how the **accounting information system** transforms raw data into useful economic information. The inputs of the system are the economic events into which the firm enters. However, as we will see, only those economic events that meet certain criteria become inputs of the system. The transformation process is the accountant's application of a set of rules and conventions used to record, classify, and summarize the inputs. The outputs of the accounting system are the accounting reports intended for a variety of users. Most importantly, these outputs include financial statements for external users and internal management.

THE ACCOUNTING INFORMATION SYSTEM

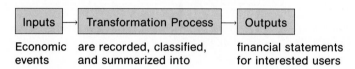

Economic   are recorded, classified,   financial statements
events   and summarized into   for interested users

Lisa Bowman's Law Firm

To illustrate how accounting operates as an information system, let us assume that we wish to account for the activities of a person who is starting a law practice. Lisa Bowman is currently earning $40,000 per year as an attorney for a large midwestern city. She has always wanted to be in business for herself and has decided to work only part time at her present job in order to begin a small law practice of her own. Her employer has agreed to this arrangement and Lisa has begun the preparations necessary to open her own firm. She plans to use the current and following months, April and May, to continue organizing her firm. She hopes to begin practicing law on her own by June. Lisa has an extra room at home that she will use as an office until her practice grows. Lisa has purchased a license for $120 from the, city which entitles her to use her home in this way. In addition, she has purchased various items of stationery for $200, office supplies for $180, and a used typewriter for $75. To announce the location of her practice and the type of law she will specialize in, Lisa has 1,000 announcements printed at a cost of $100. After a couple of weeks of preparation she has already begun to attract a number of potential clients.

At present, Lisa accounts for her business with a checkbook. She pays all of her bills by check and deposits all money received by her firm into the business checking account. So far this has seemed reasonably satisfactory, but although Lisa knows what she has spent in total, she is not certain of how much was spent on various items such as supplies, stationery, and telephones. She could, of course, go through her checkbook and classify each check according to different business categories and then aggregate or total the categories; however, she feels there must be a better way of keeping track of her business activities.

When Lisa officially begins business in June she will have to figure out whether or not her firm is able to earn a profit. Furthermore, Lisa feels that her practice has the potential to grow, and she expects the firm may need a loan from the local bank to finance this growth. She knows that her banker is going to want to see some financial statements before her firm can be granted a loan.

She is also concerned that she may have used the firm's checkbook once or twice to cover a purchase for her own use.

Given this information Lisa has to decide how to set up an accounting system for her business. The first step is to decide what the inputs are to her accounting system. Should she treat all data, economic and noneconomic, as inputs? If not all data, should all economic data be regarded as inputs? As we will see, only specific economic data should be input into the system. Also, at what particular point in time should these inputs be recorded or recognized in Lisa's records?

Data Input into the Accounting System

In order for economic data to be an input of the law firm's accounting system, it must:

1. Be a transaction or event for the business entity, Lisa Bowman's Law Firm.
2. Be quantifiable or measurable in monetary terms.
3. Be verifiable.

Business Entity Assumption

An accounting system deals with a particular business entity. This is called the **business entity assumption** of accounting and requires that we adhere to the concept that the business is independent and distinct from its owners, even though they clearly have a residual interest in the net assets of the business.

Because the accounting system is intended for a specified business entity, only the transactions and events concerning its economic activities should be included in the system. In our example, this means that only business transactions, not Lisa's personal transactions, can be admitted into the accounting system. For example, Lisa's purchase of stationery for personal use is a transaction that should be excluded from her business's accounting system. If we fail to distinguish between Lisa's business and personal expenditures, even though she owns the business, our accounting for the business will be distorted.

Quantifiability

The accounting system admits as inputs only those transactions and events that can be represented in numerical (primarily monetary) terms. This characteristic is known as **quantifiability.** If it is not possible to express an event in numerical terms, the event is not treated as an input of the accounting system. For example, Lisa has spent considerable time and effort in developing a legal specialty. She feels that specializing will greatly increase her clientele. She wonders if all her time and effort in this regard should be recorded in the accounting system. Unless there is some reasonable way to translate her own time and effort into numerical terms, it will not be an input of the system.

Verifiability

In addition to being quantifiable, an economic event should be verifiable before it is input into the accounting system. **Verifiability** means that the data pertaining to the transaction or event must be available, and if two or more qualified persons examined the same data, they would reach essentially the same conclusions about these data's accounting treatment. Verifiability adds to the usefulness and thus the reliability of the accounting information. For example, Lisa uses part of her home for her business. She also uses part of her home for personal purposes. If there is no reasonable way for her to verify the cost of using her home or to keep her business space separate from her living space, the cost of using her home should not be an input of the accounting system.

Applying these input criteria to Lisa's law firm, we may analyze the events and transactions pertaining to her operations. The following table shows that there are three categories of events and transactions:

1. Those that clearly are admissible to the accounting system (Numbers 3–6).
2. Those that are not admissible (Number 1).
3. Those that might be admissible if they can be quantified and verified (Number 2).

Analysis of Events and Transactions of Lisa Bowman's Law Firm Admitted into the Accounting System

Event and Transaction	Input	Explanation
1. Lisa's salary as a city attorney	No	Not related to the business entity
2. Use of house as office	Maybe	Yes, if can be quantified and verified
3. Lisa's investment in her new law firm	Yes	Yes, business receives funds
4. City license	Yes	Related to business and quantifiable
5. Cost of stationery	Yes	Related to business and quantifiable
6. Cost of announcements	Yes	Related to business and quantifiable

Recognizing Transactions

Once an event meets the necessary criteria to become an input of the system, one still must determine when to recognize that event in the accounting records.

Accountants recognize transactions only at specified points in the system. For example, assume that Lisa's law firm placed an order at its local computer store for a personal computer. At that time, the law firm sent the computer store a purchase order, which is a document indicating what it would like to order and the anticipated price. The computer was delivered to the law firm a week later, and two days after that the law firm received the invoice, or bill. Two weeks later the invoice was paid in full. In this example, there have been several distinct events:

1. An order was placed, and a purchase order was generated.
2. The computer was delivered.
3. An invoice was received.
4. The invoice was paid in full.

Which of these events, all related to the purchase of the computer, are recognized as accounting transactions in the accounting system? Generally, accountants do not recognize in the accounting records mutual promises to perform. For example, in the first event the computer store promised to deliver the computer, and the law firm promised to pay, but neither party had yet performed. Such mutual promises are often referred to as *executory contracts* and are not recorded as assets or liabilities. Yet records and documents are generated. The law firm sent the computer store a purchase order, which it used to keep track of what items it would receive in the future and when it could expect to receive them.

The transaction was recorded in both the law firm's and the computer store's accounting records when legal title to the computer passed from the computer store to the law firm. This occurred either when the computer left the store or when it arrived at Lisa's office. As we will see in Chapter 5, the exact point at which title exchanges hands depends on the terms of the shipping agreement. In any event, when title does pass, the law firm records the purchase and the computer store records the sale. At that point the store had performed its part of the agreement by delivering the computer, but the law firm had promised only to pay in the future; nevertheless, that transaction should be recorded in the law firm's accounting records as a payable and in the computer store's records as a receivable.

The receipt of the invoice does not cause a transaction to be recorded in the law firm's accounting records, because the purchase was already recorded when the computer was received. However, the invoice does enter the system and generates paperwork that will result in the payment of the invoice. The actual payment of the invoice is the second transaction that is recorded in the system. At that point the law firm is fulfilling its promise to pay. It is important to keep in mind that the purchase of the computer first entered the accounting system at the time the firm received the computer, two weeks and two days before it paid for it.

Effects of Transactions on the Accounting Equation

In Chapter 1 we introduced you to the following accounting equation:

$$\text{Assets} = \text{Liabilities} + \text{Owner's Equity}$$

This equation, which is a condensation of the balance sheet, represents the assets, liabilities, and owner's equity of a business at a point in time. Let us return to the example of Lisa Bowman's law firm to see how the transactions that are admissible into the accounting system affect the assets, liabilities, and owner's equity of that business.

First, all transactions are recorded in accounts. An **account** is a record that summarizes all transactions that affect a particular category of asset, liability, or owner's equity. Companies set up specific accounts depending on their own specific needs and type of business. Accounts are added or deleted over time as the company grows and changes.

Second, in order for the accounting equation to remain in balance each transaction must involve a change in at least two accounts. For example, for the accounting equation to remain in balance if an asset is increased by $20, either another asset must be decreased by that amount, a liability must be increased by that amount, or owner's equity must be increased by that amount. Keep this fundamental relationship in mind as we trace the transactions of Lisa Bowman's law firm through the accounting system.

Lisa started her own law firm by investing $1,000 of her cash on April 1. She decided to organize the business as a sole proprietorship. The effect of investing $1,000 was to provide the firm with an asset—cash. The source of that asset is Lisa's own investment in the firm. Thus, an asset account, Cash, is increased, and an owner's equity account, L. Bowman, Capital, is increased.

	Assets	= Liabilities + Owner's Equity
	Cash =	L. Bowman, Capital
4/1	+1,000	+1,000

On April 2, Lisa purchased a license from the city for $120 cash in order to do business at her home. This transaction resulted in a decrease in the Cash account, but at the same time a new asset, the license, was acquired. The license is an asset because it provides future economic benefits, namely, the right to use her home to conduct business:

	Assets		= Liabilities + Owner's Equity
	Cash + License =		L. Bowman, Capital
4/1	1,000	=	1,000
4/2	−120	+120	
Bal.	880 +	120 =	1,000

On April 3, Lisa bought a used typewriter for $75 cash, to be used to type legal papers. This transaction also decreased Cash by $75 and resulted in a new asset, the typewriter, which is put in the Office Equipment account. Notice that each transaction affects at least two items and that after they are recorded, the accounting equation is still in balance.

	Assets			= Liabilities + Owner's Equity
	Cash + License +		Office Equipment =	L. Bowman, Capital
4/2	880 + 120		=	1,000
4/3	−75		+75	
Bal.	805 + 120	+	75 =	1,000

On April 4, Lisa then purchased a variety of stationery and office supplies for $380. Because she felt it would be wise to conserve cash, she bought these items on credit. This transaction resulted in a liability, Accounts Payable, and an asset, Office Supplies. (Lisa decided to combine the stationery and office supplies into one account.)

	Assets				= Liabilities + Owner's Equity	
	Cash + License +		Office Equipment +	Office Supplies =	Accounts Payable +	L. Bowman, Capital
4/3	805 + 120	+	75		=	1,000
4/4				+380	+380	
Bal.	805 + 120	+	75	+ 380 =	380 +	1,000

After working for two weeks, Lisa felt that the typewriter she had purchased was not large enough for the amount of typing she had to do. She sold it for $75 to a friend, who asked to pay for it over the next month and a half. This transaction resulted in the loss of an asset, the typewriter, and the creation of a new asset, Accounts Receivable:

		Assets				= Liabilities + Owner's Equity	
	Cash +	Accounts Receivable +	License +	Office Equipment +	Office Supplies =	Accounts Payable +	L. Bowman, Capital
4/4	805 +		+ 120	+ 75	+ 380 =	380	+ 1,000
4/15		+75		−75			
Bal.	805 +	75	+ 120	+ 0	+ 380 =	380	+ 1,000

On April 16, Lisa purchased a large typewriter on credit for $600. This transaction increased assets and liabilities:

		Assets				= Liabilities + Owner's Equity	
	Cash +	Accounts Receivable +	License +	Office Equipment +	Office Supplies =	Accounts Payable +	L. Bowman, Capital
4/15	805 +	75	+ 120	+	+ 380 =	380	+ 1,000
4/16				+600		+600	
Bal.	805 +	75	+ 120	+ 600	+ 380 =	980	+ 1,000

At the end of the month, Lisa paid half of her bill, or $190, to the store where she purchased the stationery and office supplies. This decreased both the asset, Cash, and the liability, Accounts Payable.

		Assets				= Liabilities + Owner's Equity	
	Cash +	Accounts Receivable +	License +	Office Equipment +	Office Supplies =	Accounts Payable +	L. Bowman, Capital
4/16	805 +	75	+ 120	+ 600	+ 380 =	980	+ 1,000
4/30	−190					−190	
Bal.	615 +	75	+ 120	+ 600	+ 380 =	790	+ 1,000

On the same day, Lisa also received partial payment of $40 for the typewriter she had sold. This transaction affected only assets, as Cash increased and Accounts Receivable decreased:

		Assets				= Liabilities + Owner's Equity	
	Cash +	Accounts Receivable +	License +	Office Equipment +	Office Supplies =	Accounts Payable +	L. Bowman, Capital
4/30	615 +	75	+ 120	+ 600	+ 380 =	790	+ 1,000
4/30	+40	−40					
Bal.	655 +	35	+ 120	+ 600	+ 380 =	790	+ 1,000

The table on the top of page 30 summarizes all of the transactions we have described so far:

Lisa Bowman's Law Firm
Summary of Transactions

	Assets					= Liabilities + Owner's Equity	
	Cash +	Accounts Receivable +	License +	Office Equipment +	Office Supplies =	Accounts Payable +	L. Bowman, Capital
4/1	+1,000					=	1,000
4/2	−120		+120				
Bal.	880 +		120			=	1,000
4/3	−75			+75			
Bal.	805 +		120 +	75		=	1,000
4/4					+380	+380	
Bal.	805 +		120 +	75 +	380 =	380 +	1,000
4/15		+75		−75			
Bal.	805 +	75 +	120 −	0 +	380 =	380 +	1,000
4/16				+600		+600	
Bal.	805 +	75 +	120 +	600 +	380 =	980 +	1,000
4/30	−190					−190	
Bal.	615 +	75 +	120 +	600 +	380 =	790 +	1,000
4/30	+40	−40					
Bal.	655 +	35 +	120 +	600 +	380 =	790 +	1,000

Shown below is the balance sheet, or statement of financial position, that Lisa made up for her firm at the end of April.

Lisa Bowman's Law Firm
Balance Sheet
April 30, 1987

Assets

Cash	$ 655
Accounts receivable	35
License	120
Office supplies	380
Office equipment	600
Total assets	$1,790

Liabilities and Owner's Equity

Liabilities:	
Accounts payable	$ 790
Owner's equity:	
L. Bowman, Capital	1,000
Total liabilities and owner's equity	$1,790

Note that when Lisa began her business, she invested $1,000, and thus at that time owner's equity, or assets minus liabilities, was $1,000. As the table shows, at the end of April owner's equity is still $1,000 (assets of $1,790 less liabilities of $790). The firm's assets have increased to $1,790 from the $1,000 originally contributed by Bowman. In addition, instead of being all in cash the business now has a variety of assets. The additional $790 in assets was financed by the creditors. Thus, during April the owner's equity of the firm was not changed from Lisa's original investment.

However, as we noted, owner's equity is affected not only by what the owner invests, but by the profitability of the business as well. Because the firm's first month of business activity was spent preparing for starting legal work, no actual legal work was performed. Thus, an income statement that would show whether the firm is profitable or not is not prepared. In Chapter 3 we deal with transactions involving the providing of legal services, showing their effects on assets, liabilities, and owner's equity, and the preparation of an income statement.

It would be very difficult and costly for a business to draw up a balance sheet or accounting equation after each transaction, as we have done here. Therefore, accountants have developed a means for storing and classifying transactions so that a balance sheet is prepared only periodically. The next part of this chapter, as well as Chapters 3 and 4, shows how accounting systems store and classify information for this purpose.

The Components of the Accounting System

The major components of the accounting system are illustrated in Exhibit 2–1. Most transactions are written on business documents, such as sales invoices, purchase invoices, cash register tapes, and checks. These documents then serve as inputs into journals and ledgers, the two basic components of any accounting system, whether manual or computerized.

EXHIBIT 2–1
Components of the Accounting System

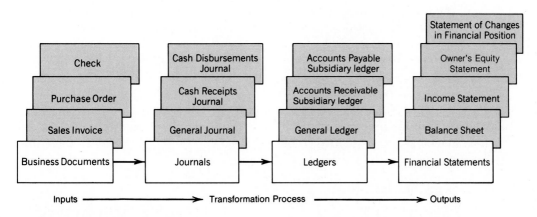

The Journal

The **journal** is the record or book in which each transaction is originally recorded. For this reason it is often referred to as the book of original entry. The journal is in effect a chronological list of each transaction the firm has entered into. There are several types of journals, ranging from a general journal to specialized journals. General journals can be used to record all types of transactions, whereas specialized journals are used to record a specific type of transaction, such as the receipt or the disbursement of cash.

The Ledger

A **ledger** is a book or computer record of specific accounts. As noted, an account is a record that summarizes all transactions affecting a particular asset, liability, or owner's equity item. A **general ledger** contains a specific account for each item listed on the financial statements and shows how each transaction changes the balances of these accounts. **Subsidiary ledgers** contain back-up or more-detailed accounts. For example, the primary account, Accounts Receivable, is in the general ledger, whereas the individual accounts for each customer are contained in the Accounts Receivable subsidiary ledger. Transactions are first recorded in the journal, and at specified intervals the same transactions are recorded in both the general and, when appropriate, subsidiary ledger accounts. The balances in the general ledger are then used to prepare financial statements.

The accounts used by a particular firm depend on its needs and the nature and size of the business. For example, a large, publicly owned corporation may have hundreds of accounts, whereas a small business may have a dozen or so accounts. Most firms maintain a **chart of accounts,** which is a list of all the accounts a firm uses. Accounts in the chart are sequentially numbered. The chart of accounts for Lisa Bowman's Law Firm is illustrated on page 33. Notice that there are numbers not currently being used, which gives Lisa the flexibility to add new accounts as needed.

Asset Accounts

A firm is likely to have a number of asset accounts. The major ones include Cash, Marketable Securities, Receivables, Inventory, Prepaid Expenses, and Property, Plant, and Equipment.

Cash

The Cash accounts include such items as coins, currency, money orders, drafts, checks, and cash on hand. In effect, any medium of exchange that the bank will accept at its face value is considered cash. The number of specific cash accounts that a firm has depends on the desires of its management.

Marketable Securities

The Marketable Securities account is used to record purchases and sales of such items as investments in the stocks and bonds of other companies. On the balance sheet, some firms combine Cash and Marketable Securities in one account.

Notes Receivable

Notes receivable are written notes from others promising to pay a specific amount of money at a specific time in the future. They may arise from cash loans or the sale of goods or services. Notes receivable usually require the borrower to pay interest to the lender, in addition to the amount owed.

Lisa Bowman's Law Firm
Chart of Accounts

100 Assets
- 101 Cash
- 103 Marketable securities
- 105 Notes receivable
- 106 Accounts receivable
- 115 Office supplies
- 120 Prepaid insurance
- 121 License
- 150 Land
- 160 Building
- 165 Office furniture and fixtures
- 167 Office equipment
- 170 Other assets

200 Liabilities
- 201 Accounts payable
- 205 Bank loan payable
- 210 Salaries payable
- 212 Interest payable

300 Owner's Equity
- 301 L. Bowman, Capital
- 311 L. Bowman, Drawing

400 Revenues
- 401 Legal fees earned
- 405 Other revenues

600 Expenses
- 601 Salaries expense
- 602 Repairs and maintenance expense
- 603 Utilities expense
- 604 Advertising expense
- 605 Licenses expense
- 607 Office supplies expense
- 611 Insurance expense
- 615 Depreciation expense

800 Other Expenses
- 801 Interest expense

1000 Income Summary

Accounts Receivable

Accounts receivable arise from sales made or services performed on credit and represent future cash collections. When a sale is made or a service performed on credit, Accounts Receivable is increased, and when customers make payments on their accounts it is decreased.

Inventory

All merchandising firms have an inventory account, and items held for re-sale are recorded in this account. A merchandising firm is one that sells products, such as a drugstore or a market. As the inventory is sold, this account is decreased and an expense account, Cost of Goods Sold, is increased. A service firm such as a travel agency or a law firm would not have an inventory account because it sells services rather than products.

Prepaid Expenses

Asset accounts such as Office Supplies, Prepaid Insurance, and Licenses all represent payment for goods or services purchased for future use. As a group these items are often called prepaid expenses. At the time these goods or services are purchased they are considered assets, but as they are used or consumed in the business they become expenses. Thus, for each of these asset accounts there is a related expense listed in the chart of accounts. Although these asset accounts usually expire daily, the assets account is decreased, and the related expense account is increased at specified intervals, generally monthly.

Property, Plant, and Equipment

Land, Buildings, Equipment, and Furniture and Fixtures are often referred to as *operating,* or *fixed assets* and provide long-term benefits to the firm. It is important to separate land from the rest of these accounts because all of these types of assets, except land, are subject to wear and tear, obsolescence, or use that will eventually decrease their future benefits to the firm. As these assets lose their benefits, their cost must be allocated to future periods. This process is called depreciation and is discussed in Chapters 4 and 12.

Liability Accounts

Liability accounts represent the enterprise's obligations to make payments or to provide goods or services in the future. The principal liability accounts are Accounts Payable and Notes and Loans Payable.

Accounts Payable

Accounts payable arise from purchases of goods and services from vendors and suppliers for which the firm has not yet made payment. These payments are usually due within a short period, normally 30 days. When one company has an account payable, the company to which the cash or service is owed will have a corresponding account receivable.

Notes and Loans Payable

Notes and loans payable generally result from cash borrowings from banks and other creditors. These notes are either short term and due within a short period of time, a month or so, or long term and due after one year. Like notes receivable, notes and loans payable usually have an interest element that must be paid in addition to the original amount borrowed.

Other Liabilities

Finally, a firm is likely to have a variety of other short-term payable accounts including Taxes Payable, Interest Payable, and Salaries Payable. These all are the result of the firm's incurring an expense for which it has not yet made a cash payment.

Owner's Equity

Because Lisa Bowman's law firm is organized as a sole proprietorship, her owner's equity accounts include L. Bowman, Capital and L. Bowman, Drawing. As we noted, the Capital account represents the owner's original investment in the business plus any accumulated profits of the business less any withdrawals made by the owner. As we will see later, the Drawing account is first used to record the owner's withdrawals and later is combined with the Capital account.

Revenues and Expenses

Revenues are the dollar value of goods sold or services rendered by a firm. **Expenses** are the cost of the assets and services used by the firm in obtaining revenues. **Net income** is the excess of revenues earned over expenses incurred. Although revenues and expenses respectively increase and decrease owner's equity, revenue and expense transactions are not directly recorded in the owner's equity accounts. Rather, they are first recorded in separate revenue and expense accounts and, at appropriate times, are transferred to the

Owner's Capital account. This enables the owner or manager to gather timely information and maintain control over the firm's profitability.

The exact nature and title of the revenue and expense accounts depend on the nature, size, and complexity of the business, and the needs of the owner or manager. The primary revenue account for Lisa Bowman's law firm is Legal Fees Earned. Other revenue accounts might include Interest and Rental Revenue. A firm is likely to have a variety of different expense accounts. For a service business such as a law firm, salaries and office expenses are likely to be major expenses. For a merchandising firm that sells retail goods, cost of goods sold is the major expense.

The Recording Process

In order to record economic transactions, accountants have developed a set of standardized procedures that are performed in sequence during every accounting period. Accounting periods can be monthly, quarterly, or yearly, depending on the needs of the business. This set of procedures is generally known as the **accounting cycle** and is outlined in Exhibit 2–2. The accounting system in which the accounting cycle takes place can range from handkept sets of records to complex computerized systems. Yet the basic nature of the system remains the same. Thus, although our discussion will be based on a simple system, the concepts and procedures in the accounting cycle that you will learn are also applicable to larger, more complex systems.

EXHIBIT 2-2
Steps in the Accounting Cycle

During the Period

Record transactions in the journal.
Periodically post entries to ledger accounts.

At End of Period

Prepare the unadjusted trial balance.
Prepare the worksheet—optional.
Prepare adjusting entries.
Post adjusting entries to the ledger accounts, balance the accounts, and prepare the adjusted trial balance.
Prepare the financial statements.
Prepare closing entries, post to the ledger accounts, and prepare a post-closing trial balance.

As Exhibit 2–2 illustrates, the first step in the accounting cycle is to record transactions in the journal as they occur. These entries are then periodically transferred to the ledger accounts. From a learning standpoint, however, it is most effective to start our discussion of the accounting cycle by explaining how transactions are recorded in the ledger because the rules for recording transactions in the accounting records are based on how they are recorded in the ledger accounts. Our discussion will then turn to how transactions are recorded in the journal. The remaining parts of the cycle are covered in Chapters 3 and 4.

Recording Transactions in a Ledger Account

The ledger is used to accumulate the effects of many transactions on specific accounts. In practice, a ledger book contains a separate page for each account. Throughout this book, **T accounts** are used to represent individual ledger items. A sample T account looks like this:

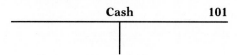

Cash   **101**

Depending on whether it is an asset account or is an equity account (which includes liability and owner's equity accounts), one side is used to record increases and the other side is used to record decreases. For all asset accounts, increases are recorded on the left side of the ledger account and decreases are recorded on the right side. Conversely, in all equity accounts, increases are recorded on the right side of the ledger account and decreases are recorded on the left side. These points are illustrated in the following T accounts.

Assets		**Equities** **(Liabilities and Owner's Equity)**	
Increases	Decreases	Decreases	Increases
+	−	−	+

Because of these conventions, each time an entry is made on the left side of an account, a corresponding entry or set of entries is made on the right side of another account. This is a direct reflection of the self-balancing accounting equation. For example, an increase in an asset account can result only from a decrease in another asset account or an increase in an equity account. This means that when an entry is recorded on the left side of an asset account to increase that account, there will be either a corresponding entry on the right side of another asset account to record a decrease in that account, or an entry on the right side of an equity account to record an increase in that account.

This is illustrated in the following two examples taken from the transactions of Lisa Bowman's law firm. On April 1, Lisa started her law firm by investing $1,000 cash. This transaction increases both an asset account, Cash, and a owner's equity account, L. Bowman, Capital. It results in an entry on the left side of the Cash account, which represents an increase of $1,000 in this account. There is a corresponding entry on the right side of the owner's equity account, L. Bowman, Capital, which represents an increase in that account. The T accounts reflecting these transactions are:

Cash		**L. Bowman, Capital**	
4/1 1,000			4/1 1,000

A second example is the transaction on April 16 in which the law firm purchased a new typewriter for $600 on account. The increase in the asset account, Office Equipment, is recorded on the left side of the T account and the increase in the liability account, Accounts Payable, is recorded on the right side of that account.

Office Equipment	Accounts Payable
4/16 600	4/16 600

As is evident from these transactions, the system for recording transactions maintains the equality of the accounting equation: For every increase in asset accounts there is a corresponding decrease in another asset account or an increase in an equity account. In addition, for every entry on the left side of an account, there is always a corresponding entry on the right side of another account.

Debits and Credits

Accountants have developed other conventions to help them record transactions easily and efficiently. Debits (Dr.) and credits (Cr.) are examples of these conventions. To **debit** an account means to make an entry on the left side of any ledger account. Therefore, to debit an account means that you are increasing an asset account and that you are decreasing an equity account. To credit an account means just the opposite. That is, a **credit** is an entry on the right side of any ledger account. It represents a decrease in an asset account and an increase in an equity account. You should understand that debit and credit are just shorthand ways of saying that you are making an entry on the debit (left) side or credit (right) side of any ledger account. They have no other meanings and do not imply a favorable or unfavorable condition. These accounting conventions are summarized in the following T accounts:

Assets		Equities (Liabilities and Owner's Equity)	
Increase	Decrease	Decrease	Increase
+	–	–	+
Debit	Credit	Debit	Credit

Referring back to the previous example, in order to record the $1,000 cash investment in the law firm, you would debit the asset account, Cash, and credit the owner's equity account, L. Bowman, Capital. To record the $600 purchase of a typewriter on account, you would debit the asset account, Office Equipment, and credit the liability account, Accounts Payable.

Debits Must Equal Credits

The correct application of the debit and credit rules ensures that the accounting equation will always stay in balance. For example, if an asset account is increased (debited), there must be a corresponding decrease in another asset account (a credit) or an increase in a liability or owner's equity account (a credit). For this reason, this system of accounting is often referred to as **double entry accounting** because each transaction will have equal debit and credit effects on the accounting equation. However, the fact that debits must equal credits does not necessarily mean that a particular transaction was correctly recorded. For example, Cash could be credited by mistake when, in fact, Accounts Payable should have been credited. As long as a credit is recorded in either account, the accounting equation will remain in balance.

Balancing T Accounts

After all transactions for a specified period have been entered in the individual ledger accounts, these accounts are totaled and balanced. As an example, all of the cash transactions for the month of April for Lisa Bowman's law firm are shown in the following T account. As is indicated, each side of the account is totaled. These totals are referred to as *footings*, and in this example are marked in color. In this example, the beginning balance plus debits or increases equals $1,040, and the credits or decreases equal $385. Subtracting the decreases or credits of $385 on the right side from the balance of $1,040 on the left leaves us with a balance of $655. This is the ending balance on April 30 and will become the beginning balance for the period beginning May 1. In future examples, the footings will be eliminated, and only the new balance will be shown. It is customary that only the date and the amount be entered in the ledger account. The specific transaction is described fully in the journal.

Cash

4/1	Beginning balance	0	4/2	Purchase of license	120
4/1	L. Bowman's investment	1,000	4/3	Purchase of typewriter	75
4/30	Receipt of payment		4/30	Payment on account	190
	on account	40			
		1,040			385
4/30	Ending balance	655			

As you would expect, all asset accounts normally have debit balances. Remember that debits represent increases in assets, and as a result there are very few situations in which it would be possible to have a credit balance in an asset account that would represent a negative asset.

Liability and owner's equity accounts are totaled and balanced in a similar manner. Normally these accounts have credit balances. The T account for Accounts Payable for Lisa's law firm follows:

Accounts Payable

4/30	Payment on account	190	4/1	Beginning balance	0
			4/4	Purchase of various supplies	380
			4/16	Purchase of typewriter	600
		190			980
			5/1	Beginning balance	790

The Bowman Law Firm Example

As noted, on April 1, 1987, Lisa organized her new law practice. April's transactions were discussed in the first part of this chapter. The balances on the April 30, 1987 balance sheet (shown on page 30) serve as the opening balances in the ledger accounts on May 1. Although Lisa acquired a number of clients during May, she did not perform any legal work during the month. She used most of the month to set up a new office and make needed preparations.

During the month of May, the following transactions took place:

- May 2: Lisa decided to devote herself full time to her practice. As a result, she decided to increase her investment in the firm and made an additional $164,000 cash investment.

- May 7: The law firm purchased a small building and land for $140,000. The land cost $20,000 and the building $120,000. The entire purchase was made in cash.
- May 10: One thousand dollars in cash was spent on office supplies.
- May 12: The law firm purchased a variety of office furniture and fixtures for $10,000; $5,000 was paid in cash and the remainder was borrowed from the bank.
- May 18: Lisa felt that the law firm needed a personal computer. The firm purchased one at a cost of $7,500. A 20% down payment of $1,500 was made; the remainder is on open account and is due within 30 days of the date of purchase.
- May 22: The firm purchased a comprehensive insurance policy for $2,400 cash. The policy covers a two-year period from June 1, 1987 to May 31, 1989.
- May 28: The firm made a $4,000 payment on its Accounts Payable.
- May 29: The remaining $35 for the typewriter sold in April was received.

Each of these transactions is analyzed from the standpoint of how they affect various accounts, and then they are entered in the appropriate ledger accounts. In thinking about how to record these transactions you should go through a three-step process:

1. Determine the specific accounts that are affected by the transactions and whether they are asset, liability, or owner's equity accounts.
2. Decide whether each account is increased or decreased.
3. Make the appropriate debit and credit entries in the specific ledger accounts.

Analysis of Transactions

1. Transaction on May 2—Bowman's $164,000 investment in the law practice.
   a. This transaction is an exchange of cash for the owner's investment in the business. Thus the two accounts affected are Cash and L. Bowman, Capital.
   b. Cash is increased by $164,000 and the owner's equity account, L. Bowman, Capital, is increased by the same $164,000.
   c. The increase in Cash is recorded on the left side of the Cash account and is a debit. The increase in the equity account, L. Bowman, Capital, is recorded on the right side of the account and is a credit.
   d. The T accounts are:

Cash		L. Bowman, Capital	
5/1 Bal. 655			5/1 Bal. 1,000
5/2 164,000			5/2 164,000

2. Transaction on May 7—Purchase of land and building for $140,000.
   a. The three accounts affected by this transaction are Cash, Land, and Buildings.
   b. The two asset accounts, Building and Land, are increased $120,000 and $20,000, respectively. The asset account, Cash, is decreased by the same $140,000. Because more than two accounts are involved, this is referred to as a compound transaction.
   c. The increase in the building and land accounts are recorded on the left side of these accounts and are debits. The decrease in cash is recorded on the right side of the cash account and is a credit.
   d. The T accounts are:

	Cash				Building			Land	
5/1 Bal.	655	5/7	140,000	5/7	120,000		5/7	20,000	
5/2	164,000								

3. Transaction on May 10—Purchase of $1,000 worth of office supplies for cash.
   a. The accounts affected by this transaction are Office Supplies and Cash.
   b. Office Supplies is increased by $1,000 and Cash is decreased by the same amount.
   c. The increase in office supplies is recorded on the left side of the Office Supplies account and is a debit. The decrease in cash is recorded on the right side of the Cash account and is a credit.
   d. The T accounts are:

	Cash				Office Supplies	
5/1 Bal.	655	5/7	140,000	5/1 Bal.	380	
5/2	164,000	5/10	1,000	5/10	1,000	

4. Transaction on May 12—Purchase of $10,000 of office furniture and fixtures for $5,000 cash and a bank loan of $5,000.
   a. This is a compound transaction that involves two asset accounts, Office Furniture and Fixtures and Cash, and one liability account, Bank Loan Payable.
   b. The asset account, Office Furniture and Fixtures, is increased, and the asset account, Cash, is decreased. In addition, the liability account, Bank Loan Payable, is increased.
   c. The increase in the asset account, Office Furniture and Fixtures, is recorded on the left side of the account and is a debit. The decrease in the Cash account is recorded on the right side of the account and is a credit. Finally, the increase in the liability account is recorded on the right side of that account and is a credit.
   d. The T accounts are:

	Cash				Office Furniture and Fixtures			Bank Loan Payable	
5/1 Bal.	655	5/7	140,000	5/12	10,000			5/12	5,000
5/2	164,000	5/10	1,000						
		5/12	5,000						

5. Transaction on May 18—Purchase of computer for $7,500 with $1,500 paid in cash and the remainder due within 30 days.
   a. This transaction involves Cash, Office Equipment, and Accounts Payable.
   b. The asset account, Office Equipment, is increased by $7,500 and the asset account, Cash, is decreased by $1,500. The liability account, Accounts Payable, is increased by $6,000.
   c. The increase in the Office Equipment account is recorded on the left side of the ledger account and is a debit. The decrease in Cash is recorded on the right side of the account and is a credit. The increase in the liability account, Accounts Payable, is recorded on the right side of the account and is a credit.
   d. The T accounts are:

Cash					Office Equipment			
5/1 Bal.	655	5/7	140,000		5/1 Bal.	600		
5/2	164,000	5/10	1,000		5/18	7,500		
		5/12	5,000					
		5/18	1,500					

Accounts Payable		
	5/1 Bal.	790
	5/18	6,000

6. Transaction on May 22—Purchase of a comprehensive insurance policy for $2,400 cash.

   a. The two accounts involved in this transaction are the asset account, Prepaid Insurance, and the asset account, Cash.
   b. The Prepaid Insurance account is increased and the Cash account is decreased.
   c. The increase in the Prepaid Insurance account is recorded on the left side of the ledger account and is a debit. The decrease in the Cash account is recorded on the right side of the ledger account and is a credit.
   d. The T accounts are:

Cash					Prepaid Insurance		
5/1 Bal.	655	5/7	140,000		5/22 2,400		
5/2	164,000	5/10	1,000				
		5/12	5,000				
		5/18	1,500				
		5/22	2,400				

7. Transaction on May 28—$4,000 partial payment of Accounts Payable.

   a. This transaction involves the asset account, Cash, and the liability account, Accounts Payable.
   b. The asset account, Cash, is decreased and the liability account, Accounts Payable, is decreased.
   c. The decrease in the Cash account is recorded on the right side of the ledger account and is a credit. The decrease in the Accounts Payable account is recorded on the left side of the account and is a debit.
   d. The T accounts are:

Cash					Accounts Payable			
5/1 Bal.	655	5/7	140,000		5/28 4,000	5/1 Bal.	790	
5/2	164,000	5/10	1,000			5/18	6,000	
		5/12	5,000					
		5/18	1,500					
		5/22	2,400					
		5/28	4,000					

8. Transaction on May 29—$35 payment received on Accounts Receivable.

   a. This transaction involves two asset accounts, Cash and Accounts Receivable.
   b. The Cash account is increased and the Accounts Receivable account is decreased.

c. The increase in the Cash account is recorded on the left side of the ledger account and is a debit. The decrease in the Accounts Receivable account is recorded on the right side of the ledger account and is a credit.

d. The T accounts are:

Cash		Accounts Receivable	
5/1 Bal. 655	5/7 140,000	5/1 Bal. 35	5/29 35
5/2 164,000	5/10 1,000		
5/29 35	5/12 5,000		
	5/18 1,500		
	5/22 2,400		
	5/28 4,000		

The Use of Ledger Accounts in Practice

Throughout this book we often use T accounts to represent ledger accounts. In practice, however, more sophisticated accounts forms are used. The cash ledger account for Lisa's law firm is illustrated below and is an example of what an actual running balance ledger account may look like the following.

Cash   **101**

Date 19 86	Item	Ref.	Debit	Credit	Balance Debit	Balance Credit
May 1		GJ–1	655 00		655 00	
2		GJ–1	164000 00		164655 00	
7		GJ–1		140000 00	24655 00	
10		GJ–1		1000 00	23655 00	
12		GJ–1		5000 00	18655 00	
18		GJ–1		1500 00	17155 00	
22		GJ–1		2400 00	14755 00	
28		GJ–1		4000 00	10755 00	
29		GJ–1	35 00		10790 00	
	Balance				10790 00	

This ledger account is designed for easy cross-reference to the journal where the original transaction is recorded. For example, the date column is used to record the date on which the actual transaction took place. The same date will appear in the journal. The description column is generally not used unless it is necessary to make an unusual notation. Ref. is the abbreviation for reference. This column is used to indicate the page number of the journal where the transaction was recorded. The debit and credit columns are used to record the respective entries, and the balance column is used to keep a running balance.

In a ledger book the accounts are arranged in normal balance sheet order, so assets are listed first, followed by liabilities and owner's equity. As we noted, each account is given a specific number for easy identification. The specific numbering system depends on the company's size and complexity.

Recording Transactions in the Journal

The use of journals and ledgers is interrelated. By first recording an entire transaction in the journal, all the specifics of the transaction are in one place and can be referred to at any future time. Remember that in a particular ledger account only part of the transaction is recorded.

Lisa Bowman's Law Firm
General Journal

GJ–1

Date	Account Titles	Ref.	Debit	Credit
1987				
May 2	Cash	101	164,000	
	L. Bowman, Capital	301		164,000
	To record investment by L. Bowman in her law practice.			
7	Land	150	20,000	
	Building	160	120,000	
	Cash	101		140,000
	To record purchase of land and building.			
10	Office Supplies	115	1,000	
	Cash	101		1,000
	To record purchase of office supplies.			
12	Office furniture and fixtures	165	10,000	
	Cash	101		5,000
	Bank Loan Payable	205		5,000
	To record purchase of furniture and fixtures for cash and loan.			
18	Office Equipment	167	7,500	
	Cash	101		1,500
	Accounts Payable	201		6,000
	To record purchase of office equipment.			
22	Prepaid Insurance	120	2,400	
	Cash	101		2,400
	To record purchase of prepaid insurance.			
28	Accounts Payable	201	4,000	
	Cash	101		4,000
	To record payment of cash on account.			
29	Cash	101	35	
	Accounts Receivable	106		35
	To record receipt of cash on account.			

The Use of the Journal

The transactions for Lisa Bowman's law firm for the month of May are recorded in the general journal above. Although there are a variety of different journals, we will use a standard two-column general journal. There are a number of points that need to be made regarding how these transactions are recorded:

1. The date column is used to record the date on which the transaction took place. For the first entry of each month, it is customary to record both the month and day. For subsequent entries, only the specific day of the month is recorded.

2. The explanation or account title column is used to record the journal entry. Accountants follow a number of conventions that simplify the use of the journal:

   a. Debits are always listed first, with the account title beginning at the extreme left margin of the explanation column.
   b. The credit portion of the entry is then recorded, indented slightly.
   c. If the transaction is a compound entry involving more than two accounts, all the debits are recorded before the credits. The entry on May 7 is an example of a compound entry.
   d. The dollar amounts are put into their respective debit and credit columns on the same line as the account titles.
   e. Because a general journal is used for a number of different types of transactions, accountants generally write a short explanation under the entry. This makes it easier to understand the transaction if it is referred to again.

3. The Ref. (reference) column is used to cross-reference the journal to the ledger. The ledger account number to which the entry is posted is placed in this column at the time the entry is posted to the ledger accounts. (See the chart of accounts on page 33 for the account number used.)

Posting to the Ledger

After transactions are entered into the journal, they are then recorded in the specific ledger accounts. This is referred to as **posting.** The size of the company and the number of entries usually determine how often entries are posted to the ledger. Posting can take place daily, semimonthly, monthly, or even yearly. If a computer is used to record transactions, the postings can be made instantaneously. Most of the examples and problem material in this book assume that entries are posted either monthly or yearly.

There are several things to remember about posting that will help you reduce errors. Each entry should be posted in its entirety, one at a time. Using the entry on May 2 as an example, first post the debit to the Cash account and then the credit to the Capital account before going on to the next entry. If you have account numbers, as in this example, place them in the reference column in the journal on the line of the account that you posted. If you are not using account numbers, place a check mark in this column. These will indicate to you that you have posted both the debit and the credit parts of the entry. In addition, the page number of the journal in which the entry was recorded should be placed in the reference column of the ledger account. If T accounts are used, just the date or number of the transaction should be placed beside the dollar entry in the T account.

For illustrative purposes the journal entry on May 10 is posted to the appropriate ledger in Exhibit 2–3. After all of the accounts for the month have been posted, the ledger accounts for Lisa Bowman's law firm will appear as they are pictured in Exhibit 2–4 beginning on page 46.

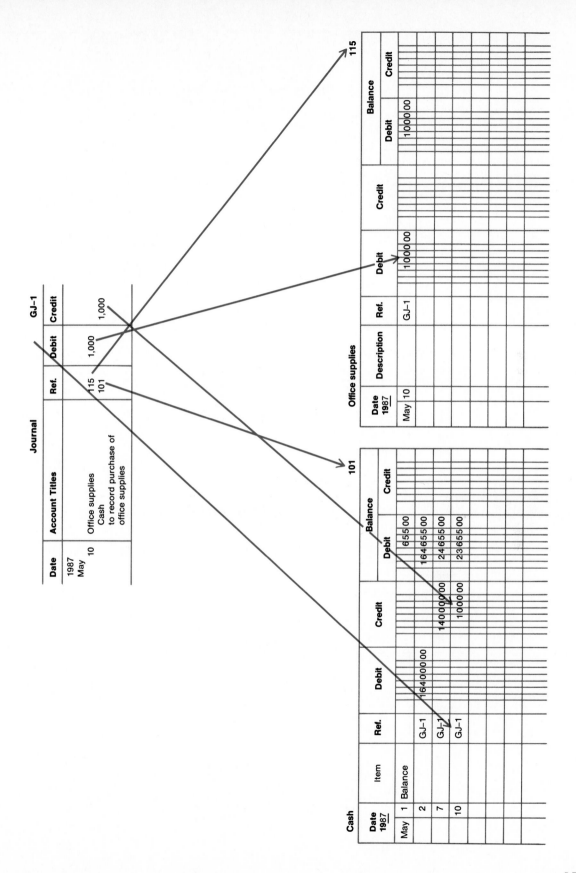

45

EXHIBIT 2–4
Lisa Bowman's Law Firm
Ledger Accounts

Cash   101

Date	Item	Ref.	Debit	Credit	Balance Debit	Balance Credit
1987						
May 1	Beg. Bal.				655	
2		GJ-1	164,000		164,655	
7		GJ-1		140,000	24,655	
10		GJ-1		1,000	23,655	
12		GJ-1		5,000	18,655	
18		GJ-1		1,500	17,155	
22		GJ-1		2,400	14,755	
28		GJ-1		4,000	10,755	
29		GJ-1	35		10,790	

Accounts Receivable   106

Date	Item	Ref.	Debit	Credit	Balance Debit	Balance Credit
1987						
May 1	Beg. Bal.				35	
29		GJ-1		35	0	

Office Supplies   115

Date	Item	Ref.	Debit	Credit	Balance Debit	Balance Credit
1987						
May 1	Beg. Bal.				380	
10		GJ-1	1,000		1,380	

Prepaid Insurance   120

Date	Item	Ref.	Debit	Credit	Balance Debit	Balance Credit
1987						
May 22		GJ-1	2,400		2,400	

License   121

Date	Item	Ref.	Debit	Credit	Balance Debit	Balance Credit
1987						
May 1	Beg. Bal.				120	

Land   150

Date	Item	Ref.	Debit	Credit	Balance Debit	Balance Credit
1987 May 7		GJ-1	20,000		20,000	

Building   160

Date	Item	Ref.	Debit	Credit	Balance Debit	Balance Credit
1987 May 7		GJ-1	120,000		120,000	

Office Furniture and Fixtures   165

Date	Item	Ref.	Debit	Credit	Balance Debit	Balance Credit
1987 May 12		GJ-1	10,000		10,000	

Office Equipment   167

Date	Item	Ref.	Debit	Credit	Balance Debit	Balance Credit
1987 May 1	Beg. Bal.				600	
18		GJ-1	7,500		8,100	

Accounts Payable   201

Date	Item	Ref.	Debit	Credit	Balance Debit	Balance Credit
1987 May 1	Beg. Bal.					790
18		GJ-1		6,000		6,790
28		GJ-1	4,000			2,790

Bank Loan Payable   205

Date	Item	Ref.	Debit	Credit	Balance Debit	Balance Credit
1987 May 12		GJ-1		5,000		5,000

L. Bowman, Capital   301

Date	Item	Ref.	Debit	Credit	Balance Debit	Balance Credit
1987 May 1	Beg. Bal.					1,000
2		GJ-1		164,000		165,000

The **trial balance** is a list of the accounts in the general ledger with their respective debit and credit balances. It is the third step in the accounting cycle and is constructed after the transactions for the accounting period are posted to the ledger accounts and these accounts have been balanced. Accounts in the trial balance are listed in the same order as they are found in the general ledger. The trial balance is a check to see whether equal amounts of debits and credits have been posted to the ledger accounts during the period. If this is the case and all accounts have been correctly balanced, then the trial balance will be in balance. That is, the dollar amount of the debits will equal the dollar amount of the credits.

The trial balance for Lisa Bowman's law firm at May 31 is shown below. In this trial balance, the Accounts Receivable account is not listed because it has a zero balance. It is important to understand the uses of a trial balance. If the trial balance is in balance, this will tell you that (1) the same dollar amount of debits and credits have been posted and (2) the accounts have been correctly balanced. However, the trial balance will not tell you that each entry has been posted to the correct account. For example, assume that in the entry on May 10, you mistakenly posted the $1,000 debit to Office Supplies to Office Equipment instead. Because both Office Supplies and Office Equipment are asset accounts, the incorrect debit to the Office Equipment account will not be picked up in the trial balance. This is because the Office Supplies account will be understated by $1,000, but the Office Equipment account will be overstated by the same $1,000. The errors would, in effect, cancel each other in the accounting equation.

Lisa Bowman's Law Firm
Trial Balance
May 31, 1987

Accounts	Debits	Credits
Cash	$ 10,790	
Office supplies	1,380	
Prepaid insurance	2,400	
License	120	
Land	20,000	
Building	120,000	
Office furniture and fixtures	10,000	
Office equipment	8,100	
Accounts payable		$ 2,790
Bank loan payable		5,000
L. Bowman, capital		165,000
Totals	$172,790	$172,790

Errors in the Trial Balance

There are a number of reasons that the total of the debits may not equal the total of the credits. Some of the more common errors that may occur in the trial balance are:

1. There simply may be an addition error in totaling the debit or credit column of the trial balance.
2. A debit may have been posted as a credit or vice versa. If this occurs, the difference between the total of the debits and credits will be twice the amount of the misposted entry. For example, if the debit of $1,000 in the Office Supplies account was posted as a credit, the total of the debits would be $171,790 and the total of the credits would be $173,790. The difference is $2,000, or twice the $1,000 error. Therefore, the way to locate this type of error is to divide the difference between the total of the debits and the credits by two and see if this number is a debit that has been posted as a credit or vice versa.
3. Part of an entry may not have been posted. For example, you may have posted the debit to Prepaid Insurance in the May 22, 1987 entry but forgot to post the credit to the Cash account. If that had happened, the total of debits would equal $175,190 and the total of the credits would equal $172,790. The difference of $2,400 is the entry that was not posted.
4. You may have misposted a dollar amount. The two most common errors of this type are transpositions and misplaced decimal points. An example of a transposition error is posting $56 as $65 or $780 as $870. If a transposition occurs, the resulting error will be divisible evenly by 9. For example, if $780 was posted as $870, the difference is $90, which is divisible by 9. Misplacing a decimal point occurs, for example, when $90 is posted as $900 or $100 is posted as $10. Such errors also result in differences in debit and credit totals that are divisible by 9.
5. Other errors in the trial balance occur when ledger accounts are incorrectly totaled or when an incorrect amount is transferred to the trial balance from a ledger account, for example, incorrectly copying the balance of $8,100 in the Office Equipment account as $8,700.

Checking for Errors

The best way to avoid errors in the trial balance is to work slowly and carefully when you are journalizing and posting. Errors inevitably occur, however. When the totals do not balance, first check to see whether you have correctly added the debit and credit columns of the trial balance. The next step is to analyze the difference in the totals of the debit and credit columns, using the techniques just described, to try to locate errors. If you still cannot locate the error, check to make sure the debits and credits for each account in the trial balance are the same as the balances in the ledger account. The next step is to recompute the balances in the ledger accounts. If you are still unable to locate your error, put your work down for a while and do something else. Then, at a later time, resume your work, and you will probably find your error quickly.

Summary of Learning Objectives

1. *How accounting functions as an information system.* Accounting is a system designed to provide certain information about economic entities.

It is made up of three parts: (1) inputs, (2) transformation process, and (3) outputs. Raw economic data are admitted into the accounting system where they are stored and classified during the transformation process in order to produce the outputs of the accounting system, financial reports for management and for external users.

2. *The characteristics of information admitted to the accounting system.* For data to be an input of the accounting system, they must:

   a. Be a transaction or event for the specified business entity for which the accounting system exists.

   b. Be measurable in monetary terms.

   c. Be verifiable.

   Economic events take place continually, and accountants must decide when to recognize and record them in the accounting system. Thus, for example, sales are not recorded until title passes from the seller to the buyer.

3. *Effects of transactions on the accounting equation.* All of the economic events that qualify as inputs for the accounting system can affect one or more of the three parts of the accounting equation. The purchase of assets for cash, for example, affects assets only, whereas the purchase of assets on account affects both assets and liabilities. Similarly, transactions that result in the receipt of cash owed by others to the firm affect only asset accounts, but the payment of a liability affects assets and liabilities. All transactions affect at least two accounts, that is, two assets, assets and liabilities, assets and owner's equity, two liabilities, or liabilities and owner's equity.

4. *The components of the accounting system.* The journal and ledger are the two primary components of the accounting system. The journal lists all transactions in the order in which they occur. At specified intervals these transactions are posted to the appropriate account in the ledger. A ledger, whether maintained by computer or manually, simply is an accumulation of all of the accounts the company has in its chart of accounts. The specific accounts used by a firm depend on the nature, size, and complexity of the business.

5. *Recording accounting transactions in the journal and ledger.* The following T accounts summarize the rules for recording changes in the balance sheet accounts:

Assets		Equities (Liabilities and Owner's Equity)	
Increases	Decreases	Decreases	Increases
+	−	−	+
Debits	Credits	Debits	Credits
Normal balance: debit			Normal balance: credit

6. *The preparation and use of a trial balance.* A trial balance is usually prepared after transactions are posted from the journal to the ledger. It lists the dollar balances of every general ledger account. If the trial balance is in balance, this will tell you that equal dollar amounts of debits and credits have been posted and that the accounts are correctly balanced. Errors still can occur, however, if the incorrect accounts have been debited or credited.

Problem for Your Review

On January 2, 1987, Bonnie Brinkley decides to open her own real estate agency, BB's Fine Properties. The following events occur during the month of January:

- January 2: Bonnie invests $100,000 cash in the business.
- January 10: The agency purchases a small building, including land, for $60,000 cash. The land has a value of $10,000, and the building a value of $50,000.
- January 15: A variety of furniture and fixtures are bought for $10,000. The agency is able to finance the purchase through a one-year bank loan.
- January 21: Various office supplies totaling $5,000 are purchased on account.
- January 30: The firm pays $3,500 on the account payable incurred on January 21.

Required:

1. Record the transactions in the general journal.
2. Post the transactions to the appropriate T accounts.
3. Prepare a trial balance at January 31.
4. Prepare a balance sheet at January 31.

Solution

1. Journal Entries

GENERAL JOURNAL   GJ–1

Date	Account Titles	Ref.	Debit	Credit
1986 January				
2	Cash		100,000	
	B. Brinkley, Capital			100,000
	To record investment by B. Brinkley.			
10	Land		10,000	
	Building		50,000	
	Cash			60,000
	To record purchase of land and building for $60,000.			
15	Furniture and fixtures		10,000	
	Bank loan payable			10,000
	To record purchase of furniture and fixtures through bank loan.			
21	Office Supplies		5,000	
	Accounts payable			5,000
	To record purchase of various office supplies on account.			
30	Accounts payable		3,500	
	Cash			3,500
	To record payment on account.			

2. T Accounts

Cash		
1/2　　100,000	1/10　60,000	
	1/30　　3,500	
1/31 Bal. 36,500		

Office Supplies	
1/21　5,000	

Furniture and Fixtures	
1/15　10,000	

Land	
1/10　10,000	

Building	
1/10　50,000	

Accounts Payable		
1/30　3,500	1/21　　　5,000	
	1/31 Bal. 1,500	

Bank Loan Payable	
	1/15　10,000

B. Brinkley, Capital	
	1/2 100,000

3. Trial Balance

BB's Fine Properties
Trial Balance
January 31, 1987

Accounts	Debit	Credit
Cash	$ 36,500	
Office supplies	5,000	
Furniture and fixtures	10,000	
Land	10,000	
Building	50,000	
Accounts payable		$ 1,500
Bank loan payable		10,000
B. Brinkley, Capital		100,000
Totals	$111,500	$111,500

4. Balance Sheet

BB's Fine Properties
Balance Sheet
January 31, 1987

Assets		Liabilities and Owner's Equity	
Cash	$ 36,500	Liabilities:	
Office supplies	5,000	Accounts payable	$ 1,500
Furniture and fixtures	10,000	Bank loan payable	10,000
Land	10,000	Total liabilities	11,500
Building	50,000		
		Owner's equity:	
		B. Brinkley, Capital	100,000
		Total liabilities and	
Total assets	$111,500	owner's equity	$111,500

Questions

1. What are the major parts of the accounting information system?

2. Explain what factors determine whether an event or transaction will be recognized as an input of the accounting system.

3. On January 20 the Gilbert Company enters into a contract to sell 100 dozen footballs to the University of California. The footballs are delivered on February 10 and February 15. The Gilbert Company receives full payment from the university on February 21. Which events are recognized in the accounting records of Gilbert and the University of California? Why?

4. Define the major components of an accounting system.

5. What is a chart of accounts? How might a chart of accounts for Carl's Market differ from that of Ohman and Rattan, attorneys?

6. Explain to your good friend, who has no knowledge of accounting, the purpose of a ledger and a journal and how they are related.

7. Complete the following chart by entering either increases or decreases on the appropriate line:

Account	Ledger Side	
	Left	Right
Assets		
Liabilities		
Owner's Equity		

8. You overheard one of your friends telling another person that all credits must be good because every time she deposits money in the bank, she gets a credit memo. Is her reasoning correct? If not, explain the meaning of *credit* in accounting.

9. For any transaction, the total of debits must equal credits. Why?

10. Complete the following chart by entering either debit or credit on the appropriate line:

Account	Increase	Decrease
Accounts receivable		
Accounts payable		
Cash		
Office supplies		
Wages payable		
L. Jones, capital		

11. What is a compound journal entry?

12. Why is it necessary to post journal entries to ledger accounts? What determines how often postings are made?

13. How do T accounts differ from the running balance ledger accounts illustrated in the text?

14. Complete the following chart by indicating whether each account is an asset, liability, or owner's equity account and its normal balance (either debit or credit):

Account	Type of Account	Normal Balance
Accounts payable		
Buildings		
Cash		
Taxes payable		
Prepaid rent		
Land		
L. Arnold, capital		

15. Put the following six items into chronological order:

    a. Enter transaction in journal.

    b. Business event occurs.

    c. Prepare trial balance.

    d. Post entries to ledger.

    e. Balance ledger accounts.

    f. Prepare balance sheet.

16. One of your accounting classmates, after spending several hours doing her accounting homework, was able to balance the trial balance. Convinced her homework must be correct, she went to bed. Should she be as confident as she is?

17. The debit and credit columns of a trial balance are not equal. What could be some of the causes for this problem?

18. What is a balance sheet, and what does it show?

19. How are accounts listed on a typical balance sheet?

20. Explain the four transactions that appear in the following T accounts:

Cash		Prepaid Insurance	
[1]100,000	40,000[2]	[3]5,000	
	5,000[3]		
	10,000[4]		

Land		Bank Loan Payable	
[2]60,000		[4]10,000	20,000[2]

L. Bean, Capital	
	100,000[1]

Exercises

1. Recognition of Inputs. John Brown started his own legal practice on January 2 of the current year. Which of the following events and transactions would be recognized as an input of the accounting system for his business?

    a. John invests $40,000 of his own money in the firm.

    b. John received $1,500 vacation pay from his previous law firm. He deposits the money in his own account.

    c. John has a computer that he purchased with personal funds. He gives the computer to his new law firm.

    d. The law firm purchases $2,500 of supplies to be paid in February. The supplies were received immediately.

    e. The law firm purchases several items of office equipment for $15,000. These purchases are financed by a local bank. Because John's law firm is new, the bank insists that John personally guarantee the loan.

2. The Accounting Equation. At the beginning of January of the current year, the Petini Association started out with total assets of $50,000. During January the firm entered into a number of transactions. State whether each of the transactions increased total assets, decreased total assets, or had no effect on total assets. Also determine the amount of total assets at the end of January.

    a. The firm purchased office supplies with a total cost of $5,000 for cash.

    b. The firm purchased a computer for office use for $10,000. It paid $4,000 in cash and borrowed the rest from a local bank.

    c. The firm was in need of additional cash and as a result the owner, J. Petini, invested an additional $50,000 cash in the firm.

    d. A business license that allowed the firm to operate within the city for the rest of the year was purchased for $500 cash.

    e. A three-year insurance policy was purchased on account. The policy cost $3,600 and took effect immediately.

    f. The owner of the business withdrew $500 of the original investment she made.

3. Analyzing Transactions. The Midway Company entered into a number of transactions during the month. State the effect each transaction had on total assets, liabilities, and owner's equity. If the effect is positive use a plus sign, if negative a negative sign, and if no effect put NE. Using the following form:

Transaction	Assets	Liabilities	Owner's Equity

Transactions during the month:

    a. Midway paid a liability.

    b. The firm purchased some stationery on account.

    c. The owner invested cash in the business.

    d. The firm collected $1,000 on an account receivable.

    e. The owner contributed a plot of land to the business.

    f. Midway purchased a building by paying cash and issuing a note payable.

    g. Midway had an account payable to the Smith Co. The Smith Co. agreed to increase the payment period and take a note payable in exchange for the account payable.

    h. Midway paid for a year's rent in advance.

Example:

Transaction	Assets	Liabilities	Owner's Equity
a	–	–	NE

4. Economic Transactions and the Entity Assumption. Indicate whether the following transactions of the Main Construction Company would increase, decrease, or have no effect on the company's total assets, liabilities, and owner's equity. Use + for increase, – for decrease, and NE for no effect. It may be that in some cases none of the accounts are affected. Refer to the table below, which is completed for the first transaction.

Transaction	Assets	Liabilities	Owner's Equity
a	+	+	NE

Transactions:

a. The firm purchased land for $100,000, $20,000 of which was paid in cash and a note payable signed for the balance.

b. The firm bought equipment for $40,000 on credit.

c. The firm paid a $15,000 liability.

d. The firm arranged for a $100,000 line of credit (the right to borrow funds as needed) from the bank. No funds had yet been borrowed.

e. The owner desired to make an additional investment in the company and arranged a $20,000 personal bank loan.

f. The firm borrowed $45,000 on its line of credit.

g. The owner in Item e invested the $20,000 in the company.

5. Analyzing Transactions. In this chapter we stated that in thinking about how to record transactions, you should go through this three-step process:

1. Determine the specific accounts that are affected.
2. Decide whether each account is increased or decreased.
3. Make the appropriate debit and credit entries in the ledger account.

For each of the following six transactions make the above analysis. Item a is done for you as an example.

a. Mr. Frazer invested $25,000 cash in the business.

b. The firm purchases some equipment for $10,000 cash.

c. Supplies worth $5,000 are purchased on account.

d. A month's rent of $1,000 is paid in advance.

e. Some of the equipment purchased in Item b at a cost of $2,000 was sold at its cost for cash.

f. Accounts Payable of $2,400 were paid.

Example (a):

1. This transaction involves an exhange of cash for a capital interest.
2. Cash is increased by $25,000 and J. Frazer, Capital is increased by $25,000.
3. The T accounts.

Cash		J. Frazer, Capital	
[a]25,000			25,000[a]

6. Recognizing Accounting Events. Crystal Kingdom, owner of Crystal Kingdom's Funland, has asked you to review the following transactions. For each event, state whether the transaction should be recorded on the books of the company, and state why.

- January 2: The firm places an order for 3 video games and 2 pinball machines at a cost of $1,300 each. The machines will be delivered next month.
- January 5: Three days later, Funland sends a deposit of $2,000 for the machines.
- February 1: The machines are delivered and Funland receives an invoice for the balance.
- February 10: As she does each business day, one of Crystal's daughters, Rainbow, goes to the local bank and exchanges $200 cash for the same amount of quarters.
- February 12: The balance due on the machines is paid.
- February 20: The demand to play video games has far surpassed anyone's expectations. As a result, Funland has negotiated a line of credit to expand the business. The line of credit allows Funland to borrow up to $100,000 as the funds are needed. As of this date, the line of credit has not been used.

7. Making Entries in T Accounts. Enter the following transactions in the appropriate T accounts. Label each transaction with the date it occurred. Balance the T accounts.

- February 1: Lewis started a CPA firm by investing $50,000 cash in the business.
- February 2: The firm rented an office and had to make a deposit of $1,500 which represented one month's rent. They will move in March.
- February 10: Supplies of $2,000 were purchased on account.
- February 15: A word processor was purchased. The cost was $2,500, of which $500 was paid in cash and the remainder was borrowed from the bank. Use the account Bank Loan Payable.
- February 22: The account payable that resulted from the purchase of supplies was paid.

8. Recognition of Accounts and Debits and Credits. Indicate whether each of the following accounts is an asset, liability, or owner's equity and whether the normal balance is a debit or credit. Arrange your answers by duplicating the following table:

Account	Type of Account	Normal Balance
a. Cash		
b. Prepaid rent		
c. Wages payable		
d. E. Weiss, Capital		
e. Land		
f. Equipment		
g. Advances received from customers		
h. Investment in ABC Corporation		
i. Patent		
j. Accounts receivable		

9. Journal Entries. J. J. Jay III has decided to open a car wash to offset his tuition to business school. Help J. J. get started by recording his first two months' transactions in his general journal. Make the appropriate explanation after each entry.

a. His three cousins, J. P., Andy, and Mary, each lent the firm $2,000 on July 1.
b. J. J. purchased an abandoned car wash for $3,000 cash on July 15.
c. On August 1, the business paid $200 for his local car wash license.
d. On August 1, the car wash also bought supplies for $760 on account.
e. After being sued in small claims court on August 15, J. J. paid $900 to buy his first customer's car since the windows were left down when it was washed. The car will be used in the business.

10. Posting to the Ledger. Post the entries that you made in Exercise 9 to the appropriate T accounts.

11. Analysis of the Accounting Equation. You have obtained the following data from the Lite Company as of December 31, 1987. However, certain figures were smeared by the duplicating machine and you are to determine the missing figures.

Lite Company	
Accounts payable	$15,630
Accounts receivable	?
Bank loan payable	6,000
Buildings	15,000
Cash	28,725
Investment in Ford Co.	14,800
Land	5,000
Licenses	225
Office supplies	1,280
Other assets	200
Prepaid insurance	2,400
Store furniture and fixtures	13,800
Total assets	91,630
Total liabilities	?
Total owner's equity	?

12. Journal Entries and Posting. Computer Calisthenics Company began business on March 1 of the current year. During the month the firm entered into the following transactions:

- March 1: The owner, M. Lasson, invested $100,000 in the business.
- March 2: Arranged a $50,000 cash loan from a local bank. The cash was immediately received.
- March 10: Purchased a small building on a downtown corner for $80,000 cash.
- March 16: Purchased various types of exercise equipment for $20,000 on account.
- March 20: Placed an order for $2,000 of various office supplies including stationery. Made a $200 deposit. All supplies will be received next month.
- March 25: Paid for equipment purchased on March 16.
- March 30: Purchased a 3-year comprehensive insurance policy for $1,500.

Required:
   a. Make the required journal entries.
   b. Create T accounts for each account and post the journal entries to the ledger accounts.

13. Correcting Errors. Some of the following journal entries are incorrect or contain missing data. Make the complete correct journal entry for each item where appropriate. (Note: Dr. = debit, Cr. = credit.)

a. Dr.
   Cr. Accounts Receivable   4,327
   To record payment received from customer on account.

b. Prepaid Rent   2,639
      Cash   2,639
   To record prepayment of rent.

c. Cash   50
      Office Supplies   50
   To record purchase of office supplies for cash.

d. Land   15,000
   Bank Loan Payable   10,000
      Cash   5,000
   To record purchase of land costing $15,000. $5,000 paid in cash, the remainder borrowed from bank.

14. Trial Balance and Effect of Errors. Which of the following posting errors would cause the debit and credit columns of the trial balance not to balance? Briefly explain your reasoning.
   a. A receipt of cash from a payment on account was posted by debiting Cash for $2,500 and crediting Accounts Receivable for $25,000.
   b. A purchase of equipment on account was posted by debiting Equipment for $1,000 and crediting Cash for $1,000.

c. When the following journal entry was posted, the debit to Accounts Payable was left out by mistake:

Accounts Payable	1,200	
Cash		1,200

d. The purchase of supplies for cash was posted as a debit to Cash and credit to Supplies for $500, respectively.

e. When the following journal was posted, the debit to Cash was actually posted as a credit:

Cash	10,000	
E. Cobb, Capital		10,000

15. Correcting Errors in the Trial Balance and Preparation of a Balance Sheet. The accountant for LFN is having trouble balancing the trial balance and asks your help. You have obtained the following trial balance as well as the additional data:

LFN
Trial Balance
December 31, 1987

Accounts	Debit	Credit
Cash	$ 5,000	
Marketable securities	1,500	
Accounts receivable	15,000	
Office supplies	2,000	
Prepaid rent	2,000	
Land	20,000	
Buildings	45,000	
Other assets		$ 5,000
Bank loans payable		10,000
Accounts payable		6,320
Mortgages payable		30,000
L. North, Capital		45,900
Totals	$90,500	$97,220

Additional Information:
a. A purchase of marketable securities for $500 was not posted to the account.
b. A cash payment on account of $570 was posted to Accounts Payable as a debit of $750. The credit was correctly posted.
c. The Prepaid Rent ledger account was footed incorrectly and overstated by $200.
d. When office supplies were purchased for $100, a credit was posted in that amount to the Office Supplies account, as well as the credit to the Cash account.
e. Although the Capital account was correctly footed in the ledger account as $49,500, it was listed in the trial balance as $45,900.

Required:
a. Prepare a corrected trial balance.
b. Prepare a balance sheet.

Problem Set A

2A–1. The Accounting Equation and Economic Transactions. At December 31, 1987 the Last In, First Out Hamburger Store had the following account balances:

Loans
Cash + Receivable + Supplies + Equipment =
$4,000 $3,500 $1,500 $7,000
Accounts Payable + Notes Payable + Owner's Equity
$5,000 $2,000 $9,000

During January 1988 the following events occurred:
  a. Supplies were purchased for $3,000; $1,000 on credit and the rest for cash.
  b. The amount of $2,500 was collected on loans receivable.
  c. The owner of the business contributed a new word processor with a cost of $1,500 to the firm.
  d. One of the old typewriters was sold for its original cost of $700, of which $200 was received in cash and the remainder on account. (Use the Loans Receivable account.)
  e. Accounts payable of $3,000 were paid.
  f. An installment payment of $500 was made on the note payable.
  g. The remainder due on the sale of the typewriter was collected.

Required:
Prepare a table similar to the one on page 30 showing the accounts and their balances at December 31 as column headings. Use a separate line on the table to show the effects of each transaction on the accounting equation. Total all columns after each transaction.

2A–2. Understanding Transactions. The balance sheet of Red's Repair Store at December 31, 1987 is shown below in equation form followed by January transactions, whose effects on the accounting equation are also shown.

Cash	+	Accounts Receivable	+	Supplies	+	Equipment	=	Accounts Payable	+	Owner's Equity
$4,000		$6,000		$1,200		$10,000		$4,500		$16,700
1. +4,000		−4,000								
8,000		2,000		1,200		10,000		4,500		16,700
2. −3,000						+3,000				
5,000		2,000		1,200		13,000		4,500		16,700
3.				−500				−500		
5,000		2,000		700		13,000		4,000		16,700
4. −2,000								−2,000		
3,000		2,000		700		13,000		2,000		16,700
5. +1,500						−1,500				
4,500		2,000		700		11,500		2,000		16,700
6. +3,000										+3,000
$7,500		$2,000		$ 700		$11,500		$2,000		$19,700

Required:
  a. Describe the nature of each of the numbered transactions that would produce the effect shown on the table.
  b. Determine the amount of net assets (assets minus liabilities or owner's equity) at the end of December and at the end of January after all the transactions have been recorded. How much have they increased or decreased? Can you determine the reason for the change?

2A–3. Recording Transactions. Alan Berg decided on the first of January 1987 to start a computer learning store called the Learning Circuit. The following transactions took place during the start-up month of January:
  1. Alan invested $75,000 cash in his business.
  2. The firm purchased a small store for $100,000. The firm made a $40,000 cash down payment and borrowed the rest from a bank.

Accounting as an Information System   59

3. Display racks and tables were purchased for $8,000 cash.
4. Computer equipment with a cost of $18,000 was purchased on account.
5. A good friend of Alan's lent the firm $20,000 for needed start-up money.
6. Five thousand dollars was paid to the suppliers of the computer equipment purchased in Transaction 4.
7. Five hundred dollars of computer equipment purchased in Transaction 4 was damaged when it arrived. The firm sent it back and received a reduction on the amount owed on its account.
8. The first installment of $10,000 was paid on the bank loan. Ignore interest at this time.
9. Some of the original display racks were replaced with sturdier models: (a) New racks with a cost of $5,000 were purchased for cash, and (b) two of the old racks with a cost of $2,000 were sold for $2,000 on account.

Required:

Prepare a table similar to the one on page 30 using the following accounts as column headings: Cash, Accounts Receivable, Store Equipment, Computer Equipment, Accounts Payable, Loans Payable, and A. Berg, Capital. Show the effect of each transaction on the accounting equation. It is not necessary to give totals after each transaction.

2A–4. Analysis of Transactions. A number of transactions for Murphy's Milk and Yogurt Shop are described below.

Required:

a. Complete the following chart by putting the amounts in the proper columns. Note that the increase/decrease columns are not necessarily intended to be in a debit/credit relationship.
b. Make the appropriate journal entries.

	Asset		Liability		Owner's Equity	
Transaction	Increase	Decrease	Increase	Decrease	Increase	Decrease
a. Purchase equipment costing $10,000 with a bank loan.						
b. Receive cash of $2,500 from Accounts Receivable.						
c. Receive cash of $20,000 from Murphy as investment in business.						
d. Receive equipment with a value of $5,000 from owner as additional investment in the business.						
e. Order supplies with a cost of $400 on account.						
f. Make a $300 payment on account.						

2A–5. Analysis of T Accounts. The T accounts for Melissa's Ballet Studio follow. These accounts reflect all the transactions for November. The firm was organized on November 1 of the current year.

Cash		Accounts Receivable		Equipment	
[1]100,000	3,600[3]	[7]2,000	2,000[10]	[11]5,000	
[10]2,000	10,000[4]				
	240[5]				
	400[9]				

Prepaid Insurance		License		Office Supplies	
[3]3,600		[5]240		[6]1,000	

Land	Buildings	Furniture and Fixtures
^{2}20,000		^{2}40,000		^{4}10,000 $\quad$ 2,000^7
		^{8}3,500	

Accounts Payable	Mortgage Payable	M. Tinker, Capital
^{9}400 $\quad$ 1,000^6	$\quad$ 60,000^2	$\quad$ 100,000^1
$\qquad$ 5,000^{11}		$\qquad$ 3,500^8

Required:

    a. For each of the numbered transactions (1 through 11), make the appropriate journal entry including a complete explanation of the transaction.

    b. Determine the balances of the T accounts and prepare a trial balance.

2A–6. Journal Entries, Ledger Accounts, and the Trial Balance. Will Miller decided to go into CPA practice for himself after three years' experience with another firm. The following events occurred in September, the date he organized his business:

    • September 1: Will began his practice with $70,000. A local bank supplied a loan to the practice for half of the $70,000 and Will invested the remaining $35,000 from his personal funds.

    • September 3: Will rented a small office for this practice. In accordance with the rental agreement, the firm prepaid the first 6 months at $2,100 per month.

    • September 10: Various typewriters, calculators, and other office equipment were purchased for $7,500 on account from a local supplier. (Record all items in the Office Equipment account.)

    • September 14: A 2-year liability insurance policy with a cost of $4,000 was purchased for cash.

    • September 18: One of the typewriters which cost $1,500 arrived damaged. It was returned to the supplier and the firm received a credit.

    • September 24: Purchased various pieces of office furniture at a cost of $4,000. All items were paid in cash.

    • September 29: Paid the remainder of the balance on the purchase of office equipment.

    • September 30: Will hired a part-time secretary who will begin work October 1. The secretary's monthly wages will be $800.

Required:

    a. Make the required journal entries.

    b. Set up the required ledger accounts and post the entries to these accounts.

    c. Prepare a trial balance at September 30.

2A–7. Journal Entries, Ledger Accounts, and the Trial Balance. Sumi Kuramoto decided to open a children's day care center called A Place for Children. The business was organized in January and during that month the following transactions occurred:

    • January 2: Sumi invested $40,000 of her own funds in the business.

    • January 3: Five of her good friends each lent $5,000 to the business and the firm issued notes in exchange.

    • January 6: The business purchased land and a small building. The total cost was $75,000 of which two-thirds was applicable to the building and one-third to the land. A 20% down payment was made and a bank loan was taken out for the remainder.

    • January 11: The building appeared to be too small for anticipated operations. The firm contracted with a local builder to add a new wing at a cost of $40,000. The work will begin next month, and the first cash payment is due February 15.

    • January 16: The firm purchased various toys to be used by the children in the day care center. They cost $2,000 and were purchased on account. The account, Toy Supplies, should be used to record this purchase.

- January 19: Various pieces of children's furniture were purchased for $15,000 cash.
- January 23: The toys purchased on January 16 were paid for in full.
- January 24: Sumi decided that she could not use one of the pieces of furniture which cost $1,000. The firm sold it to one of her friends on account for that amount.
- January 29: Office supplies of $1,200 were purchased on account.
- January 30: Her friend paid the firm for one-half of the furniture purchased on January 24.

Sumi has decided to use the following account titles and account numbers in the business:

Cash	10	Building	22
Accounts Receivable	12	Children's Furniture	24
Toy Supplies	15	Bank Loan Payable	30
Office Supplies	18	Notes Payable	31
Land	20	Accounts Payable	32
		S. Kuramoto, Capital	40

Required:

a. Make the required journal entries for January.

b. Post these entries to ledger accounts, using the running balance type shown in the text.

c. Prepare a trial balance at January 31.

2A–8. T Account Analysis. Berkeley Bizarre Shoes and Clothing, a West Coast regional firm, has the following T accounts in its general ledger. (Note that BB indicates beginning balance.)

Cash

BB	6,500	6/8	5,200
6/3	2,000	6/15	2,500
6/10	15,500	6/17	2,000
6/30	19,240	6/20	4,000
		6/28	2,700
		6/30	6,222

Accounts Payable

6/28	2,700	BB	4,200
		6/25	3,570

Store Furniture

BB	61,252	
6/8	5,200	
6/25	3,570	

Loan Payable

6/15	2,500	BB	55,000

Prepaid Rent

BB	2,000	
6/17	2,000	

Accounts Receivable

BB	3,110	6/3	2,000

Building

BB	142,000	
6/6	8,000	

Taxes Payable

6/20	4,000	BB	9,240

K. C., Capital

		BB	130,060
		6/10	15,500
		6/30	19,240

Note Payable

	BB	12,250
	6/6	8,000

Other Assets

BB 2,110	

Wages Payable

6/30	6,222	BB	6,222

Provide the following:

1. Ending balance of each account.
2. Beginning balance of assets.
3. Net change in the Cash account for June.
4. Net change in total assets for June.
5. Beginning balance of liabilities.
6. Ending balance of liabilities.
7. The amount of cash received on account.

8. The amount of net assets at the beginning of June.

9. The amount of net assets at the end of June.

10. Net change in owner's equity for June.

11. Explain the relationship between the change in net assets during June and the change in the capital account.

2A–9. Balance Sheet Analysis. The balance sheet for Susan's Advertising Agency at December 31, 1988 is as follows:

Susan's Advertising Agency
Balance Sheet
December 31, 1988

Assets		Liabilities and Owner's Equity	
Cash	$ 8,000	Accounts payable	$12,000
Accounts receivable	10,000	Note payable	5,000
Note receivable	8,000	Mortgage payable	85,000
Supplies	10,000	S. Hernandez, Capital	?
Office equipment	25,000		
Land and building	160,000		

Additional Information:

1. Forty thousand dollars worth of land shown in the Land and Buildings account was a personal purchase by Susan. She intends to develop it for resale. The remaining $120,000 in that account represents the latest market value for the land and buildings owned by the agency. They were purchased several years ago at a cost of $140,000.

2. The advertising agency recently moved. Included in the Supplies account is $2,000 worth of stationery with the old address. It will all have to be discarded.

3. The note receivable arose because one of the agency's ex-employees was in need of emergency funds. However, after receiving the loan, the employee never showed up to work again and nobody knows his current whereabouts.

4. The agency is currently being sued by the City of Rolling Oceans for $5,600 because of the company's failure to pay back taxes. The company acknowledges the debt but has not recorded it.

Required:

a. Indicate what effect, if any, each of these items would have on the balance sheet. Justify your answer.

b. Prepare a corrected balance sheet to reflect any of the changes that you think should be made.

Problem Set B

2B–1. The Accounting Equation and Economic Transactions. On June 30, 1987 Pacific Blue Computer Printing Shop had the following account balances:

	Cash	+	Notes Receivable	+	Office Supplies	+	Printing Equipment	+	Land and Building	=
	$18,000		$15,000		$5,000		$15,000		$140,000	

	Accounts Payable	+	Mortgage Payable	+	Owner's Equity
	$25,000		$110,000		$58,000

During July 1987 the following transactions occurred:

a. Five thousand dollars cash was spent on permanent additions to the building.

b. Ten thousand dollars was collected on the notes receivable.

c. Suppliers were paid $12,000 on accounts payable.

d. One of the printers in the equipment was found to be defective. It was returned to the manufacturer for a full cash refund of the purchase price of $1,200.

e. One of the display tables which cost $500 was sold for $500 cash.

f. One thousand dollars was paid on the mortgage payable.

Required:

Prepare a table similar to the one on page 30 showing the accounts and their account balances at June 30, 1987 as the column headings. Use a separate line in the table to show the effects of each transaction on the accounting equation. Total all columns after each transaction.

2B–2. Understanding Transactions. The balance sheet of Biggs's Speed Reading Center at June 30, 1987 is shown below in equation form followed by July transactions whose effect on the accounting equation is also shown.

	Cash	+	Accounts Receivable	+	Furniture & Fixtures	+	Equipment	=	Accounts & Notes Payable	+	B. Biggs Capital
	$ 2,000		$5,000		$3,000		$ 0		$ 2,000		$ 8,000
1.	+10,000										10,000
	12,000		5,000		3,000		0		2,000		18,000
2.	−2,000						+10,000		+8,000		
	10,000		5,000		3,000		10,000		10,000		18,000
3.	−1,500								−1,500		
	8,500		5,000		3,000		10,000		8,500		18,000
4.	−1,000										−1,000
	7,500		5,000		3,000		10,000		8,500		17,000
5.							+5,000				+5,000
	$ 7,500		$5,000		$3,000		$ 15,000		$ 8,500		$22,000

Required:

a. Describe the nature of each of the numbered transactions that would produce the effect shown on the table.

b. Determine the amount of net assets (assets minus liabilities or owner's equity) at the end of June and at the end of July after transactions have been recorded. How much have they increased or decreased? Can you determine the reasons for the change?

2B–3. Recording Transactions. On January 2, 1987 Roy decided to start a business that performed children's acts at birthday parties. The business was called Children Are Fun. The following transactions occurred during the start-up month of January:

1. Roy invested $50,000 cash plus toys he had personally purchased recently at a cost of $20,000 in the business. (Put the toys in the Toy Supplies account.)

2. The company leased a small store at an annual rental of $15,000, all of which was paid in advance.

3. Various items of equipment including racks, tables, and an electronic clown were purchased for $10,000. Two thousand dollars was paid in cash and the remainder was put on account.

4. Additional toys costing $15,000 were purchased on account.

5. The business secured a $20,000 loan from a local bank.

6. One thousand dollars of the toys purchased in Transaction 4 arrived damaged. They were returned to the manufacturer and the firm's account payable was decreased.

7. The remaining accounts payable from the purchase in Transaction 4 was paid by making an $8,000 cash payment and converting the remainder to a note payable.

8. A $5,000 installment was paid on the bank loan.

9. The firm decided to replace the electronic clown it had purchased with a small robot: (a) The clown, which cost $500, was sold for that amount of cash. (b) The new robot was purchased for $1,200 cash.

Required:

Prepare a table similar to the one on page 30 using the following accounts as column headings: Cash, Prepaid Rent, Toy Supplies, Store Equipment, Accounts Payable, Bank Loans Payable, and R.R., Capital. Show the effect of each transaction on the accounting equation. You do not have to give totals after each transaction.

2B–4. Analysis of Transactions. A number of transactions for Becky's Ice Parlor are described below:

Required:

Complete the chart outlined below. Note that the increase/decrease columns are not necessarily intended to be in a debit/credit relationship.

Transaction	Asset		Liability		Owner's Equity	
	Increase	Decrease	Increase	Decrease	Increase	Decrease
a. Start business by investing $50,000 cash.						
b. Purchase freezer for $20,000— $15,000 in cash, and a bank loan for the remainder.						
c. Purchase various supplies costing $1,500 on account.						
d. A bank makes a $5,000 short-term loan to the firm.						
e. Payment of $1,000 made on Accounts Payable.						
f. An older freezer which cost $2,000 is sold at its cost for cash.						

2B–5. Recognizing Transactions. The T accounts for Ray's Consulting Service follow. These accounts reflect all the transactions for March. The firm was organized on March 1 of the current year.

Cash			Marketable Securities			Accounts Receivable	
[1]60,000	2,500[3]		[9]6,000			[7]1,000	800[10]
[10]800	1,000[5]						
	5,200[8]						
	6,000[9]						

Computer Equipment		Prepaid Rent		Land	
[6]5,600		[3]2,500		[2]40,000	

Office Supplies		Office Furniture		Accounts Payable	
[4]600		[5]5,000	1,000[7]	[8]5,200	600[4]
					5,600[6]

Bank Loan Payable		A. Ray, Capital	
	4,000[5]		60,000[1]
			40,000[2]

Required:

    a. For each of the numbered transactions (1 through 10), make the appropriate journal entry. Include a complete explanation of the transaction.

    b. Determine the balances of the T accounts and prepare a trial balance.

2B–6. Journal Entries, Ledger Accounts, and the Trial Balance. Lisa Rios decided to open her own law practice after several successful years as a partner in a large local firm. The following events occurred in June, the month her practice was organized.

- June 1: Lisa began her practice with $100,000. Her brother lent the firm $40,000 and she invested the remaining $60,000 from her personal funds.

- June 3: The firm purchased a small building and the land on which it was situated for $120,000. A down payment of $24,000 was made and a mortgage was taken out for the rest. Property records indicate that 40% of the total cost should be allocated to the land and 60% to the building.

- June 4: The firm purchased a small business computer for $10,000 cash.

- June 5: The firm purchased office furniture and fixtures for $15,000 on account.

- June 18: The firm purchased various office supplies for $2,400 cash.

- June 22: One of the pieces of furniture arrived broken. It had a cost of $1,200 and was returned to the seller. The firm's account was credited for $1,200.

- June 25: Just before opening her practice, Lisa had purchased a new electronic typewriter for $2,200 with her own funds. She decided to use the typewriter in her business. She contributed the typewriter to the business in exchange for additional capital.

- June 27: The remaining balance due on the purchase of office furniture was made.

- June 30: Her first potential client came into her office. Lisa agreed to begin working on his will in July for a total fee of $250.

Required:

    a. Make the required journal entries.

    b. Set up the required ledger accounts and post the entries to these accounts.

    c. Prepare a trial balance at June 30.

2B–7. Journal Entries, Ledger Accounts, and the Trial Balance. Leon Kripki decides to open a duplicating center. He organized the business on the first of April and entered into the following transactions during the month. The center is called Kripki's Printing Center.

- April 1: Leon took all his cash out of the bank and invested it in the business as the sole owner. He invested $100,000.

- April 2: Leon found a store to buy. The previous owner had closed the store several months ago. The purchase price of $120,000 was allocated as follows:

Land	$40,000
Building	60,000
Store fixtures	20,000

A 20% down payment was made and the remainder was financed through a bank loan.

- April 4: The firm purchased 5 new self-service copy machines at a total price of $10,000 cash.

- April 10: The firm placed an order for a high-speed copy machine costing $15,000 to be delivered in 10 days. A 20% payment is due 10 days after delivery, the remainder in 30 days.

- April 13: A 2-year insurance policy was purchased for $2,400 cash.

- April 16: One of the self-service copy machines purchased on the fourth did not work properly. The firm returned it and received a refund.

- April 20: The high-speed copy machine purchased on the tenth was delivered from the warehouse. The 20% payment is due in 10 days.

- April 24: Leon realized that the firm would need additional funds. One of his close friends lent the firm $10,000 in exchange for a note.

- April 30: The firm paid the 20% due on the high-speed copy machine.
- April 30: The firm purchased a used delivery truck for $3,500 cash.

Leon decided to use the following account titles and account numbers in his business:

Cash	10	Delivery truck	46
Prepaid insurance	30	Bank loan payable	50
Land	40	Accounts payable	55
Buildings	42	Notes payable	56
Equipment	43	L. Kripki, capital	60
Store fixtures	44		

Required:

a. Make the required journal entries for April.
b. Post these entries to ledger accounts using the running balance type illustrated in the chapter.
c. Prepare a trial balance at April 30.

2B–8. T Account Analysis. Frankie's Fish Hatchery has the following T accounts in its general ledger. (Note that **BB** indicates beginning balance.)

Cash			
BB	14,000	9/1	4,500
9/15	5,426	9/12	3,500
9/20	27,000	9/28	2,460
		9/29	2,662

Supplies		
BB	19,200	
9/15	3,750	
9/29	2,662	

Livestock		
BB	78,826	
9/10	6,240	

Accounts Payable			
9/1	4,500	BB	6,927
9/28	2,460	9/5	3,750
		9/10	6,240

Other Assets	
BB	5,600

Mortgage Payable			
9/12	3,500	BB	115,000
		9/25	28,850

Accounts Receivable			
BB	10,290	9/15	5,426

F. Morel, Capital		
	BB	290,616
	9/20	27,000

Equipment		
BB	52,650	
9/26	11,200	

Land		
BB	72,100	
9/25	13,250	

Note Payable		
	BB	32,700
	9/26	11,200

Building		
BB	192,577	
9/25	15,600	

Provide the following:

1. Ending balance of each account.
2. Beginning balance of assets.
3. Net change in the Cash account for September.
4. Net change in total assets for September.
5. Beginning balance of liabilities.
6. Ending balance of liabilities.
7. Amount of cash paid on mortgage.
8. Amount of net assets at the beginning of September.
9. Amount of net assets at the end of September.
10. Net change in owner's equity for September.
11. Explain the relationship between the change in net assets during September and the change in the capital account.

2B-9. Balance Sheet Analysis. The balance sheet of Alberto's Ceramic Shop at December 31, 1987 is as follows:

Alberto's Ceramic Shop
Balance Sheet
December 31, 1987

Assets		Liabilities and Owner's Equity	
Cash	$ 12,000	Accounts payable	$ 15,000
Accounts receivable	25,000	Notes payable	5,000
Loans receivable	5,000	Taxes payable	4,000
Membership dues	1,000	A. Alberto, Capital	149,000
Inventory	25,000		
Land and buildings	95,000		
Equipment	10,000		
Total	$173,000	Total	$173,000

Additional Information:

1. The membership dues were paid several years ago to join the local chamber of commerce for one year. The membership has since expired.
2. The equipment is a one-of-a-kind oven for pottery-making purposes. It was purchased several years ago for $4,200. Alberto recently received an offer of $10,000 for the oven.
3. Included in the inventory is $5,000 of goods owned by Petro Brusima, a pottery maker. Alberto agreed to display them in his store. If they are sold, Alberto will receive a commission of $20 per item.
4. The note payable is Alberto's personal note on his own automobile.

Required:

a. Indicate what effect, if any, each of these items would have on the balance sheet. Justify your answer.
b. Prepare a corrected balance sheet to reflect any of the changes you think should be made.

Understanding Financial Statements

The following accounts have been taken from a recent annual report of Bristol-Meyers Company. The accounts have been purposely condensed to simplify the exercise. All amounts are shown in millions of dollars.

Account	Amount
Accounts Payable	$ 191.5
Accounts Receivable	559.1
Accrued Payables	292.8
Owners' Equity	1,714.4
Cash	220.0
Goodwill	90.4
Inventories	559.1
Long-term Debt	208.8
Marketable Securities	391.6
Other Assets	70.5
Other Receivables	72.5
Prepaid Expenses	139.5
Property, Plant, and Equipment	653.6
Short-term Borrowings	167.8
U.S. and Foreign Income Taxes Payable	181.0

Required:

a. What accounts do you think are included in Other Receivables? Why do you think that they are not included in Accounts Receivable?

b. Goodwill is considered an asset. What do you think it represents and why is it considered an asset?

c. What items do you think are included under the caption "Accrued Payables"?

d. Prepare a balance sheet from the above data.

Financial Decision Case

One of your close friends is opening a business that provides accounting and tax courses to teachers and school administrators. These courses are marketed to professional societies and meet the required continued education requirement of these professions. During the first month of the business's existence the following events occurred:

a. Your friend, Karen Short, invested $80,000—her entire savings—in the business.

b. The firm, which is called Tax Help, negotiated a line of credit with the bank in the amount of $50,000. A line of credit is a preapproved loan that can be used at the borrower's discretion. Presently, none of the line is used.

c. After Karen met several times with a number of professional societies, two of them agreed to use Karen's business. In three months the firm will put on a tax seminar in Las Vegas. In order to obtain the business, Karen agreed to waive any required deposits.

d. The firm made a $5,000 down payment to the Coral Sands Hotel for the use of the facilities for the seminar.

e. Karen contacted five of her associates who were professors at major universities and they agreed to teach the classes for a fee of $1,000 a week. In order to show her good faith, she sent each of them $100.

f. During the month Karen worked very hard putting together the tax course. By the end of the month she had outlined the highlights of individual taxation in over 100 typed pages. She estimates that the purchase price of similar materials would be over $1,000.

Karen was extremely pleased with the progress of her business in the first month of its existence. However, when her accountant prepared a balance sheet (which is presented below) she became very confused. She felt that the statement did not tell the true story of the business activities during the month.

Tax Help
Balance Sheet
March 31, 1987

Assets		Equities	
Cash	$74,500		
Deposits	5,500	K. Short, Capital	$80,000
Total assets	$80,000	Total equities	$80,000

Required:

Write a brief memo to Karen explaining how and why the accountant prepared the balance sheet. Be sure to detail which transactions were included and which were not and the reasons for their inclusion or lack of inclusion. Further, be sure to explain to Karen the relevant accounting concepts that are involved in this situation.

Measuring and Recording Income Statement Transactions

3

LEARNING OBJECTIVES

After reading this chapter you should be able to:

1. Discuss how accountants measure income.
2. Explain the major components of the income statement, including revenues, expenses, gains and losses, and net income.
3. Explain the important concepts in determining income.
4. Distinguish between the accrual and the cash bases of accounting.
5. Record income statement transactions.
6. Describe the relationship among the balance sheet, income statement, and statement of owner's equity.

The ability of a business enterprise to earn a profit is essential to its continued operations. The profit earned by an enterprise is a yardstick that managers, investors, and creditors use to evaluate the future prospects of the business. Thus, one of the most important parts of the accounting process is the recognition and recording of those economic transactions that affect the firm's income. These concepts are the main focus of this chapter.

The Measurement of Income

Net income is often measured by the increase in the owner's equity of the firm that results from its operations. However, economists define and measure this increase differently than accountants do for financial reporting or the Internal Revenue Service does for tax return purposes. For financial reporting purposes, income is generally realized when transactions have been completed. The accountant measures and records the transactions that occurred during the period and summarizes them on the income statement. The effect of these transactions plus additional capital contributions less withdrawals is added to the historical cost net assets at the beginning of the period in order to create historical cost net assets at the end of the period. This approach can be illustrated as follows:

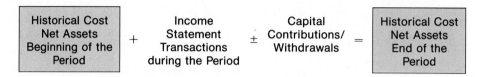

Accountants prefer this type of approach because measurements of completed transactions are objective and verifiable. Thus, the income statement that results from this process is a reliable financial statement that describes in detail the components of income: revenues and expenses, gains and losses, and net income.

The Income Statement

Although, in practice, income statements have a variety of forms, essentially they are a list of all recognized revenues and gains and expenses and losses by the firm. If revenues and gains exceed expenses and losses, net income or net profit is reported. Conversely, if there are more expenses and losses than revenues and gains, the firm would report a net loss for the period. An example of an income statement follows.

New Falcon Company
Income Statement
For the Year Ended December 31, 1987

Revenues:		
Advertising fees	$62,000	
Interest income	1,000	
Gain on sale of marketable securities	700	
Total revenues		$63,700
Expenses:		
Salaries expense	$25,700	
Rent expense	10,000	
Advertising expense	7,100	
Interest expenses	4,700	
Total expenses		47,500
Net income		$16,200

Revenues

Revenues are the price of goods sold or services rendered by a firm to others in exchange for cash or other assets. Formally, the FASB defines revenues as "inflows or other enhancements of assets of an entity or settlements of its liabilities (or a combination of both) from delivering or producing goods, rendering services, or other activities that constitute the entity's ongoing major or central operations."[1] In other words, revenues are increases in assets or decreases in liabilities caused by the firm's major business activities, such as delivering goods or providing services during a period. Revenues represent the accomplishments of an enterprise during a period and generally result from completed transactions.

Revenues cause increases in a firm's owner's equity. For example, when a firm sells a product or performs a service, it generally receives cash or an account receivable which, when collected, becomes cash. Thus, the total assets of the firm increase by the dollar amount of the sale or the service performed, and to balance the accounting equation, owner's equity increases too. In effect, when a firm sells a product or performs a service its assets increase, and this increase is assigned to owner's equity.

To illustrate, assume that the New Falcon Company is an advertising firm. The firm performs services for its customers and receives cash. At that time a completed transaction occurs—services are exchanged for cash. Advertising fees are recorded as an increase in Cash and ultimately an increase in owner's equity (the owner's Capital account). Even when the New Falcon Company does not receive cash at the time it performs a service but, instead, performs the services on account, fee revenue would still be recorded. In this case, however, Accounts Receivable rather than Cash is increased.

For service firms—such as law, accounting, real estate agencies, and advertising firms—fees earned are the major source of revenues. For retail and merchandising firms such as Safeway Stores and The Gap, sales are the major source of revenues. Other revenues for all types of firms include interest, rental, and dividends received from investments.

Expenses

Expenses for a given period are the dollar amount of the resources used by the firm in the process of earning revenues. Formally, the FASB defines expenses as "outflows or other using up of assets or incurrences of liabilities (or a combination of both) from delivering or producing goods, rendering services, or carrying out other activities that constitute the entity's ongoing major or central operations."[2] This means that expenses are decreases in assets or increases in liabilities caused by the firm's major activities, such as delivering goods or services during a period. They represent the efforts of the enterprise and also generally result from completed transactions.

Expenses cause decreases in the firm's owner's equity. In order to produce revenues, a firm must give up some of its assets or incur liabilities. These decreases in assets or increases in liabilities are recorded as decreases in owner's equity on the right side of the accounting equation.

The salary paid to its store manager by the New Falcon Company is an

---

[1]Financial Accounting Standards Board, Concepts Statement No. 6, *Elements of Financial Statements* (Stamford, Conn.: FASB, December 1985), par. 78.

[2]Ibid., par. 80.

example of an expense. To pay the store manager's salary, the company gives up cash in exchange for services. Cash and the owner's equity are decreased. Even if the store manager's salary for the current month was not paid until the following month, his or her salary would still be an expense of the current month. However, in this case, a liability, Wages Payable, would be increased in the current month, rather than decreasing the asset, Cash. In both cases, the firm's owner's equity is decreased.

Examples of expenses include cost of goods sold, salaries, rent, repairs and maintenance, interest, delivery, and advertising expense. For service firms salaries are likely to be a major expense. The major expense for retailing or merchandising firms is cost of goods sold. This represents the cost of the products sold by the firm. Thus, if an appliance store sells a stove, the cost it paid for that stove (which is included in the asset account, Inventory) becomes an expense called cost of goods sold when it is sold by the firm.

The Relationship between Receipts and Expenditures and Revenues and Expenses

An important relationship in accounting is that between receipts and expenditures and revenues and expenses. **Receipts** are inflows of cash or other assets; they do not always represent revenues. For example, a firm may receive cash from a bank loan or from a customer making a payment on account. The proceeds from a bank loan represent an increase in the asset, Cash, and an increase in a liability, Bank Loans Payable. Similarly, the collection of a receivable represents an exchange of one asset, Cash, for another asset, Accounts Receivable. In neither case is owner's equity involved. Receipts of cash or receivables that do represent revenues result primarily from products sold or services performed for customers.

Expenditures are outflows of cash or other assets or increases in liabilities. However, not all expenditures are expenses. For example, a firm may use its assets to purchase other assets such as buildings, inventories, or supplies. It may pay off a bank loan, thus reducing liabilities. These transactions do not affect owner's equity. If an expenditure is made in order to produce revenues in the current period and does not provide for future economic benefits, it is an expense that reduces owner's equity.

Gains and Losses

Gains are increases in equity (net assets) from all other activities of the firm during a period except for revenues and investments by owners. Likewise, **losses** are decreases in equity (net assets) from all other activities affecting the firm during the period except for expenses and distributions to the owner. Gains result from transactions into which the firm enters that increase or decrease owner's equity (other than the investments by the owner or the distributions to the owner) but are not directly related to selling and producing its goods and services. An example of a transaction that might result in a gain or loss is the sale of a building.

For example, the New Falcon Company sold some marketable securities at an amount greater than cost. The securities were originally purchased for $1,800 and were sold for $2,500 cash. The New Falcon Company records this transaction by increasing the asset, Cash, by $2,500; decreasing the asset, Marketable Securities, by $1,800; and recording a Gain on Sale of Marketable

Securities for the difference of $700 ($2,500 − $1,800). This gain on sale represents an increase in owner's equity because the firm received more assets than it gave up and this increase is assigned to owner's equity. You should note that only the net gain of $700 is recorded. That is, the firm does not show revenues of $2,500 and expenses of $1,800 as it does when it is selling its goods and services.

Net Income

Net income or loss is the difference between the total of revenues and gains and the total of expenses and losses. If revenues and gains exceed expenses and losses, net income is the result. If, on the other hand, expenses and losses exceed revenues and gains, a net loss is the result. Net income causes an increase in the firm's net assets during a period, whereas a net loss causes a decrease in the firm's net assets during the period.

The concept of income just described is a comprehensive one. According to the FASB, comprehensive income "is the change in equity (net assets) of a business enterprise during a period from transactions and other events and circumstances from nonowner sources."[3] That is, income includes all changes in the firm's equity during the period except those resulting from investments by its owner or distributions to its owner.

Withdrawals by the Owner

Individuals invest in a business hoping to earn a profit. In the case of a sole proprietorship, the owner invests in the business, generally works full-time in that business, and often incurs a considerable debt in the hope that the business will grow and prosper. As the business becomes profitable, the individual owner's equity or residual interest grows, and this increase represents the owner's return on investment.

Often the owner of a sole proprietorship withdraws assets, usually cash, from the business for personal use. In some cases such withdrawals are labeled salaries. However, for accounting purposes they are not considered salaries and are not recorded as an expense of the business. They represent withdrawals of cash in anticipation of profits and reduce the owner's investment in the business. Whenever the owner of a sole proprietorship invests cash or other assets in a business, his or her equity in that business increases. When the same owner withdraws cash or other assets from the business, his or her equity decreases. However, these increases and decreases only affect the balance sheet; the income statement is not involved. The income statement is only affected when the owner's equity in the business is increased or decreased (revenues earned or expenses incurred by the business), not by the owner's directly increasing or decreasing his or her investment.

When an owner withdraws cash from business the owner's equity account is directly affected, and thus the transaction could be recorded by debiting (reducing) the owner's Capital account. However, in many cases a separate owner's equity account, called a Drawing account, is established and used to record the owner's withdrawals. For example, when Lisa Bowman withdraws cash from her law practice, Cash is credited and an account called L. Bowman, Drawing, is debited. Later, in Chapter 4, we see how this Drawing account is offset against Lisa's capital account.

[3]Ibid., par. 70.

Important Concepts in Determining Income

There are a number of concepts and conventions that accountants have developed to help determine net income. The most important include the time period assumption, the matching convention, and the accrual basis of accounting.

The Time Period Assumption

Business enterprises are assumed to have an indefinite life unless there is evidence to the contrary (the going-concern assumption). However, users of financial statements, such as investors and creditors, do not wait until an enterprise ceases operating to measure the firm's performance. In order to make informed decisions, users need information, on a timely basis, about the enterprise's financial condition and performance. Thus, the enterprise's life span is divided into time periods, which can be as short as a month or a quarter and are rarely longer than a year. This division of the enterprise's life span is called the **time period assumption.**

At a minimum, firms prepare annual financial statements. If the year ends on December 31, it is considered a calendar year. However, some firms find it convenient to use a year that corresponds to their particular business cycle and so choose a year-end on the last day of another month. For example, a magazine publisher may feel that its natural business period ends on January 31 and so chooses that date as its year-end. A year that ends on the last day of a month other than December 31 is called a **fiscal year.** Publicly held corporations are required to issue quarterly financial statements, called **interim statements.** In addition, most firms prepare monthly financial statements for internal purposes.

The Matching Convention

The matching convention is the concept that accountants use to guide them in determining the net income for an accounting period. The **matching convention** simply states that the expenses incurred in one period to earn the revenues of that period should be offset against those revenues. Revenues are determined in accordance with revenue recognition principles, and the expenses incurred in earning those revenues during a period are matched against them. This is a powerful convention in accounting and is the basis for many of the accounting concepts and procedures you will learn in this book. In order to provide the best matching of expenses with revenues and the most useful income figure, the accrual basis of accounting has been developed. This method is considered to be the generally accepted method of accounting and is discussed next.

The Accrual versus the Cash Basis of Accounting

The accrual basis and the cash basis are the two basic methods of accounting. Each method identifies a different set of rules for recognizing revenues and expenses. The **accrual basis** of accounting means that revenues, expenses, and other changes in assets, liabilities, and owner's equity are accounted for in the period in which the economic event takes place, not when the cash inflows and outflows take place. Alternatively, the **cash basis** of accounting means that revenues and expenses are not recognized until the cash is received or paid.

The Accrual Basis

The best matching of revenues and expenses takes place when the accrual basis of accounting is used. This means that the financial effects of transactions and economic events are recognized by an enterprise when they occur rather than when the actual cash is received or paid by the enterprise. For example, sales are recognized as revenues when they are made, and services are recognized when they are performed, regardless of when the cash from that sale or service is actually collected. That is, a sale on account is recognized in the same manner as a cash sale is. The only difference is that Accounts Receivable rather than Cash is increased or debited at the time of sale. When the cash from the sale on account is collected, no revenue is recognized. The cash collection is just an exchange of one asset, Accounts Receivable, for another asset, Cash. At this point, the total amount of assets remains the same. The revenue and asset increases were recognized at the time the sale took place.

With the accrual basis of accounting, if cash, such as a deposit or a down payment, is received before the actual sale or the performance of a service, no revenue is recognized until the sale is made or the service performed. Instead, a liability to perform a future service or to deliver a product is recognized at the time the cash is received. This liability is usually referred to as an *unearned revenue*. When the service is finally performed or the sale is made, the revenue is then recognized and the liability is decreased. The entries associated with this particular account are discussed in Chapter 4.

Expenses are recognized in a similar manner. That is, expenses are considered to be incurred when the goods or services are consumed by the enterprise, not necessarily when the cash outflow takes place. For example, the New Falcon Company records as a June expense the salaries earned by its employees in that month, even though those salaries may not be paid until July. This is accomplished by recording Salaries Payable in June. When June's salaries are paid in July, no expense is recognized at that time. Both a payable and Cash are reduced at that time, but no expense is involved. The decrease in the firm's net assets and the corresponding expense were recorded in June.

In many cases, the cash is paid at the same time the expense is incurred. For example, plumbing repairs may be paid when the services are rendered, and Repairs and Maintenance Expense would be recorded at that time. It is not the payment of cash, however, that triggers the recognition of the expense. The expense is recognized when the plumbing services are received. Finally, using the accrual basis of accounting, if cash is paid in a period before the expense is incurred, no expense is recognized when the cash is paid. For example, if a firm prepays its June rent in May, the prepayment is considered an asset in May and is not considered an expense until June.

The Cash Basis

With the cash basis of accounting, a sale or service is recognized when the cash is collected, and an expense is recognized when the cash is paid. The cash basis of accounting thus does not properly match revenues and expenses, because the recognition of revenue and expense is contingent upon the timing of cash receipts and disbursements, and, depending on this timing, the expenses of one period could be matched against the sales or services of another period. The cash basis of accounting therefore is not considered a generally accepted accounting principle for financial reporting purposes. However, many professionals, such as doctors and lawyers, who prepare financial statements solely for themselves use the cash basis in order to simplify their record keeping. In addition, most individuals use the cash basis of accounting to determine their taxable income.

An example of the difference between the accrual and the cash bases of accounting is presented in the following table. The table shows how 10 different transactions for the month of May affect accrual basis and cash basis net income. Total accrual basis revenue is equal to services rendered for cash during the month plus all services rendered on credit during the same month. Total expenses during the month are equal to those incurred and paid in cash, plus expenses incurred on credit, during the same month. Cash basis net income is solely a function of when the cash is received and paid. In the chapters that follow we assume that the accrual basis of accounting is being utilized unless otherwise specified.

COMPARISON OF CASH AND ACCRUAL BASES		
	Revenue/Expense Amounts Recognized in May	
Transaction in May	Cash Basis	Accrual Basis
1. Cash fees earned during May $10,000	$10,000	$10,000
2. Credit fees earned during May 12,000		12,000
3. Cash collected from May's credit fees 4,000	4,000	
4. Cash collected from April's credit fees 5,000	5,000	
5. Cash deposit received in May for a service to be performed in June 1,000	1,000	
Total revenues	$20,000	$22,000
6. Cash expenses incurred and paid in May 8,000	8,000	8,000
7. Expenses incurred on account in May 7,000		7,000
8. Cash paid on May's expenses incurred on account 4,000	4,000	
9. Cash paid in May on April's expenses incurred on account 3,000	3,000	
10. Insurance expense effective June 1 paid on May 17 2,000	2,000	
Total expenses	$17,000	$15,000
Net income	$ 3,000	$ 7,000

Recording Income Statement Transactions

This section illustrates how to record income statement transactions. Following the pattern of Chapter 2, we first discuss the debit and credit rules and then discuss actual journal entries. Finally, we analyze transactions of Lisa Bowman's law firm.

Debit and Credit Rules

The debit and credit rules for income statement transactions are based on the accounting equation and the definition of revenues and expenses. Remember that the accounting equation is

$$\text{Assets} = \text{Liabilities} + \text{Owner's Equity}$$

One way to interpret this equation is to say that assets have several sources: other assets, the creditors, the owner of the business, and the business itself through profitable operations. The assets contributed by the profitable operations of the business are assigned to owner's equity. Therefore, revenues cause increases in owner's equity and expenses cause decreases in owner's equity.

Actually, it would be possible to record all income statement transactions directly in the owner's Capital account. However, if this were done, it would be very difficult to determine the dollar total of separate revenue and expense accounts, such as Fees Earned and Salaries Expense. Therefore, accountants use separate revenue and expense accounts during the period in order to capture this essential information. At the end of the period, the net effect of these accounts is transferred or closed to the owner's Capital account. Because separate revenue and expense accounts are used only during the period and have a zero beginning balance at the beginning of each period, they are often referred to as **nominal** (or **temporary**) accounts. In contrast, balance sheet accounts, including the owner's Capital account, are often referred to as **real accounts** because their balances extend beyond the accounting period.

Based upon this discussion we see that the rules for revenue and expense accounts follow the same rules as those for the owner's Capital account. These rules are illustrated below.

Owner's Capital

Debit	Credit
Decrease	Increase

Any Expense Account		**Any Revenue Account**	
Increase	Decrease	Decrease	Increase
+	−	−	+
Debit	Credit	Debit	Credit
Normal Balance:			Normal Balance:
Debit			Credit

These rules should be interpreted as follows:

1. Revenues represent increases in owner's equity. Increases in owner's equity are recorded on the right side of the ledger account and are credits. Therefore, increases in revenues are recorded on the right side of the ledger account and are credits.
2. Expenses represent decreases in owner's equity. Decreases in owner's equity are recorded on the left side of the ledger account and are debits. Therefore, because an increase in an expense represents a decrease in owner's equity, these increases are recorded on the left side of the expense ledger accounts and are debits.

Journal Entries

Journal entry rules for income statement accounts parallel the rules for balance sheet transactions. Debits are recorded first at the left margin of the journal, and then credits are recorded, indented slightly. To illustrate how revenue and expense transactions are recorded, assume that a firm has entered into the following six transactions. After each transaction the appropriate journal entry is made. For simplicity, the transaction number is entered into the date column and the reference column is not used.

1. The firm earned and collected $15,000 for services performed. The journal entry is:

Date	Account Title	Ref.	Debit	Credit
1	Cash		15,000	
	Fees earned			15,000
	To record fees earned and collected.			

The increase in the account, Fees Earned, is recorded as a credit because it represents an increase in owner's equity. The increase in Cash is recorded as a debit.

2. The firm placed an ad in the *Business Forum,* a professional journal. The ad cost $3,000 and was paid for at the time it was placed.

Date	Account Title	Ref.	Debit	Credit
2	Advertising Expense		3,000	
	Cash			3,000
	To record advertising expense incurred and paid.			

The increase in Advertising Expense is recorded as a debit because it represents a decrease in owner's equity. The decrease in Cash is recorded as a credit.

3. The firm's employees earned salaries of $1,500 but will not be paid until next month. The journal entry is:

Date	Account Title	Ref.	Debit	Credit
3	Salaries Expense		1,500	
	Salaries Payable			1,500
	To record salaries earned but not paid.			

The increase in the account, Salaries Expense, is a decrease in owner's equity and thus is recorded as a debit. The increase in the liability account, Salaries Payable, is recorded as a credit. This example shows how to record a liability that will be paid at a later date. It is essentially the same as the second transaction except that a liability account is increased rather than an asset account decreased.

4. The firm performed accounting services for a client and earned $2,000. By agreement with the client, the fee will be paid next month.

Date	Account Title	Ref.	Debit	Credit
4	Accounts Receivable		2,000	
	Fees Earned			2,000
	To record fees earned but not collected.			

In this case, the asset received was an account receivable rather than cash. However, the fees have been earned and the revenue is recognized by crediting the Fees Earned account. The transaction represents an increase in owner's equity.

5. The firm sold for $900 some marketable securities it had purchased for $1,200.

Date	Account Title	Ref.	Debit	Credit
5	Cash		900	
	Loss on Sale of Marketable Securities		300	
	Marketable Securities			1,200
	To record loss on sale of marketable securities.			

This transaction shows how to record a gain or loss. In this case the firm suffered a $300 loss which is recorded net. Cash is debited for the amount received ($900), and Marketable Securities is credited for their cost, $1,200. The $300 net difference is recorded as a loss. If a gain had occurred, it would have been recorded in the same manner except that the account Gain on Sale of Marketable Securities would have been credited.

6. The owner of the business, Jack Repcheck, withdrew $500 cash for his personal use.

Date	Account Title	Ref.	Debit	Credit
6	J. Repcheck, Drawing		500	
	Cash			500
	To record $500 withdrawal by owner.			

A withdrawal by the owner of the business' assets for personal use is not an expense. It represents a direct reduction in the owner's equity in the business. By convention, this withdrawal is originally recorded by debiting the Drawing account. Later this account will be offset against the owner's equity account, J. Repcheck, Capital.

It is important to recognize the consistent manner in which revenue and expense transactions are recorded. The revenue transactions (Nos. 1 and 4) are recorded by debiting asset accounts for what is received and crediting fee accounts to record the increase in owner's equity. The expense transactions (Nos. 2 and 3) are recorded by crediting asset accounts to record the decreases in assets or by crediting liability accounts to record increases in liabilities. Expense accounts are debited to record decreases in owner's equity.

Transactions for Lisa Bowman's Law Firm

To illustrate further how to record income statement transactions, we now examine the transactions for the first month of operations of Lisa Bowman's law firm. Remember that the firm was organized in April but did not perform any legal work until June. The trial balance as of May 31, 1987 is reproduced below, followed by June's transactions. These transactions are recorded in the general journal shown on the following page. After the journal entries have been posted to the appropriate accounts, the resulting running balance ledger accounts are illustrated (beginning on page 84). Finally, the new trial balance as of June 30 is shown.

Lisa Bowman's Law Firm
Trial Balance
May 31, 1987

Accounts	Debits	Credits
Cash	$ 10,790	
Office supplies	1,380	
Prepaid insurance	2,400	
License	120	
Land	20,000	
Building	120,000	
Office furniture and fixtures	10,000	
Office equipment	8,100	
Accounts payable		$ 2,790
Bank loan payable		5,000
L. Bowman, Capital		165,000
Totals	$172,790	$172,790

Transactions for the month of June:

- June 2: The firm placed an advertisement in a local professional listing of attorneys. A bill of $200 was received from the journal, payable within the month.
- June 15: For the first half of the month the firm performed services for various clients totaling $3,500, of which $2,000 was for cash and $1,500 was on account, due within 30 days.
- June 16: Salaries of $1,000 were paid in cash to the employees of the firm. Nothing was paid to Lisa.
- June 20: The firm purchased, on account, additional office supplies costing $1,000.
- June 23: Accounts receivable of $1,200 were collected.
- June 24: Repairs and maintenance of $400 were paid in cash.
- June 29: Accounts payable of $2,100 were paid.
- June 30: For the last half of the month the firm performed various services for clients totaling $5,000, of which $3,400 was cash and $1,600 was on credit, due within 30 days.

- June 30: The firm received its June telephone bill for $200. The bill will be paid next month and is recorded as utilities expense.
- June 30: Lisa withdrew $1,200 cash for her personal use.

Lisa Bowman's Law Firm
General Journal

GJ–3

Date	Account Titles	Ref.	Debit	Credit
1987 June				
2	Advertising Expense	604	200	
	Accounts Payable	201		200
	To record advertisement placed in newspaper.			
15	Cash	101	2,000	
	Accounts Receivable	106	1,500	
	Fees Earned	401		3,500
	To record fees for first half of June.			
16	Salaries Expense	601	1,000	
	Cash	101		1,000
	To record salaries for first half of June.			
20	Office Supplies	115	1,000	
	Accounts Payable	201		1,000
	To record purchase of inventory on account.			
23	Cash	101	1,200	
	Accounts Receivable	106		1,200
	To record collection of cash on account.			
24	Repairs and Maintenance Expense	602	400	
	Cash	101		400
	To record repairs and maintenance expense paid in cash.			
29	Accounts Payable	201	2,100	
	Cash	101		2,100
	To record payment on account.			
30	Cash	101	3,400	
	Accounts Receivable	106	1,600	
	Fees Earned	401		5,000
	To record fees for last half of June.			
30	Utilities Expense	603	200	
	Accounts Payable	201		200
	To record June's telephone bill payable in July.			
30	L. Bowman, Drawing	311	1,200	
	Cash	101		1,200
	To record withdrawal of $1,200 cash by Lisa Bowman.			

Lisa Bowman's Law Firm
Ledger Accounts

Cash   101

Date	Item	Ref.	Debit	Credit	Balance Debit	Balance Credit
June 1	Beg. Bal.				10,790	
15		GJ–3	2,000		12,790	
16		GJ–3		1,000	11,790	
23		GJ–3	1,200		12,990	
24		GJ–3		400	12,590	
29		GJ–3		2,100	10,490	
30		GJ–3	3,400		13,890	
30		GJ–3		1,200	12,690	

Accounts Receivable   106

Date	Item	Ref.	Debit	Credit	Balance Debit	Balance Credit
1987 June 1	Beg. Bal.				0	
15		GJ–3	1,500		1,500	
23		GJ–3		1,200	300	
30		GJ–3	1,600		1,900	

Office Supplies   115

Date	Item	Ref.	Debit	Credit	Balance Debit	Balance Credit
1987 June 1	Beg. Bal.				1,380	
20		GJ–3	1,000		2,380	

Prepaid Insurance   120

Date	Item	Ref.	Debit	Credit	Balance Debit	Balance Credit
1987 June 1	Beg. Bal.				2,400	

License   121

Date	Item	Ref.	Debit	Credit	Balance Debit	Balance Credit
1987 June 1	Beg. Bal.				120	

Lisa Bowman's Law Firm (cont.)
Ledger Accounts

Land   150

Date	Item	Ref.	Debit	Credit	Balance Debit	Balance Credit
1987 June 1	Beg. Bal.				20,000	

Building   160

Date	Item	Ref.	Debit	Credit	Balance Debit	Balance Credit
1987 June 1	Beg. Bal.				120,000	

Office Furniture and Fixtures   165

Date	Item	Ref.	Debit	Credit	Balance Debit	Balance Credit
1987 June 1	Beg. Bal.				10,000	

Office Equipment   167

Date	Item	Ref.	Debit	Credit	Balance Debit	Balance Credit
1987 June 1	Beg. Bal.				8,100	

Accounts Payable   201

Date	Item	Ref.	Debit	Credit	Balance Debit	Balance Credit
1987 June 1	Beg. Bal.					2,790
2		GJ–3		200		2,990
20		GJ–3		1,000		3,990
29		GJ–3	2,100			1,890
30		GJ–3		200		2,090

Bank Loan Payable   205

Date	Item	Ref.	Debit	Credit	Balance Debit	Balance Credit
1987 June 1	Beg. Bal.					5,000

(continued on next page)

Lisa Bowman's Law Firm (cont.)
Ledger Accounts

L. Bowman, Capital   301

Date	Item	Ref.	Debit	Credit	Balance Debit	Balance Credit
1987 June 1	Beg. Bal.					165,000

L. Bowman, Drawing   311

Date	Item	Ref.	Debit	Credit	Balance Debit	Balance Credit
1987 June 30		GJ–3	1,200		1,200	

Fees Earned   401

Date	Item	Ref.	Debit	Credit	Balance Debit	Balance Credit
1987 June 15		GJ–3		3,500		3,500
30		GJ–3		5,000		8,500

Salaries Expense   601

Date	Item	Ref.	Debit	Credit	Balance Debit	Balance Credit
1987 June 16		GJ–3	1,000		1,000	

Repairs and Maintenance Expense   602

Date	Item	Ref.	Debit	Credit	Balance Debit	Balance Credit
1987 June 24		GJ–3	400		400	

Utilities Expense   603

Date	Item	Ref.	Debit	Credit	Balance Debit	Balance Credit
1987 June 30		GJ–3	200		200	

Lisa Bowman's Law Firm (cont.)
Ledger Accounts

Advertising Expense   **604**

Date	Item	Ref.	Debit	Credit	Balance Debit	Balance Credit
1987 June 2		GJ–3	200		200	

Lisa Bowman's Law Firm
Trial Balance
June 30, 1987

Accounts	Debit	Credit
Cash	$ 12,690	
Accounts receivable	1,900	
Office supplies	2,380	
Prepaid insurance	2,400	
License	120	
Land	20,000	
Building	120,000	
Office furniture and fixtures	10,000	
Office equipment	8,100	
Accounts payable		$ 2,090
Bank loan payable		5,000
L. Bowman, Capital		165,000
L. Bowman, Drawing	1,200	
Fees earned		8,500
Salaries expense	1,000	
Repairs and maintenance expense	400	
Utilities expense	200	
Advertising expense	200	
Totals	$180,590	$180,590

For clarification, three points need to be made about this example. The journal entries represent summary transactions for the month. In a real situation, journal entries would be made daily to record the transactions as they occur. However, in this example, fees earned are only recorded twice a month rather than on a day-to-day basis. The Lisa Bowman's Law Firm's trial balance as of June 30, 1987, shown above, follows the order in which the accounts are listed; that is, the balance sheet accounts (assets, liabilities, and owner's equity) are listed first, followed by the income statement accounts (revenues and expense accounts). Finally, if the trial balance does not balance, you should follow the error identification suggestions made in a previous chapter.

At this point in the accounting cycle we will prepare a preliminary balance sheet, an income statement, and a statement of owner's equity. These financial statements will help Lisa Bowman evaluate the progress of her firm during its first full month of operation. However, these statements are preliminary because not all of the steps in the accounting cycle have been completed. Lisa has recorded only **external transactions,** which are the transactions with outside parties. For example, fees earned affect the firm and the client, an outside party. There are, however, a number of **internal transactions** or events not yet recorded that affect only the firm. For example, during June the firm used some of the office supplies that it purchased in May. Obviously, it is too time consuming to make journal entries every time pencils or other supplies are taken from the supply room or closet. Therefore, the cost of supplies used is determined at the end of the month, and an entry is made at that time to reflect this internal event. These transactions, called adjustments, are discussed in the next chapter.

The Bowman Law Firm Financial Statements

The financial statements for Lisa Bowman's law firm are shown on the following pages. The income statement covers a one-month period ending on June 30. The expenses are listed on the statement in order of decreasing magnitude, which also happens to be their account number order. This is just one way to list them; they could be listed alphabetically or by categories such as Selling and General and Administrative.

Lisa Bowman's Law Firm
Income Statement
For the Month Ended
June 30, 1987

Revenues		$8,500
Fees earned		
Expenses		
Salaries expense	$1,000	
Repairs and maintenance expense	400	
Advertising expense	200	
Utilities expense	200	
Total expenses		1,800
Net income		$6,700

The Statement of Owner's Equity

The cumulative increase in the net assets of the business caused by its successful operations increases the owner's equity of the business, and this is part of the residual claim of the owner. The **statement of owner's equity** shows the causes of increases in owner's equity—namely, net income and additional investments—and the causes of decreases—namely, net losses and withdrawals. The owner's equity statement for Lisa Bowman's law firm is shown next.

Lisa Bowman's Law Firm
Statement of Owner's Equity
For the Month Ended June 30, 1987

L. Bowman, Capital, June 1, 1987	$165,000
Add: Net income for the period	6,700
Subtotal	$171,700
Less: Withdrawal	1,200
L. Bowman, Capital, June 30, 1987	$170,500

The Balance Sheet

The June 30, 1987 and May 31, 1987 balance sheets for Lisa Bowman's law firm follow. Because two periods are shown, this is referred to as a **comparative balance sheet**. Except for the capital balance, the data for the June 30, 1987 balance sheet come from the June 30 trial balance shown on page 87. The balance in the capital account is taken from the owner's equity statement shown above. The data for the May 31, 1987 balance sheet are taken from the trial balance on page 48.

Lisa Bowman's Law Firm
Comparative Balance Sheet

Assets	June 30, 1987	May 31, 1987
Cash	$ 12,690	$ 10,790
Accounts receivable	1,900	0
Office supplies	2,380	1,380
Prepaid insurance	2,400	2,400
License	120	120
Land	20,000	20,000
Building	120,000	120,000
Office furniture and fixtures	10,000	10,000
Office equipment	8,100	8,100
Total assets	$177,590	$172,790

Liabilities and Owner's Equity		
Liabilities		
Accounts payable	$ 2,090	$ 2,790
Bank loan payable	5,000	5,000
Total liabilities	$ 7,090	$ 7,790
Owner's equity		
L. Bowman, Capital	170,500	165,000
Total liabilities and owner's equity	$177,590	$172,790

If you compare the owner's equity section of the two balance sheets you will see that, at June 30, owner's equity had a balance of $170,500, whereas at May 31, the balance was $165,000. The $5,500 difference represents the increase in the net assets resulting from the profits of the business of $6,700 less the withdrawal of $1,200. This important point can also be seen by comparing the net assets at June 30 and May 31 as follows:

Date	Net Assets	=	Assets	−	Liabilities
June 30	$170,500	=	$177,590	−	$7,090
May 31	165,000	=	172,790	−	7,790
	$ 5,500	=	$ 4,800	+	$ 700

Note that $5,500 represents the total increase in net assets, not just an increase in one account such as Cash. In the example of Lisa Bowman's law firm, Cash increased by $1,900 ($12,690 − $10,790). Other assets and other liabilities also increased or decreased, leading to the net increase of $5,500.

At the beginning of this chapter we stated that accountants use the transaction approach to measure income; that is, the accountant measures the income and expense transactions occurring during a period and summarizes them on the income statement. The effect of these transactions, plus any additional capital contributions and less any withdrawals, is added to the historical cost net assets at the beginning of the period in order to determine the historical cost net assets at the end of the period. Using the diagram from page 72 and the figures for Lisa Bowman's law firm we get:

Historical Cost Net Assets 5/31/87 $165,000	+	Net Income for the period $6,700	+	Capital Contributions $0 − Withdrawals $1,200	=	Historical Cost Net Assets 6/30/87 $170,500

This diagram helps explain how the financial statements are related to one another. Two consecutive balance sheets are linked by the statement of owner's equity. The owner's equity statement summarizes the factors that have caused owner's equity to change, namely, net income or net loss and additional owner investments or withdrawals. The income statement explains in detail the change in owner's equity resulting from profitable or unprofitable operations. This link between all the financial statements is referred to as **articulation** and means that all the financial statements tie into each other. For example, the net income on the income statement appears on the owner's equity statement, and the ending balance of owner's equity on the owner's equity statement is the same amount that appears as owner's equity on the balance sheet as of the end of the period.

Summary of Learning Objectives

1. *The measurement of income.* There are various ways to define income, depending on who is writing the definition. Accountants use a transaction

approach to determine income, in which generally only completed transactions affect income. Accountants feel that this provides the most objective measure of income.

2. **The major components of the income statement.** Revenues are the inflows of net assets, and expenses are the outflows of net assets, due to the primary activities of the enterprise. Gains and losses are related to other activities of the firm. Comprehensive net income or loss is the difference between the total of the revenues and the gains and the total of the expenses and the losses.

3. **Important concepts in determining income.** Accountants have developed several important concepts or conventions to help them determine income. The need for timely information requires that a firm's continuous economic activities be divided into monthly, quarterly, or yearly accounting periods. The matching convention requires that the expenses for a particular period be matched against the revenues of that period. This convention is best accomplished by using the accrual basis of accounting.

4. **The accrual versus the cash basis of accounting.** With the accrual basis of accounting, revenues are recognized when earned and expenses are recognized when incurred. With the cash basis of accounting, revenues are recognized when received and expenses are recognized when paid. The accrual basis of accounting is considered to be the generally accepted accounting method because it provides the best matching of revenues and expenses.

5. **Recording income statement transactions.** Increases in net assets from business activities are assigned to owner's equity and represent increases in that account. Conversely, decreases in net assets from business activities are also assigned to owner's equity but represent decreases in that account. Thus, the rules for revenue and expense accounts follow the same rules as do those for the owner's Capital account. These rules are illustrated in the following T accounts:

Any Expense Account		**Any Revenue Account**	
Increase	Decrease	Decrease	Increase
+	−	−	+
Debit	Credit	Debit	Credit

6. **The relationship among the financial statements.** The balance sheet, income statement, and statement of owner's equity are all related to one another. Two consecutive balance sheets are linked by the owner's equity statement. The owner's equity statement summarizes the factors (net income or net loss and owner investments and withdrawals) that cause changes in the owner's Capital account. The income statement details the changes in the owner's Capital account resulting from profitable or unprofitable operations. These relationships mean that all the financial statements are articulated.

Key Terms

Accrual Basis	Internal Transactions
Articulation	Losses
Cash Basis	Matching Convention
Comparative Balance Sheet	Net Income
Expenditures	Nominal (Temporary) Accounts
Expenses	Real Accounts
External Transactions	Receipts
Fiscal Year	Revenues
Gains	Statement of Owner's Equity
Interim Statements	Time Period Assumption

Problems for Your Review

A. Income Statement Transactions. You are the accountant for Ace World Travel, a large travel agency specializing in group tours. You obtained the following information as of January 1, 1987:

Ace World Travel
Balance Sheet
January 1, 1987

Assets		Liabilities and Owner's Equity	
Cash	$ 10,000	Liabilities	
Accounts receivable	13,000	Accounts payable	$ 4,600
Office supplies	1,500	Salaries payable	1,400
Land	25,000	Bank loan payable	10,000
Building	45,000	Total liabilities	$ 16,000
Furniture and fixtures	15,000	Owner's Equity	
		J. Hansen, capital	93,500
Total assets	$109,500	Total liabilities and owner's equity	$109,500

The following events occurred in 1987. These events are numbered because they represent summary events for the year:

1. Office supplies totaling $6,000 were purchased on account.
2. The firm purchased for cash a 2-year comprehensive insurance policy for $3,600. The policy takes affect on April 1, 1987.
3. Commissions earned for the first half of the year amounted to $28,000; $18,000 was received immediately and the remainder is due within 30 days.
4. Salaries payable of $1,400 as of January 1, 1987 were paid in full.
5. Cash collections from accounts receivable totaled $16,000.
6. There was a leak in the roof of the building. It was repaired at a cost of $500 and was paid immediately.

7. Cash payments on accounts payable were $8,000.

8. A small plot of land that the travel agency originally purchased for $5,000 was sold for $4,800 cash.

9. Commissions earned for the second half of the year amounted to $22,000; $10,000 was received in cash and the remainder is due within 30 days.

10. The following expenses were paid in cash:

Salaries	$22,000
Utilities	1,750
Automobile expense	2,250
Advertising	4,000

11. The agency rented out some excess space in its building. One month's rent of $300 was received in cash.

12. J. Hansen withdrew $1,000 cash for her personal use.

Required:

1. Make the journal entries to record these events.

2. Post the entries to ledger T accounts and open new accounts where it is appropriate to do so.

3. Prepare a trial balance.

Solution

1. Journal Entries

1. Office Supplies	6,000	
Accounts Payable		6,000
To record purchase of office supplies on account.		
2. Prepaid Insurance	3,600	
Cash		3,600
To record purchase of two-year insurance policy.		
3. Cash	18,000	
Accounts Receivable	10,000	
Commissions Earned		28,000
To record commissions earned.		
4. Salaries Payable	1,400	
Cash		1,400
To record payment of salaries payable.		
5. Cash	16,000	
Accounts Receivable		16,000
To record cash collections on account.		
6. Repairs and Maintenance Expense	500	
Cash		500
To record repairs and maintenance expense.		
7. Accounts Payable	8,000	
Cash		8,000
To record payments on account.		
8. Cash	4,800	
Loss on Sale of Land	200	
Land		5,000
To record sale of land at a $200 loss.		
9. Cash	10,000	
Accounts Receivable	12,000	
Commissions Earned		22,000
To record commissions earned.		

10.	Salaries Expense	22,000	
	Utilities Expense	1,750	
	Automobile Expense	2,250	
	Advertising Expense	4,000	
	Cash		30,000
	To record payment of various expenses.		
11.	Cash	300	
	Rental Revenue		300
	To record receipt of rental revenue.		
12.	J. Hansen, Drawing	1,000	
	Cash		1,000
	To record owner's $1,000 withdrawal.		

2. T Accounts

Cash

1/1 Bal. 10,000	(2)	3,600
(3) 18,000	(4)	1,400
(5) 16,000	(6)	500
(8) 4,800	(7)	8,000
(9) 10,000	(10)	30,000
(11) 300	(12)	1,000
12/31 Bal. 14,600		

Accounts Receivable

1/1 Bal. 13,000	(5)	16,000
(3) 10,000		
(9) 12,000		
12/31 Bal. 19,000		

Prepaid Insurance

(2) 3,600	

Office Supplies

1/1 Bal. 1,500	
(1) 6,000	
12/31 Bal. 7,500	

Land

1/1 Bal. 25,000	(8)	5,000
12/31 Bal. 20,000		

Building

1/1 Bal. 45,000	

Furniture and Fixtures

1/1 Bal. 15,000	

Accounts Payable

(7) 8,000	1/1 Bal.	4,600
	(1)	6,000
	12/31 Bal.	2,600

Salaries Payable

(4) 1,400	1/1 Bal.	1,400
	12/31 Bal.	0

Bank Loan Payable

	1/1 Bal. 10,000

J. Hansen, Capital	
	1/1 Bal. 93,500

J. Hansen, Drawing	
(12) 1,000	

Commissions Earned	
	(3) 28,000
	(9) 22,000
	12/31 Bal. 50,000

Rental Revenue	
	(11) 300

Salaries Expense	
(10) 22,000	

Advertising Expense	
(10) 4,000	

Utilities Expense	
(10) 1,750	

Automobile Expense	
(10) 2,250	

Repairs and Maintenance Expense	
(6) 500	

Loss on Sale of Land	
(8) 200	

3. Trial Balance

Ace World Travel
Trial Balance
December 31, 1987

Accounts	Debit	Credit
Cash	$ 14,600	
Accounts receivable	19,000	
Prepaid insurance	3,600	
Office supplies	7,500	
Land	20,000	
Building	45,000	
Furniture and fixtures	15,000	
Accounts payable		$ 2,600
Salaries payable		0
Bank loan payable		10,000
J. Hansen, capital		93,500
J. Hansen, drawing	1,000	
Commissions earned		50,000
Rental revenue		300
Salaries expense	22,000	
Advertising expense	4,000	
Utilities expense	1,750	
Automobile expense	2,250	
Repair and maintenance expense	500	
Loss on sale of land	200	
Totals	$156,400	$156,400

B. Income Statement Preparation. The trial balance of the Robinson Company as of December 31, 1987 is as follows:

The Robinson Company
Trial Balance
December 31, 1987

Account	Debit	Credit
Cash	$ 20,000	
Accounts receivable	14,000	
Office supplies	6,000	
Prepaid insurance	2,400	
Land	25,000	
Buildings	50,000	
Office furniture and fixtures	10,000	
Accounts payable		$ 12,000
Bank loan payable		20,000
L. Robinson, capital—1/1/87		85,400
L. Robinson, drawing	8,000	
Fees earned		100,000
Gain on sale of office furniture		1,000
Salaries expense	40,000	
Advertising expense	27,000	
Delivery expense	10,000	
Utilities expense	6,000	
Totals	$218,400	$218,400

Required:
1. Prepare an income statement for the year ended December 31, 1987.
2. Prepare a statement of owner's equity for the year ended December 31, 1987.
3. Prepare a balance sheet at December 31, 1987.

Solution

1. Income Statement

The Robinson Company
Income Statement
For the Year Ended December 31, 1987

Revenues		
Fees earned	$100,000	
Gain on sale of office furniture	1,000	
Total revenues		$101,000
Expenses		
Salaries expense	$ 40,000	
Advertising expense	27,000	
Delivery expense	10,000	
Utilities expense	6,000	
Total expenses		83,000
Net income		$ 18,000

2. Statement of Owner's Equity

The Robinson Company
Statement of Owner's Equity
For the Year Ended December 31, 1987

L. Robinson, capital, January 1, 1987	$ 85,400
Add: Net income for the year	18,000
Subtotal	103,400
Less: Withdrawals during the year	8,000
L. Robinson, capital, December 31, 1987	$ 95,400

3. Balance Sheet

The Robinson Company
Balance Sheet
December 31, 1987

Assets		Liabilities and Owner's Equity		
Cash	$ 20,000	Liabilities		
Accounts receivable	14,000	Accounts payable	$12,000	
Office supplies	6,000	Bank loan payable	20,000	
Prepaid insurance	2,400	Total liabilities		$ 32,000
Land	25,000	Owner's Equity		
Buildings	50,000	L. Robinson, capital		95,400
Office furniture and fixtures	10,000	Total liabilities		
Total assets	$127,400	and owner's equity		$127,400

Questions

1. How does the accountant measure income? When is income generally realized?

2. What are the main components of an income statement?

3. Define revenues and expenses, and explain how they differ from gains and losses.

4. How do the time period assumption and the matching concept relate to the measurement of income for the period?

5. Compare and contrast the accrual basis and the cash basis of accounting. Which method is favored by accountants, and why?

6. A friend of yours was told by his accountant that his business was profitable during the year. However, your friend is concerned because his cash decreased during the year. Explain to him how this can happen.

7. During the month, the Pfeifer Corporation fees totaled $10,000, $8,000 of which was collected in the current month and $2,000 of which will be collected in the next month. The firm also collected $1,000 during the current month from last month's fees. How much revenue is recognized using the accrual basis? How much using the cash basis?

8. Why don't accountants directly enter revenue and expense transactions in the owner's Capital account?

9. Why are revenue and expense accounts called temporary or nominal accounts?

10. Give three examples each of revenue and expense accounts. Describe the effect of a debit or a credit on each.

11. Why is an income statement reported for a specific period, whereas a balance sheet is reported at a specific time?

12. What happens to the owner's Capital account if there is a loss during a certain period? Can withdrawals be made if there is a loss during the period?

13. If net income is a summary of revenues and gains minus expenses and losses, why can't we just take "cash in" minus "cash out" to determine net income?

14. What is meant by the statement that gains and losses are net concepts?

15. Why would a deposit or down payment received before a sale be considered a liability? Why would a prepaid expense be considered an asset?

16. What is the difference between a fiscal year and a calendar year?

17. Do you think it would be more difficult to maintain books on an accrual or a cash basis? Why?

Exercises

Note: Unless otherwise specified, assume the accrual basis of accounting is used in all exercises and problems.

1. Recognizing Accounts. Examine the following accounts and indicate whether they are an asset, liability, owner's equity, revenue, or expense account. State whether a debit or credit increases the account.

a. Salary expense.
b. Prepaid insurance.
c. Buildings.
d. Interest earned.
e. Unearned rent.
f. Fees earned.
g. B. Johnson, Capital.
h. Repairs and maintenance.
i. Taxes payable.
j. Commissions paid to salespeople.

2. Recognition of Revenue and Expense Transactions. A summary of the transactions into which the Usher Company entered during October and November is reproduced below. State which of the events affected the income statement during the month of October.

a. The company needed additional funds, and the owner made an additional $50,000 investment.
b. The firm collected $40,000 on account from fees earned during September.
c. Fees earned during October totaled $8,000.
d. The firm paid its October salaries of $5,000 in early November.
e. The firm paid $40 for some plumbing repairs made in August.
f. October fees earned but not collected totaled $10,000.
g. The firm repaid a bank loan. The original amount of the loan was $5,000 and was made on October 1. At the end of October, the $5,000 was repaid, plus $50 in interest for the month.
h. A customer gave the firm a $500 deposit for services to be performed by the firm in November.
i. The owner withdrew $500 in October.

3. Recording Journal Entries. The Golden Bear Company, a consulting firm to major sports figures, entered into the following transactions during November.

• November 1: Purchased $1,000 of supplies on account.
• November 3: Placed an advertisement in the local paper for $100. Paid cash.
• November 16: Paid October's utility bill of $750. This bill was recorded as a payable at the end of October.
• November 29: Paid salaries of $7,000 for the month.
• November 30: Fees earned during the month amounted to $60,000, of which $40,000 was for cash.
• November 30: Other selling expenses amounted to $42,000 and were paid in cash.
• November 30: November's utility bill of $850 was received. It will be paid in early December.

Required:

Prepare the necessary journal entries for the month of November.

4. Income Statement Preparation. Sam Houston, owner of Houston's Fun Ranch, wants to know the bottom line from his 1987 operations. Prepare an income statement using the following information:

    a. Salaries and wages expense was $36,000.
    b. House rental revenue came to $229,000.
    c. Insurance expense was $3,000.
    d. Interest earned on invested cash was $550.
    e. Rental revenue from horseback riding totaled $13,000.
    f. Horse feed and other expenses totaled $27,600.
    g. Advertising expense totaled $2,300.

5. Income Statement Preparation. The Sandman Motor Inn has just completed its busy summer season. Taking the following facts into consideration, construct an income statement for the month ending September 30, 1987.

    a. Gross rentals were $965,312.
    b. Salary and wages equaled 30% of sales.
    c. Interest expense equaled 12% of sales.
    d. Insurance expense for the period was $1,100.
    e. Miscellaneous expenses equaled 1% of sales and wages.
    f. Advertising and promotion expenses totaled 5% of sales but were estimated to have attracted 45% of the current month's sales.

6. Income Statement Concepts. Match the following statements from Gregory Simpson, owner of Efficient Printing Services, Inc., to the relevant underlying accounting concept or concepts. There may be more than one answer for each question.

    a. Time period assumption.
    b. Matching concept.
    c. Accrual versus cash basis accounting.
    1. "I want to know how you can tell me we had income of $32,000, and the bank says we're overdrawn."
    2. "Well, I don't care. . . . How about not reporting income this year?"

7. Matching Concept. Sammy Sloppy, accountant for Good Times, Inc., has lately been ignoring the matching convention. Upon audit, you find the following trouble areas. Discuss the proper treatment of each. If Sammy did handle the issue properly, make a note of this.

    a. Good Times received $3,200 for unlimited passes to their amusement park. Although half of these passes were not valid until the following year, the entire amount was recorded currently as revenue.
    b. Two years ago Good Times paid $2,790 for a 3-year insurance policy. No insurance expense appeared on this year's income statement.
    c. At year-end, salaries earned by employees but not yet paid equaled $850. These were not recorded until they were paid in the following year.
    d. Good Times bought equipment for $11,450 in the current year. Because no payments were made, neither the equipment nor the payable was recorded on the firm's books.

8. Accrual versus Cash Basis. The Alpine Realty Company entered into the following transactions in July. Determine net income on the accrual and cash bases for the month of July.

1. Commissions earned and received in July	$7,100
2. Commissions earned in July but not yet received	2,125
3. Commissions received in advance on sale to close in August	500
4. Cash collected on commissions from May realty sales	1,000
5. Payment of June's utility and telephone bills	425
6. Payment of rent for six months, July through December	3,600
7. July's salaries paid in August	2,400
8. Received bill from plumber for services performed in July, to be paid in August	50

9. Accounting Equation and Capital Account. The following data are available for three consecutive years of the Orazco Company:

	Year 1	Year 2	Year 3
J. Orazco, capital beginning balance	$85,000	$90,000	?
Net income	?	?	$20,000
Withdrawals by owner	10,000	12,000	?
J. Orazco, capital, ending balance	?	92,000	90,000

Complete the chart by filling in the missing amounts.

10. Journal Entries. Given the following facts for Instant Tan Services, record the proper summary journal entries for the year:

a. Instant Tan sold 120 memberships for $395 each during the year. All memberships were sold for cash and are good only in the current year.

b. Rent paid by Instant Tan Services totaled $850 per month, and all 12 months' rent was paid in cash.

c. Members' guests are required to pay $10 for each visit. There were 450 guests for the first year. Forty percent of the guests' charges were placed on members' accounts, and the rest was paid in cash.

d. Instant Tan's electric bills totaled $2,695 for the year. All bills were paid in cash.

e. During the year, Ultraviolet Repair Service was called 14 times, and their bills totaled $1,420. All bills were paid in cash.

11. Cash to Accrual. The income statement that follows is based on the cash basis of accounting instead of the accrual basis. Prepare an income statement on the accrual basis.

Excavation Ltd.
Income Statement—Cash Basis
For the Year Ending December 31, 1987

Revenues		
Fees earned	$246,300	
Investment revenue	27,200	$273,500
Expenses		
Wages expense	49,400	
Insurance expense	6,490	
Interest expense	12,950	
Utility expense	11,775	
Office expense	3,195	
Miscellaneous expense	1,210	85,020
Net income		$188,480

Additional Information

a. At year-end, 12% of the fees were not yet collected.

b. In addition to investment revenue, Excavation Ltd. owned land worth $45,000; this was $16,000 more than it was appraised for last year.

c. One month's wages totaling $4,300 have not been paid yet.

d. Three years of insurance was paid this year. One year's worth was considered used in the current year.

e. Thirty-five percent of the office expense incurred during the year was unpaid at year-end.

Problem Set A

3A–1. Journal Entries. The Jaminez Company's summary transactions for April follow:

1. Paid a property tax bill of $1,800 that was recorded as a payable in March.
2. Paid its monthly rental of $1,400.
3. Fees earned during the month totaled $45,000. Thirty percent of these were for cash and the remainder was on credit.
4. Salaries expense during the month equaled $32,000. The entire amount was paid in cash.
5. Purchased additional office furniture on account for $8,200.
6. Cash collections on account were:

   $12,000 from March's fees.

   $11,000 from current month's fees.
7. The following expenses were paid in cash:

Automobile	$1,400
Repairs	1,100
Utility	800

8. The firm made a $7,000 payment on the furniture purchased in Item 5.
9. The firm sold an extra parcel of land it owned. The land cost $42,000 and was sold for $38,000 cash.
10. One of the customers was dissatisfied with the service she received, for which she had yet to pay. As a result she refused to pay the fee and the firm agreed to credit her account for $1,000.

Required:

Make the journal entries with appropriate explanations to record each of the transactions.

3A–2. Journal Entries, Posting, and the Trial Balance. Helen runs a driving school called U-Drive which was organized in January. The following events occurred during that month:

- January 2: Helen organized the business by contributing the following assets:

Cash	$40,000
Furniture and fixtures	24,000
Office equipment	10,000

- January 3: She obtained additional financing by borrowing $15,000 from a local bank for one year. (Ignore interest.)
- January 5: A word processor was purchased on account for $22,000.
- January 6: She rented an office in which to conduct business. She signed a 3-year lease and had to pay the first (January) and last months' rent of $2,000 per month.
- January 15: Fees earned for the first half of the month totaled $24,000, of which $10,000 was for cash and the remainder on account.
- January 15: Salaries incurred and paid for the first half of the month were $14,000.
- January 18: Two cars were purchased for cash and amounted to $18,000.
- January 20: Cash collections on account totaled $12,000.
- January 23: A $15,000 payment was made on the word processor purchased on January 5.
- January 30: Fees earned for the second half of January totaled $30,000, of which $22,000 was for cash and the remainder on account.
- January 30: Salaries incurred and paid for the second half of the month amounted to $21,000.
- January 31: The following expenses were paid in cash:

Legal fees	$8,000
Utilities	400
Auto repair	2,000

Required:

    a. Make the appropriate journal entries to record the transactions.

    b. Set up the appropriate ledger accounts, post the entries to these accounts, and balance the accounts.

    c. Prepare a trial balance as of January 31.

3A–3. Journal Entries, Posting, the Trial Balance, and the Income Statement. Elaine decided to open a travel agency called Heavenly Travel. All the necessary preopening arrangements were made in January, and the doors opened for business on February 1. The January 30, 1987 trial balance follows:

Heavenly Travel
Trial Balance
January 31, 1987

Accounts	Debit	Credit
Cash	$10,000	
Prepaid insurance	2,000	
Store furniture	10,000	
Store equipment	25,000	
Accounts payable		$ 8,500
Bank Note payable		8,000
E. Diamond, capital		30,500
Totals	$47,000	$47,000

In addition, the firm's chart of accounts is as follows:

Cash	10	E. Diamond, drawing	42
Investment in marketable		Fees earned	50
securities	11	Interest revenue	51
Accounts receivable	15	Gain on sale of	
Prepaid insurance	17	marketable securities	52
Interest receivable	19	Advertising expense	70
Store furniture	20	Automobile expense	71
Store equipment	22	Interest expense	72
Accounts payable	30	Repairs expense	73
Bank of note payable	32	Salaries expense	74
Interest payable	33	Rent expense	75
E. Diamond, capital	40		

During the month of February the following events occurred:

- February 1: February's rent of $1,000 was paid in cash.

- February 2: Anticipating good business, Heavenly Travel purchased an additional $5,000 of office equipment on account.

- February 4: The firm placed an advertisement in the local paper. It cost $400 and was paid in cash.

- February 15: Fees earned for the first half of the month totaled $35,000. All fees but $5,000 to a large corporate customer were for cash.

- February 16: The firm had some excess cash and invested $5,000 in marketable securities.

- February 18: The equipment purchased on February 2 was paid in full.

- February 24: Forty-two hundred dollars in cash was collected on account.

- February 25: Marketable securities with a cost of $2,000 were sold for $2,200 cash.

- February 28: Fees earned for the last half of the month were $27,000. All but $3,000 was for cash.

- February 28: The following expenses were paid in cash:

Salaries	$9,000
Automobile	1,000
Repairs	1,500

- February 28: The firm received notification from its brokers that it had earned interest of $250 on its investment in marketable securities, to be received next month.

- February 28: The bank notified the firm that interest of $155 was incurred during February and was payable immediately. However, as of the end of February it had not been paid.

- February 28: Elaine withdrew $1,500 cash for her personal use.

Required:

a. Make the required entries to record these transactions in the general journal. Assume the journal starts with page 1 and reference it by using the abbreviation GJ-1.

b. Post all entries to the running balance form of the ledger account. Use the account numbers from the chart of accounts to make the proper reference.

c. Balance the ledger accounts and prepare a trial balance.

d. Prepare an income statement for the month ended February 28, 1987.

3A–4. Preparing an Income Statement and a Balance Sheet. You have obtained the following trial balance of Tarkington Fashion Designs as of December 31, 1987.

Tarkington Fashion Designs
Trial Balance
December 31, 1987

Accounts	Debit	Credit
Cash	$ 25,000	
Loans receivable	10,000	
Accounts receivable	30,000	
Office supplies	2,000	
Prepaid insurance	2,400	
Land held for future store site	10,000	
Land	25,000	
Building	40,000	
Store equipment	15,000	
Bank notes payable		$ 30,000
Accounts payable		4,800
Wages payable		3,200
Mortgages payable		50,000
F. Tarkington, capital		61,400
Fees earned		35,000
Interest revenue		500
Gain on sale of equipment		4,000
Advertising expense	2,000	
Automobile expense	500	
Entertainment expense	1,000	
Interest expense	700	
Repairs expense	300	
Taxes expense	5,000	
Wages expense	20,000	
Totals	$188,900	$188,900

The Capital account in the trial balance represents the beginning balance at January 1987, minus the owner's withdrawals of $2,000 paid on April 1, 1987, and directly debited to the Capital account.

Required:

 a. Prepare an income statement for the year ended December 31, 1987.
 b. Verify that the balance in the Capital account at January 1, 1987 is $61,400 and that the balance at December 31, 1987 is $71,400.
 c. Prepare a balance sheet as of December 31, 1987.

3A-5. T Account Analysis. Data relating to several accounts appear below. You are to supply the entry that would most likely account for the missing information. Assume that all items are independent.

 a. The beginning balance in the Accounts Receivable account is $100,000 and the ending balance is $150,000. Assume that all the firm's sales were on credit and that they totaled $450,000 during the year.
 b. The beginning balance in the Land account is $200,000 and the ending balance is $158,000. During the year, the firm sold land with a cost of $82,000 for $89,000 cash.
 c. At the beginning of the year, interest receivable was $900. During the year the firm earned interest of $900 and the ending balance in that account is $650.
 d. The Capital account at the beginning of the year is $65,000. During the year, the firm incurred a net loss of $5,500. The ending balance in the Capital account is $49,500.
 e. The beginning balance in the Accounts Payable account is $24,000 and the ending balance is $32,000. Assume that all of the supplies purchased were on account, were the only items credited in the payable account, and totaled $86,000.
 f. Wages Payable has a beginning balance of $1,400 and an ending balance of $900. During the year the firm paid $63,500 in wages.

3A-6. Cash versus Accrual Accounting. The C. G. Ware Company was organized at the beginning of 1987 to provide management consulting services. The following represents the summary transactions for the year:

 1. The firm was organized as a sole proprietorship, and Ms. Ware invested $65,000 cash.
 2. The firm rented some office space in a prestigious building. The rental was $2,000 per month for 12 months, all of which was paid in cash. In addition, the company had to make a $5,000 prepayment to be applied to the rent at the end of a 4-year lease term.
 3. The firm purchased various supplies on account for $6,000. At the end of the year, $1,500 of the supplies remained on hand.
 4. Instead of purchasing office equipment and furniture, the Ware Company decided to lease them. Total required lease payments for the year were $16,200. However, December's payment was late and was not paid until January.
 5. The firm billed $170,000 for professional services; however, total cash collections for these services equaled $80,000.
 6. Miscellaneous administrative expenses paid in cash were $4,500.
 7. Payments on Accounts Payable for Item 3 were $6,000.
 8. Salaries paid during the year were $88,000. However, $10,000 of those wages was a prepayment for next year's service made this year in order to take advantage of the recent changes in the tax laws.

Required:

 a. Prepare an income statement for the year on the accrual basis.
 b. Prepare an income statement for the year on the cash basis.
 c. Evaluate the performance of the C. G. Ware Company. How much cash was on hand at the end of the year? Which method of accounting provides a better measure of performance? Why?

Problem Set B

3B-1. Journal Entries. The Liquid Survey Company's transactions for August follow:
 1. Received $10,000 proceeds from a bank loan.
 2. Paid July's telephone bill of $100 that was recorded as an account payable in July.
 3. Paid its monthly rental of $2,000.

4. Purchased survey equipment for $10,000 on account.

5. Professional fees earned during the month totaled $90,000, of which 35% was for cash and the remainder on credit.

6. One of the customers was dissatisfied with the survey work done and refused to pay the $1,000 fee for which he had been billed. The firm decided to adjust the customer's account for the full amount.

7. Cash collections on account were $15,000 from July's fees and $25,000 from August's fees.

8. The following expenses were paid in cash:

Wages	$52,400
Delivery	1,000
Repairs	500

9. The firm made an $8,200 payment on the survey equipment purchased in Item 4.

10. Utilities incurred but not yet paid amounted to $600.

Required:

Make the journal entries with appropriate explanations to record each of these transactions.

3B–2. Journal Entries, Posting, and the Trial Balance. Mike and Associates, a management advisory service, was organized in April of the current year. The following events occurred during April:

- April 1: Mike organized the business by contributing the following assets to the firm:

Cash	$60,000
Furniture and fixtures	20,000
Office equipment	12,000

- April 2: Mike realized that he would need additional financing, so he asked his best friend to lend the business $5,000 with no interest.

- April 4: The firm purchased various office equipment for $32,000 on account.

- April 7: The firm signed a lease on a vacant office. The lease runs for five years beginning on April 1 of the current year. The current month's rent of $1,400 plus a $4,000 deposit was paid.

- April 15: Professional fees earned for the first half of April totaled $12,000, of which $6,000 was for cash. The remaining $6,000 was on credit.

- April 17: Additional office equipment was purchased for $15,000 cash.

- April 21: Cash collections from sales on account totaled $4,000.

- April 23: A $28,000 payment was made for the office equipment purchased on April 4.

- April 25: Eight hundred dollars of the equipment purchased on April 17 was damaged. Mike returned it and received a full cash refund.

- April 30: Professional fees earned for the second half of April were $20,000, of which $12,000 was for cash, and the remainder on account.

- April 30: The following expenses were paid in cash:

Salaries	$15,000
Utilities	2,000
Taxes	4,000

Required:

a. Make the appropriate journal entries to record the transactions.

b. Set up the appropriate ledger accounts and post the entries to the accounts.

c. Prepare a trial balance at April 30.

3B–3. Journal Entries, Postings, the Trial Balance, and the Income Statement. Jon Kork decided to open a landscaping service called Looking Better. The firm was organized on May 1, but the business didn't open its doors to customers until June. The May 31, 1987 trial balance is as follows:

Looking Better
Trial Balance
May 31, 1987

Accounts	Debit	Credit
Cash	$22,000	
Garden supplies	6,000	
Prepaid insurance	5,000	
Trucks	10,000	
Equipment	5,000	
Accounts payable		$10,000
Wages payable		2,000
Bank loan payable		8,000
Capital stock		28,000
Totals	$48,000	$48,000

In addition, the firm's chart of accounts is as follows:

Cash	10	J. Kork, capital	40
Investment in		Fees earned	50
marketable securities	11	Interest revenue	51
Accounts receivable	15	Supplies used	60
Gardening supplies	16	Interest expense	61
Prepaid insurance	17	Advertising expense	62
Interest receivable	18	Delivery expense	63
Trucks	20	Salaries expense	64
Equipment	23	City tax expense	65
Accounts payable	30	Utilities expense	66
Wages payable	33	Rent expense	67
Bank loan payable	34	Loss on sale of	
Interest payable	35	marketable securities	70

During the month of June the following events occurred:
- June 1: Wages payable were paid in full.
- June 2: Rent of $1,200 for June was paid in cash.
- June 3: The firm had a number of flyers printed and distributed for advertising purposes. The total cost was $500 and was paid in cash.
- June 15: Fees earned for the first half of June were $10,000, 60% of which was cash and the remainder on account.
- June 15: Garden supplies used during the first half of June cost $4,000.
- June 18: The firm made additional garden supply purchases of $6,000 on account.
- June 20: Excess cash of $8,000 was invested in marketable securities.
- June 25: The garden supplies purchased on the eighteenth were paid for in full.
- June 26: Payments on accounts receivable totaled $3,000.
- June 26: The firm sold for $3,000 marketable securities that it had purchased for $3,600.
- June 30: Fees earned for the second half of June were $12,000, of which $8,000 was for cash and the remainder on credit.
- June 30: Garden supplies used during the second half of the month totaled $4,800.
- June 30: The following expenses were paid in cash:

Salaries	$5,000
Delivery expense	500
Utilities	500
Property taxes	600

- June 30: The firm received notification from its brokers that it had earned interest of $100, to be received next month.
- June 30: The firm was notified by the bank that interest of $80 is due on the loan payable. The firm will pay it next month.

Required:

a. Make the required entries to record these transactions in the general journal. Assume the journal starts with page 1 and reference it by using the abbreviation GJ–1.

b. Post all entries to the running balance form of ledger account. Use the account numbers from the chart of accounts to make the proper reference.

c. Balance the ledger accounts and prepare a trial balance.

d. Prepare an income statement for the month ended June 30, 1987.

3B–4. Preparing an Income Statement and Balance Sheet. You have obtained the following trial balance of the Crosby Engineering Design Company as of December 31, 1987:

**Crosby Engineering
Design Company**
Trial Balance
December 31, 1987

Accounts	Debit	Credit
Cash	$ 40,000	
Notes receivable	10,000	
Accounts receivable	50,000	
Store supplies	2,000	
Prepaid rent	5,000	
Land and building	100,000	
Store equipment	70,000	
Office equipment	3,500	
Other assets	500	
Accounts payable		$ 35,000
Notes payable		10,000
Interest payable		3,000
B. Crosby, capital		101,000
Fees earned		380,000
Rental income		20,000
Advertising expense	15,000	
Delivery expense	1,200	
Interest expense	3,000	
Maintenance expense	1,800	
Office supplies used	500	
Promotion expense	2,500	
Wages expense	240,000	
Loss on sale of land	4,000	
Totals	$549,000	$549,000

The Capital account in the trial balance represents the beginning balance at January 1, 1987, minus cash withdrawals of $10,000 made by the owner on December 15, 1987, and directly debited to the Capital account.

Required:

a. Prepare an income statement for the year ended December 31, 1987.

b. Verify that the balance in the Capital account at January 1, 1987 is $101,000 and that the balance at December 31, 1987 is $233,000.

c. Prepare a balance sheet as of December 31, 1987.

3B–5. T Account Analysis. Data relating to several accounts appear below. You are to supply the entry that would most likely account for the missing information. Assume that all items are independent.

    a. The beginning balance in the Accounts Receivable account is $65,000 and the ending balance is $56,000. All sales were made on account. Cash received on account totaled $56,000.

    b. The beginning balance in the Marketable Securities account is $70,000 and the ending balance is $88,000. During the year the firm sold some securities for $105,000, on which they had a gain of $38,000.

    c. The beginning balance in the Interest Receivable account is $5,000 and the ending balance is $5,300. During the year the firm received interest payments of $3,900.

    d. The beginning balance in the M. Burrell, Capital account is $57,000. During the year the firm earned net income of $12,000, and the ending balance in the Capital account is $53,400.

    e. The Accounts Payable account has a beginning balance of $56,000. All supplies purchases are made on account and the cash payments for the purchases totaled $83,000. The Accounts Payable account is only used to record supplies purchased on account. The ending balance in the account is $89,000.

    f. The beginning balance in the Notes Payable account is $100,000. During the year the firm borrowed an additional $40,000, and at the end of the year the balance in the Notes Payable account is zero.

3B–6. Cash versus Accrual Accounting. Webb Company was organized at the beginning of 1987 to provide contract consulting for major sports figures. The following represents the summary transactions for the year:

    1. The firm was started by Steve Webb with an investment of $60,000 cash.

    2. The firm decided it needed to have prestigious offices, so it rented a large office for $3,000 a month. The firm occupied the office for 12 months during the year; however, December's rent was not paid until January. In addition to the monthly rental payments, the firm made a $12,000 rental prepayment, to be refunded when the lease expires at the end of 5 years.

    3. Various supplies and other small office items were purchased on account for $10,000. At the end of the year $2,500 worth of supplies remained on hand.

    4. The firm leased office furniture and a computer. Total lease payments were $9,600 for the year. However, the firm was a little behind and did not make either November's or December's payment by year-end.

    5. Total billings for the year were $150,000. Seventy thousand dollars was a retainer (deposit) for work that will not be performed until the following year. Cash collections were $100,000.

    6. Miscellaneous expenses paid in cash were $6,000.

    7. Payments on account payable were $10,000.

    8. Several employees earned salaries totaling $30,000, of which $12,000 was unpaid at year-end.

Required:

    a. Prepare an income statement for the year on the accrual basis.

    b. Prepare an income statement for the year on the cash basis.

    c. Evaluate the performance of the Webb Company. How much cash was on hand at year-end? Which method of accounting provides a better measure of performance? Why?

Understanding Financial Statements

Princeville Development Corporation operates two business segments, resort operations and real estate development and sales, at the Princeville resort community located on the Hawaiian island of Kauai. In addition, the Company, through a wholly-owned subsidiary, has a significant ownership interest in a limited partnership that owns the Sheraton Princeville Hotel. Presented as follows is a consolidated statement of income.

Princeville Development Corporation
Consolidated Statement of Income

	Year Ended November 30, 1985
Revenues:	
Resort operations	$4,969,291
Sales of real estate	2,918,487
Rental income (Note 6)	750,858
Interest and other income	1,136,012
	9,774,648
Costs and expenses:	
Resort operating costs	4,067,618
Cost of real estate sales	344,284
Rental expense	250,761
Operating and selling expenses	2,104,885
Excise tax	334,805
Depreciation and amortization	193,798
	7,296,151
Operating income	$2,478,497

Required:

a. Using the data for the year ended November 30, 1985, calculate the percentage of each of the individual revenue items to total revenues. For example, resort operations of $4,969,291 are 50.8% of total revenues of $9,774,648 as calculated as follows:

$$\frac{\$4,969,291}{\$9,774,648} \times 100 = 50.8\%$$

b. Using the data for the year ended November 30, 1985 for resort operations, sales of real estate, and rental income, determine the percentage of the related expense to the revenue item. For example, resort operating costs of $4,067,618 are 81.9% of resort operation revenues of $4,969,291 as calculated as follows:

$$\frac{\$4,067,618}{\$4,969,291} \times 100 = 81.9\%$$

Perform the same calculation for cost of real estate sales and sales of real estate, and rental expense and rental income.

c. Based on the preceding information and your review of the partial income statement for the year ended November 30, 1985, which parts of the business contribute most to the overall revenues of the business? Which parts of the business appear to be the most profitable?

ncial Decision Case

The president of A&D Associates, an advertising agency, is quite concerned about the current and future financial condition of her business. After reviewing the income statement for the year ended December 31, 1987 and the balance sheets at December 31, 1986 and 1987, she relates the following to you:

"I just don't understand our cash situation. As the years go on, we seem to have less and less cash. I started the business in early 1986 with $100,000 cash and also borrowed $60,000 from the bank. During 1986 and 1987, we were profitable. In fact, our net income in 1987 was 20% greater than it was in 1986. Yet our cash balance has decreased, and the capital account has continued to increase."

She gives you the following financial statements and asks your advice:

A&D Associates
Balance Sheets

	December 31	
Assets	1987	1986
Cash	$ 15,000	$ 55,000
Accounts receivable	92,000	60,000
Advertising supplies	38,000	30,000
Prepaids	15,000	10,000
Property and equipment	130,000	90,000
Total assets	$290,000	$245,000
Equities		
Accounts payable	$ 20,000	$ 35,000
Notes payable, due March 1988	60,000	60,000
J. Parker, capital	210,000	150,000
Total equities	$290,000	$245,000

A&D Associates
Income Statement
For the Year Ended December 31, 1987

Revenues		
Advertising fees		$250,000
Operating expenses		
Salaries	$100,000	
Advertising supplies used	40,000	
Commissions paid	25,000	
General office expenses	10,000	
Other	5,000	
Total expenses		180,000
Net income		$ 70,000

Required:

Help explain the cash position of **A&D Associates** to the president by addressing the following questions:

a. Reconcile the change in owner's equity with the net income for the period. What other event appears to have occurred?

b. Explain to the president the relevance of her statement that the company's cash balance has decreased whereas its capital account has increased.

c. Explain to her the possible reasons for the continued decrease in cash since the inception of the business.

d. What future problems do you foresee for **A&D Associates**?

Completing the Accounting Cycle

4

LEARNING OBJECTIVES

After reading this chapter you should be able to:
1. Explain what adjusting entries are and why they are necessary.
2. Describe the major types of adjusting entries and be able to make these entries for different accounts.
3. Complete the accounting cycle.
4. Prepare a worksheet and describe its use.
5. Describe the purposes of reversing entries and be able to make them (Appendix).

This chapter completes our discussion of the accounting cycle. The second chapter analyzed balance sheet transactions, and the third chapter examined income statement transactions. This chapter describes the final steps in the accounting cycle. These steps are preparing adjusting entries, financial statements, closing entries, and worksheets.

Adjusting Entries

Adjusting entries are made at the end of the accounting period to update the accounts for internal transactions, such as the use of supplies or for the recognition of salaries incurred but not paid. Adjusting entries are necessary for these transactions because they affect more than one accounting period. For example, supplies purchased in one year may not be completely used up until the next year, or wages earned in one accounting period may not be paid until the next period. In order to make sure that the financial statements reflect all the events that occurred during a particular period and thus ensure the proper matching of revenues and expenses, adjusting entries are made at the end of each accounting period.

There are two major events that cause economic transactions to affect more than one accounting period, and they relate to the fact that the accrual rather than the cash basis of accounting is used. In the first instance, an economic event occurs and is recorded in one period but is recognized over several subsequent periods. For example, a firm may make an expenditure for an asset that benefits many accounting periods. The purchase of a building in the current period is an illustration of this. In the second instance, an expenditure or the receipt of an asset is not made or received until after the firm receives or provides economic benefits. For example, a firm may incur salary expense in the current period but may not pay that expense in cash until another period. The table below lists the different categories of adjusting entries and specific examples of each.

Categories of Adjusting Entries	Specific Examples
Expenditures made in one period that affect subsequent periods	Supplies, prepaid insurance
Receipts received in one period that affect subsequent periods	Unearned revenue
Expenditures made in subsequent periods	Salaries payable
Receipts received in subsequent periods	Commissions receivable

Expenditures Made in One Period That Affect Subsequent Periods

Enterprises make expenditures or incur liabilities for nonmonetary assets that affect several accounting periods. **Nonmonetary assets** are assets other than cash or legal claims to cash. They usually benefit several periods. These assets include, among others, prepaid items, office supplies, inventories, buildings, and equipment. They are recorded at their initial historical cost which represents the benefits or services that an enterprise expects to receive from these assets. As these services or benefits are consumed, the related cost must be matched against the revenues for the period. This allocation is accomplished by making adjusting entries at the end of the period.

The diagram presented on the next page illustrates this adjustment process. Note that expenditures made in the current period for assets not yet consumed are not recorded as expenses of the current period but are recorded as assets and are included in the current period's balance sheet. The portion of these assets that is consumed in a particular period is recorded as an expense and is reported on the income statement for that period. The portion of these assets that remains unused at the end of a particular period is included on that period's balance sheet.

To demonstrate this allocation process, we discuss adjusting entries for supplies, prepaid assets, and equipment. You should remember, however, that although we are looking at different accounts, the process is the same; it is to allocate the cost of an asset between the part that has been consumed or used (an expense) and the part that has remaining future economic benefits (an asset).

ALLOCATION PROCESS FOR NONMONETARY ASSETS

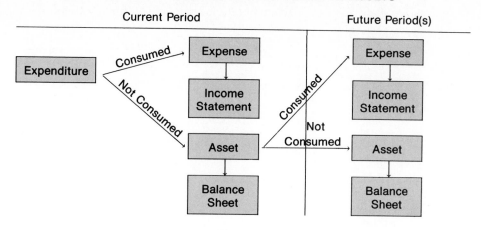

Supplies

Firms often purchase supplies at different times during the year. When these supplies are purchased, the original debit is usually made to an asset account, Office Supplies.[1] Firms generally do not record office supplies as they are used. Instead, at the end of the accounting period, the cost of the remaining supplies on hand is determined, and once this amount is known, it is easy to calculate the amount of supplies used by means of the following formula:

Formula	Amount
Beginning balance of supplies	$ 900
+ Purchases of supplies during the year	1,500
= Supplies available for use	2,400
− Ending balance of supplies	700
= Supplies used during the period	$1,700

An adjusting journal entry is necessary to record the amount of supplies used, in this case $1,700.

The journal entries to record the purchases of supplies on March 14 and on September 10, the adjusting entry at the end of the period, December 31, and the appropriate T accounts are on the next page. The figures in this example are based on the information just presented and the fact that the firm makes adjusting entries only at the end of its calendar year. After the adjusting entry is made, the balance in the Supplies account is $700, which represents

[1]It is possible to record the purchase of supplies by debiting Supplies Expense instead of the asset account, Supplies, for the amount of the purchase. In this case the journal entry would be:

Supplies Expense	XXXX	
Cash		XXXX

However, the more common practice is to debit the asset account to record the purchase of nonmonetary assets such as supplies and prepaids. This is the method followed in the text and in the problem assignments.

Completing the Accounting Cycle   113

the supplies on hand that are available for future use. The balance of $1,700 in the Supplies Expense account represents the supplies used during the period.

Purchase of Supplies

March 14	Supplies	700	
	Cash		700
	To record purchase of supplies.		
September 10	Supplies	800	
	Cash		800
	To record purchase of supplies.		
December 31	Supplies Expense	1,700	
	Supplies		1,700
	To record $1,700 of supplies used during the year.		

Supplies			Supplies Expense	
1/1/87 Bal. 900	12/31 1,700		12/31 1,700	
3/14 700				
9/10 800				
12/31 Bal. 700				

Prepaid Assets

Prepaid assets are nonmonetary assets whose benefits affect more than one accounting period. They include items such as prepaid insurance and prepaid rent and essentially represent the rights to receive future services. However, the rights to these future benefits or services rarely last more than two or three years. The matching convention requires allocation of the expenditure between the asset that represents the remaining economic benefits and the expense that represents the benefits used or consumed by the firm. The services represented by prepaid assets are a function of time, so the allocation process is closely related to the term of service.

The purchase of prepaid insurance will serve as an example. Assume that the Smith Company, which has a yearly accounting period ending on December 31, purchases on April 1, 1987 a two-year comprehensive insurance policy for $2,400. When the insurance policy is purchased, the debit is to the asset account, Prepaid Insurance. The original journal entry, as well as the adjusting entry and the relevant T accounts, is illustrated as follows.

Prepaid Insurance Entries

April 1	Prepaid Insurance	2,400	
	Cash		2,400
	To record purchase of two-year insurance policy.		
Dec. 31	Insurance Expense	900	
	Prepaid Insurance		900
	To adjust prepaid insurance for nine months.		

Amount of journal entry:

$$\frac{\text{Cost of Insurance}}{\text{Number of months benefits received}} = \frac{\$2,400}{24 \text{ months}} = \$100 \text{ per month}$$

Adjusting entry = 9 months $\times$ $100 = $900

114

Prepaid Insurance			Insurance Expense	
4/1	2,400	12/31 900	12/31 900	
12/31 Bal. 1,500				

If we assume that the entire original expenditure for insurance was recorded in the asset account, Prepaid Insurance, it is necessary on December 31 to decrease the asset account by the amount of insurance that has expired. In this case, assuming that the service represented by the asset expires equally each month, the Prepaid Insurance account must be reduced by $900. The balance of $1,500 in the Prepaid Insurance account represents the future benefits of the insurance policy, and the $900 balance in the Insurance Expense account represents the amount of benefits that have expired.

The adjusting entry for prepaid rent or other prepaid assets follows a similar process. When you begin to make adjusting entries for prepaid assets, you should follow these steps:

1. Determine the amount of the estimated monthly benefits to be received from the asset, using this general formula:

$$\frac{\text{Cost of the asset}}{\text{Total number of months benefits are to be received}}$$

2. Write off the appropriate amount of the asset used, based on the date that the asset was acquired and the length of the accounting period. The adjusting entry decreases the asset account and records an expense for the amount of benefits that have been used or have expired.

Depreciation Expense

Nonmonetary assets such as property, plant, and equipment are purchased by an enterprise because of the ability of these assets to generate future revenues. In effect, these assets represent bundles of service potentials that the enterprise gradually uses up during future operations. This occurs because of wear and tear, obsolescence, and other factors. Other than land, which does not lose its future benefits, the matching convention requires that a portion of the cost of these assets be systematically allocated against the revenues generated by these assets. **Depreciation** is the name given to this allocation process.

Although it is more difficult to imagine a building or piece of equipment giving up its benefits than it is to imagine supplies being physically used up or the term of an insurance policy expiring, the concept is the same. As the benefits from all of these assets are consumed, a portion of their cost should be written off to expense. In this sense, the term *write-off* means decreasing the asset account and increasing the expense account by the amount of benefits that have been used or have expired.

To the accountant, depreciation is an allocation process rather than a valuation concept. That is, although an asset's current market value may be increasing, accountants will still depreciate that asset because it is gradually losing its ability to generate future operating revenues. Depreciation is discussed in more detail in Chapter 12.

There are a number of acceptable depreciation methods. For our purposes, we assume that a firm uses straight-line depreciation. **Straight-line depreciation** assumes that depreciation is a constant function of time and results in an equal allocation of the asset's cost to each accounting period of its estimated service life.

In order to calculate periodic depreciation expense, the asset's life and residual (salvage) value must be estimated. Determining the life of a building or piece of equipment is much more difficult than determining the life or term of other nonmonetary assets. For example, an insurance policy has a fixed term, but there is clearly no fixed life for a building or a piece of equipment. Within broad guidelines established by the accounting profession and from past experience, management makes its best estimate of the useful life of buildings and similar assets.

Residual (salvage) value is an estimate of what the asset will be worth at the end of its life. Again, management must make this estimate based on past experience and the asset's economic characteristics. When an asset has a residual value, this amount is not depreciated. Depreciation is limited to the asset's **depreciable base,** which is its acquisition cost less its estimated residual value. The following formula can be used to calculate yearly straight-line depreciation:

$$\frac{\text{Depreciable base (acquisition cost — residual value)}}{\text{Estimated useful life}}$$

Obviously, if the asset has an estimated residual value of zero, this component would be eliminated from the formula.

To illustrate these concepts, assume that on January 2, 1987 an enterprise purchases a new piece of equipment for $75,000 cash. The company has a yearly accounting period ending every December 31 and makes adjusting entries only at that time. The firm estimates that the equipment has a service life of 10 years and that at the end of the tenth year the equipment will have a residual value of $5,000. Presented at the bottom of this page and on the top of page 117 are the journal entries to record the purchase of the equipment, the adjusting entry that is made on each December 31 of the 10-year service life to record the annual depreciation expense of $7,000, and the relevant T accounts.

Journal Entries Related to Depreciation Expense

January 2, 1987	Equipment	75,000	
	Cash		75,000
	To record purchase of equipment for cash.		
December 31, 1987 and thereafter through 1996	Depreciation Expense	7,000	
	Accumulated Depreciation—Equipment		7,000
	To record annual depreciation expense of $7,000.		

$$\text{Calculation of annual depreciation expense} = \frac{\text{Depreciable base}}{\text{Estimated useful life}}$$

$$\$7,000 = \frac{\$75,000 - 5,000}{10 \text{ years}}$$

Equipment		Accumulated Depreciation—Equipment	
1/2/87 75,000			12/31/87 7,000
			12/31/88 7,000
			12/31/89 7,000
			12/31/90 7,000
			12/31/91 7,000
			12/31/92 7,000
			12/31/93 7,000
			12/31/94 7,000
			12/31/95 7,000
			12/31/96 7,000
			70,000

Depreciation Expense	
12/31 each year 7,000	

It is important to note that the credit entry is made to an Accumulated Depreciation account rather than directly to the Equipment account. Accumulated depreciation is considered a contra-asset account. **A contra account** partially or wholly offsets another account. Crediting this account rather than the Equipment account allows the accounting system to maintain the original historical cost of the asset in one account (Equipment in this case) and also to accumulate the depreciation to date in the Accumulated Depreciation account. Both of these accounts are shown on the asset side of the balance sheet, with the Accumulated Depreciation account offset against the corresponding asset account. Going back to the original example, the proper balance sheet presentation as of December 31, 1987 is:

Property, plant, and equipment	
Equipment	$75,000
Less: Accumulated depreciation	7,000
	$68,000

The difference between these two accounts, $68,000, at the end of the first year of the asset's life is often referred to as the asset's **net book value.**

Like all other balance sheet accounts, the Accumulated Depreciation account has a cumulative balance. As a result, the balance in that account will be $14,000 at the end of 1988. The net book value of the asset will be $61,000, determined as follows:

Property, plant, and equipment	
Equipment	$75,000
Less: Accumulated depreciation	14,000
	$61,000

By the end of 1996, the Accumulated Depreciation account has a balance of $70,000, and the asset's net book value equals $5,000, its estimated residual value. Later in this chapter we demonstrate how the $7,000 yearly balance in the Depreciation Expense account is transferred to the Owner's Equity account at the end of the year.

Equipment was used for the depreciation example. The same concept applies to all operational assets except for land, which is not depreciable. Other examples are buildings, furniture and fixtures, automobiles, and machines. For each of these assets, different service lives and salvage values have to be estimated. In addition, a separate accumulated depreciation account is maintained for each major category of accounts. For example, we used an Accumulated Depreciation—Equipment account in our example. For buildings, an Accumulated Depreciation—Buildings account would be used, and so forth.

Receipts Received in One Period That Affect Subsequent Periods

The previous section examined expenditures made in one period that affect subsequent periods. In this section we consider examples in which a firm acquires receipts representing revenues that are recognized in more than one accounting period. The portion of the revenues to be recognized in subsequent accounting periods is called *unearned revenues* and is a liability. Unearned revenues arise any time an enterprise receives cash or other assets prior to a sale or the performance of a service. At the time the firm receives the asset, a liability to deliver a product or perform a service exists. For example, a firm may rent to others, on a yearly basis, part of a building it owns. The agreement calls for the tenant to pay a full year's rent of $18,000 in advance, on September 1, 1987. Assuming that the firm is on a calendar year, the revenue must be allocated between 1987 and 1988. The portion that is unearned at the end of 1987 must be reflected as a liability.

This allocation process is illustrated as follows. In reviewing this diagram, note that receipts collected in the current period that are not yet earned are not recorded as revenues of the current period, but are recorded as liabilities and are included on the current period's balance sheet. The portion of these liabilities that is earned in a particular period is recorded as a revenue and is reported on that period's income statement. The portion of these liabilities that remains unearned at the end of that particular period is included on that period's balance sheet.

ALLOCATION PROCESS FOR UNEARNED REVENUES

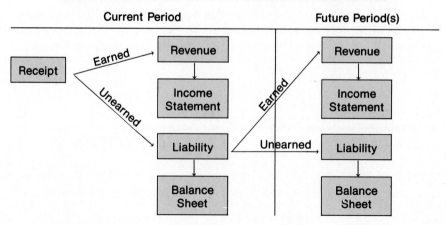

In a manner similar but opposite to that of prepaid assets, we are assuming that unearned revenues are originally recorded as liabilities.[2] As the revenues are earned, the liability account is decreased and the revenue account is increased. Using the data in the previous paragraph, the original entry, the adjusting entry, and the T accounts are illustrated next. The entire $18,000 is originally recorded as a liability. Thus, the purpose of the adjusting entry at December 31 is to reduce the liability and to record revenues for the services performed, in this case the rent earned. Earned monthly revenues total $1,500 and are determined by dividing the total rental payment of $18,000 by 12 months. The $6,000 journal entry is necessary to reduce the liability and to increase the rental revenue earned from September 1 to December 31 (4 months).

Recording Unearned Revenues

September 1	Cash	18,000	
	Unearned Rent Revenue		18,000
	To record receipt of 1 year's rent.		
December 31	Unearned Rent Revenue	6,000	
	Rent Revenue		6,000
	To adjust unearned rent for 4 months of earned revenue.		

Amount of journal entry:

$$\frac{\text{Total receipt}}{\substack{\text{Number of months} \\ \text{receipt applies}}} = \frac{\$18,000}{12\ \text{months}} = \$1,500\ \text{per month}$$

$$\text{Adjusting entry} = 4\ \text{months} \times \$1,500 = \$6,000$$

Unearned Rent Revenue			**Rent Revenue**	
12/31 6,000	9/1 18,000		12/31 6,000	
	12/31 Bal. 12,000			

Again, it is important to note the end result. The liability account has a balance of $12,000, representing the revenues yet to be earned (eight months at $1,500 per month), and the revenue account has a balance of $6,000, representing the four months of rental revenue earned by the firm. Although this example concerns rent, other unearned revenues, such as subscriptions and dues, are handled in the same manner.

Expenditures to Be Made or Receipts to Be Received in Subsequent Periods

The previous discussion focused on adjusting entries that are necessary because receipts or expenditures of net assets were received prior to the proper timing of revenue and expense recognition. In this section we discuss adjusting entries for accruals. **Accruals** recognize that certain expenses are incurred

---

[2]Again, it is possible to record this transaction by crediting a revenue account rather than the liability account for the revenue received in advance. However, this would require a change in the way the adjusting entry is made. The more common method is to credit the unearned revenue account at the time the asset is received. This is the method used in the text and in the problem assignments.

and revenues are earned over time but are recorded only periodically. As a result, adjustments must be made for revenues or expenses that continuously build up but are recorded only at the end of a specific accounting period. Payment or receipt of the asset or liability (usually cash) takes place in following accounting periods. Adjusting entries are necessary for accruals because the accrual basis of accounting requires that revenue and expenses be recognized in the period earned or incurred even if the receipt or payment of cash takes place in later periods. Common accruals, among others, include interest revenue, interest expense, and salaries expense. We must emphasize that accruals are made only for revenues or expenses earned or incurred in one period and for which the cash is received or paid in a subsequent period. If the cash is received or paid when the revenue or expense is recognized, an accrual is not made.

An illustration of the difference between asset or liability allocation (discussed previously) and accruals follows. As assets or liabilities are allocated over time to reflect benefits used or received, the prepaid or unearned portion decreases. Accruals, however, build up over the accounting period.

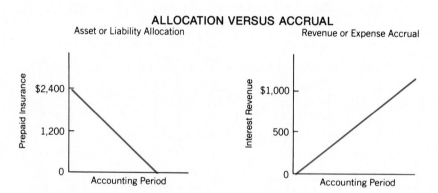

ALLOCATION VERSUS ACCRUAL

Accrued Revenues

Accrued revenues include items such as interest revenue, rental revenue, and investment revenue. Adjusting entries must be made for these items in order to recognize the revenue in the accounting period in which it is earned, even though the receipt of cash will take place in following periods. Revenues from these items occur continuously but, in order to simplify the process, they are recorded only at the end of the accounting period by recognizing an accrued receivable and a corresponding revenue item.

An Example of Accrued Interest. Interest is payment for the use of money. Most loans or notes are interest-bearing and have the following characteristics:

1. **Principal or face amount**—the amount lent or borrowed.
2. **Maturity date**—the date the loan must be repaid.
3. **Maturity value**—the total of the principal and interest at the maturity date.
4. **Interest rate**—the percentage rate of interest, which is usually stated in annual terms and must be prorated for periods shorter than a year.

In general, the correct amount of interest can be calculated by the following formula:

$$i = p \times r \times t \text{ where}$$

i = interest
p = principal of the loan
r = annual interest rate
t = applicable time period in fractions of a year.

To illustrate the use of this formula, assume that the Ozark Company borrows $100,000 at 12% for 9 months. In this example the principal of the loan is $100,000, the annual interest rate is 12%, and the maturity value is $109,000, calculated as follows:

Principal	$100,000
Interest for 9 months	
$100,000 × .12 × 9/12 =	9,000
Maturity value	$109,000

To illustrate how interest accruals are calculated and recorded, assume that on June 1, 1987 the Smith Company lent $10,000 to one of its suppliers, at 9% interest. The loan's maturity date is in nine months, February 28, 1988, at which time both the principal and the total interest are due. In this situation, 9% represents the interest for one year and must be prorated in order to determine the interest income for nine months. (In this example, as well as others, interest is based on twelve 30-day months.)

Once the loan is made, the Smith Company immediately starts earning interest revenue. However, the revenue is not recorded until the end of the accounting period, in this case December 31. It would not be correct to wait until the due date of February 28 to recognize the interest revenue earned through December 31, 1987. This would violate the matching convention because no revenue would be recognized in 1987 and too much would be recognized in 1988. Although it is possible to record the interest daily, this involves excess record keeping, and so an adjusting entry is made at the end of the accounting period, in this case year end.

In this example, the $10,000, 9% note earns interest from June 1 to December 31, 1987 (7 months, each assumed to be 30 days), which amounts to $525 and is calculated as follows:

$$i = \$10,000 \times .09 \times 7/12$$
$$= \$525$$

The total interest for the 9-month term of the loan is $675, or $10,000 × .09 × 9/12. Thus, the interest revenue recognized in 1986 is $525, and the interest earned for 1987 is $150 (total interest for 9 months of $675 less $525 earned in 1986). These relationships are illustrated in the time line below.

TOTAL INTEREST REVENUE $675

The appropriate journal entries on June 1, 1987, the date of the loan; December 31, 1987, the end of the accounting period; and February 28, 1988, the maturity date of the loan, are:

June 1, 1987	Loans Receivable	10,000	
	Cash		10,000
	To record issuance of loan.		
December 31, 1987	Interest Receivable	525	
	Interest Revenue		525
	To record 7 months' interest on $10,000, 9%, 9-month loan.		
February 28, 1988	Cash	10,675	
	Interest Receivable		525
	Interest Revenue		150
	Loans Receivable		10,000
	To record payment of principal and interest of loan.		

At the maturity date, Cash is debited for the entire value of the loan. Interest Receivable of $525 is credited for the interest recognized in the prior period. Interest Revenue is credited $150 for the interest earned during the current period. Finally, the principal of the loan of $10,000 is credited.

Accrued Expenses

Accrued expenses include such items as interest expense, salaries expense, rental expense, and any other expense incurred in one accounting period that will be paid in a subsequent period or periods. Adjusting entries must be made for these items in order to recognize the expense in the period(s) in which it is incurred, even though the cash will not be paid until the following period. Like accrued revenues, the accrued expenses occur continuously, but in order to simplify the accounting process, they are recorded only at the end of the accounting period, by recognizing an accrued payable and a corresponding expense item.

Accrued Salaries Expense. Salaries expense is an example of an accrued expense for which adjusting entries normally are made. An adjustment is necessary because the date that the salaries are paid does not necessarily correspond to the last day of the accounting period. Therefore, accrued salaries payable must be recorded for salaries earned by employees but unpaid through the end of the accounting period.

For example, assume that a firm pays its salaries every Friday for the workweek ending on that day. For simplicity's sake, also assume that the firm began operations on Monday, January 2, 1984; the first payday of the year was Friday, January 6, 1984; and weekly salaries total $1,500. (The year 1984 is used in this example, because January 2 falls on a Monday.) After the last full week of the year on December 28, 1984, the salaries T account appears as follows:

Salaries Expense

1/6	1,500
1/13	1,500
1/20	1,500
"	"
"	"
12/28	1,500
	78,000

Because the salaries for the week beginning Monday, December 31, 1984 are not paid until Friday, January 4, 1985, it is necessary to make an adjusting entry to accrue salaries through December 31, 1984. This requires an entry to debit Salaries Expense and to credit Salaries Payable. In this case, the amount of accrued salaries at December 31, 1984 is for one day's salaries, or $300 ($1,500 ÷ 5 days = $300). The salaries for the next four days of the week, or $1,200, are an expense of the next year, 1985. The following time line shows the total amount of salaries expense for the week ended Friday, January 4, 1985, and how much expense should be allocated between the two years.

TOTAL SALARIES $1,500

————$300———— ————————————$1,200————————————

Monday	Tuesday	Friday
December 31	January 1	January 4

Finally, the adjusting journal entry at December 31, 1984; the entry to record the payment of salaries on January 4, 1985; and the T accounts are:

December 31, 1984	Salaries Expense	300	
	Salaries Payable		300
	To record accrued salaries.		
January 4, 1985	Salaries Payable	300	
	Salaries Expense	1,200	
	Cash		1,500
	To record payment of salaries.		

Salaries Expense		Salaries Payable	
1/6 1,500			12/31 300
1/13 1,500			
1/20 1,500			
" "			
12/28 1,500			
12/31 300			
12/31 Bal. 78,300			

When the salaries are paid on January 4, Cash is credited for the full week's salaries. Salaries Payable is debited for the salaries recognized in the prior period, and Salaries Expense is debited for the current period's salaries.

Other Items Requiring Adjusting Entries

Other items requiring adjusting entries relate to specific items such as Accounts Receivable and estimated liabilities such as warranties and guarantees whose accounts must be adjusted to their proper balances. These items are covered in later chapters. In addition, bookkeeping errors are likely to occur and are usually corrected through adjusting entries at the end of the accounting period.

Lisa Bowman's Law Firm

Let us now examine the adjusting entries that are necessary before Lisa Bowman can complete the first (quarterly) accounting cycle for her new law firm.

The June 30, 1987 **unadjusted trial balance** follows.[3] We will assume that the firm's quarterly accounting period ends on June 30, 1987 and that adjusting entries must be made for the three-month period April (the date the firm was organized) through June 30, 1987.

Lisa Bowman's Law Firm
Unadjusted Trial Balance
June 30, 1987

Account	Debit	Credit
Cash	$ 12,690	
Accounts receivable	1,900	
Office supplies	2,380	
Prepaid insurance	2,400	
License	120	
Land	20,000	
Building	120,000	
Office furniture and fixtures	10,000	
Office equipment	8,100	
Accounts payable		$ 2,090
Bank loan payable		5,000
L. Bowman, Capital		165,000
L. Bowman, Drawing	1,200	
Fees earned		8,500
Salaries expense	1,000	
Repairs and maintenance expense	400	
Utilities expense	200	
Advertising expense	200	
Totals	$180,590	$180,590

Information containing the adjusting entries is presented next, followed by the actual adjusting entries.

1. The license purchased on April 2, 1987 has a life of one year. The appropriate expense must be recorded for April, May, and June.
2. An inventory of office supplies indicated that $880 remained on hand at the end of June.
3. Prepaid insurance must be written off. The two-year policy was purchased on May 22. However, it did not become effective until June 1. Therefore, one month must be written off.
4. The office furniture and fixtures have an estimated life of 8 years with a $400 salvage value. The firm will take depreciation on both purchases from the beginning of May.
5. The building has a life of 20 years with no salvage value. The firm will depreciate the building beginning in May.
6. The office equipment has an estimated life of five years with no salvage value. The firm will take depreciation beginning in May for two months.
7. The $5,000 bank loan to purchase office furniture and fixtures has an annual

---

[3]In past chapters we have referred to the unadjusted trial balance as just the trial balance. However, because it is produced from the general ledger prior to the adjustments, its proper name is the *unadjusted trial balance*.

interest rate of 9%. Both interest and principal are payable in one year. The loan was made on May 2. Assume an entire month's interest for May.

8. Salaries earned by employees for the second half of June totaled $1,200. These salaries will be paid the first day of July.

Lisa Bowman's Law Firm
Adjusting Journal Entries
General Journal

Date	Account Titles	Ref.	Debit	Credit
1987 June 30	License Expense	605	30	
	License	121		30
	To write off three months of license. Monthly write-off equals $10 or $120 ÷ 12 months or $30 for 3 months.			
30	Office Supplies Expense	607	1,500	
	Office Supplies	115		1,500
	To write off office supplies used during the period.			

	Balance/ Unadjusted Trial Balance	Actual Balance on Hand	Required Adjustment
Office Supplies	$2,380	$880	$1,500

Date	Account Titles	Ref.	Debit	Credit
30	Insurance Expense	611	100	
	Prepaid Insurance	120		100
	To write off one month of prepaid insurance. Monthly write-off equals $100 or $2,400 ÷ 24 months.			
30	Depreciation Expense	615	200	
	Accumulated Depreciation—Office Furniture and Fixtures	166		200
	To record two months of depreciation expense.			

$$\frac{\$10,000 - \$400}{8 \text{ years}} = \$1,200 \text{ per year, or } \$100 \text{ per month, or } \$200 \text{ for 2 months.}$$

Date	Account Titles	Ref.	Debit	Credit
30	Depreciation Expense	615	1,000	
	Accumulated Depreciation—Building	161		1,000
	To record two months of depreciation expense.			

$$\frac{\$120,000}{20 \text{ years}} = \$6,000 \text{ per year, or } \$500 \text{ per month, or } \$1,000 \text{ for 2 months.}$$

Date	Account Titles	Ref.	Debit	Credit
30	Depreciation Expense	215	270	
	Accumulated Depreciation—Office Equipment	168		270
	To record two months of depreciation expense.			

$$\frac{\$8,100}{5 \text{ years}} = \$1,620 \text{ per year, or } \$135 \text{ per month, or } \$270 \text{ for 2 months.}$$

Date	Account Titles	Ref.	Debit	Credit
30	Interest Expense	801	75	
	Interest Payable	212		75
	To record interest expense for two months.			

$5,000 × .09 × 2/12 = $75

Date	Account Titles	Ref.	Debit	Credit
30	Salaries Expense	601	1,200	
	Salaries Payable	210		1,200
	To record salaries payable for second half of June.			

Completion of the Accounting Cycle

After the adjusting entries have been recorded in the general journal, five steps remain in the accounting cycle:

1. Post the adjusting entries to the ledger accounts.
2. Prepare an adjusted trial balance.
3. Prepare financial statements.
4. Make closing entries and post to the ledger accounts.
5. Prepare a post-closing trial balance.

As we will see later in this chapter, a worksheet can be prepared that combines some of these steps.

Posting Entries to the General Ledger

After the adjusting entries have been recorded in the general journal, they must be posted to the general ledger accounts. In fact, after recording a series of journal entries in the general journal you should post them to the ledger accounts. This will allow you to find mathematical and posting errors at an early stage in the accounting cycle. The general ledger accounts for Lisa Bowman's law firm, after the adjusting entries have been posted, are illustrated next. The adjusting entries are posted to the accounts with a reference to page 4 from the general journal (GJ–4).

Lisa Bowman's Law Firm
Ledger Accounts

Cash   **101**

					Balance	
Date	Item	Ref.	Debit	Credit	Debit	Credit
1987						
June 1	Beg. Bal.				10,790	
15		GJ–3	2,000		12,790	
16		GJ–3		1,000	11,790	
23		GJ–3	1,200		12,990	
24		GJ–3		400	12,590	
29		GJ–3		2,100	10,490	
30		GJ–3	3,400		13,890	
30		GJ–3		1,200	12,690	

Accounts Receivable   **106**

					Balance	
Date	Item	Ref.	Debit	Credit	Debit	Credit
1987						
June 1	Beg. Bal.				0	
15		GJ–3	1,500		1,500	
23		GJ–3		1,200	300	
30		GJ–3	1,600		1,900	

Office Supplies 115

Date	Item	Ref.	Debit	Credit	Balance Debit	Balance Credit
1987 June 1	Beg. Bal.				1,380	
20		GJ–3	1,000		2,380	
30		GJ–4		1,500	880	

Prepaid Insurance 120

Date	Item	Ref.	Debit	Credit	Balance Debit	Balance Credit
1987 June 1	Beg. Bal.				2,400	
20		GJ–4		100	2,300	

License 121

Date	Item	Ref.	Debit	Credit	Balance Debit	Balance Credit
1987 June 1	Beg. Bal.				120	
30		GJ–4		30	90	

Land 150

Date	Item	Ref.	Debit	Credit	Balance Debit	Balance Credit
1987 June 1	Beg. Bal.				20,000	

Building 160

Date	Item	Ref.	Debit	Credit	Balance Debit	Balance Credit
1987 June 1	Beg. Bal.				120,000	

Accumulated Depreciation—Building 161

Date	Item	Ref.	Debit	Credit	Balance Debit	Balance Credit
1987 June 30		GJ–4		1,000		1,000

Office Furniture and Fixtures 165

Date	Item	Ref.	Debit	Credit	Balance Debit	Balance Credit
1987 June 1	Beg. Bal.				10,000	

(continued on next page)

Lisa Bowman's Law Firm (cont.)
Ledger Accounts

Accumulated Depreciation—Office Furniture and Fixtures   166

Date	Item	Ref.	Debit	Credit	Balance Debit	Balance Credit
1987 June 30		GJ–4		200		200

Office Equipment   167

Date	Item	Ref.	Debit	Credit	Balance Debit	Balance Credit
1987 June 1	Beg. Bal.				8,100	

Accumulated Depreciation—Office Equipment   168

Date	Item	Ref.	Debit	Credit	Balance Debit	Balance Credit
1987 June 1		GJ–4		270		270

Accounts Payable   201

Date	Item	Ref.	Debit	Credit	Balance Debit	Balance Credit
1987 June 1	Beg. Bal.					2,790
2		GJ–3		200		2,990
20		GJ–3		1,000		3,990
29		GJ–3	2,100			1,890
30		GJ–3		200		2,090

Bank Loan Payable   205

Date	Item	Ref.	Debit	Credit	Balance Debit	Balance Credit
1987 June 1	Beg. Bal.					5,000

Salaries Payable   210

Date	Item	Ref.	Debit	Credit	Balance Debit	Balance Credit
1987 June 1		GJ–4		1,200		1,200

Interest Payable 212

Date	Item	Ref.	Debit	Credit	Balance Debit	Balance Credit
1987 June 30		GJ–4		75		75

L. Bowman, Capital 301

Date	Item	Ref.	Debit	Credit	Balance Debit	Balance Credit
1987 June 1	Beg. Bal.					165,000

L. Bowman, Drawing 311

Date	Item	Ref.	Debit	Credit	Balance Debit	Balance Credit
1987 June 30		GJ–3	1,200		1,200	

Fees Earned 401

Date	Item	Ref.	Debit	Credit	Balance Debit	Balance Credit
1987 June 15		GJ–3		3,500		3,500
30		GJ–3		5,000		8,500

Salaries Expense 601

Date	Item	Ref.	Debit	Credit	Balance Debit	Balance Credit
1987 June 16		GJ–3	1,000		1,000	
30		GJ–4	1,200		2,200	

Repairs and Maintenance Expense 602

Date	Item	Ref.	Debit	Credit	Balance Debit	Balance Credit
1987 June 24		GJ–3	400		400	

Utilities Expense 603

Date	Item	Ref.	Debit	Credit	Balance Debit	Balance Credit
1987 June 30		GJ–3	200		200	

(continued on next page)

Lisa Bowman's Law Firm (cont.)
Ledger Accounts

Advertising Expense — 604

Date	Item	Ref.	Debit	Credit	Balance Debit	Balance Credit
1987 June 2		GJ–3	200		200	

License Expense — 605

Date	Item	Ref.	Debit	Credit	Balance Debit	Balance Credit
1987 June 30		GJ–4	30		30	

Office Supplies Expense — 607

Date	Item	Ref.	Debit	Credit	Balance Debit	Balance Credit
1987 June 30		GJ–4	1,500		1,500	

Insurance Expense — 611

Date	Item	Ref.	Debit	Credit	Balance Debit	Balance Credit
1987 June 30		GJ–4	100		100	

Depreciation Expense — 615

Date	Item	Ref.	Debit	Credit	Balance Debit	Balance Credit
1987 June 30		GJ–4	200		200	
June 30		GJ–4	1,000		1,200	
June 30		GJ–4	270		1,470	

Interest Expense — 801

Date	Item	Ref.	Debit	Credit	Balance Debit	Balance Credit
1987 June 30		GJ–4	75		75	

The Adjusted Trial Balance

In order to check for posting errors, it is common to prepare an adjusted trial balance. An **adjusted trial balance** is a listing of the general ledger account balances after the adjustments have been posted. The June 30, 1987 adjusted trial balance for Lisa Bowman's law firm is presented below. Often, the unadjusted trial balance and the adjusted trial balance are prepared as part of a worksheet. The purposes and preparation of a worksheet are discussed later in this chapter.

Lisa Bowman's Law Firm
Adjusted Trial Balance
June 30, 1987

Account	Debit	Credit
Cash	$ 12,690	
Accounts receivable	1,900	
Office supplies	880	
Prepaid insurance	2,300	
License	90	
Land	20,000	
Building	120,000	
Accumulated depreciation—Building		$ 1,000
Office furniture and fixtures	10,000	
Accumulated depreciation—Office furniture and fixtures		200
Office equipment	8,100	
Accumulated depreciation—Office equipment		270
Accounts payable		2,090
Bank loan payable		5,000
Salaries payable		1,200
Interest payable		75
L. Bowman, Capital		165,000
L. Bowman, Drawing	1,200	
Fees earned		8,500
Salaries expense	2,200	
Repairs and maintenance expense	400	
Utilities expense	200	
Advertising expense	200	
License expense	30	
Office supplies expense	1,500	
Insurance expense	100	
Depreciation expense	1,470	
Interest expense	75	
Totals	$183,335	$183,335

Preparing the Financial Statements

Most of the financial statements can be prepared directly from the adjusted trial balance. The income statement is usually prepared first, followed by the statement of owner's equity and then the balance sheet. The balance in the L. Bowman, Capital account on the balance sheet is taken from the ending balance on the statement of owner's equity because the Capital account on the adjusted trial balance has yet to reflect any of the income statement transactions. Later in this chapter we see that the posting of the closing entries to the general ledger makes the Capital account balance equal to the ending Capital account on the June 30 balance sheet.

Lisa Bowman's Law Firm
Income Statement
For the Three Months Ending
June 30, 1987

Revenues		
Fees earned		$8,500
Expenses		
Salaries expense	$2,200	
Office supplies expense	1,500	
Depreciation expense	1,470	
Repairs and maintenance expense	400	
Utilities expense	200	
Advertising expense	200	
Insurance expense	100	
Interest expense	75	
License expense	30	
Total expenses		6,175
Net income		$2,325

Lisa Bowman's Law Firm
Statement of Owner's Equity
For the Three Months Ending
June 30, 1987

L. Bowman, capital—April 1, 1987	$ 0
Add: Investments	165,000
Net income for the period	2,325
Subtotal	167,325
Less: Withdrawals	1,200
L. Bowman, capital—June 30, 1987	$166,125

Lisa Bowman's Law Firm
Balance Sheet
June 30, 1987

Assets			Liabilities and Owner's Equity		
Cash		$ 12,690	Liabilities		
Accounts receivable		1,900	Accounts payable	$2,090	
Office supplies		880	Bank loan payable	5,000	
Prepaid insurance		2,300	Salaries payable	1,200	
License		90	Interest payable	75	
Land		20,000	Total liabilities		$ 8,365
Building	$120,000				
Less: Accumulated depreciation	1,000	119,000	Owner's equity		
			L. Bowman, capital		166,125
Store furniture and fixtures	10,000				
Less: Accumulated depreciation	200	9,800			
Office equipment	8,100				
Less: Accumulated depreciation	270	7,830			
			Total liabilities		
Total assets		$174,490	and owner's equity		$174,490

Closing Entries

To accumulate information on the details of operations during a period, separate revenue and expense accounts are maintained. At the end of a period, this information is reported in the income statement. **Closing entries** are made at the end of the period and are used to accomplish two objectives:

1. To update the Owner's Capital account to reflect the results of operations.
2. To eliminate the balances in the revenue and expense accounts so that they may be used again in a subsequent period.

Closing Revenue Accounts

Revenue accounts such as Fees Earned and Interest Revenue have credit balances. In order to close these accounts to a zero balance, they are debited for the amount of the ending balance. The credit part of the entry is to an Income Summary account. The **Income Summary account** is a temporary holding account used in the closing process. When a firm has several revenue accounts, only one compound closing entry that debits the individual revenue accounts and credits the Income Summary account is made.

In the following example, Lisa Bowman's law firm has only one revenue account that is closed. (For simplicity, we will assume that June 30 is the end of the fiscal year.)

Fees Earned	8,500	
Income Summary		8,500
To close revenue account to income summary.		

After this entry is posted, the ledger accounts appear as follows. (Again, we will assume that the closing entries are recorded on page 4 of the general journal.)

Fees Earned   401

Date	Item	Ref.	Debit	Credit	Balance Debit	Balance Credit
June 15		GJ–3		3,500		3,500
30		GJ–3		5,000		8,500
30	Closing	GJ–4	8,500			0

Income Summary   1000

Date	Item	Ref.	Debit	Credit	Balance Debit	Balance Credit
June 30	Closing	GJ–4		8,500		8,500

Income Summary   1000

Date	Item	Ref.	Debit	Credit	Balance Debit	Balance Credit
June 30	Closing	GJ–4		8,500		
30	Closing	GJ–4	6,175			2,325

Salaries Expense   601

Date	Item	Ref.	Debit	Credit	Balance Debit	Balance Credit
June 16		GJ–3	1,000		1,000	
30		GJ–4	1,200		2,200	
30	Closing	GJ–4		2,200	0	

Repairs and Maintenance Expense   602

Date	Item	Ref.	Debit	Credit	Balance Debit	Balance Credit
June 24		GJ–3	400		400	
30	Closing	GJ–4		400	0	

Utilities Expense   603

Date	Item	Ref.	Debit	Credit	Balance Debit	Balance Credit
June 30		GJ–3	200		200	
30	Closing	GJ–4		200	0	

Advertising Expense 604

Date	Item	Ref.	Debit	Credit	Balance Debit	Credit
June 2		GJ–3	200		200	
30	Closing	GJ–4		200	0	

License Expense 605

Date	Item	Ref.	Debit	Credit	Balance Debit	Credit
June 30		GJ–4	30		30	
30	Closing			30	0	

Office Supplies Expense 607

Date	Item	Ref.	Debit	Credit	Balance Debit	Credit
June 30		GJ–4	1,500		1,500	
30	Closing			1,500	0	

Insurance Expense 611

Date	Item	Ref.	Debit	Credit	Balance Debit	Credit
June 30		GJ–4	100		100	
30	Closing	GJ–4		100	0	

Depreciation Expense 615

Date	Item	Ref.	Debit	Credit	Balance Debit	Credit
June 30		GJ–4	200		200	
30		GJ–4	1,000		1,200	
30		GJ–4	270		1,470	
30	Closing			1,470		

Interest Expense 801

Date	Item	Ref.	Debit	Credit	Balance Debit	Credit
June 30		GJ–4	75		75	
30	Closing			75	0	

Closing Expense Accounts

Expense accounts, such as Salaries and Advertising Expense, typically have debit balances. In order to close these accounts to a zero balance they are credited for the amount of their individual ending balances. The debit part of the entry is to the Income Summary account. To repeat, one compound entry is used to close all the expense accounts.

The entry to close the expense accounts for Lisa Bowman's law firm is as follows:

Income Summary	6,175	
Salaries Expense		2,200
Repairs and Maintenance Expense		400
Advertising Expense		200
Utilities Expense		200
License Expense		30
Office Supplies Expense		1,500
Insurance Expense		100
Depreciation Expense		1,470
Interest Expense		75
To close expense accounts to income summary.		

After this entry is posted, the ledger accounts appear as shown on pages 134 and 135.

Closing the Income Summary Account

The next step in the closing process is to close the Income Summary account into the Owner's Capital account. After the revenue and expense accounts have been closed into the Income Summary account, that account now shows all the effects of the income statement transactions. If the firm has made a profit, a debit will be required to close the Income Summary account. This is because more credits (revenues) have been transferred into this account than debits (expenses). The amount of this balancing debit will equal the net income for the period. Conversely, if the firm has suffered a net loss during the period, a credit will be required to close the Income Summary account. This is because more debits (expenses) have been transferred into this account than credits (revenues). The amount of this balancing credit will equal the net loss for the period. The entry to close the Income Summary account is:

Income Summary	2,325	
L. Bowman, Capital		2,325
To close income summary to capital.		

The Capital account after this entry is posted is at the top of page 137.

Closing the Drawing Account

The final step in the closing process is to close the Drawing account to the Owner's Capital account. This entry does not involve the Income Summary account because the owner's withdrawals are not an expense of the business. Because the Drawing account has a debit balance, it is closed with a credit. The corresponding debit to the Capital account reduces the owner's equity for the amount of the withdrawal.

L. Bowman, Capital   **301**

Date	Item	Ref.	Debit	Credit	Balance Debit	Balance Credit
June 1						165,000
30	Closing	GJ–4		2,325		167,325

Income Summary   **1000**

Date	Item	Ref.	Debit	Credit	Balance Debit	Balance Credit
June 30	Closing	GJ–4		8,500		8,500
30	Closing	GJ–4	6,175			2,325
30	Closing	GJ–4	2,325			0

The entry to close the Drawing account for Lisa Bowman's law firm is as follows:

```
L. Bowman, Capital                    1,200
    L. Bowman, Drawing                          1,200
To close the drawing account to capital.
```

After this entry is posted, the ledger accounts appear as follows:

L. Bowman, Capital   **301**

Date	Item	Ref.	Debit	Credit	Balance Debit	Balance Credit
June 1						165,000
30	Closing	GJ–4		2,325		167,325
30	Closing	GJ–4	1,200			166,125

L. Bowman, Drawing   **311**

Date	Item	Ref.	Debit	Credit	Balance Debit	Balance Credit
June 30		GJ–3	1,200		1,200	
30	Closing	GJ–4		1,200	0	

Post-Closing Trial Balance

The **post-closing trial balance** is prepared from the ledger accounts after the closing entries have been posted and is necessary to ensure that these entries have been correctly posted. The post-closing trial balance differs from other trial balances in two ways. First, only balance sheet accounts are included, because all of the income statement or nominal accounts have zero balances. Second, the balance in the Owner's Capital account is the balance at the end of the accounting period rather than the balance at the beginning of the period as it is in other trial balances. This is because the closing entries have put the total of all the income statement accounts and the Drawing account into the Capital account. Lisa Bowman's post-closing trial balance is shown below.

Lisa Bowman's Law Firm
Post-Closing Trial Balance
June 30, 1987

Account	Debit	Credit
Cash	$ 12,690	
Accounts receivable	1,900	
Office supplies	880	
Prepaid insurance	2,300	
License	90	
Land	20,000	
Building	120,000	
Accumulated depreciation—Buildings		$ 1,000
Office furniture and fixtures	10,000	
Accumulated depreciation—Furniture and fixtures		200
Office equipment	8,100	
Accumulated depreciation—Office equipment		270
Accounts payable		2,090
Bank loan payable		5,000
Salaries payable		1,200
Interest payable		75
L. Bowman, Capital		166,125
Totals	$175,960	$175,960

A Worksheet—A Useful Tool

A **worksheet** is a common tool used by accountants to summarize the information needed to prepare financial statements and thus complete the accounting cycle. There are several different types and forms of worksheets. The complete worksheet for Lisa Bowman's law firm, illustrated in Exhibit 4–4 is only one of the common forms used by firms. It is important to note that a worksheet does not preclude the need to make adjusting entries or closing entries or to post these entries to the ledger accounts.

Preparing a Worksheet
A worksheet can be prepared after the unadjusted trial balance is complete, the accounts analyzed, and the data are generated for the adjusting entries. The steps in the accounting cycle summarized on the worksheet are the adjusting entries, the adjusted trial balance, and the income statement and the balance sheet.

138

The Unadjusted Trial Balance

The worksheet in Exhibit 4–1 (page 140) is a portion of a 10-column worksheet. The first two columns are the unadjusted trial balance. If you compare these columns with the unadjusted trial balance on page 124 you will see that they are almost identical. Note that accounts such as Interest Payable, Salaries Payable, and Depreciation Expense are inserted into the trial balance in their proper positions, although they have zero balances. This makes subsequent work easier and guards against confusing balance sheet accounts with nominal or income statement accounts. Thus, before preparing the trial balance, you should determine what other accounts will be required and insert them in the proper place in the unadjusted trial balance columns.

The Adjustment Columns

The adjustment columns numbered 3 and 4 on the worksheet are used to enter the required adjusting entries. The eight adjusting entries for Lisa Bowman's law firm shown on page 125 are entered in the adjustment columns of the worksheet. These entries should be numbered in order to make it easier to locate errors. The debit and credit columns are then totaled to ensure that debits equal credits on the worksheet. Exhibit 4–2 (page 141) presents the worksheet after these entries have been made.

The Adjusted Trial Balance

The adjusted trial balance (columns 5 and 6) is the result of combining the adjusting entries with the corresponding account balances in the unadjusted trial balance. For example, in the unadjusted trial balance, the balance in the Office Supplies account is $2,380. Adjustment 2 credits the Office Supplies account for $1,500, and the debit balance in this account becomes $880 in the adjusted trial balance. The balance of the Office Supplies Expense account in the unadjusted trial balance is zero. This is because all purchases of office supplies are originally recorded in the asset account, Office Supplies. The debit part of adjusting entry 2 debits the Office Supplies Expense account for $880. As a result, the debit balance in the Office Supplies Expense account is $880, or the unadjusted trial balance of zero plus $880. The balances in the accounts that are not affected by the adjustments process are just carried forward to the adjusted trial balance.

The balances in the adjusted trial balance columns should equal the balances in the general ledger accounts after the adjusting entries have been posted to the ledger accounts. If you compare the adjusted trial balance on the worksheet in Exhibit 4–3 (page 142) with the adjusted trial balance on page 131, you will see that they are identical.

The Income Statement and Balance Sheet Columns

The last four columns (two for the income statement, two for the balance sheet) are used to prepare the financial statements. The real (or balance sheet) accounts are transferred to the balance sheet columns and the nominal (or income statement) accounts to the income statement columns. The accounts in the adjusted trial balance should be extended to the balance sheet and income statement columns in the order in which they are listed on the worksheet to decrease the possibility of mixing up the balance sheet and income statement accounts. After extending the accounts, check that each account has been extended to either the balance sheet or the income statement, not to both. The completed worksheet is shown in Exhibit 4–4 (page 143).

EXHIBIT 4-1
Lisa Bowman's Law Firm
Worksheet
For the Three Months Ended June 30, 1987

Account	1 Unadjusted Trial Balance Debit	2 Unadjusted Trial Balance Credit	3 Adjustments Debit	4 Adjustments Credit	5 Adjusted Trial Balance Debit	6 Adjusted Trial Balance Credit	7 Income Statement Debit	8 Income Statement Credit	9 Balance Sheet Debit	10 Balance Sheet Credit
Cash	12,690									
Accounts receivable	1,900									
Office supplies	2,380									
Prepaid insurance	2,400									
License	120									
Land	20,000									
Building	120,000									
Accumulated depreciation—Building		2,090								
Office furniture and fixtures	10,000									
Accumulated depreciation—Office furniture and fixtures										
Office equipment	8,100									
Accumulated depreciation—Office equipment										
Accounts payable		5,000								
Bank loan payable										
Salaries payable										
Interest payable										
L. Bowman, capital		165,000								
L. Bowman, drawing	1,200									
Fees earned		8,500								
Salaries expense	1,000									
Repairs and maintenance expense										
Utilities expense	400									
Advertising expense	200									
License expense	200									
Office supplies expense										
Insurance expense										
Depreciation expense										
Interest expense										
Total	180,590	180,590								
Net income										

140

EXHIBIT 4–2
Lisa Bowman's Law Firm
Worksheet
For the Three Months Ended June 30, 1987

	1	2	3	4	5	6	7	8	9	10
	Unadjusted Trial Balance		Adjustments		Adjusted Trial Balance		Income Statement		Balance Sheet	
Account	Debit	Credit	Debit	Credit	Debit	Credit	Debit	Credit	Debit	Credit
Cash	12,690									
Accounts receivable	1,900									
Office supplies	2,380			² 1,500						
Prepaid insurance	2,400			³ 100						
License	120			¹ 30						
Land	20,000									
Building	120,000									
Accumulated depreciation—Building				⁵ 1,000						
Office furniture and fixtures	10,000									
Accumulated depreciation—Office furniture and fixtures				⁴ 200						
Office equipment	8,100									
Accumulated depreciation—Office equipment				⁶ 270						
Accounts payable		2,090								
Bank loan payable		5,000								
Salaries payable				⁸ 1,200						
Interest payable				⁷ 75						
L. Bowman, capital		165,000								
L. Bowman, drawing	1,200									
Fees earned		8,500								
Salaries expense	1,000		⁸ 1,200							
Repairs and maintenance expense	400									
Utilities expense	200									
Advertising expense	200									
License expense			¹ 30							
Office supplies expense			² 1,500							
Insurance expense			³ 100							
Depreciation expense			⁴ 200 ⁵ 1,000 ⁶ 270							
Interest expense			⁷ 75							
Total	180,590	180,590	4,375	4,375						
Net income										

141

EXHIBIT 4–3
Lisa Bowman's Law Firm
Worksheet
For the Three Months June 30, 1987

Account	1 Unadjusted Trial Balance Debit	2 Credit	3 Adjustments Debit	4 Credit	5 Adjusted Trial Balance Debit	6 Credit	7 Income Statement Debit	8 Credit	9 Balance Sheet Debit	10 Credit
Cash	12,690				12,690					
Accounts receivable	1,900				1,900					
Office supplies	2,380			2 1,500	880					
Prepaid insurance	2,400			3 100	2,300					
License	120			1 30	90					
Land	20,000				20,000					
Building	120,000				120,000					
Accumulated depreciation—Building				5 1,000		1,000				
Office furniture and fixtures	10,000				10,000					
Accumulated depreciation—Office furniture and fixtures				4 200		200				
Office equipment	8,100				8,100					
Accumulated depreciation—Office equipment				6 270		270				
Accounts payable		2,090				2,090				
Bank loan payable		5,000				5,000				
Salaries payable				8 1,200		1,200				
Interest payable				7 75		75				
L. Bowman, capital		165,000				165,000				
L. Bowman, drawing	1,200				1,200					
Fees earned		8,500				8,500				
Salaries expense	1,000		8 1,200		2,200					
Repairs and maintenance expense	400				400					
Utilities expense	200				200					
Advertising expense	200				200					
License expense			1 30		30					
Office supplies expense			2 1,500		1,500					
Insurance expense			3 100		100					
Depreciation expense			4 200 / 5 1,000 / 6 270		1,470					
Interest expense			7 75		75					
Total	180,590	180,590	4,375	4,375	183,335	183,335				
Net income										

142

EXHIBIT 4-4
Lisa Bowman's Law Firm
Worksheet
For the Three Months Ended June 30, 1987

Account	Unadjusted Trial Balance Debit	Unadjusted Trial Balance Credit	Adjustments Debit	Adjustments Credit	Adjusted Trial Balance Debit	Adjusted Trial Balance Credit	Income Statement Debit	Income Statement Credit	Balance Sheet Debit	Balance Sheet Credit
Cash	12,690				12,690				12,690	
Accounts receivable	1,900				1,900				1,900	
Office supplies	2,380			² 1,500	880				880	
Prepaid insurance	2,400			³ 100	2,300				2,300	
License	120			¹ 30	90				90	
Land	20,000				20,000				20,000	
Building	120,000				120,000				120,000	
Accumulated depreciation—Building				⁵ 1,000		1,000				1,000
Office furniture and fixtures	10,000				10,000				10,000	
Accumulated depreciation—Office furniture and fixtures				⁴ 200		200				200
Office equipment	8,100				8,100				8,100	
Accumulated depreciation—Office equipment				⁶ 270		270				270
Accounts payable		2,090				2,090				2,090
Bank loan payable		5,000				5,000				5,000
Salaries payable				⁸ 1,200		1,200				1,200
Interest payable				⁷ 75		75				75
L. Bowman, capital		165,000				165,000				165,000
L. Bowman, drawing	1,200				1,200				1,200	
Fees earned		8,500				8,500		8,500		
Salaries expense	1,000		⁸ 1,200		2,200		2,200			
Repairs and maintenance expense	400				400		400			
Utilities expense	200				200		200			
Advertising expense	200				200		200			
License expense			¹ 30		30		30			
Office supplies expense			² 1,500		1,500		1,500			
Insurance expense			³ 100		100		100			
Depreciation expense			⁴ 200 ⁵ 1,000 ⁶ 270		1,470		1,470			
Interest expense			⁷ 75		75		75			
Total	180,590	180,590	4,375	4,375	183,335	183,335	6,175	8,500	177,160	174,835
Net income							2,325			2,325
							8,500	8,500	177,160	177,160

143

Totaling the Income Statement and the Balance Sheet Columns

The next step in the preparation of the worksheet is to total the income statement and balance sheet columns. The income statement columns are totaled first because net income must be determined and transferred to the Capital account before the balance sheet can be prepared. In the worksheet in Exhibit 4–4, a debit is needed to balance the two columns, thus indicating a profit (in this case $2,325) as follows:

Total of income statement credit columns	$8,500
Total of income statement debit columns	6,175
Net income for the period	$2,325

The $2,325 balance is now entered in the debit column of the income statement and the debit and credit columns are now balanced.

The balance sheet columns are now totaled. At this point, there should be more debits than credits. In Exhibit 4–4 the total of the debit column equals $177,160 and the total of the credit column equals $174,835. The difference is $2,325 ($177,160 − $174,835) and represents the increase in owner's equity for the period resulting from the net income of the business. The worksheet may now be completed by also entering $2,325 in the credit column of the balance sheet. As a result, the total debits and credits in the balance sheet columns are now equal.

If the same figure, $2,325 in this case, does not balance both the income and balance sheet columns, an error has been made. You should check to see that:

1. The account balances in the unadjusted trial balance are correct by checking them against the unadjusted trial balance.
2. The adjusting entries have been correctly entered.
3. You have correctly totaled the adjusted trial balance columns.
4. The adjusted trial balance columns have been correctly extended to the balance sheet or income statement columns.
5. The income statement and balance sheet columns have been correctly totaled and all addition and subtraction is correct.

If you still cannot find your error, we again suggest that you put your work down for a while and do something else.

After the worksheet is prepared, the income statement and the balance sheet columns can be used to prepare the formal financial statements. As shown in Exhibit 4–4, all of the necessary data are already arranged in columns 7 through 10 of the worksheet.

Net Loss Rather Than Net Income

If the firm had incurred a net loss during the period, the total of the debit column would exceed the total of the credit column in the income statement. As a result, a credit, representing a net loss for the period, would be needed to balance the debit and credit columns of the income statement. In the balance sheet, credits would exceed debits, and a debit equaling the balancing credit in the income statement columns would be needed to balance the worksheet.

144

Limitations of the Worksheet

It is worth repeating that the worksheet does not replace steps in the accounting cycle; it is only a convenient tool to summarize the information necessary to prepare financial statements. Adjusting entries must be entered in the journal and then posted to the ledger accounts, and closing entries must be made. Furthermore, there are several forms of worksheets. The type and the manner in which a worksheet is used depend on the accounting system and the needs of management.

Summary of Learning Objectives

1. *Why adjusting entries are necessary.* Adjusting entries are made at the end of the accounting period in order to update various accounts to their proper balances. They result from the need to match economic events with accounting periods.

2. *The major categories of adjusting entries and how to make these entries for different accounts.* There are several different categories of adjusting entries commonly made by enterprises. These types of entries and the accounts usually involved are:

   a. Expenditures made in one period that affect subsequent periods.
   1. Typical accounts involved:
      (i) Prepaid Assets
      (ii) Supplies
      (iii) Inventories
      (iv) Plant, Equipment, Furniture, and Fixtures
   2. Form of the adjusting entry:

Expense	XXX	
Nonmonetary Asset or		
Contra Account		XXX

   b. Receipts received in one period that affect subsequent periods.
   1. Typical accounts involved:
      (i) Unearned Rent
      (ii) Dues and Subscriptions Received in Advance
   2. Form of the adjusting entry:

Unearned Revenue	XXX	
Earned Revenue		XXX

   c. Expenditures made or receipts received in subsequent periods.
   1. Typical accounts involved:
      (i) Interest Receivable or Payable
      (ii) Salaries Payable
   2. Form of the adjusting entry:

   (i) To record accrued receivable

Receivable	XXX	
Revenue		XXX

   (ii) To record accrued payables

Expense	XXX	
Payable		XXX

3. *The accounting cycle.* The accounting cycle includes the following steps:

During the period:

a. Record business transactions in the journal.
b. Post the journal entries to the ledger.

At the end of the period:

a. Prepare the unadjusted trial balance.
b. Prepare a worksheet—an optional step.
c. Prepare adjusting entries.
d. Post adjusting entries to the ledger.
e. Prepare an adjusted trial balance.
f. Prepare financial statements.
g. Make closing entries and post to the ledger accounts.
h. Prepare a post-closing trial balance.

4. *The uses and preparation of a worksheet.* A worksheet is a convenient tool to summarize the accounting information necessary to prepare financial statements. However, it does not eliminate the need to make adjusting entries, post them to the ledger, and prepare closing entries.

Appendix: The Preparation and Uses of Reversing Entries

Reversing entries are optional entries that can be made to simplify the accounting process. They reverse adjusting entries and are made on the first day of the next accounting period. Reversing entries are not used in connection with all adjusting entries, only with those involving routine future cash payments or receipts.

To illustrate the use of reversing entries let us return to the adjusting entry pertaining to salaries payable introduced on page 122. In this example, Salaries Expense and Salaries Payable were recorded to accrue salaries earned but not yet paid at December 31, 1984. Presented below are the adjusting entry, closing entry, the entry to record the subsequent payment of salaries on January 4, 1985, and the relevant T accounts. These entries and T accounts were made without a reversing entry.

<table>
<tr><td colspan="4" align="center">Adjusting Entry for Salaries without a Reversing Entry</td></tr>
<tr><td>December 31, 1984</td><td>Salaries Expense
    Salaries Payable
To record accrued salaries.</td><td align="right">300</td><td align="right">
300</td></tr>
<tr><td>December 31, 1984</td><td>Income Summary
    Salaries Expense
To close salaries expense.</td><td align="right">78,300</td><td align="right">
78,300</td></tr>
<tr><td>January 4, 1985</td><td>Salaries Payable
Salaries Expense
    Cash
To record payment of salaries.</td><td align="right">300
1,200</td><td align="right">

1,500</td></tr>
</table>

Salaries Payable			Salaries Expense		
1/4/85	300	12/31 Adj. 300	1/6	1,500	
			1/13	1,500	
1/4/85 Bal.	0		1/20	1,500	
			"	"	
			"	"	
			"	"	
			12/28	1,500	
			12/31 Adj.	300	
				78,300	Closing 78,300
			12/31 Bal.	0	
			1/4/85	1,200	

Although these entries produce the desired result, they do cause extra problems for the accounting system, because all accounting systems, whether manual or computerized, are most efficient when routine transactions are recorded in the same way. This decreases the possibility of error or even fraud. In this particular example, each week's salaries expense was recorded by making the following entry:

Salaries Expense	1,500	
Cash		1,500
To record weekly salaries.		

However, because of the adjusting entry on December 31, 1984, the entry on January 4, 1985 is now different and does not take the same form as do all the other entries to record salaries expense during the year. The January 4, 1985 payment of $1,500 must be divided between Salaries Payable and Salaries Expense. This is not a routine entry and so must be handled differently by the bookkeeper or computer. Whenever this happens, the possibility for error increases.

Reversing entries solve this problem. To illustrate, presented next is the same set of journal entries and T accounts, only this time using a reversing entry. The reversing entry on the first day of the next accounting period, in this case January 1, 1985, is:

1/1/85	Salaries Payable	300	
	Salaries Expense		300
	To reverse 12/31/84 adjusting entry.		

This entry accomplishes two things. First, the $300 balance in the Salaries Payable account is reduced to zero. Second, the payment of salaries on January 4, 1985 can be recorded in the same manner as are all the previous weekly entries to record the payment of salaries. You should note that immediately after the reversing entry is posted, the Salaries Expense account has a temporary credit balance of $300. However, when the $1,500 payment of salaries is recorded on January 4, 1985, the balance in the Salaries Expense account becomes $1,200, which represents the actual salaries expense for the first 4 days of 1985.

If you compare the series of entries without a reversing entry with those with the reversing entry, you will see that on January 4, 1985, after all transactions have been posted, the balance in the Salaries Expense account is $1,200 and that the balance in the Salaries Payable account is zero, whether or not a reversing entry has been made. Thus, even though the results are the same, reversing entries allow the continued use of routine transactions, and as a result, reduce the potential for errors.

Adjusting Entry for Salaries with a Reversing Entry

December 31, 1984	Salaries Expense	300	
	Salaries Payable		300
	To record accrued salaries.		
December 31, 1984	Income Summary	78,300	
	Salaries Expense		78,300
	To close salaries expense.		
January 1, 1985	Salaries Payable	300	
	Salaries Expense		300
	To reverse 12/31/84 adjusting entry.		
January 4, 1985	Salaries Expense	1,500	
	Cash		1,500
	To record payment of salaries for week ended 1/2/85.		

Salaries Payable

1/1/85 300 Reversing	12/31 Adj. 300
1/1/85 Bal. 0	

Salaries Expense

1/6	1,500	
1/13	1,500	
1/20	1,500	
"	"	
"	"	
"	"	
12/28	1,500	
12/31	300	
12/31 Bal. 78,300		Closing 78,300
1/4/85	1,500	1/1 300 Reversing
1/4/85 Bal. 1,200		

Reversing entries can be made for any adjusting entry in which the expenditure or receipt of cash is made in subsequent periods. Thus, accrued expenses such as salaries, interest, taxes, and accrued revenues such as interest and commissions all are candidates for reversing entries. However, reversing entries are not required and their use depends on the design of the accounting system. Accrued salaries that are paid routinely are probably the most common example of adjusting entries that are reversed. The examples in this book and the homework assignments assume that reversing entries are not used.

Problem for Your Review

The Accounting Cycle. This problem is a continuation of Review Problem A in Chapter 3. As the accountant for Ace World Travel, you have been able to gather the following information:

Ace World Travel
Unadjusted Trial Balance
December 31, 1987

Account	Debit	Credit
Cash	$ 14,600	
Accounts receivable	19,000	
Prepaid insurance	3,600	
Office supplies	7,500	
Land	20,000	
Building	45,000	
Furniture and fixtures	15,000	
Accounts payable		$ 2,600
Salaries payable		0
Bank loan payable		10,000
J. Hansen, capital		93,500
J. Hansen, drawing	1,000	
Commissions earned		50,000
Rental revenue		300
Salaries expense	22,000	
Advertising expense	4,000	
Utilities expense	1,750	
Automobile expense	2,250	
Repairs and maintenance expense	500	
Loss on sale of land	200	
Totals	$156,400	$156,400

In addition, you have determined the following data:
1. At the end of the year, office supplies on hand totaled $3,400.
2. The prepaid insurance policy was purchased during the year for $3,600. It became effective on April 1, 1987 and has a two-year term.

3. The building and furniture and fixtures were purchased at the beginning of the year. The building has a 30-year life and no salvage value. The furniture and fixtures have a six-year life and a salvage value of $3,000.

4. Salaries accrued but unpaid at year-end were $1,500.

5. The bank loan has been outstanding all year. The interest rate is 12%. Both interest and principal are due next year.

6. A December 1987 utility bill for $50 did not arrive until early January.

Required:

1. Prepare the necessary adjusting entries.
2. Prepare a worksheet.
3. Prepare closing entries.
4. Prepare an income statement, a statement of owner's equity, and a balance sheet.

Solution

1. Adjusting Entries

1. Office Supplies Expense	4,100	
Office Supplies		4,100

To record office supplies used during the period.
$4,100 = $7,500 − $3,400

2. Insurance Expense	1,350	
Prepaid Insurance		1,350

To record insurance used during the period.
$3,600 ÷ 24 = $150/month for 9 months = $1,350.

3. Depreciation Expense	3,500	
Accumulated Depreciation— Building		1,500
Accumulated Depreciation— Furniture and Fixtures		2,000

To record depreciation expense for the period.

Building $\dfrac{\$45,000}{30 \text{ years}} = \$1,500$ per year.

Furniture and Fixtures $\dfrac{\$15,000 - \$3,000}{6 \text{ years}} = \$2,000$ per year.

4. Salaries Expense	1,500	
Salaries Payable		1,500

To record salaries payable.

5. Interest Expense	1,200	
Interest Payable		1,200

To record interest payable.
$10,000 × .12 = $1,200.

6. Utilities Expense	50	
Accounts Payable		50

To record December utility bill received in January.

2. Worksheet

(See page 151.)

Ace World Travel
Worksheet
For the Year Ended December 31, 1987

Account	Unadjusted Trial Balance Debit	Unadjusted Trial Balance Credit	Adjustments Debit	Adjustments Credit	Adjusted Trial Balance Debit	Adjusted Trial Balance Credit	Income Statement Debit	Income Statement Credit	Balance Sheet Debit	Balance Sheet Credit
Cash	14,600				14,600				14,600	
Accounts receivable	19,000				19,000				19,000	
Prepaid insurance	3,600			[2] 1,350	2,250				2,250	
Office supplies	7,500			[1] 4,100	3,400				3,400	
Land	20,000				20,000				20,000	
Building	45,000				45,000				45,000	
Accumulated depreciation—Building				[3] 1,500		1,500				1,500
Furniture and fixtures	15,000				15,000				15,000	
Accumulated depreciation—Furniture and fixtures				[3] 2,000		2,000				2,000
Accounts payable		2,600		[6] 50		2,650				2,650
Salaries payable				[4] 1,500		1,500				1,500
Interest payable				[5] 1,200		1,200				1,200
Bank loan payable		10,000				10,000				10,000
J. Hansen, capital		93,500				93,500				93,500
J. Hansen, drawing	1,000				1,000				1,000	
Commissions earned		50,000				50,000		50,000		
Rental revenue		300				300		300		
Salaries expense	22,000		[4] 1,500		23,500		23,500			
Advertising expense	4,000				4,000		4,000			
Utilities expense	1,750		[6] 50		1,800		1,800			
Automobile expense	2,250				2,250		2,250			
Repairs and maintenance expense	500				500		500			
Loss on sale of land	200				200		200			
Office supplies expense			[1] 4,100		4,100		4,100			
Insurance expense			[2] 1,350		1,350		1,350			
Depreciation expense			[3] 3,500		3,500		3,500			
Interest expense			[5] 1,200		1,200		1,200			
Totals	156,400	156,400	11,700	11,700	162,650	162,650	42,400	50,300	120,250	112,350
Net income							7,900			7,900
							50,300	50,300	120,250	120,250

3. Closing Entries

Commission Earned	50,000	
Rental Revenue	300	
Income Summary		50,300
To close revenue account.		
Income Summary	42,400	
Salaries Expense		23,500
Advertising Expense		4,000
Utilities Expense		1,800
Automobile Expense		2,250
Repairs and Maintenance Expense		500
Loss on Sale of Land		200
Office Supplies Expense		4,100
Insurance Expense		1,350
Depreciation Expense		3,500
Interest Expense		1,200
To close expense accounts.		
Income Summary	7,900	
J. Hansen, Drawing		7,900
To close income summary to drawing.		
J. Hansen, Capital	1,000	
J. Hansen, Drawing		1,000
To close drawing account to capital.		

4. Financial Statements

Ace World Travel
Income Statement

For the Year Ended December 31, 1987

Revenues		
Commission earned	$50,000	
Rental revenue	300	
Total revenues		$50,300
Expenses*		
Salaries	$23,500	
Office supplies expense	4,100	
Advertising expense	4,000	
Depreciation expense	3,500	
Automobile expense	2,250	
Utilities expense	1,800	
Insurance expense	1,350	
Interest expense	1,200	
Automobile expense	500	
Loss on sale of land	200	
Total expenses		42,400
Net income		$ 7,900

*At this point, the exact order of the expenses on the income statement is not important. Some firms list them alphabetically or in the order of their magnitude. We listed them by order of magnitude. However, once a format is selected, it is useful to consistently use it.

Ace World Travel
Statement of Owner's Equity
For the Year Ended December 31, 1987

J. Hansen, capital—January 1, 1987	$ 93,500
Add: net income for the period	7,900
Subtotal	101,400
Less: withdrawals	1,000
J. Hansen, capital—December 31, 1987	$100,400

Ace World Travel
Balance Sheet
December 31, 1987

Assets			Liabilities and Owner's Equity	
Cash		$ 14,600	Liabilities	
Accounts receivable		19,000	Accounts payable	$ 2,650
Prepaid insurance		2,250	Salaries payable	1,500
Office supplies		3,400	Interest payable	1,200
Land		20,000	Bank loan payable	10,000
Buildings	$45,000		Total liabilities	$15,350
Less: Accumulated			Owner's Equity	
depreciation	1,500		J. Hansen, capital	100,400
		43,500		
Furniture and fixtures	15,000			
Less: Accumulated				
depreciation	2,000			
		13,000	Total liabilities	
Total assets		$115,750	and owner's equity	$115,750

Questions

1. What is the relationship between the need to prepare financial statements on a timely basis and the matching convention?

2. Give three examples of an expenditure that is made in the current period but affects both the current and subsequent periods. What is the accounting problem related to these expenditures?

3. Why is it necessary to make adjusting entries? Can you think of a situation when adjusting entries would not be required?

4. Prepaid insurance amounted to $1,500 at the beginning of the year and $700 at the end of the year. The income statement for the year showed insurance expense of $2,000. How much insurance was purchased during the year?

5. During the current year the accountant for the Hamlet Company debited all purchases of office supplies to Supplies Expense. At year-end the firm still had a large amount of supplies remaining in the storeroom. Which accounts are over- or understated?

6. Explain to your friend how a building that has an increasing market value must be depreciated for financial-reporting purposes.

7. A piece of equipment was purchased several years ago. It cost $120,000 and had no salvage value. Yearly depreciation on the straight-line method was $6,000, and at the end of 1987 the accumulated depreciation account had a credit balance of $36,000. When was the equipment purchased? What is the life of the equipment?

8. Give two examples of receipts received in one period that affect current and subsequent periods.

9. At the beginning of the year, the balance in a firm's unearned subscription revenue was $1,200; at the end of the year it was $450. During the year the firm received an additional $2,000 in subscription receipts. Supply the missing entry.

10. Describe to an individual who is unfamiliar with accounting the difference between adjusting entries that involve write-offs and those that involve accruals.

11. Jones owns a 12% note receivable that was acquired on January 2, 1987. On July 30, 1987, the Interest Receivable account showed a balance of $1,400, and there have been no receipts of interest or principal. What is the principal of the note?

12. What is the purpose of closing entries? When are they made? Describe the logic of debiting revenue accounts in the closing process.

13. Describe the difference between an adjusted trial balance and a post-closing trial balance.

14. Owner's equity on January 1, 1986 were $58,000 and were $78,000 on December 31, 1986. During that time, the owner withdrew $30,000 cash which was debited to Owner's equity. Make the required closing entry that has not been made.

15. What is the purpose of a worksheet? When is it prepared?

16. The income statement columns on a worksheet are prepared before the balance sheet columns are. Why?

17. During the preparation of a worksheet, the debit column of the income statement exceeded the credit column by $5,000. Did the firm earn a profit or incur a loss? Explain your reasoning.

18. A friend of yours stated that she never has to prepare adjusting or closing entries because she prepares a worksheet at the end of each accounting period. Is this a correct technique? Why or why not?

19. What steps, if any, in the accounting cycle can a worksheet replace?

20. (*Refers to material in chapter appendix.*) A friend of yours who was taking an accounting course said that his accounting instructor stated that reversing entries are more trouble than they are worth. Do you agree? Why or why not?

21. (*Refers to material in chapter appendix.*) Which of the following types of adjusting entries are candidates for a reversing entry? Why?
   a. Recording depreciation expense.
   b. Recording unearned rent that has been earned during the period.
   c. Accrual of payroll.
   d. Accrual of interest receivable.
   e. Recording supplies used during the period.

Exercises

1. The Accounting Cycle. Following is a list of steps in the accounting cycle. Arrange them in the proper sequence by placing the appropriate number to the left of the step. The first step should be numbered 1, and so on.

_____ Preparing financial statements.

_____ Posting journal entries to the ledger.

_____ Recording transactions in the journal.

_____ Preparing an unadjusted trial balance.

_____ Preparing a post-closing trial balance.

_____ Preparing closing entries.

_____ Preparing adjusting entries.

_____ Posting adjusting entries and preparing an adjusted trial balance.

2. Making Adjusting Entries. Make the necessary entries for each of the following two independent situations:

   a. On April 1 the O'Neil Company received $5,400 for a three-year subscription to its political newsletter. The firm closes its books once a year on December 31. Make the entry to record the receipt of the subscription and the adjusting entry at December 31. The firm uses an account called Unearned Subscription Revenue.

   b. The McDonald Company pays its salaries every Friday for the five-day workweek. Salaries of $60,000 are earned equally throughout the week. December 31 of the current year is a Wednesday.

   1. Make the adjusting entry at December 31.

154

2. Make the entry to pay the week's salaries on Friday, January 2, of the next year. (Ignore reversing entries and assume that all employees are paid for New Year's Day.)

3. Making Adjusting Entries. The Deloitte Company closes its books on December 31 and makes adjusting entries once a year at that time. For each of the following items make the appropriate adjusting journal entry, if any:

a. At the beginning of the year the firm had $800 of supplies on hand. During the year another $2,400 worth was purchased on account and recorded in the asset account, Supplies. At the end of the year the firm determined that $550 of supplies remained on hand.

b. On October 1 of the current year the firm lent the Rosevsky Co. $10,000 at 12% interest. Principal and interest are due in one year.

c. Three full years ago the firm purchased a building and land for $500,000. Two-fifths of the cost was allocated to the land and three-fifths to the building. The building has a life of 20 years with no salvage value.

d. On July 1 of the current year, the firm borrowed $8,000 at 10% interest. As of December 31 of the same year, the interest expense account showed a balance of $400.

e. On March 1 of the current year, the firm rented to another firm some excess space in one of its buildings. The Deloitte Company received a year's rent, $15,000, at that time and credited the account Unearned Revenue.

4. Adjusting Entries for Interest. On October 1, 1987, the Cooper Company lent $100,000 to Lybrand Company at 14% interest. Both interest and principal are due on September 30, 1988. Both firms have a December 31 year-end and close their books annually at that time. Make the required entries for both firms at October 1, 1987; December 31, 1987; and September 30, 1988.

5. Making and Analyzing Adjusting Entries. The Brokow Company opened a news service on January 2 of the current year. The firm's year-end is December 31, and it makes adjusting entries once a year at that time. For each of the following items, make the initial entry, where appropriate, to record the transaction and, if necessary, the adjusting entry at December 31:

a. On March 31 the Brokow Company rented a new office. Before it could move, it had to prepay a year's rent of $18,000 cash.

b. On January 31, the firm borrowed $100,000 from a local bank at 12%. The principal and interest on the loan are due in one year, but no interest payments have yet been made.

c. On March 15, the firm purchased $500 of supplies for cash. On September 14, it made another cash purchase of $900. The firm's accountant determined that $1,100 of supplies had been used during the current year.

d. The firm charges its customers in advance for subscribing to its news service. During the year the firm received $120,000 cash from its customers. The firm's accountant determined that 15% of that had not yet been earned.

e. Before closing its books the Brokow Company found a bill for $1,200 from a local newspaper for an advertisement that was placed in the November paper.

f. Wages accrued but unpaid at December 31 totaled $1,400.

6. Determining the Ending Balance in Certain Accounts. The Dunesberry Company is preparing its September 30, 1987 financial statements. State at what amounts the following assets should be shown:

a. On January 2, 1986, the firm bought a three-year comprehensive insurance policy for $5,400.

b. A piece of equipment was purchased on June 30, 1985 for $125,000. It has an eight-year life with an estimated salvage value of $5,000. Depreciation is taken from July 1, 1985. Give the proper balance in the Accumulated Depreciation account.

c. On January 2, 1984, the firm bought some land for $150,000, which is currently being used as a parking lot. It expects to sell the land by the end of 1987 and feels it will get approximately $256,000 at that time. It recently received a cash offer for $187,000.

d. The firm purchases several types of supplies. During the year the firm purchased 4,250 boxes of staplers at a total cost of $14,875. On September 30, 1987 the firm had 2,250 boxes of staplers left.

e. On July 1, 1986, the firm lent $50,000 to one of its best customers at 14% interest for 2 years. Interest is due yearly, the principal at the end of two years. What amount of interest receivable should be shown on the September 30, 1987 balance sheet?

Completing the Accounting Cycle   **155**

7. Closing Entries. Some of the accounts of the Grant Company at the end of the current year are listed in alphabetical order. All accounts have normal balances, and all adjusting entries have been made.

Accounts payable	$ 8,000
Accounts receivable	7,500
Cash	5,500
Gain on sale of land	1,000
General and administrative expenses	27,500
Interest expenses	2,500
Interest payable	1,500
Land	40,000
L. Thomas, capital	91,700
Plant and equipment	72,000
Sales	52,000
Selling expenses	18,200
City tax expense	3,000
City taxes payable	2,000

Required:
a. Prepare the necessary closing entries.
b. Assuming that the owner withdrew $500 in cash during the year, what was the balance in the capital account at:
1. The beginning of the year?
2. The end of the year?

8. Closing Entries. The accountant for the Fonda Company made the following closing entries at the end of the firm's year. After reviewing these entries,
a. Discuss the errors, if any.
b. Make the correct closing entries.

1. Interest Revenue	4,200	
Accounts Payable	900	
J. Fonda, Capital	5,000	
Fees Earned	25,000	
Income Summary		35,100
To close accounts with credit balances.		
2. Income Summary	32,700	
Interest Expense		4,200
Accounts Receivable		2,000
Operating Expenses		22,000
Loss on Sale of Land		1,000
Other Assets		3,500
To close accounts with debit balances.		
3. Income Summary	2,400	
J. Fonda, Capital		2,400
To close income summary to capital.		

9. Analyzing of the Accounting Equation. For each of the following five independent situations, determine the net income or loss for the period:

a.	Net assets at the beginning of the year	$ 37,000
	Net assets at the end of the year	44,000
	Owner's withdrawals	0
	Owner's contribution	0
b.	Net assets at the beginning of the year	$ 35,000
	Net assets at the end of the year	44,000
	Owner's withdrawals	2,000
	Owner's contribution	0
c.	Net assets at the beginning of the year	$ 29,000
	Net assets at the end of the year	46,000
	Owner's withdrawals	400
	Owner's contribution	5,000

156

d. Net assets at the beginning of the year	$ 74,000
Net assets at the end of the year	125,000
Owner's withdrawals	10,000
Owner's contribution	15,000
e. Net assets at the beginning of the year	$100,000
Net assets at the end of the year	140,000
Owner's withdrawals	5,000
Owner's contribution	50,000

10. The Accounting Equation. Answer each of the following two questions:

a. You have obtained the following information for the Cal Company: Total assets were $150,000 at January 1, 1987 and $200,000 at December 31. Total liabilities at January 1, 1987 were $85,000 and were $100,000 at December 31. During the year, the firm's total revenues were $80,000. The owner made an additional capital contribution of $10,000 and made a cash withdrawal of $2,000. Determine:

1. Net income for 1987.

2. The total of all expenses for 1987.

b. Using the following data for the independent situations below, calculate the missing figures:

Year-end Amounts		G. Newton, Capital Beginning	Net Income (Loss)	Owner Withdrawal	G. Newton, Capital Ending
Total Assets	Total Liabilities				
1. $ 80,000	?	$37,000	$15,000	$7,000	?
2. ?	$65,000	?	20,000	5,000	$50,000
3. $120,000	70,000	60,000	?	4,000	?

11. Accrual to Cash Basis of Accounting. You have determined the following balance sheet data for the Oregon Company:

	1/1/87	12/31/87
Accounts receivable	$150,000	$210,000
Supplies	8,000	9,200
Salaries payable	17,000	15,000
Unearned rent revenue	8,200	7,000

The income statement data for the year showed the following data:

Sales—all credit	$570,000
Supplies used	10,000
Salaries expense	42,000
Rent revenue	23,000

You are to calculate the following information:

a. Cash received on account.

b. Cash paid for supplies—all supplies purchased for cash.

c. Salaries paid in cash.

d. Cash collected for rent.

12. Cash to Accrual Basis of Accounting. You have determined the following balance sheet data for the Washington Corporation:

	1/1/88	12/31/88
Interest receivable	$2,500	$2,800
Prepaid insurance	1,400	900
Interest payable	900	1,100

During the year the company made the following cash payments or received cash related to the items listed above:

Cash received on interest receivable	$4,000
Cash paid for additional insurance covering several periods	6,700
Interest paid	3,000

You are to calculate the following information:

a. Interest earned during the year.

b. Insurance expense for the year.

c. Interest expense for the period.

13. Preparing Adjusting Entries from Worksheet Data. The partial worksheet for the Tuggle Company is reproduced below. From this data, determine the seven adjusting entries that were made, and explain each adjusting entry.

Account	Unadjusted Trial Balance Debit	Unadjusted Trial Balance Credit	Adjusted Trial Balance Debit	Adjusted Trial Balance Credit
Cash	10,000		10,000	
Accounts receivable	14,000		14,000	
Supplies	1,200		400	
Prepaid insurance	4,100		2,200	
Land	15,000		15,000	
Building	75,000		75,000	
Accumulated depreciation—Building		12,000		13,000
Accounts payable		9,600		10,000
Interest payable		0		1,400
Salaries payable		0		3,800
Unearned rent revenue		1,800		100
J. Tuggle, capital		71,600		71,600
Fees earned		100,000		100,000
Gain on sale of land		2,500		2,500
Rental revenue				1,700
Fees paid to outside consultants	62,000		62,000	
Advertising expense	4,200		4,200	
Automobile expense	1,800		2,200	
Employee salaries	10,200		14,000	
Depreciation	0		1,000	
Supplies used	0		800	
Insurance expense	0		1,900	
Interest expense	0		1,400	
Total	197,500	197,500	204,100	204,100

14. Post-Closing Trial Balance. Using the data in Exercise 13, prepare the closing entries and a post-closing trial balance.

15. Computations and Analysis. In doing these computations, be sure to show your calculations.

a. On January 1, 1987, the Broccoli Company received a 12%, $15,000 note receivable. If accrued interest on December 31, 1987 equals $450, through what date was the interest paid?

b. On August 1, 1987, the Carrot Company received a $12,000 note. At December 31, 1987, the firm had not yet received any interest payments. If Interest Receivable had a balance of $750, what would the interest rate be?

c. The Tomato Company purchased a large machine on January 2, 1984. It is being depreciated at a straight-line rate of $9,000 per year. At the end of its useful life it will have a salvage value of $3,000. As of December 31, 1987, the machine has a remaining life of four years. What was the machine's purchase price?

d. The Onion Organization owns a small building that is being depreciated at the rate of $7,500 per year. The building has a remaining life of 24 years from December 31, 1987. Assuming that the building originally cost $235,000 and has no salvage value, determine when it was purchased.

16. Reversing Entries. (*Refers to material in chapter appendix.*) As she was closing the firm's books on December 31, 1985, the Rodriguez Company's accountant obtained the following information concerning two adjusting entries:

1. The company pays its payroll every Friday for that week's five days of work. December 31, 1985 is a Tuesday, and the entire week's wages of $18,000 will be paid on Friday, January 3, 1986. Wages are earned equally throughout the week, including January 1.

2. On February 1, 1985, the firm borrowed $15,000 from a local bank at 14% interest. The entire principal and interest are due on January 31, 1986.

Required:

a. Make the adjusting entries on December 31, 1985, and the entries on January 3 and January 31, 1986, assuming that no reversing entries are made.

b. Make the same set of entries, assuming that reversing entries are made on January 1, 1986.

c. Compare and contrast the results in (a) and (b). Which do you prefer and why?

Problem Set A

4A-1. Adjusting Entries. The accountant for the Selsun Company obtained the following information while preparing adjusting entries for the year ended December 31, 1987:

a. During the year the company made the following purchases of supplies:

February 12	$1,700
April 17	1,900
November 11	2,300

At the end of the year, it was determined that $1,450 of supplies remained on hand.

b. The Selsun Company publishes a monthly beauty newsletter. All customers are required to subscribe to 12 issues, or 1 per month for the entire year. Subscriptions are renewed annually, but the subscribers' list is staggered so that the subscribers renew at the beginning of each quarter. The following subscriptions were received during the year and credited to unearned subscription revenue:

Date	Yearly Subscription
January 1	$1,800
April 1	2,700
July 1	4,500
October 1	3,600

c. On April 1, 1987 the firm borrowed $12,000 at 12% from the South City National Bank. Principal and interest on the unpaid balance are due quarterly on:

July 1, 1987	January 1, 1988
October 1, 1987	April 1, 1988

d. As of January 1, 1987, the balance in the firm's Prepaid Rent account was $9,000 and represented four months of prepaid rent. The lease was renewed in 1987 at an increase of 10% of last year's full rent. The full year's rent was prepaid as of the beginning of the new lease term on May 1, 1987.

e. Land, buildings, and equipment all were purchased at the beginning of 1984. All depreciable assets were given a zero salvage value. As of January 1, 1987, you obtained the following account balances:

Account	Balance
Land	$80,000
Accumulated depreciation—Building	21,000
Accumulated depreciation—Equipment	36,000

Required:

Make the necessary adjusting entries at December 31, 1987.

4A–2. Adjusting Entries. The accountant for the Lloyd Company obtained the following data as she was preparing the firm's adjusting entries for the firm's fiscal year ending June 30, 1987:

1. On July 1, 1986 the balance in the firm's Prepaid Insurance account was $2,200, representing 4 months of prepaid insurance. When the policy expired, the firm purchased for cash a new three-year policy for $24,300.

2. On July 1, 1986, the balance in the firm's Supplies account was $2,400. On November 2, 1986, $8,700 of supplies were purchased on account. As of June 30, 1987, all of the original supplies and two-thirds of the supplies purchased in November had been used.

3. The Lloyd Company lent its main customer some needed cash. Analysis of the loans indicates the following:

Date of Loan	Principal	Interest Rate	Interest Paid Through
9/1/85	$10,000	9%	9/1/86
11/1/86	10,000	9	4/30/87
3/1/87	25,000	12	5/31/87

All loan due dates are after the year-end. Interest on the September/1/85 loan is paid annually.

4. The firm's rental agreement on its office and stores calls for a monthly rental of $1,200 per month plus 1% of the firm's gross revenues. The monthly portion of $1,200 is payable at the beginning of each month. The 1% portion is payable once a year, on July 15, based on the prior year's gross revenues. Gross revenues for the year ended June 30, 1987 were $675,000.

Required:

a. Make the journal entries where appropriate to record the initial transactions between July 1, 1986 and June 30, 1987.

b. Make the necessary adjusting entries at June 30, 1987.

4A–3. Completion of the Accounting Cycle from the Unadjusted Trial Balance. The bookkeeper of Financial Management Consultants gave you the unadjusted trial balance at December 31, 1987 (see page 161) and the following additional information:

Additional Information:

1. The firm was notified by its brokers that it had earned interest revenue of $850 from its various marketable securities.

2. Supplies on hand at the end of the year amounted to $300.

3. Prepaid rent of $1,200 was used during the year.

4. The building was purchased on January 2, 1985 and has no salvage value.

5. The interest rate on the note is 8%. No interest has been paid on the note since July 1, 1987.

6. Salaries payable at year-end amounted to $2,000.

7. The December 31, 1987 telephone bill of $250 arrived in January 1988 and was not included in the utilities expense of $1,000 listed in the unadjusted trial balance. Use the Accounts Payable account.

Financial Management Consultants
Unadjusted Trial Balance
December 31, 1987

Account	Debit	Credit
Cash	$ 8,000	
Investment in marketable securities	10,000	
Accounts receivable	16,500	
Interest receivable	0	
Supplies	2,800	
Prepaid rent	1,400	
Land	25,000	
Buildings	120,000	
Accumulated depreciation—Buildings		$ 8,000
Accounts payable		9,400
Bank notes payable		20,000
Salaries payable		0
Interest payable		0
R. Gorkan, capital		60,600
Fees earned		200,000
Salaries expense	90,000	
Rent expense	20,000	
Legal and accounting expense	1,800	
Utilities expense	1,000	
Delivery expense	1,500	
Totals	$298,000	$298,000

Required:

a. Set up T accounts with the December 31, 1987 balances from the unadjusted trial balance.

b. Make the adjusting entries in the general journal. Set up new accounts where appropriate.

c. Post the adjusting entries to the ledger accounts.

d. Prepare an adjusted trial balance.

e. Prepare an income statement, owner's equity statement, and balance sheet.

f. Make the closing entries.

g. Post the closing entries to the ledger accounts.

h. Prepare a post-closing trial balance.

4A–4. Accrual and Cash Basis of Accounting. The comparative December 31, 1987 and 1986 balance sheets and the income statement for the year ended December 31, 1987 for the Kennedy Realty Company are presented on page 162.

Required:

a. Prepare the necessary closing entries. You must determine the amount of owner withdrawals.

b. Prepare a statement of owner's equity for the year ended December 31, 1987.

c. Answer each of the following questions:

    1. How much cash was collected from customers on account during 1987? Assume that all fees earned were originally recorded in Accounts Receivable.

    2. If no notes receivable were repaid, by how much did the firm increase its notes receivable?

    3. How much cash was paid out for rent during 1987?

    4. Assuming that all purchases of supplies were paid in cash, how much cash was paid out for supplies during 1987?

    5. How much cash was paid out for salaries during the year?

    6. How much cash was paid out for interest during the year?

Kennedy Realty Company
Comparative Balance Sheets
December 31

Assets	1987	1986
Cash	$ 14,320	$ 6,200
Accounts receivable	10,500	3,400
Notes receivable	22,000	10,000
Prepaid rent	3,400	2,500
Supplies	2,100	4,200
Land	65,000	65,000
Buildings—net of accumulated depreciation	165,600	172,800
Other assets	42,000	35,000
Total assets	$324,920	$299,100

Liabilities and Owner's Equity		
Liabilities		
Accounts payable	$ 8,200	$ 10,000
Notes payable	20,000	25,000
Salaries payable	4,700	5,200
Interest payable	820	1,200
Other payables	4,000	0
Total liabilities	$ 37,720	$ 41,400
Owner's Equity		
E. Kennedy, capital	$287,200	$257,700
Total liabilities and owner's equity	$324,920	$299,100

Kennedy Realty Company
Income Statement
For the Year Ended December 31, 1987

Revenues		
Commissions earned	$500,000	
Interest revenue	1,500	
		$501,500
Expenses		
Salesperson's commissions	$250,000	
Office salaries	110,000	
Rent expense	50,000	
City taxes	15,000	
Depreciation	7,200	
Supplies expense	4,250	
Interest expense	3,500	
		439,950
Net income		$ 61,550

4A-5. Computations and Analysis. Make the necessary computations for each of the following independent situations. In all cases, where necessary, assume that the year-end is December 31, 1987 and that the firm has made all required adjusting entries for the year.

a. The Mynard Co. acquired an $18,000, 10% note on August 1, 1987. On December 31, 1987, the Interest Receivable account had a balance of $150. How much cash interest did the Mynard Co. collect on this note during 1987, and through what date had interest been received?

b. The Arthur Corporation borrowed $14,250 on September 30, 1987. The note is due in six months, and the total interest paid will be $855. What is the interest rate on the note?

c. On January 1, 1983 the Jackson Company bought a machine for $80,000. It has a 12-year useful life. On December 31, 1987, after the adjusting entry to record depreciation, the book value of the machine is $50,000. What is its estimated salvage value?

d. On January 1, 1984 the Hawkins Company purchased a new machine for $89,000 with a $4,000 salvage value. The machine has an estimated useful life of 10 years. What is its book value on December 31, 1987 after the adjusting entry to record depreciation is made?

e. The Waco Company purchased a building for $1,400,000. The building has a $200,000 salvage value and an estimated useful life of 30 years. On December 31, 1987, after the entry to record depreciation expense, the building's current book value is $1,300,000. When was the building purchased?

4A–6. Worksheet Preparation. The December 31, 1987 unadjusted trial balance for the International Toy Company follows:

International Toy Company
Unadjusted Trial Balance
December 31, 1987

Account	Debit	Credit
Cash	$ 10,400	
Accounts receivable	14,000	
Notes receivable	15,000	
Investments	28,000	
Supplies	3,200	
Prepaid insurance	4,200	
Land	30,500	
Building	60,000	
Accumulated depreciation—Building		$ 6,000
Equipment	18,000	
Accumulated depreciation—Equipment		9,000
Other assets	4,000	
Accounts payable		24,000
Salaries payable		0
H. Lee, capital		104,950
Fees earned		538,350
Salaries expense	430,000	
Rent expense	45,000	
Delivery expense	12,000	
Repairs and maintenance expense	6,200	
Loss on sale of land	1,800	
Totals	$682,300	$682,300

Additional Information:

1. The note receivable has a 12% interest rate and has been outstanding since Oct. 1, 1987.
2. Supplies on hand at the end of year were $670.
3. Prepaid insurance of $3,800 expired during the year.
4. The building has a life of 25 years and no salvage value. The equipment has a useful life of six years and no salvage value.
5. Salaries accrued but unpaid were $4,000 at year-end.

Required:

a. Prepare a 10-column worksheet similar to the one in the text.
b. Make the necessary closing entries in the general journal.
c. Prepare an income statement for the year ended December 31, 1987 and a balance sheet at December 31, 1987.

4A–7. Worksheet Preparation. The trial balance of the Management Consulting Agency at December 31, 1987 and additional data necessary to make adjusting entries follow:

Management Consulting Agency
Unadjusted Trial Balance
December 31, 1987

Account	Debit	Credit
Cash	$ 33,860	
Accounts receivable	27,950	
Office supplies	8,720	
Prepaid rent	3,600	
Prepaid insurance	14,000	
Office furniture	43,000	
Accumulated depreciation—Office furniture		$ 15,750
Accounts payable		7,300
Unearned fees		6,000
Salaries payable		0
M. Sciosca, capital		62,880
Consulting fees		80,000
Salaries expense	27,000	
Utilities expense	3,300	
Rent expense	4,800	
Miscellaneous expense	5,700	
Totals	$171,930	$171,930

Additional Information:

1. Office supplies on hand at the end of the year were $3,790.
2. Prepaid rent of $2,400 expired during the year.
3. The balance in the Prepaid Insurance account should be $10,500.
4. The office furniture is estimated to have a useful life of eight years and a salvage value of $1,000.
5. Two-thirds of the amount in the unearned fees account was earned during the year.
6. Accrued salaries at year-end amounted to $900.

Required:

a. Prepare a 10-column worksheet similar to the one in the text.
b. Make the necessary closing entries in the general journal.
c. Prepare an income statement for the year ended December 31, 1987 and a balance sheet at December 31, 1987.

4A–8. Summary Review Problem. The Fenton-Brenner Company was organized on January 2, 1987. During the year the following summary events occurred:

1. John Fenton-Brenner, the sole owner, invested $100,000 in the business.
2. A $50,000, 12% bank loan was obtained on February 1. The principal and interest are due in one year.
3. On April 1 the firm purchased a comprehensive two-year insurance policy for $3,600 cash.
4. Equipment costing $180,000 was purchased on account.
5. The firm signed a lease on April 30 to rent office space. Because the firm is new, the lessor required a full year's rent of $24,000, to be paid immediately.
6. Service fees during the first half of the year were $260,000, of which $180,000 was on account and the remainder was for cash.
7. Consulting fee expense for the first six months of the year accrued to outside specialists amounted to $165,000. (These fees are not yet paid.)

8. Payments on equipment purchases in Item 4 were $150,000.
9. Collections on accounts were $130,000.
10. Supplies totaling $4,300 were purchased for cash.
11. Various pieces of office furniture and fixtures were purchased for $100,000. A 20% down payment was made and the remainder was obtained through a 12% mortgage payable issued on May 1.
12. Service fees for the second half of the year were $320,000, of which $200,000 was on account and $120,000 was for cash.
13. Consulting fee expense for the second six months accrued to outside specialists totaled $195,000. (These fees are not yet paid.)
14. Cash collections on account amounted to $200,000.
15. Payments to consulting specialists on account amounted to $235,000.
16. The following expenses were paid in cash:

Salaries	$80,000
Legal and accounting	52,400
Advertising	25,000
Delivery	5,000
Repairs	4,200
Utilities	2,400

17. Fenton-Brenner withdrew $4,000 cash for his personal use.

Additional Information:

a. Interest on the bank loan and the mortgage payable must be accrued.
b. The necessary amount of prepaid insurance must be written off.
c. Prepaid rent must be written off.
d. Supplies totaling $3,500 were used during the year.
e. The office furniture and fixtures have a 10-year life and a $5,000 salvage value. The equipment has a 5-year life and a salvage value of $30,000. Take a full year's depreciation on both the office furniture and fixtures and the equipment.
f. Salaries of $1,400 must be accrued at year-end.
g. A December utility bill of $200 was received in January. This amount has not been included in the utilities expense listed on the unadjusted trial balance. Use the Accounts Payable account to record the transaction.

The firm's chart of accounts is as follows:

Cash	101	J. Fenton-Brenner, capital	310
Accounts receivable	102	J. Fenton-Brenner, drawing	311
Supplies	105	Service fees earned	400
Prepaid insurance	106	Consulting fee expense	501
Prepaid rent	107	Salaries expense	502
Office furniture and fixtures	110	Legal and accounting expense	503
Accumulated depreciation—		Advertising expense	504
Office furniture and fixtures	111	Delivery expense	506
Equipment	120	Repairs expense	507
Accumulated depreciation—		Utilities expense	508
Equipment	121	Depreciation expense	509
Accounts payable	201	Insurance expense	510
Bank loan payable	202	Rent expense	511
Mortgage payable	205	Supplies expense	512
Consulting fees payable	209	Interest expense	513
Salaries payable	210	Income summary	1000
Interest payable	212		

Required:

Depending your instructor's directions, either use T accounts or a four-column running balance ledger account to complete the following work. If required by your instructor, Item c can be prepared as part of a worksheet.

a. Make the summary journal entries for the year, and post them to the ledger accounts. As a posting reference, use the number of the account and page 1 of the general journal.

b. Prepare an unadjusted trial balance.

c. In order to complete the accounting cycle:
   1. Prepare the adjusting entries and post them to the ledger accounts.
   2. Prepare an adjusted trial balance.

d. Prepare closing entries and post them to the ledger accounts.

e. Prepare a post-closing trial balance.

f. Prepare an income statement, a statement of owner's equity, and a balance sheet.

Problem Set B

4B–1. Adjusting Entries. The following information was obtained for Angelo's Art School at year-end, August 31, 1987:

a. During the year the school made the following purchases of art supplies:

October 11, 1986	$2,500
January 16, 1987	1,750
March 1, 1987	3,200
July 5, 1987	2,300

On August 31, 1987 it was determined that $4,250 of supplies were on hand.

b. The school offers three-month courses for $300 ($100 per month) per student. Students are required to pay three months in advance of the date on which the course begins. The following payments were received and credited to Unearned Revenues:

October 1, 1986	$4,500
January 2, 1987	6,000
April 1, 1987	3,600
July 1, 1987	4,800

c. The school employs 10 full-time art teachers. They receive $1,200 a month and are paid on the first and fifteenth of each month. No journal entry has been recorded on August 31, 1987 to record salaries earned but not yet paid.

d. On September 1, 1986 the balance in the Prepaid Insurance account was $3,600 for the remaining three-month period. The policy was renewed for a full year on December 1, 1986 for $14,400 cash.

e. The school purchased the land and building in which it was located on September 3, 1984. The building has no salvage value. The following balances were obtained on September 1, 1986:

Account	Balance
Land	$50,000
Accumulated depreciation—Building	24,600

Required:

Prepare the necessary adjusting entries at August 31, 1987.

4B–2. Adjusting Entries. As the accountant for the Right Company, you have obtained the following information in order to prepare adjusting entries for the firm's fiscal year ending December 31, 1987:

a. On December 31, 1987 the balance in the prepaid insurance account is $6,200. The policy covered a three-year period beginning March 1, 1987. No expense has been recorded to date.

b. Office supplies costing $4,250 were purchased for cash during the year. On December 31, 1987 supplies on hand cost $1,575.

c. On March 1, 1987 the firm borrowed $20,000 at 16% from Pine Valley Bank. Interest on the unpaid balance is due semiannually on September 1 and March 1.

d. The firm engaged the Meyer Advertising Agency on April 1, 1987. The agency fee is $300 per month, payable at the beginning of each month, plus 2% of the estimated increase in revenue due to advertising in 1987. The 2% part of the fee is payable on January 15, 1988. Actual revenue of the Right Company for 1987 is $243,300. It is estimated that without the advertising campaign, the revenue would have been only $196,000.

Required:

a. Make the journal entries, where appropriate, to record the initial transactions during 1987. Assume that all payments were made in cash.

b. Make the necessary adjusting entries at December 31, 1987.

4B-3. Completing the Accounting Cycle from the Unadjusted Trial Balance. The unadjusted trial balance for the Lynch Accounting Firm for the fiscal year ended October 31, 1987 is presented below:

Lynch Accounting Firm
Unadjusted Trial Balance
October 31, 1987

Account	Debit	Credit
Cash	$ 19,700	
Accounts receivable	23,000	
Notes receivable	5,000	
Interest receivable	0	
Office supplies	7,200	
Prepaid rent	12,000	
Prepaid insurance	8,400	
Land	30,000	
Building	70,000	
Accumulated depreciation—Building		$ 17,500
Accounts payable		15,000
Property taxes payable		0
Salaries payable		0
J. Lynch, capital		91,160
Fees earned		104,000
Interest revenue		0
Insurance expense	0	
Advertising expense	700	
Salaries expense	8,490	
Utilities expense	550	
Rent expense	42,000	
Miscellaneous expense	620	
Totals	$227,660	$227,660

Additional Information:

1. The note receivable is a one-year note. The interest rate is 10%, and both the interest and principal are due on February 1, 1988.
2. Supplies on hand at the end of the year cost $2,500.
3. Nine hundred dollars of the prepaid rent was used during the year.
4. The prepaid insurance is for a two-year period beginning April 1, 1987.

5. The building has a useful life of 10 years with no salvage value.

6. Property taxes are based on the fair market value of the property owned by the firm, at a rate of 15% of its fair market value on July 1, 1987. At that date, the property had an estimated fair market value of $170,000. Property taxes for the year ended October 31, 1987 are payable on November 10, 1987 but are assessed as of October 31, 1987.

7. Salaries earned but not yet paid at the end of the year amounted to $3,400.

Required:

a. Set up ledger accounts with the October 31, 1987 balances from the unadjusted trial balance.

b. Make the adjusting entries in the general journal. Set up new accounts if needed.

c. Post the adjusting entries to the T accounts.

d. Prepare an adjusted trial balance.

e. Prepare an income statement for the year ended October 31, 1987 and a balance sheet at October 31, 1987.

f. Make the closing entries.

g. Post the closing entries to the T accounts.

h. Prepare the post-closing trial balance.

4B–4. Accrual and Cash Bases of Accounting. The comparative December 31, 1987 and December 31, 1986 balance sheets and the income statement for the year ended December 31, 1987 for The Clifford Company follow:

The Clifford Company
Comparative Balance Sheets
December 31

Assets	1987	1986
Cash	$ 42,000	$ 37,900
Accounts receivable	16,300	13,450
Prepaid insurance	1,400	4,200
Office supplies	1,250	1,700
Office equipment—Net of accumulated depreciation	42,000	54,000
Other assets	15,000	15,000
Total assets	$117,950	$126,250

Liabilities and Owner's Equity	1987	1986
Liabilities		
Accounts payable	$ 8,630	$ 9,750
Unearned fees	0	7,500
Salaries payable	2,900	3,500
City property taxes payable	7,300	9,900
Total liabilities	$ 18,830	$ 30,650
Owner's Equity		
C. Clifford, capital	$ 99,120	95,600
Total liabilities and owner's equity	$117,950	$126,250

The Clifford Company
Income Statement
For the Year Ended December 31, 1987

Revenues		
Fees	$58,530	
Commissions	30,435	
Total revenues		$88,965
Expenses		
Salaries	$27,000	
Advertising	15,000	
Utilities	900	
Insurance	2,800	
Supplies	1,200	
Depreciation	12,000	
City property taxes	16,275	
Total expenses		75,175
Net income		$13,790

Required:

a. Prepare the appropriate closing entry. You must determine the amount of owner's withdrawals.

b. Prepare a statement of owner's equity for the year ended December 31, 1987.

c. Answer each of the following questions:

1. Assuming that all fees earned (not commissions) are first recorded in the Accounts Receivable account, how much cash was collected from customers on account during 1987?

2. Assuming that all purchases of supplies are made for cash, how much cash was paid for supplies during 1987?

3. How much cash was paid for insurance during 1987?

4. How much cash was paid for salaries during 1987?

5. How much cash was paid for city property taxes during 1987?

4B-5. Computations and Analysis. For each of the following independent situations, make the necessary computations. For each case, assume that the year-end is December 31, 1987 and that that is the only time that adjusting entries are made.

a. Bobby Jones's Barber Shop borrowed $25,000 from a local bank on July 1, 1987. The note had an interest rate of 15%. On December 31, 1987 the Interest Payable account had a balance of $1,875. How much cash interest did the barber shop pay on this note during 1987? What was the total interest expense for 1987 for this note?

b. The Young Company borrowed $17,500 from City National Bank at 9%. The total interest expense for the year 1987 will be $525. How many months has the loan been outstanding during 1987?

c. On January 2, 1987, the Hannah Company purchased equipment at a cost of $130,000. The equipment had an estimated salvage value of $8,000. Assuming that after the December 31, 1987 adjusting entry for depreciation the book value of the equipment was $117,800, what is the estimated useful life of the equipment?

Completing the Accounting Cycle   **169**

d. On January 1, 1986, the Speedy Delivery Company purchased a new truck with an estimated useful life of five years and a salvage value of $2,000. Depreciation expense for 1987 was $2,800. What was the purchase price of the truck?

e. On July 1, 1983, the Mathy Company purchased a building for $492,000. The building has an estimated useful life of 40 years. Six months' depreciation was taken in the year of purchase, and the book value of the building on December 31, 1987 after the depreciation adjusting entry is $437,550. What is the salvage value of the building?

4B–6. Worksheet Preparation. The unadjusted trial balance at December 31, 1987 for Speedy Secretarial Service follows:

Speedy Secretarial Service
Unadjusted Trial Balance
December 31, 1987

Account	Debit	Credit
Cash	$ 24,350	
Accounts receivable	12,780	
Secretarial supplies	18,500	
Prepaid rent	8,000	
Equipment	46,500	
Accumulated depreciation—Equipment		$ 17,500
Other assets	15,000	
Accounts payable		4,940
Note payable		3,000
Interest payable		0
Salaries payable		0
T. Little, capital		62,740
Fees		92,000
Repairs and maintenance expense	8,440	
Utilities expense	3,860	
Salaries expense	25,750	
Rent expense	17,000	
Totals	$180,180	$180,180

Additional Information:
1. Secretarial supplies on hand at the end of the year were worth $7,600.
2. Prepaid rent of $5,000 should be written off in 1987.
3. The equipment has a useful life of nine years and a salvage value of $1,500.
4. The note payable has an interest rate of 15% and has been outstanding all year.
5. Earned but unpaid salaries at year-end were $2,500.

Required:
a. Prepare a 10-column worksheet similar to the one in the text.
b. Make the necessary adjusting and closing entries in the general journal.
c. Prepare an income statement for the year ended December 31, 1987 and a balance sheet at December 31, 1987.

4B–7. Worksheet Preparation. The unadjusted trial balance for T F Architects and Assoc. at year-end September 30, 1987 is presented at the top of page 171.

Architects and Assoc.
Unadjusted Trial Balance
December 31, 1987

Account	Debit	Credit
Cash	$ 34,500	
Marketable securities	25,000	
Accounts receivable	23,800	
Supplies	7,900	
Land	34,000	
Building	175,000	
Accumulated depreciation—Building		$ 15,000
Equipment	63,700	
Accumulated depreciation—Equipment		23,250
Other assets	81,500	
Accounts payable		17,500
Note payable		30,000
Unearned rent revenue		43,000
Salaries payable		0
J. Dunphy, capital		345,050
Fees earned		93,400
Rental income		6,700
Salaries expense	85,000	
Advertising expense	30,000	
Delivery expense	7,000	
Repairs and maintenance	3,900	
Utilities expense	2,600	
Totals	$573,900	$573,900

Additional Information:

1. Supplies used during the year amounted to $2,500.
2. The building has a useful life of 35 years and no salvage value. The equipment has an estimated useful life of eight years and a salvage value of $1,700.
3. The note payable has an interest rate of 13% and has been outstanding for seven months during the year.
4. Twenty-one thousand dollars of the unearned rent revenue was earned during the year.
5. Earned but unpaid salaries amounted to $6,200 at year-end.

Required:

a. Prepare a 10-column worksheet similar to the one in the text.
b. Prepare an income statement for the year ended September 30, 1987 and a balance sheet at September 30, 1987.
c. Make the necessary adjusting and closing entries in the general ledger.

4B–8. Summary Review Problem. On January 2, 1987 John Naperski started his own CPA firm. During the year the following summary events occurred:

1. Naperski invested $170,000 in cash in order to start his practice.
2. Two years' rent of $19,200 was paid in advance on January 3, 1987.
3. Office supplies of $8,200 were purchased for cash.
4. Office furniture and fixtures were purchased for $25,000 cash.
5. Office equipment of $5,000 was purchased on account.
6. Marketable securities for short-term investment were purchased for $95,000 cash.
7. Fees earned during the first half of the year were $42,000, of which $22,000 was on account and the remainder was for cash.
8. A $5,000 advance for services yet to be performed was received.

9. Utilities expense for the first half of the year amounted to $750 and was paid in cash.

10. Salaries of $19,200 were paid in cash during the first half of the year.

11. On July 1 the firm purchased a comprehensive three-year insurance policy for $6,000 cash.

12. Supplies costing $3,400 were purchased on account.

13. The firm accepted a $15,000 note receivable from a client for services rendered on August 1, 1987. The note has an interest rate of 10% and is due in a year.

14. On November 1 the firm paid $3,000 cash in advance for a three-year subscription to a professional journal.

15. The firm paid the full amount due for office equipment purchased in Item 5.

16. The firm returned $1,500 of the supplies purchased in Item 12 because they were defective. Their account was credited, and the remaining balance was paid in full.

17. Supplies costing $2,500 were purchased on account.

18. Fees earned during the second half of the year amounted to $63,000, of which 85% was on account and the remainder was received in cash.

19. One-half of the marketable securities were sold for $49,000 cash.

20. The following expenses were paid in cash during the second half of the year:

Salaries	$13,900
Utilities	950
Legal	1,500

21. Cash collections on account were $34,000.

22. Land was purchased for $25,000 cash.

23. Naperski withdrew $12,000 cash for his personal use.

Additional Information:

a. Interest on the note receivable must be accrued.

b. The necessary amount of prepaid insurance must be written off.

c. The necessary amount of prepaid subscriptions must be written off.

d. Prepaid rent must be written off.

e. Supplies on hand at December 31, 1987 amounted to $3,700.

f. The office furniture and fixtures have a seven-year life and a $4,000 salvage value.

g. The office equipment has a five-year life and no salvage value.

h. Salaries of $1,300 were earned but unpaid at year-end.

i. Fees of $2,000 were earned at year-end, for which the receivable and the revenue have not yet been recorded.

The firm's chart of accounts is as follows:

Cash	101	Accounts payable	201
Marketable securities	102	Unearned accounting fees	202
Accounts receivable	103	Salaries payable	203
Note receivable	104	J. Naperski, capital	300
Interest receivable	105	J. Naperski, drawing	310
Supplies	106	Accounting fees earned	400
Prepaid rent	107	Supplies expense	500
Prepaid insurance	108	Salaries expense	501
Prepaid subscriptions	109	Legal expense	502
Land	110	Utilities expense	503
Office furniture and fixtures	120	Subscription expense	504
Accumulated depreciation—		Insurance expense	505
Office furniture and fixtures	130	Rent expense	506
Office equipment	140	Depreciation expense	507
Accumulated depreciation—		Gain on sale of marketable securities	600
Office equipment	150	Interest revenue	610
		Income summary	1000

Required:

Depending on your instructor's directions, either use T accounts or a three-column running balance ledger account in completing the following work. If required by your instructor, Item c can be prepared on a worksheet.

a. Make the summary journal entries for the year, and post them to the ledger accounts. As a posting reference, use the number of the account and page 1 of the general journal.

b. Prepare an unadjusted trial balance.

c. In order to complete the accounting cycle:
   1. Prepare the adjusting entries and post them to the ledger accounts.
   2. Prepare an adjusted trial balance.

d. Prepare an income statement, a statement of owner's equity, and a balance sheet.

e. Prepare closing entries and post them to the ledger accounts.

f. Prepare a post-closing trial balance.

Understanding Financial Statements

The consolidated statement of income for the Anheuser-Busch Companies, Inc., and subsidiaries is reproduced below:

A N H E U S E R - B U S C H   C O M P A N I E S ,   I N C .

CONSOLIDATED STATEMENT OF INCOME
Anheuser-Busch Companies, Inc., and Subsidiaries
(In millions, except per share data)

Year Ended December 31,	1982	1981	1980
Sales	$5,185.7	$4,409.6	$3,822.4
Less federal and state beer taxes	609.1	562.4	527.0
Net sales	4,576.6	3,847.2	3,295.4
Cost of products sold	3,331.7	2,975.5	2,553.9
Gross profit	1,244.9	871.7	741.5
Marketing, administrative and research expenses	752.0	515.0	428.6
Operating income	492.9	356.7	312.9
Other income and expenses:			
Interest expense	(89.2)	(89.6)	(75.6)
Interest capitalized	41.2	64.1	41.7
Interest income	17.0	6.2	2.4
Other income (expense), net	(8.1)	(12.2)	(9.9)
Gain on sale of Lafayette plant	20.4	—	—
Income before income taxes	474.2	325.2	271.5
Provision for income taxes:			
Current	92.4	10.4	31.9
Deferred	94.5	97.4	67.8
	186.9	107.8	99.7
Net Income	$ 287.3	$ 217.4	$ 171.8
Earnings per share:			
Primary	$ 5.97	$ 4.79	$ 3.80
Fully diluted	5.88	4.61	3.80

In addition, you have gathered the following balance sheet data:

	December 31	
	1982	1981
	(in millions)	
Cash	$ 21.5	$ 49.6
Stockholders' equity	1,526.6	1,206.8

Required:

   a. Make the summary closing entries Anheuser would have made at December 31, 1982. (Income tax expense is the total of current and deferred portion.)

   b. During the year stockholders invested an additional $98.3 million in the firm. When the stockholders of a corporation withdraw assets, usually in the form of cash, it is called a dividend. From the information provided, determine the amount of dividends issued to the stockholders of Anheuser during 1982.

   c. What are the relationships, if any, between the increase in stockholders' equity and the decrease in cash during 1982?

Financial Decision Case

Statement of Cash Inflows and Outflows. Bill Gilroy is considering buying an apartment house. The building will cost $500,000, and Bill will make a 20% down payment and will finance the remainder through a 10%, 30-year mortgage. Monthly payments including principal and interest will be $3,510. Bill put together the following projected income statement for the first year. He expects this statement to reflect the operations of the apartment house for the next two years, except that interest expense will decrease very slightly.

Revenues		
Rents		$61,500
Expenses		
Interest	$39,500	
Depreciation	16,667	
Repairs and maintenance	6,000	
Insurance	2,400	
		64,567
Net loss		($ 3,067)

Bill is concerned that he will be unable to generate enough cash flow from the building to pay the necessary cash outflows. He gives you the following additional information and asks you to prepare a statement of cash inflows and outflows for the first year:

   1. All rents will be paid in cash at the beginning of each month. No prepayments or deposits are required.

   2. The building has a 30-year life and no salvage value.

   3. The insurance expense of $2,400 represents one-half the cost of the two-year comprehensive insurance policy he purchased.

   4. Finally, in preparing your statement, do not consider the 20% down payment as part of the cash outflows.

     In addition to your statement, write a brief memo to Bill explaining the differences in the two statements.

Extensions of the Basic Accounting Model

Recording Sales and Purchases of Inventory for a Merchandising Firm

5

LEARNING OBJECTIVES

After reading this chapter you should be able to:

1. Identify the elements of income statements for merchandising firms.

2. Explain how merchandising firms account for sales transactions, including trade and quantity discounts, credit card sales, and sales returns and allowances.

3. Distinguish between the perpetual and the periodic inventory systems, and the accounting entries related to each of these systems.

4. Account for purchases, including trade and quantity discounts, purchase discounts, purchase returns and allowances, and freight-in.

5. Discuss the issues involved in taking a physical inventory.

6. Prepare a worksheet for a merchandising firm using the periodic inventory system.

7. Prepare closing entries for a merchandising firm.

In the first four chapters we used a service firm, Lisa Bowman's law firm, to introduce the basic accounting cycle. This chapter describes the accounting procedures of a merchandising firm. A **merchandising firm** purchases a finished product for future sale. Examples of such firms include retail department and food stores, pharmacies, and computer stores. First we discuss accounting for sales, and then accounting for purchases of inventory. Finally, we introduce the worksheet techniques for merchandising firms and discuss how to prepare closing entries for a merchandising firm.

Income Statements for a Merchandising Firm

A condensed income statement for a merchandising firm follows. Its major elements include revenue from sales, cost of goods sold, gross margin on sales, operating expenses, and net income. The major differences between this statement and that of a service firm is in the sales and cost of goods sold sections.

Technical Computer Company
Condensed Income Statement
For the Month Ended January 31, 1987

Revenue from sales	$100,000
Cost of goods sold	60,000
Gross margin on sales	40,000
Operating expenses	30,000
Net income	$ 10,000

Revenues from **sales** are the dollar price of goods sold by the firm—in our example, $100,000. **Cost of goods sold** represents how much the firm paid for the merchandise sold—in our example, $60,000. The difference between sales and cost of goods sold is referred to as **gross margin** or **gross profit on sales** and indicates the amount of profits from sales that are available to cover operating expenses and provide for net income.

Accounting for Sales

The main concern of the merchandising firm is the sale of its product or products. The ultimate success of the firm depends on its ability to sell its goods at a higher price than that paid to its vendors or suppliers for the goods plus its operating expenses. To be profitable, the sales price charged by the firm must cover its (1) cost of goods sold, (2) operating expenses, and (3) net income.

Revenue from sales, as shown in the partial income statement on the top of page 179, consists of the gross proceeds from the sales of merchandise less sales returns and allowances and sales discounts.

Under the accrual basis of accounting, **gross sales** is the total of cash sales plus those sales made on credit during the period. It does not make any difference whether the sale is for cash or on account. In either case, an exchange has taken place and revenue is earned through the generation of cash or a receivable. The journal entry to record a day's sales of $1,000, of which $400 is for cash and $600 is on account, is:

Cash	400	
Accounts Receivable	600	
Sales		1,000
To record cash and credit sales.		

Jacob's Pet Supplies
Partial Income Statement
For the Year Ended December 31, 1987

Revenue from sales		
Gross sales		$199,300
Less: Sales returns and allowances	$ 800	
Sales discounts	3,500	4,300
Net sales		$195,000

The source of the data for this entry is the cash register or electronic point-of-sale device. In a manual system, hand postings are made to both the general ledger Accounts Receivable and the subsidiary Accounts Receivable ledger. A subsidiary ledger contains detailed information, for example, an account for each individual customer. If management desires, sales can be broken down further by department. Some electronic point-of-sale devices may be able to make these postings instantaneously as well as update inventory quantities for merchandise sold.

There are a number of issues related to accounting for sales, including trade and quantity discounts, sales discounts, credit card sales, and sales returns and allowances.

Trade and Quantity Discounts

Merchandising firms often allow reductions from their list or catalogue prices. **Trade discounts** are discounts offered to a certain class of buyers. For example, a furniture store may allow certain trade discounts to professional decorators but charge the general public the full retail price. **Quantity discounts** are reductions from the list price based on quantity purchases. For example, the price of pens may be $21 per dozen, but large discounts may be offered on the following bulk purchases:

Quantity Purchased	% Discount
below 50 dozen	0
50 to 99 dozen	5
100 to 199 dozen	10
above 200 dozen	15

Both trade and quantity discounts are price adjustments on the sales or exchange price, and generally accepted accounting principles require that transactions be recorded at the agreed-upon price, net of these discounts. Thus, there is no explicit accounting recognition given to these discounts. To illustrate, assume that an individual purchased 60 dozen pens on account for $21 per dozen. The total sales price is $1,197(60 × $21 = $1,260 × 95% = $1,197), and the transaction is recorded in the following manner:

Accounts Receivable	1,197	
Sales		1,197
To record cash sales.		

Recording Sales and Purchases of Inventory for a Merchandising Firm

Although financial reporting rules do not require explicit recognition of trade or quantity discounts, management may want to keep records of these discounts, as this will allow the firm to monitor their quantity and effectiveness. This can be important in certain retail areas such as automobile dealerships in which discounts from the list price are common and salespeople are paid commissions. The indiscriminate use of discounts may be in the salesperson's short-run best interest but not in the firm's long-run best interest. By establishing a separate discount account (offset against the sales account when external financial statements are prepared), this potential problem can be controlled.

Sales Discounts

A **sales discount** is a cash reduction offered to customers in an attempt to ensure that they promptly pay their trade accounts. In effect, the seller is willing to accept less cash than the agreed-upon sales price if the customer will pay within a specified period of time. The seller benefits because prompt payment decreases the probability of bad debts and also decreases the need for short-term financing. In a cash-tight economy, the prompt conversion of receivables into cash is essential if the company is to maintain its liquidity.

The type and amount of the sales discount depend on the credit terms set by the seller. Following are a list and an explanation of the more common types of sales discounts and credit terms. Sales discounts such as those listed are mainly offered to wholesale customers and are less often available to retail customers.

COMMON CREDIT TERMS	
Type of Credit Term	Explanation
2/10, n/30	A 2% discount is allowed if payment is made within 10 days of the invoice date. The full price is due within 30 days of the invoice date.
1/10, n/30	A 1% discount is allowed if payment is made within 10 days of the invoice date. The full price is due within 30 days of the invoice date.
5 EOM	The full invoice price is due within five days after the end of the month of the sale.
n/30	The entire invoice price is due within 30 days of the invoice date.

Unlike trade or quantity discounts, explicit accounting recognition is given to sales discounts. There are two popular methods used to record sales discounts, the gross method and the net method. The journal entries for both of these alternatives, based on a $100 sale on account with stated terms of 2/10, n/30, are:

JOURNAL ENTRIES TO RECORD SALES DISCOUNTS $100 Sale—Stated Terms 2/10, n/30					
Transaction	Gross Method			Net Method	

1. Sale of $100 of merchandise on account	Accounts Receivable
	   Sales
		100	100	Accounts Receivable
				   Sales
					98
					 98

2a. Customer pays within discount period	Cash
	Sales Discounts
	   Accounts Receivable
		98
		2
			100	Cash
				   Accounts Receivable
					98
					 98

2b. Customer *does not* pay within discount period	Cash
	   Accounts Receivable
		100	100	Cash
				   Sales Discounts
				   Not Taken
				   Accounts Receivable
					100
					
					 2
					 98

The Gross Method

The **gross method of recording sales discounts** records the sale and receivable at the gross amount before any discount. If the customer takes the discount, the Sales Discounts account must be debited. In the preceding example, a $2 debit is made to that account, Cash is debited for $98, and Accounts Receivable is credited for $100. Remember, Accounts Receivable was originally debited for the full invoice price of $100 and so must be credited for $100 in order to clear the customer's account. Sales Discounts is a contra sales account, which means that it is a deduction from total sales to arrive at a net sales figure on the income statement. If the customer fails to take the discount, the entry to record the eventual payment is straightforward. Cash is debited for $100 and Accounts Receivable is credited for $100, the full invoice price paid.

The gross method is commonly used because most manual and/or electronic systems are designed to record invoices at the billed price. Nonetheless, there are problems with this method. It is based on the assumption that the customer will not take the discount, though it is generally to the purchaser's advantage to do so. To the extent that customers eventually take the discount, both accounts receivable and sales are overstated at the time the sale is recorded. Furthermore, the gross method highlights the discounts taken, whereas management may be more interested in finding those customers who fail to take the discount. Because it generally benefits the purchaser to take the discount, the failure to take it may indicate potential credit problems with that customer. That is, those customers not paying within the discount period may be experiencing cash flow problems. Because of the shortcomings of the gross method, some firms use the net method of recording sales.

The Net Method

As the preceding journal entries illustrate, the net method records the receivable and sale net of the allowable discount. The **net method of recording sales discounts** is based on the assumption that the customer will, indeed, take the discount. As we have noted before, this is a reasonable assumption, and therefore the receivable is stated at the expected cash receipts at the time of the sale. Likewise, the sale is recorded at the lowest cash price that the seller is willing to take. If payment is made within the discount period, Cash and

Accounts Receivable are respectively debited and credited at the amount that the receivable was originally recorded. In the example, this amount is $98.

If the customer does not make the payment in the discount period, the full invoice price must be paid. The difference between the full invoice price and the net amount at which the receivable was originally recorded is credited to an account called Sales Discounts Not Taken. This is a revenue account and is generally denoted as Other Revenues and Expenses in the income statement.

The net method is theoretically preferable because accounts receivable are recorded at their net realizable value (expected cash collection) at the time of the sale. In addition, the account Sales Discounts Not Taken highlights those customers who fail to take the discount. As we noted, this is important information for management control.

Credit Card Sales

Credit card sales are a common part of American business. All sizes and types of merchandisers are likely to accept one or more of the following credit cards: VISA, MasterCard, American Express, Diners' Club, and Carte Blanche. Even large retail chains such as J. C. Penney and Montgomery Ward accept national credit cards in addition to their own charge cards. Credit cards are accepted by retailers because they stimulate business; cash is often received sooner than are payments on accounts carried by the business; and often it is cheaper to accept a national credit card than to carry individual accounts. The accounting for credit cards depends on whether a bank card or a nonbank card is accepted.

Bank Cards

Bank cards such as VISA or MasterCard are issued by banks and other financial institutions. In order to receive reimbursement on bank card sales, the retailer simply deposits the signed drafts directly into the bank with the rest of the day's receipts. Because these drafts are immediately credited to the retailer's account, they are treated just like cash.

All of the national banks or credit card companies charge for their services. This charge is based on a number of factors, such as the volume of the retailer's gross charge sales. For example, to process the sale, most credit card companies charge in the vicinity of 2–5% of the gross sales price. This charge is deducted from the total cash receipts credited to the retailer's account when the charge slips are deposited at the bank, or as a service charge at the end of the month. To illustrate, assume that Lou's Athletic Store recorded bank credit card sales of $500 for the day. The credit card company charges 4%, which is immediately deducted by the bank when the charge slips are deposited with the day's cash receipts. Based on this data, Lou's Athletic Store makes the following entry:

Cash	480	
Credit Card Fees	20	
Sales		500
To record credit card sales of $500 and a 4% ($20) fee.		

Nonbank Cards

Reimbursement on nonbank credit cards such as American Express and Diners' Club are usually handled in a different manner. Instead of being deposited directly into the retailer's bank, the drafts are periodically mailed to the credit card company, which then mails the payment, less the service charge, to the retailer.

To illustrate, assume that Lou's Athletic Store recorded nonbank credit card sales of $300 for the day. At the end of the day the store made the following entry:

Accounts Receivable, credit card company	300	
Sales		300
To record credit card sales for the day.		

By the end of the week Lou made total nonbank credit card sales of $2,000 and mailed the drafts to the credit card company. When the credit card company remitted the payment for this week's sales, less a 4% service charge, the store made the following entry:

Cash	1,920	
Credit Card Fees	80	
Accounts Receivable, credit card company		2,000
To record receipt of payment from credit card company less $80 fee.		

Most companies consider credit card fees to be a selling expense. This is based on the assumption that these fees replace the expenses that the firm incurs when it carries its own receivables. However, some individuals argue that credit card fees should be shown as a reduction of gross sales in determining net sales. Because many companies are beginning to offer discounts to customers who pay with cash rather than with credit cards, this latter treatment appears to be more appropriate. In any event, the effect is to reduce net income by the amount of the credit card fee.

Sales Returns and Allowances

Like credit cards, **sales returns and allowances** are a fact of everyday life for the retailer or merchandiser. Sales returns occur when a customer, for whatever reason, returns an item for a cash refund or a credit to his or her account. Sales allowances are a reduction in the initial sale. A retailer might allow the credit because the particular item did not perform to expectations or had other defects. Regardless of why a return is made, a Sales Return and Allowances account generally is used to record returns. Although it would be possible to debit returns and allowances directly to the Sales account, this would not provide the control that the use of a Sales Returns and Allowances account does, whereby a firm can monitor the dollar amount of returns and allowances.

To demonstrate the use of a Sales Returns and Allowances account, assume that the Lloyd Corporation purchased on account $10,000 of goods from the Austin Company. The Lloyd Corporation determined that these goods were defective and returned them for a credit. The Austin Company made the following entry to record this return:

Recording Sales and Purchases of Inventory for a Merchandising Firm

Sales Returns and Allowances	10,000	
Accounts Receivable		10,000
To record return of defective merchandise.		

If the sale had been made for cash and a cash refund granted, the credit would be made to the Cash account rather than to Accounts Receivable.

Accounting for Inventory Purchases

The purchase of inventory for resale represents the other major activity of a merchandising firm. **Inventories** are items held for resale to customers in the normal course of business, or items that are to be consumed in producing or manufacturing goods or rendering services. For merchandising and manufacturing companies, inventories often are the single largest current asset. For example, on December 28, 1985 Safeway's inventories totaled over $1.5 billion. This inventory represented 77% of its current assets and over 32% of its total assets.

The accounting information for inventory purchases must be designed to allow management to maintain the proper level of inventories and to ensure that ending inventories and cost of goods sold are properly recorded and costed. In this section we discuss the nature of inventories, the recording of inventory purchases, and the related issues of purchase discounts and purchase returns and allowances. In Chapter 11 we look at how a firm determines the cost of its ending inventory and the cost of those items sold during the period.

Two different accounting information systems have been developed to deal with accounting for inventories. They are the perpetual and the periodic inventory systems.

Perpetual Inventory System

A **perpetual inventory system** keeps a running balance of both inventory on hand and the cost of goods sold. These balances can be kept in units or in units and dollars. Management is therefore always aware of inventory levels and is able to make timely purchases that will ensure the maintenance of desired inventory levels. The use of perpetual inventory systems has been enhanced in recent years through the use of electronic point-of-sale devices and computers. However, even with such sophisticated equipment, perpetual records may be kept only in units, with the costs of ending inventories and goods sold determined by the periodic method. For example, optical scanners in markets keep track of inventory quantities, but at the end of the accounting period a physical inventory is taken to compute the cost of goods sold during the period and the appropriate cost of the ending inventory.

Accounting for Perpetual Inventories

The accounting for perpetual and later for periodic inventories is shown in the following example. Assume that a firm started the year with a beginning inventory of pens that cost $10,000. During the quarter, the following summary of transactions occurred:

Sales—All for Cash		Purchases on Account
Date	Amount of Sale	Cost of Inventory Sold*	Cost of Inventory Purchased
1/20	$12,000	$ 8,000	
1/28			$25,000
2/10	30,000	24,000	
3/28			10,000

*On a periodic system these data would not be computed; they are given here for illustrative purposes.

The appropriate journal entries for the perpetual system are presented next. As inventory is purchased, the Merchandise Inventory account is debited. As the inventory is sold, the Merchandise Inventory account is credited and Cost of Goods Sold is debited for the cost of the inventory sold. One of the features of the perpetual system is to provide the firm with information concerning its inventory levels. The system's design reflects this goal. As this series of journal entries shows, the balance in the Merchandise Inventory account at a particular time should reflect the actual cost of the goods on hand at that time. In the example, the ending balance in the Merchandise Inventory account is $13,000, which should represent the actual cost of inventory on hand.

JOURNAL ENTRIES FOR MERCHANDISE PURCHASES—PERPETUAL METHOD

Transaction	Journal Entries		
1/20 sale for $12,000 with a cost of $8,000	Cash	12,000	
	Sales		12,000
	Cost of Goods Sold	8,000	
	Merchandise Inventory		8,000
1/28 purchase for $25,000	Merchandise Inventory	25,000	
	Accounts Payable		25,000
2/10 sale for $30,000 with a cost of $24,000	Cash	30,000	
	Sales		30,000
	Cost of Goods Sold	24,000	
	Merchandise Inventory		24,000
3/28 purchase for $10,000	Merchandise Inventory	10,000	
	Accounts Payable		10,000

T Accounts

Merchandise Inventory				Cost of Goods Sold		
1/1 Bal.	10,000	1/20	8,000	1/20	8,000	
1/28	25,000	2/10	24,000	2/20	24,000	
3/28	10,000					
				3/30 Bal.	32,000	
3/30 Bal.	13,000					

We use the word *should* because the balance in the merchandise inventory account will not always equal the cost of the items remaining in the inventory. This is a result of clerical errors, spoilage, theft, and similar problems.

Recording Sales and Purchases of Inventory for a Merchandising Firm   185

Therefore, an actual physical inventory count should be made at specified intervals, usually once a year. The balance in the Merchandise Inventory account is then adjusted to the actual ending inventory as determined by the physical count.

A typical perpetual inventory record follows. The data shown in the record pertain to the journal entries on the previous page. In this perpetual record, both units and costs are maintained. Furthermore, in order to simplify the illustration, all items are assumed to have had the same cost, $2. As we noted, some perpetual records maintain only a record of units.

INVENTORY RECORD
Quarter Ended March 31, 19XX

Item **Pens**
Code No. **P-24**

Minimum Stock **1,000**
Maximum Stock **17,000**
Average Reorder Time **2 weeks**

Date	Description	Items Purchased			Items Sold			Balance Remaining		
		Units Received	Unit Cost	Total Cost	Units Sold	Unit Cost	Total Cost	Units	Unit Cost	Total Cost
January 1	Beginning Balance							5,000	2.00	10,000
January 20	Sales				4,000	2.00	8,000	1,000	2.00	2,000
January 28	Purchases	12,500	2.00	25,000				13,500	2.00	27,000
February 10	Sales				12,000	2.00	24,000	1,500	2.00	3,000
March 28	Purchases	5,000	2.00	10,000				6,500	2.00	13,000

Recap for Quarter
Purchases   17,500 $2.00 $35,000
Sales   16,000 $2.00 $32,000
Balance   6,500 $2.00 $13,000

Although the perpetual inventory system provides management with a great deal of information, it is costly and time-consuming to maintain unless the firm has completely computerized its inventory control system. Most firms, therefore, use a periodic inventory system.

Periodic Inventory Systems

Periodic inventory systems do not keep continual track of the dollar amount of ending inventories and cost of goods sold. Instead, these items are determined only periodically, at the end of each quarter, each year, or other accounting period. Although this system may be easier to use for record-keeping purposes, it results in a significant loss of information for managerial decision-making purposes. However, the sheer volume of transactions in some merchandising businesses makes it impossible to use anything but a periodic system.

Accounting under the Periodic System

The journal entries necessary to record inventories under the periodic system are shown on page 187. The data are from the example at the top of this page and are the same data used to illustrate the perpetual system. When the periodic system is used, no entry is made to record the cost of the inventory sold for a particular sale. Furthermore, as the journal entries show, inventory purchases are not debited to the Merchandise Inventory account. Rather, they are accumulated in a separate account called Purchases. As a result, there are no entries during the period to the asset account, Merchandise Inventory. Therefore, the balance in the Merchandise Inventory account will reflect the amount of inventory at the beginning of the year, as indicated in the T accounts that follow the journal entries.

JOURNAL ENTRIES FOR MERCHANDISE PURCHASES
PERIODIC METHOD

Transaction	Journal Entries		
1/20 sale for $12,000 with a cost of $8,000	Cash	12,000	
	Sales		12,000
	No entry to record cost of goods sold.		
1/28 purchase for $25,000	Purchases	25,000	
	Accounts Payable		25,000
2/10 sale for $30,000 with a cost of $24,000	Cash	30,000	
	Sales		30,000
	No entry to record cost of goods sold.		
3/28 purchase for $10,000	Purchases	10,000	
	Accounts Payable		10,000

T-Accounts

Purchases		Merchandise Inventory	
1/28 25,000		1/1 Bal. 10,000	
3/28 10,000			
3/30 Bal. 35,000			

Determining Cost of Goods Sold and Ending Inventory

Before financial statements can be prepared under the periodic system, the cost of goods sold during the period as well as the ending inventory must be calculated. This is done by taking a physical inventory, or counting the end-of-period inventory, to determine the quantity and the cost of the ending inventory and then applying this formula. (The data are from the current example.)

Beginning inventory	$10,000
+ Purchases	35,000
= Goods available for sale	45,000
− Ending inventory	13,000
= Cost of goods sold	$32,000

In effect, the total of the beginning inventory and purchases during the period represents the total of all goods that the firm had available for sale. If the ending inventory is subtracted from this total, the remaining balance represents the cost of the items sold.

As shown in the preceding calculation on page 187, the ending inventory affects the income statement by decreasing cost of goods sold. It also appears in the balance sheet as an asset. However, if the periodic method is used, only the beginning inventory is reflected in the ledger accounts. As we will see in a later part of this chapter, the ending inventory is entered into the ledger accounts through a closing entry that debits the Inventory account and credits Income Summary for the amount of the ending inventory.

Calculating the cost of the ending inventory and the resulting cost of goods sold is extremely important in determining the periodic income and financial position. Chapter 11 examines the accounting methods that have been developed to do this. At this point, assuming that we have determined these amounts, we are illustrating the journal entries to record these figures.

Issues Involved in Recording Purchases

There are several other issues in recording merchandise purchases. It is important that inventory purchases be recorded at the time title passes from the seller to the buyer and that inventory purchases be recorded in accordance with the historical cost principle. In this regard, historical cost includes the cash-equivalent price of the item plus all costs paid for freight and handling in order to deliver the merchandise to a location for its use or resale by the buyer. Specific items that affect the historical cost of inventory purchases include purchase discounts, purchase returns and allowances, and freight charges. Accounting for each of these items is explained next. Because the periodic inventory system is the one most commonly used, it is the basis for our discussion.

Accounting for **purchase discounts** is similar to accounting for sales discounts. The two methods, gross and net, are illustrated next in the journal entries at the top of page 189. The example is based on a $100 purchase with terms of 2/10, n/30.

The Gross Method of Recording Purchase Discounts

The **gross method of recording purchase discounts** records the purchase and the payable at the gross amount before any discount. If the firm takes the discount, an account titled Purchase Discounts will be credited for the amount of the discount. As we will see later, this account is eventually closed into Income Summary. The ultimate result is to reduce cost of goods sold by the amount of the discounts taken.

If the business fails to take the discount, the entry to record the payment is straightforward. Accounts Payable is debited and Cash is credited for $100, the full invoice price. Like the gross method of recording sales discounts, the gross method of recording purchase discounts is very common. However, it also suffers from the same criticisms made against recording sales at the gross amount when discounts are offered.

The Net Method of Recording Purchase Discounts

As the journal entries on the top of page 189 indicate, the **net method of recording purchase discounts** records the purchase and the accounts payable net of the allowable discount. If the payment is made within the discount period, Accounts Payable should be debited and Cash should be credited for the amount at which the payable was originally recorded. If the firm does not

JOURNAL ENTRIES TO RECORD PURCHASE DISCOUNTS
$100 Purchase—Stated Terms 2/10, n/30

Transaction	Gross Method			Net Method		
1. Purchase of $100 of merchandise on account	Purchases* Accounts Payable	100	100	Purchases Accounts Payable	98	98
2a. Firm pays within discount period	Accounts Payable Purchase Discounts Cash	100	2 98	Accounts Payable Cash	98	98
2b. Firm *does not* pay within discount period	Accounts Payable Cash	100	100	Accounts Payable Purchase Discount Lost Cash	98 2	100

*This illustration assumes the use of the periodic inventory system. If a perpetual system is used, the debit is to the Merchandise Inventory account in all places where the Purchases account is debited. All other aspects of the entry are the same.

pay within the discount period, the full invoice price is paid. The difference between the amount at which Accounts Payable is debited and Cash is credited is debited to an account titled Purchase Discounts Lost. This account is treated as either an operating expense or interest expense. The argument for treating discounts lost as interest expense is based on the fact that when a firm consciously chooses not to pay within the allowable discount period, there is an additional cost. This additional cost represents a cost for the use of money and, therefore, is considered interest.

As in the case of sales discounts, the net method is preferable. Accounts payable are recorded at their expected cash payment at the time of purchase. Furthermore, the use of the Purchase Discounts Lost account highlights the total cost of not paying within the discount period. As we noted previously, this can be a significant cost, and it is generally in the firm's best interest to pay within the discount period.

Purchase Returns and Allowances

The accounting treatment for **purchase returns and allowances** is similar to that for sales returns and allowances, except that the Purchases Returns and Allowances and Accounts Payable accounts, are involved. To illustrate, assume that the Russell Company purchased on account, for future resale, 10 television sets at a total cost of $2,800. The periodic inventory system is used, and the payable is recorded at the gross or invoice price. If one television costing $280 is found defective and is returned, the Russell Company will make the following entry:

Accounts Payable	280	
Purchase Returns and Allowances		280
Return of defective merchandise.		

The Purchase Returns and Allowances account is offset against total purchases in computing cost of goods sold. The ultimate effect is to reduce cost of goods sold. Although the Purchases account could be directly credited for any returns and allowances, the use of the Purchase Returns and Allowances account gives management more control over these items.

Freight

The cost of freight for goods purchased for resale is referred to as *freight-in*, or transportation-in. In some circumstances the seller pays the freight, and in other circumstances the purchaser pays the freight. Freight charges paid by the purchaser are debited to an account called Freight-in and are an addition to the cost of inventory purchased and ultimately to cost of goods sold. This is in accordance with the historical cost principle and ensures that the purchases carry their full cost. Freight charges paid by the seller are referred to as *freight-out*. They are considered a selling expense and as such are not included in the computation of cost of goods sold.

Deciding who pays the freight is a negotiable item in determining the terms of sale and is based on legal concepts concerning the passage of title. If the terms of the sale are **FOB (Free on Board) destination,** legal title to the goods does not pass until they reach the buyer's receiving point, and so the seller pays the freight. Conversely, when the goods are shipped **FOB shipping point,** title to the goods passes when they leave the seller's warehouse, and so the buyer pays the freight charges. The following table summarizes these points:

Terms	Who Pays Freight Charges	When Title to Goods Passes
FOB Shipping	Purchaser	When goods are shipped
FOB Destination	Seller	When goods are received

As the previous discussion pointed out, freight-in ultimately becomes an addition to cost of goods sold. There are other expenses that could be considered additional inventory costs and ultimately part of cost of goods sold, including such items as the expenses of the merchandise-receiving department, warehousing, insurance cost, and other costs of carrying inventory. Clearly, these costs are incurred because of the inventory and logically could be allocated to the cost of inventory and the cost of goods sold. However, because of the difficulty of allocating these items, accountants consider them to be period expenses and include them in either selling or general and administrative expenses. Only such items as freight-in that are directly related to the inventory are included in the cost of the inventory.

Taking a Physical Inventory

Taking a physical inventory is an important part of maintaining control over merchandising operations. When a perpetual inventory system is used, the physical inventory verifies that the firm does in fact have the inventory that its records show it has. When a periodic inventory system is used, a physical inventory is needed to determine cost of goods sold. The two steps in taking a physical inventory are the inventory count and the determination of the inventory's cost. This section briefly considers the issues pertaining to the item count; the issues pertaining to the cost of the ending inventory are studied in Chapter 11.

In taking a physical inventory, special care must be taken to ensure that all items of inventory to which the firm has legal title are counted. In addition, care must be taken to ensure that items that have been sold are not counted in the seller's year-end inventory. In this regard, items that require special analysis are goods in transit, goods on consignment, goods in public warehouses, and inventory losses.

Goods in Transit

Goods in transit are goods that have been purchased but have not yet been received by the purchaser. These goods can easily be overlooked when counting the ending inventory because they are not physically located at either the seller's or the purchaser's warehouse. In accounting for goods in transit, the main question is whether a sale has taken place resulting in the passage of title to the buyer.

As we noted, from a legal standpoint, title passes when goods reach the FOB point. Therefore, when goods are shipped FOB shipping point, title passes from the seller to the buyer at the shipping point. Because title has passed, the seller recognizes the sale, the buyer recognizes the purchase, and the inventory is included in the buyer's ending inventory. If goods are shipped FOB destination, title does not pass until the goods reach the buyer's receiving point. In this situation, goods in transit belong to the seller, and neither a sale nor a purchase is recorded until the goods reach the buyer.

Goods on Consignment

Goods on consignment are goods held by a firm for resale but to which title remains with the manufacturer. In effect, the merchandiser or retailer has agreed to display the goods but, for a variety of reasons, is not willing to purchase them. When and if the retail firm sells the consigned goods, it receives a commission. However, until the sale takes place, the title to the goods remains with the manufacturer, although they are on the premises of a different firm. The manufacturer of the items is willing to accept such an agreement in order to get new or unusual goods into the hands of retailers for possible sale. Retailers agree to this arrangement because they do not have to accept the risks of ownership and will still receive a commission if the goods are sold.

Goods in Public Warehouses

Merchandising firms often store goods in public warehouses. If the firm has title to the goods in the warehouses, they must be included in the ending inventory. Failure to count or include these items will understate the ending inventory, net assets, and profits for the period.

Inventory Losses

Many merchandising firms incur substantial inventory losses due to shoplifting, employee pilferage, spoilage, and obsolescense. When the periodic inventory system is used, these losses are automatically included in cost of goods sold. To illustrate, assume that a sporting goods store lost $1,000 worth of merchandise because of shoplifting. When the store's ending inventory is counted, the missing items obviously will not be included. Because of these missing items, the ending inventory will be understated by $1,000. Consequently, the amount of ending inventory subtracted from goods available for sale to determine cost of goods sold will be understated by $1,000. The ultimate effect is to increase cost of goods sold by the same $1,000.

Sales, Purchases, and Cost of Goods Sold Summarized

At this point we can summarize the various components of net sales and cost of goods sold by reviewing the following partial income statement. For purposes of illustration, this income statement details each account and how it affects net sales and cost of goods sold. Most published financial statements are not as detailed and usually only contain amounts for net sales and cost of goods sold.

Jacob's Pet Supplies
Partial Income Statement
For the Year Ended December 31, 1987

Gross sales			$199,300
Less: Sales returns and allowances		$ 800	
Sales discounts		3,500	
			4,300
Net sales			195,000
Cost of goods sold			
Beginning inventory		18,000	
Purchases	$146,500		
Less: Purchase returns and allowances	2,000		
Purchase discounts	4,000		
Net purchases		140,500	
Add: Freight-in		3,000	
Cost of goods available for sale		161,500	
Less: Ending inventory		25,000	
Cost of goods sold			136,500
Gross margin on sales			$ 58,500

Worksheet Techniques for a Periodic Inventory System

Chapter 4 discussed worksheet techniques for a service firm. This section explains worksheet techniques for a merchandising firm when a periodic inventory system is used. A worksheet for Jacob's Pet Supplies for the year ended December 31, 1987 is found on page 193. All the new accounts discussed in this chapter are highlighted.

The Unadjusted Trial Balance, Adjustments, and Adjusted Trial Balance Columns

The unadjusted trial balance, adjustments, and adjusted trial balance columns (Nos. 1–6) are prepared in essentially the same manner as they would be for a service firm. The amounts listed in the unadjusted trial columns come from

Jacob's Pet Supplies
Worksheet
For the Year Ended December 31, 1987

Account	Unadjusted Trial Balance Debit	Unadjusted Trial Balance Credit	Adjustments Debit	Adjustments Credit	Adjusted Trial Balance Debit	Adjusted Trial Balance Credit	Income Statement Debit	Income Statement Credit	Balance Sheet Debit	Balance Sheet Credit
	1	2	3	4	5	6	7	8	9	10
Cash	96,800				96,800				96,800	
Accounts receivable	85,000				85,000				85,000	
Merchandise inventory	18,000				18,000		18,000	25,000	25,000	
Office supplies	10,100			[1] 8,800	1,300				1,300	
Prepaid insurance	24,000			[3] 1,000	23,000				23,000	
License	10,000			[2] 300	9,700				9,700	
Accumulated depreciation—Buildings		10,000		[4] 1,250		11,250				11,250
Accumulated depreciation—Furniture and fixtures		5,000		[4] 2,000		7,000				7,000
Land	191,000				191,000				191,000	
Buildings	160,000				160,000				160,000	
Furniture and fixtures	107,000				107,000				107,000	
Accounts payable		55,200				55,200				55,200
Salaries payable				[5] 12,000		12,000				12,000
Interest payable				[6] 750		750				750
Bank loan payable		150,000				150,000				150,000
J. Daniels, capital		441,000				441,000				441,000
J. Daniels, drawing	900				900				900	
Sales		199,300				199,300		199,300		
Sales returns and allowances	800				800		800			
Sales discounts	3,500				3,500		3,500			
Purchases	146,500				146,500		146,500			
Purchase returns and allowances		2,000				2,000		2,000		
Repairs and maintenance expense	400				400		400			
Purchase discounts		4,000				4,000		4,000		
Freight-in	3,000				3,000		3,000			
Salaries expense	6,500		[5] 12,000		18,500		18,500			
Advertising expense	1,000				1,000		1,000			
Utilities expense	2,000				2,000		2,000			
Supplies expense			[1] 8,800		8,800		8,800			
Insurance expense			[3] 1,000		1,000		1,000			
Depreciation expense			[4] 3,250		3,250		3,250			
License expense			[2] 300		300		300			
Interest expense			[6] 750		750		750			
Totals	866,500	866,500	26,100	26,100	882,500	882,500	207,800	230,300	699,700	677,200
Net income							22,500			22,500
							230,300	230,300	699,700	699,700

193

the unadjusted general ledger accounts. The important points to note are that the $18,000 balance in the Merchandise Inventory account represents the amount of the beginning inventory and the inventory purchases made during the period of $146,500 are accumulated in the Purchases account.

Six adjustments to record supplies used, salaries payable, interest payable, depreciation expense, license expense, and interest expense are required for Jacob's Pet Supplies and they are entered into the adjustment columns (Nos. 3 and 4) of the worksheet. The adjusted trial balance columns (Nos. 5 and 6) can now be prepared by extending each item in the trial balance and adjustment columns.

The Income Statement Columns

The primary difference between a worksheet for a service firm and that of a merchandise firm lies in the way the income statement columns are prepared. For a merchandising firm the accounts that determine cost of goods sold must be brought together in the income statement columns of the worksheet. In our example, Jacob's Pet Supplies, these accounts include Merchandise Inventory (beginning and ending), Purchases, Purchase Returns and Allowances, Purchase Discounts, and Freight-in. Of these accounts, Purchases, Purchase Returns and Allowances, Purchase Discounts, and Freight-in accounts as well as those for Sales, Sales Returns and Allowances, and Sales Discounts are simply extended to the appropriate debit and credit columns (Cols. 7 and 8) in the income statement.

The treatment of the Merchandise Inventory account needs more explanation. In the computation of cost of goods sold, beginning inventory must be added and the ending inventory must be subtracted. This is done by extending the beginning inventory of $18,000 to the debit column of the income statement. This has the effect of adding the $18,000 of the beginning inventory to the $146,500 cost of merchandise purchases and the freight-in of $3,000 that are used to determine cost of goods available for sale.

The ending inventory of $25,000 is determined by taking a physical count. This amount is then inserted into the credit column of the income statement. As a result, the income statement column includes credits of $25,000 for the ending merchandise inventory, $2,000 for purchase returns and allowances, and $4,000 for purchase discounts. When these amounts are subtracted from the cost of goods available for sale, cost of goods sold of $136,500 results.

Cost of goods sold:			
Beginning inventory			$ 18,000
Purchases		$146,500	
Less: Purchase returns and allowances	$ 2,000		
Purchase discounts	4,000	6,000	
Net purchases		140,500	
Add: Freight-in		3,000	
Net cost of purchases			143,500
Cost of goods available for sale			161,500
Less: Ending inventory			25,000
Cost of goods sold			$136,500

The Balance Sheet Columns

The balance sheet columns of the worksheet are prepared next. The ending merchandise inventory amount of $25,000 must be inserted into the debit column of the balance sheet. This represents the amount of the asset on hand at the end of the year. If the $25,000 is not inserted into the debit column, the balance sheet will not balance.

The remainder of the balance sheet accounts can now be extended from the adjusted trial balance columns to the balance sheet columns in the manner explained in Chapter 4. The worksheet is then completed as it was for a service firm by determining net income (loss), carrying the net income figure to the credit (debit) column of the balance sheet, and totaling the balance sheet columns.

Financial Statements for Jacob's Pet Supplies

After the worksheet is completed, the adjusting entries must be entered in the general journal and posted to the ledger accounts. After financial statements and closing entries are prepared, the accounting cycle is completed. The income statement can be prepared directly from the worksheet. Following is a condensed income statement for Jacob's Pet Supplies. Following the income statement are the statement of changes in owner's equity and the balance sheet.

Jacob's Pet Supplies
Income Statement
For the Year Ended December 31, 1987

Net sales		$195,000
Cost of goods sold		136,500
Gross margin on sales*		58,500
Operating expenses:		
Salaries expense	$18,500	
Advertising expense	1,000	
Repairs and maintenance expense	400	
Utilities expense	2,000	
Supplies expense	8,800	
Insurance expense	1,000	
Depreciation expense	3,250	
License expense	300	
Interest expense	750	
Total operating expenses		36,000
Net income		$ 22,500

*See the statement on page 192 for an expanded version of this part of the income statement.

Jacob's Pet Supplies
Statement of Changes in Owner's Equity
For the Year Ended December 31, 1987

J. Daniel, capital—January 1, 1987	$441,000
Add: Net income for the year	22,500
Subtotal	463,500
Less: Withdrawals	900
J. Daniel, capital—December 31, 1987	$462,600

Jacob's Pet Supplies
Balance Sheet
December 31, 1987

Assets			Liabilities and Owner's Equity	
Cash		$ 96,800	Liabilities	
Accounts receivable		85,000	Accounts payable	$ 55,200
Inventory		25,000	Salaries payable	12,000
Supplies		1,300	Interest payable	750
Prepaid expenses		23,000	Bank loan payable	150,000
License		9,700	Total liabilities	217,950
Land		191,000		
Buildings	$160,000		Owner's equity	
Less: Accumulated depreciation	11,250	148,750	J. Daniel, capital	462,600
Furniture and fixtures	107,000			
Less: Accumulated depreciation	7,000	100,000	Total liabilities	
Total assets		$680,550	and owner's equity	$680,550

Closing Entries

When the periodic inventory system is used, the Merchandise Inventory ledger account reflects the amount of the beginning inventory. This amount must be removed from the ledger account and replaced with the amount of the ending merchandise inventory. This is most easily done through closing entries. The closing entries for Jacob's Pet Supplies are presented next.

1. Sales	199,300	
Purchase Returns and Allowances	2,000	
Purchase Discounts	4,000	
Merchandise Inventory, ending	25,000	
Income Summary		230,300

To close temporary accounts with credit balances to income summary and to establish ending merchandise inventory.

2. Income Summary   207,800

Merchandise Inventory, beginning	18,000	
Sales Returns and Allowances	800	
Sales Discounts	3,500	
Purchases	146,500	
Freight-in	3,000	
Salaries Expense	18,500	
Advertising Expense	1,000	
Repairs and Maintenance Expense	400	
Utilities Expense	2,000	
Office Supplies Expense	8,800	
Insurance Expense	1,000	
Depreciation Expense	3,250	
License Expense	300	
Interest Expense	750	

To close temporary accounts with debit balances to income summary and to remove beginning inventory.

3. Income Summary   22,500

     J. Daniels, Capital   22,500

To close income summary to capital.

4. J. Daniels, Capital   900

     J. Daniels, Drawing   900

To close drawing account to capital.

As part of the first closing entry, the ending amount of Merchandise Inventory, $25,000, is debited. As part of the second closing entry, the beginning amount of Merchandise Inventory, $18,000, is credited. The effect of these two entries is to remove the amount of the beginning merchandise inventory and replace it with the amount of the ending merchandise inventory. The remaining parts of the first and second closing entries and the third and fourth closing entries are similar to those for a service business.

Summary of Learning Objectives

1. **Elements of income statements for merchandising firms.** The major elements of an income statement for a merchandising firm includes revenue from sales, cost of goods sold, gross margin on sales, operating expenses, and net income. The major differences between this statement and that of a service firm are in the sales and cost of goods sold sections. Revenues from sales are the dollar price of goods sold by the firm; cost of goods sold represents how much the firm paid for the merchandise that has been sold.

2. **How merchandising firms account for sales transactions, including trade and quantity discounts, sales discounts, credit card sales, and sales returns and allowances.** Merchandising firms may offer their customers trade and quantity discounts and/or sales discounts. Trade and quantity discounts are adjustments to arrive at an agreed-upon price, and no accounting recognition is given to these items; that is, the sale is recorded net of any of these discounts. Sales discounts may be recorded gross or net, although in many respects the net method is preferable to the gross method. Separate accounts are maintained for credit card fees, and they

are usually considered selling expenses. Sales returns and allowances are offset against sales in order to determine net sales.

3. *The difference between the perpetual and the periodic inventory systems, and the accounting entries related to each system.* Both the perpetual and periodic inventory systems are used. The perpetual system gives management a continuous record of inventories on hand and cost of goods sold. As such, the record keeping involved is complex and, without electronic point-of-sale devices or other computer systems, can be difficult to maintain. The periodic system records only the cost of goods sold at specified times.

The entries for each system are as follows:

Transaction	Perpetual			Periodic		
1. To record sales	Accounts Receivable	XX		Accounts Receivable	XX	
	Sales		XX	Sales		XX
2. To record cost of goods sold at time of sale	Cost of Goods Sold	XX		No Entry		
	Inventory		XX			
3. To record inventory purchases	Inventory	XX		Purchases	XX	
	Accounts Payable		XX	Accounts Payable		XX

4. *How merchandising firms account for purchases, including trade and quantity discounts, purchase discounts, purchase returns and allowances, and freight-in.* The accounting for purchases parallels the accounting for sales. Accounting recognition is not given to trade or quantity discounts. The net and gross methods can be used to record purchase discounts. Although the gross method is the more common of the methods, the net method is preferable. Because freight-in is directly related to merchandise purchases, it ultimately becomes part of cost of goods sold and inventory. Other costs, such as warehouse expenses, which are only indirectly related to inventory purchases, are considered period expenses.

5. *Issues involved in taking a physical inventory.* In taking a physical inventory, special care must be taken to ensure that all items of inventory to which the firm has legal title are counted. Thus, goods in transit to which the firm has title, goods on consignment, and goods in public warehouses must be included in the ending inventory. Finally, care must be taken to ensure that items that have been sold are not counted in the seller's year-end inventory.

6. *Worksheet techniques for a merchandising firm.* The construction of a worksheet for a merchandising firm is similar to the worksheet for a service firm outlined in Chapter 4. The difference is the addition of new accounts related to sales and purchases.

7. *Closing entries for a merchandising firm.* When the periodic inventory system is used, the Merchandise Inventory ledger account reflects the amount of the beginning inventory. This amount must be removed from the ledger account and is replaced with the amount of the ending merchandise inventory. This is usually accomplished through the closing process.

Key Terms

Cost of Goods Sold

FOB Destination

FOB Shipping Point

Goods in Transit

Goods on Consignment

Gross Margin (Gross Profit) on Sales

Gross Method of Recording Purchase Discounts

Gross Method of Recording Sales Discounts

Gross Sales

Inventories

Merchandising Firm

Net Method of Recording Purchase Discounts

Net Method of Recording Sales Discounts

Periodic Inventory System

Perpetual Inventory System

Purchase Discounts

Purchase Returns and Allowances

Quantity Discounts

Sales

Sales Discounts

Sales Returns and Allowances

Trade Discounts

Problem for Your Review

Calculating Gross Method and Net Method. During the month of October, Tiny Tots (the seller) entered into the following transactions with Little Kids (the purchaser):

- October 2: Tiny Tots sold merchandise to Little Kids on account. The sale totaled $10,000 and was made under the following terms: 2/10, n/30.
- October 8: Little Kids returned $1,000 of the merchandise because it was defective.
- October 9: Tiny Tots made an additional sale of $5,000 on account to Little Kids. The terms of the sale were 2/10, n/30.
- October 10: Tiny Tots received the required payment for the October 2 sale.
- October 25: Tiny Tots received full payment on the October 9 purchase from Little Kids.

Required:

Make all the required entries on the books of both Tiny Tots and Little Kids, assuming that:

- a. Each company uses the gross method of recording sales and purchases.
- b. Each company uses the net method of recording sales and purchases.

Assume each firm uses the periodic inventory system.

Solution

A. Gross Method

	Tiny Tots (Seller)			Little Kids (Buyer)		
October 2	$10,000 sale on account, terms 2/10, n/30					
	Accounts Receivable	10,000		Purchases	10,000	
	Sales		10,000	Accounts Payable		10,000
October 8	Return of $1,000 of defective merchandise					
	Sales Returns and Allowances	1,000		Accounts Payable	1,000	
	Accounts Receivable		1,000	Purchase Returns		
				and Allowances		1,000
October 9	$5,000 sale on account, terms 2/10, n/30					
	Accounts Receivable	5,000		Purchases	5,000	
	Sales		5,000	Accounts Payable		5,000
October 10	Receipt of payment on October 2 sale					
	Cash	8,820*		Accounts Payable	9,000	
	Sales Discounts	180		Purchase Discounts		180
	Accounts Receivable		9,000	Cash		8,820*
October 25	Receipt of payment on October 9 sales					
	Cash	5,000		Accounts Payable	5,000	
	Accounts Receivable		5,000	Cash		5,000

*$8,820 = .98 × $9,000.

B. Net Method

	Tiny Tots (Seller)			Little Kids (Buyer)		
October 2	$10,000 sale on account, terms 2/10, n/30					
	Accounts Receivable	9,800*		Purchases	9,800*	
	Sales		9,800	Accounts Payable		9,800
October 8	Return of $1,000 of defective merchandise					
	Sales Returns and Allowances	980†		Accounts Payable	980†	
	Accounts Receivable		980	Purchase Returns and Allowances		980
October 9	$5,000 sale on account, terms 2/10, n/30					
	Accounts Receivable	4,900‡		Purchases	4,900‡	
	Sales		4,900	Accounts Payable		4,900
October 10	Receipt of payment on October 2 sale					
	Cash	8,820		Accounts Payable	8,820	
	Accounts Receivable		8,820	Cash		8,820
October 25	Receipt of payment on October 9 sale					
	Cash	5,000		Accounts Payable	4,900	
	Accounts Receivable		4,900	Purchase Discounts Lost	100	
	Sales Discounts Not Taken		100	Cash		5,000

*$9,800 = .98 × $10,000.
†$980 = .98 × $1,000.
‡$4,900 = .98 × $5,000.

Questions

1. What are the characteristics of a merchandising firm? How do they differ from those of a manufacturing firm?

2. Define: (a) trade discounts, (b) sales discounts, and (c) quantity discounts.

3. Why would a firm offer a sales discount to its customers?

4. What is meant by (a) 3/10, n/30, (b) 7 EOM, and (c) n/30?

5. Describe the difference between the gross method and the net method of recording sales discounts. What are the basic assumptions behind each of the methods?

6. What are the theoretical problems with the gross method of recording sales or purchase discounts?

7. Briefly discuss the difference between the perpetual inventory system and the periodic inventory system. Under what circumstances is each system used?

8. When goods are shipped FOB destination, who must pay the cost of freight? Who must pay if the goods are shipped FOB shipping point?

9. Would a hardware store be more likely to use a perpetual or periodic inventory system?

10. What costs, in addition to the initial purchase price, should be included in the inventory cost and the cost of goods sold?

11. Using the periodic method, how is the cost of goods sold determined?

12. What problems can occur with goods in transit when determining the ending inventory?

13. What is meant by goods on consignment?

14. Edward's Radio Shop sells a particular radio for $50. However, if a customer buys 10 radios, the total cost will be $450. How would such a sale be recorded? Why?

15. How are bank credit card fees usually accounted for?

16. What are sales returns and allowances and how are they accounted for?

17. What is the effect of purchase returns and allowances in computing the cost of goods sold?

18. In examining an unadjusted trial balance, how can you tell whether a firm has used the periodic or the perpetual inventory system?

19. In what ways, if any, would the cost of goods sold section of an income statement differ when a firm uses the gross method of recording sales discounts rather than the net method?

Exercises

1. Accounting for Trade and Quantity Discounts. Perry's Paint Store offers both trade and quantity discounts. Quantity discounts are given as follows:

Quantity Purchased	% Discount
1–9 cans	0
10–19 cans	2
more than 20 cans	4

In addition, professional painters also receive an additional 5% discount on the list price per gallon before any quantity discounts. Finally, cash buyers receive an additional 3% off the total price. The retail price of each can of paint is $10.

Required:
Make the entry to record the sale for each of the following two situations:
  1. Joe Kelly, a professional painter, purchases 30 cans of paint. The purchase is made on account.
  2. Al Compas, a do-it-yourself painter, purchases 15 cans. He pays cash.

2. Recording Sales Discounts. The following transactions were selected from the records of McKelvey Retailers:
  • January 2: Sold merchandise to the Vox Company for $3,000 cash.
  • January 12: Sold merchandise on account to the Chief Company for $2,000. Terms 3/10, n/30.
  • January 15: Sold merchandise on account to the Foothill Company for $6,000. Terms 2/10, n/30.
  • January 21: Received payment from Foothill Company net of the discount.
  • January 30: Received payment from the Chief Company.

Required:
Prepare the necessary entries to record these sales, assuming that McKelvey Retailers uses (a) the gross method and (b) the net method of recording sales discounts.

3. Recording Sales Discounts and Sales Returns. The PGM Company sells plumbing supplies to various plumbing stores. The gross method of recording sales discounts is used. During March the following transactions occurred:
  • March 2: Supplies with a price of $5,000 sold on account to LM Plumbing. Terms 2/10, n/30.
  • March 4: Sale of merchandise for $1,000 cash.
  • March 6: LM returned $1,000 of supplies and received a credit.
  • March 10: LM paid the amount owed to PGM.
  • March 15: Sale of $8,000 of merchandise to Ramsey Company. Sales terms are 2/10, n/30.
  • March 17: Sale of $2,000 of merchandise to Ron Company. Because this is a new customer, terms are 5 EOM.
  • March 20: Payment received from Ramsey Company.
  • March 31: Payment received from Ron Company.

Required:

Record the preceding transactions on the books of the PGM Company.

4. Credit Card Sales. During March the King Company had bank credit card sales of $5,000. The fees are 3% and are deducted when the charge slips are deposited. Also during March the firm made nonbank credit card sales of $3,000. The service charge on these sales is 5%. The drafts are mailed to the credit card firm, and the firm receives payment net of the service charge on April 10.

Required:

Make the entries to record all of these transactions.

5. The Periodic versus the Perpetual System. The Honey Company began business during the current year. The following summary of events occurred during its first month of operation:

- January 2: Merchandise costing $5,000 was purchased for cash.
- January 10: Merchandise costing $8,000 was purchased on account. Terms n/30.
- January 15: Sales for the first half of January totaled $12,000. Of this amount, $7,000 was for cash and the remaining on account. The cost of goods sold was $10,000.
- January 20: Merchandise costing $14,000 was purchased on account. Terms n/30.
- January 31: Sales for the last half of January were $15,000. Of this amount, $10,000 was for cash and the remaining on account. The cost of goods sold was $11,000.

Required:

Prepare the necessary entries to record these transactions, assuming that the firm uses (a) the periodic system and (b) the perpetual system. (Ignore closing entries.)

6. Determining Cost of Goods Sold. Given the following information, determine the missing amounts:

	Case 1	Case 2	Case 3
Sales	$20,000	$18,050	$?
Beginning inventory	5,000	7,000	10,000
Purchases	15,000	?	23,000
Purchase returns and allowances	1,500	2,000	?
Goods available for sale	?	17,000	28,500
Ending inventory	3,000	?	2,150
Cost of goods sold	?	11,000	?
Gross margin on sales	?	?	7,500

7. Accounting for Purchase Discounts. Sue's Fabric Shop entered into the following transactions during May:

- May 2: Purchased $5,000 of fabric on account. Terms 1/10, n/30.
- May 10: Purchased $7,500 of fabric on account. Terms 2/10, n/30.
- May 10: Returned $500 of goods purchased on May 2 because they were defective. The company's account was credited.
- May 11: Made the required payment on the May 2 purchase.
- May 20: Received $100 freight bill on the May 10 purchase, payable at the end of the month.
- May 30: Made the required payment on the May 10 purchase. Also paid the related freight bill received on May 20.

The company uses the periodic inventory system.

Required:

Make the necessary entries, assuming that the company used (a) the gross method and then (b) the net method of recording purchase discounts.

8. Accounting for Purchases and Transportation. On December 28, 1986, the Golden Company entered into the following transactions:

a. Merchandise costing $17,000 was purchased from Manchester Company, terms 1/10, n/30, **FOB** destination. Transportation costs were $1,200. The goods arrived on January 3, 1987. All required payments were made on January 4, 1987.

b. Merchandise costing $15,000 was purchased from the London Industries, 5 **EOM FOB** shipping point. Transportation costs were $500. The goods arrived on January 4, 1987. All required payments were made on January 5, 1987.

Required:

Assuming that the Golden Company uses the periodic inventory system and records purchases using the net method, prepare the necessary journal entries for these transactions. Assume that any transportation charges payable by the Golden Company are not subject to a discount. Which goods should be included in Golden's December 31, 1986 ending inventory?

9. Analysis. Given the following information, compute the beginning inventory:

Purchases returns and allowances	$ 7,280
Transportation-in	2,375
Purchases	134,890
Cost of goods sold	112,710
Ending inventory	38,575
Sales returns	6,250
Freight-out	1,246

10. Determining the Cost of the Ending Inventory. The Gould Antique Shop manager asks your help in determining the cost of its ending inventory at December 31. It has counted all the items in its store and determined their cost to be $102,475. In addition, the manager gives you the following information:

a. Goods costing $24,000 were held by others on consignment.

b. Goods costing $56,000 were in transit from England. They were shipped **FOB** shipping point.

c. The Gould Antique Shop held items costing $62,000 on consignment for others. These items were included in the ending inventory count.

d. Goods costing $10,000 were in transit from Spain. They were shipped **FOB** destination. What is the cost of their ending inventory?

11. Periodic Method Closing Entries. The following accounts were taken from the trial balance of the Jose Company on December 31:

Sales	$465,000
Beginning inventory	36,000
Transportation-in	4,000
Ending inventory	41,000
Sales discounts	5,000
Purchases	330,800
Purchase returns and allowances	2,400
Sales returns and allowances	15,000
Purchase discounts	7,400

Required:

    a. Prepare an income statement in good form through gross margin on sales.

    b. Prepare the appropriate closing entries.

12. Perpetual Inventory—Recording Transactions. The Conners Company is a small distributor of radiators for specialty automobiles. The firm carries only three different models and uses the perpetual inventory system. At the beginning of March, the firm had 100 radiators, Model 467, that it purchased for $27 per radiator. During March, the following cash purchases and sales took place in regard to this model:

- March 8: Purchased 40 radiators at $30 each.

- March 15: Sold 80 radiators for $50 each. (Assume that the radiators are sold in the order that they are purchased. Thus all radiators in the beginning inventory are sold before those purchased on March 8, and so forth.)

- March 20: Purchased 50 radiators at $28 each.

- March 22: Returned two of the radiators purchased on March 20 as they were defective.

- March 30: Sold 30 radiators for $50 each.

Required:

    a. Make the necessary journal entries to reflect the purchases and sales made during the month of March.

    b. Prepare an inventory record similar to the one in the text for radiator Model 467.

Problem Set A

5A–1. Recording Purchase and Sales Transactions. The Barbara Company uses the periodic inventory system. Assume that the company uses the gross method of recording sales discounts. The following transactions relating to sales and purchases occurred during the month of October:

- October 3: Purchased merchandise on account, $7,500, from the Tiger Company. Terms 2/10, n/30.

- October 4: Sold merchandise to the Sue Company for $1,150 cash.

- October 6: Sold merchandise to the Elvia Company on account, $3,620, 5 EOM, FOB shipping point.

- October 8: Made required payment to the Tiger Company on October 3 purchase.

- October 10: Purchased merchandise for $3,720 from the Kelly Company. Terms 2/10, n/30.

- October 15: Sold merchandise to the Kaufman Company on account, $2,700. Terms 1/10, n/30.

- October 17: Permitted the Kaufman Company to return for credit $700 of merchandise purchased on October 15.

- October 24: Received the required cash due from the Kaufman Company for October 15 sale.

- October 25: Made the required payment to the Kelly Company on October 10 purchase.

Required:

Prepare the necessary journal entries for the above transactions.

5A–2. Recording Purchase Transactions. Amy's Antique Shoppe made the following purchase transactions during the month of February. The firm uses the periodic inventory system and the net method to record purchase discounts.

- February 2: Five tables were purchased on account from London Furniture Company. Terms 2/10, n/30. The list price of each table is $450. Amy's Antique Shoppe was given a 5% trade discount.

- February 6: A $350 desk was delivered on consignment from the Old England Guild.

- February 7: Ten rocking chairs were purchased on account from American Company. Terms 2/10, n/30, FOB shipping point. The chairs cost $150 each. Freight charges payable to Smith Freight were $210, n/30.

- February 8: One hundred mirrors were purchased from Smithe Glass Company for $750 cash.

- February 10: Twenty-five of the mirrors purchased from Smithe Glass Company were received damaged and were returned for a cash refund.

- February 15: Three dressers costing $1,235 each were purchased from the Old England Guild on account. Terms n/30, FOB shipping point. Freight charges were $75, which was paid in cash.

- February 16: A check for the full payment due was written to the American Company.

- February 17: The Smith Freight Company was paid for the freight charges of February 7.

- February 25: A check for the full payment due was written to the Old England Guild for the February 15 purchase.

- February 28: A check for the full payment due was written to the London Furniture Company.

Required:

Record the necessary journal entries for Amy's Antique Shoppe.

5A–3. Gross and Net Methods of Recording Discounts. The Sam Sporting Goods Company entered into the following transactions during July. The firm uses the periodic inventory system.

- July 1: Purchased various inventory items for $15,000. Terms 2/10, n/30.

- July 7: Sold merchandise on account to LA Sunshine for $20,000. Terms 1/10, n/30.

- July 8: Paid $100 freight charges on items purchased on July 1.

- July 9: Made the required payment on July 1 purchases.

- July 12: Two thousand dollars of merchandise sold on July 7 was returned as defective. Accounts Receivable credited.

- July 13: Received required payment from LA Sunshine.

- July 18: Purchased $6,000 of merchandise from Knoxville Bat Company. Terms 2/10, n/30.

- July 20: Sold various merchandise to San Diego Waves for $12,000. Terms 5 EOM. Paid delivery charge of $50.

- July 24: Made required payment to Knoxville Bat Company.

Required:

  a. Make the necessary journal entries, assuming that the firm uses the gross method of recording sales and purchase discounts.

  b. Prepare the cost of goods sold section of the income statement. Assume that the beginning inventories are $5,000 and the ending inventories are $3,000.

  c. Make the necessary journal entries, assuming that the firm uses the net method of recording purchase and sales discounts.

  d. Prepare the cost of goods sold section of the income statement, using the inventory data from Item b but assuming that the net method was used.

  e. Compare and contrast the two income statements prepared using the gross and the net methods of recording discounts.

5A-4. Income Statement of a Merchandising Company. The following information was taken from the records of the Newton Company at year-end:

	Year 1	Year 2
Gross sales	$235,000	$238,430
Sales returns and allowances	5,000	?
Net sales	?	231,080
Beginning inventory	36,050	?
Purchases	101,530	?
Purchase returns and allowances	3,250	4,535
Ending inventory	?	7,254
Cost of goods sold	?	?
Gross margin on sales	103,500	?
Operating expenses	33,570	27,280
Net income	?	76,706

Required:
Supply the missing information. Show all computations, rounding them to the nearest dollar.

5A-5. Income Statement Preparation. The accounting records of the Rainbow Company are maintained on a calendar year. The adjusted trial balance is presented next.

Rainbow Company
Adjusted Trial Balance
December 31, 1987

Account	Debit	Credit
Cash	$ 38,150	
Accounts receivable	55,004	
Inventory (January 1, 1987)	45,325	
Supplies	2,925	
Land	75,000	
Furniture and fixtures	135,000	
Equipment	40,000	
Accumulated depreciation— Furniture and fixtures		$ 75,750
Accumulated depreciation—Equipment		10,000
Accounts payable		47,890
Note payable		70,000
Long-term debt		65,750
T. Grant, capital		129,265
Sales		263,140
Sales returns and allowances	23,260	
Purchases	133,160	
Purchase returns and allowances		3,785
Transportation-in	3,320	
Office, salaries, and wages	25,876	
Depreciation expense	33,000	
Supplies expense	15,530	
Rent	15,780	
Sales commissions	24,250	
Totals	$665,580	$665,580

The ending inventory was determined to be $65,725.

CHAPTER 5

Required:

a. Does the Rainbow Company use the perpetual or the periodic inventory method? How do you know?

b. Prepare closing entries.

c. Prepare an income statement for the Rainbow Company for the year ended December 31, 1987.

5A–6. Worksheet Preparation. The unadjusted trial balance of Tommy's Toy Store on September 30, 1987 is presented below. The following additional information was determined on September 30, 1987:

1. Depreciation on both the building and equipment is 10% a year.
2. Supplies on September 30, 1987 were worth $500.
3. Prepaid insurance was $900.
4. Interest has accrued for 12 months, not yet paid.
5. Ending inventory was $120,000.

Tommy's Toy Store
Unadjusted Trial Balance
September 30, 1987

Account	Debit	Credit
Cash	$ 5,000	
Accounts receivable	14,300	
Inventory	105,000	
Supplies	2,000	
Prepaid insurance	3,000	
Long-term investment	5,000	
Land	50,000	
Building	220,000	
Accumulated depreciation—Building		$ 40,000
Store equipment	90,000	
Accumulated depreciation—Equipment		17,500
Accounts payable		9,000
Mortgage payable (10%)		180,000
T. Stout, capital		125,000
Sales		250,000
Sales returns and allowance	8,000	
Sales discounts	4,500	
Purchases	110,500	
Purchase returns and allowance		7,800
Purchase discounts		2,000
Freight-in	2,000	
Salary expense	8,000	
Office rent	4,000	
Totals	$631,300	$631,300

Required:

a. Prepare a 10-column worksheet for the year ended September 30, 1987.
b. Prepare an income statement.
c. Prepare a balance sheet.
d. Make the closing entries.

5A–7. Cost of Goods Sold Analysis. Presented below is information from the income statement of Ralston Company for the year ended December 31, 1987.

Sales	$1,825,370
Purchases	987,960
Transportation-in	795
Purchase returns and allowances	4,750
Sales discounts	154,761
Ending inventory	?
Sales returns and allowances	365,074
Beginning inventory	362,820
Purchase discounts	3,820
Gross margin on sales	448,810

Required:
   a. Compute the amount of ending inventory.
   b. Prepare in good form a partial income statement using the accounts presented above.

Problem Set B

5B–1. Recording Purchases and Sales Transactions. The Davidson Company uses the periodic inventory system and the gross method of recording sales and purchase discounts. The following transactions relating to sales and purchases occurred during March:

- March 3: Purchased merchandise on account for $8,000 from the Washington Company. Terms 2/10, n/30.
- March 4: Sold merchandise to the Jefferson Company on account for $1,500. Terms 1/10, n/30.
- March 5: Sold merchandise to Adam Company on account for $3,500. Terms 7 EOM, FOB shipping point.
- March 8: Made the required payment to Washington Company for the March 3 purchase.
- March 12: Purchased merchandise on account for $6,000 from the Lincoln Company. Terms 2/10, n/30.
- March 13: Received payment from the Jefferson Company, net of the discount.
- March 16: Sold merchandise to Grant Company on account for $4,000. Terms 1/10, n/30.
- March 21: Received required payment from Adam Company for March 5 sale.
- March 31: Made payment to the Lincoln Company for the March 12 purchase.

Required:
Prepare the necessary journal entries for the above transactions.

5B–2. Recording Purchase Transactions. Sunrise Retail Store made the following purchases during December. The firm uses the periodic inventory system and the net method to record purchase discounts.

- December 4: Merchandise costing $7,500 was purchased on account from Moonlight Company. Terms 2/10, n/30.
- December 9: Five typewriters were purchased from Tony's Co. Terms 2/10, n/30, FOB shipping point. The typewriters cost $300 each. Shipping charges were $350 payable to J. C. Trucking. Terms n/30.
- December 10: Twenty desk calculators were purchased for cash from the Sunden Company for $1,600.
- December 12: Five of the calculators purchased on December 10 were received damaged and returned for a cash refund.
- December 13: A check was written for payment due to the Moonlight Company net of the discount.

- December 16: Three computers were purchased from the Orange Company on account. They cost $700 each. Terms n/30, FOB shipping point. Freight charges were $90 and were paid in cash.

- December 18: A check was written for full payment due to Tony's Co.

- December 21: Various merchandise was purchased from Tomba, Co., on account for $4,750. Terms 2/10, n/30.

- December 30: A check was written to Tomba, Co. for full payment due.

- December 31: J. C. Trucking was paid in full for freight charges of December 9.

Required:

Record the necessary journal entries for Sunrise Retail Store.

5B–3. Gross and Net Methods of Recording Discounts. The Stardust Company, which uses the periodic inventory system, entered into the following transactions during April:

- April 2: Purchased inventory items from the Lite Company for $2,400. Terms 2/10, n/30.

- April 6: Sold merchandise on account to the Mercury Company for $15,000. Terms 1/10, n/30.

- April 9: Paid freight charges of $75 in cash on items purchased on April 2.

- April 10: Made the required payment to the Lite Company on the April 2 purchase.

- April 13: One thousand dollars of the merchandise sold on April 6 was returned because of defects. Accounts Receivable was credited.

- April 15: Received required payment from the Mercury Company.

- April 20: Purchased $9,000 of merchandise from the Mars Company. Terms 2/10, n/30.

- April 23: Sold various items of merchandise to Jupiter, Inc., for $7,000. Terms 1/10, n/30.

- April 29: Made the required payment to the Mars Company.

Required:

a. Make the necessary journal entries, assuming that the firm uses the gross method of recording purchase and sales discounts.

b. Prepare the cost of goods sold section of the income statement, assuming that the beginning inventory is $6,800 and the ending inventory is $4,700.

c. Make the necessary journal entries, now assuming that the firm uses the net method of recording purchase and sales discounts.

d. Prepare the cost of goods sold section of the income statement using the data from Item b but assuming that the net method is used.

e. Compare and contrast the two income statements prepared in Items b and d.

5B–4. Income Statement of a Merchandising Company. The following information was taken from the records of the Herbert Company at year-end:

	Year 1	Year 2
Gross sales	$1,250,000	$?
Sales returns and allowances	25,000	28,000
Net sales	?	1,472,000
Beginning inventory	?	?
Purchases	950,000	?
Purchase returns and allowances	50,000	80,000
Ending inventory	340,000	269,000
Cost of goods sold	?	?
Gross margin on sales	367,500	441,600
Operating expenses	96,500	?
Net income	?	336,300

Required:

Supply the missing information. Be sure to show all of your computations.

5B-5. Income Statement Preparation. The following records of The Sunshine Company are maintained on a fiscal year ending June 30. The adjusted trial balance is presented below.

The Sunshine Company
Adjusted Trial Balance

June 30, 1987

Account	Debit	Credit
Account Cash		$ 87,000
Accounts receivable	69,000	
Inventory (July 1, 1986)	225,000	
Supplies	3,000	
Land	120,000	
Equipment	480,000	
Furniture and fixtures	125,000	
Accumulated depreciation—Equipment		$ 20,000
Accumulated depreciation—Furniture and fixtures		40,000
Accounts payable		157,000
Notes payable		60,000
R. J. Reynold, capital		620,430
Sales		1,275,000
Sales discounts	15,000	
Sales returns and allowances	73,000	
Purchases	687,650	
Purchase discounts		10,000
Purchase returns and allowances		12,340
Freight-in	8,745	
Office salaries and wages	170,000	
Depreciation expense	62,500	
Supplies expense	7,500	
Rent	38,375	
Sales commission	23,000	
Total	$2,194,770	$2,194,770

The ending inventory was determined to be $196,765.

Required:

a. Does The Sunshine Company use the perpetual or the periodic inventory system? How do you know?

b. Prepare an income statement for The Sunshine Company for the year ended June 30, 1987.

c. Make the required closing entries.

5B-6. Worksheet Preparation. The unadjusted trial balance of the Woodland Company at December 31, 1987 is presented at the top of page 211.

The following additional information was available at December 31, 1987:

1. Depreciation expense on building was $10,000.
2. Depreciation expense on equipment was $4,000.
3. Supplies on hand was $1,000.
4. Prepaid insurance was $700.
5. Interest must be accrued for 12 months.
6. Ending inventory was $90,000.

Woodland Company
Unadjusted Trial Balance
December 31, 1987

Account	Debit	Credit
Cash	$ 66,000	
Accounts receivable	24,000	
Inventory	56,000	
Supplies	2,200	
Prepaid insurance	1,400	
Land	127,000	
Building	286,000	
Accumulated depreciation—Building		$ 72,000
Equipment	75,000	
Accumulated depreciation—Equipment		17,650
Accounts payable		4,350
Mortgage payable (8%)		26,000
M. Marshall, capital		204,120
Sales		954,000
Sales returns and allowances	3,500	
Sales discounts	6,435	
Purchases	541,000	
Purchase returns and allowances		4,200
Purchase discounts		3,570
Freight-in	7,355	
Salary expense	58,000	
Rental expense	32,000	
Total	$1,285,890	$1,285,890

Required:

a. Prepare a 10-column worksheet for the year ended December 31, 1987.

b. Prepare an income statement with an expanded cost of goods sold section.

c. Prepare a balance sheet.

d. Make the required closing entries.

5B–7. Cost of Goods Sold Analysis. Following is a list of some of the accounts for Alexander & Co. for the year ended December 31, 1987:

Sales	$2,987,450
Purchases	1,848,270
Freight-in	25,000
Purchase returns and allowances	28,475
Purchase discounts	36,525
Sales discounts	54,320
Ending inventory	900,470
Sales returns and allowances	384,500
Beginning inventory	?
Gross margin on sales	264,630

Required:

a. Compute the amount of beginning inventory.

b. Prepare in good form a partial income statement using the accounts presented above.

Recording Sales and Purchases of Inventory for a Merchandising Firm

Understanding Financial Statements

The following data were taken from a recent annual report of Carter Hawley Hale Stores, Inc., a diversified North American retailer operating department stores, high-fashion specialty stores, and specialized merchandising operations:

(in thousands)	
Sales	$3,054,764
Inventories, beginning	554,701
Inventories, ending	630,169
Cost of goods sold	1,747,470

Required:

   a. Determine the amount of gross margin on sales for the year and the amount of net purchases that the firm made during the year.
   b. Do you think that Carter Hawley Hale uses the perpetual or the periodic system in accounting for inventories in its department stores? Explain your reasoning.
   c. Do you think that the firm allows its customers to take a sales discount? Why or why not?

Financial Decision Case

Inventory Systems and Accounts Receivable. David Schwartz recently decided to open a new-car dealership. The dealership will sell expensive imported cars as well as offer both engine and body repairs. David plans to organize the business into two divisions: One division will sell the cars, and the other division will provide the repair services. David has asked your advice concerning two matters:

   1. David is in the process of setting up inventory systems for both divisions. The inventory of the car division will be made up of no more than 40 to 50 new cars at any one time. The repair division inventory will be made up of over 3,000 different parts in varying quantities which must be inventoried and controlled. David is concerned about maintaining adequate quantities of fast-moving parts, about 30% of the parts in inventory.
   2. David will offer repair services on credit. He is trying to decide whether to carry his own receivable accounts or to use bank cards such as VISA or MasterCard. He estimates that his annual repair service revenues will be $300,000 per year. If he uses bank cards, he figures about 80% of the revenues will be charged on the cards. The bank card companies will charge David a 5% fee. Because of some fraud, all but .5% of total charges, less the fee, will be remitted to David. If David decides to carry his own accounts, he estimates that 70% of the revenues will be charged on account. If he carries his own accounts, he will have to hire a part-time bookkeeper at $8,000 per year. Finally, he estimates that about 3% of the charges will never be collected.

Required:

Write David a memo outlining (1) his options concerning inventory systems (periodic versus perpetual) and (2) a quantitative and qualitative analysis of whether he should carry his own accounts or use a bank card. Assume that he will not do both.

Financial Statements—
The Outputs of the System

6

LEARNING OBJECTIVES

After reading this chapter you should be able to:
1. Understand the objectives of financial statements.
2. Construct a classified balance sheet.
3. Explain the uses and limitations of a classified balance sheet.
4. Construct both forms of a classified income statement—the single-step and the multistep income statement.
5. Explain the uses and limitations of classified income statements.
6. Read and understand the basic elements of the financial statements of a major U.S. corporation.

Financial statements are the principal product of the accounting information system. The four required financial statements are the balance sheet, the income statement, the statement of changes in owner's equity, and the statement of changes in financial position. These statements communicate to external users information concerning the enterprise's financial position, strength, liquidity, and profitability, and significant changes in its resources and obligations. The goal of this chapter is to explain the objectives and concepts behind the construction of the balance sheet and the income statement. In addition, a set of actual financial statements from Safeway Stores, Inc. demonstrates these concepts. The purposes and uses of the statement of changes in financial position are introduced. However, the actual construction of this statement is discussed in detail in Chapter 20.

There are a variety of groups that are likely to use a firm's external financial statements for decision-making purposes. The groups include owners, creditors, labor unions, regulatory agencies, attorneys, educators, and management, and each uses financial statements for overlapping but somewhat different purposes. Because it is costly to prepare special purpose financial statements for each user group, the accountant prepares general purpose financial statements that, although aimed primarily at present and potential investors and creditors, meet the needs of a wide range of users.

Objectives of Financial Reporting

The Financial Accounting Standards Board (FASB) has been spending considerable time and energy in developing the **objectives of financial reporting.** The purpose of this ongoing project is to develop a broad set of principles and concepts that can be used to resolve specific accounting issues in a manner that results in financial statements that are most useful and meaningful to general purpose users. To accomplish this purpose, the FASB issues concepts Statements. To date, six such statements have been issued. They are Concepts Statements No. 1, *Objectives of Financial Reporting by Business Enterprises*, No. 2, *Qualitative Characteristics of Accounting Information*, No. 3, *Elements of Financial Statements of Business Enterprises* (replaced by Concept Statement No. 6), No. 4, *Objectives of Financial Reporting by Nonbusiness Enterprises*, No. 5, *Recognition and Measurement in Financial Statements of Business Enterprises*, and No. 6, *Elements of Financial Statements* (replacing Concept Statement No. 3).

In Concepts Statement 1, the FASB identified three major objectives of financial reporting:

1. Financial reporting should provide information that is useful to present and potential investors and creditors and other users in making rational investment, credit, and similar decisions. The information should be comprehensible to those who have a reasonable understanding of business and economic activities and are willing to study the information with reasonable diligence.
2. Financial reporting should provide information to help present and potential investors and creditors and other users in assessing the amounts, timing, and uncertainty of prospective cash receipts from dividends or interest and the proceeds from the sale, redemption, or maturity of securities or loans. Since investors' and creditors' cash flows are related to enterprise cash flows, financial reporting should provide information to help investors, creditors, and others assess the amounts, timing, and uncertainty of prospective net cash inflows to the related enterprise.
3. Financial reporting should provide information about the economic resources of an enterprise, the claims to those resources (obligations of the enterprise to transfer resources to other entities and owners' equity), and the effects of transactions, events, and circumstances that change resources and claims to those resources.[1]

The FASB considers present and potential investors and creditors to be the primary users of financial statements, and it notes that these users need

[1]Financial Accounting Standards Board, Concepts Statement No. 1, *Objectives of Financial Reporting by Business Enterprises* (Stamford, Conn.: FASB, November 1978, pars. 34, 37, and 40).

information concerning the possibility of receiving cash flows from investments or loans. These data can best be provided by giving investors and creditors information about the enterprise's resources, claims to those resources, and changes in them. However, the FASB is quite clear in noting that business and economic activities are complex and that financial statement users must be willing to study the information carefully.

Classified Financial Statements

If these objectives are to be met, financial statements must be presented in a manner that allows investors and creditors to evaluate the financial strength and profitability of business enterprises. Therefore, financial statements are often subdivided into categories that allow for meaningful interfirm and interperiod comparison. These statements are called **classified financial statements** and are discussed next in reference to Jacob's Pet Supplies and later for Safeway Stores, Inc.

Classified Balance Sheets

The purpose of the balance sheet is to present the financial position of a company at a specific date. This statement aids financial statement users in assessing a company's financial strength and liquidity and is used to answer the following types of questions:

1. What is the company's overall financial strength?
2. How liquid is the company?
3. Will the company be able to meet its short-term obligations?
4. What proportion of the company's assets has been contributed by creditors and by owners or investors, respectively?
5. How does the company's financial position compare with that of others in that industry?

The classified balance sheet for Jacob's Pet Supplies at December 31, 1988 is presented on page 217. The specific subcategories listed under the major categories of assets, liabilities, and owner's equity are the decisions of management. The classification scheme generally revolves around specific firm and industry characteristics. The statements presented in this chapter are typical of those found in major U.S. companies. However, if we were considering a French or Dutch company, the classifications used and the order of the particular elements within the balance sheet would be considerably different because accounting principles are the result of the economic and political system within particular countries and, as such, vary considerably.

In examining the balance sheet for Jacob's Pet Supplies note that balance sheet is as of a certain date. Management has the discretion to choose the year-end. Some firms have a natural business year-end when inventory, receivables, and other activities are at a relative low point. The end of the month in which the low point occurs is often picked as the year-end. If this month is other than December, the year-end is referred to as a fiscal year-end. If December 31 is picked, the year is referred to as a calendar year. Other companies choose what is referred to as a *52–53 week fiscal year*, which allows a firm to choose a year-end on the same day every year (for example, the last Saturday in December), and so some years will have 52 weeks and others will have 53 weeks.

Assets

Most balance sheets contain up to five categories within the asset section: (1) current assets, (2) long-term investments, (3) property, plant, and equipment, (4) intangible assets, and (5) other assets. Not all of these categories will be found in all balance sheets, and particular firms often use slightly different classifications and labels.

Current Assets

The Accounting Principles Board (APB) defined **current assets** as:

> ... Cash and other assets that are reasonably expected to be realized in cash or sold or consumed within the normal operating cycle of a business or within one year if the operating cycle is shorter than one year.[2]

The **operating cycle** of a business is the time that it takes a firm to go from cash back to cash. That is, an enterprise uses its cash to purchase or manufacture inventory; the inventory is then sold, and the enterprise receives cash or a receivable. The operating cycle is completed when the receivables from credit sales are collected.

Most firms have an operating cycle of less than one year. However, because some firms have operating cycles that extend for several years, assets that are used up or turned into cash during that cycle are considered current. Examples of such companies are construction companies, tobacco growers, distillers, and cattle breeders. Some firms have several operating cycles of different lengths. For example, a bank might have a short operating cycle for checking accounts and a long operating cycle for notes and mortgages.

Current assets include cash, short-term investments, accounts receivable, inventories, supplies, and various prepaid items. Only in rare situations is cash not listed as a current asset. An example of such a case occurs when a firm maintains cash in a foreign country and currency regulations prohibit the transfer of this cash to the United States. Investments can be classified as either current or noncurrent. If the security is marketable and the investment results from management's decision to invest idle cash on a temporary basis, it is classified as a current asset. If the investment does not meet the above criteria, it is classified as a noncurrent asset in the long-term investment section of the balance sheet. Short- and long-term investments are discussed in detail in Chapters 9 and 19, respectively.

Trade accounts receivable and other loans or notes receivable due within one year or the operating cycle, if longer, are classified as current. Because some accounts receivable will not be collected, a contra account called Allowance for Doubtful Accounts is established. A contra account is an account whose balance is subtracted from an associated account in the financial statements. The balance in Allowance for Doubtful Accounts represents management's estimate of the uncollectible accounts. On the balance sheet, the total in this account is offset against the total in Accounts Receivable. As a result, the net amount in Accounts Receivable represents the total that ultimately will be collected, or the net realizable value of the receivable. Receivables are discussed more fully in Chapter 9.

Inventories, supplies, and prepaid expenses are current assets because they will be sold or used during the following year or operating cycle. In some

---

[2]American Institute of Certified Public Accountants, Accounting Principles Board, Statement No. 4, *Basic Concepts and Accounting Principles Underlying Financial Statements of Business Enterprises* (New York: AICPA, 1970), par. 198.

Jacob's Pet Supplies
Balance Sheet
December 31, 1988

Assets

Current assets		
Cash	$ 68,000	
Accounts receivable	100,000	
Inventory	125,000	
Supplies	25,000	
Prepaid expenses	3,000	
License	9,000	
Total current assets		$330,000
Long-term investments		30,000
Property, plant, and equipment		
Land	$191,000	
Buildings	$160,000	
Less: Accumulated depreciation	12,500	147,500
Furniture and fixtures	$107,000	
Less: Accumulated depreciation	9,000	98,000
Total property, plant, and equipment		436,500
Intangible assets		
Patent, net of amortization		10,000
Total assets		$806,500

Liabilities and Owner's Equity

Current liabilities		
Accounts payable	$157,000	
Salaries payable	12,000	
Interest payable	1,000	
Current maturities of bank loan	50,000	
Total current liabilities		$220,000
Long-term debt		
Bank loan payable	$150,000	
Less: Current portion above	50,000	100,000
Total liabilities		320,000
Owner's equity		
J. Daniels, capital		486,500
Total liabilities and owner's equity		$806,500

situations, prepaid expenses benefit several years or operating cycles. However, because these amounts are usually not significant, the entire amount is usually shown as a current asset. If they are significant, these long-term prepaids will be listed in the other assets section of the balance sheet and are called deferred charges.

When you examine the balance sheet for Jacob's Pet Supplies on this page, you can see that current assets are listed in order of their liquidity. That

Financial Statements—The Outputs of the System

is, cash is shown first and then those items that are most easily converted into cash. Assets such as inventory, prepaids, and supplies are shown last in the current assets section.

Investments

Long-term investments include holdings in securities (stock and bonds) in which a firm may wish to establish a long-term equity position. These investments are not classified as current because either they are not easily convertible into cash or management's intention is to hold them for greater than a year. Property, plant, and equipment not used in production but held for resale or future use are often listed in this category. Other assets listed under investments include special funds, called *sinking funds,* that are established to make future purchases of property, plant, and equipment or to repay bonds and other long-term debts.

Property, Plant, and Equipment

Assets classified under property, plant, and equipment represent the productive capacity of the firm. These assets are used in the purchasing, production, selling, and delivery of the firm's goods and services. Other than land, which does not give up its future benefits, assets listed under this category are depreciated. The property, plant, and equipment section of Jacob's Pet Supplies is typical of that found on the balance sheets of many U.S. companies. As discussed in Chapter 4, plant, equipment, and other productive assets are shown net of accumulated depreciation. Although the order in which the assets are listed in this section varies, land is usually shown first, followed by plant, equipment, and similar assets. Alternative titles for this section of the balance sheet include operating assets, long-lived assets, tangible assets, and fixed assets.

Intangible Assets

Intangible assets are assets that have no physical or tangible characteristics, as do buildings and equipment. They are agreements, contracts, or rights that provide a firm with future economic benefits by giving it the right to use a certain production process, trade name, or similar right. Typical assets included in this category are patents, trademarks, copyrights, franchises, and goodwill. **Goodwill** refers to the anticipated future benefits that will accrue to a firm because of its ability to earn a rate of return on its net assets exceeding the normal return expected from firms using similar resources. Because all intangible assets eventually lose their economic benefits, their costs are written off over the shorter of their useful or economic life. This process is called **amortization.** In reference to Jacob's Pet Supplies, Jacob Daniels, the owner, developed a special vitamin-enriched dog food for which he was able to obtain a patent. The $10,000 listed in the balance sheet represents the unamortized cost of the patent.

Liabilities

Liabilities represent the economic obligations of a firm. For balance sheet purposes, they are usually classified into two categories, current liabilities and long-term liabilities or debt.

Current Liabilities

Current liabilities are those liabilities that will be paid or require the use of current assets within one year or one operating cycle, if the operating cycle exceeds one year. Current liabilities also refers to those liabilities that result in the creation of a new current liability. Typical current liabilities are short-term notes and loans payable, accounts payable, taxes payable, wages, other accrued expenses, and unearned income or advances from customers. Some liabilities, such as mortgages, are payable in equal monthly installments over a specified number of years. The portion of these liabilities that is payable within twelve months from the balance sheet date is called **current maturities of long-term debt** and is classified as a current liability. The remaining portion is classified as a noncurrent liability. Jacob's Pet Supplies has a $150,000 bank loan which is due in three equal annual installments. The $50,000 installment that is due within the next year is a current liability and is called current maturities of long-term debt. Chapter 10 describes current liabilities in more detail.

Long-term Liabilities

Liabilities that do not meet the criteria to be considered current are classified as **noncurrent** or **long-term.** Included in this category are bonds payable, mortgages payable, leases, and long-term bank loans payable. Remember that the portion of these liabilities that is due within the next twelve months is classified as current. For example, the remaining $100,000 portion of the bank loan owed by Jacob's Pet Supplies is classified as a long-term liability on the balance sheet on page 217.

Owner's Equity

The format of the owner's equity section of the balance sheet depends upon the particular form of organization. If the business is organized as a sole proprietorship or a partnership, the terms *owner's equity, proprietor's capital,* and *capital* are used. For corporations, this section of the balance sheet is referred to as *stockholders' equity.* Because the owner's equity section of the balance sheet represents assets minus liabilities, it is often referred to as net worth. This term should be used with caution, however, because assets and liabilities are recorded at net book value, not current value or worth, and so the term *net worth* can be misleading.

Sole Proprietorships

Because Jacob's Pet Supplies is organized as a sole proprietorship, owner's equity is listed on its balance sheet. The balance in the J. Daniels, Capital account represents the total investments made by Daniels in his business plus the cumulative profits of the business less any withdrawals or any net losses suffered by the business. For the pet store, the total owner's equity equals $486,500. The changes in the Capital account that occurred during the period are detailed in the statement of owner's equity.

Partnerships

The owner's equity section of a partnership is generally referred to as partners' capital. Each partner has a separate Capital account and, if necessary, a separate Drawing account. As with a sole proprietorship, the Drawing accounts are closed into the Capital accounts at the end of the period, and so all equity transactions are eventually reflected in the Capital account. A typical partners' equity section of a partnership balance sheet might appear as follows:

Kuramoto, Shiffberg, and Tse, CPA Firm
Partners' Capital

S. Kuramoto, capital	$ 58,296
T. Shiffberg, capital	103,284
M. Tse, capital	88,360
Total partners' capital	$249,940

Stockholders' Equity

The owner's equity section of a balance sheet for a corporation is called **stockholders' equity.** An example of a stockholders' equity section of a corporation follows:

The Carson Corporation
Stockholders' Equity

Common stock	$300,000
Retained earnings	100,000
Total stockholders' equity	$400,000

When the owners of a corporation invest cash or other assets in their business, they receive shares of **capital stock,** often called **common stock,** in exchange. Thus, the dollar amount of common stock on the balance sheet represents the amount invested by the owners. The owners of the Carson Corporation have invested a total of $300,000.

Individual units of common stock are called shares. When you invest in a corporation, you receive a stock certificate for the number of shares that you purchased. The more shares of stock you own, the greater is your proportionate ownership interest in the corporation. Shares of stock are easily transferable, and generally you can sell your shares to whomever you wish. The corporation itself is usually not affected by this transfer of stock except that it must update its list of shareholders.

The other component of stockholders' equity is retained earnings. Retained earnings represents the portion of stockholders' equity that results from the accumulated profits of the business that have not been distributed to the owners. In the Carson Corporation example it totals $100,000. The firm has decided to keep $100,000 of its total lifetime earnings in the business instead of distributing it in the form of cash or other assets to the owners. Monies that are not retained but are distributed are called **dividends.** The total lifetime earnings of the Carson Corporation exceeds $100,000; the $100,000 represents that portion that has not yet been distributed to the owners.

In a corporation, unlike in a sole proprietorship or partnership, there is a distinction between the amount of invested capital and the capital earned through the profitable operations of the business. This accounting distinction is required by most state laws. However, in the case of the sole proprietorship or in a partnership, this distinction does not have to be maintained. Thus, the Capital account includes both invested capital and capital earned through profitable operations.

The Uses and Limitations of Classified Balance Sheets

Previously we listed some of the questions that present and potential investors and creditors can use the balance sheet to answer. These questions usually center on measuring a company's overall financial strength. This can be accomplished through financial statement analysis, using ratios to highlight important relationships. Some of the significant ratios and other analytic data are considered next. Chapter 21 contains a complete discussion of financial statement analysis and interpretation.

Measuring Liquidity

Financial statement users are interested in liquidity. That is, they would like to know whether a firm has enough current assets to pay its current liabilities and/or to respond to changes in the business environment. Two measures, working capital and the current ratio, are commonly used to make this assessment.

Working Capital

Working Capital is defined as current assets minus current liabilities. Thus, working capital represents the amount of current assets that the firm has available to respond to its business needs after repaying all of its current liabilities. Firms need enough working capital to continue operating on a day-to-day basis. Even profitable firms that are unable to maintain a significant amount of working capital can face financial difficulties. Consequently, a firm's creditors often require it to maintain a certain level of working capital. The following footnote taken from recent Genesco financial statements illustrates such a restriction:

> Genesco's revolving credit agreement requires the Company, among other things to maintain working capital of at least $90,000,000; a current ratio of not less than 1.5:1.

Working capital is calculated for Jacob's Pet Supplies as shown on the top of page 222.

As these calculations show, the working capital for the pet store is $110,000. Several questions come to mind. How much working capital is enough? Is Jacob's Pet Supplies in strong financial shape, and how does it compare with other firms in the pet supply business? The answer to the first question depends on the company's particular needs, and the characteristics of the industry within which the firm operates. One way to answer this ques-

DETERMINATION OF WORKING CAPITAL AND THE CURRENT RATIO	
Working capital	Current Ratio
Current assets less current liabilities	$\dfrac{\text{Current assets}}{\text{Current liabilities}}$
$330,000 - $220,000 = $110,000	$\dfrac{\$330,000}{\$220,000} = 1.5{:}1$

tion is to compare the amount of working capital of a particular firm with that of other firms in the industry or with an industry average. In addition, working capital over several years also should be analyzed.

Answering the second question is more difficult. Interfirm comparisons are tentative because a firm's absolute size affects the amount of working capital it needs. Large firms are likely to have more working capital than small firms. For example, a large national chain of pet supply stores is likely to have more working capital than Jacob's Pet Supplies. Whether this chain of stores is in better financial shape than Jacob's Pet Supplies cannot be answered just by comparing the dollar amount of the two companies' working capital, however.

The Current Ratio

One way to determine the liquidity and financial strength of a company is to calculate a ratio called the current ratio. The **current ratio** is determined by dividing the total current assets by the total current liabilities. It allows meaningful comparisons among firms of different sizes because all dollar amounts are standardized by the ratio. The current ratio for Jacob's Pet Supplies is 1.5:1. This calculation is given with the working capital calculation just shown.

From these data Jacob's Pet Supplies appears to be fairly liquid. However, other items must be considered. For example, firms in some industries traditionally have higher current ratios than do firms in other industries. Thus, a firm's specific ratio should be compared with its industry average. The particular makeup of the current assets must also be considered. Cash and receivables, for example, are more liquid than inventory, supplies, or prepaids.

Long-term Measures of Financial Strength

Investors and creditors are also interested in a firm's long-term strength and financial viability. The amount of a firm's debt in relation to its total equity or total assets is an indication of its strength. Two ratios, debt to equity and debt to total assets, are often calculated to help individuals assess the firm's long-term strength.

Debt to Equity Ratio

The **debt to equity ratio** is calculated by the following formula:

$$\frac{\text{Total liabilities}}{\text{Total owner's equity}} \times 100$$

This ratio, expressed as a percentage, provides a measure of the relative risk assumed by creditors and owners. The higher this percentage is, the more difficult it will be for a firm to raise additional capital by increasing its long-term debt. The debt to equity ratio as shown next for Jacob's Pet Supplies is 65.8%.

DETERMINATION OF THE DEBT TO EQUITY RATIO AND THE DEBT TO TOTAL ASSETS RATIO	
Debt to Equity Ratio	**Debt to Total Assets Ratio**
$\dfrac{\text{Total liabilities}}{\text{Total owner's equity}} \times 100$	$\dfrac{\text{Total liabilities}}{\text{Total assets}} \times 100$
$\dfrac{\$320{,}000}{\$486{,}500} \times 100 = 65.8\%$	$\dfrac{\$320{,}000}{\$806{,}500} \times 100 = 39.7\%$

Debt to Total Assets Ratio

The **debt to total assets ratio** is determined by applying the following formula:

$$\frac{\text{Total liabilities}}{\text{Total assets}} \times 100$$

This ratio indicates the amount of assets provided by the creditors versus the amount provided by the owners. As you may recall, assets must be provided by either creditors or owners and through profitable operations. The debt to total assets ratio also indicates the relative percentage of assets contributed by each of the two groups. A higher percentage indicates that creditors have provided a larger share of the firm's assets. In this situation a prospective banker or other creditor may be unwilling to extend additional credit.

The debt to total assets ratio for Jacob's Pet Supplies is given above with the debt to equity ratio. The ratio for the pet store is 39.7%, indicating that almost 40% of the firm's assets are contributed by creditors. On the other hand, 60% of the assets are contributed by J. Daniels, the owner of the business, or by the profitable operations of the pet store.

Limitations of the Balance Sheet

This chapter has pointed out some of the ways that a balance sheet helps financial statement users evaluate a company's financial position and strength. There are, however, a number of problems inherent in the accounting model that limit the usefulness of balance sheets. These problems include the way in which accountants define assets, the use of historical cost, and the need for arbitrary cost allocations.

Definition of Assets

In Chapter 1 we defined assets as economic resources, controlled by an enterprise, that have future benefits. In order for transactions to be admitted into the accounting system, they must be quantifiable in monetary terms whose benefits are measurable and verifiable. As a result, a number of items that one might consider assets, such as good management and research and development efforts, do not meet these criteria and are not considered assets. Accordingly, not all of the real economic assets that a firm owns or controls are listed on the balance sheet.

Financial Statements—The Outputs of the System   **223**

Historical Costs

Net assets on a firm's balance sheet are recorded at their historical cost or net book value (historical cost less accumulated depreciation). Remember that accountants do not record changes in value until an external transaction occurs. Thus, except in the case of a newly formed company, the balance sheet generally does not indicate the current or market value of the company. Therefore, investors or creditors cannot use the balance sheet to determine the current cost or value of the company's net assets. This problem, to a certain extent, has been alleviated by the required footnote disclosure by large public companies of selected current cost data.[3] The entire problem of accounting for changing prices and inflation is discussed in Chapter 14.

Arbitrary Allocation

Investors and creditors need information about an enterprise on a periodic and timely basis. The matching principle ensures that the cost of assets that benefit several periods are allocated to those periods. This requires a number of allocations, such as depreciation, that are inherently estimates. To the extent to which these required estimates are arbitrary management decisions, the balance sheet is less useful to investors and creditors.

Classified Income Statements

The purpose of the income statement is to provide financial statement users with information concerning the profitability of an enterprise for a particular period of time. This statement lists all of the revenues, expenses, gains, and losses that the enterprise earned or incurred during the accounting period. The difference between the total of revenues plus gains and the total of expenses plus losses is either net income or net loss. The income statement has become very important because as Concepts Statement 1 notes, "the primary focus of financial reporting is information about . . . earnings and its components."[4]

By analyzing the income statement, the investor or creditor can answer such questions as:

1. Did the company earn a profit this year, and, if so, how does it compare with its profits from other years?
2. What is the company's gross margin on sales, and is it large enough to cover other operating expenses?
3. What are the various components of revenues and expenses, and how do they compare with those of prior years?
4. Did the firm generate enough revenues from operations to pay the current interest charges?
5. How profitable is the firm compared with others in its industry?

As with the balance sheet, management has discretion over the exact format of the income statement. There are, however, two typical formats used by most businesses in the United States, the single-step and the multistep forms. Both of these income statements for Jacob's Pet Supplies are presented on pages 225 and 226, respectively. Note that in both cases net income is the

[3]Financial Accounting Standards Board, Statement No. 33, *Financial Reporting and Changing Prices* (Stamford, Conn.: FASB, September 1979).
[4]FASB Concepts Statement 1, par. 43.

same and that only the format is different. Again, you should keep in mind that these income statements are typical of most U.S. firms but that a German or Italian firm may issue an income statement with quite a different format.

The Single-Step Statement

Usually, the **single-step income statement** has only three major categories: revenues, expenses, and net income. Individual expense accounts, other than interest, are combined into the functional categories of selling and general and administrative. Selling expenses include the costs that are directly related to the firm's efforts to sell its goods and services. Typical expenses included in this category are salespersons' salaries and commissions and advertising, promotion, and delivery. In the Jacob's Pet Supplies example, selling expenses include sales salaries, advertising, and depreciation. General and administrative expenses is a catchall category that includes general office expenses, salaries of personnel other than the sales force, and other general expenses. Because some expenses, such as depreciation and insurance expense, affect both selling and general and administrative expenses, they are often split such that a portion is allocated to each category. Most published income statements are a form of a single-step statement and, although these statements are simple to prepare, there is a significant loss of information.

Jacob's Pet Supplies
Income Statement—Single-Step
For the Year Ended December 31, 1988

Revenues		
Net sales	$405,000	
Gain on sale of land	5,000	
Total revenues		$410,000
Expenses		
Cost of goods sold	$300,000	
Selling expenses	42,500	
General and administrative expenses	21,000	
Interest expense	1,500	
Total expenses		365,000
Net income		$ 45,000

The Multistep Statement

The **multistep income statement** has several categories. The major ones include gross margin or gross profit on sales, operating expenses, income from operations, other income and expenses, and net income. (See page 226.)

Gross Margin on Sales

Gross margin on sales is sales less cost of goods sold. In a complete multistep statement all the components of cost of goods sold are listed. In a condensed multistep statement only the total cost of goods sold is presented. (For example, see the income statement for Safeway Stores on page 233.) The

Jacob's Pet Supplies
Income Statement—Multistep
For the Year Ended December 31, 1988

Gross sales			$410,000
Less: Sales returns and allowances		$ 1,000	
Sales discounts		4,000	5,000
Net sales			405,000
Cost of goods sold			
Beginning inventory		25,000	
Purchases	$403,000		
Less: Purchase returns and allowances	$2,000		
Purchase discounts	4,000	6,000	
Net purchases		397,000	
Add: Freight-in		3,000	400,000
Cost of goods available for sale		425,000	
Less: Ending inventory		125,000	
Cost of goods sold			300,000
Gross margin on sales			105,000
Selling expenses			
Sales salaries		38,000	
Advertising expense		3,000	
Depreciation expense		1,500	
Total selling expenses		42,500	
General and administrative expenses			
Salaries expense		10,500	
Supplies expense		4,350	
Depreciation expense		2,450	
Utilities expense		2,000	
Insurance expense		1,000	
Repairs and maintenance expense		400	
License expense		300	
Total general and administrative expense		21,000	
Total operating expenses			63,500
Income from operations			41,500
Other income and (expense)			
Gain from sale of land		5,000	
Interest expense		(1,500)	3,500
Net income			$ 45,000

gross margin figure is significant for financial statement users, as they evaluate the ability of a company to earn enough profit on its sales to cover its operating expenses. In addition, analysts and other financial statement users often calculate a ratio called the gross margin ratio, which provides information concerning the percentage relationship between sales and cost of goods sold, and gross margin. This ratio is examined in more detail later in this chapter.

Operating Expenses

Operating expenses are generally divided into two major subcategories, selling and general and administrative. A complete multistep income statement like that shown on page 226 lists all the individual expenses under the selling and general and administrative expense categories. Many published financial statements condense this data and report only the total expenses in each category.

Income from Operations

This is the next category on the income statement and is the difference between gross margin on sales and the total of the operating expenses. If the firm's total operating expenses exceed their gross margin on sales, the category is labeled loss from operations.

Other Income and Expenses

A firm often earns revenues from sources other than sales and incurs expenses other than for operations. On a multistep income statement, these items are listed under a category called other income and expense. Other revenue items might include investment revenue from dividends and interest, and gains from sales of noninventory assets such as property, plant, and equipment. Other expenses might include losses from sales of plant and equipment and interest expense. Accountants consider interest to be a financing charge and not an operating expense.

Net Income

Net income is determined by adding or subtracting the total of other income and expenses from income from operations. A net loss will occur if there are more expenses and losses than revenues and gains.

The Uses and Limitations of Classified Income Statements

At the beginning of this section we listed some of the questions present and potential investors and creditors could use the income statement to answer. For the most part these questions regard measuring and evaluating the profitability of a firm. Several ratios can be used to aid in this task and are discussed next.

Measuring Profitability

One way to measure and evaluate a firm's profitability is to compute percentages that compare particular income statement items, such as gross margin and net income, with sales. Two such percentages are the gross margin percentage and the profit margin percentage. These ratios for Jacob's Pet Supplies are on the top of page 228.

Gross Margin Percentage

The **gross margin percentage** is determined by dividing gross margin by sales. This ratio provides information concerning the percentage relationship of sales to cost of goods sold and gross margin on sales. For the pet store, the

DETERMINATION OF GROSS MARGIN PERCENTAGE AND PROFIT MARGIN PERCENTAGE	
Gross Margin Percentage	**Profit Margin Percentage**
$\dfrac{\text{Gross margin on sales}}{\text{Sales}} \times 100$	$\dfrac{\text{Net income}}{\text{Sales}} \times 100$
$\dfrac{\$105,000}{\$405,000} \times 100 = 25.9$	$\dfrac{\$45,000}{\$405,000} \times 100 = 11.1$

gross margin percentage is 25.9. Conversely, cost of goods sold equals 74.1% of sales. As with all ratios, individual percentages should be evaluated in terms of industry norms and specific firm trends. Nevertheless, a firm's dollar gross margin and gross margin percentage must be sufficiently high to cover operating and other expenses. Therefore, a firm's management strives to adjust sales prices to compensate for changes in the cost of goods sold, in order to maintain a stable or increasing gross margin percentage.

Profit Margin Percentage

The **profit margin percentage** relates net income to total sales and is calculated by dividing net income by sales. For the pet store, this percentage is 11.1, meaning that for every dollar of sales, Jacob's Pet Supplies nets a little over eleven cents.

Return on Investment

There are a number of ratios that can be used by investors and creditors to determine how effectively management is operating a business and the return that is accruing to the various equity holders. Two such common ratios are return on total assets and return on owner's equity. These ratios are computed next for Jacob's Pet Supplies.

DETERMINATION OF RETURN ON TOTAL ASSETS AND RETURN ON OWNER'S EQUITY RATIOS	
Return on Total Assets	**Return on Owner's Equity**
$\dfrac{\text{Net income}}{\text{Average total assets}} \times 100$	$\dfrac{\text{Net income}}{\text{Average owner's equity}} \times 100$
$\dfrac{\$45,000}{(\$680,550^* + \$806,500) \div 2} \times 100 = 6.05\%$	$\dfrac{\$45,000}{(\$462,600^* + \$486,500) \div 2} \times 100 = 9.48\%$

*Beginning total assets of $680,550 and beginning owner's equity of $462,600 are taken from Jacob's Pet Supplies' December 31, 1987 balance sheet shown in Chapter 5 on page 196.

Return on Assets

In its simplest form, the ratio **return on total assets** is determined by dividing net income by average total assets. Average total assets is determined by adding the total assets at the beginning of the year to the total at the end of the year and dividing by two. In ratios that have an income statement figure in the numerator and a balance sheet figure in the denominator, the denominator should be an average figure. This is because income and expense items take place over the entire year, and it is most appropriate to relate these items to an average asset figure. The return on assets ratio is important because it measures how efficiently a firm is using the assets at its command. A high ratio provides evidence that management is efficiently using the firm's assets or resources to produce profits. For the pet store this ratio is 6.05%.

Return on Owner's Equity

The **return on owner's equity** measures the return that the owners are receiving on their investment, and it is calculated by dividing net income by average owner's equity. This ratio is calculated above and is 9.48% for the pet store. Again, evaluation of these ratios depends on industry norms and firm trends.

Limitations of the Income Statement

As we have seen, the income statement is extremely useful to users in evaluating and measuring a firm's profitability. However, as with all financial statements, there are limitations to its usefulness. Because the income statement is linked to the balance sheet, some of the same criticisms regarding the balance sheet apply to the income statement. These include the use of historical costs and the problems associated with cost allocation. As noted, the problems inherent in using only historical costs are alleviated through the required supplemental disclosure of certain current cost data. In regard to the income statement, current cost depreciation and cost of goods sold are disclosed on a supplemental basis.

Another limitation of the income statement results from the fact that alternative generally accepted accounting principles are available under current rules. Management can therefore choose among alternatives and often does. This makes it difficult to compare the performances of firms. Consequently, the informed investor and creditor must look beyond the income statement or any one financial statement in order to analyze a firm. Other items that must be considered include the statement of changes in financial position, footnotes to the financial statements, and the auditor's report. These are presented in more detail later.

Other Financial Statements

Firms generally prepare two other financial statements. One is the statement of changes in owner's equity. The primary purpose of this statement is to summarize the transactions that caused changes in owner's equity. In a corporation, this statement is replaced by a retained earnings statement, or statement of stockholders' equity. The second statement is a statement of changes in financial position. The purpose of this statement is to describe the changes in the financial resources of a firm. When we review the statements of Safeway Stores, these two are presented in more detail.

The Financial Statements and Annual Report of Safeway Stores, Inc.

In order to introduce the basic concepts of accounting, we have used simplified illustrations involving first a service company and then a small merchandising company. Now we introduce you to a typical set of financial statements from a publicly held corporation, Safeway Stores, Inc.[5] Publicly held corporations are firms whose stock is held by many individuals and is traded on stock exchanges such as the New York Stock Exchange. There are a number of items in these financial statements that are not discussed in this book until later. However, at this point it is important that you get a glimpse of how a large U.S. corporation reports to its shareholders. Throughout this book we return to these statements many times to illustrate a variety of points.

Reporting Requirements of Publicly Held Corporations

Publicly held corporations are required to annually file a set of financial statements and other data with the Securities and Exchange Commission. This report is called the Form 10-K. In addition, every publicly held corporation is required to provide an annual report to its shareholders. Besides the financial statements and related footnotes, the annual report includes such items as the president's letter, management's discussion and analysis of operations, and the auditor's report. These items, as well as the financial statements for Safeway Stores, are discussed next. Relevant portions of Safeway's 1985 annual report are found in Appendix C.

The Consolidated Balance Sheet

Safeway's balance sheet is shown on pages 231–232. Notice that Safeway's balance sheet, like that of most publicly held companies, is comparative. That is, three years of data are presented. A number of characteristics that differentiate it from the balance sheets presented in the first part of this chapter are detailed next.

The Heading

Safeway's balance sheet is called a consolidated balance sheet because Safeway owns several other companies, and the balance sheets of these companies are combined with Safeway's. **Consolidated statements** are presented in more detail in Chapter 19.

The heading to the balance sheet also shows that Safeway's year-end is on a different date for each of the three years. Safeway has chosen as a year-end what is referred to as a 52–53 week fiscal year. As noted earlier, a 52–53 fiscal year allows a firm to choose a year-end on the same day every year. Safeway's fiscal year ends on the Saturday nearest the end of December. This means that sometimes its year ends in the last week of December and other times in the first week of January. This simplifies its accounting and closing process. Because of this choice of a fiscal year, in some years Safeway's accounting period has fifty-two weeks and in other years it has fifty-three.

[5]As this book was in its final stages of production, Safeway Stores, Inc. agreed to be purchased in a leveraged buyout. As a result, Safeway Stores is no longer a public company, and eventually its stock will no longer be traded on an exchange.

Consolidated Balance Sheets
Safeway Stores, Incorporated and Subsidiaries

As of December 28, 1985, December 29, 1984
and December 31, 1983
(in thousands, except per share amounts)

	1985	1984	1983
Assets			
Current assets:			
Cash	$ 54,593	$ 49,179	$ 51,682
Short-term investments	170,021	25,263	23,892
Receivables	111,870	105,166	91,642
Merchandise inventories:			
FIFO cost	1,878,281	1,881,525	1,722,260
Less LIFO reductions	312,715	318,281	289,006
	1,565,566	1,563,244	1,433,254
Prepaid expenses and other current assets	124,431	118,537	128,676
Total current assets	2,026,481	1,861,389	1,729,146
Property:			
Land	247,769	236,876	210,427
Buildings	431,410	345,001	305,006
Leasehold improvements	600,091	557,504	459,711
Fixtures and equipment	2,164,072	2,023,914	1,789,136
Transport equipment	186,831	186,485	173,576
Property under capital leases	1,010,277	1,144,409	1,155,493
	4,640,450	4,494,189	4,093,349
Less accumulated depreciation and amortization	2,003,752	1,894,333	1,731,138
Total property, net	2,636,698	2,599,856	2,362,211
Investments in affiliated companies	122,195	27,251	26,519
Other assets	55,237	48,733	56,487
Total assets	$ 4,840,611	$ 4,537,229	$ 4,174,363

The Assets Section

The assets section of Safeway's balance sheet is typical of that found on the balance sheets of most major U.S. corporations. The one category that we now consider further is property under capital leases.

Property held under capital leases is stores that Safeway has leased under long-term agreements. Generally accepted accounting principles require that these leases be treated as purchases, and as a result the asset Property under Capital Leases is shown in Safeway's balance sheet. Accounting for leases is discussed in Chapter 18, and accounting for property, plant, and equipment is discussed in Chapters 12 and 13.

Liabilities

Again, the liabilities section of Safeway's balance sheet is typical of that of most U.S. corporations. The items we need to consider now are obligations under capital leases and current maturities of notes and debentures.

As was previously noted, some liabilities such as mortgages and leases are payable in equal monthly or yearly installments over a specified period of time. The portion of such liabilities that is payable within twelve months from

	1985	1984	1983
Liabilities and Stockholders' Equity			
Current liabilities:			
Notes payable	$ 80,848	$ 44,913	$ 50,156
Current obligations under capital leases	43,396	45,427	45,841
Current maturities of notes and debentures	52,049	48,274	24,723
Accounts payable	1,151,426	1,038,268	1,017,094
Accrued salaries and wages	167,798	167,739	163,021
Other accrued expenses	201,357	170,905	154,373
Income taxes payable	27,827	20,431	43,081
Total current liabilities	1,724,701	1,535,957	1,498,289
Long-term debt:			
Obligations under capital leases	625,551	746,178	765,307
Notes and debentures	689,470	646,532	422,362
Total long-term debt	1,315,021	1,392,710	1,187,669
Accrued claims and other liabilities	178,275	139,539	98,051
Total liabilities	3,217,997	3,068,206	2,784,009
Stockholders' equity:			
Common stock - $1.66 ⅔ par value			
Authorized 150,000, 150,000 and 75,000 shares			
Outstanding 60,846, 59,854 and 58,760 shares	101,411	99,756	97,933
Additional paid-in capital	273,776	246,964	222,851
Cumulative translation adjustments	(164,035)	(155,994)	(114,087)
Retained earnings	1,411,462	1,278,297	1,183,657
Total stockholders' equity	1,622,614	1,469,023	1,390,354
Total liabilities and stockholders' equity	$ 4,840,611	$ 4,537,229	$ 4,174,363

the balance sheet date is often referred to as current maturities or obligations of long-term debt and is classified as a current liability. On the Safeway balance sheet, two such items—current obligations under capital leases and current maturities of notes and debentures (an unsecured bond)—are listed in the current liabilities section. The noncurrent portion of these liabilities is shown in the long-term section of the balance sheet.

Safeway lists one additional category in the liabilities section—accrued claims and other liabilities—a miscellaneous category similar in nature to the other assets category. Many firms will distribute the items in this category among the current or long-term liabilities sections of the balance sheet.

Stockholders' Equity

Included in the stockholders' equity section of Safeway's balance sheet are the accounts Common Stock, Additional Paid-in Capital, Cumulative Translation Adjustments, and Retained Earnings. The permanent investment by Safeway's stockholders at December 28, 1985, equals $375,187,000, or $101,411,000 in common stock and $273,776,000 in additional paid-in capital. The fact that this permanent investment is divided between common stock and additional paid-in capital is not significant. The reasons for this division are discussed in Chapter 16.

Without looking at Safeway's internal records, it is impossible to say how many current shareholders there are. The balance sheet does show, however, that Safeway is authorized by the state of Delaware to issue 150 million shares of common stock and has 60,846,000 shares outstanding on December 28, 1985.

Under current accounting standards, a number of items may be directly deducted from stockholders' equity. Such items include unrealized losses on long-term investments and cumulative foreign currency translation adjustments. These items are mentioned briefly in later chapters.

As noted previously, retained earnings represents the accumulated earnings of the business less any dividends issued. For Safeway Stores, the balance in the retained earnings account at December 28, 1985, is $1,411,462,000. The changes that affect the Retained Earnings account during the year (net income or loss and dividends) are described in the retained earnings statement. This statement is similar to a statement of changes in owner's equity for a sole proprietorship.

The Consolidated Statements of Income

The consolidated statements of income for Safeway Stores are shown on this page. Note again that the statement contains the accounts of Safeway and its subsidiaries. Like the balance sheet, the consolidated statement of income presents three years of data.

Safeway's income statement is typical of those published by publicly held firms. It is somewhat condensed and shows only a few subcategories such as gross profit (margin), operating profit, income before provisions for taxes, and net income. Unlike a sole proprietorship or partnership, a corporation is subject to federal and state income taxes. In a sole proprietorship or partnership, income from the business is included with the owners' other income and the business is not taxed separately. A corporation, however, is subject to taxes, and these taxes are an expense of the business. Taxes are included under the provision for income taxes category.

Consolidated Statements of Income
Safeway Stores, Incorporated and Subsidiaries

For the 52 weeks ended December 28, 1985,
December 29, 1984 and December 31, 1983

(in thousands, except per share amounts)	1985	1984	1983
Sales	$19,650,542	$19,642,201	$18,585,217
Cost of sales	14,872,247	15,004,547	14,249,843
Gross profit	4,778,295	4,637,654	4,335,374
Operating and administrative expenses	4,350,635	4,214,443	3,920,736
Operating profit	427,660	423,211	414,638
Interest expense	(172,906)	(151,263)	(134,270)
Gain on sale of foreign operations	49,046		
Other income, net	49,816	26,874	20,565
Income before provision for income taxes	353,616	298,822	300,933
Provision for income taxes	122,316	113,811	117,630
Net income	$ 231,300	$ 185,011	$ 183,303
Net income per share	$ 3.83	$ 3.12	$ 3.26

Income statements of publicly held corporations include data regarding earnings per share and may include such categories as extraordinary items, discontinued operations, and the effects of changes in accounting methods. These are unusual items and under generally accepted accounting principles must be shown separately. These items are discussed in Chapter 17.

The Statement of Stockholders' Equity

Large public corporations are likely to enter into transactions affecting a variety of stockholders' equity accounts, such as issuing additional capital stock or converting bonds into common stock. When such transactions occur, an extensive statement called the **statement of stockholders' equity** must be prepared. Safeway's statement of changes in stockholders' equity is reproduced on this page and details the changes in all the stockholders' equity accounts. In smaller firms, a simple retained earnings statement replaces the statement of changes in stockholders' equity. The retained earnings statement shows the effect of net income or loss and dividends on retained earnings.

Consolidated Statements of Stockholders' Equity

Safeway Stores, Incorporated and Subsidiaries

For the 52 weeks ended December 28, 1985, December 29, 1984 and December 31, 1983 (in thousands, except per share amounts)	Common Stock		Additional Paid-in Capital	Cumulative Translation Adjustments	Retained Earnings
	Shares	Amount			
Balance, January 1, 1983	26,150	$ 43,583	$ 64,573	$ (96,042)	$1,124,981
Net income					183,303
Cash dividends ($1.425 per share)					(80,961)
Translation adjustments				(18,045)	
Stock issued under stock option plans (pre-split)	50	84	1,841		
Stock issued in 2-for-1 split	26,200	43,666			(43,666)
Stock issued under:					
Public offering	5,500	9,167	136,729		
Dividend reinvestment plan	564	940	13,403		
Stock option plans	150	250	2,470		
Tax Reduction Act Stock Ownership Plan	146	243	3,835		
Balance, December 31, 1983	58,760	97,933	222,851	(114,087)	1,183,657
Net income					185,011
Cash dividends ($1.525 per share)					(90,371)
Translation adjustments				(41,907)	
Stock issued under:					
Dividend reinvestment plan	950	1,583	21,734		
Stock option plans	144	240	2,379		
Balance, December 29, 1984	59,854	99,756	246,964	(155,994)	1,278,297
Net income					231,300
Cash dividends ($1.625 per share)					(98,135)
Translation adjustments				(28,056)	
Translation adjustments realized on sale of foreign operations				20,015	
Stock issued under:					
Dividend reinvestment plan	753	1,256	21,899		
Stock option plans	239	399	4,913		
Balance, December 28, 1985	60,846	$101,411	$273,776	$(164,035)	$1,411,462

Consolidated Statements of Changes in Financial Position
Safeway Stores, Incorporated and Subsidiaries

For the 52 weeks ended December 28, 1985,
December 29, 1984 and December 31, 1983
(in thousands)

	1985	1984	1983
Cash provided from operations:			
Net income	$231,300	$185,011	$183,303
Charges (credits) to income not requiring (providing) cash:			
Depreciation and amortization	333,398	295,290	264,553
Gain on sale of Australian operations	(48,296)		
Equity in earnings of affiliates	(8,100)	(1,890)	(140)
Deferred income taxes	29,830	34,128	20,194
LIFO charge (credit)	(5,566)	29,275	(444)
Accrued claims and other liabilities	8,531	9,608	(11,035)
(Increase) decrease in current assets:			
Receivables	(9,233)	(13,524)	(18,537)
Inventories at FIFO cost	(59,815)	(159,265)	(94,820)
Prepaid expenses and other current assets	(8,978)	12,689	7,349
Increase (decrease) in current liabilities:			
Payables and accruals	230,035	42,424	93,761
Income taxes payable	11,510	(22,650)	31,824
Total cash provided from operations	704,616	411,096	476,008
Investment activities:			
Additions to property	(621,758)	(701,678)	(541,238)
Retirements or sales of property	131,079	113,091	90,296
Proceeds from sale of foreign operations:			
Net working capital	(26,611)		
Other net assets, at fair value	135,220		
Investments in affiliated companies	(104,272)	(2,265)	(2,432)
Exchange rate effects on property and investments	11,051	57,211	27,308
Cumulative translation adjustments	(28,056)	(41,907)	(18,045)
Other	(9,185)	6,806	(9,691)
Net investment activities	(512,532)	(568,742)	(453,802)
Financing activities:			
Additions to long-term debt	167,500	323,625	205,935
Payments on long-term debt	(174,871)	(104,008)	(266,876)
Increase (decrease) in notes payable	39,900	(5,243)	(37,872)
Exchange rate effects on long-term debt	(6,000)	(14,576)	(7,576)
Increase in current maturities of long-term debt	2,582	23,137	11,155
Cash dividends on common stock	(98,135)	(90,371)	(80,961)
Proceeds from issuance of common stock	28,467	25,936	168,962
Other	(1,355)	(1,986)	(3,207)
Net financing activities	(41,912)	156,514	(10,440)
Increase (decrease) in cash and short-term investments	150,172	(1,132)	11,766
Cash and short-term investments:			
Beginning of year	74,442	75,574	63,808
End of year	$224,614	$ 74,442	$ 75,574

The Statement of Changes in Financial Position

The **statement of changes in financial position,** now called a statement of cash flows, is the fourth required financial statement. The purpose of this statement is to describe the changes (inflows and outflows) in the resources of the enterprise. A recent FASB exposure draft now defines resources as cash and cash equivalents. The statement of changes in financial position essentially details major changes in balance sheet accounts and what caused those changes. This statement is useful in answering the following type of questions:

1. What are the sources of the firm's cash?
2. What proportion of the firm's cash is generated internally or from operations?
3. What other financing activities took place during the year?
4. Why was the firm profitable although there was only a slight increase in cash?
5. How was cash used during the year?

The statement of changes in financial position for Safeway Stores, Inc. is shown on page 235. Chapter 20 discusses the actual preparation of this statement. Our purpose here is to provide you with an introduction to the usefulness of this valuable statement.

Safeway's statement of changes in financial position is prepared on a cash basis. As the bottom line of this statement shows, by the end of 1985 Safeway's cash and short-term investments amounted to $224.6 million, and during the year Safeway's cash increased by a little over $150 million. (For purposes of discussion we assume short-term investments to be just cash.) Total cash provided from operations during 1985 amounted to over $704 million. Investing activities such as additions to properties caused cash to decrease by over $512 million. Various financing activities such as net additions to long-term debt less cash dividend payments decreased cash by almost $42 million. As noted, the net result of all activities is an increase of a little over $150 million in cash during the year.

The statement of changes in financial position is an extremely useful statement. However, because it is derived from the same accounting model as the other statements are, it also has many of the same limitations that the other statements do. In fact, the financial statements themselves do not provide all of the financial information about a firm that users require. Informed decision makers therefore look to other sources of information, some of which are discussed next.

Other Elements of an Annual Report of a Publicly Held Company

The financial statements themselves are only one aspect of the financial information that an enterprise makes available to users. This is especially true of publicly held companies, which are required to disclose various other items. In this section we discuss the footnotes to the financial statements, which are an integral part of the financial statements of all firms, the auditor's report, and other aspects of an annual report.

Footnotes to the Financial Statements

It is impossible to put into the body of the financial statements all of the important information that relates to a particular account. As a result, financial statements include **footnotes,** which are narrative explanations of the important aspects of various items. Safeway has footnotes that range from an explanation of its significant accounting policies (Footnote A) to financial information by geographic area (Footnote N). Safeway's complete financial statements, including all footnotes, are reproduced in Appendix C. As an example, Footnote I—Commitments—is shown below:

> NOTE I   COMMITMENTS
> The company has commitments under contracts for the purchase of property and equipment and for the construction of buildings. Portions of such contracts not completed at year-end are not reflected in the financial statements. These unrecorded commitments amounted to approximately $68 million at year-end 1985.

This is typical of the type of information that is often disclosed in the footnotes. These commitments are essentially executory contracts that do not meet the criteria for input into the system, as explained in Chapter 2. However, these contracts represent important information relating to the company's future activities and as such are disclosed in the footnotes.

The Auditor's Report

The managements of all public companies, as well as a number of private companies, hire independent certified public accountants (CPAs) to audit their financial statements. Public companies are required by U.S. securities laws to engage CPAs to conduct an audit. Owners-managers of private companies may want an audit for several reasons, including the desire to assure themselves that their financial statements conform with generally accepted accounting principles. Bankers and other creditors also may require such an audit. In all cases, the purpose of the audit is to assure users that the financial statements prepared by the firm's management are in conformity with generally accepted accounting principles.

The auditor's report for Safeway is shown on page 238. Most **auditor's reports** contain two paragraphs. The first paragraph often is referred to as the *scope paragraph* because it states what general procedures the CPA followed in conducting the audit. The second paragraph is referred to as the *opinion paragraph* because it states whether, in the auditor's opinion, the financial statements "present fairly." Safeway received an unqualified (or clean) opinion because, in the auditor's opinion, the financial statements present fairly Safeway's financial position and results of operations in conformity with generally accepted accounting principles applied on a consistent basis. If the auditors issue other than a clean opinion, they must state the exact reasons for such a qualified or adverse opinion.

Note that the auditors do not use the word *truth, guarantee,* or *certify.* The use of these words would be misleading because it is impossible for an outside party to make such a statement. Rather, a professional opinion is given, which meets the needs of financial statement users.

It should be emphasized that management is responsible for the data contained in the financial statements. Safeway's management explicitly notes this in a statement in the annual report, placed immediately before the auditor's report. This statement is shown on the top of page 239.

Peat, Marwick, Mitchell & Co.
To the Board of Directors and Stockholders
Safeway Stores, Incorporated:

We have examined the consolidated balance sheets of Safeway Stores, Incorporated and subsidiaries as of December 28, 1985, December 29, 1984 and December 31, 1983 and the related consolidated statements of income, stockholders' equity and changes in financial position for the years then ended. Our examinations were made in accordance with generally accepted auditing standards and, accordingly, included such tests of the accounting records and such other auditing procedures as we considered necessary in the circumstances.

In our opinion, the aforementioned consolidated financial statements present fairly the financial position of Safeway Stores, Incorporated and subsidiaries at December 28, 1985, December 29, 1984 and December 31, 1983 and the results of their operations and changes in their financial position for the years then ended, in conformity with generally accepted accounting principles applied on a consistent basis.

Peat, Marwick, Mitchell & Co.

Oakland, California
March 3, 1986

Other Aspects of the Annual Report

All public companies issue annual reports to their stockholders and other interested users. These reports contain the firm's audited financial statements, including footnotes, management's discussion and analysis of operations, the president's letter, summaries of significant financial statistics, and other data. How to effectively use this data to analyze and interpret financial statements is covered in Chapter 21. Finally, Appendix C includes relevant portions of Safeway's annual report, including all financial statements and footnotes. In addition, for your comparison, the appendix includes the financial statements of the Philips Group, a Dutch multinational firm.

Summary of Learning Objectives

1. An objective of general purpose financial statements. Financial statements are the major outputs of the accounting information system and are aimed at the general purpose user. One objective of financial statements is to provide relevant and useful information to present and potential investors and creditors that increases their ability to assess future

The consolidated financial statements of Safeway Stores, Incorporated and its subsidiaries have been prepared in accordance with generally accepted accounting principles and necessarily include amounts that are based on management's best estimates and judgments. Management is responsible for the integrity and objectivity of the data in these statements. Financial information elsewhere in this annual report is consistent with that in the financial statements.

To fulfill its responsibilities, management has developed and maintains a strong system of internal accounting controls. There are inherent limitations in any control system in that the cost of maintaining a control should not exceed the benefits to be derived. However, management believes the controls in use are sufficient to provide reasonable assurance that assets are safeguarded from loss or unauthorized use and that the financial records are reliable for preparing the financial statements. The controls are supported by careful selection and training of qualified personnel, by the appropriate division of responsibilities, by communication of written policies and procedures throughout the company, and by an extensive program of internal audits.

Peat, Marwick, Mitchell & Co., independent certified public accountants, whose report follows the consolidated financial statements, are engaged to provide an independent opinion regarding the fair presentation in the financial statements of the company's financial condition and results of operations. They obtain an understanding of the company's systems and procedures sufficient to provide them reasonable assurance that the financial statements are neither misleading nor contain material errors.

The board of directors, through its audit committee which is composed of outside directors, is responsible for assuring that management fulfills its responsibilities in the preparation of the financial statements. The board, on the recommendation of the audit committee and in accordance with stockholder approval, selects and engages the independent accountants. The audit committee meets with the independent accountants to review the scope of the annual audit and any recommendations they have for improvements in the company's internal accounting controls. To assure independence, the independent accountants have free access to the audit committee and may confer with them without management representation present.

cash flows. This is best accomplished by providing information about an enterprise's economic resources and obligations and changes in them.

2. *The construction of classified balance sheets.* Given accounting norms and conventions, the actual format of the balance sheet is at the discretion of a firm's management. However, most balance sheets of U.S. firms include at least some of these major categories: current assets; long-term investment; property, plant, and equipment; intangible assets; other assets; current liabilities; long-term liabilities; and stockholders' equity.

3. *The uses and limitations of classified balance sheets.* Investors and creditors can use a balance sheet to analyze a firm's financial position, liquidity, and strength. This can be accomplished by considering such items and ratios as working capital, the current ratio, the debt to equity ratio, and the total debt to assets ratio. However, there are limitations to the usefulness of the balance sheet because of the way in which assets are defined, the use of historical costs, the use of different accounting methods, and the need for cost allocation.

4. *The construction of classified income statements.* As with balance sheets, the usefulness of income statements can be increased by classifying items that appear on the statement. The degree of detail depends on whether a firm prepares a single-step or a multistep income statement. Both types of statements are typical of those prepared by U.S. firms.

Financial Statements—The Outputs of the System

5. *The uses and limitations of classified income statements.* Classified income statements are useful to investors and creditors in evaluating a firm's profitability and the returns that accrue to each equity group. Percentages and ratios such as the gross margin percentage, the profit margin percentage, the return on total assets, and the return on stockholders' equity are useful in this evaluation. However, as with the balance sheet, there are limitations to the usefulness of the income statement. These include the use of historical costs, cost allocations, and the availability of alternative generally accepted accounting principles.

6. *The financial statements of a major corporation.* In order to gain a full understanding of a company, an investor or creditor must look beyond the balance sheet and the income statement. The statement of stockholders' equity provides information about major changes affecting the stockholders' equity section of the balance sheet. The statement of changes in financial position is useful in evaluating significant changes in financial resources and uses of resources. In addition, items such as footnotes, summaries of financial statistics, and the auditor's report—all found in annual reports—provide essential information.

Key Terms

Amortization	Gross Margin Percentage
Auditor's Report	Intangible Assets
Classified Financial Statements	Long-term Investments
Capital Stock	Multistep Income Statement
Common Stock	Noncurrent or Long-term Liabilities
Consolidated Statements	Objectives of Financial Reporting
Current Assets	Operating Cycle
Current Liabilities	Profit Margin Percentage
Current Maturities of Long-term Debt	Return on Owner's Equity
Current Ratio	Return on Total Assets
Debt to Equity Ratio	Single-step Income Statement
Debt to Total Assets Ratio	Statement of Changes in Financial Position
Dividends	Statement of Stockholders' Equity
Footnotes (to Financial Statements)	Stockholders' Equity
Goodwill	Working Capital
Gross Margin on Sales	

Problems for Your Review

A. Classified Balance Sheet. Accounts taken from the post-closing trial balance of the Artesian Company are presented on the top of page 241 (in alphabetical order):

Artesian Company
Accounts from Post-Closing Trial Balance
December 31, 1987

Accounts payable	$10,000	Land	$40,000
Accounts receivable	12,500	L. Artesian, capital	?
Accumulated depreciation—		Marketable securities held	
Plant and equipment	20,000	for temporary investment	4,500
Bond sinking fund	15,000	Mortgage payable less	
Bonds payable	50,000	current portion	20,000
Cash	8,000	Patent, net amortization	5,000
Current maturities of		Plant and equipment	100,000
long-term debt	12,000	Prepaid insurance	2,000
Inventories	18,000	Salaries payable	5,000
Investments, long-term	5,000	Taxes payable	3,000

Required:

Prepare in good form a classified balance sheet as of December 31, 1987 for the Artesian Company.

Solution

The Artesian Company
Balance Sheet
December 31, 1987

Assets			Liabilities and Owner's Equity		
Current assets:			Current liabilities:		
Cash		$ 8,000	Current maturities of		
Marketable securities		4,500	long-term debt		$ 12,000
Accounts receivable		12,500	Accounts payable		10,000
Inventories		18,000	Salaries payable		5,000
Prepaid insurance		2,000	Taxes payable		3,000
Total current assets		45,000	Total current liabilities		30,000
Investments:			Long-term liabilities:		
Long-term investments		5,000	Bonds payable		50,000
Bond sinking fund		15,000	Mortgage payable		20,000
Total long-term investments		20,000	Total long-term liabilities		70,000
Property, plant, and equipment			Total liabilities		100,000
Land		40,000	Owner's equity		
Plant and equipment	$100,000		L. Artesian, capital		90,000
Less: Accumulated depreciation	20,000	80,000			
Total property, plant, and equipment		120,000			
Intangible assets, Patents, net of amortization		5,000			
			Total liabilities and		
Total assets		$190,000	owner's equity		$190,000

Financial Statements—The Outputs of the System

241

Points to consider:

1. The marketable securities are considered a current asset because they are marketable and held temporarily.
2. Intangible assets such as patents are usually shown net of amortization, whereas for plant and equipment both the historical costs and the accumulated depreciation are disclosed.
3. Current maturities of long-term debt must be classified as a current liability.
4. The order within the current liabilities section is not particularly significant.
5. In this example, L. Artesian, capital must be calculated. It is the amount needed to make the equities equal the assets, or $190,000 − $100,000 = $90,000.

B. Classified Income Statement. Following are the revenue, expense, and related accounts of the Artesian Company (in alphabetical order):

Artesian Company
**Revenues and Expenses
and All Related Accounts**
Year Ended December 31, 1987

Advertising expense*	$ 3,500
Beginning L. Artesian capital	79,500
Beginning inventory	21,000
Commission*	4,500
Depreciation and amortization	10,000
Ending inventory	18,000
Insurance expense	3,000
Interest expense	2,000
Owner's withdrawals	?
Purchases	164,000
Repairs and maintenance	1,000
Sales	231,500
Salespersons' salaries*	12,000

*Indicates selling expenses.

Required:

1. Prepare in good form a multistep income statement.
2. Prepare in good form a single-step income statement.
3. Prepare in good form a statement of owner's equity. (The amount of withdrawals must be determined.)

Solution _____

1.

Artesian Company
Multistep Income Statement
For the Year Ended December 31, 1987

Sales		$231,500
Cost of goods sold		
Beginning inventory	$ 21,000	
Purchases	164,000	
Cost of goods available for sale	185,000	
Less: Ending inventory	18,000	
Cost of goods sold		167,000
Gross margin		64,500

Selling expenses		
Salespersons' salaries	$12,000	
Commissions	4,500	
Advertising	3,500	
Total selling expenses		20,000
General and administrative expenses		
Depreciation and amortization	$10,000	
Insurance expense	3,000	
Repairs and maintenance	1,000	
Total general and administrative expenses		14,000
Total operating expenses		34,000
Income from operations		30,500
Other expenses		
Interest		2,000
Net income		$ 28,500

2.

Artesian Company
Single-Step Income Statement
For the Year Ended December 31, 1987

Revenues		
Sales		$231,500
Expenses		
Cost of goods sold	$167,000	
Selling	20,000	
General and administrative	14,000	
Interest	2,000	
Total expenses		203,000
Net income		$ 28,500

3.

Artesian Company
Statement of Owner's Equity
For the Year Ended December 31, 1987

L. Artesian, capital 1/1/87	$ 79,500
Added: Net income	28,500
Subtotal	108,000
Less: Withdrawals*	18,000
L. Artesian, capital 12/31/87	$ 90,000

*The withdrawal figure must be calculated. Because beginning and ending capital and net income are given, withdrawals can be determined as follows:

$ 79,500
28,500

108,000
−90,000

$ 18,000

C. Analysis. Using the data in Problems A and B, calculate the following ratios for the Artesian Company:

   a. Working capital.
   b. Current ratio.
   c. Debt to equity ratio.
   d. Total debt to total assets.
   e. Gross margin percentage.
   f. Profit margin percentage.
   g. Return on total assets. (Use year-end figures only.)
   h. Return on owner's equity. (Use year-end figures only.)

Solution

a. Working capital = current assets − current liabilities
   $$\$15,000 = \$45,000 - \$30,000$$

b. Current ratio $= \dfrac{\text{Current assets}}{\text{Current liabilities}}$ $\qquad 1.5 = \dfrac{\$45,000}{\$30,000}$

c. Debt to equity ratio $= \dfrac{\text{Total liabilities}}{\text{Total owner's equity}}$ $\qquad 1.11 = \dfrac{\$100,000}{\$\ 90,000}$

d. Total debt to total assets $= \dfrac{\text{Total liabilities}}{\text{Total assets}}$ $\qquad .526 = \dfrac{\$100,000}{\$190,000}$

e. Gross margin percentage $= \dfrac{\text{Gross margin}}{\text{Sales}}$ $\qquad .279 = \dfrac{\$\ 64,500}{\$231,500}$

f. Profit margin percentage $= \dfrac{\text{Net income}}{\text{Sales}}$ $\qquad .123 = \dfrac{\$\ 28,500}{\$231,500}$

g. Return on total assets $= \dfrac{\text{Net income}}{\text{Average total assets}}$ $\qquad .15 = \dfrac{\$\ 28,500}{\$190,000^{a}}$

h. Return on owner's equity $= \dfrac{\text{Net income}}{\text{Average owner's equity}}$ $\qquad .317 = \dfrac{\$28,500}{\$90,000^{a}}$

[a]Only year-end balance available.

Questions

1. Below are some of the common groups that are likely to use financial statements. List at least two uses each group would make of financial statements.
   a. Labor unions.
   b. Stockbrokers.
   c. Regulatory agencies such as the Securities and Exchange Commission and the Federal Trade Commission.
   d. Management.

2. If different groups use financial statements for different purposes, why are general purpose financial statements prepared?

3. Why did the FASB develop objectives of financial statements? Describe the three primary purposes of financial statements.

4. Describe classified financial statements and explain why they are prepared.

5. What are the primary purposes and uses of a balance sheet? How does it enable a user to analyze a company's financial strength?

6. What are the important limitations of a balance sheet, and what are their causes?

7. Describe the differences among a calendar year, a fiscal year, and a 52–53 week year.

8. Define and give examples of:
   a. Current assets.
   b. Long-term investments.
   c. Property, plant, and equipment.
   d. Intangible assets.
   e. Current liabilities.
   f. Long-term liabilities.
   g. Owner's equity.

9. What is the operating cycle of a business? Describe the operating cycles of the following businesses:
   a. Distillery.
   b. Savings and loan company.
   c. Gas station.
   d. Construction company.
   e. Book publisher.

10. Describe the two common measures used to assess a firm's liquidity.

11. What does the debt to equity ratio measure?

12. Why would the amount of assets provided by creditors versus the amount provided by owners be important?

13. What are the purposes of the income statement, and what information does it provide to users?

14. What are the limitations of the income statement, and what are some of their causes?

15. What are the differences between a single-step and a multistep income statement? In what circumstances should each type of statement be prepared?

16. What measures can an investor use to assess a firm's profitability?

17. What measures can an investor use to determine how effectively management is operating a business?

18. What is the purpose of the statement of changes in financial position? What information does it provide?

19. What are the footnotes to the financial statements? Describe several types of information contained in the footnotes.

20. In addition to financial statements, what other parts of a firm's annual report are useful to investors?

21. What are the purposes of an audit of financial statements conducted by CPAs? What information is contained in the auditor's report? What is management's responsibility in relation to the data contained in the financial statements?

Exercises

1. Classification of Balance Sheet Accounts. Below are the classifications commonly found on classified balance sheets. In the space next to each of the numbered items, write the letter that best indicates to which classification it belongs.

a. Current assets.
b. Long-term investments.
c. Property, plant, and equipment.
d. Intangible assets.
e. Other assets.

f. Current liabilities.
g. Long-term liabilities.
h. Owner's equity.
i. Not a balance sheet item.

_____ 1. Trucks used in business
_____ 2. Copyright owned by firm
_____ 3. Accounts payable
_____ 4. Prepaid insurance
_____ 5. Supplies on hand
_____ 6. Supplies used
_____ 7. Unearned rent
_____ 8. Bonds payable
_____ 9. Land held for future use
_____ 10. Land

_____ 11. Accounts receivable
_____ 12. L. L. Bean, capital
_____ 13. Accumulated depreciation—Truck
_____ 14. Current maturities of long-term debt
_____ 15. Inventory
_____ 16. Rent expense
_____ 17. L. L. Bean, drawing
_____ 18. Marketable securities
_____ 19. Note receivable, due in five years
_____ 20. Land held for future sale

2. Preparation of a Classified Balance Sheet. Using the following data, prepare a classified balance sheet for the Nigel Company as of December 31, 1987:

Accounts payable	$ 5,600	Equipment	$40,000
Accounts receivable	10,500	Inventory	20,000
Accumulated depreciation—Building	20,000	Long-term investments	5,000
Accumulated depreciation—Equipment	2,500	Interest payable	3,500
Building	100,000	Land	50,000
Cash	6,000	Long-term note payable	30,000
Cash in sinking fund	5,000	Marketable securities	2,500
D. B. Cooper, capital	167,000	Short-term note payable	10,400

Financial Statements—The Outputs of the System

3. Preparation of a Corporate Classified Balance Sheet. The following items were taken from the record of the Hart Corporation at the end of 1988:

Cash	$ 12,000	Patent	$ 5,000
Investment in short-term		Long-term note receivable	6,000
government securities	25,000	Accounts payable	60,000
Accounts receivable	50,000	Current maturities	
Inventory	75,000	of long-term debt	40,000
Long-term investment in securities	10,000	Long-term debt	100,000
Land	100,000	Common stock, $10 par value,	
Building	200,000	20,000 shares outstanding	200,000
Accumulated depreciation—Building	25,000	Additional paid-in capital	30,000
Equipment	60,000	Retained earnings	?
Accumulated depreciation—Equipment	10,000		

Required:

Prepare a classified balance sheet for the Hart Corporation as of December 31, 1988.

4. Balance Sheet Analysis. The balance sheet for The Mendez Company is presented next.

The Mendez Company
Balance Sheet
December 31, 1987

Assets		Liabilities and Owner's Equity	
Current assets:		Current liabilities:	
Cash	$ 7,000	Accounts payable	$10,000
Accounts receivable	14,000	Salaries payable	5,000
Total current assets	21,000	Total current liabilities	15,000
Long-term investments	24,000	Long-term liabilities:	
Property, plant, and equipment, net	40,000	Note payable—due 1/89	15,000
		Total liabilities	$30,000
		Owner's equity	
		A. Mendez, capital	$55,000
		Total liabilities and	
Total assets	$85,000	owner's equity:	$85,000

Required:

    a. Calculate the following:

       1. Working capital.

       2. Current ratio.

       3. Debt to equity ratio.

       4. Total debt to total assets ratio.

    b. If you were considering making a $20,000, 2-year loan to the firm, how would you assess its financial strength and stability? Would you make the loan?

5. Classification of Income Statement Accounts. Below are classifications commonly found on a multistep income statement. In the space next to each of the numbered items write the letter that best indicates to which classification it belongs.

      a. Revenue.   d. General and administrative expense.

      b. Cost of goods sold.   e. Other revenue and expense.

      c. Selling expenses.   f. Not an income statement item.

_____ 1. Sales
_____ 2. Purchases
_____ 3. Supplies on hand
_____ 4. Gain on sale of land
_____ 5. Sales discount
_____ 6. Interest payable
_____ 7. Depreciation expense—
      Administrative office equipment

_____ 8. Sales commissions paid
_____ 9. Freight-in
_____ 10. President's salary
_____ 11. Office rent
_____ 12. Delivery expense
_____ 13. Interest expense
_____ 14. Advertising expense
_____ 15. Prepaid insurance

6. Preparation of a Single-Step Income Statement. Given the following information, prepare a single-step income statement for the Pauline Perfume Shop for the year ended December 31, 1987.

Rent expense	$10,000
Interest expense	2,250
Sales	50,000
Selling expense	6,000
Cost of goods sold	25,000
General and administrative expense	2,500

7. Preparation of a Multistep Income Statement. You have obtained the following information for the Ponce Picke Factory. Prepare a multistep income statement for the year ended December 31, 1987.

Sales	$125,000
Sales returns and allowances	5,000
Purchases	50,000
Ending inventory	12,000
Beginning inventory	5,000
Depreciation expense*	7,000
Insurance expense*	2,500
Salaries expense*	20,000
Delivery expense	1,500
Interest expense	3,000
Rental revenue	1,000

*Split 60% general and administrative expense and 40% selling expense.

8. Income Statement and Balance Sheet Analysis. Answer each of the following two independent questions:

a. The Ching Toy Company had net income for the year ended December 31, 1987 of $25,000. Its total beginning assets were $1,000,000 and its total ending assets were $1,500,000. Its total owner's equity at January 1, 1987 was $500,000 and on December 31, 1987 was $700,000. Calculate the return on total assets and the return on owner's equity.

b. On January 1, 1987, McGinn's Book Store had current assets of $672,000 and current liabilities of $531,000. At the end of the year, its current assets increased to $783,750 and its current liabilities to $670,325. Determine the increase or decrease in working capital that occurred during the year. Did the current ratio change? If so, by how much?

9. Financial Statement Analysis. You have obtained the following data for the Marigold Company for the year ended December 31, 1987. (Some income statement items are missing.)

Cost of goods sold	$390,000
General and administrative expense	55,000
Interest expense	5,000
Net income	66,000
Sales	600,000

Answer each of the following questions:
a. What is the gross margin on sales?
b. What is the amount of income from operations?
c. What is the amount of selling expenses?

d. What is the gross margin percentage?

e. If the return on total assets is 2.5%, what was the average total assets during 1987?

f. If the return on owner's equity is 5%, what was the amount of average owner's equity during 1987?

g. What is the profit margin percentage?

10. **Balance Sheet Analysis.** Answer each of the following two independent questions:

a. State whether each of the following transactions would increase, decrease, or have no effect on (1) working capital and (2) current ratio of a business. Assume that the firm is in a positive working capital position.

1. Cash received on account.

2. Prepaid insurance is written off to expense in an adjusting entry.

3. Supplies are purchased on account.

4. An automobile is purchased. The firm makes a down payment and finances the remainder through a four-year bank loan, due in monthly installments.

5. A cash payment is made on an open account payable.

b. State whether each of the following transactions would increase, decrease, or have no effect on a debt to equity ratio which is now 32%.

1. Cash is received on account.

2. The liability, unearned rent, is written off to income in an adjusting entry.

3. The firm borrows $100,000 from a bank. The principal and interest on the loan are due in 18 months.

4. Excess land is sold; the firm recorded a $100,000 loss on the sale.

11. **Income Statement Analysis.** The Furillo Company makes both cash and credit sales. You have obtained the following data from the company's records:

Credit sales for November	$210,000
Cash received in November:	
From October credit sales	86,000
From November credit sales	43,000
From November cash sales	70,000
Gross margin on sales	30%
Profit margin	16%

Selling expenses are one-third of general and administrative expenses

Required:

Prepare a single-step income statement for the month ended November 30, 1987.

Problem Set A

6A-1. Preparation of a Classified Balance Sheet. The accounts included in the post-closing trial balance of the Vera Video Games Company are presented below (in alphabetical order):

Vera Video Games Company
Accounts in Post-Closing Trial Balance
December 31, 1987

Accounts payable	$10,000
Accounts receivable	30,000
Accumulated depreciation—Plant and equipment	25,000
Bonds payable	25,000
Cash	17,000
City taxes payable	8,000
Copyright	10,000
Current maturities of long-term debt	14,000
Inventories	60,000
Investments, long-term	5,000
Marketable securities, held for temporary investment	10,000
Mortgage payable, less current portion	20,000
Plant and equipment	70,000
Prepaid insurance	5,000
Salaries payable	5,000
Supplies on hand	1,000
Unearned commissions	10,000
V. Spraeck, capital	91,000

Required:

Prepare in good form a classified balance sheet at December 31, 1987.

6A-2. Preparation of a Classified Income Statement. The revenue, expense, and related accounts of the Weiss Company for the year ended June 30, 1987 are listed below (in alphabetical order):

Advertising expense*	$ 2,500
Beginning inventory	10,000
Delivery expense*	6,850
Depreciation expense	10,000
Ending inventory	5,000
E. Weiss, capital, beginning	42,750
Insurance expense	1,000
Interest expense	500
Purchases	20,000
Repairs and maintenance expense	2,500
Salaries expense*	5,000
Sales	75,000
Supplies expense	750

*Indicates selling expenses. Other expenses besides interest are general and administrative. Included in the salaries of $5,000 are $1,000 of withdrawals paid to the owner, E. Weiss.

Required:

a. Prepare in good form a single-step income statement.
b. Prepare in good form a multistep income statement.
c. Prepare in good form a statement of owner's equity.

6A–3. Ratio Analysis. The following financial data are for the Weldon Wire Company:

Weldon Wire Company
Comparative Balance Sheet
December 31

Assets	1987	1986
Cash	$ 25,000	$ 15,000
Accounts receivable	45,000	30,000
Inventories	140,000	120,000
Plant and equipment, net	230,000	240,000
Total assets	$440,000	$405,000

Liabilities and Owner's Equity	1987	1986
Current liabilities	$ 60,000	$ 50,000
Long-term debt	140,000	150,000
Owner's equity	240,000	205,000
Total liabilities and owner's equity	$440,000	$405,000

Weldon Wire Company
Comparative Income Statement
For the Year Ended December 31

	1987	1986
Sales	$800,000	$700,000
Cost of goods sold	600,000	550,000
Gross margin on sales	200,000	150,000
Operating expenses	98,000	75,000
Net income	$102,000	$ 75,000

Required:

a. Compute the following ratios for 1986 and 1987:
   1. Working capital.
   2. Current ratio.
   3. Debt to equity ratio.
   4. Debt to total assets.
   5. Gross margin percentage.
   6. Profit margin percentage.
   7. Return on total assets (1985 total assets, $390,000).
   8. Return on owner's equity (1985 owner's equity, $175,000).

b. Have the firm's performance and financial position improved from 1986 to 1987? Explain.

6A–4. Preparation and Analysis of Financial Statements. The following accounts have been taken from the December 31, 1987 adjusted trial balance of the Porter Press Company. They are not listed in any particular order, and all accounts have normal balances.

Notes receivable—Due in 6 months	$ 5,000
Accumulated depreciation—Building	14,000
P. Porter, capital	60,000
Sales	600,000
Beginning inventory	60,000
Salaries expense	45,000
Cash	25,000
Accounts payable	38,000
Long-term debt	39,000
Land	12,000
Building	50,000
Rent expense	22,000
Gain on sale of land	5,000
Accounts receivable	6,000
Prepaid assets	2,000
Accrued salaries and other payables	8,000
Interest payable	5,000
Depreciation expense	18,000
Machinery and equipment	20,000
Patents	6,000
Repairs and maintenance expense	6,000
Interest expense	20,000
Purchases	420,000
Ending inventory	30,000
Accumulated depreciation—Machinery and equipment	7,000
Supplies expense	9,000
Long-term investments	15,000

Required:

a. Prepare in good form the following statements:

1. Balance sheet.

2. Multistep income statement.

3. Single-step income statement.

Assume that all expenses other than interest are split into one-third selling and two-thirds general and administrative.

b. In what circumstances do you feel that a multistep income statement is more useful than a single-step?

c. Based on the above data, calculate:

1. Working capital.

2. The current ratio.

3. The debt to equity ratio.

4. Debt to total assets.

5. Gross margin percentage.

6. Profit margin percentage.

7. Return on total assets (1986 total assets, $140,000).

8. Return on owner's equity (1986 owner's equity, $58,000).

6A–5. Balance Sheet Analysis. Below is a partial list of the accounts of the Jackson Company. Referring to these figures, where appropriate, answer the following questions:

Accounts payable	$13,000	J. Jackson, capital	$10,000
Accounts receivable	25,000	Long-term investments	50,000
Accrued interest payable	2,000	Note payable, due in 15 months	20,000
Cash	20,000	Note receivable, due in 11 months	5,000
Current portion of long-term debt	5,000	Sales	40,000
Inventories	30,000		

a. What is the amount of working capital?

b. What is the current ratio?

c. For this question only, assume that the Jackson Company has a current ratio of 2:1. If the company purchased $10,000 of inventory on account, what effect (that is, increase, decrease, or no effect) would this transaction have on:
  1. Working capital?
  2. Current ratio?

d. Again for this question only, assume that the company has the same current ratio of 2:1. If the company purchased land for $3,000 cash, what effect would this transaction have on:
  1. Working capital?
  2. Current ratio?

e. Assume that the company has the same current ratio as in Item d and made the same purchase of land, except that it was on account and due three years from now. Assume that there is no interest on the note. What effect would this transaction have on:
  1. Working capital?
  2. Current ratio?

6A–6. Analysis of Financial Statements. The financial statements for the R.J.P. Company are presented below. (All accounts are listed.)

R.J.P. Company
Balance Sheet
December 31, 1987

Assets		Liabilities and Owner's Equity	
Cash	$25,000	Accounts payable	$ d
Accounts receivable	a	Total liabilities	e
Total current assets	45,000	Owner's equity	f
Property, plant, and equipment	b		
Total assets	$ c	Total liabilities and owner's equity	$ g

R.J.P. Company
Income Statement
For the Year Ended December 31, 1987

Revenues		
Sales		$ h
Expenses		
Cost of goods sold	$35,000	
Selling	20,000	
General and administrative	6,000	
Interest	900	
City taxes	1,100	
Total expenses		$ i
Net income		$ j

In addition, you have gathered the following data:

Working capital = $7,500
Current ratio = 1.2:1
Debt to equity ratio = 1.25
Gross margin percentage = 50%
Profit margin percentage = 10%

Required:

Complete the financial statements of R.J.P. Company by determining the amounts of Items a through j.

CHAPTER 6

Problem Set B

6B–1. Preparation of a Classified Balance Sheet. Presented below are selected accounts for the Stoddard Shoe Store at July 31, 1987. (All accounts have normal balances.)

Accounts payable	$10,000
Accounts receivable	12,000
Buildings, net	75,000
Cash	15,000
Current portion of long-term debt	2,000
K. Stoddard, capital	?
Interest payable	900
Inventories	10,000
Investments held for temporary investment	5,000
Long-term investments	7,000
Mortgage payable, less current portion	10,000
Furniture and fixtures, net	17,000
Prepaid insurance	1,000
Salaries payable	4,500

Required:
Prepare in good form a classified balance sheet.

6B–2. Preparation of a Classified Income Statement. Greenman Art Studio opened on January 2, 1987. During the year, sales amounted to $75,000. Expenses and related items during the year were: inventory purchases, $25,000; supplies expense, $15,000; depreciation, $5,000; salaries, $12,000; telephone and utilities, $5,000; insurance, $2,000; and ending inventory, $5,000. Greenman also has rental revenue of $13,000, and she withdrew $5,000 during the year for her own personal use. All operating expenses are split into 60% selling and 40% general and administrative.

Required:
  a. Prepare in good form a single-step income statement for the year ended December 31, 1987.
  b. Prepare in good form a multistep income statement for the year ended December 31, 1987.
  c. Prepare in good form a statement of owner's equity for the year ended December 31, 1987. Assume that Greenman opened the studio with an initial investment of $40,000.

6B–3. Ratio Analysis. The following financial data are taken from the records of the Compeq Company:

The Compeq Company
Comparative Balance Sheet
December 31

Assets	1987	1986
Cash	$ 30,000	$ 21,000
Accounts receivable	4,000	7,000
Inventory	240,000	215,000
Property, plant, and equipment, net	40,000	40,000
Total assets	$314,000	$283,000
Liabilities and Owner's Equity		
Current liabilities	$ 45,000	$ 33,000
Noncurrent liabilities	109,000	100,000
Owner's equity	160,000	150,000
Total liabilities and owner's equity	$314,000	$283,000

The Compeq Company
Comparative Income Statement
For the Year Ended December 31

	1987	1986
Sales	$500,000	$430,000
Cost of goods sold	220,000	180,000
Gross margin on sales	280,000	250,000
Operating expenses	190,000	165,000
Net income	$ 90,000	$ 85,000

Required:

   a. Compute the following ratios for 1986 and 1987:

     1. Working capital.

     2. Current ratio.

     3. Debt to equity.

     4. Debt to total assets.

     5. Gross margin percentage.

     6. Profit margin percentage.

     7. Return on total assets (1985 total assets, $251,000).

     8. Return on owner's equity (1985 owner's equity, $140,000).

   b. Have the firm's performance and financial position improved from 1986 to 1987? Explain.

6B–4. Preparation and Analysis of Financial Statements. The following accounts were taken from the June 30, 1987 adjusted trial balance of the Sun Company. They are not listed in any order, and all accounts have normal balances.

Cash	$ 30,000
Interest payable	1,500
Buildings	100,000
L. Moon, capital	205,000
Salaries expense	88,000
Ending inventory	120,000
Supplies expense	2,000
Supplies on hand	1,000
Accumulated depreciation—Buildings	25,000
Accounts payable	25,000
Marketable securities	7,000
Long-term investments	10,000
Beginning inventory	100,000
Depreciation expense	28,000
Interest expense	42,000
Sales	800,000
Bonds payable, less current portion	129,000
Copyright	20,000
Accumulated depreciation—equipment	6,000
Prepaid assets	2,000
Current portion of bonds payable	5,000
Accrued liabilities	8,500
Equipment	10,000
Land	60,000
Purchases	570,000
Rent expense	24,000
Accounts receivable	45,000

Required:

   a. Prepare in good form the following statements:

     1. Balance sheet.

     2. Multistep income statement.

3. Single-step income statement.

Assume that all expenses other than interest are split into one-quarter selling and three-quarters general and administrative.

b. In what circumstances do you think that a multistep income statement is more useful than a single-step statement?

c. Based on the above data, calculate:

1. Working capital.
2. Current ratio.
3. Debt to equity ratio.
4. Debt to total assets.
5. Gross margin percentage.
6. Profit margin percentage.
7. Return on total assets (June 30, 1986 total assets, $250,000).
8. Return on owner's equity (June 30, 1986 owner's equity, $180,000).

6B–5. Balance Sheet Analysis. Below is a partial list of the accounts for the Diamond Company. Referring to these figures, where appropriate, answer the following questions:

Accounts payable	$28,000	Investment, long-term	$ 20,000
Accounts receivable	45,000	Long-term debt	30,000
Interest payable	12,000	Notes receivable, due in 12 months	5,000
Cash	30,000	M. Diamond, capital	45,000
Current portion of long-term debt	30,000	Sales	400,000
Inventories	60,000		

Required:

a. What is the amount of working capital?

b. What is the current ratio?

c. For this question only, assume that the company has a current ratio of 3:1. If the company purchased $5,000 of inventory on account, what effect (that is, increase, decrease, or no effect) would this transaction have on:

1. Working capital?
2. Current ratio?

d. Again for this question assume that the company has a current ratio of 3:1. If the company purchased some equipment for $10,000 cash, what effect would this transaction have on:

1. Working capital?
2. Current ratio?

e. Assume the same current ratio as in Item d and the same purchase, except now assume that the equipment purchased was on account with the payable due in two years. For simplicity, assume that there is no interest on the note. What effect would this transaction have on:

1. Working capital?
2. Current ratio?

6B–6. Analysis of Financial Statements. The financial statements of the Craft Company are presented below and on the top of page 266. (All accounts are listed.)

The Craft Company
Balance Sheet
December 31, 1987

Cash	$8,000	Accounts payable	$ e
Accounts receivable	a	Long-term debt	10,000
Total current assets	b	Total liabilities	f
Plant and equipment, net	c	Owner's equity	g
Total assets	$ d	Total liabilities and owner's equity	$ h

The Craft Company
Income Statement
For the Year Ended December 31, 1987

Revenues		
Sales		$ i
Expenses		
Cost of goods sold	$ j	
Operating expenses	14,000	
Interest	k	
Repairs	5,000	
Total expenses		43,500
Net income		$ l

In addition, you have determined the following data:

Working capital	$10,000
Current ratio	3.5:1
Debt to equity ratio	0.7
Gross margin percentage	52%
Profit margin percentage	13%

Required:

Based on the above data, complete the financial statements by determining the amounts of Items a through l.

Understanding Financial Statements

A. The financial statements on pages 257 and 258 were taken from the annual report of Carter Hawley Hale Stores (a group of large department stores on the West Coast). February 1, 1986 refers to year-end 1985 and February 3, 1985 refers to year-end 1984.

Required:

Answer the following questions based on the financial statements on pages 257 and 258:
1. What type of income statement is presented?
2. Property, plant, and equipment are shown net. What does this mean?
3. Explain the difference between accounts payable and accrued liabilities.
4. Explain the term *accumulated earnings*.
5. Compute the following data for year-end 1985 and 1984:
    a. Working capital.
    b. Current ratio.
    c. Debt to equity ratio.
    d. Debt to total assets ratio.
    e. Gross margin percentage.
    f. Profit margin percentage.
    g. Return on total assets.
6. Would you say that the firm's financial performance and position have improved from 1985 to 1984? Explain.

B. The statements on pages 260–262 were taken from the annual report of Pacific Gas and Electric Company (a large West Coast utility):

Required:

a. In what ways do these statements differ from those of Safeway Stores? What do you think are the reasons for the differences in the format?

(In thousands, except per share data)	1985 52 Weeks	1984 53 Weeks	1983 52 Weeks
Sales	$3,977,913	$3,724,294	$3,101,682
Costs and expenses			
Cost of goods sold, including occupancy and buying costs	2,850,599	2,702,055	2,240,404
Selling, general, and administrative expenses	923,504	862,272	706,368
Interest expense and discount, net	131,235	117,237	92,345
	3,905,338	3,681,564	3,039,117
Earnings from continuing operations before nonoperating income and income taxes	72,575	42,730	62,565
Nonoperating income			
Loss on sale of Holt Renfrew	(2,450)		
Costs relating to unsolicited tender offer		(7,100)	
Gain on sale of joint venture interest			12,768
Gain on retirements of debentures			4,252
	(2,450)	(7,100)	17,020
Earnings from continuing operations before income taxes	70,125	35,630	79,585
Income taxes	22,100	8,500	24,200
Earnings from continuing operations	48,025	27,130	55,385
Discontinued operations			
Earnings (loss) from operations, net of income taxes of ($1,050) and $10,600		(510)	12,100
Gain on sale of Waldenbooks, net of income taxes of $29,850		63,050	
		62,540	12,100
Net earnings	$ 48,025	$ 89,670	$ 67,485
Primary earnings per common share			
Continuing operations	$ .92	$	$ 1.57
Discontinued operations		2.75	.36
	$ .92	$ 2.75	$ 1.93
Fully diluted earnings per common share			
Continuing operations	$	$ .83	$ 1.56
Discontinued operations		1.89	.34
	$ *	$ 2.72	$ 1.90

Carter Hawley Hale Stores, Inc.
Consolidated Balance Sheet

(In thousands)	February 1, 1986	February 2, 1985
Assets		
Current assets		
Cash	$ 18,147	$ 22,727
Accounts receivable, net	292,785	125,524
Merchandise inventories	776,831	717,300
Receivable on sale of Holt Renfrew	29,682	
Other current assets	41,416	39,487
	1,158,861	905,038
Property and equipment, net	855,494	823,569
Investment in finance subsidiaries	142,916	143,864
Other assets	77,496	74,735
	$2,234,767	$1,947,206
Liabilities and Shareholders' Equity		
Current liabilities		
Notes payable and current installments	$ 84,707	$ 50,370
Accounts payable	344,036	285,466
Accrued liabilities	158,967	134,562
Dividends payable	6,145	5,983
Current income taxes	8,355	16,933
Deferred income taxes	114,399	99,648
	716,609	592,962
Long term debt	551,613	396,654
Capital lease obligations	145,940	152,006
Other liabilities	57,857	55,922
Long term deferred income taxes	103,394	101,496
Redeemable preferred stock, $5 par value, stated		
at redemption value of $300 per share	300,000	300,000
Common stock, $5 par value	97,797	95,334
Other paid-in capital	149,957	140,358
Accumulated earnings	111,600	112,474
	$2,234,767	$1,947,206

b. What is the account, Construction in Progress, and why is it an asset?

c. What do you think that the account, Minority Interest in Subsidiary, is?

d. Compute the following data for 1981:
   1. Working capital.
   2. Current ratio.
   3. Return on total assets.

Financial Decision Case

Rebecca Webb is head of the loan department at Wilshire National Bank. She has been approached by two firms in the retail toy business. Each firm is requesting a nine-month term loan in order to purchase inventory for the holiday season. She must make her recommendation to the loan committee and has gathered the following data in order to make her analysis.

The Fun Toy Company was organized in early 1986. The first year of operations was fairly successful, as the firm earned net income of $45,000. Total sales for the year were $600,000, and total assets at year-end, December 31, 1986, were $350,000. A condensed balance sheet at September 30, 1987 follows. The firm is requesting a $100,000 loan.

Assets		Liabilities and Owner's Equity	
Cash	$ 60,000	Accounts payable	$ 70,000
Accounts receivable	65,000	Note payable, due 10/5/88	100,000
Inventory	125,000	Owner's equity	240,000
Prepaids	5,000		
Furniture and fixtures, net	155,000	Total liabilities	
Total assets	$410,000	and owner's equity	$410,000

The Toy Store, the other firm, has been in business for many years. The firm's net income is $100,000 on total sales of $2,000,000. Total assets at year-end, December 31, 1986, were $1,250,000. A condensed balance sheet at September 30, 1987 follows. The firm is seeking a $200,000 loan.

Assets		Liabilities and Owner's Equity	
Cash	$ 60,000	Accounts payable	$ 350,000
Accounts receivable	100,000	Current bank loan payable	150,000
Inventory	400,000	Long-term debt	400,000
Supplies	10,000	Owner's equity	500,000
Prepaids	5,000		
Property, plant, and equipment	825,000	Total liabilities	
Total assets	$1,400,000	and owner's equity	$1,400,000

Required:

a. Calculate the ratios that you think will help Rebecca Webb in her analysis.

b. Based on the above data and your further analyses, what should Rebecca Webb recommend to the loan committee regarding each firm's request? Explain your reasoning.

CONSOLIDATED BALANCE SHEETS

Pacific Gas and Electric Company

For the Years Ended December 31,	1985	1984	1983
	In Thousands (except per share amounts)		
Operating Revenues			
Electric	$5,819,983	$5,158,165	$3,905,814
Gas	2,610,998	2,671,538	2,740,885
Total Operating Revenues	8,430,981	7,829,703	6,646,699
Operating Expenses			
Operation			
Cost of Electric Energy	2,072,548	2,098,473	1,449,203
Cost of Gas Sold	1,749,207	1,823,218	1,842,571
Transmission	148,479	130,340	140,437
Distribution	173,081	171,907	177,798
Customer Accounts and Services	357,189	317,125	251,636
Administrative and General	591,926	510,015	439,436
Other	257,025	118,000	21,811
Total Operation	5,349,455	5,169,078	4,322,892
Maintenance	312,531	287,882	250,478
Depreciation	535,654	445,690	391,105
Gas Exploration	45,301	48,977	41,493
Income Taxes	652,669	637,674	555,323
Property and Other Taxes	166,012	137,014	125,536
Total Operating Expenses	7,061,622	6,726,315	5,686,827
Operating Income	1,369,359	1,103,388	959,872
Other Income and (Income Deductions)			
Allowance for Equity Funds Used During Construction	247,367	365,625	338,706
Interest Income	132,985	59,771	71,287
Minority Interest in Net Income of Subsidiary Companies	(13,525)	(14,123)	(12,552)
Reserve–Construction Projects	(6,712)	(59,137)	(103,858)
Disallowed Project Costs	(58,882)	(16,653)	(70,220)
Other–Net	32,000	101,446	101,428
Total Other Income and (Income Deductions)	333,233	436,929	324,791
Income Before Interest Expense	1,702,592	1,540,317	1,284,663
Interest Expense			
Interest on Long-term Debt	709,258	609,086	525,456
Other Interest Charges	55,588	70,960	62,201
Less Allowance for Borrowed Funds Used During Construction	(93,059)	(114,621)	(90,961)
Total Interest Expense	671,787	565,425	496,696
Net Income	1,030,805	974,892	787,967
Preferred Dividend Requirements	164,230	164,316	159,824
Earnings Available for Common Stock	$ 866,575	$ 810,576	$ 628,143
Weighted Average Common Shares Outstanding	326,838	309,367	292,107
Earnings Per Common Share	$2.65	$2.62	$2.15
Dividends Declared Per Common Share	$1.81	$1.69	$1.58

The accompanying notes to consolidated financial statements are an integral part of these statements.

CONSOLIDATED BALANCE SHEETS

Pacific Gas and Electric Company

December 31,	1985	1984*
	In Thousands	
Assets		
Plant in Service (at original cost)		
Electric	$13,591,161	$ 9,373,162
Gas	3,065,009	2,813,970
Total Plant in Service	16,656,170	12,187,132
Accumulated Depreciation	(4,806,255)	(4,314,088)
Net Plant in Service	11,849,915	7,873,044
Construction Work in Progress	2,852,691	5,471,744
Nuclear Fuel and Other Capital Leases	436,376	450,417
Gas Exploration Costs	264,865	262,672
Advances to Gas Producers	361,250	356,220
Construction Funds Held by Trustee	66,985	29,041
Investments		
LNG Partnerships	1,310	1,310
Alberta Natural Gas Company Ltd	45,802	42,703
ANGUS Chemical Company	32,981	28,979
Other Investments	26,275	16,291
Total Investments	106,368	89,283
Customer Conservation Loans Receivable (net of current portion $43,722,000 in 1985; $43,070,000 in 1984)	75,250	98,632
Current Assets		
Cash	7,759	3,220
Short-term Investments (at cost which approximates market)	374,035	75,526
Accounts Receivable		
Customers	721,606	705,197
Other	285,206	331,141
Allowance for Uncollectible Accounts	(9,899)	(10,970)
Regulatory Balancing Accounts Receivable	378,531	415,783
Inventories (at average cost)		
Fuel Oil	257,405	290,431
Gas Stored Underground	290,474	309,091
Materials and Supplies	170,301	126,431
Prepayments	27,607	18,605
Total Current Assets	2,503,025	2,264,455
Deferred Charges		
Diablo Canyon Adjustment Account	157,739	–
Project Costs Pending Regulatory Action	40,710	116,790
Unamortized Project Costs	137,865	121,837
Workers' Compensation and Disability Claims Recoverable	73,000	76,000
Unamortized Debt Expense	18,136	15,100
Other–Net	153,828	94,124
Total Deferred Charges	581,278	423,851
Total Assets	$19,098,003	$17,319,359

*Changed to conform to 1985 presentation.

The accompanying notes to consolidated financial statements are an integral part of these statements.

December 31,	1985	1984*
	In Thousands	
Capitalization and Liabilities		
Capitalization		
Common Stock	$ 1,686,741	$ 1,584,542
Additional Paid-in Capital	1,790,222	1,518,963
Reinvested Earnings	2,610,512	2,340,041
Common Stock Equity	6,087,475	5,443,546
Preferred Stock Without Mandatory Redemption Provision	1,427,451	1,427,451
Preferred Stock With Mandatory Redemption Provision	252,500	260,000
Long-term Debt	7,146,866	6,143,070
Total Capitalization	14,914,292	13,274,067
Customer Conservation Loans Funding	96,400	114,300
Other Noncurrent Liabilities		
Capital Lease Obligations	361,140	393,447
Customer Advances for Construction	119,435	117,163
Workers' Compensation and Disability Claims	73,000	76,000
Other	19,677	18,431
Total Other Noncurrent Liabilities	573,252	605,041
Current Liabilities		
Short-term Borrowings	520,435	491,225
Accounts Payable–Trade Creditors	547,304	613,664
Accounts Payable–Other	206,497	190,929
Accrued Taxes	29,648	33,846
Deferred Income Taxes–Current Portion	157,490	196,894
Long-term Debt–Current Portion	94,673	242,796
Capital Lease Obligations–Current Portion	82,796	59,651
Interest Payable	96,484	85,490
Dividends Payable	155,302	136,172
Amounts Due Customers	73,203	89,213
Other	100,038	99,362
Total Current Liabilities	2,063,870	2,239,242
Deferred Credits		
Deferred Investment Tax Credits	504,710	399,449
Deferred Income Taxes	783,316	434,840
Unamortized Gain Net of Loss on Reacquired Debt	26,769	68,603
Other	22,305	82,104
Total Deferred Credits	1,337,100	984,996
Minority Interest in Subsidiary Companies	113,089	101,713
Contingencies (Note 10)		
Total Capitalization and Liabilities	$19,098,003	$17,319,359

Internal Control, Accounting Systems, and the Role of Computers

7

LEARNING OBJECTIVES

After reading this chapter you should be able to:

1. State the principles of internal control and explain the attributes of a strong internal control system.
2. Explain the need for subsidiary ledgers for accounts receivable and accounts payable.
3. Discuss the need for specialized journals.
4. Record entries into the following specialized journals:
   a. Sales journal.
   b. Purchases journal.
   c. Cash receipts journal.
   d. Cash payments journal.
5. List the uses of computers in accounting.

In the first six chapters we explained how the accounting information system classifies, processes, and summarizes economic data. We used a simple accounting system based on a manually kept set of books. The main components of that system were the general journal and the general ledger. In this chapter we introduce you to more complex accounting systems employing specialized journals and ledgers. First we discuss the need for strong internal controls in the accounting system. Then we explore the design of accounting systems and end with the use of computers in various accounting applications.

An accounting system should be designed to meet a firm's specific information needs. Thus, the system can range from a simple manual system to a complex computerized on-line system with remote terminals spread across the entire country. Whether manual or computerized, the accounting system must process information efficiently, accurately, and on a timely basis. At the heart of any well-designed accounting system is a well-thought-out internal control system.

One of the principal responsibilities of management is to protect the assets under its control, ensure the accuracy and reliability of its accounting records, and see that its policies are carried out. **Internal control** is the organizational plan, including specific methods and procedures, that management develops to meet these responsibilities. Specifically, internal control is formally defined as:

> the plan of organization and all of the coordinate methods and measures adopted within a business to safeguard its assets, check the accuracy and reliability of its accounting data, promote operational efficiency, and encourage adherence to prescribed policies.[1]

A strong internal control system will contain both administrative and accounting controls. **Administrative controls** include the plan of organization and the procedures and records that are concerned with the decision processes leading to management's authorization of transactions. That is, management uses administrative controls to ensure that its policies and procedures are carried out.

Accounting controls are the plan of organization and the procedures and records that are concerned with safeguarding the assets and the reliability of the financial records. These controls are more specific and are designed to ensure that:

a. Transactions are executed in accordance with management's general or specific authorization.
b. Transactions are recorded as necessary (1) to permit preparation of financial statements in conformity with generally accepted accounting principles or any other criteria applicable to such statements and (2) to maintain accountability for assets.
c. Access to assets is permitted only in accordance with management's authorization.
d. The recorded accountability for assets is compared with the existing assets at reasonable intervals and appropriate action is taken with respect to any differences.[2]

In order for a firm to have a sound system of internal control, both administrative and accounting controls must be present. The administrative controls provide the overall framework in which the specific accounting controls operate. If management is not interested in maintaining administrative controls, specific accounting controls cannot ensure that the firm's assets are being safeguarded.

---

[1] *AICPA Professional Standards* (Chicago: Commerce Clearing House, 1983), vol. 1, sec. AU 320.09.

[2] Ibid., AU 320.28.

Necessity of Internal Controls

Internal controls are necessary because accounting systems are designed and run by people, and people make errors. These errors may be either true mistakes or deliberate actions. There have been numerous instances in which large corporations have restated their financial reports because of inadvertent errors in the accounting records. Recently, a large personal computer company discovered that it had not accounted for millions of dollars of inventory. Poor record keeping rather than fraud appears to have been the reason.

There are situations, however, in which individuals falsify accounting records in order to steal or embezzle. In the early 1980s, one individual stole huge sums of money from Wells Fargo Bank by daily making a simple accounting entry in the bank's computer system. A strong internal control system is necessary to minimize these events and their associated losses.

Recently, a strong impetus for internal controls resulted from payments that U.S. corporations made to foreign officials to obtain business. In many cases these payments were considered legal in the foreign country, although many in the United States considered them a violation of good business ethics. Furthermore, many of these questionable payments were made by large, decentralized multinational firms, the top executives of which did not even know about the payments.

Because of these and other events, both the American Institute of CPAs (AICPA) and the U.S. Congress mandated the maintenance of a strong system of internal control. In its auditing guidelines, the AICPA stated that the system of internal control should be under the continuing supervision of management to determine that it is functioning as prescribed and is modified as appropriate for changes in condition.[3]

Congress, alarmed by the number of questionable payments to foreign officials, passed the Foreign Corrupt Practices Act. This act holds management accountable for developing and maintaining a strong internal control system that would prevent such payments. This act requires every publicly held corporation to maintain such a system of internal control. Furthermore, the act requires that the system of internal control limit the use of corporate assets to the purposes designated by management and that the accounting records be compared with the assets owned by the firm.

Attributes of a Strong Internal Control System

The design of an internal control system and the procedures utilized should be tailored to the firm's specific needs. However, a well-designed internal control system will center on a properly designed accounting system and include sound personnel and personnel practices and the separation of duties.

A Well-Designed Accounting System

A strong internal control system is difficult to implement without a well-designed accounting system. This accounting system should provide accounting controls over the firm's assets, liabilities, revenues, and expenses. Whether the accounting system is manual or automated, it should provide for adequate management authorizations and internal checks and balances. The system should be well documented with accounting manuals. Surprise checks should be made periodically to ensure that these procedures are being carried out and that the firm's assets are being safeguarded.

[3]Ibid., AU 320.31.

Sound Personnel and Personnel Policies

Any internal control system is dependent on the people who run it. Individuals should be placed in positions commensurate with their abilities. Good personnel policies include the rotation of people in key positions, the requirement that all employees take an annual vacation, and the bonding of individuals who handle cash or other liquid assets. Bonding means checking employees and insuring the company against theft by them.

Separation of Duties

There should be a clear separation of duties within the accounting function. That is, those individuals who have responsibility for and control over a particular asset should not also account for it. For example, the individual in the organization who handles cash receipts should not also handle accounts receivable or prepare the bank reconciliation. This makes it more difficult for one individual to steal the company's assets.

Limitations to Internal Control Systems

No system of internal control can be completely foolproof. This is especially true if top management is trying to override the system. Even if possible, the costs of completely foolproofing the system would probably outweigh the benefits derived. However, a properly designed and executed system can eliminate many potential problems and offer management a reasonable assurance that its policies are being carried out and that the firm's assets are being safeguarded.

Accounting Systems Components

An accounting system must be designed to meet the needs of the specific firm. However, most accounting systems will contain a strong internal control system, discussed previously, and subsidiary ledgers and specialized journals.

The Need for Subsidiary Ledgers

The need for timely and accurate information, as well as good internal control procedures, requires that certain backup accounts be maintained. To illustrate, management needs to know not only the total of its accounts receivable but also the amount that each individual customer owes. The same type of information is needed in regard to payables. Management needs to know the total it owes its various vendors as well as how much it owes its individual vendors and when each payment is due. Similar backup information is often necessary for such items as prepaid insurance and plant and equipment.

The main, or primary, account is often called a **controlling account** and is maintained in the general ledger. For example, the general ledger contains an account called Accounts Receivable. It shows summary information about the beginning balance, the total of all sales on account for the period, the total cash collected on account during the period, and the total owed by all of the firm's customers at the end of the period.

Backup accounts for each individual customer are also maintained. These are called **subsidiary accounts** and are placed in a subsidiary accounts receivable ledger. A subsidiary ledger is separate from the general ledger. It contains a set of related accounts whose balances in total will equal the balance in the controlling account. Each individual account in the subsidiary accounts receivable ledger should show the customer's name, address, credit rating, credit limit, and other vital collection information. An example of such a subsidiary account follows. The account in this example is a three-column ledger account; that is, there's only one column for the balance. This represents the fact that those accounts that normally have debit balances do not need to be specified as debits. Furthermore, those accounts that normally have credit balances, do not need to be specified as credits.

ACCOUNTS RECEIVABLE SUBSIDIARY LEDGER

Name: Thomas Hunter   Account No.   4

Address: 125 East 55th Street   Credit Limit: $2,500

East Rutherford, NJ 01908   Sale Terms: 2/10

Date	Post Ref.	Debit	Credit	Balance
June 1				201.48
2	SJ-1	1,500.00		1,701.48
12	CR-5		1,500.00	201.48

Similar subsidiary accounts are maintained for payables and, depending on the firm's needs, for other accounts such as Property, Plant, and Equipment. For example, the general ledger account Equipment shows the historical cost of the total equipment owned by the firm. Often, backup cards are maintained for each item of equipment. These cards show such information as the cost of each item; its estimated life; its salvage, or residual value; and its insurance coverage. These individual cards serve as a subsidiary ledger to the controlling Equipment account. The number and detail of the subsidiary accounts depend on the needs of the firm's management.

Posting to Subsidiary Accounts

When subsidiary accounts are maintained, it is necessary to post journal entries to both the general ledger or controlling account and the subsidiary account. Thus, if an entry is made to record a sale on account, two postings must be made, one to the general ledger receivable account and the other to the individual subsidiary Accounts Receivable. To maintain control, postings to subsidiary accounts should be made daily. Postings to general ledger accounts need to be made only periodically. Similar posting procedures are followed for subsidiary Accounts Payable and any other subsidiary accounts that are maintained.

To demonstrate these procedures, we will record and post three representative entries related to accounts receivable, sales on account, a sales return, and collections on account. Assume that at the beginning of the current year, in this case 1987, The LA Company's accounts receivable totaled $6,000 and comprised five customers with the following account balances:

Customer	Account No.	Account Balance
A. Abbot	001	$1,250
B. Battle	002	750
L. Lloyd	003	2,000
O. Ort	004	400
Q. Quint	005	1,600
Total		$6,000

Sales for January 2, 1987 were $1,500 and were recorded in the general journal as follows:

Date	Explanation		Ref.	Debit	Credit
1987					
Jan. 2	Accounts Receivable		200	1,500	
	Sales		600		1,500
	To record credit sales to the following customers:				
	B. Battle	$700	002		
	O. Ort	300	004		
	Q. Quint	500	005		

On January 10, O. Ort returned $100 of the merchandise that she purchased on account on January 2. This entry is recorded as follows:

Date	Explanation	Ref.	Debit	Credit
1987				
Jan. 10	Sales Returns and Allowances	610	100	
	Accounts Receivable	200		100
	To record return of merchandise by O. Ort.	004		

Finally, on January 12, the firm received $5,300 of cash on account from various customers. The following entry was made to record these collections:

Date	Explanation		Ref.	Debit	Credit
1987					
Jan. 12	Cash		100	5,300	
	Accounts Receivable		200		5,300
	To record collections on account from the following customers:				
	A. Abbot	$1,250	001		
	B. Battle	750	002		
	L. Lloyd	1,500	003		
	O. Ort	600	004		
	Q. Quint	1,200	005		

The general ledger account Accounts Receivable and the subsidiary accounts are shown on the top of page 269. T accounts, rather than the running balance form, are used for convenience. Each entry is posted to both the appropriate general ledger accounts and the individual customer accounts. Postings to the subsidiary ledger accounts are indicated by noting the customer's account number in the Ref. column. Postings to the general ledger accounts are likewise indicated by noting the general ledger accounts in the Ref. column.

At the end of the accounting period, after the postings have been completed, a list is made of all the individual subsidiary accounts. This **accounts receivable trial balance,** often called a **schedule of accounts receivable,** is totaled, and the total should equal the balance in the related general ledger account. If these totals are not equal, this indicates a posting or similar error. The schedule of accounts receivable for the customers in our example is shown following the general ledger and subsidiary ledger accounts on page 269.

General Ledger				Subsidiary Ledger			

General Ledger

Accounts Receivable   **200**

1/1/87 Bal. 6,000	1/10 100
1/2 1,500	1/12 5,300
1/12 Bal. 2,100	

Subsidiary Ledger

A. Abbot   **001**

1/1/87 Bal. 1,250	1/12 1,250
1/12 0	

B. Battle   **002**

1/1/87 Bal. 750	1/12 750
1/2 700	
1/12 Bal. 700	

L. Lloyd   **003**

1/1/87 Bal. 2,000	1/12 1,500
1/12 Bal. 500	

O. Ort   **004**

1/1/87 Bal. 400	1/10 100
1/2 300	1/12 600
1/12 Bal. 0	

Q. Quint   **005**

1/1/87 Bal. 1,600	1/12 1,200
1/2 500	
1/12 Bal. 900	

The LA Company
Schedule of
Accounts Receivable
January 31, 1987

Accounts		Amount
A. Abbot	001	$ 0
B. Battle	002	700
L. Lloyd	003	500
O. Ort	004	0
Q. Quint	005	900
Total		$2,100

Specialized Journals

The need for subsidiary accounts and the need to process information efficiently and on a timely basis necessitate the use of specialized journals. A **specialized journal** is one that is designed to handle certain transactions such as cash receipts or sales. As we will see, the use of specialized journals significantly reduces the amount of time necessary to record transactions and post them to the ledgers.

Most of the firm's transactions can be classified into four groups. These groups, as well as the specialized journal used to record the appropriate transactions, are shown below:

Transaction	Specialized Journal	Posting Abbreviation
Sales of merchandise on credit	Sales journal	SJ
Purchase of merchandise on credit	Purchases journal	PJ
Receipts of cash	Cash receipts journal	CR
Payments of cash	Cash payments journal	CP

If a particular transaction does not fit into one of these groups, it is recorded in the general journal. This is the type of journal we have been using up to this point. However, for many firms, most transactions can be recorded in specialized journals.

For illustrative purposes, the following discussion is based on a manual accounting system. This means that one or more individuals must record the transactions by hand in the appropriate journals. These transactions must then be posted by hand to the appropriate general and subsidiary ledgers. The widespread use of microcomputers has enabled even small firms to automate their accounting systems. Later we describe how the accounting system can be computerized.

The specialized journals that we illustrate are examples of those found in many manually kept sets of books, but they are not the only types used. Many firms design their own specialized journals to meet their particular needs.

The Sales Journal

The **sales journal,** sometimes called the credit sales journal, is used to record all sales made on account. The sales journal for the Fortune Retail Store is shown in Exhibit 7–1 on page 271. All the sales on account for the month of June are shown in this journal; cash sales are recorded in the cash receipts journal. Sales invoices are the primary inputs into this journal. In this example, we assume that all sales are made on terms of 2/10, n/30 and that the gross method is used to record sales discounts. This way, each account receivable is shown at its full amount. Because the sales journal is used exclusively to record credit sales, the last column, labeled amount, represents both a debit to Accounts Receivable and a credit to Sales.

The use of the sales journal is illustrated by reviewing the June 2 entry. A sale made to Thomas Hunter is recorded by recording the date, his name, the sales invoice number, and the amount of the sale in the appropriate columns. No explanations are necessary; the sales journal records only one type of transaction, credit sales. The post reference (Ref.) column is completed when the entry is posted to Thomas Hunter's subsidiary Accounts Receivable ledger account.

Posting from the Sales Journal. Exhibit 7–1 also shows how postings are made from the sales journal to both the subsidiary and the general ledger accounts. Each individual sale is posted to its appropriate subsidiary account. After the posting is made, the account number or a check is placed in the Post Ref. column. The Post Ref. in the subsidiary ledger and controlling accounts is labeled SJ-1 to represent page 1 of the sales journal. Postings to the subsidiary

EXHIBIT 7–1
Sales Journal

Sales Journal					Page 1
Date	Account Debited	Invoice Number	Ref.	Amount	
June 2	Thomas Hunter	614	4	→ 1,500.00	
5	Arnold Hackett	615	10	→ 2,612.85	
9	A. B. Nolan	616	19	→ 589.75	
14	Jerry Myers	617	26	→ 1,450.00	
18	William Young	618	15	→ 3,799.90	
23	Frank Sills	619	23	→ 1,200.00	
				$11,152.50	Posted monthly
			Posted daily	1110/4011	

Accounts Receivable Subsidiary Ledger

Thomas Hunter   4

Date	Ref.	Debit	Credit	Balance
June 1				201.48
2	SJ-1	1,500.00		1,701.48

Arnold Hackett   10

Date	Ref.	Debit	Credit	Balance
June 1				156.90
5	SJ-1	2,612.85		2,769.75

Continue posting to other accounts

General Ledger

Accounts Receivable   1110

Date	Ref.	Debit	Credit	Balance
June 1				12,445.50
30	SJ-1	11,152.50		23,598.00

Sales   4011

Date	Ref.	Debit	Credit	Balance
June 30	SJ-1		11,152.50	11,152.50

ledger should be made daily to ensure that management has up-to-date knowledge of how much each customer owes. This knowledge can be used to make sure that individual customers have not exceeded their credit limits.

At the end of the month, the amount column in the journal is totaled. This total is then posted as a debit in the Accounts Receivable control account and as a credit to the general ledger Sales account. In the illustration shown in Exhibit 7–1, this amount is $11,152.50. The numbers under this amount are the account numbers for accounts receivable (1110) and sales (4011). Finally, at the end of the month, the accounts receivable trial balance is prepared.

Advantages of the Sales Journal. Using a sales journal significantly decreases the amount of work needed to record transactions in a manual system.

As noted, only one line is needed to record each transaction. It also is not necessary to write out an explanation of the transaction because only credit sales are recorded in the sales journal. Finally, the amount of time needed to post entries is reduced. Although each transaction must be posted to the subsidiary accounts receivable ledger, only the totals for the month have to be posted to the general ledger accounts. If a general journal were used to record credit sales, each transaction would have to be posted to both the subsidiary and the general ledger accounts. Even for a firm with only several hundred sales a month, using a sales journal can save considerable time.

Other Forms of the Sales Journal. Depending on the needs of the firm, other columns can be added to the sales journal. For example, if the seller offers a variety of credit terms to various customers, a credit terms column should be added. If the seller is subject to sales taxes, a column for sales taxes should be added. If this column is added, its total must be posted at month-end as a credit to the Sales Taxes Payable general ledger account.

The Purchases Journal

The **purchases journal,** sometimes called the credit purchases journal, is used mainly to record merchandise inventory purchases on credit. If these are the only transactions recorded in the purchases journal, then the journal would be similar to the one in Exhibit 7–2 on page 273. Purchase invoices are used to enter data into the journal. We are assuming that a periodic inventory system is in use and that all purchases are recorded at their gross amounts. Therefore, the amount column represents a credit to Accounts Payable and a debit to Purchases at the full invoice price.

Each purchase invoice is entered in the purchases journal on a single line. In Exhibit 7–2 the June 1 purchase is recorded by entering June 1 in the date column, the supplier's name (Super Cola) in the account credit column, and the purchase terms, invoice date, and amount in the appropriate columns. No explanations are necessary; the purchases journal only records one type of transaction, purchases on account.

Posting from the Purchases Journal. Postings from the purchases journal follow the same pattern as that of postings from the sales journal. Each day the individual purchases should be posted to the vendor's account in the accounts payable subsidiary ledger. At the end of the month the amount column in the journal is totaled, and this amount is posted as a debit in the general ledger Purchases account and as a credit in the general ledger Accounts Payable account. Finally, at the end of the month, a list of the individual subsidiary accounts is made. This list is often called an **accounts payable trial balance** or a **schedule of accounts payable.** The balance in this list is compared with the balance in the general ledger Accounts Payable account. This procedure helps verify that all the postings have been correctly made.

Other Forms of the Purchases Journal. Depending on the needs of the firm, other columns can be added to the purchases journal. For example, if a firm commonly pays freight and insurance on its purchases, columns can be added for these items. If used, the total of these columns would be posted to the general ledger accounts at the end of the month.

Cash Receipts Journal

The **cash receipts journal** is used to record all transactions involving the receipt of cash, including such transactions as cash sales, the receipt of a bank

EXHIBIT 7–2
Purchases Journal

Purchases Journal					Page 12
Date	Account Credited	Terms	Invoice Date	Ref.	Amount
June 1	Super Cola Bottling	2/10, n/30	6/1 /83	5	→ 1,700.00
6	Jones Farm	2/10, n/30	6/6 /83	11	→ 1,000.00
18	Mrs. Smith's Bakeries	n/30	6/17/83	8	→ 1,294.60
25	Wholesale Grocery Co.	2/10, n/30	6/25/83	15	→ 2,800.90
30	Jim's Snacks	n/30	6/30/83	16	105.00
					$6,900.50
			Posted daily		5011/2010

Accounts Payable Subsidiary Ledger

Super Cola Bottling   5

Date	Ref.	Debit	Credit	Balance
June 1				784.84
1	PJ-12		1,700.00	2,484.84

Jones Farm   11

Date	Ref.	Debit	Credit	Balance
June 1				0
6	PJ-12		1,000	1,000

General Ledger

Accounts Payable   2010

Date	Ref.	Debit	Credit	Balance
June 1				10,246.81
30	PJ-12		6,900.50	17,147.31

Purchases   5011

Date	Ref.	Debit	Credit	Balance
June 30	PJ-12	6,900.50		6,900.50

Continue posting to other accounts

loan, the receipt of a payment on account, and the sale of other assets such as marketable securities. An example of a common type of cash receipts journal is shown in Exhibit 7–3 on page 274. As this exhibit shows, a typical cash receipts journal has many columns. This is necessary because there are numerous transactions that result in a receipt of cash. The debit columns will always include a cash column and most likely a sales discounts column. Other debit columns could be used if the firm routinely entered into a particular transaction. In the journal shown in Exhibit 7–3, another debit column is the other accounts column. This column is divided into three parts—one for the name of the account; one for the post reference, in this case labeled Ref.; and one for the amount. If desired, the area for the name of the account in this column can be replaced by just an area for account numbers.

EXHIBIT 7–3
Cash Receipts Journal

Date		Explanation	Debits					Account Credited	Credits				
			Cash	Sales Discounts	Other Accounts				Accounts Receivable		Sales	Other Accounts	
					Account Title	Ref.	Amount		Ref.	Amount		Ref.	Amount
June	1	Cash sales	506.00								506.00		
	2	Invoice of May 18	184.61					Perry Alexander	17	184.61			
	10	Sale of marketable securities	2,000.00					Marketable securities Other income				1528 8021	1,800.00 200.00
	12	Invoice of June 1, less 2%	1,470.00	30.00				Thomas Hunter	4	1,500.00			
	15	Cash sales	1,200.00								1,200.00		
	20	Invoice of June 14, less 2%	1,421.00	29.00				Jerry Myers	26	1,450.00			
	22	Repayment— Employee adv.	200.00					Employee advances				1130	200.00
	30	Invoice of June 18	3,947.27					William Young	15	3,947.27			
			10,928.88	59.00						7,081.88	1,706.00		2,200.00
			(1010)	(8531)						(1110)	(4011)		(✔)

Monthly totals posted at end of month

General Ledger

Cash   1010

Date	Post Ref.	Debit	Credit	Balance
June 1				16,056.50
30	CR-8	10,928.88		26,985.38

Accounts Receivable   1110

Date	Post Ref.	Debit	Credit	Balance
June 1				12,445.50
30	SJ-1	11,152.50		23,598.00
30	CR-8		7,081.88	16,516.12

Marketable Securities   1528

Date	Post Ref.	Debit	Credit	Balance
June 1				5,000.00
10	CR-8		1,800.00	3,200.00

> Continue posting to other general ledger accounts

Subsidiary Accounts Receivable Ledger

Perry Alexander   17

Date	Post Ref.	Debit	Credit	Balance
June 1				184.61
2	CR-8		184.61	∅

Thomas Hunter   4

Date	Post Ref.	Debit	Credit	Balance
June 1				201.48
2	SJ-1	1,500.00		1,701.48
12	CR-8		1,500.00	201.48

> Continue posting to other subsidiary ledger accounts

The credit columns in a cash receipts journal will most often include both accounts receivable and sales. Again, other columns can be used depending on the type of routine transactions into which the firm enters. In our example in Exhibit 7–3, the only other credit column is for all other accounts. It is set up in the same way that the other column on the debit side is, except that the account title area is replaced by just a ref. column.

Other Subsidiary Ledger Accounts

To demonstrate the use of the cash receipts journal, assume that during June the Fortune Retail Store entered into the following transactions involving cash receipts:

- June 1: Cash sales totaled $506.
- June 2: Collected from Perry Alexander (account no. 17) $184.61 from sale made in May. No sales discount allowed.
- June 10: The firm sold marketable securities for $2,000 that it purchased for $1,800.
- June 12: Collected $1,470 on account from Thomas Hunter (account no. 4). Sales discount of $30 allowed.
- June 15: Cash sales totaled $1,200.
- June 20: Collected $1,421 on account from Jerry Myers (account no. 26). Sales discount of $29 allowed.
- June 22: Repayment of employee advances of $200.
- June 30: Collection on account from William Young (account no. 15). Total collected is $3,947.27 which represents outstanding balance of $147.37 on June 1 and subsequent sale on June 18. No discount allowed.

Each of these transactions is entered sequentially into the cash receipts journal in the appropriate column. For example, the cash sale on June 1 is recorded in the cash receipts journal by first entering June 1 in the date column. "Cash sales" are entered in the explanation column. The amount of $506 is then placed in both the cash debit column and the sales credit column. It is not necessary to make an entry in the account credited column, because the entry in the cash and the sales columns makes it clear that this is a cash sale. Other entries are made in a similar fashion.

Posting the Cash Receipts Journal to the Ledgers. As with the other journals, the cash receipts journal is posted in two stages. Any entries in the accounts receivable column should be posted daily to the subsidiary accounts receivable ledger. This ensures that the individual customers' accounts are up to date and accurately reflect the balance owed at that date. As these accounts are posted, the account number is entered into the post reference column. In the subsidiary ledger, the post reference is CR-8, which indicates that the entries came from page 8 of the cash receipts journal.

At the end of the month the different columns in the cash receipts journal are totaled. The totals from all the amount columns except for the other accounts column are posted to the appropriate general ledger accounts. Again, in the general ledger accounts the post reference CR-8 is made to indicate that these entries came from page 8 of the cash receipts journal.

The amounts in the other accounts column must be posted separately. Although these amounts are often posted at the end of the month, they could be posted more frequently. As each amount is posted, the account number is placed in the post reference column. A check is placed under the total of this column, as this total is not posted. The postings are shown in Exhibit 7–3 for the general ledger accounts Cash, Accounts Receivable, and Marketable Securities, and two selected subsidiary ledger accounts receivable accounts, Perry Alexander and Thomas Hunter.

The Cash Payments Journal

The **cash payments journal** is used to record the cash disbursements made by check, including payments on account, cash payments for merchandise purchases, payments for various expenses, and other loan payments.

A typical cash payments journal is shown in Exhibit 7–4 on page 276. This journal has a date column, a check number column, an explanation column, and at least two credit columns, one for cash and one for purchase discounts.

EXHIBIT 7–4
Cash Payments Journal

Page 6

Date	Check No.	Explanation	Credits		Other Accounts			Account Debited	Debits			Other Accounts	
			Cash	Purchases Discounts	Account Title	Ref.	Amount		Accounts Payable Ref.	Amount	Purchases	Ref.	Amount
June 1	498	Store lease	1,500.00					Lease expense				6531	1,500.00
1	499	Invoice of May 17	76.00					Ricco's Pizza	12	76.00			
2	500	Merchandise purchased	1,250.00								1,250.00		
3	501	Invoice of May 21	784.84					Super Cola	5	784.84			
9	502	Purchase of equipment	2,000.00		Loans payable	2620	8,000.00	Machinery—equipment				1520	10,000.00
10	503	Invoice of June 1, less 2%	1,660.00	40.00				Super Cola	5	1,700.00			
15	504	Paid managers' salary	2,200.00					Salaries				6011	2,200.00
16	505	Invoice of June 6, less 2%	980.00	20.00				Jones Farms	11	1,000.00			
25	506	Merchandise purchased	1,400.00								1,400.00		
30	507	Invoice of June 18	1,294.60					Mrs. Smith's Bakeries	8	1,294.60			
30	508	Loan repayment	120.00					Interest Notes payable				6641 2620	30.00 90.00
			13,265.44	60.00			8,000.00			4,855.44	2,650.00		13,820.00
			(1010)	(8031)			(✔)			(2010)	(5011)		(✔)

General Ledger

Cash 1010

Date		Post Ref.	Debit	Credit	Balance
June	1				16,056.50
	30	CR-8	10,928.88		26,985.38
	30	CP-6		13,265.44	13,719.94

Accounts Payable 2010

Date		Post Ref.	Debit	Credit	Balance
June	1				10,246.81
	30	PJ-12		6,900.50	17,147.31
	30	CP-6	4,855.44		12,291.87

Continue posting to other general ledger accounts

Subsidiary Accounts Payable Ledger

Ricco's Pizza 12

Date		Post Ref.	Debit	Credit	Balance
June	1				76.00
	1	CP-6	76.00		0

Super Cola 5

Date		Post Ref.	Debit	Credit	Balance
June	1				784.84
	1	PJ-12		1,700.00	2,484.84
	3	CP-6	784.84		1,700.00

Continue posting to other subsidiary ledger accounts

In the journal in Exhibit 7–4, the other credit column is for other accounts. If necessary, other specific account columns could be added if they were used routinely. The debit columns will include at least an accounts payable column, a purchases column, and an other accounts column. Again, other specific account columns could be added if needed. The main source of entries for this journal are check stubs and payment requests.

To demonstrate how entries are recorded in the cash payments journal, we assume that the Fortune Retail Store made the following cash payments during the month of June:

- June 1: Payment of store lease, $1,500.
- June 1: Paid Ricco's Pizza (account no. 12) for $76 invoice dated May 17. No discount taken.
- June 2: Cash purchase of $1,250.

- June 3: Paid to Super Cola (account no. 5) $748.84 for invoice dated May 21. No purchase discount taken.
- June 9: Purchase of equipment for $10,000 with 20% down payment.
- June 10: Paid to Super Cola $1,660 for invoice dated June 1. Discount taken.
- June 15: Paid manager's salary, $2,200, for first half of June.
- June 16: Paid $980 to Jones Farm for invoice dated June 6. Discount taken.
- June 25: Cash purchase of $1,400.
- June 30: Paid $1,294.60 to Mrs. Smith's Bakeries for invoice dated June 18. No discount allowed.
- June 30: Loan payment of $120, of which $30 is interest.

The entries in the cash payments journal are recorded and posted in a similar manner to those in the cash receipts journal. Thus, the entries are entered sequentially into the cash payments journal as they occur. The cash payments journal is also posted in two stages. Entries to the Accounts Payable account should be posted daily to the subsidiary accounts payable ledger. At the end of the month all amount columns are summed. All the totals, except those in the other columns, are posted to the appropriate general ledger accounts. The accounts in the other columns must be posted individually. They can be posted daily, monthly, or at other convenient intervals. Because the basic posting procedures are the same as those for the other journals, the actual postings are not shown in the exhibit.

The General Journal

The special-purpose journals just described can be used to record most of the transactions into which the firm is likely to enter. However, there are some transactions that do not involve sales, purchases, cash receipts, or cash payments or are too complex to fit conveniently into these journals. Examples are a sales or purchase return, a compound entry involving several accounts, and adjusting entries. These entries are most easily made in the general journal.

To illustrate, assume that the Fortune Retail Store entered into the following three transactions:

- June 5: Purchased $500 worth of wine from the Neuman Wine Company that arrived damaged. It was returned, and Fortune's account was reduced.
- June 17: A. Waller, a customer, returned some merchandise because it did not meet her needs. She received a $200 credit on her account.
- June 30: Depreciation expense for the month is $1,200.

These entries are recorded in the following general journal:

	General Journal			Page 6
Date	Explanation	Ref.	Debit	Credit
June 5	Accounts Payable—Neuman Wine	2010/23	500	
	Purchase Returns and Allowances	8040		500
	To record return of damaged merchandise.			
17	Sales Returns and Allowances	8541	200	
	Accounts Receivable—A. Waller	1110/12		200
	To record refund to customer for damaged goods.			
30	Depreciation Expense	6781	1,200	
	Accumulated Depreciation	1550		1,200
	To record monthly depreciation expense.			

The form of this journal is the same as what we used throughout the first six chapters of this book. You should note that the Receivables and Payables accounts must be posted twice. That is, the entry must be posted to both the appropriate subsidiary account and the controlling account. This posting is shown by noting both the particular controlling account number in the post reference column and the subsidiary ledger account number.

Internal Control and Special Journals

As we noted, separation of duties is an important aspect of internal control. In regard to special journals, if possible, different individuals should record transactions in each of the journals. Depending on the size and the complexity of the accounting department, a total separation of duties may not be possible. However, not all accounting personnel should have access to the general journal. Nonroutine transactions are recorded in this journal, and many of these transactions should be approved by the head of the accounting department or by someone with similar authority. On the other hand, routine transactions are recorded in the special journals and do not require authorization.

The Use of Computers in Accounting

In the last twenty years, there has been a tremendous increase in the use of computers in accounting, primarily to automate accounting systems. Computerized accounting systems are now found in businesses of all sizes and complexities. This development is due to the growth of data-processing services and the widespread use of microcomputers. Computers also perform analysis for management and provide word processing and communications for the timely dissemination of financial reports. In addition, computers are beginning to play an important role in all aspects of the public accounting profession.

Computerized Versus Manual Accounting Systems[4]

A computerized accounting system differs procedurally from a manual system. For example, an accounting information system consists of three phases:

INPUT
Economic events

PROCESSING
record, classify, and summarize

OUTPUT
financial statements

[4]This section draws heavily upon *On Guard Inc.: A Computerized Accounting Information System,* by Earl Weiss and Donald L. Raun, Macmillan Publishing Co., 1986, pp. 33–34.

The difference between a manual and a computerized system exists in the processing and output phases. The accounting procedures performed in a manual accounting system are described as follows.

INPUT

- **ANALYZE TRANSACTIONS (SOURCE DOCUMENTS)**

PROCESSING

- **RECORD JOURNAL ENTRIES**
- **POST TO GENERAL LEDGER**
- **ADJUST AND CLOSE**

OUTPUT

- **PREPARE TRIAL BALANCE**
- **PREPARE FINANCIAL STATEMENTS**
- **ANALYZE AND INTERPRET**

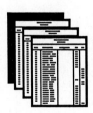 

A computerized accounting system makes use of the same input of raw data from source documents as does a manual accounting system, but the remaining procedures are performed automatically with total accuracy. Hours of manual processing can be accomplished in minutes. Current output is available on a continuous basis, and up-to-date financial statements can be prepared as often as needed without concern for time or cost. These benefits also extend to the very important function of analyzing and interpreting financial statements.

Data-processing Services

Data-processing services emerged when it became possible to input data from remote terminals. In effect, the data-processing service has a computer at its service center. Clients of the service lease or purchase terminals which are located on their premises. These terminals are used to input the various transactions into the main computer. This computer processes the data; the necessary journals are generated; the postings are made; and the financial statements are produced. In addition, such services as inventory control and payroll are often provided by these data-processing companies.

Microcomputers

The development of the microcomputer has made in-house computerized accounting systems available to even the smallest of companies. Software companies have devised accounting programs to run on various personal computers. These programs are easy to use and can handle the bookkeeping chores for firms of various sizes and complexities.

To illustrate how these systems work, we duplicated the transactions used to describe a manual system on a common accounting software program.[5] A sample of the output is presented in Exhibits 7–5 and 7–6. Exhibit 7–5 shows the sales journal, while Exhibit 7–6 shows the purchases journal. In a similar manner, cash receipts, cash purchases, and general journals are generated by the accounting program.

EXHIBIT 7–5

Fortune Retail Store
Sales Journal

SALES JOURNAL

Date	A/R Subs. Ref.	Customer	Invoice#	Amount
06/02	4	THOMAS HUNTER	614	1,500.00
06/05	10	ARNOLD HACKETT	615	2,612.85
06/09	19	A. B. NOLEN	616	589.75
06/14	26	JERRY MYERS	617	1,450.00
06/18	15	WILLIAM YOUNG	618	3,799.90
06/23	23	FRANK SILLS	619	1,200.00
TOTALS				11,152.50

EXHIBIT 7–6

Fortune Retail Store
Purchases Journal

PURCHASES JOURNAL

Date	A/P Subs. Ref.	Supplier	Invoice#	Terms	Amount
06/01	5	SUPER COLA BOTTLING	3142	2/10,n/30	1,700.00
06/06	11	JONES FARMS	217	2/10,n/30	1,000.00
06/18	8	MRS. SMITH'S BAKERIES	912	n/30	1,294.60
06/25	15	WHOLESALE GROCERY CO.	128	2/10,n/30	2,800.00
06/30	16	JIM'S SNACKS	618	n/30	105.00
TOTALS					6,900.50

[5]The software package used in this example was developed by IBM and BPI. However, for consistency, the form of the journals has been altered.

These software programs are relatively inexpensive and have a number of advantages over manual systems. The programs are extremely accurate, and if transactions are entered correctly, computational errors can be eliminated. Most of these software programs have subroutines that post entries after a set of transactions has been recorded. This means that both general and subsidiary ledger accounts can be updated daily. Thus management has up-to-date information on such accounts as Cash and Receivables. This information is valuable in providing data on receivable collections and cash flows.

The more sophisticated software programs have the ability to generate checks on the firm's printer. As these checks are printed, appropriate entries are made in the cash payments journal. Many of these same programs have payroll routines that are able to determine the firm's periodic payroll, generate the necessary payroll journals and ledgers, and supply the firm with the information required to prepare a variety of payroll tax forms.

Although these accounting software programs are usually versatile, they do have drawbacks. In many cases, the financial statement formats are fixed and cannot easily be changed. Since not all programs are designed to meet the needs of all firms, what is appropriate for a typical merchandising firm may not be best suited for a service or merchandising firm. Furthermore, these programs are limited by disk space as to the number of functions they can perform. Firms with complex accounting needs might require sophisticated office computers that can run more intricate programs.

Financial Analysis Program

The development of spreadsheet programs that can be used on personal computers has greatly enhanced the financial analysis capability of management. A **spreadsheet** is an empty matrix of rows and columns that are individually labeled by the user. Programs such as Visicalc, Supercalc, and Lotus 1-2-3 enable individuals to perform a variety of functions, including cash flow projections, depreciation schedules, inventory management, receivables and payables management, sales projections, and product line summaries. An example of an accounts payable management worksheet that was developed using a common spreadsheet program is reproduced in Exhibit 7–7. The purpose of this program is to show when payables should be paid in order to receive the discount and the amount of savings if the discount is taken.

EXHIBIT 7–7
Mike's Restaurant
Accounts Payable Schedule
October, 1987

Account Name	Invoice Amount	Invoice Day	Date Month	Year	Discount Percent	Days for Discount	Date to Get Discount	Discount Amount	Net Payable
Kojack Corp.	$ 1,200.00	2	10	85	2%	10	12-Oct.-85	$ 24.00	$ 1,176.00
Lite Co.	675.00	2	10	85	2	10	12-Oct.-85	13.50	661.50
LaJolla Corp.	1,575.00	3	10	85	2	0	03-Oct.-85	0.00	1,575.00
Luga Inc.	700.00	5	10	85	2	10	15-Oct.-85	14.00	686.00
Olympic Co.	3,000.00	5	10	85	1	10	15-Oct.-85	30.00	2,970.00
Ripech Corp.	788.00	7	10	85	2	15	22-Oct.-85	15.76	772.24
Levins Inc.	3,277.50	9	10	85	2	10	19-Oct.-85	65.55	3,211.95
Laird Walls	908.00	10	10	85	0	0	10-Oct.-85	0.00	908.00
Hours Corp.	2,200.00	13	10	85	1	15	28-Oct.-85	22.00	2,178.00
Industrial Co.	200.00	16	10	85	1	10	26-Oct.-85	2.00	198.00
Sonics	2,567.89	20	10	85	2	10	30-Oct.-85	51.36	2,516.53
Entertainment Co.	675.00	21	10	85	2	5	26-Oct.-85	13.50	661.50
Potporri Plus	3,567.00	24	10	85	2	10	03-Nov.-85	71.34	3,495.66
Cellular Co.	2,098.25	25	10	85	2	10	04-Nov.-85	41.96	2,056.29
Devices Corp.	1,990.00	29	10	85	1	10	08-Nov.-85	19.90	1,970.10
Totals	$25,421.64							$384.87	$25,036.77

Communications and Word Processing

Communications and word processing programs allow for the efficient preparation of reports as well as the communication of these reports to various users. In addition, advanced integrated software programs such as Framework and Symphony have greatly expanded the capabilities of personal computers in this area. These programs combine spreadsheets with data base management, communications, and word processing. They allow for the creation of a data base that can be used in several applications. Specific reports can be generated and then communicated to various users, either electronically or through print.

The importance of computers to accounting and the communication of financial information is illustrated in this *Forbes* interview with John C. (Sandy) Burton, former chief accountant of the Securities and Exchange Commission (SEC).

> He began by predicting that in 10 to 15 years corporate financial statements will be supplanted by a steady flow of computer-generated information. Under the present system, investors and analysts generally must wait until the end of a quarter for earnings information, and frequently to the end of a year for crucial balance-sheet information. This existing system reflects pre-computer-era difficulties in gathering data, Burton says. It took so long and cost so much back then that everyone settled for one common format. But, today, generating information is no problem, so the best method is to present the information to users—institutional analysts, mainly—via computer, as often as they wish and in as many formats as possible.
>
> In short, he thinks, investors shouldn't have to wait until July to learn about a sales or earnings slippage that may have begun in April.[6]

In addition to the continuous data base accounting predicted by Burton, the SEC's EDGAR (Electronic Data Gathering, Analysis, and Retrieval System) project will, in the near future, allow firms to file their traditional financial statements with the SEC electronically rather than by print. Eventually, individuals will have electronic access to this data base.

The Use of Computers in Public Accounting

The use of micro- and personal computers is beginning to have a significant impact on public accounting. CPA firms of all sizes are beginning to use these computers in various tax, audit, and management-consulting functions. For example, for many years tax return preparation has been automated. However, with the use of personal computers, tax planning is greatly enhanced. Furthermore, the ability to access data bases containing the latest tax laws and court cases will increase the efficiency and effectiveness of tax research.

Personal computers are playing a larger role in the audit function. Audit work papers can be standardized and stored on hard disks. This greatly reduces the time currently required for their preparation. Electronic spreadsheets can be used to facilitate account analysis, and word processing programs can be used to prepare audit programs and financial statements. Finally, communications programs assist auditors in transferring data between remote audit locations. These same programs are used to transfer data to the CPA firm's central computer, to be used in automated audit programs.

---

[6]Geoffrey Smith, "Toward a More Perfect Market," *Forbes*, December 17, 1984, p. 73.

1. *Designing accounting systems and the role of internal control.* Accounting systems should be designed to meet the needs of individual firms. These systems should process information efficiently, accurately, and on a timely basis. The system also must be designed to meet the firm's internal control needs, including the duplication of records and the separation of duties. Internal control is the plan of organization and all the methods and measures adopted by a business to safeguard its assets, check the reliability of its accounting data, promote operational efficiency, and encourage adherence to management policies. Such a system should ensure that:

   a. Only those transactions that are authorized by management are entered into.
   b. Transactions are properly recorded and allow the preparation of financial statements that are in accordance with generally accepted accounting principles.
   c. There is a separation of duties and only those individuals with proper authorization are given access to assets.
   d. Assets are periodically verified and differences reconciled.

2. *The need for subsidiary ledgers.* Management needs comprehensive backup information for certain accounts such as receivables and payables. This information is contained in the subsidiary ledgers. For example, the accounts receivable subsidiary ledger contains all the individual customer accounts. The balance in these accounts should equal the balance in the general ledger accounts receivable account. This general ledger account is often called a controlling account.

3. *Common specialized journals.* Specialized journals are used to record routine transactions of the same type. These transactions and the related specialized journals are:

Transaction	Specialized Journal
Sales of merchandise on credit	Sales journal
Purchase of merchandise on credit	Purchases journal
Receipts of cash	Cash receipts journal
Payments of cash	Cash payments journal

Transactions that do not conveniently fit into any one of these journals are recorded in the general journal. Although there are standard forms for these journals, they can be designed to meet the needs of a particular firm.

4. *Recording transactions into specialized journals.* In a manual system, transactions must be recorded by hand in specialized journals. In most cases, transactions that affect subsidiary accounts are posted daily, whereas transactions that affect general ledger accounts are posted monthly. At the end of the month, subsidiary trial balances are made, and the totals in these reports are compared with the balances in the related controlling or general ledger accounts.

Internal Control, Accounting Systems, and the Role of Computers

5. *The use of computerized systems.* The recent development of micro-computers has made computerized accounting systems available to firms of all sizes. There are many software packages available to run on various makes of personal or business computers. These systems post transactions as they are recorded and supply management with up-to-date reports as needed. Spreadsheet, word processing, data base management, and integrated software programs have increased the financial analysis ability of private and public accountants. This trend will continue into the future and will enhance the efficiency of the accounting information system.

Key Terms

Accounting Controls	Controlling Account
Accounts Payable Trial Balance	Internal Control
(Schedule of Accounts Payable)	Purchases Journal
Accounts Receivable Trial Balance	Sales Journal
(Schedule of Accounts Receivable)	Specialized Journal
Administrative Controls	Spreadsheet
Cash Payments Journal	Subsidiary Accounts
Cash Receipts Journal	

Problem for Your Review

Special Sounds. Business World entered into the following transactions during April:

- April 1: Cash sales amounted to $1,500.
- April 2: Sales to G. M. Smith on account amounted to $2,000. Terms are 2/10, n/30. The invoice number is 126.
- April 8: Collected $2,600 from A. L. Ford on sale made on March 2. No discount allowed.
- April 10: Sales to A.M.R. for $5,000 on account. Terms are 2/10, n/30. The invoice number is 127.
- April 11: Collected from G. M. Smith amount due from April 2 sale less appropriate discount.
- April 18: Sold marketable securities with a cost of $2,500 for $2,200 cash.
- April 22: Collected from A.M.R. amount due from April 10 sale. Discount not taken.
- April 25: Cash sales amounted to $2,700.
- April 29: A customer returned some items, as they were defective, and received a cash refund of $500.
- April 30: Sale to N. B. Honda for $6,000. Terms are n/30. The invoice number is 128.

Required:

1. Record these transactions in (1) the sales journal, (2) the general journal, or (3) the cash receipts journal, depending on the nature of the transaction.
2. Explain how these transactions should be posted to the subsidiary and general ledgers. It is not necessary to make the postings.

Solution _____

1.

Sales Journal

Date	Account Debited	Invoice Number	Post Ref.	Amount
April 2	G. M. Smith—2/10, n/30	126	✔	$ 2,000
10	A.M.R.—2/10, n/30	127	✔	5,000
30	N. B. Honda—n/30	128	✔	6,000
				$13,000

General Journal

Date	Explanation	Post Ref.	Debit	Credit
April 29	Sales returns and allowances	✔	500	
	Cash	✔		500
	To record cash refund to customer.			

Cash Receipts Journal

Page 2

Date	Explanation	Debits Cash	Debits Sales Discounts	Debits Other Accounts Account Title	Debits Other Accounts Ref.	Debits Other Accounts Amount	Account Credited	Credits Accounts Receivable Ref.	Credits Accounts Receivable Amount	Credits Sales	Credits Other Accounts Ref.	Credits Other Accounts Amount
April 1	Cash sales	1,500.00								1,500.00		
8	Invoice from March 2	2,600.00					A. L. Ford	✔	2,600.00			
11	Invoice of April 2, less 2%	1,960.00	40.00				G. M. Smith	✔	2,000.00			
18	Sale of marketable securities	2,200.00		Loss on sale of securities	✔	300.00	Marketable securities					2,500.00
22	Invoice of April 10	5,000.00					A.M.R.	✔	5,000.00			
25	Cash sales	2,700.00								2,700.00		
		15,960.00	40.00			300.00			9,600.00	4,200.00		2,500.00
		✔	✔						✔	✔		

2. At the end of each day, postings from the sales journal and the cash receipts journal should be made to the appropriate customer accounts in the subsidiary ledger. Because account numbers were not given, these postings are shown by a check mark. At the end of the month, postings should be made to the general ledger accounts. Again, these postings are shown by a check mark.

Questions

1. Why must internal control needs be considered when designing accounting systems?

2. The ABCO Company is a medium-sized business with several individuals in the accounting department. Under current job assignments, the employee who makes entries in the cash receipts journal is also the individual who makes the daily bank deposit. Does this represent good internal control? Why or why not?

3. One of your fellow students was overheard saying that if all people were honest, there would be no need for internal control systems. Do you agree? Why or why not?

4. What is the difference between administrative controls and accounting controls? Give an example of each type of control.

5. What are subsidiary ledgers, and what purpose do they serve?

6. Name five general ledger accounts that are likely to be supported by subsidiary accounts. State why this is the case.

7. How are subsidiary accounts related to the controlling accounts? What purpose does the subsidiary trial balance serve in this regard?

8. What are specialized journals, and what purpose do they serve?

9. List the four most common specialized journals

and the transactions that would be recorded in them.

10. Explain when and what postings are made from the sales journal to the appropriate ledgers. How might you detect an error in this posting process?

11. The purchases journal described in the text had only one amount column for purchases and accounts payable. If the journal were to be expanded to a multicolumn form, what additional columns might be included? What determines their selection?

12. One of your fellow students stated that all sales are recorded in the sales journal. Do you agree? Why or why not?

13. The Nett Company sells all its goods on a 2/10, n/30 basis. Its practice is to record all sales invoices net. Describe how this would affect the format of the cash receipts journal described in the text.

14. The Firegate Company makes its inventory purchases both by cash and on account. In what journals

would these transactions be recorded? Would it be possible to record both these transactions in one journal? If so, which one?

15. Given the widespread use of specialized journals, is it still necessary to use a general journal? Why or why not?

16. A small retail store has always kept its accounting records manually. However, the company is thinking about trying to increase the efficiency and accuracy of its records. The president of the company is always complaining that the records he gets are often late and full of errors. What alternatives are available to the firm to upgrade its accounting system?

17. What is an electronic spreadsheet? Describe three accounting-related uses of such spreadsheets.

18. Mildred Jones is about to open her own CPA firm. She is considering purchasing a personal or office computer. List four functions for which such a computer could be used in her firm.

Exercises*

1. Internal Control. The Allowance Company recently redesigned its accounting department to increase its efficiency. Several employees were terminated, and several jobs were combined. As a result of the reorganization, two employees now have the following jobs:

- Employee A: Makes entries in the purchases journal and the cash payments journal.
- Employee B: Makes entries in the sales journal and the cash receipts journal. Employee B also has access to the general journal.

Furthermore, the head of the accounting department will allow all employees to receive overtime pay instead of taking their regularly scheduled vacations.

Required:

What internal control problems, if any, might result from the reorganization?

2. Internal Control. The Discount Warehouse is a discount apparel store in southern California. The company has a small accounting department made up of three individuals who must perform the following functions:

  a. Record purchases from suppliers in the purchases journal.

  b. Record sales on account in the sales journal and cash sales in the cash receipts journal.

  c. Make cash payments to suppliers and record these payments in the cash payments journal.

  d. Record customers' payments on accounts in the cash receipts journal and make the daily deposits.

  e. Make entries in the general journal for purchase returns and allowances, and sales returns and allowances.

Required:

List the tasks for which each employee should be responsible. Use good internal control techniques. If necessary, each employee may have more than one task.

3. Transactions and Special Journals. The Grant Company uses a one-column sales journal, a one-column purchases journal, multicolumn cash receipts and cash payments journals, and a general journal. For each of the following transactions, state in which journal it should be recorded:

  a. Purchase of inventory for cash.

  b. Receipt of a $5,000 bank loan.

      *Unless otherwise noted, assume that all sales and purchases are recorded gross of any allowable sales or purchase discounts.

c. Sales on account.

d. Receipt of interest revenue for the month.

e. Cash withdrawal by the owner.

f. Purchase of inventory on account.

g. Payment of monthly rent.

h. Sale of an old delivery truck for cash. There was a loss on the sale.

i. Cash sales for the day from the cash register.

j. Return of merchandise purchased on account because it arrived damaged.

4. Characteristics of Special Journals. The Feel-Rite Drugstore uses the following specialized journals: a single-column sales journal, a single-column purchases journal, a multicolumn cash receipts journal, a multicolumn cash payments journal, and a general journal. Answer each of the following questions regarding these journals:

a. At the end of the period, the total in the sales journal should be posted to which ledger accounts?

b. What subsidiary ledgers would most likely be associated with the cash payments and cash receipts journals?

c. In which journal would the fewest transactions most likely be recorded?

d. The firm takes all available purchase discounts. In what journal would the purchase discounts be recorded?

e. At the end of the period, the total in the purchases journal should be posted to which ledger accounts?

f. In which journal are adjusting entries and closing entries made?

g. In which journal would sales discounts be recorded?

5. Characteristics of Specialized Journals and Subsidiary Ledgers. A fellow student made the following statements. State whether each statement is true or false and explain your reasoning.

a. All general ledger accounts must have subsidiary accounts.

b. All entries in the cash receipts journal should be posted daily.

c. The purchases journal can be used to record cash purchases.

d. Daily postings in the sales journal are made to the subsidiary accounts payable ledger.

e. Not all the column totals in the cash receipts journal are posted to specific ledger accounts.

f. Computerized accounting systems have eliminated the need for internal controls.

6. Making Entries in Specialized Journals. During the month of October the Kwan Company entered into the following selected transactions:

- October 1: Purchased merchandise on account from the White Co., $10,000. Terms are 1/10, n/30.

- October 3: Purchased merchandise for cash, $1,000.

- October 5: Paid invoice of the ABC Co. from September, $8,000 less 2% discount.

- October 12: Purchased merchandise on account from the Brown Co., $6,000. Terms are n/30.

- October 15: Paid $1,000 for advertising expense.

- October 24: Returned $400 of merchandise purchased on October 12 because it was defective.

- October 30: Paid the remaining balance on the October 12 purchase.

Required:

Record these transactions in the appropriate journals. Use journals similar in form to those used in the chapter.

7. Making Entries in Specialized Journals. During November the Spartan Company entered into the following transactions:

- November 1: Sales to The Express on account amounted to $5,000. Terms are n/30. The invoice number is 156.

- November 5: Collected $3,822 from the Raider Company from sale on October 30. The amount received represents the total invoice less the 2% discount. All sales are recorded gross.

- November 15: Cash sales for the first half of the month amounted to $10,000.

- November 18: Sales to the Invader Company on account amounted to $15,000. Terms are 2/10, n/30. The invoice number is 157.

- November 20: Three hundred dollars' worth of the merchandise sold to the Invader Company was defective and returned. Its account was credited.

- November 27: Collected the remaining balance due from the Invader Company, less the appropriate discount.

- November 30: Received an $8,000 bank loan from First City Bank.

- November 30: Cash sales for the remainder of the month were $13,000.

Required:

Record these transactions in the appropriate journals. Use forms similar to those in the chapter. Number checks beginning with check no. 1.

8. Posting to Ledger Accounts. The Michigan State Company uses a general journal, a one-column sales journal, a one-column purchases journal, multicolumn cash receipts and cash payments journals, and subsidiary accounts receivable and payable ledgers. As of September 30 of the current year, the following balances were in these controlling accounts:

Accounts receivable	$180,000
Accounts payable	140,000

After the October transactions were recorded in the specialized journals, certain columns had the following totals:

Sales journal		$160,000
Purchases journal		190,000
Cash receipts journal	—Accounts receivable column	135,000
	—Sales column	40,000
Cash payments journal	—Accounts payable column	200,000
	—Purchases column	30,000

Required:

Answer each of the following questions:

a. To which ledger accounts would the $160,000 column total of the sales journal be posted?

b. To which ledger accounts would the $190,000 column total of the purchases journal be posted?

c. Where would the accounts receivable total of $135,000 in the cash receipts journal be posted?

d. Where would the accounts payable total of $200,000 in the cash payments journal be posted?

e. What was the total sales for the month of October?

f. What was the total purchases for the month of October?

g. What are the balances in the controlling accounts receivable and the accounts payable accounts at the end of October?

9. Posting to Subsidiary Accounts. The Raleigh Company started business on the first of January. At the end of January, the accounts receivable subsidiary trial balance appeared as follows:

Customer Name	Account Number	Balance
B. F. Good	001	$ 2,500
C. L. Cooper	002	3,000
P. M. Marwick	003	5,500
A. Y. Young	004	2,400
Total		$13,400

The sales journal for February appeared as follows:

Date	Account Debited	Invoice Number	Amount
February 2	C. D. Badd	749	$ 2,200
5	A. A. Andersen	315	6,000
14	C. L. Cooper	828	2,400
22	P. M. Marwick	170	3,000
29	P. W. Waterhouse	1,357	2,500
			$16,100

The accounts receivable column of the cash receipts journal contained the following:

B. F. Good	$2,500
C. L. Cooper	3,000
C. D. Badd	2,000
P. M. Marwick	8,000
C. L. Cooper	2,000

Required:
a. Post entries from the sales journal and the cash receipts journal to the appropriate accounts receivable subsidiary accounts. Where necessary, open new accounts beginning with account number 005. Use T accounts.
b. Post the entries to the controlling Accounts Receivable and Sales accounts. Assume that the balance in the Sales account at February 1 is $70,000.
c. Prepare an accounts receivable trial balance at February 29.

10. Errors in Special Journals. The Budget Company records all sales on account in a one-column sales journal. During the month of July the bookkeeper made the following errors in recording and posting in the sales journal:
a. The amount column of the sales journal was incorrectly totaled.
b. A sale on account to the Brinkley Company was correctly recorded in the sales journal as $100 but was posted to the subsidiary account as $1,000.
c. A sales return of $200 was recorded in the general journal as a debit to Sales Returns and Allowances and a credit to Accounts Receivable. By mistake, the credit to Accounts Receivable was not posted to the controlling Accounts Receivable account.
d. A mathematical error was made in determining a balance in one of the subsidiary Accounts Receivable accounts.
e. A sale on account to the Dominici Company was posted in error to the account of the Hamm Company.

Required:
Determine how each of these errors could be detected, assuming that they are independent.

Problem Set A*

7A-1. Sales Journal and Subsidiary Ledgers. Martinez Toys is a small toy company in the Midwest. Its business is primarily cash and carry. However, it does sell on account to selected customers. At the beginning of January of the current year, the controlling Accounts Receivable account (account no. 200) has a balance of $1,600. Analysis of the subsidiary accounts receivable ledger indicated the following:

Customer	Account No.	Balance
C. Chow	2-001	$450
L. Gean	2-002	300
M. Nee	2-003	600
D. Pest	2-004	20
S. West	2-005	230

*Unless otherwise noted, assume that all purchases and sales are recorded gross of any allowable sales or purchases discounts.

During the month of January the following sales were made on account to these customers:

Customer	Account No.	Sales
C. Chow	2-001	$200
L. Gean	2-002	100
M. Nee	2-003	300
S. West	2-005	50

Collections on account during January were as follows:

Customer	Account No.	Amount
C. Chow	2-001	$450
L. Gean	2-002	400
M. Nee	2-003	700
D. Pest	2-004	10
S. West	2-005	130

On January 12, D. Pest returned a small toy that he had purchased on account. His account was credited for $5.

Required:

    a. Set up the Sales and the controlling Accounts Receivable accounts and the appropriate accounts in the accounts receivable subsidiary ledger. Use T accounts.

    b. Record the above transactions in a cash receipts journal and a single-column sales journal, as shown in the text. Record the sales return in the general journal. The specific days of the month may be omitted.

    c. Post the entries to the controlling Accounts Receivable account and the subsidiary accounts.

    d. Prepare a schedule of accounts receivable (accounts receivable trial balance) as of January 31.

7A–2. Identifying Transactions in Specialized Journals. The following is an excerpt from one of the specialized journals used by the Erwin Company. Describe the transaction that resulted in each entry. In addition, describe the postings that should be made daily and at the end of the month.

Date		Check No.	Explanation	Credits					Account Debited	Debits				
				Cash	Purchases Discounts	Other Accounts				Accounts Payable		Purchases	Other Accounts	
						Account Title	Ref.	Amount		Ref.	Amount		Ref.	Amount
May	1	101	Invoice of April 23	980	20				Lester, Inc.	002	1,000			
	5	104		2,000								2,000		
	12	105		2,400		Note payable	31	9,600	Equipment				21	12,000
	18	106	Invoice of May 1	3,000					Doctors, Inc.	007	3,000			
	23	107		2,000					Marketable securities				11	2,000
	29	108		400					Note payable				31	100
									Interest expense				100	300
	30	109		4,000					Salaries				90	4,000
				14,780	20			9,600			4,000	2,000		18,400
				(10)	(51)			(✔)			(30)	(50)		(✔)

7A–3. Recording Transactions in the Sales and Purchases Journals. The Okida Company uses a sales and purchases journal in its accounting system. All sales and purchases are recorded net. The company entered into the following selected transactions during May:

    • May 1: Purchased merchandise on account from the Arnold Company for $1,000. Terms are 2/10, n/30.

    • May 3: Purchased inventory for $2,000 cash.

    • May 5: Sold on account to the Green Company $1,500 of merchandise. Terms are 2/10, n/30. The invoice number is 729.

- May 14: Sold on account to the Pear Company $2,000 of merchandise. Terms are n/30. The invoice number is 730.

- May 22: Purchased inventory on account from the Clausen Company, $3,000. Terms are n/30.

- May 30: Sold on account to the Gallary Company $5,000 of merchandise. Terms are 1/10, n/30. The invoice number is 731.

Required:

a. Open all the necessary general ledger accounts and accounts receivable and payable subsidiary ledger accounts. Use the following general ledger account numbers:

Accounts receivable	200	Sales	500
Accounts payable	400	Purchases	800

Assume that there are no beginning balances in any accounts.

b. Record the above transactions in the appropriate journal.

c. Post the transactions from the journals to the appropriate general and subsidiary ledgers. Use a check mark to indicate a posting to a subsidiary account.

d. Prepare an accounts receivable and an accounts payable trial balance as of the end of the month.

e. In this problem, the Okida Company recorded purchases and sales net. Because of this practice, what changes were made in the cash receipts and cash payments journals from those illustrated in the text?

7A–4. Recording Transactions in the Sales and Cash Receipts Journals. The Nakasone Specialty Shop began business in January of the current year. The following selected transactions took place during January:

- January 2: The owner, O. Nakasone, invested $100,000 in the business.

- January 5: The firm received a $25,000 bank loan.

- January 7: Sales on account to the Mahoney Company amounted to $4,000. Terms are 2/10, n/30. The invoice number is 001.

- January 10: Sales on account to the Eastern Export Co. were $12,000. Terms are n/30. The invoice number is 002.

- January 15: Cash sales for the first half of January are $14,000.

- January 17: The firm sold one of its typewriters that it purchased earlier in the month. No depreciation had ever been taken on the typewriter. The typewriter cost $1,500 and was sold for $1,500. Five hundred dollars was received in cash, the remainder on account. The purchaser is Henry's Used Typewriters.

- January 17: Received payment from the Mahoney Company, less the appropriate discount.

- January 20: Sales on account to the Milford Company amounted to $2,200. Terms are 2/10, n/30. The invoice number is 003.

- January 23: Received a $6,000 payment on account from the Eastern Export Co.

- January 25: The Milford Company returned $200 of merchandise purchased on January 20, because it was defective. Milford's account was credited for $200.

- January 29: Received a refund of $500 from the state of Nebraska for overpayment of taxes paid to open business.

- January 30: Received remaining payment due from the Milford Company.

Required:

a. Enter the above transactions in the sales journal, the cash receipts journal, or the general journal.

b. Set up the following general ledger and subsidiary accounts:

General Ledger Accounts

Account	Account No.
Cash	100
Accounts receivable	200
Office equipment (balance prior to entry, $6,000)	300
Bank loan payable	400
O. Nakasone, capital	500
Sales	600
Sales discounts	650
Tax expense (balance prior to entry, $1,900)	900

Assume all accounts other than Office Equipment and Tax Expense have a zero balance prior to the preceding transactions. Open a subsidiary ledger for each customer. Begin with account 001 for the first customer. The second customer should be 002, and so forth.

c. Foot and rule the specialized journals and post all entries to the appropriate ledger accounts.

7A–5. Recording Transactions in the Purchases and Cash Payments Journals. The Bench Company's chart of accounts includes the following accounts:

Cash ($36,000)	100	Purchase returns and	
Investment in marketable securities	200	allowances	920
Office furniture ($12,000)	500	Purchase discounts	930
Accounts payable ($10,000—Rule Co.)	600	Rent expense	1000
Notes payable	700	Salary expense	2000
Purchases	900	Interest expense	3000

The amounts listed in parentheses represent the beginning balance on these accounts as of January 1, 1987. If no amount appears, the balance is zero.

The following transactions occurred during January:

- January 2: Purchased merchandise from the Perlberg Company for $4,000 with an invoice date of January 2. Terms are 2/10, n/30.
- January 5: Made a $2,000 cash purchase from the Oslo Company.
- January 6: Purchased merchandise from the Lins Company for $6,000. The invoice is dated January 5. Terms are 2/10, n/30.
- January 7: Returned $200 of merchandise to the Perlberg Company because it arrived damaged. Received an adjustment on its account.
- January 8: Paid monthly rent of $2,500.
- January 10: Made required payment to the Perlberg Company.
- January 14: Purchased marketable securities for $2,000 cash.
- January 15: Cash purchases totaled $1,000.
- January 15: Made appropriate payment to the Lins Company.
- January 16: Purchased merchandise from the Window Company for $4,000. The invoice is dated January 14. Terms are 2/10, n/30.
- January 20: Purchased additional office equipment for $5,000. Made a 20% down payment and the remainder was financed by the bank.
- January 24: Purchased merchandise from the Rule Co. for $1,000. The invoice is dated January 24. Terms are n/30.
- January 28: Made appropriate payment to the Window Company.
- January 30: Made a $50 monthly payment on the bank loan of January 20. The interest portion is $40.
- January 30: Monthly salaries of $4,000 had accrued; payment will be made on February 1.

Required:

a. Record the transactions in the appropriate journals. Use journals similar to those shown in the text and a two-column general journal. Make all the required postings to the general ledger and subsidiary accounts. Use check marks to show the postings to the subsidiary accounts. Number checks beginning with check no. 1.

b. Balance the subsidiary accounts and the accounts payable general ledger account. Prepare an accounts payable trial balance. Make sure that the total in this trial balance agrees with the control account.

7A-6. Recording Transactions in Several Journals. The Great Western Company began operations on August 1 of the current year. The company's accounting system is based on a general journal, a one-column sales journal, a one-column purchases journal, a multicolumn cash receipts journal, and a multicolumn cash payments journal. The forms are similar to the ones used in the text. The following chart of accounts was set up:

Cash	10	Sales discounts	45
Accounts receivable	11	Sales returns and allowances	46
Inventory	12	Purchases	50
Supplies	15	Purchase discounts	55
Office furniture and equipment	18	Purchase returns and allowances	56
Accounts payable	20	Rent expense	60
Notes payable	21	Supplies used	70
Interest payable	25	Salaries expense	80
D. Western, capital	30	Interest expense	90
Sales	40		

During August the following events occurred:

- August 1: D. Western supplied $20,000 cash.
- August 2: Borrowed $8,000 from Marina National for 2 years at 12%.
- August 3: Monthly rent of $1,200 paid in cash.
- August 5: Purchased merchandise for cash, $3,000.
- August 5: Purchased merchandise on account from the Lee Company, $2,000. The invoice was dated August 4. Terms are 2/10, n/30.
- August 6: Purchased merchandise on account from the A Company, $800. The invoice was dated August 5. Terms are 2/10, n/30.
- August 8: Purchased office furniture and fixtures for cash, $1,200.
- August 8: Sold merchandise on account to the East Indian Co., $1,500. Terms are 2/10, n/30. The invoice number is 001.
- August 9: Some of the merchandise purchased from the A Company arrived damaged. It was returned and the Great Western account was credited $100.
- August 12: The merchandise purchased from the Lee Company was paid for.
- August 14: The appropriate payment was made to the A Company for the outstanding balance of the payable.
- August 15: Cash sales for the first half of the month totaled $300.
- August 16: Office supplies of $800 were purchased for cash.
- August 17: Received balance owed from the East Indian Co.
- August 18: Purchased merchandise on account from the Honig Co., $1,400. The invoice was dated August 18. Terms are n/30.
- August 20: Cash purchases, $200.
- August 21: Purchased merchandise on account from the Jackson Co., $400. The invoice was dated August 20. Terms are 2/10, n/30.
- August 23: Sold merchandise on account to Naguchi, Inc. for $700. Terms are 2/10, n/30. The invoice number is 002.
- August 25: Paid the Honig Co. $700 on account.
- August 27: Sold merchandise to the Software Co. for $1,100. Terms are 2/10, n/30. The invoice number is 003.
- August 30: Salaries for the month of $1,000 were paid in cash.

- August 30: The Software Co. returned some merchandise and received a credit of $100.
- August 30: Cash sales for the second half of the month were $1,500.

In addition, the following adjustments must be made:

a. Supplies on hand at the end of the month were $300.

b. Interest for one month must be accrued on the bank loan.

Required:

a. Set up the general ledger accounts using the accounts from the chart of accounts. As necessary, set up appropriate subsidiary receivable and payable accounts.

b. Enter the above transactions in the appropriate journals. Assume that all journals begin with page 1. Number checks beginning with check no. 1.

c. Total the journal and make the appropriate postings to the general ledger accounts and subsidiary accounts. Use check marks to indicate a posting to the subsidiary accounts.

d. Prepare subsidiary trial balances and check to see that they agree with the controlling accounts.

7A-7. Using Specialized Journals and Completing the Accounting Cycle. The UTLA Company uses a one-column sales journal, a one-column purchases journal, a multicolumn cash receipts journal, a multicolumn cash payments journal, and a general journal. Subsidiary accounts receivable and accounts payable ledgers are also maintained. On page 295 are the May 31, 1987 post-closing trial balance and the subsidiary trial balances. The revenue and expense accounts are listed in order to present their account numbers.

During the month of June the following events occurred:

- June 1: Received a check for the balance due from the Applegate Company, less 2% discount.
- June 1: Purchased equipment from the Dole Co., $10,000. Made a 20% down payment; the remainder was borrowed from the bank at 12% interest.
- June 2: Sold merchandise on account to the Cheetah Co. (account no. 005), $850. Terms are 2/10, n/30. The invoice number is 601.
- June 3: Paid monthly rent of $500. Considered a G&A expense.
- June 4: Purchased merchandise on account from the Porta Co. (account no. 140), $1,000. The invoice date was June 4. Terms are 2/10, n/30.
- June 5: Paid the English Company the full amount due. No discount was allowed.
- June 9: Received payment from the Cheetah Co. from the June 2 sale, less discount.
- June 10: Paid the Mayor Company $2,000 on account.
- June 13: Paid the Porta Co. the amount due from the June 4 purchase.
- June 15: Cash sales for the first half of the month were $3,000.
- June 16: Received a check from the Domino Company, $1,500 for payment on account.
- June 17: Sold merchandise on account to the Applegate Company, $1,000. Terms are 2/10, n/30. The invoice number is 602.
- June 18: Purchased merchandise from the Mayor Company, $1,500. The invoice was dated June 17. Terms are 2/10, n/30.
- June 19: Sold merchandise on account to the Scheiner Co. (account no. 006), $500. Terms are n/30. The invoice number is 603.
- June 22: Full payment on account was made to the Price Company; no discount was taken.
- June 26: Received payment due from the Applegate Company from the June 17 sale.
- June 27: Made required payment to the Mayor Company for the June 18 purchase.
- June 30: Selling expenses paid in cash, $800.
- June 30: General and administrative expenses paid in cash, $1,000.
- June 30: Cash sales for the second half of the month, $1,800.
- June 30: Cash purchases for the month, $3,800.

UTLA Company
Post-Closing Trial Balance
May 31, 1987

Account		Debit	Credit
100	Cash	$16,000	
120	Accounts receivable	7,000	
140	Inventory	20,000	
150	Equipment	35,000	
155	Accumulated depreciation		$ 5,000
200	Accounts payable		10,000
210	Notes payable		0
300	A. Cherry, capital		63,000
400	Sales		
410	Sales discounts		
420	Sales returns and allowances		
500	Purchases		
510	Purchase discounts		
520	Purchase returns and allowances		
600	Selling expenses		
700	General and administrative expenses		
800	Interest expense		
	Totals	$78,000	$78,000

Accounts Receivable Subsidiary Ledger

001	Applegate Company	$1,700
002	Brenner Company	1,400
003	Domino Company	2,000
004	Yates Company	1,900
	Total	$7,000

Accounts Payable Subsidiary Ledger

100	English Company	$ 1,400
110	Mayor Company	4,000
120	Price Company	2,600
130	Turnkey Company	2,000
	Total	$10,000

In addition, the following adjusting and closing entries must be made:
   a. One month's interest on the note must be recorded.
   b. Depreciation expense of $500 must be recorded. Considered a G&A expense.
   c. Ending inventory equals $21,551. This and other closing entries must be made.

Required:
   a. Set up the appropriate general ledger and subsidiary accounts, entering the beginning balance as of June 1.
   b. Record all the above transactions in the appropriate journals. Number checks beginning with check no. 1. Journals begin with page 6.
   c. Post all the transactions to the appropriate general and subsidiary ledgers.
   d. Prepare a trial balance and the appropriate subsidiary trial balances.
   e. Prepare a balance sheet at June 30, 1987, and an income statement for the month then ended.

Problem Set B*

7B-1. Purchases Journal and Subsidiary Ledgers. Stuart's Supplies is an office supplies company in New Haven. Most of the company's purchases are made from five vendors. At the beginning of July of the current year, the controlling Accounts Payable (account no. 500) had a balance of $12,000. Analysis of the subsidiary accounts payable ledger indicated the following:

Supplier	Account No.	Balance
A. Doe	3-001	$2,800
L. Link	3-002	3,200
F. Owl	3-003	3,450
C. Roet	3-004	2,150
Z. Xu	3-005	400

During July the following purchases were made on account from these suppliers. (No discounts are allowed on purchases.)

Supplier	Account No.	Sales
A. Doe	3-001	$2,600
L. Link	3-002	4,300
F. Owl	3-003	1,400
C. Roet	3-004	2,150

Payments on account during July were as follows:

Supplier	Account No.	Amount
A. Doe	3-001	$2,800
L. Link	3-002	5,000
F. Owl	3-003	1,500
C. Roet	3-004	4,300
Z. Xu	3-005	170

On July 22 the company returned some staplers to Z. Xu that it previously purchased on account. The company's account was debited for $100.

Required:

a. Set up the controlling Accounts Payable account and the appropriate accounts in the accounts payable subsidiary ledger. Use T accounts.

b. Record the above transactions in a single-column purchases journal, as shown in the text. Record the purchase returns and the payment to suppliers in the general journal. The specific days of the month may be omitted.

c. Post the entries to the controlling Accounts Payable account and the subsidiary accounts.

d. Prepare a schedule of accounts payable (accounts payable trial balance) as of July 31.

7B-2. Identifying Transactions in Specialized Journals. The following is an excerpt from one of the specialized journals used by the Moses Company. Describe the transaction that resulted in each entry. In addition, describe the postings that should be made daily and at the end of the month.

---

*Unless otherwise noted, assume that all sales and purchases are recorded gross of any allowable sales or purchase discounts.

Date	Explanation	Debits		Other Accounts			Account Credited	Credits			Other Accounts	
		Cash	Sales Discounts	Account Title	Ref.	Amount		Ref.	Accounts Receivable Amount	Sales	Ref.	Amount
September 1		3,000.00								3,000.00		
6		10,000.00					Securities						8,000.00
							Gain on sale					2,000.00
10		500.00	10.00				C.W. Poat		510.00			
14		5,500.00								5,500.00		
21		1,200.00					J. C. Ray		1,200.00			
27		100.00					Interest revenue					100.00
29		2,450.00	50.00				P. Chain		2,500.00			
30												
		6,000.00					E. Capital					6,000.00
		28,750.00	60.00						4,210.00	8,500.00		16,100.00

7B–3. Recording Transactions in the Sales and Purchases Journals. The Fashion Coordinates Company uses a sales and purchases journal in its accounting system. The following selected transactions took place during July:

- July 1: Purchased merchandise on account from the Dimension Company for $3,000. Terms are 2/10, n/30. The invoice date 7/1.
- July 3: Purchased inventory for $5,000 cash. Check number is 701.
- July 5: Sold on account to the Elite Company $3,500 of merchandise. Terms are 2/10, n/30. The invoice number is 927.
- July 15: Sold on account to the Large Sizes Co. $4,000 of merchandise. Terms are n/30. The invoice number is 928.
- July 22: Purchased inventory on account from the New Fashions Company, $4,500. Terms are n/30. The invoice date is 7/21.
- July 29: Sold on account to the Merton Company $7,000 of merchandise. Terms are 1/10, n/30. The invoice number is 929.

Required:
a. Open all the necessary general ledger accounts and accounts receivable and payable subsidiary ledger accounts. Use the following general ledger account numbers:

Accounts receivable	200	Sales	500
Accounts payable	400	Purchases	800

Assume that there are no beginning balances in any accounts.
b. Record the above transactions in the appropriate journals.
c. Post the transactions from the journals to the appropriate general and subsidiary ledgers. Use a check mark to indicate a posting to a subsidiary account.
d. Prepare an accounts receivable and accounts payable trial balance as of the end of the month.
e. Now assume that the sales and purchases are recorded net rather than gross. Describe the differences that would have to be made in the design of the sales journal, the purchases journal, the cash receipts journal, and the cash payments journal. How would this practice affect the way the entries are made in these journals?

7B–4. Recording Transactions in the Sales and Cash Receipts Journals. The Molokai Company began business in January of the current year. The following selected transactions took place during the month of January:

- January 2: The owner, H. Molokai, invested $100,000 cash in the business.
- January 5: The firm sold short-term investments with a cost of $15,000 for $25,000 cash.
- January 7: Sales on account to the Lanai Co. amounted to $8,000. Terms are 2/10, n/30. The invoice number is 100.

Internal Control, Accounting Systems, and the Role of Computers

- January 9: Sales on account to the New Japan Co. for $22,000. Terms are n/30. The invoice number is 101. New Japan's account balance was $4,000 prior to the sale.
- January 15: Cash sales for the first half of January are $8,000.
- January 16: The Big Island Company had an outstanding account receivable balance of $10,000. Because of financial difficulties, Big Island was having trouble paying. The Molokai Company agreed to exchange the account receivable for a $10,000, 12% note receivable due in one year.
- January 17: Received payment from Lanai Company less appropriate discount.
- January 21: Sales on account to the Kanapalli Co. amounted to $2,600. Terms are 2/10, n/30. The invoice number is 103.
- January 22: Twelve-thousand dollars payment on account from the New Japan Co.
- January 23: The Kanapalli Co. returned $400 of merchandise purchased on January 21 because it was defective. The company's account was credited for $400.
- January 30: Received a check for $1,000 representing rental revenue on a small building the firm owns.
- January 30: Received the amount due from the Kanapalii Co.

Required:

a. Enter the above transactions in either the sales journal, the cash receipts journal, or the general journal.
b. Set up the following general ledger and subsidiary accounts:

General Ledger Accounts

Account	Account Number
Cash	100
Short-term investments (balance prior to entry, $15,000)	150
Accounts receivable (balance prior to entries, $14,000)	200
Notes receivable	250
H. Molokai, capital	500
Sales	600
Sales returns and allowances	650
Sales discounts	660
Rental revenue	900
Gain on sale of securities	950

Unless otherwise noted, assume that the account has a zero balance.

Open a subsidiary ledger for each customer. Begin with account 001 for the first customer. The second customer should be 002, and so forth.

c. Foot and rule the specialized journals and post all entries to the appropriate ledger accounts.

7B–5. Recording Transactions in the Purchases and Cash Payments Journals. The Rose Company's chart of accounts includes the following accounts:

Cash ($48,000)	100	Purchases	800
Office furniture ($12,000)	400	Purchase returns and allowances	920
Land	500	Purchase discounts	930
Accounts payable	600	Selling expenses	1000
Notes payable	700	General expenses	2000
Accrued expenses payable	750	Interest expense	3000

The amounts listed in parentheses represent the beginning balance on these accounts as of March 1, 1987. If no amount appears, the balance is zero.

The following transactions occurred during March:

- March 1: Purchased merchandise from the Zorn Company for $8,000 with an invoice date of March 1. Terms are 2/10, n/30.
- March 4: Made a $6,000 cash purchase from the Seaver Company.

- March 5: Purchased merchandise from the Plunkett Co. for $9,000. Terms are 2/10, n/30. The invoice is dated March 4.
- March 6: Returned $500 of merchandise to the Plunkett Co. because it arrived damaged. Received an adjustment on their account.
- March 8: Purchased a plot of land for $50,000. Made a 10% down payment and financed the rest through a 12% bank loan.
- March 10: Made required payment to the Zorn Company.
- March 15: Cash purchases totaled $1,000.
- March 18: Made appropriate payment to the Plunkett Co.
- March 19: Purchased merchandise from the Wodin Company for $8,000. Terms are 2/10, n/30. The invoice is dated March 18.
- March 22: Purchased additional office furniture for $2,000 cash.
- March 23: Purchased merchandise from the Huie Co. for $3,000. Terms are n/30. The invoice is dated March 23.
- March 27: Made appropriate payment to the Wodin Company.
- March 30: Made a $500 monthly payment on the bank loan of March 8. The interest portion is $450.
- March 30: Paid selling expenses of $3,000 and general expenses of $1,000.
- March 31: Accrued additional selling expenses of $500.

Required:
  a. Record the transactions in the appropriate journals. Use journals similar to those shown in the text, and a two-column general journal. Make all the required postings to the general ledger and subsidiary accounts. Use check marks to show the postings to the subsidiary accounts. Number the checks beginning with check no. 1.
  b. Balance the subsidiary accounts and the accounts payable general ledger account. Prepare an accounts payable trial balance. Make sure that the total in this trial balance agrees with the control account.

7B–6. Recording Transactions in Several Journals. The Federal Company began operations on June 1 of the current year. The company's accounting system is based on a general journal, a one-column sales journal, a one-column purchases journal, a multicolumn cash receipts journal, and a multicolumn cash payments journal. The forms are similar to the ones used in the text. The following chart of accounts was set up:

Cash	10	Sales discounts	45
Accounts receivable	11	Sales returns and allowances	46
Prepaid rent	15	Purchases	50
Office furniture and equipment	18	Purchase discounts	55
Accounts payable	20	Purchase returns and allowances	56
Loan payable	21	Interest expense	59
Interest payable	25	Rent expense	60
C. Fazzi, capital	30	Advertising expense	70
Sales	40	Salaries expense	80

During June the following events occurred:
- June 1: The owner, C. Fazzi, invested $50,000 cash in the business.
- June 3: Borrowed $20,000 from a group of potential investors at 12%.
- June 3: Leased a store. A full year's rent of $4,800 was paid in advance.
- June 5: Purchased merchandise for cash, $6,000.
- June 6: Purchased merchandise on account from the Loutus Company, $4,000. Terms are 2/10, n/30. The invoice is dated June 5.
- June 7: Purchased merchandise on account from the Micro Co., $1,000. Terms are 2/10, n/30. The invoice is dated June 7.
- June 9: Purchased office furniture and fixtures, $5,000. Made a cash payment of $1,000; the rest on open account payable to the Furniture Company.

- June 9: Sold merchandise on account to the Chee Chee Co., $3,500. Terms are 2/10, n/30. The invoice number is 100.
- June 10: Some of the merchandise purchased from the Loutus Company arrived damaged. It was returned and the Federal Company account was reduced $200.
- June 12: The merchandise purchased from the Micro Co. was paid for.
- June 14: The appropriate payment was made to the Loutus Company for the outstanding balance of the payable.
- June 15: Cash sales for the first half of the month totaled $2,000.
- June 16: Advertising expense of $1,000 was incurred and paid for.
- June 18: Received balance owed from the Chee Chee Co.
- June 19: Purchased merchandise on account from the Rafferty Co., $1,800. Terms are n/30. The invoice is dated June 19.
- June 21: Cash purchases, $700.
- June 21: Purchased merchandise on account from the Quincy Co., $900. Terms are 2/10, n/30. The invoice is dated June 20.
- June 23: Sold merchandise on account to Carroll Co. for $4,000. Terms are 2/10, n/30. The invoice number is 102.
- June 25: Paid the Rafferty Co. $900 on account.
- June 27: Sold merchandise to the Discount Drug Store for $3,200. Terms are 2/10, n/30. The invoice number is 103.
- June 30: Salaries for the month of $2,000 were paid in cash.
- June 30: The Discount Drug Store returned some merchandise and received a credit of $200.
- June 30: Cash sales for the second half of the month, $4,500.

In addition, the following adjustments must be made:
  a. One month's prepaid rent must be written off.
  b. Interest for one month must be accrued on the loan.

Required:
  a. Set up the general ledger accounts using the accounts from the chart of accounts. As necessary, set up appropriate subsidiary receivable and payable accounts.
  b. Enter the above transactions in the appropriate journals. Assume that all journals begin with page 1. Number checks beginning with check no. 1.
  c. Total the journal and make the appropriate postings to the general ledger accounts and subsidiary accounts. Use check marks to indicate a posting to the subsidiary accounts.
  d. Prepare subsidiary trial balances and check to see that they agree with the controlling accounts.

7B-7. Using Specialized Journals and Completing the Accounting Cycle. The King Company uses a one-column sales journal, a one-column purchases journal, a multicolumn cash receipts journal, a multicolumn cash payments journal, and a general journal. Subsidiary accounts receivable and accounts payable ledgers are also maintained. The April 30, 1987 post-closing trial balance and subsidiary trial balances are presented on page 301. The revenue and expense accounts are listed in order to present their accounts numbers.

During the month of May the following events occurred:
- May 1: Received a check from the Brink Company less 2% discount.
- May 1: Purchased equipment from the Hole Company, $20,000. Made a 10% down payment; the remainder was borrowed from bank at 12% interest which is due in two years.
- May 2: Sold merchandise on account to the Deedly Company (account no. AR5), $1,500. Terms are 2/10, n/30. The invoice number is 701.
- May 3: Paid monthly rent of $600 (to be included as G&A expense).
- May 3: Received full amount from the Acqua Company. No discount was taken.

King Company
Post-Closing Trial Balance
April 30, 1987

Accounts		Debit	Credit
100	Cash	$12,000	
120	Accounts receivable	15,000	
140	Inventory	25,000	
150	Equipment	40,000	
155	Accumulated depreciation		$10,000
200	Accounts payable		18,000
210	Notes payable		0
220	Interest payable		0
300	B. J. King, capital		64,000
400	Sales		
410	Sales discounts		
420	Sales returns and allowances		
500	Purchases		
510	Purchase discounts		
520	Purchase returns and allowances		
600	Selling expenses		
700	General and administrative expenses		
800	Interest expense		
	Total	$92,000	$92,000

ACCOUNTS RECEIVABLE SUBSIDIARY LEDGER

AR1	Brink Company	$ 2,800
AR2	Coates Company	3,400
AR3	Rios Company	3,000
AR4	Zeros Company	5,800
	Total	$15,000

ACCOUNTS PAYABLE SUBSIDIARY LEDGER

AP1	Denmark Company	$ 4,500
AP2	Mace Company	5,000
AP3	Ripcheck Company	4,700
AP4	Ski Company	3,800
	Total	$18,000

- May 4: Purchased merchandise on account from the Acqua Co. (account no. AP5), $2,200. Terms are 2/10, n/30. The invoice is dated May 4.

- May 5: Paid Mace Company the amount due less 2% discount.

- May 9: Received payment from the Deedly Company less discount.

- May 10: Paid the Denmark Company full amount due. No discount was allowed.

- May 13: Paid the Acqua Company the amount due.

- May 15: Cash sales for first half of month, $5,000.

- May 15: Cash purchases, $3,500.

- May 16: Received a $3,500 check from the Zeros Company for payment on account.

- May 17: Sold merchandise on account to the Brink Company, $1,000. Terms are 2/10, n/30. The invoice number is 702.

- May 18: Purchased merchandise from the Mace Company, $3,500. Terms are 2/10, n/30. The invoice is dated May 17.

- May 19: Sold merchandise on account to the Spiceland Company, $1,500 (account no. AR6). Terms are n/30. The invoice number is 703.
- May 22: Payment in full on account to the Ski Company. No discount was taken.
- May 26: Received payment due from the Brink Company.
- May 27: Made required payment to the Mace Company.
- May 31: Selling expenses paid in cash, $900.
- May 31: General and administrative expenses paid in cash, $1,800.
- May 31: Cash sales for second half of month, $4,800.
- May 31: Cash purchases, $5,800.

In addition, the following adjusting and closing entries must be made:

a. One month's interest on the note must be recorded.

b. Depreciation expense of $800 must be recorded (to be included as G&A expense).

c. Ending inventory equals $22,500. This and other closing entries must be made.

Required:

a. Set up the appropriate general ledger and subsidiary accounts entering the beginning balance as of May 1.

b. Record all the above transactions in the appropriate journals. Journals begin with page 10. Number checks beginning with check no. 1.

c. Post all the transactions to the appropriate ledgers.

d. Prepare a general ledger trial balance and appropriate subsidiary trial balances.

e. Prepare a balance sheet at May 31, 1987 and an income statement for the month then ended.

Using the Computer

A. Electronic Spreadsheet—Cash Receipts Journal. The Stickney Candy Company records all of its cash receipts in a cash receipts journal similar to that in the text. During August the company entered into the following transactions:

- August 1: Cash sales amounted to $2,000.
- August 6: Sold a parcel of land for $10,000, which was purchased several years ago for $8,000.
- August 8: Received payment on account from C. W. Chang. Amount after 2% discount was $490. Receivables were recorded gross.
- August 15: Cash sales amounted to $3,500.
- August 19: Received payment on account from J. Donohoo. Amount received was $1,000. No discount was taken.
- August 24: Monthly interest revenue of $300 was received on note receivable. No monthly accruals were made.
- August 29: Received payment on account from P. Lockett. The receivable was originally recorded at a gross amount of $2,500. The 2% discount was taken.
- August 30: C. Stickney, the owner of the business, made an additional cash investment in the business of $5,000.

Required:

Using an electronic spreadsheet, create a cash receipts journal similar to the one in the text. Debit columns should include cash, sales discounts, and other accounts. Credit columns should include receivables, sales, and other accounts. Enter the above transactions, and total the columns at the end of the month.

B. Electronic Spreadsheet—Cash Payments Journal. Davidson's Donuts uses a cash payments journal similar to the one in the text to record all of its cash purchases. During October the following events occurred:

- October 1: The firm paid its monthly rent of $1,500.
- October 3: Cash purchases totaled $3,700.
- October 9: Paid $2,000 account payable to Edwards Flour Company, less 2% discount.
- October 12: Purchased 100 shares of B. R. Communications marketable securities at a total price of $2,200.
- October 15: Cash purchases totaled $3,500.
- October 19: Paid $1,200 on account to Simole Sugar Corporation. No discount was taken.
- October 22: Paid $500 to National Journal for monthly advertising expense. No previous accrual was made.
- October 27: Purchased a new stove for $12,000. The company made a 20% down payment and took out a 12% note for the remainder.
- October 30: Paid $2,000 on account to Lincoln Ice, less 2% discount.

Required:

Using an electronic spreadsheet, create a cash payments journal similar to the one in the text. Credit columns should include cash, purchase discounts, and other accounts. Debit columns should include accounts payable, purchases, and other accounts. Make the entries in the journal, and total the columns.

Understanding Financial Statements

The following excerpt was taken from a recent annual report of Safeway Stores, Inc.:

> We also believe strongly in the potential of technology to help us increase efficiency, improve productivity and reduce costs.
>
> With store scanner installations expected to number nearly 500 by the end of this year, we are on the threshold of reaping huge benefits from the vast data they generate. The greatest potential of computer-assisted checkout systems lies in the development of more sophisticated methods of applying that data.
>
> Safeway is among 13 pilot companies involved in the development of the Uniform Communication System (UCS), an electronic means of placing orders with vendors and receiving invoices. No paperwork is prepared until the transaction is complete.

Required:

a. State how computer-assisted checkout systems can be used in Safeway's accounting system. Address issues such as recording sales and purchases as well as inventory control.
b. Describe how the Uniform Communication System might work. What paperwork will be avoided? What advantages and/or disadvantages do you see in such a system?

Financial Decision Case

Discount Fashions Ltd. is a high-volume clothing store. About 40% of its sales are on credit, the remainder for cash. Because of the nature of its business, sales returns and allowances run about 10% of sales. Any customer who returns an item receives cash in return if the original sale was for cash; if the original sale was on account the customer's account is credited. Discount Fashions includes an interest charge on all accounts that are not paid within 30 days. Discount Fashions rents out a small portion of its store to a fast-food restaurant. Under the terms of the lease agreement the restaurant must pay its rent weekly.

The firm is presently redesigning its special journals to make them more useful. The controller asks your help in this project. There are no set formats except that the controller does not want sales returns and allowances recorded in either the general or the cash payments journal, but in the journals where the sales are recorded.

Required:

Design the sales and cash receipts journal for the controller. Include the columns that you think are most appropriate.

Measuring and Reporting
Assets and Liabilities

The Control and Accounting for Cash Transactions

8

LEARNING OBJECTIVES

After reading this chapter you should be able to:
1. **Determine what items are considered cash.**
2. **Discuss the purpose of management control procedures relating to cash.**
3. **Explain the specifics of internal control procedures for cash transactions including cash receipts and disbursements.**
4. **Discuss bank checking transactions and prepare a bank reconciliation.**
5. **Establish and account for a petty cash fund.**
6. **State the purposes of a voucher system and make entries in the system.**

The purpose of this chapter is to discuss the control and accounting for cash transactions. Our primary emphasis is on how to develop, implement, and maintain a strong internal control system over cash transaction. We apply the general internal control procedures we introduced in Chapter 7 to the specific area of cash, and discuss the important role of the bank reconciliation in the internal control system. Finally, we introduce you to the workings of a voucher system.

In the broadest sense, **cash** is any medium of exchange that a bank will accept for deposit and, as such, includes coins, paper money, money orders, checks, certified and cashier's checks, and money on deposit in a bank. However, IOUs, postdated checks (the date on the checks is beyond the present date), and postage stamps are not considered cash, and a bank would not accept any of them for deposit. Cash in savings accounts, certificates of deposit, commercial paper, and money market accounts are cash equivalents because they can quickly be converted into cash. Those equivalents that can immediately be converted into cash are usually included in the cash category on the balance sheet. Most savings accounts and money market accounts fall into this category. However, if there are restrictions on withdrawals, such as those on certain certificates of deposits and Treasury certificates, the item should not be included in the cash category. It should be shown as a short-term or long-term investment. For practical purposes, though, many firms combine cash and all cash equivalents into one account.

Cash and cash equivalents are current assets and are the first item shown on the balance sheet. Although a firm will have separate ledger accounts for each of its individual bank accounts, savings accounts, and so forth, they all are combined into one account for balance sheet presentation. There are, however, a number of situations in which cash may be excluded from the current assets section of the balance sheet. They all relate to cases in which there are restrictions on the cash that make it unavailable for current use. For example, a firm may set aside cash in a special fund to repay bonds or for the future purchase of a building. The funds are often called *sinking funds* and are shown in the long-term investment section of the balance sheet. In other situations a firm may have cash balances in banks in foreign countries that cannot be returned to the United States. Again, in this case, the cash is not shown as a current asset. Finally, there are situations in which the company overdraws its bank account and has a cash overdraft. Cash overdrafts are not shown as a negative item in the current assets section but as a liability in the current liabilities section of the balance sheet.

Management Control over Cash

The management and control of cash are essential managerial functions. The primary responsibility of those individuals in charge of overseeing cash transactions is to develop, implement, and maintain a cash management and control system that:

1. Prevents losses, theft, and the misappropriation of cash.
2. Provides accurate records of all cash receipts, disbursements, and other cash transactions.
3. Offers accurate and timely information concerning cash balances in order to enable management to control the amount of cash on hand at any time.

The first and second objectives pertain to the internal control of cash transactions and are the items discussed in this chapter. However, in recent years the third objective has become more and more important. In a credit- and cash-tight economy, management must make maximum use of its cash resources, which means that the control system must provide information that can be used to prepare cash budgets and projections. These budgets can then be used to ensure that only minimal amounts of cash are held in non-interest-bearing accounts or to enable a firm to establish lines of credit with banks to provide for future cash shortfalls. The preparation of cash budgets and other problems related to managerial control of cash are discussed in Chapter 26.

Internal Control over Cash

Most business transactions involve cash receipts and disbursements, and many employees play a role in the collection and payment of cash. Furthermore, cash is a firm's most liquid asset, and thus it is the most difficult to control. As the following excerpt from *The Wall Street Journal* (May 10, 1982) points out, these two features make it imperative that a firm devise a strong internal control system to prevent losses from theft, fraud, and misappropriation.

HOW TO PREVENT AN EMPLOYE FROM RIPPING OFF THE FIRM[1]

By SANFORD L. JACOBS   *Staff Reporter of* THE WALL STREET JOURNAL

Could someone be ripping off your business? What about the bookkeeper, that godsend who relieves you of the accounting stuff that bores you stiff? How about the old-timer who is so darn good at filling orders you let him run the shipping department with an iron fist? Not them, you say, they're trusted employes. Well, consider how a few "trusted" employes cheated small companies recently.

A bookkeeper diverted $750,000 of bill payments to her bank account in three years. Another bookkeeper made off with $80,000 in less than a year by drawing checks to herself and forging the owner's signature on them. A fellow in charge of paying bills paid himself $250,000 of company money. An employe of 28 years, who was a crackerjack at filling and shipping orders, shipped thousands of dollars of merchandise to himself.

Small companies can be easy prey. Their accounting systems usually lack tight controls because of the extra expense involved. A few employes normally do a number of critical jobs, weakening the first line of defense against employe dishonesty: segregating duties.

The bookkeeper who makes bank deposits, opens the mail and draws checks—even for someone else's signature—can divert receipts or forge checks and doctor the books to hide the loss.

Some simple precautions can make larceny difficult. "Segregation of duties is the biggest single deterrent," says Thomas Frey, of Arthur Andersen & Co., accountants. For example, the person who makes accounts-receivable entries shouldn't be the one who receives checks, because that person could divert the checks and cover up by juggling the records. One juggling method is to credit customer accounts for fictitious returns of goods or price adjustments.

Another employe should open the mail, list, endorse and total incoming checks, and, perhaps, make up a bank deposit. If that person diverts checks, receivables won't be adjusted to hide the fraud, and eventually customers will squawk about being billed or dunned for sums they already have paid. Complaints about statement balances from customers can signal something wrong: bookkeeping may be sloppy, someone may be embezzling—or both.

Sloppy record-keeping invites cheating, for employes know when money or merchandise can disappear without immediate detection. "Eventually you may know there is a shortage," says Al Roberts of the accounting firm of Arthur Young & Co., "but the records are such that you can't track the shortage."

Good controls mean nothing moves in or out of inventory without documents, such as purchase orders, receiving tickets, bills of lading, invoices, sales orders and shipping tickets. Different people should process forms to act as a check on one another. Then fraud could be covered up only by collusion of two or more employes. Prenumbered forms provide some protection if access is limited and someone checks to assure that the correct numerical order is being kept.

---

[1]Reprinted by permission of *The Wall Street Journal.* © Dow Jones & Company, Inc., 1982. All Rights Reserved.

The Control and Accounting for Cash Transactions

The design of an internal control system over cash depends on the firm's specific size, complexity, and nature. For example, separation of duties is an important cornerstone of any control system. Yet, the smaller the size of the organization and/or the accounting staff is, the more difficult it will be to separate duties properly. Thus, the controls described next are meant to be general in nature and cannot be applied to all firms in all situations.

If possible, the control system over cash should contain the following procedures or steps:

1. The duties of those handling cash and keeping records of cash transactions should be segregated. For example, the individual who prepares the bank reconciliation should not handle cash receipts and/or disbursements.
2. Only a limited number of clearly designated and bonded employees should have access to cash.
3. All procedures relating to cash receipts and disbursements should be clearly stated in the accounting manual. Compliance checks should be made regularly, and surprise audits should be made randomly.
4. All cash receipts should be deposited intact daily in the bank account. Only a small amount of cash in a petty cash fund should be maintained on hand. All but minor cash payments should be made by check.
5. All cash expenditures should be approved and the amounts verified by an employee not involved in the disbursement process.

Cash Receipts

The primary sources of cash receipts are collection of accounts receivable, cash sales, and other sources such as interest, collection of notes, and proceeds from the sale of assets. The overall cash receipts system is illustrated in Exhibit 8–1. As we will see, each step should be handled by a different individual.

Collection of Accounts Receivable

Collection of accounts receivable represents a major source of cash. Exhibit 8–2 (on page 312) illustrates a detailed schematic of the cash receipts system as it primarily relates to cash received through the mail. As the schematic illustrates, three individuals, all with different but clearly defined duties, should be involved if possible.

A designated employee should receive all the mail containing payments on accounts or other cash receipts. This individual should open the mail and prepare, in triplicate, a list of remittance advices. A **remittance advice** is a document that is attached to the sales invoice that is mailed to the customer. The purpose of the remittance advice is to ensure that the proper customer account is credited for the cash received. In many cases, the remittance advice is a copy of the sales invoice or a detachable part of the seller's invoice. This remittance advice is then returned with the cash payment to the seller. If a remittance advice is not returned, the individual who receives the cash should prepare one.

The list of the remittances serves to show the amount of cash received in the day's mail. One copy of the list along with the checks is given to the individual in charge of handling cash (often designated as the cashier). The cashier then combines the checks with the cash received from over-the-counter sales, if any, and prepares a deposit slip. All of the receipts are then deposited in the bank, intact, at the end of the day.

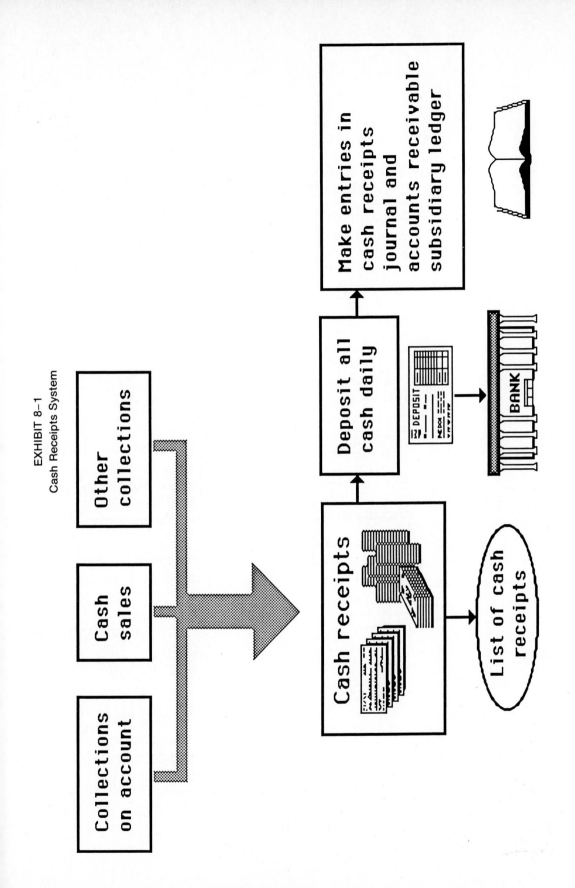

EXHIBIT 8–1
Cash Receipts System

Collections on account | Cash sales | Other collections

Cash receipts

List of cash receipts

Deposit all cash daily

DEPOSIT

BANK

Make entries in cash receipts journal and accounts receivable subsidiary ledger

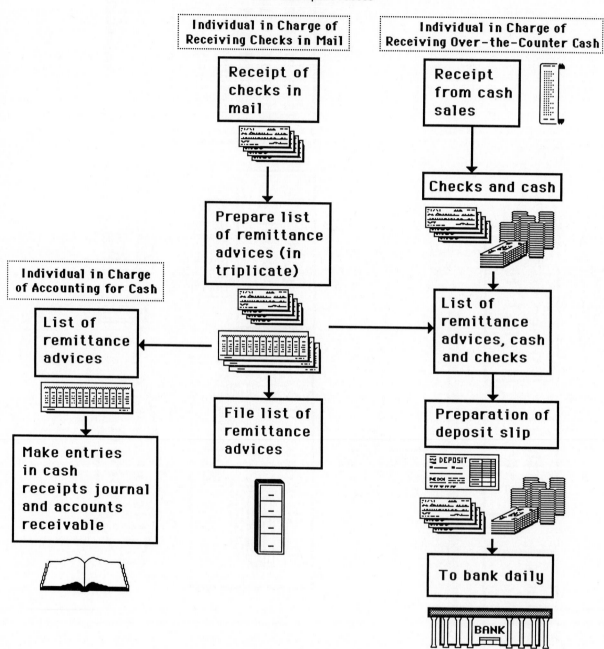

EXHIBIT 8–2
Cash Receipts Process

Individual in Charge of Receiving Checks in Mail

Receipt of checks in mail

Prepare list of remittance advices (in triplicate)

Individual in Charge of Accounting for Cash

List of remittance advices

Make entries in cash receipts journal and accounts receivable

File list of remittance advices

Individual in Charge of Receiving Over-the-Counter Cash

Receipt from cash sales

Checks and cash

List of remittance advices, cash and checks

Preparation of deposit slip

DEPOSIT

To bank daily

BANK

The second copy of the list of the remittance advices is sent to the accounting department. The accounting department uses this list to make entries in the cash receipts journal and the accounts receivable subsidiary ledger. The third list remains with the individual who opens the mail. The manager of the accounting department (or his or her designee) should check daily to ensure that the total of the cash received in the mail and through over-the-counter sales equals the amount of cash deposited by the cashier and also equals the amounts recorded in the cash receipts journal.

Cash Received from Over-the-Counter Sales

Some businesses, such as retail stores, collect a large portion of their cash receipts through over-the-counter sales. Two devices, cash registers and prenumbered sales tickets, are used independently or in conjunction with each other to control cash received on over-the-counter sales.

The conversion of cash registers into electronic point-of-sale devices has greatly improved the control of cash receipts from over-the-counter sales. These devices, which are linked to a central computer, instantaneously record cash transactions as well as keeping inventory records. Any type of cash register, however, should be prominently displayed so the customer can easily see the amounts of the cash transactions, and all cash sales should be recorded on the register. (In most stores, point-of-sale devices also are used to record credit sales.) At the end of the day, the cash received in the register is reconciled with totals maintained by the cash register. This reconciliation should not be performed by the individual in charge of the register. The figures from the register, reconciled with cash receipts, are then used to make the entries in the cash receipts journal.

The internal control over cash receipts from over-the-counter sales can be enhanced by using prenumbered sales tickets. In this situation, each salesperson receives prenumbered duplicate sales tickets at the beginning of the day. As a sale is made, the ticket is filled out in duplicate. The customer receives one of the tickets and takes it to a central cashier, who rings up the sale on the register. However, in many situations the salesperson also acts as the cashier. The other copy of the ticket is retained by the salesperson. In this system, the total of the cash receipts at the end of the day is compared with the total of the salesperson's duplicate tickets. Further, all numbered tickets must be accounted for. This ensures that all sales are rung up on the register. As we noted, the cash received from over-the-counter sales is combined with cash received through the mail and is deposited daily.

Cash Over or Short

When there are numerous cash transactions, errors are likely to occur. Individuals ringing up cash transactions on a cash register are human and will make errors. These errors are detected when the total cash received is compared with the reading on the cash register or prenumbered sales tickets.

To illustrate how to account for cash overages and shortages, assume that the cash register tape shows total sales of $1,510, but the actual cash count totals only $1,506. As a result, there is a $4 shortage which is recorded as follows:

Cash	1,506	
Cash Over and Short	4	
Sales		1,510
To record day's sales and cash shortage of $4.		

EXHIBIT 8–3
Purchase and Disbursements System

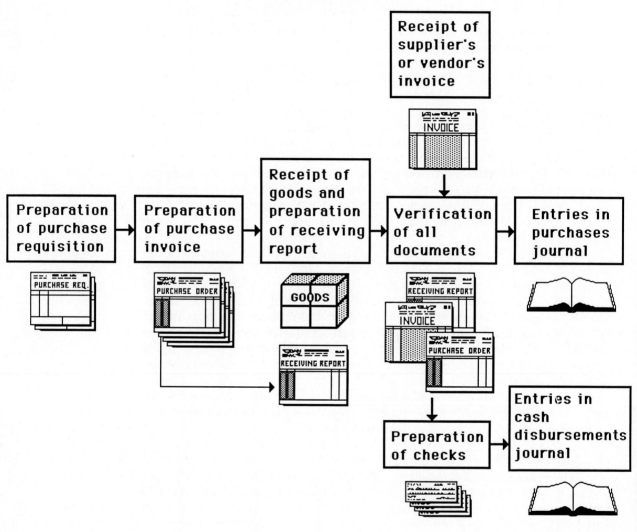

As the journal entry at the bottom of page 313 illustrates, the Cash Over and Short account is debited for cash shortages and credited for cash overages. At the end of the accounting period, this account will have either a debit or credit balance. A debit balance represents a cash shortage and is usually shown as a miscellaneous expense. A credit balance represents a cash overage and is generally shown as a miscellaneous revenue. Any consistent cash shortages and overages or a pattern in shortages and overages should be examined in order to determine their cause.

Cash Disbursements

Cash disbursements are made for a variety of reasons, including the payment of inventory purchases made on account, payments for services received, and for payroll. Failure to provide good internal control in this area can lead to the diversion of cash through the preparation and disbursement of unauthorized checks. An adequate internal control system over cash disbursements should be based on segregation of duties and the use of checks to make all cash disbursements. In most cases, a voucher system provides the greatest internal control. This system is illustrated in the last section of this chapter. At this point, we will use the purchase of inventory on account to illustrate internal control over cash disbursements.

The Purchase and Disbursement Cycle

An overview of the purchase and disbursement cycle is illustrated in Exhibit 8–3. The primary documents involved in the system are the purchase requisition, purchase order, purchase invoice, and receiving report. The purpose of this system and the documents are to ensure that only properly authorized purchases are made, that purchases are received, and that correct payment is made. A more detailed schematic picturing the interaction between the buyer and the seller is shown in Exhibit 8–4 on pages 316–317.

To illustrate how this system works, assume that on November 29 the inventory control department of Norris Plumbing Supply notices that Norris is running short of flexible gas hoses, one of its main products. As a result, the inventory control clerk prepares a purchase requisition for 50 dozen 6-foot flexible gas hoses and forwards it to the purchasing section of the accounting department. The **purchase requisition** is a document sent to the purchasing department requesting that it purchase a certain quantity and type of item. A purchase requisition is illustrated on page 318.

After receiving the requisition, the purchasing department reviews its list of vendors and places an order with a particular supplier. A purchase order, illustrated on page 318, is prepared and forwarded to the supplier. A **purchase order** is a document prepared by the purchaser which indicates to the seller the quantity, type, and estimated price of the items the buyer wishes to purchase. The policy of Norris Plumbing is that no invoice will be paid unless accompanied by a purchase order and receiving report.

After receiving the purchase order, the vendor (in this case Kwik Gas Lines) will either ship the goods or back order them. If changes are required because the goods are either not available or substitute goods are not on hand, Kwik should immediately notify Norris Plumbing.

When the goods are shipped by Kwik, a packing slip is enclosed. This packing slip is used by the receiving department to verify the amount of goods shipped. The packing slip is attached to a receiving report, which is prepared

EXHIBIT 8–4

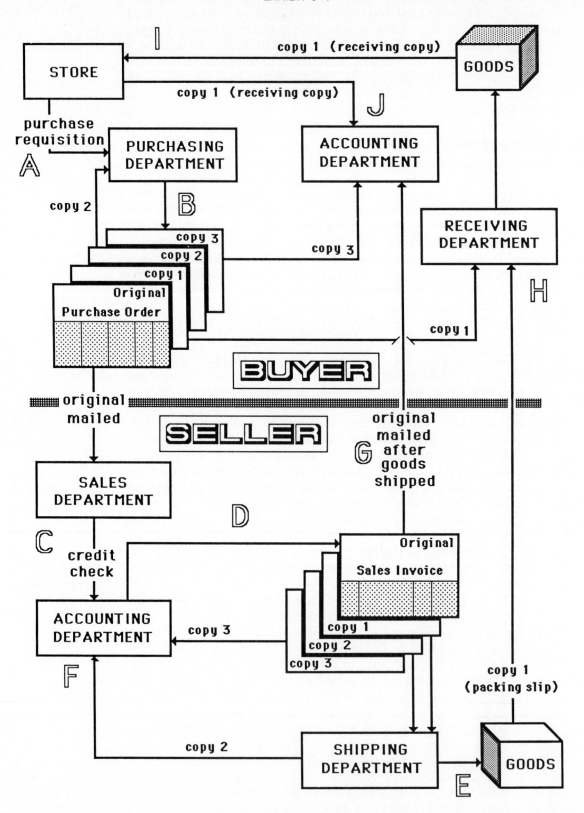

A The buyer's **retail store** forwards a purchase requisition to the **purchasing department** requesting the purchase of merchandise.

B The buyer's **purchasing department** prepares a **purchase order** (original and 3 copies):
- Original is mailed to the seller;
- Copy 1 goes to the buyer's **receiving department**;
- Copy 2 is filed;
- Copy 3 goes to the buyer's **accounting department**.

C When the purchase order is received by the seller, the buyer's credit is approved before the order is processed.

D The seller's **accounting department** prepares a sales invoice (original and 3 copies):
- Original and copy 3 is held by the seller's **accounting department**;
- Copy 1 and Copy 2 go to the seller's **shipping department**.

E The seller's **shipping department** packs the goods and encloses Copy 1 (**packing slip**). Copy 2 is sent back to the seller's **accounting department** listing the items shipped.

F The seller's **accounting department** completes the original invoice and Copy 3 using information entered on Copy 2 by the **shipping department**. THE SALE IS THEN RECORDED USING COPY 3 AS THE SOURCE DOCUMENT.

G The original sales invoice is dated and mailed to the buyer. This date begins the discount period.

H The buyer's **receiving department** unpacks the new merchandise, checking both the quality and quantity and noting any discrepancies. Copy 1 of the purchase order and the goods are then sent to the **store**.

I The **store** again checks the quality and quantity noting any discrepancies that might necessitate a return. Copy 1 of the purchase order is then forwarded to the buyer's **accounting department**.

J The sales invoice received from the seller and Copy 1 and Copy 3 of the purchase order are matched to verify that the merchandise ordered has been received in good condition. THE PURCHASE IS THEN RECORDED USING THESE AS SOURCE DOCUMENTS.

PURCHASE REQUISITION

No. R 123   Norris Plumbing Supply
                     Purchase Requisition

FROM: Inventory Control, LD Mgm.   DATE: Nov. 29

TO: Purchasing Department   Suggested Vendor: Kwik Gas Lines

QUANTITY	ITEM NUMBER	DESCRIPTION
50 Doz.	FG 6	6' Flexible Gas Line Hose

REASONS FOR PURCHASE

Replenish Supply

APPROVED _____
DATE ORDERED 12/1
P.O. NUMBER P0254

PURCHASE ORDER

ORDER NO.

0254

Norris Plumbing Supply
120 So. LaPeer Dr.
Los Angeles, CA 90021

TO   Kwik Gas Lines   SHIP TO   Norris Plumbing Supply

ADDRESS 192 So. Leonard Street   ADDRESS   see above

CITY   Los Angeles, CA 90081   CITY

FOR	REQ. NO.	HOW SHIP	DATE REQUIRED	TERMS		DATE
Inventory	R 123	United Parcel	12/10/87	2/10, n/30		12/1/87

	QUANTITY ORDERED	RECEIVED	PLEASE SUPPLY ITEMS LISTED BELOW	PRICE		UNIT
1	50 doz		6' Flexible gas line hose — FG6	75.	20	doz.
2						
3						
4						
5						
6						
7						

IMPORTANT

OUR ORDER NUMBER MUST APPEAR ON ALL INVOICES, PACKAGES, ETC.

PLEASE NOTIFY US IMMEDIATELY IF YOU ARE UNABLE TO SHIP COMPLETE ORDER BY DATE SPECIFIED.

PLEASE SEND 2 COPIES OF YOUR INVOICE WITH ORIGINAL BILL OF LADING.

PURCHASING AGENT

by the receiving department of Norris and indicates the amount and condition of the goods. Both items are then forwarded to the accounting department.

Upon shipment, Kwik will prepare a sales invoice and send it to Norris. (See below.) The accounting department of Norris will then compare the invoice to the purchase order, packing slip, and receiving report. Further, Norris's accounting department will verify the prices and the calculations on the invoice. After all verifications and reconciliations are made, the purchase is then recorded in the accounting records. When payment is due, the complete set of documents with a check authorization form is forwarded to the cash disbursement section of the accounting department for payment, less the appropriate discount.

SALES INVOICE

Kwik Gas Lines
192 So. Leonard Street
Los Angeles, CA 90081

Invoice 863   Customer's Order R123   Date 12/8/87

SOLD TO   •   Norris Plumbing Supply
120 So. LaPeer Dr.
Los Angeles, CA 90021

SHIPPED TO   •   Same

DATE SHIPPED		SHIPPED VIA	TERMS	F.O.B.	SALESMAN			
12/8/87		United Parcel	2/10, n/30		B.P. Farn			
50	doz	6' Flexible Gas line hose — FG6			75	20	3,760	00

The procedures just outlined represent the ideal. Not all firms need nor can afford the checks and balances built into the system. However, the closer the internal control system is to the one described, the better will be the system.

Most firms have a policy that requires all disbursements except minor petty transactions to be made by check. This requires the maintenance of a checking account and the implementation of controls over that account.

The Checking Account

All business firms maintain at least one checking account. When a business opens a checking account, the bank will require certain information such as proof of a business name and a business license. If the business is a corporation, certain other data may also be required, such as a resolution by the board of directors authorizing certain individuals to sign checks. A signature card listing those authorized to sign checks, as well as their signatures, must be completed. This is used by the bank to verify the signatures on checks presented for payment. Large firms often have an automatic check imprinter that signs all checks.

Once a checking account is opened, the firm receives personalized deposit tickets and checks. It is imperative that these personalized documents be used because they contain magnetic numbers that identify both the company and the bank. These magnetic numbers help facilitate the quick collection and payment of funds between banks.

The Deposit Slip

At the end of each business day, the designated individual in the accounting department should prepare a deposit slip in duplicate. This **deposit slip,** which is illustrated below and on the top of page 321, lists the cash and checks to be deposited. Each check is listed on the deposit slip by the bank identification number printed on the checks. This slip shows that A & D Associates deposited currency and checks totaling $7,101.83 on November 24, 1987. The bank officer who receives the deposit slip initials the duplicate slip and returns it to the depositor. The duplicate slip is used to verify the amount deposited at the bank and that all the day's receipts have been deposited and recorded in the cash receipts journal.

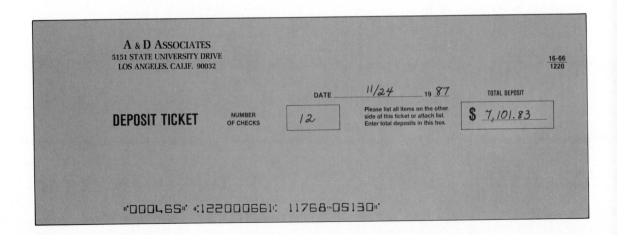

A & D ASSOCIATES
5151 STATE UNIVERSITY DRIVE
LOS ANGELES. CALIF. 90032

16-66
1220

DEPOSIT TICKET

NUMBER OF CHECKS: 12

DATE 11/24 19 87

Please list all items on the other side of this ticket or attach list. Enter total deposits in this box.

TOTAL DEPOSIT: $ 7,101.83

⑈000465⑈ ⑆122000661⑆ 11768⑈05130⑈

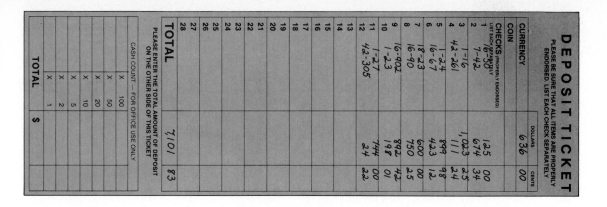

Checks

A **check** is a negotiable instrument signed by the authorized employee of the depositor to pay a specified sum of money to a certain individual or organization. The maker (or drawer) signs the check and the payee is the person to whom the check is written. An example of a check from A & D Associates is illustrated below. The important elements of the check are highlighted in that illustration. After the check is written, it is recorded in the cash payments journal. If a computer system is used, the computer can print the check and automatically make the entry in the cash payments journal.

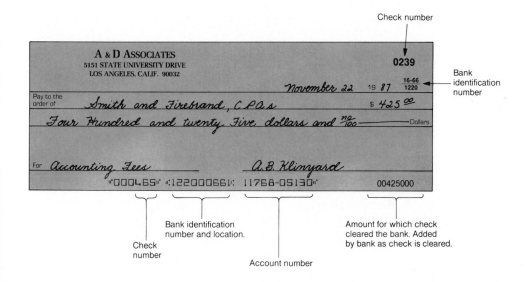

The Bank Statement

Every month the bank prepares a **bank statement** and mails it to the depositor. The statement should be addressed to a designated individual in the depositor's organization and should be opened only by that individual. The statement lists the beginning balance in the account, all deposits received, checks paid, other debits (charges) and credits (receipts), and the ending balance in the account.

In recent years, bank statements have become more complex as banks have begun to handle a variety of different types of transactions as their data-processing capabilities have increased. The bank statement for A & D Associates for the month of November is shown on page 323. It contains four sections. The first section summarizes all the transactions during the month. As indicated, the beginning balance on November 1 is $2,156.43. During the month, total credits (only deposits in this case) of $27,883.87 increased the balance, and total debits (checks paid of $28,099.26 plus a $108.00 NSF returned check) of $28,207.26 were paid, which decreased the balance. Interest of $18.50 earned on the average balance in the checking account was added to the balance, and service charges of $15.00 were deducted, resulting in an ending balance of $1,836.54.

The second section lists all the checks that the bank paid during the period. Each check is listed in order of check number. The checks can be listed this way because the check number is magnetically listed on the check, and this magnetic number is used in preparing the bank statement. The date on which the check cleared the bank is also listed on the statement.

The third section lists all the deposits made by A & D Associates and received by the bank. In this case, A & D does not make deposits daily. We did this in order to simplify our illustration. These deposits are listed on the statement by date.

The last section of this statement lists other transactions. These usually consist of service charges such as check-printing fees and monthly maintenance charges. In this illustration there are two service charges: $5.00 for printing checks and $10.00 for processing a deposit that was returned because of nonsufficient funds (NSF). That is, in the deposit of 11/23, a check for $108.00 was included that, when presented for payment at the payer's bank, was returned because the party who wrote the check had insufficient funds. The $108.00 debit is included with the total debits of $28,207.26 in the first section of the statement.

Other miscellaneous credits are also included in the fourth section of the statement. An example is the bank's collection of a note for a customer that the bank deposited directly in the customer's account. Other examples are interest on checking account balances and proceeds from bank loans. In our illustration, A & D earned $18.50 interest.

The Bank Reconciliation

A **bank reconciliation** is an essential part of any cash internal control system. If the cash balance per the bank statement can be reconciled with the cash balance per the firm's general ledger, this will ensure the accuracy of the firm's cash receipts and disbursement journal. This is so because the bank statement is prepared by the bank and is completely independent of the firm's accounting system. Whenever a third party's records can be used to verify internal records, the firm has good evidence as to the accuracy of its records. However, in order to maintain this independence, the bank reconciliation must be prepared by a designated individual within the firm who neither handles cash nor maintains the firm's cash accounting records.

At the end of the month or any period, the balance on the bank statement will not equal the balance shown in the firm's cash general ledger account because the bank and the depositor are likely to record certain transactions at

BANK STATEMENT

A & D Associates

5151 State University Dr.
Los Angeles, CA 90032

Checking Account Number

11768-05130

From: 11/1/87
Through: 11/30/87

1

Beginning Balance	+ Total Credits	− Total Debits	+ Interest	− Service Charge	= Ending Balance
2,156.43	27,883.87	28,207.26	18.50	15.00	1,836.54

2

Check Activity

Check	Date	Amount	Check	Date	Amount
221	11/4	683.24	235	11/22	147.75
222	11/4	500.00	236	11/30	386.25
223	11/7	1,246.32	237	11/29	152.40
224	11/9	1,056.22	238	11/21	2,456.20
226	11/12	247.32	239	11/29	425.00
227	11/7	1,022.28	240	11/30	2,167.67
228	11/12	746.46	241	11/25	843.13
229	11/21	1,000.01	243	11/22	52.30
230	11/15	4,331.00	245	11/24	1,105.00
231	11/17	2,456.56	246	11/27	785.15
232	11/19	1,132.24	250	11/30	42.40
233	11/30	1,010.00	251	11/30	542.36
234	11/27	3,562.00			

3

Deposits

Date	Amount	Date	Amount
11/1	1,050.25	11/16	725.00
11/4	4,200.01	11/23	1,022.43
11/7	653.24	11/25	7,101.83
11/8	1,524.87	11/26	500.24
11/11	2,220.00	11/27	603.36
11/12	2,600.24	11/28	1,050.23
11/15	532.15	11/30	4,100.02

4

Other Transactions

Date	Amount	Explanation
11/5	−5.00	Check Printing Fee
11/21	−10.00	NSF Check Return Charge
11/28	−108.00	NSF Check
11/30	+18.50	Interest

different times. On one hand, the depositor will record certain events prior to the time they are recorded by the bank. The examples are:

1. **Outstanding checks**—checks written by the depositor but yet to be paid by the bank. These occur because, when the check is written by the depositor, it is immediately deducted from the general ledger Cash account. However,

The Control and Accounting for Cash Transactions

there is a lag of a few days due to the mailing and so forth before the bank pays the check and deducts the amount from the depositor's account.

2. **Deposits in transit**—deposits made by the depositor but not yet recorded by the bank. These result because, once a deposit is made by the depositor, it is added to the general ledger Cash account, but because of lag time, the bank has yet to credit the depositor's account.

Conversely, the bank may record certain transactions prior to the time they are recorded by the depositor. There are a variety of such items, but the most common are service charges, charges for NSF checks, and interest earned.

1. The service charge is the amount the bank charges depositors for maintaining their account. The amount of the charge is usually based on a number of factors including the average balance in the depositor's account and the number of checks written.

2. NSF (nonsufficient funds) checks are checks that had been deposited by the company but were not paid by the drawer's bank when presented by the depositor's bank. The bank then charges the depositor's account and returns the check for future collection.

3. Interest earned is the amount of interest paid by the bank to the depositor based on the depositor's average daily balance.

Finally, both the bank and the depositor may make errors. If the bank makes an error, such as charging the depositor's account for a check drawn on a different account, the balance from the bank statement must be adjusted. If the error is in the depositor's records, the cash general ledger balance must be adjusted.

Preparing the Bank Reconciliation

There are several methods used to prepare bank reconciliations. For example, the balance per the bank statement may be reconciled to the general ledger cash balance or the general ledger cash balance may be reconciled to the bank's balance. However, the best method is to reconcile both the balance per the bank and the balance per the books or general ledger to an actual adjusted balance. This is accomplished by focusing on items that are recorded at different times by the bank and the depositor. The following steps should be followed in preparing such a bank reconciliation:

1. Determine deposits in transit. As we noted, deposits in transit are deposits recorded by the firm but not yet recorded by the bank. Deposits in transit can be determined by comparing the deposits listed in the cash receipts journal with those on the bank statement. By simply placing a check mark by the deposits listed in the cash receipts journal that agree with those listed on the bank statement, you will quickly be able to note which deposits have yet to be received by the bank. They will most likely be the deposits close to or at the end of the month. These deposits in transit must be added to the bank's balance to arrive at the corrected cash balance. It is important to be sure that any deposits in transit at the beginning of the month have been recorded on this month's bank statement.

2. Review all checks returned by the bank. All checks returned by the bank with the bank statement should be reviewed to make sure that they are the company's checks, they have been properly charged to the account, and they include an authorized signature.

3. Determine outstanding checks. As we noted, outstanding checks are checks written by the depositor but not yet paid by the bank. Outstanding checks can be determined by comparing the checks listed in the cash payments journal with those paid by the bank as shown on the bank statement. When making

this comparison you should make sure that the amount of the check written in the cash disbursements journal equals the amount for which the check was paid as evidenced by the magnetic number on the bottom of the check. By simply placing a check mark by the checks on the cash disbursements journal that agree, you will quickly be able to find the outstanding checks. These outstanding checks must be subtracted from the balance per the bank statement to arrive at the corrected cash balance.

4. Determine items debited or credited by the bank but not yet recorded in the accounting records. Included are service charges and interest earned. These items are evidenced by debit and credit memos issued by the bank. Debits must be deducted from the cash balance per the books and credits must be added to the cash balance per the books.

5. Determine if any errors were made by the bank or the firm. Depending on the nature of the error, it must either be added to or subtracted from the bank's balance or the balance per the books.

6. Make journal entries to record items recorded by the bank but not yet by the firm and for errors, if any, made by the firm.

An Example of a Bank Reconciliation

To illustrate the preparation of a bank reconciliation, we will use the November 30 bank statement for A & D Associates, shown on page 326. As this statement indicates, the balance per the bank at November 30 is $1,836.54. In addition, you have determined that the general ledger cash balance is $2,414.47, as indicated in the following cash T account:

Cash

11/1 Bal.	2,023.44		
Cash receipts	28,482.81	Cash disbursements	28,091.78
11/30 Bal.	2,414.47		

The bank reconciliation is presented on page 326. The balance, taken from the bank statement, is $1,836.54. The deposits in transit of $1,524.31 and $124.88 are determined by comparing the deposits on the cash receipts journal with the deposits listed on the bank statement.

The outstanding checks listed on the bank reconciliation are determined in a similar manner. All the checks listed in the cash payments journal are compared with the checks paid by the bank. As a result, eight checks totaling $1,193.76 are determined to be outstanding.

When the deposits in transit are added to the bank balance and the outstanding checks are subtracted, the actual (or corrected) balance of $2,291.97 is determined. There are no bank errors that need adjustment.

The balance in the cash general ledger account is $2,414.47, as shown in the T account. Interest revenue of $18.50 credited by the bank has not been recorded in the cash receipts journal and must be added to the balance per the books. The service charges of $15.00 and the NSF check for $108.00 must be subtracted. Finally, check number 236 was written for $386.25 and cleared the bank for that amount. However, by mistake it was recorded as $368.25 in the cash payments journal. Automobile expense was originally debited for the incorrect amount. Thus, the cash disbursements per the general ledger are un-

A & D Associates
Bank Reconciliation
November 30, 1987

Balance per Bank, November 30		$1,836.54
Add: Deposits in transit		
11/29	$1,524.31	
11/30	124.88	1,649.19
Less: Outstanding checks		
225	100.00	
242	158.10	
244	91.78	
247	100.25	
248	31.41	
249	22.12	
252	601.29	
253	88.81	(1,193.76)
Adjusted Balance		$2,291.97
Balance per Books, November 30		2,414.47
Add: Interest revenue		18.50
Less: Service charges	$ 15.00	
NSF check	108.00	
Error check no. 236	18.00	(141.00)
Adjusted Balance		$2,291.97

derstated by $18.00 ($386.25 − $368.25), and this amount must be deducted on the bank reconciliation. When these adjustments are made, the adjusted balance equals $2,291.97, and the bank account is reconciled.

The last step in the bank reconciliation process is to make adjusting entries for all the items required to adjust A & D Associates' general ledger cash account to the adjusted balance as determined on the bank reconciliation (that is, the items on the bottom half of the bank reconciliation). These entries are:

Nov. 30	Cash	18.50	
	Interest Revenue		18.50
	To record interest revenue earned on bank account.		
	Service Charge	15.00	
	Accounts Receivable	108.00	
	Automobile Expense	18.00	
	Cash		141.00
	To record adjustment from bank reconciliation, NSF check from Grant Co. recorded as a receivable and automobile expense debited for error in recording check no. 236.		

After these adjusting entries are posted, the cash T account will appear as follows:

Cash

11/1			
Bal.	2,023.44		
Cash		Cash disburse-	
receipts	28,482.81	ments	28,091.78
Adj.	18.50	Adj.	141.00
11/30			
Bal.	2,291.97		

If these entries are not made, the general ledger will never be adjusted to the correct balance as determined by the bank reconciliation.

Petty Cash

Although it would be preferable if all disbursements were made by check and all receipts were deposited intact, most firms usually maintain a small amount of cash on hand for miscellaneous expenditures. These expenditures include such items as postage, delivery expense, and minor office supplies such as coffee. The greatest degree of internal control can be maintained when a petty cash fund under the control of one individual is established to handle these expenditures. A **petty cash fund** is a small fund whose purpose is to make small disbursements of cash.

Creating a Petty Cash Fund
In order to create a petty cash fund, a check is written to cash for a set amount, such as $75 or $100. The size of the fund depends on the firm's needs but should be large enough to last at least three to four weeks. The check is cashed and the money put under the control of one designated individual. This ensures that one individual can be held responsible for all the cash in the fund. The entry to record the establishment of a $100 petty cash fund is:

Petty Cash	100	
Cash		100
To establish petty cash fund.		

Making Disbursements from the Fund
The custodian of the petty cash fund is in charge of approving and making all disbursements from the fund and must make out a petty cash voucher for all expenditures. This voucher indicates the purpose of the expenditure, the date, and the name of the person receiving the cash. The voucher is attached to the receipt, which has been stamped "paid" to ensure that it is not used again. Because a petty cash voucher is made out for all disbursements, the total of the vouchers and the remaining cash should always equal the amount of the fund, in this case $100.

Replenishing the Fund
During the month the custodian will make various disbursements from the petty cash fund, and at some time the fund will have to be replenished. For example, assume that during April disbursements totaling $84.32 were made from the $100 petty cash fund previously established. Analysis of the petty cash

The Control and Accounting for Cash Transactions   327 vouchers indicates that the disbursements were for the following expenses: postage, $24.10; delivery expense, $16.31; supplies, $15.39; and taxi fares, $28.52. Actual cash remaining on hand is $15.48, which indicates a shortage of $.20 ($100 − $84.32 = $15.68, the amount that should be on hand; because only $15.48 is on hand, there is a $.20 shortage). The shortage is recorded in a Cash Over and Short account.

In order to replenish the petty cash fund to its $100 balance, a check is drawn for $84.52 and is cashed. The following entry is made:

Postage Expense	24.10	
Delivery Expense	16.31	
Supplies Expense	15.39	
Taxi Expense	28.52	
Cash Over and Short	.20	
Cash		84.52
To record replenishment		
of petty cash fund.		

Notice that the appropriate expense accounts are debited and that cash is credited. There is no need to make an entry to the petty cash account because it still shows a balance of $100. Another entry to petty cash is not made unless the firm wants to increase or decrease the fund above or below $100. For example, if the firm decided to increase the petty cash from $100 to $150, it would make the following entry:

Petty Cash	50	
Cash		50
To increase petty cash		
fund to $150.		

The petty cash fund is replenished as needed. However, it should be replenished at the end of the accounting period in order to ensure that all expenses are properly recorded. Finally, surprise petty cash counts should be made to maintain good internal control over the fund.

The Voucher System

A **voucher system** is a highly formalized, structured system aimed at maintaining internal control over all expenditures and payables. This system combines the features of the purchase and cash disbursement journals and the internal control procedures over payables. The central element of a voucher system is a **voucher**—a preprinted document that, when properly filled out and approved, provides approval to the accounting department to issue a check. Thus, before any check can be issued, a voucher must be completed by an individual not involved in the cash disbursements transaction. Other elements of a voucher system include a voucher register and a check register.

The Voucher

A typical voucher is illustrated on the following page. The face amount of the voucher lists all the information relating to the liability. Included are such data as the invoice number, invoice date, date due, payee, terms of the invoice, and the invoice amount. Vouchers are sequentially numbered and prepared by

VOUCHER
Face of Voucher

A & D ASSOCIATES
LOS ANGELES, CA

PAY TO: Welcome Products   VOUCHER NO.   212

                 1801 S. Florence Ave.   DATE PREPARED: 2/21

                 Twin Cities, PA 26215   DATE DUE: 3/1

DATE of INVOICE: 2/21   GROSS AMOUNT: $2,400

INVOICE NO.   P-4683   LESS: CASH DISCOUNT   48

TERMS: 2/10, n/30   NET AMOUNT   2,352

APPROVED: M. L. Fernback   APPROVED: _____
                                              Controller*

*Approval required if over $5,000.

Reverse of Voucher

Account Debited	Account No.	Amount
Purchases	400	2,400
Freight-in	401	———
Rent Expense	501	———
Commissions	502	———
Salaries	503	———
Advertising	600	———
Delivery Expense	601	———
Repairs/Maintenance	602	———
Utilities	603	———
TOTAL		2,400

Account Distribution by: *S. a. M.*

VOUCHER NO.   121

DATE DUE   3/1

PAY TO: Welcome Products

             1801 So. Florence Ave.

             Twin Cities, PA 26215

GROSS AMOUNT OF
INVOICE $2,400

LESS: CASH DISCOUNT   48

NET AMOUNT   2,352

CHECK NO.

DATE PAID

ENTERED IN VOUCHER
REGISTER   *M. a. F*

The Control and Accounting for Cash Transactions

individuals not involved in the payable or cash disbursement area. The voucher—with the relevant invoices, receiving reports, and other documents, if necessary—is sent to another individual who verifies extensions and footings and then approves the voucher. The voucher is then sent to an individual in the accounting department who fills out the reverse side by indicating which accounts are to be debited. Notice that this procedure assures a separation of duties because the following steps are all performed by different individuals:

1. Preparation of voucher.
2. Approval for payments.
3. Account distribution.
4. Entry in voucher register.
5. Payment of check.

The Voucher Register

Immediately after approval, the voucher is entered in the **voucher register.** An example of a voucher register is presented on page 331. The voucher register contains all of the features of a purchases journal and some of the features of a cash disbursements journal. Thus, a voucher register is used to record all cash disbursements, not just those arising from inventory purchases. Such items as rent, repairs and maintenance, purchase of property, plant, and equipment, and repayment of loans all are recorded in the voucher register.

A voucher register has two other differences from a purchase journal. An account, Vouchers Payable, instead of Accounts Payable is credited and payment columns are added to the register. The payment columns are not completed until the check is prepared. Thus entries in the voucher register for which the payment columns have not been completed represent unpaid vouchers, a liability at any point in time.

Other than Vouchers Payable, the specific accounts assigned columns in the voucher register depend on the needs of the specific firm. The last column is used as a general column to handle all other accounts. The voucher register shown has specific columns for purchase, freight-in, commission, salaries, advertising, delivery, repairs, and maintenance of utilities.

Vouchers are entered in the voucher register in numerical order. Vouchers Payable is always credited and the appropriate account is debited. As we noted, the payment columns are not completed until the check is drawn. At the point the check is drawn, the payment date and check number are entered in the appropriate columns.

Two of the entries need further elaboration. The entry on February 14, voucher no. 209, records the entire payroll. Firms often pay their employees from a separate payroll account. On each payroll payment date a voucher is prepared and paid to cover the entire payroll. The check is then deposited in the special payroll account against which the payroll checks are drawn. Thus, the company does not have to keep funds in the payroll account until they are needed.

Voucher no. 212, entered on February 21 to Welcome Products, is the voucher illustrated on page 329. This voucher has not been paid as of the end of February and thus the payment columns are not yet completed. As we will see shortly, this voucher appears on the list of unpaid vouchers. Immediately after the vouchers are entered on the voucher register, they are filed in the unpaid voucher file by payment date rather than payee. This is because the

VOUCHER REGISTER

Voucher No.	Date	Payee	Payment Date	Check No.	Credit Vouchers Payable	Purchases	Freight-in	Commissions	Salaries	Advertising	Delivery	Repairs/Maintenance	Utilities	Other Accounts Name	No.	Amount
200	Feb. 1	Smith Development	Feb. 2	821	800									Rent Exp	501	800
201	2	Welcome Products	6	823	1,000	1,000										
202	2	Loa Freight	7	824	50		50									
203	4	So. Cal. Water & Power	5	822	124								124			
204	7	West Bank	7	825	5,200									Note Payable / Interest	202 / 701	5,000 / 200
205	8	L.L. Bean II	8	826	150			150								
206	10	O&L Agency	13	829	1,200					1,200						
207	11	First-Rate	12	828	3,800	3,800										
208	11	Commercial Telephone	12	827	160								160			
209	14	Payroll	14	830	6,200				6,200							
210	17	G. Orwell	18	831	100			100								
211	20	Air Express			75						75					
212	21	Welcome Products	21		2,400	2,400										
213	24	Loa Freight	24		80		80									
214	26	Petty Cash	26	832	64						24			Office Supplies / Postage / Miscellaneous	450 / 491 / 700	18 / 10 / 12
215	28	Link Plumbing			740							740				
					22,143 (201)	7,200 (400)	130 (401)	250 (502)	6,200 (503)	1,200 (600)	99 (601)	740 (602)	284 (603)			6,040 (✓)

331

firm is interested in controlling the timing of cash disbursement in order to take advantage of discounts or to avoid interest penalties.

The entries on the voucher register are posted to the general ledger accounts at specified intervals, but at least monthly. The procedures used are similar to posting any specialized journal in that only column totals need be posted for all columns but the general or other column. The posting notation in the general ledger accounts will be VR,P or something similar.

The Check Register

The **check register** presented below is used in conjunction with a voucher register and is a simplified cash disbursements journal with only three debit/credit columns, vouchers payable, purchase discounts, and cash. Remember, all the other columns often found on a normal cash disbursements journal are on the voucher register.

CHECK REGISTER

| | | | | | Debits | Credits | |
| | | | | | | | |
Date	Check No.	Payee	Voucher No.	Voucher Payable	Purchase Discount	Cash
Feb 2	821	Smith Development	200	800		800
5	822	So. Cal. Water & Power	203	124		124
6	823	Welcome Products	201	1,000	20	980
7	824	Loa Freight	202	50		50
7	825	West Bank	204	5,200		5,200
8	826	L.L. Bean II	205	150		150
12	827	Commercial Telephone	208	160		160
12	828	First-Rate	207	3,800	38	3,762
13	829	O&L Agency	206	1,200		1,200
14	830	Payroll	209	6,200		6,200
18	831	G. Orwell	210	100		100
26	832	Petty Cash	214	64		64
				18,848	58	18,790
				(201)	(402)	(101)

The vouchers are paid in the order of their payment date, which was the order in which they were filed. At the appropriate date, a member of the accounting department pulls the voucher and a check is written. The check number and date are noted on the reverse side of the original voucher as well as in the voucher register. When an entry is made on the check register, Vouchers Payable is debited, Cash is credited, and, if appropriate, Purchase Discounts is credited. At the end of the month the totals of each of the three columns in the check register are posted to the appropriate general ledger accounts.

In order to maintain good internal control, the accounting department is not authorized to sign the checks. All the checks, along with the supporting vouchers and documents, are forwarded to the treasurer's office. They are examined to ensure that they are complete and have been signed by the appropriate individual. The voucher, supporting documents, and often a duplicate of the check are then perforated with a paid stamp and filed by the payee. Stamping "paid" on the voucher and related documents ensures that they are not used to make a duplicate payment.

Schedule of Unpaid Vouchers

At the end of each accounting period, a schedule of unpaid vouchers is prepared. The schedule is developed by listing all the vouchers from the voucher register for which a check has not yet been written. This list for **A & D Associates** is presented below. The total of unpaid vouchers is $3,295 and should be verified by two calculations. First, all the vouchers remaining in the unpaid voucher file should be totaled and should, as in this case, equal $3,295. Furthermore, as a proof, the total debits to the Vouchers Payable account for the month should be subtracted from the total credits to the Vouchers Payable account. The resulting figure in the example should also equal $3,295. The proof is shown below.

SCHEDULE OF UNPAID VOUCHERS
February 28

Voucher No.	Payee	Amount
211	Air Express	$ 75
212	Welcome Products	2,400
213	Loa Freight	80
215	Link Plumbing	740
	Total Unpaid Vouchers	$3,295

Proof:

Vouchers payable credit from voucher register	$22,143
Vouchers payable debit from check register	18,848
Total unpaid vouchers	$ 3,295

This schedule of unpaid vouchers serves the same purpose as the accounts payable trial balance discussed in Chapter 7. Yet it is much easier to prepare and does not require the maintenance of an accounts payable subsidiary ledger for each vendor or supplier. However, data pertaining to individual creditors such as total invoices outstanding for each vendor or total purchases made from each vendor are lost when accounts payable subsidiary ledgers are not maintained.

A Voucher System—A Summary

A voucher system is an elaborate, structured system developed to provide maximum internal control over all disbursements. One of the primary features of the voucher system is the high degree of separation of duties. For example, all of the following functions are likely to be performed by different individuals at different times:

1. Preparation of voucher.
2. Approval for payment.
3. Account distribution.
4. Entry in voucher register.
5. Preparation of check.
6. Signing of check.

However, a complete voucher system is neither feasible nor necessary for every firm. The system needs a large accounting staff, and in some cases the cost of maintaining a voucher system outweighs its benefits. This is especially true in smaller, owner-managed businesses, where in order to maintain internal control it is often necessary for the owner to take a more active role in the internal control system.

Summary of Learning Objectives

1. *What is included in the balance sheet account Cash?* Cash is any medium of exchange that a bank will accept for deposit. Thus, cash includes coins, paper money, money orders, checks, certified and cashiers' checks, and money on deposits in a bank. IOU's and postdated checks are not included in cash. Cash, unless it is unavailable for current use, is considered a current asset.

2. *Management control over cash.* Management is very concerned with the control of cash. A system must be developed to:
   1. Prevent losses, theft, and misappropriation of cash.
   2. Provide accurate records of all cash receipts, disbursements, and other cash transactions.
   3. Provide accurate and timely information concerning cash balances.

3. *The specifics of internal control procedures over cash.* Internal control over cash is important in order to prevent theft or misappropriation. The design of a particular internal control system must meet the needs of the specific firm. However, if possible, the following steps or procedures should be incorporated into the system:
   1. Segregation of duties.
   2. A limited number of bonded individuals who actually handle cash.
   3. Procedures that are clearly written and documented.
   4. All cash receipts deposited, intact, daily; all but minor cash disbursements made by check.
   5. All cash disbursements verified and approved.

4. *Bank checking transactions, including the purpose and preparation of the bank reconciliation.* All but petty cash disbursement should be made by check. A bank reconciliation should be prepared monthly by a designated individual who neither handles cash transactions nor has access to cash-related accounting records. A bank reconciliation is prepared by recording both the bank's and the ledger cash balance to an adjusted correct amount. A bank reconciliation takes the following general form:

Balance per bank	$7,500
Add: Deposits in transit	2,000
Less: Outstanding checks	(3,500)
Plus or minus bank errors	0
Adjusted balance	$6,000
Balance per books	$5,875
Add: Interest	75
Collection on notes	260
Less: Service charge	(10)
NSF checks	(200)
Other charges	0
Plus or minus firm errors	
Adjusted balance	$6,000

Adjusting journal entries must be made for any item required to reconcile the general ledger balance to the adjusted balance.

5. *The accounting procedures for the establishment and maintenance of petty cash fund.* All cash disbursements not made by check should be made from a petty cash fund. The fund should be under the control of a single individual. The following entries pertain to petty cash accounts:

Petty Cash	100	
Cash		100
To establish the fund.		
Delivery Expense	20	
Freight-in	15	
Postage	30	
Office Supplies	22	
Cash		87
To replenish the fund.		

6. *The purpose and procedures relating to a voucher system.* A voucher system is an elaborate system aimed at controlling all cash expenditures. The main elements of the system are:

1. Vouchers.
2. A voucher register.
3. A check register.

However, such systems are costly to maintain and should be tailored to the specific needs of the firm.

Key Terms

Bank Reconciliation	**Petty Cash Fund**
Bank Statement	**Purchase Order**
Cash	**Purchase Requisition**
Check	**Remittance Advice**
Check Register	**Voucher**
Deposits in Transit	**Voucher Register**
Deposit Slip	**Voucher System**
Outstanding Checks	

Problem for Your Review

Bank Reconciliation. As the accountant for Hall Ltd., you are to prepare its March 31 bank reconciliation. You have obtained the following data:

1. The ending balance on the March 31 bank statement is $8,975.

2. During your examination of the bank statement, you noticed that the bank charged Hall's account for $170 for a check that should not have been charged to the account. Furthermore, you find that the bank credited the firm's account for a note it collected on its behalf. The credit was for $1,090. The principal of the note is $1,000, and the interest for the month is $100. The bank charged a fee for making the collection. This note has not yet been recorded in the firm's accounts.

3. The balance in the cash general ledger account is $7,258. You determined that the deposits on 3/30 and 3/31 for $1,567 and $432, respectively, have not yet been credited to the account by the bank.

4. Analysis of the cash payments journal indicated that the following checks have not yet been paid by the bank:

No.	Amount
842	$ 170
863	243
867	190
868	586
869	320
870	1,450

While verifying checks, you discovered that check no. 832, written to Smith Janitorial Service, was recorded in the cash disbursements journal as $57. The actual amount of the check was $75, and that is the amount paid by the bank.

5. A debit memo for $20 for monthly maintenance fees and a debit memo for $125 for an NSF check from A. Spielberg were included in the returned checks. These items have not yet been recorded on Hall's books.

Required:

1. Prepare a bank reconciliation at March 31.
2. Make the required adjusting journal entry.

Solution

1. Bank Reconciliation

Hall Ltd.
Bank Reconciliation
March 31

Balance per Bank Statement			$8,975
Add: Deposit in transit 3/30		$1,567	
3/31		432	1,999
Bank error check charged against wrong account			170
Less: Outstanding checks	No.	Amount	
	842	$ 170	
	863	243	
	867	190	
	868	586	
	869	320	
	870	1,450	(2,959)
Adjusted Balance			$8,185

Balance per General Ledger		$7,258
Add: Note collection and interest less collection charge		1,090
Less: Maintenance fee	$ 20	
NSF check	125	
Error on check no. 832 ($75 — $57)	18	(163)
Adjusted Balance		$8,185

2. Journal Entries

Cash	1,090	
Service Charge	10	
Note Receivable		1,000
Interest Revenue		100
To record collection of notes.		
Service Charge	20	
Accounts Receivable	125	
Repairs and Maintenance	18	
Cash		163
To record service charge, NSF check by		
Spielberg, and error in check no. 832.		

Questions

1. Which of the following item(s) would not be included in the current assets section under cash when preparing a December 31, 1987 balance sheet?

   a. Certified checks.

   b. Cash on hand.

   c. A check dated January 2, 1988.

   d. Cash held in a building fund.

   e. Petty cash.

2. What are the purposes of a management control system over cash?

3. Is it possible to have too much cash? Explain.

4. How many ledger accounts should a firm maintain for the balance sheet item cash?

5. Why do you think it is important that those authorized to handle cash also do not do the record keeping for cash?

6. What is the purpose of having duplicate prenumbered sales tickets for over-the-counter sales?

7. What is a remittance advice? What purpose does it serve?

8. What is the purpose of keeping the purchase order, purchase invoice, and receiving report with each other?

9. List and explain three items that may be required to adjust the bank balance to a corrected balance when performing a bank reconciliation.

10. Why is it usually necessary to adjust the cash general ledger balance when preparing a bank reconciliation?

11. What items may cause the difference between the total debits charged against a depositor's account and the depositor's total cash disbursements for the month?

12. What items may cause the difference between the total credits on a depositor's bank account and the total cash receipts in the depositor's cash receipts journal?

13. Why would a firm establish a petty cash fund? Why should the fund be replenished at the end of each accounting period, regardless of the amount of cash remaining in the fund at that time?

14. What is the purpose of a voucher system? Should every firm establish such a system?

15. What is a voucher register? A check register? How do they differ from a purchase journal and a cash disbursements journal?

16. Is the following statement true? Why or why not?

   The dollar total of unpaid vouchers in the open voucher file should equal the balance in the vouchers payable account at any point of time.

17. Is the following statement true? Why or why not?

   Only large businesses can have an adequate internal control system.

Exercises

1. Internal Control. The Boston Company is about to establish a $400 petty cash fund. The following guidelines have been developed: The fund will be under the control of Henry Winkler except when he goes to lunch or is on break. During those times Katie McKiven will handle the fund. In addition to normal petty cash transactions, the fund will be used to make loans of under $25 to employees. When employees need a loan they will write checks to the Boston Company. The employee receives the cash and the check remains uncashed with other items in petty cash. When the employee repays the loan, the check is returned.

Required:

    a. Evaluate the internal control guidelines over petty cash.

    b. What improvements can you suggest?

2. Internal Control. Eric Tracey handles the cash receipts and accounts receivable area of Commonwealth Products' accounting section. On Thursday, because of temporary financial difficulties, Tracey took $2,500 from the cash drawer. This represents the bulk of the week's cash receipts from over-the-counter sales. All cash receipts are deposited weekly on Friday. In order to conceal this, he then took two checks totaling $2,500 from the next day's incoming mail, which represented customer payments on purchases. Tracey did not record anything in the cash receipts journal. He then deposited these two checks, totaling $2,500, in the week's deposit on Friday to take the place of the $2,500 he took. Finally, in order to keep the customers from disputing their accounts, he made the following entry in the general journal:

Sales Returns and Allowances	2,500	
Accounts Receivable—Y Company		1,240
Accounts Receivable—Z Company		1,260

    1. How do these actions of Tracey affect the balance in the general ledger accounts Cash and Accounts Receivable and the subsidiary ledger accounts receivable?

    2. Evaluate the internal control of Commonwealth Products. Make suggestions for improvement.

3. Internal Control. The B. B. Dean Company is a mail order catalog firm. The firm's business has expanded greatly in the last few years, and the president is concerned about maintaining strong internal control. She tells you that after an order is received, the merchandise is pulled from the warehouse shelves and sent to the shipping department, where it is shipped. After shipment an invoice is prepared and mailed to the customer with credit terms of 2/10, n/30. Because of the nature of the business, about 30% of the items are returned for either a cash refund or a credit on account.

Required:

    a. What are some of the potential internal control problems with such a business?

    b. Outline the procedures the firm should follow when filling an order. Start with the receipt of the order and continue through shipment, billing, and possibly the receipt of returned goods.

4. Bank Reconciliation. From the following data prepare the bank reconciliation for the E. O. Smith Company as of April 30, 1987: balance per bank statement April 30, $1,150.25; balance per books April 30, $1,048.34; outstanding checks, $342.85; interest income earned on average balance, $12.40; deposit in transit, $246.34; check printing charge, $7.00. In addition, prepare any necessary journal entries.

5. Bank Reconciliation—Determining Missing Data. In preparing the bank reconciliation for the Hopie Company, you obtained the following information: balance per bank, $10,465; balance per books, $10,072; outstanding checks, $1,058; notes collected by bank for firm, $125; service charge, $6. What was the amount of the deposits in transit?

6. Bank Reconciliation—Determining Missing Data. The Kenney Company conducts all of its cash transactions by check. Thus all receipts and payments are received or made by checks. You obtained the following information:

Bank Reconciliation
September 30

Balance per bank	$10,025
Add: Deposits in transit	2,150
Less: Outstanding checks	(1,825)
Balance per books	$10,350

Data from October

	Per Bank	Per Books
September deposits	$10,650	$11,985
September checks	9,940	9,175

Given the above information, determine as of October 31:

1. Deposits in transit.
2. Outstanding checks.

7. Petty Cash Transactions. The Harvey Company maintains a petty cash fund of $100. At the end of March the fund contained the following:

Cash and currency	$ 17.57
Expense vouchers	
Postage	20.00
Delivery expense	34.30
Office supplies	15.65
Parking	12.48
Total	$100.00

Prepare the necessary journal entry at March 31 to replenish the fund.

8. Petty Cash Transactions. The Corona Company currently maintains a petty cash fund of $200.00. At December 31 the fund contained the following items:

Cash and currency	$ 9.10
Expense vouchers	
Delivery expense	22.30
Office supplies	105.00
Postage	20.00
Taxi (debit travel)	15.00
Parking	18.50
Donation to Cancer Fund	10.00
Total	$199.90

Recent experience indicates that $200.00 is not enough money for the fund and the firm decides to increase the fund to $300.00. Make the necessary journal entries to replenish and to increase the fund.

9. Establishing a Petty Cash Fund. On May 1 the Goldsmith Company decides to establish a $200.00 petty cash fund. At May 31, the end of its fiscal year, the following items were in the fund:

Cash and currency	$163.25
Expense vouchers	
Donations	5.00
Salary advance to employee	20.00
Office supplies	11.75
Total	$200.00

Required:

a. There is currently $163.25 in the fund. Why is it necessary to replenish the fund at May 31?
b. Prepare the entry to replenish the fund.

10. Voucher System. The Telecopter Corporation uses a voucher system. Following are several transactions. For each transaction, indicate whether it would be recorded in the voucher register, check register, or both.

   a. Prepared voucher no. 606 to purchase merchandise inventory from Wade Co. in the amount of $1,200. Terms are 2/10, n/30. The firm uses the periodic inventory system and all items are recorded gross.

   b. Prepared voucher no. 607 to purchase typewriter from Klein Office Supply for $842.

   c. Issued check no. 1023 to Wade Company within discount period.

   d. Prepared voucher no. 608 to Hawkins Realty in amount of $1,200 for rent.

   e. Issued check no. 1024 to Klein Office Supply to pay voucher no. 607.

   f. Issued check no. 1025 to Hawkins Realty to pay voucher no. 608.

   g. Prepared voucher no. 609 to replenish $100 petty cash fund which contains $36 cash and the following receipts: postage, $12; delivery, $25; parking, $27.

Problem Set A

8A–1. Internal Control. William Stolen works in the accounting department of Computech, a retail minicomputer store. He is in charge of the purchasing function, as well as accounts payable. Many of the computers purchased by Computech are delivered by the manufacturer directly to Computech's clients without first being delivered to the Computech store.

Stolen decided to divert the firm's computers to his own use in the hope of opening his own store. In order to do this, Stolen did the following: He first prepared fake purchase orders under Computech's name for computers and peripheral equipment. He had the suppliers deliver the merchandise to a little store he rented called Specialty Computer Sales. When the order arrived at Specialty, Stolen entered them in the purchases journal as:

Purchase
Accounts Payable

When the invoices were due, Stolen prepared the checks and sent them to the treasurer for signature. Based on a purchase order and vendor's invoice, the checks were signed and mailed to the vendor.

Required:

   a. Discuss the weaknesses in internal control, if any, in the system described above.

   b. What suggestions would you make?

8A–2. Bank Reconciliation. Using the information below, prepare a bank reconciliation for the month ended July 31, 1987 for Video Fun Co. In addition, make any required journal entries.

   1. The bank statement showed an ending balance of $8,742 at July 31. The general ledger cash account showed an ending balance of $10,121 at that date.

   2. Your examination showed that included with the bank statement were:

      a. A credit memo indicating that the bank collected a $540 note for you. The interest portion was $525. The bank charged a $5 collection fee.

      b. A debit memo for a $125 NSF check received by R. Cavett for payment on open account.

      c. A debit memo for $5 for printing checks.

   3. The deposit of $2,149 representing July 31 cash receipts was taken to the bank after 3:00 P.M. As a result it was not posted by the bank until August 1.

   4. Your review of the bank statement and cash disbursements journal indicated that the following checks, which were written in July, were not returned with the paid checks: no. 208 for $175, no. 209 for $83, no. 212 for $197, and no. 213 for $742.

   5. The bank charged Video's account for an $832 check. Because no check was returned with the statement and Video did not write a check for that amount, further inquiry was made. It was determined that the account of Televideo Co. should have been charged for that amount.

8A-3. Bank Reconciliation. Lenore Gonzales is a successful consultant. She asks you, her accountant, to prepare her November 30 bank reconciliation. You have obtained the following data:

1. The November 30 bank statement showed an ending balance of $2,463. The general ledger cash account showed a balance of $3,988 as of that date.

2. All deposits are made by mail. Examination of the bank statement indicated that the deposits made at the end of the month were not credited to Lenore's account. These deposits are:

November 29	$1,400
November 30	700

3. The following items were returned with the bank statement:
   a. A credit memo in the amount of $24 for interest earned on the average daily balance.
   b. A debit memo for $156 for an NSF check written by L. Dootle, a client paying on account.
   c. A debit memo for $963 for an automatic repayment of a bank loan. The principal portion is $874.
   d. A debit memo for $7 for monthly service charges. Lenore's accountant makes a monthly general journal entry to record this recurring fee prior to preparing the bank reconciliation. Other items have not been recorded.

4. The following checks were written by Lenore but have not yet been paid by the bank: no. 243 for $124, no. 244 for $37, no. 246 for $641, no. 247 for $932, and no. 249 for $107.

5. In reconciling the credits to the cash receipts journal, you determined that a deposit properly credited for $854 was recorded in the cash receipts journal for only $845. The check was for services performed at that time.

6. In reconciling the bank debits to the cash disbursements journal, you find that check no. 212 was written and properly cleared the bank for $972. It was recorded in the cash disbursements journal for $792. It was written to pay a repair person for work performed at that time.

Required:
   a. Prepare a bank reconciliation at November 30.
   b. Make any necessary journal entries.

8A-4. Bank Reconciliation—Missing Data. Computer Software Co. makes all cash receipts and disbursements by check. You have obtained the following information for February and March of the current year:

Computer Software Co.
Bank Reconciliation
February 28

Balance per Bank Statement	$10,683
Add: Deposits in transit	1,867
Less: Outstanding checks	(2,438)
Adjusted Balance	$10,112
Balance per Books	$10,119
Less: Printing charge	(7)
Adjusted Balance	$10,112

Transactions During March

	Per Bank Statement	Per Accounting Records
Balance, March 31	$ 7,717	$ 9,212
March deposits	15,792	15,100
March checks	17,248	16,000
Note payable to bank automatically charged against account (not included in March cash disbursements per accounting records)	1,500	
Monthly service charge	10	

Required:

a. Determine the following as of March 31:

1. Deposits in transit.

2. Outstanding checks.

b. Prepare a bank reconciliation at March 31.

c. Make the necessary adjusting entries. Assume that the interest portion on the note is $200.

8A–5. Bank Reconciliation—Using Cash Receipts and Disbursements Journals. As the accountant for the Marx Company, you have obtained the following information in preparing to do the bank reconciliation for June 30, 1987:

Cash Receipts Journal		Cash Disbursements Journal		
Date	Debit Cash	Date	Check No.	Credit Cash
6/1	$ 1,540	6/1	206	$ 154
6/8	786	6/3	207	633
6/12	2,210	6/6	208	1,054
6/18	3,152	6/10	209	2,201
6/24	1,400	6/12	210	1,564
6/29	1,256	6/16	211	25
6/30	1,001	6/21	212	31
	$11,345	6/22	213	789
		6/23	214	432
		6/26	215	1,891
		6/27	216	2,001
		6/29	217	1,984
		6/30	218	102
				$12,861

GENERAL LEDGER

Cash   Account No. 101

Date	Item	Ref.	Debit	Credit	Balance	
					Debit	Credit
May 31	Balance				1,914	
June 30		CR42	11,345		13,259	
June 30		CD81		12,861	398	

CHAPTER 8

BANK STATEMENT—MARX COMPANY

			Account No: 1006-54-9342	
Long Beach National Bank				
Account Name: Marx Corporation			Date: June 30, 1987	
Date	Checks and Misc. Debits		Deposits and Misc. Credits	Balance
Beginning Balance				$4,132
June				
1	980	1,020	482	2,614
2	700		1,540	3,454
3	154			3,300
5	633			2,667
10	1,054	2,201	768	180
11	150 NSF			30
14	1,564		2,210	676
15				
16	25			651
24	432	31	3,152	3,340
25			1,400	4,740
26				
28	2,001			2,739
30	10 SC		141 CM	2,870

Code: I = Interest; NSF = Not sufficient funds; SC = Service charge; DM = Debit memo; CM = Credit memo.

In addition, you determined the following data:

a. The deposit of $768 credited by the bank on 6/10 was correctly credited for $768. It represented an immediate payment for professional fees. It was recorded in the cash receipts journal on 6/8.

b. The NSF check was from Mr. Edwards and was a payment on an open account.

c. The credit memo is for a note receivable collected by the banks. The interest portion is $41.

d. At the end of May, checks no. 203 for $980, no. 204 for $700, and no. 205 for $1,020 were outstanding. The deposit in transit at the end of May was $482.

Required:

a. Prepare a bank reconciliation at June 30, 1987.

b. Make any necessary adjusting journal entries.

8A–6. Petty Cash Transactions. The Boggs Farm Equipment Corporation decided in November to establish a $200 petty cash fund. The following transactions affected the fund during November and December:

• November 1: A check for $200 is drawn to establish the fund.

• November 30: Examination of the fund indicates that $72.40 in cash is on hand. The following expense vouchers are also on hand:

Donations	$12.00
Office supplies	47.56
Parking	24.32
Delivery expense	30.42
Repairs	15.60

A check is drawn to replenish the fund.

• December 31: Examination of the fund indicates that $12.36 is on hand. The following expense vouchers are also on hand:

Travel	$48.00
Freight-out	17.00
Postage	23.46
Store supplies	96.18

The Control and Accounting for Cash Transactions

The firm decides to increase the fund to $300. A check is drawn to replenish and to increase the fund.

Required:

Make all the necessary journal entries to record these transactions.

8A–7. Voucher System. The Ironside Company uses a voucher that includes a voucher register and a check register similar to the ones illustrated in the text.

VOUCHERS PREPARED BY THE ACCOUNTING DEPARTMENT DURING APRIL

Date	Voucher No.	Payee	Amount	Terms	Account Distribution
April					
1	231	AB Realty Co.	$ 1,500	2/10, n/30	Rent
2	232	Freeze Corp.	8,400	2/10, n/30	Purchases
4	233	Best Repair Service	100		Repairs
5	234	Airborne Freight	75		Freight-in
8	235	Al Smith, Inc.	2,800	2/10, n/30	Purchases
11	236	Dees Temporary Service	1,200		Outside Lbr.
15	237	First Westwood Bank	10,250		Payroll
16	238	CD Advertising Agency	1,100		Advertising
21	239	Best Office Supplies	600	2/10, n/30	Var. off. sup.
24	240	Hand Made Furniture	2,300	n/30	Office furn.
25	241	High Priced Gas Co.	245		Utility
27	242	Old Iron Works	4,200	2/10, n/30	Purchases
28	243	Tired Phone Co.	150		Utility
30	244	First Westwood Bank	10,300		Payroll
30	245	Federal Loan Co.	2,500		Note pay–$2000 Interest– $ 500

CHECKS PAID IN APRIL

Date	Check No.	Payee	Voucher No.	Amount
April				
2	483	Douglas Smith Inc.	207	$ 1,850
2	484	D. D. Plant Co.	229	75
3	485	AB Realty Co.	231	1,500
4	486	Pull Inc.	230	1,960
5	487	Best Repair Service	233	100
9	488	Airborne Freight	234	75
10	489	Freeze Corp.	232	8,232
14	490	Dees Temporary Service	236	1,200
15	491	Payroll	237	10,250
21	492	Al Smith, Inc.	235	2,800
26	493	High Priced Gas Co.	241	245
27	494	Best Office Supplies	239	588
30	495	Tired Phone Co.	243	150
30	496	Payroll	244	10,300
30	497	Federal Loan Co.	245	2,500

The following items were in April's paid voucher file but were unpaid as of March 31:

Date	Voucher No.	Payee	Date of Invoice	Terms	Amount
April					
2	207	Douglas Smith, Inc.	March 21		$1,850
2	229	D. D. Plant Co.	March 15		75
4	230	Pull Inc.	March 25	2/10, n/30	2,000

Required:

a. Record the total of unpaid vouchers as of March 31 in the general ledger account Vouchers Payable, no. 201.

b. Enter the vouchers prepared in April in a voucher register similar to the one on page 321 in the text.

c. Enter the checks written in April in a check register similar to the one on page 322 in the text.

d. Foot the voucher and check register. Post the appropriate amounts to the Vouchers Payable account. Prepare a list of unpaid vouchers and ensure that it agrees with the April 30 balance in Vouchers Payable.

Problem Set B

8B–1. Internal Control. The Lovable Egg Museum operates a small museum in Minneapolis. Members of the Lovable Egg Society are allowed to enter the museum free of charge. Non-members pay a $2 entrance fee which is collected by two clerks who are stationed at the museum entrance.

At the end of each day one of the clerks takes the proceeds to the museum treasurer. The treasurer then counts the cash in the presence of the clerk and puts the cash in the safe. On Friday of each week the clerk takes the cash to the bank and receives a signed deposit slip from the bank clerk, which serves as the basis for the weekly entry to the cash receipts journal.

Required:

a. Identify the weaknesses in the internal control system.

b. What recommendations would you make?

8B–2. Bank Reconciliation. Using the following information, prepare a bank reconciliation for the month ended December 31 for Southern California, Inc. In addition, make any required journal entries.

1. The bank statement showed an ending balance of $6,719.79 at December 31. The general ledger cash account showed an ending balance of $6,385.96 at December 31.

2. Your examination showed that included with the bank statement was a credit memo indicating that the bank collected $1,100 in accounts receivable for you. The bank charged a $5 fee.

3. A credit memo showed $33.74 interest earned on average balance.

4. A debit memo showed a $3 monthly service charge.

5. A deposit of $1,374.29 representing December 31 cash receipts was not posted in the bank statement.

6. Your review of the bank statement and cash disbursements journal indicated that the following checks written in December were not returned: no. 1034 for $125.27; no. 1036 for $83.78; no. 1037 for $378.54; no. 1040 for $21.79.

7. Check no. 1030, issued for monthly rent, properly paid by the bank for $596, was recorded in the book for $569.

8B–3. Bank Reconciliation. As the accountant for Central Communication Co., you are preparing the bank reconciliation as of September 30, 1987. You have obtained the following data:

1. The bank statement showed an ending balance as of 9/30/87 of $3,785. The general ledger cash account showed a balance of $5,303 as of that date.

2. Deposits of $769 and $338 representing cash receipts of 9/28 and 9/30 were not posted by the bank.

3. The following items were returned with the bank statement:

   a. A credit memo in the amount of $17 for interest earned in September.

   b. A debit memo for $176 for a NSF check written by GEE Company.

   c. A debit memo for $1,300 for an automatic repayment of a bank loan. The interest portion is $1,245.

   d. A debit memo for $5 for monthly service charge.

4. The following checks were written by Central Communication Co. but not yet paid by the bank: no. 3479 for $126; no. 3480 for $374; no. 3483 for $29; no. 3485 for $273; no. 3487 for $137; no. 3488 for $114.

The Control and Accounting for Cash Transactions   **345**

Required:

    a. Prepare a bank reconciliation at September 30, 1987.

    b. Make any required journal entries.

8B–4. Bank Reconciliation—Missing Data. Standard Company makes all cash receipts and disbursements by check. You have obtained the following information for November and December 1987:

Standard Company
Bank Reconciliation
November 30, 1987

Balance per bank	$14,785
Add: Deposit in transit	1,756
Less: Outstanding checks	(3,574)
Adjusted balance	$12,967
Balance per book	$12,972
Less: Service charge	(5)
Adjusted balance	$12,967

Transactions during December:

	Per Bank Statement	Per Book
Balance, December 31	$17,595	$18,388
December deposits per book		24,599
December deposits per bank, includes a collection on accounts receivable of $1,771 less collection fee of $15	23,574	
December checks	20,759	19,178
Service charge	5	

Required:

    a. Determine the following as of December 31:

        1. Deposits in transit.

        2. Outstanding checks.

    b. Prepare a bank reconciliation at December 31.

    c. Make the required adjusting entries, if any. Assume there is no interest income involved in accounts receivable collected.

8B–5. Bank Reconciliation Using Cash Receipts and Disbursements Journals. As the accountant for the Western Co., you have obtained the following information in preparing the bank reconciliation for December 31, 1987:

Cash Receipts Journal		Cash Disbursements Journal		
Date	Debit Cash	Date	Check No.	Credit Cash
		12/1	1470	$ 684
12/6	$1,881	12/4	1471	934
12/9	2,038	12/7	1472	213
12/20	1,964	12/8	1473	445
12/26	1,573	12/10	1474	297
12/29	1,038	12/13	1475	663
12/31	1,453	12/15	1476	733
	$9,947	12/20	1477	577
		12/21	1478	179
		12/22	1479	380
		12/24	1480	423
		12/27	1481	193
		12/29	1482	554
		12/31	1483	295
				$6,570

GENERAL LEDGER

Cash   Account No. 101

Date 1987	Item	Ref.	Debit	Credit	Balance Debit	Balance Credit
11/30	Balance				4,331	
12/31		CR14	9,947		14,278	
12/31		CR16		6,570	7,708	

BANK STATEMENT—WESTERN COMPANY

Downtown National Bank
Account Name: Western Company

Account No: 1006-54-9342
Date: December 31, 1987

Date	Checks and Misc. Debits		Deposits and Misc. Credits	Balance
Beginning Balance				$4,784
December				
1	484	593		4,784
2	378			3,329
	133	254		2,942
4			$1,398	4,331
7	684			3,647
8			1,881	5,528
10	934			4,594
11			2,038	6,632
12	445	213		5,974
15	375 NSF			5,599
17	297		375	5,677
19	663			5,014
21	733			4,281
22			1,964	6,245
25	577	179		5,489
28			1,573	7,062
31	5 SC		31 I	7,088

Code: NSF = Not sufficient funds; SC = Service charge; I = Interest.

In addition, you determined that the NSF check was from Stardust Company and was later redeposited and cleared. This was not entered in the cash receipts journal for the second time. November checks that were paid by the bank consisted of check no. 1462 for $593, check no. 1464 for $378, check no. 1465 for $484, check no. 1468 for $254, and check no. 1469 for $133. The deposit in transit at the end of November was $1,398.

Required:

a. Prepare a bank reconciliation at December 31, 1987.

b. Make any required adjusting journal entries.

8B–6. Petty Cash Transactions. The Eastern Corporation decided in May to establish a $300 petty cash fund. The following transactions affected the fund during May and June:

• May 1: A check for $300 was drawn to establish the fund.

• May 31: Examination of the fund indicated that $180.40 of cash on hand. The following expense vouchers were also on hand:

Stationery	$32.45
Repair parts	45.00
Coffee (for office)	17.35
Gas (car for sales manager)	23.50

The Control and Accounting for Cash Transactions   347

A check was drawn to replenish the fund.

- June 30: Examination of the fund indicated that $106.02 of cash was on hand. The following expense vouchers were also on hand:

Stationery	$28.75
Travel (sales manager)	75.00
Postage	12.70
Freight-in	43.28
Repair parts	37.80

A check was drawn to replenish the fund.

Required:

Make all required journal entries to record these transactions.

8B-7. Voucher System. The Holland Company began operations in January of the current year. In order to control its disbursements as tightly as possible, the firm has decided to use a voucher system with a voucher register and a check register. During January the Holland Company entered into the following transactions:

- January 2: Prepared voucher no. 001 payable to Trump Realty for January rent, $2,000.
- January 4: Prepared voucher no. 002 payable to the Price Company for merchandise purchased for $1,000. Terms are 2/10, n/30.
- January 5: Prepared voucher no. 003 payable to Reese Stationery for purchase of supplies, $500. Terms are n/30.
- January 6: Issued check no. 100 in payment of voucher no. 001.
- January 10: Prepared voucher no. 004 payable to the Padre Company for merchandise purchased, $2,500. Terms are 1/10, n/30.
- January 12: Issued check no. 101 in payment of voucher no. 002.
- January 13: Prepared voucher no. 005 for payroll, $3,000. Payroll is paid through first bank.
- January 14: Issued check no. 102 in payment of voucher no. 003.
- January 15: Issued check no. 103 in payment of voucher no. 005.
- January 19: Prepared voucher no. 006 payable to the Sante Fe Times for advertising, $200. Terms are n/30.
- January 22: Prepared voucher no. 007 payable to Inteck for merchandise purchased, $1,200. Terms are 2/10, n/30.
- January 23: Prepared voucher no. 008 payable to Southwestern Electric for utility bill, $140.
- January 25: Issued check no. 104 in payment of voucher no. 004.
- January 27: Prepared voucher no. 009 for payroll, $3,200.
- January 28: Prepared voucher no. 010 payable to Contel for telephone bill (use Utility account), $100.
- January 30: Issued check no. 105 in payment of voucher no. 007.
- January 30: Issued check no. 106 in payment of voucher no. 009.

Required:

a. Prepare a voucher register and check register similar to those shown in the text on page 321 and 322, respectively. Use separate debit columns in the voucher register for purchases, salaries, and utilities.
b. Make the necessary posting to the Vouchers Payable account (account no. 301).
c. Prepare a schedule of unpaid vouchers.

Using the Computer

Refer to the data in problem 8A–7. With this data prepare a voucher register using an electronic spreadsheet. Use separate columns for all accounts other than Notes Payable and Interest Expense. For these two accounts use the "other" column.

Understanding Financial Statements

The following statement was taken from Safeway's annual report:

MANAGEMENT'S RESPONSIBILITY FOR FINANCIAL STATEMENTS

The consolidated financial statements of Safeway Stores, Incorporated and its subsidiaries have been prepared in accordance with generally accepted accounting principles applied on a consistent basis and include amounts that are based on Management's best estimates and judgments. Management is responsible for the integrity and objectivity of the data in these statements. Financial information elsewhere in this Annual Report is consistent with that in the financial statements.

To fulfill its responsibilities, Management has developed and maintained a strong system of internal accounting controls. There are inherent limitations in any control system in that the cost of maintaining a control should not exceed the benefits to be derived. However, Management believes the controls in use are sufficient to provide reasonable assurance that assets are safeguarded from loss or unauthorized use and that the financial records are reliable for preparing the financial statements. The controls are supported by careful selection and training of qualified personnel, by the appropriate division of responsibilities, by communication of written policies and procedures throughout the Company, and by an extensive program of internal audits.

Peat, Marwick, Mitchell & Co., independent certified public accountants, whose report follows the consolidated financial statements, are engaged to provide an independent opinion regarding the fair presentation in the financial statements of the Company's financial condition and operating results. They obtain an understanding of the Company's systems and procedures and perform tests of transactions and other procedures sufficient to provide them reasonable assurance that the financial statements are neither misleading nor contain material errors.

The Board of Directors, through its Audit Committee composed of outside Directors, is responsible for assuring that Management fulfills its responsibilities in the preparation of the financial statements. The Board, on the recommendation of the Audit Committee and in accordance with stockholder approval, selects and engages the independent public accountants. The Audit Committee meets with the independent accountants to review the scope of the annual audit and any recommendations they have for improvements in the Company's internal accounting controls. To assure independence, the independent accountants have free access to the Audit Committee and may confer with them without Management representatives present.

Required:

a. Do you agree with the statement that "there are inherent limitations in any control system in that the cost of maintaining a control should not exceed the benefits to be derived." Provide specific examples in which the cost of maintaining such a system in a market may outweigh the benefits derived.

b. Safeway's management lists a number of items that support their controls. Do these items meet the attributes a good internal control system should have?

c. In what ways do you think the Audit Committee influences the system of internal control at Safeway?

Financial Decision Case

The Metro Gold Store is owned by two partners, Ed Roebuck and Sharon Sears. Their primary business is the purchase and resale of gold bars and gold coins. Each day a large number of cash receipts and disbursements are made. All transactions are conducted by check. The company has grown in recent years and the firm has been able to obtain a $200,000 line of credit from the bank.

Controlling the daily cash balance is an important aspect of their business. Ed is primarily in charge of this aspect of the business. At the end of each day he calls the bank and finds out what the current balance is in their account. He then adds the amount of the day's deposits, and this gives him the amount of cash available to use. He then writes checks for that amount, and in some cases in excess of that amount. He feels comfortable writing checks in excess of the amount available because he knows that it will take a few days before those checks are paid.

As the firm's business has expanded, the available cash balance has continued to decrease and they have been forced to use most of their line of credit. They are both happy in the increase in sales as the price of gold has increased, but they are concerned with their cash position.

Required:

a. Comment on the procedures that Ed uses to control the firm's cash. Explain to him why he may not be getting an accurate cash figure.

b. What circumstances could cause their cash problems as their sales continue to rise?

c. Describe several procedures the firm could institute to gain better control over the daily cash balance.

Accounting for Short-term Monetary Assets

9

LEARNING OBJECTIVES

After reading this chapter you should be able to:
1. Differentiate between short-term and long-term investments.
2. Account for short-term investments and understand the lower-of-cost-or-market rule for equity investments.
3. Explain the nature of accounts receivable.
4. Explain the nature of uncollectible accounts, and apply the accounting procedures related to the allowance method of accounting for uncollectible accounts, including the percentage-of-sales and the aging methods.
5. Evaluate management controls over receivables.
6. Explain the nature of notes receivable and the elements of a promissory note.
7. Describe how a firm uses receivables to generate cash.
8. Classify receivables on a balance sheet.

The purpose of this chapter is to discuss the accounting concepts and procedures related to short-term monetary assets other than cash. **Monetary assets** are considered to be cash and those items that represent claims to specific amounts of cash. These assets are liquid, can be quickly converted into cash when needed, and include cash, many investments, and accounts and notes receivable. In contrast, **nonmonetary assets** are generally used in the productive cycle of the business and include such assets as inventories, long-term investments, and property, plant, and equipment. Cash was discussed in the prior chapter. Short-term investments and receivables are discussed in this chapter.

One of the purposes of a cash management control system, discussed in the previous chapter, is to ensure that the firm maintains adequate cash balances to meet its working capital needs. However, a firm does not want to let excess cash lie idle and not earn interest. Thus, it is likely to invest cash that is in excess of its working capital needs in marketable securities such as stocks, government securities, and corporate bonds. These are called **short-term investments** because management generally does not intend to hold them longer than one year. If the investments are not marketable or management intends to hold them for an indefinite period, they should be excluded from the current assets section and included under the caption "long-term investments."

Accounting for Short-term Investments

When short-term investments are acquired they are recorded at cost, which includes all commissions, fees, taxes, and other items that must be incurred to acquire the investment. When dividends or interest are received, investment revenue is credited.

To illustrate, assume that the Able Corporation purchases 1,000 shares of Safeway Stores, Inc. at $28 per share including all commissions. Able Corporation would make the following entry to record this investment:

Short-term Investments	28,000	
Cash		28,000
To record purchase of 1,000 shares of		
Safeway Stores, Inc. at $28 per share.		

Subsequently Safeway Stores, Inc. declares a quarterly dividend of 75 cents per share. Able records the receipt of this $750 dividend as follows:

Cash	750	
Investment Revenue (or Dividend Revenue)		750
To record receipt of 75¢ per share		
dividend (1,000 × 75¢ = $750).		

When some or all of the shares of stock are sold, Able will record a gain or loss equal to the difference between the sales price and the recorded cost of the securities. To illustrate, assume that Able sells 500 shares of Safeway for $30 per share, net of commission. The firm makes the following entry to record this transaction:

Cash	15,000	
Gain on Sale of Short-term Investment		1,000
Short-term Investment		14,000
To record $1,000 gain on sale of 500		
shares of Safeway stock at $30 per share.		

In this case a $1,000 gain (or $2 per share) is recorded. If a loss had occurred, the account Loss on Sale of Short-term Investments would be debited for the amount of the loss.

Valuation of Short-term Investments

Under current accounting practices, short-term marketable equity investments (i.e., stocks as opposed to bonds, which are debt investments) must be valued at the lower of their cost or market at each balance sheet date.[1] This means that if the market value of the securities on the balance sheet date is below their cost, they must be written down to that amount. The amount of the write-down is shown on the income statement as an unrealized loss. Conversely, if the market value is above the cost of the securities, they are left at the lower (cost) amount. The lower-of-cost-or-market standards in FASB Statement 12 do not have to be applied to debt securities such as bonds or government securities. However, a firm may, if it wishes, value these securities at the lower of cost or market.

Application of the Lower-of-Cost-or-Market Rule

To illustrate the application of the lower-of-cost-or-market rule, assume that on December 31 Able still holds the remaining 500 shares of the Safeway stock. At that date the current market value of Safeway Stores, Inc. is $27 per share. Because the total market value of the shares—$13,500 ($27 × 500 shares)—is less than their remaining cost—$14,000 ($28 × 500 shares)—the shares must be shown at market. After this write-down, the Short-term Investments account appears on the balance sheet as follows.

Current assets	
Cash	10,000
Short-term Investments (at market, which is below cost)	13,500

The loss of $500 ($14,000 − $13,500) is shown on the income statement as an unrealized loss.

Actually, the accounting procedures related valuing equity securities at the lower of cost or market can be more complicated than just illustrated. However, because these procedures parallel those used for long-term investments, they are discussed in greater detail in Chapter 19.

Accounting for Receivables

Accounts receivable arise from credit sales, and the accounting issues related to the recognition of credit sales and accounts receivable were discussed in Chapter 5. In this section of the chapter we focus on accounting for subsequent cash collections and uncollectible accounts. **Uncollectible accounts** are receivables that the firm is unable to collect in the full amount due from the customer.

Credit Sales

A major portion of wholesale and retail sales in the United States are on credit. As a result, some firms have a substantial portion of their current assets in the form of accounts receivable. For example, at the end of 1985, Sears, Roebuck and Company's accounts receivable totaled over $12 billion, and IBM's totaled over $9 billion. The ability of these firms, as well as others, to collect these amounts affects their cash liquidity and financing needs. In a cash-tight economy this is an essential aspect of overall cash management.

[1]*Financial Accounting Standards Board, Statement No. 12, Accounting for Certain Marketable Securities* (Stamford, Conn.: FASB, 1975).

The ability of a firm to collect its credit sales depends on (1) the initial decision about to whom to extend credit, (2) the particular credit policies of the firm such as the use of sales discounts or interest charges on unpaid accounts, and (3) general economic conditions. A firm obviously has more control over the first two factors than over the third.

In large firms the credit department is charged with the responsibility of granting credit as well as subsequently collecting unpaid accounts. In smaller firms this responsibility often lies with the owner-manager. In deciding whether originally to grant credit or to extend credit limits, the firm must obtain information about customers, such as their financial condition and past credit history. This information can be obtained through credit applications and the services of credit-rating bureaus.

Credit Policies

A firm could adopt a very conservative credit policy and extend credit only to customers with excellent credit ratings. Although this type of policy virtually eliminates bad debts or uncollectible accounts, the firm can lose sales and profits by not extending credit to individuals or firms with less-than-perfect credit histories that still might fully pay their accounts. In theory a firm should extend credit to any particular class of credit customers from which the ultimate cash collected (through either partial or full payment on account) exceeds the total of the cost of goods sold to all customers in that class, plus other incremental selling and general and administrative expenses. If a firm follows such a credit policy, it can expect still to incur some bad debts or uncollectible accounts. However, as long as these uncollectible accounts do not exceed the incremental profits from sales to other customers in this credit class, the firm will be better off.

For large firms the cost of administering a credit department and the associated bad debts can be substantial. In an attempt to reduce the cost of their products, some firms have decided to eliminate retail credit sales. For example, Arco decided in 1982 to eliminate its retail gas credit cards in the hope of saving $73 million.

Uncollectible Accounts

The primary accounting issue regarding accounting for uncollectible accounts is matching the bad debts with the sales of the period that gave rise to the bad debts. That is, the bad-debt expense should be recognized in the period in which the sale took place and the receivable was generated, not in the period in which management determined that the customer was unable or unwilling to pay. The accounting problem arises because it may be the following year before management discovers that a sale made in the current year will not be collectible. Waiting to record the bad-debt expense in the year following the sale would violate the matching convention.

In order to provide the best matching, the allowance method is used. Under the **allowance method,** the uncollectible accounts expense for the period is matched against the sales for that period. This requires estimating the uncollectible accounts expense in the period of the sale. An estimate is required because it is impossible to know with certainty which outstanding accounts at the end of the year will become uncollectible during the next year. This estimate is usually recorded through an adjusting journal entry at year-end. Although estimates are uncertain, accountants feel that the benefits of applying the matching convention outweigh the uncertainties associated with estimates.

Using the Allowance Method to Record Uncollectible Accounts Expense

To demonstrate the application of the allowance method, we first discuss the journal entries that must be made, and then we examine the different methods used to make the required estimates.

In order to understand the required journal entries used with the allowance method, assume that during 1987, Delta Company's first year in business, sales totaled $1 million. All sales were made on credit, and cash collections on account totaled $750,000. After analyzing the ending balance of $250,000 in Accounts Receivable, management estimated that $12,500 of these accounts would ultimately become uncollectible.

Journal Entries to Record Original Estimate. The summary journal entries required to record the sales, cash collections, and the $12,500 in uncollectible accounts are:

Summary entry for the year:

Accounts Receivable	1,000,000	
Sales		1,000,000
To record sales during the year.		

Summary Entry		
Cash	750,000	
Accounts Receivable		750,000
To record cash collected on account during the year.		

December 31, 1987—Adjusting entry

Uncollectible Accounts Expense	12,500	
Allowance for Uncollectible Accounts		12,500
To record estimated uncollectible accounts.		

The first two entries are the usual ones to record sales on account and the subsequent collection of cash. However, the adjusting entry on December 31, 1987 to record the estimated uncollectible accounts needs to be explained.

The debit part of the adjusting entry is made to the Uncollectible Accounts Expense account. Another title for this account is Bad Debt Expense. This account is closed to Income Summary and is generally shown as a selling expense on the income statement. However, some firms show this item as a deduction from gross sales in arriving at net sales. The credit part of the entry is to an account called Allowance for Uncollectible Accounts. This account, rather than Accounts Receivable, is credited because the firm is only making a total dollar estimate of uncollectible accounts and does not know with certainty which particular account will ultimately prove uncollectible. If a firm knows that a particular account is, in fact, uncollectible, it should already have been written off.

The **Allowance for Uncollectible Accounts** account is a contra-asset account in that it is an asset account with a credit balance. Other titles for this account include Allowance for Doubtful Accounts and Allowance for Bad Debts. In preparing a balance sheet, the dollar balance in the Allowance account is netted against the dollar balance of gross accounts receivable. This amount represents management's estimate of the net realizable value of the firm's receivables. Following is the current assets section of the Delta Company's balance sheet at December 31, 1987 after the adjusting entry has been made. Because this is the first year of the firm's operations, the balance in the Allowance account equals the amount of the journal entry. However, in future years this may not be the case.

Delta Company
Partial Balance Sheet
December 31, 1987

Current assets		
Cash		$ 15,000
Temporary investments		5,000
Accounts receivable	$250,000	
Less: Allowance for uncollectible accounts	12,500	237,500
Inventory		180,000
Prepaids		2,500
Total current assets		$440,000

To extend this illustration, assume that the following events occur in 1988:

1. On April 14, the Corona Company, one of Delta's customers, informs Delta that it is entering bankruptcy proceedings. Because Delta's management feels that it is unlikely that it will be able to collect the $6,000 balance in Corona's account, it decides to write off the entire balance.
2. On November 29, Delta receives $400 from the bankruptcy court as the final settlement of Corona's account.

Journal Entries to Record Actual Write-Off. Based on these data, Delta makes the following entry on April 14, 1988 to write off the $6,000 account:

Apr. 14, 1988	Allowance for Uncollectible Accounts	6,000	
	Accounts Receivable—Corona		6,000
	To write off balance in Corona Company's account receivable.		

As this entry shows, the debit part of the entry is to the Allowance account. The entry is not to the Uncollectible Accounts Expense account because we are assuming that the $6,000 is included in the $12,500 debit to expense as part of the December 31, 1987 adjusting entry. The credit part is to Accounts Receivable—Corona. This part of the entry must be posted to both the general ledger accounts receivable and to Corona's account in the accounts receivable subsidiary ledger.

After the $6,000 entry to write off the specific account, the net amount of accounts receivable (Accounts Receivable less Allowance for Uncollectible Accounts) remains the same, as illustrated on the top of page 357.

Account	Balances	
	Before Write-off of Accounts	After Write-off of Accounts
Accounts receivable	$250,000	$244,000
Less: Allowance for uncollectible accounts	12,500	6,500
Net accounts receivable	$237,500	$237,500

These identical balances result from the fact that the adjustment that actually decreased the balance in the net receivables took place on December 31, 1987. The entry on April 14, 1988 just decreases the Allowance account and the Accounts Receivable account by the same amount, $6,000. In effect, once a particular account is determined to be bad, the balance that pertains to that account is taken out of both the Allowance account and the Accounts Receivable account, and there is no effect on net receivables.

Journal Entries to Record Subsequent Collection of Accounts Previously Written Off. In some cases, a customer whose account has been written off will subsequently pay part or all of his or her account. For example, in the Corona case, Delta's management decided it was prudent to write off the entire balance when Corona entered bankruptcy proceedings because in Delta's opinion the outcome of such proceedings is uncertain. In November 1988, when Delta received $400 as its full settlement, it had to make the following two entries:

Nov. 29, 1988	Accounts Receivable—Corona	400	
	Allowance for Uncollectible Accounts		400
	To reinstate $400 of Corona's account receivable.		
	Cash	400	
	Accounts Receivable—Corona		400
	To record receipt of $400 cash.		

The first entry reinstates Corona's account receivable in the amount of $400. This entry is a reversal, in the amount of $400, of the entry to write off the receivable. The second entry records the receipt of the $400.

These two entries should not be combined. First, there may be a lag between the notification of the intention to pay and the actual receipt of the cash. Second, the two entries create a complete record in Corona's subsidiary accounts receivable account of the actual bad debt. A combined entry would not accomplish this. Finally, an entry that debits Cash and credits an Allowance account cannot arise from normal external transactions. For internal control purposes, therefore, unusual entries or combination of entries should be avoided.

The previous entries demonstrate the entries made to write off an account declared uncollectible and reinstate an account that had previously been written off. During the year, similar entries are made to record other accounts declared uncollectible. At the end of 1988, the Delta Company would again make an estimate of its uncollectible accounts for 1988 and make the necessary adjusting entry to Uncollectible Accounts Expense and the Allowance for Uncollectible Accounts to record this amount. How this estimate is made will be considered next.

Accounting for Short-term Monetary Assets

357

How to Estimate Uncollectible Accounts Expense

As we have shown, the allowance method is based on the accountant's ability to estimate future uncollectible accounts that result from current year's sales. The percentage-of-net-sales method and the aging method are the two methods that have been developed to make this estimate.

Percentage-of-Net-Sales Method. The **percentage-of-net-sales method** determines the amount of uncollectible accounts expense by analyzing the relationship between net credit sales and the prior years' uncollectible accounts expense. This method is often referred to as the income statement approach because the accountant attempts, as accurately as possible, to measure the expense account Uncollectible Accounts. As we will see later the balance in the Allowance for Uncollectible Accounts is simply a result of the entry to record the estimated uncollectible accounts expense for the period.

To demonstrate the application of the percentage-of-net-sales method, assume that you have gathered the following data, prior to any adjusting entries, for the Porter Company at the end of 1987. This assumes that all accounts determined to be uncollectible during the period have already been written off against Accounts Receivable and the Allowance account.

Account	Balance 12/31/87
Credit sales	$1,020,000
Sales returns and allowances (relating to credit sales)	15,000
Sales discounts (relating to credit sales)	5,000
Accounts receivable	200,000
Allowance for doubtful accounts—credit balance	2,000

The management of the Porter Company has analyzed the relationship of the prior years' losses from uncollectible accounts and net credit sales for the last five years and feels that uncollectible accounts expense will be approximately 2% of credit sales. This analysis, based on five years' prior data, is as follows:

Year	Credit Net Sales	Losses Resulting from Uncollectible Accounts
1982	$ 650,000	$12,000
1983	680,000	15,000
1984	780,000	14,820
1985	850,000	17,850
1986	940,000	18,330
	$3,900,000	$78,000

Average percentage
$78,000 ÷ $3,900,000 = 2%

Based on this data, the debit to the Uncollectible Accounts Expense is 2% of net credit sales of $1 million ($1,020,000 − $15,000 − $5,000), or $20,000. The correct adjusting entry at December 31, 1987 to record this estimate is:

Uncollectible Accounts Expense	20,000	
Allowance for Uncollectible Accounts		20,000
To record uncollectible accounts expense		
based on 2% of net sales.		

After this entry is posted, the relevant T accounts appear as on the top of page 359.

Allowance for Uncollectible Accounts			Uncollectible Accounts Expense		
	12/31/87 Bal.	2,000	12/31/87 Adj.	20,000	
	12/31/87 Adj.	20,000			
	12/31/87 Adj. Bal.	22,000			

The balance in the Uncollectible Accounts Expense account represents 2% of net credit sales. The balance in this account will always be a function of a predetermined percentage of credit sales when the net-sales method is used. The balance in the Allowance for Uncollectible Accounts account is $22,000—$2,000 for the prior years' sales that have not yet been written off as uncollectible and $20,000 from 1987 sales. At the end of any particular year, the credit balance in this account will fluctuate, but only by coincidence will it be equal to the debit balance in the account Uncollectible Accounts Expense.

To continue with this illustration, assume that during 1988 the following events related to accounts receivable took place:

1. The accounts receivable balance at December 31, 1988, prior to any receivable write-offs or adjusting entries is $230,000.
2. Management determined that $20,600 of accounts actually became uncollectible during the year and had to be written off.
3. Net credit sales for year (after deducting sales returns and allowances and discounts) totaled $1,350,000, and 2% of these are estimated to be uncollectible.

The entries to record the write-off of the actual uncollectible accounts and the adjusting entry at the end of the year to record the estimated uncollectible accounts are as follows:

Summary entry for the year:

Allowance for Uncollectible Accounts	20,600	
Accounts Receivable		20,600
To record accounts written off during the year.		

December 31, 1988—Adjusting entry

Uncollectible Accounts Expense	27,000	
Allowance for Uncollectible Accounts		27,000
To record estimated uncollectible accounts expense for the year.		

$$.02 \times \$1,350,000 = \$27,000$$

After these entries are posted, the relevant T accounts are as follows:

Allowance for Uncollectible Accounts				Uncollectible Accounts Expense		
During year	20,600	12/31/87 Bal.	22,000	12/31/88 Adj.	27,000	
		12/31/88 Adj.	27,000			
		12/31/88 Adj. Bal.	28,400			

The balance in the Allowance account is now $28,400, which represents $1,400 ($22,000 − $20,600) for the prior years' sales and $27,000 for 1987 sales. At December 31, 1988 the accounts receivable would be shown as follows in the current assets section of the balance sheet.

Accounts receivable	$209,400
Less: Allowance for uncollectible	
accounts	28,400
	$181,000

The Aging Method. The **aging method** is based on determining the desired balance in the account Allowance for Uncollectible Accounts. The accountant attempts to estimate what percentage of outstanding receivables at year-end will ultimately not be collected; this amount becomes the desired ending balance in the Allowance for Uncollectible Accounts, and a credit entry to this account is made to adjust the previous balance to the new, desired balance. The debit part of this entry is to the account Uncollectible Accounts Expense. The aging method is often referred to as the balance sheet approach because the accountant attempts to measure, as accurately as possible, the net realizable value of Accounts Receivable, a balance sheet figure.

The method to estimate the desired balance in the allowance account is called an aging of accounts receivable. This is done by dividing the balance in the Accounts Receivable account into age categories based on the length of time they have been outstanding. Categories such as current, 31–60 days, 61–90 days, and over 90 days are often used. On the assumption that the longer an account is outstanding, the less likely its ultimate collection is, an increasing percentage is applied to each of these categories. The total of these figures represents the desired balance in the account Allowance for Uncollectible Accounts.

To demonstrate the application of the aging method, we will use the data from the Porter Company on page 358. At the end of 1987 the balance in Accounts Receivable was $200,000, and an aging schedule of the accounts is presented at the top of page 361. For the sake of simplicity we are assuming that the entire $200,000 balance in Accounts Receivable consists of only 5 customers.

Based on the data in the exhibit on page 361, the Porter Company makes the following adjusting entry at December 31, 1987 to record the uncollectible accounts expense:

Uncollectible Accounts Expense	17,700	
Allowance for Uncollectible Accounts		17,700
To record uncollectible accounts expense		
based on the aging method.		

After this entry is posted, the relevant T accounts appear as follows:

Allowance for Uncollectible Accounts		**Uncollectible Accounts Expenses**	
	12/31/87 Bal. 2,000	12/31/87 Adj. 17,700	
	12/31/87 Adj. 17,700		
	12/31/87 Adj. Bal. 19,700		

Porter Company
Aging of Accounts Receivable
12/31/87

Customer	Total	Current	31–60 Days	61–90 Days	Over 90 Days
A. B. Dick	$ 30,000	$ 10,000	$15,000	$ 5,000	
T. V. Marsh	65,000	45,000	15,000	5,000	
J. Ong	45,000	30,000	5,000	5,000	$5,000
L. Tse	10,000	9,000			1,000
M. S. Worth	50,000	40,000	5,000	5,000	
	$200,000	$134,000	$40,000	$20,000	$6,000
Percentage estimated to be uncollectible		✕ 5%	✕ 10%	✕ 30%	✕ 50%
Desired balance in Allowance account	$ 19,700 =	$ 6,700 +	$ 4,000 +	$ 6,000 +	$3,000
Current credit balance	2,000				
Required entry	$ 17,700				

A number of points need to be made about this illustration. First, the dollar amount of the required journal entry is the amount needed to bring the Allowance account to the desired balance of $19,700. Because the Allowance account had a $2,000 credit balance prior to adjustment, the required entry is for $17,700, or the difference between $19,700 and $2,000. In some situations, the Allowance account may have a debit balance before the adjustment. This may occur if during the year more accounts were written off as uncollectible than had been estimated for in the prior year. In this situation the debit balance should be added to the desired credit balance in the Allowance account to figure the correct amount of the entry. For example, if the Porter Company's Allowance account had a $300 debit balance before the entry to record the uncollectible accounts expense was made, the Allowance account would require a credit entry of $20,000 in order to establish the necessary ending balance of $19,700.

The second issue is how the accountant determines the percentages to apply to each age category. Generally, these percentages are based on past experience adjusted for current economic and credit conditions. These percentages should be evaluated on a regular basis and adjusted when necessary.

Finally, in some cases the aging of the accounts receivable will indicate that a particular account has no possibility of collection. If this occurs, this account should be written off by debiting the Allowance account and crediting Accounts Receivable before figuring the desired ending balance in the Allowance account. In effect, this particular account is eliminated from the aging process, as it is already considered uncollectible.

To continue with this illustration, again assume that the following events occurred during 1988. (These are the same items used in the previous illustration on page 359 relating to the percentage-of-sales method). That is:

1. The accounts receivable balance prior to any receivable write-offs or adjusting entries is $230.000.
2. Management determined that $20,600 of accounts actually became uncollectible during the year and had to be written off.
3. In addition, accounts receivable at December 31, 1988 total $209,400.

The aging schedule of the accounts receivable as of Dec. 31, 1988 are:

Porter Company
Aging of Accounts Receivable
12/31/88

Customer	Total	Current	Age of Receivables		
			31–60 Days	61–90 Days	Over 90 Days
A. B. Dick	$ 40,000	$ 13,000	$21,000	$ 6,000	
T. V. Marsh	60,400	42,000	15,400	3,000	
J. Ong	52,000	38,000	4,000	7,000	$3,000
L. Tse	12,900	8,000	1,000	2,000	1,900
M. S. Worth	44,100	36,000	5,100	3,000	
	$209,400	$137,000	$46,500	$21,000	$4,900
Percentage estimated to be uncollectible		✕ 5%	✕ 10%	✕ 30%	✕ 50%
Desired balance in Allowance account	$ 20,250	= $ 6,850	+ $ 4,650	+ $ 6,300	+ $2,450
Current debit balance		900 debit (see T account below)			
Required entry	$ 21,150				

Allowance for Uncollectible Accounts

Write-off during year	20,600	12/31/87 Bal.	19,700
Bal. before adj.	900		

As the schedule illustrates, the accounts receivable balance at December 31, 1988 is $209,400. This is the amount after the $20,600 write-off for uncollectible accounts during 1988 has been posted. The $209,400 is split among the firm's five customers. The computation shows that the amount of required entry is $21,150 because the balance in the Allowance account prior to the adjusting entry is a debit of $900. Remember, the $20,600 write-off has also been posted as a debit to this account and causes this account to temporarily have a debit balance. The journal entries to record these events are:

Summary entry for the year:

Allowance for Uncollectible Accounts	20,600	
Accounts Receivable		20,600
To record write-off of accounts receivable.		

December 31, 1988—Adjusting entry

Uncollectible Accounts Expense	21,150	
Allowance for Uncollectible Accounts		21,150
To record estimate of uncollectible accounts expense per aging schedule.		

After these entries are posted, the relevant T accounts are as follows:

Allowance for Uncollectible Accounts		Uncollectible Accounts Expense	
During year 20,600	12/31/87 Bal. 19,700	12/31/88 Adj. 21,150	
	12/31/88 Adj. 21,150		
	12/31/88 Adj. Bal. 20,250		

Comparison of the Methods.   Both the percentage-of-net-sales and the aging methods are generally accepted accounting methods, in that they both attempt to match revenues and expenses. The percentage-of-net-sales method is aimed at determining the amount of uncollectible accounts expense, and the aging method is aimed at determining the balance in the account Allowance for Uncollectible Accounts. These methods thus will show different balances in both the expense and contra-asset accounts. This is illustrated below using the data from the 1987 Porter Company example.

	Balance—12/31/87	
Method	Allowance for Uncollectible	Uncollectible Accounts Expense
Percentage of Net Sales	$22,000	$20,000
Aging	$19,700	$17,700

These differences point out that management can choose among methods of applying generally accepted accounting principles and that these choices affect the firm's financial statements. Once a method of estimating bad debts is chosen, it should be consistently followed. This will enhance the comparability of the financial statements.

Both the aging and the percentage-of-net-sales methods are found in practice. Although the percentage-of-net-sales method is easier to apply, the aging method forces management to analyze the status of their accounts receivable and credit policies annually. Some firms use both methods. The percentage-of-net-sales method is used to prepare monthly and quarterly statements, but the aging method is used to make the final adjustment at year-end.

Difference between Estimates and Actual Experience

Regardless of which method is used, the actual accounts written off seldom exactly equal the estimates made in the prior year. However, this presents no problem in accounting for accounts receivable. If fewer accounts in dollars are written off than previously estimated, the Allowance account will have a credit balance prior to the adjustment. The adjustment will then increase this balance to reflect management's new estimate of the uncollectible accounts. If more accounts are written off than previously estimated, the Allowance account will have a temporary debit balance prior to the year-end adjustment. This debit balance will be eliminated when the new adjusting entry is made.

Estimates are inherent in accounting because the accountant attempts to match revenues and expenses. Most individuals feel that the benefits of this proper matching outweigh the disadvantages of using estimates. Furthermore, for stable companies, the amount of receivables and uncollectible accounts tends to be steady from year to year.

J. C. PENNEY

This point can be illustrated by looking at the following data taken from a recent annual report of J. C. Penney:

The following table presents key operating data relative to credit operations:

(In millions)	1983	1982	1981
Customer receivables			
Regular plan	$2,560	$2,474	$2,269
Time payment plan	$ 925	$ 976	$ 914
Total customer receivables	$3,485	$3,450	$3,183
Finance charge revenue	$ 569	$ 528	$ 411
Net bad debts written off	$ 81	$ 83	$ 79
Percent of credit sales	1.6	1.8	1.7
Accounts 90 days or more past due as a % of customer receivables	2.0	2.2	2.2

The Company's policy is to write off accounts when the scheduled minimum payment has not been received for six consecutive months, or if any portion of the balance is more than 12 months past due, or if it is otherwise determined that the customer is unable to pay. Collection efforts continue subsequent to write off, and recoveries are applied as a reduction of bad debt losses.

As we have seen, reasonable errors in a prior year's estimates are adjusted in current and future years; the accountant does not retroactively change a prior year's statement. However, if estimates such as uncollectible accounts are consistently incorrect, management should reevaluate the method used to make the estimate.

Management Control and Analysis of Receivables

Management control and analysis of receivables are important parts of the overall cash management system. In a previous chapter we discussed various aspects of internal control of cash transactions. An additional point regarding the proper authorization of receivables written off as uncollectible must be emphasized. Only the controller or an individual who does not have day-to-day operational control over receivables or cash should authorize a write-off of a receivable due to a bad debt or a sales return. In addition, a written authorization should be attached to the customer's subsidiary ledger or file. This separation of duties and these control procedures will ensure that an employee is not able to steal a cash payment on account and conceal the theft by writing off the customer's account as a bad debt or a sales return.

Other control procedures in this area include monitoring the age and size of the Accounts Receivable balance. Being able to convert receivables into cash quickly is important in maintaining the firm's cash liquidity. A regular aging of accounts receivable and a review of credit policies are important to helping ensure that the collections of receivables do not lag.

To help management monitor receivables, two figures, the **receivable turnover** and the **average collection period** in days, are often calculated. The receivable turnover is figured by dividing credit sales by the average accounts receivable for the period. For example, a firm with annual credit sales of $2.5 million and average accounts receivable of $500,000 has a receivable turnover of 5 times, calculated as follows:

$$\text{Receivable turnover} = \frac{\text{Credit sales}}{\text{Average accounts receivable}}$$

$$5 = \frac{\$2,500,000}{\$\ 500,000}$$

This turnover figure can easily be converted into the average number of days that the receivables are outstanding, by dividing 365 days by the turnover. In this case, receivables are outstanding an average of 73 days (365 days ÷ 5). Within the constraints of the firm's credit policies, management is interested in reducing the turnover period and thus quickly turning receivables into cash.

Notes Receivable

A **note receivable** is a written, unconditional promise by an individual or business to pay a definite amount at a definite date or on demand. The individual or business that signs the note is referred to as the **maker** of the note, and the person to whom the payment is to be made is called the **payee.** Below is a common form of a note receivable, in which J. Hart is the maker and C. Brecker is the payee.

Promissory Note Receivable

$5,000   April 5   , 19 87

_____ Ninety days _____ after date,

for value received, _____ J. Hart _____ promise(s) to

pay to _____ C. Brecker _____ , or order,

at _____ San Francisco, Calif. _____

the sum of _____ Five Thousand _____ dollars

in lawful money of the United States of America, with interest thereon, at the rate of

___12___ % per _____ annum _____ from date

J. Hart

In this illustration, C. Brecker records the note as an asset, and J. Hart records the note as a payable. The journal entries to record the note for each individual on April 5, 1987, the date of note, are on the top of page 366.

C. Brecker

Note Receivable	5,000	
Cash		5,000

To record $5,000 note receivable at 12% interest.

J. Hart

Cash	5,000	
Note Payable		5,000

To record $5,000 note payable at 12% interest.

Although in this chapter we are primarily concerned with accounting for notes receivable, the concepts that we shall consider apply equally well to notes payable, which are the topic of Chapter 10.

There are several types of notes receivable that arise from different economic transactions. For example, trade notes receivable result from written obligations by a firm's customers. In some industries it is common for a seller to insist on a note rather than an open account for certain types of sales, for example, the sale of equipment or other personal or real property in which payment terms are normally longer than is customary for an open account. In other cases, a particular customer's credit rating may cause the seller to insist on a written note rather than relying on an open account. Further, if a particular customer is delinquent in paying his or her account, the seller may insist that the customer sign a note for the balance. Other notes receivable result from cash loans to employees, stockholders, customers, or others. For the purposes of our discussion, we refer to all notes as **promissory notes.**

Elements of Promissory Notes

There are several elements of promissory notes that are important to the full understanding of the accounting for these notes. These are the note's principal, maturity date, duration, interest rate, and maturity value.

The Principal

The principal of the note is the amount that is lent or borrowed. It does not include the interest portion. The principal of the note shown on page 365 is $5,000. Together, the principal and interest portions represent the note's maturity value. The principal portion is often referred to as the face amount or face value.

Maturity Date

The maturity date is the date that the note becomes due and payable. This date either is stated on the note or can be determined from the facts stated on the note. For example, a note may have a stated maturity date, such as December 31, or be due in a specific number of days or months, such as three months after the note's date. The note shown above is due in 90 days from its date (April 5), or on July 4. This July 4 maturity date is computed as follows:

Days remaining in April (30 − 5)	25
Days in May	31
Days in June	30
Days in July (number of days	
required to make 90 days)	4
	90 days

Duration

The **duration of the note** is the length of time that the note is outstanding, or the number of days called for by the note. This period of time is important in figuring the interest charges related to the note. In order to determine the duration of the note, both the date of the note and its maturity date must be known. For example, a note dated July 15 with a maturity date of September 15 has a duration of 62 days.

Days remaining in July (July 31 — July 15; date of origin not included)	16
Days in August	31
Days in September (date of payment included)	15
	62 days

In this example, interest is based on the note's being outstanding for 62 days.

Interest Rate

Interest is the revenue or expense from lending or borrowing money. To the lender or payee, interest is revenue, and to the maker or borrower, it is an expense. The total interest related to a particular note is based on the note's principal, rate of interest, and duration and can be calculated by using the following formula:

$$i = P \times R \times T$$
$$\text{Interest} = \text{Principal} \times \text{Interest rate} \times \text{Time}$$

In applying this formula, interest rates are assumed to be stated in annual terms. For example, the total interest related to a $10,000, 12% note that is due in one year is $1,200, or

$$\$1,200 = \$10,000 \times .12 \times 1$$

If this same note had a term of only 5 months, the interest would be $500, calculated as follows:

$$\$500 = \$10,000 \times .12 \times 5/12$$

In some cases the term of the note is expressed in days, and the exact number of days should be used in the interest computation. However, for simplicity we will assume a 360-day year. For example, the interest related to a $10,000, 12% note with a 90-day term is $300, computed as follows:

$$\$300 = \$10,000 \times .12 \times 90/360$$

Accounting for Notes Receivable

When a note is received from a customer, the account Notes Receivable is debited. The credit can be to Cash, Sales, or Accounts Receivable, depending on the transaction that give rise to the note. In any event, the Notes Receivable account is debited at the face, or principal, of the note. No interest revenue is recorded at the date of the issue because no interest has yet been earned. Interest is recorded at the maturity date or at the end of the accounting period through an adjusting entry if the note extends beyond one period.

Receipt of the Note

To show the initial recording of a note receivable, assume that on July 1 the Fenton Company accepts a $2,000, 12%, four-month note receivable from the Zoe Company in settlement of an open account receivable. The entry on the top of page 368 is made to record this transaction.

July 1	Notes Receivable—Zoe	2,000	
	Accounts Receivable—Zoe		2,000
	To record 12%, 4-month note.		

In some situations the receipt of the note results from a sale of merchandise. For example, assume that a $5,000 sale is made to a customer for a trade note receivable. In this case the following two entries are made:

Accounts Receivable	5,000	
Sales		5,000
To record $5,000 sale.		

Notes Receivable	5,000	
Accounts Receivable		5,000
To record receipt of note in exchange		
for open account receivable.		

The previous two entries can be combined by debiting Notes Receivable and crediting Sales. However, to do so will result in a loss of information because not all the sales made to a particular customer are recorded in the customer's accounts receivable subsidiary ledger.

Payment of the Note

When the payment on the note is received, Cash is debited, Notes Receivable is credited, and Interest Revenue is credited. For example, assume that the $2,000 note from the Zoe Company recorded on July 1 is paid in full on October 31. The entry is:

October 31	Cash	2,080	
	Notes Receivable—Zoe		2,000
	Interest Revenue		80
	To record full payment of note and interest of $80.		

$$\$80 = \$2,000 \times .12 \times 4/12$$

In some cases the note is received in one accounting period and collected in another. In these situations, interest must be accrued at year-end. For example, assume that the Bullock Company received a three-month, 18% note for $5,000 on November 1, 1987 in exchange for cash. The firm's year-end is December 31, and the note matured on January 31, 1988. The entries that the Bullock Company made on November 1, 1986, December 31, 1987, and January 31, 1988 are:

November 1, 1987	Notes Receivable	5,000	
	Cash		5,000
	To record receipt of $5,000, 18%,		
	3-month note.		

December 31, 1987	Interest Receivable	150	
	Interest Revenue		150
	To record interest revenue for November		
	and December 1986.		

$$\$150 = \$5,000 \times .18 \times 2/12$$

January 31, 1987	Cash	5,225	
	Interest Receivable		150
	Notes Receivable		5,000
	Interest Revenue		75
	To record full collection of loan as follows:		

Total Interest = $5,000 × .18 × 3/12	$225
Interest accrued to 12/31/86	150
Interest revenue for 1/87	$ 75

Defaulted Notes Receivable

When the borrower, or maker of the note, fails to make the required payment at maturity, the note is considered to be **defaulted.** At that point the note should be transferred to an open account receivable. Accounts Receivable is debited for the full maturity value, including the principal and the unpaid interest. For example, if the Zoe Company defaults on its $2,000, 12%, note, the Fenton Company will make the following entry on October 31:

Accounts Receivable—Zoe	2,080	
Notes Receivable—Zoe		2,000
Interest Revenue		80
To record default by the Zoe Company on $2,000,		
12%, 4-month loan, including interest of $80 =		
($2,000 × .12 × 4/12)		

Although it may seem strange to record interest revenue on a defaulted note receivable, the Zoe Company is still obligated to pay both the interest and the principal. The account receivable is just as valid a claim as are the note receivable and the interest. Furthermore, by transferring the note to Accounts Receivable, the remaining balance in the note receivable general ledger contains only the amounts of notes that have not yet matured. The Fenton Company should also indicate the default on the Zoe Company's subsidiary accounts receivable ledger. Subsequently, if the account receivable proves uncollectible, it should be written off against the Allowance account.

Using Receivables to Generate Cash

Both accounts and notes receivable can be used to generate immediate cash. Accounts receivable can be assigned, pledged, or factored. Essentially, in all these situations the company that owns the receivable either sells it to a bank or other lender or borrows against it to obtain immediate cash. The ability to raise cash in this manner is especially important to small- and medium-sized businesses, which are often strapped for cash. Accounting for the assigning, pledging, or factoring of accounts receivable are topics covered in an intermediate accounting text.

Discounting Notes Receivable

Notes receivable can also be used to obtain immediate cash. This is done by discounting the note to a bank or other lender prior to its maturity date. Discounting means selling or pledging a customer's note receivable to the bank at some point prior to the note's maturity date. The term **discount** is used because the bank deducts the interest it charges from the note's maturity value and thus discounts the note. The note is usually discounted with recourse. This means that the company discounting the note, called the *endorser*, guarantees the eventual full payment of its maturity value. If the maker fails to make the required payments, the bank will present the note to the endorser and demand full payment.

By discounting a note with recourse, the endorser has contingent liability. **A contingent liability** is a possible liability that may or may not occur depending on some future event. In many cases these liabilities are not included in the balance sheet with other liabilities. Rather, they are usually referred to in the footnotes to the financial statements. If the maker pays the bank, the contingent liability will end; if the maker defaults, the contingent liability will become a real liability. Because most discounted notes are reviewed for their creditworthiness by both the bank and the endorser, this type of contingent liability rarely turns into a real liability. (Contingent liabilities are discussed in more detail in Chapter 11.)

Accounting for a Discounted Note

When the note is discounted, the endorser obtains an amount of cash less than the maturity value. This amount of cash is called the proceeds of the note and is computed by applying the interest rate charged by the bank (the discount rate) to the note's maturity value for only the time between the date of the discount and the maturity date.

For example, assume that on April 1 the Schwartz Company receives a $10,000, 12%, 90-day note from Ruth, Inc. The note's maturity date is June 30. Because of the need for immediate cash, the Schwartz Company discounts the note at the Second National Bank with recourse on April 16. (At this point the note has 75 days until maturity.) The bank charges an interest rate, often called the discount rate, of 16%. The Schwartz Company will receive proceeds of $9,957, computed as follows:

Principal of note	$10,000
Add: Interest on note from date of issue to maturity date	
$10,000 × .12 × 90/360 =	300
Maturity value	$10,300
Less: Bank discount charge—16%	
$10,300 × .16 × 75/360 =	343*
Proceeds	$ 9,957

*Rounded off—actual amount equals $343.33.

The journal entry to record this transaction is:

Cash	9,957	
Interest Expense	43	
Note Receivable		10,000
To record discounting of note receivable at a 16% rate.		

In this case the firm incurs net interest expense of $43, the difference between the principal of $10,000 and the proceeds of $9,957, or the difference between the interest expense of $343 and the total interest of $300. In other situations, the proceeds may exceed the principal, and the endorser records interest revenue in the amount of the difference. Whether interest expense or interest revenue results depends on the interest rate on the note, the discount rate, and the time remaining on the note when it is discounted.

After the note is discounted, the Second National Bank will notify Ruth, Inc. that it is now the holder of the note. As a result, Ruth will be instructed to pay the bank the maturity value of $10,300 when the note matures on June 30. When Ruth makes the payment, the bank will notify the Schwartz Company that the note has been fully paid.

If Ruth, Inc. fails to make the required payment, the bank will notify Schwartz of this and demand payment. The Schwartz Company must pay the bank and so makes the following entry:

```
Accounts Receivable—Ruth          10,300
    Cash                                    10,300
To record account receivable from
Ruth, Inc. due to default on note.
```

When the note is defaulted, a bank will often charge a protest fee that must be paid by the endorser. If this occurs, the protest fee is added to the accounts receivable and the cash payment.

Classification of Receivables

This portion of the chapter has examined several types of receivables. Trade accounts receivable that arise from ordinary sales are usually collected within a year or the operating cycle and thus are classified as current assets. Other receivables that arise from loans to outsiders, employees, or stockholders should be shown separately from trade receivables. If the receivable is due within a year or the operating cycle, it should be classified as current. If the receivable arises from a loan to a stockholder or employee and there is no definite due date, it should be considered noncurrent. It is included in either the long-term investment or other asset section of the balance sheet.

J. C. Penney's annual report provides a good example of how receivables are presented in corporate financial statements. In the current asset section of its January 31, 1983 balance sheet, total receivables are listed net at $3,673 million. However, in the footnotes to the statement, this figure is disaggregated, as shown below:

J. C. PENNEY

Receivables were as follows:

(In millions)	1983	1982	1981
Customer receivables............................	$3,485	$3,450	$3,183
Less allowance for doubtful accounts			
(2% of customer receivables).................	70	69	64
Customer receivables, net........................	3,415	3,381	3,119
Other receivables, net	258	243	165
Receivables, net	$3,673	$3,624	$3,284
Company	$1,793	$1,710	$1,617
Financial......................................	$1,880	$1,914	$1,667

When receivables are discounted with recourse, the issue arises as to whether the transfer should be treated as a sale or as collateral for a loan. The FASB has rules beyond the scope of this book that are related to this issue. In any event, any contingent liability arising from discounted notes treated as sales should be disclosed in the notes to the financial statements.

Summary of Learning Objectives

1. *The difference between short-term and long-term investments.* Short-term investments are investments in such marketable securities as stocks, government securities, and bonds. These are considered short-term because management generally does not intend to hold them longer than

one year. If the investment is not marketable or management intends to hold them for an indefinite period, they should be considered long-term.

2. *Accounting for short-term investments.* When short-term investments are acquired they are recorded at cost, which includes all commissions, fees, and other items. Subsequently, equity securities are recorded at the lower of cost or market at each balance sheet date. Any write-downs to market are recorded on the income statement as unrealized losses.

3. *Accounts receivable.* Accounts receivable result from credit sales, and for many retailing firms accounts receivable represent a substantial portion of current assets. The function of the credit department is to establish and enforce credit policies. Credit policies should protect the firm against excessive bad debts but should not be so restrictive as to eliminate customers who, although they do not have a perfect credit rating, are likely to pay.

4. *Accounting for uncollectible accounts.* Uncollectible accounts are a fact of life in business. The allowance method attempts to match the uncollectible accounts expense against the sale in the period the sale takes place. This is accomplished by estimating uncollectible accounts in the period of the sale.

   Both the percentage-of-net-sales and the aging methods are acceptable alternative methods used to estimate uncollectible accounts. The percentage-of-net-sales method is often called the income statement approach because it attempts to estimate the amount of Uncollectible Accounts expense. The aging method is often called the balance sheet method because it attempts to estimate the desired balance in the account Allowance for Uncollectible Accounts.

5. *Management and control and analysis of receivables.* To help management monitor receivables, two figures—the receivable turnover and the average collection period in days—are often calculated. The receivable turnover is figured by dividing credit sales by the average accounts receivable for the period. This turnover figure can easily be converted into the average number of days that the receivables are outstanding by dividing 365 days by the turnover.

6. *Notes receivable.* Notes receivable are unconditional promises in writing to pay a definite amount at a definite time. Notes arise from a variety of transactions. The major accounting issue relates to the computation of interest.

7. *Using receivables to generate cash.* Both accounts and notes receivable can be used to generate immediate cash. Accounts receivable can be pledged, assigned, or factored. Notes receivable can be discounted at banks or with other secured lenders.

8. *Classification of receivables.* Different types of receivables should be classified separately. Trade accounts receivable are not mixed with loans to employees, stockholders, or others. Interest receivable is also shown separately.

Key Terms

Aging Method	Monetary Assets
Allowance for Uncollectible Accounts	Nonmonetary Assets
Allowance Method	Note Receivable
Average Collection Period	Payee
Contingent Liability	Percentage-of-Net-Sales Method
Default	Promissory Note
Discount	Receivable Turnover
Duration of the Note	Short-term Investments
Maker	Uncollectible Accounts

Problems for Your Review

A. Uncollectible Accounts. During your review of the financial statements of the SBC Company you have gathered the following data relating to receivables as of December 31, 1987 (prior to any adjusting entries):

Net sales, all on credit	$5,000,000
Accounts receivable balance	800,000
Allowance for uncollectible account—Debit balance	5,000

Required:

1. Assuming the firm estimates that 1½% of all credit sales will become uncollectible,
   a. Make the required adjusting entry at 12/31/87.
   b. What are the balances in the (1) Uncollectible Accounts Expense account and (2) Allowance for Uncollectible Accounts account after the 12/31/87 adjusting entry?

2. Assume that an aging of accounts receivable at 12/31/87 reveals the following:

Age	Total	Estimated Percentage Uncollectible
Current	$450,000	5%
30–60 days	150,000	10
61–90 days	75,000	15
91–120 days	100,000	20
past 120 days	25,000	50
Total	$800,000	

   a. Make the required adjusting entry at 12/31/87.
   b. What are the balances in the (1) Uncollectible Accounts Expense account and (2) Allowance for Uncollectible Accounts account after the 12/31/87 adjusting entry?

Solution

1. Percentage-of-Net-Sales Method

   a. Estimate of uncollectible accounts expense

$5,000,000 × .015 = $75,000

Adjusting Entry, 12/31/87		
Uncollectible Accounts Expense	75,000	
Allowance for Uncollectible Accounts		75,000

b. Balance in accounts

Uncollectible Accounts Expense		Allowance for Uncollectible Accounts	
		12/31/87 5,000	
Adj. 75,000		Adj. 75,000	
12/31/87 Bal. 75,000		12/31/87 Bal. 70,000	

2. Aging Method

a. Estimate of uncollectible accounts expense

Age	Total	Estimated Percentage Uncollectible	Total
Current	$450,000	5%	$22,500
31–60 days	150,000	10	15,000
61–90 days	75,000	15	11,250
91–120 days	100,000	20	20,000
Past 120 days	25,000	50	12,500
		Required balance	$81,250
		Unadjusted balance—debit	5,000
		Amount of adjusting entry	$86,250

Adjusting entry—12/31/87
Uncollectible Accounts Expense   86,250
    Allowance for Uncollectible Accounts   86,250

b. Balance in accounts

Uncollectible Accounts Expense		Allowance for Uncollectible Accounts	
		12/31/87 5,000	
Adj. 86,250		Adj. 86,250	
		12/31/87 Bal. 81,250	

B. Discounting. The Weiss Corporation discounted a $2,000, 12%, 60-day, note receivable of the Cobb Company, dated April 1, 1987. The note was discounted on April 21, 1987 at a discount rate of 14%.

1. What are the proceeds of the note to Weiss?
2. Make the journal entry that Weiss should make to record the discount.

Solution

1. Maturity Value

Face Value	$2,000.00
Interest	
$2,000 × .12 × 60/360	40.00
Maturity value	$2,040.00
Discount	
$2,040 × .14 × 40[a]/360	31.73
Proceeds	$2,008.27

[a]The remaining term of the loan is 40 days.

2. Journal Entry

Cash	2,008.27	
Interest Revenue		8.27
Note Receivable		2,000.00
To record discount of note receivable.		

Questions

1. What are monetary assets? Give three examples.

2. What factors determine whether an investment is classified as short-term or long-term?

3. The Smith Company purchased 100 shares of IBM at $135 per share. In addition, the company paid a brokerage commission of $100 and a state transfer tax of $50. What is the recorded historical cost of the investment?

4. On April 1, 1987 the Zahary Company purchased 2,000 shares of Murphy's Milk Company at a total cost of $8,500. On December 31, 1987, the Zahary Company's year-end, the stock had a market value of $7,900. At what amount would these securities be shown on the December 31, 1987 balance sheet?

5. What factors affect a firm's ability to collect its credit sales?

6. The controller for Switch and Save Stores is proud of herself because she has eliminated all bad debts by giving credit to only a small number of customers. Do you think this is a good policy? Why or why not?

7. Briefly describe the allowance method of accounting for uncollectible receivables. Include a discussion of the two methods of estimating uncollectible accounts expense.

8. The Allowance for Uncollectible Accounts is a contra-asset account. Explain what this means to your friend, who has no knowledge of accounting.

9. What is the accounting procedure that a firm should use to reinstate a receivable that has previously been written off as uncollectible?

10. In estimating the amount of future uncollectible accounts, a business may use the balance sheet approach or the income statement approach. Briefly describe these two approaches.

11. In what situation would there be a debit balance in the account Allowance for Uncollectible Accounts?

12. Prior to the year-end adjustment, the Grant Co. had a debit balance in its Allowance for Uncollectible Accounts of $1,500. If the firm uses the aging method and estimates $10,000 of the accounts to be uncollectible, what should be the amount of the entry? If the firm uses the percentage-of-sales method and determines that uncollectible accounts expense should be $11,000, what should be the amount of the entry?

13. Define the following terms regarding notes receivable:
   a. Payee.
   b. Maker.
   c. Face value.
   d. Maturity value.
   e. Duration of note.
   f. Interest rate.

14. List four examples in which a promissory note might be issued.

15. How can accounts and notes receivable be used to generate cash?

Exercises

1. Accounting for Short-Term Investments. The Kline Company has been very profitable over the last few years and has accumulated a large amount of cash. Management decided to invest some of the excess cash in short-term investments. On June 1 the company purchased 1,000 shares of Liqco Company at $50 per share and 500 shares of International Equity at $120 per share. On July 1 the firm received cash dividends of $2.00 per share from Liqco and $2.50 per share from International Equity. On November 1 the Kline Company sold all the shares of International Equity for $100 per share. At year-end the market value of the Liqco Company shares was $60 per share.

Required:
   a. Make the required entries to record the above events.
   b. Show how the short-term investments should be shown on the year-end balance sheet.

2. Uncollectible Accounts Journal Entries. During your examination of the Paton Co., you discovered the following series of journal entries:

1986	a.	Uncollectible Accounts Expense	2,500	
		Allowance for Uncollectible Accounts		2,500
	b.	Allowance for Uncollectible Accounts	250	
		Accounts Receivable		250
1987	c.	Accounts Receivable	100	
		Allowance for Uncollectible Accounts		100
	d.	Cash	100	
		Accounts Receivable		100

Describe the events that caused these entries. What effect did each of these transactions have on net income, gross accounts receivable, allowance for uncollectible accounts, and net accounts receivable?

3. Recording Sales and Uncollectible Accounts. During 1987 Baker's Department Store had total sales of $750,000, of which 65% were on credit. During the year $421,500 was collected on credit sales. Management uses the allowance method and estimates that $15,750 of accounts receivable will be uncollectible.

Prepare the journal entries to record:
  a. Sales during the year.
  b. Cash collected on account.
  c. The establishment of the account Allowance for Uncollectible Accounts.

4. Recording Sales and Uncollectible Accounts. On March 15, 1987 the Hernandez Company purchased on account from the Stepanskie Manufacturing Company merchandise costing $32,000. On December 31, 1987 the accounts receivable of the Stepanskie Manufacturing Company showed a balance of $750,000, including $32,000 owed to it by the Hernandez Company. Stepanskie's management estimates that 4% of the accounts receivable will be uncollectible. At December 31, 1987 there is no balance in either the Uncollectible Accounts Expense account or in the Allowance for Uncollectible Accounts account.

On February 4, 1988 the Hernandez Company enters into bankruptcy proceedings. The Stepanskie Manufacturing Company feels that only 10% of Hernandez's outstanding receivable balance will ever be collected.

On November 12, 1988 Stepanskie receives $4,000 from Hernandez in payment of the receivable. No other funds will be received on this account.

Prepare the necessary journal entries on Stepanskie's books:
  a. March 15, 1987.
  b. December 31, 1987.
  c. February 4, 1988.
  d. November 12, 1988.

5. Accounting for Uncollectible Accounts. The following data were taken from the unadjusted trial balance of the Yokotake Company:

	Debit	Credit
Accounts receivable	$200,000	
Allowance for uncollectible accounts		$ 1,950
Total Sales—40% for cash		642,000

Actual uncollectible accounts written off during the year amounted to $2,300.

Required:

If the firm uses the allowance method to record uncollectible accounts, compute uncollectible accounts expense under each of the following assumptions:
  a. Two percent of total sales.
  b. Three percent of credit sales.
  c. The Allowance for Uncollectible Accounts account is increased to 5% of the ending receivable balance.

6. Uncollectible Accounts—Percentage-of-Sales Method. The following information has been taken from the records of the Lord Company prior to any adjusting entries on December 31, 1987:

Account	Balance—12/31/87
Credit sales	$3,675,000
Sales returns and allowances	23,000
Sales discounts	7,500
Accounts receivable	365,000
Allowance for uncollectible accounts, credit balance	3,400

All accounts have normal balances.

Management uses the percentages of net credit sales to estimate uncollectible accounts. Actual credit sales and uncollectibles for the five previous years have been:

Year	Net Credit Sales	Uncollectible Accounts
1982	$ 450,000	$11,250
1983	532,000	17,500
1984	950,000	25,050
1985	1,300,000	42,060
1986	2,200,000	39,940

Using the above information, prepare the adjusting entry to record the uncollectible accounts expense for 1987. What is the balance in the Allowance for Uncollectible Accounts account after the adjusting entry?

7. Uncollectible Accounts—Aging Method. On December 31, 1987 the balance in the Accounts Receivable account of the McClain Company is $217,820. The company sells highly specialized products to a small number of customers. The following aging schedule was prepared by the company's bookkeeper:

Customer	Totals	Current	Age of Accounts Receivable 31–60 Days	61–90 Days	Over 90 Days
M. A. Pagano	$ 30,500	$ 500	$12,000	$18,000	$ 0
G. M. Wright	52,700	3,100	24,000	15,000	10,600
J. E. Francis	65,950	0	33,450	0	32,500
S. A. Chent	68,670	60,000	0	8,670	0
Totals	$217,820	$63,600	$69,450	$41,670	$43,100

Based on past experience, management makes the following estimate of uncollectible accounts:

Age	%
Current	4
31–60 days	11
61–90 days	25
Over 90 days	60

Prior to any adjustment, the Allowance for Uncollectible Accounts account has a debit balance of $1,700.

Prepare the necessary journal entry to record the uncollectible accounts expense at December 31, 1987.

8. Receivables Management. K & J Electronics had total credit sales of $1,940,000 during 1987. The beginning balance in the Accounts Receivable account was $340,000, and the ending balance in the account was $630,000.

Figure the receivable turnover rates and the average number of days that the receivables

Accounting for Short-term Monetary Assets

377

were outstanding. Explain what these figures mean. What advice can you give to management to improve these figures?

9. Notes Receivable. On March 12, 1987 the Griffith Company received a 90-day note receivable for $30,000, with a stated interest rate of 15%. Determine the following amounts or items:

    a. The principal of the note.

    b. The interest revenue computed on a 360-day year.

    c. The maturity value of the note.

    d. The date the note is due.

10. Notes Receivable. On October 1, 1987 the Jackson Co. sold a piece of fine furniture to the LuLu Company for $2,000. One month later Jackson took a three-month, 12% note in exchange for the full account receivable. Jackson's accounting period ends on December 31. LuLu makes the appropriate payment when the note becomes due on February 1, 1988.

    Make all the necessary entries to record these events on Jackson's books.

11. Defaulted Notes Receivable. The Stover Company was the payee on a $3,000, 14%, 60-day promissory note due on May 4, 1987 from the sale of merchandise. The maker of the note was the Rau Company, a steady customer. The Rau Company began to experience financial difficulties and on May 5 defaulted on the note. The Stover Company still feels that there is some possibility it will ultimately be able to collect the funds.

    Prepare the necessary journal entries to record the receipt and subsequent default on the note. How would your answer differ, if at all, if the Stover Company felt that it would never be able to collect on the note?

12. Discounted Notes Receivable. On November 1, 1987 Rainbow Oil Company received a $56,000, 13%, 90-day note from Spenser, Inc. On December 1, 1987 Rainbow discounted the note at the First City Bank with recourse. The bank's discount rate at that time was 18%.

    Figure the amount of cash Rainbow Oil Company will receive from discounting the note, and prepare the necessary journal entry.

Problem Set A

9A–1. Accounting for Short-Term Investments. The Porter Chip Company entered into the following transactions related to short-term investments.

- April 1: Purchased 500 shares of Poco's at $25 per share.

- June 30: Purchased 1,000 shares of Optical Inc. at $45 per share.

- September 1: Received cash dividends of $2 per share on Poco's stock.

- November 20: Sold all of its shares of Poco's at $28 per share.

- December 31: The market value of Optical Inc.'s stock is $40 per share.

Required:

    a. Make the necessary journal entries to record the above transactions.

    b. Show how the securities would be shown on the December 31 balance sheet.

9A–2. Uncollectible Accounts Expense. The YU Company operates in an industry that has been experiencing a high rate of bad debts caused by the recession. On December 31, 1987, before the company made any year-end adjustments, the balance in the YU Company's Accounts Receivable account was $5 million, and the Allowance for Uncollectible Accounts account had a normal balance of $250,000. The Allowance for Uncollectible Accounts account will be adjusted using the aging method and applying the schedule shown below:

Days Account Outstanding	Amount	Probability of Collection
Less than 15 days	$3,000,000	.98
Between 16 and 30 days	1,000,000	.90
Between 31 and 45 days	500,000	.80
Between 46 and 60 days	300,000	.70
Between 61 and 75 days	100,000	.60
Over 75 days	100,000	.00

CHAPTER 9

Required:

   a. What is the appropriate balance for the Allowance for Uncollectible Accounts account at December 31, 1987?

   b. Make the journal entry or entries to record the required adjustment.

   c. Show how Accounts Receivable would be presented on the balance sheet prepared at December 31, 1987.

   d. What is the dollar effect of the year-end uncollectible accounts expense adjustment on the income for 1987?

9A–3. Uncollectible Accounts Expense. The following items were taken from the financial statements of Hard-Rock Wholesale Grocery Company at year-end before adjustments, except as noted.

1.	Accounts receivable balance, beginning of the year	$ 560,000
2.	Allowance for uncollectible accounts—debit balance	2,400
3.	Sales—all on credit	1,700,000
4.	Sales returns and allowances	2,500
5.	Cash received from customers on account, net of sales discounts of $4,500	1,737,500

The company uses the gross method to record accounts receivable.

Required:

   a. Make the necessary journal entries to record the summary events in Items 3 through 5.

   b. Assuming that the firm decides to estimate its uncollectible accounts expense as 2% of net sales before discounts, make the appropriate adjusting entry.

   c. Independent of your answer to (b), now assume that the firm decides to use the aging method to estimate the balance in the allowance for uncollectible accounts. After aging the accounts, the firm decides that the Allowance for Uncollectible Accounts account should have a balance of $34,800. Make the appropriate entry.

   d. Prepare partial balance sheets showing Accounts Receivable and Allowance for Uncollectible Accounts for each of the methods used to estimate uncollectible accounts described in (b) and (c). Compare and contrast the two.

9A–4. Accounting for Notes Receivable. During the current year the Green, Patrick, and Kiley Company entered into the following transactions pertaining to notes receivable:

• March 1: One of the firm's customers, the O'Leary Company, which purchased a large amount of inventory on open account, was unable to pay the bill. As a result Green, Patrick, and Kiley took a $10,000, 12%, 180-day note in exchange.

• April 5: In order to obtain immediate cash, the firm discounted the note with recourse at the Third Bank of Berkeley, at 14%. Assume the note has 145 days remaining until its maturity.

• May 1: Green, Patrick, and Kiley lent $25,000 to one of its best customers. The terms of the note call for interest of 10%. Principal and interest are due in one year.

• July 15: The firm sold some merchandise to the Blarney Company. Because the Blarney Company is a poor credit risk, Green, Patrick, and Kiley insisted on a note. The principal of the note is $9,000, is due in 90 days, and has an interest rate of 15%.

• July 31: The note from Blarney was discounted at the bank at a discount rate of 16%. Assume the note has 75 days remaining until its maturity.

• September 1: Green, Patrick, and Kiley received notice from the Third Bank of Berkeley that the note discounted on April 5 was paid in full.

• September 10: A note was due from Bad Way Company. However, Bad Way informed Green, Patrick, and Kiley it could not pay the note at this time. The note had a face value of $15,000 with accrued interest of $2,925 as of September 1.

• October 20: The firm received notice from the bank that the Blarney Company had defaulted on its note. Green, Patrick, and Kiley made the required payment plus a $10 protest fee.

• November 1: The firm lent another customer $5,000 cash. The note is due in 90 days and has an interest rate of 14%.

Required:
   a. Make all the entries to record these transactions.
   b. Make any required adjusting entries at December 31. (For purposes of adjusting entries, assume a 360-day year.)

9A–5. Accounting for Notes Receivable. The Inaco Company's treasurer was reviewing its accounts and notes receivable as the firm's year-end approached. As a result of this review the treasurer decided to take the following actions:

   1. An open account amounting to $10,000 from the Dickens Company was 60 days overdue. The treasurer insisted that the Dickens Company sign a 60-day, 12% note. The note was signed on December 1, 1986.
   2. The treasurer decided to discount the existing notes. The relevant data for each of these notes follow:

Company	Principal of Note	Length of Note	Date of Note	Interest Rate	Discount Date	Discount Rate
Lost Co.	$10,000	90 days	Nov. 1	12%	Dec. 1	15%
Winner Co.	$60,000	60 days	Dec. 1	15%	Dec. 15	18%

The Lost Co. paid the note to the bank when it was due. However, the Winner Co. defaulted on the note. The bank charged the Inaco Company a protest fee of $20.

Required:
Make the necessary entries to record the above events.

9A–6. Analysis of Uncollectible Accounts. You have gathered the following data regarding the Accounts Receivable balance at 12/31/87 of the Bream Company:

   1. Sales for 1987 $1,250,000
   2. Accounts Receivable balance—12/31/87   346,000
   3. The T accounts for the Uncollectible Accounts Expense and the Allowance for Uncollectible Accounts are presented below:

Uncollectible Accounts Expense

12/11/87	Sales returned for credit	1,200	Various times during 1987	Accounts written off during 1987	18,600
12/31/87	2.5% of credit sales	25,000			

Allowance for Uncollectible Accounts

Various times during 1987	Accounts written off	18,600	1/1/87	Bal.	22,500
			12/11/87	Sales returned for credit	1,200
			12/31/87	2.5% of total credit sales	25,000

Owing to past experience, you feel that the Bream Corporation should now use the aging method. Your analysis of the accounts receivable before corrections indicates the data on the top of page 381.

Required:
   a. Make the summary journal entry to record sales for the year.
   b. Make the necessary analyses and journal entries to correct, and then adjust, the accounts using the aging method.

Age	Net Balance	% Considered Uncollectible
Current	$103,800[b]	1
31–60 days	96,500	5
61–90 days	76,120	10
91–120 days	50,080[a]	20
Over 120 days	19,500[a]	100
Total	$346,000	

[a]Sixty % of the accounts written off in 1987 were over 120 days, and remaining 40% were from the 91–120 day category.

[b]Sales returned for credit made on December 1, 1987, and returned on December 11, 1987.

Problem Set B

9B–1. Accounting for Short-Term Investments. The Gar Oil Company entered into the following transactions related to short-term investments.

- February 12: Purchased 1,500 shares of Crunchy Nut at $40 per share.
- May 30: Purchased 2,000 shares of Diversified Inc. at $80 per share.
- September 20: Received cash dividends of $3 per share on Crunchy Nut stock.
- December 1: Sold all of its shares of Diversified at $90 per share.
- December 30: Received special $1 per share dividend on Crunchy Nut stock.
- December 31: The market value of Crunchy Nut's stock is $45 per share.

Required:

a. Make the necessary journal entries to record the above transactions.

b. Show how the securities would be shown on the December 31 balance sheet.

9B–2. Uncollectible Accounts Expense. The Europe Company has been experiencing a high rate of bad debts in the last few years. On December 31, 1987, before the company made any year-end adjustments, the balance in Europe's Accounts Receivable account was $800,000 and the Allowance for Uncollectible Accounts had a debit balance of $4,000. The Allowance for Uncollectible Accounts account will be adjusted using the aging method and applying the following schedule:

Days Account Is Outstanding	Amount	Probability of Default
Current	$450,000	.05
Between 30 and 60 days	240,000	.10
Between 61 and 90 days	80,000	.20
Between 91 and 120 days	20,000	.30
Over 121 days	10,000	1.00

Required:

a. Make the journal entry or entries to record the required adjustment.

b. What is the appropriate balance for the Allowance for Uncollectible Accounts on December 31, 1987?

c. Show how Accounts Receivable would be presented on the balance sheet prepared on December 31, 1987.

d. What is the dollar effect of the year-end uncollectible accounts expense adjustment on income for 1987?

9B–3. Accounting for Uncollectible Accounts. The following items were taken from the financial records of the Bean Ball Company at year-end before any adjustments, unless noted otherwise:

1. Accounts receivable balance, beginning of the year	$ 800,000
2. Allowance for doubtful accounts—credit balance	4,500
3. Sales—all on credit	2,000,000
4. Sales returns and allowances	3,500
5. Cash received from customers on open accounts net of sales discounts of $5,000	1,800,000

The company uses the gross method to record accounts receivable.

Required:

a. Make the necessary journal entries to record the summary events in Items 3 through 5.

b. Assuming the firm decides to estimate its uncollectible accounts expense as 1.5% of net sales before sales discounts, make the appropriate adjusting entry.

c. Independent of your answer to (b), now assume that the firm decides to use the aging method to estimate the balance in the allowance for uncollectible accounts. After aging the accounts, the firm estimates that the allowance for uncollectible accounts should have a balance of $45,000. Make the appropriate entry.

d. Prepare partial balance sheets showing accounts receivable and the allowance for doubtful accounts for each of the methods of estimating uncollectible accounts as described in (b) and (c). Compare and contrast the two.

9B–4. Accounting for Notes Receivable. During the current year the Jones Company entered into the following transactions relating to notes receivable:

- February 1: The Jones Company lent one of its best customers $50,000. The terms of the note call for interest of 12%. Principal and interest are due in one year.

- April 1: One of the firm's customers, which purchased a large amount of inventory on open account, was unable to pay its debt. As a result, the Jones Company took a 10%, $20,000, 90-day note in exchange for the receivable.

- May 1: In order to obtain immediate cash the firm discounted the note with recourse at the Far West Bank at a discount rate of 12%.

- June 16: The firm sold some merchandise to the Glasson Company. Because Glasson is a poor credit risk, Jones insisted on a note for $12,000. The note is due in 6 months and has an interest rate of 12%.

- July 15: The note from Glasson was discounted at the bank at a rate of 15%.

- July 16: The Jones Company received notice from the Far West Bank that the note discounted on May 1 was paid in full.

- August 1: A note was due from the Huang Company. However, the firm informed Jones that it could not pay the note at this time. The note had a face value of $18,000 with accrued interest to August 1 of $3,000.

- November 1: The firm loaned one of its customers $7,000 cash. The note is due in 90 days and has an interest rate of 12%.

Required:

a. Make all the entries to record these transactions.

b. Make any required adjusting entries required at December 31.

9B–5. Accounting for Notes Receivable. The Dream Company needed a considerable amount of cash to undertake production expansion next year. The firm decided to take the following actions relative to its accounts and notes receivable:

1. An open account amounting to $50,000 from the Ray Company was 60 days overdue. The Dream Company insisted that the Ray Company sign a 90-day, 15% note. The note was signed on November 1, 1986.

2. The treasurer decided to discount the existing notes. The relevant data for each of these notes follow:

Company	Principal of Note	Length of Note	Date of Note	Interest Rate	Discount Date	Discount Rate
Ray Co.	$50,000	90 days	Nov. 1	15%	Dec. 1	15%
Almost Inc.	90,000	60 days	Dec. 1	12	Dec. 16	15
West Inc.	40,000	120 days	Dec. 1	12	Dec. 16	15

Ray and Almost paid their notes to the bank when they were due. However, West defaulted on its note. The bank charged the Dream Company a protest fee of $20.

Required:

Make the necessary entries to record the above events.

9B–6. Analysis of Uncollectible Accounts. You have obtained the following data relative to the accounts receivable balance at 6/30/87 of The Sandman, Inc.

1. Sales for the year ended 6/30/87 — $2,450,000
2. Accounts Receivable — 389,500
3. The T accounts for Uncollectible Accounts Expense and Allowance for Uncollectible Accounts are presented below:

Uncollectible Accounts Expense

6/20/87	Sales returned for credit	5,000	Various times	Accounts written off	25,000
6/30/87	3% of total credit sales	55,125	during the year		

Allowance for Uncollectible Accounts

Various times during the year	Accounts written off	25,000	7/1/86	Beg. Bal.	42,875
			6/20/87	Sales returned for credit[a]	5,000
			6/30/87	3% of total credit sales	55,125

Due to past experience, you feel that The Sandman, Inc. should now use the aging method. Your analysis of the accounts receivable indicates the following:

Age	Net Balance	% Considered Uncollectible
Current	$147,000[a]	2%
31–60 days	117,600	6
61–90 days	70,560[b]	15
91–120 days	31,040[b]	30
Over 120 days	23,300[b]	70
Total	$389,500	

[a]Sale that was returned for credit was made on June 15, 1987 and returned on June 20, 1987.

[b]Fifty % of the accounts written off during the year were over 120 days, 30% were in the 91–120 day category, and 20% were in the 61–90 day category.

Required:

a. Make the summary journal entry to record sales for the year.

b. Make the required analysis and journal entries and then adjust the accounts to the aging method.

Using the Computer

The controller of the Computer Graphics Company has asked you to prepare an aging of accounts receivable on a common computer spreadsheet software program. She provides you with the following data concerning outstanding accounts receivable as of December 31:

Customer	Sales Date	Amount
Atwater Co.	October 5	$4,000
	December 8	6,000
Beckweth Corp.	November 20	2,000
	December 15	6,000
Lotuse Inc.	October 16	1,000
	November 22	500
	December 2	3,000
Perset Ltd.	August 17	5,000
Visiadd Co.	September 13	5,000
	October 22	2,500
	November 12	1,000

The controller estimates that the following schedule should be used in estimating the necessary amount for the journal entry to record uncollectible accounts as of December 31:

Days Account Outstanding	Probability of Default
Current	.02
Between 31 and 60 days	.05
Between 61 and 90 days	.10
Between 91 and 120 days	.25
Over 120 days	.50

Finally, prior to any adjustment, the balance in the Allowance for Uncollectible Accounts account was a credit balance of $1,000.

Required:

a. Using a spreadsheet program available at your school, prepare an aging of accounts receivable that determines the amount of the required adjusting entry at December 31. Use a format similar to that in the text.

b. The controller now tells you that she feels the economy may not be as good as she originally thought. She would like you to repeat the analysis using the following estimates of uncollectible accounts:

Days Account Outstanding	Probability of Default
Current	.05
Between 31 and 60 days	.10
Between 61 and 90 days	.25
Between 91 and 120 days	.50
Over 120 days	1.00

Understanding Financial Statements

The following note was taken from the 1982 and 1981 consolidated balance sheets of Caesar's World, Inc.:

NOTE 4. RECEIVABLES, NET

	(in thousands)	
	1982	1981
Accounts receivable		
Casino	$141,828	$107,558
Hotel	4,290	6,183
Other	7,568	15,094
	153,686	128,835
Less: Allowance for doubtful accounts	73,554	49,296
Net Accounts Receivable	$ 80,132	$ 79,539
In addition, net revenues (in thousands) for each year were	$556,618	$596,031

Required:

   a. Under what circumstances do you think the casino receivables arise?

   b. Compute the ratio of the Allowance for Doubtful Accounts to gross Accounts Receivable and to net revenues. What do these figures tell you about the collectibility of receivables?

   c. During 1982 the uncollectible accounts expense amounted to $46,227 (in thousands). What was the net amount of receivables that Caesar's World, Inc. wrote off as uncollectible during 1982?

Financial Decision Case

The Muppett Computer Store sells computers and software to individuals and to businesses. Because of the high price of the goods it sells, Muppett has always had a very stringent credit policy and will sell on credit only to customers with a AAA credit rating. However, the president of the company has begun to notice that many of the firm's competitors have begun to advertise that they welcome credit sales. As a result, the president is concerned that the firm's profits are suffering by its insisting on such a tough credit policy. She gives you the following data and asks your advice as to whether the firm's credit policies should be relaxed:

   Current sales are running about $10 million a year, of which only 10% are currently made on credit. The firm's gross margin on sales is 30% or, correspondingly, cost of goods sold equals 70% of sales. Current uncollectible accounts amount to only 1% of credit sales. The firm has analyzed its potential customers and feels that there are three additional classes of credit customers to which it could extend credit. If it does, the firm expects to increase sales and to incur the following amount of uncollectibles and additional selling expenses for each of the three classes:

Class Rating	Additional Sales	Percent Uncollectible	Additional Expenses
A	$100,000	5	$10,000
B	60,000	10	11,000
C	90,000	20	13,000

Required:

   a. Advise the president as to whether the firm's credit policies should be revised and, if so, to what extent. Include a discussion of what effect there will be on profits if sales are made to the additional customers.

   b. What else should the president take into consideration before making a final decision on extending credit to these potential customers?

Accounting for Current Liabilities and Payrolls

10

Liabilities represent the economic obligations of an enterprise. In recent years, as many firms have struggled to maintain an adequate level of liquidity, issues related to the determination, measurement, and recognition of liabilities have become more important. This chapter discusses the accounting concepts and procedures related to current liabilities. In addition, we introduce the topic of payroll accounting and related internal controls.

Definition and Recognition of Liabilities

The FASB defines liabilities as "probable future sacrifices of economic benefits arising from present obligations of a particular entity to transfer assets or provide services to other entities in the future as a result of past transactions or events."[1] To recognize a liability, a firm need not know the actual recipient of the assets that are to be transferred or for whom the services are to be performed. For example, when General Motors guarantees or warrants an automobile, a liability must be recorded, even though at the time of sale GM does not know which particular customer's automobile may require repair.

In order for a liability to exist, an event or transaction must already have occurred. In effect, only present—not future—obligations are liabilities. For example, the exchange of promises of future performance between two firms or individuals does not result in the recognition of a liability or the related asset. The signing of a labor contract between a firm and an individual does not cause the firm to recognize a liability. Rather, the liability is recognized when the employees perform services for which they have not yet been compensated. In the automobile warranty case, the liability occurs at the time of sale because at that time the firm obligates itself to make certain repairs. Thus, the event has occurred and a present obligation is incurred.

Classification of Liabilities

In preparing a balance sheet, liabilities are classified as either current or long-term. **Current liabilities** require the use of existing resources that are classified as current assets or require the creation of new current liabilities. Current liabilities include such accounts as Accounts Payable, Short-term Notes Payable, Current Maturities of Long-term Debt (the principal portion of a long-term liability due within the next 12 months), Taxes Payable, and other Accrued Payables. **Long-term liabilities,** discussed in Chapter 18, are those liabilities that will not be satisfied within one year or the operating cycle, if longer than one year. Included in this category are Mortgages Payable, Bonds Payable, and Lease Obligations. As noted, however, the current portion, if any, of these long-term liabilities is classified as current liabilities.

Measurement and Valuation of Current Liabilities

Like assets, liabilities are originally measured and recorded according to the cost principle. That is, when incurred, the liability is measured and recorded at the current market value of the asset or service received. Because current liabilities are payable within a relatively short period of time, they are recorded at their face value, which is the amount of cash needed to discharge the principal of the liability. No recognition is given to the fact that the present value of these future cash outlays is less. **Present value** is related to the idea of the time value of money. Essentially it means that cash received or paid in the future is worth less than the same amount of cash received or paid today. This is true because cash on hand today can be invested and thus can grow to a greater future amount. Thus, the value of the liability at the time incurred is actually less than the cash required to be paid in the future.

In connection with current liabilities, the difference between value today and future cash outlay is not material because of the short time span between

---

[1]Financial Accounting Standards Board, Concepts Statement No. 6, *Elements of Financial Statements* (Stanford, Conn.: FASB, December 1985), par. 35.

the time the liability is incurred and when it is paid. Current liabilities, therefore, are shown at the amount of the future principal payment. However, present value concepts are applied to long-term liabilities, liabilities with no stated interest, and liabilities with a stated interest rate materially different from the market rate for similar transactions. Some of these cases are explored in Chapter 18.

Types of Current Liabilities

Liabilities are often divided into three categories: (1) those that are definitely determinable in amount, (2) collections for third parties and those liabilities conditioned on operations, and (3) contingent liabilities.

Liabilities That Are Definitely Determinable

Definitely determinable current liabilities are those liabilities that are known and are definite in amount. Included in this category are accounts such as Accounts Payable, Trade Notes Payable, Current Maturities of Long-term Debt, and Interest Payable. The major accounting problems associated with these liabilities are determining their existence and ensuring that they are recorded in the proper accounting period. For example, if the cost of an item is included in the ending inventory but a corresponding payable and/or purchase is not recorded, there will be an understatement of both cost of goods sold and total liabilities.

Accounts Payable

Accounts payable, or **trade accounts payable,** are monies owed to the enterprise's suppliers or vendors for the purchase of goods and services. Most purchases take place on credit, and under the accrual basis of accounting, the liability must be recorded at the time title passes for the assets purchased or when the services are received. Proper internal control procedures require using subsidiary accounts payable ledgers or a voucher register. Internal control procedures for accounts payable utilizing a voucher system are discussed in Chapter 8.

Notes Payable

As with notes receivable, **notes payable** can result from different types of transactions, but the most likely sources are from purchases of goods and services through trade notes payable or from bank loans through notes payable. We concentrate here on notes payable to banks. The concepts related to these notes can easily be applied to other forms of notes payable.

Notes Issued to Banks

Bank loans are a major source of funding for all types and sizes of businesses. There are two different types of notes that can be issued to banks: One type is drawn to include the principal or face amount and a separate interest element, and the other type is drawn in such a way that the face amount also includes the interest charge. Exhibit 10–1 on page 390 shows both types of notes.

| $5,000 | | October 1 | 19 87 |

four months _____ after date, for value received

S. F. Giant _____ promise(s) to pay to

L. A. Dodger _____, order of,

at _____ Los Angeles, California _____

the sum of _____ Five thousand _____ dollars

in lawful money of the United States of America, with interest thereon,

at the rate of _____ 12 _____ percent per _____ annum _____ from date

S. F. Giant

EXHIBIT 10–1. continued
Case 2—Interest Element Included

| $5,200 | | October 1 | 19 87 |

four months _____ after date, for value received

S. F. Giant _____ promise(s) to pay to

L. A. Dodger _____, order of,

at _____ Los Angeles, California _____

the sum of _____ Five thousand two hundred _____ dollars

in lawful money of the United States of America.

S. F. Giant

The note in Case 1 is drawn in the principal amount of $5,000. The interest element of 12% is stated separately. The note in Case 2 is drawn for $5,200, but the interest element is not stated separately. The interest of $200 (12% of $5,000 for 120 days) is included in the face of the note at the time it is issued but is deducted from the proceeds at the time the note is issued. Thus, S. F. Giant receives only $5,000 instead of $5,200, the face value of the note. The second case is an example of a discounted note payable.

Issuance of the Note

The journal entries to record this note under each of the two cases are:

CASE 1:			CASE 2:		
INTEREST STATED SEPARATELY			INTEREST NOT STATED SEPARATELY		
October 1, 1987			October 1, 1987		
Cash	5,000		Cash	5,000	
Notes Payable		5,000	Discount on Notes Payable	200	
To record $5,000, 12%			Notes Payable		5,200
120-day note payable.			To record $5,200, 12%, 120-day		
			discounted note payable.		

The entry in Case 1 is straightforward. Cash is debited and Notes Payable is credited for $5,000. In Case 2, Notes Payable is credited for $5,200, the maturity value of the note, but S. F. Giant receives only $5,000 cash. The $200 difference is debited to the account Discount on Notes Payable. This is a contra-liability account and is offset against the Notes Payable account on the balance sheet. Interest expense is not debited because interest is a function of time. The discount simply represents the total potential interest expense to be incurred if the note remains unpaid for the full 120 days. Over the life of the note, the discount is written off as interest expense is recognized. The partial balance sheets for both cases as of the date of the note are presented below:

CASE 1:		CASE 2:		
PARTIAL BALANCE SHEET		PARTIAL BALANCE SHEET		
Current liabilities:		Current liabilities:		
Notes payable	$5,000	Notes payable		$5,200
		Less: Discount on notes payable		200
				$5,000

Interest Accrual

Because the interest on the notes is not payable until maturity, an interest accrual must be made at year-end. This accrual is for three months, as adjusting entries are assumed to be made only at year-end, December 31. The entry in each case is:

CASE 1: DECEMBER 31, 1987			CASE 2: DECEMBER 31, 1987		
Interest Expense	150		Interest Expense	150	
Interest Payable		150	Discount on Notes Payable		150
To record 3 months of			To amortize discount on straight-line		
accrued interest.			basis for 3 months.		
$150 = \$5,000 \times .12 \times 90/360$			$150 = \$200 \times 3/4$		

The adjusting journal entry in Case 1 is similar to the entries to accrue interest made in Chapter 4. Interest Expense is debited and Interest Payable is credited for three months of accrued interest. The entry in Case 2 needs additional explanation. At the origin of the note, the account Discount on Notes Payable represents interest charges related to future accounting periods. At the end of the note's term, all of these interest charges have been recognized, and so the balance in this discount account becomes zero. To accomplish this process, the Discount on Notes Payable account is written off over the life of the note. This write-off is referred to as amortization of the discount.

In the journal entry in Case 2, the discount is amortized on a straight-line basis.[2] That is, an equal amount of the discount ($200 ÷ 4 = $50) is charged

---

[2]Under the straight-line basis, interest expense is the same each period. This is similar to straight-line depreciation. In Chapter 18 we see that in some cases a method called the effective interest method is preferable.

each month to interest expense. The entry is for $150 because the amortization entry is for a three-month period. After the entry on December 31, the Discount account has a balance of only $50. This increases the net liability to $5,150, which represents the $5,000 proceeds from the note plus $150 of interest incurred since the inception of the loan. Partial balance sheets at December 31, 1987 for Cases 1 and 2 appear as follows:

CASE 1: PARTIAL BALANCE SHEET		CASE 2: PARTIAL BALANCE SHEET	
Current liabilities:		Current liabilities:	
Notes payable	$5,000	Notes payable	$5,200
Interest payable	150	Less: Discount on notes payable	50
	$5,150		$5,150

As these partial balance sheets show, the total liability related to notes and interest is $5,150 in both cases.

Payment at Maturity of the Note

When the note matures on January 31, 1988, S. F. Giant must pay the entire principal and, in the first case, the accrued interest. In both cases, the final month's interest expense, $50, is recognized. The journal entries for both cases are presented below.

CASE 1: JANUARY 31, 1988		
Notes Payable	5,000	
Interest Payable	150	
Interest Expense	50	
Cash		5,200

To record payments of $5,000 principal and $150 of interest payable and to record interest expense for 1 month of $50.

CASE 2: JANUARY 31, 1988		
Notes Payable	5,200	
Interest Expense	50	
Discount on Notes Payable		50
Cash		5,200

To record payment of $5,200 note and to amortize discount of $50 on note payable for 1 month.

In summary, both cases represent different ways in which notes can be written. In the first case, the firm receives the total face value of $5,000 and ultimately repays principal and interest of $5,200. In the second case, the firm receives the same $5,000, but the note is written for $5,200. The interest is deducted from the note at the time of its origin. Eventually, however, the firm must repay the full $5,200.

Current Portion of Long-term Debt

Current maturities of long-term debt are those portions of long-term liabilities that are payable within one year of the balance sheet date and thus are classified as current. For example, the principal portion of the next 12 payments due on a 30-year mortgage following the balance sheet date is classified as current. The remaining portion is considered long-term.

Other Definitely Determinable Liabilities

Other definitely determinable liabilities include accrued liabilities such as interest and wages payable and unearned revenues. Recognition of accrued liabilities requires periodic adjusting entries. Failure to recognize accrued liabilities overstates income and understates liabilities.

A firm may receive cash in advance of performing some service or providing some goods. Because the firm has an obligation to perform the service or provide the goods, this advance payment is a liability. These advance payments are termed *unearned revenues* and include such items as subscriptions or dues received in advance, prepaid rent, and deposits. These liabilities are generally classified as current because the goods or services are usually delivered or performed within one year or the operating cycle, if longer than one year. If this is not the case, they should be classified as noncurrent liabilities.

Liabilities That Represent Collections for Third Parties or Are Conditioned on Operations

Firms are often required to make collections for third parties such as unions and governmental agencies. For example, taxes are levied on the consumer and/or the firm, and the firm is required to collect the tax on behalf of the taxing agency. Included in this category are sales and excise taxes, social security taxes, withholding taxes, and union dues. Other liabilities such as federal and state corporate income taxes are conditioned or based on the results of the enterprise's operations.

Sales Taxes

Most states and some counties and cities impose sales or excise taxes. These taxes are usually imposed on the consumer, but the retailer usually must collect these taxes and remit them to the taxing authority. The tax when collected by the retailer is a liability and is not included in total sales. For example assume that the Lottery Corporation makes a $500 sale on account that is subject to a 6% sales tax. The entry to record this sale is:

Accounts Receivable	530	
Sales		500
Sales Taxes Payable		30
To record $500 sales on account		
plus 6% sales tax.		
$30 = $500 × .06		

When the sales tax is remitted to the taxing agency, usually on a monthly or quarterly basis, the Sales Taxes Payable account is debited and Cash is credited.

Payroll Tax Liabilities

As employees earn wages, certain federal and state taxes are incurred by the employee and the employer. Included are federal and state withholding taxes, social security taxes, and unemployment taxes. The employer must account for these taxes and file appropriate tax returns on a quarterly or yearly basis. Payroll accounting is discussed in detail in a later part of this chapter.

Compensated Absences

Although compensated absences do not represent collections for third parties, they are closely related to payroll taxes and thus are covered here. As employees work, they accrue certain fringe benefits that allow them time off with full or partial pay. These are called **compensated absences** and include such benefits as vacation and sick pay.

Under current accounting practices, a firm should accrue the liability for these benefits as they are earned. For example, many employees receive a two-week paid vacation every year. As the employee works throughout the year, he or she earns a portion of that vacation and an estimated liability should be accrued for that amount. To illustrate, assume that during the current quarter a firm estimates that its employees have earned 20 vacation days at an average salary of $200 per day. As a result, the firm should accrue a $4,000 ($200 × 20 days) liability as follows:

Vacation Pay Expense	4,000	
Accrued Vacation Pay		4,000
To record an estimated liability		
of $4,000 for vacation pay.		

As the employees take their vacation and they are paid the liability, Accrued Vacation Pay is debited and Cash is credited. For example, assume that one employee, Mary Lelani, is paid $400 for a two-week vacation she took ending June 30. The following entry is made to record this payment:

Accrued Vacation Pay	400	
Cash or Wages Payable		400
To record payment of wages of		
employee on vacation.		

Corporate Federal Income Taxes

Corporations are taxed by the federal as well as many state governments. These taxes are based on the results of the firm's operations as defined by the Internal Revenue Code. However, during the year corporations are required to make quarterly payments based on their estimated tax for the entire year. At the end of the year the corporation must record a liability for the remaining taxes due based on the firm's operations for the year. To illustrate, if the Winwrich Corporation's unrecorded federal income tax liability at December 31, 1987 is $42,000, the following entry would be made:

Federal Income Tax Expense	42,000	
Federal Income Tax Payable		42,000
To record estimated federal income		
tax liability.		

Contingent Liabilities

Contingent liabilities are potential future liabilities whose existence is contingent on some future event. In effect, a contingent liability is the result of an existing condition or situation whose final resolution depends on some future event. Generally, the amount of these liabilities must be estimated; the actual amount cannot be determined until the event that confirms the liability occurs. Furthermore, in many cases the actual payee of the liability is not known until the future event occurs.

Examples of contingent liabilities include product warranties and guarantees, pending or threatened litigation, and the guarantee of others' indebtedness. In all these situations, a past event has occurred that may give rise to a liability depending on some future event. For example, when General Motors sells a car, it gives the purchaser a 12,000-mile or 12-month guarantee against defects. Thus the event, the sale of a car, has taken place. However, the actual amount of the liability and the person to whom it will be paid depend on some future action, the customer's presenting the automobile for repair.

Contingent Liabilities That Are Accrued

Under generally accepted accounting principles, contingent liabilities are recorded as actual liabilities only if the potential liability is probable and its amount can be reasonably estimated.[3] An automobile guarantee or other product warranties are examples of contingent liabilities that are usually recorded on a company's books. Past experience indicates that a certain percentage of products will be defective, and past experience can also be used to reasonably estimate the amount of the future expenditure required by the warranty. The matching convention requires the expense to be recorded in the period of the sale, not when the repair is made.

To illustrate, assume that the Micro Printing Company manufactures and sells high-speed laser printers for personal computers. The retail price per unit is $1,200, and each printer is guaranteed for three years; that is, the firm will repair the unit free of charge during this period. During the 1986 calendar year, the firm sold 2,000 printers. Past experience indicates that Micro Printing will incur an average of $40 in repair expense for each of the printers sold. Finally, during 1986 the company actually incurred $35,000 of warranty expenditures related to these printers. The following summary journal entries were made by Micro Printing Company in 1986 to reflect these events:

Cash or Accounts Receivable	2,400,000	
Sales		2,400,000
To record sales for the year.		
$2,400,000 = 2,000 units × $1,200		
Product Guarantee Expense	80,000	
Estimated Liability for Product Guarantees		80,000
To record estimated liability for product guarantees.		
$80,000 = 2,000 units × $40		
Estimated Liability for Product Guarantees	35,000	
Cash, Supplies, Accrued Wages, etc.		35,000
To record actual expenditures incurred for product guarantees during the year.		

Each accounting period in this cycle is repeated. As the firm makes sales, an estimated liability is accrued. And as the guarantee expenditures are made by the firm, the liability is debited, and the appropriate accounts are credited.

Contingent Liabilities That Are Not Accrued

Contingent liabilities that are not probable and/or whose amount cannot be reasonably estimated are not accrued on the company's books. Instead, they are usually disclosed in the footnotes to the financial statements. These types of contingencies usually include pending litigation and guarantees of indebtedness that exist when a company guarantees the collectibility of a receivable that it has discounted at the bank.

The following example taken from a recent annual report of Sears, Roebuck and Co. shows how such contingent liabilities are disclosed:

SEARS, ROEBUCK AND CO.

> Various legal actions and governmental proceedings are pending against Sears, Roebuck and Co. and its subsidiaries, many involving ordinary routine litigation incidental to the business engaged in. Other matters contain allegations which are nonroutine and involve compensatory, punitive or antitrust treble damage claims in very large amounts, as well as other types of relief. The consequences of these matters are not presently determinable but, in the opinion of management, the ultimate liability resulting, if any, will not have a material effect on the shareholders' equity of the company.

[3]Financial Accounting Standars Board, No. 5 *Accounting for Contingencies* (Stanford, Conn.: FASB, March 1975).

Balance Sheet Presentation of Current Liabilities

The particular order in which current liabilities are presented on the balance sheet is a management decision. The current liability section of Safeway Stores, Inc. is typical of those found in the balance sheets of many U.S. companies. That is, notes and loans are usually listed first, then accounts payable, and finally accrued liabilities and taxes.

Safeway Stores, Inc.
Partial Balance Sheet
(in thousands)

Liabilities	1985	1984	1983
Current liabilities:			
Notes payable	$ 80,848	$ 44,913	$ 50,156
Current obligations under capital leases	43,396	45,427	45,841
Current maturities of notes and debentures	52,049	48,274	24,723
Accounts payable	1,151,426	1,038,268	1,017,094
Accrued salaries and wages	167,798	167,739	163,021
Other accrued expenses	201,357	170,905	154,373
Income taxes payable	27,827	20,431	43,081
Total current liabilities	$1,724,701	$1,535,957	$1,498,289

Accounting for Payrolls

Payroll and related payroll costs including payroll taxes and fringe benefits represent a major expense for most companies. As our economy becomes more and more automated, service-oriented personnel costs of all types will continue to increase. For some industries, such as airlines, retail grocery stores, and professional organizations, personnel costs are already 50% of total operating costs.

Creating and maintaining an efficient payroll department and system are important tasks. Employers are required to comply with a variety of laws governing minimum pay, payroll taxes, hiring practices, and working conditions. The payroll system must be able to compute, process, and distribute each employee's pay and paycheck. This must be done on a timely basis, often weekly. Furthermore, because of the high volume of activity and dollars that flow through the system, internal controls must be developed to ensure against fraud.

The accounting issues related to payrolls include (1) determining employee compensation, (2) determining liabilities for employee payroll withholding, (3) recording the payment of wages and employees' take-home pay, (4) determining the employer's payroll tax expense, (5) paying the payroll and payroll taxes, and (6) developing internal controls for payrolls.

Determining Employee Compensation

Before employee compensation can be determined, it is necessary to distinguish a firm's employees from its independent contractors. Independent contractors are not regular employees of the firm and often are not part of the regular payroll system. Furthermore, independent contractors are not subject to the same payroll taxes that the employees of the firm are. Individuals acting as independent contractors offer their services to a firm in order to accomplish a particular assignment or job for a set fee. As a result, these independent contractors are not under the direct supervision of the firm, and as noted they are not subject to payroll taxes or withholding taxes. However, firms employing these individuals must report to the Internal Revenue Service the amount of fees paid to each independent contractor who does not have a separate business on a form 1099. An example of an independent contractor is an outside management consultant.

Employees of a firm receive pay that is subject to payroll taxes, withholding taxes, and other fringe benefits. Employees who receive a wage often receive an hourly wage rate or are paid on a per-work basis. Employees who receive a salary usually are paid a set monthly or yearly salary regardless of hours worked or work produced. Employees in either category may or may not be unionized.

Employee salaries are set by union contract, individual negotiation between employee and employer, or perhaps by minimum wage laws determined by the Fair Labor Standards Act. In addition, wages and salaries may or may not include overtime premiums. Pay periods may be weekly, biweekly, semimonthly, or monthly. These issues again depend on union contracts and management decisions.

To illustrate, assume that Michele Duffy works for the Brer Rabbit Grocery Store. Under the current union contract Michele's regular wages are $6 per hour. In addition, she receives time and one-half for work over eight hours a day and double time for work on Saturday and Sunday regardless of actual hours worked on the weekend. During the workweek ended Sunday, January 25, 1987 she worked 48 hours as follows:

Day	Hours Worked	Regular Time	1 1/2 Overtime	Double Overtime
Monday	10	8	2	
Tuesday	8	8		
Wednesday	8	8		
Thursday	10	8	2	
Friday				
Saturday	8			8
Sunday	4			4
Total	48	32	4	12

Duffy's total wages for the week are determined as follows:

Regular time	32 hours × $ 6 =	$192
1 1/2 overtime	4 hours × 9 =	36
Double overtime	12 hours × 12 =	144
Total wages		$372

Recording Liabilities for Employee Payroll Withholdings

When an employee earns a wage, certain federal and state taxes are incurred by both the employee and the employer. In addition to these taxes, employees might approve certain other deductions from their paychecks. These include union dues, medical insurance, parking, and charitable contributions. After the monies are withheld from the employees' paychecks, the employer has the responsibility of remitting these funds to the appropriate organizations.

FICA Taxes

FICA taxes are the result of the Federal Insurance Contributions Act and commonly are referred to as social security taxes. The coverage provided by these taxes has grown over the years and now includes Old Age Survivors and Disability Insurance (OASDI) and Medicare Insurance. Equal taxes are levied on both the employee and the employer on a varying salary base. The FICA rate levied against both employees and employers is scheduled to be 7.15% of the first $42,600 of wages in 1987. However, this rate is subject to change by Congress.

Because of the drain on the Social Security System, FICA taxes have risen dramatically since the late 1970s. This increase has occurred mainly through an increase in the taxable salary base. Because a majority of wage earners currently do not earn more than the maximum in any one year, all their wages are subject to FICA taxes. In fact, some individuals pay more in social security taxes than in federal income taxes. If we assume for purposes of our example that all of Michele Duffy's wages of $372 are taxable for FICA purposes at a rate of 7%, taxes of $26.04 would be levied on Duffy and on her employer, the Brer Rabbit Grocery Store. (Seven percent is used in this illustration for ease of computation.)

Federal and State Income Tax

The federal government and many states have adopted pay-as-you-go requirements for the collection of individual income taxes. These rules require employers to withhold income taxes from employees' paychecks and then remit these taxes to the federal and state governments on a timely basis.

The amount of income taxes withheld depends on the employee's income level and the number of exemptions claimed by the employee. Exemptions ultimately reduce an individual's taxable income so that the higher the number of exemptions claimed, the lower the amount of the taxes withheld. In effect, each individual is entitled to one exemption for him- or herself, one for each dependent, and additional exemptions based on the estimated amount of itemized deductions and other factors such as age. Employees file a tax form called a W-4 which indicates the number of exemptions claimed for the year. Once the number of exemptions is determined, the amount of periodic income tax withheld is calculated by referring to withholding tables provided by federal and state governments. Exhibits 10–2 and 10–3, respectively, present examples of a W-4 form and federal withholding tables.

To illustrate the use of these tables assume that Michele Duffy, a single parent, claims two exemptions, one for herself and one for her dependent. Based on her pay of $372 for the week ended January 25, withholding for federal income taxes is $51. (See Exhibit 10–3.) In addition, for purposes of our example we will assume withholding for state income taxes is $7.50.

EXHIBIT 10-2

Form **W-4** (Rev. January 1986)	Department of the Treasury—Internal Revenue Service **Employee's Withholding Allowance Certificate**		OMB No. 1545-0010 Expires: 11-30-87

1 Type or print your full name		**2** Your social security number	

Home address (number and street or rural route)	**3** Marital Status	☐ Single ☐ Married ☐ Married, but withhold at higher Single rate **Note:** If married, but legally separated, or spouse is a nonresident alien, check the Single box.
City or town, state, and ZIP code		

4 Total number of allowances you are claiming (from line F of the worksheet on page 2) . . . .

5 Additional amount, if any, you want deducted from each pay . . . . $

6 I claim exemption from withholding because (see instructions and check boxes below that apply):

  a ☐ Last year I did not owe any Federal income tax and had a right to a full refund of **ALL** income tax withheld, **AND**

  b ☐ This year I do not expect to owe any Federal income tax and expect to have a right to a full refund of   Year
    ALL income tax withheld. If both a and b apply, enter the year effective and "EXEMPT" here ▶ **19**

  c If you entered "EXEMPT" on line 6b, are you a full-time student? . . . . ☐Yes ☐No

Under penalties of perjury, I certify that I am entitled to the number of withholding allowances claimed on this certificate, or if claiming exemption from withholding, that I am entitled to claim the exempt status.

Employee's signature ▶   **Date ▶**   , 19

7 Employer's name and address (**Employer: Complete 7, 8, and 9 only if sending to IRS**)	**8** Office code	**9** Employer identification number

-------------------- Detach along this line. Give the top part of this form to employer; keep the lower part for your records. --------------------

EXHIBIT 10-3

SINGLE Persons–WEEKLY Payroll Period
(For Wages Paid After December 1985)

And the wages are–		And the number of withholding allowances claimed is–										
At least	But less than	0	1	2	3	4	5	6	7	8	9	10
		The amount of income tax to be withheld shall be–										
$0	$32	$0	$0	$0	$0	$0	$0	$0	$0	$0	$0	$0
32	34	1	0	0	0	0	0	0	0	0	0	0
34	36	1	0	0	0	0	0	0	0	0	0	0
36	38	1	0	0	0	0	0	0	0	0	0	0
38	40	1	0	0	0	0	0	0	0	0	0	0
40	42	2	0	0	0	0	0	0	0	0	0	0
42	44	2	0	0	0	0	0	0	0	0	0	0
44	46	2	0	0	0	0	0	0	0	0	0	0
46	48	2	0	0	0	0	0	0	0	0	0	0
48	50	2	0	0	0	0	0	0	0	0	0	0
50	52	3	0	0	0	0	0	0	0	0	0	0
52	54	3	1	0	0	0	0	0	0	0	0	0
54	56	3	1	0	0	0	0	0	0	0	0	0
56	58	3	1	0	0	0	0	0	0	0	0	0
58	60	4	1	0	0	0	0	0	0	0	0	0
60	62	4	1	0	0	0	0	0	0	0	0	0
62	64	4	2	0	0	0	0	0	0	0	0	0
64	66	4	2	0	0	0	0	0	0	0	0	0
66	68	5	2	0	0	0	0	0	0	0	0	0
68	70	5	2	0	0	0	0	0	0	0	0	0
70	72	5	3	0	0	0	0	0	0	0	0	0
72	74	5	3	0	0	0	0	0	0	0	0	0
74	76	6	3	1	0	0	0	0	0	0	0	0
76	78	6	3	1	0	0	0	0	0	0	0	0
78	80	6	4	1	0	0	0	0	0	0	0	0
80	82	6	4	1	0	0	0	0	0	0	0	0
82	84	7	4	2	0	0	0	0	0	0	0	0
84	86	7	4	2	0	0	0	0	0	0	0	0
86	88	7	4	2	0	0	0	0	0	0	0	0
88	90	8	5	2	0	0	0	0	0	0	0	0
90	92	8	5	2	0	0	0	0	0	0	0	0
92	94	8	5	3	0	0	0	0	0	0	0	0
94	96	8	6	3	1	0	0	0	0	0	0	0
96	98	9	6	3	1	0	0	0	0	0	0	0
98	100	9	6	3	1	0	0	0	0	0	0	0
100	105	9	7	4	1	0	0	0	0	0	0	0
105	110	10	7	4	2	0	0	0	0	0	0	0
110	115	11	8	5	3	0	0	0	0	0	0	0
115	120	12	9	6	3	1	0	0	0	0	0	0
120	125	12	9	6	4	1	0	0	0	0	0	0
125	130	13	10	7	4	2	0	0	0	0	0	0
130	135	14	11	8	5	2	0	0	0	0	0	0
135	140	15	11	9	6	3	1	0	0	0	0	0
140	145	15	12	9	6	4	1	0	0	0	0	0
145	150	16	13	10	7	4	2	0	0	0	0	0
150	160	17	14	11	8	5	3	0	0	0	0	0
160	170	19	16	13	10	7	4	1	0	0	0	0
170	180	20	17	14	11	8	5	3	0	0	0	0
180	190	22	19	16	12	9	6	4	1	0	0	0
190	200	24	20	17	14	11	8	5	2	0	0	0
200	210	25	22	19	15	12	9	6	4	1	0	0
210	220	27	24	20	17	14	11	8	5	2	0	0
220	230	29	25	22	18	15	12	9	6	4	1	0
230	240	31	27	23	20	17	14	11	8	5	2	0
240	250	32	29	25	22	18	15	12	9	6	4	1
250	260	34	31	27	23	20	17	14	10	8	5	2
260	270	36	32	29	25	22	18	15	12	9	6	3
270	280	38	34	30	27	23	20	17	13	10	7	5
280	290	40	36	32	28	25	21	18	15	12	9	6
290	300	43	38	34	30	27	23	20	16	13	10	7
300	310	45	40	36	32	28	25	21	18	15	12	9
310	320	47	42	38	34	30	26	23	20	16	13	10
320	330	49	45	40	36	32	28	24	21	18	15	12
330	340	52	47	42	38	34	30	26	23	19	16	13
340	350	54	49	45	40	36	32	28	24	21	18	15
350	360	56	52	47	42	38	34	30	26	23	19	16
360	370	59	54	49	44	40	36	32	28	24	21	18
370	380	62	56	51	47	42	38	34	30	26	23	19
380	390	64	59	54	49	44	40	36	31	28	24	21

Accounting for Current Liabilities and Payrolls

Other Types of Withholding

Depending on individual circumstances, employees may be subject to a variety of other withholdings, including forced contributions to retirement plans, pension plans, and union dues as well as voluntary withholdings. The payroll system must be designed to ensure that the proper amounts are withheld from each employee and that these amounts are forwarded to the proper organizations on a timely basis.

For purposes of our example we will assume that Duffy has the following amounts withheld from her paycheck:

Organization	Amount
Health insurance	$ 5.00
Union dues	10.00
Employer's pension fund	20.00
Community Chest charity	5.00

If we combine these data with the previous withholdings, Duffy's take-home pay is $231.56, calculated as follows:

Gross earnings		$372.00
Payroll withholdings		
FICA taxes	$26.04	
Federal income taxes payable	51.00	
State income taxes payable	7.50	
Health insurance payable	5.00	
Union dues payable	10.00	
Payable to pension fund	20.00	
Due to Community Chest	5.00	
Total withheld		124.54
Net take-home pay		$247.46

Recording the Payment of Wages

The previous example illustrated how to determine the gross and net pay of one individual employee. However, most payroll departments and systems must process anywhere from several dozen to several hundred thousand employees. This requires maintaining a variety of payroll records. The records that we describe relate to a manual system. However, all these records and documents can easily be computerized. Most large companies have computerized these systems, while smaller companies often take advantage of computer payroll services.

Compensation Record

A **compensation record** must be maintained for each employee. A sample of such a record is reproduced in Exhibit 10–4. Its purpose is to accumulate all the payroll data relating to an individual employee. For employees receiving a wage, the entries for the hours worked most likely come from time cards or other timekeeping documents. The entry for salaried employees will generally come from time reports indicating the time worked on various projects. At the end of the calendar year the data on the compensation records are used to prepare the W-2 statements. The W-2 statement indicates the total wages earned and taxes withheld, and is sent to the employees so that they can prepare their individual income tax returns. Other copies of the W-2 are sent to the Internal Revenue Service and to the state taxing authorities.

EXHIBIT 10-4

Compensation Record

NAME _____ Michele Duffy _____

ADDRESS _____ 85 So. Leo Way _____

_____ Oakland, CA 94617 _____

Male _____
Female __F__ U.S. Citizen? __Y__ Date of Birth __11/19/48__

Date Employed: __9/81__ Date Terminated _____ Reason _____

S.S. ACCT. NO. _____ 557-56-9832 _____

1st Quarter	DATE		EARNINGS			DEDUCTIONS						PAID	
Period Ends 1987	Paid 1987	Regular	Overtime	Total	FICA @ 7%	Federal Income Tax	State Income Tax	Health Insurance	Union Dues	Pension	Charities	Net Amount	Check No.
Jan	Jan												
3	6	185.00	125.00	310.00	21.70	49.40	6.80	5.00	10.00	20.00	5.00	192.10	182
10	13	196.00	140.00	336.00	23.52	55.20	7.00	5.00	10.00	20.00	5.00	210.28	207
17	20	180.00	176.00	356.00	24.92	61.00	7.40	5.00	10.00	20.00	5.00	222.68	219
25	27	192.00	180.00	372.00	26.04	51.00	7.50	5.00	10.00	20.00	5.00	247.46	228

The Payroll Register

A **payroll register** is a list of the firm's payroll and is prepared each payday. An example of a payroll register is found in Exhibit 10–5 on page 403. It has major headings for earnings, deductions, the net amount paid, and distribution of the payroll. The distribution columns grocery, meat, and produce are necessary so that the market can keep track of employee wages in various departments. In order to fully understand the relationship between a compensation record and the payroll register, compare the January 25 entry for Michele Duffy in the compensation record with the entry for her in the payroll register.

Recording the Payroll

The data in the payroll register are used to make the journal entry to record the periodic payroll. Based on the payroll register in Exhibit 10–5, the entry to record the payroll for the week ended January 25 is:

Wages Expense, Grocery	1,037.00	
Wages Expense, Meat	345.00	
Wages Expense, Produce	180.00	
FICA Taxes Payable		109.34
Federal Income Taxes Payable		282.15
State Income Taxes Payable		31.40
Health Insurance Payable		35.00
Union Dues Payable		50.00
Payable to Pension Fund		106.00
Due to Community Chest		20.00
Wages Payable		928.11

To record wages expense for the week ended January 24, 1987.

Wages Payable rather than Cash is credited in this entry. This is due to the fact that the Brer Rabbit Grocery Store, as do most companies, pays its payroll sometime after the pay period ends. This delay is necessary in order to allow the company to accumulate the payroll information and prepare the checks. In our example, the market's pay period ends every Sunday; however, the checks are not distributed until the following Wednesday.

Determining the Employer's Payroll Tax Expense

In addition to the payroll taxes levied against the employee, certain payroll taxes are levied directly against the employer. These include the employer's share of FICA taxes and federal and state unemployment taxes.

FICA Taxes

As already noted, FICA taxes are levied equally on the employee and the employer. In our example, Brer Rabbit incurred FICA taxes of $109.34 for the week ended January 25, 1987.

Federal and State Unemployment Taxes

In addition to their share of social security taxes, employers must also pay federal unemployment taxes. These taxes are the result of the **Federal Unemployment Tax Act (FUTA)** and at the time of this writing are 6.2% of the employees' first $7,000 of wages. However, the employer receives a maximum

EXHIBIT 10-5
Payroll Register

PAYROLL PERIOD FROM January 19, 1987 to January 25, 1987

Employee	EARNINGS			DEDUCTIONS							PAID		DISTRIBUTIONS		
	Regular	Over-time	Total	FICA @7%	Federal Income Tax	State Income Tax	Health Insurance	Union Dues	Pension	Charities	Net Amount	Check No.	Grocery	Meat	Produce
Scully	260.00	140.00	400.00	28.00	72.45	9.20	12.00	10.00	22.00	10.00	236.35	225	220.00		180.00
Weiss	145.00	35.00	180.00	12.60	42.40	2.50	—	10.00	18.00	—	94.50	226	180.00		
Porter	185.00	160.00	345.00	24.15	74.00	8.20	10.00	10.00	26.00	—	192.65	227		345.00	
Duffy	192.00	180.00	372.00	26.04	51.00	7.50	5.00	10.00	20.00	5.00	247.46	228	372.00		
Lefkowitz	190.00	75.00	265.00	18.55	42.30	4.00	8.00	10.00	20.00	5.00	157.15	229	265.00		
Totals	972.00	590.00	1,562.00	109.34	282.15	31.40	35.00	50.00	106.00	20.00	928.11		1,037.00	345.00	180.00

credit of 5.4% against these federal unemployment taxes for state unemployment taxes incurred. As a result, if the maximum credit is received, federal unemployment taxes can be reduced to 0.8%. In most states the tax rate varies from firm to firm depending on the unemployment claims made by the specific firm's ex-employees. In the following example, we will assume that state unemployment taxes are 2.7%.

Recording the Employer's Portion of Payroll Taxes

At the same time that the liability for employees' wages and taxes withheld are recorded, an entry is made to record the employer's portion of the payroll taxes. Again, the payroll register is the source of this entry. Referring to the data in Exhibit 10–5, Brer Rabbit makes the following entry to record its share of the payroll taxes:

Payroll Tax Expense	164.01	
FICA Taxes Payable		109.34
State Unemployment Taxes Payable		42.17[a]
Federal Unemployment Taxes Payable		12.50[b]
To record employer's portion of payroll taxes.		

[a]$42.17 = \$1,562 \times .027$.

[b]$12.50 = \$1,562 \times .008$.

This entry assumes that all employees are still under the payroll tax limits, and as such all wages are subject to the full amount of taxes.

The Payment of Payroll and Payroll Taxes

As we noted, there is generally a delay between the end of the payroll period and the actual distribution of the payroll checks. This delay is necessary to accumulate the data necessary to prepare the payroll. In our example, payday is each Wednesday, following a pay period that ends on Sunday. At that time Wages Payable is debited and Cash is credited. The entry to record the payment of the payroll is:

Wages Payable	928.11	
Cash		928.11
To record payment of previous week's wages.		

In order to improve internal control, some firms maintain a separate payroll bank account. A check equal to the amount of employees' total take-home pay is drawn against the firm's regular account and deposited in a special payroll account. The employees' checks are then issued against this special account.

The employer must remit both shares of the FICA taxes and the federal income tax withheld to the IRS on a timely basis. Depending on the size of the payroll, these payments must be made either weekly, monthly, or quarterly. At the end of each quarter the employer must file a Form 941, Employer's Quarterly Federal Tax Return. This form summarizes all the firm's wage and tax data for a particular quarter. Similar reporting requirements are made by state taxing authorities.

The timing of federal unemployment taxes depends on their amount. Generally, these taxes are due quarterly. State unemployment taxes are paid at least quarterly, but payment dates vary among individual states. The entry to record the payables recorded above is:

FICA Taxes Payable	218.68	
Federal Income Taxes Payable	282.15	
State Income Taxes Payable	31.40	
Health Insurance Payable	35.00	
Union Dues Payable	50.00	
Payable to Pension Fund	106.00	
Due to Community Chest	20.00	
State Unemployment Taxes Payable	42.17	
Federal Unemployment Taxes Payable	12.50	
Cash		797.90

To record payment of various payroll taxes payable and other withholdings.

Internal Control for Payrolls

Proper internal controls are essential for the efficient functioning of a payroll system. Because a great deal of money is usually involved with payrolls, the temptation for fraud is increased. Fraud occurs if individuals not employed by the company receive paychecks, excess overtime not worked is paid, or excess vacation pay or bonuses are paid. Furthermore, failure to comply with government regulations related to payroll can result in large penalties and fines imposed on the employer.

As with other systems, one of the best ways to increase internal control over the payroll system is to build the system around a separation of duties. Thus, if possible, the following functions should be separated: the personnel department, timekeeping, the accounting or payroll department, and the distribution of paychecks. In smaller firms all these functions may not be clearly differentiated. In that event, more responsibility falls on the owner-manager to oversee the payroll functions.

The Personnel Department

The personnel department is charged with hiring and terminating all employees. This department should ensure that proper records are maintained for all employees; all employees are evaluated on a timely basis; government hiring practices and regulations, if required, are followed; and all terminated employees are promptly removed from the payroll. This last point ensures that terminated employees do not continue to receive paychecks.

Timekeeping

Accurate timekeeping ensures that employees receive the correct amount of pay for the time worked. For hourly employees this is essential. All salaried employees should prepare weekly or monthly time sheets approved by the appropriate supervisor. Besides ensuring that individuals receive pay only for time worked, control over timekeeping helps management allocate employee costs to the appropriate jobs or departments.

The Accounting or Payroll Department

The main function of the payroll department is to maintain employee compensation records and payroll registers, issue paychecks, and file appropriate tax returns. Failure to accurately perform any of these functions can lead to fraud or fines and penalties. If at all possible, the payroll department should be separated from those approving the records.

The Distribution of Paychecks

The accounting or payroll department should not distribute the paychecks. If possible, the paychecks should be distributed in person to employees. In the event, occasional spot checks should be made and all employees should be required to provide identification and sign a receipt prior to receiving their paycheck.

Summary of Learning Objectives

1. *Definition and recognition of liabilities.* Liabilities are probable future sacrifices of economic benefits arising from present obligations to transfer assets or provide services. Liabilities, as are assets, are classified as either current or noncurrent. Current liabilities are shown on the balance sheet at their face value.

2. *Types of current liabilities.* Current liabilities can be classified into three major categories. They are summarized as follows:

Category	Example
Definitely determinable	Accounts and notes payable and accrued liabilities
Collection for third parties and liabilities conditioned on operations	Sales taxes payable, payroll taxes, and corporate income taxes
Contingent liabilities	Warranties, guarantees, and litigations

3. *Payroll accounting.* Payroll costs are a major expense to most firms. In many cases taxes and other fringe benefits amount to 30 to 40% of the base salary. A firm's employees are subject to various payroll taxes including FICA taxes, federal income taxes, and in many cases state and local income taxes. In addition, the firm is also subject to FICA taxes and federal and state unemployment taxes.

4. *Internal control for payroll systems.* Proper internal control is essential for the efficient functioning of a payroll system. The best way to increase internal control is to build the system around separation of duties. Thus, if possible, the following functions should be separated: the personnel department, timekeeping, the accounting or payroll department, and the distribution of paychecks.

Key Terms

Accounts Payable
Compensated Absences
Compensation Record
Contingent Liabilities
Current Liabilities
Current Maturities of Long-term Debt
Dividends
Federal Unemployment Tax Act (FUTA)

FICA (Federal Insurance Contributions Act) Taxes
Long-term Liabilities
Notes Payable
Payroll Register
Present Value
Trade Accounts Payable

Problems for Your Review

A. Notes Payable. On November 1, 1986 the British Company signed a $10,000 note to the French Co. The note has an interest rate of 12% and is due in six months, on April 30, 1987. The British Company has a December 31 year-end. Make the appropriate journal entries on the books of the British Company (the borrower) on November 1, 1986, on December 31, 1986, and on April 30, 1987, assuming that:

1. The note contains a separate interest element so that British receives proceeds of $10,000.
2. The note is discounted so that it is written for $10,600, but the British Corporation receives only an amount less the discount.

Solution

CASE 1: **SEPARATE INTEREST ELEMENT**			**CASE 2:** **NO SEPARATE INTEREST ELEMENT**	

November 1, 1986

Cash	10,000		Cash	10,000	
Notes Payable		10,000	Discount on Notes Payable	600	
			Notes Payable		10,600
To record issuance of			To record issuance of $10,600,		
$10,000, 12%, 6-month note.			12%, 6-month discounted note		
			payable. Discount of		
			$600 = $10,000 \times .12 \times 6/12		

December 31, 1986

Interest Expense	200		Interest Expense	200	
Interest Payable		200	Discount on Notes Payable		200
To record accrued interest			To amortize discount on notes		
from 11/1 to 12/31.			payable for 2 months on		
$200 = $10,000 \times .12 \times 2/12			a straight-line basis.		
			$200 = ($600 \div 6 \text{ months}) \times 2		

April 30, 1987

Notes Payable	10,000		Notes Payable	10,600	
Interest Payable	200		Interest Expense	400	
Interest Expense	400		Discount on Notes Payable		400
Cash		10,600	Cash		10,600
To record payment of			To record payment of loan and		
loan and interest			discount amortization for		
expense for 4 months.			4 months.		

B. Payroll. The Sparkey Corporation has four hourly employees and one salaried manager:

Names	Cumulative Wages to December	Wages for December	Federal and State Taxes Withheld
B. Furillo	$10,500	$1,500	$300
T. Hawkins	33,000	3,000	650
L. Bowman	10,500	800	200
R. Steamer	40,000	4,000	800

The current payroll taxes are as follows:

Employee and employer's FICA = 7.0% on first $35,000 of wages
Unemployment taxes = 3.4% of first $12,000 of wages

Required:

1. Make the entry to record the firm's wages for the month of December. Assume that all wages are paid in cash.
2. Make the entry to record the company's payroll tax expense assuming the taxes will be paid at a later date.
3. Make the entry to record the payment of December's payroll taxes and withholdings.

Accounting for Current Liabilities and Payrolls   407

Solution

Name	Wages	FICA Wages	Unemployment Tax Wages
Furillo	$1,500	$1,500	$1,500
Hawkins	3,000	2,000[a]	0
Bowman	800	800	800
Steamer	4,000	0[b]	0
Total	$9,300	$4,300	$2,300
Tax rate		× .07	× .034
Taxes		$ 301	$78.20

[a]Only $2,000 taxable before $35,000 limit reached.
[b]Already over limit.

Journal Entries:

```
1. Wages Expense                              9,300
       FICA Taxes Payable                                301
       Federal and State Withholding
         Taxes Payable                                 1,950
       Cash                                            7,049
   To record payment of monthly wages.

2. Payroll Tax Expense                         379.20
       FICA Taxes Payable                              301.00
       Unemployment Taxes Payable                       78.20
   To record accrual of payroll tax
   expense of FICA of $301 and
   unemployment taxes of $78.20.

3. FICA Taxes Payable                          602.00
   Unemployment Taxes Payable                   78.20
   Federal and State Withholding
     Taxes Payable                            1,950.00
       Cash                                          2,630.20
   To record payment of tax liability.
```

Questions

1. In your own words, define *liabilities*.

2. Distinguish current liabilities from noncurrent liabilities. Why is the classification of liabilities important to an enterprise?

3. What is meant by *present value*? Discuss the application of present value concepts to the valuation of current liabilities.

4. The Santa Cruz Co. entered into an agreement with the Los Padres Co. to purchase 100,000 tons of iron ore. The first delivery is to be made in one month. No cash or other consideration has changed hands. Should Santa Cruz recognize a liability? Why or why not?

5. What are the characteristics of liabilities that are classified as definitely determinable in nature? Give three examples of liabilities in this category. What are the important accounting problems related to this liability?

6. Define the following terms relating to notes payable:
   a. Payee.
   b. Maker.
   c. Face value.
   d. Maturity date.
   e. Duration of note.
   f. Interest rate.

7. What is a discount on notes payable and how does it arise?

8. What are contingent liabilities and how do they differ, if at all, from other types of liabilities?

9. Give an example of a contingent liability that is accrued and one that is just disclosed in the financial statements. Explain what criteria are used in deciding whether to accrue a liability.

10. In December 1986, an accident occurred at the No Nuke Nuclear Power Plant. As a result, personal

injury suits totaling $10 million have been filed against the company owning the plant. Although it appears that the company will lose several of the lawsuits, there is no way to reasonably determine the amount of the ultimate loss. In preparing its December 31, 1986 financial statements, how do you think these facts should be accounted for? Would your answer be different if the accident took place in early January 1987 but before the firm's December 31, 1986 financial statements were prepared?

11. How does an independent contractor differ from an employee?

12. How is the amount of income taxes withheld from an employee's paycheck determined?

13. What is the purpose of a compensation record and a payroll register?

14. Define and explain the following terms:
   a. FICA taxes.
   b. Federal and state withholding taxes.
   c. Federal and state unemployment taxes.

15. State the internal control principles related to payrolls.

Exercises

1. Recording Notes Payable. On January 31, 1987 the Lynch Co. purchased equipment from the Andersen Company for $375,000. A one-year, 12% note was signed. Assuming Lynch has a December 31 year-end, make all the appropriate entries related to this note.

2. Notes Payable. The Maxwell Company signed on March 1, 1987 a $232,000, one-year, 16% discounted note payable to the Olympic National Bank. What cash proceeds did the Maxwell Company receive? Make the necessary journal entries related to this note assuming that the firm has a December 31 year-end. In addition, show how the note payable would be disclosed on a December 31, 1987 balance sheet.

3. Notes Payable. The Reds Company borrowed $10,000 at 12% from Wilshire West National Bank. The loan was made on September 1 and is due in one year. Assume that the firm closes its books once a year on December 31. Make the entries to record (1) the note, (2) the adjustment at year-end, and (3) the payment of the note, assuming the note:
   a. Is drawn in the principal amount of $10,000 and interest is stated separately.
   b. Is drawn in the face amount of $11,200, is discounted, and does not contain a separate interest element.

4. Sales Taxes. M & T Shoes had $21,000 of sales during the first quarter of 1987. The sales tax for the state in which the store operates is 6%. All sales are on account. Prepare the necessary entries to record the sales and subsequent payment of the sales taxes on May 1, 1987.

5. Compensated Absences. The Holmes Company's policy regarding paid vacations is as follows: Each employee is allowed 15 days paid vacation after working for the company one full year. After reviewing payroll records, the controller estimates that 60% of the individuals employed during November will qualify for vacation pay. Total payroll for November is $100,000 and vacation pay is accrued monthly.

Compute the amount of estimated vacation pay liability for November and make the entry to record the liability.

6. Accounting for Warranties. The Ring Company manufactures and sells executive telephones. The telephones sell for $100 and are warranted for two years. Any defects during this period will be fixed by the company without charge. During the year the firm sold 50,000 telephones. Past experience indicates that 10% of the telephones will need some type of repair during the warranty periods. In the past the firm has incurred expenditures of $7 on each telephone in need of repair. At the beginning of the year, the Estimated Liability for Warranties account had a credit balance of $4,000. Actual expenditures for warranties amounted to $36,000 during the year, including $4,000 for items sold in previous years.

Prepare the journal entries to record the transactions regarding the warranties. What is the balance in the Estimated Liability for Warranties account at the end of the year, and where should it be disclosed on the balance sheet?

7. Payroll and Payroll Taxes. The payroll expense for the Ziggy Corporation for the week ending August 15, 1986 is $7,500. The entire payroll is subject to FICA taxes of 7%, but only 75% is subject to state unemployment taxes of 2.7% and federal unemployment taxes of 0.8%. Federal income taxes of $1,300, state income taxes of $600, and $250 payable to the pension fund were withheld.

Prepare the necessary journal entries to record the payroll and the payroll taxes.

8. Payroll Entries and Calculation of Net Pay. Jean Yu is an attorney with a large firm. She receives a wage of $25 per hour plus time and one-half for overtime. For the week ended June 15, 1987, Jean worked 40 regular hours and 10 overtime hours. Jean is single and claims a total of three dependents on her W-4 form. In addition to her payroll taxes, Jean has $10 per pay period withheld for parking and $5 per period withheld for health insurance. Before this pay period, Jean's total wages for 1987 were $41,700. Her federal and state income tax withheld was $108.

Required:

    a. Determine the following items relative to Jean's pay:

        1. Gross pay.

        2. FICA taxes (7% of the first $42,600 of wages).

        3. Net pay.

    b. Prepare the journal entry to record the payment of Jean's wages including all related employer liabilities.

Problem Set A

10A-1. Accounting for Notes Payable. The Deferral Company's fiscal year ends on June 30. During the year ended June 30, 1987 and the next two months of the next fiscal year, the firm entered into the following transactions regarding various notes payable. All adjusting entries are made once a year on June 30.

- December 31, 1986: Signed an agreement with Filmore National Bank establishing a $500,000 line of credit at 12% interest. Immediately borrowed $200,000.

- March 1, 1987: Signed a six-month, 15% term loan. The face value of the note was $107,500, but the firm received net proceeds of only $100,000 because the note was discounted.

- April 1, 1987: Repaid $100,000 of the line of credit, including all accrued interest to date.

- April 30, 1987: The firm was granted a 90-day extension on an open trade account payable in exchange for signing an $8,000 note at 10%. The interest element was stated separately.

- May 15, 1987: The Deferral Company was notified by the bank that its $20,000, 10% one-year loan was discounted by the payee. The note that is due on June 30, 1987 should now be paid to Adams-Madison National Bank.

- June 1, 1987: Borrowed an additional $300,000 under the terms of the revolving line of credit.

- June 30, 1987: Made the required payment to the Adams-Madison National Bank. No interest has been accrued on the note.

- June 30, 1987: Made all adjusting entries.

- July 31, 1987: Repaid the April 30 loan.

- August 31, 1987: Repaid the March 1 loan.

Required:

Make all the journal entries to reflect the above transactions. Assume that the firm does not make reversing entries.

10A-2. Analysis of Notes Payable and Receivable. The accountant for the Chambliss Company prepared the partial balance sheet at September 30, 1987 (shown at the top of page 411). However, the accountant failed to make the required *quarterly* adjusting entries for the last quarter. Company policy requires that adjusting entries be made quarterly.

    During your analysis you obtained the following additional data:

    a. The $150,000 accounts receivable general ledger balance includes an account with a credit balance of $2,500 which resulted from an overpayment by an occasional customer.

    b. The interest payable pertains to the $14,000 note that was signed nine months ago. Interest is due annually.

    c. The balance in the Mortgage Payable account represents the total outstanding balance in that account. The principal payments for the next 12 months amount to $2,400.

Chambliss Company
Partial Balance Sheet
September 30, 1987

Current assets		
Accounts receivable	$150,000	
Allowance for uncollectible accounts	(800)	
		$149,200
Note receivable		20,600
Current liabilities		
Accounts payable		$ 60,000
Interest payable		630
Notes payable		14,000
Mortgage payable		125,000

Required:
  a. Make the necessary adjusting entries at September 30, 1987.
  b. Prepare a revised partial balance sheet at September 30, 1987.

10A–3. Accounting for Current Liabilities. Super O Discount Stores entered into the following transactions during the current fiscal year:
  a. On March 1 the store purchased a delivery truck for $20,000 at the beginning of the fiscal year. A 20% down payment was made, and the firm signed a 12% one-year note for the balance. Both principal and interest are due at the maturity date.
  b. The firm purchased inventory for $60,000 on account. (Use the periodic system.)
  c. The store purchased some additional office equipment for $10,000 subject to credit terms of 2/10, n/30.
  d. One thousand dollars of the inventory purchased in (b) above arrived damaged and was returned to the manufacturer. Super O's account was credited.
  e. The office equipment purchased in (c) above was paid for within the discount period.
  f. Sales for the year amounted to $130,000, of which 40% was on account and the remainder was for cash. State and local sales taxes amounted to 5%.
  g. The department store rents part of its space to Tasty Croissants. The agreement calls for Tasty to pay a year's rent in advance. Tasty began business on October 1 and made the $4,800 required payment to Super O on that date.
  h. Super O's payroll for the year amounted to $30,000, all of which was paid in cash. Applicable payroll taxes and related items were as follows: federal and state income taxes withheld, $2,400 and $800, respectively; FICA taxes, 7% for both employee and employer on entire payroll; state unemployment taxes of 2.7% on $20,000 of the payroll; and federal unemployment taxes of 0.8% on $20,000 of the payroll.
  i. Sales and payroll taxes were fully paid before year-end.

Required:
  a. Make the necessary journal entries to record the above transactions.
  b. Make any necessary adjusting entries at February 28 other than depreciation.

10A–4. Product Warranty. The Micro Jet Stove Company manufactures and sells combination microwave and convection stoves. The retail price is $1,500 per stove. Parts on the stove are warrantied for three years, but labor is warrantied for only one year. During 1987 the firm sold 6,000 stoves. Past experience indicates that 15% of the stoves will require warranty work and that average replacements will cost Micro $50 per unit and labor costs will be $70 per unit. During the year the firm incurred $50,000 for replacement parts and $30,000 for labor while performing warranty work. Also during the year it collected $25,000 in labor service revenue while performing warranty work on stoves for which the labor warranty had expired. At the end of 1987, before any adjusting entries, the balance in the Estimated Liability for Warranties account was a debit of $4,000.

Accounting for Current Liabilities and Payrolls

Required:

a. How can there be a debit balance in the estimated liability account at the end of 1987 prior to any adjusting entries? What was the balance in that account at the beginning of 1987?

b. Prepare the summary journal entries to record the above events related to warranties and the required adjusting entry. Assume that all sales were made on account.

c. Determine the balance in the estimated liability for warranties at the end of 1987, after all adjusting entries have been made.

10A-5. Payroll Taxes and Compensated Absences. The Meaty Meat Company had five employees on its payroll for the fourth quarter of 1987. Because of a favorable rate, the company is allowed a 1% unemployment rate by the state; the federal unemployment rate is 0.8%. The maximum unemployment wage for each employee is $7,000 for both federal and state purposes. Meaty has determined the federal and state income tax rate for each employee to be 10% and 5%, respectively. Current FICA taxes are 7% of the first $42,600 of the current year's salary. Each employee is entitled to two weeks' compensated vacation pay yearly. This pay is based on the average salary for the year, assuming a 50-week year. Each quarter the firm accrues 25% of that amount as an estimated liability.

During your review of Meaty Meat, you have obtained the following information:

Name	Earnings to 9/30/87	Earnings 4th Quarter 1987
H. Lover	$ 4,600	$ 2,400
I. Hyper	38,800	7,000
Y. Good	16,000	5,100
D. Left*	3,400	800
B. Hote	33,100	9,700
Totals	$95,900	$25,000

*Terminated on 11/7/87, so not entitled to vacation pay.

Required:

a. For each employee, determine the correct amount of payroll taxes for the fourth quarter.

b. As stated before, the federal income tax withheld and the state income tax withheld equaled $2,500 and $1,250, respectively, for the quarter. Make the journal entries to record the payroll and related expenses for the fourth quarter.

c. Determine the amount of vacation pay that each employee is entitled to. Make the journal entry to record the estimated liability for the fourth quarter.

10A-6. Comprehensive Payroll. The CPA firm of Merva, Lee, and O'Rourke employs eight staff accountants. The employees are paid every other Friday. All accountants are paid an hourly wage and time and one-half for overtime. All employees and the firm are subject to FICA taxes of 7% of the first $42,600 of wages. Unemployment taxes are 2.7% at the state level and 0.8% at the federal level, and are levied on the employer based on the first $7,000 of each employee's wages. The firm withholds an additional 2% of each employee's wages for health, life, and disability insurances. This applies to the employee's total gross wages and is matched by the firm.

The data relating to the October 31, 1987 payroll (the last Friday in October) follow:

Employee	Hours Worked Regular	Hours Worked Overtime	Hourly Pay Rate	Gross Pay to Date Excluding Current Two-Week Period	Federal and State Income Tax Withheld
N. Becker	80	—	$ 7.00	$38,500	$115
M. Dauberman	80	10	7.50	40,000	130
L. Eaton	80	12	6.00	26,120	65
H. Vernon	80	—	12.00	42,500	145
J. Kiley	80	30	10.00	39,500	275
C. Lewis	80	20	12.00	40,560	230
L. Southern	70	—	6.00	26,260	55
M. Wilson	60	—	5.50	22,700	64

Required:

a. Prepare a payroll register similar to the one in Exhibit 10–5. Use the following columns:

Employee	Deductions
Earnings	FICA
Regular	Federal and State Income Tax Withheld
Overtime	Health Insurance
Total	Amount Paid

b. Prepare the general journal entry to record the payroll and payroll tax liabilities for the two weeks ended October 31, 1987.

c. Prepare the general journal entry to record the employer's payroll tax expense and share of health insurance.

Problem Set B

10B–1. Accounting for Notes Payable. The Smith Company's fiscal year ends on March 31. During the year ended March 31, 1988, the firm entered into the following transactions relating to notes payable. Adjusting entries are made once a year on March 31. Assume a 360-day year.

- April 15, 1987: Signed an agreement with Hollywood National Bank establishing a $100,000 line of credit at 10% interest. Immediately borrowed $10,000.
- May 10, 1987: Signed a nine-month, 12%, $109,000 term loan. The note was discounted and the firm received $100,000.
- June 15, 1987: Repaid $5,000 of the line of credit including all interest accrued to date.
- July 1, 1987: The firm was granted a one-year extension on an open trade account payable in exchange for signing a $60,000, one-year note at 12%.
- August 1, 1987: The firm was notified by Santa Ana National Bank that its $50,000, 12%, one-year-term loan payable was discounted by Grannett Company, the payee. The note (which is due on November 1, 1987) should now be paid to Santa Ana.
- September 15, 1987: Borrowed an additional $50,000 under the terms of its revolving line of credit.
- November 1, 1987: Made the required payment on the note now owed to Santa Ana National Bank. Interest has been accrued to March 31, 1987.
- February 10, 1988: Paid the May 10, 1987 loan.
- March 1, 1988: Borrowed $100,000 on a 10% loan from First Savings and Loan. The note is due and payable on September 1, 1988.
- March 31, 1988: Made all adjusting entries.

Required:

Make all the journal entries to reflect the above transactions. Assume that the firm does not make reversing entries.

10B–2. Analysis of Notes Payable and Receivables. The accountant for the Papaya Company prepared the partial balance sheet at October 31, 1987 (shown at the top of page 414). However, the accountant failed to make the required monthly adjusting entries. Company policies require that these entries be made monthly.

During your analysis, you have obtained the following additional information:

1. The $200,000 accounts payable general ledger balance includes an account with a debit balance of $3,975, which resulted when the Papaya Company returned some defective goods. Papaya has asked the vendor to refund its money.
2. The interest payable relates to a $60,000 note that was signed six months ago.
3. When the firm records its sales, applicable sales taxes are included in the sales account. At the end of each month an adjusting entry is made to reverse out the amount of the sales taxes and to set up a payable account. During October Sales were $212,000 including sales taxes of 6%.

Required:

a. Make the necessary adjusting entries at October 31, 1987.

b. Prepare a revised partial balance sheet as of October 31, 1987.

Accounting for Current Liabilities and Payrolls   413

Papaya Company
Partial Balance Sheet
October 31, 1987

Current assets		
Accounts receivable	$243,875	
Less allowance for uncollectible accounts	1,250	
		$242,625
Note receivable		32,700
Current liabilities		
Accounts payable		$200,000
Interest payable		2,500
Notes payable		60,000

10B–3. Accounting for Current Liabilities. Tracy's Tennis Stores entered into the following transactions during the current calendar year:

1. Inventory purchases of $50,000 were made on account. (Assume periodic system.)
2. On April 1 a light truck was purchased for $10,000 at the beginning of the year. A 25% down payment was made and a 10% note was signed for the balance. Principal and interest are due in one year.
3. The inventory purchased in Item 1 was paid in full.
4. On July 31 the firm signed a $78,400 note at a local bank. It received proceeds of $70,000 at that time. The note is due in one year.
5. Sales for the year amounted to $180,000. All sales are for cash. State sales taxes are 6%.
6. During the holiday season the firm issues gift certificates. Gift certificates totaling $5,000 were sold for cash. By the end of the calendar year, only 30% of the certificates had been redeemed. Sales of certificates are credited to the Sales Revenue account.
7. Wages of $30,000 were paid during the year. Federal and state income taxes withheld amounted to $4,400 and union dues of $200 were also withheld. The FICA rate is 7% for both the employee and employer, and all wages but $5,000 are subject to these taxes. State unemployment taxes of 2.7% are levied on $10,000 of wages.
8. Sales, union dues, and payroll taxes were paid in full prior to year-end.

Required:

a. Make the necessary journal entries to record these events.
b. Make the necessary adjusting entries, other than depreciation.

10B–4. Product Warranty. The Wolfer Company manufactures and sells high-quality stereo equipment. It has a special line of speakers which it sells at $1,000 a piece. The parts on the speaker are guaranteed for three years. During the first year all labor for repairs is performed free of charge. During the next two years of the guarantee, there is a set labor charge of $40 per repair. During 1988 the firm sold 500 of these speakers. Past experience indicates that 20% of these units will need repair within the guarantee period and that average replacement parts will cost $80 and labor costs will be $50. During the year the firm incurred $5,000 in labor costs and $6,000 in replacement costs. Also during the year the firm collected $2,800 in revenue from labor performed on guarantee work. At the end of 1988, before any adjustments were made, the account Estimated Liability for Guarantee Work had a credit balance of $500.

Required:

a. Would it be possible for the account Estimated Liability for Guarantee Work to have a debit balance prior to the adjusting entry at the end of the year? If so, how would this occur? What was the actual balance in this account at the beginning of 1988?
b. Prepare the summary journal entries to record the above events related to guarantees. Assume that all sales are made on credit.
c. Determine the balance in the estimated liability for guarantee work at the end of 1988 after all adjusting entries have been made.

10B–5. Payroll Taxes and Compensated Absences. The Bubble Laundry Company had four employees on its payroll for the fourth quarter of 1987. The unemployment compensation at the state level is 2.7%; the federal unemployment rate is 0.8%. The maximum unemployment wage is $7,000 for both federal and state unemployment taxes. Current FICA taxes are 7% of the first $42,600 of the current year's wages. Each employee is entitled to two weeks' compensated vacation pay yearly. The pay is based on the average salary for the year assuming a 50-week year. Each quarter the firm accrues 25% of that amount as an estimated liability.

During your review of Bubble Laundry's records, you have obtained the following information:

Name	Earnings to 9/30/87	Earnings 4th Quarter 1987
J. Korman	$ 35,920	$11,490
O. Jones	24,280	6,890
T. Glasson	16,230	2,780
R. Sato	40,500	15,000
Totals	$116,930	$36,160

Required:

a. For each employee determine the correct amount of payroll taxes for the fourth quarter.

b. Assume that the federal income tax withheld and state income tax withheld equaled $3,800 and $1,300, respectively, for the quarter. Make the journal entries to record the payroll and related expenses for the fourth quarter.

c. Determine the amount of vacation pay each employee is entitled to. Make the journal entry to record the estimated liability for the fourth quarter.

10B–6. Comprehensive Payroll. The law firm of Morfeld, Schnyder, Smith and Co. employ six people. The employees are paid every Friday. All are paid an hourly wage and time and one-half for overtime. All employees and the firm are subject to FICA taxes of 7% of the first $42,600 of wages. Unemployment taxes are 2.7% at the state level and 0.8% at the federal level, and are levied on the employer based on the first $7,000 of each employee's wage. The firm withholds an additional 4% of each employee's wages for health insurance and $5 for parking fees.

The data relating to the December 26, 1988 payroll follow:

Name	Hours Worked Regular	Overtime	Hourly Pay Rate	Earnings to Date Excluding Current Period	Federal and State Income Tax Withheld
T. Johnson	40	5	$ 8.50	$27,040	105
J. Collins	40	7	8.00	26,390	105
D. Lee	40	3	7.25	24,750	90
S. Warner	40	0	10.50	30,800	107
C. Conners	35	0	12.25	36,200	110
A. Williams	30	0	14.00	44,140	107

Required:

a. Prepare a payroll register similar to the one in Exhibit 10–5. Use the following columns:

Employee	Deductions
Earnings	FICA
Regular	Federal and State Income
Overtime	Tax Withheld
Total	Health Insurance
	Parking
	Amount Paid

b. Prepare the general journal entry to record the payroll and payroll tax deductions for the week ended December 26, 1988.

c. Prepare the general journal entry to record the employer's payroll tax expense.

Accounting for Current Liabilities and Payrolls **415**

Using the Computer

The law firm of Simmer, Smith, and Sental employs six administrative employees in addition to its professional staff. The administrative staff is paid on an hourly basis and receives time and one-half for overtime. Employees are paid every Friday for the week's work. All employees are subject to FICA wages of 7% of their first $38,100 of wages. The firm is subject to FICA taxes of 7% on the same basis. State unemployment taxes are 2.7% and federal unemployment taxes are 0.8% on the first $7,000 of each employee's wages. In addition, the firm withholds 5% of each employee's wages for health insurance and $5 for parking.

The data relating to the December 22, 1986, payroll are as follows:

Name	Hours Worked Regular	Hours Worked Overtime	Hourly Pay Rate	Earnings to Date prior to Current Period	Federal and State Income Tax Withheld
T. Johnson	40	5	$ 8.50	$17,000	$180
J. Collins	40	7	8.00	16,500	140
J. C. Ray	40	3	7.25	14,000	100
E. Weiss	40	0	20.00	39,000	278
M. Tofukagi	35	0	18.00	38,000	190
R. Williams	40	2	15.00	30,000	210

Required:
Using an electronic spreadsheet, prepare a payroll register similar to the one on page 403. Use the following format:

PAYROLL REGISTER

Payroll Period: December 22–29, 1986

Employee	Earnings Regular	Earnings Overtime	Earnings Total	Deductions FICA—7%	Deductions Withholdings	Deductions Total	Amount Paid

Understanding Financial Statements

The following note was taken from Safeway's 1985 financial statements:

> There are pending against the company, as of March 3, 1986, various claims and lawsuits arising in the normal course of the company's business, some of which seek damages in very large amounts, as well as other relief which, if granted, would require very large expenditures. Included are suits claiming violation of certain civil rights laws, some of which purport to be class actions.
>
> Although the amount of liability at year-end 1985 with respect to all of the above matters cannot be ascertained, management is of the opinion that any resulting liability will not materially affect the company's consolidated income or financial position.

Required:
a. What is meant by contingent liabilities, and what accounting problems are associated with them?
b. Safeway decided to disclose these contingent liabilities through a footnote rather than to actually record a liability on the balance sheet. Is this the correct accounting treatment? Why or why not?
c. Assume that one of the above-mentioned lawsuits was settled as of year-end 1985 and Safeway agreed to pay damages of $5 million early in June 1987. How should this event be recorded and/or disclosed?

Financial Decision Case

Big Eight Stores is a large sporting goods retailer. The firm's business is rather cyclical, with large increases in sales the last week of every month when the company runs special promotions. Currently, the firm employs 10 full-time salespersons. However, for month-end promotions, the firm hires five part-time salespeople for five 8-hour days each. Currently, each full-time employee earns an hourly rate of $10, while part-time employees earn $8 an hour. In addition, the firm pays FICA taxes of 7.15% on all employee wages, state and federal unemployment taxes of 6.2% on the first $7,000 of each employee's wages, and $40 a month per employee (full- or part-time) for health insurance.

The We-Help Temporary Personnel Service has contacted Big Eight and has suggested that Big Eight lay off its part-time staff. In their place We-Help will provide five temporary salespeople for five days each month. We-Help will charge Big Eight $9 per hour for each temporary employee.

The controller of Big Eight asks you to evaluate We-Help's proposal. He tells you that after a quick analysis it appears that the proposal would not save the firm any money, as the hourly rate We-Help would charge is greater than the $8 per hour Big Eight pays its part-time employees.

Required:
   a. From a cost standpoint, should Big Eight accept the proposal from We-Help?
   b. What other factors other than costs should Big Eight consider?

Accounting for Inventories

11

LEARNING OBJECTIVES

After reading this chapter you should be able to:

1. Explain the relationship between inventories and income determination.
2. Discuss inventory valuation principles.
3. Determine the cost of ending inventories.
4. Apply the four methods of assigning prices to the ending inventory.
5. Apply the lower-of-cost-or-market rule as it relates to inventories.
6. Use the gross margin and retail inventory methods to estimate ending inventories.
7. Use inventory data in decision making.
8. Use inventory costing methods with the perpetual inventory system (Appendix).

In this chapter we focus on how accountants determine both the cost of ending inventories and the cost of the goods sold during the period. The problems involved in this allocation are typical of those found with all nonmonetary assets. In addition, using inventories as an example, we examine how management chooses among alternative accounting methods. Finally, we look at other issues related to inventories, including the use of estimation procedures such as the gross margin and the retail methods to determine the cost of ending inventories.

Inventories and Income Determination

Inventories are nonmonetary assets. As noted in Chapter 4, one of the major accounting issues regarding nonmonetary assets is determining the cost of the current benefits that have been used or consumed (the expense of the period) and the cost of the future benefits that remain (the cost of the asset at the end of the period). This process helps ensure that the costs of these assets are matched against the revenues they produce. For inventories, this requires allocating the cost of all goods available for sale between the cost of the items sold and the cost of the items remaining in ending inventory. The AICPA stated:

> A major objective of accounting for inventories is the proper determination of income through the process of matching appropriate costs against revenues.[1]

The following diagram and formula illustrate this allocation process for inventories:

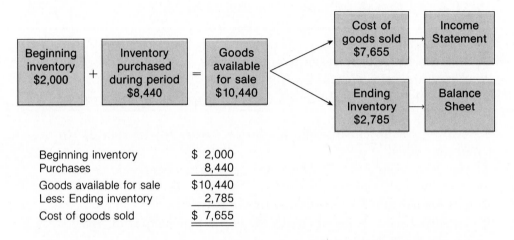

Beginning inventory	$ 2,000
Purchases	8,440
Goods available for sale	$10,440
Less: Ending inventory	2,785
Cost of goods sold	$ 7,655

As the formula indicates, the ending inventories on hand at the end of the period are determined first, and the cost of goods sold then is derived by subtracting the ending inventory from the goods available for sale. Although it is not as feasible to do so, cost of goods sold could be determined first, and then the ending inventory would become a derived figure. The accounting methods and procedures that accountants use to make this allocation are the main focus of this chapter.

Measuring Ending Inventories and Income

The allocation of the cost of the goods available for sale between the cost of the ending inventories and the cost of the goods sold affects both the balance sheet and the income statement. Ending inventories are usually the most material current asset, and an improper allocation of costs to the ending inventory can cause a serious error in the amount of current assets, total assets, working

---

[1]American Institute of Certified Public Accountants, Committee on Accounting Procedure, Accounting Research Bulletin No. 43, *Restatement and Revision of Accounting Research Bulletins* (New York: AICPA, 1961), Chap. 4, Statement 2.

capital, and the current ratio. The cost of goods sold is most likely the largest item on the income statement. For some firms this figure can reach 75 to 80% of total sales. A measurement error in cost of goods sold affects the gross margin figure, the gross margin percentage, and the net income. Furthermore, a measurement error in determining the amount of ending inventory has a two-period effect, because the ending inventory for one period becomes the beginning inventory for the next period.

The effects of inventory on the determination of income can be demonstrated by analyzing the effect of an inventory measurement error. The first column in the following table presents the data used to illustrate these effects. The data in Column 1 show the correct amount of ending inventory as well as all other items. As the statements show, the gross margins for years 1 and 2 are $25,000 and $20,000, respectively. The total gross margin for the two-year period is $45,000.

EFFECT OF INVENTORY ERRORS

Column 1			Column 2 (Case A)			Column 3 (Case B)		
Correct Ending Inventory in Year 1			Ending Inventory in Year 1 Overstated by $5,000			Ending Inventory in Year 1 Understated by $5,000		
Year 1			**Year 1**			**Year 1**		
Sales		$110,000	Sales		$110,000	Sales		$110,000
Cost of goods sold			Cost of goods sold			Cost of goods sold		
Beginning inventory	$ 10,000		Beginning inventory	$ 10,000		Beginning inventory	$ 10,000	
Purchases	90,000		Purchases	90,000		Purchases	90,000	
Goods available for sale	100,000		Goods available for sale	100,000		Goods available for sale	100,000	
Less:			Less:			Less:		
Ending inventory	15,000		Ending inventory	20,000		Ending inventory	10,000	
Cost of goods sold		85,000	Cost of goods sold		80,000	Cost of goods sold		90,000
Gross Margin		$ 25,000	Gross Margin		$ 30,000	Gross Margin		$ 20,000
Year 2			**Year 2**			**Year 2**		
Sales		$135,000	Sales		$135,000	Sales		$135,000
Cost of goods sold			Cost of goods sold			Cost of goods sold		
Beginning inventory	$ 15,000		Beginning inventory	$ 20,000		Beginning inventory	$ 10,000	
Purchases	120,000		Purchases	120,000		Purchases	120,000	
Goods available for sale	135,000		Goods available for sale	140,000		Goods available for sale	130,000	
Less:			Less:			Less:		
Ending inventory	20,000		Ending inventory	20,000		Ending inventory	20,000	
Cost of goods sold		115,000	Cost of goods sold		120,000	Cost of goods sold		110,000
Gross Margin		$ 20,000	Gross Margin		$ 15,000	Gross Margin		$ 25,000
Total for 2 Years		$ 45,000	Total for 2 Years		$ 45,000	Total for 2 Years		$ 45,000

Ending Inventory Overstated

Case A in Column 2 shows the effect of an overstatement by $5,000 of ending inventory in year 1. We will assume that this error is the result of miscounting the items in the ending inventory. You should keep in mind that this is the only error and that all other items remain the same. The effect of this error in year 1 is to decrease the cost of goods sold by $5,000, from $85,000 to $80,000. Thus there is a corresponding increase in the gross margin from $25,000 to $30,000. Generally, everything else being equal, the higher the ending inventory is, the higher the gross margin will be.

In year 2 the ending inventory from year 1 becomes the beginning inventory. As a result, the beginning inventory in year 2 is increased by $5,000, from $15,000 to $20,000. Therefore, goods available for sale and cost of goods sold are increased by $5,000, and gross margin is decreased by $5,000. Again, everything else being equal, the higher the beginning inventory is, the lower the gross margin will be.

Comparing Columns 1 and 2, we see that over a two-year period, the gross margin in both cases is $45,000. In effect, the error of $5,000 in the ending inventory of year 1 and the beginning inventory of year 2 cancel each other out, and so by the end of year 2 the ending inventory and the owner's equity are correctly stated. However, there are important differences within each period. In year 1, ending inventory and gross margin are overstated, and in year 2, beginning inventory is overstated and gross margin is understated. Thus, although inventory errors can be self-correcting, there are serious allocation errors between the accounting periods that affect gross margin and income trends.

Ending Inventory Understated

Case B in Column 3 illustrates the effect of an understatement by $5,000 of the ending inventory in year 1. Again, keep in mind that this is the only error and that all other items remain the same. The effect of this error in year 1 is to increase cost of goods sold by $5,000, from $85,000 to $90,000, and to decrease the gross margin by the same $5,000. Generally, all else being equal, the lower the ending inventory is, the lower the gross margin will be.

In year 2 the ending inventory from year 1 becomes the beginning inventory. As a result, the cost of goods sold decreases by $5,000, from $115,000 to $110,000, and there is a corresponding $5,000 increase in the gross margin, from $20,000 to $25,000. Again, everything else being equal, the lower the beginning inventory is, the higher the gross margin will be.

Comparing Columns 1, 2, and 3, you can see that over a two-year period, the total gross margin in all three cases is $45,000. This emphasizes that a single inventory error is self-canceling over a consecutive two-year period, but that serious allocation errors take place during each year. The data and the relationships in this illustration are summarized next.

| | EFFECT OF INVENTORY MEASUREMENT ERRORS | | | | | |
| | Cost of Goods Sold | | | Gross Margin | | |
Year 1 Ending Inventory	Year 1	Year 2	Total	Year 1	Year 2	Total
Correct	$85,000	$115,000	$200,000	$25,000	$20,000	$45,000
Overstated $5,000	80,000	120,000	200,000	30,000	15,000	45,000
Understated $5,000	90,000	110,000	200,000	20,000	25,000	45,000

1. The higher the ending inventory, the higher the gross margin.
2. The lower the ending inventory, the lower the gross margin.
3. The higher the beginning inventory, the lower the gross margin.
4. The lower the beginning inventory, the higher the gross margin.

Determining the Cost of Ending Inventories

In order for a firm to calculate the total cost of its ending inventories, it is necessary first to determine the actual quantity of items in the ending inventory and then to attach a price to these items. This is usually done by taking a physical inventory at least once a year, usually at year-end. A physical inventory is required, regardless of whether a firm uses the perpetual or the periodic inventory system. After the quantity of items is determined, a particular cost flow pattern is assumed and prices are assigned to each item in the inventory. The total of the prices times the quantity equals the cost of the ending inventory.

Ending Inventory Quantities

Determining the actual quantity of items in the ending inventory usually requires a physical count. This count can take more than a day and often requires the firm to cease operations. For example, imagine the effort in counting the ending inventory of a large department store. For these reasons some firms, especially those in the retail sales business, use estimation procedures, some of which are discussed later in this chapter.

When the ending inventory is counted, the firm must ensure that all the items to which it has legal title are part of the count, including goods stored in public warehouses and goods in transit. Goods in transit include both sales on an FOB destination basis and purchases on an FOB shipping basis. Goods sold but still on hand should not be included.

Costs Included in the Ending Inventory

Under generally accepted accounting principles, the presumption is that inventories should be recorded at cost. The AICPA defines cost as "the price paid or consideration given to acquire an asset. As applied to inventories, cost means in principle the sum of the applicable expenditures and charges directly or indirectly incurred in bringing an article to its existing condition and location."[2] For the retailer this means that acquisition costs include the purchase price less any sales discounts, plus other freight charges, insurance in transit, and sales taxes that are incurred to have the product ready for sale. However, costs such as freight charges and insurance are usually small, and the cost of trying to allocate them to individual items outweighs the benefit. Thus most firms will use just the invoice price when attaching a cost to an individual item in the ending inventory. These other costs then become part of cost of goods sold. Indirect costs such as selling and warehouse expenses are not included in the cost of inventory because of the difficulty in reasonably allocating them to particular items. They are therefore treated as period expenses and reduce the current period's income.

However, even after determining the quantity of the ending inventory

---

[2]Ibid., Statement 3.

and deciding what to include in the acquisition cost, a major accounting problem for inventories still has not been resolved. That is, the decision still must be made as to what price to attach to the particular items in the ending inventory. In other words, the problem is how the accountant determines the acquisition cost or price paid for each item in the ending inventory when the items have been purchased at different times for different prices.

Methods of Assigning Prices to the Ending Inventory

At first glance, it would seem easy to determine the acquisition cost of each item sold or the acquisition cost of the items in ending inventory. However, imagine a firm that sells identical products, such as molded plastic chairs, that have been purchased at different prices. Or imagine a large department store that sells a variety of products in different sizes and styles, again purchased at different prices. Even with a well-developed electronic record-keeping system, it is difficult, if not impossible, for these types of businesses to determine the acquisition price of each item remaining in the ending inventory.

If all items are purchased at the same price, there will be no problem in determining the cost of either the ending inventory or the items sold. However, prices do not remain stable, and so accountants have developed alternative methods to assign costs to inventory items. These methods use cost flow assumptions, in contrast with physical flow assumptions. That is, an assumption is made that costs flow in any one of four different patterns, regardless of how the goods physically move into and out of the firm. These cost flow assumptions are (1) first-in, first-out (FIFO), (2) last-in, first-out (LIFO), and (3) average cost. In some limited situations an actual flow approach, called specific identification, can be used.

First-in, first-out assumes that the costs assigned to the first goods purchased are the costs of the first goods sold. In effect, the items are assumed to be sold in the order that they were purchased, and thus the cost of the ending inventory is that of the most recent purchases. **Last-in, first-out** makes the opposite assumption about the flow of costs. Thus, the costs attached to the last purchases made are assumed to be the cost of the first items sold. In effect, items are assumed to be sold in the opposite order in which they were purchased, and thus the cost of the ending inventory is that of the earliest purchases made. **Average cost** attaches an average cost, determined by dividing the total cost of goods available for sale by the number of units available for sale, to both the cost of goods sold and the ending inventory. Finally, the **specific identification method** determines the actual acquisition cost of each item in the ending inventory. The firm's management is free to choose any one of these cost flow patterns, regardless of the physical flow of goods.

Applying Different Cost Flow Assumptions

The data for the Cerf Company shown on page 425 are used to demonstrate the computations required to apply the three cost flow assumptions and the specific identification method. Three points should be made about this example. First, it is simplistic in that only six purchases are made during the year. However, the procedures in this example hold for more complex, real purchasing patterns. Second, we are using a periodic inventory system, which for cost flow purposes does not require that we keep track of the particular dates on which actual sales are made. In a perpetual system (which is discussed in the appendix to this chapter), the dates of the particular sales and purchases are important. Third, each of these methods is an alternative under generally accepted accounting principles.

First-in, First-out (FIFO)

Under the FIFO method, the costs attached to the first goods purchased are assumed to be the costs of the first goods sold; the cost of the ending inventories consists of the costs of the latest goods purchased. FIFO refers to a means of determining the cost of goods sold during the period. We will see, however, that when applying the FIFO method, the cost of the ending inventory is determined first, after that the cost of the goods sold is easily derived.

Cerf Company
Data for Cost Flow Illustration
Year Ended December 31, 1987

	Unit	Acquisition Cost	Total Cost
Beginning inventory	500	$4.00	$ 2,000
Purchases during year			
January 24	200	4.10	820
March 18	400	4.20	1,680
May 5	300	4.50	1,350
July 31	350	4.50	1,575
September 27	400	4.60	1,840
November 29	250	4.70	1,175
Goods available for sale	2,400		$10,440
Less: Items in ending inventory	600		
Items sold	1,800		
Total dollar value of sales	$10,800		

Using the data just presented, the cost of the ending inventory under FIFO is $2,785, and the cost of goods sold is $7,655. These figures are determined as follows:

Cost of goods available for sale			$10,440

Cost of Ending Inventory—FIFO

Date Purchased	Units	Acquisition Cost	Total Cost	
November 29	250	$4.70	$1,175	
September 27	350	$4.60	1,610	
Total	600			2,785
Cost of goods sold				$7,655

As the preceding figures indicate, the 600 units in the ending inventory consist of (1) the 250 units purchased on November 29 and (2) 350 of the 400 units purchased on September 27. The 50 items remaining from the September 27 purchase, as well as the units from prior purchases and the beginning inventory, are assumed to have been sold. However, we could directly calculate the cost of goods sold as follows:

Date Purchased	Units	Acquisition Cost	Total Cost of Goods Sold
Beginning inventory	500	$4.00	$2,000
January 24	200	4.10	820
March 18	400	4.20	1,680
May 5	300	4.50	1,350
July 31	350	4.50	1,575
September 27	50	4.60	230
	1,800		$7,655

This approach is rarely used because firms sell many more goods than they have on hand at the end of the year, and so it is easier to cost the smaller number—what is left.

In 1988, the 1987 ending inventory of $2,785 becomes the beginning inventory. Although this inventory consists of 2 distinct layers of 250 and 350 units, respectively, each purchased at different prices, it is usually not necessary to maintain these layers. The inventory can be brought forward as 600 units at a cost of $2,785. The reason that we can merge these two layers is that under the FIFO method, these goods will be assumed to be the first ones sold in the next year. When they become part of the goods sold, the cost becomes part of a large pool in which the identity of the layers is not important.

Although a number of goods physically move on a FIFO basis, this is not a necessary criterion for its use. For example, think of a large barrel of nails in a hardware store. As additional nails are added to the barrel, they are placed on top of the older nails, and when the nails are sold, the top nails are sold first. In this situation, the nails move in a last-in, first-out pattern. Nonetheless, the management of the hardware store is free to choose the FIFO method of pricing its inventories.

Last-in, First-out (LIFO)

Under the LIFO method of pricing inventories, the cost attached to the last goods purchased is assumed to be the cost of the first goods sold. Therefore, the cost of the ending inventory consists of the cost of the items of the earliest purchases.

Using the previous data, the cost of the ending inventory under LIFO is $2,410, and the cost of goods sold is $8,030. These figures are determined as follows:

		Cost of goods available for sale		$10,440

Cost of Ending Inventory—LIFO

Date Purchased	Units	Acquisition Cost	Total Cost	
Beginning inventory	500	$4.00	$2,000	
January 24	100	4.10	410	
Total	600			2,410
Cost of goods sold				$8,030

As the preceding illustration indicates, the 600 units in the ending inventory are assumed to consist of (1) 500 units from the beginning inventory and (2) 100 units from the January 24 purchases. As we did in the previous example, we could directly calculate the cost of the goods sold as $8,030 instead of deriving it by subtracting the ending inventory of $2,410 from the goods available for sale of $10,440.

When the LIFO method is used, it is important to maintain separate layers of costs of ending inventory. Therefore, in our illustration, the beginning inventory for the following period is carried forward in two layers comprising 500 units at $4.00 and 100 units at $4.10. If next year's ending inventory falls below 600 units, the 100 units represented by the January 24 purchase would be included in cost of goods sold before the 500 units represented by the beginning inventory. That is, inventory is decreased in the order that it was originally added, and because the January 24 layer was added last, under the LIFO method it is considered to be sold first.

Average Cost

Under the average cost method, a weighted average cost per unit is calculated by dividing the total cost of the goods available for sale by the number of units available for sale. For the Cerf Company this calculation is:

$$\frac{\text{Cost of goods available for sale}}{\text{Units available for sale}} = \frac{\$10,440}{2,400} = \$4.35 \text{ per unit}$$

This $4.35 cost per unit is applied to both the ending inventory and the goods available for sale and is as follows:

$$
\begin{aligned}
\text{Ending inventory} &= 600 \text{ units} \times \$4.35 &&= \$\ 2,610 \\
\text{Cost of goods sold} &= 1,800 \text{ units} \times \$4.35 &&= \underline{\ \ 7,830} \\
& && \$10,440
\end{aligned}
$$

In 1988 the beginning inventory, consisting of 600 units at a total cost of $2,610, is included in the computation of the weighted average unit cost of goods available for sale.

Specific Identification

In some situations, it is practical to determine the specific acquisition cost of the items remaining in the ending inventory. For example, an automobile dealer has records of the exact cost of every car sold and every car remaining in inventory at the end of the year. Other examples of such firms are furniture companies, antique stores, and coin and stamp dealers. Depending on the costs and benefits, other firms might want to maintain such records.

To illustrate this method, assume that the Cerf Company is able to determine that the 600 items in the ending inventory are from the specific purchases listed below and thus computed the cost of the ending inventory to be $2,640 and the cost of goods sold to be $7,800.

Cost of goods available for sale			$10,440

Cost of Ending Inventory—Specific Identification

Date Purchased	Units	Acquisition Cost	Total Cost	
March 18	250	$4.20	$1,050	
July 31	200	4.50	900	
September 27	150	4.60	690	
Total	600			2,640
Cost of goods sold				$7,800

In addition to the practical problems of keeping track of the costs of the specific items in the inventory, there are theoretical problems with the specific identification method. For example, assume that a firm produces only one type of item, and that all items are identical (fungible). Wheat and other commodities are examples of fungible goods. Buyers of such products are indifferent as to which specific item or lot they buy, and so the firm's management is free to sell the specific lot(s) it desires. That is, the buyer of 10 ounces of gold does not care which lot the gold comes from, as long as all the gold is of the same quality. Thus the firm's management can sell the gold from any lot it chooses.

Management is able to manipulate income by selling lots with certain acquisition costs. To demonstrate this point, assume that the management of the Cerf Company wants to maximize its income for the current year. In this situation the firm sells those goods with the lowest acquisition costs (that is, the items purchased at $4.00 and $4.10). Next year, if management decides to minimize its income, it will sell those products with the highest acquisition prices. Each year management could make such decisions without having to maintain a consistent pattern from year to year. Therefore, it has some ability to manipulate the firm's income.

Comparing the Methods

Presented on page 429 is a comparison of the effect of the FIFO, average cost, and LIFO cost flow assumptions on ending inventory, cost of goods sold, and gross margin for the Cerf Company.[3] The highest gross margin and ending inventory and lowest cost of goods sold result when FIFO is used; the lowest gross margin and ending inventory and highest cost of goods sold result when LIFO is used. Average cost falls between these two extremes for all three accounts. This is because the acquisition price of the inventory consistently rises during the year, from $4.10 to $4.70. We deliberately constructed this example to reflect rising prices because in today's economy, rising prices are more common than are falling prices. However, in some sectors of the economy, such as electronics, prices have been falling. In this case, the income state-

---

[3]We have not included specific identification in this comparison because of its limited use.

ment and balance sheet effects of LIFO and FIFO would be the opposite of the rising-price situation. That is, LIFO would produce the highest gross margin and the highest ending inventory cost.

	FIFO	Average Cost	LIFO
CERF COMPANY			
Comparison of Three Cost Flow Assumptions			
Sales	$10,800	$10,800	$10,800
Cost of goods sold	7,655	7,830	8,030
Gross margin	$ 3,145	$ 2,970	$ 2,770
Ending inventory	$ 2,785	$ 2,610	$ 2,410

Rising Prices and FIFO

In a period of rising prices, FIFO produces the highest gross margin and the highest ending inventory. The high gross margin is produced because the earliest and thus the lowest costs are allocated to cost of goods sold. Thus, cost of goods sold is the lowest of the three inventory costing methods, and gross margin is correspondingly the highest of the three methods. Ending inventory reflects the highest cost under FIFO because the latest and highest costs are allocated to ending inventory. These results are logical, given the relationship between ending inventories and gross margin.

Many accountants approve of using FIFO because ending inventories are recorded at costs that approximate their current acquisition or replacement cost. Thus, inventories are realistically valued on the firm's balance sheet. On the other hand, accountants criticize FIFO because it matches the earliest cost against sales and results in the highest gross margin. Some accountants argue that these profits are overstated because, in order to stay in business, a going concern must replace its inventory at current acquisition prices or replacement costs. These overstated profits are often referred to as **inventory profits.**

To illustrate the concept of inventory profits, assume that a firm enters into the following transactions:

- January 2: Purchases one unit of inventory at $60.
- December 15: Purchases a second unit of inventory at $85.
- December 31: Sells one unit at $100. Current replacement cost of inventory, $85.

On a FIFO basis, the firm reports a gross margin of $40 ($100 − $60). However, if it is to stay in business, the firm will not have $40 available to cover operating expenses. This is because it must replace the inventory at a cost of at least $85. Thus, in reality the firm has only $15 ($100 − $85) available to cover its operating expenses. The $25 difference between the $85 replacement cost and the $60 historical cost is the inventory profit and is considered a holding gain that is caused by the increase in the acquisition price of the inventory between the time that the firm purchased the item and when it was sold. This holding gain is not available to cover operating costs because it must be used to repurchase inventory at new, higher prices.

Rising Prices and LIFO

In a period of rising prices, LIFO results in the lowest gross margin and the lowest ending inventory. The low gross margin results when the latest and highest costs are allocated to cost of goods sold. Thus, cost of goods sold is the highest of the three inventory costing methods, and gross margin is the lowest of the three methods. Too, under LIFO, the ending inventory is recorded at the lowest cost of the three methods because the earliest and lowest prices are allocated to it. In fact, if a company had switched to LIFO 20 years ago, the original LIFO layers, if unsold, would be costed at 20-year-old prices.

LIFO has the opposite effect of FIFO on the balance sheet and income statement. Consequently, LIFO is criticized because the inventory cost on the balance sheet is often unrealistically low. Therefore, working capital, the current ratio, and current assets tend to be understated.

SAFEWAY

This possible effect can be significant, as illustrated by the following excerpt from the 1985 Safeway annual report:

> Consolidated working capital decreased $23.6 million to $301.8 million in 1985 from $325.4 million in 1984, compared with $230.9 million in 1983. The current ratio also decreased to 1.17 from 1.21 and 1.15 in those years. Had the company valued its inventories using the FIFO method, its current ratio would have been 1.36, 1.42, and 1.35, and working capital would have been $614.5, $643.7, and $519.9 million at year-ends 1985, 1984, and 1983, respectively.

Many accountants argue, however, that LIFO provides a more realistic income figure because it eliminates a substantial portion of inventory profit. If you refer back to the simple example on page 429, you will see that on a LIFO basis, the firm's gross margin is $15 because the December 15 purchase is matched against the $100 sale. In this case, the acquisition price of the inventory did not change between the last purchase on December 15 and its sale on December 31, and so all the inventory profits are eliminated. In reality, LIFO will not eliminate all inventory profits but will substantially reduce them.

The elimination of these inventory profits on the income statement can be drastic. For example, according to the Safeway annual report, the application of the LIFO inventory method reduced gross profits by $29.3 million in 1984. This is a substantial figure, considering that Safeway's net income for 1984 was $185.0 million.

In summary, in a period of rising prices, FIFO and LIFO have opposite effects on the balance sheet and income statement. LIFO usually provides a realistic income statement at the expense of the balance sheet. Conversely, FIFO provides a realistic balance sheet at the expense of the income statement. In a period of falling prices, the opposite is true. In either case, average cost will provide figures between those of FIFO and LIFO.

How Current Cost Can Alleviate the Problem

A current cost accounting system can alleviate the need for a cost flow method and can thus help solve the problem of having either a realistic income statement or a realistic balance sheet, but not both. In general, current cost is the cost of currently acquiring an item. Under such a system, cost of goods sold is recorded at the current cost of the item at the time of its sale. Thus, the gross margin figure, which is the difference between sales and the current cost of goods sold, represents income available to the firm to cover operating expenses after maintaining its ability to purchase new inventory. On the balance sheet, ending inventory is recorded at the current cost as of the end of the accounting period. The difference between the current cost of the ending inventory and its historical cost is considered an unrealized holding gain. Thus, figures on the income statement and balance sheet represent realistic amounts.

Current cost accounting is not a generally accepted accounting principle for primary financial statements. However, because of the perceived importance of these data to present and potential investors and creditors, the FASB requires that certain companies disclose selected current cost data on a supplemental basis. In regard to inventories, FASB Statement No. 33 requires firms having inventories and property, plant, and equipment of more than $125 million, or total assets exceeding $1 billion, to disclose income from continuing operations on a current cost basis, and the current cost amounts of inventory and property, plant, and equipment at the end of the year. For an example of such disclosures, see Footnote L in Safeway's financial statements in Appendix C. Current cost accounting is examined in detail in Chapter 14.

Selecting an Inventory Cost Method

The management of a firm can choose any of the four cost flow methods to determine the cost of its ending inventory and its cost of goods sold. Further, within limits set by the accounting profession, a firm can switch from one method to another. The Internal Revenue Code (Code), however, does contain a provision called a LIFO conformity rule, which requires a company to use LIFO for financial reporting purposes if LIFO is used for tax purposes. This is one of the few situations in which the choice of accounting principles for tax and financial reporting purposes cannot be made independently. This rule was inserted in the Code by Congress to keep businesses in a period of rising prices from reporting low earnings to the government while at the same time reporting high earnings to stockholders and other financial statement users.

The popularity of LIFO for tax purposes and the LIFO conformity rule have led to the increasing use of LIFO for financial reporting purposes. An AICPA survey indicates that 66% of the 600 firms sampled use LIFO.

| | AICPA INVENTORY COST* | | | | | | | |
| | 1984 | | 1983 | | 1982 | | 1981 | |
Method	Number	%	Number	%	Number	%	Number	%
LIFO	400	67	408	68	407	68	408	68
FIFO	377	63	366	61	373	62	371	62
Average cost	223	37	235	39	238	40	241	40
Other	54	9	52	9	53	9	52	9
Totals**	1,054		1,061		1,071		1,072	

*AICPA, *Accounting Trends and Techniques*, 39th ed. (New York: AICPA, 1985), p. 116.

**Totals and percentages are more than 600 and 100%, respectively, because many firms use more than one method of inventory costing. For example, a firm with three different classes of inventory may elect to use a different cost flow method for each class. (Percentages based on total sample of 600.)

Accounting for Inventories   431

Inventory Valuation—Lower of Cost or Market

The previous paragraphs explained how to determine the cost of a firm's ending inventory. As we noted, under generally accepted accounting principles, the presumption is that inventories will be recorded at cost. If, however, the utility of the goods in the inventory is not as great as their cost is, the goods must be written down to the **lower of cost or market.** Although this is a violation of the historical cost principle, accountants feel that losses should be recorded as soon as they become evident. Thus, in this case, the concept of conservatism takes precedence over the historical cost convention. Approximately 90% of the 600 companies in the AICPA survey reported their inventory at the lower of cost or market.[4]

The Theory of Lower of Cost or Market

In applying the lower-of-cost-or-market rule, cost is determined by one of the cost flow methods; market, in this case, generally means replacement cost, or the cost to purchase a similar inventory item. The use of lower of cost or market is based on the theory that if an item's replacement cost decreases in the current period, its sales price will ultimately decrease. Because accountants feel that all losses should be recognized when they occur, this loss is recognized in the period that it occurs—that is, when the price declines—not in a later period—when the item is eventually sold.

The Application of Lower of Cost or Market

The application of lower of cost or market is a two-step process. In the first step, **market,** defined as the item's replacement cost, is determined. This can usually be done by examining vendors' invoices at the end of the year. In the second step, market or replacement cost is compared with cost, and if necessary, the inventory is reduced to the lower of cost or market (LCM). Under generally accepted accounting principles, this comparison can be made (1) on an item-by-item basis, (2) on a group-of-items basis, or (3) for the inventory as a whole.

The LCM comparison on all three bases is shown on page 433. When the item-by-item basis is used, individual comparisons for all items must be made. This results in an inventory value of $24,000. Under the group basis, the inventory is divided into a luxury group and a standard group, and the comparison is then made for each group total. For example, in the luxury group the cost of $22,500 is compared with the market of $22,000, and so the value of the group is determined to be $22,000. The same comparison is then made for the standard group, and its value is $2,750. This results in a total inventory value of $24,750. On a total-inventory basis, the cost and the market of the entire inventory are compared, resulting in an inventory value of $24,800.

Comparing all three methods, we see that the item-by-item method is the most conservative; that is, it results in the lowest inventory value. This is because increases in the value of one item cannot offset decreases in other items, as is the case under the group and total inventory methods.

[4]AICPA, *Accounting Trends and Techniques,* p. 122.

| | | Lower of Cost or Market (LCM) | | | | | | |
| | | Per Unit | | Total | | LCM | | |
	Quantity	Cost	Market	Cost	Market	Item-by-Item	Group	Total Inventory
Luxury group								
Item A	100	$50	$40	$ 5,000	$ 4,000	$ 4,000		
Item B	250	70	72	17,500	18,000	17,500		
Total luxury group				$22,500	$22,000		$22,000	
Standard group								
Item C	50	$25	$20	$ 1,250	$ 1,000	1,000		
Item D	100	15	18	1,500	1,800	1,500		
Total standard group				$ 2,750	$ 2,800		2,750	
Total inventory				$25,250	$24,800			$24,800
Inventory value—Item by item						$24,000		
Inventory value—Group basis							$24,750	
Inventory value—Total								$24,800

Estimating Ending Inventories

In some situations it is impossible to determine the actual cost of the ending inventory. For example, a firm's inventory may be destroyed by fire or flood, and the cost of the inventory lost must be estimated. The gross margin method can be used in such circumstances. For a retail store, taking inventory at cost is difficult, if not impossible. The inventory is thus valued at retail and then converted to cost. This is referred to as the retail inventory method.

The Gross Margin Method

The **gross margin method** is used when a firm wishes to estimate its ending inventory without actually taking a count. For example, firms that wish to determine their ending inventories on a monthly basis certainly do not want to take a physical inventory. Some firms have inventories in so many locations that a complete physical count would be impossible. And when there are losses from such disasters as fire or flood, it may be impossible to take an ending inventory. In all these cases, the gross margin method can be used to estimate ending inventories.

The gross margin method is based on the fact that most firms have a gross margin percentage that remains stable. The firm's past gross margin percentage therefore can be used to estimate ending inventories. To illustrate, assume that the Wong Company began the month of January with an inventory of $20,000 and made net purchases of $170,000 during January. Net sales for the month totaled $200,000 and the firm's gross margin percentage has remained at 20%. A 20% gross margin implies that cost of goods sold is 80% of sale.

If we put these data into the normal formula to calculate cost of goods sold, we can easily show how to use the gross margin percentage. Goods available for sale of $190,000 can be determined from existing records by adding the amount of beginning inventory to the purchases for the period. Cost of goods sold is equal to 80% of sales, or $160,000. The ending inventory of $30,000 is the difference between the cost of goods available for sale of $190,000 and the cost of goods sold of $160,000.

Sales		$200,000
Cost of goods sold		
Beginning inventory	$ 20,000	
Net purchases	170,000	
Goods available for sale	190,000	
Less: Ending inventory	?	
Cost of goods sold (80% of sales)		160,000
Gross margin (20% of sales)		40,000

The Retail Inventory Method

Retail firms such as department stores and grocery stores use the **retail method** to determine their ending inventories. In essence, the inventory is taken at retail prices and then converted to cost. Because the inventories that are displayed on the shelves are priced at retail, the entire inventory for a store, such as a large market, can be taken at retail in just a few hours. Two or three individuals read the quantity of the items and their retail prices into tape recorders. The tapes are then transcribed and extended, and the result is the total inventory at retail prices. That is, a listing of the tape noting the quantity and prices is made. When the prices and quantities are multiplied, the total inventory at retail is determined. This inventory is then converted to cost by using a cost-to-retail percentage. This process is considerably less time-consuming than trying to determine the cost of each particular item, even using some cost flow assumption.

The heart of the retail method is determining a cost-to-retail percentage. This percentage is often calculated by dividing goods available for sale at cost by goods available for sale at retail. This means that a firm using the retail method must keep track of both inventories and purchases at cost and at retail. This is not as difficult as it seems because most retailers know the retail prices they are going to set on the goods they buy.

The retail method can be used to estimate ending inventories even if a physical inventory has not been taken. This is done by first determining goods available for sale at retail and then subtracting sales which are at retail. The result is an estimated ending inventory at retail. The ending inventory at cost is then determined by applying a cost-to-retail percentage to the ending inventory at retail. This procedure (see page 435) is illustrated for the Martinez Grocery Store. In this case the cost-to-retail percentage is 80%, or goods available for sale at cost of $190,000 divided by goods available for sale at retail of $237,500. The ending inventory at retail of $37,500 is multiplied by this ratio to determine the ending inventory at cost of $30,000.

Although this example is a simplified version of the retail method, it does indicate the theory behind its application. In practice, different cost percentages can be used to cost inventories at FIFO, LIFO, and average cost. This and other complications, such as LCM valuation, are considered in intermediate accounting textbooks.

| **Martinez Grocery Store** | | |
| **Retail Inventory Method** | | |
	Cost	Retail
Beginning inventory	$ 20,000	$ 26,000
Net purchases	168,000	211,500
Freight-in	2,000	—
Goods available for sale	$190,000	$237,500
Ratio of cost to retail		

$$\frac{\$190,000}{237,500} = 80\%$$

Less: Net sales during period		200,000
Ending inventory, at retail		37,500
Ratio of cost to retail		.80
Ending inventory at cost		$ 30,000

Using Inventory Data for Decision Making

Because inventories have a substantial effect on both the balance sheet and the income statement, they offer important data to investors and managers in evaluating a firm's financial performance and position. Two ratios are often used in this evaluation—the gross margin percentage and the inventory turnover. As we noted, the gross margin percentage is gross margin on sales divided by sales and has several uses, including estimating inventories.

Inventory turnover indicates how quickly a firm is able to convert its inventory into receivables and/or ultimately cash. In effect, the quicker the inventory turns over, the less cash the firm has tied up in inventory and the less need there is for inventory financing. Furthermore, the quicker the turnover is, the less of a problem that obsolescence or spoilage will be. But too quick an inventory turnover may indicate that certain items are not available to meet consumer demands, and as a result sales may be lost. The optimal inventory turnover therefore depends on the firm's characteristics and policies.

The inventory turnover is computed by dividing cost of goods sold by average inventory. Generally, the average inventory is determined by taking the inventory at the beginning of the year plus the inventory at the end of the year, and dividing by 2. For example, if a firm had cost of goods sold of $1.2 million and average inventories of $100,000, the inventory would turn over 12 times during the year, calculated as follows:

$$\frac{\text{Cost of goods sold}}{\text{Average inventory}} = \frac{\$1,200,000}{\$100,000} = 12 \text{ times}$$

If the inventory turnover is divided into 365 days, the result will be the average number of days that the inventory is on hand. In this case the average time is about 30 days, or a month.

In one annual report, Safeway's management made the following point concerning inventory turnover:

> Inventory turnover is an important liquidity factor in the retail industry. On the average the Company turns over its merchandise inventory every 5½ weeks, minimizing the need for borrowed funds to finance them.

When evaluating inventory data and ratios, remember that they are sensitive to the cost flow method adopted. For example, inventory turnover under LIFO is apt to be higher than under FIFO because under LIFO, cost of goods sold (the numerator) is higher, and average inventories (the denominator) is lower. The result is higher turnover. Thus, accounting data must be used carefully when evaluating one firm or comparing several firms.

Summary of Learning Objectives

1. *The relationship between inventories and income determination.* Inventories are nonmonetary assets and, as such, the major accounting issue is allocating the cost of goods available for sale between the ending inventory and the cost of goods sold. The process of matching these costs against revenues helps ensure the proper determination of income. The measurement of ending inventories affects two accounting periods, because the ending inventory for the first year becomes the beginning inventory of the second year. Although a single measurement error is self-canceling, there is an improper allocation of income between the two accounting periods.

2. *Inventory valuation principles.* The primary basis for reporting inventories on the balance sheet is the cost. However, conservatism requires using lower of cost or market if the market price or utility of the goods falls below their cost.

3. *How the cost of ending inventories is determined.* The cost of ending inventory is determined by multiplying the quantity on hand by the acquisition cost of the items. The quantity on hand is usually determined by taking a physical inventory. Cost is the price paid to bring the item to its existing condition ready for sale. But when items are purchased at different prices, the accountant must still use a specific cost flow assumption to attach acquisition prices to the ending inventory.

4. *The four methods of attaching prices to the ending inventory.* There are four generally accepted accounting methods of attaching costs to inventory quantities: (1) FIFO, (2) LIFO, (3) average cost, and (4) specific identification. FIFO assumes that the costs attached to the first goods purchased are the costs of the first goods sold. The cost of the ending inventory is that of the most recent purchase. LIFO makes the opposite assumption, and so the costs attached to the latest purchase are assumed to be the cost of the first item sold. Thus, the cost of the ending inventory is that of the earliest purchases made. Average cost attaches a weighted

average cost, determined by dividing the total cost of the goods available for sale by the number of units available for sale, to both the cost of goods sold and the ending inventory. Specific identification determines the actual acquisition cost of each item in the ending inventory. Because of practical problems, this method is not often used. In a period of changing prices, the selection of a particular cost flow assumption may have a drastic effect on a firm's balance sheet and income statement.

5. *The lower-of-cost-or-market rule.* Generally accepted accounting principles assume that inventories should be valued at cost, unless the replacement cost of the items falls below cost. In applying the lower-of-cost-or-market rule, market, which is generally considered replacement cost, is compared with cost, and if necessary, the inventory is written down to the lower of cost or market. This comparison can be made on an item-by-item basis, a group basis, or a total inventory basis. The lower-of-cost-or-market rule is an excellent example of the conservatism convention in accounting.

6. *The gross margin and retail methods of estimating inventories.* For some merchandising firms, it is difficult, if not impossible, to determine the cost of their ending inventories. For such cases, two methods have been developed to estimate inventories. The gross margin method can be used to estimate the ending inventory on a monthly basis when the inventory is destroyed or when it is otherwise impractical to physically count and cost the inventory. This method is based on the fact that most firms have a relatively stable gross margin percentage. The retail inventory method is used by retail firms such as grocery stores. The retail value of the ending inventory is first determined and then a cost-to-retail percentage is applied to reduce this value to its cost.

7. *Using inventory data for decision making.* Because inventories and cost of goods sold are substantial components of the balance sheet and the income statement, they provide important data for evaluating a firm's financial position and profitability. In this respect, two common ratios used are the gross margin percentage and the inventory turnover. However, because these ratios are very sensitive to the cost flow assumption adopted, they must be used with caution.

Appendix: Cost Methods and the Perpetual Inventory System

This Appendix shows how to apply the FIFO, LIFO, and average cost flow methods when a perpetual inventory system is used. The data for the Cerf Company from the example on page 425 are used to demonstrate these methods and are reproduced on the top of page 438. With the perpetual system, the date of the particular sale is important and therefore is inserted along with the other data.

Cerf Company Data

Date	Purchase	Sales	Balance
Beginning inventory			500 units
January 24	200 @ $4.10		700 units
March 1		400 units	300 units
March 18	400 @ $4.20		700 units
May 5	300 @ $4.50		1,000 units
May 29		650 units	350 units
July 31	350 @ $4.50		700 units
September 27	400 @ $4.60		1,100 units
October 9		750 units	350 units
November 29	250 @ $4.70		600 units

To review, the main difference between the periodic and perpetual methods is the timing of the recognition of the cost of goods sold. Under the perpetual method, an entry to recognize cost of goods sold is made at the point of each sale. Application of the various cost flow systems will be different under the perpetual method. To illustrate the application of the perpetual system, refer to the January 24 purchase of inventory on account and the March 1 sale on account. Assume that each unit is sold for $6. Under the perpetual system, the entries to record this inventory purchase and sale and cost of goods sold (assuming **FIFO**) are:

January 24	Inventory (200 × $4.10)	820	
	Accounts Payable		820
	To record inventory purchase on account.		
March 1	Accounts Receivable (400 × $6)	2,400	
	Sales		2,400
	To record sales on account.		
March 1	Cost of Goods Sold (400 × $4)	1,600	
	Inventory		1,600
	To record cost of goods sold.		

FIFO Perpetual

When the FIFO perpetual system is used the inventory must be layered after each purchase and sale. After each sale, the earliest layers are assumed to have been sold first. To illustrate the application of FIFO perpetual, refer to the perpetual inventory record for the data from the Cerf Company on a FIFO basis on page 439. After the purchase on January 24, the total inventory of $2,820 now contains two layers: 500 units at $4.00 (the beginning inventory) and 200 units at $4.10 (the January 24 purchase). When the cost of goods sold for the March 1 sale is recorded, 400 units from the beginning inventory are assumed to have been sold. This is in line with the first-in, first-out assumption. Thus cost of goods sold is recorded at $1,600. The remaining inventory of $1,220 now contains the following two layers:

$$100 \text{ units (beginning inventory)} @ \$4.00 = \$400$$
$$200 \text{ units (January 24 purchase)} @ 4.10 = \underline{820}$$
$$\phantom{200 \text{ units (January 24 purchase)} @ 4.10 = }\underline{\$1,220}$$

FIFO Perpetual

Date	Purchase Units	Acquisition Cost	Total	Sales Units	Acquisition Cost	Balance Units	Acquisition Cost	Total
Beginning inventory						500 @	$4.00 =	$2,000
January 24	200 @	$4.10	= $ 820			500 @	$4.00 =	$2,000
						200 @	$4.10 =	820
						700		$2,820
March 1				400 @	$4.00	100 @	$4.00	$ 400
						200 @	$4.10 =	820
						300		$1,220
March 18	400 @	$4.20	= $1,680			100 @	$4.00 =	$ 400
						200 @	$4.10 =	820
						400 @	$4.20 =	1,680
						700		$2,900
May 5	300 @	$4.50	= $1,350			100 @	$4.00 =	$ 400
						200 @	$4.10 =	820
						400 @	$4.20 =	1,680
						300 @	$4.50 =	1,350
						1,000		$4,250
May 29				100 @	$4.00	50 @	$4.20 =	$ 210
				200 @	$4.10	300 @	$4.50 =	1,350
				350 @	$4.20	350		$1,560
				650				
July 31	350 @	$4.50	= $1,575			50 @	$4.20 =	$ 210
						300 @	$4.50 =	1,350
						350 @	$4.50 =	1,575
						700		$3,135
September 27	400 @	$4.60	= $1,840			50 @	$4.20 =	$ 210
						300 @	$4.50 =	1,350
						350 @	$4.50 =	1,575
						400 @	$4.60 =	1,840
						1,100		$4,975
October 9				50 @	$4.20	350 @	$4.60 =	$1,610
				300 @	$4.50			
				350 @	$4.50			
				50 @	$4.60			
				750				
November 29	250 @	$4.70	= $1,175			350 @	$4.60 =	$1,610
						250 @	$4.70 =	1,175
						600		$2,785

At the end of the period, FIFO perpetual results in the same inventory cost as does FIFO periodic because the first goods acquired are assumed to have been the first goods sold. This order remains the same throughout the period; therefore, whether the cost of goods sold is recorded when the sales are made or at the end of the period, the result will be the same.

LIFO Perpetual

Unlike FIFO, LIFO perpetual results in a different amount of ending inventory than does LIFO periodic because LIFO perpetual matches each sale with the immediately preceding LIFO layers, whereas LIFO periodic matches sales after it is assumed that all purchases for the period have been made. The inventory record for the Cerf Company on a LIFO perpetual basis is presented on page 441.

As there was after the January 24 purchase, there now are two layers: 500 units at $4.00 and 200 units at $4.10. Under LIFO perpetual, the March 1 sale first wipes out 200 units from the January 24 layer, as this was the last layer added. The remaining 200 units sold are assumed to have come from the beginning inventory, thus reducing that layer to 300 units at $4. At this point, this layer makes up the total inventory of $1,200. After the next purchase on March 18, an additional layer of 400 units at $4.20 is added. On May 5, another layer of 300 units at $4.50 is added. Because this is the last layer added, the 650 units sold on May 29 are first assumed to have come out of this layer and then from the March 18 layer. At the end of the year, the cost of the ending inventory under LIFO perpetual is $2,585, compared with $2,410 under LIFO periodic.

Average Cost Perpetual

Average cost perpetual is often referred to as a moving average method. Under this method, a new average must be computed after each additional purchase. The perpetual record using the weighted moving average method is shown on page 442. To illustrate how the weighted average is calculated, refer to the January 24 purchase. After this purchase, a new moving average of $4.03 per unit is computed as follows:

$$
\begin{array}{ll}
500 \text{ units @ } \$4.00 = & \$2,000 \\
200 \text{ units @ } 4.10 = & 820 \\
\hline
700 \text{ units} & \$2,820 \\
\end{array}
$$

$$
\text{Average cost per unit} = \frac{\$2,820}{700} = \$4.03
$$

On the perpetual record, all per-unit costs are rounded off to two decimal points, and the total inventory costs are rounded off to whole dollars.

When the March 1 sale is recorded, Cost of Goods Sold is debited for 400 units at $4.03 per unit, or $1,612. This leaves 300 units in the ending inventory at an average cost per unit of $4.03, or a total of $1,209. After the next purchase of 400 units at $4.20 on March 18, a new moving average must be calculated as follows:

$$
\begin{array}{ll}
300 \text{ units @ } \$4.03 = & \$1,209 \\
400 \text{ units @ } 4.20 = & 1,680 \\
\hline
700 \text{ units} & \$2,889 \\
\end{array}
$$

$$
\text{Average cost per unit} = \frac{\$2,889}{700} = \$4.13
$$

Under the moving average method, the ending inventory is $2,736, versus $2,610 under the average cost periodic.

LIFO Perpetual

Date	Purchase Units	Acquisition Cost	Total	Sales Units	Acquisition Cost	Balance Units	Acquisition Cost	Total
Beginning inventory						500 @	$4.00 =	$2,000
January 24	200 @	$4.10 =	$ 820			500 @ 200 @ 700	$4.00 = $4.10 =	$2,000 820 2,820
March 1				200 @ 200 @ 400	$4.10 $4.00	300 @	$4.00 =	$1,200
March 18	400 @	$4.20 =	$1,680			300 @ 400 @ 700	$4.00 = $4.20 =	$1,200 1,680 $2,880
May 5	300 @	$4.50 =	$1,350			300 @ 400 @ 300 @ 1,000	$4.00 = $4.20 = $4.50 =	$1,200 1,680 1,350 $4,230
May 29				300 @ 350 @ 650	$4.50 $4.20	300 @ 50 @ 350	$4.00 = $4.20 =	$1,200 210 $1,410
July 31	350 @	$4.50 =	$1,575			300 @ 50 @ 350 @ 700	$4.00 = $4.20 = $4.50 =	$1,200 210 1,575 $2,985
September 27	400 @	$4.60 =	$1,840			300 @ 50 @ 350 @ 400 @ 1,100	$4.00 = $4.20 = $4.50 = $4.60 =	$1,200 210 1,575 1,840 $4,825
October 9				400 @ 350 @ 750	$4.60 $4.50	300 @ 50 @ 350	$4.00 = $4.20 =	$1,200 210 $1,410
November 29	250 @	$4.70 =	$1,175			300 @ 50 @ 250 @ 600	$4.00 = $4.20 = $4.70 =	$1,200 210 1,175 $2,585

Average Cost Perpetual

Date	Purchase Units	Acquisition Cost	Total	Sales Units	Acquisition Cost	Balance Units	Acquisition Cost	Total
Beginning inventory						500 @	$4.00	= $2,000
January 24	200 @	$4.10	= $ 820			700 @	$4.03*	= $2,821
March 1				400 @	$4.03	300 @	$4.03	= $1,209
March 18	400 @	$4.20	= $1,680			700 @	$4.13	= $2,891
May 5	300 @	$4.50	= $1,350			1,000 @	$4.24	= $4,240
May 29				650 @	$4.24	350 @	$4.24	= $1,484
July 31	350 @	$4.50	= $1,575			700 @	$4.37	= $3,059
September 27	400 @	$4.60	= $1,840			1,100 @	$4.45	= $4,895
October 9				750 @	$4.45	350 @	$4.45	= $1,558
November 29	250 @	$4.70	= $1,175			600 @	$4.56	= $2,736

*All average cost figures rounded off to two decimal places.

Key Terms

Average Cost

First-in, First-out (FIFO)

Gross Margin Method

Inventory Profits

Inventory Turnover

Last-in, First-out (LIFO)

Lower of Cost or Market

Market

Retail Method

Specific Identification Method

Problems for Your Review

A. Cost Flow Assumption. The following data relates to the beginning inventory and purchases of the Gooden Company:

Date	Purchases Units	Cost	Sale Units	Balance Units
Beginning Inventory	200	$ 9.75		200
January 3	50	$10.00		250
January 10	100	$10.50		350
January 15			175	175
January 20	225	$10.80		400
January 31			150	250

Required:

Assuming that the Gooden Co. uses a periodic inventory system, calculate the ending inventory and cost of goods sold as of January 31, based on the following methods:

1. FIFO.   2. LIFO.   3. Average cost.

Solutions

Total goods available for sale are calculated as follows:

	Units	Acquisition Cost	Total Cost
Beginning Balance	200	$ 9.75	$1,950
Purchases			
January 3	50	10.00	500
January 10	100	10.50	1,050
January 20	225	10.80	2,430
	575		$5,930
Sales	325		
Ending inventory	250		

1. FIFO

Cost of goods available for sale	$5,930.00
Ending inventory—FIFO	
225 × $10.80 = $2,430.00	
25 × $10.50 = 262.50	
Ending inventory	2,692.50
Cost of Goods Sold	$3,237.50

2. LIFO

Cost of goods available for sale	$5,930.00
Ending inventory—LIFO	
200 × $ 9.75 = $1,950.00	
50 × $10.00 = 500.00	
Ending inventory	2,450.00
Cost of Goods Sold	$3,480.00

3. Average Cost

$$\frac{\text{Cost of goods available for sale}}{\text{Units available for sale}} = \frac{\$5,930.00}{575} = \$10.31^* \text{ Unit}$$

Ending inventory	250 @ $10.31 = $2,577.50
Cost of goods sold	325 @ $10.31 = 3,352.50[†]
Cost of goods Available for Sale	$5,930.00

*Rounded off.
†Rounded off so that ending inventory and cost of goods sold equal cost of goods available for sale.

B. Lower of Cost or Market. The Duffy Company uses the lower-of-cost-or-market convention in valuing its inventory. The company has divided its products into two groups, with two types within each group. The following schedule presents the relevant data as of December 31, 1987:

	Group 1		Group 2	
	Type A	Type B	Type C	Type D
Number of units	50	100	100	200
Selling price per unit	$30	$40	$35	$20
Replacement cost per unit—				
12/31/87	20	28	26	16
Cost per unit	19	29	27	15

Accounting for Inventories   443

Required:

Determine at what amount the ending inventory should be shown, assuming that the firm applies the lower-of-cost-or-market rule on

1. An item-by-item basis.
2. A group basis.
3. A total inventory basis.

Solution

Group 1

Type A	Cost = 50 × $19 = $ 950	Market = 50 × $20 = $1,000
Type B	Cost = 100 × $29 = 2,900	Market = 100 × $28 = 2,800
Total group 1	$3,850	$3,800

Group 2

Type C	Cost = 100 × $27 = $2,700	Market = 100 × $26 = $2,600
Type D	Cost = 200 × $15 = 3,000	Market = 200 × $16 = 3,200
Total group 2	5,700	5,800
Total inventory	$9,550	$9,600

1. Item-by-item = $9,350 = $950 + $2,800 + $2,600 + $3,000.

2. Group basis = $9,500 = $3,800 + $5,700.

3. Total inventory = $9,550.

Questions

1. What is the main accounting issue regarding inventories, and why is it so important?

2. Assume that the ending inventory in year 1 is overstated by $1,000 and that all other items in the cost of goods sold computation are correct. What is the impact on:

  a. Beginning inventory in year 2?

  b. Gross margins for years 1 and 2?

  c. Owner's Capital balance at the end of year 2?

3. One of your fellow students stated, "Determining the quantity of items in the ending inventory is easy—you just count the number of items in the storeroom." Do you agree? Why or why not?

4. What costs should be included in the ending inventory? In practice, how are these costs handled?

5. Explain to a friend who knows nothing about accounting why it is necessary to make cost flow assumptions that often differ from the actual physical flow of the goods.

6. Explain the four cost flow methods that are considered generally accepted accounting principles.

7. Safeway Stores, Inc. uses the LIFO method of determining the cost of its inventories. Another large grocery chain uses the FIFO method. In a period of rising prices, how does this affect each firm's (a) total assets and (b) net income?

8. Why do some accountants feel that the specific identification method is not appropriate in many circumstances?

9. The Quick Chip Company is in an industry in which material prices have been declining. If the firm wants to report the highest gross margin and ending inventory and lowest cost of goods sold, what inventory cost method should it use?

10. For a number of years, the Jackson Co. has been using the FIFO method of costing its inventories. During the last few years the prices of its inventory have been steadily rising. The controller is concerned that the firm's reported gross margin may not reflect its economic ability to repurchase future inventories for resale. Do you agree or disagree with the controller? Why?

11. Describe the concept of inventory profits.

12. The Financial Accounting Standards Board requires large companies to disclose the current cost of their inventories. Why do you think the Board adopted this policy? If inventories are reported on a current cost basis, how do you think the inventory account and cost of goods sold would be affected?

13. How do the regulations contained in the Internal Revenue Code affect management's choice of inventory methods for financial reporting purposes?

14. If you were the president of a newly formed high-tech firm, what inventory method would you choose? Why?

15. What is the accounting concept behind the lower-of-cost-or-market rule? Should lower of cost or market be applied in all circumstances?

16. The Regal Company began business at the beginning of the current year. The firm has decided to use the FIFO method of inventory costing. If LIFO inventory costing had been used, the cost of the ending inventory would have been higher. Can you determine the direction that the cost of the purchases moved in during the year? If so, in what direction did they move?

17. What is the gross margin method of estimating inventories? When is its use most appropriate?

18. What is the retail method of estimating inventories? When is its use most appropriate?

19. In applying the retail method, how does the accountant convert the retail price of the inventory to its cost?

20. (This applies to material covered in the Appendix.) Briefly describe the difference in applying the following inventory costing methods when a perpetual system rather than a periodic system is used:

a. FIFO.   b. LIFO.   c. Average cost.

Exercises*

1. Inventory Errors. During 1987 the Edward Company had sales of $660,000 and made inventory purchases of $370,000. Inventories on January 1, 1987 amounted to $123,000, and inventories at December 31, 1987 were $75,000.

Required:

a. Compute cost of goods sold and the gross margin for 1987.

b. Now assume that an error was made in determining the ending inventory in 1986, and as a result the inventory was overstated by $25,000. What is the effect of this error on the gross margin for 1986 and 1987? What is the effect on the balance in the Retained Earnings account at the end of 1987?

2. Inventory Errors. Following are condensed income statements for the TG Company for two consecutive years:

	Year 1	Year 2
Sales	$800,000	$850,000
Cost of goods sold	560,000	612,000
Gross margin on sales	240,000	238,000
Operating expenses	140,000	125,000
Net income	$100,000	$113,000

At the beginning of the third year the new controller of the TG Company found that there had been two inventory errors in year 1. She determined that the beginning inventory had been overstated by $4,000 and that the ending inventory had been understated by $6,000. At the end of year 2 the Owner's Capital account had a balance of $290,000.

Required:

a. Determine the correct amount of net income for both years 1 and 2.

b. Compute the correct balance in the retained earnings account at the end of year 2.

3. Comparison of Inventory Costing Methods. The Robinson Football Equipment Company gives you the data (on the top of page 446) regarding one of its inventory items, football helmets:

---

*Where appropriate, work all exercises and problems based on the periodic inventory system unless otherwise noted.

Date	Quantity	Cost per Unit
Beginning	40 units	$125
2/28 purchase	100	122
6/24 purchase	85	120
10/4 purchase	110	118

The ending inventory consisted of 50 units.

Required:
  a. Determine the cost of the:
     1. goods available for sale,
     2. ending inventory, and
     3. goods sold
     under the FIFO, LIFO, and average cost inventory methods.
  b. Explain the relationship between the cost of goods sold figure under each of the methods. That is, which is higher and lower and what are the reasons for this relationship?

4. Determining the Cost of Ending Inventories. The Brenner Brin Company uses the periodic inventory method system. During March the following sales and purchases of inventories were made:

	Number of Units	Cost per Unit	Total Cost
March 1 inventory	100	$13.50	$1,350
March 3 sale	75		
March 15 purchase	250	15.00	3,750
March 20 sale	125		
March 29 purchase	150	16.00	2,400
March 30 sale	110		

Determine the ending inventory and cost of goods sold for the Brenner Brin Company under the following methods:
  a. First-in, first-out.
  b. Last-in, first-out.
  c. Average cost.

5. Determining the Cost of Ending Inventories. The following data were taken from the records of the Imdieke Co. regarding the purchases of its main inventory item, instant gold:

April 1:	Beginning inventory	300 units @ $10.00 per unit
April 4:	Purchase	800 units @ $10.20 per unit
April 10:	Purchase	600 units @ $10.25 per unit
April 18:	Purchase	800 units @ $10.25 per unit
April 30:	Purchase	500 units @ $10.40 per unit

At the end of the month there were 800 units remaining in the ending inventory.

Determine the cost of the ending inventory and the cost of goods sold under each of the following methods:
  a. First-in, first-out.
  b. Last-in, first-out.
  c. Average cost.

6. Specific Identification Method. Smith's Specialty Desk Company uses the specific identification method of inventory costing. You obtained the following inventory records for the year ended December 31, 1987:

Quantity Purchased	Purchase Price per Unit	Units on Hand at End of the Year
10	$120.00	1
15	130.00	5
12	124.50	4
20	122.00	0
15	128.00	5

Required:

a. Determine the cost of the ending inventory using the specific identification method.

b. Assume that all the desks are substantially identical and that their selling price is $200 each. Determine the gross margin from the sales. How would your answer differ if the entire inventory of 15 units was from the items purchased at $122 per unit? What does this suggest about some of the conceptual problems with the specific identification method?

7. Effects of Different Inventory Costing Methods. The president of Pete's Pickles is confused about the effects of different inventory costing methods on income. The firm has been in business since the beginning of 1985, and the president gives you the following inventory data for 1985 through 1987:

Date	LIFO Cost	FIFO Cost	Average Cost
12/31/85	$6,000	$6,500	$6,300
12/31/86	5,200	5,400	5,325
12/31/87	5,800	5,600	5,540

Required:

a. Which inventory costing method will show the highest net income in each of the years?

b. Which inventory costing method will show the lowest net income in each of the years?

8. Lower of Cost or Market. The following information pertains to the ending inventory of the Great Dane Company:

Item	Cost per Unit	Replacement Cost per Unit
A	$50	$65
B	80	75
C	75	67
D	25	19
E	45	46

The firm values its inventory using lower of cost or market on an item-by-item basis.

Required:

a. At what value should the ending inventory be shown on the balance sheet?

b. Can you think of a situation when it would not be appropriate to use lower of cost or market?

9. The Gross Margin Method. On August 15 of the current year, the entire inventory of Youngblood's Bookstore was destroyed in a freak tornado in San Diego. In order to file a claim with the insurance company, the owner of the store compiled the following information regarding the purchases and sales of inventory for the month of August just prior to the tornado:

Beginning inventory	$15,000
Purchases	45,000
Sales	50,000

During the last few years the gross margin percentage has been averaging 25%.

Compute the amount of inventory destroyed in the tornado. Also compute the cost of goods sold from August 1 to August 15.

10. Retail Inventory Method. Sunset Drug Store uses the retail inventory method to estimate its ending inventory. You have been able to determine the following information for the year ended December 31, 1987:

	Cost	Retail
Beginning inventory	$12,000	$20,000
Net purchases	30,000	40,000
Net sales		42,000

Determine the cost of the ending inventory and the cost of goods sold during the year.

11. Inventory Turnover. The following information was taken from the records of the McGinnis Company:

Beginning inventory—1/1/87	$ 42,000
Net purchases	195,000
Ending inventory—12/31/87	20,000

Determine the inventory turnover and the average number of days that the inventory is on hand.

12. Inventory Costing Methods—Two-Period Analysis. The Marshall Company began business on January 1, 1987. During 1987 and 1988 the firm made the following purchases:

1987:

January 2	75 units @ $2.00
February 5	50 units @ $2.10
April 14	125 units @ $2.20
July 14	100 units @ $2.20
September 28	80 units @ $2.25
November 29	70 units @ $2.30

1988:

January 14	100 units @ $2.35
March 25	600 units @ $2.40
August 19	400 units @ $2.38
December 4	60 units @ $2.36

During 1987 and 1988 the firm sold 360 units and 1,200 units, respectively.

Required:

Determine the amount of cost of goods sold and the ending inventories for 1987 and 1988 under both the FIFO and the LIFO methods.

13. Determining the Cost of Ending Inventories—Perpetual System. (This applies to material covered in the Appendix.) The Payton Company uses the perpetual inventory system. During March the following sales and purchases of inventories were made:

	Number of Units	Cost per Unit
March 1 inventory	200	$8.00
March 8 sale	150	
March 11 purchase	220	8.10
March 20 sale	240	
March 25 purchase	150	8.15
March 31 sale	140	

All sales are made at $14 per unit. Prepare a condensed income statement through gross margin on sales, assuming the firm uses (a) the FIFO method and (b) the LIFO method.

Problem Set A

11A–1. Inventory Errors. You have just been hired as the accountant for Youngsters, Inc., the makers of Murfs. During your review of the records, you found that the following errors were made in calculating the year-end inventory amounts:

	Overstated	Understated
12/31/83	0	
12/31/84	$8,500	
12/31/85	9,200	
12/31/86		$5,000
12/31/87		4,500
12/31/88	2,000	
12/31/89	0	

Required:

For each year, determine the dollar error on (1) total assets and (2) net income.

11A–2. Inventory Errors. The Gilded Antique Store uses the periodic inventory system. Its accountant prepared the following condensed income statements for the years ended December 31, 1987 and 1988:

	1987	1988
Net sales	$500,000	$625,000
Cost of goods sold:		
Beginning inventory	$120,000	$125,000
Purchases, net	330,000	402,500
Goods available for sale	450,000	527,500
Less: Ending inventory	125,000	140,000
Cost of goods sold	$325,000	$387,500
Gross margin on sales	$175,000	$237,500
Operating expenses	125,000	162,500
Net Income	$ 50,000	$ 75,000

During 1989 the accountant discovered that several errors had been made in determining the amount of the ending inventories.

1987:

1. At the end of 1987 the store had several pieces of furniture that it was holding on consignment for others. These items were included in the ending inventory at their selling price of $5,000. These items were not included in 12/31/88 inventory.

2. A sale was made on December 31, 1987 to an out-of-town customer. The merchandise was shipped FOB shipping point on that date. However, the item was included in the ending inventory at its cost of $2,500. The selling price of the item was $3,200. Through an oversight, the sale and the receivable were not recorded until early January.

1988:

3. At the end of December 1988, the store made a purchase of several antique desks from England. The desks were shipped in late December, FOB shipping point, for delivery in early January 1989. The items cost $5,000. Because they were not on hand as of the end of 1988, they were not included in the ending inventory, nor were they recorded as purchases in December.

4. At the end of December an antique table was lent to an interior decorator on the condition that if the decorator sold the table, it would be purchased from the store at a price of $1,000. The item had a cost of $600. Because the item was not on hand when the inventory was taken, it was not included in the cost of the ending inventory.

Required:

a. Prepare a correct set of income statements for the years ended December 31, 1987 and 1988.

b. Assume that the firm had net assets of $1 million and $1,050,000 at December 31, 1987 and 1988, respectively, prior to any corrections for the preceding items. Determine the correct amount of net assets after you have made the necessary corrections.

11A-3. Inventory Determination. The Hawk Steamer Company uses the periodic inventory system and prepares financial statements every December 31. You have gathered the following data regarding the main item in the inventory:

	Number of Units	Unit Cost	Total Cost
1987			
Beginning inventory	0		
Purchases: January	600	$2.00	$1,200.00
April	400	2.10	840.00
July	400	2.25	900.00
Total for year	1,400		
Less items sold	800		
Ending inventory	600		
1988			
Beginning inventory	600		
Purchases: February	400	3.00	1,200.00
June	800	3.10	2,480.00
November	200	3.20	640.00
Total for year	2,000		
Less items sold	1,600		
Ending inventory	400		

Required:

Determine the cost of the ending inventory and the cost of goods sold for each year, assuming the firm uses the following inventory costing methods:

a. FIFO.

b. LIFO.

c. Average cost.

11A-4. Inventory Determination. Ekbog Inc. stocks and sells a single product. During 1987 and 1988 the firm made the following inventory purchases:

	1987		
	Quantity	Price	Total
Beginning inventory	200	$ 5.00	$1,000
Purchases: 2/20	300	9.00	2,700
5/20	200	9.50	1,900
8/15	300	9.25	2,775
11/15	400	9.20	3,680
Ending inventory	450	?	?

	1988		
Beginning inventory	450	?	?
Purchases: 3/15	600	$ 9.50	$5,700
6/15	200	10.00	2,000
9/15	200	10.50	2,100
12/15	300	10.20	3,060
Ending inventory	400	?	?

Required:
Determine the cost of the ending inventory and cost of goods sold for 1987 and 1988 under each of the following methods:

a. FIFO.

b. LIFO.

c. Average cost.

11A–5. Lower of Cost or Market. The Rimbau Company sells home and office telephones. It has divided its product into a basic and a luxury group and has two different telephones in each group. The firm uses the lower-of-cost-or-market rule in determining the value of its ending inventory. Data pertaining to their December 31 inventory is presented as follows:

| | Luxury Group | | Basic Group | |
	Type 1	Type 2	Type 3	Type 4
Number of units	50	100	100	200
Selling price per unit	$60	$80	$75	$40
Replacement cost	40	56	52	32
Purchase cost	38	58	54	30

Required:
Determine the value of the December 31 ending inventory, applying the lower-of-cost-or-market rule under each of the following independent assumptions:

a. Applied individually to each item.

b. Applied to each group of products.

c. Applied to the inventory as a whole.

11A–6. Gross Margin Method. The Winrich Company has been taking a physical inventory every quarter in order to prepare its quarterly financial statements. Because this process is very time-consuming, the president of the company is wondering whether there is a more efficient way to determine the cost of inventories for its quarterly reports.

You have been provided with the following information and asked to figure a better way to determine quarterly inventories:

The Winrich Company
Partial Income Statement
For the Year Ended December 31, 1987

Net sales		$655,000
Cost of goods sold:		
Beginning inventory	$ 80,000	
Purchases, net	575,000	
Goods available for sale	655,000	
Less: Ending inventory	223,000	432,000
Gross margin on sales		$223,000

You have obtained the following additional data:

a. In early 1988 it was determined that a sale for $5,000 recorded in late 1987 was actually an item provided to a good customer on consignment. The cost of the item was $3,000 and was not included in the ending inventory. The item was subsequently returned unsold in early 1988.

b. Gross margin percentages for the previous years were 1983, 32%; 1984, 35%; 1985, 33%; and 1986, 36%.

c. Data for the first quarter of 1988 were sales, $280,000; net purchases, $130,000.

Required:

    a. Explain to the president how the ending inventory for the first quarter of 1988 can be estimated.

    b. Estimate the ending inventory at the end of the first quarter of 1988.

    c. Explain other uses for the gross margin method.

11A–7. Retail Inventory Method. The Weiss Drugstore uses the retail method to determine its cost of goods sold and ending inventory. You have been able to gather the following data for the month of April:

	Cost	Retail
Beginning inventory	$20,650	$ 32,790
Purchases	65,870	102,510
Purchase returns	2,460	5,000
Freight-in	635	
Sales		99,400
Sales returns		1,120

Required:

Determine the cost of the ending inventory and cost of goods sold for April.

11A–8. Perpetual Inventory System. (This applies to material covered in the Appendix.) The Z-Image Company sells X-ray machines. The firm uses the perpetual inventory system to keep track of its major product, Unit 145. The record of inventory purchases and sales during the current year is as follows:

Beginning inventory		10 units @ $400 per unit
Purchases and sales		
February 1:	Purchase	30 units @ $450 per unit
March 15:	Sale	35 units
May 2:	Purchase	20 units @ $460 per unit
June 4:	Purchase	25 units @ $470 per unit
August 8:	Sale	20 units
September 1:	Sale	15 units
November 12:	Purchase	60 units @ $480 per unit
December 1:	Purchase	10 units @ $485 per unit
December 31:	Sale	55 units

Required:

Determine cost of goods sold and ending inventory, assuming the firm uses the following inventory methods:

    a. FIFO.

    b. LIFO.

    c. Moving average.

Where necessary, round off unit costs and total inventory costs to two decimal points.

Problem Set B

11B–1. Inventory Errors. You are the accountant for Good, Inc. During your review of the firm's records, you found that the following errors were made in calculating the year-end inventory. The firm has a June 30 fiscal year-end.

	Overstated	Understated
6/30/84	$1,000	
6/30/85		$1,500
6/30/86		2,500
6/30/87	3,200	
6/30/88	2,700	
6/30/89	0	

Required:
For each year, determine the dollar error on (1) total assets and (2) net income.

11B–2. Inventory Errors. The Taktech Company uses the periodic inventory system. The accountant for the company prepared the following condensed income statements for the years ended June 30, 1987 and 1988.

	1987	1988
Net sales	$700,000	$950,000
Cost of goods sold		
Beginning inventory	80,000	110,000
Purchases, net	580,000	770,000
Goods available for sale	660,000	880,000
Less: Ending inventory	110,000	150,000
Cost of goods sold	550,000	730,000
Gross margin on sales	150,000	220,000
Operating expenses	70,000	100,000
Net income	$ 80,000	$120,000

During 1989 the accountant found that several errors were made in determining the amount of ending inventories:

1987:

1. On June 30 the company had several personal computers that were not included in Taktech's ending inventory, held on consignment by some retailers. These computers had a cost of $5,000.

2. A sale was made in late June; the customer did not take delivery of the equipment until some time in July. As a result, ending inventory was overstated by $3,200, and sales were understated by $4,300.

1988:

3. A purchase was made on June 25, 1988; the merchandise did not arrive until July. The purchase had been recorded properly in the purchases journal, but the item was not included in the ending inventory. The merchandise had a cost of $10,000.

4. Some equipment that was held on consignment for others was included in Taktech's ending inventory. As a result, ending inventory was overstated by $2,000.

Required:
a. Prepare a correct set of income statements for the years ended June 30, 1987 and 1988.
b. Assume that the firm had net assets of $250,000 and $300,000, respectively, prior to any corrections for the preceding items. Determine the correct amount of net assets after you have made the necessary corrections.

11B–3. Inventory Determination. The Kline Company uses the periodic inventory system and prepares financial statements every December 31. The information relative to its main inventory item (on the top of page 454) has been gathered by the firm's accountant:

Required:
Determine the cost of the ending inventory and the cost of goods sold for each year, assuming the firm uses the following inventory methods:
a. FIFO.
b. LIFO.
c. Average cost.

	Number of units	Unit Cost	Total Cost
1987			
Beginning inventory	0		
Purchases: February	1,000	$3.00	$3,000
July	800	3.15	2,520
October	1,200	3.40	4,080
Total available	3,000		
Less items sold	1,600		
Ending inventory	1,400		
1988			
Beginning inventory	1,400		
Purchases: March	800	3.60	2,880
September	1,100	3.75	4,125
November	700	3.70	2,590
Total available	4,000		
Less items sold	2,800		
Ending inventory	1,200		

11B–4. Inventory Determination. Eddite, Inc. is a one-product merchant. During 1987 and 1988 the firm made the following purchases:

	1987		
	Quantity	Unit Price	Total
Beginning inventory	1,000	$3.98	$ 3,980
Purchases: 1/15	1,500	5.00	7,500
4/15	2,300	5.30	12,190
7/15	2,700	5.50	14,850
10/15	1,500	5.40	8,100
Ending inventory	1,200	?	?
	1988		
Beginning inventory	1,200	?	?
Purchases: 2/1	1,700	$5.35	$ 9,095
5/1	2,100	5.45	11,445
8/1	2,500	5.50	13,750
11/1	2,000	5.60	11,200
Ending inventory	1,500	?	?

Required:

Determine the cost of the ending inventory and the cost of goods sold for 1987 and 1988 under each of the following methods:

a. FIFO.

b. LIFO.

c. Average cost.

11B–5. Lower of Cost or Market. The Mini Company sells desk calculators. It has divided its product into a basic and a fancy group and has three different calculators in each group. The firm uses the lower-of-cost-or-market rule in determining the value of its ending inventory. Data pertaining to their March 31, 1987 inventory is presented as follows:

	Fancy Group			Basic Group		
	Type 1	Type 2	Type 3	Type 4	Type 5	Type 6
Number of units	100	120	150	200	180	150
Selling price per unit	$165	$130	$100	$ 80	$ 60	$ 40
Replacement cost	120	80	66	65	48	25
Purchase cost	125	75	70	50	45	30

Required:

Determine the value of the March 31, 1987 ending inventory, applying the lower-of-cost-or-market rule under each of the following independent assumptions:

a. Applied individually to each item.

b. Applied to each group of calculators.

c. Applied to the inventory as a whole.

11B–6. The Gross Margin Method. The Baker Company uses the gross margin method to determine the cost of goods sold and its ending inventory.

You have been provided with the following partial income statement:

The Baker Company
Partial Income Statement
For the Year Ended June 30, 1987

Net sales		$1,105,000
Cost of goods sold:		
Beginning inventory	$ 350,000	
Purchases, net	750,000	
Goods available for sale	1,100,000	
Less: Ending inventory	492,250	607,750
Gross margin on sales		$ 497,250

You have obtained the following additional information:

a. In July, 1987 it was determined that a sale for $95,000 made on June 30 was not included in sales, and that the cost of $52,250 was erroneously included in ending inventory.

b. Gross margin percentages for the four preceding years were: 42%, 43%, 47%, and 48%.

c. Data for the month of July 1987 were sales, $150,000 and net purchases, $90,000.

Required:

a. Explain the basic assumptions needed for use of the gross margin method.

b. Estimate the cost of goods sold and the ending inventory for the Baker Company at the end of July, 1987.

11B–7. Retail Inventory Method. The Diamond Computer Store uses the retail method to determine its cost of goods sold and ending inventory. You have gathered the following information for the month of July:

	Cost	Retail
Beginning inventory	$100,000	$135,000
Purchases	450,000	600,000
Purchase returns	5,100	6,800
Freight-in	1,250	
Sales		586,200
Sales returns		7,000

Required:

Determine the cost of the ending inventory and cost of goods sold for July.

11B–8. Perpetual Inventory System. (This applies to material covered in the Appendix.) The Copy-It Company sells duplicating machines. The firm uses the perpetual inventory system to keep track of its major product, the Image Maker. The record of inventory purchases and sales during the current year is as follows:

Beginning inventory		20 units @	$1,000 per unit
Purchases and sales			
February 10:	Purchase	50 units @	980 per unit
March 25:	Sale	45 units	
April 29:	Purchase	25 units @	975 per unit
June 12:	Purchase	25 units @	970 per unit
July 30:	Sale	35 units	
September 15:	Sale	25 units	
November 12:	Purchase	100 units @	965 per unit
December 9:	Purchase	40 units @	960 per unit
December 24:	Sale	130 units	

Required:

Determine cost of goods sold and ending inventory, assuming the firm uses the following inventory methods:

a. FIFO.

b. LIFO.

c. Moving average.

Where necessary, round off unit costs and total inventory costs to two decimal points.

Using the Computer

The EDP manager of the Clean Washing Machine Company is considering computerizing the firm's inventory valuation system and asks your help. The firm wholesales two types of washers, the Super Wash model and the Clean Wash model. Data regarding the cost, market, and units on hand for each model are given below.

	Super Wash		Clean Wash	
	Model A	Model B	Model C	Model D
Units on hand	200	300	100	80
Cost per unit	$300	$325	$225	$250
Replacement cost per unit:				
Optimistic	340	320	220	255
Conservative	315	308	215	251

Required:

Using an electronic spreadsheet available at your university, prepare a lower-of-cost-or-market analysis using the format shown in your text on page 433. Prepare a separate analysis using first the optimistic replacement cost and then the conservative value.

Understanding Financial Statements

After analyzing one of Safeway's recent annual reports, you obtained the following information (all figures in thousands):

Purchases	$13,193,000
Cost of sales	12,966,000
Beginning inventory, FIFO	1,268,000
Ending inventory, FIFO	1,495,000

In discussing and analyzing operations, management noted that the current cost of the ending inventory was $1,501,000 and that cost of goods sold on a replacement cost basis was $13,020,000.

Required:

a. Determine the amount of inventory profits included in Safeway's reported net income of $115,000,000.

b. How do you think your analysis would differ if Safeway reported its inventories on the LIFO basis?

Financial Decision Case

In mid-December, the Diamond Gold Company is reviewing its financial and tax position prior to year-end. The price of gold has been falling, and the company is considering making an additional purchase of 5,000 ounces of gold prior to year-end. The following data reflect inventory purchases and sales through mid-December:

	Ounces of Gold	Cost per Ounce	Total Cost
Beginning inventory	6,000	$200	$1,200,000
Purchases during year			
First	10,000	400	4,000,000
Second	8,000	380	3,040,000
Third	12,000	350	4,200,000

During the year the company sold 34,000 ounces of gold and does not expect to make any additional sales prior to year-end. The company has been offered 5,000 ounces of gold at $340 per ounce. Although this price appears attractive, the company feels that the price of gold will continue to decline and will finally stabilize at $300 per ounce at the beginning of the next year. The company uses the LIFO method of inventory cost and has an average tax rate of 30%.

Required:

a. Determine cost of goods sold assuming that (1) the purchase is not made and (2) the purchase is made.

b. Assume that the 34,000 oz. of gold were sold at $450 per ounce and that all expenses other than taxes amounted to $1 million. Determine net income, assuming that (1) the purchase is not made and (2) the purchase is made.

c. Determine the difference in cash flows to the firm if the purchase is made in December at $340 per ounce or in January at $300 per ounce.

d. What course of action would you suggest that the firm take?

Property, Plant, and Equipment

12

LEARNING OBJECTIVES

After reading this chapter you should be able to:

1. Explain the accounting concepts and issues related to noncurrent, nonmonetary assets.
2. Discuss the importance of differentiating between capital and revenue expenditures.
3. Measure the acquisition cost of property, plant, and equipment and record their original acquisition.
4. Explain the accounting concept of depreciation.
5. Compute depreciation expense under four different methods.
6. Identify depreciation problems relating to partial-year's depreciation, revision of depreciation rates, and depreciation and inflation.

This chapter considers the accounting concepts and procedures related to noncurrent, nonmonetary assets. Specifically, we concentrate on accounting for property, plant, and equipment and the related concept of depreciation. The next chapter examines the accounting for the disposition of these assets as well as natural resources, intangible assets, and the related concepts of depletion and amortization.

Noncurrent, Nonmonetary Assets

Noncurrent, nonmonetary assets are often broken down into two categories: tangible and intangible. **Tangible assets** include property, plant, and equipment and other similar productive assets acquired by a company. These assets have physical substance and capabilities. Natural resources also are considered tangible assets. **Natural resources** are physical substances that, when taken from the ground, produce revenues for a firm. Included in this category are oil, natural gas, coal, iron ore, uranium, and timber.

Intangible assets have no physical substance or properties. They benefit a firm because they give the enterprise the right of ownership or use. Included in this category are patents, copyrights, leaseholds, trademarks, and franchises.

All noncurrent, nonmonetary assets have the following common characteristics:

1. They represent bundles of future economic services that are acquired for use in the business and as such are usually not held for resale.
2. The future services will benefit a firm for several accounting periods.
3. The cost of consuming these services is systematically allocated to the periods in which the revenues are earned (except for land).

Bundles of Future Services Not Held for Resale

Property, plant, and equipment, as well as other noncurrent, nonmonetary assets, are acquired by an enterprise because of their ability to generate future revenues. In effect, these assets are viewed as bundles of future service potentials that are consumed in the firm's merchandising or production cycle. For example, accountants are not concerned with the physical properties of a lathe but rather with its ability to produce a product and thus provide future benefits.

Assets that are not used in the merchandising or production process (including assets that are held for resale) are not included in this category. For example, a warehouse that is no longer being used or land held for speculation is not classified under the category of property, plant, and equipment. Rather, these assets are included in the long-term investment category of the balance sheet. Similarly, land held for resale by a real estate firm is shown in the inventory section of the balance sheet.

Long-term Nature of the Assets

The economic or service life of a noncurrent, nonmonetary asset is the period of time that a firm expects to receive benefits from the asset and depends on economic and legal factors. A building generally has an economic life of at least 20 to 30 years; a delivery truck may have a life of 100,000 miles. Intangible assets have a legal life as well as an economic life. For example, a patent has a legal life of 17 years in addition to its economic life, which may be shorter than 17 years. Generally, any asset that has a life of over one year is included in the noncurrent section of the balance sheet.[1]

Allocation of Benefits for Accounting Periods

The matching convention requires that the cost of expired benefits be matched with the revenues they helped produce. Accountants do this for all nonmonetary assets (other than land), whether classified as current or noncurrent. For example, prepaid assets such as insurance are written off to ensure that as their benefits expire or are consumed, the asset is reduced and an expense is recorded. Further, as we noted in Chapter 11, various cost flow assumptions

---

[1]Long-term prepaid expenses represent an exception to this. In Chapter 6 we noted that prepaid expenses that benefit several years are still classified as current, because these items are not material and thus the financial statements are not distorted.

are used to allocate cost of total goods available for sale to ending inventory and cost of goods sold. In this chapter we consider how the cost of noncurrent, nonmonetary assets, other than site land, is systematically allocated to future accounting periods. Land is not depreciable because its benefits are considered to last indefinitely.

Following are the major categories of noncurrent, nonmonetary assets and the expenses associated with the cost allocation process:

Asset Category	Expense
Tangible assets	
Land	None
Plant, buildings, equipment, and other similar assets	Depreciation
Natural resources (e.g., oil and gas)	Depletion
Intangible assets	Amortization

Major Accounting Issues Associated with Noncurrent, Nonmonetary Assets

The major accounting issues related to noncurrent, nonmonetary assets include:

1. Distinguishing between capital and revenue expenditures.
2. Measuring and recording their acquisition cost.
3. Measuring the cost of using the assets in future periods related to depreciation expense.
4. Recognizing the effect of inflation in measuring the current cost and depreciation of these assets.
5. Measuring the cost of using the assets in future periods related to repairs, maintenance, and improvements.
6. Accounting for the disposal of property, plant, and equipment.
7. Maintaining management control over plant assets.

The following sections of this chapter are concerned with the first four of these issues as they relate to property, plant, and equipment. Chapter 13 discusses the last three issues, as well as the accounting concepts for natural resources and intangibles.

Capital versus Revenue Expenditure

Throughout this book we have used the term *expenditure* to refer to a payment of an asset or the incurrence of a liability in exchange for another asset or for a service rendered. That is, the expenditure is made in cash or on credit and results in the firm's receiving another asset, such as a delivery truck, or in using a service, such as a repair to a delivery truck. When the expenditure produces another asset, it is called a **capital expenditure.** Thus, the term *capitalize,* when used in this sense, means to consider an expenditure as an asset. When the expenditure results in a service whose benefits are consumed in the current period, it is called a **revenue expenditure.** Revenue expenditures are current expenses and include ordinary repairs, maintenance, fuel, and other items required to keep the asset in normal working condition. The following diagram illustrates the difference between capital and revenue expenditures:

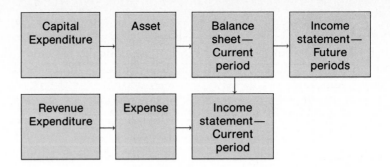

The distinction between capital and revenue expenditures is important in determining periodic net income, because capital expenditures affect several accounting periods, whereas revenue expenditures affect only the current period's income. If an error is made and a capital expenditure, such as an equipment purchase, is recorded as a revenue expenditure, both the current period's and future periods' net income will be misstated. The current period's income will be understated because the entire expenditure was expensed when only a portion of it, the current year's depreciation, should have been expensed. Future periods' income will be overstated because no depreciation expense is recorded in these years. Although over the useful life of the asset the error is self-correcting, in the interim the income is misstated.

How do firms decide what is a capital and what is a revenue expenditure? Clearly, the purchase of a delivery truck is a capital expenditure, whereas an engine tune-up is a revenue expenditure. But what about the purchase of a wastepaper basket or a major engine overhaul that practically constitutes a new engine? In order to have consistent accounting policies that can be followed from year to year, firms develop guidelines or formal policies to handle these items. Materiality considerations play a large part in the design of such policies. Most firms put some minimum dollar limit for capital expenditures. The minimum can range from one hundred dollars for small companies to several thousand dollars for large companies.

This problem is further complicated by the fact that the same item can sometimes be considered a capital expenditure and at other times a revenue expenditure. For example, the labor cost to adjust a new machine during installation is considered a capital expenditure and is thus part of the acquisition cost of the machine. This is because the expenditure is necessary to make the machine ready for use. On the other hand, the same labor cost subsequent to the operation of the machine is a revenue expenditure because at that time it is a normal and recurring repair. Thus, the purpose as well as the nature of the expenditure must be considered when deciding whether an item is a capital or a revenue expenditure.

Measuring and Recording the Acquisition Cost of Property, Plant, and Equipment

According to the FASB, "the historical cost of acquiring an asset includes the costs necessarily incurred to bring it to the condition and location necessary for its intended use."[2] In terms of property, plant, and equipment, this means that all the reasonable and necessary costs required to get the asset to its location and ready for use are included in the acquisition cost. For example, the acquisition cost of equipment includes any transportation charges, insurance in transit, installation, testing costs, and normal repairs before putting the asset into service. All of these costs are necessary to bring the equipment to a location and condition to make it ready for its intended use. However, the acquisition cost does not include unexpected costs, such as the cost of repairing damage incurred in transportation, purchase discounts lost, or, in most cases, interest costs. These costs, as well as normal repairs and maintenance expenses incurred in subsequent periods, are considered period expenses when incurred.

Each type of asset within the property, plant, and equipment category has special conventions regarding which particular items should be included in the asset's acquisition cost. For example, when land is purchased, various incidental costs that must be included in its total acquisition cost include real estate commissions; title fees; legal fees; draining, grading, and clearing costs; and delinquent property taxes. However, in many cases the accountant's judgment must be used to determine which items should be capitalized.

Cash Acquisitions

When property, plant, and equipment are purchased for cash, the acquisition price is easy to determine. It is the asset's net cash equivalent price paid plus all other costs necessary to get the asset ready to use. To illustrate, assume the Miller Company purchases a lathe from the Arnold Company. The price of the lathe is $15,000, and the terms of sale are 2/10, n/30. Sales tax is 6%; freight charges are $850; and installation costs are $150. The total acquisition cost of the equipment is $16,600, computed as follows:

Purchase price		$15,000
Less: Discount of 2%		(300)
Net price		14,700
Add: Sales tax (6% of $15,000)	$900	
Freight charges	850	
Installation charges	150	1,900
Total acquisition cost		$16,600

If the discount is not taken, the $300 should not be included in the cost of the equipment but instead should be considered as interest expense.

Other Methods of Acquiring Property, Plant, and Equipment

There are a variety of ways in which an enterprise can acquire property, plant, and equipment other than by a direct cash purchase. These include basket purchases, deferred payment plans, noncash exchanges such as in exchange for other productive assets, and self-construction. The determination of cost in

[2]Financial Accounting Standards Board, Statement No. 34, *Capitalization of Interest Cost* (Stamford, Conn.: FASB, October 1979), par. 6.

these types of acquisitions is often more difficult than in straightforward cash exchanges and thus warrants special attention.

Basket or Group Purchases

Whether or not the purchase is for cash, a firm's property, plant, and equipment are often purchased together in one lump sum. For example, when an existing building is purchased, the land on which that building is situated also is usually purchased. The agreed-upon purchase price represents the total cost of both the building and the land, and in many cases the total purchase price is more or less than the individual fair market values of the building and the land. As a result, the total purchase price must be allocated between the individual assets. This is especially important because the building is subject to depreciation, but the land is not. The allocation is often based on appraisals or property records.

To illustrate, assume that the H. Jones Company purchases an existing office building and the site land. The total purchase price is $1 million. An independent appraiser determines that the building and land have fair market values of $900,000 and $300,000, respectively. The $1 million purchase price is allocated as follows:

	Appraised Value	Relative Percentage of Total Appraised Value[a]	Purchase Price	Allocation of Cost
Building	$ 900,000	75% ×	$1,000,000	$ 750,000
Land	300,000	25 ×	1,000,000	250,000
Total	$1,200,000	100		$1,000,000

[a]$900,000 ÷ $1,200,000 = 75%.

As this example illustrates, acquisition cost is the basis for recording assets, even though their individual appraised values may be higher.

Deferred Payment Plans

Because of the high cost involved, property, plant, and equipment often are purchased through a cash down payment and the issuance of a note or a **mortgage.** A mortgage is long-term debt secured by real property and is usually paid in monthly installments. Generally, there are no particular accounting problems in recording these transactions. The asset is debited for the agreed-upon purchase price, Cash is credited for the down payment, and Mortgage or Note Payable is credited for the remainder. Subsequent interest payments are considered a period expense. For example, if an enterprise purchases an acre of land for $100,000 by making a 20% down payment and issuing a 30-year, 10% mortgage note, the firm makes the following journal entry:

Land	100,000	
Mortgage Payable		80,000
Cash		20,000
To record purchase of land for 20% down and the remainder through a mortgage.		

As the mortgage is paid monthly, the accounts Interest Expense and Mortgage Payable are debited and Cash is credited. In effect, the interest on the mortgage is recorded as a period expense and is not included as part of the acquisition cost of the equipment. This is because interest is considered to be cost of using money and thus is an expense during the period the money is being used. However, in very limited circumstances, it is appropriate to include some interest expense in the acquisition cost of certain property, buildings, or equipment. This issue is discussed later in this chapter.

Noncash Exchanges

The exchange of one productive asset for another is the primary type of noncash exchange in which a firm is likely to enter. Because this transaction involves the disposal of an asset, it is discussed in the next chapter when the accounting for the disposal of property, plant, and equipment is illustrated.

Self-constructed Assets

In some circumstances, a building or a piece of equipment is constructed by the enterprise itself. The assets are called self-constructed assets, and their acquisition costs include materials and labor used directly in the construction process as well as a portion of overhead. Overhead costs include supervisory labor, utilities, and depreciation on the factory building.

Capitalization of Interest. Interest is the time value of money and, as such, generally is considered an expense in the period incurred. Thus, when property, plant, or equipment is purchased through the issuance of a note, the interest related to that note is expensed when incurred. However, in 1979 the FASB issued Statement 34, which requires that in limited circumstances interest be capitalized and thus be included in the acquisition cost of certain noncurrent, nonmonetary assets.[3] In particular, Statement 34 requires that when an enterprise constructs its own assets, or has another entity construct an asset for it, and there is an extended period to get it ready for use, interest incurred in the construction period should be capitalized as part of the acquisition or production cost of the asset. The rules relating to capitalized interest are complex and are discussed in intermediate accounting texts.

The Accounting Concept of Depreciation

Depreciation is probably the most misunderstood and yet one of the most important of all the accounting concepts that we will study. Perhaps the best way to understand the nature of depreciation is to explore what depreciation is and what it is not.

The Nature of Depreciation

Noncurrent, nonmonetary assets are purchased because they represent bundles of future benefits. All of these assets, with the exception of site land, eventually give up these benefits as the firm uses them to produce revenues. Depreciation, as noted in Chapter 4, is the process of allocating the cost of plant and equipment to the period in which the enterprise receives the benefit

[3]Ibid.

from these assets. **Depletion** refers to the allocation of the cost of natural resources, and **amortization** refers to intangible assets. Next, we analyze the concept of depreciation, but the theoretical concepts are the same, and the analysis applies equally well to depletion and amortization, which are discussed in the next chapter.

Depreciation Is an Allocation Process

From an accounting perspective, depreciation is an allocation process. That is, the cost of the asset is allocated to the periods in which the enterprise receives benefits from the asset. Theoretically, when an enterprise buys an asset such as delivery equipment, it can account for it in three different ways. It can:

1. Write off to expense the entire cost of the asset at the time of purchase, that is, consider it a revenue expenditure.
2. Record the expenditure as an asset at the time of purchase and make no further adjustment until the asset is sold, abandoned, or otherwise disposed of, at which time the entire cost of the asset is written off to expense.
3. Record the expenditure as an asset at the time of purchase and systematically allocate the cost to the periods in which the asset benefits the firm (depreciation).

Clearly, the third option provides the best matching of revenue and expense and is the only one considered to be a generally accepted accounting principle. Although estimates such as useful lives and salvage value must be made, accountants believe that the benefits of the depreciation process outweigh the subjectivity of these estimates.

Depreciation Is Not a Valuation Concept

Unfortunately, many individuals think that depreciation represents a decrease in the value of an asset.[4] Accounting records do not attempt to show the current value of an asset, and depreciation is not used to value plant or equipment. For example, because of market conditions, the value of a building may substantially increase over a specific period of time. However, accountants would continue to depreciate the building because they know that eventually the building will give up its benefits to the firm, and the matching concept requires that as these benefits expire, they should be offset against the revenues they help produce. The assumption also is made that productive assets will not be sold but will be consumed in the operations of the business (the going-concern assumption). Thus, depreciation is used to allocate the cost of an asset over its estimated useful life, regardless of current market value.

Depreciation Is Not a Direct Source of Cash

Another common misconception regarding depreciation is that it is a source of cash. Depreciation is a noncash expense in that it does not require a cash payment at the time the expense is recorded. This is no different from the write-off of prepaid insurance or rent. The cash outlay takes place when the payment for the related asset is made. As a result, depreciation does not result in a direct cash outflow or inflow, nor does the balance in the Accumulated Depreciation account represent cash. The balance in this account represents only the total of the expired costs of the particular asset and is recorded as a

---

[4]From an economic viewpoint, this may be the case. However, from an accounting perspective, depreciation is strictly an allocation process.

debit to Depreciation Expense and a credit to the Accumulated Depreciation account. Neither cash nor any other current asset or current liability account is involved. Unless a company purposely sets aside cash by taking it out of its regular cash account and putting it into a special fund, there is no guarantee that the firm will have the funds to replace its plant and equipment.

There is one way, however, in which depreciation is an indirect source of cash to a firm. Depreciation is a noncash expense that reduces taxable income. The lower the firm's income is, the lower the cash outflows due to tax payments will be. Thus, the higher the depreciation expense for tax purposes is, the more cash the firm will be able to retain through lower tax payments. Only in this way does depreciation affect cash flow. As we will see later in this chapter, using depreciation for tax purposes is closely tied to reducing taxable income.

What Causes Depreciation?

There are two factors that cause a tangible asset to give up its economic benefits: deterioration and obsolescence.

Physical Deterioration

Tangible assets deteriorate because of use, the passage of time, and exposure to the elements such as weather and other climatic factors. Clearly, a good maintenance policy can keep a firm's tangible assets in good repair and performing according to expectations. However, eventually even the best-maintained asset will wear out and need to be replaced. Thus, depreciation is recorded for all tangible assets other than land, no matter how well maintained. In addition, depreciation is recorded for those items included in the Plant and Equipment account, even if they are temporarily not in use. This is because as time passes, physical deterioration takes place to a certain extent, regardless of use.

Obsolescence

Obsolescence refers to the process of becoming outdated, outmoded, or inadequate. Certain high-tech equipment, such as computers and other electronic devices, are subject to rapid obsolescence. Although these assets continue to perform, new technology makes them outdated in a relatively short period of time. Some assets, although technologically sound, become obsolete because they are no longer able to produce at the increased levels required as a result of expanded growth and sales.

Physical deterioration and obsolescence are factors that cause depreciation. However, it is not necessary to distinguish between them in determining depreciation. They are primarily related to determining the economic useful life of assets, and no attempt is made to separate these joint factors in that determination.

Recording Period Depreciation

In Chapter 4, we introduced you to the process of recording periodic depreciation. Before describing the various methods of computing depreciation, we will review the recording process. When a tangible asset is purchased, an asset account is debited. The credit part of the entry depends on how the asset is acquired. Periodic depreciation expense is recorded by debiting Depreciation Expense and crediting the contra-asset account, Accumulated Depreciation.

To illustrate, assume that a firm purchases a delivery truck for $8,500 cash on January 2 of the current year. Yearly depreciation is determined to be $1,700. The necessary journal entries to record these events and the correct balance sheet presentation at December 31 are:

Jan. 2	Delivery Truck	8,500	
	Cash		8,500
	To record purchase of delivery truck.		
Dec. 31	Depreciation Expense	1,700	
	Accumulated Depreciation—Delivery Truck		1,700
	To record depreciation for the year.		

December 31
Partial Balance Sheet

Delivery truck	$8,500
Less: Accumulated depreciation	1,700
	$6,800

Two points should be emphasized when studying this example. The $6,800 figure is referred to as the asset's book value, or carrying value, and is calculated by subtracting the balance in the asset's Accumulated Depreciation account from its historical cost. In addition, separate accumulated depreciation ledger accounts are maintained for each asset or group of asset accounts, such as buildings, delivery equipment, and office equipment. However, for balance sheet presentation, large companies often combine all of these balances into one accumulated depreciation account.

Methods of Computing Periodic Depreciation

As is the case with determining the cost of ending inventory, there are acceptable alternative methods of computing periodic depreciation. The primary guideline is that the method be rational and systematic. The four most common depreciation methods are straight-line, units-of-production, and two accelerated methods, declining-balance and sum-of-the-years-digits. Management is free to choose any of these methods and can depreciate one class of assets using one method and another class of assets using a different method. As we will see later, another form of depreciation is usually calculated for tax purposes.

Factors in Computing Depreciation

Regardless of which depreciation method is used, certain factors must be considered: (1) the asset's acquisition cost, (2) its residual or salvage value, (3) its depreciable cost, and (4) its estimated useful or economic life.

Acquisition Cost

The previous portions of this chapter explained how the acquisition cost of tangible assets is determined. The proper determination of this figure is important because it serves as a foundation for many other figures on which periodic depreciation is based.

Residual or Salvage Value

The residual or salvage value is management's best estimate of what an asset will be worth at the time of its disposal. That is, it is the amount that the firm expects to receive or recover from the asset, less any cost to dispose of it. In many cases, a firm will assume that the cost to dispose of the asset is about equal to what it will recover and thus gives the asset a zero residual value. The residual value is obviously an estimate and is often based on management's past experience. Assets are not depreciated below their salvage value.

Depreciable Cost

Depreciable cost is determined by subtracting an asset's estimated residual value from its acquisition cost. The starting point for most depreciation methods is the asset's depreciable cost. Often this amount is referred to as the asset's depreciable base.

Estimated Useful or Economic Life

The asset's estimated useful or economic life is a measure of the service potential that the current user may expect from the asset. Thus when a used asset is purchased, it is assigned a life based on its use to the new owner, regardless of the life assigned to it by the former owner. It can be in years, percentage rates, or units produced, such as expected miles. For example, a delivery truck may have a five-year life. A five-year life represents a 20% per-year depreciation rate ($1 \div 5 = 20\%$). In the case of a delivery truck, it may be appropriate to express its estimated life in terms of expected miles, such as 150,000 miles. All of these methods of expressing useful or economic lives are used for various assets.

Of the factors that affect the depreciation computation, the estimated useful life of an asset is perhaps the most difficult to estimate. Information such as past experience, the asset's physical condition, the firm's maintenance policy, and the state of technology all are used to help estimate an asset's life.

Methods of Computing Depreciation

To demonstrate the previous concepts, as well as the various depreciation methods, we use the following data:

Equipment purchase date	January 2, 1987
Cost	$40,000
Residual value	$ 4,000
Depreciable cost	$36,000
Useful life	5 years

Straight-line Depreciation

Straight-line depreciation is the simplest of the various depreciation methods. Under this method, yearly depreciation is calculated by dividing an asset's depreciable cost by its estimated useful life. For example, using the above data, yearly straight-line depreciation is $7,200, calculated as follows:

$$\frac{\text{Cost} - \text{Salvage value}}{\text{Useful life}} = \frac{\$40{,}000 - \$4{,}000}{5} = \$7{,}200$$

When the straight-line method is used, the depreciable cost of the asset is spread evenly over its life, in this case at a uniform rate of 20% (1 ÷ 5 = 20%). Therefore, depreciation expense is the same each year, and by the end of the fifth year, the asset's book value has been reduced to its estimated residual value of $4,000. Even if the equipment is still being used past the fifth year, it is left at its book value of $4,000. These points are summarized in the following schedule:

Year	Acquisition Cost	Yearly Depreciation	Accumulated Depreciation	Book Value
1987	$40,000	$7,200	$ 7,200	$32,800
1988	40,000	7,200	14,400	25,600
1989	40,000	7,200	21,600	18,400
1990	40,000	7,200	28,800	11,200
1991	40,000	7,200	36,000	4,000

This example assumes that an entire year's depreciation is taken in the year of acquisition. However, a firm purchases assets at different times during the year, and a full year's depreciation need not be taken on a partial-year's usage. Furthermore, depreciation is often calculated monthly or quarterly for the preparation of interim statements. To illustrate the calculation of partial-year's depreciation, assume that in the previous example the asset was purchased on April 1 rather than on January 2. In this case, only 9 months of depreciation expense, or $5,400 ($7,200 × 9/12), is recorded on December 31.

Straight-line depreciation is widely used because of its simplicity and the fact that it allocates an equal amount of expense to each period of the asset's life. Even though from a conceptual perspective straight-line depreciation is most appropriate for assets that give up their benefits on a fairly uniform basis, management can choose straight-line depreciation regardless of the pattern in which the asset gives up its benefits.

Units-of-Production Method

The cost of some assets can be more easily allocated according to their estimated production or output, rather than their life. The **units-of-production method** assumes that the primary depreciation factor is use rather than the passage of time and so is appropriate for assets such as delivery trucks and equipment, when there are substantial variations in use. To illustrate, assume that the equipment described above is estimated to produce 120,000 units over its useful life. In this case, depreciation per unit is $0.30, determined as follows:

$$\frac{\text{Cost} - \text{Salvage value}}{\text{Estimated production in units}} = \frac{\$40{,}000 - \$4{,}000}{120{,}000 \text{ units}} = \$0.30 \text{ per unit}$$

This cost per unit is then applied to the units produced during the year. For example, the following schedule shows yearly depreciation over the equipment's life:

Date	Acquisition Cost	Units Produced	Yearly Depreciation	Accumulated Depreciation	Book Value
1987	$40,000	22,000	$6,600	$ 6,600	$33,400
1988	40,000	24,000	7,200	13,800	26,200
1989	40,000	18,000	5,400	19,200	20,800
1990	40,000	26,000	7,800	27,000	13,000
1991	40,000	30,000	9,000	36,000	4,000
		120,000			

We assumed that the 120,000 units produced by the equipment are spread over five years. However, when the units-of-production method is used, the life in years is of no consequence.

The units-of-production method requires that the production base, or output measure, be appropriate to the particular asset. For example, miles driven or flown might be most appropriate for a delivery truck or airplane, whereas units produced is most appropriate for a lathe or other equipment. The units-of-production method meets the criterion of being rational and systematic and provides a good matching of expenses and revenues for those assets for which use is an important factor in depreciation. However, for static assets such as buildings, the units-of-production method is inappropriate.

Accelerated Depreciation Methods

Accelerated depreciation methods allocate a greater portion of an asset's cost to the early years of its useful life and consequently less to later years. These methods are based on the theoretical assumption that some assets produce greater benefits or revenues in their earlier years, and thus a greater portion of their cost should be allocated to those earlier years. The two most common accelerated methods found in practice are the declining-balance and sum-of-the-years-digits.

Declining-Balance Method   Under the **declining-balance method,** yearly depreciation is calculated by applying a fixed percentage rate to an asset's remaining book value at the beginning of each year. Because twice the straight-line rate is generally used, this method is often referred to as double-declining-balance depreciation.

In our equipment example, the equipment has a five-year life. This results in an annual straight-line percentage rate of 20% (1 ÷ 5 = 20%). The double-declining-balance rate is 40% (2 × 20%). This rate is applied to the asset's remaining book value at the beginning of each year. When applying the double-declining-balance method, the asset's residual value initially is not subtracted from the asset's acquisition cost to arrive at a depreciable cost, as it is when applying the straight-line method, the units-of-production method, and (as we will see later) the sum-of-the-years-digits method. Residual value is considered only in the last year of the asset's life, when that year's depreciation is limited to the amount that will reduce the asset's book value to its residual value. These points are illustrated in the following schedule, which computes yearly depreciation for the equipment:

| Year | Cost | Yearly Depreciation | | Accumulated Depreciation | Book Value |
		Computation	Expense		
1987	$40,000	$40,000 × .40 =	$16,000	$16,000	$24,000
1988	40,000	24,000 × .40 =	9,600	25,600	14,400
1989	40,000	14,400 × .40 =	5,760	31,360	8,640
1990	40,000	8,640 × .40 =	3,456	34,816	5,184
1991	40,000	*	1,184	36,000	4,000

*Depreciation expense in 1991 is the amount required to reduce the equipment's book value to its residual value of $4,000 ($5,184 − $4,000 = $1,184).

Partial-year depreciation also can be calculated by using the declining-balance method. For example, if the equipment in the previous illustration is purchased on October 1 rather than on January 2, depreciation for the period between October 1 and December 31 is $4,000 ($16,000 × 3/12). In the second year, depreciation is calculated in the regular manner by multiplying the remaining book value of $36,000 ($40,000 − $4,000) by 40%.

In the previous example we assumed a depreciation rate equal to twice the straight-line rate. However, many firms use a rate equal to one and one-half the straight-line rate. This is called 150% declining-balance depreciation and is calculated in the same manner as is double-declining-balance depreciation, except that the rate is 150% of the straight-line rate.

Sum-of-the-Years-Digits The **sum-of-the-years-digits** method is another variation of accelerated depreciation. Under this method, the asset's depreciable base is multiplied by a declining rate. Note that the asset's residual value is subtracted from its acquisition cost to determine its depreciable base. This rate is a fraction, in which the numerator is the number of years remaining in the asset's life at the beginning of the year and the denominator is the sum of the digits of the asset's useful life. To demonstrate how this fraction is computed, assume that an asset has a five-year life. In the first year, the rate is a fraction that has a numerator of 5, the number of years remaining at the beginning of the year. The denominator is 15, or $1 + 2 + 3 + 4 + 5$.[5] In the second year the fraction is 4/15, and so forth.

The depreciation schedule using the sum-of-the-years-digits method for the equipment is shown at the top of the next page.

[5]The denominator of the fraction can easily be computed from the following formula:

$$N \frac{(N + 1)}{(2)}$$

where N equals the asset's life. In the above illustration the denominator is calculated as follows:

$$5 \frac{(5 + 1)}{(2)} = 5(3) = 15$$

If the asset's life is 10 years the denominator is 55, calculated as follows:

$$10 \frac{(10 + 1)}{(2)} = 10(5.5) = 55$$

Year	Cost	Depreciation Calculation Depreciable Cost × Fraction = Expense				Accumulated Depreciation	Book Value
1987	$40,000	$36,000	×	5/15	= $12,000	$12,000	$28,000
1988	40,000	36,000	×	4/15	= 9,600	21,600	18,400
1989	40,000	36,000	×	3/15	= 7,200	28,800	11,200
1990	40,000	36,000	×	2/15	= 4,800	33,600	6,400
1991	40,000	36,000	×	1/15	= 2,400	36,000	4,000

As with the double-declining-balance method, the sum-of-the-years-digits method allocates more depreciation in early years and less in later years. However, unlike the double-declining-balance method, the sum-of-the-years-digits method is calculated by applying a declining rate to a constant base, the asset's depreciable cost.

Partial-year depreciation also can be calculated under the sum-of-the-years-digits method. For example, now assume that the equipment is purchased on October 1 of the current year. In this case, the equipment is in use for only three months during the year, and the sum-of-the-years-digits depreciation is $3,000, calculated as follows:

$$\$3,000 = 3/12 \times \$12,000, \text{ or } 3/12 \times (\$36,000 \times 5/15)$$

In the second year, the depreciation expense of $11,400 must be calculated in two steps, as follows:

$$9/12 \times (\$36,000 \times 5/15) = \$\ 9,000$$
$$3/12 \times (\$36,000 \times 4/15) = \underline{\ \ 2,400}$$
$$\underline{\underline{\$11,400}}$$

In the second year, all 12 months must be accounted for. The first nine months is based on the fraction 5/15 and the next three months on the fraction 4/15. Depreciation expense for the remaining three years is calculated in a similar manner.

Both declining-balance and sum-of-the-years-digits are examples of accelerated depreciation. From a conceptual perspective, these methods are most appropriate for assets that give up a greater portion of their benefits in their early years. As such, most of the cost of these assets should be allocated to these same early years. High-tech products are examples of assets in which the decline of benefits is likely to follow such a pattern. Accelerated depreciation is also appropriate for assets that have a greater amount of repair expense in later years. This results in a reasonably constant expense related to the asset because depreciation expense declines as repair expense increases.

Regardless of these conceptual arguments, the management of a firm can choose either accelerated depreciation method for any depreciable asset. The only guideline is that the depreciation method be systematic and rational, and as we noted, all of the depreciation methods discussed so far meet this requirement. Furthermore, management can choose straight-line depreciation for financial reporting purposes and a special form of accelerated depreciation for tax purposes. This allows a firm to report higher income for financial statement purposes and lower income for tax return purposes.

Comparison of Various Depreciation Methods

Exhibit 12–1 compares the four depreciation methods discussed in this chapter. One of the most important points to note is that in all cases total depreciation expense over all 5 years is $36,000. As a consequence, the balance in the Accumulated Depreciation account at the end of the fifth year is also $36,000 in all four cases. This shows that we are dealing with various ways to allocate the same depreciable cost of $36,000 and that each method results in a different expense pattern within the five-year period. These differences are significant and can have a great effect on earnings for each year. For example, in the first year, double-declining depreciation is $16,000, and depreciation under the units-of-production method is only $6,600. These differences tend to lessen in the middle years of the asset's life and again increase in the last years of the asset's life. However, in the last years the differences reverse. That is, straight-line and units-of-production depreciation is greater than depreciation under either of the accelerated methods. Of course, the pattern under the units-of-production method could differ greatly in different situations.

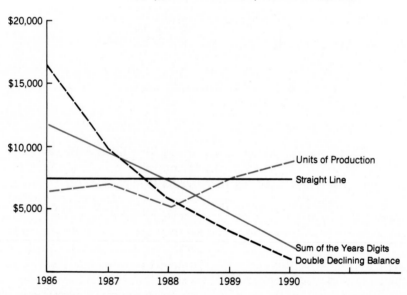

EXHIBIT 12–1
Comparison of Four Depreciation Methods

COMPARISON OF FOUR DEPRECIATION METHODS

| | Depreciation Expense | | | | Accumulated Depreciation | | | |
Year	Straight-Line	Units-of-Production	Double-Declining-Balance	Sum-of-the-Years-Digits	Straight-Line	Units-of-Production	Double-Declining-Balance	Sum-of-the-Years-Digits
1986	$ 7,200	$ 6,600	$16,000	$12,000	$ 7,200	$ 6,600	$16,000	$12,000
1987	7,200	7,200	9,600	9,600	14,400	13,800	25,600	21,600
1988	7,200	5,400	5,760	7,200	21,600	19,200	31,360	28,800
1989	7,200	7,800	3,456	4,800	28,800	27,000	34,816	33,600
1990	7,200	9,000	1,184	2,400	36,000	36,000	36,000	36,000
Total	$36,000	$36,000	$36,000	$36,000				

474

Selecting a Depreciation Method for Financial Reporting Purposes

Because all four of the depreciation methods are generally accepted accounting methods, management has the option of selecting any of them for financial reporting purposes. In fact, it is possible to use one method to depreciate equipment and another method to depreciate buildings. All of these methods are used in practice. However, the following survey of 600 companies shows that the straight-line method is the most popular.

DEPRECIATION METHODS USED BY 600 MAJOR COMPANIES[a]				
	Number of Companies[b]			
	1984	1983	1982	1981
Straight-line	567	564	562	565
Declining balance	54	57	57	57
Sum-of-the-years-digits	15	17	20	25
Accelerated method—Not specified	76	74	69	68
Units-of-production	60	65	62	52
Other	13	12	—	—

[a]Source: AICPA, *Accounting Trends and Techniques*, 39th ed. (New York: AICPA, 1985), p. 268.
[b]Adds up to more than 600, as some companies use more than one method.

Theoretically, the best depreciation method is the one that allocates the cost of the individual asset to the years of its useful life in the same pattern as do the benefits or revenues that the asset produces. Because different assets have different revenue patterns, all of the methods are appropriate in specific circumstances. The theoretical soundness of a depreciation method is not, however, an absolute requirement for its use. In choosing a particular method for financial reporting purposes, management is usually more concerned with practical reasons, such as simplicity and financial statement effects. To a large extent, this explains the popularity of straight-line depreciation. It is easy to compute and results in a constant expense spread over the asset's useful life.

Because the choice of depreciation methods can have a significant effect on a firm's financial statements, current accounting rules require that a firm disclose how it depreciates its assets. This disclosure is usually made in the footnote to the financial statements that summarizes the firm's accounting policies.

An excerpt from the footnote included in Safeway's 1985 financial statements reads as follows:

SAFEWAY

> Property and Depreciation:
> Property is stated at historical cost. Interest incurred in connection with construction in progress is capitalized. Depreciation is computed for financial reporting purposes under the straight-line method using the following lives:
>
> | | |
> |---|---|
> | Stores and other buildings | 20–40 years |
> | Fixtures and equipment | 3–20 years |
> | Transport equipment | 6–14 years |

Depreciation and amortization expense for property of $331.3 million in 1985, $293.7 million in 1984, and $263.4 million in 1983 included amortization of property under capital leases of $53.8, $54.9, and $55.2 million, respectively.

Choosing a Depreciation Method for Tax Purposes

The Economic Recovery Act of 1981 made substantial changes in the depreciation rules for tax purposes. Essentially, the traditional depreciation system was replaced by a new concept called the **Accelerated Cost Recovery System (ACRS).**

In late 1986, President Reagan signed into law a major tax reform act. This act, which is explained in Appendix B, made some changes in the ACRS system. These changes relate to assets placed into service in 1987 and thereafter and, basically, revise some of the class lives. However, the concept behind ACRS depreciation remains the same. The discussion that follows incorporates, where appropriate, these changes. In most usual circumstances, ACRS must be used for tax purposes. However, ACRS is not considered a generally acceptable accounting principle and cannot be used for financial reporting purposes.

Under the ACRS, the cost of depreciable property placed in service prior to 1987 is recovered over a 3-, 5-, 10-, or 18-year period of time, depending on the nature of the asset. For example, automobiles, light trucks, and certain machinery and equipment have been assigned a three-year life. Most production line equipment, delivery trucks, office furniture, aircraft, and so forth were assigned a five-year life. Certain public utility property was assigned a 10-year life, and most real property such as buildings are now assigned an 18-year life. In addition to allowing a write-off over lives that in some cases are substantially shorter than economic lives, the ACRS incorporates the benefits of the accelerated-depreciation methods. For assets placed in service in 1987 and thereafter, the class lives range from 3 to 31 1/2 years. Interestingly, automobiles that were previously in the 3-year category were placed in the 5-year category.

In order to determine ACRS depreciation for an asset, multiply the acquisition cost (residual value is not considered) of the property by a statutory percentage. This percentage depends on when the asset is purchased, its class life, and the number of years since the asset was placed in service. The relevant percentages for tangible personal property such as equipment placed in service prior to 1987 are:

	ACCELERATED COST RECOVERY TABLE		
Recovery Year	3-Year	Property Class 5-Year	10-Year
1	25%	15%	8%
2	38	22	14
3	37	21	12
4		21	10
5		21	10
6			10
7			9
8			9
9			9
10			9

To demonstrate the use of this table and how ACRS compares with depreciation for financial reporting purposes, assume that at the beginning of 1986 a company purchases a piece of equipment at a cost of $40,000. For tax purposes the asset has an ACRS class life of five years, but management estimates that for financial reporting purposes its economic life is eight years (a 12.5% rate). Depreciation expense for 1986, 1987, and 1988 for both tax and financial reporting purposes is calculated next.

| COMPARISON OF ACRS AND STRAIGHT-LINE DEPRECIATION |||
| ACRS |||
Year	Computation	Depreciation Expense
1986	$40,000 × .15	$6,000
1987	40,000 × .22	8,800
1988	40,000 × .21	8,400
Straight-line		
Year	Computation	Depreciation Expense
1986	$40,000 × .125	$5,000
1987	40,000 × .125	5,000
1988	40,000 × .125	5,000

Under the straight-line method, a full year's depreciation was taken, because the asset was placed in service at the beginning of the year. However, for assets such as equipment, the ACRS table allows for only one-half of a year's depreciation in the acquisition year regardless of when the asset is placed in service. The 15% rate is a half-year rate; therefore, this rate is applied to the equipment even though it was purchased at the beginning of the year.

Clearly, the ACRS provides substantial tax benefits in the asset's first years. That is, the firm's taxable income and thus its tax payments are reduced when ACRS is used instead of straight-line. In years 1991–1993, these benefits reverse when the asset is still being depreciated for financial reporting purposes but no depreciation is being taken under ACRS. However, the fact that tax payments are being deferred until later years benefits the firm, as it is able to earn interest on the money that is saved in the early years. Although the table for assets placed in service after 1987 will be different, the basic concepts just illustrated will remain the same.

Other Problems Related to Depreciation

In order to explain depreciation concepts, we have purposely simplified our examples and illustrations. Actual businesses confront a number of practical problems related to depreciation, which include depreciation for partial years, revision of depreciation patterns, and the effects of inflation on depreciation.

Depreciation for Partial Years

Productive assets are purchased and disposed of at various times during the year. When this occurs, firms often calculate annual depreciation expense

Property, Plant, and Equipment

for the number of nearest full months since the purchase and up to the full month closest to its disposal. In explaining how depreciation is calculated under the four depreciation methods, we showed how partial-year depreciation could be computed. Unless other methods were indicated, partial-year depreciation should be computed based on the nearest full month since the purchase or up to the full month closest to the time of disposal.

But, because depreciation is inherently an estimate, many firms do not feel that it is necessary to calculate partial-year's depreciation so precisely. As a result, two common conventions are often used. Under one convention, depreciation expense is calculated for the entire year if the asset is purchased in the first half of the year. If the asset is purchased in the last half of the year, no depreciation is taken. Under another convention, six months of depreciation is taken in the year of purchase and six months in the year of retirement or disposal, regardless of the date when the asset is actually purchased or disposed of. This six-month convention is built into the ACRS table for assets other than real estate.

Revision of Depreciation Patterns

Factors such as economic lives and residual values are estimates made at the time the asset is purchased. There may be later events that require that these original estimates be revised. For example, improved maintenance techniques may increase the life of an airplane an additional five years beyond the estimate made at the time it was purchased. Failure to revise these estimates for the new information will cause a mismatching of revenue and expense.

A change in estimate is not an error correction. As noted, new events or new information may require a revision of the original estimates. Because of this, changes in depreciation estimates, such as a revision in useful life, are handled by spreading the remaining undepreciated base (undepreciated cost or book value less estimated residual value) of the asset over the years of the new remaining useful life. That is, there is no correction of prior years' statements; only current year's and future years' depreciation are affected. This treatment is required by the accounting profession in APB Opinion No. 20.

To illustrate, assume that on January 2, 1984 the Pen and Ink Company purchases a piece of equipment for $12,000 with a $2,000 residual value. The firm estimates that the equipment will have a useful life of 10 years and elects to use straight-line depreciation. At the beginning of the asset's fourth year of life, January 2, 1987, management decides the asset still has a remaining life of 10 years instead of 7 years. Further, it is estimated that the asset's residual value will be $1,000 at the end of its new remaining useful life. The first step in determining the revised depreciation pattern is to calculate the asset's undepreciated cost, or book value, at the beginning of the fourth year, January 2, 1987. From that value, $9,000 in this case, the new estimated residual value of $1,000 is subtracted. The resulting amount is the remaining depreciable base which is then spread over the remaining new life. This is done as follows:

Asset's historical cost:	$12,000
Asset's depreciable cost: $12,000 − $2,000 = $10,000	
Yearly depreciation: $10,000 ÷ 10 years = $1,000	
Accumulated depreciation as of 1/2/87: $1,000 × 3 =	(3,000)
Book value at January 2, 1987	$ 9,000

Remaining depreciable base: ($9,000 − $1,000 residual value)	$ 8,000
Remaining life based on new estimate	10 years
Yearly depreciation for 1987 and afterwards ($8,000 over 10 years)	$ 800

A change in depreciation method is another event that will revise the future depreciation pattern. Under current accounting rules a change in method, such as a change from sum-of-the-years-digits to straight-line depreciation, requires a catch-up adjustment that affects the current period's income. The accounting procedures for this type of depreciation revision are outlined in Chapter 17.

Inflation and Depreciation

Historical cost is the primary method of recording assets. As such, periodic depreciation is based on the historical cost of productive assets. Many individuals feel that when price levels rise in the economy, historical cost depreciation overstates profits and does not provide a reasonable picture of a firm's financial position.

To illustrate, assume that a firm purchases a piece of equipment for $2 million in 1978. Over the asset's 10-year life, straight-line depreciation is used. In 1988, the firm purchases a similar asset as a replacement. However, the cost of the new machine is now $4 million. In this situation many accountants feel that the $2 million of depreciation is not adequate and that depreciation expense should have totaled $4 million. This represents the expenditure that the firm must ultimately make to maintain its productive capacity and as such should be charged to expense over the life of the original asset. That is, depreciation expense is based on the asset's replacement cost rather than on its historical cost. This means that depreciation expense increases as the asset's replacement cost increases.

Because of the difficulty in obtaining objective data on replacement costs, it is not the primary method of recording assets. Rather, the historical cost of the assets is maintained in the records. But because of the conceptual importance of replacement cost data, the FASB suggests the supplemental disclosure of certain current cost data.[6] In respect to productive assets, large firms may disclose the current cost of their property, plant, and equipment and the related depreciation expense based on current costs. Accounting for inflation is discussed in Chapter 14.

Summary of Learning Objectives

1. *The accounting concepts and issues related to noncurrent, nonmonetary assets.* Noncurrent, nonmonetary assets include both tangible and intangible assets. Tangible assets include property, plant, and equipment and

---

[6]Financial Accounting Standards Board, Statement No. 33, *Financial Reporting and Changing Prices* (Stamford, Conn.: FASB, September 1979), par. 30. Although not exactly the same, current cost and replacement cost are similar concepts. However, an exposure draft was recently issued amending Statement No. 33 to make voluntary these disclosures.

natural resources. Intangible assets have no physical substance and include such assets as patents, franchises, and goodwill. All noncurrent, nonmonetary assets:

a. Are bundles of future economic services.
b. Affect several accounting periods.
c. Are systematically allocated over the periods in which the benefits are received (except for land).

2. *Differentiating between capital and revenue expenditures.* When a firm makes an expenditure and it results in the acquisition of an asset, it is called a capital expenditure. When the expenditure results in a service whose benefits are consumed in the current period, it is called a revenue expenditure. The distinction between capital and revenue expenditures is important when determining periodic net income, because capital expenditures affect several periods, whereas revenue expenditures affect only current period's income.

3. *Measuring the acquisition cost of property, plant, and equipment.* The historical cost of plant assets includes all the costs incurred that are necessary to get the assets to their location and in condition to be used. Included are such costs as transportation charges, insurance in transit, and installation and testing costs. When the purchase is made for cash, the acquisition cost is the net cash equivalent price. When a noncash acquisition is made, the acquisition cost is equal to the cash given, plus the fair market value of the noncash consideration given. If it is difficult or impossible to obtain the fair market value of the noncash consideration given, the transaction should be recorded at the fair market value of the asset received.

4. *The accounting concept of depreciation.* Depreciation is the process of allocating the cost of plant and equipment to the period in which the enterprise receives the benefits from the assets. Depreciation is not a valuation concept, nor is it a direct source of cash. Rather, it is caused by such factors as physical deterioration and obsolescence.

5. *Methods of computing periodic depreciation.* There are several alternative methods of computing depreciation, all of which meet the criteria of being systematic and rational. The four most common methods are straight-line and units-of-production and two accelerated methods, declining-balance and sum-of-the-years-digits. Management is free to choose any of these methods for financial reporting purposes. For tax purposes, depreciation is calculated under the ACRS. The tax reform act of 1986 made significant changes in the ACRS system.

6. *Other problems related to accounting for depreciation.* There are several other problems related to accounting for depreciation. Included are depreciation for partial years, revision of depreciation rates, and the effects of inflation.

Key Terms

Accelerated Cost Recovery System (ACRS)
Accelerated Depreciation
Amortization
Capital Expenditure
Declining-Balance Method
Depletion
Depreciable Cost
Intangible Assets

Mortgage
Natural Resources
Obsolescence
Revenue Expenditure
Sum-of-the-Years-Digits Method
Tangible Assets
Units-of-Production Method

Problems for Your Review

A. Acquisition Cost of Assets. During 1987 the C. Price Company purchased the following assets:

- January 15: Purchase of land and building in which to conduct business. The entire cost was $5,000,000, and was purchased for cash. The assets were appraised at the following individual values:

Land	$1,500,000
Buildings	4,500,000

- April 14: Store equipment with a list price of $10,000 is purchased on account. The terms are 2/10, n/30. Other costs incurred for cash are:

Shipping	$500
Insurance in transit	50
Installation	100
Repair for damage in transit	200

Required:

Make all the required journal entries. It is not necessary to make the December 31, 1987 depreciation entries for the plant's assets still on hand.

Solution

January 15	Land	1,250,000	
	Buildings	3,750,000	
	Cash		5,000,000
	To record purchase of land and buildings, allocated as follows:		

Account	Fair Market Value	%	Total Purchase Price	Allocation of Total Purchase Price
Land	$1,500,000	25% × $5,000,000 =		$1,250,000
Building	4,500,000	75% × $5,000,000 =		3,750,000
	$6,000,000			$5,000,000

April 14	Store Equipment	10,450	
	Repair	200	
	Accounts Payable		9,800
	Cash		850
	To record purchase of store equipment on account.		

Acquisition cost is determined as follows:

List price		$10,000
Less 2% discount		(200)
		$ 9,800
Add: Shipping	$500	
Insurance	50	
Installation	100	650
		$10,450

Cost to repair damage in transit is not capitalizable into the cost of the equipment.

B. Depreciation Methods. Commute Air, a small commuter airline, purchased an airplane for $6 million. The president of the company is trying to decide how to depreciate the plane. She asks you to calculate the annual depreciation for each of the next three years under each of the following methods:

1. Straight-line.
2. Units-of-production.
3. Double-declining-balance.
4. Sum-of-the-years-digits.

In each case the asset has a 10-year life, or a 110 millior -mile life. Miles flown are:

Year	Miles Flown
1	8,800,000
2	10,000,000
3	15,000,000

The plane has an estimated residual value of $500,000.

Solution

	Year 1	Year 2	Year 3
Straight-line^a	$ 550,000	$550,000	$550,000
Units-of-production^b	440,000	500,000	750,000
Double-declining-balance^c	1,200,000	960,000	768,000
Sum-of-the-years-digits^d	1,000,000	900,000	800,000

a $\dfrac{\$6,000,000 - \$500,000}{10 \text{ years}} = \$550,000$ per year

b $\dfrac{\$6,000,000 - \$500,000}{110,000,000 \text{ miles}} = \$.05$ per mile

c Year 1 $\$6,000,000 \times .20^* =$ $1,200,000
   Year 2 $(\$6,000,000 - \$1,200,000) \times .20 =$ 960,000
   Year 3 $(\$4,800,000 - \$960,000) \times .20 =$ 768,000

   *Straight-line rate = 10%; twice the straight-line rate = 20%. Salvage value is not considered until the last year.

d Year 1 $(\$6,000,000 - \$500,000) \times 10/55^\dagger =$ $1,000,000
   Year 2 $(\$6,000,000 - \$500,000) \times 9/55 =$ 900,000
   Year 3 $(\$6,000,000 - \$500,000) \times 8/55 =$ 800,000

$\dagger N \dfrac{(N+1)}{2} = 10 \dfrac{(11)}{2} = 55$

Questions

1. What are the similarities and differences between tangible and intangible assets? Give three examples of each.

2. Why must the cost of noncurrent, nonmonetary assets be allocated to future accounting periods?

What are some of the problems involved in this allocation process?

3. Smith Company purchased a computer for $500,000. Freight charges amounted to $750 and were paid by Smith. Smith also incurred costs of

$1,500 to have the old computer taken out and $2,500 to have the new one installed. Subsequently, the old computer was sold for $20,000. At what amount should Smith record the new computer?

4. In your own words, explain the meaning of capital expenditure. How does it differ from a revenue expenditure? From an accounting perspective, describe the consequences of recording a capital expenditure as a revenue expenditure.

5. If interest of $80,000 is capitalized as part of the acquisition cost of self-constructed assets, what effect does this have on current and future periods' income?

6. Explain the accountant's concept of depreciation. Why do accountants insist on depreciating a building whose fair market value is increasing?

7. Your best friend, who knows very little about accounting, made the following statement after purchasing a new car: "I just bought this car for $8,500 and as soon as I drove it off the lot it depreciated by one-third." How would you respond?

8. What is meant by each of the following terms, and how are they estimated?

   a. Residual or salvage value.
   b. Economic or useful life.
   c. Depreciable amount.

9. What are the main factors that cause each of the following items to give up their economic benefits?

   a. A minicomputer.
   b. A truck.
   c. A warehouse.
   d. A piece of heavy equipment.
   e. An airplane.

10. How is straight-line depreciation calculated? From a conceptual perspective, when is its use most appropriate?

11. What is the basic assumption behind units-of-production depreciation? From a conceptual perspective, when is its use most appropriate?

12. What is the basic assumption behind the accelerated depreciation methods? From a conceptual perspective, when are these methods most appropriate?

13. What is ACRS depreciation? How does it compare with depreciation methods used for financial reporting purposes? Why do you think that it is included in the Internal Revenue Code?

14. In examining the annual reports of the Flemming and José companies, you notice that the Flemming Company uses straight-line depreciation while the José Company uses double-declining balance. Both firms are in the same industry, are about the same size, and purchase similar assets. Isn't one firm's depreciation policy incorrect? Why or why not?

15. Why would a company change its original estimate of an asset's useful life? How is this change accounted for?

16. The Southern Iowa Utility Company is in the process of building a nuclear power plant. The cost of the plant is $25 million. Under current Iowa laws, the plant must be dismantled after 50 years. Southern Iowa estimates that it will cost $10 million to dismantle the plant. How should this $10 million be handled from an accounting perspective? What is the depreciable cost of the nuclear plant?

17. Many individuals argue that in a period of inflation, historical cost depreciation overstates earnings. What do they mean and how can this problem be overcome?

Exercises

1. Revenue versus Capital Expenditures. Identify each of the following items as a revenue or capital expenditure. If you cannot make a clear distinction, state why not.
   a. Immediately after the purchase of a new warehouse and before its use, it was painted at a cost of $50,000.
   b. Immediately after the purchase of a used delivery truck, new tires were purchased at a cost of $200.
   c. Purchased a wastepaper basket for the office at a cost of $7.
   d. Installed air conditioning in an office building that had been owned for several years. The cost of the air conditioning was $24,000.
   e. Purchased land for possible future use as a site for a new building. Paid a guard $200 per week to protect the site.
   f. Acme Freight Company decided to overhaul one of its trucks instead of purchasing a new one. Total overhaul cost is $3,500, including a new drive train.

2. Determining Acquisition Cost. For each of the following independent situations, determine the appropriate acquisition cost:

  a. Coral, Co. purchased a tract of land for $320,750 as a potential building site. In order to acquire the land, the firm paid a $15,000 commission to a real estate agent. Additional costs of $17,000 were incurred to clear the land.

  b. On August 15 the Nigerian Export Company purchased a tract of land for $675,000. Additional expenses incurred by the company were a $25,000 commission paid to a real estate agent, $75,000 clearing fees, and $60,000 in delinquent property taxes. This property was adjacent to the Nigerian Export Company's present warehouse, and two months later the company incurred expenses of $60,000 for paving and $3,500 for fencing in order to turn the land into a parking lot.

3. Determining Acquisition Cost. New office equipment was purchased by the Davenport Corporation. The equipment had a list price of $75,000. Terms of purchase were 2/10, n/30. State taxes are 6%. Davenport incurred the following additional costs in connection with the purchase:

Transportation	$360
Installation	480
Removal of old equipment	200
Testing of new equipment	500
Repair of damage incurred in transit	240

Determine the acquisition cost of the new equipment assuming that (1) payment is made within the discount period and (2) payment is not made within the discount period.

4. Lump-sum Purchase. On November 15 the Hutch Company acquired four pieces of machinery for a lump sum of $643,000. The company then paid $4,000 to have the machines installed. Hutch Company also paid $2,500 to determine the appraised value of the machinery. These appraised values were:

Machine 1	$ 200,000
Machine 2	300,000
Machine 3	400,000
Machine 4	100,000
Total	$1,000,000

Determine the acquisition cost of each machine.

5. Depreciation Concepts. You overheard the following conversation about depreciation among five of your friends:

  • Sumi—As generally used in accounting, depreciation applies to all items of property, plant, and equipment.

  • Helene—No, depreciation does not apply to land and is used to value operational assets.

  • Jay—You both are wrong. Depreciation records only the decline in value of nonmonetary assets other than land. Accountants do not record increases in value.

  • Michelle—No, depreciation is essentially an allocation process used to match revenues and expenses. And it does not apply to land.

  • Ernesto—You all are wrong. Depreciation has nothing to do with cost or value. It is used solely to generate cash for the firm.

Evaluate each of their comments.

6. Calculating Depreciation. The Brett Aviation Company at the beginning of the current year purchased a 12-passenger commuter plane for $3.5 million. The plane has an estimated salvage value of $500,000.

Required:

  a. If the airplane has a useful life of eight years and the firm uses straight-line depreciation, calculate the annual depreciation for the first four years of the asset's life.

  b. Now assume that the firm believes that the plane will fly 2 million miles and it has decided to use the units-of-production method of calculating depreciation. What is the depreciation for each of the first four years, assuming the plane flew the following miles:

Year 1	300,000
Year 2	250,000
Year 3	275,000
Year 4	240,000

7. Calculating Depreciation. Equipment with a useful life of five years was purchased by Hondo, Co. on January 2, 1987 for $29,000. Salvage value is estimated to be $2,000. Compute annual depreciation expense relating to this equipment for the next five years using the following methods:

a. Straight-line.

b. Double-declining-balance.

c. Sum-of-the-years-digits.

8. Analysis of Depreciation Calculations. Answer each of the following independent questions:

a. At the beginning of 1986 the Lombardi Company purchased a heavy-duty power generator for $240,000. The firm estimates that the generator will have a $30,000 salvage value at the end of its useful life. The firm uses sum-of-the-years depreciation, which was as follows for years 1986 and 1987:

Year	Annual Depreciation
1986	$56,000
1987	42,000

What would be depreciation for 1988, assuming that the straight-line basis was always used?

b. Jigs' Self-Service Storage bought a warehouse for $23 million. It estimates that this building will have a useful life of 35 years and a salvage value of $2 million. On the firm's December 31, 1987 financial statements, the warehouse's book value was $20.6 million. Assuming that the firm uses straight-line depreciation, when was the warehouse purchased?

c. On January 2, 1987 Smile Cosmetics bought a machine that liquifies certain chemicals. The firm estimates that the machine will have a useful life of 12 years and a salvage value of $1,800. On December 31, 1992 the machine has a book value of $22,300 based on straight-line depreciation. If the firm had used double-declining-balance depreciation rather than straight-line, what would be the depreciation expense for the years ended December 31, 1987 and December 31, 1988?

9. Partial-Year's Depreciation. On March 1, 1987 Radar Enterprises purchased a machine for $350,000. The machine has a useful life of eight years and a salvage value of $20,000. The policy of Radar Enterprises is to calculate depreciation expense from the beginning of the month the asset was purchased.

Calculate depreciation expense for 1987 and 1988 assuming that the firm uses (a) sum-of-the-years-digits depreciation and (b) double-declining-balance depreciation.

10. Comparing Depreciation for Accounting and Tax Purposes. On April of the current year the West Valley Company purchased for $7,000 a new light truck to use for delivery purposes. For financial reporting purposes, the asset was given a five-year life with a $500 residual value and will be depreciated using the straight-line method. The firm's policy is to take six months' depreciation in the year of purchase. For tax purposes the truck falls into the three-year life class.

Required:

a. Prepare a five-year schedule comparing annual depreciation expense for financial reporting purposes and for tax purposes. Use the ACRS table on page 476 for tax depreciation.

b. Explain the benefit the firm received, if any, from using ACRS depreciation for tax purposes.

11. Revision of Depreciation Estimates. At the beginning of 1987 the Porter-Fitch Company purchased a piece of heavy equipment for $600,000. The firm estimates that the asset will have a $60,000 residual value at the end of its 15-year life. The firm uses straight-line depreciation. At the beginning of 1990 the firm decides the machine has a remaining life of only 10 years. Calculate depreciation for 1990, given the new estimate of the asset's economic life.

12. Inflation and Depreciation. Becky Aguilar decided to start her own word processing business. She invested $70,000 and immediately purchased a sophisticated minicomputer and word processing software for $50,000. She kept the remaining $20,000 in the business. The equipment and software have a useful life of 10 years, no salvage value, and are depreciated on the straight-line basis. Becky feels that it is necessary to keep at least $20,000 in the business and as a result feels that she can withdraw cash equal to her reported net income each year.

Required:

a. At the end of 10 years, how much cash will remain in the business? Ignore taxes.

b. If the cost of the computer equipment needed by Becky increases about three times over the 10-year period, will she have enough cash available in the business to purchase the new equipment? Why or why not?

c. Is there any way she could ensure herself of having enough cash to replace her equipment at the end of 10 years?

Problem Set A

12A–1. Acquisition of Nonmonetary Assets. The following transactions are made during 1987 by Dawson Enterprises, a manufacturer of novelty tee-shirts:

a. A tract of land was acquired for $250,000. In addition, commissions of $25,000 were paid to two real estate agents and a special assessment for late taxes of $5,000 was also incurred. The taxes and fees were paid in cash. A 15% down payment was made and a 20-year mortgage was used to finance the project.

b. A small building and tract of land were purchased for a lump sum of $635,000 cash. The property was appraised for tax purposes near the end of 1986 as follows: building, $322,000; land, $378,000. The building has an estimated useful life of 20 years and a salvage value of $25,000. The company will be using double-declining-balance depreciation and takes a full year's depreciation in the year of purchase.

c. Computerized files were purchased for a total cost of $100,000. Terms of purchase were 1/10, n/30. State sales taxes were 6%. In addition, the following costs were incurred in connection with the purchase:

Transportation	$500
Installation	300
Removal of old files	100

There is no salvage value and the estimated life is ten years. A full year's depreciation on the straight-line method is taken.

Required:

a. Prepare the necessary journal entries to record the above acquisitions.

b. Make the required adjusting entries for depreciation expense for 1987. Make a separate entry for each depreciable asset.

12A–2. Calculating Depreciation. Washington, Co. purchased an automated conveyer belt on April 1, 1987 at a cost of $175,000. The machine had an estimated useful life of 10 years and a $10,000 salvage value. Washington estimates that the machine will be able to handle 3.3 million units before it must be scrapped. Actual output in the first three years was: year 1, 900,000 units; year 2, 750,000 units; and year 3, 600,000 units.

Required:

a. Determine the annual depreciation expense and book value of the conveyer belt under each of the following methods at the end of the first three years of the asset's life. Assume that the firm takes a full year's depreciation in the year of purchase.

1. Straight-line.
2. Units-of-production.
3. Sum-of-the-years-digits.
4. Double-declining-balance.

b. Repeat requirement (a) for years 1 and 2, assuming that the firm calculates depreciation from the date of the purchase.

12A–3. Depreciation Calculations and Adjusting Entries. CompuStores sells personal computers, video games, and software. You have obtained the following data regarding their depreciable assets:

	Building	Store Furniture and Fixtures	Office Equipment	Delivery Equipment
Date acquired	6/1/84	6/9/84	1/2/85	8/14/86
Cost	$450,000	$65,000	$12,000	$16,400
Salvage value	25,000	2,000	2,000	1,400
Useful life	40 years	6 years	5 years	4 years
Method of depreciation	Straight-line	Sum-of-the-years-digits	Double-declining	Sum-of-the-years-digits

Depreciable assets purchased at the beginning of the year are depreciated for the entire year in the year of purchase. Assets purchased at other times during the year are depreciated for only six months in the year of purchase.

Required:

a. For each asset group, determine the balance in the accumulated depreciation account as of 1/1/87.

b. Make the adjusting entries to record depreciation expense for the year ended December 31, 1987. Make a separate entry for each asset group.

12A–4. Revision of Depreciation Rates. Webber Company owns a machine that was purchased at a cost of $95,000. It is being depreciated on a straight-line basis with a 16-year estimated life and a salvage value of $7,200. At the end of 1987 the equipment was one-fourth depreciated. In January 1988 new information was gathered that made Webber Company change the total estimated useful life from 16 to 20 years with no residual value.

Required:

a. Compute the amount of depreciation expense that should be recorded in 1987 and the book value of the equipment on December 31, 1987.

b. Compute the amount of depreciation expense for 1988. Show all computations and round to the nearest dollar if necessary.

12A–5. Selecting Depreciation Methods. The president of a high-tech company has asked you to help her choose a depreciation method for financial reporting and for tax purposes. The firm has purchased a depreciable asset for $120,000. The asset has no salvage value and an estimated useful life of eight years. She is primarily interested in the allocation of the expense over the asset's eight-year life. She asks you the following questions:

a. I know that double-declining-balance depreciation will give me the highest depreciation expense in the asset's first years. At what point in the asset's life does sum-of-the-years-digits depreciation exceed double-declining-balance?

b. I know that straight-line depreciation results in an even depreciation each year. However, at what point does straight-line exceed both sum-of-the-years-digits and double-declining-balance depreciation?

c. Explain ACRS depreciation to me. I understand that the asset will fall into the five-year class life. Using the table on page 476, what would the depreciation be for tax purposes for each of the next five years?

d. Assuming that I desire to smooth earnings for financial reporting and to increase cash flows by decreasing tax payments, which method or methods should I choose? Why?

Required:

Answer the president's questions.

12A–6. Analyzing Depreciation Calculations. Answer each of the following independent questions:

a. On January 2, 1984 Pagano, Co. purchased a specialized drilling machine with an estimated useful life of 10 years and a salvage value of $2,500. For the year ended December 31, 1986 depreciation expense for this machine totaled $24,000. Determine the acquisition cost of the machine, assuming the firm uses straight-line depreciation.

b. On January 2, 1983 the Eddows Company purchased a machine with an estimated useful life of five years and a salvage value of $2,000. Depreciation expense for 1984 was $18,000. The company uses the double-declining-balance method of depreciation for financial reporting. Determine the acquisition cost of the machine on January 2, 1983.

c. On January 2, 1985 Heller Manufacturing Products bought a lathe that cost $140,000. The firm estimates that the lathe will have a useful life of six years. The company uses straight-line depreciation. At December 31, 1986 the lathe had a book value of $95,000. What was the asset's estimated salvage value?

12A–7. Purchase and Depreciation of Equipment. During your examination of the records of the Current Deterrent Company, you obtained the following information concerning the purchase of a new piece of equipment called an Exionic:

Acquisition date	4/1/86
Purchase price	$154,000
Terms	2/10, n/30
Installation costs	$7,500
Freight costs	$ 500
Repairs required for damage while in transit	$ 200
Normal repairs and maintenance, 12/1/86	$1,000
Estimated useful life	10 years
Salvage value	$ 0
Depreciation method	Straight-line

Required:

a. Determine the acquisition cost of the equipment.

b. Assuming that depreciation is calculated from the month of purchase, determine the depreciation expense for 1986 and 1987.

c. Now assume that on January 2, 1988 the firm performs a complete rebuilding of the machine for $40,000. Because of this, the firm believes that the asset's life will be extended an additional 10 years from the beginning of 1988. Determine the correct amount of depreciation expense for 1988.

Problem Set B

12B–1. Acquisition of Nonmonetary Assets. As the accountant for the H. G. Company, you found the following transactions relating to the acquisition of nonmonetary assets were made during 1986:

a. A building and tract of land were purchased for $1 million. In addition to the purchase price, commissions of $60,000 were paid in cash to the real estate broker. No other acquisition costs were incurred. A 20% down payment was made and a 30-year mortgage was used to finance the acquisition. The latest property tax records appraised the land and building at $900,000 and $300,000, respectively. The building has an estimated useful life of 30 years and a salvage value of $45,000. The company uses sum-of-the-years-digits depreciation, and a full year's depreciation is taken in 1986.

b. A rotary power inhibitor was acquired on July 1 for $50,000. A 20% down payment was made and a 5-year, 12% note was signed for the balance. Interest is due and payable each year. The equipment is expected to produce 5 million units during its useful life. During 1986, 200,000 units were actually produced.

c. A new mainframe computer was acquired at a cost of $500,000. In order to install the computer, the floor in the room in which the computer was to be housed had to be strengthened at a cost of $50,000. In addition, insurance costs during shipping amounted to $500. Shipping costs were paid by the seller. The computer was purchased for cash. At the time of purchase, various software programs were acquired at a cost of $25,000. The computer has an estimated life of 10 years and is depreciated on the double-declining-balance method. The software has an estimated life of five years and is depreciated on the straight-line method. In both cases, a full year's depreciation is taken in the current year.

Required:

 a. Prepare the necessary journal entries to record the above acquisitions.

 b. Make the required adjusting entries for depreciation and interest expense for 1986. Assume that accrued interest on the mortgage in transaction amounts to $8,000. You must calculate the interest on the note payable in Item (b).

12B–2. Calculating Depreciation. Jefferson, Co. owns several radio stations and recently acquired some new broadcasting equipment for $550,000. The equipment has a useful life of eight years and a salvage value of $50,000. Jefferson estimates that the equipment will work 5 million hours over its useful life. Actual hours used during the first two years were: year 1, 800,000 hours; year 2, 600,000 hours.

Required:

Determine the annual depreciation expense and book value of the equipment under each of the following methods at the end of the first two years of the asset's life. Assume that the firm takes a full year's depreciation in the year of purchase.

 a. Straight-line.

 b. Units-of-production.

 c. Sum-of-the-years-digits.

 d. Double-declining-balance.

12B–3. Depreciation Calculations and Adjusting Entries. Cooper and Sons Ltd. is an automobile parts importer. You have obtained the following data relative to their depreciable assets:

	Building	Furniture	Equipment	Trucks
Date acquired	7/1/81	1/2/84	7/6/85	10/3/86
Cost	$250,000	$16,500	$8,000	$16,000
Salvage value	$10,000	$0	$800	$1,000
Useful life	30 years	10 years	8 years	5 years
Method of depreciation	Straight-line	Sum-of-the-years-digits	Double-declining	Sum-of-the years-digits

The policy of Cooper and Sons is to calculate depreciation expense from the beginning of the month the asset is purchased.

Required:

 a. For each asset group, determine the balance in the Accumulated Depreciation account as of January 1, 1987.

 b. Make the adjusting entries to record depreciation expense for the year ended December 31, 1987. Make a separate entry for each asset group.

12B–4. Revision of Depreciation Rates. Rick Monday's Sports Manufacturing Co. owns a special machine that makes baseballs. The machine was purchased at the beginning of 1986 for a price of $200,000. The machine is being depreciated on the straight-line basis. It has an estimated life of 15 years and a salvage value of $20,000. At the beginning of 1988, new information was presented that made the firm change the estimated life to 20 years instead of 15. Salvage value was also reduced from $20,000 to $5,000.

Required:

 a. Compute the amount of depreciation expense that should be recorded in 1987 and the book value of the machine on December 31, 1987.

 b. Compute the amount of depreciation expense for 1988. Show all computations and round to the nearest dollar, if necessary.

12B–5. Selecting Depreciation Methods. You are the controller of the J. C. Ray Company. The firm has just purchased a specialized piece of equipment for $300,000. The equipment has a salvage value of $12,000 and an estimated useful life of eight years. In order to choose the most beneficial depreciation method, you have been asked to determine the following data:

 a. At what point in the equipment's life does sum-of-the-years-digits depreciation exceed double-declining-balance depreciation?

 b. At what point in the equipment's life does straight-line exceed both sum-of-the-years-digits and double-declining-balance depreciation?

c. If the equipment falls into the five-year class life under ACRS depreciation (use the table on page 476), what would annual depreciation be for the next five years?

d. Assuming the firm desires to smooth earnings for financial reporting purposes and to increase cash flows by decreasing tax payments, which method or methods should the firm choose?

12B–6. Analyzing Depreciation Calculations. Answer each of the following independent questions:

a. On July 1, 1983 Kickson, Co. acquired equipment with an estimated useful life of eight years and a residual value of $5,000. On December 31, 1985 the Accumulated Depreciation account for this equipment amounted to $37,500 including the depreciation expense for 1985. If the firm only took six months' depreciation in 1983, determine the acquisition cost of the equipment. The firm uses straight-line depreciation.

b. On January 2, 1984 Pinky, Co. purchased a building with an estimated useful life of 20 years and a residual value of $20,000. Depreciation expense for the year ended December 31, 1986 was $16,200. The firm uses double-declining-balance depreciation. Determine the acquisition cost of the building.

c. On January 2, 1985 the Bingo Company acquired a machine with a cost of $300,000. The firm estimated that the machine would have an estimated life of seven years. The policy of Bingo is to use straight-line depreciation. On December 31, 1987 the book value of the machine was $180,000. Determine the residual value of the machine.

12B–7. Purchase and Depreciation of Machinery. Diversionics recently purchased a new machine called an Ionofire to produce its main product. You obtained the following information relative to the purchase:

Acquisition date	10/1/87
Purchase price	$18,000
Terms	2/10, n/30
Installation costs	$3,000
Freight costs	$1,000
Repairs required for damage while in transit	$500
Normal repairs and maintenance, 12/31/87	$600
Estimated useful life	8 years
Salvage value	$1,000
Depreciation method	Double-declining-balance

The machine was purchased by making a 40% down payment on the net price including freight and installation charges. The remaining 60% was financed through a five-year, 12% term loan. Interest is due every October 1. The firm's year-end is December 31.

Required:

a. Determine the acquisition cost of the machinery. Make the journal entry to record the purchase.

b. Assuming that depreciation is calculated from the month of purchase, make the entry to record the depreciation expense for 1987 and 1988.

c. Make the entry to record the accrued interest on December 31, 1987.

Using the Computer

At the beginning of the current year, the Macmillan Company purchased three depreciable assets. Information pertaining to these assets follows:

	Asset A	Asset B	Asset C
Cost	$10,000	$25,000	$55,000
Depreciation data for financial reporting purposes:			
Method	SL	DDB	SYD
Residual value	0	0	0
Life	5 yrs.	10 yrs.	10 yrs.
ACRS depreciation for tax purposes:			
Class life	3 yrs.	5 yrs.	5 yrs.

Other Data:

For financial reporting purposes, a full year's depreciation is taken in the year of purchase.

The controller asks you to develop an electronic spreadsheet program that calculates for each asset the annual depreciation expense for both financial reporting purposes and tax purposes. She suggests that you develop a table like the following:

YEARLY DEPRECIATION

	Financial Reporting				Tax Purposes			
Year	Asset A	Asset B	Asset C	Total	Asset A	Asset B	Asset C	Total
1								
2								
3								
.								
.								
.								
10								
Totals								

Understanding Financial Statements

The Pacific Lighting Corporation is the parent company of the Southern California Gas Co., which is a major utility in Southern California. According to its 1982 annual report, the company reported profits of over $128 million. In presenting data relating to the effects of inflation on its company, the management of Pacific Lighting noted that the historical cost depreciation amounted to $87 million during 1982. They went on to disclose that depreciation adjusted for general price level changes (i.e., inflation) would have been over $200 million.

Required:

   a. If there are no other changes between historical cost net income and inflation-adjusted net income, what would have been the reported profit of Pacific Lighting Corporation for 1982?
   b. Because the utility industry is very capital-intensive (that is, the major portion of the company's assets is tied up in plant and equipment), how do these inflation-adjusted depreciation and net income figures influence your thoughts about the firm's reported net income in a period of inflation?
   c. During 1982 Pacific Lighting declared dividends totaling over $87 million. What do you think about the amount of the dividends, given your previous analysis? What can you say about the ability of Pacific Lighting to replace its utility plants?

Financial Decision Case

The Oldham Corporation is in the paper products industry. This industry is very capital-intensive, and it has been using the standard industry policy to calculate depreciation on the straight-line basis. The company is contemplating the purchase of a large milling machine that will cost $3 million. The machine will probably have a useful life of 10 years, at which time the machine's salvage value will be negligible. However, the machine is most productive in its first five years. After that, increasing repairs and maintenance requirements will increase the machine's down-time and decrease its efficiency. Prior experience indicates that repairs and maintenance expense will be $40,000 in the first year and will increase at a rate of 10% per year.

Required:

The president is contemplating the use of different depreciation methods and asks you, his financial adviser, the following questions:

   a. I have read in a business magazine that for this type of asset an accelerated depreciation method such as double-declining-balance is conceptually the most appropriate method. Why is that so? If you disagree, please let me know why.
   b. Most firms in the industry use straight-line depreciation. Prepare a comparative schedule for me showing the annual expense related to this machine if (1) straight-line or (2) dou-

ble-declining-balance depreciation is used. Include both depreciation and repairs and maintenance expense in your schedule. (Round off to whole dollars where appropriate.)

c. I am concerned that if I use double-declining-balance depreciation, the earnings of the company, especially in the early years, will not look good in comparison with firms using straight-line depreciation. Because I am interested in selling the company in the near future, how will a potential buyer view our earnings, in comparison with those of other companies in the industry?

d. Our present machine is fully depreciated, and although not as productive as the new one would be, it is still working. I understand there would be some tax benefits to buying the new machine. Explain to me how depreciation is calculated for tax purposes and what the potential tax benefits are. (Assume the equipment falls into a five-year-life class.)

Property, Plant, and Equipment (Continued), Natural Resources, and Intangible Assets

13

LEARNING OBJECTIVES

After reading this chapter you should be able to:
1. Account for subsequent expenditures related to plant and equipment.
2. Account for the disposal of plant assets.
3. Explain the management control systems for plant assets.
4. Explain accounting concepts related to natural resources and depletion.
5. Describe the accounting concepts related to intangible assets and the amortization of these assets.

This chapter continues our discussion of the accounting issues related to property, plant, and equipment. Specifically, we concentrate on accounting for subsequent expenditures such as repairs, maintenance, and improvements; accounting for the disposal of property, plant, and equipment; and management control over plant assets. In addition, the chapter introduces you to the accounting concepts for natural resources and intangible assets.

Accounting for Subsequent Expenditures

Subsequent expenditures made on property, plant, and equipment can be in the form of either capital or revenue expenditures. As we noted in Chapter 12, the distinction between the two is often hazy and depends on the accounting policies developed by management. However, the distinction is important because it affects the determination of current and future periods' income.

Revenue Expenditures

Revenue expenditures are expenditures whose benefits are used up or consumed in the period of the expenditure. In terms of plant and equipment, revenue expenditures usually are called repairs and maintenance. Technically, a repair or maintenance is an expenditure that maintains the asset's expected level of service or output and neither extends its useful life nor increases the quantity or quality of its output. These expenditures are expensed in the current period by debiting the expense account Repairs and Maintenance or a similar account.

Capital Expenditures Subsequent to Purchase

Capital expenditures are those that benefit several accounting periods. In terms of plant and equipment, capital expenditures made in periods subsequent to an asset's acquisition are considered additions, betterments, or extraordinary repairs. **Additions** are enlargements, such as the addition of a new wing to an existing plant. **Betterments** are improvements to existing assets, such as the installation of a computer-controlled, temperature-monitoring system in a department store. **Extraordinary repairs** are a major reconditioning or overhaul of existing assets, such as a major overhaul or the installation of a new engine. Regardless of how these expenditures are described, they either extend the asset's useful life or increase the quantity or quality of its output.

Accounting for these expenditures is accomplished by debiting the asset's Accumulated Depreciation account, or in the case of an addition, debiting the Asset account itself. To illustrate the accounting for an extraordinary repair, assume a firm purchases a machine on January 2, 1982 for $40,000. The machine has a 10-year life, has no salvage value, and is depreciated on the straight-line basis. At the beginning of the seventh year of the machine's life, in 1988, a major overhaul costing $6,000 is undertaken. Because management feels that this overhaul will extend the machine's useful life 4 years beyond its original estimate of 10 years, this expenditure is considered an extraordinary repair.

At the time just prior to the extraordinary repair, the machine's book value is $16,000 ($40,000 − $24,000), which is illustrated in the following T accounts:

Machinery		Accumulated Depreciation—Machinery	
1/2/82 40,000			12/31/82 4,000
			12/31/83 4,000
			12/31/84 4,000
			12/31/85 4,000
			12/31/86 4,000
			12/31/87 4,000
			24,000

The extraordinary repair is recorded by debiting Accumulated Depreciation by $6,000, thus increasing the asset's book value to $22,000 ($16,000 + $6,000). The appropriate entry is:

Accumulated Depreciation	6,000	
Cash		6,000
To record extraordinary repair of $6,000.		

Because the asset's life has been extended four years, its new remaining life at the beginning of year 7 is now eight years (four years remaining on old life, plus four additional years). As a result, depreciation in year 7 and there-after is $2,750, or $22,000 ÷ 8 years. At the end of the machine's new remaining life, the credit balance in the Accumulated Depreciation account will be $40,000, which gives the asset a zero book value. However, the total credits to the Accumulated Depreciation account and the corresponding total debits to the Depreciation Expense account equal $46,000. This $46,000 figure represents the depreciation on the machinery, which is equal to the total of the machine's original acquisition cost of $40,000 plus the extraordinary repair of $6,000. These points are illustrated in the T accounts presented next:

Machinery

1/2/82 40,000	

Accumulated Depreciation—Machinery

1/2/88 6,000	12/31/82 4,000
	12/31/83 4,000
	12/31/84 4,000
	12/31/85 4,000
	12/31/86 4,000
	12/31/87 4,000
	12/31/88 2,750
	12/31/89 2,750
	12/31/90 2,750
	12/31/91 2,750
	12/31/92 2,750
	12/31/93 2,750
	12/31/94 2,750
	12/31/95 2,750
6,000	46,000
	12/31/95
	Bal. 40,000

Disposal of Property, Plant, or Equipment

Disposals of plant assets can occur through a retirement of discarded assets, sales, or trade-ins. No matter how the disposal is accomplished, the accounting procedures are quite similar. Depreciation must be recorded up to the date of disposal and, where appropriate, a gain or loss must be recorded on the disposal.

Retirement of Discarded Plant Assets

At some point, any long-term asset becomes obsolete or worn out and must be discarded. If the asset cannot be sold or scrapped for some value, the entry to record the disposal is straightforward. To illustrate, asume that a fully depreciated piece of equipment that originally cost $60,000 with no salvage value is discarded. Because the asset is fully depreciated and no cash is received, there is no gain or loss and the entry is:

Accumulated Depreciation	60,000	
Equipment		60,000
To record the retirement of fully		
depreciated equipment.		

If the asset is not fully depreciated or is fully depreciated but has a salvage value, and the firm cannot sell or scrap the asset, a loss will occur when it is discarded. For example, assume that the equipment in the previous example was discarded when its book value was $4,000. In that case a $4,000 loss is recorded as follows:

Accumulated Depreciation	56,000	
Loss on Disposal of Asset	4,000	
Equipment		60,000
To record loss on retirement of		
equipment with no salvage		
value.		

Sale of Plant Assets

In many cases plant assets are sold rather than disposed of for no value in return. An asset can be sold during its useful life when it has a positive book value or at the end of its life when it is fully depreciated. In either situation, a gain or loss will usually result. A gain occurs if the cash or other assets received (referred to as consideration) are greater than the asset's book value at the time of sale. Conversely, a loss occurs if the consideration received is less than the asset's book value at the time of sale.

To illustrate, assume that a delivery truck with a historical cost of $35,000 and accumulated depreciation to date of $30,000 (book value of $5,000) is sold for cash—in Case 1 for $7,000 and in Case 2 for $4,000.

Case 1: Sale Price $7,000

Cash	7,000	
Accumulated Depreciation	30,000	
Delivery Truck		35,000
Gain on Disposal of Asset		2,000
To record $2,000 gain on disposal of asset:		

Cash received	$7,000
Book value of delivery truck	5,000
Gain	$2,000

Case 2: Sale Price $4,000

Cash	4,000	
Accumulated Depreciation	30,000	
Loss on Disposal of Asset	1,000	
Delivery Truck		35,000
To record a $1,000 loss on disposal of asset:		

Cash received	$4,000
Book value of delivery truck	5,000
Loss	($1,000)

As shown in these journal entries, both the asset and its related Accumulated Depreciation account are removed from the books at their full amounts. Furthermore, these examples assumed that depreciation had been recorded up to the date of the disposal of the delivery truck. However, in most cases, assets are sold or otherwise disposed of at various dates throughout the year. If depreciation normally is recorded at a date (quarter or year-end) other than the sale date, an entry is required to record the depreciation expense from the date of the previous depreciation entry to the date of the sale.

For example, assume a piece of machinery is sold for $10,000 on April 1 of the current year. Depreciation has been recorded only through December 31 of the previous year, and as of that date the balances in the relevant accounts are as follows:

Machinery	$60,000
Accumulated Depreciation	48,000

Depreciation is based on the straight-line method with a five-year life and no residual value. As a result, yearly depreciation is $12,000 ($60,000 ÷ 5 years).

In order to record the sale of this asset, the following two entries must be made:

April 1	Depreciation Expense	3,000	
	Accumulated Depreciation		3,000
	To record depreciation expense for the period January 1 to April 1. $12,000 × 3/12 = $3,000.		
	Cash	10,000	
	Accumulated Depreciation	51,000	
	Gain on Disposal of Asset		1,000
	Equipment		60,000
	To record gain of $1,000 on disposal of machinery, calculated as follows:		

Cash		$10,000
Book Value of Machinery		
Cost	$60,000	
Accumulated depreciation to December 31	(48,000)	
Depreciation expense in current year	(3,000)	
Book Value as of April 1		9,000
Gain on disposal		$ 1,000

Trade-in of Plant Assets

Depreciable assets, such as automobiles, computers, and copy machines, are often traded in for new assets of a similar kind. In most cases, the trade-in allowance on the asset might be considerably different from its book value. If the trade-in allowance is higher than the asset's book value, a gain will be realized on the trade-in. Conversely, if the trade-in allowance is less than the asset's book value, a loss will be realized. However, care must be exercised when using a trade-in allowance to measure a gain or loss on this type of transaction. Dealers such as automobile companies often set an unrealistically high list price in order to offer the customer an inflated trade-in allowance. This is done in order to make the transaction appear more attractive to the buyer.

The accounting procedures that govern trade-ins are quite complex. However, for our purposes they can be stated as follows:

1. Realized gains on the trade-in of assets for similar assets are not usually recognized as accounting gains. The cost basis of the new asset is the book value of the old, plus the additional cash or other consideration paid.
2. Realized losses on the trade-in of similar assets are always recognized.[1]

Both of these situations will be described next.

Gain Realized But Not Recognized

To illustrate the accounting procedures when a realized gain on a trade-in occurs, assume that the Jackson Company trades in a delivery truck for a new one. At the time of the trade-in, the old delivery truck has a historical cost

[1]American Institute of Certified Public Accountants, Accounting Principles Board, Opinion No. 2a, *Accounting for Nonmonetary Transactions* (New York: AICPA, 1973), par. 22.

of $40,000 and accumulated depreciation to date of $30,000 (book value equals $10,000). The new truck has a list price of $65,000, and the dealer gives the Jackson Company a trade-in allowance of $14,000 on the old truck, which is assumed to be equal to its fair market value at that time. Thus, a cash payment of $51,000 ($65,000 − $14,000) is made for the difference. Because the asset was traded in for a similar one, the realized gain of $4,000 (trade-in allowance of $14,000 less book value of $10,000) is not recognized in the accounting records, and the cost basis of the new truck is $61,000, computed as follows:

Book value of old truck	$10,000
Cash paid	51,000
Cost basis of new truck	$61,000

The entry to record this trade-in is

Delivery Truck, New	61,000	
Accumulated Depreciation	30,000	
Delivery Truck, Old		40,000
Cash		51,000
To record trade-in of old delivery truck and purchase of new delivery truck.		

At first it may seem strange that a realized gain is not recognized in the accounting records. The Accounting Principles Board (APB) felt that revenue should not be recognized merely because one productive asset is exchanged or substituted for a similar one. According to the APB, revenue flows from the production and sale of the goods and services are made possible by the new asset, not from the exchange of one asset for another.[2] In effect, the realized gain of $4,000 is just postponed. It is ultimately realized through lower depreciation charges in future years because the asset is recorded at $61,000, rather than at its list price of $65,000. Furthermore, because the new asset has a lower book value than if the realized gain of $4,000 had been recognized, a larger gain or a smaller loss will be recognized if and when it is finally disposed of other than by another trade-in.

Loss Realized and Recognized

Because of the conservatism concept in accounting, any realized loss on a trade-in must be recognized in the accounting records. In this sense, conservatism means that the accountant anticipates all losses but not gains. For example, assume the same facts as in the previous example, but now the dealer offers a trade-in allowance of only $8,000, which is now assumed to be equal to the asset's fair market value. As a result, a loss of $2,000 ($10,000 book value less $8,000 trade-in allowance) is both realized and recognized. Because the trade-in allowance is only $8,000, a cash payment of $57,000 also must be made by the Jackson Company. Finally, the new asset is recorded at the list price of $65,000. The appropriate entry is:

[2]Ibid., par. 16.

Delivery Truck, New	65,000	
Accumulated Depreciation	30,000	
Loss on Disposal	2,000	
Delivery Truck, Old		40,000
Cash		57,000

To record $2,000 loss on trade-in
and purchase of new delivery truck.

Income Tax Rules for Trade-ins. Income tax rules for trade-ins do not completely correspond to the accounting rules that we just analyzed. Under current Internal Revenue Code regulations, neither gains nor losses are recognized on exchanges for similar productive assets if a strict exchange is made and no cash is involved. Whether cash is involved or not, a loss is not recognized for tax purposes. This means that for tax purposes, the $2,000 loss in the previous example is not recognized. As the following journal entry illustrates, for tax purposes the new asset is recorded at $67,000, or its list price of $65,000 plus the $2,000 loss not recognized.

Delivery Truck, New	67,000	
Accumulated Depreciation	30,000	
Delivery Truck, Old		40,000
Cash		57,000

To record trade-in of delivery
truck on tax basis.

Interestingly, this means that for tax purposes the asset has a cost of $67,000, but for financial reporting purposes the asset's cost is $65,000. Consequently, future years' depreciation and any gain or loss on disposal will differ for both tax and financial reporting purposes.

Management Control for Plant and Equipment

Management must maintain proper internal control over plant and equipment, which includes ensuring that proper authorization is obtained for purchases of depreciable assets; that once purchased, they are properly identified, recorded, maintained, and depreciated; and that the proper authorizations and entries are received and made when management disposes of assets. For example, if a plant manager is contemplating the purchase of a new delivery truck, he or she must include the proposed purchase in a capital budgeting plan. If the plan is approved, the final purchase of the delivery truck must be approved as to the vendor and method of payment. Once the firm takes delivery of the vehicle, it must be properly identified with a company number, and records must be maintained to ensure that proper licenses are obtained, depreciation is taken, and the vehicle is maintained at proper intervals.

Failure to maintain these management controls can lead to unauthorized purchases of assets, or purchase of assets with company funds for personal use. In addition, failure to maintain proper records might result in the misstatement of the asset accounts, the accumulated depreciation accounts, and the depreciation expense accounts. Errors in these accounts will affect periodic income and result in a mismatching of income and expense.

In order to maintain proper control in this area, the accounting system is designed to use subsidiary ledger accounts in conjunction with the controlling accounts. For example, the general ledger will contain a separate asset account and related accumulated depreciation accounts for each major asset account. To illustrate, a restaurant may have five controlling accounts for (1) land, (2) buildings, (3) cooking equipment, (4) restaurant furniture and fixtures, and (5) delivery equipment. For each of these major groups a controlling asset account, accumulated depreciation account, and depreciation expense account is maintained. Of course, the specific number and type of controlling accounts depend on the nature and size of the particular business.

In conjunction with each controlling account, subsidiary ledger accounts are maintained. This subsidiary ledger maintains information related to each particular unit of the assets found in the controlling account. In the restaurant example, separate subsidiary ledgers should be maintained for the two delivery trucks owned by the firm. Whether maintained on a computer or a manual system, this ledger should contain the following data about the asset: name, identification number, date of purchase, acquisition cost, salvage value (if any), useful life, depreciation method for financial reporting purposes, insurance coverage, maintenance schedule, yearly depreciation, disposal records, and so forth.

Each time entries are posted to the controlling accounts, they also must be posted to the appropriate subsidiary ledger accounts. If all entries are properly posted, the total of all the amounts in the subsidiary ledgers will equal the balance in the controlling accounts. Further, periodic inspection should be made of all plant and equipment items and the data obtained from that inspection should be compared with that in the subsidiary ledger. These procedures will help ensure that management's policies and guidelines are being followed.

Natural Resources

Natural resources are physical substances that when extracted from the ground are converted into inventory and when sold produce revenues for the firm. Natural resources include oil, natural gas, coal, iron, uranium, and timber. These assets are often referred to as wasting assets, because once they are removed from the ground or physically consumed, they cannot be replaced.

Natural resources give up their benefits as the resources are removed. This process is called **depletion** and essentially follows the same process as units-of-production depreciation. That is, in order to determine the cost per unit of output, the capitalized cost of the natural resources is divided by the estimated output. This per-unit cost is then charged to depletion expense as the resources are removed.

To show how depletion is calculated, assume that the JDD Company pays $18 million for land on which to drill oil. Other capitalized costs relating to exploration and development are $14 million, and so the total cost is $32 million. The company estimates that there will be a $2 million residual value at the end of the project, and so the total depletable cost is $30 million. Geologists estimate that the oil field will produce 15 million barrels of oil over the project's life. The depletion charge is $2 per barrel, calculated as shown at the top of the next page.

$$\frac{\text{Accumulated cost} - \text{Residual value}}{\text{Estimated barrels of oil to be produced}}$$

$$\frac{\$32,000,000 - \$2,000,000}{15,000,000 \text{ barrels}} = \$2.00 \text{ per barrel}$$

Assuming that 4.5 million barrels were produced in the current year, the depletion charge is $9 million (4,500,000 × $2), and the required journal entry is:

Depletion Expense	9,000,000	
Oil Field		9,000,000
To record depletion expense of $9,000,000 based on production of 4,500,000 barrels of oil during the period.		

By convention, the credit is made directly to the asset account rather than a contra-asset account. The depletion expense ultimately becomes part of the cost of the oil inventory that eventually will be sold. This allocation can be accomplished by making the following journal entry:

Inventory of Oil	9,000,000	
Depletion Expense		9,000,000
To transfer depletion expense to inventory of oil.		

Other production costs such as transportation and direct labor must be included as part of the inventoriable cost of the oil. To continue our example, assume that during the year these costs amounted to $7.5 million. They would be recorded as follows:

Inventory of Oil	7,500,000	
Cash, Accounts Payable, etc.		7,500,000
To record production costs of $7,500,000.		

After these entries, and assuming that no sales have yet taken place, the relevant section of JDD's balance sheet would be as follows:

JDD Company
Partial Balance Sheet

Current assets:	
Inventory of oil	$16,500,000
Natural resources:	
Oil fields, net	23,000,000

The inventory of oil is recorded in the current assets section, and the book value of the oil fields is shown in the noncurrent section under natural resources. Finally, when the barrels of oil are sold, the sale and cost of sale are recorded in the usual manner.

Establishing A Depletion Basis—
Successful Efforts versus Full Cost

In recent years there has been considerable controversy related to determining the proper cost for an oil well. Once the firm obtains exploration rights, it will incur certain exploration costs. These exploration costs can be immense for companies such as ARCO and Exxon, and the way they are accounted for can have a significant effect on an oil company's financial statements.

Most large oil companies use what is called the **successful efforts method** of accounting. Under this method, only the exploration costs of successful finds are capitalized into the natural resource asset account. Exploration cost of unsuccessful activities are immediately written off to expense in the current period. Because of the immediate expensing of the costs associated with dry wells, many accountants consider the successful efforts method to be the more conservative method.

Some firms follow what is referred to as the **full cost method.** Under this method, all exploration costs are capitalized into the cost of the natural resource asset account. Thus the cost of producing oil wells includes the exploration cost of those wells in addition to the costs of the dry wells. Depletion is then based on this full cost. Because exploration costs of unsuccessful wells are capitalized instead of written off in the current period, the full cost method tends to improve earnings in early years. Although each method will produce considerably different periodic income figures, they are both acceptable under current accounting practices.

In 1977 the FASB issued Statement 19, which required all firms to use the successful efforts method. This Statement generated considerable controversy, and strong opposition arose from smaller oil companies, many of which were using the full cost method. These smaller oil companies felt that if they were forced to switch to successful efforts, their earning performance would decline and their ability to raise capital for further exploration would be hurt. Because of this controversy and the intervention of the Securities and Exchange Commission, the FASB suspended that Statement and, as noted, both methods currently are acceptable.

Intangible Assets

Intangible assets are noncurrent assets that have no physical properties. They generate revenues because they offer a firm value in future revenue production or exchange because of the right of ownership or use. However, there generally is a higher degree of uncertainty concerning the benefits generated from intangible assets than that concerning tangible assets. In addition, intangible assets are differentiated from nonphysical assets, such as accounts receivable or prepayments, because intangible assets are long-term in nature and contribute to the production or operating cycle of a business.

Intangible assets generally are divided into two categories: those that are specifically identifiable and those that are not. **Specifically identifiable intangible assets** are those intangibles whose costs can easily be identified as part of the cost of the asset and whose benefits generally have a determinable life. Examples include patents, trademarks, franchises, and leaseholds. Conversely, intangibles that are not specifically identifiable represent some right or benefit that has an indeterminate life and whose cost is inherent in a continuing business. The primary example of such an intangible is goodwill. Exhibit 13–1 contains a list of the most common intangible assets.

| | EXHIBIT 13–1
Common Intangible Assets | |
Type of Intangible Asset	Description	
Specifically Identifiable	
Patent	An exclusive right to use, manufacture, process, or sell a product granted by the U.S. Patent Office. Patents have a legal life of 17 years; however, their economic life may be shorter.
Copyright	The exclusive right of the creator or heirs to reproduce and/or sell an artistic or published work. Granted by the U.S. government for the period of the life of the creator plus 50 years.
Leaseholds	A contractual agreement between a lessor (owner of the property) and a lessee (user of the property) that gives the lessee the right to use the lessor's property for a specific period of time in exchange for cash payments.
Leasehold improvements	Improvements that are made by the lessee that at the end of the lease term revert to the ownership of the lessor.
Trademark and trade name	A symbol or name that allows the holder to use it to identify or name a specific product or service. A legal registration system allows for an indefinite number of 20-year renewals.
Organization cost	Costs incurred in the creation of a firm, including legal fees, registration fees, and fees to underwriters.
Franchise	An exclusive right to use a formula, design, technique, or territory.
Not Specifically Identifiable	
Goodwill	Present value of expected excess earnings of a business above average industry earnings. Recorded only when a business is purchased at a price above the market value of the individual net assets of the business.

Accounting Problems Related to Intangible Assets

The accounting treatment of intangible assets parallels the accounting treatment of tangible noncurrent assets. Thus it is necessary to (1) measure and capitalize their acquisition cost; (2) amortize their cost over the shorter of their legal life, if any, or their economic life (in no case can the amortization period exceed 40 years); and (3) account for any gain or loss on their disposition.

Determining Acquisition Cost

Intangible assets are originally recorded at cost. As with tangible assets, cost includes all the expenditures necessary to get the intangible asset ready for its intended use. Included in the acquisition cost are the purchase price and any legal fees. If an intangible asset such as a trademark or goodwill is acquired without a cost, it is not shown on the balance sheet. Subsequent valuation of intangibles is at net book value, that is, at cost less accumulated amortization to date.

Operating Expenses and Intangible Assets. Because intangible assets are characterized by a lack of physical qualities, it is difficult to determine their existence, the value of their future benefits, and the life of these benefits. As a consequence, it is difficult to separate expenditures that are essentially operating expenses from those that give rise to intangible assets. For example, advertising and promotion campaigns and training programs provide future benefits to the firm. If this were not the case, firms would not spend the millions of dollars on these programs that they do. However, it is extremely difficult to measure the amount and life of the benefits generated by these programs. As a result, expenditures for these and similar items are written off as an expense in the period incurred. When recurring expenditures are made for these items in approximate equal amounts, the effect on periodic income is not much different than if they were capitalized and then amortized over their estimated life.

Research and Development Costs. Research and development costs are expenditures incurred in discovering, planning, designing, and implementing a new product or process. Accounting for these costs has presented the accounting profession with significant problems. They clearly provide the firm with some future benefits. The billions of dollars spent by firms such as IBM result in new successful products but also in products that never reach the marketplace or are unsuccessful in the marketplace. Thus, it is difficult to measure the ultimate benefits that accrue from research and development expenditures that are made in 1982 but that may not result in a product until 1990. Furthermore, in today's highly competitive world economy, it is almost impossible to measure how long any of the benefits produced by research and development expenditures will last. The failure of IBM's PC Jr. is a good example of this. Because of these problems and the diversity of accounting practices that existed, the FASB now requires that all research and development costs be expensed in the period incurred.[3]

Amortization of Intangible Assets

For accounting purposes, intangible assets do not have an indefinite life, and so their cost must be systematically written off to expense over their useful life.[4] This generally is done by debiting the Amortization Expense account and crediting the Intangible Asset account directly. By convention, an accumulated amortization account is not used, although there is no reason it could not be.

Estimating the useful life of intangible assets is quite difficult. Some assets, such as patents, have legal lives, whereas others, such as trademarks, have indefinite lives. If a legal life exists, the intangible asset should be amortized over its useful economic life or legal life, whichever is shorter. The APB ruled that if an intangible asset has a legal life of over 40 years or has an indetermi-

---

[3]Financial Accounting Standards Board, Statement No. 2, *Accounting for Research and Development Costs* (Stamford, Conn.: FASB, October 1974), par. 12.

[4]In previous years some accountants argued that some intangibles had as indefinite life. This view was rejected by both the AICPA and the FASB.

nate economic life, the period of amortization should not exceed 40 years.[5] In practice, straight-line amortization is used, although any systematic, rational method can be used.[6]

Gains and Losses on Disposition

When intangible assets are sold or otherwise disposed of, a gain or a loss equal to the difference between the amount received for the asset, if any, and its book value is recorded. If there has been a substantial or permanent decline in the value of an intangible asset still on hand, the unamortized cost should be reduced or written off as an expense of the current period.

Accounting for Specific Intangible Assets

Exhibit 13–1 listed some of the more common intangible assets. The following section outlines the accounting for the more significant intangible assets.

Patents

A **patent** is an exclusive right to use, manufacture, process, or sell a product and is granted by the U.S. Patent Office. Patents can either be purchased from the inventor or holder or be generated internally. When a patent is purchased from the inventor, its capitalized cost includes its acquisition cost and other incidental costs, such as legal fees. The legal costs of successfully defending a patent are also capitalized as part of its cost.

If a patent results from successful research and development efforts, its cost is only the legal or other fees necessary to patent the invention, product, or process. This is because all the research and development costs expended to develop the patent, including those in the year the patent is obtained, must be written off to expense in the period incurred.

A patent has a legal life of 17 years. In many cases, however, its useful economic life is less than 17 years. As a result, patents should be amortized over their remaining legal life or economic life, whichever is shorter. For example, assume that a patent is purchased from its inventor for $240,000. At that time the patent has a remaining legal life of 10 years but has an estimated economic life of 8 years. In this case the patent should be amortized on a straight-line basis over 8 years, with the following journal entry each year:

Amortization Expense	30,000	
Patent		30,000
To amortize the patent at $30,000 per year ($240,000 ÷ 8 years).		

Copyrights

Copyrights are the exclusive right of the creator or his or her heirs to reproduce and/or sell an artistic or published work. The copyright is granted by the U.S. government for the life of the creator plus 50 years. The cost to the creator of obtaining a copyright from the government is the modest sum of $10. For this reason, the cost to the creator to obtain a copyright is usually charged to an expense account when incurred. But when a copyright is pur-

---

[5]American Institute of Certified Public Accountants, Accounting Principles Board, Opinion No. 17, *Intangible Assets* (New York: AICPA, 1970), par. 29.

[6]Under current Internal Revenue Code regulations, goodwill or other intangible assets that the IRS feels resemble goodwill cannot be amortized for tax purposes. Therefore, amortization of those intangibles does not reduce taxable income.

chased by someone other than the creator, its cost may be substantial and should be capitalized. The capitalized cost should then be amortized over its remaining economic life, which is usually substantially shorter than its original legal life.

Leaseholds and Leasehold Improvements

A **lease** is a contractual agreement between the lessor (the owner of the property) and the lessee (the user of the property) that gives the lessee the right to use the lessor's property for a specific period of time in exchange for stipulated cash payments. The rights contained in this agreement usually are called leaseholds.

Leases are classified into two types: operating leases and capital leases. Capital leases, which are complex financing arrangements, are briefly discussed in Chapter 18. **Operating leases** usually require regular monthly payments by the lessee, but the lessor retains control and ownership of the property. The property or equipment always reverts to the lessor at the end of the lease term. Renting office space on a monthly or yearly basis is an example of an operating lease. Leases of this type do not result in a leasehold. The lessee records the lease by debiting Rent or Lease Expense and crediting Cash. The leased property remains on the books of the lessor.

Some operating lease payments require the prepayment of the final month's rent. When this occurs, this payment is classified as a prepaid expense or other asset, and remains on the books until the lease is terminated. Some leases may also require a lump-sum rental payment that represents additional rent over the life of the lease. This is usually a significant amount in relation to the monthly payment and should be written off over the life of the lease.

Leasehold improvements are improvements made by the lessee to leased property. They consist of such items as air conditioning, partitioning, and elevators. These improvements are permanent in nature and become the property of the lessor when the leased property reverts to the lessor at the termination of the operating lease. These expenditures should be recorded in an asset account called Leasehold Improvements and amortized over the shorter of their useful life or the remaining term of the lease.

Franchises

A **franchise** is a right to use a formula, design, or technique or the right to conduct business in a certain territory. Franchises can be granted by either a business enterprise or a governmental unit. Many businesses, such as fast food restaurants and convenience markets, are operated as franchises. For example, the parent company of 7–Eleven Markets sells franchises to individual owner-operators. Cities and municipalities also often grant franchises, such as a taxi franchise that allows a company to operate in a specified territory for a designated period of time.

If the cost of a franchise is substantial, it should be capitalized and amortized over its useful life, not to exceed 40 years. If the cost is insignificant, the expenditure can be treated as an expense and immediately written off.

Goodwill

Goodwill has a very specific meaning in accounting. It represents the value today of the excess earnings of a particular enterprise. Excess earnings represent earnings above the normal earnings of an industry. That is, the firm is able to earn a rate of return on its net assets above the industry average.

These excess earnings are the result of a number of factors, including superior management, well-trained employees, good location, and manufacturing efficiencies. Unlike the other intangible assets we have discussed, goodwill is not specifically identifiable and is not separable from the firm. Thus, goodwill can only be recorded when purchased. The existence of internally generated goodwill is verified only when a firm is purchased by another party, and it is at that time that the goodwill, if any, is recorded.

To illustrate the concept of goodwill, assume a group of investors is contemplating the purchase of an electronic components manufacturing business. At the time of purchase, the fair market value of the firm's identifiable net assets (assets, excluding goodwill, minus liabilities) is $10 million. The normal rate of return on net assets in this industry is 10%. This rate of return is generally based on an industry average or similar figure. Further, the investors have been able to determine that the firm's average net income over each of the last 5 years is $1.4 million. In this case, excess earnings are $400,000, calculated as follows:

Fair market value of net identifiable assets	$10,000,000
Normal rate of return	.10
Normal earnings	$ 1,000,000
Average net income for each of the past five years	$ 1,400,000
Normal earnings (from above)	1,000,000
Excess earnings	$ 400,000

Estimating Goodwill. Once excess earnings are calculated, there are a number of alternative methods that are used to determine goodwill. The buyer and seller may reach a negotiated total for goodwill. For example, in our illustration the investors who are considering the purchase of the electronic components business know that the excess earnings of $400,000 will not last indefinitely, and they want to limit the amount paid for goodwill to only a few years of excess earnings. After negotiation, the buyers and seller agree that goodwill should be equal to 5 times excess earnings, or $2 million. Therefore, the total purchase price of the business is $12 million—$10 million for net identifiable assets and $2 million for goodwill.

Another method to estimate goodwill is to capitalize excess earnings; that is, to determine what dollar total of goodwill is giving rise to the excess earnings. For example, the parties could agree on a capitalization rate of 25%. This rate is divided into the excess earnings of $400,000 to obtain a goodwill figure of $1 million, as follows:

$$\frac{\$400,000}{.25} = \$1,600,000$$

Essentially, this is saying that there are $1.6 million of additional assets above the identifiable ones, and they are producing a 25% rate of return. Because a higher rate of return will produce a lower goodwill figure, a capitalization rate above the normal industry rate of return is used. This is so because excess earnings are considered more risky than normal earnings.

Conceptually, the best way to estimate goodwill is to determine the present value of the excess earnings. This means calculating in today's dollars the value of the excess earnings. In order to accomplish this, an estimate must be made of both the number of years the excess earnings will last and the appropriate discount rate. Discounting and present value are discussed in Appendix A. Regardless of how goodwill is estimated, the actual amount of goodwill in any purchase is negotiated by buyer and seller.

Recording Goodwill. Once the purchase price is agreed upon, it is first allocated to the identifiable net assets. Any remaining portion is considered goodwill and is recorded by a debit to the Goodwill account. Subsequently, goodwill is amortized over a period not exceeding 40 years. Again, although internally generated goodwill may be an important economic asset to a firm, it is not recorded until a business is sold.

Summary of Learning Objectives

1. *Accounting for subsequent expenditures.* Expenditures made on plant and equipment consist of either revenue expenditures or capital expenditures. Revenue expenditures are generally for repairs and maintenance that maintain the asset's expected level of service. They neither extend the asset's useful life nor increase the quantity or quality of its output. Capital expenditures after acquisition benefit several accounting periods and are additions, betterments, or extraordinary repairs.

2. *Disposal of plant assets.* Disposal of plant assets occurs through retirements, sales, or trade-ins. In most cases a firm will realize a gain or loss on disposal. The gain or loss is measured by the difference between the book value of the disposed asset and the consideration, if any, received for it. Accountants also recognize in the financial records the gains and losses on retirements or sales. However, when the plant asset is traded in for a similar one, a gain is not recognized, though a loss is always recognized. The following table summarizes these concepts:

Method of Disposal	Is the Gain/Loss to Be Recognized for Accounting Purposes?
Sale of asset for realized gain	Yes
Sale of asset for realized loss	Yes
Trade-in of asset for similar asset for realized gain	No
Trade-in of asset for similar asset for realized loss	Yes

3. *Management control for plant assets.* Management must maintain proper control over plant and equipment. This ensures that asset accounts and the related accumulated depreciation and depreciation expense accounts are properly recorded in the financial statements. This usually is accomplished by maintaining subsidiary ledger accounts in connection with controlling accounts.

4. *Accounting for natural resources.* Natural resources are physical substances that are extracted from the ground. They are often called wasting assets, and as such their cost must be allocated on a prorated basis over the units produced. This process is called depletion. The

depletable base of natural resources includes the acquisition cost of the site land, exploration costs, and development costs.

5. *Intangible assets.* Intangible assets have no physical properties. They generate revenue for the firm because they give it the right of ownership or use. Intangible assets include patents, trademarks, franchises, leaseholds, and goodwill. (See Exhibit 13–1.) Intangible assets have a definite life and must be amortized over the shorter of their legal life or economic life. In no case, however, can the amortization period exceed 40 years.

Key Terms

Additions	Lease
Betterments	Leasehold Improvements
Copyrights	Natural Resources
Depletion	Operating Leases
Extraordinary Repairs	Patents
Full Cost Method	Research and Development Costs
Franchises	Specifically Identifiable Intangible Assets
Intangible Assets	Successful Efforts Method

Problems for Your Review

A. Accounting for Plant and Equipment. The property, plant, and equipment section of the Ken and Bob Company's December 31, 1987 balance sheet contained the following items:

Property, plant, and equipment		
Land		$1,000,000
Radio studio	$5,000,000	
Less accumulated depreciation	250,000	4,750,000
Radio and broadcasting equipment	$ 600,000	
Less accumulated depreciation	120,000	480,000
Total property, plant, and equipment		$6,230,000

In addition, you gathered the following information:
1. All assets were acquired on January 2, 1986.
2. The firm depreciates all assets on a straight-line basis with no residual value and with the following lives:
   a. Radio studio   40 years
   b. Radio and broadcasting equipment   10 years
3. The following transactions occurred during 1988:
   - April 1: A new additional broadcasting studio was finished. The studio had a cost of $1 million and the new equipment a cost of $50,000. All items were paid for in cash.
   - July 15: Repairs of $5,000 were made for cash on certain pieces of radio equipment.
   - September 30: Radio equipment with a cost of $100,000 and accumulated depreciation of $20,000 (as of 12/31/87) was sold for $82,000 cash.
   - December 30: Radio equipment with a cost of $50,000 and accumulated depreciation of $10,000 (as of 12/31/87) was traded in for new equipment. The firm received a trade-in allowance of $32,000. The list price of the new equipment is $85,000.

Required:

Make all the required journal entries. It is not necessary to make the December 31, 1988 depreciation entries for the plant assets still on hand.

Solution _____

April 1	Radio Studio	1,000,000	
	Radio and Broadcasting Equipment	50,000	
	Cash		1,050,000
	To record addition to radio studio and purchase of new equipment.		

July 15	Repair and Maintenance Expense	5,000	
	Cash		5,000
	To record $5,000 repair on radio equipment.		

Sept. 30	Depreciation Expense	7,500	
	Accumulated Depreciation—Radio and Broadcasting Equipment		7,500
	To record depreciation for 9 months on radio and broadcasting equipment to be sold.		
	$100,000 \times .10 \times 9/12 = \$7,500$		

	Cash	82,000	
	Accumulated Depreciation—Radio and Broadcasting Equipment	27,500	
	Gain on Sale of Radio and Broadcasting Equipment		9,500
	Radio and Broadcasting Equipment		100,000
	To record gain on sale of equipment of $9,500, computed as follows:		

Historical cost		$100,000
Accumulated:		
to 12/31/87	$20,000	
from 1/2/87 to 9/30/88	7,500	27,500
Book value on 9/30/88		72,500
Cash received		82,000
Gain		$ 9,500

Dec. 30	Depreciation Expense	5,000	
	Accumulated Depreciation—Radio and Broadcasting Equipment		5,000
	To record depreciation for the year 1988 on equipment trade-in.		
	$50,000 \times .10 = \$5,000$		

	New Radio and Broadcasting Equipment	85,000	
	Accumulated Depreciation—Radio and Broadcasting Equipment	15,000	
	Loss on Trade-in	3,000	
	Old Radio and Broadcasting Equipment		50,000
	Cash		53,000
	To record trade-in of radio equipment, computed as follows:		

Historical cost		$50,000
Accumulated depreciation		
to 12/31/87	$10,000	
from 1/2/87 to 12/31/88	5,000	15,000
Book value at 12/31/88		35,000
Trade-in allowance		32,000
Loss		($ 3,000)

Because the trade-in resulted in a loss, it must be recognized. If a gain had occurred, it would not be recognized.

B. Accounting for Goodwill. You are considering the purchase of a restaurant. You have determined the following information:

Identifiable net assets:	
Book value	$1,500,000
Fair market value	$2,000,000
Average yearly net income over past five years	$ 270,000
Average industry rate of return on identifiable net assets	12%

Goodwill is to be determined if capitalizing excess of earnings at 20%.

Required:

Determine how much you would pay for the restaurant.

CHAPTER 13

Solution _____

Determination of Goodwill

Average earnings	$270,000
Normal earnings $2,000,000 × .12	240,000
Excess earnings	$ 30,000

Capitalization at 20%

$$\frac{\$30,000}{.20} = \text{Goodwill} \qquad\qquad \$150,000$$

Total Purchase Price

Identifiable net assets	$2,000,000
Goodwill	150,000
Total	$2,150,000

Questions

1. Define the following terms:
   a. Additions.
   b. Betterments.
   c. Extraordinary repairs.
   d. Revenue expenditures.

2. Briefly describe the accounting procedures for the sale or retirement of plant assets.

3. How is the gain or loss on the sale or retirement of plant assets determined?

4. Briefly describe the accounting procedures when a trade-in allowance is given on the purchase of a new asset. Does it make any difference whether a similar or dissimilar asset is acquired?

5. Why is a gain not recognized when an asset is traded in for a similar one? What is the ultimate effect of not recognizing the gain on the firm's financial statements over the life of the new asset?

6. Which accounting concept requires the recognition of any realized loss that results from trade-ins?

7. Describe the current Internal Revenue Code regulations regarding the recognition of gains and losses resulting from trade-ins of similar assets. Why do you think these regulations differ from financial reporting rules under generally accepted accounting principles?

8. Why is it important to maintain adequate internal control over plant assets? Describe the controls that should be used.

9. Why are natural resources often referred to as wasting assets?

10. What costs are commonly included in the acquisition of natural resources? Give an example of each type of cost.

11. What is depletion and how is it calculated?

12. The Found-It Gas Company recognized $1.50 depletion for each metric ton of mine taken from the wellhead. During the year the firm produced 1 million metric tons of gas, of which 750,000 tons were delivered to customers. The remaining was stored for future delivery. How much depletion expense should Found-It recognize in the current year?

13. The Canyon Mining Company produces ore from a strip mining site. The acquisition costs including development and exploration costs were $5 million. The mine is estimated to produce 20 million tons of ore over the next 10 years. Under state laws, Canyon must reclaim the land after the mine closes. The reclamation costs are estimated to be $1 million, after which time the salvage of the land should be $750,000. Determine the depletion cost per ton of ore.

14. Compare and contrast the successful efforts and full cost methods of accounting for oil exploration.

15. Briefly define and describe intangible assets. How do these assets provide future benefits to the firm?

16. What are research and development costs? Under current accounting principles, how are these costs accounted for? Do you agree with this treatment? Why or why not?

17. Why must intangible assets be amortized? What factors should you consider in determining the useful life of intangible assets?

18. The Alfredo Invention Company recently acquired two patents. The first patent was purchased from the Klein-Smith Corporation for $2.5 million. The second patent was developed internally. The prior year's research and development costs were $1.5 million. During the current year, additional R & D costs amounted to $750,000. Also during the year,

legal fees of $250,000 were incurred to obtain the patent. How should each of these patents be recorded on Alfredo's books?

19. One of your good friends owns a fashionable restaurant. In recent years the restaurant has been extremely profitable. As a result, your friend has decided to recognize goodwill by debiting Goodwill and crediting Owner's Equity. Is this in accordance with generally accepted accounting principles? Why or why not?

20. The Jackson Company recently purchased Way-Out Video Games for $1 million. The appraisers for Jackson estimated that the fair market value of Way-Out's 10 tangible assets were $850,000. How much goodwill, if any, should Jackson recognize on this transaction? How should the goodwill, if any, be subsequently accounted for?

Exercises

1. Revenue versus Capital Expenditures. The following expenditures were made by the R & G Corporation. For each item, indicate whether the expenditure is a capital expenditure, a revenue expenditure, or neither. If you cannot make a clear-cut decision, so state and explain why.

a. Paid $500 for a small machine.
b. Paid $600 for ordinary repairs to a large machine.
c. Paid premiums of $760 for insurance for the firm's officers.
d. Paid $1,500 for a patent.
e. Paid $10 for an electric pencil sharpener.
f. Paid $1,750 to overhaul a large delivery truck.
g. Removed a wall during installation of a new computer, $500.

2. Extraordinary Repairs. Hollis Answering Service began operations on January 2, 1984. At that time the firm purchased switchboard equipment for $23,000 cash. The equipment had an estimated useful life of 10 years and a salvage value of $2,000. The company uses straight-line depreciation. During 1987 ordinary repairs totaling $500 were made and paid in cash. At the beginning of 1988 an employee spilled coffee on the equipment. As a result, a major overhaul of the equipment was made. The equipment was upgraded at the same time. The total cost was $8,000, which was paid in cash. These expenditures will increase the total useful life of the equipment from 10 years to 15.

Required:

a. Prepare the required entries to record the $500 expenditure in 1987 and the depreciation expense in 1987.
b. Prepare the required entries to record the $8,000 expenditures in 1988 and the depreciation expense in 1988.

3. Retirement of Plant Assets. On March 31, 1987 Flip Pockets, Co., retired a machine used in manufacturing designer jeans. The machine was acquired on May 1, 1984. Straight-line depreciation was used. The asset had an estimated salvage value of $200 and a 5-year life. On December 31, 1986 the balance in the Accumulated Depreciation account was $3,200. The machine was scrapped without Flip Pockets' receiving any consideration.

Required:

a. Make the entry to record the depreciation expense for the period January through March 1987. Depreciation is calculated from the date of acquisition. (*Hint:* You must first determine the acquisition cost of the machine.)
b. Make the entry to record the retirement of the asset on March 31, 1987.

4. Sale of Plant Assets. On September 30, 1987 Schneider's Maintenance Service sold one of its vans. The acquisition cost of the van was $9,500. It had an estimated useful life of 5 years and a salvage value of $500. Straight-line depreciation was used. The balance in the Accumulated Depreciation account at December 31, 1986 was $4,950.

Required:

a. Calculate the gain or loss on the sale assuming that the asset is sold for either (1) $4,000 or (2) $2,500. In both cases the sale is for cash.

b. Make the necessary journal entries to record the transaction for each of the cases in requirement (a).

c. Now assume that the van was scrapped without any consideration. Make the journal entry to record the retirement.

5. Asset Sale. On December 31, 1986 the records of the Benson Company showed the following information with regard to one of the company's delivery trucks.

Delivery truck	$8,500
Accumulated depreciation—12/31/86	5,000

Depreciation is based on a 4-year useful life, a $2,500 salvage value, and straight-line depreciation. On February 1, 1987 the truck is sold for $4,000 cash.

Required:

a. How old was the truck on January 1, 1987? Show your computations.

b. Prepare the necessary journal entries to record the sale of the truck.

c. Prepare the necessary journal entries to record the sale, now assuming a cash sale price of $2,000.

6. Asset Trade-in. On July 1, 1987 Drake, Co. traded a machine used in the production of bottle caps for a newer model. Drake received a trade-in allowance of $10,000 on the new machine, which had a list price of $65,000. The old machine was purchased 7 years and 3 months ago at a price of $42,000. It had an estimated useful life of 10 years and a salvage value of $3,000. Straight-line depreciation was used.

Required:

a. How much cash did Drake have to pay for the new machine?

b. Make the necessary journal entry to record the acquisition of the new machine.

c. What is the cost basis for the new machine for tax purposes? Explain why it is different from the accounting basis.

7. Asset Disposition. The Yangtse Company acquired an asset that had a cost of $130,000. The asset is being depreciated over five years using the sum-of-the-years-digits method of depreciation. The asset has an estimated salvage value of $10,000. Make the journal entry to record the disposition of the asset under each of the following independent assumptions:

a. At the end of the third year, the asset was sold for $38,000 cash.

b. At the end of the second year, the asset was traded in for a similar one. The new asset had a list price of $150,000. The firm received a trade-in allowance of $60,000. Assume that the trade-in allowance represents the fair market value of the old asset.

c. At the end of the sixth year, the asset was retired and given to a scrap dealer in exchange for $1,000.

d. At the end of the third year, the asset was traded in for a similar one with a list price of $80,000. The firm paid $62,000 cash. The trade-in allowance represented the fair market value of the old asset.

8. Depletion. During 1987 Fortune Company purchased a mine for $14.8 million. In addition, the firm capitalized exploration and development costs of $6,450,000. The firm estimates that the property will have a salvage value of $8 million when the mine is finally closed. A geological survey indicates that 25 million units of the mineral can be extracted over the life of the mine. If 1.2 million units are extracted in 1987 and 2 million are extracted in 1988, determine the depletion expense for each year.

9. Intangible Assets. The Imagination Company has the following intangible assets on December 31, 1987, which is the end of the firm's year:

a. A patent was purchased on January 2, 1987 for $5,896 cash. This patent had beeen registered with the U.S. Patent Office on January 2, 1981 and is to be amortized over its remaining legal life.

b. On January 2, 1986 the company purchased a copyright for $12,600 cash. The remaining legal life is 20 years; however, management estimates that the copyright will have no value at the end of 15 years.

c. On July 1, 1987 the company received a patent on a product developed by the firm. Expenses of $26,500 were incurred in the development of the product. Legal fees and costs associated with obtaining the patent amounted to $5,100. The company will amortize the patent over its legal life beginning on the date of obtaining the patent.

d. Imagination hired a public relations firm to develop a trademark for the company. The fees to that firm amounted to $25,000. Legal fees associated with the trademark amounted to $5,000. The acquisition date is January 1, 1987.

Required:

Determine the amortization expense for 1987 and the book value of each of the intangible assets that should be shown on the December 31, 1987 balance sheet.

10. Determining Excess Earnings. A & M Company is interested in investing in a particular type of industry. After much investigation, the owners narrowed their choice to two companies. The first one, the Andrews Company, has net identifiable assets (at fair market value) of $1 million and average net income for the past 5 years of $130,000 per year. The second company, the Bedford Company, has net identifiable assets (at fair market value) of $1.1 million and average net income for the past 5 years of $132,000 per year. The normal rate of return for the industry is 12%.

Required:

Determine the amount of excess earnings of each company.

11. Determining Goodwill. The Mann Company is negotiating the purchase of the Horace Company. The Horace Company's tangible net assets have a book value of $2.6 million. Independent appraisers indicate that the fair market value of the net assets approximate $3 million. In addition, the firm has been able to earn average profits of $390,000 per year for the past 5 years. Industry norms indicate that the normal rate of return for the industry is 12%.

Required:

Determine the total purchase price, assuming:
a. Goodwill is determined by capitalizing excess earnings at 20%.
b. Goodwill is negotiated to be three times excess earnings.

Problem Set A

13A–1. Disposal of Plant Assets. The Corona Company purchased a metal crusher for $140,000 on January 2, 1985. The asset has a 5-year useful life and a salvage value of $5,000. The firm uses sum-of-the-years-digits depreciation.

Required:

Make the entry to record the disposition of the asset under each of the following independent situations. Assume that depreciation has been recorded to the date of sale. (You do not have to make the depreciation entry unless so instructed.)
a. The asset is retired without consideration at the end of its useful life.
b. The asset is sold for $5,500 cash at the end of its useful life.
c. The asset is sold for cash on March 31, 1988 for (1) $60,000 and (2) $20,000. Depreciation for the period January 1, 1988 to March 31, 1988 must be recorded.
d. The asset is traded in for a similar one on January 2, 1989. A trade-in allowance of (1) $35,000 and (2) $5,000 is received. In both Cases 1 and 2, assume that the trade-in allowance represents the fair market value of the asset given up at that time. The list price of the new machine is $100,000.

13A–2. Asset Trade-in. A tractor with an estimated useful life of 5 years was acquired by the Parish Farm Company at a cost of $12,000. Straight-line depreciation is used, and the salvage value is estimated to be $2,400. The tractor had been used by the company for several years when Parish decided to trade it in on a new one. The new tractor had a list price of $15,000, and a $4,500 trade-in allowance was received on the old tractor. The remainder of the cost was paid in cash. At December 31, prior to sale on March 1 of the following year, the Accumulated

Depreciation account related to the old tractor had a balance of $6,240. No depreciation had been recorded during the period from January 1 to March 1.

Required:

Prepare the necessary journal entries to record the following:

a. Depreciation of the old tractor for the period January 1 to March 1 in the year of the trade-in. (Hint: Determine monthly depreciation.)

b. The acquisition of the new tractor on March 1 using the rules acceptable for financial reporting purposes.

c. The acquisition of the new tractor on March 1 using the rules acceptable for income tax purposes.

d. Assuming that the new tractor has an estimated life of 4 years, a salvage value of $5,000, and straight-line depreciation is used for both financial accounting and tax purposes. Discuss the difference in depreciation for tax purposes and for financial reporting purposes due to the trade-in transaction. Assume that a full year's depreciation is taken in the year of acquisition.

e. If the trade-in allowance was for $6,000, how would your answers to (b) and (c) differ?

13A–3. Plant Asset Transactions. During 1987 the Travis Company entered into the following transactions related to various items of property, plant, and equipment:

- January 2: A delivery truck owned by the firm was overhauled at a cost of $4,000, which was paid in cash. The truck had been purchased on January 2, 1985 at a price of $13,000. At that time the firm estimated that the truck would have a salvage value of $1,000 and a five-year life with no salvage value. After the overhaul, Travis estimated that the life of the truck should be extended two more years from the date of the overhaul.

- February 1: Sold a used machine which had a book value of $2,500 on the date of the sale. The machine had a historical cost of $72,000 and the firm received $2,300 cash.

- March 31: A fully depreciated machine purchased several years ago was scrapped for no consideration. The machine had an original cost of $15,000, a useful life of 6 years, and a salvage value of $1,500.

- July 1: Travis sold one of its computers for $8,000. The computer, which was purchased on January 2, 1986 for $25,000, had a useful life of 5 years and a $4,000 salvage value. The firm uses sum-of-the-years-digits depreciation on this asset. No depreciation has been taken since December 31, 1986. Of the $8,000 selling price, the firm received 20% down and a 12%, 1-year note for the remainder.

Required:

a. Make the journal entries to record the above transactions.

b. Make any necessary adjusting entries for depreciation and interest. Assume that the firm closes its books once a year on December 31. The firm calculates depreciation from the beginning of the month in which the asset is purchased.

13A–4. Purchase and Disposal of Equipment. On January 2, 1985 the Lewis Company purchased a piece of equipment for $80,000. The asset is depreciated based on the double-declining-balance method with a life of 10 years and a $5,000 salvage value. On January 2, 1987 the asset was traded in for a similar one. The new equipment had a list price of $100,000, but after the trade-in allowance, which approximated the fair market value of the old asset at that time, Lewis paid only $40,000 in cash. The Lewis Company decided the new asset should have a life of 5 years and a salvage value of $10,000. The double-declining-balance method was again used. Depreciation expense for 1987 on the new machine amounted to $40,000.

Required:

a. From your analysis of the above facts, did Lewis properly record the trade-in of the old equipment? Why or why not? Assume that the depreciation calculation on the new asset is mathematically correct.

b. Make one entry to correct the books at January 2, 1987 and another to correct the depreciation expense for 1987.

13A–5. Purchase and Disposal of Equipment. On January 2, 1984 the Perkins Company purchased a piece of high-tech equipment for cash. The equipment, which cost $200,000, had a 5-

year life and a $20,000 salvage value. Straight-line depreciation is used. Installation costs were $10,000. At the beginning of 1986 the firm decided to upgrade the equipment and spent $50,000 in the process. The asset's Accumulated Depreciation account was debited for this amount. As a result, its useful life was extended an additional three years from that date. In addition, the salvage value was increased by $5,000. However, at the end of 1987 a new machine came on the market that made the old equipment obsolete. As a result, Perkins traded in the old piece of equipment for a new one. The trade-in was made on December 31, 1987, prior to any adjusting entries. The list price of the new equipment was $180,000 and Perkins received a $40,000 trade-in allowance on the old equipment. The trade-in allowance was equal to the asset's fair market value at that time.

Required:

    a. Record the purchase of the equipment on January 2, 1984.

    b. Record depreciation expense for 1984 and 1985.

    c. Record the relevant entries for 1986, including the depreciation expense.

    d. Record all the relevant entries for 1987, including the depreciation expense.

13A–6. Natural Resources and Depletion. Western Oil purchased three sites during 1986 for possible drilling. Cost data relative to each site are as follows:

	Site		
Costs Incurred in 1986	South Dakota Red	Wyoming Black	California Gold
Acquisition costs	$750,000	$1,200,000	$1,000,000
Exploration costs	100,000	500,000	400,000
Costs Incurred in 1987			
Exploration costs	0	200,000	600,000
Development costs*			
Well equipment			500,000
Intangible costs			200,000
Production costs, direct labor, etc.			750,000

*Development costs are accumulated in a separate account and are not part of the depletable cost of the well. These costs are assumed to have a five-year life and are depreciated on the straight-line basis with no salvage value. For depletion purposes, the cost of the well includes only acquisition and exploration costs of successful wells; that is, the successful efforts method of accounting is used.

By the end of 1986 it was clear to Western Oil that South Dakota Red was not going to produce any oil. The firm decided to immediately write it off. However, preliminary tests indicated that Wyoming Black and California Gold would be successful.

    In 1987 Western continued exploration. However, Wyoming Black proved to be dry and all costs were written off at the end of 1987. California Gold was successful and actual production started in mid-1987. Geologists estimated that over the next 8 years the well would produce 5.5 million barrels. No salvage value for the well was assumed. During 1987 516,000 barrels of oil were produced, of which 387,000 were sold at $20 a barrel.

Required:

    a. Prepare all the journal entries to record these transactions during 1986 and 1987. Assume all transactions were conducted in cash, where appropriate.

    b. At what amount should the remaining inventory of oil be shown on the December 31, 1987 balance sheet?

13A–7. Patents. The Think Company manufactures state-of-the-art electronic products. Its products are being manufactured under two patents. The first patent, No. 106–235, was developed by the firm. During 1986 and 1987 the firm incurred research and development costs of $600,000 and $200,000, respectively. In addition, in 1987 the firm incurred $100,000 of legal and other related costs to have its work patented. Management estimates that the patent will have a 10-year economic life, although the legal life is 17 years.

    The second patent, No. 203–589, was purchased at the beginning of 1985 from its inventor for $120,000. The firm decided to amortize it over 15 years. During 1986 the firm was sued for patent infringement in connection with this patent. Think was able to successfully defend the suit. Legal costs were $56,000. As a result of this suit, management decided that beginning in 1987 the remaining useful life of the patent should be reduced to 10 years.

Required:

a. Make all the journal entries for 1986 and 1987 relative to each patent. Make separate sets of entries for each patent. Assume that the firm's year-end is December 31 and adjusting entries are made yearly at this time.

b. At what amount should each patent be shown on the firm's December 31, 1987 balance sheet?

13A–8. Determination of Goodwill. Brenner Electronics is considering the purchase of one of its competitors, Kress Technology. Kress Technology has been very profitable and has been averaging an annual net income of $88,500 since its inception 6 years ago. Under the terms of the proposed purchase agreement, Brenner will pay a price equal to the fair market value of Kress's net identifiable assets plus goodwill as of December 31, 1987. Goodwill is to be determined by capitalizing excess earnings at 20%. Excess earnings are the amount by which Kress's average annual earnings exceed the industry norm of 10% of net identifiable assets at their fair market value. Brenner will make the purchase by paying cash.

The balance sheet of Kress Technology at December 31, 1987 is as follows:

Kress Technology
Balance Sheet
December 31, 1987

Assets		
Current assets		$100,000
Property, plant, and equipment		
Land	$200,000	
Buildings, net	320,000	
Plant and equipment, net	100,000	620,000
Other assets		10,000
Total assets		$730,000
Liabilities and Owner's Equity		
Current liabilities		$ 75,000
Long-term liabilities		140,000
Total liabilities		$215,000
Owner's equity		$515,000
Total liabilities and owner's equity		$730,000

The following additional information is available:

a. The fair market value of the current assets approximates their book value.

b. The fair market value of the property, plant, and equipment is as follows:

Account	Amount
Land	$300,000
Buildings, net	360,000
Plant and equipment, net	140,000

c. The other assets consist of an advance to Kress's owner. The debt is being forgiven when the purchase is made, so the owner has no intention of repaying it.

d. Kress has a patent which was developed internally. As a result, all costs related to this patent have been expensed. The management of Brenner feels that the fair market value of this patent is $50,000.

e. The fair market values of all liabilities approximate their book values.

Required:

a. Determine the amount of excess earnings.
b. Determine the amount of goodwill involved in the transaction.
c. Determine the total purchase price Brenner will pay to Kress.
d. Make the entry on Brenner's books to record the purchase of the assets and the assumption of the liabilities of Kress. Assume that all assets and liabilities are recorded at fair market value.

Problem Set B

13B–1. Disposal of a Plant Asset. The Southern California Company purchased a mainframe computer for $250,000 on January 2, 1984. The computer was given a 5-year useful life and a salvage value of $10,000. The firm uses double-declining-balance depreciation.

Required:

Make the entry to record the disposition of the asset under each of the following independent situations. (Assume that depreciation is recorded through the date of disposal. However, you do not need to make the depreciation entry.)

a. The computer is retired without consideration at the end of its useful life.
b. The computer is sold for $12,000 cash at the end of its useful life.
c. The asset is sold for cash on June 30, 1987 for (1) $50,000 and (2) $15,000.
d. The asset is traded in for a similar one on January 1, 1987. A trade-in allowance of (1) $70,000 and (2) $20,000 is received. The list price of the new computer is $150,000. In both cases, assume that the trade-in allowance represents the fair market value of the asset at the time of the trade-in.

13B–2. Asset Trade-in. On July 1, 1987 Yuki Yogurt Company decided to replace its obsolete refrigeration system with a more efficient one. The old system was acquired on January 1, 1981 at a cost of $125,000. It had an estimated useful life of 8 years and a salvage value of $5,000. Straight-line depreciation was used. Yuki's new refrigeration system has a fair market value of $214,000; Yuki paid $189,000 after permitting the contractor to keep the old refrigeration equipment. Depreciation on the old system was recorded since the month of purchase through December 31, 1986.

Required:

Prepare the necessary journal entries to record the following:

a. Depreciation of the old system for the year of the trade-in.
b. The acquisition of the new system on July 1 using the rules acceptable for financial reporting purposes.
c. The acquisition of the new system on July 1 using the rules acceptable for tax purposes.
d. Assuming that the new system has an estimated life of 5 years and a salvage value of $10,000 and that straight-line depreciation is used for financial reporting purposes and five-year ACRS depreciation for tax purposes, discuss the differences between income for financial reporting purposes and tax purposes due to the depreciation computation and the trade-in transaction. Assume that half-year depreciation is taken in the year of acquisition for financial reporting purposes. (Use the ACRS table on page 476.)

13B–3. Plant Asset Transactions. The Smith Company entered into the following transactions related to items of property, plant, and equipment during 1987:

- January 1: The firm made an extraordinary repair on equipment to upgrade its quality at a cost of $6,000 cash. The equipment was originally purchased on January 1, 1984 at a price of $25,000. At that time the company estimated that the equipment had a useful life of 5 years and a salvage value of $5,000. After the repair, the estimated useful life will be extended two more years from the date of the repair. The Accumulated Depreciation account was debited to record the repair.

- March 31: The company sold an old truck for $3,000 cash. The truck was acquired on January 2, 1983 at a cost of $12,000 and had an estimated useful life of 6 years with no salvage value. The company used straight-line depreciation.

- April 30: An obsolete machine was retired without consideration. The machine was purchased on July 1, 1982 at an original cost of $35,000 and had a book value of $7,000 and was fully depreciated at the date it was retired.

- July 1: The firm had a computer which it acquired at an original cost of $8,000 several years ago. On July 1, 1987 the computer had a net book value of $3,600. At that date the computer was traded in for a new one that had a list price of $10,000. The company received a $2,000 trade-in allowance, which represented its fair market value at that time. The new computer was given a four-year life and no salvage value. Straight-line depreciation is used.

Required:

a. Make the journal entries to record the above transactions.

b. Make the adjusting entries at December 31 to record depreciation expense. The company calculates depreciation from the beginning of the month in which the asset was purchased.

13B–4. Purchase and Disposal of Equipment. On January 2, 1985 the Jackson Steel Company purchased a blast furnace for $123,000. The furnace is depreciated using the sum-of-the-years-digits method of depreciation with a life of 10 years and a salvage value of $2,000. On January 2, 1987 the furnace was traded in for a new, similar one. The new furnace had a list price of $150,000, but after the trade-in allowance, the Jackson Company paid only $33,400 cash. The trade-in allowance was equal to the fair market value of the old furnace at the time it was traded in. The new machine was given a 10-year life and a salvage value of $7,000. The sum-of-the-years-digits method was again used. Depreciation expense for 1987 on the new furnace was $26,000.

Required:

a. From your analysis of the above facts, did the Jackson Company properly record the trade-in of the old furnace? Why or why not?

b. Make one entry to correct the books at January 2, 1987 and another to correct the depreciation expense for 1987.

13B–5. Purchase and Disposal of Equipment. On January 2, 1983 the Hawkins Company acquired for cash a robot to work on its assembly line. The robot cost $100,000 and had an estimated useful life of 8 years. The company estimated that the robot would have a salvage value of $5,000 at the end of its useful life. Straight-line depreciation is used to depreciate all of the firm's depreciable assets. At the beginning of January 1985 the company decided to upgrade the capabilities of the robot and spent $10,000 cash doing so. As a result, the useful life of the robot was extended from 8 years to 10 years. Further, its salvage value was increased by $1,000.

During 1986 new technologies made the company's robot obsolete. As a result, the Hawkins Company traded in the old robot for a new one on January 2, 1987. The new one cost $130,000 and Hawkins received a trade-in allowance of $50,000, which was equal to the old robot's fair market value at that time.

Required:

a. Record the purchase of the robot on January 2, 1983.

b. Record depreciation expense for 1983 and 1984.

c. Record the relevant entries for 1985 including depreciation expense.

d. Make the journal entry to record the trade-in in 1987.

13B-6. Natural Resources and Depletion. Energy Gas Company acquired three sites during 1985 for possible drilling. Cost data relative to each site are as follows:

	Site		
Costs Incurred in 1985	Washington White	Texas Tan	California Clear
Acquisition costs	$1,000,000	$1,500,000	$2,000,000
Exploration costs	300,000	500,000	600,000
Costs Incurred in 1986			
Exploration costs			
Well equipment*	0	300,000	400,000
Intangible costs			700,000
Production costs, direct labor, etc.			1,000,000

*Development costs are accumulated in a separate account and are not part of the depletable cost of the well. These costs are assumed to have a seven-year life and are depreciated on the straight-line basis with no salvage value. For depletion purposes, the cost of the well includes only acquisition and exploration costs of successful wells. That is, the successful efforts method of accounting is used.

By the end of 1985 Energy Gas determined that the Washington site was not going to produce enough gas to warrant further exploration. As a result, the well was written off. At that time it appeared that the other two sites would produce substantial amounts of gas.

In 1986 the company continued its exploration work. However, the Texas site proved dry and all costs were written off at the end of 1986. The California site did prove successful and actual production started in the middle of 1986. It was estimated that over the next 5 years the well would produce 1 billion cubic feet of gas. At the end of five years the company assumed that the well would be abandoned with no salvage value. During 1986 150 million cubic feet of gas were produced and sold at $20 per thousand cubic feet.

Required:

  a. Prepare all the journal entries to record these transactions during 1985 and 1986. Assume that, where appropriate, all transactions are conducted in cash.

  b. List the income statement and balance sheet accounts that are affected by these transactions, and the balances in these accounts.

13B-7. Patents. Tryco, an electronics components manufacturer, possesses two patents. Patent A was developed by the firm during 1986 and 1987. The firm incurred research and development costs of $500,000 and $100,000 during 1986 and 1987, respectively. In addition, in 1987 the firm incurred and paid $50,000 in legal fees in connection with getting the item patented. Compac, Inc. estimates that the patent will have an economic life of 12 years.

Patent B was purchased at the beginning of 1987 from its inventor for $100,000 cash. The firm decided to amortize it over 10 years. During December 1987 an additional $20,000 was spent to enhance the electronic process involved in the patent. As a result, management decided that beginning in 1988 the remaining useful life of the patent should be increased two additional years.

Required:

  a. Make all the journal entries for 1986 through 1988 relative to each patent. Make a separate set of entries for each patent. Assume that the firm's year-end is December 31 and adjusting entries are made yearly at this time.

  b. At what amount should each patent be shown on the firm's December 31, 1988 balance sheet?

13B-8. Determination of Goodwill. The Cobb Company is considering the purchase of one of its competitors, David, Ltd. David, Ltd. has been averaging an annual net income of $100,000 since its inception 4 years ago. This amount is considerably better than other firms in the industry. Under the terms of the proposed purchase agreement, Cobb will pay a price equal to the fair market value of David's net identifiable assets plus any goodwill as of December 31, 1987. Goodwill is to be determined by capitalizing excess earnings at 10%. Excess earnings are the amount by which David's average annual earnings exceed the industry norm of 10% of net identifiable assets at fair market value. Cobb will make the purchase by making a 40% down payment and taking on a 14% note payable for the remainder.

David, Ltd.'s balance sheet as of December 31, 1987 is as follows:

David, Ltd.
Balance Sheet
December 31, 1987

Assets

Current assets		$180,000
Property, plant, and equipment		
Land	$300,000	
Buildings, net	400,000	
Equipment, net	160,000	860,000
Total assets		$1,040,000

Liabilities and Owner's Equity

Current liabilities	$ 120,000
Long-term liabilities	300,000
Total liabilities	$ 420,000
Owner's equity	$ 620,000
Total liabilities and owner's equity	$1,040,000

The following information is also available:

1. The fair market value of the current assets approximates their book value.
2. The fair market values of the property, plant, and equipment are as follows:

Account	Amount
Land	$400,000
Buildings, net	420,000
Plant and equipment, net	180,000

3. The fair market value of all the liabilities approximate their book value.

Required:
   a. Determine the amount of excess earnings.
   b. Determine the amount of goodwill.
   c. Determine the total purchase price Cobb will pay for David.

Using the Computer

At the beginning of 1987 the Ruby Goldmine Company acquired three active mines. The following data related to each mine:

	Cost	Salvage Value	Estimated Tons of Gold to Be Mined
1.	$1 million	none	4 million
2.	$5 million	½ million	9 million
3.	$8 million	$2 million	15 million

The actual production schedule for each mine for each of the next five years is as follows:

Year	Mine No.	Actual Production
1987	1	1 million
1988	1	1.5 million
1989	1	1 million
1990	1	.5 million
1991	1	0
1987	2	2 million
1988	2	2.5 million
1989	2	1 million
1990	2	1.5 million
1991	2	1 million
1987	3	2 million
1988	3	3 million
1989	3	2.5 million
1990	3	1.5 million
1991	3	4 million

Required:

Using an electronic spreadsheet, determine the annual amount of depletion. Use the following format:

	Mine No. 1		Mine No. 2		Mine No. 3	
Year	Annual Depletion	Book Value*	Annual Depletion	Book Value	Annual Depletion	Book Value
1987						
1988						
1989						
1990						
1991						

*Book value at the end of each year (cost less depletion to date).

Understanding Financial Statements

The financial statements of the Times Mirror Company (a large newspaper publishing company) contained the following item relating to timberlands:

NOTE F
TIMBERLANDS
Timberlands, less depletion, consist of the following
(in thousands of dollars):

	1982	1981
Owned	$ 92,479	$ 82,097
Capitalized timber harvesting rights	38,185	33,901
	$130,664	$115,998

Required:

a. Why do you think a firm like Times Mirror owns timberlands?

b. What do you think the account Capitalized Timber Harvesting Rights is?

c. How do you think Times Mirror accounts for the costs of timberlands owned. For example, how do you think the cost of forests that are planted and cultivated are determined?

d. How do you think Times Mirror determines the depletion on the timberlands?

e. In what section of the balance sheet do you think that Times Mirror lists its timberlands?

Financial Decision Case

Brent Mumberg recently purchased a professional football team. He paid $20 million, roughly broken down as follows:

Franchise rights	$ 8 million
Player contracts	11 million
Equipment and so forth	1 million

In addition, Brent is dissatisfied with the current name of the team, the Diablos, and has undertaken a citywide contest to rename the team. The contest cost $500,000 and the winning name is the Golden Eagles. After Brent officially named the team the Golden Eagles, a local university sued the school for infringement of its trade name. It seems that the university had legally registered the name Golden Eagles for its sports teams. As a result, Brent had to pay the university $100,000 to use the name.

Required:

    a. Do the items *franchise rights* and *player contracts* represent assets in the accounting sense? If so, how should they be accounted for?

    b. How should Brent account for the $500,000 he spent on the contest to find a name for the team?

    c. How should Brent account for the $100,000 he had to pay the local university to use the name Golden Eagles?

Accounting Concepts and Accounting for Changing Prices

14

LEARNING OBJECTIVES

After reading this chapter you should be able to:

1. **Explain the development of accounting concepts and standards.**
2. **Discuss the purposes and uses of the conceptual framework.**
3. **State the main accounting concepts and conventions.**
4. **Explain the need for and concepts related to accounting for changing prices.**
5. **Do the basic procedures involved in accounting for changing prices, including accounting for purchasing power gains and losses and current cost accounting.**

Throughout the first 13 chapters of this book, we often used the term *generally accepted accounting principles* (GAAP). What are the sources of GAAP and what are the important principles and concepts? These are the questions we focus on in this chapter. The final portion of the chapter introduces you to the effects that changing prices have on financial reports, and the concepts accountants have developed to deal with these effects.

Development of Accounting Concepts and Standards

The concepts and standards underlying accounting for financial information are governed by generally accepted accounting principles (GAAP), which represent the consensus at a particular time as to how economic resources and obligations should be recorded, what information should be disclosed and how it should be disclosed, and which financial statements should be prepared. Generally accepted accounting principles are required in order to help ensure the integrity and credibility of financial information reported by business enterprises to external users.

The "consensus" at a particular time as to the concepts and standards that make up GAAP is influenced by several different sources, including the Securities and Exchange Commission (SEC); the Financial Accounting Standards Board (FASB) and its predecessor, the Accounting Principles Board (APB) of the American Institute of Certified Public Accountants (AICPA); managements of publicly held corporations; and the members of the academic accounting community. The role of each was examined in Chapter 1.

The Conceptual Framework Project

In addition to issuing specific standards and rules, the FASB has spent considerable time and energy working on developing broad accounting concepts. These concepts provide a framework within which specific standards can be developed. The attempt to develop this framework is called the conceptual framework project. The purpose of the **conceptual framework project** is to develop objectives and concepts that the FASB will use in deciding on standards of financial accounting and reporting. According to a former research director of the FASB:

> A conceptual framework is the backbone of a standard-setting activity in the private enterprise system. Without a conceptual framework to guide its accounting policy, the FASB could not be distinguished from a government agency that would be forced to follow the policies and politics of the government in power, thereby setting accounting standards that would undoubtedly be inconsistent through time.[1]

In order to accomplish this objective the FASB has issued six Concepts Statements. Concept Statement No. 2, *Qualitative Characteristics of Accounting Information,* is the basis for much of the discussion of the accounting concepts that follows.

Accounting Concepts and Conventions

Exhibit 14–1 summarizes 13 of the more important accounting concepts and conventions. It is broken down into three major categories: basic assumptions about the accounting environment, qualitative characteristics of accounting information, and the generally accepted conventions that result from the above. These classifications are not meant to be rigid but are used to provide a general framework for the discussion.

Basic Assumptions about the Accounting Environment

The accounting procedures that constitute generally accepted accounting principles and practices are built around two basic assumptions about busi-

---

[1] Michael O. Alexander, "After Eight Years, Is the End in Sight?" *FASB Viewpoints,* June 2, 1982, p. 2.

EXHIBIT 14–1
Accounting Concepts and Conventions

Basic Assumptions about the Accounting Environment

Business Entity	Business entities are separate economic units that control resources and obligations and that have separate and distinct records.
Going Concern	There is an assumption that a particular business enterprise will continue in existence for a long enough period of time to carry out its objectives and commitments.

Qualitative Characteristics of Accounting Information

Quantifiability	Money is the basic measuring unit. This means that in the United States items included in the accounting system must be quantifiable into dollars.
Relevance	Accounting information is relevant if it is capable of making a difference in a decision by a user.
Reliability	Accounting information is reliable if it measures without bias what it is supposed to. Verifiability is a prime ingredient of reliability.
Comparability and Consistency	Accounting information is comparable if it enables users to identify similarities and differences between two sets of economic events. Consistency refers to using the same accounting principles in different periods.
Conservatism	Uncertainties in accounting are resolved by choosing among the alternatives of equal likelihood, the one that produces the lowest asset valuation or the least amount of income.
Materiality	Accounting information is material if the judgment of a reasonable user would have been changed or influenced by the omission or misstatement of the information.
Full Disclosure	All information that would be useful to an informed decision maker should be disclosed.

Generally Accepted Conventions

Historical Cost	Historical cost is the primary valuation basis used in financial statements. Assets are recorded at their acquisition cost and are usually not adjusted for increases in value until a sale has occurred.
Time Period	Although we assume a business enterprise has an indefinite life, measurement of the enterprise's financial condition and operations must be made at relatively short intervals such as quarterly or yearly.
Matching	Under the matching concept, expenses must be offset against the revenues earned in the period. Thus, expenses of the period are matched against the revenues of the same period, and the result is net income or loss for the period.
Revenue Recognition	Revenue is recognized for accounting purposes when it is realized. For the vast majority of enterprises revenue is realized when the sale occurs.

ness enterprises: They are the business-entity and the going-concern assumptions.

The Business-Entity Assumption

According to the business-entity assumption, separate accounting records are kept for individual entities. A business or accounting entity is a separate and distinct unit which controls economic resources and is responsible for economic obligations. For example, a firm—whether organized as a sole proprietorship, partnership, or corporation—is a separate entity from its owner(s). As such, the net assets of the business are accounted for separately from the net assets of the owner(s).

Some accounting entities are combinations of individual entities that are jointly owned. They are combined and reported as one entity because the common ownership results in one economic unit. For example, Safeway, Inc. issues consolidated financial statements that include the accounts of Safeway plus those companies in which Safeway has an ownership interest of over 50%.

In some instances an economic entity can be difficult to determine. For example, Sears, Roebuck & Company buys a good deal of the merchandise from outside suppliers that it sells under the Sears label. In some instances substantially over 50% of the business generated by these suppliers is with Sears. From an economic standpoint it could be argued that Sears has control over these suppliers. However, consolidated statements would not be prepared in this instance if Sears did not actually have an ownership interest of over 50% in these suppliers.

The entity assumption is basic to the accounting system and principles developed in the United States. The accounting equation, assets = liabilities + owner's equity, is built around this concept. The equation is self-contained and always in balance because we keep separate records for distinct business entities.

The Going-Concern Assumption

According to the going-concern assumption, a business enterprise will continue in existence for a period of time long enough to carry out its objectives and commitments. This does not mean that accountants ignore the fact that some enterprises do not make profits or ultimately go out of business. However, generally we can realistically assume that an individual business will continue to operate in the future.

The going-concern assumption allows accountants to use historical costs and to ignore liquidation values. For example, when a firm purchases office supplies, they are recorded at cost and are subsequently written off to expense in the accounting period that they are used. Inherent in this process is the assumption that the firm will be in existence over a period of time long enough to use the supplies. If, however, shortly after the purchase of the supplies the firm were to go out of business, the historical cost of these supplies would not be relevant. Instead of using historical costs, accountants would record these supplies at their liquidation value, which may be substantially lower than their historical cost.

Previously, we indicated that the going-concern assumption is a reasonable one for most businesses. However, if circumstances indicate that a business may not be a going concern, the auditors must indicate in their report that the financial statements based on historical cost may not fairly present the financial position of the company. An example of an auditor's report containing such a going-concern exception is shown as follows:

To The Stockholders and Board of Directors
of Pentron Industries, Inc.:

We have examined the consolidated balance sheets of Pentron Industries, Inc. and subsidiaries as of June 30, 1984 and 1983 and the related consolidated statements of operations, changes in stockholders' equity (deficit), and changes in financial position for each of the three years in the period ended June 30, 1984. Our examinations were made in accordance with generally accepted auditing standards and, accordingly, included such tests of the accounting records and such other auditing procedures as we considered necessary in the circumstances.

As shown in the consolidated financial statements, the Company incurred substantial losses in 1984, 1983, and 1982 and has an excess of liabilities over assets at June 30, 1984. As described in Note 1, the Company's violation of a loan agreement, which would have permitted the acceleration of substantially all long-term debt, was waived by the bank through June 30, 1985, subject to monthly defined minimum tangible net worth requirements. The Company's 1985 business plan contemplates reduced operating losses and the infusion of additional capital into the Company. The Company's ability to achieve the foregoing elements of its business plan, which may be necessary to permit the realization of assets and satisfaction of liabilities in the ordinary course of business, is uncertain. *The financial statements do not include any adjustments relating to the recoverability and classification of recorded assets or the amounts and classification of liabilities that might be necessary should the Company be unable to continue in its present form* (emphasis added).

In our opinion, subject to the effects on the 1984 consolidated financial statements of such adjustments, if any, as might have been required had the outcome of the uncertainties referred to in the preceding paragraph been known, the financial statements referred to above present fairly the consolidated financial position of Pentron Industries, Inc. and subsidiaries as of June 30, 1984 and 1983 and the consolidated results of their operations and consolidated changes in financial position for each of the three years in the period ended June 30, 1984, in conformity with generally accepted accounting principles applied on a consistent basis.

Qualitative Characteristics of Financial Information

The primary purpose of financial statements is to provide information that is useful in decision making. To be useful, the FASB feels that accounting information must possess certain qualitative characteristics including quantifiability, relevance, and reliability.

Quantifiability

In order to be admitted into the accounting system, transactions and events must be represented in numerical and monetary terms. This characteristic is known as quantifiability and was briefly discussed in Chapter 2. Items that appear on the face of financial statements are quantifiable into dollars, and the dollar serves as the primary measuring unit. Because of the necessity to represent events in monetary terms, not all items that may be considered economic assets are considered accounting assets. An example of such an asset is good management. Because many accountants feel that it is impossible to quantify the benefits provided by good management, this asset does not appear anywhere on the balance sheet.

An important corollary to quantifiability is the assumption that the measuring unit—the dollar—is a stable unit of value. With certain exceptions this assumption has been a fairly reasonable one. However, from the late 1970s through the mid-1980s double-digit inflation became a chronic problem for the U.S. economy. Many accountants and financial analysts argue that providing only historical cost–based information in a period of significantly changing prices does not provide users with relevant information. Thus, the accounting profession has been pressured by the SEC and others to develop alternative methods of accounting. These methods are the topics of the second half of this chapter.

Relevance and Reliability

According to the FASB, **relevance** and **reliability** are the two primary qualities that make accounting information useful. "Relevant accounting information is capable of making a difference in a decision by helping users to form predictions about the outcome of past, present, and future events or to confirm or correct prior expectations."[2] That is, information is relevant if it has predictive and/or feedback value to users. This means the information helps users predict the future or evaluate past decisions. Further, timeliness is an important ingredient of relevance. If information is not given to users when it is capable of influencing their decision, it loses its relevance.

Reliability is an indication of whether the information measures what it should. From an accounting perspective, information is reliable if users can depend on it to represent the economic conditions or events that it purports to represent. For example, if receivables are shown on the balance sheet at $500,000, this figure will be reliable only if the real collectibility of these receivables closely approximates $500,000. We use the word *approximate* because informed users of accounting information know that estimates and approximations rather than exact measures must often be made.

Verifiability is an important ingredient of reliability. Verifiability is similar to objectivity and means that several individuals or measurers would reach similar conclusions. For example, the $500,000 balance in Accounts Receivable is verifiable if several individuals could agree that the net realizable value of the receivables is in fact $500,000. Verifiability is important because external users do not have access to a firm's accounting records and must rely on published financial statements as well as other public data in making their decisions. Verifiable and objective information increases users' confidence in accounting information.

In their attempt to provide useful information, accountants often are forced to make a trade-off between relevance and reliability. In many cases, the more relevant the information is, the less reliable it becomes. The controversy surrounding the use of certain current cost data is an example of a debate that involves this trade-off. Many individuals feel that current cost data is more relevant than historical cost data to users in decision making. For example, if you were to measure your net worth and owned a plot of land, its current cost might be more relevant to you than its historical cost would be.

[2]Financial Accounting Standards Board, Concepts Statement No. 2, *Qualitative Characteristics of Accounting Information* (Stamford, Conn.: FASB, May 1980), Summary.

However, current cost data is less reliable. You may have several individuals appraise the land and receive a different appraisal value from each of them. There might be no measurement consensus. Accountants often are confronted with this trade-off and, as with other issues in accounting, there is no single solution; the accountant's judgment is required.

Comparability and Consistency

Comparability and consistency are important factors in evaluating the usefulness of accounting information. Accounting information is comparable if it allows users to identify similarities and differences between two sets of economic events. When accounting information is comparable, it can be used to evaluate the financial position and performance of one firm over time or for comparison with other firms. However, comparability does not imply that accounting procedures or methods should be the same for all firms. This would disguise real differences that exist in the economic circumstance reported.

Consistency is related to comparability and is an important quality of accounting information. **Consistency** means that a firm uses the same accounting procedures and policies from one period to the next. It presumes that once an accounting principle has been adopted, it will not be changed in accounting for similar events. For example, once a firm selects a certain depreciation method, it should not change the method in one period and then switch back to the original method in the following period. However, as the FASB notes, such consistency should not inhibit necessary changes in accounting principles and practices. If such a change is made, the full disclosure principle requires that the effect of this change on net income be fully noted.

Conservatism

Although conservatism may qualify more as a convention than as a qualitative characteristic of accounting information, it has been a pervasive factor in U.S. accounting for over 50 years. Generally, **conservatism** means prudence in financial reporting because of the uncertainty surrounding business and economic activities. According to APB Statement 4,

> Frequently, assets and liabilities are measured in a context of significant uncertainties. Historically, managers, investors, and accountants have generally preferred that possible errors in measurement be in the direction of understatement rather than overstatement of net income and net assets. This has led to the convention of conservatism. . . .[3]

This convention developed in the early stages of financial reporting when bankers and lenders were the main users of financial reports, especially balance sheets. To the banker, the further the understatement of assets, the greater the margin of safety the assets provided as security for loans. The valuation of certain assets at lower-of-cost-or-market is an example of conservative accounting that gives the banker such security. As we discussed in Chapter 11 and will discuss in Chapter 19, the lower-of-cost-or-market rule is applied to certain assets such as inventories and marketable securities and means that these items are reported at their market values should market values fall below historical costs.

However, in Concepts Statement 2 the FASB clearly stated: "Conserva-

---

[3]American Institute of Certified Public Accountants, Accounting Principles Board, Statement No. 4, *Basic Concepts and Accounting Principles Underlying Financial Statements of Business Enterprises* (New York: AICPA, 1970), par. 171.

tism in financial reporting should no longer connote deliberate, consistent understatement of net assets and profits."[4] The Board correctly noted that understatement in one period leads to overstatement in another period. To demonstrate how this works, assume that an enterprise started operating on January 2, 1984 and ceased operating three years later, on December 31, 1986. At the end of the 3-year period, we are able to determine, with certainty, that the firm earned net income of $300,000. However, during the life of the firm, we do not know with certainty its income in each one of these years. Accountants thus must make estimates and allocations in order to match income and expense in each year. If income in years 1 and 2 is deliberately understated by a total of $50,000, income in year 3 must be overstated by $50,000 for total income over the 3-year period to equal $300,000.

Nonetheless, conservatism is still a reasonable reaction to the uncertainties inherent in business and economic events. For example, if two estimates of the amounts to be collected on an account receivable are equally likely, the less optimistic estimate should be used. However, if the two estimates are not equally likely and the more optimistic one is more likely, it would be an incorrect application of conservatism to use the less optimistic one.

Materiality

In an accounting context, **materiality** refers to the relative importance or significance of an item to an informed decision maker. An item or event is material if it is probable that the judgment of a reasonable person, relying on that information, would have been changed or influenced by its omission or misstatement. If a particular item or transaction is not considered material, it does not make any difference whether it is accounted for in the theoretically correct manner. For example, if a firm purchases a wastepaper basket for $2.50, this item theoretically should be considered an asset and be depreciated over its lifetime. However, because of the immaterial nature of the amount, a firm would most likely consider the entire $2.50 an expense of the current period. Clearly this decision would not affect the decisions of informed financial statement users.

Many decisions regarding materiality are not as clear-cut as the above example is and call for the careful application of the accountant's judgment. The application of materiality often depends on the size of the particular item in relation to the overall size of the firm. Obviously, what is material to Smith's Shoe Store is not material to General Motors. Because of the difficulty in applying the materiality concept, a rule of thumb is often used. For example, an accountant may decide that an item is material if it equals or exceeds 5% of net income or 10% of total assets. Although such yardsticks are helpful, they do not replace the accountant's judgment.

Full Disclosure

The **full disclosure principle** requires that a firm's financial reports provide users with all of the relevant information about the various transactions into which the firm has entered. In implementing the full disclosure principle, accountants are faced with a trade-off between providing information in sufficient detail to be useful in decision making and yet still making the information understandable to informed readers. The footnotes to the financial state-

---

[4]FASB Concepts Statement 2, par. 93.

ments are often used in this regard to more fully explain certain aspects of more important events.

Generally Accepted Conventions

The assumptions and qualitative characteristics just discussed provide a framework within which specific accounting conventions have developed over the last 50 years or so. These conventions are certainly not immutable and, in fact, have changed and will continue to change over time.

Historical Cost

Historical cost has been and continues to be the primary valuation basis used in financial statements. Under this convention, assets are recorded at their acquisition cost and are not adjusted for increases in value until a sale has occurred. However, the costs of appropriate assets are written off as their benefits are consumed. The primary modification to the historical cost convention is conservatism. For example, as we discussed in Chapter 11, inventory is recorded at the lower of cost or market. Thus assets may be recorded below their acquisition cost but may not be written up above their cost.

This historical cost convention is based on the going-concern assumption and verifiability or objectivity. As we noted, because we assume that an enterprise will stay in existence long enough to meet its objectives, liquidation values are not relevant. Verifiability comes into play because many accountants feel that historical cost is the most verifiable or objective of the possible valuation methods. Thus, historical costs are considered more reliable than current costs.

However, a number of accountants and users of financial statements are becoming increasingly concerned that historical cost data, while reliable, is not relevant in a period of significant inflation or changing price levels. They feel that either current cost or current market value should become the primary valuation basis. This is based on the premise that current values are more relevant in evaluating the financial position of the firm and its ability to generate enough profit to maintain its productive capacity. Professional accounting bodies in the United States do not completely accept this view, although as we will see, the FASB does suggest certain current cost to be voluntarily disclosed on a supplemental basis.

Time Periods

Business enterprises are assumed to have an indefinite life unless there is evidence to the contrary (the going-concern assumption). However, users of financial statements, such as investors and creditors, cannot wait until an enterprise ceases operating to measure the firm's performance. In order to make informed decisions, users need information on a timely basis about the enterprise's financial condition and performance. Thus, the enterprise's life span is divided into time periods, which can be as short as a month or a quarter and are rarely longer than a year. This division of the enterprise's life span is called the **time period assumption.**

The legitimate requirements to provide financial data on a timely basis cause many of the accounting problems we have studied. In order to determine periodic income, accountants need to make estimates such as the lives of depreciable assets and the likely percentage of bad debts, and they must choose appropriate inventory cost flow assumptions and depreciation methods. The shorter the accounting period, the more arbitrary these allocations become, and the less reliable the figures become. Yet information must be provided to users, and accountants must use their judgment in making these allocations.

The Matching Convention

We introduced the matching convention in Chapter 3 and have made several references to it subsequently. As we noted, the matching convention simply states that the expenses of one period should be matched against the revenues of that period. A vast majority of accountants feel that the accrual method of accounting results in the best matching and consequently the most useful income figure. The accrual basis of accounting means that revenues are recognized when they are earned and that expenses are recognized when they are incurred.

Revenue and Expense Recognition

In determining when revenue should be recognized, accountants follow what is often referred to as the **realization principle.** In short, this principle states that revenue is earned and therefore should be recognized when two events occur:

1. The earnings process is essentially complete.
2. There is objective evidence as to the exchange or sale price.

Depending on a firm's particular business and industry, these two events can take place at different points in the earnings cycle. The following diagram depicts the different points at which these events may occur:

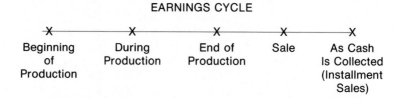

However, the earnings process is continuous, and for most firms it is difficult to state at what exact point the earnings process is complete. At each point in the process, some earnings take place as the firm adds value to products before their actual sale. A flower shop provides a good example of this problem. Assume that the shop purchases some marigold seeds for $10. The seeds are planted and eventually grow into plants that are sold for $25. At what point should we recognize the $15 earned on the production and eventual sale of the plants? Another way of looking at the issue is to ask, "When should the value of the plants be increased from their historical cost of $10 to their sales price of $25?"

Sale As the Point of Revenue Recognition

The application of the revenue recognition principle to most firms leads to the conclusion that the point of sale is the most realistic point at which to recognize revenue. Thus in the above example, no revenue would be recognized until the marigold plants were sold. There are two reasons for this. First, at the point of sale an actual exchange takes place that provides objective evidence as to the amount of revenue that is actually realized. That is, a transaction has been completed. Second, most accountants feel that the earnings process is not complete until an actual sale is made. The sale, therefore, represents the culmination of the earnings process, and so revenue should not be recognized before this point. For these reasons, the sale is considered to be the critical event in the earnings process.

For a service firm, revenues are normally considered earned when the services have been performed. Revenues from allowing others to use the firm's assets include interest, rents, and royalties. Revenues from these items are considered to be earned as time passes or as the assets are used up. Finally, gains or losses from disposing of other assets are recognized as of the date of disposition.

Alternative Recognition Points

The earnings cycle diagram points out that there are other times when revenue recognition can take place. These exceptions are based on industry characteristics that make it reasonable to recognize revenue at a time different from that of the actual sale. We will briefly examine the percentage of completion, the completion of production, and the installment methods of revenue recognition.

Percentage of Completion. Large-scale construction projects can take several years to complete. The primary issue faced by accountants is whether to delay recognizing the revenue from the project until it is complete or to recognize a portion of the revenue in each of the years it takes to complete the project. In the completed contract method, all of the profits earned from the contract are recognized in the year that the project is completed. An alternative method is the percentage of completion method. Under this method revenue is recognized in proportion to the amount of work completed on the project, and thus by its end, all revenue has been recognized. Because of the reliability principle, the percentage of completion method should be used only if reasonable estimates of construction progress and future costs can be made.

End of Production. In some situations it is reasonable to recognize revenue at the point at which the production cycle is complete, but before sale. These situations occur when indistinguishable goods are sold in large, well-developed markets. Examples include certain agricultural products, such as wheat, and precious metals. Because the market can absorb all of the production of these products, a sale is ensured at harvest or mining, and an objective price can be obtained from the marketplace. Because the sale is ensured, the earnings process is complete at the end of production rather than at the point of sale.

Installment Basis. In a few situations, accountants will delay the recognition of revenue until the cash is collected from the sale. These sales are long-term payment plans in which the buyer makes a relatively low down payment and the payments are spread over a number of years. In earlier years, many companies, such as land development firms, recognized all the revenue from their sales at the time of sale but collected only a small portion of the receivable before the buyer defaulted on the arrangement. As a result, accountants require the installment method of accounting to be used in certain circumstances. Under the installment method, which is used only when there is a great deal of uncertainty regarding the collection of the receivable, revenues will be recognized only in proportion to the cash collected.

Expense Recognition

Expense recognition is the other essential ingredient of the matching convention. With the accrual basis of accounting, expenses are recognized when incurred and at that point are matched against revenues. This matching is accomplished by relating the expense to either (1) a particular product sold or a service rendered or (2) a particular time period in which the revenue is recognized.

Some expenses can be related directly to the product that the firm sells or the service it renders. Cost of goods sold is probably the most obvious example. Inventory costs are accumulated in the asset account Inventory and when the inventory is sold, these costs are written off as expenses of Cost of Goods Sold in direct proportion to the units sold. Sales commissions are another example of an expense that is matched against revenues as the revenues are earned. This is so because the amount of the commission is a direct function of the amount of the sale.

Most expenses of a business cannot be directly related to a product or service. These expenses are called **period expenses** and are matched against revenues in the period during which the expenses are incurred. Included in period expenses are what we normally think of as selling and general expenses. Examples include salaries other than direct commissions, insurance, and rent expense.

Accounting for Changing Prices

During the 1970s and the early 1980s, inflation was a persistent problem for the U.S. economy. Unfortunately, double-digit inflation became common. These inflation rates distorted normal business patterns as well as personal purchasing and savings patterns. Although inflation rates have moderated to about 2–4% in recent years, the potential for increasing inflation rates is still in the U.S. economy.

Not only does inflation affect the aggregate U.S. economy, but it can have substantial effects on the reported profits of specific companies.

SAFEWAY

As an example, the following data was taken from the Safeway Stores, Inc. 1985 financial statement (in millions):

	As Reported in the Statement of Income	Adjusted for Changes in Specific Prices (Current Costs)
Sales	$19,650	$19,650
Cost of sales	14,872	14,903
Other expenses, net	4,425	4,461
Income (loss) before provision for income taxes	353	286
Provision for taxes	122	122
Net Income	$ 231	$ 164

As this example points out, changing price levels can have a material effect on earnings that are reported on a historical cost basis. But what do we mean by changing prices, and why are earnings adjusted for changes in specific prices different from historical cost earnings? What did Safeway really earn in 1985, and which of the income figures is most useful to present and potential investors and creditors? Such questions have caused considerable debate both within and outside of the accounting profession and are the subject of the next part of this chapter.

Different Types of Changing Prices

Inflation has become a common word in our daily language. Yet accountants do not speak of accounting for inflation; they speak of accounting for changing prices. This is because *changing prices* is a broader term which considers the two types of price changes that affect any economy: general price level changes and specific price level changes. Both of the changes affect historical cost statements in a different manner, and therefore it is important to understand the distinction between them.

General Price Level Changes

General price level changes measure changes in the ability of the dollar to purchase a variety of goods and services. As the general price level increases, the purchasing power of the dollar declines. Thus, when people talk about inflation they are talking about a rise in the general price level and a corresponding decline in the purchasing power of the dollar. Conversely, deflation occurs when the general price level declines and the purchasing power of the dollar increases. During the early part of 1986, the U.S. economy actually enjoyed a period of deflation due to low oil prices and a sluggish economy.

General price level changes are measured by such indexes as the Consumer Price Index for All Urban Consumers (CPI-U) and the Gross National Product Deflator. These indexes take a representative basket of goods and services and compare its current year's price to its base year's price. This ratio of the current year's price to the base year's price forms the index that measures the weighted-average general price changes in the economy.

The following table shows how a general price level index is calculated. The five commodities in the illustration are assumed to be a representative basket of goods and services, and their prices at the beginning of 1987 are compared with their prices at the end of 1987. Because we assumed that the beginning of 1987 is the base year, the index at that time is 100, and the index at the end of the year is 102. Thus, there has been a 2% increase in the general price level. This means that dollars at the end of 1987 will buy 2% less than the same number of dollars at the beginning of 1987.

Commodity	January 1, 1987	December 31, 1987	Percentage Changes in Individual Items
CALCULATION OF GENERAL PRICE LEVEL CHANGES			
Diesel oil—gallon	$1.10	$1.05	−4.5
Butter—pound	1.80	1.88	+4.4
Hamburger—pound	2.40	2.60	+8.3
Wheat—bushel	1.28	1.20	−6.3
Cotton fabrics—yard	1.93	1.95	+1.0
	$8.51	$8.68	

Price index at December 31, 1987
(Assuming January 1, 1987 index is 100) $\dfrac{\$8.68}{\$8.51} \times 100 = 102$

Specific Price Level Changes

Specific price level changes reflect the change in the value of a specific good or service vis à vis other goods or services. Therefore, specific price changes reflect an adjustment in the price of a particular item such as a building or a gallon of gasoline rather than average change in prices of all items in the economy. In addition to general inflation, specific price changes are caused by market dynamics and distortions such as decreased supply or increased demand or both.

Specific prices are measured by looking at the change in the current cost or value of the individual item under consideration. In the previous table we also calculated the specific price changes of the individual items in the general index. These individual changes ranged from a 6.3% decrease to an 8.3% increase. The U.S. government's Bureau of Labor Statistics as well as other public and private agencies publishes a number of specific price indexes.

The Relationship between General and Specific Price Changes

As the previous table also shows, price changes for all goods and services in the economy do not move together. In this example, the prices of diesel oil and wheat fell while the prices of other commodities rose. This situation occurs all the time, such as the continued decrease in the prices of small calculators and personal computers while the general price level has continued to increase.

To illustrate this concept further, let's assume that an acre of land is purchased at the beginning of the year for $10,000. At the end of the year the current value of the land is determined to be $15,000. Further, during the year the general price level increased 15%. Thus, of the $5,000 increase, $1,500 ($10,000 $\times$ .15) is due to an increase in the general price level, while the remaining $3,500 is due to a specific price increase above the general price level increase. In this example both price changes moved in the same direction, but this is not always the case.

Problems with Financial Statements Not Adjusted for Price Changes

Traditional financial statements in the United States are based on historical costs and are not adjusted for either general or specific prices. The FASB refers to these statements as historical cost/nominal dollar statements. For ease of discussion we refer to these as historical cost statements. In a period of fluctuating prices, many users question the relevance of these statements. As we saw from the Safeway example, when earnings are adjusted for specific price changes, they can be significantly different from earnings reported on a historical cost basis.

General Price Level Changes Ignored

When statements are not adjusted for general price level changes, dollars of different purchasing power are aggregated. This is so because assets such as land, buildings, and inventories were all purchased at different times and thus with dollars of different purchasing power. Many individuals feel that when this occurs the dollar value of total assets on the balance sheet loses its significance. Furthermore, it is difficult to measure a firm's performance in relation to other firms' performance when price levels are changing, because general price level changes do not affect all firms in the same way.

Even more important, historical cost financial statements do not measure

purchasing power gains or losses, which result from holding monetary assets (cash and rights to receive cash) and monetary liabilities (all liabilities other than those requiring the performance of a service). In a period of inflation a firm that holds net monetary assets suffers a purchasing power loss. For example, if you started the year with $5,000 in cash and held those dollars all year while the general price level rose 10%, you suffered a $500 purchasing power loss. This occurs because you would need $5,500 at the end of the year to purchase the same goods as $5,000 had purchased at the beginning of the year, but you still have only $5,000 on hand. Conversely, a firm in a net liability position will incur a gain in a period of inflation because it pays back a fixed amount of dollars whose purchasing power is declining. This gain or loss is not measured by historical cost statements, and as a result income can be over- or understated. These gains or losses can be significant. For example, during 1985 Safeway showed a $103 million purchasing power gain.

If financial statements are adjusted for general price level changes, they can overcome some of the limitations of historical cost statements. The FASB refers to these general price level adjusted statements as historical cost/constant purchasing power dollar statements. (Again, for ease of discussion, we will refer to these as **constant dollar statements.**) These statements are prepared by adjusting historical dollars to dollars of the same or constant purchasing power by using a general price index such as the CPI-U. Although complete constant dollar statements were never required by the FASB, certain supplementary constant dollar disclosures were required. After experimenting with these disclosures, in late 1984 the FASB decided to eliminate all constant dollar disclosures other than the reporting of purchasing power gains and losses.

Specific Price Level Changes Ignored

Historical cost statements are based on the realization principle discussed in Chapter 3. This means that assets and liabilities are recorded at their historical cost and are not adjusted until an exchange has taken place. As a result, current values are not reflected in the financial statements and revenue generally is not recognized until a sale takes place.

To illustrate, assume that one item of inventory is purchased at a cost of $100. This inventory is held until the end of the year, at which time its replacement cost increases to $125. At the beginning of the next year the item is sold for $135. Assuming the firm entered into no other transactions, a traditional income statement would show no income for the first year but would show income of $35 ($135 − $100) in the second year. A number of accounting theorists argue that this is misleading because the increase in value was not reported when it occurred. These individuals feel that a holding gain of $25 occurred during the first year as the inventory increased in value from $100 to $125. In the second year, an operating gain of $10 occurred when the inventory with a current value of $125 was sold for $135. Thus, the total income over the 2-year period is still $35, but it is allocated as a $25 holding gain in year 1 and a $10 operating gain in year 2. Further, at the end of the first year the inventory is recorded on the balance sheet as $125, its current cost.

The FASB refers to financial statements adjusted for specific price changes as current cost/nominal dollar. For ease of discussion, we will refer to these as **current cost statements.** Although the FASB does not require firms to prepare complete current cost statements, it does require certain current cost disclosures. These disclosures are discussed later.

Statements Adjusted for Both General and Specific Prices

Many individuals feel that to reflect economic reality properly, financial statements should be adjusted for both specific and general price level changes. These statements, referred to as **current cost/constant purchasing power dollar statements** by the FASB, combine the attributes of both current cost and constant dollar statements.

FASB Statements 33 and 82

After years of controversy and debate, the FASB decided that the effects of changing prices were significant enough to require some recognition in the financial statements. As a result, in September 1979 the FASB issued Statement 33, which requires large firms to disclose on a supplemental basis certain financial information adjusted for changing prices. After studying the effects of this statement for five years, the Board issued Statement 82, which reduced the supplemental disclosures required under Statement 33. Recently, the FASB reduced these requirements further by making all disclosures voluntary. Specifically, Statement 33, as amended by these other statements encourages the voluntary disclosure of the following items:

1. Information on income from continuing operations for the current fiscal year on a current cost basis.
2. The purchasing power gain or loss on net monetary items for the current fiscal year.
3. The current cost amounts of inventory and property, plant, and equipment at the end of the current fiscal year.
4. Increases or decreases for the current fiscal year in the current cost amounts of inventory and of property, plant, and equipment, net of inflation.
5. A summary of selected data for the five most recent fiscal years.[5]

Prior to the change made by Statement 82, firms also had to disclose information on income from continuing operations on a constant dollar as well as a current cost basis. However, the Board felt that these constant dollar figures were not used by financial statement readers and were not as meaningful as current cost figures. Thus, under current rules only income from continuing operations on a current cost basis has to be disclosed if supplemental disclosures are to be made.

In these Statements, the FASB suggests the disclosure of only selected constant dollar and current cost information. That is, complete current cost statements are not required. Adjustments are made to only the inventory; cost of goods sold; property, plant, and equipment; and depreciation expense accounts. This is so because the Board felt that the major effects of changing prices are on these accounts and, in addition, the Board wanted to ease some of the implementation problems.

The disclosures required by Statements 33 and 82 (which are prior to the new voluntary rules) are illustrated in Exhibit 14–2, which presents changing prices data for Safeway Stores, Inc.

---

[5]FASB Statement No. 33, *Financial Reporting and Changing Prices* (Stamford, Conn.: FASB, September 1979), pars. 29 and 30.

EXHIBIT 14–2

Note L–Supplementary Information on Inflation and Changing Prices (Unaudited)

The company's primary financial statements are stated on the basis of historical costs. The statements reflect the actual transactions expressed in the number of dollars earned or expended without regard to changes in the purchasing power of the dollar. The following supplementary information attempts to measure the effect of changes in specific prices on the results of operations by restating historical costs to amounts which approximate the current costs to the company of producing or replacing inventories and property.

The computed net income for 1985 under current cost accounting includes restatements of merchandise costs, depreciation and amortization expense. The effects of inflation on merchandise costs have already been recognized in the historical financial statements to the extent that the LIFO method of accounting is used for approximately 68 percent of merchandise inventories.

The provision for income taxes has not been restated to a current cost basis because inflation adjustments are not deductible for income tax purposes.

The purchasing power gain results from an excess of net monetary liabilities over monetary assets. In periods of general inflation monetary assets lose purchasing power because such assets will buy fewer goods. Conversely monetary liabilities gain purchasing power since the liabilities will be repaid with dollars of reduced purchasing power.

In 1985, the current costs of merchandise inventories and property increased by $418.7 million, whereas those assets increased by $225.4 million as a result of general inflation. Thus, the year's increase in inventories and property due to current cost exceeded the increase in general inflation by $193.3 million, indicating a greater increase in the company's specific price indices than the rate of general inflation. At year-end 1985, the current cost of merchandise inventories was $1.9 billion and the current cost of net property was $3.8 billion.

Current cost accounting methods involve the use of assumptions, estimates and subjective judgments, and the results should not be viewed as precise measurements of the effects of inflation.

Supplementary Financial Data Adjusted for the Effects of Changing Prices *(in millions)*

	1985	
	As Reported in the Consolidated Statement of Income (Historical Cost)	Adjusted for Changes in Specific Prices (Current Cost)
Sales	$19,650	$19,650
Cost of sales	14,872	14,903
Other expenses, net	4,425	4,461
Income before provision for income taxes	353	286
Provision for income taxes	122	122
Net income	$ 231	164
Gain from the change in purchasing power of net monetary liabilities		103
Net income including purchasing power gain		$ 267
Depreciation and amortization expense*	$ 333	$ 422

*Allocated between cost of sales and other expenses in the determination of net income.

The following amounts for 1985 reflect the current cost assumption discussed in the preceding. Prior year amounts are adjusted to reflect the relationship between the average CPI-U for each of the years indicated as measured against the average CPI-U for 1985.

Five-Year Comparison of Selected Financial Data Adjusted for the Effects of Changing Prices
(in dollars of 1985 average purchasing power)

	1985	1984	1983	1982	1981
Sales	$19,650	$20,343	$20,068	$19,652	$19,611
Net income (loss)	164	57	22	23	(50)
Net income (loss) per share of common stock	2.72	.96	.40	.45	(.96)
Gain from the change in purchasing power of net monetary liabilities	103	100	96	93	216
Net income including gain in purchasing power	267	158	118	116	166
Increase in the current costs of merchandise inventories and property over (under) the increase due to general inflation	193	(140)	83	(161)	(280)
Net assets at year-end	3,034	2,951	3,045	2,762	2,913
Cash dividends per share of common stock	1.625	1.579	1.539	1.477	1.538
Market price per share of common stock at year-end	36.62	28.48	27.80	25.49	15.67
Average Consumer Price Index (CPI-U)	322.2	311.1	298.4	289.1	272.4

Note: Dollars in millions except per share amounts.

The Theory behind Constant Dollar Accounting

The primary objective of constant dollar accounting is to prepare financial statements that are adjusted for general price level changes. This means that the items on the financial statements are stated in dollars of the same purchasing power. In all other respects the historical cost model is maintained. However, the measuring unit becomes a constant dollar rather than the nominal dollar. The traditional realization principle is not changed. That is, historical costs are adjusted to dollars of equal purchasing power, but they are not adjusted for current costs. For example, on page 538 we provided an example of land purchased for $10,000. During the year the inflation rate was 15% and the current cost of the land at year-end was $15,000. On a constant dollar statement, the land would be shown at a constant dollar amount of $11,500, or $10,000 + ($10,000 × .15), not its current cost of $15,000 nor its historical cost of $10,000.

The primary constant dollar disclosure that is presently required by the FASB is purchasing power gain or loss. The first step in determining this gain or loss is to distinguish between monetary and nonmonetary assets and liabilities. As we have noted, monetary assets and liabilities are subject to purchasing power gains and losses. However, nonmonetary assets and liabilities do not represent fixed claims on dollars, and as the general price level increases, nonmonetary items retain their purchasing power.

To illustrate the concepts involved, we will assume that the Instant Gold Company was organized on December 31, 1987. At that time the inventory, land, and buildings were purchased. Business commenced January 2, 1988. The financial statements reflecting the first year of operations (1988) are presented in Exhibit 14–3. Other relevant data are also presented in that exhibit.

EXHIBIT 14–3

Instant Gold Company
Historical Cost Balance Sheet
December 31,

Assets:	1988	1987	Liabilities and owner's	1988	1987
Cash	$ 6,500	$ 3,000	equity:		
Accounts receivable	8,000	0	Accounts payable	$ 10,000	$ 0
Inventory	12,000	4,000	L. Morton, capital	90,000	82,000
Land	30,000	30,000			
Buildings, net	43,500	45,000	Total liabilities and		
Total assets	$100,000	$82,000	owner's equity	$100,000	$82,000

Instant Gold Company
Historical Cost Income Statement
For the Year Ended December 31, 1988

Sales		$100,000
Cost of goods sold		
Beginning inventory	$ 4,000	
Purchases	68,000	
Cost of goods available for sale	72,000	
Less: Ending inventory	12,000	
Cost of goods sold		60,000
Gross margin on sales		40,000
Operating expenses		
Selling and general and administrative, excluding depreciation	$28,500	
Depreciation	1,500	30,000
Net income		$ 10,000

Other Data
Relevant General Price Level Indexes:

Date	Index	Event, Where Appropriate
December 31, 1987	150	Company formed; inventory, land, and buildings purchased
Average for 1988*	165	Used for monetary asset and liability inflows and outflows
December 31, 1988	175	Date owner withdrew cash
Inflation Rate	16.67%†	

*The average for the year is a monthly average and does not necessarily equal the average of the beginning and ending price indices.

†$\frac{(175 - 150)}{150} = 16.67\%$

The monetary assets on Instant Gold's balance sheet are cash and receivables. The monetary liability is the accounts payable. In order to determine the purchasing power gain or loss, monetary assets and liabilities must be restated to dollars of current purchasing power. This is accomplished by multiplying the historical cost of these items by a conversion factor—the current year's price index divided by the index that existed when the monetary asset or liability was recorded in the accounts. Specifically, the formula is:

$$\begin{array}{c} \text{Constant dollar} \\ \text{amount} \end{array} = \begin{array}{c} \text{Historical} \\ \text{cost} \end{array} \times \dfrac{\begin{array}{c} \text{Index at end} \\ \text{of the year} \end{array}}{\begin{array}{c} \text{Index when the} \\ \text{item was acquired} \end{array}}$$

Following is a schedule showing how the purchasing power loss of $713 suffered by the Instant Gold Company during 1988 is determined.

Instant Gold Company
Schedule of Purchasing Power Loss
For the Year Ended December 31, 1988

Net monetary assets, 1/1/87	$ 3,000[a] × 175/150 =	$ 3,500*
Add: Sales	100,000 × 175/165 =	106,061
	$103,000	$109,561
Less:		
Purchases	$ 68,000 × 175/165 =	$ 72,121
Selling and general administrative expenses	28,500 × 175/165 =	30,227
Owner's withdrawals	2,000 × 175/175 =	2,000
	$ 98,500	$104,348
Net monetary position, 12/31/88, restated		5,213
Net monetary position, 12/31/88, actual	4,500[b]	4,500
Purchasing power loss		(713)

*Rounded to whole dollars where appropriate.

[a]Net monetary position, 1/1/88

Cash	$3,000

[b]Net monetary position, 12/31/88

Cash	$ 6,500
Receivables	8,000
	14,500
Less: Accounts payable	10,000
	$ 4,500

The following procedures were used in calculating the loss:

1. Restate the net monetary assets or liabilities at the beginning of the year to their value in terms of year-end purchasing power. This is done by multiplying the conversion factor of 175/150 by the net monetary asset position at the beginning of the year. The denominator is 150 because these assets were on hand at the beginning of the year, and they are assumed to be held all year.
2. Restate all transactions during the year that increased monetary items so that they reflect year-end value. These items will include sales and the proceeds

from the sale of other assets, if any. In this situation, only sales increased monetary items and they are assumed to take place evenly throughout the year so that the conversion factor is 175/165.[6] This restated figure is added to the amount calculated in Step 1.

3. Restate all transactions that decreased monetary items so that they reflect year-end values. These items are subtracted from the total in Step 2. Included are purchases and selling and administrative expenses and taxes. They are restated using the conversion factor, 175/165, because they are assumed to take place evenly throughout the year.

In this case the owner's withdrawal must also be subtracted. However, no restatement is necessary because it was paid on December 31, 1988. Depreciation expense is ignored because it does not affect any monetary items. That is, the depreciation entry just affects two nonmonetary accounts, Depreciation Expense (Owner's Equity) and Accumulated Depreciation. Only the purchases component of cost of goods sold is adjusted because this amount represents a net monetary asset outflow in the current period.

4. Subtract the excess of monetary assets or liabilities based on actual historical costs from the figure in Step 3 to arrive at a purchasing power gain or loss.

A $713 loss occurred because, in order to maintain its purchasing power, the Instant Gold Company needed to have net monetary assets of $5,213 at the end of the year. Since there was only $4,500 of net monetary assets on December 31, 1988, the company suffered a loss of $713 ($5,213 − $4,500).

In this example a loss occurred because the firm held net monetary assets in a period of inflation. However, in reality, a gain or loss may occur depending on a firm's particular monetary position and the rate and direction of general price level changes. The following table illustrates when a purchasing power gain or loss results:

	Actual Monetary Position	
Restated Amount	Net Assets	Net Liability
Exceeds actual	Loss	Gain
Less than actual	Gain	Loss

Interpreting Purchasing Power Gains and Losses

The Instant Gold Company suffered a $713 purchasing power loss due to the effect of general price level changes or inflation upon the purchasing power of its net monetary assets. This purchasing power loss is in addition to the results of the firm's operations computed on either a historical cost or constant dollar basis. In effect, if a firm had no revenues or expenses but held net monetary assets during a period of inflation, it would suffer a purchasing power loss.

On the other hand, Safeway had a purchasing power gain of $103 million. This results from the fact that Safeway had an excess of monetary liabilities over monetary assets. Safeway's assets are primarily nonmonetary due to the fact that it has few receivables and has large amounts of inventory. Yet most of its liabilities are monetary. Other companies with different financial characteristics are likely to incur heavy purchasing power losses. For example, Sears incurred a $56 million purchasing power loss during 1985, because Sears has large amounts of receivables and other monetary assets.

There is some controversy as to whether the purchasing power gain or

[6]It is important to note that all sales, whether for cash or on account, increase net monetary assets because both cash and receivables are monetary items.

loss should be included as part of income. For example, Safeway includes its $103 million purchasing power gain in a figure called Net Income Including Gain in Purchasing Power. (See Exhibit 14–2 on page 544.) Some individuals argue that this treatment is potentially misleading. They note that the gain is more the result of Safeway's financial characteristics than the successful efforts of management. Further, they argue that these purchasing power gains do not provide funds for dividends, wages, and other uses. Sears' 1985 supplemental price level disclosures show its $56 million purchasing power loss as a separate line item, and it is not included in an adjusted net income figure.

Current Cost Financial Statements

Current value accounting represents a departure from historical cost accounting in that the attribute being measured is current value rather than historical cost, whether or not adjusted for general price level changes. In this context, when accountants speak of current value they generally mean current cost.

Current Cost is the current replacement cost of an asset in its current condition with a similar asset. Current replacement cost measurements can be difficult to obtain for operational assets in which the value of the service potential of the asset rather than the asset itself is being measured. Nevertheless, in most circumstances the FASB uses current cost to measure current value. The FASB suggests the use of specific price indexes, current price lists, or appraisals in determining current costs.

The Theory behind Current Cost Financial Statements

To illustrate the basic theory behind current cost financial statements, we will return to the example on page 539. In the example, an item of inventory was purchased during year 1 for $100. At the end of the year the item's current cost increased to $125. An unrealized holding gain of $25 is calculated as follows:

Current cost	$125
Less: Historical cost	100
Unrealized holding gain	$ 25

Under current cost accounting, the inventory on the balance sheet at the end of the year is shown as $125. The $25 holding gain is shown as a separate component of current cost net income.

When the inventory is sold in January of the next year for $135, operating income of $10 is reported, calculated as follows:

Sale	$135
Less: Current cost of inventory	125
Operating income	$ 10

Under historical cost accounting, income of $35 ($135 − $100) is reported in the second year. Note that the $35 figure is equal to the $25 unrealized holding gain plus the $10 operating profit. Proponents of current cost accounting argue that because it takes $125 to replace the item of inventory just sold, $10 is the real operating profit. This is the amount that remains after the company has maintained its capital in terms of productive capacity because $25 of the historical cost profit must be reinvested in inventory if the firm is to remain a going concern.

Preparing Current Cost Statements

Preparing current cost statements involves a number of complex procedures that are beyond the scope of a principles of accounting course. Following are a current cost balance sheet and an income statement for the Instant Gold Company and, because the FASB requires certain current cost disclosures, we will briefly discuss how they are prepared.

Instant Gold Company
Current Cost Balance Sheet
December 31, 1988

Assets		Liabilities and Owner's Equity	
Cash	$ 6,500	Accounts payable	$ 10,000
Accounts receivable	8,000	L. Morton, capital	94,400
Inventory	13,500		
Land	30,000		
Building, net	46,400	Total liabilities and	
Total assets	$104,400	owner's equity	$104,400

The Current Cost Balance Sheet

A current cost balance sheet lists all the accounts at their current cost. In the Instant Gold example, we assumed that the only items whose current costs differ from their historical costs are the inventory and the building. The current cost of the inventory is $13,500 while the gross current cost of the building before depreciation is $48,000. By the end of 1988, one year's depreciation has been taken, and on a current cost basis it equals $1,600 ($48,000 ÷ 30 years).[7] This assumes a 30-year life, no salvage value, and straight-line depreciation. Therefore, the net current cost at December 31, 1988 is $46,400, or $48,000 − $1,600. The Capital account supplies the amount needed to balance the balance sheet.

The Current Cost Income Statement

A current cost income statement for the Instant Gold Company follows. Net operating income of $7,400 is equal to sales less all expenses at current cost. In the Instant Gold Company example, only cost of goods sold and depreciation expense are different on a current cost basis. Cost of goods sold on a current cost basis is assumed to be $62,500, while current cost depreciation is $1,600 as just calculated. The $7,400 net operating income represents the income available to the company after maintaining its productive capacity. This is the figure the FASB requires to be disclosed on a supplemental basis.

---

[7]In reality, the calculation of current cost depreciation is quite complex. For example, the FASB argues that the expense should be based on the asset's average current cost for the year. For simplicity, we calculated depreciation expense on the year-end current cost.

Instant Gold Company
Current Cost Income Statement
For the Year Ended December 31, 1988

Sales		$100,000
Cost of goods sold		62,500
Current cost gross margin		37,500
Operating expenses		
Selling, general, and administrative	$28,500	
Depreciation	1,600	30,100
Net operating income		$ 7,400

Consistent with FASB disclosures, in this income statement we have not included unrealized holding gains or losses (the increase or decrease in the current value of assets and liabilities still on hand). Instead, they are indirectly included in the L. Morton, Capital account, since the number in this account is the amount needed to balance the balance sheet. Some accountants argue that these unrealized gains and losses should be included in that income.

Interpreting Current Cost Statements

The current cost model rests on a particular theory of capital maintenance. The purpose of current cost accounting is to maintain capital in terms of the firm's productive capacity, that is, the ability of the firm to continue to produce goods and services. As a result, income is not earned until the firm's productive capacity at the end of the period is at least as great as it was at the beginning of the period.

Referring to the Safeway example on page 541, net income on a historical cost basis was $231 million, while on a current cost basis, before unrealized gains and losses and the addition of the purchasing power gain, the net income is only $164 million. The causes of this difference are the excess of current cost depreciation and cost of goods sold over historical cost depreciation and cost of goods sold. Essentially, these figures indicate that Safeway has been able to earn enough income to maintain its productive capacity, but only by $164 million. Considering that Safeway paid over $98 million in dividends during 1985, many would argue that its productive capacity actually increased by only $66 million.

Current Cost/Constant Dollar Statements

Complete current cost/constant dollar statements also can be prepared. The advantage of these statements is that they combine the benefits of both current cost and constant dollar statements. To illustrate the complete preparation of these statements is beyond the scope of an introductory course. Rather, a simple example can illustrate the concept behind current cost/constant dollar statements.

In the example on page 539 we assumed that an item of inventory was purchased in year 1 for $100. At the end of the year the item's current cost increased to $125. Now assume that during that period the general price level increased 4%. In this case, the holding gain, net of inflation, is only $21, calculated as follows:

Current cost	$125
Historical cost adjusted for 4% Inflation ($100 × 1.04)	104
Holding gain, net of inflation	$ 21

In effect, $4 of the original holding gain of $25 is the result of inflation and does not represent real income available to the firm to maintain its productive capacity.

The FASB requires only limited current cost/constant dollar disclosures. Under the present rules, firms must disclose the increase in the current cost of inventories and property net of the effect of inflation. Using the above data, the firm would report a $21 increase in the current cost of its inventory net of the $4 effect of inflation. Referring again to Exhibit 14–2, Safeway reports that 1985's increase in inventories and property due to current cost exceeded the increase in general inflation by $193.3 million, indicating a greater increase in the company's specific price indexes than the rate of general inflation. That is, during the year the current cost of inventories and property increased $193.3 due to specific price increases and another $225.4 million as a result of general inflation.

Accounting for Inflation—A Summary

Accounting for changing prices has been and continues to be a controversial subject both inside and outside the accounting profession. The requirements of Statement 33, as amended by Statement 82, are complex and in some cases costly to implement. Whether this data is useful to present and potential investors and creditors is a question for research. Recognizing this, the FASB considers the requirements of Statement 33 to be experimental. As a result, the FASB is constantly reassessing the impact of the data and has begun to make changes such as those in Statement 82 and the recent statement which makes the disclosures voluntary.

Summary of Learning Objectives

1. *The development of accounting concepts and standards.* The development of accounting concepts and standards is necessary to ensure the integrity and credibility of financial statements. The two major groups that currently are involved in setting accounting standards are the SEC and the FASB.

2. *The conceptual framework project.* The FASB has been working on the conceptual framework project since its inception in 1973. The purpose of this project is to develop objectives and concepts that the FASB will use in setting specific accounting standards and procedures. In this regard, the FASB has issued six Concept Statements.

3. *The main accounting concepts and conventions.* There are a number of accounting concepts and conventions that represent a consensus as to what is useful accounting information and what qualitative character-

istics this information should have. Exhibit 14–1 lists 13 of the more important of these concepts.

4. *The need for and concepts related to accounting for changing prices.* Traditional financial statements are based on historical costs. However, in a period of changing prices, these statements no longer present all the relevant information informed users need to make resource allocation decisions. The following table presents the alternatives to accounting for changing prices that have been developed:

Type of Price Change	Accounting Alternatives Available
None or slight	Historical cost/nominal dollar accounting
General	Historical cost/constant purchasing power accounting
Specific	Current cost/nominal dollar accounting
General and specific	Current cost/constant purchasing power accounting

FASB Statements 33 and 82 require the supplemental disclosure of purchasing power gains and losses, current cost information, and limited current cost/constant dollar information for large companies.

5. *The basic procedures involved in accounting for changing prices.* The primary constant dollar disclosure that is presently required by the FASB is a purchasing power gain or loss. In order to determine a purchasing power gain or loss, monetary assets and liabilities must be restated to dollars of current purchasing power. Monetary assets or liabilities based on historical costs are subtracted from the restated amount to arrive at a purchasing power gain or loss.

On a current cost balance sheet, all items other than owner's equity are shown at their current cost. A current cost income statement is prepared by subtracting expenses at their current cost from revenues recognized during the period.

Key Terms

Comparability
Conceptual Framework Project
Conservatism
Consistency
Constant Dollar Statements
Current Cost
Current Cost/Constant Purchasing Power
  Dollar Statements
Current Cost Statements
Full Disclosure Principle

General Price Level Changes
Materiality
Period Expenses
Purchasing Power Gains or Losses
Realization Principle
Relevance
Reliability
Specific Price Level Changes
Time Period Assumption
Verifiability

Problems for Your Review

A. Accounting Concepts. Each of the following statements describes an independent transaction:

1. The Smith Grocery Store has been on the FIFO method of inventory valuation since it commenced business 20 years ago. This year the company changed to the LIFO method in order to reduce its taxes. The effect was to reduce income by $2.5 million in the current year.

2. Andrea Levini decided to open a home decorating service. After the business started, she saw a sofa which she wanted for her personal use. She purchased the sofa with business funds. The sofa was recorded on the firm's books although it was used solely by Andrea.

3. The Watch Clock Company makes watches with spring mechanisms. Recent digital mechanisms have made a good part of the company's inventory obsolete. The inventory has a cost of $10 million although its fair market value is only $7.5 million. The company still carries the inventory on its books at $10 million.

4. The Newton Take-Out Pizza Parlor purchased a delivery truck. The truck had a cost of $7,500 and was expensed in the current period.

5. H. Stein has owned a successful delicatessen for many years. Stein just hired a famous chef and feels business will increase 20% per year. As a result, he instructs his accountant to debit goodwill and credit contributed capital for $40,000.

Required:

For each independent statement, discuss the accounting assumption(s) or convention involved.

Solution

1. The consistency and disclosure conventions or principles are involved. There is a presumption that once an accounting method is selected, it should not be changed unless a change is made to a preferable one. In this case, the firm's financial statements in the current year will not be consistent with previous years' statements. Full disclosure is also involved because once the change is made, the company must disclose the effect on income in the current year.

2. The entity assumption is involved. The sofa should not be shown on the books of the company because it is used solely for Andrea's personal use.

3. The conservatism convention is involved in this situation. The inventory is obsolete and should be written down to market because market is lower than cost. The matching principle is also involved because by not taking the loss in the period in which it occurred, revenues and expenses are not properly matched.

4. This situation involves the matching convention. Here a capital expenditure was treated as a revenue expenditure. Thus revenue and expenses will not be properly matched in the individual years over the entire life of the delivery truck.

5. This situation involves quantifiability and objectivity. Under current accounting practices, accountants feel there is no objective way to quantify the benefits provided by the new chef. Thus, goodwill should not be recognized at this time. Goodwill is only recognized when it is purchased.

B. Accounting for Changing Prices. The historical cost income statement for Nikolai's Shoe Store follows:

Nikolai's Shoe Store		
Historical Cost Income Statement		
For the Year Ended December 31, 1988		
Sales		$400,000
Cost of goods sold		
Beginning inventory	$ 30,000	
Purchases	270,000	
Cost of goods available for sale	300,000	
Ending inventory	40,000	260,000
Gross margin on sales		140,000
Operating expenses		
Selling and general and administrative	87,000	
Depreciation	5,000	92,000
Net income		$ 48,000

Additional Information:

1. Relevant price indexes:

Date	Index	Event
January 1, 1988	130	
Average for 1988	140	
September 30, 1988	145	Date owner made a cash withdrawal
December 31, 1988	150	

2. The owner of the company withdrew $5,000 on September 30, 1988.
3. The firm held a net monetary asset position of $5,000 on January 1, 1988. All items affecting the position are described above. (Hint: The net monetary asset position at 12/31/88 is $43,000.)
4. Unless otherwise indicated, assume all items of income and expense took place evenly throughout the year.

Required:

Prepare a schedule computing a purchasing power gain or loss. Round off to whole dollars where appropriate.

Solution

Nikolai's Shoe Store
Schedule of Purchasing Power Gain or Loss
For the Year Ended December 31, 1988

Net monetary position 1/1/88	$ 5,000 × 150/130[a] =	$ 5,769
Increases:		
Sales	400,000 × 150/140 =	428,571
	$405,000	$434,340
Decreases:[b]		
Purchases	$270,000 × 150/140 =	$289,286
Selling, general, and administrative expenses	87,000 × 150/140 =	93,214
Owner's withdrawals[c]	5,000 × 150/145 =	5,172
	$362,000	$387,672
		46,668
Net monetary position 12/31/88	43,000	43,000
Purchasing power loss		($ 3,668)

Notes: [a]Beginning of year index; items are held all year.

[b]Depreciation not included as it does not affect monetary item.

[c]September 30, 1988 index used, as this is when the owner withdrew cash. All other items adjusted using 1988 average index.

Questions

1. What does the term *generally accepted accounting principles* mean? Why are such principles or standards necessary?

2. What are the two groups that have the greatest influence over the development of generally accepted accounting principles? Briefly describe their function.

3. What is the conceptual framework project and what does it hope to accomplish?

4. What is meant by the business-entity and going-concern assumptions? What accounting procedures are affected by these assumptions about the economic environment?

5. Due to the special selection and training of the upper management of the Roberto Company, the board of directors believes that management should be considered an asset. What advice would you give the board concerning recording management as an asset? What accounting concept supports your conclusion?

6. Many individuals feel that accounting information must possess certain qualitative characteristics to be useful. In many cases there are trade-offs among these characteristics. Discuss each of the following trade-offs:
   a. Relevance versus reliability.
   b. Full disclosure versus information overload.

7. Define *reliability*. How does the concept of verifiability impact on reliability?

8. What do accountants mean by conservatism? Why do you think that this characteristic of financial information has been part of accounting for so long? Are there situations where it is possible to be too conservative? When?

9. Due to a change in economic conditions, a firm decides to switch from one accounting method to another. What principle is being violated, and what principle would require that the change be noted in the financial statements?

10. The Winwrich Co., a large conglomerate, has a policy of expensing all items under $1,000. Do you agree with this policy? What accounting characteristic is involved?

11. Why has the historical cost convention played such a central role in accounting in the United States? Can you think of any countries where historical cost would be clearly inappropriate? If so, list them and discuss why.

12. Distinguish between general price level changes and specific price level changes. Why is it important to make this distinction when accounting for changing prices?

13. What do people mean by *inflation*? Name two common indexes used to measure inflation.

14. How are specific price level changes measured?

15. Define the following terms:
   a. Monetary assets.
   b. Monetary liabilities.
   c. Constant dollar accounting.
   d. Purchasing power gain or loss.

16. Financial statements that are not adjusted for changing prices are called historical cost/nominal dollar statements. Some individuals contend that these statements are no longer relevant for decision makers. What are the reasons for this contention?

17. What are the basic provisions of FASB Statement No. 33? What changes were made by FASB Statement No. 82? What is the current status of disclosures related to changing prices?

18. At the beginning of the year, the Lynch Co. purchased a downtown office building for $1 million. At the end of the year the building was appraised at $1,150,000. During the year the inflation rate was 8%. Determine the amount of price increase due to inflation and the amount due to the specific price change.

19. What are the basic theoretical differences between current cost accounting and current cost/constant purchasing power accounting?

20. For many large U.S. companies, the difference between historical cost and current cost or constant dollar cost of goods sold is not as great as the difference in historical cost depreciation and the current cost and constant dollar measures of depreciation. Why do you think that this is the case?

21. Name an industry, besides those mentioned in the text, in which firms are likely to have a large purchasing power gain. Name an industry in which firms are likely to incur large purchasing power losses.

Exercises

1. Accounting Conventions and Principles. For each of the following independent situations, describe the accounting assumptions, characteristics, or conventions that are violated. There may be more than one answer for each situation.

   a. Hillary Wong is the sole proprietor of Wong Jewelry Imports. During March the following items were recorded as expenses on the firm's books:

Rent on office	$500
Employees' wages	700
Supplies for personal use	100
Advertising	250
Pleasure travel	800

   b. The Wright Company began business in 1986. The company used the LIFO method of inventory valuation. In 1987 the firm used the FIFO method. When the 1986 and 1987 comparative financial statements were issued, no mention was made of this change.

c. The Weiss Company spent $200,000 in employee training during the current year. This amount was included under the intangible assets section of the balance sheet with the caption "Investment in employees."

d. During 1987 the Sunshine Furniture Company filed suit against Robert's, Inc. for $325,000 for damages caused by Robert's to merchandise delivered to Sunshine. Sunshine's lawyers are very confident that they will win the suit and collect the full amount. Based on this opinion, Sunshine recorded a receivable for $325,000 on its 1987 balance sheet.

e. A fancy stapling machine costing $125 was debited to the Office Equipment account and will be depreciated over 10 years.

2. Accounting Conventions and Principles. For each of the following independent situations, state the accounting convention, characteristic, or assumption that is involved. There may be more than one answer for each question.

a. Earth Airlines has suffered huge losses in recent years and may not be able to continue to operate in the future. The firm's public accountants feel that this information should be disclosed in their opinion.

b. The following footnote was taken from an annual report of General Motors:

There are various claims and pending actions against the Corporation and its subsidiaries with respect to commercial matters, including warranties and product liability, governmental regulations including environmental and safety matters, civil rights, patent matters, taxes and other matters arising out of the conduct of the business. Certain of these actions purport to be class actions, seeking damages in very large amounts. The amounts of liability on these claims and actions at December 31, 1982 were not determinable but, in the opinion of the management, the ultimate liability resulting will not materially affect the consolidated financial position or results of operations of the Corporation and its consolidated subsidiaries.

c. The president of the Crazy Accounting Supply Co. consistently switches accounting methods in order to improve the profit picture of the company. Because these changes are consistently made, the president does not feel he is violating any accounting rules.

3. Accounting for Changing Prices. During 1987 the Prudential Plaza Company purchased a plot of land for $100,000. At the end of 1987 the land was appraised at $160,000. During the year the general price level rose 12%. How would the land be listed on the December 31, 1987 balance sheet under each of the following methods:

a. Historical cost.

b. Constant dollar.

c. Current cost.

4. Determining a Price Index. As an accountant in the cost accounting department of Shop Here Markets, you are asked by the controller to determine the effect of inflation on the market's products based on a representative basket of groceries. You have gathered the following data:

	Prices	
Item	January 1	December 31
Butter (pound)	$1.70	$1.79
Hamburger (pound)	1.65	1.60
Lettuce (head)	.40	.60
Diapers (dozen)	2.35	2.59
Coffee (pound)	2.20	2.14
Milk (gallon)	1.05	1.05

Required:

a. Determine the December 31 price index for the market, assuming that the January 1 index equals 100.

b. What does this new price index mean when some prices are rising, some are falling, and some remain stable?

5. Purchasing Power Gain or Loss. The Hernandez Company was formed at the beginning of 1987. Cash of $100,000 and computer equipment with a fair market value of $500,000 were contributed by the owner to the company. The company spent all of 1987 in start-up preparations and did not actually begin sales until 1988. The only transaction that occurred in 1987 was a $55,000 bank loan the firm received on July 1, 1987. At the beginning of 1987 the consumer price index was 100; it was 110 on July 1, 1987, and 120 at year-end. Determine the purchasing power gain or loss incurred by Hernandez during the year. (Round to whole dollars.)

6. Calculating a Purchasing Power Gain or Loss. The Pao Company was formed several years ago. The president of the company is concerned about how the recent high rates of inflation have affected the company. She provides you with the following financial data and asks you to prepare a schedule calculating the firm's purchasing power gain or loss:

The Pao Company
Historical Cost Income and Owner's Equity Statements
For the Year Ended December 31, 1987

Sales		$320,000
Cost of goods sold		
Beginning inventory	$ 20,000	
Purchases	280,000	
Cost of goods available for sale	300,000	
Less ending inventory	60,000	240,000
Gross margin on sales		80,000
Operating expenses, except depreciation	$ 56,000	
Depreciation	10,000	66,000
Net income		14,000
Beginning owner's equity		80,000
Withdrawals		(8,000)
Ending owner's equity		$ 86,000

Additional Information:

a. Relevant price indexes:
  1. January 1, 1987   125
  2. average for the year   130
  3. December 31, 1987   135
b. The withdrawals were made at the end of the year.
c. All other items were earned or incurred evenly throughout the year.
d. Net monetary asset position:

January 1, 1987	$50,000
December 31, 1987	26,000

Round to whole dollars where appropriate.

7. Purchasing Power Gains and Losses. The following selected accounts were taken from the records of Wingit Company:

Beginning inventory	$12,000	Sales	$50,000
Salaries expense	16,000	Depreciation expense	4,000
Sales returns	2,000	Purchases	30,000
L. Wingit, drawing	1,000	Rent expense	1,500
Ending inventory	14,000		

In addition, the company purchased a plot of land for $50,000 cash during the year.

Required:

Which of these accounts would be involved in the computation of the purchasing power gain or loss of the Wingit Company? Why?

8. Current Cost Income Statements. The Beta Byte Company began operations at the beginning of 1987. At that time the firm purchased 2,000 bytes, its main inventory item, at a cost of $20 per unit. Also at that time, the firm purchased all of its equipment at a cost of $20,000. All the equipment has an estimated useful life of 10 years with no salvage value, and the firm uses the straight-line method of depreciation. During the year the firm sold 1,400 bytes at $35 per unit. In addition, you have been able to gather the following data:

a. The current cost of goods sold is $25 per unit.

b. The current cost of the equipment is $22,000. This is the amount on which current cost depreciation should be calculated.

c. Other operating expenses totaled $2,000.

Required:

Prepare a current cost income statement for the year ended December 31, 1987. Do not include the unrealized increase in the value of the equipment in net income.

9. Current Cost Balance Sheet. The following trial balance was prepared from the records of the Falk Company at December 31, 1988:

Account	Debit	Credit
Cash	$ 150,000	
Accounts receivable	190,000	
Inventory	250,000	
Plant and equipment, net	450,000	
Other assets	40,000	
Accounts payable		$ 200,000
Bank loan payable		100,000
E. Falk, capital		780,000
Totals	$1,080,000	$1,080,000

You have been able to determine that the following items had fair market values at December 31, 1988:

Inventory	$275,000
Plant and equipment, net	510,000
Other assets	30,000

All other items have a fair market value equal to their recorded amounts.

Required:

Prepare in good form a current cost balance sheet at December 31, 1988.

10. Current Cost/Constant Purchasing Power Accounting. The Alberto Realty Co. purchased a plot of land for speculation at the beginning of 1987. The purchase price was $500,000. At the end of the year the land was appraised at $600,000. Also during that period, the general price level rose 5%.

Required:

a. Determine the holding gain, net of inflation, during 1987.

b. At what amount would the land be listed on December 31, 1987 current cost/constant dollar balance sheet?

Problem Set A

14A-1. Accounting Concepts. For each of the following independent situations, state which accounting concept, if any, is violated. If more than one concept is violated, say so. If you feel the item has been appropriately handled, say so. Be sure to explain your answer.

a. Recently, Cardulucci's Fine Restaurant hired one of the country's outstanding chefs. Based on the anticipated increased earnings, the firm debited Goodwill and credited Owner's Capital for $100,000.

b. For years the Watts Equipment Company has been using straight-line depreciation on its plant and equipment for both financial reporting and tax purposes. However, with recent changes in the tax laws, the firm will now use ACRS depreciation for tax purposes while retaining straight-line for accounting purposes.

c. The Ecological High-Tech Company began operations early in 1986. Because of high start-up costs, the firm suffered a large loss during 1986. However, the company's prospects appear to be very good for 1987 and beyond. In order not to discourage the firm's owners, the president of Ecological High-Tech decides not to issue financial statements until 1987, or until the firm can show a profit.

d. Natural Foods, Co. is a large producer of natural foods. During the last half of 1987, the firm undertook a large advertising campaign in an attempt to increase its market share. Because the firm believes that the expenditures for advertising will benefit several years, management has decided to capitalize the advertising costs and write them off over five years.

e. The Colossas Oil Co. has always used the FIFO method of inventory costing. However, because of changing economic conditions in the oil industry, the firm now believes that the LIFO method will provide more relevant financial statements and has decided to make the change to LIFO.

f. The president of the BSAF Company is a firm believer in accounting conservatism. Although the company sells a profitable product, the president feels that there may be a price decline in this product in the next year. As a result, the president has decided to write down the inventory 20% in order to cover the anticipated price decline.

14A–2. Constant Dollar Accounting. At the beginning of 1986, Dennis Chambliss decided to open his own CPA firm after working many years with a national firm. Presented below is his firm's comparative balance sheet for January 2, 1987 and December 31, 1987 as well as a condensed income statement for the year then ended.

Dennis Chambliss, CPA
Comparative Balance Sheet

	January 2, 1987	December 31, 1987
Assets:		
Cash	$ 40,000	$ 30,000
Accounts receivable	0	60,000
Supplies	5,000	5,000
Furniture and equipment, net	55,000	50,000
Total assets	$100,000	$145,000
Equities:		
Bank loan payable	$ 30,000	$ 20,000
Accounts payable	0	25,000
D. Chambliss, capital	70,000	100,000
Total equities	$100,000	$145,000

Dennis Chambliss, CPA
Income Statement
For the Year Ended December 31, 1987

Revenues from accounting services		$200,000
Expenses:		
Operating expenses other than depreciation	$145,000	
Depreciation	5,000	
		150,000
Net income		$ 50,000

Dennis is concerned about how inflation may be affecting his practice and asks you to prepare a schedule determining the purchasing power gain or loss for the year. He provides you with the additional following data:

a. During 1987 the price level increased evenly from 100 to 120, with the average for the year being 110.

b. Dennis withdrew $20,000 cash on December 31.

c. All revenues earned and expenses (except for depreciation) were incurred evenly throughout the year.

Required:

a. Prepare a schedule computing the purchasing power gain or loss for the year. Round to whole dollars where appropriate.

b. Explain to Dennis how the 20% inflation rate has affected his business.

14-3. Determining Purchasing Power Gains and Losses. As the treasurer for the Muffin Company, you are asked to prepare a schedule determining the firm's purchasing power gain or loss. You are presented with the following historical cost income statement and additional data:

Muffin Company
Historical Cost Income Statement
For the Year Ended December 31, 1987

Sales		$300,000
Cost of goods sold:		
Beginning inventory	$ 75,000	
Net purchases	250,000	
Cost of goods available for sale	325,000	
Ending inventory	125,000	
Cost of goods sold		200,000
Gross margin on sales		100,000
Operating expenses:		
Selling, general, and administrative	$ 55,000	
Depreciation	20,000	75,000
Net income		$ 25,000

In addition, you are able to gather the following data relative to corporate events and general price indexes:

	Price Index
December 31, 1986	140
September 30, 1987—purchase of land for $50,000	155
December 31, 1987	160
Average for 1987	150

The firm's net monetary position:

December 31, 1986	$200,000
December 31, 1987	145,000

Finally, assume that sales and expenses other than the cost of goods sold and depreciation were earned or incurred evenly throughout the year.

Required:

Determine the purchasing power gain or loss for the year. Round off to whole dollars where appropriate.

14A-4. Current Cost Financial Statements. Los Angeles Period Furniture completed its first year of business at the end of 1987. Although the firm has been fairly successful, the president is concerned about the effects of specific price level changes in the furniture business and asks you to prepare a current cost statement. She presents you with the following historical cost statements:

Los Angeles Period Furniture
Historical Cost Balance Sheet
December 31, 1987

Assets		Equities	
Cash	$160,000	Bank loan payable	$150,000
Accounts receivable, net	115,000	Accounts payable	75,000
Inventory	170,000	J. Brandler, capital	320,000
Property and plant	100,000		
Total assets	$545,000	Total equities	$545,000

Los Angeles Period Furniture
Historical Cost Income Statement
For the Year Ended December 31, 1987

Sales	$500,000
Cost of goods sold	220,000
Gross margin on sales	280,000
Operating expenses	160,000
Net income	$120,000

In addition, you obtained the following data:
a. Depreciation expense is included in operating expenses. On a historical cost basis it equals $10,000, and on a current cost basis it equals $16,000. Thus, current cost operating expenses were $166,000.
b. Cost of goods sold on a current cost basis equals $235,000.
c. The current cost of the plant and equipment, net, is $120,000.
d. Current cost of the inventory at year-end is $180,000.
e. For all other items, the current cost is the same as historical cost.

Required:
a. Prepare a current cost income statement for the year ended December 31, 1987. Do not include the unrealized increase in the value of the plant and equipment and inventory in net income.
b. Prepare a current cost balance sheet at December 31, 1987. The balance in the J. Brandler Capital account is the amount needed to make the current cost balance sheet balance.
Round off to whole dollars where appropriate.

14A-5. Current Cost Accounting Data. The investment management firm of Mason, Magee and Murphy began business on December 31, 1986. The firm provides investment management services as well as speculating in real estate. The financial statements of the firm at the end of its first year in operation follow:

Accounting Concepts and Accounting for Changing Prices 559

Mason, Magee and Murphy
Historical Cost Balance Sheet
December 31

Assets	1986	1987
Cash and marketable securities	$ 15,000	$ 65,000
Accounts receivable, net	0	55,000
Land held for resale	30,000	45,000
Other assets	55,000	55,000
Total assets	$100,000	$220,000

Equities	1986	1987
Bank loans payable	$ 7,500	$ 22,500
Accounts payable	12,500	17,500
M. Mason, capital	80,000	180,000
Total equities	$100,000	$220,000

Mason, Magee and Murphy
Historical Cost Income Statement
For the Year Ended December 31, 1987

Revenues		
Fees earned	$600,000	
Revenues from sales of real estate	400,000	
Total revenues		$1,000,000
Expenses		
Cost of land sold	$200,000	
Operating expenses	700,000	
Total expenses		900,000
Net income		$ 100,000

In addition, you have gathered the following data at the end of 1987:

Account	Current Cost
Cost of land sold	$230,000
Land	50,000
Cash and marketable securities	66,000

Required:
  a. What is the amount of the current cost net operating income for 1987?
  b. At what amount would land be shown on a current cost balance sheet at December 31, 1987?
  c. At what amount would cash and marketable securities be shown on a current cost balance sheet at December 31, 1987?
  d. What is the amount of the purchasing power gain or loss to be reported on the current cost income statement for 1987?
  e. At what amount would the total owner's equity be shown on the December 31, 1987 current cost balance sheet?

Problem Set B

14B–1. Accounting Concepts. For each of the following independent situations, state which accounting concept, if any, is violated. If more than one concept is violated, say so. If you feel the item has been appropriately handled, say so. Be sure to explain your answer.

   a. Industrial Technology, Inc. has just completed a new project. Based on the anticipated increased earnings on the new product, Industrial Technology capitalized all expenses for this project.

   b. Due to the economic situation, Tommy's Restaurant chain suffered a great loss in 1987. As a result, current liabilities exceed current assets by $20 million. In anticipation of future losses, Tommy's has already sold or closed many restaurants. Tommy's prepares financial statement using historical costs.

   c. Doggy and Kathy Corporation has just changed depreciation policy from the double-declining-balance method to the straight-line method. In order to show a better result for this year, the firm did not mention this change in its financial statements.

   d. At the year-end, the president of Jack and Sons Company found that the inventory on hand has increased in value over 50%. He decided to give this information to the firm's creditors by writing up inventory to fair market value.

   e. Graham and Sons Company has experienced an extremely profitable year. In order to smooth out earnings, the president decided to expense all merchandise when purchased during the year rather than when it was sold.

14B–2. Constant Dollar Accounting. At the end of 1986, Dianna Simpson opened her own law office. Shown below and at the top of page 562 are the firm's comparative balance sheet for January 2, 1987 and December 31, 1987 as well as a condensed income statement for the year then ended. Supplies, furniture, and fixtures were purchased when the firm was formed.

Additional Information:

   a. During 1987, the price level increased evenly from 120 to 130, with the average for the year being 125.

   b. Dianna withdrew cash of $20,000 on March 31, 1987 when the price level was 122.

   c. All revenues earned and expenses incurred were evenly distributed throughout the year except for depreciation.

Required:

   a. Prepare a schedule computing the purchasing power gain or loss. (Round off to whole dollars.)

   b. Explain the effects of inflation.

Dianna Simpson, Attorney at Law
Comparative Balance Sheet

Assets	January 2, 1987	December 31, 1987
Cash	$10,000	$ 20,000
Accounts receivable	0	45,000
Supplies	5,000	5,000
Furniture and fixtures	45,000	40,000
Total assets	$60,000	$110,000

Equities		
Accounts payable	$ 0	$ 15,000
Bank loans payable	40,000	35,000
D. Simpson, capital	20,000	60,000
Total equities	$60,000	$110,000

Dianna Simpson, Attorney at Law
Income Statement
For the Year Ended December 31, 1987

Revenues		$150,000
Expenses		
Operating expenses other than depreciation	$85,000	
Depreciation	5,000	
		90,000
Net income		$ 60,000

14B-3. Determining a Purchasing Power Gain or Loss. You are the controller for Ultimate System, Ltd. You are asked by the president of the company to determine the purchasing power gain or loss incurred by the firm. The following historical cost income statement and other data are available to you:

Ultimate System, Ltd.
Historical Cost Income Statement
For the Year Ended December 31, 1988

Sales		$1,000,000
Cost of goods sold		
Beginning inventory	$450,000	
Net purchases	450,000	
Cost of goods available for sale	900,000	
Ending inventory	400,000	
Cost of goods sold		500,000
Gross margin on sales		500,000
Operating expenses		
Selling, general, and administrative	$300,000	
Depreciation	50,000	350,000
Net income		$ 150,000

In addition, you are able to gather the following data relative to corporate events and general price indexes:

	Index
December 31, 1987	140
December 31, 1988	150
Average for 1988	148

The firm's net monetary position:

December 31, 1987	$500,000
December 31, 1988	750,000

Assume that sales and expenses other than the cost of goods sold and depreciation were earned and incurred evenly throughout the year.

Required:

Determine the purchasing power gain or loss for the year. Round to whole dollars where appropriate.

14B–4. Current Cost Financial Statements. Rose Florist has just completed its first year of operations at the end of 1987. Due to the excess demand over supply, there is a tendency for the cost of flowers to increase faster than the general price index. The owner of the florist shop was concerned about the effects of specific level changes in the flower business. You are asked to prepare current cost financial statements. The historical cost financial statements are provided for you.

Rose Florist
Historical Cost Balance Sheet
As of December 31, 1987

Assets		Equities	
Cash	$ 30,000	Bank loan payable	$ 20,000
Accounts receivable, net	20,000	Accounts payable	10,000
Inventory	10,000	D. Bug, capital	70,000
Furniture and fixtures, net	40,000		
Total assets	$100,000	Total equities	$100,000

Rose Florist
Historical Cost Income Statement
For the Year Ended December 31, 1987

Sales	$150,000
Cost of goods sold	80,000
Gross margin on sales	70,000
Operating expenses	30,000
Net income	$ 40,000

In addition, you obtained the following data:

a. Depreciation expense was included in operating expenses. On a historical cost basis, it equals $8,000 and on a current cost basis it equals $10,000. Thus, current cost operating expenses are $32,000.

b. Cost of goods sold on a current cost basis equals $100,000.

c. The current cost of the furniture and fixtures, net, is $50,000.

d. Current cost of inventory is $18,000.

e. For all other items, the current cost is the same as historical cost.

Required:

a. Prepare a current cost income statement for the year ended December 31, 1987. Do not include the unrealized increase in the value of the furniture and fixtures and inventory in net income.

b. Prepare a current cost balance sheet at December 31, 1987. The balance in the D. Bug Capital account is the amount needed to make the current cost balance sheet balance.

14B–5. Current Cost Accounting Data. Southern California Property Management began business on December 31, 1986. The firm offers property management for property owners as well as speculating in real estate. The financial statements of the firm at the end of its first year of operations are shown on page 564.

Required:

a. What is the amount of current cost net operating income for 1987?

b. At what amount would buildings and land be shown on a current cost balance sheet at December 31, 1987?

c. At what amount would cash and marketable securities be shown on a current cost balance sheet at December 31, 1987?

d. What is the amount of the purchasing power gain or loss to be reported on the current cost income statement for 1987?

e. At what amount would the total owner's equity be shown on the December 31, 1987 current cost balance sheet?

Southern California Property Management
Historical Cost Balance Sheet
As of December 31

Assets	1986	1987
Cash and marketable securities	$ 400,000	$ 500,000
Accounts receivable, net	0	80,000
Building and land held for resale	1,000,000	1,050,000
Other assets	100,000	120,000
Total assets	$1,500,000	$1,750,000

Equities		
Bank loans payable	$ 980,000	$1,080,000
Accounts payable	20,000	70,000
L. Bean, capital	500,000	600,000
Total equities	$1,500,000	$1,750,000

Southern California Property Management, Inc.
Historical Cost Income Statement
For the Year Ended December 31, 1987

Revenues:		
Management fees earned	$ 400,000	
Gross revenues from sales of real estate	1,350,000	
Total revenues		$1,750,000
Expenses:		
Cost of real estate sold	$1,000,000	
Operating expenses	450,000	
Total expenses		$1,450,000
Net income		$ 300,000

In addition, you have gathered the following data at the end of 1987:

Accounts	Current Cost
Cost of real estate sold	$1,200,000
Buildings and land	1,300,000
Cash and marketable securities	550,000

Using the Computer

The Melody Company began business at the beginning of 1985. The income statement for the year ended December 31, 1986 follows, as well as certain other information.

The Melody Company
Income Statement
For the Year Ended December 31, 1986

Sales		$840,000
Cost of goods sold		
Inventory, beginning	$210,000	
Purchases	480,000	
Cost of goods available for sale	690,000	
Inventory, ending	250,000	
Cost of goods sold		440,000
Gross margin on sales		$400,000
Operating expenses		
Expenses other than depreciation	$258,000	
Depreciation	70,000	
Total expenses		328,000
Net income		$ 72,000

Other Information:

a. Net monetary liability position at 1/1/86 = $220,000.

b. Net monetary liability position at 12/31/86 = $302,000.

c. No fixed assets were acquired during the year.

d. The owner withdrew $20,000 cash on June 30, 1986.

e. The company's sales, purchases, and expenses were earned or incurred evenly throughout the year.

f. Relevant price indexes:

January 1, 1986	120
June 30, 1986	125
December 31, 1986	130

Required:

Using an electronic spreadsheet, prepare a schedule determining the firm's purchasing power gain or loss.

Understanding Financial Statements

Following is a schedule of income adjusted for changing prices taken from an annual report of General Motors:

EFFECTS OF INFLATION ON FINANCIAL DATA

The accompanying schedules display the basic historical cost financial data adjusted for changes in specific prices (current cost) for use in the evaluation of comparative financial results.

One method by which to analyze the effects of inflation on financial data (and thus the business) is by adjusting the historical cost data to the current costs for the major balance sheet items which have been accumulated through the accounting system over a period of years and which thus reflect different prices for the same commodities and services.

The current cost of inventories was estimated based on costs in effect at December 31, 1984. Cost of sales for inventories maintained on a first-in, first-out basis was restated to a current cost basis using the specific level of prices at the time the goods were sold.

The current cost of property owned and the related depreciation and amortization expense for U.S. operations were calculated by applying (1) selected producer price indices to historical book values of machinery and equipment and (2) the Marshall Valuation Service index to buildings, and the use of assessed values for land. For locations outside the United States, such amounts were calculated generally by applying indices closely related to the assets being measured and translating the resulting amounts using year-end foreign currency exchange rates.

The purpose of this type of restatement is to furnish estimates of the effects of price increases for replacement of inventories and property on the potential future net income of the business and thus assess the probability of future cash flows. Although these data may be useful for this purpose, they do not reflect specific plans for the replacement of property. A more meaningful estimate of the effects of such costs on future earnings is the estimated level of future capital expenditures which is set forth on page 16 in the Financial Review: Management's Discussion and Analysis.

Under the current cost method, the net income of General Motors is lower (or the net loss is higher) than that determined under the historical cost method. This means that businesses, as well as individuals, are affected by inflation and that the purchasing power of business dollars also has declined. In addition, the costs of maintaining the productive capacity, as reflected in the current cost data (and estimate of future capital expenditures), have increased, and thus management must seek ways to cope with the effects of inflation through accounting methods such as the LIFO method of inventory valuation, which matches current costs with current revenues, and through accelerated methods of depreciation and amortization.

It must be emphasized that there is a continuing need for national monetary and fiscal policies designed to control inflation and to provide adequate capital for future business growth which, in turn, will mean increased productivity and employment.

Schedule of Income Adjusted for Changing Prices
For the Year Ended December 31, 1984
(Dollars in Millions Except Per Share Amounts)

	As Reported in the Financial Statements (Historical Cost)	Adjusted for Changes in Specific Prices (1984 Current Cost)
Net Sales and Revenues	$83,889.9	$83,889.9
Cost of sales	70,217.9	70,270.1
Depreciation and amortization of property	4,899.9	4,999.5
Other operating and nonoperating items—net	2,450.5	2,450.5
United States and other income taxes	1,805.1	1,805.1
Total costs and expenses	79,373.4	79,525.2
Net Income	$ 4,516.5	$ 4,364.7
Earnings per share of $1-2/3 par value common stock	$14.22	$13.74
Earnings per share of Class E common stock	$1.03	$1.03
Accumulated foreign currency translation adjustments	($ 127.7)	($ 161.0)
Unrealized gain from decline in purchasing power of dollars of net amounts owed		$ 157.2
Excess of increase in general price level over increase in specific prices of inventories and property		$ 998.1*

*At December 31, 1984, current cost of inventories was $9,535.2 million, and current cost of property (including special tools), net of accumulated depreciation and amortization, was $27,042.0 million.

Based on the information contained in this schedule, answer the following questions:

   a. Did the current cost of General Motors' inventory and depreciable assets increase at a greater or slower rate than the general price level?

   b. Which net income figure do you think is more representative of General Motors' actual operations during the year? Why?

   c. What is the general cause of the unrealized purchasing power gain? What can you say about the relationship of net monetary assets to net monetary liabilities?

   d. Given the data on pages 565–566, what can you say about the prospects of General Motors and similar companies if inflation reaches high levels?

Financial Decision Cases

The owner and president of Silicon Inc., Sue Weinreb, has just reviewed the financial statements prepared by the firm's accountant and is distressed by the fact that the firm suffered a $1 million loss in the current year. This has been a very tough year for high-tech firms. Demand has slowed for Silicon's product, competition has increased, and prices have fallen.

    The firm was created several years ago and was funded primarily by venture capital. Prior to this year the firm had been profitable. As the firm's financial condition deteriorated this year, it was forced to borrow heavily from a local bank at 15%. At the beginning of the year the firm was in a small net liability position, but by the end of the year monetary liabilities exceeded monetary assets by $5,000,000.

    As Sue was preparing for a presentation to the board of directors, she noticed that in the footnotes to the financial statements the accountant had determined that the firm had a purchasing power gain of $1.5 million for the current year. When added to the $1 million net loss for the period, Sue figured, the firm had positive net income of $.5 million. She feels that with this new information she will be able to satisfy the members of the board. In fact, she feels that the firm may now be able to declare the dividends it was planning to omit.

Required:

   a. What do you think is the likely cause of the purchasing power gain?

   b. As a member of the board of directors, how would you respond to Sue's logic that the income for the year amounted to $.5 million?

   c. Do you think that Sue is correct in now planning to declare the dividend?

**Measuring and Reporting
Owners' Equity and
Special Problems Related
to Corporations**

Accounting for Partnerships

15

LEARNING OBJECTIVES

After reading this chapter you should be able to:

1. List the main concepts behind partnerships, including the advantages and disadvantages of this form of business organization.
2. Account for issues related to partnership operations including:
   a. Partnership formation.
   b. Subsequent investment of partners.
   c. Distribution of profit and losses.
3. Account for partnership dissolutions.
4. List the reasons for and be able to account for partnership liquidations.

Throughout this book, we have used a sole proprietorship to illustrate various accounting principles. However, many businesses are organized as partnerships or corporations. For example, large service businesses such as law and CPA firms are organized as partnerships. Most major merchandising and manufacturing companies in the United States are organized as corporations. In this and the next two chapters we turn our attention to the specific accounting issues related to the owners' equity section of partnership and corporation balance sheets.

Partnership—The Main Concepts

The Uniform Partnership Act defines a **partnership** as "an association of two or more persons to carry on as co-owners of a business for a profit." Traditionally, many professional firms such as law firms and CPA firms have been organized as partnerships. This is due to the fact that until the mid-1970s, most states prohibited professionals from incorporating. However, this prohibition has been lifted and many professional firms are now incorporated.

Features of a Partnership

Partnerships have several features or characteristics that are both advantageous and disadvantageous. Included in these features are voluntary association, ease of formation, limited life, mutual agency, unlimited liability, co-ownership of property, and participation in partnership profits and losses.

Voluntary Association

A partnership is a voluntary association between two or more individuals. It is not a legal entity and thus no federal or state income taxes are levied against the partnership. However, as in the case of the sole proprietorship, the partnership is a distinct accounting entity. Because the partnership does not represent a separate legal entity, each partner has unlimited liability for partnership debts and is bound by the actions of his or her partners on behalf of the partnership (mutual agency).

Ease of Formation

Because a partnership is a voluntary association rather than a separate legal entity, it is relatively easy to form. In fact, any two competent individuals can verbally agree to organize a partnership. No state approval such as is required to form a corporation is needed.

When individuals agree to form a partnership, a partnership agreement results. This agreement constitutes a contract between the partners and states the details of the partnership. Although this document does not have to be in writing, it certainly makes good sense to have a written partnership agreement, containing the following points:

1. The name, location, and purpose of the business.
2. The names and addresses of the original partners.
3. The investment to be made by each partner.
4. The respective duties of each partner.
5. The method in which profits and losses are to be distributed.
6. The amount and timing of the withdrawals allowed to the partners.
7. Procedures for the admission or withdrawal of partners.
8. Procedures for the orderly dissolution of the partnership.

Limited Life

Because of the voluntary association aspect of a partnership, the partnership is ended every time there is a change in partners. For example, the admission of a new partner or the withdrawal or death of an old partner automatically terminates the old partnership and creates a new one. Business does not necessarily have to cease when a partnership ends; it is likely to continue as the new partnership is formed. Other events causing the termination of a partnership are the bankruptcy of a partner, incapacitation due to illness or other factors of a partner, or by the mutual consent of all the partners.

Mutual Agency

Mutual agency means that each partner can make binding agreements for the partnership as long as the individual partner acts within the normal scope of partnership business. In effect, each partner is an agent of the partnership and has authority to act in behalf of the partnership. Mutual agency clearly means that individuals must be very careful in selecting partners.

Unlimited Liability

Unlimited liability means that each partner is personally liable for the debts of the partnership. Thus, an individual partner's liability is not limited to the amount of that partner's investment in the partnership. For example, if a partnership is bankrupt, the creditors may seek relief from the individual partners. Furthermore, if an individual partner does not have enough personal assets to meet his or her share of these debts, the creditors are able to make a claim against the personal assets of the remaining solvent partners.

In recent years, primarily for tax reasons, a form of partnership called a **limited partnership** has evolved. The primary difference between a limited partnership and a regular partnership (often referred to as a **general partnership**) revolves around the individual partner's liability for partnership debts. In a limited partnership there are generally one or two general partners and several limited partners. In this type of partnership, only the general partners have unlimited liability; the liability of the other partners is limited to their investment in the partnership. However, the management control of the partnership lies with the general partners. Limited partnerships have definite advantages for tax shelter investments, but not necessarily for the usual general business operation. As a result, we assume that a general partnership exists in our future examples.

Co-ownership of Property and Participation in Partnership Profits and Losses

The property of the partnership is jointly owned by all partners. This means that if an individual partner contributes property to the partnership, the property becomes jointly owned by all partners. Furthermore, each partner has the right to share in partnership profits and losses. The distribution of profits and losses among partners can be in any manner agreed upon by the partners and should be clearly stated in the partnership agreement. As we will see, it is possible for the partners to agree to split profits in one manner and losses in a different manner.

Advantages and Disadvantages of Partnerships

The characteristics of partnerships described above result in both advantages and disadvantages. Partnerships are advantageous because they are easy to form or dissolve. Because partnerships are not separate legal entities, they are not subject to income tax or to the same state and federal regulations as corporations are. Generally, a partnership is a convenient way to pool capital and managerial skills.

However, there are three serious disadvantages to a partnership. These result from unlimited liability, mutual agency, and limited life. The unlimited liability and limited life aspects of a partnership make it very difficult for partnerships to raise the amounts of capital that are needed to finance large businesses. This is further complicated by the fact that it is difficult to transfer a partnership interest in the same way that a person can purchase and sell a share of capital stock. Finally, mutual agency means that individual partners are subject to the actions of all their partners.

The only major difference in accounting for a partnership from what we discussed in the previous chapters of this book is in the owners' equity section of the balance sheet. Instead of just one Capital account, the owners' equity section of a partnership contains a Capital account for each partner. The Capital account is a running total of all of the individual partners' investments and their share of partnership profits less their share of partnership losses and withdrawals. In addition, a Drawing account which is closed into the Capital account yearly is maintained for each partner.

The primary issues related to partnerships include accounting for (1) the formation of the partnership, (2) subsequent investments and withdrawals by partners, and (3) distribution of profits and losses. Each of these items is discussed in the following sections.

Accounting for the Formation of a Partnership

In order to illustrate the accounting procedures required when a partnership is formed, we will assume that Jim Levitas and Teri Brown decide to leave their positions with a large CPA firm and open their own practice on January 2, 1987. The partnership agreement states that each partner is to contribute $60,000 in cash or other assets to the partnership. Levitas contributes $60,000 in cash and Brown contributes $30,000 in cash plus other assets including office equipment and office furniture and fixtures having fair market values of $12,000 and $18,000, respectively.

The entry to record Levitas's cash investment is straightforward: Cash is debited and J. Levitas, Capital, is credited for $60,000. The entry to record Brown's capital investment is more complicated. As is the case with sole proprietorships, assets other than cash that are contributed to the partnership are recorded at their current fair market values. Thus, the cost of the office equipment and the office furniture and fixtures to Teri Brown or even their current book value is not relevant. The current fair value of these assets must be determined and those values become the basis to the partnership.

The following entries are made to record the original investment in the partnership of Levitas and Brown:

Jan. 2, 1987	Cash	60,000	
	J. Levitas, Capital		60,000
	To record $60,000 cash investment by Levitas.		
	Cash	30,000	
	Office Equipment	12,000	
	Office Furniture and Fixtures	18,000	
	T. Brown, Capital		60,000
	To record investment in cash and assets by Brown.		

Subsequent Investments and Withdrawals

Subsequent investments by partners are quite common. When that occurs, Cash or Other Assets is debited and the partners' Capital accounts are credited. Occasionally, a partner (or partners) will make loans to the partnership instead of making a capital investment. This may occur if the funds are needed only for a short period of time or when only one of the several partners is willing to provide additional funds to the partnership. These loans are recorded by a debit to Cash and a credit to a Partners' Loan account. However, in most states these loans are considered part of the partners' capital. In effect, liabilities to third parties always take precedence over partners' loans, and in case of liquidation, these third-party liabilities must be paid in full before any partners' loans are repaid.

Partners often withdraw cash or other assets and a drawing account is established for each partner to record these transactions. This account is used to record cash or asset withdrawals made by the partners, payments by the partnership of individual partner debts or expenses, or partnership cash collected and held by individual partners. Again, as was the case with the sole proprietorship, partners' salaries are not considered an expense but are withdrawals in anticipation of partnership profits. As a result, all partners' withdrawals are debited to this Drawing account regardless of whether or not they are referred to as salaries.

Recording Profits and Closing Entries

In order to continue with our example, assume that the firm of Levitas and Brown was successful during its first year. The income statement for the year ended December 31, 1987, on the bottom of this page, is similar to that of any service business. One added feature to a partnership income statement is the bottom portion showing the distribution of profits. In this case, the net income of $80,000 is split evenly. As we will see, however, profits can be split in any manner the partners desire.

Partnership Net Income and Income Taxes

As we noted, partnerships are not required to pay income taxes on their profits. As a result, there is no line item called income tax expense on a partnership income statement. However, both partners must include their share of profits or losses in their individual tax returns. These profits and losses must be included in the partners' income in the year earned, regardless of when they are distributed in cash or other assets to the partners. In order to ensure the proper reporting of partnership profits, the partnership must file an information tax return with the Internal Revenue Service showing the partnership net income or loss and each partner's share of that net income or loss.

Levitas and Brown, CPAs
Income Statement
For the Year Ended December 31, 1987

Revenues		
Fees		$210,000
Expenses		
Employee salaries	$75,000	
Rent	25,000	
Travel	12,000	
Depreciation	10,000	
Supplies used	6,500	
Delivery	1,500	130,000
Net income		$ 80,000
Distribution of net income		
Jim Levitas, 50%	$40,000	
Teri Brown, 50%	40,000	$ 80,000

Closing Entries

The entries to close the income statement accounts into the partners' Capital accounts are:

Dec. 31, 1987	Fees	210,000	
	Income Summary		210,000
	To close revenue accounts.		
	Income Summary	130,000	
	Employee salaries		75,000
	Rent		25,000
	Travel		12,000
	Depreciation		10,000
	Supplies used		6,500
	Delivery		1,500
	To close expense accounts.		
	Income Summary	80,000	
	J. Levitas, Capital		40,000
	T. Brown, Capital		40,000
	To close income summary into the capital accounts.		
	J. Levitas, Capital	24,000	
	T. Brown, Capital	24,000	
	J. Levitas, Drawing		24,000
	T. Brown, Drawing		24,000
	To close drawing accounts into the capital accounts.		

These entries are based on the income statement as well as the fact that each partner withdrew $2,000 a month.

After the closing entries are made, a balance sheet and a statement of partners' capital are prepared. These statements are shown on page 577. Again, the balance sheet is similar to that of any service business. The only feature that distinguishes it as a partnership balance sheet is the owners' equity section. The statement of partners' capital shows all the changes that occurred during the period in each individual partner's Capital account.

Distribution of Partnership Profits

The partners can agree to share profits and losses in any manner they wish. In fact, profits can be distributed in one ratio and losses in another. The distribution of profits and losses should be clearly stated in the partnership agreement. If the agreement fails to mention how the profits are to be divided, generally the law requires an equal split among the partners. If the agreement mentions the ratio in which profits are to be split but fails to mention losses, losses will usually be split in the same ratio as profits or, in some cases, equally.

Dividing Partnership Net Income or Loss

As we noted, partners can agree to divide partnership profit and losses in any manner they desire. However, most agreements take one of three general types:

1. A fixed ratio. For example, a three-person partnership can agree to divide income and losses equally so that each partner is allocated one-third of the profits or losses. In other instances, the profits can be split 40%, 35%, and 25% and the losses, 33⅓%, 33⅓%, and 33⅓%.

Levitas and Brown, CPAs
Balance Sheet
December 31, 1987

Assets		Liabilities and Owners' Equity	
Current assets:		**Liabilities:**	
Cash	$ 13,000	Accounts payable	$ 13,400
Accounts receivable	56,500	Salaries payable	3,600
Office supplies	9,500		
Total current assets	79,000	Total liabilities	17,000
Noncurrent assets:		**Owners' equity:**	
Store equipment, net	20,000	Jim Levitas, capital	76,000
Office equipment and		Teri Brown, capital	76,000
fixtures, net	4,000	Total owners' equity	152,000
Other assets	66,000		
Total noncurrent assets	90,000	Total liabilities and	
Total assets	$169,000	owners' equity	$169,000

Levitas and Brown, CPAs
Statement of Partners' Capital
For the Year Ended December 31, 1987

	Levitas	Brown	Total
Capital, 1/1/87	$ 0	$ 0	$ 0
Add: Investment during the year	60,000	60,000	120,000
Net income	40,000	40,000	80,000
	100,000	100,000	200,000
Less: Withdrawals	24,000	24,000	48,000
Capital, 12/31/87	$ 76,000	$ 76,000	$152,000

2. A set salary to partners with the remaining net income split in any agreed-upon fixed ratio. For example, each of three partners agrees to a salary of $12,000 and the remaining net income, if any, is split 35%, 35%, and 30%.

3. Salaries to partners, interest on partners' Capital accounts, and the remaining income, if any, split in a fixed ratio. Thus, in addition to salaries, each partner is allocated a stated percentage rate on his or her Capital balance. This type of agreement combines the features of each of the previous types of profit allocation.

However, it must be remembered that these examples are not all-inclusive; they are just representative of the types of profit-sharing arrangements that can be made.

The components found in these types of profit-sharing arrangements grew out of the nature of partnership profits. For example, partnership profits are assumed to be composed of three distinct elements: (1) a return on the partners' invested capital, (2) a salary or compensation for services performed by the partner for the partnership, and (3) an economic or pure profit for taking the risk of running a business. Different profit-sharing arrangements are necessary because partners are apt to contribute in different ways to the components of partnership profits. For example, one partner may make a larger investment in the business but may perform few services for the partnership. The other partner may make a smaller investment in the partnership but may perform a greater portion of personal services to the partnership. A profit-sharing agreement that is based on capital investments, salaries, and a fixed ratio for the remaining profits is flexible enough to handle these situations.

To illustrate the calculations required for each of the three major types of profit-sharing agreements, we assume the following data. The partnership of Maynard and Arthur has been in existence for several years. At the end of 1987, the following data is available:

	Maynard	Arthur	Total
Capital balances, 1/1/87	$124,800	$115,200	$240,000
Additional contribution, 4/1/87	15,650		15,650
Additional contribution, 7/1/87		9,350	9,350
Capital balance, 12/31/87	$140,450	$124,550	$265,000
Net income for 1987*			$100,000

*Before partners' salaries or interest on Capital balances.

Fixed Ratio. One of the simplest ways to divide partnership profits is on some fixed ratio. This ratio can be based on any criteria the partners agree upon. For example, Maynard and Arthur may decide to allocate profit and losses in the ratio 60% to Maynard and 40% to Arthur, recognizing the fact that Maynard devotes more time to the partnership. If that were the case, the $100,000 profit would be split as follows:

$$\text{Maynard} \quad \$100,000 \times .60 = \underline{\$60,000}$$

$$\text{Arthur} \quad \$100,000 \times .40 = \underline{\$40,000}$$

The journal entry to close the Income Summary account is:

Income Summary	100,000	
K. Maynard, Capital		60,000
B. Arthur, Capital		40,000
To close income summary account to partners' capital.		

In many situations, the amount invested in the partnership is an important component of partnership profits. In this case, profits are divided according to each partner's capital investment. In this way, the partner or partners who maintain the highest capital balance receive the highest portion of the profits. The two most common ways to divide profits in this situation are to use the ratio of partners' Capital balances at the beginning of the year or to use a ratio based on the weighted average capital balance during the year. These are both illustrated using the data from our example above.

The ratio of Maynard's and Arthur's beginning Capital balances is 52% to 48%, determined as follows:

Partner	Beginning Capital	Capital Ratio	%
Maynard	$124,800	$124,800/$240,000	52
Arthur	115,200	$115,200/$240,000	48
	$240,000		100

Each partner's share of the $100,000 profit is therefore calculated as:

Partner	Profit	%	Share
Maynard	$100,000	52	$ 52,000
Arthur	100,000	48	48,000
			$100,000

The journal entry to close the Income Summary account is:

```
Income Summary                          100,000
     K. Maynard, Capital                            52,000
     B. Arthur, Capital                             48,000
   To close income summary account
   to partners' capital.
```

Distributing profits based on Capital balances at the beginning of the year is fine as long as there have not been significant withdrawals or additional investments by the partners during the year. If these withdrawals or investments occur, then the partners' weighted average capital balances should be used. In our illustration, both Maynard and Arthur made additional capital investments during the year, but neither partner withdrew any funds. The ratio of the weighted average capital balances are 53% and 47%, calculated as follows:

Partner	Period	Capital Balance		Fraction of Year Outstanding		Weighted Average Capital Balance	Capital Ratio		%
Maynard	1/1/87–3/31/87	$124,800	×	3/12	=	$ 31,200	$136,538	=	53
	4/1/87–12/31/87	140,450	×	9/12	=	105,338	$256,413		
				12/12		$136,538			
Arthur	1/1/87–6/30/87	$115,200	×	6/12	=	57,600	$119,875	=	47
	7/1/87–12/31/87	124,550	×	6/12	=	62,275	$256,413		
				12/12		$119,875			
	Total					$256,413		=	100

Profits of $100,000 are distributed to Maynard and Arthur as follows:

Partner	Profit	%	Partner's Share
Maynard	$100,000	53	$ 53,000
Arthur	100,000	47	47,000
			$100,000

The partners' weighted average capital balances are calculated by first determining the various balances in the Capital accounts during the year and then multiplying these balances by the fraction of the year they were unchanged. For example, Maynard's beginning Capital balance of $124,800 was unchanged 3 months, January 1 to March 31 or 3/12 of a year. After the additional investment of $15,650, the balance on April 1 was $140,450 and was unchanged for the remainder of the year, 9/12 of the year. Arthur's weighted average capital balance of $119,875 is calculated in a similar manner. In both cases there were no withdrawals. However, they would be handled in the same way as additional investments, only they would reduce the Capital balance.

Once the weighted average capital balance is calculated, a percentage ratio is determined, and that ratio is used to distribute the profits. Based on these weighted average capital balances, the ratio is 53% to 47%. In this case, the ratio is little different from that based on the opening Capital balances. However, this occurs because, for simplicity's sake, we assumed that each partner only made one additional investment. If several investments or withdrawals were made during the year, the ratio could change significantly.

Set Salary to Partners and Remainder in a Fixed Ratio. Each partner in a partnership is apt to contribute different degrees of personal service to the partnership. For example, assume that the agreement between Maynard and Arthur requires that Arthur is to work full time in the partnership while Maynard works only three-quarters of the time. One way to compensate partners for personal work performed is to allocate part of the profits based on a set salary and divide the remaining profits in a fixed ratio.

To illustrate, now assume that Arthur draws a salary of $2,000 per month (or $24,000 per year) and Maynard draws a salary of $1,500 per month (or $18,000 per year). The profits in excess of $42,000, the combined yearly salaries, are to be split equally. (See table below.) It is important to remember that these salaries are not expenses of the partnership and are not reflected in the net income of $100,000. The salaries, when withdrawn monthly, are debited to the respective partner's Drawing account.

DISTRIBUTION OF PARTNERSHIP NET INCOME			
	Maynard	Arthur	Net Income
1987 net income			$100,000
Allocation of salaries	$18,000	$24,000	(42,000)
Remaining to be allocated in a fixed ratio			58,000
Maynard = 50%	29,000		(29,000)
Arthur = 50%		29,000	(29,000)
Total share to each partner	$47,000	$53,000	0

580

The salaries are first allocated in the agreed-upon manner and then the remaining $58,000 is divided equally. The closing entries to reflect this allocation are:

Income Summary	100,000	
K. Maynard, Capital		47,000
B. Arthur, Capital		53,000
To record distribution of		
$100,000 net income.		
K. Maynard, Capital	18,000	
B. Arthur, Capital	24,000	
K. Maynard, Drawing		18,000
B. Arthur, Drawing		24,000
To close drawing accounts		
into the capital accounts.		

Salaries, Interest on Capital Balance, and the Remainder in a Fixed Ratio. In order to reflect the fact that partners should be adequately compensated for the amount of invested capital they keep in the partnership, some agreements require interest to be paid on Capital balances. This interest is not an expense of the business but, as with partners' salaries, it is a way to allocate partnership profits among the partners. However, unlike partners' salaries, interest is usually not withdrawn prior to the end of the current year.

To illustrate, now assume that the agreement between Maynard and Arthur calls for them to receive (1) salaries of $18,000 and $24,000, respectively, (2) 10% interest on their Capital balances at the beginning of the year, and (3) any remaining income on an equal split. Again, assuming partnership net income was $100,000, the following schedule illustrates how this income is distributed between Maynard and Arthur:

DISTRIBUTION OF PARTNERSHIP NET INCOME			
	Maynard	Arthur	Net Income
1987 net income			$100,000
Allocation of salaries	$18,000	$24,000	(42,000)
Remaining to be allocated			58,000
Interest on beginning capital balance			
Maynard ($124,800 × .10)	12,480		(12,480)
Arthur ($115,200 × .10)		11,520	(11,520)
Remaining to be allocated in a fixed ratio			34,000
Maynard, 50%	17,000		(17,000)
Arthur, 50%		17,000	(17,000)
Total share to each partner	$47,480	$52,520	0

The closing entry to reflect this distribution is shown at the top of page 582.

```
Income Summary                          100,000
    K. Maynard, Capital                              47,480
    B. Arthur, Capital                               52,520
To close net income for the
year to partners' capital.

K. Maynard, Capital                      18,000
B. Arthur, Capital                       24,000
    K. Maynard, Drawing                              18,000
    B. Arthur, Drawing                               24,000
To close drawing accounts
into the capital accounts.
```

In any particular period, the partnership's net income may be less than the partners' salaries and the interest on their Capital balances. If this occurs, the salaries or the interest on invested capital that is called for in the partnership agreement must still be allocated in the prescribed manner. Any deficit then must be allocated in the same ratio in which any positive remainder would have been allocated.

To illustrate, now assume the same facts as before, except that the partnership's net income for 1987 is only $58,000. The following schedule shows how the $58,000 is distributed between Maynard and Arthur:

DISTRIBUTION OF PARTNERSHIP NET INCOME			
	Maynard	Arthur	Total
1987 net income			$58,000
Allocation of salaries	$18,000	$24,000	(42,000)
Remaining to be allocated			16,000
Interest on beginning capital balance			
Maynard ($124,800 × .10)	12,480		(12,480)
Arthur ($115,200 × .10)		11,520	(11,520)
Deficit after salaries and interest			(8,000)
allocated in a fixed ratio			
Maynard, 50%	(4,000)		4,000
Arthur, 50%		(4,000)	4,000
Total share to each partner	$26,480	$31,520	0

The closing entry to record this distribution is:

```
Income Summary                           58,000
    K. Maynard, Capital                              26,480
    B. Arthur, Capital                               31,520
To close net income for the
year to partners' capital.

K. Maynard, Capital                      18,000
B. Arthur, Capital                       24,000
    K. Maynard, Drawing                              18,000
    B. Arthur, Drawing                               24,000
To close drawing accounts
into capital accounts.
```

From a legal standpoint, a **dissolution of a partnership** occurs when there is any change in the partners that constitute it. When a new partner is admitted or when one withdraws or dies, the old partnership ceases. However, it is quite likely that in most cases, business operations will continue while a new legal partnership is formed.

Admission of a New Partner

The admission of a new partner dissolves the old partnership and results in the creation of a new one. A new partner can be admitted by either purchasing an interest from one or more of the existing partners or by investing additional assets in the existing partnership. In either case, all existing partners must agree to the new partner and the partnership agreement should state under what circumstances and how a new partner is to be admitted.

Purchase of an Existing Interest

When a new partner purchases an interest from one or more partners, no additional assets are contributed to the partnership. In fact, the transaction is between the existing partner or partners, and the only effect on the partnership is a change in the Capital accounts.

To illustrate, assume that Williams has a $100,000 equity in the accounting firm of Fisher, Dennis, and Williams. After obtaining the agreement of the other partners, Williams sells his entire interest to Holder for $150,000. In order to reflect this sale, the partnership simply makes the following entry:

Williams, Capital	100,000	
Holder, Capital		100,000
To record transfer of Williams'		
capital to Holder's capital.		

As this journal entry indicates, the only thing that the partnership does is to transfer Williams' capital to Holder. Since no assets were contributed directly to the partnership, there is no increase in total partnership equity, just a reclassification of the existing equity.

The fact that Holder paid Williams $150,000 for her $100,000 interest does not affect the partnership; it is a transaction between Williams and Holder. Obviously, Williams has a gain of $50,000 ($150,000 − $100,000), which she must report on her individual income tax return.

This example can easily be expanded to a situation in which the incoming partner purchases an interest from more than one partner. To illustrate, now assume that Holder purchases a 25% interest in the equity of each partner. Assume that immediately before the purchase, each partner had the following Capital balance:

Fisher	$140,000
Dennis	150,000
Williams	100,000

Because Holder will purchase her interest directly from the existing partners, the actual purchase price is not relevant. The following entry is made to transfer the capital to Holder from the existing partners:

Fisher, Capital	35,000	
Dennis, Capital	37,500	
Williams, Capital	25,000	
Holder, Capital		97,500

To record transfer of 25% interest
of existing partners' capital
to Holder.

Investment in the Partnership

In many cases, a new partner is admitted into the partnership only after he or she makes an investment of cash or other assets in the firm. In this situation, there is a direct transaction involving the new partner and the partnership. Because of the new investment of assets, the total owners' equity of the partnership is increased. In the simple case, the new partner receives a partnership interest equal to his or her investment. In the more complex situation, the new partner's interest in the partnership is less or more than the assets he or she invests.

Partnership Interest Equal to Investment. To illustrate this situation, let's assume the CPA partnership of Levitas and Brown has been very successful and decides to admit a new partner, D. Eddows, at the end of 1988. At that time, Levitas has a Capital balance of $200,000 and Brown has a Capital balance of $250,000. As a result, the total partnership equity before Eddows is admitted is $450,000. Eddows invests $150,000 cash for a 25% interest in the partnership. As the following calculation illustrates, Eddows' $150,000 investment exactly represents a 25% share in the partnership equity after the $150,000 investment.

Levitas and Brown, Capital	$450,000
Eddows' investment	150,000
New partnership equity	600,000
25% interest	$\times$ .25
Eddows' interest	$150,000

The entry to record this investment by Eddows is:

Cash	150,000	
D. Eddows, Capital		150,000

To record D. Eddows' 25%
interest in the partnership.

The fact that Eddows now has a 25% interest in the partnership's equity does not mean that she is entitled to a 25% interest in the profits. As we indicated previously, partnership profits can be split in any manner the partners desire.

Partnership Interest Less Than Investment.[1] In many cases, a new partner receives a partnership interest percentage less than his or her investment would indicate. This situation occurs when a partnership has been very profitable and the existing partners, in effect, demand a bonus from the entering partner. This bonus results from the fact that a new partner, for example,

---

[1]The examples that follow assume that the investment in the partnership is accounted for by the bonus method. As an alternative, the goodwill method could be used. This method is quite complex and is a subject of an advanced accounting text.

purchases a $150,000 interest for $200,000. The bonus is distributed to the old partners' Capital accounts in the same manner that profits and losses are.

To illustrate, assume now that Eddows purchases an interest in the partnership of Levitas and Brown for $150,000, but now she receives only 20% rather than the 25% interest in the previous example. The following calculation illustrates how the $30,000 bonus is distributed to Levitas and Brown:

Levitas and Brown, Capital before admission of Eddows	$450,000
Investment of Eddows	150,000
New partnership equity	$600,000
Eddows' purchase price	$150,000
Eddows' share in the partnership equity ($600,000 × .20)	120,000
Bonus to Levitas and Brown	$ 30,000
Levitas' share ($30,000 × 60%*)	18,000
Brown's share ($30,000 × 40%*)	12,000
	$ 30,000

*Based on profit and loss ratio existing at the time of Eddows' admission.

The entry to record this purchase is:

Cash	150,000	
Levitas, Capital		18,000
Brown, Capital		12,000
Eddows, Capital		120,000
To record the purchase by Eddows of a 20% interest in the partnership with a bonus allocated to Levitas and Brown.		

Partnership Interest More Than Investment. In some cases, a new partner will receive a greater percentage share of the partnership than his or her investment warrants. This situation generally occurs when the existing partnership is experiencing financial difficulties or needs the expertise of the entering partner. As a result, the existing partners are willing to give a bonus to the entering partner.

To illustrate this situation, let's now assume that Levitas and Brown agree to give Eddows a 30% interest in the new partnership for an investment of $150,000, but all other facts remain the same. This agreement, as illustrated below, means that Levitas and Brown are giving Eddows a bonus of $30,000.

Levitas and Brown, Capital before admission of Eddows	$450,000
Investment of Eddows	150,000
New partnership equity	$600,000
Eddows' share in the partnership equity ($600,000 × .30)	$180,000
Eddows' purchase price	150,000
Bonus to Eddows	$ 30,000
Bonus allocated from Levitas and Brown	
Levitas ($30,000 × .60)	$ 18,000
Brown ($30,000 × .40)	12,000
	$ 30,000

The entry to record this purchase is:

Cash	150,000	
Levitas, Capital	18,000	
Brown, Capital	12,000	
Eddows, Capital		180,000
To record Eddows' purchase of		
30% interest in partnership with		
$30,000 bonus.		

Withdrawal of a Partner

A withdrawal of a partner can occur when (1) an existing partner sells his or her interest to other partners or to an outsider, (2) an existing partner leaves the partnership and receives partnership assets in return, or (3) the partner dies.

Sale to Existing or New Partner

Sale of a partnership interest to an existing or new partner is handled in the same manner as the admission of a new partner through a sale by existing partners. The partnership is only involved indirectly through a capital transfer. No partnership asset or liabilities are involved.

To illustrate this type of withdrawal, assume that Hinge is a partner in the firm of Ball, Stone, and Hinge. With the agreement of the other partners, Hinge sells his $100,000 interest to Brace for $120,000. The partnership need only make the following entry to record a capital transfer:

Hinge, Capital	100,000	
Brace, Capital		100,000
To record transfer of Hinge's		
interest to Brace.		

Payment to Withdrawing Partner from Partnership Assets

Quite often, a partner will retire from the partnership through withdrawing a portion of partnership assets. Essentially, the partnership buys out the withdrawing partner. The payment from the partnership's assets may be more or less than the withdrawing partner's Capital balance.

Payment Exceeds Partner's Capital Balance

The current value of the net assets of a successful partnership that has been in existence for several years will probably exceed their historical cost. This is especially true in a period of inflation and when the partnership owns real estate. In this situation, the fair value of the withdrawing partner's share of the partnership's net assets (Capital balance) is likely to be greater than his or her actual Capital balance reflected on the partnership's books at historical cost.

One way to handle this situation is to revalue partnership assets to their fair market value and distribute that increase to all the partners' Capital accounts per their profit-sharing ratio. After that distribution, the fair market value of the withdrawing partner's Capital account would be equal to his or her share of the fair market value of the partnership's net assets. However, this procedure violates the historical cost convention. In addition, if there are numerous changes in the partnership, this procedure is expensive and time-consuming.

A more efficient way to handle this situation is to give the withdrawing partner a bonus that is charged to the remaining partners' Capital accounts per the agreed-upon ratio of distributing profits and losses. To illustrate, assume that when Hinge withdraws from the partnership of Ball, Stone, and Hinge, the partnership purchases his $100,000 Capital balance for $150,000 consisting of $90,000 cash and a $60,000 note payable. If the remaining partners split profit and losses equally, the following journal entry is made to record this purchase:

Ball, Capital	25,000	
Stone, Capital	25,000	
Hinge, Capital	100,000	
Cash		90,000
Note Payable to Retiring Partner		60,000
To record retirement of Hinge with		
$50,000 bonus allocated against		
capital accounts of Ball and Stone.		

As is evident from this entry, Hinge's Capital account is debited for $100,000, but he receives cash and a note amounting to $150,000. The difference of $50,000 is the bonus given to Hinge and is allocated equally against the remaining partners' Capital accounts.

Payment Less Than the Partner's Capital Balance

Occasionally a withdrawing partner will accept an amount less than his or her Capital balance. This might occur if there are disputes within the partnership and the retiring partner just wants out. In this situation, the withdrawing partner gives a bonus to the remaining partner(s). To illustrate, assume that Hinge is willing to accept $70,000 cash in full payment of his $100,000 Capital balance and now the profit and loss ratios before Hinge's withdrawal are Ball 40%, Stone 20%, and Hinge 40%. Therefore, the relative profit and loss ratio is Ball 40%, Stone 20%. As a result, the $30,000 bonus is allocated to Ball and Stone in a ratio of 40/60 to 20/60, or 2/3 to 1/3. The entry to record this withdrawal is:

Hinge, Capital	100,000	
Ball, Capital		20,000
Stone, Capital		10,000
Cash		70,000
To record withdrawal of Hinge		
for $70,000: $30,000 allocated		
to Ball and Stone, 2/3 to 1/3.		

Death of a Partner

The death of a partner causes a dissolution of the partnership. The partnership agreement, if properly drawn, will contain explicit procedures to cover this contingency. These procedures may include a certified audit by a CPA firm or an appraisal of partnership assets by an independent third party. However, in all cases, the partnership's books must be closed as of the date of the partner's death. Financial statements are prepared and the partners' Capital account balances are credited for income earned and debited for withdrawals made to the dissolution date.

At this point, the partnership may be liquidated. That is, the partnership ceases operations and its net assets are distributed to the remaining partners and the estate of the deceased partner. As an alternative, the remaining partners may buy out the interest of the deceased partner. This can be done easily if the partners have taken out insurance policies on each other's lives.

The Liquidation of a Partnership

A dissolution of a partnership is the result of a change in the partners who make up the partnership. Usually, a new partnership is formed and the partnership business continues. A **liquidation of a partnership** results in a cessation of the firm's business, the selling of assets, the payment of liabilities, and the distribution of the remaining assets, if any, to the partners.

A well-drawn partnership agreement will contain procedures for the orderly liquidation of the partnership. Generally, the partnership first ceases operations and financial statements are prepared from the beginning of the accounting period to the date operations ceased. The partners' Capital accounts are adjusted for their share of profit and losses for that period. As the partnership's assets are sold, the partners' Capital accounts are credited or debited for their share of the gain or loss. After all partnership assets are sold and all liabilities paid, the remaining cash, if any, is distributed to the partners, which reduces their Capital balances to zero.

All Partners with a Positive Capital Balance

We first illustrate the liquidation of a partnership in which all partners have a positive Capital balance after the liquidation of all assets and the payment of all liabilities. For example, assume that the partnership of Ball, Stone, and Hinge decides to liquidate. After the business ceases operations on May 1, 1987 and the profit to that point has been distributed to the partners' Capital accounts, the May 1, 1987 balance sheet appears as follows:

Ball, Stone, and Hinge
Balance Sheet
May 1, 1987

Assets		Liabilities and Owners' Equity	
Cash	$ 60,000	Accounts payable	$150,000
Accounts receivable	40,000	Ball, Capital	140,000
Inventory	120,000	Stone, Capital	100,000
Property, plant, and		Hinge, Capital	80,000
equipment (net)	250,000		
Total	$470,000	Total	$470,000

According to the partnership agreement, Ball, Stone, and Hinge now divide profits and losses 40:40:20.

The partnership begins the liquidation process on May 2, 1987. All receivables are sold to a local bank, and the firm receives $30,000 in full settlement. On May 5 and 8, respectively, the inventory is sold for $140,000 and the property, plant, and equipment for $265,000. Finally, on May 15, all liabilities are paid and the remaining cash is distributed to the partners. The journal entries to record these liquidation transactions are:

Transaction Number					
1.	May 2, 1987	Cash		30,000	
		Gain or Loss from realization		10,000	
		Accounts Receivable			40,000
		To record sale of receivable to bank for $30,000.			
2.	May 5, 1987	Cash		140,000	
		Gain or Loss from Realization			20,000
		Inventory			120,000
		To record sale of inventory for $140,000.			
3.	May 8, 1987	Cash		265,000	
		Gain or Loss from Realization			15,000
		Property, Plant, and Equipment			250,000
		To record sale of property, plant, and equipment.			
4.	May 15, 1987	Accounts Payable		150,000	
		Cash			150,000
		To record payment of partnership liabilities.			
5.	May 15, 1987	Gain or Loss from Realization		25,000	
		Ball, Capital			10,000
		Stone, Capital			10,000
		Hinge, Capital			5,000
		To distribute gain on asset liquidation to partners' capital accounts.			
6.	May 15, 1987	Ball, Capital		150,000	
		Stone, Capital		110,000	
		Hinge, Capital		85,000	
		Cash			345,000
		To record final distribution of cash to partners.			

When a partnership liquidates, a statement of liquidation is often prepared. Such a statement for Ball, Stone, and Hinge is presented at the top of page 590. For convenience, all assets other than cash are combined and shown under the column labeled "Other assets." Each journal entry has a transaction number which is tied into the liquidation schedule. As is evident, after the final distribution of cash to the partners, all accounts have a zero balance.

A Partner with a Negative Capital Balance

In some situations, losses on the liquidation of assets are large enough to cause one or more of the partners to end up with a negative Capital balance. At that point, the partner with the negative balance must either put additional cash into the partnership or the other partners must cover the deficit.

To illustrate this situation, assume that on May 1, just prior to the liquidation of assets, the balance sheet of the firm of Ball, Stone, and Hinge is as it appears on page 588. However, let us now assume that when the partnership's assets other than cash are liquidated, a loss of $300,000 results. The journal entries to record these transactions are illustrated in the middle of page 590 and the liquidation statement is presented at the top of page 591.

Ball, Stone, and Hinge
Statement of Partnership Liquidation
For the Period May 1–15, 1987

Trans-action		Explanation	Cash	Other Assets	Accounts Payable	Ball, Capital (40%)	Stone, Capital (40%)	Hinge, Capital (20%)	(Gain) or Loss from Realization
	5/1	Balances	$ 60,000	$410,000	$150,000	$140,000	$100,000	$80,000	
1	5/2	Sale of receivables for $30,000	30,000	(40,000)					$10,000
2	5/5	Sale of inventory for $140,000	140,000	(120,000)					(20,000)
3	5/8	Sale of property, plant, and equipment	265,000	(250,000)					(15,000)
4	5/15	Payment of accounts payable	(150,000)		(150,000)				
5	5/15	Distribution of gain or loss from realization				10,000	10,000	5,000	25,000
			345,000	0	0	150,000	110,000	85,000	0
6	5/15	Cash distribution to partners	(345,000)	0	0	(150,000)	(110,000)	(85,000)	0
			0	0	0	0	0	0	0

Transaction Number				
1.	May 2, 1987	Cash	110,000	
		Loss from Realization	300,000	
		Accounts Receivable		40,000
		Inventory		120,000
		Property, Plant, and Equipment		250,000
		To record loss on sale of partnership assets.		
2.	May 15, 1987	Accounts Payable	150,000	
		Cash		150,000
		To record payment of liabilities.		
3.	May 15, 1987	Ball, Capital	120,000	
		Stone, Capital	120,000	
		Hinge, Capital	60,000	
		Loss from Realization		300,000
		To record distribution of loss from realization.		
4.	May 15, 1987	Cash	20,000	
		Stone, Capital		20,000
		To record additional capital contribution by Hinge to erase deficit.		
5.	May 15, 1987	Ball, Capital	20,000	
		Hinge, Capital	20,000	
		Cash		40,000
		To record final distribution of cash to partners.		

After the sale of assets in this example, Stone has a deficit of $20,000 in his Capital account. Because Stone is personally solvent, he makes an additional capital contribution of $20,000, which eliminates his deficit. The remaining cash of $40,000 is then distributed to Ball and Hinge.

Ball, Stone, and Hinge
Statement of Partnership Liquidation
For the Period May 1–15, 1987

Trans-action		Explanation	Cash	Other Assets	Accounts Payable	Ball, Capital (40%)	Stone, Capital (40%)	Hinge, Capital (20%)	(Gain) or Loss from Realization
	5/1	Balances	$ 60,000	$410,000	$150,000	$140,000	$100,000	$80,000	
1	5/2	Sale of assets for $110,000	110,000	(410,000)					300,000
2	5/15	Payment of liabilities	(150,000)		(150,000)				
3	5/15	Distribution of loss				(120,000)	(120,000)	(60,000)	(300,000)
			20,000	0	0	20,000	(20,000)	(20,000)	
4	5/15	Additional payment by Stone	20,000				20,000		
			40,000	0	0	20,000	0	20,000	0
5	5/15	Cash distribution to partners	(40,000)			(20,000)	0	(20,000)	
			0	0	0	0	0	0	0

There are situations in which a partner with a deficit Capital balance is personally insolvent and cannot make additional cash contributions. Because of the unlimited-liability feature of partnership, the other partners must make up that deficit. Let's now assume that Stone is insolvent and cannot make the additional $20,000 investment. In that case, Ball and Hinge must absorb the loss on a ratio of 2/3 to 1/3. Remember that before Hinge dropped out, they shared profit and losses in a ratio of 40% to 20%. Assuming that this now represents 100%, the new ratios are 40/60 and 20/60, or 2/3 to 1/3. The entries to record these events are:

May 15, 1987	Ball, Capital	13,330	
	Hinge, Capital	6,667	
	Stone, Capital		20,000
	To offset deficit in Stone's capital account against Ball's and Hinge's capital accounts.		

May 15, 1987	Ball, Capital	13,330	
	Hinge, Capital	6,667	
	Cash		20,000
	To record final distribution to partners.		

At this point, Ball and Hinge have a personal claim of $20,000 against Stone. Whether or not they are able to collect depends on Stone's financial situation.

Summary of Learning Objectives

1. **The Main Concepts behind Partnerships.** A partnership is an association of two or more persons to carry on as co-owners of a business for a profit. Partnerships have certain characteristics that make them advantageous. Included are their ease of formation and dissolution and the fact that they

are not separate legal entities, which means they are not taxed. On the other hand, there are certain disadvantages to a partnership, including unlimited liability, mutual agency, and limited life. These characteristics tend to make it more difficult to raise capital than it is for a corporation.

2. *Accounting Issues Related to Partnership Operations.* Except for the owners' equity section of the balance sheet, accounting for a partnership is similar to the accounting for other business organizations. The Partners' Capital account reflects the individual partners' equity in the partnership. It is used to record initial investments, subsequent investments, and the partners' share of profit or losses. Partners' withdrawals are eventually closed into their Capital accounts.

The partners can agree to share partnership profit and losses in any manner they wish. However, the profit-sharing agreement should be clearly spelled out in the partnership agreement. Generally, the distribution of profit and losses is based on one or more of the following items:

1. Partners' salaries.
2. Interest on capital balances.
3. A fixed ratio.

3. *Accounting Issues Related to Partnership Dissolution.* A partnership is dissolved every time there is a change in the individual partners constituting the partnership. This occurs when there is an admission of a new partner or the withdrawal, retirement, or death of an existing partner. In most cases, a dissolution does not result in the cessation of business; however, from a legal standpoint, a new partnership is formed.

Admissions and withdrawals can take place either by individual partners' buying and selling interest to each other or by investing and withdrawing assets from the partnership. If the agreement is between individual partners, the partnership is not involved and total partnership equity remains the same. There is just a transfer between partners. If assets are invested or withdrawn, overall partners' equity changes, and there is usually a bonus to the existing or retiring partner or the new or existing partners.

4. *Issues Related to Partnership Liquidation.* A partnership liquidation involves a selling of partnership assets, the payment of partnership liabilities, and the distribution of any remaining cash to the partners. Any gain or loss on the sale of partnership assets is distributed to the partners. If one of the partners is in a deficit capital position, he or she must make an additional investment or the deficit must be made up by the other partners.

Key Terms

Dissolution of a Partnership
General Partnership
Limited Partnership

Liquidation of a Partnership
Mutual Agency
Partnership

Problem for Your Review

Accounting for Partnership Operations. The partnership of Webb, Gernon, and Rios commenced business on January 2, 1987. The financial statements at the end of 1987 are shown below and at the top of page 594.

In addition, you have obtained the following information:

The partnership agreement calls for profit and losses to be split as follows:

1. Webb is to receive a salary of $1,500 per month.
2. Gernon and Rios are to receive salaries of $2,000 per month.
3. All partners will receive interest of 10% on their opening Capital balances (in this case, the investment made on 1/2/87). The remainder of income is to be distributed as follows: Webb 40%, Gernon 30%, and Rios 30%.

Required:

1. Make the journal entries to record the partners' investment in the partnership on 1/2/87. Assume all partners contributed cash.
2. Show how the profit distribution was calculated.
3. Make all the required closing entries.
4. If net income for the year was only $75,000, recalculate the profit distribution.

Webb, Gernon, and Rios, Attorneys
Income Statement
For the Year Ended December 31, 1987

Revenues		
Fees earned		$330,000
Expenses		
Salaries	$140,000	
Rent	75,000	
Depreciation	15,000	
Insurance	2,500	
Office supplies	2,000	
Delivery	1,500	236,000
Net income		$ 94,000
Distribution of net income		
Webb		$ 29,200
Gernon		32,400
Rios		32,400
		$ 94,000

Webb, Gernon, and Rios, Attorneys
Statement of Partners' Capital
For the Year Ended December 31, 1987

	Webb	Gernon	Rios	Total
Capital, 1/1/87	$ 0	$ 0	$ 0	$ 0
Add: Investment during year	60,000	45,000	45,000	150,000
Net income	29,200	32,400	32,400	94,000
Less: Withdrawals	(18,000)	(24,000)	(24,000)	(66,000)
Capital, 12/31/87	$71,200	$53,400	$53,400	$178,000

Webb, Gernon, and Rios, Attorneys
Balance Sheet
December 31, 1987

Assets		Liabilities and Partners' Equity	
Cash	$ 29,000	Liabilities	
Accounts receivable	42,600	Accounts payable	$ 5,200
Office supplies	8,200	Wages payable	1,500
Prepaid insurance	9,700	Total liabilities	6,700
Office equipment, net	38,400		
Office furniture, net	56,800	Partners' equity	
		Webb, Capital	71,200
		Gernon, Capital	53,400
		Rios, Capital	53,400
			178,000
Total assets	$184,700	Total liabilities and partners' equity	$184,700

Solution

1. Entries to record original investment

1/2/87	Cash	150,000	
	Webb, Capital		60,000
	Gernon, Capital		45,000
	Rios, Capital		45,000
	To record original investment in partnership.		

2. Distribution of profits

Webb, Gernon, and Rios, Attorneys
Distribution of Income for 1987

	Webb	Gernon	Rios	Total
1987 net income				$94,000
Allocation of salaries	$18,000	$24,000	$24,000	(66,000)
Remaining to be allocated				28,000
Interest on beginning capital balance:				
Webb ($60,000 × .10)	6,000			(6,000)
Gernon (45,000 × .10)		4,500		(4,500)
Rios (45,000 × .10)			4,500	(4,500)
				13,000
Remaining to be allocated in a				
fixed ratio: Webb, 40%	5,200			(5,200)
Gernon, 30%		3,900		(3,900)
Rios, 30%			3,900	(3,900)
	$29,200	$32,400	$32,400	$ 0

3. Closing entries

12/31/87	Fees Earned	330,000	
	Income Summary		330,000
	To close fees earned to income summary.		

Income Summary	236,000		
Salaries		140,000	
Rent		75,000	
Depreciation		15,000	
Insurance		2,500	
Office Supplies		2,000	
Delivery		1,500	
To close expenses to income summary.			
Income Summary	94,000		
Webb, Capital		29,200	
Gernon, Capital		32,400	
Gios, Capital		32,400	
To close income summary to capital.			
Webb, Capital	18,000		
Gernon, Capital	24,000		
Rios, Capital	24,000		
Webb, Drawing		18,000	
Gernon, Drawing		24,000	
Rios, Drawing		24,000	
To close drawing into partners' capital.			

4. Distribution of profits—Net income $75,000

Webb, Gernon, and Rios, Attorneys
Distribution of Income for 1987

	Webb	Gernon	Rios	Total
1987 Net income				$75,000
Allocation of salaries	$18,000	$24,000	$24,000	(66,000)
Remaining to be allocated				9,000
Interest on beginning capital balance:				
Webb ($60,000 × .10)	6,000			(6,000)
Gernon ($45,000 × .10)		4,500		(4,500)
Rios ($45,000 × .10)			4,500	(4,500)
Deficit				(6,000)
Deficit allocated in profit-sharing ratio				
Webb ($6,000 × .40)	(2,400)			2,400
Gernon ($6,000 × .30)		(1,800)		1,800
Rios ($6,000 × .30)			(1,800)	1,800
	$21,600	$26,700	$26,700	$ 0

Questions

1. Describe the primary features of a partnership. Discuss the advantages and disadvantages of the partnership form of business organization.

2. Until recently, many personal service business in the United States that had more than one owner were organized as partnerships. Why do you think that was the case?

3. What is a partnership agreement and what items should be included in the document?

4. In forming the partnership of Scully and Porter, Scully contributed only cash and Porter contributed various assets other than cash. How should these assets be recorded on the partnership books? What is the relevance of the book value of these assets on Porter's records?

5. Describe the nature of partnership profits and how they should be taken into consideration in developing a scheme to divide partnership profits or losses.

6. You and a potential partner are considering starting a partnership to practice law. What factors should be considered in deciding how to divide profits and losses. Is it necessary that profits and losses be divided in the same manner?

7. The partnership of Arnold and Cherry earned $50,000 during the current year. During the year, Arnold withdrew $30,000 and Cherry withdrew $24,000. The partnership agreement calls for Arnold and Cherry to split profit and losses equally. How much income must Arnold and Cherry report on their income tax returns for the current year?

8. How does a dissolution of a partnership differ from a liquidation of a partnership? When is each appropriate?

9. Martinelle purchases all of Loa's one-third interest in the Tiny Tim partnership directly from Loa. At the time of the purchase, Loa's Capital balance is $120,000. The interest is purchased for $150,000 cash with the consent of the remaining partners. What amount is Martinelle's Capital account credited for? How would your answer differ, if at all, if the purchase was for $100,000 instead of $150,000?

10. Describe in your own words how the accounting differs when a new partner makes an investment in a partnership rather than purchasing an existing interest of one or more of the partners.

11. Under what circumstances would a new partner be willing to receive a partnership interest less than his or her investment? Under what circumstances would an existing partner be willing to accept a payment or withdrawal that is less than his or her interest in the partnership?

12. Does the death of an existing partner cause the dissolution and/or liquidation of the partnership? Why or why not?

13. Describe the procedures that take place when a partnership is liquidated. Is it true that all partners will receive in cash the balance in their Capital account before liquidation?

14. The partnership of Able, Better, and Cannis is developing procedures to ensure the continuation of the partnership in the event of the death of one of the partners. What actions and procedures can they agree to in order to meet their desires?

15. The three partners in a partnership split profits and losses in the ratio of 4:4:2. During liquidation, all of the partnership assets are converted to cash and all of the liabilities are paid. After this process, one of the partners with a 40% interest has a deficit Capital balance. Assuming the partner is personally solvent, what actions must be taken? If the partner with a deficit balance is not personally solvent, what actions must the other two partners take?

Exercises

1. Accounting for the Formation of a Partnership. Emily Chang ran a small but successful CPA firm as a sole proprietorship for a number of years. During the current year, she decides to expand the firm and admit a partner, Ken Cobb. The partnership agreement calls for Cobb to contribute $100,000 and for Chang to contribute the assets of her existing practice. The partnership agreement provides the following information concerning the assets contributed by Chang:

Account	Book Value	Fair Value
Cash	$ 5,000	$ 5,000
Accounts receivable	25,000	20,000
Supplies	8,000	8,000
Office equipment	50,000	67,000

During the first year, the partnership's net income was $50,000. All profit and losses are split equally, and during the year each partner was paid a salary of $20,000.

Required:

    a. Make the necessary summary journal entries to record these events.

    b. What is the amount of each partner's Capital account at the end of the first year of operations?

2. Partnership Operations. Make the journal entries to record each of the following independent situations relating to a partnership:

    a. H. Aber contributes cash of $20,000 and assets with a book value of $40,000 and a fair market value of $25,000 to a partnership.

    b. T. O'Keefe withdraws $8,000 cash from the partnership.

    c. H. Gernon borrows $5,000 cash from the partnership.

    d. A. Zapata, one of the partners in a local CPA firm, collects a $1,000 receivable from one of the partnership clients and deposits the funds in his own bank account for his personal use.

e. B. Crocker purchased one-half of the interest of one of the existing partners in the Express Co. for $50,000. The total Capital balance of the partner, BA America, was $80,000 before the purchase.

3. Statement of Partners' Capital Accounts. At the beginning of the current year, 1987, the total capital of the JAR partnership was $120,000. During the year the partnership's net income was $100,000. The following salaries were paid to each of the partners: J, $18,000; A, $24,000; R, $15,000. The partners split profit and losses as follows: J, 30%; A, 30%; R, 40%. The partners have also agreed to maintain Capital balances in that ratio, and they agree that the total capital of the partnership at the end of the year should be $130,000. Prepare a statement of the partners' capital accounts at the end of the current year.

4. Division of Partnership Profits. The beginning capital of the Furillo and Lombardi partnership was $200,000. Furillo's Capital balance was $120,000 and Lombardi's was $80,000. Determine how profit and losses should be split in each of the following independent situations:

a. Partnership net income was $51,000 and the profits are split one-third to Furillo and two-thirds to Lombardi.

b. Partnership net loss was $60,000 and profit and losses are split in the ratio of the beginning Capital balances.

c. Partnership net income was $120,000. Each partner draws a salary of $25,000 a year. Partnership profits in excess of salaries are split 55% to Furillo and 45% to Lombardi.

d. Partnership net income was $40,000. Each partner draws a salary of $25,000 a year. The partnership agreement is silent as to how profit and losses are to be split.

5. Distribution of Partnership Profits. R. Eskew and D. Jensen are partners in the Wangler Co. During the year the following activity took place in each of their Capital accounts:

	Eskew	Jensen
Beginning balance	$60,000	$80,000
Additional investments		
4/1	20,000	
6/1		20,000
Withdrawals		
8/1	10,000	
12/1		10,000

During the year the partnership's net income amounted to $100,000. The partnership agreement calls for profit and losses to be distributed based on the weighted average capital balance during the year. Determine how the $100,000 net income should be allocated between the two partners. (If necessary, round off percentages to whole numbers.)

6. Admission of a New Partner. The partnership of Houston and Vegas splits profit and losses 60% to Houston and 40% to Vegas. At the beginning of the current year, each partner had the following Capital balance:

Houston	$250,000
Vegas	300,000

Make the appropriate journal entry on the partnership's books assuming a new partner is admitted under each of the following independent situations:

a. Dantana purchases all of Houston's interest for $200,000.

b. Dantana purchases a 45% interest in the partnership for $450,000.

c. Dantana purchases a 45% interest in the partnership for $500,000.

d. Dantana purchases a 45% interest in the partnership for $400,000.

7. Withdrawal of a Partner. At the beginning of the current year, the partners' Capital balances in the partnership of Heilkamp, Smith, and Schwartz are as follows:

Heilkamp	$100,000
Smith	125,000
Schwartz	150,000

Accounting for Partnerships   **597**

According to the partnership agreement, profit and losses are split according to the following formula: Heilkamp, 25%; Smith, 30%; and Schwartz, 45%. Make the appropriate journal entry to record the withdrawal of Heilkamp under each of the following independent situations:

a. Smith and Schwartz each purchase one-half of Heilkamp's interest for $75,000.

b. Heilkamp withdraws from the partnership, and the partnership purchases her interest for $140,000. The terms of the buy-out call for Heilkamp to receive a cash payment of $100,000 and a $40,000, 12% note.

c. Heilkamp withdraws from the partnership, and the partnership purchases her interest for $80,000 cash.

8. **Determining Missing Figures.** Answer each of the following independent questions:

a. At the beginning of the year, the Capital balances of Welsch, Anthony, and Thomas were:

Welsch	$504,000
Anthony	252,000
Thomas	84,000

The partnership has decided to expand and the partners agree to admit Meigs with a 25% interest. Assuming Meigs neither receives nor pays a bonus, how much must he contribute to the partnership?

b. Jones is a partner in the Jedi partnership. She has a 30% interest in partnership profits and losses. During the current year, her Capital account decreased $30,000. During the same year, Jones drew a salary of $65,000 and contributed equipment to the partnership with a fair market value of $12,500. Determine the net income of the Jedi partnership for the current year.

9. **Liquidation of a Partnership.** Jigs and Poco are the two partners in the Dogey Store. Because of disagreements, the partners decided to liquidate the business. Just prior to liquidation, the condensed balance sheet of the company was as follows:

Cash	$ 60,000
Other assets	330,000
Liabilities	90,000
Jigs, Capital	150,000
Poco, Capital	150,000

Under the terms of the partnership agreement, Jigs receives 55% of the profits and Poco receives 45% of the profits. During the liquidation process the other assets were sold for $420,000.

Required:

a. Prepare the necessary journal entries to record the sale of the assets, the payment of the liabilities, and the distribution of any remaining cash to the partners.

b. Prepare the necessary journal entries to record the sale of assets, the payments of the liabilities, and the distribution of the remaining cash to the partners now, assuming the other assets were sold for $300,000.

10. **Liquidation of a Partnership.** The condensed balance sheet of the Blitz partnership is as follows:

Cash	$ 180,000
Other assets	1,640,000
Accounts payable	420,000
West, Capital	540,000
Wiley, Capital	400,000
Kent, Capital	460,000

Required:

a. The partners have agreed to share partnership profit and losses in the ratio of 40%, 30%, and 30%. The partners have decided to liquidate the partnership and have been able to sell the other assets for $1.2 million. Determine how much cash should be distributed to each of the partners.

598

b. Now assume that the profits and losses are split in the ratio of 30%, 50%, and 20% and that the other assets are sold for $640,000. Determine how much cash should be distributed to each of the partners.

Problem Set A

15A–1. Accounting for the Formation of Partnerships. Helene Blanc and Henry Lee each operated their own CPA firm for several years before deciding to form a partnership at the beginning of the current year, 1987. The partnership agreement stipulated that Blanc and Lee were to contribute the net assets of their individual practices. In addition, because Blanc was to be the managing partner, she was to receive 55% of the profits and Lee was to receive 45%. All losses were to be split equally.

Just prior to the merger, the individual balance sheets for Blanc and Lee were as follows:

Assets	Blanc's Practice		Lee's Practice	
	Book Value	Fair Value	Book Value	Fair Value
Cash	$ 5,000	$ 5,000	$10,000	$10,000
Accounts receivable, net	25,000	22,000	34,000	30,000
Office supplies	2,500	2,500	1,500	1,000
Office equipment, net	50,000	60,000	40,000	48,000
Total	$82,500	$89,500	$85,500	$89,000
Equities				
Accounts payable	$12,000	$12,500	$ 1,500	$ 1,500
Blanc, Capital	70,500	77,000		
Lee, Capital			84,000	87,500
Total	$82,500	$89,500	$85,500	$89,000

At the end of the firm's first year of operations, these accounts showed the following balances:

Income Summary	$80,000 credit
Blanc, Drawing	30,000 debit
Lee, Drawing	25,000 debit

No additional capital contributions were made.

Required:
a. Prepare the journal entries to open the partnership's books.
b. Prepare a balance sheet on the first day of partnership operations, January 2, 1987.
c. Prepare the closing entries at the end of 1987.
d. Prepare a statement of partners' capital accounts on December 31, 1987.

15A–2. Partnership Operations. Bill Garrison, the managing partner of a partnership that owns a large department store, prepared the income statement on page 600.

In addition, the following data are also available:
1. Included in general and administrative expenses are partners' salaries of $50,000, split as follows: Garrison, $25,000; Smith, $20,000; Beaver, $5,000.
2. During the year Al Smith, one of the partners, took some merchandise home from the department store for his personal use. The bookkeeper did not record this and as a result the merchandise, with a cost of $5,000, was not counted in the ending inventory.
3. One of the other partners, B. Beaver, paid off a partnership bank loan of $10,000 and the related interest of $1,500. No interest accrual had been made. The bookkeeper was not notified of this transaction and as a result it was not recorded on the partnership books.

Accounting for Partnerships   599

4. Partners' Capital balances per books at December 31, 1986 and drawings during 1987 were:

	Amount	Profit and Loss %
Garrison, Capital	$100,000	40%
Garrison, drawing during 1987	5,000	
Smith, Capital	125,000	35
Smith, drawing during 1987	0	
Beaver, Capital	90,000	25
Beaver, drawing during 1987	10,000	

Buy-Rite Department Store
Income Statement
For the Year Ended December 31, 1987

Net sales		$2,500,000
Cost of goods sold		1,625,000
Gross margin on sales		875,000
Operating expenses		
Selling	$435,000	
General and administrative	240,000	675,000
Net income		$ 200,000

Required:

a. Based on the information provided, make any necessary correcting entries.

b. Prepare a revised income statement. Include a schedule showing the distribution of net income.

c. How much income should each partner include in his income tax for 1987?

d. Prepare a statement of partners' capital accounts for the year ended December 31, 1987.

15A–3. Distribution of Partnership Income. P. Crack and C. Pot are partners in a very successful medical practice. According to the partnership agreement, profit and losses are divided according to the partners' weighted average capital balances during the year. Partnership net income amounted to $200,000 during the current year. Your analysis of the partners' capital account revealed the following:

Partner	Date	Transaction	Amount
P. Crack	1/2/87	Beginning balance	$200,000
	4/1/87	Capital investment	50,000
	6/1/87	Capital investment	30,000
	11/1/87	Withdrawal	40,000
C. Pot	1/2/87	Beginning balance	$220,000
	3/1/87	Withdrawal	20,000
	6/1/87	Withdrawal	20,000
	10/1/87	Capital investment	50,000

Required:

a. Determine how partnership profits should be divided between the two partners. (Where necessary, round to whole dollars and whole percentages.)

b. Now assume that the partnership profits are to be split based on the beginning Capital balances. Determine how the profits should now be split. Which arrangement do you think is more equitable? Why?

15A-4. Distribution of Partnership Profits. Lotus has three partners—Padilla, Doggett, and Kari. Their beginning Capital balances as well as certain provisions of the partnership agreement are provided below:

Partner	Capital Balance	Annual Salary	Residual Profit and Loss %
Padilla	$100,000	$24,000	20%
Doggett	150,000	36,000	40
Kari	200,000	48,000	40

Under the partnership agreement, profit and losses are split in the following manner: Each partner receives an annual salary and then 10% interest on the beginning Capital balance. Any residual profits shall be split per the above percentages.

Required:

Prepare schedules indicating how the partnership profit or losses should be split under each of the following independent situations:

   a. Partnership income—$600,000.
   b. Partnership income—$140,000.
   c. Partnership loss—$100,000.

15A-5. Admission of a New Partner. Education for Professionals has been in existence for several years. The existing partners decided to admit a new partner, Jennifer Steele. Just prior to the admission of Steele, the partners' Capital balances and profit and loss ratios were:

Partner	Capital Balance	Profit and Loss %
Gonzales	$200,000	35%
Schroeder	180,000	35
Williams	222,000	30

Required:

For each of the following independent situations, make the necessary journal entry on the partnership books to record the admission of Steele. Assume that all existing partnership assets are recorded as costs close to their fair value.

   a. Steele purchases all of Gonzales's share for $200,000.
   b. Steele purchases one-half of Schroeder's interest for $85,000 and one-third of Williams' interest for $70,000. All payments are made directly to the partners.
   c. Steele invests $125,000 for a 15% interest in the partnership.
   d. Steele invests $163,000 for a 30% interest in the partnership.
   e. Steele invests $150,500 for a 20% interest in the partnership.

15A-6. Retirement of a Partner. Because of disagreements with his partners, Riggins decides to withdraw from the partnership of Riggins, Dinelly, and Cook. Just prior to his retirement, each partner's Capital balance and profit and loss ratio are as follows:

Partner	Capital Balance	Profit and Loss %
S. Riggins	$300,000	40%
D. Dinelly	340,000	40
I. Cook	260,000	20

Required:

Under each of the following independent situations, make the entry on the partnership books to record the retirement of Riggins. Assume that partnership assets are not revalued.

   a. Dinelly and Cook each buy one-half of Riggins' interest directly from him for $200,000 each.
   b. The partnership purchases Riggins' interest from him for $320,000. Riggins receives $100,000 cash and a note for the remainder.

c. The partnership purchases Riggins' interest from him for $250,000. Riggins receives $170,000 cash and a piece of partnership equipment with a book value of $80,000.

15A–7. Partnership Liquidation. On December 31, 1987 the partners in the Golden Eagle Company decide to liquidate the partnership. A condensed balance sheet as of that date appears as follows:

Golden Eagle Company
Balance Sheet
December 31, 1987

Assets		Equities	
Cash	$ 50,000	Accounts payable	$ 80,000
Other assets	150,000	Rosser, Capital	50,000
		Numrich, Capital	40,000
		Greenly, Capital	30,000
Total assets	$200,000	Total equities	$200,000

Partnership profits and losses are shared equally.

Required:

Prepare liquidation schedules similar to the ones illustrated in the chapter under each of the following independent situations:

a. The other assets are sold for $210,000.
b. The other assets are sold for $120,000.
c. The other assets are sold for $54,000 and all partners are personally solvent and will contribute any necessary cash to the partnership.
d. The other assets are sold for $45,000 and Greenly is personally insolvent.

15A–8. Comprehensive Partnership Problem. At the beginning of the current year, 1987, Susan Brentano and Sam Perez form a partnership that will run a travel agency, called the Ultimate Trip. The partnership agreement states that Brentano is to have a 60% share in profit and losses and Perez a 40% share. During the next three years the following events occurred:

• January 2, 1987: The partners contributed the following assets to the partnership:

Asset	Book Value	Fair Value
Brentano:		
Cash	$10,000	$10,000
Office equipment	50,000	70,000
Furniture and fixtures	10,000	30,000
Perez:		
Cash	80,000	80,000

• December 31, 1987: The partnership concluded a moderately profitable year with net income of $40,000. During the year Brentano drew a salary of $30,000 and Perez a salary of $12,000.

• January 2, 1988: In order to expand their business, Brentano and Perez decided to admit Joe Murphy into the partnership. Murphy purchased a 20% interest in the partnership for $60,000. In addition, the partnership agreement was amended so that each partner is to receive 10% interest on the beginning Capital balances with the remaining profits split 40% to Brentano, 40% to Perez, and 20% to Murphy. Each partner was allowed a salary of $2,000 a month in cash. (Include Murphy's investment in the partnership on January 2 as part of the beginning Capital balances.)

• December 31, 1988: Partnership profits during 1988 amounted to $200,000.

• January 2, 1989: Brentano decides to withdraw from the partnership. Under an agreement with the remaining two partners, she took $200,000 cash plus a note for $100,000 in exchange for her partnership interest.

Required:

a. Prepare summary journal entries, including those to close the partners' capital and drawing accounts, to record the above events.

b. Prepare a statement of partners' capital accounts at the end of 1987 and 1988.

Problem Set B

15B-1. Accounting for the Formation of a Partnership. Mary Hong and Mimi Segal each operated her own medical clinic for several years prior to deciding to form a partnership at the beginning of 1987. The partnership agreement required that Hong and Segal each contribute the net assets of their individual clinics to the new partnership. Profit and losses were to be split 60% to Hong and 40% to Segal. However, Segal was to receive $1,000 a month salary for running the new clinic. Hong was not to receive a salary.

Just prior to the merger, the individual balance sheets for Hong and Segal were as follows:

	Hong's Practice		Segal's Practice	
Assets	Book Value	Fair Value	Book Value	Fair Value
Cash	$ 10,000	$ 10,000	$ 12,000	$ 12,000
Accounts receivable, net	45,000	42,000	38,000	35,200
Clinic supplies	7,000	6,500	6,000	5,800
Medical equipment, net	80,000	91,500	75,000	82,000
Total	$142,000	$150,000	$131,000	$135,000
Equities				
Accounts payable	$ 15,000	$ 15,000	$ 15,000	$ 15,000
Loans payable	5,000	5,000	0	0
Capital	122,000	130,000	116,000	120,000
Total	$142,000	$150,000	$131,000	$135,000

The company's first year of operations was very profitable. The firm's net income for the year was $400,000. In addition to Segal's monthly salary, Hong withdrew a piece of medical equipment from the partnership for her own use. The equipment had a book value and a fair market value of $5,000. No other drawings or capital contributions were made.

Required:

a. Prepare the journal entries to open the partnership books.

b. Prepare a balance sheet on first day of operations, January 2, 1987.

c. Prepare the closing entries at the end of 1987.

d. Prepare a statement of partners' capital accounts on December 31, 1987.

15B-2. Partnership Operations. Javier Bitar, the managing partner of a partnership that owns a large grocery store, prepared the income statement for the year ended December 31, 1987 shown on page 604.

In addition, you have been able to gather the following information:

1. Included in selling expenses are partners' salaries, split as follows: Bitar, $45,000; Cluff, $35,000; Wylie, $20,000.

2. During the year one of the partners, Cody Cluff, collected one of the firm's accounts receivable and deposited it in his personal account for his own use. The receivable amounted to $10,000. The bookkeeper was not notified of the cash collection.

3. One of the other partners, Sara Wylie, took $5,000 worth of groceries for her personal use. These groceries were not counted in the ending inventory.

Accounting for Partnerships 603

4. Partners' Capital balances per the partnership books at December 31, 1986 and drawings during 1987 were as follows:

	Amount	Profit and Loss %
Bitar, Capital	$200,000	40%
Bitar, drawings, 1987	10,000	
Cluff, Capital	150,000	25
Cluff, drawings, 1987	8,000	
Wylie, Capital	400,000	35
Wylie, drawing, 1987	12,000	

Green Grocery Store
Income Statement
For the Year Ended December 31, 1987

Net sales		$4,000,000
Cost of goods sold		2,800,000
Gross margin on sales		1,200,000
Operating expenses		
Selling	$750,000	
General and administrative	250,000	1,000,000
Net income		$ 200,000

Required:

a. Based on the information provided make any necessary correcting entries.

b. Prepare a revised income statement. Include a schedule showing the distribution of net income.

c. How much income should each partner include in his or her income tax for 1987?

d. Prepare a statement of partners' capital accounts for the year ended December 31, 1987.

15B–3. Distribution of Partnership Income. B. Beck and A. Chan are partners in a successful law practice. According to a newly revised partnership agreement, profits are to be divided according to the partners' weighted average capital balances. Losses are to be split equally. During the year partnership income amounted to $500,000. Your analysis of the partners' Capital accounts revealed the following contributions and withdrawals:

Partner	Date	Transaction	Amount
B. Beck	1/2/87	Beginning balance	$100,000
	3/1/87	Capital investment	10,000
	9/1/87	Withdrawal	20,000
	10/1/87	Withdrawal	10,000
A. Chan	1/2/87	Beginning balance	$ 70,000
	4/1/87	Capital investment	10,000
	7/1/87	Capital investment	10,000
	10/1/87	Withdrawal	10,000

Required:

a. Determine how partnership profits should be split between the two partners. (Round to whole dollars and percentages where necessary.)

b. Now assume that the partnership profits are to be split based on the beginning Capital balances. Determine how that split should be made. Compare your answer with that in (a) above. Which do you think more equitable? Why?

15B–4. Distribution of Partnership Profits. Butler and Associates, a law firm, has three partners, A. Butler, C. Collins, and G. Goldman. Their beginning Capital balances and the provisions of the partnership agreement related to the profit and loss ratio are provided below:

Partner	Capital Balance	Annual Salary	Residual Profit %	Loss %
Butler	$100,000	$50,000	50%	35%
Collins	70,000	30,000	40	35
Goldman	30,000	25,000	10	30

Under the partnership agreement, profits are to be split in the following manner: Each partner receives an annual salary and then 12% interest on the beginning Capital balance. Any residual profits shall be split per the above profit percentages. All losses will be split per the above loss percentages.

Required:

Prepare schedules indicating how the partnership profit or losses should be split under each of the independent situations:

a. Partnership income—$200,000.

b. Partnership income— 110,000.

c. Partnership loss   — 100,000.

15B–5. Admission of a New Partner. Ziegler, Hechler and Co. is a very successful CPA firm. The existing partners decide to admit a new partner, Janet Cooper. Just prior to the admission of Cooper, the partners' Capital balances and profit and loss ratios are:

Partner	Capital Balance	Profit and Loss %
Ziegler	$300,000	45%
Hechler	250,000	35
Johnson	150,000	20

Required:

For each of the following independent situations, make the necessary journal entry on the partnership books to record the admission of Cooper. Assume that all existing partnership net assets are recorded at costs close to their fair values.

a. Cooper purchases all of Johnson's share for $180,000.

b. Cooper purchases one-third of Ziegler's interest for $120,000 and one-half of Johnson's interest for $100,000. All payments are made directly to the partners.

c. Cooper invests $200,000 for a 15% interest in the partnership.

d. Cooper invests $100,000 for a 20% interest in the partnership.

e. Cooper invests $300,000 for a 30% interest in the partnership.

15B–6. Retirement of a Partner. Because of health problems, Tommy Ngo decides to retire from the partnership of Ngo, Hsu, and Label. Just prior to his retirement, each partner's Capital balance and profit and loss split are as follows:

Partners	Capital Balance	Profit and Loss %
T. Ngo	$200,000	40%
C. Hsu	180,000	30
D. Label	170,000	30

Required:

Under each of the following independent situations make the entry on the partnership's books to record Ngo's retirement. Assume that partnership net assets are not revalued unless otherwise stated.

a. Hsu and Label each buy one-half of Ngo's interest directly from him for $120,000 each.

b. The partnership purchases Ngo's interest from him for $250,000. Ngo receives $150,000 cash and a note for the remainder.

Accounting for Partnerships

c. The partnership purchases Ngo's interest from him for $180,000. Ngo receives $100,000 cash and a piece of equipment with a book value of $50,000.

15B–7. Partnership Liquidation. The partners of the Western International Co. decided to liquidate the partnership on December 15, 1987. A condensed balance sheet as of that date, immediately before the liquidation, appears as follows:

Western International Company
Balance Sheet
December 15, 1987

Assets		Equities	
Cash	$200,000	Accounts payable	$220,000
Other assets	600,000	Tune, Capital	250,000
		Miller, Capital	180,000
		Williams, Capital	150,000
Total assets	$800,000	Total equities	$800,000

Profits and losses are shared equally.

Required:

Prepare liquidation schedules similar to the ones illustrated in the chapter under each of the following independent situations:
   a. The other assets are sold for $800,000.
   b. The other assets are sold for $400,000.
   c. The other assets are sold for $80,000 and all partners are personally solvent and will contribute any necessary cash to the partnership.
   d. The other assets are sold for $60,000 and Williams is personally insolvent.

15B–8. Comprehensive Partnership Problem. At the beginning of 1986, Eve Cordova and Michele Kemp formed a partnership to market multicolored computer disks. The partnership agreement stated that Cordova is to receive a 55% share in the profit and losses and Kemp is to receive a 45% share. During the next three years the following events occurred:
   • January 2, 1986: The partners contributed the following assets to the partnership:

Assets	Book Value	Fair Value
Cordova		
Cash	$100,000	$100,000
Office equipment	200,000	250,000
Furniture and fixtures	150,000	200,000
Kemp		
Cash	$450,000	$450,000

   • December 31, 1986: The partnership determined that the net income for the year was $100,000. During the year Cordova drew a salary of $60,000 and Kemp a salary of $50,000.
   • January 2, 1987: In order to expand their business, Cordova and Kemp decided to admit Bobby Jones into the partnership. Jones purchases a 30% interest in the partnership for $600,000. In addition, the partnership agreement is amended so that each partner is to receive 10% interest on the beginning Capital balance, with the remaining profits split 40% to Cordova, 30% to Kemp, and 30% to Jones. Each partner will draw $30,000 a year as salary. (Include Jones's contribution on January 2 as part of the beginning Capital balance.)
   • December 31, 1987: Partnership net income during 1987 amounted to $250,000.

- January 2, 1988: Cordova decides to withdraw from the partnership. Under an agreement with the remaining partners, she agrees to take $400,000 cash plus a note for $400,000 in exchange for her partnership interest.

Required:

a. Prepare summary journal entries, including those to close the partners' Capital and Drawing accounts, to record the above events.
b. Prepare a statement of partners' capital at the end of 1986 and 1987.

Using the Computer

Yolo has three partners—Zachery, Silver, and Pecora. Their beginning Capital balances as well as certain provisions of the partnership agreement are provided below:

Partner	Capital Balance	Annual Salary	Residual Profit and Loss %
Zachery	$200,000	$48,000	40%
Silver	300,000	72,000	20
Pecora	400,000	96,000	40

Under the partnership agreement, profit and losses are split in the following manner: Each partner receives an annual salary and then 12% interest on the beginning Capital balance. Any residual profit are split per the above percentages.

Required:

Using an electronic spreadsheet, prepare schedules indicating how the partnership profit or losses should be split under each of the following independent situations:

a. Partnership income—$500,000.
b. Partnership income—$250,000.

Understanding Financial Statements

Following is a statement of partner's equity at December 31, 1983 for Transco Exploration Partners, Ltd. The general partners have unlimited liability while the limited partners have liabilities limited to their investment.

	Transco Exploration Partners, Ltd.		
	General Partners	Limited Partners	Total
Transfer of net assets of TXC	$ —	$ 914,925,579	$ 914,925,579
General Partners' cash contributions	10,303,030	—	10,303,030
Sale of depositary units	—	120,000,000	120,000,000
Add (deduct):			
Syndication costs	(18,467)	(1,828,202)	(1,846,669)
Net income	104,812	10,376,424	10,481,236
Distribution	(257,576)	(28,500,000)	(28,757,576)
Reinvestment	227,273	22,500,000	22,727,273
Balance at December 31, 1983	10,359,072	1,037,473,801	1,047,832,873

During the year ended December 31, 1984 the following events occurred:

Syndication costs	$ 67,568
Net income	47,107,552
Distributions	108,433,714
Reinvestments	98,168,636

a. Determine the distribution ratio between the general and limited partners for the syndication costs, net income, distribution, and reinvestment for the year ended December 31, 1983.

b. Applying these ratios for 1984, prepare the statement of partners' equity at December 31, 1984 in the same format as on the preceding page.

Financial Decision Case

For several years, Lin and Rusbarsky have operated a partnership that develops high-tech products for the Defense Department. The business is very risky in that their profit levels depend largely on the contracts received from the Defense Department. Thus, some years are very profitable and others are not. Each partner's current Capital balance and other partnership data are presented below:

	Capital Balance	Annual Salary	Profit (Loss) Sharing Ratio
Lin	$300,000	$40,000	50%
Rusbarsky	400,000	50,000	50

Partnership profits during the last six years have been:

1982	$180,000
1983	(50,000)
1984	120,000
1985	(40,000)
1986	160,000
1987	90,000

Because of prior losses and uncertainty, the partners often make additional capital contributions.

One employee, C. Purvis, is being considered for admittance to the partnership. She currently receives an annual salary of $35,000. The terms of the new partnership agreement are as follows:

a. Purvis will purchase a 15% interest in the partnership for $200,000.

b. She will receive an annual salary of $30,000 plus her share of partnership profits. Partnership profits will now be split as follows:

Lin	42.5%
Rusbarsky	42.5
Purvis	15.0

The original two partners will receive their same yearly salaries.

Purvis is concerned about joining the partnership and asks your advice on a number of issues.

Required:

a. Explain to Purvis the advantages and disadvantages of the partnership form of business organization, especially as related to the current partnership under consideration.

b. Explain to Purvis the advantages and disadvantages of the proposed partnership agreement outlined above.

Corporate Organization and Capital Stock Transactions

16

LEARNING OBJECTIVES

After reading this chapter you should be able to:

1. List the major characteristics of a corporation in comparison to partnerships and sole proprietorships.
2. Explain how corporations are formed and organized.
3. List the characteristics of the two major types of capital stock, common and preferred.
4. Discuss the components of stockholders' equity.
5. Make the journal entries related to the issuance of capital stock.
6. Use stock information in making decisions.
7. State the internal control procedures over stock transactions.

Perhaps more than any other symbol, the corporation characterizes U.S. business. Although sole proprietorships and partnerships outnumber corporations, the corporation is the dominant form of organization in the United States. Most major businesses other than service-oriented businesses such as large accounting firms are organized as corporations. The purpose of this chapter is to introduce you to corporate organizations, their formation, and related capital stock transactions. In the next chapter we discuss other issues related to corporations such as retained earnings, treasury stock transactions, and corporate income statements.

Characteristics of a Corporation

A corporation is a separate body, authorized by law, owned by one or more persons, which has its own rights, privileges, and obligations distinct from those of its owner(s). In effect, under court rulings, a corporation is a separate legal entity with a continuous life which has similar rights and obligations to those of an individual in the United States. This means that a corporation can sue or be sued and does not go out of existence with the death of an owner or a change in ownership.

Advantages of a Corporation

A corporation has certain characteristics that give it a number of advantages over sole proprietorships and partnerships. These advantages include limited liability for the shareholders, transferability of ownership, ease of capital formation, and professional management.

Limited Liability

A corporation is responsible for its own obligations. Its creditors can look only to the assets of the corporation to satisfy their claims. The owners' total liability generally is limited to the amount they invested in the corporation. Thus, if you invested $5,000 in a corporation, your liability is limited to that investment regardless of the debts the corporation may eventually incur. However, in many smaller corporations owned by families or a few individuals, the shareholders often are required to guarantee corporation loans from banks and other creditors.

The limited liability feature of the corporation is considerably different from the legal liability of the sole proprietor. Sole proprietors have unlimited liability in that the creditors of the business can look to the personal assets of the owners of the business to satisfy claims against the business.

Related to the concept of limited liability is the corporation's lack of mutual agency. This means that an individual owner who is not part of operating management cannot act on behalf of the corporation. In effect, a corporation is not bound by the actions of its individual owners. In contrast, mutual agency exists in a partnership, which means that if any individual partner signs a contract on behalf of the partnership, the partnership and the other partners are bound by that contract.

Transferability of Ownership

Ownership in a corporation is evidenced by shares of stock. These shares generally are transferable without any restriction. Large exchanges such as the New York and American stock exchanges, as well as regional exchanges, exist to facilitate the exchange of stock between individuals. Once the stock of a corporation is issued, the corporation is not affected by subsequent stock transactions among individual shareholders, other than the fact that its list of shareholders will change.

Again, this is considerably different from a partnership. Generally, a partnership agreement requires that all the other partners approve the sale of a partnership interest. Further, there are no exchanges to facilitate the sale of a partnership interest or a business owned by a sole proprietor.

Ease of Capital Formation

Limited liability and transferability of ownership make it relatively easy for a corporation to raise capital. A large number of individuals can invest small amounts of capital that, in total, will meet the large capital needs of major corporations. It is attractive to individuals to invest in corporations because they know the amount of their total risk and usually are able to liquidate their investment when they desire.

Professional Management

In a large corporation, the owners have no direct management control. They give this control to the corporation president and other senior officers. This separation between ownership and control allows corporations to attract top-level professional management. In most sole proprietorships and partnerships, the owner is also the manager. Consequently, an owner who has considerable engineering skills may not have the proper management skills to successfully operate a business.

Disadvantages of Corporations

Some of the same corporate characteristics that provide certain advantages to incorporating may also result in some disadvantages. These disadvantages are especially relevant to smaller businesses.

Double Taxation

Double taxation is one of the major disadvantages of a corporation. The earnings of a corporation are subject to taxes under the new tax reform act of up to 34%. When corporate earnings are distributed to stockholders in the form of cash dividends, these dividends are not deductible by the corporation but are taxable to the recipient. In effect, corporate earnings are taxed twice, once at the corporate level and once at the individual shareholder level.

Government Regulation

Corporations must be chartered by a state and thus must comply with various state as well as federal regulations. Several reports and documents must be filed with state and federal agencies. For smaller companies, the cost of complying with these regulations may outweigh the benefits of the corporate form of business organization. Although government regulation applies to all forms of business enterprise, generally it is not as great a factor for sole proprietorships and partnerships.

Limited Liability

For smaller companies, the limited liability feature of a corporation may be a disadvantage in raising capital. Because of this feature, creditors have claims against only the assets of a corporation. Thus, if a corporation defaults, the creditors have no recourse against the owners. As a result, loans from bankers and other creditors are often limited to the amount of security offered by the corporation, or in other cases, the shareholders may have to sign an agreement pledging their own assets as security.

In other situations, the owners of a small corporation may raise capital with the help of venture capitalists. A *venture capitalist* is an individual or group of individuals who provide capital to growing and emerging firms. In return for their capital, these individuals usually demand an equity position in the firm. Thus, the original owners may have to give up their control of the corporation as the price of obtaining capital.

Exhibit 16–1 summarizes and compares the characteristics of a corporation with those of a sole proprietorship and a partnership.

EXHIBIT 16–1
Characteristics of Corporations, Partnerships and Sole Proprietorships

| | Type of Business Organization | | |
Characteristics	Corporation	Partnership	Sole Proprietorship
Limited liability	Yes	No	No
Mutual agency	No	Yes	—
Transferability of ownership	Yes	No*	No
Ease of capital formation	Yes	No	No
Centralization, professional management	Yes	No**	No**
Continuity of existence	Yes	No	No
Payment of taxes by the entity	Yes	No	No

*As noted, partnerships' interests can be transferred; however, the process can be considerably more difficult than with corporations.

**Clearly, any large business can have centralized professional management; however, this feature is considerably more common in corporations.

The Formation and Organization of a Corporation

The procedures to form a corporation and subsequently to conduct business are a function of state law, and as you might expect, all states have somewhat different laws. For example, historically it has been easier to incorporate in some states such as Delaware than in other states such as California. To a large extent this has been because of the regulatory environment in California. The following discussion is thus based on the general procedures found in most states.

Forming a Corporation

The first step in forming a corporation is for at least three individuals, generally the corporate president, vice-president, and secretary-treasurer, to file an application with the appropriate state official, often called the Secretary of State. Among the items included in the application are the articles of incorporation which list:

1. The name and place of business of the corporation.
2. The main purpose of the business.
3. The names of the principal officers of the corporation.

4. The names of the original stockholders.

5. The type of stock to be issued; the number of authorized shares; their par value, if any; and their dividend and voting rights.

Once the articles of incorporation have been approved by the appropriate state official, they are often referred to as the corporate charter.

Organization Costs

During the organization process, a corporation incurs certain costs. These include filing and incorporation fees to the state, attorney's fees, promotion fees, printing and engraving fees, and similar items. These costs all are necessary to get the corporation started. Because they are considered to have future benefit, they are capitalized and are referred to as **organization costs.** These organization costs are usually listed in the other assets section of the balance sheet.

Although these costs benefit the corporation over its entire life (considered to be indefinite under the going-concern assumption), they are normally written off over a five-year period of time. This is so because the income tax laws allow these costs to be written off over a minimum of five years. Although accountants do not necessarily follow tax laws in setting accounting principles, they do so in this case because organization costs are usually not material.

Organizing the Corporation

Immediately after the corporation's charter is issued, the shareholders must organize the firm in order to conduct future business. A board of directors must be elected which in turn appoints the new officers of the corporation. Corporate bylaws are drafted that establish rules of order for the operation of the new corporation. The diagram below, which presents a typical corporate organization chart, shows the relationship among the stockholders, the board of directors, and senior corporate management.

TYPICAL CORPORATE ORGANIZATION CHART

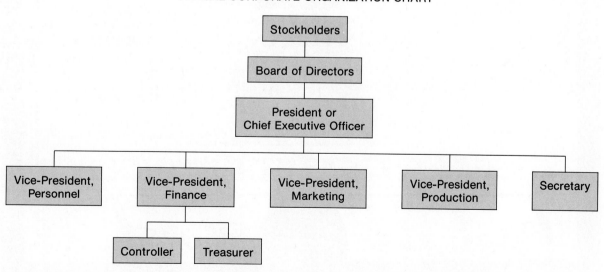

Stockholders

The stockholders are the owners of the corporation, and this ownership is evidenced by stock certificates. A sample stock certificate from Macmillan, Inc., is reproduced in Exhibit 16–2. A stock certificate is a legal document that shows the number, type, and par value, if any, of the shares issued by the corporation. Stock certificates are serially numbered and may include other data required by state laws.

In large corporations, the shareholders do not participate in the day-to-day operation of the business. They do elect the board of directors and vote on important issues at the annual stockholders' meeting. The **board of directors** is charged with establishing broad corporate policies and appointing senior corporate management. However, stockholders do have certain rights, which include:

1. The right to attend all stockholders' meetings, to vote for the board of directors, and to vote on major corporate policies and decisions such as proposed mergers and consolidations. The number of votes is based on the number of shares owned. Stockholders who do not attend the meetings are able to vote through a proxy. A **proxy** gives another individual or individuals, usually the current management, the right to vote the shares in the manner they deem best.

2. The right to receive a proportionate share of all dividends declared by the board of directors.

EXHIBIT 16–2

3. The right to a proportionate share of remaining corporate assets upon the liquidation of the corporation. Remember that the stockholders' interest is a residual one and that they are entitled to the remaining assets only after all the claims of the creditors and other equity holders have been satisfied.

4. The preemptive right. This gives the existing stockholders the right to purchase shares from a new stock issue in proportion to the shares already owned. This right ensures that the ownership of the current stockholders is not diluted by the issue of additional shares. To illustrate, assume that Mark Wilson owns 5% of the outstanding shares of the Ironside Corporation. If the corporation decides to issue 100,000 new shares, Wilson will have the right to purchase 5,000 (100,000 $\times$ .05) additional shares. Of course, Wilson does not have to purchase these shares. Stockholders often waive this right in order to facilitate mergers that require the issuance of additional shares.

5. The right to dispose of or transfer their shares if and when they desire. In some situations this right of free transferability is limited. Such limitations, if and when they exist, are clearly noted on the stock certificate.

The Board of Directors and Senior Management

The board of directors and the chairperson of the board are elected by the stockholders. The board usually consists of senior management and outside members. Outside members are individuals who are not otherwise employed by the company and thus are independent of senior management. In recent years it has become commonplace for a majority of the board to be made up of these outside members. The board's primary function is to determine general corporate policies and to appoint senior management. The board is also charged with protecting the interest of stockholders and creditors.

The corporation's senior management is appointed by the board. Obviously, the primary function of senior management is to conduct the day-to-day operations of the company. The organization chart on page 613 shows some of the typical officers found in general management. Clearly, the designations and functions of these individuals depend on the specific needs and organization of the company.

Types of Capital Stock

The term *capital stock* is used to refer to the stock issued by a corporation. In reality, there are at least two major types of capital stock, common stock and preferred stock.

Common Stock

Common stock is capital stock that must be issued by all corporations. Common stockholders have all of the rights listed on page 614 and above. Generally, because common stock is the only type of stock with voting rights, common stockholders control the corporation. However, they have only a residual interest in its net assets. This means that in the event of a corporate liquidation, common shareholders will not receive any assets until the claims of the creditors and the preferred stockholders are satisfied.

Some states allow different classes of common stock. For example, a corporation may issue Class A and Class B common stock. Depending on state laws and the corporate charter, Class A stock may be voting, whereas Class B is not. However, it is relatively rare for large, publicly held corporations to issue two classes of common stock.

Preferred Stock

In addition to common stock, a corporation may issue a type of stock called **preferred stock.** Preferred stock does not necessarily mean better; the term *preferred* means that this type of stock has certain preferences over common stock. Preferred stock generally has the following preferences and characteristics:

1. Preference as to dividends.
2. Preference over common stockholders upon liquidation.
3. No voting rights.
4. Cumulative and callable.

Preferred Dividends

Preferred stock has a preference in regard to dividends, which means that the preferred stockholders must receive all of the dividends to which they are entitled before any dividends can be declared and paid to the common stockholders. Unlike common stock, the amount of preferred dividends is normally stated on the stock certificate. This is done in one of two ways. The actual dollar amount of the dividend may be stated on the stock certificate. For example, the preferred stock for Nabisco Brands is stated at $3.50 per share. This means that if a dividend is declared by the board of directors, each preferred stockholder will receive a dividend of $3.50 per share. In the second case, the dividend is stated as a percentage of par value. Par value is a stated amount printed on the stock certificate. For example, Koppers, another publicly held corporation, has issued 150,000 shares of $100 par value, 4% preferred stock. This means that if and when declared, an annual per-share dividend of $4, or 4% × $100, will be received by the preferred stockholder. Because the amount of preferred dividends is stated, many individuals feel the stock is more stable and less risky than common stock is.

Cumulative versus Noncumulative Dividends

A corporation does not have to issue a dividend. Only when the board of directors declares a dividend does it become an actual liability of the corporation. Because of this, many issues of preferred stock are cumulative. This means that preferred stockholders do not lose their claim to undeclared dividends. The right to receive these undeclared dividends accumulates over time and must be fully paid before common stockholders can receive any dividends. This is an attractive feature, and so most preferred issues are cumulative. Conversely, if the stock is noncumulative, any dividends not declared in the current year will lapse, and preferred stockholders will lose their claim to these dividends.

To demonstrate, assume that the Place Publishing Corporation issued 10,000 shares of $3 cumulative preferred stock. As of the beginning of 1986, all stated preferred dividends were declared and paid. During 1986, profits were down, and so Place decided to declare only $20,000 of dividends. As a result, there was a shortfall of $10,000, calculated as follows:

Required dividend, $3.00 × 10,000	$30,000
Dividends declared	20,000
Dividends in arrears	$10,000

This shortfall is called **dividends in arrears.** Although this $10,000 is not a liability of the Place Publishing Corporation, if dividends are declared the next year, 1987, the dividends in arrears of $10,000 plus 1987's preferred dividends of $30,000 must be paid before common stockholders will receive anything.

To continue our illustration, assume that in 1987 Place decided to declare total dividends of $75,000 to preferred and common stockholders. In this case, preferred stockholders would receive $40,000, and common stockholders would receive $35,000, calculated as follows:

Total dividend		$75,000
Preferred dividends:		
Dividends in arrears	$10,000	
1987 current year's dividend	30,000	
Total to preferred stockholders		40,000
Total to common stockholders		$35,000

As we noted, dividends in arrears are not liabilities of the corporation. However, full disclosure requires that any such dividends be disclosed in the footnotes to the financial statements.

For example, the following note was taken from an annual report of Western Airlines:

> The company has omitted payment of the quarterly dividends on the Series A (cumulative) Preferred Stock beginning the first quarter of 1982. The total amount of the dividends in arrears at January 1, 1984 was $4,785,000. Various loan agreements currently prohibit payment of dividends on preferred stock. Because more than six quarterly dividends have been omitted, holders of preferred stock have the right (unless all dividend arrearages have been cured) to elect two additional members to the Company's Board of Directors at the next annual meeting of the shareholders.

Participating versus Nonparticipating

In some limited situations, preferred stock has a participating feature. This means that in addition to the stated dividend, preferred stockholders also will participate with common shareholders in additional dividends. This participation feature can range from limited to full. When full participation exists, the common shareholders receive dividends per share equal to the stated preferred rate, and all excess dividends are split on a proportionate basis between common and preferred shareholders.

Most preferred stock, however, is not participating. Thus, the preferred stockholder receives only the stated dividend rate, regardless of how profitable the company is. This is one of the major disadvantages of preferred stock. After the stated preferred dividend rate is paid, all of the benefits of above-average profitable years may accrue to the common stockholders through higher dividends. In effect, the stockholder who has purchased cumulative nonparticipating preferred stock trades off a possible higher return for less risk.

Preference on Liquidation

Normally, preferred stock has preference in the event of corporate liquidation. This means that after the creditors are satisfied, preferred shareholders must be fully satisfied before common stockholders can receive any assets. Furthermore, dividends in arrears are included in this liquidation preference.

Most preferred stock has an actual stated liquidation value per share that the shareholder will receive if liquidation occurs. Current accounting practices require that this liquidation value be disclosed in the stockholders' equity section of the balance sheet.

Other Features of Preferred Stock

In some situations a corporation may issue **convertible preferred stock.** This enables preferred stockholders to convert their preferred stock at a stated rate and time to common stock. This conversion feature allows preferred stockholders to enjoy the stability of preferred dividends, and, if it becomes advantageous, they can convert to common stock and benefit from increases in the price of the common shares. The issuing corporation also benefits from the conversion feature because it can issue preferred stock with a lower stated dividend rate than it otherwise could have.

Preferred stock can be redeemable or callable. Under certain conditions, **redeemable preferred stock** can be returned, for a stated price, to the issuing corporation by the owner of the stock. Some preferred stock has mandatory redemption requirements by which the corporation can force redemption at a certain price and time.

Callable preferred stock gives the issuing corporation, at its option, the right to retire the stock at a specified price. The specified price (call price) usually is above the stated par value of the stock, and the difference between the call price and the par value is called the **call premium.** To illustrate, $100 par value preferred stock with a call price of $108 has a call premium of $8. When the issuing corporation calls the stock, the total price paid is the call price plus any dividends in arrears.

There are several reasons that a corporation may wish to issue callable, or redeemable, preferred stock. If the stock is also convertible, the call provision will allow the corporation to force conversion by threatening to call the stock. In addition, if interest and investment rates change in the economy, the call provision will give the corporation flexibility by allowing it to retire preferred stock with a high dividend rate and replace it with new stock at a lower rate. Finally, if the corporation has considerable amounts of excess cash, it may wish to retire its preferred stock and thus avoid paying dividends in the future.

The Components of Stockholders' Equity

Stockholders' equity represents the stockholders', or equity investors', residual interest in the corporation's assets. Although terminology and form differ among firms, the shareholders' equity section of the Stride Rite Corporation's (a major manufacturer of children's shoes) consolidated balance sheet presented in Exhibit 16–3 is typical of those found in most U.S. corporate balance sheets. Although not specifically designated as such in most published balance sheets, stockholders' equity consists of the following components: (1) contributed capital, including preferred and common stock and additional paid-in capital; (2) retained earnings; (3) treasury stock; and, in some situations, (4) certain debit items. You should keep in mind that the total of these categories represents owners' claims; they are subdivided only for legal and accounting purposes.

EXHIBIT 16–3
The Stride Rite Corporation
Stockholders' Equity
November 29, 1985

Stockholders' Equity:
Preferred stock, $1 par value—1,000,000 shares authorized;
  Issued—none
Common stock, $1 par value—15,000,000 shares authorized;

Issued—7,603,000	$ 7,603,000
Capital in excess of par value	30,112,000
Retained earnings	74,276,000
	111,991,000
Less cost of 74,586 shares of common stock held in treasury	(465,000)
Total stockholders' equity	$111,526,000

Contributed Capital

Contributed capital represents the total capital contributed by all stockholders as well as others. This capital comes from the original issue of common and preferred, from subsequent issues, and from other sources such as donations to the corporation. Contributed capital consists of two major components, the legal or stated capital of the corporation and additional paid-in capital. The total contributed capital of Stride Rite at November 29, 1985 is $37.715 million, consisting of legal capital of $7.603 million and capital in excess of par of $30.112 million.

Legal Capital or Stated Capital

The definition of **legal (stated) capital** depends on the laws of the state in which the corporation is chartered. Generally, it pertains to the number of shares of common and, if any, preferred stock, and their par values, stated values, or issue price if no par stock is issued. Thus, the legal capital of Stride Rite is $7.603 million consisting of the par value of the common stock. Although Stride Rite lists preferred stock, none has yet been issued. The definition and determination of legal capital have important legal implications. Many courts have ruled that if a corporation's legal capital is reduced through dividend payments or actions other than unprofitable operations, its creditors have a claim against the current stockholders to the extent of that reduction. As noted, the amount of legal capital is closely tied to the concept of par value, which we explore next.

Par Value

Par value is an accounting term that often is misunderstood. The **par value** of common or preferred stock is an amount designated in the articles of incorporation or by the board of directors and is printed on the stock certificate. For example, the Macmillan common stock certificate presented in Exhibit 16–2 shows a par value of $1 per share. It does not represent the amount that the board feels the stock will sell for when issued or in the future. In fact, it does not represent value at all.

Par value is a concept developed in the 1900s in order to protect the creditors and investors of corporations. It was meant to provide an amount of assets that could not be distributed to shareholders if there were other creditors' and investors' claims that would be impaired by this distribution. However, the concept of par value has lost much of its significance today. The board of directors has the right to set the par value of the stock at any amount it desires. Because it is unlawful in most states to issue stock below its par value, the board usually sets a relatively low par value, such as $1, $5, or $10. For example, the par value of Stride Rite's common stock is $1 per share. From an accounting perspective, the main significance of par value is that it often is a basis on which the amount of the preferred stock dividends is derived.

No Par Stock

Many states now allow corporations to issue no par stock. True **no par stock** has no stated value placed on it by the board of directors. In some situations, the board of directors will place a stated value on the no par stock. No par stock with a stated value is treated in the same way that par value stock is.

Shares Authorized and Issued

Under current accounting practices, the par value or stated value of a firm's capital stock and the number of shares authorized, issued, and outstanding must be disclosed in its financial statements. The number of shares authorized is stated in the articles of incorporation and is simply the number of shares that the corporation is allowed to issue. For example, Stride Rite is authorized to issue 1 million and 15 million shares of preferred and common stock, respectively. The number of shares authorized in Stride Rite's articles of incorporation is clearly large enough to meet its present and future needs.

Shares issued represents the number of shares the corporation has actually issued to date. As of November 29, 1985 Stride Rite had issued 7,603,000 shares of common stock. Since 74,586 shares have been repurchased and held in the treasury, only 7,528,414 (7,603,000 − 74,586) shares are still outstanding. Stock that is authorized but unissued, such as Stride Rite's preferred stock, has no rights associated with it.

Additional Paid-in Capital

Because par value or stated value is arbitrary and often a low figure, the concept of contributed capital is more meaningful. **Contributed capital** is equal to the legal capital plus any additional capital contributed by the stockholders or others. One of the primary sources of **additional paid-in capital** is from the issue of stock in excess of the par or stated value. For example, if you want to know how much a corporation received from the issuance of other than true no par common stock, you must combine both the balance in the Common Stock account and the additional paid-in capital account Paid-in Capital from the Issue of Common Stock in Excess of Par. Other sources of additional paid-in capital include donated capital and the resale of treasury stock (stock repurchased by the corporation) above its cost. Stride Rite's additional paid-in capital equals $30.112 million, and as we noted, the total contributed capital equals $37.715 million, consisting of common stock and additional paid-in capital.

Retained Earnings

The second category in the stockholders' equity section is retained earnings. Retained earnings result from a business's profitable operations and represent part of the owners' residual claim. Dividends reduce retained earnings. Transactions that affect this account are discussed in the next chapter.

Treasury Stock

The stockholders' equity section of Stride Rite shows the category, treasury stock. **Treasury stock** represents the cost of Stride Rite's own stock that the company itself repurchased. We consider treasury stock in the next chapter.

Debit Items in Stockholders' Equity

Under current accounting standards, there are a number of items other than treasury stock that are treated as direct deductions to stockholders' equity. These include unrealized losses on long-term investments and cumulative foreign currency translation adjustments. Those items are discussed in future chapters.

Accounting for the Issuance of Stock

When a corporation is formed, it must issue common stock and, in addition, it may issue preferred stock. Subsequently, if the corporation needs additional capital, it may decide to issue common stock, preferred stock, or bonds. Large public corporations often issue stock through **underwriters**—brokerage firms such as Merrill Lynch or groups of firms that purchase the entire stock issue for a stated price. The underwriters assume the risks in marketing the stock to their clients. Some firms sell their stock directly to the public. Smaller firms that are going to issue only limited amounts of stock often do so through private solicitations and private placements. The decision as to how to market a stock issue is an important management decision but does not affect the way in which the stock is recorded in the firm's books and records.

Stock Issued for Cash

Large public corporations usually issue stock in exchange for cash. To illustrate the accounting entries, we will assume that on January 2, 1987 The Jackson Corporation decides to issue 5,000 of the 20,000 authorized shares of common stock and receives $25 per share. We will consider the following three independent cases:

1. The stock has a par value of $10 per share.
2. The stock is no par with no stated value.
3. The stock is no par but has a stated value of $5 per share.

Although we are using common stock in these examples, the same concepts apply to preferred stock.

Exhibit 16-4 presents the appropriate journal entries for all three cases as well as the stockholders' equity section of the balance sheet immediately after the stock issue. In the first case, as in all of the cases, Cash is debited for the total proceeds received, of $125,000 (5,000 × $25 = $125,000). When com-

EXHIBIT 16–4

Issue of 5,000 Shares of Stock at $25 per share

Case (1)
$10 Par Value Stock

January 2, 1986
Cash	125,000	
Common Stock		50,000
Paid-in Capital from Issue of		
Common Stock in Excess of Par		75,000

To record issue of 5,000 shares of $10 par value stock at $25 per share.

The Jackson Corporation
Partial Balance Sheet
January 2, 1987

Contributed capital
Common stock, $10 par value,		
20,000 shares authorized, 5,000		
shares issued and outstanding	$ 50,000	
Additional paid-in capital	75,000	
Total stockholders' equity		$125,000

Case (2)
No Par, No Stated Value

Cash	125,000	
Common Stock		125,000

To record issue of 5,000 shares of no par stock at $25 per share.

The Jackson Corporation
Partial Balance Sheet
January 2, 1987

Contributed capital
Common stock, no par value,	
20,000 shares authorized, 5,000	
shares issued and outstanding	$125,000
Total stockholders' equity	$125,000

Case (3)
No Par, $5 Stated Value

Cash	125,000	
Common Stock		25,000
Paid-in Capital from Issue of		
Common Stock in Excess of		
Stated Value		100,000

To record issue of 5,000 shares of no par, $5 stated value stock at $25 per share.

The Jackson Corporation
Partial Balance Sheet
January 2, 1987

Contributed capital
Common stock, no par with		
$5 stated value, 20,000 shares		
authorized, 5,000 shares issued		
and outstanding	$ 25,000	
Additional paid-in capital	100,000	
Total stockholders' equity		$125,000

ª Assumed figure.

mon stock has a par value, the Common Stock account is credited for the par value of the total stock issued, or $50,000 (5,000 × $10 = $50,000), and the paid-in capital account Paid-in Capital from Issue of Common Stock in Excess of Par is credited for the difference of $75,000 (5,000 × [$25 − $10] = $75,000). The partial balance sheet pictured under Case 1 in the exhibit shows that the corporation's contributed capital is divided into the legal capital of $50,000 (the par value of the stock) and the additional paid-in capital of $75,000. Total stockholders' equity, which does not include retained earnings (because the corporation has just been organized), equals $125,000.

In Case 2, the stock is no par and has no stated value. Again, Cash is debited for the entire proceeds of $125,000. However, in this case, Common Stock is also credited for the entire proceeds of $125,000. There is no entry to an additional paid-in capital account. Because different stock issues are apt to be sold at different prices, there is no uniform price per share recorded in the capital stock, as it is for par value stock. In this case, the corporation's legal capital is $125,000; the total stockholders' equity is still $125,000.

In Case 3, the stock is no par but has a stated value of $5 per share. As before, Cash is debited for $125,000, but now Common Stock is credited for only $25,000 (5,000 × $5 = $25,000), or the stated value of the entire issue. The account Paid-in Capital from Issue of Common Stock in Excess of Stated Value is credited for the difference of $100,000 (5,000 × [$25 − $5] = $100,000). Assuming that the stock's stated value remains the same, there will be a uniform amount per share recorded in the Capital Stock account. Most states consider that the corporation's legal capital is the stock's total stated value, in this case $25,000. Total stockholders' equity, as with the other two cases, is $125,000.

There are a number of points to keep in mind when reviewing these examples. In all cases, total stockholders' equity remains the same. The difference is just in the manner in which contributed capital is divided between legal capital and other paid-in capital. Although the distinction between legal capital and contributed capital may have important legal ramifications, especially on liquidation, it has little accounting significance.

Stock Issued for Noncash Assets

There are some circumstances in which stock is issued for noncash assets or for services. For example, in payment for their services, attorneys and other promoters may accept stock in a corporation instead of cash. In other circumstances, a corporation may receive land, buildings, or other assets in exchange for its stock. In either case, the transaction should be recorded in accordance with the cost principle. This means that the assets or services acquired should be recorded at the fair market value of the stock issued at the date of the transaction, that is, the consideration given. In those transactions for which it is not feasible to reasonably determine the fair market value of the stock that has been issued, the fair market value of the assets or services received should be used.

To illustrate, assume that Rebecca Webb, the attorney for the Secco Corporation, agrees to take 1,000 shares of the corporation's $5 par value stock in exchange for the services she performed in organizing the corporation. Her normal fee for such work is $7,500. Because the corporation is owned by only a few individuals and is not traded on an exchange, its market value cannot be determined, and so the value of the services performed will be used to value the transaction. The entry to record this transaction is:

Organization Costs	7,500	
Common Stock		5,000
Paid-in Capital from Issue of Common Stock in Excess of Par		2,500
To record issue of 1,000 shares of $5 par value stock in		
exchange for attorney's services valued at $7,500.		

The intangible asset account Organization Costs is debited for the fair market value of the attorney's service, Common Stock is credited for the par value of the stock, and Additional Paid-in Capital is credited for the difference.

If stock is exchanged for noncash assets such as land or buildings, the entry would be similar. For example, now assume that the Secco Corporation issues 5,000 shares of its $100 par value preferred stock in exchange for land and a building. At the time of the transaction, the preferred stock has a fair market value of $120 per share, and so the total transaction is valued at $600,000 (5,000 × $120 = $600,000). Assume that the land and the building are valued at $200,000 and $400,000, respectively. The entry to record this transaction is:

Land	200,000	
Building	400,000	
Preferred Stock		500,000
Paid-in Capital from Issue of Preferred Stock in		
Excess of Par		100,000
To record issue of 5,000 shares of $100 par value preferred		
stock in exchange for land and building. Market value of pre-		
ferred stock is $120 per share.		

If it is impossible to determine the fair market value of the stock, the fair market value of the land and building should be used to value the transaction. If this figure cannot be determined, then the board of directors would have to set a value for the transaction.

Donated Capital

There are several transactions that give rise to donated capital. Included are donated assets, stock contributed back to the corporation by stockholders, and forgiveness of corporate debt of a stockholder. A very common situation involving donated assets occurs when a city or municipality offers a corporation site land on which to locate its plant at no cost. Cities do this in the hope of improving local employment and increasing tax revenues.

To illustrate, asume the Orange Company acquires a parcel of land from the City of Orange at no cost. At the time of donation, the land is appraised at a fair market value of $200,000. To record this transaction, the Orange Company makes the following entry:

Land	200,000	
Donated Capital		200,000
To record donated loan at		
fair market value.		

In some situations, stockholders will donate a portion of their capital stock to the corporation. The firm can then resell their stock and use the funds in the operations of the business. When the stock is donated, the dollar amount of stockholders' equity is not affected. However, the number of shares outstanding is reduced. A memorandum journal entry (an entry without amounts which is not posted to the general ledger) can be made to record this decrease. When the shares are resold, Cash is debited and the paid-in capital account Paid-in Capital from Sale of Donated Stock is credited.

To illustrate, assume that on April 1, one of the major stockholders of the Home Corporation donates 1,000 shares of no par common stock back to the corporation. On April 15, Home sells all of the shares for $25 per share. The memorandum entry on April 1 and the journal entry on April 15 are:

April 1

      Received donation of 1,000 shares of no par
      common stock

April 15

Cash	25,000	
Paid-in Capital from Sale of		
Donated Stock		25,000
To record resale of 1,000 shares of donated stock at $25 per share.		

Occasionally, stockholders will forgive debts owed to them by the corporation. This is likely to occur if the corporation is experiencing financial difficulties. When this happens, the debt is written off by a debit to the appropriate liability account and Donated Capital is credited.

Conversion of Preferred Stock to Common

As we noted, some issues of preferred stock are convertible into common shares after some specified date. When this occurs, the convertible preferred stock is originally recorded in the normal way. That is, the Preferred Stock account is credited for the par value of the shares, and Paid-in Capital is credited for the difference, if any, between the issue price and the par value. When the stock is converted, it is done so at its book value. No gain or loss is recorded.

To illustrate, assume that the BAFS Corporation issues 5,000 shares of $100 par value convertible stock at $130. Each preferred share is convertible into 5 shares of $1 par value common. Subsequently, 1,000 shares of preferred are converted into 5,000 shares of common. The journal entries to reflect these transactions are:

Cash	650,000	
Preferred Stock		500,000
Paid-in Capital from Issue of Preferred Stock in Excess of Par		150,000
To record issue of 5,000 shares of $100 convertible preferred stock at $130 per share.		

Preferred Stock	100,000	
Paid-in Capital from Issue of Preferred Stock in Excess of Par	30,000	
Common Stock		5,000
Paid-in Capital from Issue of Common Stock in Excess of Par		125,000
To record conversion of 1,000 shares of preferred stock into 5,000 shares of $1 par value common.		

Notice that when the preferred stock is converted, the Preferred Stock account is debited for the total par value of the converted stock. The Paid-in Capital account also is debited for the amount per share credited to that account when the stock is originally issued. In this case, that amount is $30,000, or $30 × 1,000 shares. Common Stock is credited at par, and Paid-in Capital is credited for the difference. Although total stockholders' equity remains the same, its components have changed.

Use of Stock Information

After the stock of a major corporation is issued, it trades on a national exchange such as the New York or the American stock exchange or possibly on a regional exchange. To help them evaluate a corporation, present and potential investors and creditors look at the market price of the stock as well as other indicators.

Market Value

The market value per share refers to the price at which a particular stock is currently trading. Clearly, this market price is most objective when there is a large market for the stock on a national exchange. In effect, the price is set by many individuals all acting independently as they buy and sell shares of stock. Such factors as general economic conditions, interest rates, the perceived risk of the company, expectations concerning future profits, and present and expected dividends all contribute to the stock's current market price.

The Stock Page

The current market price of stocks traded on a major exchange are listed in major newspapers. A recent stock-page listing for IBM is reproduced as follows:

52-week

High	Low	Stock	Dividend	Yield	P-E Ratio	Sales 100's	High	Low	Last	Change
161	117⅜	IBM	4.40	2.7	15	13146	161⅜	158½	161⅜	+1⅞

The 52-week high and low columns show the highest and lowest price of the stock during the previous 52 weeks, plus the current week. In this situation, IBM's high for the previous year was $161, and its low was $117.375. The dividend column shows the latest annual dividend, which, in IBM's case, is $4.40.

The yield column indicates the rate of return that a stockholder would receive if the stock was purchased at its latest price. In the IBM example, an annual dividend of $4.40 on an investment of $161.375 (last price; ⅛ = $.125) represents a yield of 2.7%, calculated as follows:

$$\text{Yield} = \frac{\text{Annual dividend}}{\text{Current market price}}$$

$$2.7\% = \frac{\$4.40}{\$161.375} \times 100$$

The **price-earnings ratio** (P-E) is a ratio used by many investors and analysts to compare stocks. The P-E ratio is calculated by means of the following formula:

$$\frac{\text{Current market price}}{\text{Earnings per share}}$$

Earnings per share (EPS), which is discussed in detail in the next chapter, shows the amount of current earnings available to common shareholders on a per-share basis. It is calculated by dividing the earnings available to common stockholders (net income less preferred dividends) by the average number of shares outstanding. The P-E ratio uses this data to help investors compare firms having different market prices and earnings. For IBM, based on an EPS of $10.76 per share, the P-E ratio of 15 is calculated as follows:

$$15 = \frac{\$161.375}{10.76}$$

This means that IBM was selling at a multiple of 15, or 15 times its EPS. This can be used to compare alternative investments. For example, Burroughs, a somewhat comparable company, had a P-E ratio of 13.

The last five columns are relatively straightforward. The sales column, which is in 100s, indicates the total sales for the day. During the day we are considering, 1,314,600 shares of IBM stock changed hands. The high and low columns show the highest and lowest price at which the stock traded during the day. The next column indicates the price of the last trade of the day, and the change column shows the net change from the prior day's last trade. In this case, the stock rose $1.875.

Book Value per Share

Book value per share of common stock indicates the net assets represented by one share of common stock. Thus, book value is the equity that the owner of one share of common stock has in the net assets (assets — liabilities) or stockholders' equity of the corporation. It is the amount that each share would receive if the firm were liquidated and the firm received the amount actually shown on the balance sheet for the various assets less the liabilities. It is important to remember, however, that the term *value* in this sense does not mean market value or current value. Because the firm's net assets are recorded at historical cost less the write-offs to date, value is in terms of these historical costs, not in terms of market value or liquidation value. Thus, there is no particular reason that book value and market value per share should be related.

Book Value When Only Common Stock Is Issued

When a firm has only common stock outstanding, the book value per share is equal to

$$\frac{\text{Total stockholders' equity}}{\text{Number of common shares outstanding}}$$

To illustrate, the 1985 stockholders' equity section of the Safeway Stores' balance sheet is reproduced on page 628.

Safeway Stores, Inc.
Stockholders' Equity
December 28, 1985
(in thousands)

Common stock—$1.66 2/3 par value; authorized 150,000 shares; outstanding 60,846	$ 101,411
Additional paid-in capital	273,776
Cumulative translation adjustments	(164,035)
Retained earnings	1,411,462
Total stockholders' equity	$1,622,614

The book value per share of $26.67 is calculated as follows:

$$\$26.67 = \frac{\$1,622,614,000}{60,846,000}$$

In comparison, during 1985 the price of Safeway's common stock ranged between $26.875 and $37.625.

Book Value When Both Common and Outstanding Preferred Stock Are Outstanding

Book value refers to the common stockholders' interest in the firm's net assets. Thus, when preferred stock is outstanding, total stockholders' equity must be reduced by the preferred stockholders' claims, in order to arrive at the common stockholders' equity. This is usually done by subtracting the liquidation or redemption value of the preferred stock and any dividends in arrears from total stockholders' equity.

To demonstrate, selected items from the 1985 stockholders' equity section of Baxter Travenol Laboratories, Inc., a large health-care products firm, follow:

Total stockholders' equity	$2,963,000,000
Redemption value of preferred stock	880,373,650
Common shares outstanding at year-end	211,258,248

The book value per common share of $9.86 is calculated as follows:

$$\$9.86 = \frac{\$2,963,000,000 - \$880,373,650}{211,258,248 \text{ shares}}$$

At year-end 1985, Baxter Travenol's common stock was selling at $15.75, about one and a half times its book value.

Maintaining Internal Control over Stock Records

Maintaining internal control over stock certificates and stock records is an important management control function. Corporations must have an up-to-date and accurate list of stockholders to ensure that the proper stockholders receive dividends, the firm's financial statements, proxy data, and other materials. Further, old stock certificates must be promptly canceled and new ones issued to guard against individuals' gaining access to unauthorized stock certificates.

Large corporations have hundreds of thousands of stockholders, who trade stock daily. As a result, internal control over stock records becomes quite complex. Such firms often employ a stock transfer agent and a stock registrar to control stock transfers among stockholders. **A stock transfer agent,** usually a large bank, handles all the transfers by canceling the old certificate, issuing a new one, and updating the stockholders' ledger. **A stock registrar,** if also used, maintains an independent record of the number of shares outstanding. In effect, the individuals who maintain the records of the stockholders have no access to corporate assets.

Smaller corporations often cannot afford, nor do they need, the services of a transfer agent or registrar. Rather, they maintain their own records, which include a stock certificate book and a subsidiary stockholders' equity ledger. The stock certificate book contains serially numbered certificates and stubs. The stock is signed by the proper authority officer when it is issued, and a notation is made on the stub. The stubs thus serve as a stock register of all outstanding stock. In addition, an independent subsidiary stockholders' ledger is usually maintained. Each shareholder, the number of shares owned, certificate numbers, and transaction data are listed in the subsidiary ledger. The total shares outstanding in the certificate book must be reconciled with the total shown in the subsidiary ledger.

Summary of Learning Objectives

1. *The main characteristics of corporations.* Corporations are separate legal entities with a continuous life. Corporations are characterized by the following features:
   a. Limited liability.
   b. Transferability of ownership.
   c. Ease of capital formation.
   d. Centralization of management.
   e. Continuity of existence.

2. *The formation and organization of a corporation.* Corporations are chartered by individual states and must comply with state and federal regulations. Although control of a corporation lies ultimately with the common stockholders, they give this power to the board of directors. The board is responsible for setting broad corporate policies and appointing senior management.

3. *Types of capital stock.* Common and preferred stock are the two major types of capital stock. All corporations must issue common stock, and common shareholders have the following rights:
   a. The right to vote.
   b. The right to a proportionate share of dividends when declared.
   c. The right to a proportionate share of assets upon liquidation.
   d. The preemptive right.
   Preferred stockholders have certain preferences over common shareholders with respect to dividends and assets upon liquidation.

4. *Components of stockholders' equity.* Stockholders' equity consists of contributed capital; retained earnings; treasury stock, if any; and, possibly, special debit items. Contributed capital is often divided into legal capital and additional paid-in capital. Legal capital is based on the par or stated value of the issued and outstanding shares. If true no par stock is issued, the legal capital will be the entire issue price of the stock. Sources of additional paid-in capital include the issue of capital stock in excess of par, the sale of treasury stock above par, and donated capital.

5. *The accounting concepts and procedures regarding the issuance of capital stock.* If par value or no par stock with a stated value is issued, the Capital Stock account should be credited for the par or stated value. Additional Paid-in Capital from the Sale of Capital Stock in Excess of Par or Stated Value is credited for the difference between the issue price and the par or stated value. If true no par stock is issued, the capital stock should be credited for the entire amount.

6. *Uses of stock information.* Present and potential investors use stock information in their evaluation of a particular company. Included are such data as the stock's current market price, its P-E ratio, and EPS. Book value per share is also used, but it does not provide data on market or liquidation values.

7. *Maintaining internal control over stock records.* Maintaining internal control over stock certificates and stock rcords is an important management control function. Corporations need to have an up-to-date list of stockholders. Generally this control is maintained through a stock transfer agent and a stock registrar.

Key Terms

Additional Paid-in Capital	Organization Costs
Board of Directors	Par Value
Book Value	Preferred Stock
Callable Preferred Stock	Price-Earnings Ratio
Call Premium	Proxy
Common Stock	Redeemable Preferred Stock
Contributed Capital	Stock Register
Convertible Preferred Stock	Stock Transfer Agent
Dividends in Arrears	Treasury Stock
Legal (Stated) Capital	Underwriters
No Par Stock	

Problem for Your Review

Accounting for Stock Transactions. The Square Pizza Corporation was organized in 1987 to manufacture and distribute square pizzas. The corporation was authorized to issue 5 million shares of $5 per value common stock and 1 million shares of $100, 6% par value convertible preferred stock. The following transactions took place during 1986:

- January 25: Issued 100,000 shares of common stock at $20 per share.
- April 10: Issued 1,000 shares of common stock to the firm's attorneys in connection with organizing the corporation. The fair market value of the fees was $25,000.

- July 1: Issued 10,000 shares of preferred stock at par.
- November 20: Converted 5,000 shares of preferred stock into common shares at the rate of 2 common shares for each preferred. At the time of conversion, the common stock was selling at a price of $30 per share.

Required:

1. Make the journal entries to record these events.
2. Assuming net income for the year equaled $500,000 and no dividends were declared, prepare the stockholders' equity section of the balance sheet at December 31, 1987.

Solution

1. Journal Entries.

Jan. 25, 1987	Cash	2,000,000	
	Common Stock (100,000 × $5)		500,000
	Paid-in Capital from Issue of Common		
	Stock in Excess of Par		1,500,000
	To record issue of 100,000 shares of $5 par value common stock at $20 per share.		
Apr. 10, 1987	Organization Costs	25,000	
	Common Stock (1,000 × $5)		5,000
	Paid-in Capital from Issue of Common		
	Stock in Excess of Par		20,000
	To record issue of 1,000 shares of common stock in connection with organization costs.		
July 1, 1987	Cash	1,000,000	
	Preferred Stock		1,000,000
	To record issue of 10,000 shares of preferred stock at par.		
Nov. 20, 1987	Preferred Stock	500,000	
	Common Stock*		50,000
	Paid-in Capital from Issue of Common		
	Stock in Excess of Par		450,000
	To record conversion of 5,000 shares of preferred stock into 10,000 shares of common stock.		

*Note: The conversion to common is made at the book value of the preferred. The market value of the common stock is not relevant.

2. Partial Balance Sheet.

The Square Pizza Corporation
Partial Balance Sheet
December 31, 1987

Preferred stock, 6%, $100 par value, 1,000,000 shares authorized and 5,000 shares issued and outstanding	$ 500,000
Common stock, $5 par value, 5,000,000 shares authorized and 111,000 shares issued	555,000
Paid-in Capital from Issue of Common Stock in Excess of Par	1,970,000
Retained earnings[a]	500,000
Total stockholders' equity	$3,525,000

[a]Note: Retained earnings equals income for the year. The corporation was organized at the beginning of the year and no dividends were declared.

Questions

1. List and discuss the major characteristics of a corporation.

2. Why have corporations become the dominant form of business organization in the United States?

3. A famous business school professor recently stated that all businesses should be organized as corporations in order to take advantage of their special tax and legal treatment. Do you agree with this statement? Why or why not?

4. Describe the purposes or functions of each of the following:
   a. Articles of incorporation.
   b. Board of directors.
   c. Senior management.

5. Shareholders have certain rights. Describe and discuss these rights and how they differ between common and preferred shareholders.

6. You overheard a fellow student say that he had recently invested in the preferred stock of a major corporation because his stockbroker told him that preferred stock is a better investment than common stock because it is less risky. Do you agree? Why or why not?

7. You recently purchased 100 shares of cumulative preferred stock, which has a stated dividend of $2 per share. Because the current year's operations were barely profitable, the firm did not declare any dividends. How much in dividends will you be entitled to in the next year?

8. Describe the major components of stockholders' equity.

9. One of your friends invests only in stock that has a par value above $10, because she feels that this will guarantee that the price of the stock will not fall below this amount. Do you agree with her investment strategy? Why or why not?

10. Recently a number of states have allowed corporations to issue stock that does not have a par value. What factors do you think have led to this policy?

11. Which of the following statements, if any, regarding par value is correct? Explain your answer.
   a. All stock must be issued at its par value.
   b. When stock has a par value, the total issue price is credited to the Capital Stock account.
   c. Par value differs from stated value because the par value is set by the board of directors and the stated value is set by the stock market.
   d. When stock has a par value, the Capital Stock account is credited for the par value, and the Paid-in Capital account is credited for the excess of the issue price over the par value.

12. In some circumstances a corporation issues stock in exchange for services or other assets such as land and buildings. In these situations, what factors must the accountant consider in assigning a dollar value to the exchange?

13. Describe the yield on common stock and the P–E ratio and how they are used by investors.

14. Explain how the book value per share of common stock is calculated (a) when a corporation has only common shares outstanding and (b) when it has both common and preferred shares outstanding.

15. Discuss the meaning and usefulness of book value per share of common stock. Does it provide a good measure of the stock's current or market value?

16. Would you purchase stock in a company just because the price of the stock was below its book value? Why or why not?

17. Describe the functions of a stock transfer agent and a stock registrar.

18. Describe a stock certificate book and a subsidiary stockholders' equity ledger.

Exercises

1. **Identification of Accounts.** State whether each of the following items should be classified as an asset, liability, stockholders' equity, revenue, or expense:
   a. Organization costs.
   b. Paid-in capital from issue of common stock in excess of par.
   c. Common stock.
   d. Cumulative foreign currency adjustments.
   e. Preferred stock.
   f. Donated capital.
   g. Dividends declared.
   h. Interest paid on notes.
   i. Dividends received on investments.

2. Dividends on Preferred and Common Stock. The El Tota Corporation has the following shares of stock outstanding:

Common stock, no par	50,000 shares
Preferred stock, cumulative, stated dividend $2	10,000 shares

The company had been very profitable until 1984, when its business and profits fell. As a result, in 1984, for the first time in its history, the company was unable to pay all of its usual dividends. The board of directors made the following funds available for dividends during 1984, 1985, and 1986:

1984	$12,000
1985	25,000
1986	30,000

Determine the amount of dividends that the preferred and common shareholders will receive each year.

3. Issuance of Stock. The Software Corporation is authorized to issue 50,000 shares of common stock. During the current year it decides to issue 10,000 shares. Make the required entry to record the issuance of the common stock under each of the following independent situations:

a. The shares have a $5 par value and were sold for $20 per share.

b. The shares are no par but have a stated value of $10. The total issue price was $300,000.

c. The shares are no par and have no stated value. They were issued at $25 per share.

d. The shares are no par and have no stated value. They were issued to an attorney in exchange for services rendered in connection with organizing the corporation. The attorney normally charges $40,000 for these services. There is no reasonable way to determine the fair market value of the stock.

4. Preparation of the Stockholders' Equity Section. The Baker Corporation was formed in early 1985. At that time the corporation was authorized to issue 100,000 shares of $5 par value common stock and 50,000 shares of 6%, $100 par value cumulative preferred stock. At the time the corporation was formed, 20,000 shares of common stock were issued at $25 per share. Net income during 1985 amounted to $10,000.

At the beginning of 1986 the firm issued 5,000 shares of the preferred stock at par. Net income during 1986 amounted to $50,000. In addition to the preferred dividends, the firm declared common dividends of $5,000. Prepare the stockholders' equity section of the balance sheet as of December 31, 1986, the end of the firm's year.

5. Determining Missing Value. The stockholders' equity section on the December 31, 1987 balance sheet of Advanced Technologies follows. Answer each of the following questions:

a. How many preferred shares were issued?

b. What was the total issue price of the preferred shares?

c. What amount should be recorded in the common stock account?

d. What was the total issue price per share of the common shares?

e. What is the amount of required preferred dividends?

f. What is the amount of required common dividends?

g. What is the amount of total stockholders' equity?

Preferred stock, 5%, $100 par value, cumulative, 50,000 shares, authorized ___ ? ___ issued	$2,000,000
Common stock, $5 par value, 100,000 shares authorized, 25,000 issued	?
Paid-in capital from sale of common stock in excess of par	750,000
Retained earnings	650,000

6. Stock Issued for Noncash Consideration. On July 1, 1987 the West Corporation exchanged 1,500 shares of its $5 par value common stock for site land. A few months ago, the land was appraised by an independent appraiser for $100,000.

Required:

Make the required journal entry to record this transaction, given the two following independent assumptions:

a. West Corporation's stock is currently trading on the New York Stock Exchange at $65 a share.

b. West Corporation is a privately held corporation whose stock is owned by five family members.

7. Donated Capital. During 1987 the following two transactions affected the stockholders' equity accounts of the Belverd Corporation:

- April 23: The firm acquired as a donation 100 acres to land from the city of Link. The land was acquired by the city several years ago at a cost of $250,000. Its current fair market value is estimated to be $400,000.

- October 4: One of the firm's stockholders donated 1,000 shares of no par common stock back to the corporation.

- November 1: The firm sold all the donated shares at a price of $40 per share.

Required:

Make the necessary journal entries to record these events.

8. Conversion of Preferred Stock to Common. The capital structure of the Santa Anita Corporation is as follows:

Preferred stock: 5%, $100 par value convertible preferred stock, 10,000 shares authorized, issued, and outstanding	$1,000,000
Common stock: $1 par value common stock, 100,000 shares authorized, issued, and outstanding	100,000
Paid-in capital from sale of common stock in excess of par	500,000

Each preferred share is convertible into five shares of common stock. During the current year, 5,000 shares of the preferred shares were converted into common shares.

Required:

a. Make the required journal entry to record the conversion.

b. Now make the entry assuming that (1) the common stock is no par and has no stated value and (2) the common stock is no par and the stock has a $10 stated value.

9. Book Value per Share. You have gathered the following data from the 1987 annual report of the STN Corporation:

Total common stockholders' equity	$2,380,000
Net income from 1987	$1,120,000
Number of common shares outstanding	560,000
Dividends declared during 1987	$1.25 per share
Market price at end of 1987	$10.00 per share
EPS for 1987	$2.00

Determine each of the following at the end of 1987:

a. Dividend yield.

b. P-E ratio.

c. Book value per share.

10. Book Value per Share—Preferred Stock Outstanding. Stockholders' equity of the Logus Corporation as of December 31, 1987 follows. Determine book value per common share, given the following two independent assumptions:

a. All preferred dividends are fully paid.

b. The preferred shares are cumulative, and the board of directors has decided to forgo the declaration of all dividends this year.

Preferred stock, 5%, $100 par value, 20,000 shares authorized and issued (total liquidation value $2,100,000)	$2,000,000
Common stock, no par value, 50,000 shares authorized and issued	1,000,000
Donated capital	500,000
Retained earnings	4,500,000
Total stockholders' equity	$8,000,000

Problem Set A

16A–1. Preparation of the Stockholders' Equity Section. At the beginning of the current year, 1987, the Softlite Corporation was formed. The firm issued 50,000 of the 100,000 shares that were authorized of $5 par value common stock for $30 per share. In addition, the firm issued all 1,000 authorized shares of 6%, $100 par value preferred. During the year the firm's net income amounted to $60,000. All dividends on the preferred shares were declared; no dividends on the common were declared. Finally, at the end of the year, the city of Westbridge donated a plot of land to the firm. The land was originally purchased by the city for $100,000 and had a fair market value of $60,000 at the time it was donated to Softlite.

Required:

Prepare in good form the stockholders' equity section of Softlite's balance sheet at the end of 1987.

16A–2. Issuance of Stock. In early 1987 Gerald Weinstein and several associates formed the Pico National Bank. The corporation was authorized to issue 500,000 shares of $100, 6% par value preferred stock and 1 million shares of $10 par value common stock. The following transactions occurred during 1987:

- March 1: Sold 100,000 shares of common stock to a group of investors at $40 per share.

- March 9: Issued 4,375 shares of the preferred stock to an individual in exchange for a building. The building was appraised at $525,000. It was impossible to determine the fair market value of the stock.

- April 1: Issued 1,000 shares of common stock to the bank's attorney in exchange for services rendered in forming the corporation. The stock was currently selling at $50 a share. All parties agreed that this represented the value of the attorney's services.

- December 1: Issued an additional 625 shares of preferred stock at $130 per share.

Required:

a. Make the journal entries to record these transactions.

b. Assuming that net income for the year amounted to $2 million, prepare the stockholders' equity section of the balance sheet at the end of December.

16A–3. Preparation of the Stockholders' Equity Section. The following events occurred during the first three years of the LaGrange Corporation's existence:

Year 1:

a. Issued 20,000 shares of 50,000 authorized of no par, no stated value common stock at $40 per share.

b. The net loss for the year was $100,000, and no dividends were declared.

Year 2:

c. Issued an additional 10,000 shares of the common stock at $30 per share.

d. Issued 5,000 shares of 10,000 authorized of $100, 4% cumulative preferred stock at $120 per share.

e. The net loss for the year was $20,000, and no dividends were declared

Year 3:

    f. Net income for the year amounted to $400,000.

    g. Common dividends for the year of $75,000 were declared. In addition, all required pre-ferred dividends were paid.

Required:

Prepare in good form the stockholders' equity section of the balance sheet as of December 31, Year 3.

16A–4. Formation of a Corporation. Dennis Murphy is a successful computer programmer and has decided to begin a business that develops and markets computer learning games for young children. The corporation, called Learn with Computers, was authorized to issue the following stock:

- 100,000 shares of 10% convertible $100 par value preferred stock.

- 500,000 shares of $2 par value common stock.

The following events occurred during the first quarter of 1986:

- January 2: Murphy issued 5,000 shares of common stock to himself in exchange for com-puters and various software with fair market values as follows:

Computers	$25,000
Software	15,000

- January 30: Twenty of Murphy's friends each purchased 2,000 shares of common stock at $10 per share.

- February 1: The attorney submitted a bill for $5,000 in connection with services per-formed in organizing the corporation. The attorney agreed to take half of the payment in cash and 250 shares of common stock. The stock in Learn with Computers is not traded on an exchange, so it is difficult to determine its fair market value.

- February 15: A venture capitalist purchased 10,000 shares of the convertible preferred stock at $100 per share.

- March 31: The venture capitalist converted 5,000 shares of preferred stock into 20,000 shares of common stock.

Required:

a. Make the necessary journal entries to record these transactions.

b. Prepare in good form the stockholders' equity section of the firm's balance sheet. Net income for the first quarter amounted to $100,000, and no dividends were issued.

c. Why does a firm such as Learn with Computers issue convertible preferred stock, and why would the venture capitalist purchase it?

16A–5. Determining Missing Figures. Recently, California Valley Federal Savings and Loan con-verted from a depositor-owned savings and loan association to a publicly held one. The stock-holders' equity section of its 1987 balance sheet appears as follows (after conversion and with certain details omitted):

Stockholders' equity	
5% preferred stock, $100 par value, authorized 100,000 shares (liquidation value $110 per share)	$1,000,000
Common stock, no par value, stated value $5, authorized 1,000,000, issued 500,000	?
Paid-in capital from sale of common stock in excess of stated value	4,000,000
Retained earnings	8,000,000

Required:

Based on the above information, answer the following questions:

a. How many shares of preferred stock are outstanding?

b. At what price was the preferred stock issued?

c. What is the total of stockholders' equity?

d. What was the average issue price of the common stock?

e. What is the total contributed capital of the savings and loan association?

f. What is the total legal capital of the savings and loan association?

g. What is the book value per share of common stock?

h. What is the total dividend requirement on the preferred stock?

i. What is the total dividend requirement on the common stock?

16A–6. Common and Preferred Dividends. The KABC Corporation began operations in January 1983. During the first five years of operations, it reported the following net loss or income:

1983	$ 300,000 loss
1984	260,000 loss
1985	240,000 loss
1986	1,500,000 income
1987	1,120,000 income

At December 31, 1987 KABC's capital accounts were as follows:

Common stock, par value $10 per share; authorized, issued, and outstanding 100,000 shares	$1,000,000
4% nonparticipating, noncumulative preferred stock, par value $100 per share; authorized, issued, and outstanding 2,000 shares	200,000
8% nonparticipating, cumulative preferred stock, par value $100 per share; authorized, issued, and outstanding 20,000 shares	2,000,000

KABC has never paid a cash dividend or any other type of dividend. KABC is incorporated in California, and under California law, dividends can be paid only if there is a positive balance in retained earnings. There has been no change in the capital structure since the firm's inception.

Required:

a. Determine the maximum amount of dividends that can be paid each year and how it would be distributed between common and preferred shareholders.

b. What does the participating feature of preferred stock mean? Without recalculating your figures, explain how your answer to (a) would be different if the 8% preferred stock were fully participating.

Problem Set B

16B–1. Preparation of the Stockholders' Equity Section. At the beginning of 1986 the Maine Water Company was formed. At that time the firm was authorized to issue 100,000 shares of no par $2 stated value common stock and 50,000 shares of 6% convertible $100 par value preferred stock. Each share of preferred stock is convertible into five shares of common. In 1986 20,000 shares of common were issued at $10 per share and 5,000 preferred shares were issued at $120 per share. Net income during 1986 amounted to $70,000.

During 1987 an additional 5,000 shares of common were issued in exchange for a plot of land. At the time of the transaction, the firm's common shares were actively traded on a regional exchange at a market price of $25 per share. Holders of 1,000 preferred shares converted their shares into common when the market price of the common was $27 per share. Net income for 1987 amounted to $100,000.

Required:

Prepare in good form the stockholders' equity section of the Maine Water Company's balance sheet at the end of 1987.

16B–2. Issuance of Stock. Jackson Corporation was authorized to issue 800,000 shares of $100, 8% par value preferred stock and 1.5 million shares of no par $10 stated value common stock. The following transactions occurred during 1987:

- January 2: Twenty thousand shares of common stock were sold to a group of investors at $20 per share.

- January 15: Five thousand shares of preferred stock were issued to an individual in exchange for a plot of land to be held for future development. The land was appraised at $750,000. The preferred stock was not actively traded.

- March 31: Fifteen hundred shares of common stock were issued to an attorney in exchange for services rendered in forming the corporation. The stock was currently trading at $30 a share. All parties agreed that this represented the value of the attorney's services.

- October 20: An additional 5,000 shares of common stock were issued at $45 per share.

- November 15: An additional 1,000 shares of preferred stock were issued at $125 a share.

Required:

a. Make the journal entries to record these transactions.

b. Assuming that net income for the year amounted to $100,000, prepare the stockholders' equity section of the balance sheet at the end of December.

16B–3. Preparation of the Stockholders' Equity Section. Adventure, Inc. was formed in early 1986. The following events occurred from 1986 through 1988:

a. Issued 500,000 shares of 1,000,000 authorized of no par, no stated value common stock at $20 per share.

b. Issued 10,000 shares of 20,000 authorized of $100, 5% cumulative preferred stock at $105 per share.

c. The net loss for the year was $200,000. No dividends were declared.

1987

d. An additional 10,000 shares of common stock were issued at $15 per share.

e. Issued 5,000 shares of 10,000 authorized of $100, 8% preferred stock at par.

f. The net income for the year was $10,000. No dividends were declared.

1988

g. A plot of land was donated to the corporation by the city. The land was appraised at $100,000.

h. Net income for the year amounted to $800,000. A $.10 per share dividend was paid on common stock. In addition, all required preferred dividends were declared and paid.

Required:

Prepare in good form the stockholders' equity section of the balance sheet as of December 31, 1988.

16B–4. Formation of a Corporation. Charley is a mechanical engineer who has designed a high-speed lathe which he feels will have a large demand. He decides to form a corporation to manufacture and distribute the lathe. The corporation, called Charley's Lathe, was authorized to issue the following stock:

> 200,000 shares of 6% convertible $100 preferred stock
> 200,000 shares of 10% nonconvertible $50 preferred stock
> 1,000,000 shares of $10 par value common stock

The following events occurred during the first quarter of 1987:

- January 2: Charley issued 10,000 shares of common stock to himself in exchange for the prototype high-speed lathe and various equipment. The fair values were:

> | Lathe | $50,000 |
> |-------|---------|
> | Equipment | 50,000 |

- February 10: Five of Charley's friends decided to purchase 5,000 shares of common stock at $20 per share.

- February 28: The firm's attorney submitted a bill for $10,000 in connection with services performed in forming the corporation. Twenty-five hundred dollars was paid in cash; the remainder was paid with 300 shares of common stock. Ten thousand dollars was considered the fair value of the services received.

- March 10: An investor purchased 6,000 shares of the convertible preferred stock at $120 per share. Each share is convertible into four shares of common stock.
- March 15: Another investor purchased 5,000 shares of 10% nonconvertible preferred stock at $53 per share.
- March 30: The investor who purchased the convertible preferred stock converted 3,000 shares of the preferred stock into 12,000 shares of common stock.

Required:
   a. Make the necessary journal entries to reflect the above transactions for the quarter.
   b. Prepare in good form the stockholders' equity section of the firm's balance sheet at the end of March. Assume that net income for the quarter was $10,000 and no dividends were declared.
   c. Why do you think that the firm issued two different types of preferred stock? What would be the motivation for people to purchase each type of stock?

16B–5. Determining Missing Figures. The following stockholders' equity section was taken from the 1987 balance sheet of Southern Oil Co.:

Stockholders' equity	
8% preferred stock, $50 par value authorized	
100,000 shares (liquidation value $53 per share)	$3,500,000
Common stock, $10 par value, authorized	
800,000 shares, issued 700,000 shares	?
Paid-in capital from issue of common	
stock in excess of par	2,800,000
Retained earnings	5,000,000

Required:
Based on the above information, answer each of the following questions:
   a. How many shares of preferred stock are outstanding?
   b. At what price was the preferred stock issued?
   c. What is the total of stockholders' equity?
   d. What is the total contributed capital of the company?
   e. What is the total legal capital of the company?
   f. What was the average issue price of the common stock?
   g. What is the book value per share of common stock?
   h. What is the total dividend requirement on the preferred stock?
   i. What is the total dividend requirement on the common stock?

16B–6. Common and Preferred Dividends. The Peggy Corporation was formed in January 1984. During the first five years of operations, it reported the following net income or loss:

1984	$100,000 loss
1985	280,000 loss
1986	150,000 income
1987	10,000 loss
1988	400,000 income

At December 31, 1988 Peggy's capital accounts were as follows:

Common stock, $5 par value; authorized	
1,000,000 shares; issued and outstanding	
500,000 shares	$2,500,000
7% nonparticipating, noncumulative preferred	
stock, $50 par value; authorized, issued, and	
outstanding 10,000 shares	500,000
5% nonparticipating, cumulative preferred	
stock, $50 par value; authorized, issued, and	
outstanding 5,000 shares	250,000

Peggy has never paid a cash dividend or any other type of dividend. Under the law, dividends can only be paid up to the amount of retained earnings.

Required:

Determine the maximum amount of dividends that can be paid each year and how they would be distributed between common and preferred stockholders.

Using the Computer

The European Corporation has 100,000 shares of preferred stock and 300,000 shares of common stock outstanding. The preferred stock has a stated dividend rate of $2 per share and is cumulative and nonparticipating. As of the beginning of the year there were no preferred dividends in arrears. Using an electronic spreadsheet, determine the amount of dividends distributed to preferred and common shareholders under each of the following independent cases:

	Total Dividends Distributed	
	Current Year	Next Year
Case 1	$ 50,000	$100,000
2	150,000	300,000
3	300,000	400,000

Use the following format in preparing your spreadsheet:

	Case 1	Case 2	Case 3
Current Year			
Preferred dividends			
Common dividends			
Total dividends			
Next Year			
Preferred dividends			
Common dividends			
Total dividends			

Understanding Financial Statements

The following stockholders' equity section was taken from the 1985 and 1984 comparative balance sheets of Lockheed Corporation:

Dollar figures in millions	1985	1984
Redeemable $9.50 senior preferred stock		13
Common shareholders' equity		
Common stock, $1 par value, 100,000,000 shares authorized; 65,222,110 shares issued and outstanding (64,674,725 in 1984)	65	65
Additional capital	454	446
Retained earnings (since November 29, 1981)	992	641
Total common shareholders' equity	1,511	1,152
	$3,022	$2,317

Additional Information:

	1985	1984
Cash dividends per share of common stock	$ 0.75	$ 0.45
EPS	6.10	5.28
Year-end market price—Common shares	48.00	41.00
Liquidation value of preferred shares		13 million

Required:

    a. Calculate the dividend yield on the common stock at the end of 1985 and 1984.

    b. Determine the P–E ratio at the end of both years.

    c. Determine the book value per share of common stock for both years.

    d. Describe the relationship, if any, between book value and the market price of the stock.

    e. If the average number of common shares outstanding for 1985 was 65,737,705, what was the net income for 1985?

Financial Decision Case

The Myers Corporation is a successful company owned solely by the members of the Myers family. The company manufactures and distributes animal care products. It has recently developed a new antiflea pill that will protect animals from fleas for up to one year. The formula is patented, and it appears that if the company can finance its manufacturing and distribution, the product will dominate that part of the animal care market.

    The firm has been in existence for several years. There are currently 1,000 shares of $1 par value common stock outstanding, all of which are held by family members. The stockholders' equity section of the June 30, 1986 balance sheet is as follows:

Common stock, $1 par value, 1,000 shares authorized and issued	$ 1,000
Additional paid-in capital from issue of common stock in excess of par	499,000
Retained earnings	3,450,000
Total stockholders' equity	$3,950,000

    Although the company has been profitable, it needs additional cash in order to finance the production and distribution of the new product. Maintaining adequate cash has always been a problem for the firm. L. D. Myers, the current president of the company, tells you that the company is considering three alternatives to raising additional capital:

    1. Borrowing $3 million in a 5-year term loan from the bank at a 12% interest rate. Interest is due annually; the principal at the end of five years.

    2. Issuing 30,000 shares of 8%, $100 par value cumulative convertible preferred stock to a venture capitalist. Each share could be converted into five shares of common stock, beginning in five years.

    3. Going public by issuing 50,000 shares of common stock at an estimated price of $6 per share. At their discretion, family members could purchase some of this stock at the $6 price.

Myers tells you that the family has two considerations. The first has to do with forced cash payments due to interest and/or dividends. He reminds you that maintaining adequate cash has always been a problem for the firm. He informs you that interest is deductible for tax purposes but dividend payments are not. The firm is currently in a 46% tax bracket. The second consideration has to do with family control. The company has always been family owned, and Myers is concerned that the family may have to relinquish that control.

Required:

Write a memo to Myers outlining the advantages and disadvantages of each proposal. Be sure to consider the issues the family has raised.

Stockholders' Equity— Retained Earnings and Dividends

17

LEARNING OBJECTIVES

After reading this chapter you should be able to:

1. Prepare a corporate income statement.
2. Calculate earnings per share and understand its uses.
3. Prepare the entries to record corporate dividends.
4. Differentiate between stock splits and stock dividends and be able to record them.
5. Make prior period adjustments and appropriate retained earnings.
6. Record treasury stock transactions.
7. Record retirements of capital stock.
8. List the purposes of the statement of stockholders' equity.
9. Account for corporate income tax expense and understand the need for interperiod income tax allocation (Appendix).

This chapter continues our discussion of the stockholders' equity section of a corporate balance sheet. Specifically, we concentrate on those transactions that affect retained earnings, including corporate net income, dividends, and treasury stock transactions. In addition, you will be introduced to the concepts behind earnings per share. Accounting for corporate income tax expense is discussed in the Appendix.

The statement of retained earnings for General Electric Company is illustrated on page 644. As this statement shows, net earnings and dividends are the two primary events that affect retained earnings. Obviously, net earnings increase retained earnings, and a net loss and dividends decrease retained earnings. As we will see in later sections of this chapter, retained earnings can also be affected by prior period adjustments and certain treasury stock transactions. Because net income is the single largest source of change in retained earnings, corporate income statements are discussed first, and then dividends.

**General Electric Company
and Consolidated Affiliates**
Statement of Retained Earnings
For the Years Ended December 31 (in millions)

	1985	1984	1983
Retained earnings, January 1	$11,667	$10,317	$ 9,145
Net earnings	2,336	2,280	2,024
Dividends declared	(1,020)	(930)	(852)
Adjustment for pooling of interests	11	0	0
Balance, December 31	$12,994	$11,667	$10,317

Corporate Income Statements

A corporation or even a large private enterprise probably derives income and incurs expenses from many sources. Since the mid-1960s, the accounting profession has felt that net income should be a comprehensive figure. That is, comprehensive net income "includes all changes in equity during a period except those resulting from investments by owners and distributions to owners [dividends]."[1]

The notion of comprehensive income, however, does present a problem for users of the income statement. One of the primary purposes of this statement is to help users predict future income patterns. Yet when a firm derives income from various types of transactions, it is difficult to separate recurring from nonrecurring transactions, and thus the predictive ability of the income statement may be decreased. As the FASB noted:

> . . . Characteristics of various sources of comprehensive income may differ significantly from one another, indicating a need for information about various components of comprehensive income.[2]

In order to meet this need, generally accepted accounting principles require that the major components of income be segregated on the income statement. These major components are:

1. Income from continuing operations.
2. Discontinued operations.
3. Extraordinary items.
4. Cumulative effect of changes in accounting methods or principles.

An example of an income statement that includes all of these components is shown in Exhibit 17–1. In reviewing this income statement, you should keep in mind that it is unlikely that an enterprise would have income from all of these

[1]Financial Accounting Standards Board, Concepts Statement No. 6, *Elements of Financial Statements* (Stamford, Conn.: FASB, December 1985), par. 76.

[2]Ibid., par. 61.

EXHIBIT 17–1

The Exacto Computer Corporation
Comparative Income Statement
For the Years Ended December 31 (in millions)

	1987	1986
Net sales	$6,000	$5,700
Cost of goods sold	3,900	3,648
Gross margin	2,100	2,052
Selling and general and administrative expenses	1,260	1,230
Operating income	840	822
Other income		
Gain on sale of building	15	0
Interest income	5	2
	860	824
Other expenses		
Interest expense	10	6
Income from continuing operations, before taxes	850	818
Provision for income taxes	340	327
Income from continuing operations	510	491
Discontinued operations		
Loss from operations of discontinued segment, net of tax savings of $18 in 1987 and $14 in 1986	(27)	(16)
Gain on disposal of business segment, net of applicable taxes of $27	33	0
Income before extraordinary items and cumulative effect of accounting change	516	475
Extraordinary item—Gain on expropriation of subsidiary, net of applicable taxes of $45	0	55
Cumulative effect of change in accounting method for depreciation, net of taxes of $23	27	0
Net income	$ 543	$ 530
Earnings per share		
Income from continuing operations	$2.04	$1.96
Discontinued operations	.02	(.06)
Income before extraordinary items and cumulative effect of accounting change	2.06	1.90
Extraordinary gains	0	.22
Cumulative effect of accounting change	.11	0
Net income	$2.17	$2.12

sources in any one year; they all are presented for illustrative purposes only. Furthermore, if all these categories do in fact exist, they must be listed in the manner and order shown in the exhibit.[3]

[3]In December 1984 the FASB issued Concepts Statement No. 5, *Recognition and Measurement in Financial Statements of Business Enterprises* (Stamford, Conn.). In that Statement the FASB suggested reformulating the income statement. The major change would be differentiating earnings from comprehensive net income. Cumulative effect of changes in accounting methods would not be included in earnings, but they would be included in net income. These changes are only suggestions and the Board expects only gradual change.

[4]American Institute of Certified Public Accountants, Accounting Principles Board, Opinion No. 30, *Reporting the Results of Operations* (New York: AICPA, 1973), par. 13.

Income from Continuing Operations

Income from continuing operations includes all of the recurring and usual transactions that the firm enters into as it produces its goods and services. Thus, such items as sales, cost of goods sold, operating expenses, and other income and expense items all are included in income from continuing operations. For 1987 and 1986, income from continuing operations for The Exacto Computer Corporation is $510 million and $491 million, respectively. The significance of these amounts is that as decision makers use the income statement to make predictions about the future, these items indicate how profitable the corporation has been and how profitable it might be on a recurring and continuing basis.

There are two important points that need to be made about this example. First, either a single-step or multistep format (shown in Chapter 6) can be used. Regardless of which form is used, income from continuing operations must be the same. Second, unlike a sole proprietorship or partnership, a corporation is subject to income tax and, thus, the item, tax expense, appears in the income statement. However, the total income tax expense is divided among the four components of the income statement. This is called **intraperiod income tax allocation** and means that the total income tax expense for the period is related to the proper component that caused the income. Conversely, **interperiod income tax allocation,** discussed in the appendix to this chapter, refers to the allocation of income taxes among different accounting periods. Intraperiod income tax allocation is necessary in order to maintain an appropriate relationship between income tax expense and income from continuing operations, discontinued operations, extraordinary items, and cumulative effects of accounting changes.

To illustrate, the total income tax expense for 1987 for Exacto is $372 million, computed as follows:

	Before-Tax Amount	Tax (Tax Savings)
	(in millions)	
Income from continuing operations before taxes	$850	$340
Discontinued operations		
Loss from operations	(45)	(18)
Gain on sale	60	27
Cumulative effect of accounting change	50	23
	$915	$372
Net income ($915 − $372) = $543		

Instead of showing just one figure for taxes, $372 million, this amount is allocated to the various components of net income. Thus, the reader of the income statement knows how each item affected the firm's total tax expense and what the income tax expense can be expected to be in the future on a recurring basis.

At first glance, it may seem strange that a loss is reduced by a tax savings. For example, as noted in Exhibit 17–1, the firm suffered a loss on discontinued operations of $45 million in 1987. Because a loss reduces income, income tax is less by a portion of the loss. Thus, in this example, total taxes are reduced by

$18 million because of this loss, and this tax savings is netted against the before-tax loss of $45 million to arrive at the net loss of $27 million. By convention, discontinued operations, extraordinary items, and cumulative effects of accounting changes are shown net of their tax effects, whereas income from continuing operations is shown both before and after taxes.

Discontinued Operations

The Accounting Principles Board stated in Opinion 30 that results from discontinued operations and the gain or loss from the disposal of the discontinued segment should be shown separately from income from continued operations. These figures should be disclosed immediately below income from continuing operations.

According to professional pronouncements, a **segment** of a business is a "component of an entity whose activities represent a separate major line of business or class of customer."[4] A segment may be a subsidiary, a division, or a department, as long as its activities can be clearly distinguished from other assets both physically and operationally for financial reporting purposes. For example, in 1982 CBS discontinued its CBS Cable division which produced certain cable programming. This represents a discontinued operation. However, if CBS sold one of its corporate-owned television stations, this would not be considered a discontinued operation because it still owns several other stations and has several hundred affiliates.

The discontinued operations segment of the income statement of The Exacto Computer Corporation that is illustrated in Exhibit 17–1 is reproduced below:

The Exacto Computer Corporation
Partial Income Statement
For the Years Ended December 31 (in millions)

	1987	1986
Income from continuing operations	$510	$491
Discontinued operations		
Loss from operations of discontinued segment, net of tax savings of $18 in 1987 and $14 in 1986	(27)	(16)
Gain on disposal of business segment, net of applicable taxes of $27	33	0
Income before extraordinary items and cumulative effect of accounting change	516	475

As this partial income statement shows, the two types of events listed under the discontinued operations segment are income or loss from operations and the gain or loss on the actual disposal of the segment. As noted before, each item is shown net of its tax effect. Income or loss from operations represents the net of the revenues and the expenses related to that particular segment. In our example, there is a loss of $27 million, net of taxes, in 1987.

The treatment for 1986 in the comparative 1987 and 1986 income statement is important to understand. In this example, the segment was disposed of in 1987, and so if one looked at the comparative income statement covering 1985 and 1986, the entire discontinued operations segment would not exist. All income and expenses from this particular segment were included with the regular income and expense categories found in income from continuing operations. However, when the comparative statement covering 1986 and 1987 was prepared in 1987, the 1986 statement was changed. The relevant revenues and expenses were pulled out of their regular categories, netted, and shown after their tax effects, at a loss of $16 million. This was done in order to make the 1987 and 1986 statements comparative.

The second item under the discontinued segment category is a gain or loss on the actual disposal. In our example, The Exacto Computer Corporation incurred a $33 million gain, net of taxes. There is no comparable gain shown in 1986 because the disposal did not occur until 1987.

Extraordinary Items

Extraordinary items are gains and losses that result from transactions that are both unusual in nature and infrequent in occurrence. Because these transactions are unusual and infrequent, they need to be separated from continuing operations so that investors can better use the income statement to predict future income.

Criteria for Determining Extraordinary Items

The criteria for determining whether an item is extraordinary have caused much controversy. Prior to the issuance of Opinion 30 in 1973, the management of a firm had considerable discretion in determining whether an item was extraordinary. Thus, several items were considered extraordinary when, under current accounting principles, they would be included in income from continuing operations. For example, there was considerable controversy over Penn Central's decision in 1969 to consider the sale of certain real estate as an ordinary gain rather than an extraordinary gain. Many individuals felt that this classification was made in order to conceal operating losses during the year.[5] In order to limit the number and type of extraordinary items, current accounting pronouncements restrict them to those transactions that are both unusual and infrequent.

An unusual event or transaction is one that is highly abnormal or is clearly or only incidentally related to the enterprise's ordinary and typical activities, taking into account the environment in which the entity operates. For an event to be infrequent in occurrence, it should be of a type that would not reasonably be expected to recur in the foreseeable future, again taking into account the environment in which the entity operates.

Although an event or transaction must meet both of these criteria to be extraordinary, considerable judgment is still needed to apply them. For example, in order to determine a business's ordinary and typical activities, the specific characteristics of the entity, such as its scope of operations and line of business, should be considered. The entity's environment includes such factors as the characteristics of the industry in which the entity operates, its geographical location, and the extent of governmental regulation. Thus, an item

---

[5]Abraham Briloff, *Unaccountable Accounting* (New York: Harper & Row, 1972), p. 194.

may be unusual and/or infrequent for one enterprise but not for another, because of the differences in their environments.

To demonstrate the judgment required in this area, assume that a Florida citrus grower's crop of oranges is destroyed by frost. Is this an extraordinary item? No. Frost damage in Florida is normally experienced every three to four years, and thus, given the environment in which the entity operates, the infrequency-of-occurrence criterion has not been met.[6] However, if we were dealing with a California grower, would the answer be different? Most likely yes, because damage from frost is unusual and infrequent in California, and thus any loss would be extraordinary.

Examples of Extraordinary Items

Because of the judgment involved in determining extraordinary items, the APB and the FASB both have stated that certain items or transactions definitely either are or are not extraordinary items. The more important ones are listed in Exhibit 17–2 on page 650. Some of the items that are not considered extraordinary in the exhibit are classified that way because they are unusual or infrequent but not both. In these cases, the item should be recorded as a separate component of income from continuing operations.

The income statement in Exhibit 17–1 on page 645 shows how both extraordinary items and transactions that do not meet both criteria are disclosed. The extraordinary item in this example is a gain from an expropriation of a subsidiary. The gain occurred because the firm received compensation in excess of the book value of its subsidiary. The 1986 gain of $55 million is shown net of tax. Thus, the actual gain of $100 million is reduced by the related taxes of $45 million. It is disclosed on the income statement immediately after discontinued operations, if any. If there were no discontinued operations, extraordinary items would follow income from operations. The gain on the sale of the building, which does not meet both criteria, is shown before taxes in the continuing operations section of the income statement.

Types of Accounting Changes

Over a period of time, a firm is likely to make two different types of accounting changes, a change in accounting methods and a change in accounting estimates. A **change in accounting method** results when a firm changes from one generally accepted accounting principle or method to another generally accepted one. A **change in accounting estimate** occurs when a firm changes a particular estimate, such as an asset's depreciable life, as a result of new information that was not available when the original estimate was made.

A Change in Method or Principle

Throughout this book we have noted several instances in which management can choose among acceptable accounting methods. For example, there are different methods of determining bad debts, cost of goods sold, and depreciation expense. Once a particular method is chosen, accountants feel that it should be consistently used unless a change to a different method is preferable, or a particular accounting standard is changed that mandates the switch. When there is a change in accounting method, current accounting rules generally require that the cumulative effect of the change be included in income of

---

[6]American Institute of Certified Public Accountants, Accounting Principles Board, Accounting Interpretations of APB Opinion 30, *Reporting the Results of Operations* (New York: AICPA, 1973).

EXHIBIT 17–2

Illustration of Extraordinary Items*

Considered Extraordinary	Not Considered Extraordinary
1. Destruction by an earthquake of one of the oil refineries owned by a large, multinational oil company.	1. Write-downs or write-offs of receivables, equipment, or similar items.
2. Destruction of a large portion of a tobacco manufacturer's crops by a hailstorm in an area in which severe damage from hailstorms is rare.	2. Gains and losses from a disposal of a segment.
3. Expropriation of assets by a foreign government.	3. Gains and losses from the sale or abandonment of property, plant, or equipment.
4. Gains or losses due to a prohibition under a newly created law.	4. Effects of strikes against the firm and/or competitors and major suppliers.
5. Gains and losses on early extinguishment of debt.[†]	5. Changes in accounting estimates and methods.

*Sources:
1. APB Opinion No. 30, *Reporting the Results of Operations* (New York: AICPA, 1973).
2. Accounting Interpretations of APB Opinion No. 30, *Reporting the Results of Operations* (New York: AICPA, 1973).

[†]FASB Statement 4 requires these gains and losses, if material, to be treated as extraordinary, regardless of the criteria set forth by Opinion 30.

---

the current period.[7] The cumulative effect is the amount required to adjust the asset or liability to what it would have been had the new accounting method always been used. This amount, which is either a gain or a loss, is shown on the income statement, net of taxes, immediately before net income.

To illustrate, assume that on January 2, 1986 a firm purchased a piece of equipment at a cost of $100,000. The equipment has a useful life of 10 years with no residual value. In 1986 and 1987, the firm used double-declining-balance depreciation, but at the beginning of 1988, the third year of the asset's life, the firm switched to straight-line. The difference of $16,000 between what the depreciation was for the first two years on double-declining-balance and what it would have been had the straight-line method been used is a cumulative effect of an accounting change and is calculated at the top of page 651.

The cumulative effect of $16,000 can be calculated either by comparing the difference in the total depreciation expense for the two years or by comparing the asset's net book value under each of the depreciation methods. For example, at the beginning of year 3, 1988, the asset had a book value of $64,000 under the double-declining-balance method. If straight-line depreciation had been used for the two previous years, the asset would have had a book value of $80,000. Thus, a cumulative gain of $16,000 is needed to increase the book value of the asset from $64,000 to $80,000. The gain, net of any tax effect, is

---

[7]American Institute of Certified Public Accountants, Accounting Principles Board, Opinion No. 20, *Accounting Changes* (New York: AICPA, 1971). There are several exceptions to this general rule. For example, when a firm changes from FIFO to LIFO, a cumulative effect *is not calculated*, because the layering process of LIFO makes it impossible to calculate the cumulative effect. FASB Concepts Statement 5 recommends that cumulative-effect-of-accounting changes be included in comprehensive income but not earnings.

Calculation of Cumulative Effect of Change in Depreciation		
Difference in Depreciation		
Double-declining-balance	Straight-line	Difference
Year 1, 1986		
$20,000[a]	$10,000[c]	$10,000
Year 2, 1987		
16,000[b]	10,000	6,000
$36,000	$20,000	$16,000

Difference in Book Value		
Double-declining-balance	Straight-line	Cumulative Effect of Accounting Change
Historical cost	$100,000	$100,000	$ 0
Accumulated depreciation	36,000[d]	20,000[d]	16,000
Book value	$ 64,000	$ 80,000	$16,000

[a]$100,000 × .20 = $20,000.
[b]($100,000 − $20,000) × .20 = $16,000.
[c]$100,000 × .10 = $10,000.
[d]From previous schedule.

shown on the 1988 income statement. Depreciation expense for 1988 is calculated on the straight-line method and is $10,000. If it were necessary to decrease the book value of the asset, a loss would be recorded.

In our example in Exhibit 17–1, there is a gain resulting from the cumulative effect of a change in depreciation method. The total gain is $50 million but is shown at $27 million, or net of the tax effect of $23 million. Full disclosure requires that the effect of this change be reported in the footnotes to the financial statements as well as in the auditor's report.

A Change in Estimate

In order to make the allocations required under the matching convention, accountants must make estimates. Examples of some of these estimates are service lives, uncollectible receivables, residual value, and warranty costs. Because an estimate is inherently uncertain, new information may require a change in the original estimate. This is quite common in accounting and does not require a cumulative catch-up. A change in estimate affects only the current period in which the change is made and future periods.

To demonstrate, assume that an enterprise purchases equipment at a cost of $40,000 on January 2, 1986. The asset, with no residual value, is depreciated over an estimated life of 10 years using the straight-line method. At the beginning of 1988, year 3 of the asset's life, the firm decides to decrease the total service life of the equipment from 10 years to 8 years. Thus, with a new total life of eight years, there are only six years remaining at the beginning of 1988 (eight years less the two years that expired in 1986 and 1987). This change in estimate is handled by now spreading the book value of $32,000 at January 2,

1988 over the remaining 6 years. This depreciation expense in 1988 and for each of the next 5 years is $5,333, calculated as follows:

Yearly depreciation from 1/2/86 to 12/31/87: $\dfrac{\$40,000}{10 \text{ yrs.}} = \underline{\$4,000}$ per year

Book value
1/2/88:

Historical cost	$40,000
Accumulated depreciation, 1/2/86 to 12/31/87	8,000
	$32,000

Depreciation expense, 1988 and thereafter: $\dfrac{\$32,000}{6 \text{ yrs.}} = \underline{\$5,333}$

Thus, depreciation expense in 1988 is $5,333, and there is no cumulative effect of a change in accounting method on the income statement.

Earnings per Share

Earnings per share (EPS) is one of the most popular, if not the most popular, financial statistic reported in financial publications. The relationship between EPS and the stock's market price is called the price-earnings ratio (P-E ratio) and is presented for most stocks listed on the stock page of newspapers. Thus, an understanding of how EPS is calculated and its uses and limitations is necessary in order to be an informed user of financial information.

Calculating EPS—The Basics

The rules regarding the calculation of EPS are complex and are spelled out primarily in APB Opinion 15.[8] Our purpose here is to present an overview of the calculation. In the simplest sense, EPS is calculated by dividing net income available to common shareholders by the weighted average number of outstanding common shares.

$$\text{EPS} = \frac{\text{Net income available to common shareholders}}{\text{Weighted average number of common shares outstanding}}$$

EPS is meaningful only in regard to common stockholders. This is so because preferred shareholders have claims to only the stipulated dividend.

Net Income Available to Common Shareholders

Net income available to common shareholders is equal to net income less preferred stock dividends declared.[9] If there is no preferred stock, the numerator of the formula will be simply net income. To illustrate, assume that the Mori Corporation earned net income of $1,562,500 for the year ended December 31, 1987. The firm declared the following dividends during 1987:

---

[8]American Institute of Certified Public Accountants, Accounting Principles Board, Opinion No. 15, *Earnings per Share* (New York: AICPA, 1969).

[9]If the preferred stock is cumulative, the dividends relating to the stock must be deducted from net income whether or not they are declared, because preferred shareholders do not lose their claim to undeclared dividends on cumulative stock.

Common dividends	$125,000
Preferred dividends	62,500

In this case, net income available to common shareholders is $1,500,000, or $1,562,500 − $62,500. The common dividends declared are ignored because all the earnings after preferred dividends are theoretically available to common shareholders, whether or not returned in the form of dividends.

Weighted Average Number of Common Shares Outstanding

If a corporation has not issued any additional common stock, the denominator of the EPS formula will be simply the number of common shares outstanding at the end of the year. In many cases, however, firms issue additional shares of common stock at various times during the year. In these cases, it is incorrect to take the total number of shares outstanding at the end of the year, because the firm did not have benefit of the cash or other assets generated from the additional stock issue for the entire year. Therefore a weighted average number of shares must be calculated based on the number of months that the shares were outstanding.

To demonstrate, assume that the Mori Corporation has 1 million shares of common stock outstanding on January 1, 1987. During the year, the firm issued the following additional common stock:

Beginning		1,000,000
April 1, 1987	250,000	
September 30, 1987	150,000	400,000
Ending		1,400,000

The weighted average number of common shares outstanding is 1,225,000, calculated as follows:

Number of Shares		Fraction of Year Outstanding		Weighted Average Number of Shares
1,000,000	×	3/12	=	250,000
1,250,000	×	6/12	=	625,000
1,400,000	×	3/12	=	350,000
		12/12		
Weighted average number of common shares outstanding				1,225,000

In effect, the number of shares outstanding for any part of the year is multiplied by the fraction of the year in which they were outstanding. In a full year, 12/12ths must be accounted for.

Based on these data, EPS for the Mori Corporation is $1.22 (rounded), determined by the following calculation:

$$\frac{\$1,500,000}{1,225,000} = \$1.22$$

EPS of $1.22 is more realistic than a figure determined by using 1.4 million shares, the number of common shares outstanding at year-end. Using 1.4 million shares would decrease EPS and would be based on the assumption that the firm had use for the entire year the cash from the additional stock issued on April 1 and September 30.

Calculating EPS for More Complex Capital Structures

Many large corporations have what is referred to as complex capital structures. A **complex capital structure** contains certain types of bonds, preferred stock, or other securities that are convertible into common shares. These types of convertible securities are often dilutive, because if they were converted into common stock, increasing the number of common shares outstanding, EPS could be reduced. Accounting rules require that when a firm has a complex capital structure, two separate EPS figures must be calculated, primary and fully diluted EPS.

Primary EPS

Primary earnings per share is calculated by dividing net income available to common shareholders by the weighted average number of shares outstanding plus those dilutive securities that meet the definition of a common stock equivalent. A **common stock equivalent** is a dilutive security that because of the terms or circumstances at the time of its issue is essentially equivalent to common stock. That is, a common stock equivalent is not common stock *per se*, but it does allow the holder to become a common stock holder at some future date. Therefore, the market value of the common stock equivalent tends to vary in relation to the common stock to which it is related.[10] Because these securities so closely resemble common stock, they are treated as common stock in the EPS calculation. Thus, the formula to calculate primary EPS is:

$$\text{Primary EPS} = \frac{\text{Net income available to common shareholders}}{\text{Weighted average number of common shares outstanding plus common stock equivalents}}$$

Fully Diluted EPS

Fully diluted EPS is calculated by dividing net income available to common shareholders by the weighted average number of common shares outstanding plus all dilutive securities, whether or not they are considered common stock equivalents. The purpose of presenting fully diluted EPS is to show the worst possible case, which assumes that all the dilutive securities were converted. Thus, present and potential investors can see what their earnings per share would be, assuming maximum dilution. The formula to calculate fully diluted EPS is:

$$\text{Fully diluted EPS} = \frac{\text{Net income available to common shareholders}}{\text{Weighted average number of common shares outstanding and common stock equivalents and all other dilutive securities}}$$

[10]The accounting profession has definite rules governing which dilutive securities are common stock equivalents. These rules are far beyond the scope of this book, though they can be found in APB Opinion 15 and FASB Statements 55 and 85.

Although the numerator in both cases represents net income available to common shareholders, the actual dollar amounts are likely to be different. This distinction is discussed next.

EPS Example

To illustrate the calculation of both primary and fully diluted EPS, assume that The GAAP Corporation, which earned net income of $2.5 million during 1987, has the capital structure portrayed in Exhibit 17–3. There are two separate issues of convertible preferred stock. Both are potentially dilutive, but we are assuming that only the 8% preferred stock is considered a common stock equivalent under the current accounting pronouncements. The 6% preferred stock is not a common stock equivalent.

EXHIBIT 17–3

The GAAP Corporation
Partial Balance Sheet
December 31, 1987

Stockholders' equity	
Preferred stock, 8%—$100 par value convertible stock, 1,000,000 shares authorized, 20,000 shares issued and outstanding	$ 2,000,000
Preferred stock, 6%—$100 par value convertible stock, 500,000 shares authorized, 15,000 shares issued and outstanding	1,500,000
Common stock, $5 par value stock, 4,000,000 shares authorized, 1,000,000 shares issued and outstanding	5,000,000
Additional paid-in capital	2,000,000
Retained earnings	40,000,000
Total stockholders' equity	$50,500,000

Additional information:

1. All shares of preferred and common stock were outstanding for the entire year.
2. Each share of the 8% preferred stock is convertible into five common shares and *is a common stock equivalent.*
3. Each share of 6% preferred stock is convertible into 10 common shares and *is not a common stock equivalent.*

Exhibit 17–4 on page 656 shows how primary and fully diluted EPS are calculated. In calculating primary EPS, net income available to common shareholders is determined by subtracting only the dividends on the 6% preferred stock—which is not a common stock equivalent—from the reported net income. The 8% preferred stock—which is a common stock equivalent—is assumed to be converted into shares of common stock, and thus these dividends need not be subtracted from net income. As a result, net income available to common shareholders is $2,410,000. The weighted average number of common shares at year-end is determined by adding the 1 million outstanding in shares of common to the number of common shares that would be issued if the 8% preferred shares were converted. (Conversion is assumed to take place at the beginning of the year.) Because each of the 20,000 preferred shares is

EXHIBIT 17–4

The GAAP Corporation
Computation of Primary and Fully Diluted EPS

	Primary EPS	Fully Diluted EPS
Net income as reported	$2,500,000	$2,500,000
Dividend on 6% preferred stock, 6% × $1,500,000	(90,000)	0
Net income available to common shareholders	$2,410,000	$2,500,000
Weighted average number of common shares outstanding	1,000,000	1,000,000
Common stock equivalent—8% preferred stock, 20,000 shares convertible into 100,000 common shares	100,000	100,000
Dilutive security—not common stock equivalent— 6% preferred stock, 15,000 shares convertible into 150,000 shares		150,000
Adjusted number of common shares	1,100,000	1,250,000

$$\text{Primary EPS} = \frac{\$2,410,000}{1,100,000} \qquad \$2.19$$

$$\text{Fully diluted EPS} = \frac{\$2,500,000}{1,250,000} \qquad \$2.00$$

convertible into 5 common shares, an additional 100,000 shares would be issued. Thus the adjusted number of common shares is 1.1 million, and primary EPS is $2.19.

In calculating fully diluted EPS, we assume that all the convertible preferred shares, whether or not common stock equivalents, are converted into common shares. Thus, no adjustment is made to reported net income because now we assume that no preferred dividends will be paid because all the preferred stock is assumed to have been converted. The weighted average number of common shares is determined by adding the 1 million outstanding shares of common to the number of shares that would be issued if both the 8% and 6% preferred shares were converted at the beginning of the year. The adjusted number of common shares is 1.25 million, and fully diluted EPS is $2.

Presenting EPS on Corporate Income Statements

All publicly held corporations are required to present EPS data on their income statements.[11] Primary EPS must be disclosed, and if fully diluted EPS is at least 3% less than primary EPS, fully diluted EPS also must be disclosed. EPS data also should be presented for major categories on the income statement, such as income from continuing operations and discontinued operations. Exhibit 17–1 on page 645 shows the EPS presentation for our hypothetical company, The Exacto Computer Corporation, and Exhibit 17–5 presents

[11]Financial Accounting Standards Board, Statement No. 21, *Suspension of the Reporting of Earnings per Share and Segment Information by Nonpublic Enterprises* (Stamford, Conn.: FASB, April 1978). Before the issuance of this Statement, all corporations had to disclose EPS data, which was of limited use to nonpublic entities.

the income statement for Optical Coating Laboratory, Inc., a manufacturer of multilayer thin film-coated products.

Uses and Limitations of EPS Data

EPS is a popular financial statistic that provides useful comparisons among companies. It also provides a basis for other ratios such as the price-earnings ratio. However, one must be extremely careful in using these data. As we noted, the rules for calculating EPS are complex, and it is often impossible for even a sophisticated user to calculate EPS from just looking at published financial data. Furthermore, if you are relying on published EPS data, you still must be careful. For example, are the published P-E ratios based on primary or fully diluted EPS? Is EPS from continuing operations used, or is the figure based on other income statement categories? Generally, the P-E ratio is based on primary EPS calculated on income from continuing operations. These are only a few examples of the issues that must be considered in using EPS data.

EXHIBIT 17–5

Optical Coating Laboratory, Inc. and Subsidiaries
Consolidated Statements of Operations
Years Ended October 31, 1985, 1984, and 1983

(Amounts in thousands, except per share data)	1985	1984	1983
Net Sales and Other Revenues	$58,601	$80,158	$64,748
Costs and Expenses:			
Cost of sales	43,461	49,947	40,422
Research and development	6,666	4,969	3,397
Selling and administrative	18,405	17,598	15,046
Total Costs and Expenses	68,532	72,514	58,865
Earnings (Loss) from Operations	(9,931)	7,644	5,883
Interest income, net of expense	3,454	3,980	2,540
Earnings (Loss) from Continuing Operations before Taxes	(6,477)	11,624	8,423
Taxes on income (credit)	(3,305)	4,683	3,553
Earnings (Loss) from Continuing Operations	(3,172)	6,941	4,870
Discontinued Operations:			
Income from discontinued operations, net of taxes		722	1,274
Gain on sale of investment, net of taxes of $3,985 in 1985 and $2,512 in 1983	3,055		4,643
Net Earnings (Loss)	$ (117)	$ 7,663	$10,787
Earnings (Loss) per Common and Common Equivalent Share:			
Continuing operations	$ (.54)	$ 1.18	$ .92
Discontinued operations		.12	.24
Gain on sale of investment	.52		.88
Net Earnings (Loss)	$ (.02)	$ 1.30	$2.04
Average Common and Common Equivalent Shares Used to Compute Earnings (Loss) Per Share	5,839	5,866	5,275

Corporate income is the principal means by which retained earnings are increased. Other than losses, dividends are the principal cause of retained earnings decreases. Dividends, which represent a distribution of assets to shareholders, can be in the form of cash, other assets, or, in some cases, the corporation's own stock.

Cash Dividends

Most investors purchase either common or preferred stock with some expectation of receiving cash dividends. The amount and regularity of cash dividends are two of the factors that affect the market price of a firm's stock. Many corporations, therefore, attempt to establish a regular quarterly dividend pattern that is maintained or slowly increased over a number of years. In profitable years, the corporation may issue a special year-end dividend in addition to the regular dividends. Such stable dividend policies increase the attractiveness of the firm's stock.

GENERAL ELECTRIC

The following, taken from a General Electric Company annual report, shows how one corporation implements this policy:

> • Dividends declared totaled $1.020 billion in 1985. At $2.23 per share (up 18 cents), 1985 marked the 10th consecutive year of increased dividends for share owners. GE's policy is to maintain dividend growth while at the same time retaining sufficient earnings to enhance productive capability and to provide adequate financial resources for growth opportunities.

As this quote indicates, management gives considerable thought to the amount and timing of dividends. In addition to the desire to maintain a stable dividend policy, other factors also affect the amount of cash dividends declared in any one year, for example, the amount of retained earnings or the firm's cash position and business needs.

From a theoretical and practical point of view, there must be a positive balance in retained earnings in order to issue a dividend. If there is a deficit (negative balance) in retained earnings, any dividend would represent a return of invested capital and is called a *liquidating dividend*. A corporation can still issue a normal dividend (a dividend other than a liquidating one) even if it incurred a loss in any one particular year, as long as there is a positive balance in retained earnings.

Because there must be a positive balance in retained earnings before a normal dividend can be issued, the phrase "paying dividends out of retained earnings" developed. But this phrase is a misstatement, dividends are not paid out of retained earnings; they are a distribution of assets and are paid in cash, or, in some circumstances, in other assets or even stock. Retained earnings are the increase in the firm's net assets due to profitable operations and represent the owners' claim against net assets, not just cash.

The maximum amount of dividends that can be issued in any one year is the total amount of retained earnings. However, this is rarely, if ever, done. Again, in order to pay a cash dividend, a firm must have the necessary cash available, and the amount of cash on hand is not directly related to retained earnings. Furthermore, as is evident from the statement in the GE annual report, a firm has other uses for its cash. Most mature and stable firms restrict their cash dividends to about 40% of their net earnings. Returning to the GE example, in 1985 it paid dividends of $1.020 billion, which represented 44% of its net income.

Declaring Dividends

All dividends must be declared by the board of directors before they become a liability of the corporation. There are three dates that are significant to the declaration and payment of dividends. They are the declaration date, the date of record, and the payment date.

The **declaration date** is the date on which the board of directors declares the dividend. It is at that time that the dividend becomes a liability of the corporation and is recorded on its books. The declaration date is usually several weeks prior to the payment date. A typical dividend announcement may be:

The Board of Directors on December 1 declared a $1.20 per share dividend payable on January 4 to common shareholders of record on December 21.

Only the stockholders as of the **date of record** are eligible for the dividend. Because of the time involved in compiling the list of stockholders at any one date, the date of record usually is two to three weeks after the declaration date, but before the actual payment date.

The **payment date** is the date that the dividend is actually paid. It usually occurs about a month after the declaration date.

Journal Entries to Record Cash Dividends

To demonstrate the journal entries required when a cash dividend is declared and paid, we will return to the above example in which the board of directors declared on December 1 a $1.20 per-share dividend payable on January 4 to the common shareholders of record on December 21. Because there are 100,000 common shares outstanding, the total cash dividends will be $120,000.

Dec. 1	Declaration date		
	Retained Earnings	120,000	
	Dividends Payable		120,000
	To record declaration of $1.20 per-share dividend on 100,000 shares of outstanding common stock. Dividend is payable on January 4 to shareholders of record on December 21.		
Dec. 21	Date of record		
	No entry		
Jan. 4	Payment date		
	Dividends Payable	120,000	
	Cash		120,000
	To record payment of $1.20 per-share dividend declared on December 1.		

When recording the declaration of a dividend, some firms debit an account titled Dividends Declared, rather than debit Retained Earnings. There is nothing wrong with this procedure, except that a closing entry must be made to close the Dividends Declared account into Retained Earnings. As a result of this entry, the ultimate effect is to reduce retained earnings by the amount of the dividend.

Noncash Dividends

Occasionally a firm will issue a dividend in which the payment is in an asset other than cash. Noncash dividends, which are called property dividends, are more likely to occur in private corporations than in publicly held ones. Under current accounting pronouncements, the property is revalued to its current market value, and a gain or loss is recognized on the disposition of the asset.[12]

To illustrate, assume that the Ironside Corporation declared a property dividend on December 1 to be distributed on January 4. Marketable securities held by the firm that have a cost of $750,000 and a fair market value (FMV) of $1 million are to be distributed to the shareholders. The journal entries to reflect these transactions are:

Dec. 1	Date of declaration		
	Investment in Marketable Securities	250,000	
	Gain on Revaluation of Marketable Securities		250,000
	To record revaluation of marketable securities		
	FMV = $1,000,000		
	Cost 750,000		
	$ 250,000		
	Retained Earnings	1,000,000	
	Property Dividends Payable		1,000,000
	To record declaration of property dividend payable on January 4.		
Jan. 4	Distribution of property dividend		
	Property Dividends Payable	1,000,000	
	Investment in Marketable Securities		1,000,000
	To record distribution of property dividend.		

Stock Dividends

Many corporations issue stock dividends instead of, or in addition to, cash dividends. **A stock dividend** is a distribution to current shareholders on a proportional basis of the corporation's own stock. That is, the current holders of stock receive additional shares of stock in proportion to their current holdings. For example, if you own 10,000 shares of common stock in a corporation and it issues a 15% stock dividend, you will receive an additional 1,500 shares (15% $\times$ 10,000 = 1,500). Most stock dividends are given to common stockholders.

When investors receive a stock dividend, the cost per share of their original shares is reduced accordingly. For example, assume that an individual owns 1,000 shares of South Gulf Oil Company. These shares were purchased at $60 per share, for a total cost of $60,000. Subsequently, South Gulf issues a 20% stock dividend, and so the investor will receive an additional 200 shares (1,000 $\times$ .20). Therefore, the cost per share to the investor is reduced to $50 per share ($60,000 ÷ 1,200 shares), from the original $60 per share. Thus, no income is recognized on the stock dividends when they are received. The reduced cost per share will increase the gain or decrease the loss on subsequent sales of the stock.

Why Stock Dividends Are Issued

There are a number of reasons that a corporation may issue a stock dividend rather than a cash dividend. Clearly, a stock dividend conserves cash and

[12]American Institute of Certified Public Accountants, Accounting Principles Board, Opinion No. 29, *Accounting for Nonmonetary Transactions* (New York: AICPA, 1973), par. 18.

thus allows the firm to use its cash for growth and expansion. Corporations experiencing growth generally are more likely to issue a stock dividend than are stable, mature firms. In addition, stock dividends transfer a part of retained earnings to permanent capital. This is referred to as **capitalizing retained earnings** and makes that part of retained earnings transferred to permanent capital unavailable for future cash dividends.

Recording Stock Dividends

When a stock dividend is declared and issued, the corporation debits Retained Earnings for the total fair market value of the stock dividend. Assuming that the stock is immediately issued, the Common Stock account is credited for its par value, if any. Additional Paid-in Capital from the Issue of Common Stock in Excess of Par is credited for the difference between the market value and par value. If the stock has neither a par nor a stated value, Common Stock is credited for the entire market value.[13]

After all these entries have been made, total stockholders' equity remains the same, because there has not been a distribution of cash or other assets. The only difference is in the components of stockholders' equity. Retained earnings is decreased, and contributed capital is increased. As noted, this is often referred to as capitalizing retained earnings, because a portion of retained earnings becomes part of the firm's permanent invested capital. In effect, after the stock dividend, each individual shareholder owns the same proportionate share of the corporation as he or she did before.

To demonstrate the journal entries to record stock dividends, assume that the stockholders' equity section of the Korean Export Corporation immediately before the issue of a 10% stock dividend appears as follows:

Korean Export Corporation	
Stockholders' Equity	
Before Stock Dividend	
Common stock, $5 par value, 1,000,000 shares authorized, 60,000 shares issued and outstanding	$ 300,000
Paid-in capital from issue of common stock in excess of par	800,000
Retained earnings	1,900,000
Total stockholders' equity	$3,000,000

On November 30, 1987 the corporation issues a 10% stock dividend distributed immediately. At the time of the declaration, the stock is selling at $40 per share. As a result of the 10% dividend, a total of 6,000 shares (10% × 60,000 = 6,000) are issued. Based on these data, the following journal entry is made:

---

[13]In this example we assumed that the dividend was declared and issued at the same time. In reality, a period of time may elapse before the declared stock dividend is actually issued to the stockholders. Although this slightly changes the required journal entries, it does not change the effect of the dividend when either declared or issued.

Nov. 30, 1987	Retained Earnings	240,000	
	Common Stock		30,000
	Paid-In Capital from Issue of Common Stock		
	in Excess of Par		210,000

To record declaration of 10% stock dividend; 6,000 shares distributed. FMV of stock at time of declaration is $40 per share.

The stockholders' equity section of the Korean Export Corporation's balance sheet at November 30, immediately after the issuance of the stock dividend, appears as follows:

Korean Export Corporation
Stockholders' Equity
After Stock Dividend

Common stock, $5 par value, 1,000,000 shares authorized, 66,000 shares issued and outstanding	$ 330,000
Paid-in capital from issue of common stock in excess of par	1,010,000
Retained earnings	1,660,000
Total stockholders' equity	$3,000,000

The most important thing to note by comparing the stockholders' equity section in both balance sheets is that the total is $3 million in both cases. The only difference is the total of the various accounts within stockholders' equity.

Large versus Small Stock Dividends

Up to this point, we have been discussing small stock dividends, which range up to 20 or 25%. Occasionally a corporation will issue a large stock dividend. The accounting profession defines a large stock dividend as one in excess of 20 to 25%. Some stock dividends are as large as 100%, and these have the effect of proportionately reducing the market price of the corporation's stock. Large stock dividends are recorded by debiting Retained Earnings and crediting Common Stock for the total par value of the stock issued by the stock dividend. The market value of the stock is ignored.

Stock Splits

A **stock split** happens when a corporation increases the number of its common shares and proportionally decreases their par or stated value. The end result is a doubling, tripling, or quadrupling of the number of outstanding shares and a corresponding decrease in the market price per share of the stock. This price decrease is the main reason that a corporation decides to split its stock. When the market price per share is too high, the stock loses its attractiveness to many investors, because it is most economical to purchase stock in round lots of 100. A stock price that is too high makes round-lot purchases impossible for some potential investors. For example, if a firm's stock is currently selling for $240, and the firm splits its stock 4 for 1, the price

662

per share will fall to around $60. Thus, it takes only $6,000 rather than $24,000 to purchase 100 shares.

To demonstrate the accounting for stock splits, assume that the Moreno Corporation's stockholders' equity accounts are:

Moreno Corporation
Stockholders' Equity
Before Stock Split

Common stock, $15 par value, 1,000,000 shares authorized, 50,000 shares issued and outstanding	$ 750,000
Additional paid-in capital	1,450,000
Retained earnings	1,800,000
Total stockholders' equity	$4,000,000

The corporation's stock is currently selling at $90 per share. The firm decides to issue a 3-for-1 stock split. As a result, the corporation reduces the par value of its stock from $15 to $5 and increases the number of shares issued and outstanding from 50,000 to 150,000. Although no journal entry is required, some firms will make a memorandum entry noting the stock split. Immediately after the stock split, the Moreno Corporation's stockholders' equity accounts are:

Moreno Corporation
Stockholders' Equity
After Stock Split

Common stock, $5 par value, 3,000,000 shares authorized, 150,000 shares issued and outstanding	$ 750,000
Additional paid-in capital	1,450,000
Retained earnings	1,800,000
Total stockholders' equity	$4,000,000

As you can see by comparing the corporation's stockholders' equity accounts before and after the stock split, there is no change in either total stockholders' equity or the individual components. Only the par value and the number of issued and outstanding shares are different.

From the investor's viewpoint, each stockholder receives two additional shares for each share owned. In effect, the old shares are canceled and shares with the new par value are issued. Because the price of the firm's stock is likely to fall to about $30, the total market value of each stockholder's investment immediately after the split will be about the same as it was before the split.

Stock splits and large stock dividends are quite similar. They both serve to reduce the market price per share and increase the number of shares issued and outstanding. In each circumstance, total stockholders' equity remains the same because there has been neither an increase nor a decrease in the entity's net assets. For example, a 2-for-1 stock split is similar to a 100% stock dividend. In both cases, the number of shares issued and outstanding doubles, and the market price per share will fall accordingly. However, if this event is a stock dividend, there will be no change in the stock's par or stated value, but there will be a decrease in the Retained Earnings account and an increase in the Common Stock account. If this event is a stock split, there is no change in either Retained Earnings or Common Stock, just a decrease in par value and an increase in the number of issued and outstanding shares.

Stock dividends and stock splits affect the number of common shares issued and outstanding, which in turn affects the EPS calculation. The current year's EPS is calculated by using the number of common shares after any stock dividends and stock splits. This means that when comparative statements are issued, or 5- and 10-year summaries are presented, the number of common shares on which EPS is determined in these statements must be retroactively adjusted for these dividends or splits. This ensures that the EPS figures will be comparable.

AMP

These points regarding stock splits and EPS are illustrated in the following footnote taken from the AMP annual report:

> At the April 26, 1984 annual meeting, shareholders increased the number of authorized shares from 50,000,000 to 150,000,000 and approved a 3-for-1 stock split effective on a May 7, 1984 record date. The stated value of the no par stock was changed from \$.33⅓ per share to \$.11⅑ per share. All per share earnings and dividends and references to AMP common stock have been retroactively restated to reflect the increased number of AMP common shares outstanding.

Prior Period Adjustments, Appropriations, and Treasury Stock

To this point we have been discussing the two major events that affect retained earnings—net income or loss and dividends. There are three other events that can affect retained earnings—prior period adjustments, appropriations, and treasury stock transactions.

Prior Period Adjustments

Under the all-inclusive concept of income, with a few exceptions, all items of profit and loss recognized during the period are included in net income for the period. These exceptions mainly relate to **prior period adjustments** and are accounted for by an adjustment to the beginning balance of retained earnings. There has been considerable controversy, however, about what causes an event to qualify as a prior period adjustment. Only two events are considered prior period adjustments:

1. Correction of an error in the financial statements of a prior period.
2. Adjustments that result from realization of income tax benefits of pre-acquisition operating loss carryforwards of purchased subsidiaries.[14]

Because the realization of tax benefits is a specialized topic, we will examine only prior period adjustments that relate to error corrections.

Occasionally, a firm will discover a material error in a prior year's financial statements. Material errors are very rare, especially when a firm's financial statements are audited by a CPA firm. However, when they do occur and are discovered, the manner in which the error is corrected depends on whether the firm publishes single-year or comparative financial statements and on the year in which the error was made.

When single-year statements are published, the error is corrected by adjusting the beginning balance of retained earnings on the retained earnings statement. To demonstrate accounting for prior period adjustments in a single-year statement, we assume that during the audit of its 1987 statements, the Mondrian Corporation discovered that depreciation in 1986 had been understated by $100,000, net of tax. Because this is a material error, a prior period adjustment is required. The following journal entry is made at year-end to correct this error:

Dec. 31, 1987	Retained Earnings	100,000	
	Accumulated Depreciation—Building		100,000
	To record error in 1985 through a prior period adjustment.		

The 1987 statement of retained earnings would appear as follows:

Mondrian Corporation
Statement of Retained Earnings
For the Year Ended December 31, 1987

Retained earnings, January 1, 1987	$5,000,000	
Less: Prior period adjustment for error correction, net of tax	(100,000)	
Retained earnings, January 1, 1987, restated		4,900,000
Net income for 1987		650,000
Less: Dividends		(150,000)
Retained earnings, December 31, 1987		$5,400,000

In addition, the prior period adjustment is explained in the footnotes to the financial statement.

When comparative financial statements are presented, the procedure is different. If the error is in an earlier financial statement that is being presented for comparative purposes, that statement should be revised to correct the er-

[14]Financial Accounting Standards Board, Statement No. 16, *Prior Period Adjustments* (Stamford, Conn.: FASB, June 1977), par. 11.

ror. As a result, net income will be corrected, and after that corrected net income figure is reflected on the retained earnings statement, no further adjustment is required. If the error is in a year for which the financial statements are not being presented, the correction is made through a prior period adjustment to the earliest retained earnings balance presented.

Appropriation of Retained Earnings

An **appropriation of retained earnings** occurs when the board of directors transfers a portion of the Retained Earnings account into a separate Appropriated Retained Earnings account. The sole purpose of such a transfer is to indicate to stockholders and others that the balance in the Appropriated Retained Earnings account is not available for dividends. Thus, by appropriating retained earnings, the firm limits the amount of dividends it can declare.

The board may appropriate retained earnings in order to limit dividends voluntarily in the hope of conserving cash for projects such as the purchase of new buildings. In other cases, creditors may force the board to appropriate retained earnings and thus limit dividends. The creditors do so in the hope that the firm will not use its cash to pay dividends rather than make timely interest and principal payments.

In order to appropriate retained earnings, the firm debits Retained Earnings and credits Appropriated Retained Earnings. For example, if the Clayborn Corporation decides to appropriate retained earnings of $1 million for future plant expansion, out of a total of $7,435,000 in retained earnings, it will make the following entry:

Retained Earnings	1,000,000	
Appropriated Retained Earnings—Plant Expansion		1,000,000
To appropriate $1,000,000 of retained earnings for future plant expansion.		

Immediately after this entry, the stockholders' equity section of the Clayborn Corporation appears as on page 667. If the appropriation is no longer needed or required, the Retained Earnings account will be credited and Appropriated Retained Earnings will be debited.

These entries point out the problem with the appropriation of retained earnings and some of the confusion surrounding it. If you review the entry to appropriate retained earnings, you will see that no cash is involved. Thus, retained earnings can be appropriated each year, but there is no guarantee that the cash will be there for its intended use. Although the amount of dividends is limited by appropriating retained earnings, cash can still be used for other purposes. The only way to ensure the availability of cash is to create a special cash fund and to set aside a certain amount each year. To the extent that users believe that appropriated retained earnings ensure that cash in that amount is available, it is a misleading concept.

Because of these issues, corporations seldom appropriate retained earnings. Instead, voluntary or required dividend restrictions are disclosed in the footnotes to the financial statements. For example, the following footnote was in the financial statement of the Adams-Mills Corporation:

> The debt agreements contain provisions regarding working capital requirements, other borrowings, acquisitions, redemption of the Company's stock and dividends. Under these provisions, retained earnings of $29,788,000 at December 30, 1984, are restricted as to the payment of dividends.

Common stock, no par, 1,000,000 shares authorized, 500,000 shares issued and outstanding	$2,465,000
Unappropriated retained earnings	6,435,000
Appropriated retained earnings, future plant expansion	1,000,000
Total stockholders' equity	$9,900,000

Footnotes such as this accomplish the same purpose as does appropriating retained earnings, but they do not involve the misunderstandings that may result from appropriating retained earnings.

Treasury Stock

Treasury stock is the corporation's own capital stock, either common or preferred, that has been issued and subsequently reacquired by the firm, but not canceled. Such stock, held in the corporate treasury, loses its right to vote, receive dividends, or receive assets upon liquidation. In computing EPS, treasury stock is not considered outstanding and must be deducted when computing the weighted average number of shares outstanding.

There are a number of valid business reasons that a firm may reacquire its own capital stock. For example, a firm may need to acquire additional shares (1) for employee stock option or bonus plans, (2) for mergers and acquisitions, (3) in order to support the price of its stock, (4) to increase EPS, or (5) because the firm may believe the stock is a good investment at its current price.

Accounting for Treasury Stock

Treasury stock is not considered an asset; it is a reduction in stockholders' equity. A firm cannot record a profit on the subsequent sale of treasury stock. Any difference between the reacquisition price and the selling price is either an increase in paid-in capital if the shares sold at a gain, or a decrease in paid-in capital and/or retained earnings if the shares sold at a loss.

Recording the Purchase of Treasury Stock. To show how the purchase of treasury stock is recorded, assume that the stockholders' equity section at September 30, 1987 of the Linefsky Corporation is as shown on page 668.

On October 1 the corporation repurchased 1,000 shares of its common stock at $24 per share. This transaction is recorded by debiting the stockholders' equity account Treasury Stock and crediting Cash for the cost of the purchase as follows:

Oct. 1, 1987	Treasury Stock	24,000	
	Cash		24,000
	To record purchase of 1,000 shares of treasury stock at $24 per share.		

Linefsky Corporation
Stockholders' Equity
September 30, 1987

Common stock, $5 par value, 100,000 shares authorized, 10,000 shares issued and outstanding	$ 50,000
Additional paid-in capital from issue of common stock above par	150,000
Retained earnings	700,000
Total stockholders' equity	$900,000

Immediately after this purchase, the stockholders' equity section of the Linefsky Corporation appeared as follows:

Linefsky Corporation
Stockholders' Equity
October 1, 1986

Common stock, $5 par value, 100,000 shares authorized, 10,000 shares issued, of which 9,000 are outstanding	$ 50,000
Additional paid-in capital from sale of common stock above par	150,000
Retained earnings	700,000
Less 1,000 shares of treasury stock at cost	(24,000)
Total stockholders' equity	$876,000

As this partial balance sheet shows, treasury stock is not shown as an asset but as a negative item in stockholders' equity. The effect of the transaction is to reduce both assets and stockholders' equity by $24,000.

The corporation can sell its treasury stock any time that it desires. The subsequent resale can be either above or below its repurchase price. However, in no case is net income for the current period affected.

Recording Resale above Cost. When treasury stock is resold above its cost, Cash is debited for the entire proceeds; Treasury Stock is credited for the total cost of the shares sold, and the account Additional Paid-in Capital from the Sale of Treasury Stock above Cost is credited for the difference. The Additional Paid-in Capital account is credited for the economic gain because current accounting and tax rules do not allow a corporation to record a profit and thus to increase retained earnings by dealing in its own stock.

To demonstrate, now assume that on November 29, 1987, 500 shares of the treasury stock purchased at $24 per share were sold at $30 per share. To record this sale, the Linefsky Corporation made the following entry:

Nov. 29, 1987	Cash	15,000	
	Treasury Stock		12,000
	Paid-in Capital from Sale of Treasury Stock above Cost		3,000
	To record sale of treasury stock. Cost of treasury stock, $12,000 = 500 × $24.		

Recording Resale below Cost. If treasury stock is resold below cost, there will be an economic loss. This loss does not affect the current period's income but reduces the credit balance in the paid-in capital account that resulted from other treasury stock transactions. If there are no previous treasury stock transactions or if the balance in this paid-in capital account is not large enough to cover the loss or if there is no other Paid-in Capital account from the same class of stock, Retained Earnings is debited.

To illustrate, now assume that the remaining 500 shares of treasury stock were resold on December 24 at $15 per share. The following journal entry is made to record this sale:

Dec. 24, 1987	Cash	7,500	
	Paid-in Capital from Sale of Treasury Stock above Cost	3,000	
	Paid-in Capital from Sale of Common Stock above Par	1,500	
	Treasury Stock		12,000
	To record sale of 500 shares of treasury stock at $15 per share.		

In this case, Paid-in Capital from Sale of Treasury Stock above Cost is debited for only $3,000, the balance in this account that resulted from the previous resale. The remaining $1,500 difference of the $4,500 economic loss is charged to Paid-in Capital from Sale of Common Stock above Par. If there had not been a credit balance in this paid-in capital account, the difference would have been debited to Retained Earnings.

Restrictions of Retained Earnings and Treasury Stock

Like cash dividends, treasury stock purchases return cash to stockholders. The essential difference between dividends and treasury stock is that all shareholders receive cash when dividends are issued, but only the stockholders who resell the stock to the corporation receive cash from treasury stock transactions. Thus, one way the corporation can avoid dividend restrictions is to purchase treasury stock. As a result, when creditors require restrictions on dividend payments, they also often require restrictions on treasury stock purchases. If you review the footnote from the Adams-Mills Corporation on page 656, you will see that the restriction includes both dividends and treasury stock transactions.

Retirement of Capital Stock

Occasionally, a corporation may repurchase its stock with the intent to retire it rather than to hold it in the treasury. Essentially, a corporation retires its stock for some of the same reasons that it purchases treasury stock. Like treasury stock transactions, income or loss for the current period is not affected, nor are retained earnings increased when capital stock is retired.

Accounting for stock retirements depends on the original issue price and the price that must be paid to retire it. For example, assume that the Kishi Corporation issued 10,000 shares of $10 par value common stock at $25 per share and made the following entry to record this issue:

Cash	250,000	
Common Stock		100,000
Paid-in Capital from Issue of Common Stock		
in Excess of Par		150,000
To record issue of common stock.		

Several years later, the firm repurchased and retired 1,000 shares of its stock at a price of (1) $25 per share, (2) $20 per share, and (3) $30 per share. The journal entries to record each of these three independent cases are:

Case 1—Repurchase price, $25 per share

Common Stock	10,000	
Paid-in Capital from Issue of Common Stock in Excess of Par	15,000	
Cash		25,000

To record retirement of 1,000 shares of $10 par value stock originally issued at $25 per share and retired at $25 per share.

Case 2—Repurchase price, $20 per share

Common Stock	10,000	
Paid-in Capital from Issue of Common Stock in Excess of Par	15,000	
Paid-in Capital from Retirement of Common Stock		5,000
Cash		20,000

To record retirement of 1,000 shares of $10 par value stock originally issued at $25 per share and retired at $20 per share.

Case 3—Repurchase price, $30 per share

Common Stock	10,000	
Paid-in Capital from Issue of Common Stock in Excess of Par	15,000	
Retained Earnings	5,000	
Cash		30,000

To record retirement of 1,000 shares of $10 par value common stock originally issued at $25 per share and retired at $30 per share.

In each case, both the Common Stock account and the Paid-in Capital from Issue of Common Stock in Excess of Par account are debited for the amounts per share for which they were originally credited. In the first case, when the retirement price is equal to the original issue price, the only remaining entry is a credit to Cash. In the second case, when the stock is retired at a price below its original issue price, Paid-in Capital from the Retirement of Common Stock is credited. In the third case, when the stock is retired at a price above its original issue price, Retained Earnings is debited for the difference.

Statement of Stockholders' Equity

In today's corporate environment, many corporations enter into complex transactions that directly affect stockholders' equity. A simple statement of retained earnings does not adequately disclose all of the information needed by financial statement users. As a result, many corporations are substituting a broader statement, called a statement of stockholders' equity, which presents the changes that affected all of the stockholders' equity accounts. If this statement is not presented as a fourth financial statement, information regarding changes in stockholders' equity accounts can be found in the footnotes to the financial statements. An example of a statement of stockholders' (shareholders') equity is shown next.

Triad Systems Corporation
Consolidated Statements of Shareholders' Equity
For the Years Ended September 30, 1985, 1984 and 1983
(Amounts in thousands)

	Common Stock	Retained Earnings	Translation Adjustments	Total
Balances, September 30, 1982	$34,361	$23,058	$ 28	$57,447
Issuance of common stock:				
Nonqualilfied stock option plan	88	—	—	88
Stock purchase plan	901	—	—	901
Income tax benefits resulting from exercises				
of nonqualified stock options	7	—	—	7
Collection of notes receivable	8	—	—	8
Translation adjustments	—	—	39	39
Net income	—	2,142	—	2,142
Balances, September 30, 1983	35,365	25,200	67	60,632
Issuance of common stock:				
Nonqualified stock option plan	11	—	—	11
Stock purchase plan	724	—	—	724
Collection of notes receivable	8	—	—	8
Translation adjustments	—	—	69	69
Net income	—	4,807	—	4,807
Balances, September 30, 1984	36,108	30,007	136	66,251
Issuance of common stock:				
Stock purchase plan	836	—	—	836
Collection of notes receivable	20	—	—	20
Translation adjustments	—	—	136	136
Net loss	—	(5,507)	—	(5,507)
Balances, September 30, 1985	$36,964	$24,500	$272	$61,736

Summary of Learning Objectives

1. *Construction of the corporate income statement.* Large businesses generally earn income and incur expenses from a variety of sources. Because financial statement users want to use the income statement to make predictions about future income flows, the various income sources must be segregated. There may be up to four separate categories on the income statement: (1) income from continuing operations, (2) discontinued operations, (3) extraordinary items, and (4) cumulative effect of a change in accounting principles. Intraperiod income allocation requires that the income tax expense that relates to each of the categories be allocated to it.

2. *Calculation, use, and limitations of EPS.* Earnings per share is one of the most widely used of the financial statistics. In simple situations, EPS is calculated by the following formula:

$$\frac{\text{Net income available to common shareholders}}{\text{Weighted average number of common shares outstanding}}$$

Firms that have complex capital structures generally must make a dual presentation of EPS that discloses both primary and fully diluted EPS. The primary EPS calculation includes only common stock equivalents, whereas the fully diluted EPS calculation includes all dilutive securities.

3. *Corporate dividends.* The amount and type of dividend to issue is a financial decision made by a corporation's board of directors. Firms attempt to establish a stable dividend policy. Although most firms issue cash dividends, they can also declare stock and property dividends.

4. *Stock splits and their relationship to stock dividends.* Stock splits are used by firms to decrease the price of their stock in order to make round-lot purchases more attractive to investors. Neither stock dividends nor stock splits change the firm's total net assets or total stockholders' equity. Stock dividends do, however, change the balances in Retained Earnings and Common Stock and possibly Additional Paid-in Capital.

5. *Prior period adjustments and appropriation of retained earnings.* In recent years the accounting profession has limited the items that qualify as prior period adjustments. Under current pronouncements, only error corrections and certain tax benefits qualify. Prior period adjustments are generally handled by adjusting the beginning balance of retained earnings on the retained earnings statement.

   The appropriation of retained earnings is either voluntary or required in order to restrict dividend payments. However, the balance in the Appropriated Earnings account does not imply that an equal amount of cash is available. Instead of appropriating retained earnings, most firms just disclose dividends and/or other restrictions in the footnotes to the financial statements.

6. *Accounting for treasury stock transactions.* A firm may repurchase its own stock for a number of reasons. This stock is called treasury stock. These transactions result neither in an asset nor affect the current period's income. Any economic gain on the subsequent resale of treasury stock is credited to Additional Paid-in Capital, and any economic loss is debited to Additional Paid-in Capital and/or Retained Earnings.

7. *Retirement of capital stock.* Occasionally a firm will repurchase and then retire its capital stock. When this occurs, the Capital Stock and Additional Paid-in Capital accounts, if any, are debited for the original amounts per share for which they were credited. If the stock is retired at a price below its original purchase price, Additional Paid-in Capital is credited. Conversely, if the stock is retired at a price above its original issue price, Retained Earnings is debited.

8. *Purpose of the statement of stockholders' equity.* Because of the importance and complexity of transactions that affect stockholders' equity, many firms are replacing the retained earnings statement with a more comprehensive statement called a statement of stockholders' equity, which summarizes all of the items that have changed the stockholders' equity accounts.

Appendix: Accounting for Corporate Income Taxes

At various points in this book we have pointed out differences between generally accepted accounting principles (GAAP) and the provisions of the Internal Revenue Code (IRC). These differences result from the varying objectives of GAAP and the IRC. The objectives of GAAP are aimed at providing investors and other users of financial statements with reliable and relevant financial information. The objectives of the tax law contained in the IRC include social equity, ease of administration, political considerations, and ensuring that individuals and corporations are taxed when they have the ability to pay. Furthermore, there are many cases when the management of a firm will use one accounting method, such as straight-line depreciation, for accounting purposes and another method, such as ACRS-based depreciation, for tax purposes. Thus, often a prudent management will select accounting methods allowed by the IRC that will minimize the firm's taxable income and thus reduce its cash outflow due to taxes. On the other hand, the same management may select a different set of accounting principles for financial reporting purposes. This Appendix discusses the accounting that arises when different accounting methods are used for financial and tax reporting. Appendix B, at the end of the book, discusses current provisions of the IRC.

Sources of Differences between Accounting and Taxable Income

Differences between accounting income and taxable income can be classified into permanent and timing differences. *Permanent differences* enter into the determination of accounting income but never into the determination of taxable income or vice versa. They are, in effect, statutory differences between GAAP and the IRC. An example of a permanent difference is interest on state and local bonds. Although interest on these items represents revenue from an accounting perspective, it is not included in taxable income in either the year received or the year earned. Congress did this in order to make it easier for states and local governments to raise revenues by making the interest on their obligations nontaxable. Because these differences are indeed permanent, we are not concerned with them.

Timing differences are the other reason that accounting income in any year may be different from taxable income. Timing differences result from the fact that some transactions affect taxable income in a different period from when they affect pretax accounting income. However, over the life of a particular transaction, the amount of income or expense for accounting and tax purposes is the same; it is just that it is different within the various periods.

An example of a timing difference is the use of straight-line depreciation based on the asset's economic life for financial reporting purposes and the use of ACRS depreciation for tax purposes. Generally, in the first few years of the asset's life, ACRS depreciation exceeds straight-line depreciation, and pretax accounting income is reduced less than taxable income as the result of depreciation expense. However, in later years the timing difference reverses. Straight-line depreciation now exceeds ACRS depreciation, causing a greater reduction in accounting income than in taxable income as the result of differences in depreciation expense.

To illustrate, assume that a firm purchased a light truck in the beginning of 1986 for $10,000 and decided to use straight-line depreciation for accounting purposes, with a 5-year life and no salvage value. The firm takes an entire year's depreciation in the first year so that annual depreciation is $2,000, or $10,000 ÷ 5 years. For tax purposes, the asset has a 3-year class life, and under ACRS the depreciation percentages are 25% in the first year, 38% in the second year, and 37% in the third year.[15] The following table compares the annual and total depreciation under each method:

| Method | Years | | | | | Total |
	1986	1987	1988	1989	1990	
Straight-line	$2,000	$2,000	$2,000	$2,000	$2,000	$10,000
ACRS	2,500	3,800	3,700	0	0	10,000
Difference	($ 500)	($1,800)	($1,700)	$2,000	$2,000	$ 0

As this table shows, over the life of the asset, in both cases the total depreciation is $10,000. In the first three years, ACRS depreciation exceeds straight-line depreciation, but in the last two years, straight-line depreciation exceeds ACRS depreciation, which has been reduced to zero.

There are several other timing differences between taxable income and accounting income. Some of the more important ones are summarized below. You should remember two points. Timing differences affect two or more periods: the period in which the timing difference originates and the later periods when it turns around or reverses. However, over the life of a single transaction, the amount of accounting and taxable income or expense related to that transaction will be the same. It is just a question of when timing differences affect accounting and taxable income.

SUMMARY OF TIMING DIFFERENCES		
Transaction	Accounting Method	Tax Method
Rent received in advance	Recognized when earned	Recognized when cash received
Installment sales	Recognized at point of sale	Installment basis; income recognized as cash collected
Construction contracts	Percentage-of-completion	Completed contract
Inventories	FIFO	Average cost
Depreciation	Straight-line	ACRS

The Need for Income Tax Allocation

The liability, income taxes payable, is based on taxable income. This is the amount a firm will have to pay the federal government as the result of its operations, as defined by the IRC. The question is, IF the firm's pretax accounting income is different from its taxable income because of timing differences,

---

[15]See Chapter 12 for a discussion of ACRS depreciation.

what should be the amount of its tax expense? That is, should it be based on the firm's pretax accounting income or on its taxable income?

The accounting profession feels that a firm's tax expense should not be based on its taxable income. Rather, the matching principle requires that the tax expense for the period be based on accounting income before taxes. In order to do this, current accounting practice requires the use of interperiod income tax allocation.[16] The purpose of interperiod income tax allocation is to allocate the income tax expense to the periods in which revenues are earned and in which expenses are incurred. Thus, when tax expense is based on pretax accounting income rather than on taxable income, all applicable taxes are allocated against the income for the period, regardless of when the taxes are actually paid. This concept is no different from accruing a liability for wages in the current period as they are incurred, although the wages are not paid until the next period.

To demonstrate the application of interperiod income tax allocation, assume that the Price Corporation uses the same accounting principles for financial reporting purposes as it does for tax purposes, except for depreciation methods. For financial reporting purposes the firm uses straight-line depreciation, and for tax purposes it uses ACRS. At the beginning of 1986, the firm purchased the light truck described on page 674. As we noted, the truck has a five-year life for accounting purposes and falls into the three-year class life for ACRS purposes. The annual depreciation under each method is also calculated on page 674. The required calculations necessary to compute tax expense and taxes payable are shown below.

Price Corporation
Determination of Tax Expense and Tax Payable
Year

	1986	1987	1988	1989	1990	Total
Accounting income before depreciation and taxes	$10,000	$11,000	$14,000	$16,000	$20,000	$71,000
Depreciation expense— straight-line	(2,000)	(2,000)	(2,000)	(2,000)	(2,000)	(10,000)
Income before taxes	8,000	9,000	12,000	14,000	18,000	61,000
Tax expense—40%	(3,200)	(3,600)	(4,800)	(5,600)	(7,200)	(24,400)
Net income	$ 4,800	$ 5,400	$ 7,200	$ 8,400	$10,800	$36,600
Taxable income before depreciation and taxes	$10,000	$11,000	$14,000	$16,000	$20,000	$71,000
Depreciation—ACRS	(2,500)	(3,800)	(3,700)	–0–	–0–	(10,000)
Taxable income	7,500	7,200	10,300	16,000	20,000	61,000
Tax payable—40%	(3,000)	(2,880)	(4,120)	(6,400)	(8,000)	(24,400)
Income after taxes	$ 4,500	$ 4,320	$ 6,180	$ 9,600	$12,000	$36,600

[16]American Institute of Certified Public Accountants, Accounting Principles Board, Opinion No. 11, *Accounting for Income Taxes* (New York: AICPA, 1967).

The top part of the table shows how the annual tax expense is calculated. Income before taxes is based on straight-line depreciation of $2,000 per year. Given a constant tax rate of 40%, income tax expense ranges from $3,200 in 1986 to $7,200 in 1990. The bottom part of the table indicates how taxes payable are calculated each year. In this case, taxable income is based on ACRS depreciation. Because the truck falls into the three-year class life, all depreciation is taken in the first three years of the asset's life. Income tax payable ranges from $3,000 in 1986 to $8,000 in 1990.

It is important to note that total depreciation expense, total taxes, and total net income over the five-year period are the same in both cases. The total depreciation in both cases is $10,000; it is just being allocated differently among the 5 years. This is typical of a single-asset case in which salvage values are ignored and the asset is held for its entire life.

Journal Entries to Record Income Tax Expense

The journal entries to record the income tax expense and the related payable are:

	1986		1987		1988		1989		1990	
Tax Expense	3,200		3,600		4,800		5,600		7,200	
Deferred Income Tax		200		720		680	800		800	
Income Tax Payable		3,000		2,880		4,120		6,400		8,000

As these entries show, the expense in all periods is based on pretax accounting income, whereas the payable is based on taxable income. In 1986, the difference of $200 is a credit to the Deferred Income Tax account. At this point the account is called a deferred tax credit. If the Deferred Income Tax account has a debit balance at the end of any accounting period, it is called a deferred tax charge. Similar entries are made in 1987 and 1988, both of which increase the credit balance in the Deferred Income Tax account. Because the timing difference reverses in 1989 and 1990, the Tax Payable is greater than the Tax Expense account. The Deferred Income Tax account therefore is debited for $800 in each year. In this case, the timing difference completely reverses by the end of 1990, so that by the end of that year the balance in the Deferred Income Tax account is zero. This point is shown in the following Deferred Income Tax T account:

Deferred Income Tax

12/31/89	800	12/31/86	200
12/31/90	800	12/31/87	720
		12/31/88	680
Bal.	0		

When the Deferred Income Tax account has a credit balance, it is shown on the liability section of the balance as a deferred tax credit. On the other hand, if the Deferred Income Tax account has a debit balance, it is shown on the asset side of the balance sheet as a deferred tax charge. A related question is whether the Deferred Income Tax account should be shown as a current or a noncurrent asset liability. The FASB decided that the classification of the deferred charge or credit depends on the asset or liability that gave rise to it. Thus, if the timing difference is related to a current asset such as inventory, the resulting deferred income tax charge or credit should be classified as current. On the other hand, if the timing difference is related to a noncurrent asset such as equipment, the resulting deferred income tax charge or credit should be classified as noncurrent.

The Controversy Surrounding Interperiod Income Tax Allocation

There is still much controversy surrounding interperiod income tax allocation. Many research studies have shown that deferred tax credits have increased over the years and, for many firms, represent a large item in the liability section of their balance sheets. The primary reasons for this are the current use of ACRS depreciation and, before that, the use of accelerated depreciation methods for tax purposes. A company with a relatively stable or growing investment in depreciable assets that uses straight-line depreciation in determining pretax accounting income but uses ACRS in determining taxable income will be likely to have an increasing credit balance in its Deferred Income Tax account. This is so because the continued investment in higher-priced assets indefinitely postpones the total reversal of the timing difference, even though differences due to individual assets completely reverse. That is, as the effect of ACRS depreciation reverses on assets purchased in earlier years, it is offset by the effect of higher-priced assets purchased in the current year. If this is the case, then the deferred tax credits may not meet the definition of a liability. Remember that a liability is defined as a probable future sacrifice of economic benefits. However, if the deferred tax credit is not reduced because the timing difference does not turn around, then the future sacrifice of cash, due to higher income taxes payable, will never take place.

The controversy surrounding interperiod income tax allocation has not been settled. The FASB decided to review the issues regarding income tax allocation and in late 1983 issued a Discussion Memorandum on the subject. Since then, public hearings have been held, and the FASB has issued an exposure draft. The FASB expects to issue a new statement in late 1987. It appears, that some changes will be made in the way deferred taxes are calculated. However, the basic concepts will remain the same.

Key Terms

Appropriation of Retained Earnings	Date of Record	Intraperiod Income Tax Allocation
Capitalizing Retained Earnings	Declaration Date	Payment Date
	Earnings per Share (EPS)	Primary Earnings per Share
Change in Accounting Estimate	Extraordinary Items	Prior Period Adjustments
	Fully Diluted EPS	
Change in Accounting Method	Income from Continuing Operations	Segment
Common Stock Equivalent		Stock Dividend
Complex Capital Structure	Interperiod Income Tax Allocation	Stock Split
		Treasury Stock

Problem for Your Review

Corporate Income Statements. As the treasurer of the Gernon Airline Corporation, you have been asked to prepare the firm's 1987 income statement and retained earnings statement. Your assistant has provided you with the following data:

1. Income before taxes, $5 million.
2. Included in the above figure are the following items:
   a. One of the firm's planes crashed. No one was hurt, and the crash resulted in a $500,000 gain from the insurance proceeds.
   b. One of the planes was struck by lightning at an airport in southern California. Lightning very rarely occurs in this area, and the firm suffered a $400,000 loss.
   c. The corporation had been incurring substantial losses in its catering business. It therefore sold that part of the business and now operates only the airline. Losses from operation totaled $600,000 for 1987, and there was a gain of $100,000 on disposal of the segment.
   d. All amounts are before taxes, which are currently 40% on all transactions.
3. Retained earnings at the beginning of 1986 equaled $18 million. The firm had 100,000 shares of $5 par value common stock outstanding and issued the following dividends:
   a. April 15, 1987—10% stock dividend. At the time of the stock dividend, the price per share was $20.
   b. December 15, 1987—$1 per-share cash dividend declared.

Required:

1. Prepare an income statement for 1987; begin with income from continuing operations before taxes. Ignore earnings per share.
2. Prepare a statement of retained earnings for 1987.

Solution

1.

Gernon Airline Corporation
Partial Income Statement
For the Year Ended December 31, 1987

Income from continuing operations, before taxes		$5,900,000
Provision for taxes		2,360,000
Income from continuing operations		3,540,000
Discontinued operations		
Loss from operations, net of tax savings of $240,000	($360,000)	
Gain on disposal of segment, net of taxes of $40,000	60,000	(300,000)
Income before extraordinary items		3,240,000
Extraordinary items—Loss on destruction of airplane, net of tax savings of $160,000		(240,000)
Net income		$3,000,000

Notes:

1. Catering business is treated as a discontinued operation.
2. Plane crash does not meet criteria of extraordinary—not unusual or infrequent in airline business.
3. Plane destroyed by lightning is extraordinary because unusual and infrequent, given the environment.

4. Income from continuing operations =

Income before taxes (as given)	$5,000,000
Plus: Loss on operations of discontinued segment	600,000
Loss on destruction of airplane	400,000
Less: Gain on disposal of segment	(100,000)
	$5,900,000

Proof:	
Income before taxes	$5,000,000
Less total taxes (40% × 5,000,000)	2,000,000
Net income	$3,000,000

2.

Gernon Airline Corporation
Statement of Retained Earnings
For the Year Ended December 31, 1987

Retained earnings, beginning balance		$18,000,000
Add: Net income for the year		3,000,000
Less: Stock dividends[a]	$200,000	
Cash dividend[b]	110,000	(310,000)
Retained earnings, ending balance		$20,690,000

[a]100,000 × 10% = 10,000 shares
× $20 per share
$200,000

[b]100,000 × 110% = 110,000 shares
× $1 per share dividend
$110,000

Questions

1. What is the statement of retained earnings, and what items are likely to affect the balance in the Retained Earnings account?

2. Describe the major components of a corporate income statement. Are they all likely to be found on a single-year income statement? Why is it necessary to distinguish among these components?

3. What items are included in the category *loss from continuing operations,* and what is the significance of this figure?

4. One of your fellow students stated that income tax expense was income tax expense, and he did not understand the need to go to all the trouble to apply intraperiod income tax allocation. How would you respond?

5. On the income statement of the Jigs Corporation you noticed the following item:

Extraordinary item—Loss on early extinguishment
of debt, net of tax savings of $25,000 $50,000

Explain the concept of a tax savings. What is the amount of the loss before the tax savings?

6. What constitutes a segment for purposes of disclosing a discontinued operation? Explain how the operations and the gain or loss on the disposition of a discontinued operation must be disclosed on the income statement.

7. What are the criteria for determining whether an item should be classified as extraordinary? Why do you think that the environment in which the entity operates must be considered?

8. Recently an airplane of a large airline slid off the runway. Although no one was seriously injured, the plane was completely destroyed. The airline received insurance proceeds in excess of the book value of the airplane. How should this item be classified on the income statement? Why?

9. Recently the IAC Corporation changed the way it calculates its bad debts expense, from the percentage-of-sales method to the aging method. What type of

accounting change is this, and how should it be disclosed on the income statement? How would your answer differ if the firm had remained on the percentage-of-sales method but changed the percentage from 2% of net credit sales to 3% of net credit sales?

10. Two years ago the Peters Corporation purchased a new machine for $100,000. The machine had a 10-year useful life and no salvage value. At the beginning of the third year, the firm changed from the double-declining-balance method of depreciation to the straight-line method. Determine the amount of depreciation for the third year, and show how this change should be disclosed on the income statement for the third year. Assume a tax rate of 40%.

11. Earnings per share is one of the most looked-at of all the financial statistics. Describe earnings per share. Why do you think so many financial statement users attach such importance to it?

12. What are the basic components that go into the earnings-per-share calculation? How are they affected by additional issues of common stock during the year?

13. What is the essential difference between primary and fully diluted earnings per share? Under what circumstances is it necessary to disclose both, and what is the purpose of this dual disclosure?

14. What is a complex capital structure, and what is its importance in the calculation of earnings per share?

15. Describe common stock equivalents. How do they affect the calculation of primary and fully diluted earnings per share?

16. A famous stock market adviser suggests that all of his clients make their stock purchase and sales decisions solely on whether a stock EPS is increasing or decreasing. Do you think that is good advice? Why or why not?

17. What significance does each of the following dates have to the declaration and payment of cash dividends?
   a. Declaration date.
   b. Date of record.
   c. Payment date.

18. What is a stock dividend? What are the benefits of stock dividends, if any, to the issuing corporation and the existing stockholders?

19. After a stock dividend is issued, what changes occur in total stockholders' equity and within the individual components of stockholders' equity?

20. You overheard a friend of yours saying that stock dividends and stock splits are essentially the same. Do you agree or disagree? Why or why not?

21. What items are currently considered prior period adjustments, and how are they accounted for?

22. What does the appropriation of retained earnings accomplish?

23. The purchase of treasury stock is recorded by a debit to the Treasury Stock account and a credit to Cash. Treasury stock is shown as an asset on the balance sheet. Comment on these statements.

24. Why does a firm purchase its own stock? Once the purchase is made and the stock is resold, how is the economic gain or loss on the transaction, if any, recorded?

25. What is a statement of stockholders' equity, and how does it differ from a statement of retained earnings?

The following questions relate to material in the Appendix:

26. In your opinion, what is the primary objective of determining pretax accounting income according to GAAP? How does this objective differ from the objectives of determining taxable income as defined by the IRC?

27. What are timing differences, and how do they relate to interperiod income tax allocation?

28. There are several instances when the management of a firm can use one accounting method in determining pretax accounting income and a different method in computing taxable income. Give four examples.

29. The books of the Bowmant Co. for the year ended December 31, 1987 showed pretax income of $200,000. In computing taxable income for federal tax purposes, Bowmant deducted $10,000 of depreciation in excess of depreciation recorded on the books. Assuming the current tax rate is 40%, make the entry to record the tax expense and the taxes payable.

Exercises

1. Corporate Income Statements. The controller of Moreno Technical Systems gave you the following information for the year ended December 31, 1987:

Sales	$4,000,000
Cost of goods sold	2,800,000
Selling expenses	500,000
General and administrative expenses	200,000

Income from discontinued operations	100,000
Loss on disposal of discontinued operations	40,000
Extraordinary loss from earthquake damage	70,000
Tax rate on all items	30%

Prepare in good form the income statement for the year ended December 31, 1987.

2. Extraordinary Items. During a very eventful year, the following events happened to the Bacuall Corporation:

a. The first hurricane in 100 years occurred in the area where the corporation's headquarters was located, and its headquarters building was completely destroyed.

b. The company recorded a loss on the abandonment of some equipment formerly used in the business.

c. Uncollectible accounts of $20,000 were written off during the year.

d. One of the company's major employee unions went on strike, and the firm was shut down for several weeks. Management estimates that profits of $500,000 were lost.

Required:
Which of the above items should be classified as extraordinary, and why?

3. Change in Accounting Methods. Air North is a small commuter airline. At the beginning of the current year, 1987, it made the following accounting changes:

a. The firm decided to change the method of depreciation on one of its newer airplanes. The plane was purchased at the beginning of 1985 at a price of $2 million. The plane has a useful life of 10 years and no salvage value. The firm had been using double-declining-balance depreciation but now has decided to change to straight-line.

b. The firm decided to change the remaining life of one of its older aircraft. The plane was purchased at the beginning of 1983 at a cost of $1 million. At that time the firm estimated that the aircraft would have a useful life of 20 years and no salvage value. At the beginning of 1987, the firm estimated that the aircraft would have a remaining useful life of only 10 years. However, the firm estimated the plane would now have a salvage value of $10,000. Straight-line depreciation has always been used on this particular aircraft.

Required:
Assuming these are the only depreciable items, determine the amount of depreciation expense for 1987 and the cumulative effect of the change in accounting principle. Ignore taxes.

4. Earnings per Share. At the beginning of the current year, the Batitta Corporation had 120,000 shares of common stock outstanding. During the year, the following stock transactions occurred:

- March 1: 30,000 additional common shares were issued.

- July 1: 60,000 additional common shares were issued.

- November 1: 30,000 common shares were repurchased and held in the treasury for the rest of the year.

- December 1: The firm issued 10,000 shares of nonconvertible preferred stock. This was the first issue of preferred stock.

Net income during the year amounted to $650,000. The firm issued preferred dividends of $20,000 and common dividends of $40,000.

Required:
Determine the weighted average number of common shares outstanding and the earnings per share for the year.

5. Earnings per Share. At the beginning of the current year, 1987, the Totita Corporation had 450,000 common shares outstanding. On April 1, 1987 the company issued an additional 200,000 common shares of stock for cash. All 650,000 shares were outstanding on December 31, 1987.

At the beginning of 1987, Totita issued 5,000 shares of 8%, $100 par value convertible preferred stock at par. Each share of preferred stock is convertible into eight shares of common. As of the end of the year, none of the preferred stock had been converted. Net income during the year amounted to $1.2 million.

Required:

    a. Assuming the preferred stock is a common stock equivalent, calculate earnings per share for 1987.

    b. Assuming the preferred stock is not a common stock equivalent, calculate (1) primary earnings per share and (2) fully diluted earnings per share.

6. Cash Dividends. Informatics has 100,000 shares of $5 par value common stock outstanding and 50,000 shares of 5%, $100 par value preferred stock outstanding. During December the board of directors made the following dividend declarations:

    On December 1 the board of directors declared that the preferred dividend would be paid on January 4 to preferred shareholders of record on December 25.

    On December 10 the board of directors declared a $2 per-share dividend payable on January 4 to common shareholders of record on December 25.

Required:

    a. Make all the necessary entries related to the declaration and payment of the preferred dividends.

    b. Make all the necessary entries related to the declaration and payment of the common dividends.

7. Property Dividends. The Klinger Company is a closely held family corporation. On December 10, 1987 the board of directors decided to declare a property dividend. The dividend was to consist of a plot of land held by the corporation. The land was purchased several years ago at a cost of $140,000. Recently, the land was appraised at $250,000. On January 2, 1988 title to the land was transferred to the Klinger Family Trust.

Required:

Make the entries to record the property dividend.

8. Stock Dividends. The Mister Mo Mart has 100,000 shares of $5 par value common stock outstanding. Although the company has been profitable, it has decided to issue stock dividends instead of cash dividends in order to conserve cash for future expansion. On December 10, when the common stock was selling at $25 per share, the board of directors declared a 5% stock dividend to be distributed immediately.

Required:

    a. Make the entries to record the stock dividend.

    b. Assume that you own 100 shares of Mister Mo stock that you purchased at $12 per share. How would the stock dividend affect your investment, and how would you account for it?

    c. Independent of (a) and (b), now assume that Mister Mo declared a 30% stock dividend instead of the 5% dividend. Make the necessary entry to record the stock dividend.

9. Stock Dividends and Stock Splits. On December 31, 1987, the stockholders' equity section of the Price-Aker Corporation appeared as follows:

Price-Aker Corporation
Partial Balance Sheet
December 31, 1987

Stockholders' equity	
Common stock, no par $10 stated value, 500,000 shares authorized, 200,000 shares issued and outstanding	$2,000,000
Paid-in capital from issue of common stock in excess of par	1,000,000
Retained earnings	5,000,000
Total stockholders' equity	$8,000,000

Required:

   a. Assume that on January 2, 1988 the board of directors declared and issued a 10% stock dividend. At that time the stock was selling at $25 per share. Prepare the stockholders' equity section of the balance sheet after the declaration.

   b. Now assume that instead of issuing a stock dividend, the board of directors declared a 2-for-1 stock split on January 2. Prepare the stockholders' equity section of the balance sheet after the stock split.

10. Prior Period Adjustments. At the beginning of 1987 Newtonian Incorporated's retained earnings balance was $500,000. During the year the firm's net income amounted to $100,000, and dividends of $30,000 were paid. During the preparation of the 1987 financial statements, it was discovered that a piece of equipment that had been purchased at the beginning of 1986 at a cost of $50,000 had been entirely expensed in that year. Management feels the equipment has a five-year life and should be depreciated on the straight-line basis with no salvage value.

Required:

   a. Assuming that the current year's books have not been closed and that reported income of $100,000 does not reflect the depreciation on the equipment, make the necessary entries to correct the error. Ignore taxes.

   b. If single-year statements are published, prepare the retained earnings statement for 1987, based on the corrections made in (a).

   c. If comparative 1987 and 1986 statements were prepared, explain how you would handle the error correction. Do not actually prepare new statements.

11. Appropriation of Retained Earnings. The Oops Chemical Corporation has been producing an insect spray for a number of years. Recently it has discovered that this spray is very dangerous, and the company has been sued over the illness of a number of individuals. The board of directors, on December 31, 1987, decided to appropriate retained earnings in the amount of $50 million to cover future lawsuits. Just before the appropriation, the firm had 100,000 shares of no par, no stated value common stock outstanding that had been issued at an average price of $15 per share. In addition, total retained earnings at that time amounted to $120 million. Several years later, when all the lawsuits had been settled (the ultimate cost to the company was $47 million), the appropriation was removed by the Board.

Required:

   a. Make the entry to record the appropriation.

   b. Prepare the stockholders' equity section of the balance sheet immediately after the appropriation.

   c. Make the journal entry to record the removal of the appropriation.

   d. Did the appropriation ensure that the firm had the cash to pay the lawsuits? What other method besides appropriation of retained earnings is available to handle situations such as these?

12. Treasury Stock Transactions. Make the appropriate journal entries to record the following treasury stock transactions:

- January 5: The Truly Modern Corporation repurchases 500 shares of its $5 par value common stock at its current price of $30 per share.

- April 15: The company resells 200 shares of the treasury stock at $40 per share.

- November 29: The firm resells 200 additional treasury shares at $24 per share.

- December 15: The firm sells the remaining 100 shares still held in the treasury at $18 per share.

The following exercises relate to material in the Appendix:

13. Income Tax Allocation Procedures. The MacKnee Corporation's accounting income before depreciation and taxes for 1985, 1986, and 1987 was $200,000, $250,000, and $270,000, respectively. The depreciation expense pertains to an asset that was purchased at the beginning of 1984 for $100,000. for financial accounting purposes, the firm uses straight-line depreciation with a five-year life and no salvage value. The firm took a full year's depreciation in the year of purchase. The machine has a three-year class life under ACRS depreciation which is used for tax purposes. (see the table on page 476 in Chapter 12.) This is the only difference between accounting income and taxable income.

Prepare the journal entries to record the tax liability and tax expense for 1985 through 1987. Assume the tax rate is a flat 40% in all three years. What is the balance in the Deferred Tax account at the end of 1987, and how should it be disclosed on the balance sheet?

14. Interperiod Income Tax Allocation. The Barter Corporation reported the following taxable income and pretax accounting income for 1985 through 1987:

	1985	1986	1987
Taxable income	$360,000	$400,000	$580,000
Pretax accounting income	440,000	410,000	480,000

Assume that the tax rate is 40% in all years and that the differences between taxable income and pretax accounting income are due to timing differences in the recognition of an installment receivable.

Prepare the required journal entries for 1985 through 1987 to record the company's tax expense and tax liability. What is the balance in the Deferred Tax account at the end of 1987? Assume that the balance in that account at the beginning of 1985 was zero.

Problem Set A

17A-1. Income Statement Construction. During the current year, 1987, the Fullerton Manufacturing Company sold its carpet manufacturing division because of consistently poor performance. In addition, you obtained the following information about the events that affected the firm during 1987:

	Continuing Operations	Discontinued Operations
Sales	$4,500,000	$1,800,000
Expenses:		
Cost of goods sold	3,000,000	1,500,000
Operating expenses	500,000	500,000
Loss on disposal of discontinued operations		(300,000)
Gain on expropriation of assets by foreign country	300,000	
Gain on sale of building	100,000	
Cumulative effect (gain) of change from average cost to FIFO	50,000	

All of the above items are shown prior to any tax effect. Assume that a tax rate of 30% applies to all items. In addition, assume that the firm had 200,000 shares of common stock outstanding for the entire year.

Required:

Prepare an income statement in good form for the year ended December 31, 1987. Include earnings per share.

17A-2. Income Statement Construction. Shelly Grant is the accountant for Air Churchill, a successful commuter airline. Because Shelly is just beginning to learn accounting, she asks for your help in preparing the firm's income statement. She has prepared the following condensed statement of income and retained earnings for the year ended December 31, 1987 (page 685).

In addition, you have obtained the following information:

a. The firm changed the estimated lives of its airplanes at the beginning of 1987. The effect was to decrease this year's depreciation expense by $50,000. The decrease is reflected in the depreciation expense shown on the income statement. If the company had always used the new lives, the effect on all prior years' income would have been an increase of $100,000.

b. Included in selling and general and administrative expense is a $25,000 cash dividend issued by the company in July 1987.

Air Churchill
Condensed Statement of Income and Retained Earnings
For the Year Ended December 31, 1987

Revenues:		
Ticket revenue	$1,000,000	
Gain on sale of used airplane	50,000	
Gain on sale of hotels	150,000	$1,200,000
Expenses:		
Selling, general, and administrative	$ 600,000	
Depreciation	300,000	
Interest	100,000	1,000,000
Income before extraordinary item		200,000
Extraordinary item		300,000
Income before taxes		500,000
Taxes—30%		150,000
Net income		350,000
Retained earnings, January 1		700,000
Retained earnings, December 31		$1,050,000

c. The extraordinary gain is the result of a plane crash in which no one was injured or killed, though the plane was completely destroyed. The insurance proceeds exceeded the book value of the plane by $300,000.

d. On January 2, 1985 the company acquired some maintenance machinery at a cost of $150,000. The company adopted the double-declining-balance method of depreciation for this machinery and had been recording depreciation over an estimated useful life of 10 years with no salvage value. At the beginning of 1987, a decision was made to adopt the straight-line method of depreciation for this machinery. Depreciation was recorded on the straight-line method for 1987.

e. Air Churchill sold one of its older airplanes. Because this is a relatively new company, it is the first sale of this kind. The pretax gain as indicated on the income statement is $50,000.

f. At the end of 1987 Air Churchill decided to sell its small chain of hotels. In the past this segment of the company had been unprofitable. The sale of the hotel chain resulted in a pretax gain of $150,000. The company determined that its loss from operations on hotels during 1987 amounted to $20,000. This amount was included in selling and general and administrative expenses. The company intends to restrict all of its future operations to the airline business.

Required:

Prepare a revised income statement and retained earnings statement. Assume a tax rate of 30% on all items. Ignore earnings per share.

17A–3. Earnings per Share. Following is information regarding the Bowman Construction Company:

a.	Net income	$500,000

b. Transactions related to common shares

	January 1, 1987 Beginning balance	300,000
	March 1, 1987 Issuance of shares	30,000
	October 1, 1987 Purchase of treasury stock	10,000

c. Preferred stock
   1. Convertible 5% preferred stock, $100 par value, 2,000 shares issued and outstanding. Each share is convertible into 10 shares of common stock. This issue is considered a common stock equivalent.
   2. Convertible 7% preferred stock, $100 par value, 5,000 shares issued and outstanding. Each share is convertible into 20 shares of common stock. This issue is not considered a common stock equivalent.

Stockholders' Equity—Retained Earnings and Dividends

Required:

Calculate primary and fully diluted earnings per share.

17A–4. Stockholders' Equity Transactions. The stockholders' equity section of Federated Markets' balance sheet at December 31, 1987 is as follows:

Common stock $10 stated value stock, authorized	
1,000,000 shares, issued 60,000 shares	$ 600,000
Paid-in capital in excess of stated value	400,000
Paid-in capital from sale of treasury stock	
in excess of cost	25,000
Retained earnings	700,000
Total stockholders' equity	$1,725,000

The following events occurred during 1988:

- January 2: Sold 10,000 shares of unissued common stock for $20 per share.
- January 20: Declared a cash dividend of $.20 per share, payable on February 20 to shareholders of record on February 10.
- February 5: Exchanged 5,000 shares of authorized but unissued common stock for 600 acres of land. The stock had a fair market value of $25 per share.
- February 20: Dividend declared on January 20 paid.
- March 1: A 2-for-1 stock split was declared: per share market value $40.
- July 1: Federated Markets purchased 1,000 shares of its own stock at the current market price of $35 per share.
- July 18: A 10% stock dividend was declared and issued. Market value is currently $30 per share.
- August 20: Sold 600 shares of treasury stock at $30 per share.
- August 30: Declared a cash dividend of $.10 per share, payable on September 10.

Required:

a. Make the appropriate journal entries to record these transactions. It may be useful to use T accounts as you proceed.
b. Prepare the stockholders' equity section of the balance sheet at December 31, 1988. Assume that net income during the year amounted to $200,000.

17A–5. Stock Splits and Stock Dividends. Several years ago, Bruce Schneider purchased 100 shares of the common stock of E. Kennedy Cobb, Inc. for a total price of $9,000. In the intervening years the company has been profitable, and at the end of 1987 the stockholders' equity section of the balance sheet was as appears below.

E. Kennedy Cobb, Inc.
Partial Balance Sheet
December 31, 1987

Stockholders' equity	
Common stock $10 par value, 100,000 shares	
authorized, 50,000 shares outstanding	$ 500,000
Paid-in capital from issue of common stock	
in excess of par	800,000
Retained earnings	3,000,000
Total stockholders' equity	$4,300,000

Required:

For each of the following situations, make the appropriate journal entries or answer the required questions:

a. On April 1, 1988, the firm decided on a 4-for-1 stock split. Just before the stock split, the stock had been selling at $200 per share.
   1. What entry should the firm make to record the stock split?
   2. What effect do you think that the split will have on Schneider's investment?
   3. If Schneider decided to sell some shares at $60 per share, how much gain or loss per share would he record?

b. On June 30, 1988, after the stock split, the firm decided to declare a $1 per-share cash dividend. Assuming the dividend is paid directly on June 30:
   1. Make the entry required on the books of E. Kennedy Cobb, Inc.
   2. After the cash dividend is recorded, what will be the balance of the retained earnings account, and what will be the total stockholders' equity?

c. On December 30, 1988 the firm decided to declare and issue a 10% stock dividend. At the time of declaration, the stock had a market value of $80 per share.
   1. Make the required entry on the firm's books.
   2. What effect will this dividend have on stockholders' equity and its various components?

17A–6. Stockholders' Equity—Comprehensive Problem. The stockholders' equity section of The Duffy Corporation is shown below:

The Duffy Corporation
Partial Balance Sheet
December 31, 1987

Stockholders' equity	
Common stock, $10 par value, authorized 200,000 shares,	
issued and outstanding 90,000 shares	$ 900,000
Paid-in capital from issue of common stock	
in excess of par	1,500,000
Retained earnings	4,000,000
Total stockholders' equity	$6,400,000

During the month of January 1988, the following events occurred:
- January 10: The board of directors declared a 3-for-1 stock split. At the time of the split, the market price per share was $70.
- January 15: The board of directors declared and issued a 10% stock dividend. At the time of the dividend, the stock had a market price of $25 per share.
- January 20: The corporation repurchased 5,000 shares of its common stock at a price of $28 per share.
- January 25: The board of directors declared a cash dividend of $1 per share to be paid on February 12.
- January 29: The board of directors declared and issued a 30% stock dividend. At the time of the dividend, the stock's market value was $26 per share.
- January 30: The net income for the month of January was $135,000.

Required:
Answer each of the following questions:
a. After the stock split on January 10, what was the amount of total stockholders' equity?
b. After the stock split on January 10, what was the balance in the common stock account?
c. After the stock dividend on January 15, what was the balance in the retained earnings account?
d. After the stock dividend on January 15, what was the amount of the firm's total net assets?
e. After the treasury stock purchase, by how much did the firm's assets increase or decrease, if at all?
f. What was the total balance in retained earnings after all transactions in January were completed?

17A-7. Stockholders' Equity—Comprehensive Problem. The stockholders' equity section on the December 31, 1987 balance sheet of the Sandy Bean Corporation appeared as follows (certain details omitted):

Sandy Bean Corporation
Partial Balance Sheet
December 31, 1987

Preferred stock, 5%, $40 par value authorized 100,000 shares; ? issued	$2,400,000
Common stock, $5 par value, authorized 100,000 shares; ? issued of which 1,000 are held in treasury	250,000
Paid-in capital in excess of par, common	750,000
Paid-in capital from sale of treasury stock	10,000
Donated capital	20,000
Retained earnings	560,000
Cost of treasury stock, common	22,000

Required:

Answer each of the following questions:

a. How many shares of preferred stock were issued?

b. Was the preferred stock issued at par, above par, or below par?

c. How many shares of common stock were issued?

d. How many shares of common stock are outstanding?

e. What was the average issue price of the common stock?

f. Have the treasury stock transactions increased or decreased the firm's net assets, and by what amount?

g. How much did the treasury stock cost per share?

h. What is the total amount of dividends, both preferred and common, that the board of directors could legally declare? How would they be divided between preferred and common shareholders?

i. What is the amount of the corporation's total contributed capital?

j. What is the amount of total stockholders' equity?

17A-8. Statement of Changes in Stockholders' Equity. The stockholders' equity section on the June 30, 1987 balance sheet of the Learning Circuit is shown below. For the year ended June 30, 1988, the following events regarding stockholders' equity are listed in chronological order:

a. Converted 5,000 shares of the convertible preferred stock into common. Each share is convertible into two shares of common.

b. A 10% stock dividend was declared and issued. At that time the common stock was selling at $40 per share.

Preferred stock, 6%, $100 par value convertible preferred stock, 100,000 shares authorized, 10,000 shares issued and outstanding	$ 1,000,000
Common stock, $1 par value, 5,000,000 shares authorized, 120,000 shares issued, of which 10,000 are held in the treasury	120,000
Paid-in capital from issue of common stock in excess of par	5,280,000
Paid-in capital from sale of treasury stock in excess of cost	5,000
Retained earnings	6,000,500
Treasury stock, at cost	(245,000)
Total stockholders' equity	$12,160,500

c. Sold 5,000 shares of treasury stock at $50 per share.

d. Declared and paid $50,000 of dividends.

e. Net income for the year amounted to $1.4 million.

Required:

Prepare a statement of changes in stockholders' equity similar in form to the one illustrated in the text.

17A–9. Interperiod Income Tax Allocation. (This problem relates to material in the Appendix.) Below are the condensed income statements for the Morango Corporation for the last four years:

	1984	1985	1986	1987
Revenues	$300,000	$320,000	$360,000	$450,000
Expenses	210,000	240,000	290,000	370,000
Pretax accounting income	$ 90,000	$ 80,000	$ 70,000	$ 80,000

At the beginning of 1984 the firm purchased a new piece of equipment that cost $100,000. For financial accounting purposes, the firm uses straight-line depreciation based on a four-year life with no salvage value. A full year's depreciation was taken in the first year. Depreciation is included in expenses in the condensed income statements. For tax purposes, the firm uses ACRS depreciation, and the asset falls into the three-year class life. (See the ACRS table in Chapter 12.) The tax rate is a flat 40%.

Required:

a. For each year, determine the amount of taxable income and the actual tax liability.

b. For each year and the total over four years, determine net income, assuming that interperiod income tax allocation is used.

c. Prepare the journal entries to record the income taxes payable and income tax expense, assuming that interperiod income tax allocation is used. What is the balance in the deferred tax account at the end of 1987? Comment on the figure you determined.

Problem Set B

Alpha Corporation sold its auto parts division in 1987 due to consistent poor performance. The following information about the events that affected the firm during 1987 has been provided to you:

	Continuing Operations	Discontinued Operations
Sales	$7,000,000	$2,000,000
Expenses		
Cost of goods sold	2,800,000	900,000
Operating expenses	1,200,000	1,200,000
Gain on sale of disposal of discontinued operations		700,000
Gain on sale of land	500,000	
Cumulative effect of change from FIFO to LIFO	100,000	

All items shown are prior to any tax affect. Assume that a tax rate of 30% applies to all items. In addition, assume that the firm has 500,000 shares of common stock outstanding the entire year.

Required:

Prepare an income statement in good form for the year ended December 31, 1987, including earnings per share.

17B–2. Income Statement Construction. You are the accountant for Camus Manufacturing Company. The condensed statement of income and retained earnings for the year ended December 31, 1987 has been provided for you.

Camus Manufacturing Company
Condensed Statement of Income and Retained Earnings
For the Year Ended December 31, 1987

Revenues:		
Sales	$5,000,000	
Gain on sale of used equipment	150,000	$5,150,000
Expenses:		
Cost of goods sold	2,700,000	
Selling, general, and administrative	1,200,000	
Depreciation	300,000	
Interest	300,000	4,500,000
Income before extraordinary item		650,000
Extraordinary item		(100,000)
Income before taxes		550,000
Taxes, 40%		220,000
Net income		330,000
Retained earnings, 1/1/87		150,000
Retained earnings, 12/31/87		$ 480,000

In addition, the following information is available to you:

a. The firm changed the estimated lives of its equipment at the beginning of 1987. The effect was to decrease this year's depreciation by $20,000. The decrease is reflected in the depreciation expense shown on the income statement. If the company had always used the new lives, the effect on all prior years' income would have been $120,000.

b. Included in selling, general, and administrative expense is a $400,000 cash dividend issued by the company in December of 1986.

c. The extraordinary item is the result of a lawsuit that was brought to court by a group of consumers due to product defects.

d. On January 2, 1985 the company acquired a piece of machinery at a cost of $110,000. The company adopted the sum-of-years-digits method of depreciation to depreciate this machinery over a useful life of 10 years with no salvage value. At the beginning of 1987, a decision was made to adopt the straight-line method of depreciation for this machinery. Depreciation was recorded on the straight-line method for 1987.

Required:

Prepare a revised income statement and retained earnings statement. Assume a tax rate of 40% on all items. Ignore earnings per share.

17B–3. Earnings per Share. Following is information relating to United International, Inc., a trading company:

a.	Net income		$800,000

		Shares
b.	Transactions related to common shares	
	January 1, 1987 Beginning balance	500,000
	April 1, 1987 Issuance of shares	100,000
	August 1, 1987 Purchase of treasury stock	20,000

c. Preferred stock
1. Convertible 6% preferred stock, $50 par value, 4,000 shares issued and outstanding. Each share is convertible into 10 shares of common stock. This issue is considered a common stock equivalent.
2. Convertible 10% preferred stock, $100 par value, 7,000 shares issued and outstanding. Each share is convertible into 20 shares of common stock. This issue is *not* considered a common stock equivalent.

Required:
Calculate primary and fully diluted earnings per share.

17B–4. Stockholders' Equity Transactions. The stockholders' equity section of the Crikos Company's balance sheet as of December 31, 1987 is as follows:

Common stock, par value $10 per share; authorized 1,000,000 shares, issued and outstanding 200,000 shares	$2,000,000
8% convertible preferred stock, par value $100 per share; 10,000 shares authorized, issued, and outstanding. Each share is convertible into five shares of common stock	1,000,000
Paid-in capital in excess of par, common stock	2,000,000
Paid-in capital in excess of par, preferred stock	2,000,000
Retained earnings	800,000
Total stockholders' equity	$7,800,000

The following events occurred during 1988:

- January 2: Twenty thousand shares of common stock were issued and sold for $45 per share.
- January 31: A cash dividend on preferred stock was declared. In addition, a cash dividend of $.10 per share on common stock was declared.
- February 15: Both preferred and common dividends were paid.
- June 1: The Crikos Company purchased 3,000 shares of its own stock at the current price of $50 per share.
- August 1: A 5% common stock dividend was declared and issued. Market value is currently $40 per share.
- September 1: Issued 10,000 shares of common stock in exchange for a building. At the time, the stock had a fair market value of $45 per share.
- October 1: A 2-for-1 stock split was declared. The market value of the stock is currently $50 per share.

Required:
a. Make the appropriate journal entries to record these transactions. It may be useful to use T accounts as you proceed.
b. Prepare the stockholders' equity section of the balance sheet at December 31, 1988. Assume that net income during the year amounted to $500,000.

17B–5. Stock Splits and Stock Dividends. Jerry Dunphy purchased 1,000 shares of common stock of the Little Corporation for a price of $20,000 several years ago. At the end of 1987, the stockholders' equity section of the balance sheet is as follows:

Little Corporation
Partial Balance Sheet
December 31, 1987

Stockholders' equity	
Common stock, $10 par value, 100,000 shares authorized, 80,000 shares outstanding	$800,000
Paid-in capital from issue of common stock in excess of par	450,000
Retained earnings	700,000
Total stockholders' equity	$1,950,000

Required:

For each of the following situations, make the appropriate journal entries or answer the required questions:

a. On June 30, 1988 the firm decided on a 2-for-1 stock split. At the time, the stock was trading at $30 per share.

1. What entry should the firm make to record the stock split?
2. What effect do you think that the split will have on Jerry's investment?
3. If Jerry decided to sell some shares at $12 per share, how much gain or loss would he record per share?

b. On September 30, 1988 the firm declared a cash dividend of $.50 per share payable October 31.

1. Make the entry required on the book of the Little Corporation.
2. After the cash dividend is declared, what is the balance of the retained earnings account and what is the total stockholders' equity?

c. On December 31, 1988 the firm declared and distributed a 5% stock dividend. At the time of declaration, the stock was trading at $20 per share.

1. Make the required entry on the books of the Little Corporation.
2. What effect does this dividend have on stockholders' equity and its various components?
3. Assuming Jerry Dunphy has never sold any shares of stock, what is his new basis per share after all of the above transactions?

17B–6. Stockholders' Equity—Comprehensive Problem. The stockholders' equity section of Davison's, Inc. follows:

Davison's, Inc.
Partial Balance Sheet
December 31, 1987

Stockholders' equity	
Common stock, $20 par value, authorized 500,000	
shares, issued and outstanding 100,000 shares	$2,000,000
Paid-in capital from issue of common stock in excess of par	1,500,000
Retained earnings	2,000,000
Total stockholders' equity	$5,500,000

During the month of January 1988, the following events occurred:

• January 12: A 2-for-1 stock split was declared by the board of directors. At the time of split, the market price was $100 per share.

• January 20: A 5% stock dividend was declared and issued by the board of directors. At the time of the declaration, the market price of the stock was $45 per share.

• January 22: The corporation repurchased 4,000 shares of its common stock at a price of $40 per share.

• January 28: A cash dividend of $.40 per share was declared by the board of directors, payable February 28.

• January 30: A 25% stock dividend was declared and issued. At the time of declaration, the market price of the stock was $42 per share.

• January 31: The net income for the month amounted to $100,000.

Required:

Answer each of the following questions:

a. After the stock split on January 12, what was the amount of total stockholders' equity?
b. After the stock split on January 12, what was the balance in the Common Stock account?

c. After the stock dividend on January 20, what was the balance in the Retained Earnings account?

d. After the stock dividend on January 20, what was the amount of the firm's total net assets?

e. After the treasury stock purchase, by how much did the firm's assets increase or decrease, if at all?

f. Make the journal entry for stock dividend on January 30.

g. What was the total balance in retained earnings after all transactions for January were completed?

17B-7. Stockholders' Equity—Comprehensive Problem. The stockholders' equity section on the December 31, 1987 balance sheet of the Hilliard Corporation appeared as follows:

Hilliard Corporation
Partial Balance Sheet
December 31, 1987

Common stock, $10 par value, authorized	
1,000,000 shares, ___ ? ___ issued of which	
4,000 shares are held in treasury	$2,000,000
Preferred stock, 8% $50 par value, authorized	
200,000 shares, ___ ? ___ issued	4,000,000
Paid-in capital in excess of par, common	1,000,000
Paid-in capital in excess of par, preferred	240,000
Paid-in capital from sale of treasury stock	100,000
Retained earnings	1,500,000
Treasury stock, common, at cost	80,000

Required:

Answer each of the following questions:

a. How many shares of common stock were issued?

b. How many shares of common stock were outstanding?

c. What was the average issue price of the common stock?

d. How many shares of preferred stock were issued?

e. What was the average issue price of the preferred stock?

f. Have the treasury stock transactions increased or decreased the firm's assets, and by what amount?

g. How much did the treasury cost per share?

h. What is the total amount of dividends, both preferred and common, the board of directors could legally declare? How would they be divided between preferred and common shareholders?

i. What is the amount of the total contributed capital of the corporation?

j. What is the amount of total stockholders' equity?

17B-8. Statement of Changes in Stockholders' Equity. The stockholders' equity section on the December 31, 1987 balance sheet of Valley International, Inc. is as follows:

Preferred stock, 8%, $50 par value, convertible preferred stock; 500,000 shares authorized, 10,000 shares issued and outstanding	$ 500,000
Common stock, $10 par value; 1,000,000 shares authorized, 100,000 shares issued of which 5,000 shares are held in the treasury	1,000,000
Paid-in capital from issue of common stock in excess of par	500,000
Paid-in capital from sale of treasury stock in excess of cost	10,000
Retained earnings	2,000,000
Treasury stock, at cost	(110,000)
Total stockholders' equity	$3,900,000

During the year ended December 31, 1988, the following events relating to stockholders' equity occurred in chronological order:

a. Converted 3,000 shares of the convertible preferred stock into 9,000 shares of common stock.

b. A 15% stock dividend was declared and issued. At the time, the market value of common stock was $22 per share.

c. Sold 4,000 shares of treasury stock at $25 per share.

d. Dividends of $100,000 were declared and paid.

e. Net income for the year amounted to $1 million.

Required:

Prepare a statement of changes in stockholders' equity similar in form to the one illustrated in the text.

17B–9. Interperiod Income Tax Allocation. (This material relates to the material in the Appendix.) You have obtained the following tax information from the records of the Marshall Co.:

	1984	1985	1986	1987
Taxable income	$110,000	$140,000	$125,000	$150,000

At the beginning of 1984 the firm purchased a new piece of equipment for $120,000. For tax purposes the firm uses ACRS depreciation and the asset falls into the three-year class life. (See the ACRS table in Chapter 12.) However, for financial statement purposes, the firm uses straight-line depreciation based on a four-year life with no salvage value. A full year's depreciation was taken in 1984. The tax rate is a flat 40%.

Required:

a. For each year, determine the amount of pretax accounting income and income tax expense.

b. For each year and the total over four years, determine net income assuming interperiod income tax allocation is used.

c. Prepare the journal entries to record the income taxes payable and income tax expense assuming that interperiod income tax allocation is used. What is the balance in the Deferred Tax account at the end of 1987? Comment on the figure that you determined.

Using the Computer

The stockholders' equity section on the December 31, 1986 balance sheet of News Company, Incorporated, is as follows:

Preferred stock, 5%, $100 par value, 500,000 shares authorized, 100,000 shares issued and outstanding	$10,000,000
Common stock, $5 par value, 1,000,000 shares authorized, 200,000 shares issued, of which 10,000 are held in treasury	1,000,000
Paid-in capital from issue of common stock in excess of par	12,000,000
Retained earnings	14,000,000
Treasury stock, at cost	(200,000)
Total stockholders' equity	$36,800,000

During 1987 and 1988 the following events occurred:

1987

- Issued 1,000 shares of preferred stock at $100 per share.

- Net income for the year amounted to $4 million.

- Dividends declared during the year amounted to $1 million.

News Company, Incorporated
Statement of Changes in Stockholders' Equity
For the Years Ended December 31, 1987 and 1988

	Preferred Stock	Common Stock	Paid-in Capital Sale of Common	Paid-in Capital Sale of Treasury Stock	Retained Earnings	Treasury Stock	Total
January 1, 1987	$10,000,000	$1,000,000	$12,000,000	$0	$14,000,000	($200,000)	$36,800,000
Transactions during 1987							
.							
.							
.							
Transactions during 1988							
.							
.							
.							
Totals							

1988

- Issued 10,000 shares of common stock at $25 per share.
- Sold 5,000 shares of treasury stock at $30 per share.
- Net income for the year amounted to $5 million.
- Dividends declared during the year amounted to $2 million.

Required:

Using an electronic spreadsheet, prepare a statement of changes in stockholders' equity using the format on page 695.

Understanding Financial Statements

The following data were taken from the 1982 annual report of the Stop & Shop Companies, Inc.:

Earnings per share:	
Primary	$6.87
Fully diluted	6.57

Required:

a. Why did the company report both primary and fully diluted EPS? What type of securities do you think would cause primary EPS to differ from fully diluted EPS?

b. According to the footnotes to the financial statements, EPS is computed on the basis of the weighted average number of shares outstanding. The company reported that for 1982 the weighted average number of shares used to compute primary EPS was 5,071,446. Determine the amount of net income for the year.

c. The following two footnotes were taken from the same annual report:

1. During 1981 the Company disposed of 19 of 20 stores in the New Jersey Supermarket Division, including one in New York, by leasing and subleasing the stores and selling the fixed assets to other area supermarket operators. Total cash proceeds of approximately $20,000,000 were received and resulted in the realization of net gains on the divestiture of $6,611,000 ($1.30 per share) in the third quarter of 1981 after recognition of operating losses during the closeout period and after provisions for income taxes and other post-closing expenses, including the present value of expected future payments to union pension plans.

2. The company approved a plan in September, 1980 to discontinue the operation of its unprofitable meat processing facility located in Marlboro, Massachusetts. The plan provided for the disposal of facility assets by sale or lease.

How should each of these two items be shown on the company's income statement? That is, how should they be classified, and why?

Financial Decision Case

Michael Day is president of Day's Donuts, a chain of successful doughnut shops. Until recently, Day owned all of the company's stock. However, last year the company issued a significant amount of stock to the public, and the stock is now trading on a major exchange. At the end of the current year, the stockholders' equity section of the firm's balance sheet appeared as follows:

Common stock, $10 par value, 100,000 shares issued and outstanding	$1,000,000
Paid-in capital from issue of common shares in excess of par	1,000,000
Retained earnings	2,000,000
Total stockholders' equity	$4,000,000

In addition, total assets amounted to $7 million.

Michael tells you that the stock of Day's Donuts has recently been selling around $100 a share. He is somewhat mystified by the high price of the stock in comparison with its book value. He is considering several courses of action to reduce the price of the stock, to make it more attractive to potential stockholders:

1. A 20% stock dividend.
2. A 100% stock dividend.
3. A 2-for-1 stock split.

Required:

a. What is the relationship between the book value per share and the market price per share?
b. Write a memo to Michael Day outlining how each of the above alternatives would affect stockholders' equity and book value per share and describing the likely effect on the stock's market price. Calculate the new totals for stockholders' equity and book value per share under each alternative.

Accounting for Long-term Liabilities and Investments in Bonds

18

LEARNING OBJECTIVES

After reading this chapter you should be able to:
1. Explain the nature and features of bonds payable.
2. Account for bonds issued at par value.
3. Account for bonds issued at either a discount or a premium.
4. Amortize a discount or premium on both the straight-line and the effective-interest methods.
5. Discuss the other issues related to bonds payable, including bonds issued between interest dates, year-end accruals, and bond issue costs.
6. Account for the retirement of bonds.
7. Account for bonds purchased by the investor.
8. Account for other forms of long-term debt, including notes payable, mortgages, and leases.

The focus of this chapter is accounting for long-term liabilities and investments in bonds. Long-term liabilities are the obligations of an enterprise that are not due within the next 12 months or the business's operating cycle, if longer than a year. Included in the long-term liabilities section of a typical balance sheet are accounts such as Bonds Payable, Mortgages Payable, Long-term Notes Payable, and Leases. Because bonds are a common form of long-term debt, they are used to explain the key accounting procedures for long-term liabilities. Because of their similarities with long-term liabilities, investments in bonds are also covered in this chapter.

A **bond** is a written agreement between a borrower and lenders in which the borrower agrees to repay a stated sum on a future date and to make periodic interest payments at specified dates. Although bonds can be issued by local, state, or federal governments, we are concentrating on bonds issued by corporations to public investors.

Features of Bonds

If you purchase a bond, you will receive a bond certificate. This certificate spells out the terms of agreement between the issuer and the investor. These terms include the denomination or principal of the bond, its maturity date, the stated rate of interest, the interest payment terms, and any other agreements made between the borrower and lenders.

Denomination of the Bond

Individual bonds usually have a **denomination** of $1,000, although in recent years $5,000 and $10,000 bonds have become more common. In this chapter and the homework assignments, we assume that all bonds are in $1,000 denominations unless otherwise stated. The denomination, or principal, of a bond is often referred to as its face value, maturity value, or par value, and it is always on this amount that the required interest payment is calculated.

A total bond issue usually contains several hundreds or thousands of individual bonds. For example, a $10 million bond issue might be made up of 10,000 individual $1,000 bonds. Investors can purchase as many of these individual bonds as they wish. After bonds are issued by a large publicly held company, they trade on the New York Bond Exchange. This enables present and potential investors to sell and purchase bonds after their initial issue, just as they do with shares of stock.

Maturity Date

The date that the principal of the bond is to be repaid is called the maturity date. Bonds usually mature in from 5 years to more than 30 years from their date of issue. Bonds whose entire principal is due in one payment are called **term bonds,** and bonds that are payable on various dates are called **serial bonds.**

Stated Interest Rate and Interest Payment Dates

Most bonds have a **stated interest rate** which is part of the bond agreement. This rate is often referred to as the **nominal interest rate** and is specified on the bond at the time it is issued. This rate does not change over the life of the bond. The stated rate of interest is fixed by the firm's management in conjunction with its financial advisers. They attempt to set the rate as close as they can to the **market interest rate** that exists at the time the bond is issued. The market rate is the interest rate that the money market establishes through hundreds of individual transactions and depends on such factors as prevailing interest rates in the economy and the perceived risk of the individual company.

Most bonds pay interest semiannually, or every six months. However, the stated interest rate is an annual rate based on the face value of the bond. For example, a $1,000, 12% bond that pays interest on January 2 and July 1 will pay interest of $60 ($1,000 × .12 × 6/12) on each of these dates until it matures. In effect, the bond in this example pays 6% interest every 6 months.

Other Agreements

Bondholders are unable to vote for corporate management or otherwise participate in corporate affairs in the way that common shareholders do. As a result, bondholders often insist on written covenants as part of the bond agreement. These agreements are often referred to as **bond indentures,** and although they can take a variety of forms, they usually include restrictions as to dividends, working capital, and the issuance of additional long-term debt. The purpose of these agreements is to ensure that the borrower will maintain a strong enough financial position to meet the interest and principal payments.

Types of Bonds

There are several different types of bonds, including term, serial, coupon, registered, secured, unsecured, convertible, and callable bonds.

Term versus Serial Bonds

As noted, term bonds are bonds whose entire principal amount is due at a single date. Most corporate bonds are term bonds. In contrast, serial bonds have principal payments that are required at specific intervals. Serial bonds are often issued by state or local municipalities. To illustrate, assume that the city of San Francisco issues $5 million of serial bonds whose terms require that $500,000 of the bonds are to be repaid every 5 years beginning 5 years after the date of issue. Thus, for the first 5 years, $5 million of bonds will be outstanding, and for the second 5 years, $4.5 million will be outstanding, and so forth. From both the investors' and the issuer's point of view, serial bonds help ensure that the issuer will be able to repay the entire principal.

Coupon versus Registered Bonds

Some bonds are bearer or **coupon bonds.** This means that the bonds are not registered in the name of individual holders but are negotiable by whoever holds them. In order to receive their interest payments, the current holders simply clip off a coupon and redeem it at an authorized bank. Because coupon bonds do not offer much safety to the holder, most currently issued bonds are registered. This means that the bonds are registered in the name of the holder and that all interest payments are made by the issuing company directly to the current bondholder.

Secured versus Unsecured Bonds

Unsecured bonds, called debentures, are issued without any security to back them. Investors purchase them based on the creditworthiness of the company. Some bonds are secured by the borrower's collateral or specified assets. These secured bonds are often referred to as *mortgage bonds.*

Convertible Bonds

Convertible bonds are convertible at some future specified date into the firm's common stock; thus they enable the bondholder eventually to obtain an equity interest in the firm. This conversion feature allows the firm to issue the bond at a lower interest rate. Convertible bonds are usually callable, which means that the borrower, or issuer, is able to call the bonds prior to their maturity. Thus, the bondholder is forced either to convert the bonds or to have them called prior to their maturity.

Bond Prices

Traditionally bond prices are quoted in terms of 100. A price of 100 means the bond is quoted at 100% of its face value, or $1,000. Often this is referred to as the bond's selling at par. If a bond is quoted at 104, this means its price is $1,040, or $1,000 × 104%. Any time the bond's price is above 100, the bond is selling at a premium. Conversely, if the bond is quoted at 97½, its price is $975, or $1,000 × 97.5%. Any time the bond's price is below 100, the bond is selling at a discount.

Bond Quotations on the Bond Exchange

Exhibit 18–1 on page 703 presents a portion of the bond page from *The Wall Street Journal*. The listing for AT&T, underlined in the exhibit, is reproduced below.

Bond		Cur yld	Vol	High	Low	Close	Net Change
AT&T	10⅜90	10.3	379	100¼	100⅛	100¼	—

As can be seen from the exhibit, there are several issues of AT&T bonds. The issue underlined has a stated interest rate of 10⅜% and is due in 1990. Its current yield is 10.3%, which means that if the bonds were purchased at their closing price of 100¼, the investor would earn a 10.3% rate of return to maturity. To illustrate, the bond pays interest of 10⅜% on stated value of $1,000, or $103.75 per bond. If the bond sells for 100¼, or $1,002.50, the return is 10.3% ($103.75 ÷ $1,002.50). During the day, 379 bonds were traded. The high and low for the day were 100¼ and 100⅛, respectively, and the closing price was 100¼. The closing price represented no change from yesterday's closing price.

How Bond Prices Are Determined

Bond prices at the issue date and during subsequent trading are the result of the interaction among the stated interest rate, the prevailing market rate, and the length of time to maturity. When a bond is issued, the company will receive the full face amount of the bond only if the stated rate of interest equals the market rate at the time of issue. That is, when $100,000, 12%, 10-year bonds are issued, the company will receive $100,000 only if the prevailing market rate is 12% for bonds of that duration and perceived risk. If the prevailing market rate is above 12%, say 14%, the bond will be issued at a discount, and the firm will receive less than $100,000. Conversely, if the market rate of interest for such bonds is below 12%, say 10%, the bonds will be issued at a premium, and the firm will receive more than $100,000 at the time of issue. The amount of the discount or the premium is the difference between the face value of the bond and the amount for which the bond was actually issued. You should keep in mind that the issuing company is obligated to repay the full face amount of the bond, regardless of whether the bond is issued at a discount or at a premium. Furthermore, all interest payments are based on this face value.

To demonstrate further this relationship between interest rates and bond prices, assume that you are considering investing in a $1,000, 5-year, 10% bond that pays 5% interest semiannually. Therefore, you will receive $50 every 6

EXHIBIT 18–1
Portion of the Bond Page from *The Wall Street Journal**

Bonds	Cur Yld	Vol	High	Low	Close	Net Chg.
AMR 10¼06	10.4	2	99	99	99	...
Advst 9s08	cv	225	115	113	114¾	−1¼
AetnLf 8⅛07	8.6	10	95	95	95	+1¾
AlaP 9s2000	9.3	7	97¾	96⅞	96⅞	+ ½
AlaP 7¾s02	8.9	20	87¼	87⅛	87⅛	...
AlaP 8⅞s03	9.3	20	95¾	95¾	95¾	+ ⅜
AlaP 10⅞05	10.6	4	103	103	103	...
AlaP 10½05	10.2	9	103⅜	103⅜	103⅜	+ ½
AlaP 8¾07	9.3	17	94⅜	94⅛	94⅜	+1⅜
AlaP 9¼07	9.3	12	99	99	99	+ ⅛
AlaP 9½08	9.5	40	99¾	97⅛	99¾	+1⅛
AlaP 9⅝08	9.7	11	98¾	98¾	98¾	− ¼
AlaP 9⅝08	13.	74	75¼	74½	75¼	+ ¾
AlaP 12⅝10	11.6	6	109¼	109¼	109¼	− ¼
AlaP 15¼10	13.6	96	112¼	112¼	112¼	...
AlaP 18¼89	16.9	42	108	107½	108	+1
AlskA 9s03	cv	10	114	114	114	−3
AlskH 16¼99	14.4	13	113	113	113	...
AlskH 17¾91	14.8	13	119¾	119¾	119¾	−1¼
AlskH 18⅜01	16.4	190	115	110⅜	111⅞	−3⅛
AlskH 15¼92	14.5	28	105	105	105	
....						
AlskH 12⅞93	12.3	10	105	105	105	+1
Alco 8½10	cv	10	113	113	113	−1½
AllgWt 4s98	6.8	3	59⅛	59⅛	59⅛	+ ⅝
Allgl 10.4s02	12.5	27	83⅞	83¼	83¼	− ⅝
Allgl 9s89	9.8	4	91⅜	91⅜	91⅜	+ ⅞
AlldC 6.6s93	7.3	1	90¼	90¼	90¼	...
AlldC 7⅞96	8.2	25	96½	96½	96½	−1½
AlldC zr87	...	30	90⅞	90⅞	90⅞	...
AlldC zr92	...	16	58⅝	58⅜	58⅜	− ⅝
AlldC zr96	...	40	43½	43	43	−1⅜
AlldC zr98	...	3	33½	33½	33½	+ ⅛
AlldC zr2000	...	45	27¾	27⅜	27¾	+ ⅛
AlldC d6s88	6.3	5	94⅞	94¾	94⅞	+ ⅛
AlldC d6s90	6.5	8	92½	92½	92½	+1¾
AlldC zr91	...	50	64	64	64	−1
AlldC zr95	...	50	44⅛	44⅛	44⅛	+ ⅛
AlldC zr05	...	5	17¾	17¾	17¾	+ ¼
AlldC zr09	...	65	13	13	13	+ ⅛
AlsCha 16s91	14.3	27	111½	111½	111½	...
Alcoa 7.45s96	8.2	1	91⅜	91⅜	91⅜	− ⅛
AMAX 8½96	10.3	20	82⅝	82⅝	82⅝	...
AMAX 14¼90	13.3	60	107⅝	107⅜	107⅜	− ¼
AMAX 14½94	13.2	46	110⅛	110	110	− ⅝
AAirl 4¼92	5.6	4	76⅛	76	76	+ ¾
ABrnd 4⅝90	5.2	1	88⅛	88⅛	88⅛	+ ⅛
ABrnd 5⅞92	6.6	2	89⅜	89⅜	89⅜	+ ⅜
ACan 6s97	7.6	6	79⅛	79	79	− ½
ACan 11⅜10	10.5	4	108	108	108	+1
ACan 13¼93	12.0	25	110½	110½	110½	+ ½
ACeM 6¾91	cv	10	67½	67½	67½	−2⅞
AExC 14¾92	12.4	17	119	119	119	...
AmGn 11s07	cv	3	210	210	210	+1
AHoist 5½93	cv	38	73	73	73	...
AmMed 9½01	cv	170	106	105	105	−1
AmMed 8¼08	cv	37	96¾	96½	96¾	...
AmMot 6s88	cv	4	89½	89¼	89½	+ ⅛
ASmel 4⅝88	5.1	1	90⅛	90⅛	90⅛	...
ATT 2⅝s86	2.6	5	99⅛	99⅛	99⅛	...
ATT 2⅞s87	3.0	17	96⅛	96⅛	96⅛	+ ⅛
ATT 3⅞s90	4.3	10	90	90	90	+ ½
ATT 8¾00	8.9	403	99⅛	98¾	98¾	− ⅛
ATT 7s01	8.0	152	87¾	87¼	87½	− ¼
ATT 7⅛s03	8.1	40	87¾	87½	87¾	− ¼
ATT 8.80s05	9.0	195	98½	97⅜	98⅛	+ ¼
ATT 8⅝s07	9.0	60	96¾	96¼	96¼	− ⅛
ATT 10⅜90	10.3	379	100¼	100⅛	100¼	...
Amfac 5¼94	cv	16	90	90	90	...
Amoco 6s91	6.5	15	92⅞	92⅜	92⅞	+1
Amoco 6s98	7.1	16	84⅝	84⅝	84⅝	− ¼
Amoco 8¼89t	8.2	5	100½	100½	100½	+ ⅛
Amoco 7⅞07	8.6	30	92	92	92	+ ⅜
Amoco 14s91	12.6	70	111½	111	111	− ¼
Ancp 13⅞02f	cv	19	100	99½	99½	−1½
Anhr 6s92	6.8	1	87⅝	87⅝	87⅝	− ⅜
Anxtr 8¼03	cv	15	110	109	109	− ½
ArizP 12⅛09	11.2	5	108⅝	108⅝	108⅝	...
ArmS 8.7s95	9.8	5	89	89	89	+1⅞
ArmS 9.2s00	11.0	5	84	84	84	...
Arms 8½01	10.8	5	78¾	78¾	78¾	+1¼
AshO 8.2s02	9.4	21	87	87	87	− ½
AsCp 12⅜89	12.0	10	103¼	103¼	103¼	− ¾
Atchsn 4s95	5.6	10	71¼	71¼	71¼	...
ARich 11⅜10	10.4	10	109	109	109	+1
ARich 13⅝11	11.8	35	115¼	115¼	115¼	...
ARch 11⅛15	10.5	100	106	106	106	−1
ARch 10⅜95	9.4	10	110¾	110¾	110¾	+ ½
AutDt 6½11	cv	109	107	106	106¼	− ¾
AvcoC 5½93	cv	7	91	91	91	...
Avnet 8s13	cv	75	109	108	108	...

*From *The Wall Street Journal,* May 2, 1986. Reprinted by permission of *The Wall Street Journal,* © Dow Jones & Company, Inc., 1986. All rights reserved.

months ($1,000 × 5%). Because this stated interest rate will not change, you will receive this $50 every 6 months for 5 years, regardless of what happens to future interest rates. However, assume that you have an alternative $1,000, 5-year investment that represents the same risk as the bond investment. The alternative investment pays 14%, or 7% every 6 months. Clearly, the second alternative is more valuable because it pays a semiannual interest of $70, versus $50 for the first investment. If you wanted to purchase the first investment, one way to equalize the difference between the two investments would be to pay less than $1,000 for the first investment. By paying less than $1,000 and still receiving $50 every 6 months, your rate of return would increase. In effect, as a rational economic person, you would pay only an amount for the first investment that would provide a return of 14%. Such an amount would be less than $1,000.

This is exactly what happens with bonds. Bonds having a stated rate less than the prevailing market rate for investments of similar risk will attract investors only if they are issued at a discount. In effect, the price of the bonds will be bid down until they yield a rate of return equal to the prevailing market rate of return for investments of similar risk. Conversely, if the stated rate is higher than the market rate, the demand for these bonds will cause their price to be bid up, and they will be issued at a premium. The actual rate at which the bond is issued is referred to as the **yield rate** or **effective rate.**

The same relationships hold after the bonds are issued and are trading in the marketplace. Remember that the stated rate is specified on the bond and does not change over its life. Market rates of interest, however, constantly change as economic conditions change. Thus, taken as a whole, when there is a general rise in interest rates, the bond market declines, and when interest rates decline, bond prices tend to rise. But, because of the historical cost principle, subsequent price changes in the bonds are not reflected in the accounting records.

Determining Interest Rates

Obviously, interest rates play an important role in determining bond prices. As we noted, the stated interest rate is set by management and in some cases by the underwriters. Underwriters help the issuing company market the bond. They often agree to purchase the entire bond issue at a certain price and then assume the risks involved in selling them to institutions and/or private investors. Management and the underwriters attempt to set the stated or face interest rate as close as possible to the prevailing market rate. The stated rate must be decided on far enough in advance of the actual issue date to allow regulatory bodies such as the Securities and Exchange Commission to approve the issue and then to allow the firm to have the bond certificate printed. Thus, there is a lag time between the time the decision must be made concerning the stated interest rate and the time the bonds are actually issued. A number of economic and financial events can occur during this period that may cause the prevailing market rate to change. Thus, there is likely to be a difference between the two interest rates, and so bonds are often issued at a discount or a premium.

The determination of market interest rates is as difficult to understand as it is to predict. They are affected by the federal government's economic policies, the Federal Reserve Board, investors' expectations about inflation, the risk of the particular investment, and various other factors. In recent years these rates have been very volatile and have reached new heights in the process. For example, the cost of borrowing through traditional debt instruments, such as bonds, rose sharply in the early 1980s, and the number of new bond issues at that time dropped correspondingly.

Determining the Risk of a Bond

As we noted, there are different market rates of interest for bonds of different risk. All else being equal, investors will demand a higher interest rate on investments that are perceived to be riskier than other investments are. One way in which a bond's risk can be measured is through bond ratings. Financial advisory services such as Standard and Poor's and Moody's rate the bonds of major corporations, states, and cities. The higher the rating is, the less risky the bond will be in the opinion of the rating service. Thus, firms with high ratings can issue bonds with a lower stated interest rate than can firms with lower ratings.

Issuers' (Borrowers') Accounting for Bonds

Accounting for the issuance of bonds by the issuer and the purchase of bonds by the investor closely parallel each other. We first discuss, in detail, the accounting procedures from the issuer's, or borrower's, point of view and then we turn to accounting from the investor's point of view.

The decision to issue bonds represents a major financial commitment by an enterprise. Approval must be obtained by its board of directors, regulatory agencies, and often stockholders. The bond issue can be made through underwriters or issued directly to the public and private institutions without the aid of underwriters. Regardless of the method used to issue the bonds or whether the bonds are issued at par, discounted, or at a premium, the accounting issues are similar.

Bonds Issued at Par or Face Value

Bonds will be issued at par or face value if the stated interest rate equals the prevailing rate for similar investments at the issue date. Because bonds can be issued on an interest date or between interest dates, both cases are discussed.

Bonds Issued on an Interest Date

If bonds are issued at par or face value on an interest date, the entry is straightforward. Cash is debited and Bonds Payable is credited for the total dollar amount of the bond issue. For example, assume that on January 2, 1987 the Valenzuela Corporation issues $100,000, 5-year term bonds with a stated interest rate of 12%. The bonds pay interest every January 2 and July 1. The bonds were issued to yield 12%, which is another way of saying that they were issued at par, and thus the company received the full $100,000. The entry to record this bond issue is:

Jan. 2, 1987	Cash	100,000	
	Bonds Payable		100,000
	To record the issuance of $100,000, 12%,		
	5-year bonds at face value.		

The Valenzuela Corporation is required to make semiannual interest payments of $6,000, or $100,000 × 6%. The entry on July 1, 1987 is:

July 1, 1987	Interest Expense	6,000	
	Cash		6,000
	To record payment of semiannual interest of $6,000.		

The next interest payment is due on January 2, 1988. The corporation's year-end is December 31, and the firm must make an adjusting entry to record interest expense for the six-month period, July 1 to December 31. This adjusting entry and the entry to record the subsequent payment are:

Dec. 31, 1987	Interest Expense	6,000	
	Interest Payable		6,000
	To record interest accrual for 6 months on $100,000, 12%, 5-year bonds.		
Jan. 2, 1988	Interest Payable	6,000	
	Cash		6,000
	To record payment of 6 months' accrued interest.		

In this case the interest accrual is for the entire six-month period, because the last interest payment was on July 1. If the year-end were other than December 31, the interest accrual would be for less than six months.

Bonds Issued at Par between Interest Dates

Bonds are often issued between interest dates. When this occurs, the investors pay the issuing corporation for the interest that has accrued since the last interest date. This is so because the investors receive the entire six months' interest on the next interest payment date, regardless of how long they held the bonds. This procedure has definite record-keeping advantages for the issuer, whether or not the bonds are registered. If the bonds are registered, the corporation does not have to maintain records of when each of the particular bonds in the bond issue was purchased or to compute individual partial interest payments. Interest on unregistered or coupon bonds is paid by authorized banks upon presentation of the coupon. Banks, however, will not honor a partial coupon. These problems are alleviated by the fact that the accrued interest is collected from the investors when the bonds are sold, thus allowing the corporation to pay all of the investors the full six months' interest.

For example, now assume that the Valenzuela Corporation issues $100,000, 5-year, 12% bonds on March 1, 1987. The bonds, dated January 2, 1987, pay interest semiannually on January 2 and July 1. In this situation the investor must pay the Valenzuela Corporation for 2 months of accrued interest (from January 2 to February 28), or $2,000 ($100,000 × .06 × 2/6 = $2,000). The entry to record this transaction is:

Mar. 1, 1987	Cash	102,000	
	Interest Payable		2,000
	Bonds Payable		100,000
	To record issuance of $100,000, 5-year, 12% bonds on March 1 plus accrued interest of $2,000.		

Several points should be emphasized about this entry. Bonds Payable is always credited for the face amount of the issue, and so the accrued interest element must be accounted for separately. This is done by crediting Interest Payable for the two months of accrued interest, or $2,000. Interest Payable is credited because these funds will be repaid on the next interest date. Cash is debited for the entire proceeds.

When the next interest payment is made on July 1, the following entry is recorded:

July 1, 1987	Interest Expense	4,000	
	Interest Payable	2,000	
	Cash		6,000
	To record interest payment for 6 months' interest on 7/1/87.		

In this entry, Cash is credited for $6,000, Interest Payable is debited for $2,000, and Interest Expense is debited for $4,000. The result is that there is a zero balance in the Interest Payable account and a $4,000 balance in the Interest Expense account. This $4,000 balance represents the actual interest expense that the Valenzuela Corporation incurred from March 1, 1987 to July 1, 1987 ($100,000 × .06 × 4/6). These relationships are illustrated in the diagram below and in the relevant T accounts.

$$\$2,000 \quad + \quad \$4,000 = \$6,000$$

accrued interest	interest expense	total paid
1/2/87	3/1/87	7/1/87
Start of interest period	Date bonds issued	First interest payment date

Interest Payable			Interest Expense	
7/1 2,000	3/1 2,000		7/1 4,000	
	0		4,000	

Bonds Issued at Other Than Face Value

As we noted, bonds are often issued above or below their face value. If the prevailing market interest rate is above the stated rate, the bonds will be issued at a discount. Conversely, if the prevailing interest rate is below the stated rate, the bonds will be issued at a premium.

Recording Bonds Issued at a Discount

To illustrate the entries to record a bond issued at a discount, assume that on January 2, 1987 the Valenzuela Corporation issues $100,000, 12%, 5-year term bonds. Interest is payable semiannually on January 2 and July 1. The bonds were issued when the prevailing market interest rate for such investments was 14%. Thus the bonds were issued at a discount to yield 14%. As noted, this rate is also called the effective interest rate. Based on this effective rate, the bonds would be issued at a price of 92.9764, or $92,976. This price can be determined independently using present value techniques illustrated in Appendix A. Bond tables that calculate bond prices based on different yield and maturity dates also are available. The entry to record this bond issue is:

Jan. 2, 1987	Cash	92,976	
	Discount on Bonds Payable	7,024	
	Bonds Payable		100,000
	To record issuance of $100,000, 12%, 5-year bonds for $92,976.		

As this entry illustrates, Cash is debited for the actual proceeds received and Bonds Payable is credited for the face value of the bonds. The difference of $7,024 is debited to an account called Discount on Bonds Payable.

This Discount on Bonds Payable account is a contra-liability account in that it is offset against the Bonds Payable account on the balance sheet in order to arrive at the bonds' carrying value. To illustrate, a balance sheet prepared on January 2, 1987, immediately after the bonds were issued, would show the following under the long-term liabilities section:

Valenzuela Corporation
Partial Balance Sheet
January 2, 1987

Long-term liabilities		
Bonds payable, 12% due 1/2/92	$100,000	
Less: Discount on bonds payable	7,024	
	$ 92,976	

The Nature of the Discount Account

It is important to understand the nature of the Discount on Bonds Payable account. In effect, the discount should be thought of as additional interest expense that should be amortized over the life of the bond. Remember that the bond was issued at a discount because the stated rate was below the market rate. The bondholders are receiving only $6,000 every 6 months, whereas comparable investments yielding 14% are paying $7,000 every 6 months ($100,000 × .07). The discount of $7,024 represents the present value (the value today of money to be received or paid in the future) of that $1,000 difference that the bondholders are not receiving over each of the next 10 interest periods (5 years' interest paid semiannually). Essentially the company incurs that additional interest expense of $7,024 at the time of issuance by receiving only $92,976 rather than $100,000. But, because of the matching concept, this cost of $7,024 cannot be expensed when the bonds are issued but must be written off over the life of the bond.

As a result of issuing the bonds at a discount, the total interest expense incurred by the Valenzuela Corporation over the 5-year life of the bond is $67,024, calculated as follows:

Interest expense paid in cash to bondholders:	
Face value of bond	$100,000
Semiannual stated interest rate	.06
Semiannual interest	6,000
Number of interest periods	× 10
Total cash interest	60,000
Discount on issuance	7,024
Total interest expense incurred	$ 67,024

Another way to view this is to look at the difference between the cash that the company will eventually repay the bondholders versus what it received at the time of issuance. This calculation is:

Total cash repaid to bondholders		
Principal	$100,000	
Cash interest—see above	60,000	
	160,000	
Total cash received at issuance	92,976	
Total interest expense incurred	$ 67,024	

Amortizing the Discount

The discount of $7,024 must be written off or amortized over the life of the bond. There are two methods used to do this, the straight-line method and the effective-interest method. The effective-interest method is conceptually preferable, and accounting pronouncements require its use unless there is no material difference in the periodic amortization between it and the straight-line method. However, the straight-line method is easy to compute and understand and so it is examined first in order to aid in your understanding of the concepts. The effective-interest method is discussed later in the chapter.

The Straight-line Method. The straight-line method simply allocates the discount evenly over the life of the bond. Thus there is a constant interest charge each period. An entry is usually made on every interest date, and if necessary, an adjusting journal entry is made at the end of each period to record the discount amortization.

To demonstrate the application of the straight-line method, we return to the Valenzuela Corporation example. In this case the discount of $7,024 will be amortized over 10 interest periods at a rate of $702 per interest period ($7,024 ÷ 10). The total interest expense for each period is $6,702, consisting of the $6,000 cash interest and the $702 amortized discount. Another way to calculate the $6,702 is to divide the total interest cost, $67,024, as shown on page 710, into the 10 interest periods of the bond's life. The journal entry at July 1, 1987 and each interest payment date thereafter is:

July 1, 1987	Interest Expense	6,702	
	Discount on Bonds Payable		702
	Cash		6,000
	To record cash interest payment and amortization of discount on the straight-line method.		

As the bonds approach maturity, their carrying value increases, and the result of this and subsequent entries is to reflect this increase in the carrying value of the bonds. This is so because the discount account, which is offset against bonds payable in arriving at the bonds' carrying value, is decreased each time a credit entry is made to that account. To illustrate, the relevant T accounts and a partial balance sheet as of July 1, 1987 are presented next:

Bonds Payable		Interest Expense	
	1/2/87 100,000	7/1/87 6,702	

Discount on Bonds Payable		
1/2/87	7,024	7/1/87 702
7/1/87 Bal.	6,322	

Valenzuela Corporation
Partial Balance Sheet
July 1, 1987

Long-term liabilities		
Bonds payable		$100,000
Less: Discount on bonds payable		6,322
		$ 93,678

In each interest period, the bond's carrying value will be increased by $702, so that by the time the bond matures, the balance in the Discount on Bonds Payable account will be zero, and the bond's carrying value will be $100,000. Exhibit 18–2 presents an amortization schedule for this bond on the straight-line method. When the company repays the principal it makes the following entry:

Jan. 2, 1992	Bonds Payable	100,000	
	Cash		100,000
	To record the repayment of $100,000, 5-year bonds.		

EXHIBIT 18–2
Discount Amortization—Straight-line

Date	Cash Interest	Discount Amortization	Total Interest Expense	Carrying Value of Bonds
	(1)	(2)	(3)	(4)
1/2/87				$ 92,976
7/1/87	$6,000	$702	$6,702	93,678
1/2/88	6,000	702	6,702	94,380
7/1/88	6,000	702	6,702	95,082
1/2/89	6,000	702	6,702	95,784
7/1/89	6,000	702	6,702	96,486
1/2/90	6,000	702	6,702	97,188
7/1/90	6,000	702	6,702	97,890
1/2/91	6,000	702	6,702	98,592
7/1/91	6,000	702	6,702	99,294
1/2/92	6,000	706	6,706	100,000

(1) $6,000 = $100,000 × .06.

(2) $702 = $\dfrac{\$7,024}{10 \text{ periods}}$ = $702.40 rounded to $702.

(3) $6,702 = $6,000 + $702.

(4) Carrying value at beginning of period plus discount amortization for period ($93,678 = $92,976 + $702). Last year's interest expense rounded to make carrying value $100,000.

Bonds Issued at a Premium

To show how to account for bonds issued at a premium, we now assume that on January 2, 1987 the Valenzuela Corporation issues $100,000, 5-year, 12% term bonds. Interest is payable semiannually on January 2 and July 1. In this case, however, the bonds are issued when the prevailing market interest rate for such investments is 10%. The bonds therefore are issued at a premium to yield 10% and are sold at a price of 107.7215, or $107,722. The entry to record this bond issue is:

Jan. 2, 1987	Cash	107,722	
	Premium on Bonds Payable		7,722
	Bonds Payable		100,000
	To record issuance of $100,000, 5-year,		
	12% bonds at 107,722.		

This entry is similar for recording bonds issued at a discount, except that a premium account is involved. Cash is debited for the entire proceeds and Bonds Payable is credited for the bonds' face amount. The difference in this case is a credit to the Premium on Bonds Payable account of $7,722.

The Premium on Bonds Payable is called an **adjunct account** because it is added to the Bonds Payable account in determining the bonds' carrying value. To illustrate, the Valenzuela balance sheet prepared on January 2, 1987, immediately after the bonds were issued, shows the following under the long-term liabilities section:

Valenzuela Corporation
Partial Balance Sheet
January 2, 1987

Long-term liabilities	
Bonds payable, 12% due 1/2/92	$100,000
Plus: Premium on bonds payable	7,722
	$107,722

The Nature of the Premium Account

In effect, the premium should be thought of as a reduction in interest expense that should be amortized over the life of the bond. The bonds were issued at a premium because the stated interest rate was higher than the prevailing market rate. The bondholders are receiving $6,000 ($100,000 × .06) every 6 months when comparable investments were yielding only 10% and paying $5,000 ($100,000 × .05) every 6 months. The premium of $7,722 represents the present value of that extra $1,000 difference that the bondholders will receive in each of the next 10 interest periods. Because the bond is an attractive investment, its price is bid up to $107,722, and the premium of $7,722 is considered a reduction of interest expense. Although the borrower receives all of the funds at the time of the issue, the matching convention requires that it be recognized over the life of the bond.

After issuing the bonds at premium, the total interest expense incurred by the Valenzuela Corporation over the 5-year life of the bonds is $52,278, calculated as follows:

Interest expense paid in cash to bondholders:	
Face value of bonds	$100,000
Semiannual interest rate	.06
Semiannual interest	6,000
Number of interest periods	× 10
Total cash interest	60,000
Premium upon issuance	(7,722)
Total interest expense	$ 52,278

Again, another way to view this is to consider what the company will ultimately repay the bondholders versus what it received at the time of issuance. This calculation is shown next:

Total cash repaid to bondholders	
Principal	$100,000
Cash interest	60,000
	160,000
Total cash received at issuance	107,722
Total interest expense incurred	$ 52,278

Amortizing the Premium

The premium of $7,722 is amortized by using either the straight-line method or the effective-interest method. Again, the straight-line method is discussed first, then the effective-interest method is discussed for both the discount and premium examples.

The Straight-line Method. Under the straight-line method, the premium of $7,722 is amortized over 10 interest periods at a rate of $772 ($7,722 ÷ 10) per period. Thus the total interest expense for each period is $5,228, consisting of the $6,000 cash interest less the premium amortization of $772. Another way to calculate the $5,228 is to divide the total interest cost of $52,278, as just calculated, into the 10 interest periods of the bond's life. Exhibit 18–3 (page 713) presents an amortization schedule for this bond issue, on a straight-line basis. The journal entry at July 1, 1987 and each interest payment date thereafter is:

July 1, 1987	Interest Expense	5,228	
	Premium on Bonds Payable	772	
	Cash		6,000
	To record cash interest payment and amortization of the premium on the straight-line method.		

The effect of this and subsequent entries is to decrease the carrying value of the bonds as the premium account is reduced each period. By the time the bonds reach maturity, their carrying value will have been reduced to their face value of $100,000. The relevant T accounts and partial balance sheet as of July 1, 1987 are presented next:

Premium on Bond Payable		**Bonds Payable**
7/1/87 772	1/2/87 7,722	1/2/87 100,000
	7/1/87 Bal. 6,950	

Interest Expense

7/1/87 5,228	

Valenzuela Corporation
Partial Balance Sheet
July 1, 1987

Long-term liabilities	
Bonds payable	$100,000
Premium on bonds payable	6,950
	$106,950

The Effective-Interest Method

Although the straight-line method is simple to use, it does not produce the accurate amortization of the discount or premium. It makes the unrealistic assumption that the interest cost for each period is the same, even though the carrying value of the liability is changing. For example, under this method, each period's dollar interest expense is the same, but as the carrying value of the bond increases or decreases, the actual percentage interest rate correspondingly decreases or increases. For example, the Valenzuela bonds issued

---

EXHIBIT 18-3
Premium Amortization—Straight-line

Date	Cash Interest Payment	Premium Amortization	Total Interest Expense	Carrying Value of Bond
	(1)	(2)	(3)	(4)
1/2/87				$107,722
7/1/87	$6,000	$772	$5,228	106,950
1/2/88	6,000	772	5,228	106,178
7/1/88	6,000	772	5,228	105,406
1/2/89	6,000	772	5,228	104,634
7/1/89	6,000	772	5,228	103,862
1/2/90	6,000	772	5,228	103,090
7/1/90	6,000	772	5,228	102,318
1/2/91	6,000	772	5,228	101,546
7/1/91	6,000	772	5,228	100,774
1/2/92	6,000	774	5,226	100,000

(1) $6,000 = $100,000 \times .06$.

(2) $772 = \dfrac{\$7,722}{10 \text{ interest periods}} = \$772.20$ rounded off to $772.

(3) $5,228 = \$6,000 - \$772$.

(4) Carrying value = carrying value at beginning of period, less premium amortized during period ($106,950 = $107,722 - $772). 1/2/92 rounded to equal $100,000.

---

at a discount (see Exhibit 18–2 on page 710) had a carrying value of $92,976 at the date of their issue. The interest expense based on straight-line amortization for the period between January 2, 1987 and July 1, 1987 is $6,702. This results in an actual percentage interest rate of 7.2%, or $6,702 ÷ $92,976. In the next interest period this rate falls to 7.15% because the interest expense for the period remains at $6,702, but as shown in Exhibit 18–2, the bond's carrying value has increased to $93,678. As a result, the percentage interest rate is now 7.15% or $6,702 ÷ $93,678. Over the life of the bond, this percentage interest rate continues to decrease until January 2, 1992, when it reaches 6.7%, or $6,702 ÷ $99,294.

In the premium example, the same conceptual problem occurs, except that the percentage rate continuously increases as the carrying value of the bond decreases from $107,722 to $100,000, whereas the semiannual interest expense remains constant at $5,228.

Because of the conceptual problem with the straight-line method, the Accounting Principles Board (APB) required that the effective interest method be used unless there are no material differences between the two.[1] Under the **effective-interest method,** a constant interest rate equal to the market rate at the time of issue is used to calculate periodic interest expense. Thus, the interest rate is constant over the term of the bond, but the actual interest expense changes as the carrying value of the bond changes. Furthermore, when the effective-interest method is used, the carrying value of the bonds will always be equal to the present value of the future cash outflow at each amortization date. We will illustrate the effective-interest method for both the discount and the premium cases.

Discount Amortization—Effective-Interest Method. As illustrated, the $100,000, 5-year, 12% bonds issued to yield 14% were sold at a price of $92,976, or at a discount of $7,024. Exhibit 18–4 shows how this discount is amortized using the effective-interest method over the life of the bond.

In Exhibit 18–4 on page 715, the effective periodic bond interest expense is calculated by multiplying the bond's carrying value at the beginning of each period by the semiannual yield rate determined at the time the bond was issued. In this case the interest expense of $6,508 in Column 2 at July 1, 1987 is equal to $92,976 multiplied by 7%. The difference between the required cash interest payment of $6,000 in Column 3 ($100,000 × 6%) and the effective-interest expense of $6,508 is the required discount amortization of $508 in Column 4. Finally, the unamortized discount of $6,516 at July 1, 1987 in Column 5 is equal to the original discount of $7,024, less the amortized discount of $508. The carrying value of the bond in Column 6 is thus increased by $508, from $92,976 to $93,484. Alternatively, the bond's carrying value on July 1, 1987 is equal to $100,000 less the unamortized discount of $6,516.

The information for each period's journal entry to record the semiannual interest expense can be drawn directly from the amortization schedule. The entry on July 1, 1987 is:

Interest Expense	6,508	
Discount on Bonds Payable		508
Cash		6,000

To record semiannual interest expense based on the effective-interest method.

---

[1]Accounting Principles Board, Opinion No. 21, *Interest on Receivables and Payables* (New York: AICPA, 1971), par. 15.

EXHIBIT 18–4
Discount Amortization Table—Effective-Interest Method

| | (1) | Debit | Credit | | (5) | (6) |
| | | (2) | (3) | (4) | | |
Date	Carrying Value at Beginning of the Period	Effective Bond Interest Expense, 7% of Carrying Value from Col. 1	Cash Interest Paid, 6% of $100,000	Discount Amortization Col. 2 − Col. 3	Unamortized Discount Balance at End of the Period—Previous Balance less Col. 4	Carrying Value of Bond at End of the Period Col. 1 + Col. 4
1/2/87					$7,024	
7/1/87	$92,976	$ 6,508[a]	$ 6,000	$ 508	6,516	$ 93,484
1/2/88	93,484	6,544	6,000	544	5,972	94,028
7/1/88	94,028	6,582	6,000	582	5,390	94,610
1/2/89	94,610	6,623	6,000	623	4,767	95,233
7/1/89	95,233	6,666	6,000	666	4,101	95,899
1/2/90	95,899	6,713	6,000	713	3,388	96,612
7/1/90	96,612	6,763	6,000	763	2,625	97,375
1/2/91	97,375	6,816	6,000	816	1,809	98,191
7/1/91	98,191	6,873	6,000	873	936	99,064
1/2/92	99,064	6,936[b]	6,000	936	—	100,000
		$67,024	$60,000	$7,024		

[a]Rounded to whole dollars.
[b]Rounded to balance.

The following table compares the two different methods of discount amortization for the first 3 interest periods and for the total over all 10 periods:

| | Interest Expense | |
Date	Straight-line	Effective-Interest
July 1, 1987	$ 6,702	$ 6,508
January 2, 1988	6,702	6,544
July 1, 1988	6,702	6,582
.	.	.
January 2, 1992	6,702	6,936
Total for all 10 interest periods	$67,024	$67,024

As the table indicates, under the straight-line method the interest expense for each period is $6,702, and the total over all 10 periods is $67,024. Under the effective-interest method the semiannual interest expense is $6,508 in the first period and increases thereafter as the carrying value of the bond increases. With the effective-interest method, as with the straight-line method, the total interest expense is $67,024. The important point is that there is no difference in the total interest expense but only in the allocation within the five-year period of time.

Accounting for Long-term Liabilities and Investments in Bonds

Premium Amortization—Effective-Interest Method. To illustrate premium amortization using the effective-interest method, we return to the $100,000, 5-year, 12% bonds issued to yield 10%. These bonds were issued at a price of $107,722, or at a premium of $7,022. The schedule in Exhibit 18–5 shows how the premium is amortized under the effective-interest method. This schedule is set up in the same manner as the discount amortization schedule in Exhibit 18–4 except that the premium reduces the cash interest expense every period. For each period, the interest expense in Column 2 is the semiannual yield rate at the time of issue (5%) multiplied by the carrying value of the bonds. The difference between this amount and the cash interest in Column 3 is the premium amortization in Column 4. The carrying value of the bond at the end of the period in Column 6 is reduced by the premium amortization for the period.

The journal entry to record the semiannual interest expense can be drawn directly from this schedule. The entry on July 1, 1987 is:

July 1, 1987	Interest Expense	5,386	
	Premium on Bonds Payable	614	
	Cash		6,000
	To record semiannual interest expense based on the effective-interest method.		

As with the discount example, the total interest expense over the life of the bond under the straight-line and the effective-interest methods is the same. However, it is allocated differently among periods. In both the discount and the premium examples, the difference between the straight-line and the effec-

---

EXHIBIT 18–5
Premium Amortization Table—Effective-Interest Method

	(1)	Debit (2)	Credit (3)	Debit (4)	(5)	(6)
Date	Carrying Value at Beginning of the Period	Effective Bond Interest Expense, 5% of Carrying Value from Col. 1	Cash Interest Paid, 6% of $100,000	Premium Amortization, Col. 3 − Col. 2	Unamortized Premium Balance at End of the Period—Previous Balance less Col. 4	Carrying Value of Bond at End of the Period Col. 1 − Col. 4
1/2/87					$7,722	
7/1/87	$107,722	$ 5,386[a]	$ 6,000	$ 614	7,108	$107,108
1/2/88	107,108	5,355	6,000	645	6,463	106,463
7/1/88	106,463	5,323	6,000	677	5,786	105,786
1/2/89	105,786	5,289	6,000	711	5,075	105,075
7/1/89	105,075	5,254	6,000	746	4,329	104,329
1/2/90	104,329	5,216	6,000	784	3,545	103,545
7/1/90	103,545	5,177	6,000	823	2,722	102,722
1/2/91	102,722	5,136	6,000	864	1,858	101,858
7/1/91	101,858	5,093	6,000	907	951	100,951
1/2/92	100,951	5,049[b]	6,000	951	—	100,000
		$52,278	$60,000	$7,722		

[a]Rounded to whole dollars.
[b]Rounded to balance.

tive-interest amortization methods is not significant, but for large bond issues the difference between these two methods can become significant. If this is the case, generally accepted accounting principles require that the effective-interest amortization be used.

Other Issues Related to Bonds Payable

Besides the basic concepts and procedures related to the issuance and subsequent accounting for bonds payable, there are other issues concerning bonds which are important.

Bonds Issued at a Premium or Discount between Interest Dates

Bonds are likely to be sold between interest dates at either a discount or a premium. When this occurs, the discount or premium and the accrued interest must be accounted for separately. To demonstrate, assume that the Valenzuela Corporation issues $100,000, 12%, 5-year term bonds on March 1, 1987. The bonds are dated January 1, 1987. They are issued at a discount to yield 14% and pay interest semiannually on January 2 and July 1. The price of the bonds net of the discount is 93.0939, and the accrued interest is $2,000 ($100,000 × .06 × 2/6 = $2,000). The entry to record this issue is:

Mar. 1, 1987	Cash	95,094	
	Discount on Bonds Payable	6,906	
	Interest Payable		2,000
	Bonds Payable		100,000
	To record the issue of $100,000,		
	12%, 5-year bonds on March 1, 1987, to yield		
	14%. The discount equals $6,906		
	($100,000 − $93,094).		

In this example the cash proceeds that the firm receives of $95,094 consist of the proceeds from the bond of $93,094 plus the accrued interest of $2,000. The discount of $6,906 is the difference between the face value of $100,000 and the issue price net of the interest of $93,094. The bonds payable are recorded at their face value of $100,000.

When the first interest payment is made, the entry at the bottom of this page is made (assuming straight-line amortization). You should note that the discount is amortized over only 58 months, or 4 years and 10 months, not 5 years, because the bonds had a remaining life of only 58 months when they were issued on March 1, 1987. Subsequent interest payments and discount amortization should be made in the usual way.

July 1, 1987	Interest Expense	4,476	
	Interest Payable	2,000	
	Discount on Bonds Payable		476
	Cash		6,000
	To record semiannual interest payment and		
	amortize discount on a straight-line basis.		

Discount amortization:

$$\frac{\$6,906}{58 \text{ months}} = \$119^*/\text{month} \times 4 \text{ months} = \underline{\$476}$$

Interest expense: $100,000 × .06 × 4/6 = $4,000
$4,000 + $476 = \underline{\$4,476}$

*Rounded to whole dollars.

Year-end Accruals of Interest Expense

It is likely that the issuing firm's year-end will not coincide with an interest payment date. We showed the proper accounting procedures to handle this situation when bonds are issued at par. It is a simple extension to handle premiums or discounts in this situation. To demonstrate, we use the data from the Valenzuela Corporation from the previous example. However, we will assume that the company's year-end is September 30. An adjusting entry must be made on this date to record an interest accrual of three months since the last interest payment date on July 1, 1987. This entry, assuming straight-line amortization, is:

Sept. 30, 1987	Interest Expense	3,357	
	Discount on Bonds Payable		357
	Interest Payable		3,000
	To record interest expense on bonds payable from 7/1/87 to 9/30/87.		

Interest payable: $100,000 \times .06 \times 3/6 = \$3,000$

Discount amortization:

$$\frac{\$6,906}{58 \text{ months}} = \$119/\text{month} \times 3 \text{ months} = \qquad 357$$

Total interest expense $\underline{\$3,357}$

As this entry shows, the interest must be accrued and the discount must be amortized for three months.

On January 2, 1988, when the interest is paid, the following entry is made:

Jan. 2, 1988	Interest Expense	3,357	
	Interest Payable	3,000	
	Discount on Bonds Payable		357
	Cash		6,000
	To record interest payment and 3 months' discount amortization.		

Discount amortization: $\$119 \times 3 = \$ \quad 357$
Cash interest expense: $\$100,000 \times .06 \times 3/6 = \underline{\quad 3,000}$
Total interest expense $\underline{\$3,357}$

In this entry, the Interest Payable account is debited and Interest Expense is recorded for the three-month period from October 1, 1987 to January 2, 1988. The Discount on Bonds Payable is also amortized for the same three-month period.

Bond Issue Costs

When a corporation issues bonds, various expenses are incurred. Examples are printing and engraving, and legal and accounting costs. Furthermore, many bonds are marketed through investment bankers, who receive a commission for underwriting the bond issue. These costs result in the issuer's receiving less cash than it otherwise would. Under current accounting principles, these costs are accumulated in a noncurrent asset account called Bond Issue Costs and are amortized over the life of the bond on a straight-line basis.

Accounting for the Retirement of Bonds

Bonds can be retired in a number of ways, including repayment at maturity, early extinguishment of the debt before maturity, and conversion into common stock.

Retirement of Bonds at Maturity and Bond Sinking Funds

When bonds are repaid at maturity, the journal entry is straightforward. Bonds Payable is debited and Cash is credited. There are no problems with discounts or premiums, as they have been amortized to zero by the time of the last interest payment just prior to maturity.

In order to ensure the repayment of the principal, some bond agreements require that the issuing corporation create and maintain a sinking fund. A **sinking fund** is a collection of cash or perhaps other assets such as marketable securities that is set apart from the firm's other assets and is used only for a specified purpose. This fund generally is under the control of a trustee or agent who is independent of the enterprise that established the fund. The issuing corporation makes periodic payments to its bond sinking fund. These monies are then invested by the trustee and eventually are used to pay the interest and to repay the principal of the bond. The amount of periodic payments to the fund is based on the expected return that the trustee can earn on the assets in the fund.

The sinking fund is shown under the investment section on the balance sheet of the issuing corporation. The accounting procedure regarding interest expense recognition and other aspects of bonds is not affected by the existence of a bond sinking fund.

Early Extinguishment of Debt

Early extinguishment of debt occurs whenever a firm's long-term debt is retired before maturity. Management can accomplish this extinguishment by repurchasing the bonds in the market. Other bonds are callable and give the issuing corporation the right to buy back the bonds before maturity at a specified price. This price is usually set above the par or face value of the bond because the bondholder will be forgoing future interest income. The amount above par is often referred to as a *call premium*.

The early extinguishment of long-term debt is a financing decision of management and depends on such factors as cash flows and past, existing, and anticipated interest rates. For example, it may be advantageous for a firm to repurchase bonds if market interest rates have risen since the original bond issue date. To demonstrate, assume that the Tracy Hospital Company issued $50,000, 6%, 20-year bonds at face at the beginning of 1977. Because the bonds were issued at face or par, we can assume that at that time the market interest rates were equivalent to the stated rates for this type of bond. By the beginning of 1986, interest rates rose to 10%, and as a result the market value of the bonds decreased to $36,201. Therefore the Tracy Hospital Company repurchased for that amount, all the bonds on the open market and was able to liquidate a $50,000 debt for only $36,201. This situation occurred often in the late 1970s and early 1980s when market interest rates rose, and many firms did retire their debt early.

When a firm extinguishes its debt prior to maturity, there will be a gain or loss. This gain or loss is the difference between the reacquisition price and the carrying value of the bonds. In the example of the Tracy Hospital bonds, the firm would record a gain of $13,799, or $50,000 less the reacquisition price of $36,201. Prior to recording the gain or loss, the carrying value must be adjusted for any discount or premium amortization up to the date the bonds are retired. If the carrying value exceeds the reacquisition price there is a gain, and conversely, if the reacquisition price exceeds the carrying value there is a loss. Under current accounting practices, this gain or loss is considered extraordinary and must be shown as a separate item on the income statement.[2]

To illustrate the accounting for the early extinguishment of debt, assume that $100,000, 12%, 5-year term bonds that were issued at a discount of $7,024 by the Valenzuela Corporation (see page 707) were called on July 1, 1989. The bonds were reacquired at a price of 104. The firm uses the straight-line method of amortization. The entries to record (1) the payment of interest and the amortization of the discount and (2) the retirement of the bonds are as follows (see Exhibit 18–2 on page 710 for the necessary data):

July 1, 1989	Interest Expense	6,702	
	Discount on Bonds Payable		702
	Cash		6,000
	To record semiannual interest payment and discount amortization.		

July 1, 1989	Bonds Payable	100,000	
	Extraordinary Loss on Early Extinguishment of Debt	7,514	
	Discount on Bonds Payable		3,514
	Cash		104,000
	To record early retirement of bonds at 104.		

Reacquisition price ($100,000 × 1.04)	$104,000
Carrying value—See Exhibit 18–2	96,486
Loss on reacquisition	$ 7,514

The first entry records the interest payment and the discount amortization from January 2, 1989 to July 1, 1989. The second entry records the actual extinguishment of the debt. There is a loss in this case because the reacquisition price exceeds the carrying value of the bonds.

Conversion of Bonds into Capital Stock

As we noted previously, many corporations issue convertible bonds because of the advantages that accrue to the bondholders and to the issuing corporation. When convertible bonds are issued, no recognition is given to the conversion feature. That is, the entire issue is treated as debt. For example, assume that the Farr Corporation issues $500,000, 10-year, 10% bonds. Each bond is convertible into 50 shares of capital stock and is issued at a price of 95. The entry to record the bond issue on January 2, 1987 is:

Jan. 2, 1987	Cash	475,000	
	Discount on Bonds Payable	25,000	
	Bonds Payable		500,000
	To record issuance of $500,000 convertible bonds.		

---

[2]Financial Accounting Standards Board, Statement No. 4, *Reporting Gains and Losses on Extinguishment of Debt* (Stamford, Conn.: FASB, 1975).

When the bonds are converted into capital stock, the capital stock is recorded at the carrying value of the bonds, and no gain or loss is recognized on the conversion. For example, assume that all the bonds of the Farr Corporation are converted into 25,000 shares on July 1, 1991, when the unamortized discount is $13,750 and the carrying value of the bonds is $486,250. Twenty-five thousand shares are issued because 500 ($500,000 ÷ $1,000) bonds were converted and the conversion agreement calls for each bond to be converted into 50 shares of stock. The entry to record this conversion is:

July 1, 1991	Bonds Payable	500,000	
	Discount on Bonds Payable		13,750
	Capital Stock		486,250
	To record issuance of 25,000 shares of capital stock in exchange for outstanding bonds.		

Bonds Payable is debited for the face value of the converted bonds. The unamortized discount of $13,750 is written off. The 25,000 shares of capital stock are recorded at the bonds' carrying value at the date of conversion.

Investor's (Lender's) Accounting for Bonds

The investor's accounting for bonds is similar to that by the issuer, except that the investor records an asset, Investment in Bonds, rather than a liability, Bonds Payable. The Investment in Bonds account can be classified as either a current asset or a long-term investment, depending on the marketability of the bonds and management's intention as to when the bonds will be converted into cash. Thus, bonds can be purchased in order to invest idle cash on a short-term basis, to make a long-term investment in another company, or to accumulate funds for future expansion plans. The accounting procedures followed by investors in long-term bonds is outlined in the next section.

Accounting for the Acquisition of Bonds

The acquisition price of bonds includes their purchase price, brokerage commission, and any other costs related to the purchase. Bonds may be purchased at their face value or at a discount or premium, and at or between interest dates. In practice, the debit to the Investment in Bonds account is made at cost, including all acquisition costs but excluding the accrued interest element. A separate account is not maintained for the premium or discount. This practice varies from the accounting procedures used by the issuer and the recommendation found in official pronouncements.[3] However, the investor seldom purchases an entire bond issue, and the amount of the discount or premium is not material. We do not use a separate discount or premium account in accounting for investments in the remaining portion of the chapter or in homework assignments for these particular problems.

If bonds are purchased between interest dates, the investor must pay the issuer or the previous bondholder for any interest accrued since the last interest date, because the purchaser will collect the full six months' interest on the next interest date. To illustrate these procedures, assume that the Cinzano

[3]Opinion No. 21.

Corporation purchased twelve $1,000, 10%, 5-year bonds on March 1, 1987. The bonds are dated January 1, 1987. The total face value of the bonds was $12,000. The bonds pay interest semiannually on January 2 and July 1 and were purchased at a price of 98. The following entry is made to record this investment:

Mar. 1, 1987	Investment in Bonds	11,760	
	Interest Receivable	200	
	Cash		11,960
	To record purchase of $12,000 bonds at 98 plus accrued interest of $200.		

Cash payment required
  Acquisition cost
    $12,000 × .98   = $11,760
  Interest receivable
    $12,000 × .05 × 2/6 =   200
                          $11,960

The Investment in Bonds account is recorded at $11,760, net of the discount of $240 ($12,000 − $11,760). The $11,760 also represents the carrying value of the bonds at their purchase date. Interest Receivable is debited for the two months' interest that has accrued since the last payment date on January 2. The receivable is debited because the investor will receive all six months' interest on July 1, 1987.

Amortizing the Discount or Premium

The straight-line method or the effective-interest method can be used to amortize the bond discount or premium. As we noted, if there are material differences between the two methods, the effective-interest method should be used. However, for ease of illustration, we use the straight-line method in this part of the chapter. Regardless of which method is used, the discount is amortized by debiting the Investment in Bonds account, and the premium is amortized by crediting the Investment in Bonds account. This procedure ensures that after the discount or premium is fully amortized, the investment account will reflect the bond's maturity value.

To demonstrate these concepts, we continue with the Cinzano Corporation example. The first interest payment day is on July 1, 1987, and the following entry would be made to record the receipt of the cash interest and the amortization of the discount:

July 1, 1987	Cash	600	
	Investment in Bonds	17	
	Interest Receivable		200
	Interest Revenue		417
	To record semiannual interest payment and discount amortization.		

In this entry, Cash is debited for $600, which is the full 6 months' interest payment ($12,000 × .05). The Investment in Bonds account is debited for four months of discount amortization. The total discount is $240 and is amortized over the remaining 58 months of the bond's life at the time of issue. This equals $4.14 ($240 ÷ 58 months = $4.14) per month, and 4 months' amortization from March 1, 1987 to July 1, 1987 is $16.56 ($4.14 × 4). This is rounded off to $17 in the journal entry. Interest revenue is credited for $417, which consists of 4 months' cash interest plus $17 of the amortized discount. Note that from the investor's perspective, the discount increases interest revenue, and from the issuer's point of view, it increases interest expense.

Thereafter the Cinzano Corporation would make the following set of journal entries each year until the bonds mature or until they are sold. The corporation has a December 31 year-end.

Dec. 31	Interest Receivable	600	
	Investment in Bonds	25	
	Interest Revenue		625
	To record accrual of 6 months' interest plus the amortization of 6 months' interest. ($4.14 × 6 = $24.84, rounded off to $25)		
Jan. 1	Cash	600	
	Interest Receivable		600
	To record receipt of accrued interest receivable.		
July 1	Cash	600	
	Investment in Bonds	25	
	Interest Revenue		625
	To record receipt of 6 months' interest and amortization of discount.		

These examples illustrate the accounting procedures for discounts. Premiums are handled in a similar manner except that the premium decreases interest revenue and is recorded by crediting the Investment in Bonds account.

Sale of Bonds Prior to Maturity

Investors often sell bonds prior to their maturity. The sale is recorded by debiting Cash for the net proceeds received (sale price less commission and fees). The Investment in Bonds account is credited for the net carrying value of the bonds, and a gain or loss is recorded for the difference between the cash proceeds and the carrying value of the bonds. If the bonds are sold between interest dates, the seller also receives the interest that has accrued since the last interest date.

To illustrate, assume that the Cinzano Corporation decides to sell its bonds on October 1, 1989 for $11,500 plus accrued interest. As of the last interest date, July 1, 1989, the balance in the Investment in Bonds account is $11,877, as shown in the T account below:

Investment in Bonds

3/ 1/87 11,760	
7/ 1/87 17	
12/31/87 25	
7/ 1/88 25	
12/31/88 25	
7/ 1/89 25	
Bal. 11,877	

The first step is to record the discount amortization for the three months from July 1 to October 1, 1989. This amounts to $12 ($4.14 × 3 = $12.42, rounded to $12) and is recorded as follows:

Oct. 1, 1989	Investment in Bonds	12	
	Interest Revenue		12
	To record discount amortization for 3 months.		

After this entry the Investment in Bonds account now has a balance of $11,889 ($11,877 + $12). Because the firm sold the bonds for $11,500, it suffered a $389 loss, recorded as follows:

Oct. 1, 1989	Cash	11,800	
	Loss on Sale	389	
	Investment in Bonds		11,889
	Interest Revenue		300
	To record sale of bonds and interest income for 3 months.		

The cash proceeds of $11,800 represents the sale price of $11,500 plus 3 months' accrued interest of $300 ($12,000 × 5% × 3/6) that the buyer is paying the Cinzano Corporation. There is a corresponding credit of $300 to the Interest Revenue account. This represents the cash portion of the interest revenue, and the $12 from the previous October 1, 1989 entry represents the amortized discount portion. Thus over the 3-month period from July 1 to October 1, interest revenue of $312 is earned by the Cinzano Corporation. Again, the loss is the difference between the carrying value of the bond and the sale price of $11,500, excluding interest.

Other Forms of Long-term Debt

This chapter primarily has been concerned with accounting problems related to bonds. There are, however, other types of long-term debt including notes payable, mortgages payable, and leases.

Notes Payable

A firm may issue long-term notes payable for a variety of reasons. For example, notes may be issued to purchase equipment or other assets or to borrow money from the bank for working capital purposes. Generally, as long as the note bears a reasonable rate of interest, there are no particular problems with accounting for these notes.[4] Accounting procedures related to long-term notes payable are similar to those for short-term notes discussed in Chapter 10; that is, the asset received is debited and the note is credited. As interest accrues it is periodically recorded and eventually paid.

Mortgages Payable

A **mortgage** is a promissory note secured by an asset whose title is pledged to the lender. Mortgages generally are payable in equal installments consisting of interest and principal. To demonstrate the accounting procedures, assume that on January 2, 1987 the Grant Corporation purchases a small building for

---

[4]A problem does arise, however, when obligation has no stated interest or the interest rate is substantially below the current rate for similar notes. The accounting issues in this case are rather complex and are the topic of intermediate textbooks.

$1 million and makes a down payment of $200,000. The mortgage is payable over 30 years at a rate of $8,229 monthly. The annual interest rate is 12%, and the first payment is due on February 1, 1987.

The entry to record the purchase of the building is:

Jan. 2, 1987	Building	1,000,000	
	Mortgage Payable		800,000
	Cash		200,000
	To record purchase of building and issuance of 12%, 30-year mortgage.		

Subsequent entries are based on dividing the monthly payment of $8,229 between principal and interest. A mortgage amortization table can be used for this purpose, and such a table for the first five months of 1987 follows:

MORTGAGE AMORTIZATION TABLE				
Date	Total Payment	1% monthly Interest	Principal	Carrying Value of Mortgage
January 1				$800,000
February 1	$8,229	$8,000	$229	799,771
March 1	8,229	7,998	231	799,540
April 1	8,229	7,995	234	799,306
May 1	8,229	7,993	236	799,070
June 1	8,229	7,991	238	798,832

Each month the total payment of $8,229 is divided into interest and principal. The interest is based on 1% (12% ÷ 12 months) of the note's carrying value at the beginning of the month. Therefore, on February 1 the interest is $8,000, or $800,000 × 1% and the principal portion of the payment is thus $229, or $8,229 − $8,000. In March the interest is $7,998, or 1% of $799,771, and this pattern continues monthly. The journal entry for February 1987 is:

Feb. 1, 1987	Interest Expense	8,000	
	Note Payable	229	
	Cash		8,229
	To record February mortgage payment of $8,229.		

Because most mortgages are payable in monthly installments, the principal payments for the next 12 months following the balance sheet date must be shown in the current liability section as a current maturity of long-term debt. The remaining portion is, of course, classified as a long-term liability.

Leases

A lease is a contractual agreement between the **lessor** (the owner of property) and the **lessee** (the user of property) that gives the lessee the right to use the lessor's property for a specific period of time in exchange for stipulated cash payments. The accounting treatment of leases has long been a controversial subject. The basic controversy centers on the classification and accounting treatment for capital leases that are essentially equivalent to installment purchases.

Types of Leases

From the lessee's point of view, there are two types of leases: *operating leases* and *capital leases*. The distinction between them is important because a different accounting treatment is required for each. Thus there are substantial balance sheet and income statement effects based on whether a lease is classified as a capital or an operating lease.

According to FASB Statement No. 13, *Accounting for Leases*, a lease should be classified as a capital lease if the lease meets one or more of the following criteria:

1. The lease transfers ownership of the property to the lessee at the end of the lease term.
2. The lease contains a bargain purchase option (the asset can be purchased by the lessee at a price significantly lower than its then fair market value).
3. The lease term is 75 percent or more of the leased property's estimated economic life.
4. The present value of the minimum lease payments is 90 percent or more of the fair market value of the property to the lessor at the inception of the lease.[5]

Capital leases are accounted for as essentially purchases of property. A lease rather than a bank loan is used to finance the purchase. Accounting for these types of leases requires the lessor (the individual or firm leasing the asset) to record an asset called Leased Property under Capital Lease, and a corresponding liability called Obligation under Capital Lease. At the inception of the lease, the asset and liability are recorded at the present value of the future lease payments. In addition, the leased property as long as it is not land must be depreciated over its useful life. Finally, each period's lease payment must be allocated between interest and principal.

A lease that does not meet any of the above criteria is considered an operating lease. With this type of lease, the lessor retains control and ownership of the property, which subsequently reverts back to the lessor at the end of the lease term. Accounting for this type of lease requires only that the lessee record an expense for the periodic lease payments as they are made. You should keep in mind that these two types of leases are not alternatives for the same transaction. If the terms of the lease agreement meet any of the previously enumerated four criteria, the lease must be accounted for as a capital lease.

The Lease Controversy

Prior to the issuance of FASB Statement No. 13, companies had a good deal of latitude in deciding whether a lease should be classified as an operating or a capital lease. Most companies felt that it was in their best interest to classify as many leases as possible as operating leases, and some obvious purchases that were being financed through leases were considered operating leases when they should have been considered capital leases.

If a lease is considered an operating lease, no liability is recorded on the balance sheet for the required lease payments. This means that the lessee's working capital position or current ratio is not affected by the lease agreement. Remember, if a liability is recorded on a balance sheet, the next 12

[5]Paragraph 7.

payments would have to be considered current while the entire balance in the account Leased Equipment under Capital Lease is considered a noncurrent asset. The fact that the lessee was in substance making an installment purchase but did not have to record the asset or liability on the balance sheet is referred to as **off balance sheet financing.** Off balance sheet financing may make some individuals feel that the firm has incurred less debt than it actually has. Further, the annual expense associated with an operating lease is less in the first few years of the lease term than with the capital lease. Because of these facts and the fear that creditors might react adversely if leases were capitalized on the balance sheet, management had a definite bias to classify leases as operating leases.

The criteria set forth in Statement No. 13 corrected a number of obvious situations in which agreements that were in substance capital leases were being accounted for as operating leases. The four criteria contained in this Statement ensure that leases that are in fact installment purchases are recorded as capital leases. Thus, the appropriate asset and liability, interest expense, and depreciation are recorded. In addition, current accounting rules require substantial footnote disclosure concerning lease terms and agreements.

Summary of Learning Objectives

1. ***The nature and features of bonds payable.*** A bond is a written agreement between a borrower and a lender in which the borrower agrees to repay a stated sum on a future date and to make periodic interest payments. Most bonds are in $1,000 denominations and pay interest semiannually. There are various types of bonds, including term, serial, secured, convertible, and callable bonds.

   The issue price of bonds and subsequent trading prices depend on the relationship between the stated rate of interest and the prevailing market rates. For investments of similar risk, these two rates are often different, so that if the prevailing interest rate is above the stated interest, the bond will be issued or subsequently traded at a discount. Conversely, if the prevailing rate of interest is below the stated rate, the bond will be issued or traded at a premium.

2. ***Accounting for bonds issued at par.*** Bonds will be issued at par or face value if the stated interest rate equals the prevailing market rate. In this situation the journal entry to record the issuance of the bonds is straightforward and takes the following form:

Cash	XXXX	
Bonds Payable		XXXX

   If the bond is issued between interest dates, the accrued interest element is accounted for separately by crediting Interest Payable.

3. ***Bonds issued at other than face value.*** Bonds are often issued at other than face or par value. Any discount or premium should be accounted for separately and should be thought of as an additional interest expense or a reduction of interest expense to be amortized over the life of the bond. The journal entries to record bond issues in these cases take the following form:

Discount			Premium		
Cash	XXX		Cash	XXX	
Discount on Bonds Payable	XXX		Premium on Bonds Payable		XXX
Bonds Payable		XXX	Bonds Payable		XXX

4. **The straight-line and effective-interest methods.** The straight-line and effective-interest methods are different methods used to amortize the discount or premium. Unless there is little difference between the two, the effective-interest method should be used. The following table summarizes each:

Method	Calculation/Interpretation
Straight-line	Amortization is determined by dividing discount or premium by life of bonds since issue date. Result is equal dollar amount of interest expense each period.
Effective-interest	Amortization is determined by multiplying semiannual yield or effective interest rate by bonds' carrying value at beginning of period. Thus interest expense is a constant percentage rate, although dollar amount changes with bond's carrying value.

5. **Other issues related to bonds payable.** If bonds with a discount or premium are issued between interest dates, the interest element also must be accounted for separately. This is done by crediting Interest Payable for the amount of interest that has accrued since the last interest date. If the issuing company's year-end is not an interest date, an adjusting entry must be made to record the interest accrual and the appropriate discount or premium amortization. Finally, any bond issue costs incurred by the issuing firm are generally accumulated in a deferred charge account and amortized on the straight-line basis over the bond's life.

6. **Accounting for the retirement of bonds.** When bonds mature, they are repaid by the firm. The journal entry is simply a debit to Bonds Payable and a credit to Cash. The premium or discount account has already been amortized to zero. If a bond is retired prior to its maturity, a gain or loss will usually result. This gain or loss is the difference between the reacquisition price and the carrying value of the bonds and is considered to be extraordinary.

   Some bonds are convertible into capital stock. At the time these bonds are issued, the proceeds are considered debt. At the time of conversion, the stock is recorded at the carrying value of the converted bonds.

7. **The investor's accounting for bonds.** The investor's accounting for bonds generally parallels the issuer's accounting for bonds. However, by convention, a separate account is not maintained for the discount or premium account. The discount account increases the investor's periodic interest revenue, and the premium reduces the investor's periodic interest revenue.

8. **Other forms of long-term debt.** Other common types of long-term debt include bank loans and notes payable, mortgages payable, and leases. Other than leases, the concepts that apply to bonds payable apply equally well to other forms of long-term debt.

Accounting for leases centers on whether the lease is classified as an operating lease or a capital lease. Lease payments related to operating leases are expensed when paid. Lease payments related to capital leases are recorded at their present value on the lessee's books as both an asset and a liability. If a lease meets the criteria established by the FASB, it is a capital lease; if not, it is an operating lease.

Key Terms

Adjunct Account	Effective-Interest Method	Off Balance Sheet Financing
Bond	Effective Rate	Serial Bonds
Bond Indentures	Lessee	Sinking Fund
Convertible Bonds	Lessor	Stated Interest Rate
Coupon Bonds	Market Interest Rate	Term Bonds
Denomination	Mortgage	Unsecured Bonds
Early Extinguishment of Debt	Nominal Interest Rate	Yield Rate

Problem for Your Review

Accounting for Bonds. On January 2, 1987 the Garvey Corporation issued $200,000 of 14%, 10-year term bonds. The bonds were issued at a premium to yield 12%. The issue price was 111.4699, and the bonds pay interest every January 2 and July 1.

Required:

1. Make the journal entry to record the issue of the bonds on January 2, 1988.
2. Make the journal entry to record the first interest payment on July 1 and premium amortization, assuming that:
   a. Straight-line amortization is used.
   b. Effective-interest amortization is used.
3. If the Garvey Corporation has an August 31 year-end, make the appropriate journal entries at August 31, 1987, assuming that:
   a. Straight-line amortization is used.
   b. Effective-interest amortization is used.
4. The Garvey Corporation repurchased all bonds on January 2, 1990 at a price of 107. Assume that all interest payments and premium amortization for January 2, 1990 have been made and that the firm uses the straight-line method of amortization.

Solution _____

1. January 2, 1987

Cash	222,940	
Premium on Bonds Payable		22,940
Bonds Payable		200,000

To record issuance of $200,000 bonds at a price of 111.4699.

	$200,000
	× 1.114699
Issue price	$222,940
Face value	− 200,000
Premium	$ 22,940

2. July 1, 1987
a. Straight-line Method

Interest Expense	12,853	
Premium on Bonds Payable	1,147	
Cash		14,000

To record interest payment and premium amortization
on a straight-line basis, calculated as follows:

Cash interest $200,000
$\times .07$
$ 14,000

Premium amortization

$$\frac{\$22,940}{20 \text{ interest periods}} = \$1,147 \text{ per period}$$

b. Effective-Interest Method

Interest Expense	13,376	
Premium on Bonds Payable	624	
Cash		14,000

To record interest payment and premium amortization
on effective-interest basis, calculated as follows:

Carrying value, 1/2/87	$222,940
Yield rate	.06
Effective interest	$ 13,376
Cash interest	14,000
Premium amortization	(624)
Carrying value, 1/2/87	222,940
Carrying value, 7/1/87	$222,316

3. 8/31/87—Year-end Accruals (2 months from 7/1 to 8/31/87)
a. Straight-line Method

Interest Expense	4,285	
Premium on Bonds Payable	382	
Interest Payable		4,667

To record 2 months' interest accrual and premium amortization, calculated as follows:

Interest payable = $200,000 $\times$ .07 $\times$ 2/6 =	$4,667
Premium amortization = $1,147 $\times$ 2/6 =	(382)
Interest expense	$4,285

b. Effective-Interest Method

Interest Expense	4,446	
Premium on Bonds Payable	221	
Interest Payable		4,667

To record 2 months' interest accrual and premium amortization, calculated as follows:

Carrying value 7/1/87	$222,316	See Item (b) above
Yield rate	.06	
	13,339*	
Two-months' adjustment	$\times$ 2/6	
Interest expense	$ 4,446	
Interest payable	4,667	
Premium on bonds payable	$ 221	

*Rounded to whole dollars.

4. 1/2/90 Repurchase of Bonds

Bonds Payable	200,000	
Premium Bonds Payable	16,058	
Extraordinary Gain		2,058
Cash		214,000

To record repurchase of bonds at 107. Gain, which is extraordinary, is calculated as follows:

Carrying value of bonds on 1/2/90

Face value	$200,000
Unamortized premium	
(See T account, below)	16,058
	216,058
Repurchase price	214,000
Gain	$ 2,058

Premium on Bonds Payable

7/1/87	1,147	1/2/87	22,940
1/2/88	1,147		
7/1/88	1,147		
1/2/89	1,147		
7/1/89	1,147		
1/2/90	1,147		
	6,882		
		1/2/90	16,058

Note: We have ignored year-end accruals in this T account and have recorded just the July and January 2 entries.

Questions

1. What is a term bond? Describe the common features of bonds.

2. Define the following terms regarding bonds:
   a. Face value.
   b. Maturity value.
   c. Maturity date.
   d. Stated interest rate.
   e. Market interest rate.

3. Describe the following types of bonds:
   a. Serial bonds.
   b. Term bonds.
   c. Bearer bonds.
   d. Coupon bonds.
   e. Debentures.
   f. Convertible bonds.

4. What are written covenants, and why are they included in certain bond agreements?

5. Several months ago, you purchased a $1,000, 8% bond of the Marlow Corporation at a price of 102. You recently looked in the paper and noticed that the latest price was 98.
   a. How much did you pay for the bond?
   b. How much interest will you receive every six months?
   c. If you sold the bond today, how much would you receive? (Assume all interest has been paid.)

6. What factors are considered in setting the stated rate of interest on a bond? How does this stated rate affect the bond's issue price?

7. One of your fellow students does not understand how a bond with a stated rate of interest of 10% set by management can be issued at a discount. Explain how this can happen.

8. Explain the relationship among the stated interest rate, the market interest rate, and the price at which the bond is issued.

9. Several years ago the Newburyport Corporation issued bonds with a stated interest rate of 12%, which

approximated the market rate at the time. However, in recent years interest rates in the economy have fallen to about 8%. What effect will this have on the current price of the bonds? Why?

10. What is the proper method of presenting bonds payable and any related premium or discount on the balance sheet?

11. Recently the Diome Corporation issued 100 $1,000, 8% bonds at 98. Were the bonds issued at a premium or a discount, and what is the amount of that premium or discount? How much cash did the firm receive from the issue? (Assume the bonds were issued on an interest date.)

12. The Jiffy Computer Corporation recently issued $100,000 of 10% bonds at 103. Interest is paid semiannually. The bonds were issued on an interest date.
  a. Were the bonds issued at a premium or a discount?
  b. How much cash did the company receive from the issue?
  c. What was the amount of interest expense in the first 6-month period, assuming the firm uses the straight-line method of amortization and the bond will mature in 10 years?

13. Describe the straight-line and the effective-interest amortization methods. Which method is considered preferable?

14. What are bond issue costs, and how are they handled under current accounting practices?

15. What is a bond sinking fund, and what is its purpose?

16. In some situations, notes are issued with no interest rate or with an interest rate that is unreasonably low. Under current accounting practices, how should these notes be handled?

17. Define leases and describe the different types.

18. Many individuals consider capital leases to be essentially purchases. Why? In answering the question, also include the characteristics of capital leases.

19. Why would a business wish to classify a lease as an operating lease rather than as a capital lease?

20. The Always Late Delivery Company recently leased one of its trucks. Under the terms of the lease, the company had to make monthly payments of $500 for the next 5 years. At the end of the lease term, Always Late can purchase the truck for $100. What type of lease is this, and why?

Exercises*

1. The Issuance of Bonds. The Rugless Corporation issued $1 million of bonds on an interest date at a price of 105.
  a. Determine the total cash the company received from the bond issue.
  b. Did the bonds sell at par, at a discount, or at a premium?
  c. Make the journal entry to record the issue of the bonds.

2. Recording the Issuance of Bonds. On January 2, 1987 the Alpha Beta Corporation issued $100,000 of 10-year term bonds with a stated rate of interest of 14%. The bonds pay interest semiannually on January 2 and July 1. At the time of the issue, the current market interest rate was also 14%. Prepare the necessary journal entries to record:
  a. The issue of the bonds on January 2, 1987.
  b. The interest payment on July 1, 1987.
  c. The necessary adjusting entry on December 31, 1987—the firm's year-end.
  d. The interest payment on January 2, 1988.

3. Bonds Issued between Interest Dates. The Homestead Corporation issued $100,000 of 20-year, 9% term bonds on March 1, 1987. The bonds were issued at par and pay interest semiannually every January 2 and July 1. Prepare the necessary journal entries to record:
  a. The issuance of the bonds on March 1, 1987.
  b. The interest payment on July 1, 1987.
  c. The adjusting entry on December 31, 1987—the firm's year-end.

4. Issue of Bonds Not at Face Value. On January 2, 1987 Vacation Cruises sold 10-year term bonds with a face value of $250,000. The bonds had a stated interest rate of 13%, payable semiannually on January 2 and July 1. The bonds were sold to yield 15%, and as a result were issued at a price of $224,513.

*****Note:** Unless otherwise indicated, assume all premiums and discounts are amortized at each interest date and at each adjustment date.

a. Prepare the journal entry to record the issuance of the bonds.

b. Show how the bonds would be disclosed on the balance sheet immediately after their issue.

c. Make the entry to record the interest payment on July 1, 1987. Assume that straight-line amortization is used.

d. Show how the bonds would be disclosed on the balance sheet immediately after the interest payment on July 1, 1987.

5. Issue of Bonds Not at Face Value. El Cholos Restaurants, a franchiser of Mexican restaurants, issued $100,000 of 10-year, 12% bonds on January 2, 1987. Interest is payable on January 2 and July 1. These bonds were issued to yield 10% and were sold at a price of $112,462.

a. Prepare the journal entry to record the issuance of the bonds.

b. Show how the bonds would be disclosed on the balance sheet immediately after their issue.

c. Assuming the firm uses the straight-line amortization method, make the required journal entry to record the interest payment on July 1, 1987.

d. Show how the bonds would be disclosed on the balance sheet on July 1, 1987, after the payment of the interest.

6. Effective Interest Method of Amortization. Using the data from (a) Exercise 4 and (b) Exercise 5, prepare the journal entries to record the payment of interest on July 1, 1987 and the interest accrual on December 31, 1987, assuming the firms use the effective-interest method of amortization.

7. Bonds Issued between Interest Dates above Face Value. On March 1, 1987 the Downing Manufacturing Corporation issued $200,000 of 12%, 10-year term bonds dated January 2, 1987. The bonds were issued to yield 14% and pay interest semiannually on January 2 and July 1. The bonds were issued at a price of 89.44389 net of the discount. The firm uses the straight-line method of amortization. Prepare the entries to record:

a. The issuance of the bonds on March 1, 1987.

b. The interest payment on July 1, 1987.

c. The interest accrual on December 31, 1987—the firm's year-end.

8. Early Extinguishment of Bonds. On January 2, 1984 South Central Airlines issued $500,000 of 20-year, 12% bonds at 102. The bonds pay interest every January 2 and July 1. On July 1, 1987, immediately after the interest payment, the bonds were called at a price of 105. The firm uses the straight-line method of amortization. Prepare the journal entries at:

a. January 2, 1984—the date of issue.

b. July 1, 1987—to record the interest payment and premium amortization.

c. July 1, 1987—to record the extinguishment of the bonds.

9. Conversion of Bonds. On April 1, 1984 the Orwell Company issued $100,000 of 8%, 5-year convertible bonds at 98. The bonds pay interest every April 1 and October 1. Each bond is convertible into 5 shares of capital stock. On April 1, 1987, immediately after the required interest payment, all the bonds were converted into capital stock. Make the required entries to record:

a. The issuance of the bonds.

b. The interest payment on April 1, 1987 (using straight-line amortization).

c. The conversion of the bonds into capital stock.

10. Investment in Bonds. On March 1, 1987 the Vargo Specialty Manufacturing Company purchased $15,000 of 12%, 5-year bonds. The bonds were dated January 1, 1987. They pay interest semiannually on January 2 and July 1. The company purchased the bonds for $16,160. Straight-line amortization is used. Prepare the journal entries to:

a. Record the initial investment on March 1.

b. Record the receipt of the first interest collection on July 1.

c. Assume that the company sold the bonds at 104 on April 1, 1988. Make the entry to record the sale.

11. Analysis Relating to Bond Amortization. On January 2, 1987 the Old Time Brewer Co. issued $100,000 of 12%, 20-year bonds at a price of 86.667 that resulted in a 14% yield. The bonds pay interest semiannually on January 2 and July 1.

Required:

    a. How much cash did the firm receive from the issue of the bonds?

    b. Assuming the firm uses the straight-line method of amortizing any discount or premium:

        1. How much cash did the firm expend for interest from January 2, 1987 to January 2, 1988?

        2. How much interest expense did the firm incur from January 2, 1987 to January 2, 1988?

        3. How much interest expense did the firm incur because of the bond over its 20-year life?

    c. Assuming that the firm uses the effective-interest method of amortizing any discount or premium:

        1. How much cash did the firm expend for interest from January 2, 1987 to January 2, 1988?

        2. How much interest expense did the firm incur from January 2, 1987 to January 2, 1988?

        3. How much interest expense did the firm incur because of the bond over its 20-year life?

12. Accounting for Mortgages. The Gar Company recently purchased a new office building. The building cost $500,000. The firm made a 20% down payment and financed the remainder through a 30-year 12% mortgage with monthly payments of $4,114.

Required:

    a. Prepare an amortization table similar to the one on page 725 for the first four monthly payments.

    b. Make the entries to record the purchase of the building and the first two monthly mortgage payments.

13. Accounting for Leases. On January 1, 1987 the Greenblatt-Falk Corporation entered into a five-year agreement to lease a special typesetting machine. The lease calls for 10 annual payments of $17,698 to begin on December 31, 1987. At the end of the lease term, Greenblatt-Falk can purchase the machine for $100, substantially below its estimated fair market value at that time.

Required:

    a. Is this agreement considered an operating or a capital lease? Why?

    b. Assuming that it is considered an operating lease, make the entry to record the first payment on December 31, 1987.

    c. Assuming that it is a capital lease and its value on January 1, 1987 is $100,000, make the entry to record the lease agreement on January 1, 1987.

Problem Set A

18A-1. Accounting for Bonds. The Hemsted Corporation is considering issuing bonds and has asked your advice concerning several matters. The firm plans to issue $500,000 of 20-year 10% bonds. Bond interest payments are on April 1 and October 1. The firm has a December 31 year-end.

Required:

    a. If the bonds are issued on April 1 at a price of 91.977 to yield 11%, how much cash will the firm receive? Explain to the president of the corporation the difference in interest expense the firm will incur during the first year if the effective-interest method of amortization rather than the straight-line method is used. How will the firm's cash flow be affected in the first year?

    b. If the bonds are issued on April 1 at a price of 109.201 to yield 9%, how much cash will the firm receive? Explain to the president of the corporation the difference in interest expense the firm will incur during the first year if the effective-interest method rather than the straight-line method of amortization is used. How will the firm's cash flow be affected in the first year?

    c. If the bonds are issued on June 1 at par, how much cash will the firm receive? Determine for the president the amount of interest expense the firm will incur relative to the bonds for the period between June 1 and April 1 of the following year. Ignore the 12/31 year-end.

18A-2. Bond Transactions—Straight-line Amortization. At the beginning of 1986, the long-term debt section of the China Export Corporation's balance sheet appeared as follows:

Long-term debt:	
10% bonds payable	$200,000
Premium on bonds payable	3,600
	$203,600

The bonds were issued on January 2, 1985 and will mature in 10 years from that date. The firm uses the straight-line method of amortization for bond issues. Interest on these bonds is payable semiannually on January 2 and July 1. During 1986 and 1987 the following transactions regarding bonds took place:

- January 2, 1986: The interest payment on the 10% bonds was made. Assume that the company has a December 31 year-end and that all proper accruals were made at that time.
- March 1: The firm issued $100,000 of 8%, 10-year bonds dated February 1, 1986 at 97. The bonds pay interest semiannually on February 1 and August 1 of every year.
- July 1: The interest payment on the 10% bonds was made, and the premium was amortized.
- August 1: The interest payment on the 8% bonds was made, and the discount was amortized.
- December 31: The firm's year-end, and all interest accruals must be made.
- January 2, 1987: The interest payment on the 10% bonds was made.
- February 1: The interest payment on the 8% bonds was made, and the discount was amortized.
- July 1: Immediately after the interest payment was made on the 10% bonds, they were called at a price of 104.
- August 1: The interest payment on the 8% bonds was made, and the discount was amortized.
- December 31: Year-end interest accruals were made.

Required:
- a. Make the necessary journal entries for 1986 and 1987.
- b. Prepare the long-term debt section of the firm's balance sheet at December 31, 1986 and 1987.
- c. Make the entry to record the last interest payment on the 8% bonds and their repayment at maturity.

18A-3. Bond Transactions—Effective-Interest Amortization. The AB-Smith Corporation is about to undertake a major business expansion. On July 1, 1986 the firm issued $100,000 of 10% bonds to yield 11%. As a result, the issue price was $94,025. The bonds mature on July 1, 1996 and pay interest semiannually on July 1 and January 2. The firm uses the effective-interest method of amortization. The long-term debt section of the firm's December 31, 1986 balance sheet appeared as follows:

Long-term debt:	
10% bonds payable	$100,000
Less: Unamortized discount	5,804
	$ 94,196

During 1987 and 1988, the following events occurred regarding the bonds:

- January 2, 1987: The firm's year-end is December 31. The interest accrual made on that date for the 10% bonds was paid.
- July 1: The semiannual interest payment on the 10% bonds was made, and the discount was amortized.
- September 1: The firm issued $500,000 of 10% bonds at 106.5040 to yield 9%. The bonds mature in 10 years and pay interest every September 1 and March 1.

Accounting for Long-term Liabilities and Investments in Bonds   **735**

- December 31: Year-end interest accruals and amortizations were made.
- January 2, 1988: The interest payment on the $100,000 bonds was made.
- March 1: The interest payment on the $500,000 bonds was made, and the proper amount of premium was amortized.
- July 1: The interest payment on the $100,000 bonds was made, and the proper amount of discount was amortized. Immediately thereafter, all of these bonds were called at a price of 101.
- September 1: The interest payment on the $500,000 was made, and the proper amount of premium was amortized.
- December 31: The proper interest accruals and amortizations were made at year-end.

Required:

a. Prepare the journal entries to record the above transactions.
b. Prepare the long-term debt section of the firm's balance sheet at December 31, 1987 and 1988.

18A–4. Interest Amortization Tables. On April 1, 1985 the E. Dills Corporation issued $150,000 of 5-year bonds. The stated interest rate on the bonds is 7% and the bonds were issued at a price of 92.2209 to yield 9%. Interest is payable *annually* on April 1 of each year.

Required:

Prepare an amortization table for the bonds, assuming (a) the straight-line method of discount amortization is used and (b) the effective-interest method is used. You should use the following headings for your tables:

a. Date.
b. Carrying value of bonds at the beginning of the period.
c. Interest expense.
d. Cash interest paid.
e. Discount amortization.
f. Unamortized discount at the end of the period.
g. Carrying value of bonds at the end of the period.

18A–5. Bond Analysis. The accountant for Early Games, Inc. prepared the following partial amortization table for $200,000 of 5-year bonds on which interest is payable every July 1 and January 2:

Date	Interest Expense	Interest Paid	Amortization	Unamortized Amount	Carrying Value of Bonds
1/02/84				$15,444	$215,444
7/01/84	$10,772	$12,000	$1,228	14,216	214,216
1/02/85	10,711	12,000	1,289	12,927	212,927

Required:

a. Were these bonds issued at a discount, at a premium, or at par?
b. What is the stated rate of interest on the bonds?
c. At what interest rate were the bonds issued to yield?
d. Is the firm using the straight-line or the effective-interest method of amortization? Explain the reasoning behind your answer.
e. Continue the table through 1986.

18A–6. Investment in Bonds. On May 1, 1986 the Price-Fischer Corporation issued $100,000 of 5-year, 10% bonds dated January 2, 1986 at a price of 98. All of these bonds were purchased by Helen Chen. The bonds pay interest every July 1 and January 2.

Required:

a. Assuming that both Price-Fischer and Chen use the straight-line method of interest amortization, make the entries for these bonds for both parties through January 2, 1987. Assume that both have a December 31 year-end.

b. On July 1, 1987, after the interest payment, Price-Fischer calls one-half of the bonds at a price of 102. Make the entries to record this event on the books of both Price-Fischer and Chen.

18A-7. Mortgage and Note Payable Transactions. During 1986 the West Corporation entered into the following transactions:

- April 1: The corporation borrows $100,000 from the local bank. The loan is payable in full in five years. Interest of 10% is payable annually on April 1.

- December 31: The firm purchased a building for $600,000. A $100,000 down payment was made, and a 30-year mortgage was taken out for the remaining $500,000. Under the terms of the mortgage, payments of $71,408 are to be made annually for 30 years, beginning on December 31, 1987. The mortgage has a stated interest rate of 14%.

Required:

a. Make the journal entries for the note and the mortgage for 1986 and 1987. Assume that the firm has a December 31 year-end.

b. Assuming that these are the firm's only long-term liabilities and that the only recorded short-term payables other than interest are accounts payable of $20,000, prepare the liabilities section of the firm's December 31, 1986 balance sheet.

Problem Set B

18B-1. Accounting for Bonds. Weiss Corporation plans to issue $1 million of 10-year, 9% term bonds. Interest is payable semiannually on January 2 and July 1. The firm has a December 31 year-end.

Required:

a. If the bonds were issued on January 2 at a price of 93.769 to yield 10%, how much cash will the firm receive? Explain the difference in interest expense the firm will incur during the first year if the effective-interest method rather than the straight-line method of amortization is used. How much is the firm's cash flow affected in the first year?

b. If the bonds are issued on January 2 at a price of 106.795 to yield 8%, how much cash will the firm receive? Explain the difference in interest expense the firm will incur during the first year if the effective-interest method rather than the straight-line method of amortization is used. How is the firm's cash flow affected in the first year?

c. If the bonds are issued on March 1 at par, how much cash will the firm receive? Determine the amount of interest expense the firm will incur relative to the bonds for the period March 1 to December 31 of the first year.

18B-2. Bond Transactions—Straight-line Amortization. At the beginning of 1987, the long-term debt section of Julia International, Inc. appeared as follows:

8% bonds payable	$300,000
Less: Discount on bonds payable	4,800
	$295,200

The bonds were issued on January 2, 1985 and mature in 10 years from that date. The firm uses the straight-line method of amortization for all bond issues. Interest on these bonds is payable semiannually on January 2 and July 1. During 1987 and 1988 the following transactions relative to bonds took place:

- January 2, 1987: The interest payment on the 8% bonds was made.

- April 1: The firm issued $500,000 of 10%, 10-year bonds at 104. The bonds pay interest semiannually on April 1 and October 1.

- July 1: The interest payment on the 8% bonds was made and the discount was amortized.

- October 1: The interest payment on the 10% bonds was made and the premium was amortized.

- December 31: The firm's year-end and all interest accruals are made.

- January 2, 1988: The interest payment on the 8% bonds was made.

- April 1: The interest payment on the 10% bonds was made and the premium was amortized.
- July 1: Immediately after the interest payment was made on the 8% bonds, they were called at a price of 99.
- October 1: The interest payment on the 10% bonds was made and the premium was amortized.
- December 31: The firm's year-end and all interest accruals are made.

Required:

a. Make the necessary journal entries for 1987 and 1988 to record these events.
b. Prepare the long-term debt section of the firm's balance sheet at December 31, 1987 and 1988.
c. Make the entry to record the last interest payment on the 10% bonds and their repayment at maturity.

18B-3. Bond Transactions—Effective-Interest Amortization. Bill Smith and Associates needs additional financing in order to begin a new product line. The board of directors authorizes the company to issue $400,000 of 10% bonds on September 1, 1987. The bonds mature on September 1, 1997 and pay interest semiannually on September 1 and March 1. Because of market conditions, the bonds were issued to yield 12%. The firm uses the effective-interest method of amortization for all bond issues. The long-term debt section of the firm's balance sheet at December 31, 1987 appears as follows:

10% bonds payable	$400,000
Less: Discount on bonds payable	45,050
	$354,950

During 1988 and 1989 the following events relative to the bonds occurred:
- March 1, 1988: The interest payment on the $400,000 10% bonds was made and the discount was amortized.
- July 1: The firm issued $200,000 of 10% bonds at 113.59 to yield 8%. The bonds mature in 10 years and pay interest on January 2 and July 1.
- September 1: The interest payment on the $400,000 10% bonds was made and the discount was amortized.
- December 31: The firm's year-end and interest accruals and amortizations were made.
- January 2, 1989: The interest payment on the $200,000 10% bonds was made.
- March 1: The interest payment on the $400,000 10% bonds was made and the discount was amortized.
- July 1: The interest payment on the $200,000 10% bonds was made and the premium was amortized.
- September 1: The interest payment on the $400,000 10% bonds was made and the discount was amortized. Immediately thereafter, all the bonds were called at a price of 95.
- December 31: The firm's year-end and interest accruals and amortizations were made.

Required:

a. Prepare the journal entries to record the above bond transactions during 1988 and 1989.
b. Prepare the long-term debt section of the firm's balance sheet at December 31, 1988 and 1989.

18B-4. Interest Amortization Tables. On January 2, 1987 the Peacock Corporation issued $500,000 of 5-year bonds. The bonds have a stated rate of interest of 10% and were issued at 107.986 to yield 8%. Interest is payable *annually* on January 2 of each year.

Required:

Prepare an amortization table for the bonds assuming (a) the straight-line method of premium amortization is used and (b) the effective-interest method of premium amortization is used. You should use the following headings for your table:

a. Date.

b. Carrying value of bonds at the beginning of the period.

c. Cash interest paid.

d. Interest expense.

e. Premium amortization.

f. Unamortized premium at the end of the period.

g. Carrying value of the bonds at the end of the period.

18B–5. Bond Analysis. The accountant for J. C. Lee Enterprises prepared an amortization table for a $500,000, 10-year bond issue. The interest payments are made on March 1 and September 1.

Date	Interest Expense	Interest Paid	Amortization	Unamortized Amount	Carrying Value of Bonds
3/1/86				$57,352	$442,648
9/1/86	$26,559	$25,000	$1,559	55,793	444,207
3/1/87	26,652	25,000	1,652	54,141	445,859

Required:

a. Were the bonds issued at a premium, at a discount, or at par?

b. What is the stated rate of interest on the bonds?

c. At what interest rate were the bonds issued to yield?

d. Is the firm using the straight-line or the effective-interest method of amortization? Explain the reasoning behind your answer.

e. Continue the table through 9/1/88.

18B–6. Investment in Bonds. On March 1, 1987 T, R, & T Enterprises issued $300,000 of 10-year, 9% bonds at 102. All of the bonds were purchased by the S, T, & S Corporation. The bonds pay interest every January 2 and July 1.

Required:

a. Assuming that both parties use the straight-line method of interest amortization, make the entries relative to these bonds for both. Assume that both parties have a December 31 year-end.

b. On July 1, 1988, after the interest payment, T, R, & T Enterprises called one-third of the bonds at a price of 103. Make the journal entries to record this event on the books of both parties.

18B–7. Mortgage and Note Payable Transactions. During 1987 the Johnston Corporation entered into the following transactions:

• May 1: The corporation borrows $500,000 from Nance National Bank. The loan is fully payable on April 30, 1988. Interest is 12% and is payable every six months.

• November 1: The firm purchased land and a building for $200,000. A 20% down payment was made and a 30-year mortgage was taken out for the remainder. Under the terms of the mortgage, payments of $1,646 are paid monthly beginning December 1. The mortgage has an annual interest rate of 12%.

Required:

Make the journal entries for the note and mortgage from May 1, 1987 through April 30, 1988. Assume that the firm has a December 31 year-end.

Using the Computer

A. The Carey Corporation borrowed $500,000 at 15%. The note is to be repaid in 60 equal monthly installments, beginning at the end of the first month. Prepare a loan amortization table using an electronic spreadsheet similar to the mortgage table on page 725 of the text. Use the following format:

LOAN AMORTIZATION TABLE

Data Entry Area

Principal	$250,000
Interest	15%
Term	60 months

Month	Total Payment	Interest Portion	Principal Portion	Carrying Value of Mortgage

Now repeat the amortization schedule, assuming that the interest is only 12%.

B. The Star Gazer Corporation issued $700,000 of 10-year, 14% term bonds to yield 12%. Interest is payable semiannually on January 2, the issue date, and July 1. Using an electronic spreadsheet, prepare a premium amortization table similar to the one on page 716 using the effective interest method. Use the same column headings.

Understanding Financial Statements

Following is the comparative balance sheet for the Priam Corporation:

Consolidated Balance Sheets

June 30, 1983 and 1982	1983	1982
	(Dollars in thousands)	
ASSETS		
Current assets:		
Cash and temporary cash investments	$58,606	$ 125
Accounts receivable, net of allowance for doubtful accounts of $719 ($367 in 1982)	15,187	8,752
Inventories	12,203	12,221
Prepaid expenses	1,317	142
Total current assets	87,313	21,240
Net property and equipment	7,539	2,110
Other assets	84	929
	$94,936	$24,279
LIABILITIES AND SHAREHOLDERS' EQUITY		
Current liabilities:		
Notes payable to bank	$ —	$ 4,050
Accounts payable	7,214	5,664
Accrued payroll and related benefits	1,100	256
Accrued liabilities	1,199	851
Current obligations under capital leases	672	72
Total current liabilities	10,185	10,893
Noncurrent obligations under capital leases	5,045	1,363
15% convertible subordinated notes	—	3,570
Shareholders' equity		
Preferred stock, no par value;		
4,000,000 shares authorized;		
issued and outstanding 1,708,531 at June 30, 1982.	—	14,381
Common stock, no par value;		
25,000,000 shares authorized;		
issued and outstanding 15,178,824 and 3,057,089 at June 30, 1983 and 1982, respectively.	81,440	353
Accumulated deficit	(1,734)	(6,281)
Total shareholders' equity	79,706	8,453
	$94,936	$24,279

Required:

    a. The 15% convertible subordinated notes were issued in April 1982, due in 1992. Why do you think that they were extinguished early? (The notes were not converted into common stock.)

    b. According to the income statement, the firm incurred a $384,000 loss in the early extinguishment of these notes. Determine how much the corporation paid in order to pay off the notes.

    c. Make the journal entry to record the early extinguishment of debt.

Financial Decision Case

On January 2, 1975 the Lafler Corporation issued $600,000 of 20-year, 8% bonds to yield 10%. The bonds were issued at a price of 82.8413. The bonds pay interest semiannually on January 2 and July 1. By January 2, 1985 interest rates in the economy had risen, and current market rates for investments of risk similar to that of the Lafler Corporation were 12%. As a result, the current aggregate market value of the bonds on January 2, 1985 ($500,000) was below their carrying value. The president of the firm is considering repurchasing all these bonds in the open market at that price. However, to do that the firm will have to issue new 30-year bonds with a stated rate of interest of 12%. Bonds with a face value of $500,000 would be issued at par. The president asks your advice on the feasibility of this proposed repurchase.

Investment in Corporate Equity Securities

19

LEARNING OBJECTIVES

After reading this chapter you should be able to:

1. Discuss the nature and role of publicly held corporations and security exchanges.
2. Measure and record investments in current marketable securities, including:
   a. Equity securities.
   b. Debt securities.
3. Measure and report long-term investments.
4. Account for investments when there is no significant influence or control.
5. Account for ownership interests when there is significant influence but no control.
6. Account for majority ownership interests including:
   a. The difference between the purchase and the pooling-of-interests methods of accounting for acquisitions.
   b. The preparation of consolidated financial statements.

The securities of business firms are purchased by many groups and individuals, including corporations, mutual funds, bank trust departments, and individual investors. There are several reasons that individuals or other entities may invest in the securities of other firms. The investment may be made in order to invest idle cash in the hope of realizing a gain or in order to have significant influence or control over another corporation. For example, Allied Chemical Company recently purchased large blocks of Bendix Corporation in a takeover fight. Eventually, Allied gained control over Bendix, and Bendix became a subsidiary of Allied.

Equity and debt securities are the two major types of securities purchased by investors. **Equity securities** refer to preferred and common stock, and **debt**

securities refer to bonds. Accounting for investments in long-term bonds was discussed in Chapter 18. In this chapter we focus on accounting for both short- and long-term investments in equity securities.

Most investors purchase the securities of publicly held corporations. A **publicly held corporation** is one whose stock is owned by outside investors and whose stock and/or bonds are listed on national and regional exchanges. National exchanges include the New York Stock Exchange, the American Stock Exchange, and the national over-the-counter market. The stocks of the largest publicly held corporations are listed on the New York Stock Exchange, and the stocks of smaller corporations are listed on the American Stock Exchange or regional exchanges such as the Pacific Stock Exchange. The stocks of some corporations are not listed on an organized exchange but on the over-the-counter market. The over-the-counter market is maintained by numerous brokerage firms buying and selling securities for their customers. Corporations whose stock is traded on this market are generally smaller corporations or corporations that have recently issued stock for the first time (often referred to as "going public").

Publicly held corporations must comply with regulations of both the Securities and Exchange Commission (SEC) and the exchange on which its stock is listed. For example, these companies must file an annual report, called a 10-K, with the SEC. In effect, this report is an expanded version of the financial data contained in the annual report to shareholders. The 10-K form must contain the corporation's financial statements, which have been audited by a certified public accounting firm. These same corporations must also file condensed quarterly reports, called 10-Qs. Stock exchanges also have certain filing requirements. For example, the listing agreement between the New York Stock Exchange and member companies provides for the timely disclosure of earnings statements, dividend notices, and other financial information that might reasonably be expected to materially affect the market for a firm's securities.

Accounting for Current Marketable Securities

Investment in securities refers to investments in equity and debt securities of corporations as well as the debt securities of federal and local governments and agencies. If these investments are made in publicly held corporations or governmental agencies, they are usually readily marketable and thus can easily be turned into cash. Conversely, if the investment is in a nonpublicly held or closely held corporation, it may not be liquid. Depending on their marketability and management's intention, investments are classified as either current assets or long-term investments. In this section of the chapter we examine accounting for marketable securities that are considered current. Later we discuss accounting for marketable securities and other investments that are classified as long term.

In order for an investment in securities to be considered a current asset, it must meet two criteria:

1. It must be readily marketable, which means there must be an established market for the security.
2. It must be management's intention to convert the securities into cash within the normal operating cycle of the business or one year, whichever is longer.

If both of these criteria are not met, the investment cannot be considered a current asset and is classified as long term.

Marketable securities are usually purchased in order to invest idle cash. Management needs to maintain a certain level of cash in order to meet its current obligations and working capital requirements. Excess cash is often invested in securities to provide a return. The ability to turn these investments into cash quickly is important, as management constantly monitors its immediate cash needs.

Marketable securities include both equity and debt securities. When more than one security of either or both types is purchased, the investor is considered to be holding a portfolio, which is made up of several different securities and which allows the investor to decrease his or her risk through diversification. Because the accounting treatment differs slightly for equity and debt securities, both of them will be discussed.

Accounting for Current Equity Securities

When equity securities are purchased, they are recorded at cost in an account titled Investment in Marketable Securities. Under the historical cost convention, cost includes all brokerage commissions, other costs, and taxes incurred at acquisition. To illustrate, assume that during the first year of business on October 1, 1986, the EFP Corporation made the following purchases of current marketable equity securities:

Security	Number of Shares	Price per Share*	Total Cost
Kahn, Inc.—Common	100	$ 75	$ 7,500
Webb Construction—Preferred	100	200	20,000
Stern-Price Piano—Common	50	60	3,000
Total cost			$30,500

*Includes all brokerage commissions.

In order to record this purchase, the EFP Corporation made this entry:

Oct. 1, 1986	Investment in Current Marketable Securities	30,500	
	Cash		30,500
	To record purchase of marketable securities.		

All the securities are recorded in one general ledger account, Investment in Marketable Securities. Subsidiary ledger accounts are also maintained for each security. In most cases, the subsidiary ledger account consists of a separate card for each security which shows the acquisition date, the total cost, the number of shares or bonds owned, the dividends or the interest received, and the gain or the loss on disposition.

Accounting for Subsequent Events

Investors purchase the stock of another company in the hope of realizing a return on their investment. Their return is in the form of dividends received while the stock is held and/or a gain or loss when the securities are sold.

An investor usually records the dividends as income when the dividend checks are received, rather than when they are declared by the issuing company. Although this is not in accordance with strict accrual accounting, the financial statements usually are not materially misstated and it does simplify the accounting records. To demonstrate, assume that the Best Eastern Corporation owns 100 shares of Electric General. On December 1, Electric General declares a $0.75 per-share dividend payable on December 20. On December 20, Best Eastern makes the following entry:

```
Dec. 20, 1986   Cash                                    75
                    Dividend Revenue                        75
                To record dividend received of $75.
                ($0.75 × 100 shares)
```

Besides expecting to receive dividends, investors expect to sell their stock in the future at a price above their original purchase price. The market price of equity securities reacts to general economic conditions as well as to specific events that affect the firm. Thus the market price of the investor's stock may rise or fall during a particular accounting period. The investor may choose to sell the stock and realize a gain or loss on the transaction or to hold the stock and incur an unrealized gain or loss. (The gain or loss is unrealized because the stocks have not been sold.) One of the issues confronting the accounting profession is how to account for unrealized gains or losses on marketable equity securities.

The Lower-of-Cost-or-Market Rule

In 1975 the FASB issued Statement 12, which requires that after acquisition, investments in marketable equity securities must be valued at the lower of cost or market and that the necessary adjustments must be made on each balance sheet date. Essentially, this Statement requires that firms divide their marketable equity securities into a current portfolio and a noncurrent portfolio and that each portfolio be shown on the balance sheet at the lower of its aggregate cost or market value. Thus, if the total market value of the securities in a portfolio is below its cost, an unrealized loss must be recognized. An Allowance account, similar to the Allowance for Doubtful Accounts, is used to reduce the securities to market. This reduction is made whether the price decline is temporary or permanent. But if the market price of the stock rises above its cost, the stock cannot be written up above its original cost.

To illustrate the application of the lower-of-cost-or-market rule (LCM rule) as applied to current marketable equity securities, we will continue with the EFP example. (See page 745 for initial data.) Because EFP prepares its balance sheet once a year on December 31, it must apply the LCM rule at that date. At December 31, 1986, the end of the firm's first year in business, the cost and market value of the portfolio are as shown at the top of page 747.

The total market value of the portfolio, $29,500, is $1,000 below its cost of $30,500. Notice that the valuation is based on the total portfolio, not just on the two stocks that decreased in value. Thus the $1,400 increase in the Webb Construction stock offsets the combined $2,400 decreases in the prices of the other two stocks. The following adjusting entry is made for the purpose of recording the unrealized loss at December 31, 1986:

```
Dec. 31, 1986   Unrealized Loss on Marketable Securities        1,000
                    Allowance to Reduce Marketable Securities
                        to Market                                    1,000
                To record the unrealized loss on marketable
                securities.
```

Current Marketable Equity Security Portfolio
December 31, 1986

Security	Total Cost	Total Market Value	Unrealized Gain or (Loss)
Kahn, Inc.—Common	$ 7,500	$ 6,000	$(1,500)
Webb Construction—Preferred	20,000	21,400	1,400
Stern-Price Piano—Common	3,000	2,100	(900)
Total	$30,500	$29,500	$(1,000)
Present balance in allowance account			0
Required adjustment			$ 1,000

It is important to understand the nature of the two accounts involved in the adjusting journal entry. The Allowance account works just as the Allowance for Doubtful Accounts does when the aging method is used. That is, the amount of the adjusting entry is that amount necessary to bring the Allowance account to a predetermined balance. That balance is the difference between the cost and the market value of the portfolio at the balance sheet date. In this case, because this is the first year of the firm's operations, the balance in the Allowance account before adjustment is zero; the required balance is $1,000, and so the adjusting entry is made for that amount.

The Unrealized Loss account is an income statement account and is included in the other income and expense category. However, because the loss is unrealized, it should be shown as a separate item in order to distinguish it from actual realized gains or losses on the sale of securities.

Balance Sheet Presentation

The account Allowance to Reduce Marketable Securities to Market is a contra-asset account and is offset against the Marketable Securities account. The partial December 31, 1986 balance sheet for EFP appears as follows:

EFP CORPORATION
Partial Balance Sheet
December 31, 1986

Current assets:		
Cash		$124,000
Marketable securities	$30,500	
Less: Allowance to reduce marketable securities to market	(1,000)	29,500
Accounts receivable	89,000	
Less: Allowance for uncollectible accounts	(4,000)	85,000

As we noted, the Unrealized Loss account appears on the income statement under the other income and expense category.

To continue our example, assume that two events occurred in 1987 involving current marketable securities: (1) On April 17, 1987 EFP sold 50 shares of Kahn, Inc. at $65 per share, and (2) an adjustment was made at December 31, 1987 to value the portfolio at the lower of cost or market.

The entry to record the sale of 50 shares of Kahn, Inc. is:

April 17, 1987	Cash	3,250	
	Realized Loss on Sale	500	
	Investment in Marketable Securities		3,750
	To record sale of 50 shares of Kahn, Inc. at $65 per share.		

Notice that a loss of $500 is recorded. This loss is the difference between the recorded cost of the securities of $3,750 ($75 per share $\times$ 50 shares) and the sales price of $3,250 ($65 per share $\times$ 50 shares). The Allowance account is not involved because this account is not directly associated with any specific security in the portfolio. Remember that the Allowance account reduces the entire cost of the portfolio to market but has no effect on the individual securities in the portfolio.

The cost and market of the portfolio at December 31, 1987 are shown as follows. Again, the fact that the makeup of the portfolio has changed over the year is not important. The amount of the required adjusting entry is based on only the total cost and market value of the portfolio.

Current Marketable Equity Security Portfolio
December 31, 1987

Security	Total Cost	Total Market	Unrealized Gain or (Loss)
Kahn, Inc.—Common	$ 3,750	$ 3,600	$ (150)
Webb Construction—Preferred	20,000	21,000	1,000
Stern-Price Piano—Common	3,000	1,800	(1,200)
Total	$26,750	$26,400	$ (350)
Balance in allowance account, 1/1/87			1,000
Required entry to reduce allowance account to balance based on market value on 12/31/87			$ 650

At the end of 1987 the total market value of the securities is only $350 below their cost. Because the Allowance account currently has a balance of $1,000, it must be reduced by $650 to reflect the new balance of $350. The following adjusting entry is made to accomplish this:

Dec. 31, 1987	Allowance to Reduce Marketable Securities to Market	650	
	Reduction in Unrealized Loss on Marketable Securities		650
	To reduce allowance account to required balance of $350.		

The Allowance account is debited and an income statement account, Reduction in Unrealized Loss, is credited. This account can be considered an unrealized gain, though we have chosen not to label it as that. In effect, the firm is simply reducing a loss recorded in the prior year. This account is shown as an income item in the other income and expense category of the income statement.

The correct balance sheet and income statement presentations follow. As before, the Allowance account is offset against the Investment account. Both the realized loss and the unrealized gain are shown separately on the income statement.

EFP Corporation
Partial Balance Sheet
December 31, 1987

Current assets		
Cash		$150,000
Marketable securities	$ 26,750	
Less: Allowance to reduce		
marketable securities to market	350	26,400
Accounts receivable	120,000	
Less: Allowance for uncollectible accounts	8,000	112,000

EFP Corporation
Partial Income Statement
For the Year Ended December 31, 1987

Income from continuing operations		$240,000
Other income (expense)		
Rental income	$24,000	
Reduction of unrealized loss on marketable securities held	650	
Loss on sale of marketable securities	(500)	24,150

Securities Cannot Be Recorded above Cost

According to Statement 12, marketable securities cannot be valued above cost. Thus, the Allowance account will have either a zero or a credit balance. To demonstrate, assume that the entire portfolio is held throughout 1988 and that at the end of 1988 the market value of the portfolio has increased to $30,000. In this case, market exceeds the cost of $26,750, and so the balance in the Allowance account should be zero. Because the balance before any adjustment is $350, the following adjusting entry should be made at December 31, 1988:

Dec. 31, 1988	Allowance to Reduce Marketable Securities		
	to Market	350	
	Reduction in Unrealized Loss on Marketable		
	Securities		350
	To reduce allowance account to a zero balance.		

In effect, this entry writes the securities back up to their cost, but no accounting recognition is given to the fact that the market value now exceeds the cost by \$3,250 (\$30,000 − \$26,750).

In summary, Statement 12 should be applied to marketable equity securities. If the total price of the current portfolio is below cost, an Allowance account should be established for the entire portfolio, regardless of the composition of the securities in the portfolio. Any changes in the Allowance account should be included in net income in the period in which they occur. According to Statement 12, no accounting recognition is given to an increase in market value above cost. Finally, under the full disclosure principle, both the cost and the market value of the securities should be disclosed in the financial statements or in the footnotes.

Evaluation of Lower of Cost or Market

Many accountants feel that the accounting profession was correct in moving away from the strict use of cost in valuing marketable securities. However, many of these same individuals feel that lower of cost or market is too conservative and that marketable equity securities should be valued at market, regardless of whether market is below or above cost. This is so because market values are objectively determined in the capital market; gains and losses occur when the value of the security changes, not when the investment is sold; and the market price can be realized at any time management desires. The main argument given by those against the use of market is that fluctuations in earnings that have not or may not become realized must be recorded in the accounting records. Furthermore, market fluctuations are outside the control of management.

Accounting for Current Debt Securities

The accounting treatment for current investments in debt securities is slightly different from that for current equity securities. First, at acquisition, accounting recognition must be given to any interest that has accrued since the last interest date. This interest is recorded in an Interest Receivable account. This is not the case with dividends on stock. Dividends do not accrue, and no accounting recognition is given to dividends until declared by the board of directors of the issuing company. Second, the lower-of-cost-or-market rule of Statement 12 as it applies to temporary price declines does not have to be applied to investments in debt securities.

To illustrate the accounting issues related to investments in current debt securities, assume that on May 1, 1987 the Doggett Corporation purchases 20 \$1,000, 12% bonds that pay interest every January 2 and July 1. The bonds are purchased at a price of 102 plus \$100 in brokerage commissions. The total cash outlay is \$21,300, which is calculated by adding the cost of the bonds of \$20,500 (\$20,000 × 1.02 = \$20,400 + \$100 brokerage commission = \$20,500) to the accrued interest of \$800 (\$20,000 × .12 × 4/12 = \$800). The following entry is made on May 1, 1987 to record this purchase:

```
May 1, 1987   Investment in Marketable Securities        20,500
              Interest Receivable                            800
                 Cash                                                 21,300
              To record purchase of 20 $1,000 bonds at 102
              plus brokerage commissions and accrued
              interest.
```

On July 1, 1987 the Doggett Corporation receives interest of $1,200, and the following entry is made to record the interest:

```
July 1, 1987   Cash                                         1,200
                  Interest Receivable                               800
                  Interest Revenue                                  400
               To record receipt of six months' interest.
```

The Interest Receivable account is reduced to zero, and 2 months' interest revenue representing May and June is recorded ($20,000 × .12 × 2/12 = $400).

Recording a Gain or Loss

In Chapter 18 we considered the need to amortize the premium or discount on long-term bond investments. The premium or discount is amortized on long-term investments because it is assumed that they will be held to maturity. In effect, the market price of the bond will move toward the maturity or face value as the bond nears maturity. Thus, it makes sense to amortize the discount or premium over the life of the bond, by using the effective-interest method.

Short-term bond investments, however, are usually not held to maturity. The investment account therefore is carried at cost, and any difference between the cost of the bonds and their current selling price represents a gain or loss in the period of sale. Because these investments are held for a relatively short period of time, amortizing a discount or premium would not provide a more meaningful measurement basis than would leaving the investment at cost.

To show how a gain or loss on a sale of a short-term bond investment is measured and recorded, assume that on December 1, 1987 ten of the $1,000, 12% bonds purchased on May 1, 1987 were sold at a price of 104, less brokerage commissions of $50. The total cash received for the bonds was $10,350, or $10,000 × 1.04 − $50. A gain of $100, or $10,350 minus $10,250 (one-half of the acquisition cost of $20,500), is recognized. Finally, because the bonds were sold between interest dates, the seller will receive the interest accrued since July 1. This amounts to $500, or $10,000 × .12 × 5/12. Therefore, the total cash received is $10,850, or $10,350 plus $500. The following entry is made to record the sale:

```
Dec. 1, 1987   Cash                                        10,850
                  Interest Revenue                                  500
                  Gain on Sale of Bonds                             100
                  Investment in Marketable Securities            10,250
               To record gain on sale of 10 $1,000, 12% bonds.
```

LCM Not Required

In addition to the fact that no recognition is given to discount or premiums on short-term debt investments, the LCM rule in Statement 12 need not be applied. Thus, no accounting recognition need be given to a temporary decline in the market value of a bond below its recorded cost. We use the term *need be* because Statement 12 does not prohibit a firm from valuing the debt securities at lower of cost or market; it just requires this treatment for equity securities. Nonetheless, in order to simplify their accounting process, many firms treat current debt and equity investments in the same way and thus apply the LCM rule to all short-term investments.

Financial Statement Presentation of Current Marketable Securities

Marketable securities are shown in a variety of ways on the balance sheets of major corporations. For example, some companies include these temporary investments with cash. Other companies show their investment in marketable securities as a separate item immediately following cash. These two approaches are illustrated by the following two excerpts taken from annual reports:

BR COMMUNICATIONS

BR Communications

	Year End	
	1985	1984
Current assets		
Cash including short-term investments of $3,100,000 and $3,400,000	$3,507,985	$4,384,965

SAFEWAY

Safeway Stores, Inc.

	Year End	
	1985	1984
Current assets		
Cash	$ 54,593,000	$49,179,000
Marketable securities	170,921,000	25,263,000

There are two interesting points about these disclosures. First, note in each case the relative proportion of cash and investments. These firms are practicing good cash management by maintaining small amounts of cash relative to their temporary investments. Second, in both reports no separate disclosure is made of any allowance account. This is so because there is no material difference between the cost and the market value of the securities. This treatment is very common in published financial statements.

Long-term Investments

Investments that do not meet the criteria to be considered current assets are shown in the long-term investment section of the balance sheet. Thus, either these securities are not readily marketable, or management's intention is to hold them for a long period of time or for purposes of control. Accounting for long-term debt investments was explained in Chapter 18. This portion of the chapter considers accounting for long-term equity investments.

Exhibit 19–1 summarizes the accounting treatment for long-term equity investments. The correct accounting treatment depends on the degree of the investor's control over the investee (the firm whose stock has been purchased). The accounting pronouncements differentiate among three levels of control: no significant influence or control, significant influence but not control, and control.[1]

EXHIBIT 19–1

Accounting for Long-term Equity Investments

Amount of Influence or Control	Percentage of Common Stock Owned	Accounting
1. No significant influence or control	Less than 20%	Cost method and lower-of-cost-or-market valuation
2. Significant influence but not control	20% to 50%	Equity method—no LCM valuation
3. Controlling interest	more than 50%	Consolidated financial statements

---

No significant influence or control exists when the investor is unable to have an important impact on either the financing or operating policies of the investee. The accounting pronouncements presume that ownership of less than 20% of the voting stock or any amount of the investee's nonvoting stock will not result in any significant influence or control. This presumption can be overcome, however, if economic circumstances dictate.

Significant influence but not control exists when an investor can influence, but cannot control, the operating and financing policies of the investee. In many situations this influence is evidenced by the investor's having a seat on the board of directors of the investee company, other participation in the policymaking process, material intercompany transactions, the interchange of

[1]Three related pronouncements govern accounting for long-term investments: American Institute of Certified Public Accountants, Accounting Principles Board, Opinions No. 16, *Business Combinations* (New York: AICPA, 1970), and No. 18, *The Equity Method of Accounting for Investments in Common Stock* (New York: AICPA, 1971); and Financial Accounting Standards Board, Statement No. 12, *Accounting for Certain Marketable Securities* (Stamford, Conn.: FASB, December 1975).

management personnel, and technological interdependencies. The accounting pronouncements presume that significant influence but not control exists when the investor holds at least 20% but not more than 50% of another company. In this situation an investor can influence the investee's operating policies but cannot control them because the investor does not have majority control.

Finally, a controlling interest exists when an investor is able to determine both the financial and the operating policies of the other company. Control is presumed when the investor owns more than 50% of the stock of another company.

No Significant Influence or Control

When the ownership interest is less than 20%, the investor is presumed not to have significant influence or control over the operations of the investee company. Under current practices the cost method of accounting is used to account for these types of investments.[2] Thus, at acquisition, the investment is recorded at cost and is subsequently valued at lower of cost or market. Income from the investment is recognized when dividends are received by the investor. With the exception of a few variations in applying the LCM rule, measuring and recording long-term investments of ownership interests of less than 20% are the same as for short-term marketable equity securities.

Accounting at Acquisition

Like short-term equity securities, acquisition cost includes whatever expenditures are necessary to acquire the securities. Thus, brokerage fees, commissions, and taxes all are included in the initial acquisition cost. For example, assume that on July 1, 1987 the Popper Company purchased 100 shares of Bailey, Inc. at $40 per share and 100 shares of Essence, Inc. at $60 per share. The Popper Company made the following entry at July 1, 1987:

July 1, 1987	Long-term Investments in Securities	10,000	
	Cash		10,000
	To record purchase of long-term investments.		

Accounting for Subsequent Events

Under the cost method of accounting for investments, dividends are recorded as income when they are received. Furthermore, at each balance sheet date the securities must be valued at the lower of cost or market.

To illustrate, assume that on December 1, 1987 the Popper Company received cash dividends of $2 per share on the 100 shares of Essence. The entry to record the receipt of the dividends is:

Dec. 1, 1987	Cash	200	
	Dividend Revenue		200
	To record dividends of $2 per share of Essence stock.		

On the balance sheet date, the securities must be valued at lower of cost or market. Assume that on December 31 the Bailey stock was selling at $34 per share, and the Essence stock at $62 per share. Because the aggregate market value of $9,600 is $400 below its $10,000 cost and the Allowance account

[2]Opinion 18.

currently has a zero balance (assuming first purchase of securities), this account must be credited for this amount. Accordingly, the Popper Company would make the following entry on December 31:

Dec. 31, 1987   Unrealized Loss on Long-term Investment   400
                 Allowance to Reduce Long-term Equity
                 Investments to Market   400
                 To record decrease in market value of securities.

The Allowance account is a contra-asset account that is offset against the Investment account on the balance sheet. This is the same treatment as for short-term investments.

The Unrealized Loss account, however, is not an income statement account, as it is when short-term investments are involved. For long-term investments, the Unrealized Loss account is a debit item in stockholders' equity (a contra-equity account) and is shown immediately after retained earnings. Thus both accounts in the adjusting entry are balance sheet accounts. This treatment is based on the view that long-term investments will not be sold in the near future, and so unrealized losses will not immediately affect income.

In most other respects, the application of LCM requirements is the same as for short-term equity investments.[3] That is, if the securities subsequently increase in value so that market exceeds cost, the contra-equity account can be eliminated. Because the investments cannot be valued at higher than cost, the Unrealized Loss on Long-term Investment account cannot have a credit balance.

Ownership Interest between 20 and 50 Percent

Significant influence but not control is presumed to exist when an investor holds an interest in the investee of at least 20% but not more than 50%. In this situation the investor can influence the investee's operating and financial policies but cannot completely control them. For example, the investor may control one or two seats on the investee's board of directors, which were gained through the exercise of a large block of stock, but the investor is unable to control the investee completely.

When this relationship exists between the investor and the investee, dividends paid to the investor by the investee no longer are a proper measure of income received. This is so because the investor is able to influence the investee's dividend policy. Thus an investor may pressure an investee to pay dividends in an amount that has little to do with the investee's profitability. For example, this may occur if the investee is forced to issue a large dividend that otherwise would not be issued. In this situation the cost method of accounting is not appropriate, and the equity method should be used.

The Equity Method of Accounting

The primary differences between the equity and cost methods of accounting are the way in which income from the investment is recognized and the fact that LCM is not applied when the equity method is used. Under the **equity method** of accounting, the investment is first recorded at its acquisition cost. Subsequently, however, the Investment account is adjusted to reflect the proportionate increase or decrease in the investee's stockholders' equity that re-

---

[3]There are other variations in applying LCM to long-term investments. For example, if the decline is considered permanent, realized loss is recorded. This, as well as other complexities, is a topic for intermediate accounting textbooks.

Investment in Corporate Equity Securities

sults from the investee's net income or loss for the period. That is, as the investee earns net income, its stockholders' equity increases, and so the investor recognizes its proportionate share of the increase as investment income. If the investee suffers a loss, the investor will recognize a proportionate share of the loss.

Under the equity method of accounting, dividends declared are not considered revenue but reduce the Investment account. A cash dividend reduces the net asset or stockholders' equity of the investee, and thus the investor records a proportionate decrease in its Investment account. In effect, dividends received represent a conversion of the investment into cash. Thus, under the equity method, investors recognize revenue as the investee earns it rather than at the time dividends are declared.

Illustration of the Equity Method

Accounting for the equity method is illustrated by the following example. Assume that at the beginning of the year, the Jackson Corporation purchased for $300,000 a 30% interest in Wildcat Ventures. At the time of purchase, Wildcat Ventures' net assets totaled $1 million, so the $300,000 purchase equaled exactly a 30% interest in Wildcat's net assets.[4] During the year Wildcat Ventures reported net income of $70,000 and declared cash dividends of $25,000. Jackson Corporation would make the following entries to reflect these events:

At time of acquisition:

Investment in Wildcat Ventures	300,000	
Cash		300,000
To record 30% interest in Wildcat Ventures.		

At Jackson's year-end:

Investment in Wildcat Ventures	21,000	
Investment Income		21,000
To record increase in investment from 30% share of net income earned by Wildcat, $70,000 × 30% = $21,000.		

Cash	7,500	
Investment in Wildcat Ventures		7,500
To record decrease in investment due to receipt of dividends, $25,000 × 30% = $7,500.		

Note that after these events, Wildcat Ventures' net assets or stockholders' equity is $1,045,000, or the amount of $1 million at acquisition plus the net income of $70,000 less the dividends of $25,000. The balance in the investment account is now $313,500, or the original investment of $300,000 plus Jackson's share of the net income, $21,000 less its share of the dividend, $7,500. Thus, the balance in the investment account equals 30% of the net assets of Wildcat Ventures ($1,045,000 × 30% = $313,500). The equity method ensures that the balance in the investment in the investee account equals the investor's proportionate share of the net assets purchased. These points are illustrated in the following T accounts:

[4]In reality, the purchase price rarely equals the book value of the investee's net assets. We have made this assumption in order to simplify the illustration. Although beyond the scope of an introductory book, adjustments can be made if the purchase price is more or less than the book value.

| WILDCAT BOOKS | | | JACKSON'S BOOKS | | |
Stockholders' Equity, Wildcat Ventures			Investment in Wildcat Ventures		
Dividends 25,000	1,000,000			300,000	7,500 Dividends
	70,000 Net income		Net income 21,000		
	1,045,000			313,500	

To summarize, the equity method of accounting for long-term investments ensures that the investor reflects in its statements during the period earned the income or loss of the company in which it invested. The lower-of-cost-of-market method is not applied, and therefore no adjustments are made for declines, if any, in the investment's market value.

Ownership Interest above 50 Percent

Often a corporation owns more than 50% of the stock of another corporation. The corporation that owns the majority of stock is called the **parent company,** and the corporation that is wholly or partially owned is called a **subsidiary.** In fact, one parent often owns several subsidiaries. The degree of ownership interest in these subsidiaries may vary between 50 and 100%.

Once a corporation owns more than 50% of the stock of another company, the parent corporation can elect the board of directors of the subsidiary and can control its operating and financial policies. In effect, the parent and subsidiary or subsidiaries represent one economic unit, and the entity assumption requires that it be accounted for as such.

Both the parent company and the subsidiary or subsidiaries are separate legal entities, and so they each maintain separate records and prepare separate financial statements for internal purposes and, under some circumstances, for external purposes. On the parent's books, the investment in the subsidiary is accounted for by the equity method of accounting. Because the parent and subsidiary represent one economic unit, the parent company prepares consolidated financial statements to be distributed to external users. These consolidated balance sheets and income statements show the financial position and operating results of the entire economic unit.

Consolidated Financial Statements

Consolidated financial statements should not be confused with combined financial statements. Although the assets, liabilities, and revenues and expenses of all the entities are combined to provide a single set of financial statements, certain eliminations and adjustments are made. These eliminations are necessary to ensure that only arm's-length transactions between independent parties are reflected in the consolidated statements. For example, a parent and subsidiary may make intercompany sales and/or loans and borrowings. Viewed independently, the transactions represent sales and expenses or assets and liabilities on the books of the respective entities. When consolidated statements are prepared, these intercompany transactions must be eliminated. This ensures that only arm's-length transactions between independent parties are reflected in the consolidated statements, and so transactions between related parties are not counted.

When to Use Consolidated Financial Statements

If one company owns more than 50% of the voting stock of another company, the presumption is that consolidated financial statements should be prepared. Sometimes, however, it does not make sense to consolidate the financial statements of companies even if one owns more than 50% of another. For example, the operations of certain companies are not compatible, and so consolidated financial statements would not be useful to stockholders or other users.

This occurs when a manufacturing company owns a financing subsidiary. Thus General Motors does not consolidate its financing subsidiary, GMAC. Unconsolidated subsidiaries are accounted for by using the equity method. To demonstrate these concepts, the following footnote was taken from a financial statement of General Motors:

> The consolidated financial statements include the accounts of the Corporation of all domestic and foreign subsidiaries which are more than 50% owned and engaged principally in manufacturing or wholesale marketing of General Motors products. General Motors' share of earnings or losses of nonconsolidated subsidiaries and of associates in which at least 20% of the voting securities is owned is generally included in consolidated income under the equity method of accounting.

Methods of Accounting for Consolidations

There are various ways in which a parent may acquire a controlling interest in a subsidiary. For example, the investor may acquire it by paying cash, by issuing stock for stock, or through a combination of stock and cash. How the investment is made and other circumstances surrounding the investment or business combination determine the correct accounting method of consolidation. Either the **purchase method** or the **pooling-of-interests method** must be used. They each will produce significantly different consolidated statements. These methods are not interchangeable, and the circumstances of the acquisition determine which method should be used. We first explain the purchase method, which is appropriate when the investment is made for cash, through the issue of stock or bonds, or a combination of these. Later in the chapter we discuss the pooling-of-interests method, which is appropriate only when stock of the parent company is exchanged for substantially all of the stock of its subsidiary.

Preparing Consolidated Financial Statements

Accounting procedures for consolidation are quite complex and, in fact, occupy many chapters in advanced accounting texts. Our purpose here is to introduce you to the basics so that you will be able to interpret and understand consolidated financial statements. We first consider consolidation of a 100% owned subsidiary acquired at book value and then move on to more complex situations. In most cases, we illustrate consolidations only at the date of acquisition.

Consolidation of a 100% Owned Subsidiary at Date of Acquisition

To illustrate the preparation of consolidated financial statements, assume that on January 2, 1987 Scientific Instruments purchased 100% of the common stock of Technical Tools, Inc. The purchase price was $100,000 and represented the book value of Technical Tools' net assets at that time. Before the purchase, Scientific Instruments had made a $25,000, non-interest-bearing loan to Technical Tools. The individual balance sheets of the two companies immediately after the purchase are shown in Exhibit 19–2.

EXHIBIT 19–2
Scientific Instruments and Technical Tools
Balance Sheets
January 2, 1987

Accounts	Scientific Instruments	Technical Tools
Cash	$ 20,000	$ 18,000
Notes receivable from Technical Tools	25,000	—
Accounts receivable, net	60,000	22,000
Investment in Technical Tools	100,000	—
Other assets	165,000	140,000
Total assets	$370,000	$180,000
Notes payable to Scientific Instruments	—	25,000
Accounts payable	10,000	5,000
Other liabilities	60,000	50,000
Common stock	175,000	55,000
Retained earnings	125,000	45,000
Total liabilities and stockholders' equity	$370,000	$180,000

The worksheet to prepare consolidated financial statements immediately after acquisition is shown in Exhibit 19–3 on page 760. Remember that each firm maintains separate books and records. Thus, a worksheet is needed to prepare a consolidated balance sheet. However, the elimination entries on the worksheet are not made in the individual accounting records of the parent or subsidiary but are made for consolidation purposes only.

As we noted, certain elimination entries must be made before a consolidated balance sheet is prepared. Typical intercompany eliminations pertain to intercompany stock ownership, intercompany debt, and intercompany revenue and expenses. Because we are constructing a consolidated balance sheet in this example, only the first two elimination entries will be shown. Intercompany eliminations for revenue and expense items are discussed later.

Elimination of Intercompany Stock Ownership. The first entry eliminates the Investment in Technical Tools account. This entry is necessary in order to keep from double counting the amount of the investment. Before the consolidation, the $100,000 investment in Technical Tools was shown in the Investment account. However, the purpose of the consolidated balance sheet is to combine the individual accounts of the parent and subsidiary. Thus, the $100,000 investment account must be eliminated so that the individual assets and liabilities of Technical Tools that net to $100,000 can be added to the respective accounts of Scientific Instruments to form the consolidated balance sheet.

EXHIBIT 19-3

Consolidated Balance Sheet Worksheet

January 2, 1987—Acquisition Date

Accounts	Scientific Instruments	Technical Tools	Intercompany Eliminations		Consolidated Balance Sheet
			Debit	Credit	
Cash	20,000	18,000			38,000
Notes receivable from Technical Tools	25,000	—		25,000[b]	
Accounts receivable, net	60,000	22,000			82,000
Investment in Technical Tools	100,000	—		100,000[a]	
Other assets	165,000	140,000			305,000
Total assets	370,000	180,000			425,000
Notes payable to Scientific Instruments	—	25,000	25,000[b]		—
Accounts payable	10,000	5,000			15,000
Other liabilities	60,000	50,000			110,000
Common stock	175,000	55,000	55,000[a]		175,000
Retained earnings	125,000	45,000	45,000[a]		125,000
Total liabilities and stockholders' equity	370,000	180,000	125,000	125,000	425,000

[a]To eliminate investment in Technical Tools against stockholders' equity of Technical Tools.
[b]To eliminate intercompany debt.

The elimination of the Investment account is made against the stockholders' equity accounts of Technical Tools. Essentially there are no external stockholders of Technical Tools. All the stock is owned internally by the consolidated entity. Ownership of a company's own stock does not give rise to either an asset or stockholders' equity. Thus the purpose of the entry is to eliminate the Investment account on Scientific Instruments' books against the stockholders' equity accounts of Technical Tools.

Elimination of Intercompany Debt. Before Scientific Instruments purchased Technical Tools, it lent the firm $25,000. Scientific Instruments thus recorded a note receivable, and Technical Tools recorded a note payable. From a consolidated entity point of view, this transaction results only in the transfer of cash from one part of the entity to another and does not give rise to a receivable or a payable. Thus, in preparing a consolidated balance sheet, an entry must be made to eliminate the notes receivable and payable.

Preparation of a Consolidated Balance Sheet. After the two elimination entries are posted to the worksheet, the remaining assets and liabilities and stockholders' equity accounts are combined to prepare the consolidated balance sheet columns in the worksheet shown in Exhibit 19-3. The actual consolidated balance sheet is presented in Exhibit 19-4.

Acquisition of Less Than 100% Interest at Book Value

There are instances in which the parent company does not purchase a 100% interest in a subsidiary. But as long as the parent owns 51% of the subsidiary's stock it has control, and according to current accounting practices, con-

EXHIBIT 19-4

Scientific Instruments, Inc.
Consolidated Balance Sheet
January 2, 1987

Assets		Liabilities and Stockholders' Equity		
Cash	$ 38,000	Liabilities:		
Accounts receivable	82,000	Accounts payable		$ 15,000
Other assets	305,000	Other liabilities		110,000
		Stockholders' equity:		
		Common stock	$175,000	
		Retained earnings	125,000	300,000
		Total liabilities and		
Total assets	$425,000	stockholders' equity		$425,000

solidated statements must be prepared. When these statements are prepared, 100% of the subsidiary's net assets are consolidated with the parent's net assets. It is necessary, therefore, to give recognition to the interests of the minority stockholders who own the remaining outstanding stock. The interest of the minority shareholders is generally shown in the stockholders' equity section of the consolidated balance sheet at an amount equal to the percentage ownership in the book value of the subsidiary's net assets.[5]

To demonstrate, we will return to the example on pages 758 and 759 and in Exhibit 19–2. We will now assume that Scientific Instruments purchases only an 80% interest in Technical Tools. The purchase price is $80,000, which represents 80% of the book value of Technical Tools' net assets.

The worksheet showing the eliminations necessary to prepare a consolidated balance sheet at January 2, 1987 is illustrated in Exhibit 19–5. The following entry is made to eliminate the investments in Technical Tools against its stockholders' equity and to establish a minority interest:

Common Stock	55,000	
Retained Earnings	45,000	
Investment in Technical Tools		80,000
Minority Interest		20,000

As this entry indicates, the entire stockholders' equity of Technical Tools—$100,000—is offset against the $80,000 investment account. The $20,000 difference represents the 20% minority interest of the other stockholders. The stockholders' equity section of the consolidated balance would appear as follows:

Stockholders' equity	
Minority interest	$ 20,000
Common stock	175,000
Retained earnings	125,000
Total stockholders' equity	$320,000

[5]Many accountants prefer to show the minority interest's share of the stockholders' equity of the acquired company as a special item between liabilities and stockholders' equity. Both methods are followed in practice.

EXHIBIT 19–5
Consolidated Balance Sheet Worksheet
January 2, 1987—Acquisition Date

Accounts	Scientific Instruments	Technical Tools	Intercompany Eliminations		Consolidated Balance Sheet
			Debit	Credit	
Cash	40,000	18,000			58,000
Notes receivable from Technical Tools	25,000	—		25,000[b]	
Accounts receivable, net	60,000	22,000			82,000
Investment in Technical Tools	80,000	—		80,000[a]	
Other assets	165,000	140,000			305,000
Total assets	370,000	180,000			445,000
Notes payable to Scientific Instruments	—	25,000	25,000[b]		
Accounts payable	10,000	5,000			15,000
Other liabilities	60,000	50,000			110,000
Common stock	175,000	55,000	55,000[a]		175,000
Retained earnings	125,000	45,000	45,000[a]		125,000
Minority interest				20,000[a]	20,000
Total liabilities and stockholders' equity	370,000	180,000	125,000	125,000	445,000

[a]To eliminate investment in Technical Tools against stockholders' equity of Technical Tools and to establish minority interest.
[b]To eliminate intercompany debt.

Purchase above or below Book Value

In order to simplify our discussion, we have assumed that the purchase price has been equal to the book value of the net assets acquired. Usually this will not be the case. The price that an investor is willing to pay for a business depends on several factors, such as general economic conditions, market prices, estimates of future anticipated earnings, and the relative bargaining position of the buyer and seller. The book value of a subsidiary's net assets therefore often bears little relation to what a buyer may be willing to pay for them. For example, a parent will pay more for a business if it feels that the potential subsidiary's assets are undervalued, that there is a potential for future excess earnings, or perhaps that the subsidiary owns a valuable patent needed by the parent. The parent may pay less than the book value for a potential subsidiary's net assets, however, if these assets are overvalued, the firm is in a declining industry, or it has suffered losses in the past.

The Accounting Principles Board developed a number of guidelines to be used when the purchase method is used and when the purchase price differs from the book value of the net assets acquired.[6] Briefly, the purchase method follows the principles normally found under historical cost accounting in regard to the purchase of assets. Thus when the purchase price exceeds the book value of the net assets acquired, the purchase price is first allocated to the identifiable assets acquired and liabilities assumed, based on their respective

[6]Opinion 16.

fair market values. The excess cost of the acquired company over the amounts assigned to the identifiable assets, less liabilities assumed, should be recorded as goodwill. In effect, the acquired net assets of the acquired company are recorded at their fair market value, and any excess cost is considered goodwill. This is based on the assumption that the reason the parent is willing to pay more for a subsidiary than the fair market value of its identifiable net assets is the existence of goodwill.

In some circumstances the parent will purchase the subsidiary at a price below the book value of the subsidiary's net assets. This implies that some assets are recorded at amounts above their current values. In this situation the assets of the company are written down to their fair market value. Negative goodwill is rarely recorded.

Purchase above Fair Market Value. To demonstrate the preparation of a consolidated balance sheet when the parent pays more than the book value of the subsidiary's net assets, assume that on December 31, 1987 the Peter Corporation purchased 100% of the Mary Company for $140,000. The book value of Mary Company's net assets on the date of acquisition is $130,000, as shown in Exhibit 19–6. The Peter Corporation paid $10,000 in excess of the book value of Mary's net assets. The Peter Corporation evaluated the fair market value of the Mary Company's net assets and decided to increase the property, plant, and equipment by $7,500. The remaining $2,500 is allocated to goodwill.

EXHIBIT 19–6

Mary Company
Balance Sheet
December 31, 1987

Assets		Equities	
Cash	$ 10,000	Current liabilities	$ 20,000
Accounts receivable, net	15,000	Long-term debt	15,000
Inventory	40,000	Common stock	50,000
Property, plant, and		Paid-in capital	25,000
equipment, net	100,000	Retained earnings	55,000
		Total liabilities and	
Total assets	$165,000	stockholders' equity	$165,000

The consolidated worksheet is shown in Exhibit 19–7. The following entry is made to write off the investment account against the stockholders' equity accounts of the Mary Company, to increase the property, plant, and equipment account to fair market value, and to record goodwill.

Property, Plant, and Equipment	7,500	
Goodwill	2,500	
Common Stock	50,000	
Paid-in Capital	25,000	
Retained Earnings	55,000	
Investment in Mary Company		140,000

EXHIBIT 19-7
Consolidated Balance Sheet Worksheet
December 31, 1987

Accounts	Peter Corporation	Mary Company	Eliminations		Consolidated Balance Sheet
			Debit	Credit	
Cash	24,000	10,000			34,000
Accounts receivable	36,000	15,000		6,000[b]	45,000
Inventory	80,000	40,000			120,000
Investment in Mary Company	140,000	0		140,000[a]	0
Property, plant, and equipment, net	200,000	100,000	7,500[a]		307,500
Goodwill	0	0	2,500[a]		2,500
Total assets	480,000	165,000			509,000
Current liabilities	60,000	20,000	6,000[b]		74,000
Long-term debt	100,000	15,000			115,000
Common stock	100,000	50,000	50,000[a]		100,000
Paid-in capital	50,000	25,000	25,000[a]		50,000
Retained earnings	170,000	55,000	55,000[a]		170,000
Total liabilities and stockholders' equity	480,000	165,000	146,000	146,000	509,000

[a]To eliminate investment account and to increase property, plant, and equipment to fair market value and to record goodwill.
[b]To eliminate intercompany debt of $6,000.

Goodwill must be amortized over a maximum of 40 years, whereas the plant and equipment will be depreciated over their useful lives. The allocation between goodwill and other assets will affect future periods' income. The other entry is made to eliminate intercompany receivables and payables.

Purchase below Book Value of Net Assets. Occasionally a parent will purchase a subsidiary at a price below the book value of the subsidiary's identifiable net assets. As we noted, this may occur if the book value of the subsidiary's net assets is greater than their current fair market value and/or the acquired firm has suffered heavy losses in the immediate past. In this case the book value of the subsidiary's assets must be written down by the amount of the excess of the book value of the acquired identifiable net assets over the purchase price. Rarely, if ever, is this excess used to record negative goodwill.

Consolidated Income Statements

To this point we have illustrated only the preparation of consolidated balance sheets at the date of acquisition. Consolidated income statements and statements of retained earnings also are prepared. Essentially, a consolidated income statement is prepared by combining the revenues and expenses of the parent and subsidiary companies after eliminating intercompany revenue and expense transactions such as sales, cost of goods sold, interest income, and interest expense.

The preparation of consolidated income statements can be extremely complex. To illustrate their preparation in a simplified case we assume that on January 2, 1987 the Nekro Corporation purchased 100% of the Pena Company for the book value of Pena's net assets. During the year Nekro sold $200,000 of goods at cost to Pena. All of these goods were subsequently sold to outsiders. In addition, Pena paid Nekro $5,000 in interest on intercompany borrowings.

The consolidating worksheet for the year ended December 31, 1987 is shown in Exhibit 19–8. The first elimination entry reduces the parent's sales and the subsidiary's cost of goods sold. The second entry eliminates intercompany interest income and expense. The purpose of these entries is to ensure that only revenues and expenses made to outside parties are included in the consolidated income statement and to avoid double counting of revenues and expenses. Notice that the net income of the consolidated entity—$623,000—is equal to the total of the net incomes of the parent and the subsidiary ($623,000 = $360,000 + $263,000). The effect of the elimination entries is to reduce the consolidated revenues and expenses by equal amounts.

EXHIBIT 19–8

Consolidated Income Statement Worksheet

For the Year Ended December 31, 1987

Accounts	Nekro Corporation	Pena Company	Eliminations Debit	Eliminations Credit	Consolidated Income Statement
Revenue					
Sales	2,500,000	1,800,000	200,000[a]		4,100,000
Interest	70,000	8,000	5,000[b]		73,000
Total revenue	2,570,000	1,808,000			4,173,000
Expenses					
Cost of goods sold	1,750,000	1,170,000		200,000[a]	2,720,000
Interest expense	60,000	25,000		5,000[b]	80,000
Other expenses	400,000	350,000			750,000
Total expenses	2,210,000	1,545,000			3,550,000
Net income	360,000	263,000	205,000	205,000	623,000

[a]To eliminate intercompany sales and purchases.
[b]To eliminate intercompany interest income and expenses.

Pooling-of-Interests versus Purchase Methods

In all of the examples to this point, we have assumed that the purchase method of accounting has been used. The purchase method must be used when the acquisition is made for cash and/or if the parent company issues debt or equity securities to the previous shareholders of the subsidiary. This method assumes that the company's shareholders have sold out their interest to the parent company. As a result, accounting principles applied to any purchase of assets are followed, and the acquired assets are recorded at their fair market value. Any goodwill resulting from the excess of the purchase price over the fair market value of the identifiable net assets is amortized over a maximum of 40 years.

In some situations the acquisition is structured in a different manner. Substantially all of the subsidiary's stock may be acquired in exchange for the parent's common stock. If this occurs and if certain other restrictive requirements are met, the acquisition must be considered a pooling of interests rather than a purchase. Essentially, a pooling of interests assumes that the subsidiary's stockholders are now stockholders of the parent company and that a mutual pooling of interests rather than an outright purchase has taken place.

If in fact a pooling of interests has taken place, then there has not been a sale of the subsidiary's net assets. The subsidiary's net assets therefore are not revalued to their fair market value as they are when the purchase method is used. Thus, when a consolidated balance sheet is prepared under the pooling-of-interests method, the book value of the parent's assets and liabilities is combined with the respective book value of the subsidiary's assets and liabilities. As a result, no goodwill is recognized and there is no subsequent goodwill amortization.

There is another difference between the purchase and the pooling-of-interests methods of consolidating financial statements. Under the purchase method, only the subsidiary's earnings after the acquisition date are combined with the parent's earnings. Thus if a purchase took place on October 1, only the subsidiary's earnings from that date to the year-end would be consolidated with the parent's earnings for the entire year.

Under the pooling-of-interests method, however, in the year of acquisition the subsidiary's earnings for the entire year would be combined with the parent's earnings, regardless of the date of the acquisition. Thus even if an acquisition took place on October 1, the subsidiary's earnings for the entire year would be consolidated with the parent's earnings when preparing a consolidated income statement for the year ending December 31. This is based on the idea that the two companies have merely combined their resources and operations.

These factors explain the popularity of the pooling method of accounting with the managements of many companies. If the pooling-of-interests method is used when the purchase price exceeds the value of the acquired assets, the consolidated net assets will be recorded at lower amounts than if the purchase method is used. Furthermore, in the year of acquisition, earnings can be consolidated for the entire year. As a result, ratios such as return on investment and earnings per share will be better when the pooling-of-interests method is used than if the purchase method is used. The following table summarizes the major differences between these two methods of accounting for acquisitions.

	Method of Consolidation	Recording of Net Assets	Subsidiary's Earnings
Purchase Method	Acquisition of more than 50% of subsidiary's voting stock for cash and/or other assets, debt, or securities.	Subsidiary's assets are revalued to fair market value. Excess of cost over fair market value, if any, is considered goodwill. Goodwill is amortized over a maximum of 40 years.	In year of acquisition, earnings of parent are combined with those of subsidiary from date of acquisition.
Pooling-of-Interests Method	Acquisition of substantially all (90% or more) of the subsidiary's voting stock for voting stock of parent.	Subsidiary's net assets are shown on consolidated balance sheet at book value. As a result, no goodwill is recognized. Retained earnings of subsidiary are usually carried over.	In year of acquisition, earnings of subsidiary are combined with those of the parent for the entire year.

Because of the dramatic effect that the pooling-of-interests method can have on consolidated statements, as well as its abuse during the 1960s, the APB set certain conditions that must be met if that method is to be used. There are 12 requirements that basically revolve around the fact that the transaction must be structured as an exchange of the parent's stock for substantially all of the subsidiary's stock. If all 12 requirements are not met, the purchase method must be used. In effect, the purchase and pooling-of-interest methods are not alternatives for the same acquisition, and the correct accounting treatment depends on the nature of the transaction.

To demonstrate the pooling-of-interests method, we return to the Peter Corporation's acquisition of 100% of the Mary Company for a total price of $140,000. (See Exhibit 19–7 on page 764.) But we now assume that instead of making the acquisition for cash, the Peter Corporation issues 10,000 shares of its $10 par value common stock, which currently has a fair market value of $14, for all of the shares of the Mary Company. Under the pooling-of-interests method, the Investment in Mary Company is recorded at the book value of the net assets acquired—$130,000—not at the fair market value of the stock exchanged—$140,000—as it would be if the purchase method were used. The journal entry to record this acquisition under the pooling-of-interests method is:

Investment in Mary Company	130,000	
Common Stock, $10 Par		100,000
Paid-in Capital from Issue of		
Common Stock in Excess of Par		30,000
To record investment in Mary Company		
under the pooling-of-interests method.		

EXHIBIT 19–9
Consolidated Balance Sheet Worksheet—Pooling of Interests
December 31, 1987—Acquisition Date

Accounts	Peter Corporation	Mary Company	Eliminations Debit	Eliminations Credit	Consolidated Balance Sheet
Cash	164,000	10,000			174,000
Accounts receivable	36,000	15,000		6,000[b]	45,000
Inventory	80,000	40,000			120,000
Investment in Mary Company	130,000	0		130,000[a]	0
Property, plant, and equipment, net	200,000	100,000			300,000
Total assets	610,000	165,000			639,000
Current liabilities	60,000	20,000	6,000[b]		74,000
Long-term debt	100,000	15,000			115,000
Common stock	200,000	50,000	50,000[a]		200,000
Paid-in capital	80,000	25,000	80,000[a]		25,000
Retained earnings	170,000	55,000			225,000
Total liabilities and stockholders' equity	610,000	165,000	136,000	136,000	639,000

[a]To eliminate investment account.
[b]To eliminate intercompany debt.

The worksheet to consolidate these companies under the pooling-of-interests method is shown in Exhibit 19–9 on page 767. The investment elimination entry is reproduced below.

Common Stock	50,000	
Paid-in Capital	80,000	
Investment in Mary Company		130,000
To eliminate investment account		
against capital accounts.		

In this entry the investment account is first eliminated against Mary Company's common stock and then against the paid-in capital account. However, under the theory of a pooling of interests, the Mary Company's retained earnings are carried over in total. It is assumed that the two companies have always been one. Finally, because all the net assets of the Mary Company are carried over at their net book value, no revaluation of assets is made, nor is goodwill recorded. The consolidated balance sheet under the pooling-of-interest method, compared with the purchase method, follows:

Peter Corporation
Consolidated Balance Sheets
December 31, 1987

Assets	Purchase	Pooling of Interests
Cash	$ 34,000	$174,000
Accounts receivable	45,000	45,000
Inventory	120,000	120,000
Property, plant, and equipment, net	307,500	300,000
Goodwill	$ 2,500	
Total	$509,000	$639,000

Liabilities and Stockholders' Equity		
Current liabilities	$ 74,000	$ 74,000
Long-term debt	115,000	115,000
Common stock	100,000	200,000
Paid-in capital	50,000	25,000
Retained earnings	170,000	225,000
Total	$509,000	$639,000

Under the purchase method the Investment in Mary Company account is recorded at $140,000, the fair value of the shares exchanged. The $10,000 paid in excess of the book value of the net assets required is allocated $7,500 to the property, plant, and equipment, and $2,500 to goodwill. After the elimination entry, the stockholders' equity of the subsidiary is completely eliminated, and consolidated retained earnings is equal to the parent's retained earnings of $170,000.

1. *The nature of publicly held corporations and security exchanges.* Publicly held corporations are those whose securities are owned by outside investors and whose stocks and/or bonds are listed on a national or regional stock exchange. These exchanges include the New York Stock Exchange, the American Stock Exchange, and the over-the-counter market. Publicly held corporations are required to file certain reports with the Securities and Exchange Commission and various exchanges.

2. *The accounting issues regarding accounting for current marketable securities.* Investments in securities are listed as current assets if they are readily marketable and management's intention is to turn them into cash within the operating cycle of the business. Investments in current marketable securities include both equity and debt securities.

   a. Current equity securities are originally recorded at their acquisition costs and at each balance sheet date valued at lower of cost or market (LCM). A valuation account is established to reduce the securities to market when market falls below cost. The unrealized loss is shown as a separate item in the current period's income statement. Prior years' losses can be recaptured, but the securities are never valued above cost.

   b. Debt securities are recorded at cost. However, the interest that has accrued since the last interest date must be accounted for separately. Because of materiality, there is no subsequent amortization of any discounts or premiums. Furthermore, debt securities do not have to be valued at lower of cost or market, though for simplicity's sake, many firms do so.

3. *Long-term investments and the differences in control exercised by the investor.* Long-term investments are those investments that do not meet the criteria to be classified as current. The accounting for long-term investments is based on the degree of control exercised by the investor over the investee. This degree of control is based on whether the investor owns less than 20% of the investee's stock, between 20% and 50% of its stock, or more than 50% of its stock.

4. *Accounting for investments when there is no significant influence or control.* No significant influence or control is presumed to exist when the investor owns less than 20% of the investee's stock. In this circumstance, the investment is originally recorded at cost and is subsequently valued at lower of cost or market. When applying the LCM rule, unrealized losses are shown as a debit item in stockholders' equity. Dividends are recorded as income when received.

5. *Accounting for ownership interest between 20 and 50%.* Significant influence but not control is presumed to exist when an investor owns between 20 and 50% of an investee's stock. Because the investor can influence the operating policies of the investee, the cost method of accounting is not appropriate; rather, the equity method is used. Under the equity method, the investor records as income the proportionate share of the investee's income. Dividends declared serve to decrease the investment account. Thus the investment account is carried at an amount

equal to the investor's proportionate share of the purchased net assets of the investee.

6. *Accounting for ownership interest above 50%.* Complete control exists when the investor owns more than 50% of the investee's stock. In these situations there is a presumption that consolidated financial statements should be prepared. The preparation of these statements requires using certain elimination entries. These entries eliminate the investment account against the subsidiary's stockholders' equity as well as all intercompany transactions.

   a. Acquisitions must be accounted for by using either the purchase or the pooling-of-interests method. These methods are not alternatives for the same acquisition; rather, the use of a particular one depends on how the acquisition is structured.

   b. When the purchase method is used, all assets and liabilities are revalued to their fair market values, and any remaining excess cost is considered goodwill. When the pooling-of-interests method is used, all of the assets and liabilities of the subsidiary are combined with the parent's assets and liabilities at their net book value. Furthermore, under a pooling of interests, in the year of acquisition the subsidiary's earnings for the entire year are combined with the parent's earnings.

Key Terms

Consolidated Financial Statements	**Pooling-of-Interests Method**
Debt Securities	**Publicly Held Corporation**
Equity Method	**Purchase Method**
Equity Securities	**Subsidiary**
Parent Company	

Problems for Your Review

A. Lower of Cost or Market. At the beginning of the current year, West Coast Silicon held the following portfolio of current marketable equity securities:

Security	Number of Shares	Total Cost	Market Value
Allied, Inc.	50	$ 4,000	$ 4,600
Gora Company	100	2,500	2,300
Leaky Oil and Gas	200	6,000	5,400
		$12,500	$12,300

During the current year, West Coast Silicon entered into the following transactions:

1. Sold 100 shares of Leaky Oil and Gas for $2,800 net of commissions.
2. Purchased 100 shares of EG & P for $40 per share, including commissions.
3. Current market values at the end of the year are as shown at the top of page 771.

Required:

1. Prepare all the necessary journal entries for the year.
2. How would the marketable securities be shown on the balance sheet?

Stock	Total Market Value
Allied, Inc.	$ 4,400
Gora Company	2,200
Leaky Oil and Gas	2,000
EG & P	4,100
	$12,700

3. Assume that all securities were held throughout the next year and that at the end of the year their market values totaled $14,000. Make the required entry at year-end.

Solution

1. Journal Entries

1. Cash	2,800	
Loss on Sale of Marketable Securities	200	
Investment in Marketable Securities		3,000
To record loss on sale of securities.		
2. Investment in Marketable Securities	4,000	
Cash		4,000
To record purchase of 100 shares of EG & P at $40 per share.		
3. Unrealized loss on Marketable Securities	600	
Allowance to Reduce Marketable Securities to Market		600
To record unrealized loss.		

Current market value	$12,700
Cost ($4,000 + $2,500 + $3,000 + $4,000)	13,500
Required balance in allowance account	800
Current balance in allowance account ($12,500 − $12,300)	200
Amount of adjusting entry	$ 600

2. Balance Sheet Presentation

Investment in marketable securities	$13,500
Less: Allowance to reduce marketable securities to market	(800)
	$12,700

3. Next Year's Journal Entry

Allowance to Reduce Marketable Securities to Market	800	
Reduction in Unrealized Loss on Marketable Securities		800
To reduce allowance account to zero as market exceeds cost.		

B. Equity Method. Several years ago, the Anger Company purchased a 25% interest in the Zebra Corp. The purchase price was $50,000, which represented a 25% interest in the book value of Zebra's net assets at that time. At the beginning of the current year, the book value of Zebra's net assets was $350,000. During the current year Zebra reported the following:

Net Income	$75,000
Dividends Paid	40,000

Required:

1. Make the appropriate entries on Anger's books to reflect these events during the current year.
2. What is the balance in the Investment in Zebra account at end of the year?

Investment in Corporate Equity Securities

771

Solution

1.

Investment in Zebra	18,750	
Investment Revenue		18,750
To record investment revenue		
($75,000 × .25 = $18,750).		
Cash	10,000	
Investment in Zebra		10,000
To record receipt of dividend		
($40,000 × .25 = $10,000).		

2.

Balance in investment account

Net book value at beginning of year	$350,000
Anger's interest	.25
Current year's transaction	$ 87,500
Income	18,750
Dividend received	(10,000)
Net book value at end of year.	$ 96,250

Questions

1. What is a publicly held corporation? How does one acquire stock in such a corporation?

2. Investment in securities can be classified as either a current asset or a long-term investment. What criteria are used in making this distinction?

3. Marketable securities include both debt and equity securities. What is the distinction between these types of securities? Why would an investor hold a portfolio that includes both debt and equity securities?

4. In order to invest idle cash, the Orleans Corporation purchased 100 shares of General Motors stock at $65 per share, plus brokerage commissions of $100 and state taxes of $50. At what amount should this investment be shown on the balance sheet? Where should it be classified on the balance sheet?

5. At the beginning of the current year, the Juarez Co. purchased 1,000 shares of California Federal Savings stock at $20 per share, including brokerage commissions. During the year the firm received dividends of $1.50 per share. At the time Juarez was preparing its year-end balance sheet, California Federal Savings stock was selling at $18 per share. Assuming that this is the only stock Juarez owns, how much income or loss should the firm record regarding this stock?

6. Lower-of-cost-or-market is applied to various situations in accounting. Compare and contrast the application of lower-of-cost-or-market to marketable securities with its application to inventories.

7. Malibu Publishing Co. owns several stocks classified as current marketable securities. At the end of 1985 the firm had a credit balance of $2,500 in the account Allowance to Reduce Marketable Securities to Market. By the end of 1986 the market value of the firm's stock investments had risen and now exceeds

its cost by $1,000. Make the appropriate entry at the end of 1986 to record this fact.

8. Some accountants argue that marketable securities should be valued at market, regardless of whether market is above or below cost. What is the basis for their argument? Do you agree or disagree? Why?

9. To what types of investments does FASB Statement 12 apply?

10. Briefly describe the difference in accounting for current equity securities and for current debt securities.

11. Describe the accounting treatment for long-term equity investments of less than 20%. How is the lower-of-cost-or-market rule applied to these investments?

12. When the market value of a portfolio of either current marketable securities or long-term investments is less than its cost, an account titled Allowance to Reduce Marketable Securities to Market is credited. How does this account differ if the portfolio consists of long-term investments rather than current investments?

13. Briefly describe the equity method of accounting, why it is used, and when it is used.

14. Explain to a fellow accounting student why dividends received are not considered income when the equity method of accounting for long-term investments is applied.

15. At the beginning of 1986 the Metro Co. owned 30% of the Freeway Corporation. At that time the balance in the investment in the Freeway account was $200,000. During the year Freeway issued cash dividends totaling $100,000 and earned net income of $400,000. What should be the balance in the invest-

ment in the Freeway account after these events are considered?

16. Under what circumstances should consolidated statements be prepared? How do these consolidated statements differ from just combining the financial statements of two companies?

17. List and describe at least three different elimination entries. Why must these entries be made?

18. At the beginning of the current year Symphony, Inc. purchased an 80% interest in Software Centers, Inc. for $400,000 cash. At the time of the purchase, Software's stockholders' equity accounts were as follows: common stock, no par $350,000; retained earn-

ings $150,000. Make the entry on a consolidated worksheet to eliminate Symphony's investment in Software Centers, Inc.

19. Often when one company purchases another, the purchase is made at a price above the net book value of the assets acquired. Describe the accounting procedures to handle this when the purchase method of accounting is used.

20. Compare and contrast the purchase method of accounting for acquisitions with the pooling-of-interests method. If you were the manager of a company that was about to acquire another company, what factors would you consider in deciding which method to use?

Exercises

1. Accounting for Current Marketable Equity Securities. On February 2, 1986 the Chaise Lounge Co. purchased 100 shares of Pops Brewery at $45 per share, plus brokerage commissions of $1 per share. During 1986 and 1987 the following events occurred regarding this investment:

- December 15, 1986: Pops Brewery declares and pays a $1.50 per-share dividend.
- December 31, 1986: The market price of Pops Brewery's stock is $40 per share at year-end.
- December 1, 1987: Pops Brewery declares and pays a dividend of $1 per share.
- December 31, 1987: The market price of Pops Brewery's stock is $42 per share at year-end.

Required:

Assuming that this is the only investment that Chaise Lounge made during 1986 and 1987, record the entries to reflect these events. How would the investment in marketable securities be disclosed on the December 31, 1987 balance sheet?

2. Accounting for Current Marketable Equity Securities. The following items were taken from the December 31, 1986 balance sheet of the Simmonds Company:

Simmonds Company
Partial Balance Sheet
December 31, 1986

Current assets	
Cash	$ 50,000
Investment in Akro Corporation, less allowance to reduce	
marketable equity securities to market of $1,000	15,000
Accounts receivable, less allowance for uncollectible accounts of $6,000	120,000

The investment in Akro Corporation consisted of 1,000 shares of Akro common stock purchased on November 29, 1986.

Required:

a. What was the purchase price per share of the Akro Corporation common stock?

b. What was the market price per share of the Akro Corporation common stock on December 31, 1986?

c. On April 1, 1987 the Simmonds Company sold 500 shares of Akro at $18 per share. Make the necessary journal entry to record this sale.

d. Simmonds held the remaining 500 shares of Akro throughout the remaining year. At December 31, 1987 Akro was selling at $15.75 per share. Make the necessary entry, if any, to value the securities at lower of cost or market at December 31, 1987.

3. Application of the Lower-of-Cost-or-Market Rule. During 1986 the Ambrosia Corp. made several purchases of current marketable equity securities. No securities were owned prior to 1986. None of these purchases represented an interest of 20% or more. The cost and market value of these securities are as follows:

Securities	Total Cost	Market value—December 31,		
		1986	1987	1988
BPOE Inc.	$ 1,500	$ 1,200	$ 1,100	$ 1,600
Laird, Inc.	5,600	5,700	5,600	5,500
Showboat Co.	4,900	4,400	4,300	4,600
Total	$12,000	$11,300	$11,000	$11,700

Required:

    a. Make the adjusting entries at December 31 of each year to reflect these changes in market values.

    b. How should the account Investment in Marketable Equity Securities be disclosed on the December 31, 1988 balance sheet?

4. Accounting for Debt Securities. On September 1, 1987 the Thesaurus Co. purchased 10 $1,000, 12% bonds of Webster Corporation. The bonds were purchased at 97 plus $100 of brokerage commissions and accrued interest. The bonds pay interest every January 2 and July 1. Because the Thesaurus Co. intends to hold these bonds as a short-term investment, it does not plan to amortize any discount or premium. On February 1, 1988 the firm sold all the bonds at 102 less $125 brokerage commissions plus accrued interest.

Required:

    a. Make the required journal entries on September 1, 1987, December 31, 1987 (the firm's year-end), January 2, 1988, and February 1, 1988 to record these bond transactions.

    b. If the price of the bonds had declined below their cost at December 31, 1987, would the Thesaurus Co. have to make an entry to reflect this fact?

5. Accounting for Current and Long-term Equity Investments. At the end of 1986 CIJI Corporation owned two equity investments that it classified as current marketable securities. The relevant cost and market data at December 31, 1986 is as follows:

Security	Cost	Market
Lockness, Inc.	$6,700	$6,200
Scottish Co.	5,400	5,500

During 1987 CIJI Corporation sold all of its holdings in Lockness, for $6,500 after commissions. In addition, the firm purchased 500 shares of English Inc. on November 1, 1987 at a price of $27 per share including commissions. CIJI considers this to be a long-term investment.

At December 31, 1987 Scottish Co. had a market value of $6,000, and English Inc. had a market value of $13,200.

Required:

    a. Prepare the journal entries to record the transactions that took place during 1987.

    b. How much income or loss would CIJI report during 1987 regarding these stock transactions? How would this income or loss be classified?

    c. Determine the December 31, 1987 balances in the balance sheet accounts regarding these stock investments.

6. Cost and Equity Methods of Accounting for Long-term Investments. At the beginning of 1987, the El Paso Corp. purchased two long-term investments. The first purchase was a 30% interest (30,000 shares) in the common stock of Houston Inc. for $1.5 million. The second pura 15% interest (15,000 shares) in the common stock of Lubbock Inc. for $495,000. The following data is available regarding these companies:

Company	Reported Income	Dividends Declared and Paid	Market Price per Share 12/31/87
Houston	$ 500,000	$100,000	$45
Lubbock	$1,000,000	$300,000	$35

Required:

   a. Which of these investments should be accounted for on the cost or on the equity method? Why?

   b. As a result of these two investments, what should be the income reported by El Paso for the year ended December 31, 1987?

   c. As a result of these two investments, what should be the balance in the investments account for El Paso at December 31, 1987?

7. Equity Method of Accounting. At the beginning of the current year the Bond Company purchased for $300,000 as a long-term investment common stock representing a 30% interest in Spy Corporation. This represented a 30% interest in the book value of Spy's net assets. During the year Spy declared and issued dividends totaling $80,000. Spy reported net income of $200,000 during the current year.

Required:

   a. Make the required journal entries on the Bond Company's books to record these events.

   b. What is the balance in the Investment in Spy Corporation account at the end of the current year?

8. Accounting for Long-term Investments. For several years Southworth Corporation has held a 40% interest in the Corona Co. At the time of purchase, Corona's net assets were $1 million and Southworth paid $400,000 for its interest. At the end of 1986 Southworth reported a balance of $1.6 million in its Investment in Corona account.

During 1987 Corona reported a loss of $100,000. Because management considered this loss to be temporary, Corona declared dividends of $20,000.

Required:

   a. Does Southworth use the cost or the equity method of accounting for its investment in Corona? Explain your answer.

   b. Make the appropriate journal entries to record the events that occurred during 1987.

   c. As a result of these transactions, what is the December 31, 1987 balance in the Investment in Corona account?

9. Elimination Entries—Date of Acquisition. During the year, First Air purchased 100% of the common stock of Royal Hotels for $600,000 in cash. At the time of the purchase, the book value of Royal Hotels' net assets was $600,000, consisting of common stock of $200,000 and retained earnings of $400,000. Also at the time of acquisition, First Air had an accounts receivable on its books in the amount of $10,000 from Royal Hotels. Royal Hotels had a corresponding accounts payable.

Prepare the elimination entries that would be made on the worksheet required for the preparation of a consolidated balance sheet.

10. Elimination Entries—Minority Interest. During June 1987, Oniix Inc. purchased 80% of the common stock of Praim for $400,000 cash and a note of $112,000. At the time of the purchase, Praim's stockholders' equity accounts were common stock of $450,000 and retained earnings of $190,000. Included in Oniix's accounts payable at the time of acquisition was a $5,000 liability to Praim. A corresponding receivable was on Praim's books.

Required:

   a. Prepare the journal entry to record Oniix's purchase of Praim.

   b. Prepare the elimination entry that would appear on a worksheet necessary to prepare a consolidated balance sheet at the date of acquisition.

11. Accounting for Consolidations and Goodwill. On April 1, 1987 the Pual Co. purchased 100% of the common stock of Santos Inc. for $175,000 cash. Immediately after the purchase, the balance sheet of each company appeared as follows:

Assets	Pual Co.	Santos Inc.
Cash and receivables	$ 50,000	$ 20,000
Inventory	80,000	35,000
Investment in Santos	175,000	—
Property, plant, and equipment, net	240,000	200,000
Total	$545,000	$255,000

Equities		
Accounts payable	$ 60,000	$ 15,000
Long-term debt	80,000	85,000
Common stock, no par	200,000	60,000
Retained earnings	205,000	95,000
Total	$545,000	$255,000

After evaluating the assets of Santos, Pual decided that the fair market value of the inventory was $40,000 and that the fair market value of the property, plant, and equipment was $210,000. The remaining cost of the acquisition over the net assets acquired should be considered goodwill.

Required:

    a. Prepare the entry to record the acquisition of Santos by Pual.

    b. Prepare the elimination entry that would be made on the worksheet required to prepare a consolidated balance sheet at the date of acquisition.

    c. After consolidation, what will be the amount of the total assets of the consolidated entity?

    d. After consolidation, what will be the amount of the total stockholders' equity of the consolidated entity?

12. Consolidation Worksheet. On November 1, 1987 the Rosenberg Rose Co. purchased 100% of the stock of the Seedy Seed Co. for $180,000 cash. Immediately after the purchase, the condensed balance sheets of the two companies were as follows:

	Rosenberg Rose	Seedy Seed
Receivable from Seedy	$ 10,000	$ 0
Other assets	800,000	250,000
Investment in Seedy	180,000	0
Total assets	$990,000	$250,000
Payable to Rosenberg	$ 0	$ 10,000
Other liabilities	300,000	100,000
Capital stock, no par	400,000	100,000
Retained earnings	290,000	40,000
Total equities	$990,000	$250,000

After a detailed analysis, Rosenberg has decided that the fair market value of Seedy's assets approximates their book value, and so any excess of the cost of the investment over the book value of the acquired net assets should be considered goodwill.

Required:

Prepare a worksheet consolidating the two companies as of the date of acquisition.

13. Purchase versus Pooling. On March 1, 1987 Northstar Tech purchased 100% of Tahoe Limited by exchanging 10,000 shares of its $5 par value common stock for all of Tahoe's common stock. Tahoe's common stock is no par and has a balance of $100,000. At the acquisition date, Northstar's common stock was selling at $21 per share. At the time of the purchase, the book value and fair market value of Tahoe's net assets appeared as follows:

	Book Value	Fair Market Value
Monetary assets	$ 50,000	$ 50,000
Inventory	75,000	85,000
Property, plant, and equipment, net	150,000	175,000
Total assets	$275,000	$310,000
Total liabilities	$100,000	$100,000

Tahoe's net income during the year amounted to $150,000, earned as follows:

January 2, 1987 to February 28, 1987	$ 40,000
March 1, 1987 to December 31, 1987	110,000

Required:

a. Assuming that the purchase method of accounting is used, make the required journal entries and answer the following questions:

1. Make the entry to record the acquisition.
2. Make the elimination entry that would be made on the date of acquisition.
3. At what dollar amount would Tahoe's net assets be consolidated with Northstar's assets?
4. How much income would Northstar report on its consolidated income statement from Tahoe's operations?

b. Make the required journal entries and answer the preceding questions, assuming that the pooling-of-interests method of accounting is used.

Problem Set A

19A–1. Accounting for Current Marketable Securities. At the beginning of 1987 the Rose Corporation held the following current marketable equity securities:

Security	Number of Shares	Total Cost	Total Market
MG, Inc.	1,000	$35,000	$30,000
Drof Co.	500	10,000	12,000

During 1987 the following transactions took place:

- March 1: Purchased 200 shares of Joellen Inc. at $45 per share including commissions.
- March 31: Received dividends of $1.50 per share on MG, Inc. stock.
- May 2: Sold all of the shares in Drof Co. for $22 per share.
- September 1: Sold 500 shares of MG, Inc. for $29 per share.
- September 30: Received cash dividends of $1.50 per share on MG, Inc. stock.
- December 1: Purchased 10 $1,000, 12% bonds of United Inc. at 98 plus accrued interest for 5 full months. The company does not intend to amortize any discounts or premiums.
- December 31: Received the semiannual interest payment on the United Inc. bonds.
- December 31: You have obtained the following market values as of December 31:

Joellen	$46 per share
MG, Inc.	34 per share
United, Inc.	97

The company applies the lower-of-cost-or-market rule to debt as well as equity securities.

Required:

a. Prepare the journal entries to record the above transactions regarding the marketable securities.

b. Show how the marketable securities would be disclosed on the December 31, 1987 balance sheet.

19A-2. Valuation of Marketable Equity Securities. Included in the information contained in the footnotes to the financial statements of Diamond Green Corporation at December 31, 1987 is the following regarding current marketable equity securities:

	1987	1986
Marketable securities—at cost	$125,000	$50,000
Gross unrealized gains	5,600	2,100
Gross unrealized losses	(10,500)	(5,500)
Marketable securities—at market	$120,100	$46,600

During 1987 the firm sold for $18,500 securities with a cost of $14,000.

Required:

Based on the above information, answer the following questions:

a. At what amount should the marketable equity securities be shown on the balance sheet for 1987 and 1986?

b. What should be the balance, if any, for 1987 in the account titled Allowance to Reduce Marketable Equity Securities to Market, and where is this account disclosed?

c. What is the amount of the unrealized gain or loss for 1987 that should be disclosed, and where should this amount be disclosed?

d. What is the amount of realized gain or loss for 1987 that should be disclosed, and where should this amount be disclosed?

e. What is the cost of the securities purchased by Diamond Green during 1987?

19A-3. Investment in Long-term Securities. During 1986 and 1987 the Hubbard Scientific Corporation entered into the following transactions regarding long-term investments. All investments represent less than a 20% interest in the related companies. Prior to 1986 Hubbard Scientific had no long-term investments.

1986

- January 15: Purchased 500 shares of Saco Industries for $25 per share.
- April 14: Purchased 100 shares of Listo Lecon for $80 per share.
- September 30: Received a $1 per-share cash dividend on Saco Industries stock.
- November 29: Purchased 1,000 shares of Inca Ink for $30 per share.
- December 15: Received a 10% stock dividend on Listo Lecon stock.
- December 31: The market value per share of stocks was:

Saco Industries	$22
Listo Lecon	84
Inca Ink	28

1987

- February 1: Purchased an additional 500 shares of Saco Industries at $26 per share.
- April 28: Sold all the shares in Listo Lecon for $81 per share.
- October 1: Received $1 per-share dividend on Saco Industries stock.
- December 31: The market value of the stocks held at December 31, 1987 was as follows:

Saco Industries	$22 per share
Inca Ink	32 per share

Required:

a. Make the appropriate journal entries for 1986 and 1987.

b. Prepare the long-term investment section of the balance sheet at December 31, 1986 and 1987.

19A–4. Equity Method of Accounting. At the beginning of 1987 Kaput Inc. purchased as a long-term investment a 30% interest (representing 30,000 shares) in Daloon Co. for $510,000 cash. Daloon had a very successful year during 1987 and reported net income of $150,000. In addition, the firm declared and paid dividends totaling $100,000. At year-end the price per share of Daloon stock was $20.

During 1988 business slowed significantly, and Daloon reported a net loss of $80,000 for the year. However, in order to keep its stockholders happy, the firm declared and paid dividends of $.10 per share. Because of the firm's poor performance, the price per share of its stock at year-end dropped to $15.

Required:

a. Make the journal entries to record these transactions during 1987 and 1988.

b. How much income would Kaput report from this investment during 1987 and 1988?

c. Prepare the long-term investment section of Kaput's balance sheet at December 31, 1987 and 1988.

d. If this investment was accounted for under the cost method of accounting, how much income would Kaput report from this investment during 1987 and 1988?

19A–5. Cost versus Equity Method of Accounting. During 1987 the RFD Company made the following two investments:

- January 2: RFD purchased for cash and notes 40% of the 500,000 shares of common stock of the Marina Trading Co. The purchase was made for $1 million cash and notes of $600,000. Marina's net income for the year ended December 31, 1987 was $300,000. In addition, Marina paid total dividends of $.50 per share. At December 31, 1987 the market price of Marina's stock was $10.50 per share.

- July 1: RFD purchased 25,000 shares of Mitsui Inc. for $300,000 cash. This purchase represented a 15% interest in Mitsui. Mitsui's net income during 1987 was $400,000, and Mitsui paid dividends of $.40 on the last day of each quarter during 1987. At December 31, 1987 the market price of Mitsui's stock was $11 per share. However, RFD considers this to be a temporary price decline.

These were the only two long-term investments made by RFD.

Required:

a. Make the journal entries to record these investments.

b. At the end of 1987, what was the balance in RFD's investment account?

c. What should be the 1987 income reported by RFD regarding these two investments?

19A–6. Consolidated Worksheet and Balance Sheet. On April 1, 1987 the Canfield Corporation purchased an 80% interest in the Skinner Company for $150,000 cash. At the date of acquisition, the condensed balance sheets of each company were as follows:

Assets	Canfield Corporation	Skinner Company
Cash	$ 50,000	$ 12,000
Accounts receivable	72,000	18,000
Inventory	165,000	112,500
Investment in Skinner	150,000	0
Property, plant, and equipment, net	400,000	130,000
Total assets	$837,000	$272,500

Equities	Canfield Corporation	Skinner Company
Current liabilities	$140,000	$ 85,000
Long-term debt	100,000	0
Common stock, no par	400,000	100,000
Retained earnings	197,000	87,500
Total equities	$837,000	$272,500

Included in the accounts receivable and current liabilities is intercompany debt amounting to $5,000.

Required:

   a. Prepare a worksheet to consolidate Canfield and Skinner.

   b. Prepare a consolidated balance sheet at the date of acquisition.

19A–7. Consolidated Worksheet and Balance Sheet. On November 1, 1987 the Pepper Corporation purchased for $240,000 cash a 90% interest in the Salt Company. The condensed balance sheets of each company at the date of acquisition are presented below:

Assets	Pepper Corporation	Salt Company
Cash	$ 48,000	$ 25,000
Accounts receivable	70,000	35,000
Inventory	95,000	75,000
Investment in Salt	240,000	0
Property, plant, and equipment, net	230,000	150,000
Total assets	$683,000	$285,000

Equities		
Current liabilities	$ 74,000	$ 30,000
Long-term debt	125,000	45,000
Common stock $1 par value	200,000	60,000
Paid-in capital	120,000	25,000
Retained earnings	164,000	125,000
Total equities	$683,000	$285,000

Pepper decided to allocate the 60% excess of the purchase price over the book value of the net assets acquired to increase to fair market value Salt's property, plant, and equipment. The remaining amount of the excess is considered goodwill. Included in the accounts receivable and current liabilities is $10,000 of intercompany debt.

Required:

   a. Prepare a worksheet to consolidate the two companies at the date of acquisition.

   b. Prepare a consolidated balance sheet at the date of acquisition.

19A–8. Consolidated Income Statement. At the beginning of 1985 the Mikla Corporation purchased 100% of the assets of the Stillwill Company at an amount equal to the book value of Stillwill's net assets at that time. The condensed income statements for both companies for the year ended December 31, 1987 are presented below.

	Mikla Corporation	Stillwill Company
Sales	$1,000,000	$600,000
Cost of goods sold	650,000	420,000
Gross margin on sales	350,000	180,000
Operating expenses		
Selling	80,000	45,000
General and administrative	60,000	50,000
Total operating expenses	140,000	95,000
Income from operations	210,000	85,000
Interest revenue (expense)	12,000	(5,000)
Income before taxes	222,000	80,000
Taxes	62,000	20,000
Net income	$ 160,000	$ 60,000

During 1987 Stillwill purchased $50,000 of inventory at cost from Mikla. All of this inventory had been sold to outside customers by year-end. In addition, included in interest income and expense is $5,000 of interest expense paid by Stillwill to Mikla.

Required:

Prepare a consolidated income statement worksheet for Mikla and Stillwill for the year ended December 31, 1987.

19A–9. Purchase versus Pooling of Interests. The Minneapolis Company intends to merge with the St. Paul Corporation by exchanging 10,000 shares of its common stock for 100% of the shares of the St. Paul Corporation. At the time of the merger, the Minneapolis Company's common stock was selling for $18 per share. Following are the condensed balance sheets of the two firms immediately prior to the acquisition:

Assets	Minneapolis Company	St. Paul Corporation
Current assets	$100,000	$ 45,000
Property, plant, and equipment, net	250,000	150,000
Total assets	$350,000	$195,000

Equities		
Current liabilities	$ 40,000	$ 30,000
Long-term debt	140,000	45,000
Common stock, $1 par value	75,000	50,000
Paid-in capital	40,000	25,000
Retained earnings	55,000	45,000
Total equities	$350,000	$195,000

Required:

a. Prepare journal entries to record the acquisition of St. Paul by Minneapolis, assuming that (1) the pooling-of-interests method is used and (2) the purchase method is used.

b. Prepare a worksheet as of the date of acquisition, assuming that (1) the pooling-of-interests method is used and (2) the purchase method is used. (Apply the excess cost over the book value of net assets acquired to goodwill.)

c. Prepare a consolidated balance sheet at the date of acquisition for the two different methods. Compare and contrast the two balance sheets.

Problem Set B

19B–1. Accounting for Current Marketable Securities. At the beginning of 1988, the Modem Corporation held the following current marketable equity securities:

Security	Number of Shares	Total Cost	Total Market
Tele Inc.	2,000	$80,000	$74,000
Byte Co.	800	16,000	29,000

During 1988 the following transactions took place:

- February 1: Purchased 300 shares of Alexis Inc. at $60 per share including commissions.

- March 31: Received dividends on $1 per share of Tele Inc. stock.

- April 14: Sold 400 of the shares in Byte Co. for $22 per share.

- August 14: Sold 1,000 shares of Tele Inc. for $39 per share.

- September 30: Received cash dividends of $1 per share on Tele Inc. stock.

- November 1: Purchased 20 $1,000, 10% bonds of Americo, Inc. at 102 plus accrued interest for 4 full months. The company does not intend to amortize any discounts or premiums.

- December 31: The company receives the semiannual interest payment on the Americo, Inc. bonds.
- December 31: You have obtained the following market values as of December 31, 1988:

Alexis	$61 per share
Tele Inc.	38 per share
Byte Co.	23 per share
Americo bonds	100

The company applies the lower-of-cost-or-market rule to debt as well as equity securities.

Required:

a. Prepare the journal entries to record the above transactions related to the marketable securities.

b. Show how the marketable securities would be disclosed on the December 31, 1988 balance sheet.

c. Describe how the income statement accounts relative to these transactions would be shown on the income statement.

19B–2. Valuation of Marketable Equity Securities. Included in the information contained in the footnotes to the financial statements of Grenada Corporation at December 31, 1987 is the following related to current marketable equity securities:

	1987	1986
Marketable securities, at cost	$160,000	$75,000
Gross unrealized gains	14,300	5,100
Gross unrealized losses	(17,200)	(2,300)
Marketable securities, at market	$157,100	$77,800

During 1987 the firm sold securities with a cost of $30,000 for $38,500.

Required:

Based on the above information answer the following questions:

a. At what amount should the marketable equity securities be shown on the balance sheet for 1987 and 1986?

b. What should be the balance, if any, for 1987 and 1986 in the account titled Allowance to Reduce Marketable Equity Securities to Market, and where is this account disclosed?

c. What are the amounts of the unrealized gains and/or losses, if any, for 1987 and 1986 that should be disclosed, and where should these amounts be disclosed?

d. What is the amount of realized gain or loss for 1987 that should be disclosed, and where should this amount be disclosed?

e. What is the cost of the securities purchased by the Grenada Corporation during 1987?

19B–3. Investment in Long-term Securities. During 1986 and 1987 the Crafty Tool Corporation entered into the following transactions related to long-term investments. All investments represent less than a 20% interest in the related companies. Prior to 1986 Crafty Tool had no long-term investments.

1986:

- January 29: Purchased 200 shares of Fast Industries for $60 per share.
- March 24: Purchased 300 shares of Celeste at $45 per share.
- September 30: Received a $2 per-share cash dividend on Fast Industries' stock.
- October 13: Purchased 2,000 shares of Cool Pen for $20 per share.
- December 30: Received a 20% stock dividend on Celeste stock.
- December 31: The market value per share of stocks was:

Fast Industries	$63
Celeste	35
Cool Pen	19

1987:

- February 12: Purchased an additional 100 shares of Fast Industries at $65 per share.
- May 29: Sold 200 shares in Celeste for $34 per share.
- September 30: Received a $2 per-share dividend on Fast Industries' stock.
- December 31: The market value of the stocks held at December 31, 1987 was as follows:

Fast Industries	$66.00 per share
Celeste	32.00 per share
Cool Pen	19.25 per share

Required:

   a. Make the appropriate journal entries for 1986 and 1987.

   b. Prepare the long-term investment section of the balance sheet at December 31, 1986 and 1987.

19B–4. Equity Method of Accounting. At the beginning of 1987 Eastbound Inc. purchased a 40% interest (representing 40,000 shares) in Earth Co. for $1,008,000 cash. Earth had a good year during 1987 and reported net income of $250,000. In addition, on June 30, 1987 the firm declared and issued a 5% stock dividend. On December 30, 1987 the firm also declared and paid a $1 per-share dividend. At year-end the price per share of Earth's stock was $22 per share.

During 1988 business increased significantly and Earth reported a net income of $400,000 for the year. The firm declared and paid dividends of $1.50 per share. Because of the firm's strong performance, the price per share of its stock at year-end increased to $30.

Required:

   a. Make the journal entries to record these transactions during 1987 and 1988.

   b. How much income would Eastbound report from this investment during 1987 and 1988?

   c. Prepare the long-term investment section of Eastbound's balance sheet at December 31, 1987 and 1988.

   d. If this investment was accounted for under the cost method of accounting for long-term investment, how much income would Eastbound report from this investment during 1987 and 1988?

19B–5. Cost versus Equity Method of Accounting. During 1987 the Strawberry Company made the following two investments:

- January 2: Strawberry purchased for cash and notes 30% of the 1 million shares of common stock of the Adam Computer Co. The purchase was made for $2 million cash and notes of $1 million. Adam Computer Co.'s net income for the year ended December 31, 1987 was $500,000. In addition, Adam Computer paid total dividends of $1.50 per share. At December 31, 1987 the market price of Adam Computer's stock was $31.50 per share.

- April 1: Strawberry purchased 50,000 shares of Chow Inc. for $600,000 cash. This purchase represented a 10% interest in Chow. Chow's net loss during 1987 was $100,000 and Chow paid dividends of $.10 the last day of each quarter during 1987. At December 31, 1987 the market price of Chow's stock was $5 per share. However, Strawberry considers this to be a temporary price decline.

These are the only two long-term investments made by the Strawberry Company.

Required:

   a. Make the journal entries to record these investments.

   b. At the end of 1987, what is the balance in the investment account of the Strawberry Company?

   c. What should be the income reported by the Strawberry Company related to these two investments during 1987?

19B–6. Consolidation Worksheet and Balance Sheet. On June 1, 1987 the Upbeat Corporation purchased a 90% interest in the Deadbeat Co. for $225,000 cash. At the date of acquisition the condensed balance sheets of each company are as shown at the top of page 784.

Included in the accounts receivable and current liabilities is intercompany debt amounting to $8,000.

Investment in Corporate Equity Securities

Assets	Upbeat Corporation	Deadbeat Company
Cash	$ 85,000	$ 15,000
Accounts receivable	107,000	24,000
Inventory	300,000	126,000
Investment in Deadbeat	225,000	0
Property, plant, and equipment, net	525,000	180,000
Total assets	$1,242,000	$345,000

Equities		
Current liabilities	$ 220,000	$ 95,000
Long-term debt	150,000	0
Common stock, no par	600,000	100,000
Retained earnings	272,000	150,000
Total equities	$1,242,000	$345,000

Required:
  a. Prepare a worksheet to consolidate Upbeat and Deadbeat.
  b. Prepare a consolidated balance sheet at the date of acquisition.

19B-7. Consolidated Worksheet and Balance Sheet. On September 1, 1988 the Button Corporation purchased an 80% interest in the Zipper Co. for $300,000 cash. The condensed balance sheets of each company at the date of acquisition are presented below:

Assets	Button Corporation	Zipper Company
Cash	$ 65,000	$ 75,000
Accounts receivable	85,000	45,000
Inventory	178,000	85,000
Investment in Zipper	300,000	0
Property, plant, and equipment, net	360,000	200,000
Total assets	$988,000	$405,000

Equities		
Current liabilities	$105,000	$ 50,000
Long-term debt	180,000	55,000
Common stock, $2 par value	400,000	100,000
Paid-in capital	80,000	25,000
Retained earnings	223,000	175,000
Total equities	$988,000	$405,000

Button decided to allocate the 70% excess of the purchase price over the book value of the net assets acquired to increase the inventory of Zipper to its fair market value. The remaining amount of the excess is considered goodwill. Included in the accounts receivable and current liabilities is $4,000 of intercompany debt.

Required:
  a. Prepare a worksheet to consolidate the two companies at the date of acquisition.
  b. Prepare a consolidated balance sheet at the date of acquisition.

19B-8. Consolidated Income Statement. At the beginning of 1987, the Rogers Corporation purchased 100% of the assets of the Maryann Company at an amount equal to the book value of the net assets of Maryann at that time. The condensed income statements for both companies for the year ended December 31, 1987 are presented at the top of page 785.

During 1987 Rogers purchased $70,000 of inventory from Maryann. All of this inventory had been sold to outside customers by year-end. In addition, included in interest income and expense is $7,000 of interest expense paid by Maryann to Rogers.

	Rogers Corporation	Maryann Company
Sales	$3,000,000	$950,000
Cost of goods sold	2,160,000	665,000
Gross margin on sales	840,000	285,000
Operating expenses		
Selling	320,000	65,000
General and administrative	240,000	55,000
Total operating expenses	560,000	120,000
Income from operations	280,000	165,000
Interest income (expense)	25,000	(8,000)
Income before taxes	305,000	157,000
Taxes	122,000	47,100
Net income	$ 183,000	$109,900

Required:

Prepare a consolidated income statement worksheet for Rogers and Maryann for the year ended December 31, 1987.

19B–9. Purchase versus Pooling of Interests. The Moran Company intends to merge with the Aker Corporation by exchanging 10,000 shares of its common stock for 100% of the shares of the Aker Corporation. At the time of the merger the Moran Company's common stock was selling for $50 per share. Following are the condensed balance sheets of the two firms immediately prior to the acquisition.

Assets	Moran Company	Aker Corporation
Current assets	$ 400,000	$180,000
Property, plant, and equipment, net	850,000	520,000
Total assets	$1,250,000	$700,000

Equities		
Current liabilities	$ 250,000	$100,000
Long-term debt	350,000	165,000
Common stock, $10 par value	400,000	150,000
Paid-in capital	50,000	125,000
Retained earnings	200,000	160,000
Total equities	$1,250,000	$700,000

Required:

a. Prepare journal entries to record the acquisition of Aker by Moran assuming that (1) the pooling-of-interests method is used and (2) the purchase method is used.

b. Prepare a worksheet as of the date of acquisition assuming that (1) the pooling-of-interests method is used and (2) the purchase method is used. (Apply the excess cost over the book value of net assets acquired to goodwill.)

c. Prepare a consolidated balance sheet at the date of acquisition for the two different methods. Compare and contrast the two balance sheets.

Using the Computer

The Horn Corporation acquired 80% of the Gren Company on July 1, 1986 for $550,000 cash. At the date of acquisition, the condensed balance sheets of the two companies were as follows:

Assets	Horn Corporation	Gren Company
Cash	$ 165,000	$175,000
Accounts receivable	185,000	145,000
Inventory	278,000	185,000
Investment in Gren Company	550,000	0
Property, plant, and equipment, net	460,000	400,000
Total assets	$1,638,000	$905,000

Equities		
Current liabilities	$ 205,000	$150,000
Long-term debt	280,000	155,000
Common stock, $2 par value	500,000	300,000
Paid-in capital	180,000	125,000
Retained earnings	473,000	175,000
Total equities	$1,638,000	$905,000

The excess purchase price over the book value of the net assets acquired is allocated as 60% to the property, plant, and equipment on Gren's books and the remainder to goodwill.

Required:

Using an electronic spreadsheet, prepare a worksheet to consolidate the two entities' balance sheets at the date of acquisition.

Understanding Financial Statements

The following footnote appeared in the financial statements of the Sunshine Mining Company:

3. Investments:

Investments are comprised of the following noncurrent marketable securities at December 31, 1983 (dollar amounts in thousands):

Issuer	Number of Shares	Cost	Market
Gulf Corporation	1,374,502	$61,470	$59,282
Consolidated Silver Corporation	1,512,387	1,361	6,050
Other mining company stocks	4,999,658	4,279	2,928
Other corporate stocks	4,444	51	70
		$67,161	$68,330

At December 31, 1982, investments were comprised of current and noncurrent marketable securities with a cost of $7,067,000 and $6,158,000, respectively, and market value of $4,601,000 and $8,807,000, respectively.

Realized gain on the sale of noncurrent marketable securities was $1,570,000 in 1983. Realized and unrealized losses on marketable securities totaled $5,534,000 in 1982. Unrealized losses on marketable securities totaled $10,267,000 in 1981.

Required:

a. At what amount would the noncurrent marketable securities be shown on the December 31, 1982 and 1983 balance sheets? At what amount would current marketable securities be shown on the December 31, 1982 balance sheet?

b. On what financial statement would the 1983 realized gain on the sale of marketable securities of $1,570,000 be shown? Assume all realized gains relate to noncurrent securities.

c. On what financial statement would the 1981 unrealized losses on noncurrent marketable securities of $10,267,000 be shown? Assume all unrealized losses relate to noncurrent securities.

d. Assuming that the firm received proceeds of $5 million on the sale of noncurrent marketable securities in 1983, what was the cost of noncurrent marketable securities purchased in 1983?

Financial Decision Case

The Space Parts Company has been in business for several years. However, in the last couple of years, growth in the industry has slowed down and the company is facing its first net loss. In order to increase its future prospects, the company is considering purchasing 100% of a competing company called High Tech Parts.

The president of Space Parts asks your advice concerning the contemplated purchase of High Tech. He tells you that it is now December 1, and it appears that Space Parts will have a loss of $300,000 for the year ended December 31, 1987. On the other hand, High Tech has had a successful year with estimated profits through November of $500,000. Profits for December are estimated to be another $75,000. Further, the president of Space Parts feels that the net assets of High Tech are substantially undervalued. The purchase price will be substantially above the net book value of High Tech's net assets and probably above the fair value of the net assets.

The president of Space Parts had heard about purchase and pooling-of-interests accounting, but he is confused about the difference between them. He asks your advice on the following points:

a. In structuring the contemplated purchase of High Tech, do I have a choice between using purchase accounting and pooling-of-interests accounting?

b. I am considering either purchasing High Tech entirely with cash or exchanging common stock of Space Parts for all the common stock of High Tech. What effect does this have, if any, on whether I can use the purchase or pooling method of accounting? Compare for the possible other effects on Space Parts' financial statements of using the two different methods.

c. Prepare a schedule for me that compares the effect on Space Parts' current period's income of using the pooling-of-interests method versus the purchase method.

Required:

Answer the president's questions.

V

Analysis of Accounting Information

The Statement of Changes in Financial Position* 20

LEARNING OBJECTIVES

After reading this chapter you should be able to:
1. Describe a statement of changes in financial position and give its purpose.
2. Describe what is meant by financial resources.
3. Differentiate between operating and financial changes.
4. Prepare a working capital–based statement of changes in financial position using a worksheet.
5. Prepare a cash-based statement of changes in financial position.
6. Discuss the overall importance of the statement of changes in financial position.

When a large commuter airline in California filed for bankruptcy, the president of the airline stated, "We just ran out of money."[1] This statement underlines the importance of the statement of changes in financial position. While a balance sheet and income statement provide important information about the enterprise, the statement of changes in financial position provides essential information about the sources and uses of the enterprise's financial resources. Thus, by studying this statement, present and potential investors and creditors can assess possible current and future working capital and cash flow problems. The purpose of this chapter is to discuss the uses and the preparation of the statement of changes in financial position.

*The material in this chapter is based on accounting standards in place as of the end of 1986. It appears quite likely that the FASB will issue in the second half of 1987 a standard called *The Statement of Cash Flows*. This standard will substantially alter the material in the first part of this chapter. Once the actual standard is issued, appropriate revisions will be made immediately.

[1]*Los Angeles Times*, April 26, 1983, p. 1, part iv.

The Purpose of a Statement of Changes in Financial Position

The statement of changes in financial position is a required financial statement along with the balance sheet, income statement, and retained earnings statement or statement of changes in stockholders' equity. The purpose of this statement, illustrated in Exhibit 20–1, is to describe the changes (inflows and outflows) in the resources of the enterprise. This statement is useful to present and potential investors and creditors because it helps answer such questions as:

1. What are the sources of the firm's financial resources?
2. What proportion of the firm's financial resources is generated internally or from operations?
3. What other investing and financing activities took place during the year?
4. Why was the firm profitable although there was only a slight increase in working capital or cash?
5. How was working capital or cash used during the year?

For example, ETR Sound Systems (Exhibit 20–1) was able to obtain financial resources (in this case defined as working capital) from operations, the sale of noncurrent assets, and the issuance of long-term debt and common stock. In this case the total source of working capital amounted to $166,500, of which only $16,500 was provided from operations. The issuance of equities—either long-term liabilities or common stock—provided the bulk of the firm's working capital during the year. As its outside sources of resources become less available in the future, ETR must begin to generate additional working capital from operations.

ETR used its working capital primarily to purchase noncurrent assets and secondarily to retire long-term debt and to issue cash dividends. Looking at

---

EXHIBIT 20–1

ETR Sound Systems
Statement of Changes in Financial Position
For the Year Ended December 31, 1987

Sources of working capital		
From operations		$ 16,500
Sale of equipment	$ 20,000	
Issuance of bonds	80,000	
Issuance of common stock	50,000	150,000
Total sources		$166,500
Uses of working capital		
Purchase of building	$120,000	
Retirement of note payable	20,000	
Dividends	6,000	146,000
Net increase in working capital		$ 20,500

---

this statement as a whole, it appears that ETR is expanding and is financing this expansion through issuing long-term debt and common stock.

In summary, the purpose of the statement of changes in financial position is to show in detail the sources and uses of the firm's financial resources and thus help to explain the changes that took place in the firm's financial position over the accounting period. In many circumstances this information cannot be obtained from comparing two consecutive balance sheets. Let's assume that at the beginning of the year the balance in a firm's land account was $750,000 and at the end of the year the balance in the account was $800,000. The net increase of $50,000 does not tell the entire story. The cause of this net increase was a cash purchase of land for $600,000 and a sale of existing land for $550,000. The terms of the sale called for the firm to receive a small down payment and a large long-term note receivable. These transactions represent significant events and are fully disclosed only in the statement of changes in financial position.

Financial Resources Defined

We stated that the statement of changes in financial position shows changes in the financial resources of the firm. However, what do we mean by financial resources? In the context of this statement, **financial resources** means either working capital or cash. Working capital, the difference between current assets and current liabilities, has been the most common definition of financial resources. This is so because firms buy and sell on credit and are constantly turning their cash into inventories and then into receivables. Thus, the amount of working capital represents the stock of liquid resources that the firm has to work with, and information concerning the sources and uses of these resources is necessary to evaluate the ability of the business to operate on a daily basis.

In the last few years more and more firms have begun to define financial resources as cash, and thus the statement of changes in financial position essentially becomes a statement of changes in cash. The movement toward a cash-based statement is the result of a feeling by financial statement users that in a cash-tight economy the amount of working capital may not be a good indicator of a firm's liquidity. Due to the accumulation of unsold inventories or uncollected receivables, a firm may have substantial working capital but at the same time may be facing serious cash flow problems. As a result, investors and creditors feel that they need information concerning the sources and uses of the firm's cash. In response to these views, the FASB in September 1986 issued an exposure draft that would require companies to present a statement of cash flows as part of a full set of financial statements. This cash flow statement would replace the present statement of changes in financial position. This exposure draft, if adopted, would likely be effective for fiscal years ending after June 30, 1987.

Causes of Changes in Financial Position

Regardless of whether financial resources are defined as cash or working capital, there are certain activities that cause changes in financial resources. These activities can be grouped into two major categories—operating and financial.

Operating activities relate to the purchase, production, and sale of the firm's goods and services. The results of these activities produce either a net income or a net loss and are summarized on the income statement. These same transactions also cause changes in the stock of the firm's financial resources. For example, sales result in increases in cash and receivables and/or decreases in liabilities while expenses decrease inventory, cash, and/or other assets or increase liabilities. As a result, these operating activities, when netted, produce either a source of resources or a use of these resources.

Financial activities are all those activities that are not considered operating ones and generally relate to changes in noncurrent assets, noncurrent liabilities, and stockholders' equity accounts. Again, these financial activities can result in either a source or a use of financial resources. The following three major types of financial activities result in sources of financial resources:

1. *Decreases in Noncurrent Assets.* When a firm sells a noncurrent asset such as property, plant, and equipment, financial resources are increased. The sale of these assets results in an increase in cash and/or receivables. An inflow of assets takes place whether a firm incurs a gain or a loss on the sale of the asset. Obviously, a gain will produce a higher asset inflow than will a loss.

2. *Increases in Long-term Debt.* Issue of long-term notes, bonds, and other credit instruments represents major financial decisions made by a firm's management. When a firm increases its long-term debt to banks or other creditors, its financial resources are increased through the infusion of cash or other assets into the firm.

3. *Increases in Capital Stock.* The issue of common and/or preferred stock is another way in which the firm can increase its financial resources through the infusion of cash and/or other assets into the firm.

On the other hand, uses of financial activities result from the following activities:

1. *Purchases of Noncurrent Assets.* When a firm purchases or otherwise increases its noncurrent assets, it uses its financial resources. For example, the purchase of land either decreases the firm's cash or increases its payables.

2. *Decreases in Long-term Payables.* When a firm repays or retires its long-term payables, financial resources are used. That is, the repayment of bonds or other notes generally causes a decrease in the firm's cash.

3. *Decrease in Capital Stock.* Occasionally a firm repurchases its own stock. These treasury stock transactions decrease the firm's financial resources generally through a decrease in cash.

4. *Cash Dividends.* The issuance of cash dividends is clearly a reduction in the financial resources of the firm. As we noted, the issuance of dividends is not an operating activity and does not affect net income. Rather, it is related to the financing activities and decisions of the firm's management.

The diagram on the top of page 795 outlines the sources and uses of financial resources:

Statement of Changes in Financial Position— Working Capital Basis

As we noted, the working capital basis is still a common form of the statement of changes in financial position. This type of statement defines the stock of financial resources as working capital and explains the causes for the changes in the stock of these resources.

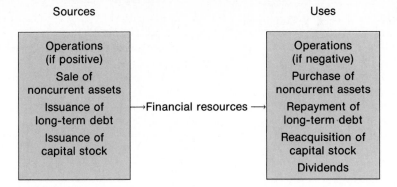

SOURCES AND USES OF FINANCIAL RESOURCES

Sources | | Uses

Operations (if positive)		Operations (if negative)
Sale of noncurrent assets		Purchase of noncurrent assets
Issuance of long-term debt	→Financial resources →	Repayment of long-term debt
Issuance of capital stock		Reacquisition of capital stock
		Dividends

The following diagram shows how a balance sheet can be partitioned into two major categories—working capital and other net assets. The other accounts are further divided into three categories—noncurrent assets, noncurrent liabilities, and stockholders' equity. During a particular period of time a firm enters into a variety of different types of transactions, some of which affect working capital and some of which do not. The following diagram helps explain which types of transactions cause an increase or decrease in working capital:

WORKING CAPITAL	
Current Assets (a)	— Current Liabilities (b)
Noncurrent Assets (c)	Noncurrent Liabilities (d) Stockholders' Equity (e)

Transactions That Affect Working Capital

Any transaction that crosses the major working capital–nonworking capital partition causes a change in working capital. These transactions can be further divided into operating and financial changes.

Operating Changes

As noted, **operating changes** result from the production, purchase, and sale of the firm's goods and services. These transactions affect working capital, category (a) or (b), and ultimately retained earnings, category (e), and are often called income statement transactions. To illustrate, each of the four transactions (on the top of page 796) affects a working capital account and ultimately retained earnings.

The great majority of income statement transactions are of this type. If all these transactions are netted together and result in an increase in working capital, they are labeled as a source of working capital from operations. On the

Transaction	Categories	Journal Entry	Effect on Net Working Capital
1. Sale on account	a e	Cash or Accounts Receivable Sales	increase
2. Cost of goods sold	e a	Cost of Goods Sold Inventory	decrease
3. Recognition of unearned revenue	b e	Unearned Revenue Earned Revenue	increase
4. Wages paid in cash	e a	Wages Expense Cash	decrease

other hand, if they result in a decrease in working capital, they are labeled as a use of working capital from operations.

We said that the great majority of income statement transactions are of this type. The major exceptions are depreciation and amortization. These transactions do not affect working capital because they affect only categories (c) and (e), noncurrent assets and retained earnings. The following journal entries illustrate these points; other examples will be discussed later.

Transaction	Categories	Journal Entry	Effect on Working Capital
1. Recognition of depreciation	e c	Depreciation Expense Accumulated Depreciation	none
2. Recognition of amortization	e c	Amortization Expense Patent	none

To summarize, the majority of income statement transactions affect one or more working capital accounts and retained earnings and are one of the major causes of changes in financial resources. In the ETR example in Exhibit 20–1 on page 792, working capital from operations totaled $16,500.

Financial Changes

Financial changes are changes in working capital from other than operating transactions. As noted, they result from the purchase and sale of noncurrent assets, the issuance and retirement of long-term debt, and the issuance and reacquisition of capital stock and from the declaration of cash dividends. All of the transactions illustrated on page 797 cross the partition between working capital and nonworking capital accounts, and represent the major types of financial changes that affect the stock of working capital.

Transactions That Do Not Affect Working Capital

There are two major types of transactions that do not cause a change in working capital—transactions that affect only working capital accounts and transactions that affect only nonworking capital accounts.

Transaction	Categories	Journal Entry	Effect on Working Capital

1. Sale of land	a
	e
	c
		Cash or Receivable
		  Gain on Sale of Land
		  Land
			increase

2. Issuance of bonds	a d	Cash Bonds Payable	increase
3. Issuance of capital stock	a e	Cash Capital Stock	increase
4. Purchase of building	c a	Building Cash	decrease
5. Repayment of long-term debt	d a	Notes Payable Cash	decrease
6. Reacquisition of common stock	e a	Treasury Stock Cash	decrease
7. Declaration of cash dividend	e b	Retained Earnings Dividends Payable	decrease

Transactions Affecting Only Working Capital Accounts

A vast number of transactions a firm enters into affect only working capital accounts. Thus, while the individual working capital accounts change, the total working capital remains unchanged. Examples include the purchase of inventory on account, the purchase of supplies for cash, and the collection or payment of cash on account. These transactions affect either two current asset accounts or a current asset and a current liability account and, as a result, have no effect on the total of working capital. None of these transactions is relevant to a statement of changes in financial position prepared on a working capital basis because they do not cause a change in the total amount of working capital.

Transactions Affecting Only Two Nonworking Capital Accounts

There are two major types of transactions that affect two nonworking capital accounts. The first type, depreciation and amortization, was discussed previously. The second type involves transactions that affect only noncurrent assets, noncurrent liabilities, and capital stock. That is, they are all within the noncurrent section of the balance sheet. These transactions, although not common, have an important effect on the firm's financial position and because of that cannot be ignored in the preparation of the statement of changes in financial position. The **all financial resources concept** was developed to deal with these changes.

The All Financial Resources Concept

Most changes in noncurrent asset and liability and capital stock accounts are accompanied by a change in a working capital account. For example, a building is purchased with cash, or capital stock is issued for cash. Occasionally, however, a firm enters into a direct exchange in which a noncurrent account is affected without a corresponding change in a working capital account. For example, a firm may issue common stock in exchange for land or purchase a building solely through the issuance of long-term debt. These transactions alter the financial position of the firm without actually affecting working capital.

Because these transactions do not change total working capital, they could be ignored in the preparation of the statement of changes in financial position. However, to do so would ignore important changes in the composition of the firm's noncurrent assets, liabilities, and capital stock accounts. As a result, accountants employ the all financial resources concept, which requires that all material changes in noncurrent assets, long-term debt, and capital stock accounts be reported on the statement of changes in financial position regardless of whether they resulted in changes in the total of working capital.

To illustrate, assume that a firm purchases a plot of land from one of its stockholders by issuing 1,000 shares of no par common stock. At the time of the purchase the stock had a fair market value of $125,000. This direct transaction can be viewed as two intermediate transactions: the issuance of capital stock for cash and the subsequent immediate purchase of land for cash. In effect, this one transaction can be viewed as two as follows:

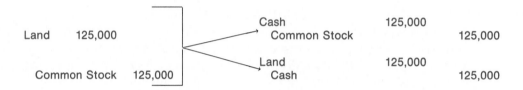

In this sense the first part of the transaction is considered a source of working capital and the second a use of working capital. This treatment ensures that all the significant transactions affecting the firm's financial resources are disclosed in the statement of changes in financial position.

Preparing a Statement of Changes in Financial Position—Working Capital Basis

A statement of changes in financial position can be prepared by identifying, from all the transactions the firm entered into, only those transactions that caused changes in working capital plus those changes included because of the all financial resources concept. This would be rather tedious because it would be necessary to review all the transactions the firm entered into during the period. Instead, the information contained in the balance sheet, income statement, and statement of changes in stockholders' equity can be utilized to prepare the statement of changes in financial position. Thus, this statement is usually the last one prepared and, as we will illustrate, a worksheet is often used to facilitate its preparation.

Determining Working Capital from Operations

A key to the preparation of the statement of changes in financial position is using net income to determine working capital from operations. As we noted, net income includes all transactions that affect net income, while working capital from operations includes only those income transactions that affect a working capital account. Thus, our starting point is to use net income as presented on the income statement and then to make any adjustments for items that are included in that figure but do not affect working capital.

Expenses That Do Not Reduce Working Capital

There are a number of expenses that reduce net income but do not reduce working capital. These expenses involve transactions between a noncurrent account and retained earnings, and include such items as depreciation, amortization of intangible assets, and amortization of discounts on bonds payable. The accounts related to these expenses are noncurrent assets or liabilities and ultimately retained earnings; no working capital accounts are involved. The following two journal entries illustrate these points:

Transaction	Categories	Journal Entry			Effect on	
					Net Income	Working Capital
1. Depreciation	e	Depreciation Expense	10,000			
	c	Accumulated Depreciation		10,000	(10,000)	0
2. Amortization of	e	Interest Expense	2,500			
bond discount	d	Discount on Bonds Payable		2,500	(2,500)	0

Thus, to determine working capital from operations, net income must be *increased* for all the expenses that reduced net income but did not reduce working capital.

Before we continue, one additional point must be emphasized. Items that are added back to net income to determine working capital from operations are not sources of working capital. They are added back because they were deducted in calculating net income, which is used as the starting figure to determine working capital from operations. Because depreciation is a very common example of this, many people consider depreciation as a source of funds, which is an incorrect interpretation. Depreciation is just one of the expenses that have no effect on working capital.

Income Items That Do Not Increase Working Capital

Occasionally a firm will earn revenue or have an expense reduced by an item that does not increase working capital. Perhaps the most common example is the amortization of a premium on a bond. The following entry decreases interest expense and thus increases income without affecting a working capital account:

        Premium on Bonds Payable   500
            Interest Expense   500

To determine working capital from operations, these items must be subtracted from net income.

Nonoperating Gains and Losses

Working capital from operations includes just items generated from the operating activities of the firm. Gains and losses from nonoperating or financial changes, such as the sale or disposal of noncurrent assets or the early extinguishment of debt, are not included in income from operations. Rather, the proceeds from these transactions are included, in total, in the financial section of the statement of changes in financial position.

Assume that a firm sold a parcel of land for $120,000. The land had a historical cost of $100,000, so the $20,000 gain was included in the net income for the period. In preparing the statement of changes in financial position, the entire $120,000 is included in the section called Proceeds from the Sale of Noncurrent Assets. As a result, the $20,000 gain must be deducted from net income in determining working capital from operations. If this is not done, the $20,000 would be double counted, because the full $120,000 is included in other sources.

In a similar manner, nonoperating losses must be added back to net income in determining working capital from operations. Again assume a firm sold land for $100,000 cash but now assume the land had a historical cost of $120,000. The $100,000 cash is included in the Proceeds from the Sale of Noncurrent Assets section of the statement. The $20,000 must then be added back to net income. This assures that the $20,000 loss is not double counted and working capital from operations includes only transactions resulting from the regular operating activities of the firm.

The following diagram illustrates the typical items that must be added back to or subtracted from net income in determining working capital from operations:

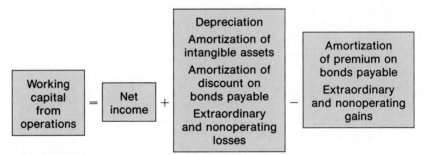

Using a Worksheet to Prepare a Statement of Changes in Financial Position

A worksheet is commonly used to prepare the statement of changes in financial position. It is a convenient way to analyze those transactions that affected working capital and thus would be part of the statement. The essence of the worksheet approach is to explain all the changes in working capital accounts by detailing the changes in nonworking capital accounts. Because there are fewer transactions affecting noncurrent accounts than those affecting current accounts, it is easier to concentrate on the noncurrent accounts.

The following steps are used in this approach:

1. Determine the change in working capital for the year.
2. Set up the worksheet.
3. Analyze the changes in the noncurrent accounts using the balance sheet, income statement, and, if necessary, the statement of changes in stock-

holders' equity. Determine whether these transactions resulted in a source or a use of working capital. Use these data to complete the worksheet.

4. Prepare the statement of changes in financial position and a schedule of changes in working capital accounts.

Exhibit 20–2 on pages 802 and 803 presents a comparative balance sheet and an income statement for BMI Computers. These data will be used to illustrate worksheet techniques for preparing the statement of changes in financial position.

Determining the Net Change in Working Capital

The first step in preparing the statement is to determine the change in working capital that occurred during the year. In this case there is an increase of $53,000 in working capital. The individual changes in the working capital accounts are:

	December 31,		Increase (Decrease) in Working Capital
	1987	1986	
Current assets			
Cash	$ 33,000	$ 20,000	$13,000
Accounts receivable, net	85,000	60,000	25,000
Inventory	150,000	140,000	10,000
Prepaids	4,000	5,000	(1,000)
	$272,000	$225,000	$47,000
Current liabilities			
Current maturities of long-term notes payable	$ 90,000	$ 80,000	($10,000)
Accounts payable	52,000	60,000	8,000
Dividends payable	15,000	20,000	5,000
Other accrued liabilities	7,000	10,000	3,000
	$164,000	$170,000	$ 6,000
Working capital	$108,000	$ 55,000	$53,000

The statement of changes in financial position should therefore show an increase in working capital of $53,000.

Setting Up the Worksheet

An illustrative worksheet for BMI Computers is presented in Exhibit 20–3 on page 804. This worksheet has two major parts: The first has a line for working capital and a list of the individual noncurrent accounts; the second is a skeleton statement of changes in financial position.

The first part of the worksheet can be set up by using the comparative balance sheet in Exhibit 20–2 on page 802 and the schedule of changes in working capital accounts prepared above. An item called Working Capital as well as the noncurrent accounts should be placed in the first column of the worksheet. The account balances at the end of the prior year, 1986 in this case, should be placed in the next column. The $55,000 in working capital at the end of 1986 comes from the Schedule of Changes in Working Capital accounts. The balances for the noncurrent accounts come from the comparative balance sheet in Exhibit 20–2. At this point columns C and D, which are used to analyze the interim transactions during the year, are not filled in. The relevant account

EXHIBIT 20-2
BMI Computers
Comparative Balance Sheet
December 31,

Assets	1987	1986
Current assets:		
Cash	$ 33,000	$ 20,000
Accounts receivable, net	85,000	60,000
Inventory	150,000	140,000
Prepaids	4,000	5,000
Total current assets	$ 272,000	$225,000
Property, plant, and equipment:		
Land	$ 375,000	$200,000
Building	400,000	400,000
Less: Accumulated depreciation	(40,000)	(30,000)
Equipment	135,000	120,000
Less: Accumulated depreciation	(21,000)	(24,000)
Total property, plant, and equipment	$ 849,000	$666,000
Other assets:		
Goodwill, net	$ 8,000	$ 9,000
Total other assets	$ 8,000	$ 9,000
Total assets	$1,129,000	$900,000

Liabilities and Stockholders' Equity	1987	1986
Current liabilities:		
Current maturities of notes payable	$ 90,000	$ 80,000
Accounts payable	52,000	60,000
Dividends payable	15,000	20,000
Other accrued liabilities	7,000	10,000
Total current liabilities	$ 164,000	$170,000
Long-term liabilities:		
Notes payable, long-term	170,000	260,000
Bonds payable	175,000	100,000
Total liabilities	$ 509,000	$530,000
Stockholders' equity:		
Common stock, $10 par	$ 100,000	$ 80,000
Paid-in capital in excess of par	200,000	120,000
Retained earnings	320,000	170,000
Total stockholders' equity	$ 620,000	$370,000
Total liabilities and stockholders' equity	$1,129,000	$900,000

EXHIBIT 20-2 (Continued)

BMI Computers
Income Statement
For the Year Ended December 31, 1987

Revenues		
Sales	$2,500,000	
Gain on sale of equipment	10,000	
Total revenues		$2,510,000
Expenses		
Cost of goods sold	$1,625,000	
Selling	240,000	
General and administrative	300,000	
Interest	52,000	
Taxes	93,000	
Total expenses		2,310,000
Net income		$ 200,000

balances at the end of the current year, 1987 in this case, are then inserted in column E.

The second part of the worksheet contains a skeleton statement of changes in financial position. The first major heading is sources of working capital. The major subheadings are from operations and other sources. After these subheadings several blank spaces should be left, leaving enough room for various items under each category. At this point in the analysis the specific sources of working capital are not yet determined.

The second major heading is uses of working capital. Again, several lines should be left blank to leave room for listing the various uses. The final major heading is change in working capital, in this case an increase. Finally, a total column is provided. In setting up this skeletal statement, make sure that you leave yourself enough room to insert all the necessary sources and uses of working capital.

At this point the $53,000 change in working capital should be put in column C on the working capital line. It is a debit because working capital increased during the year. The $53,000 is also inserted in column D on the line called increase in working capital. This $53,000, which was taken from the schedule of changes in working capital accounts, should make the skeletal statement balance. A check mark is used for reference.

Analyzing the Changes in Various Noncurrent Accounts

The next step in completing the worksheet is to analyze the changes in the various noncurrent accounts. Essentially we are trying to recreate the summary journal entries that caused the noncurrent accounts to change. These journal entries are then inserted on the worksheet. The first part of the entry goes on the top part of the worksheet and details the changes in the noncurrent accounts. The second part of the entry classifies the change as a source or use of working capital and is placed on the bottom portion of the worksheet with the appropriate description in column A.

The Statement of Changes in Financial Position   **803**

EXHIBIT 20-3
BMI Computers
Statement of Changes in Financial Position Worksheet
For the Year Ended December 31, 1987

A	B	C	D	E
	Account	Analysis of Interim		Account
	Balances	Transactions for 1987		Balances
Description	12/31/86	Debit	Credit	12/31/87
Debits				
Working capital	55,000	✔ 53,000		108,000
Land	200,000	4b) 175,000		375,000
Building	400,000			400,000
Equipment	120,000	3b) 70,000	3a) 55,000	135,000
Goodwill	9,000		2c) 1,000	8,000
Total debits	784,000			1,026,000
Credits				
Accumulated depreciation—building	30,000		2a) 10,000	40,000
Accumulated depreciation—equipment	24,000	3a) 15,000	2b) 12,000	21,000
Notes payable—Long-term	260,000	5) 90,000		170,000
Bonds payable	100,000		4a) 75,000	175,000
Common stock—$10 par	80,000		7) 20,000	100,000
Paid-in capital in excess of par	120,000		7) 80,000	200,000
Retained earnings	170,000	6) 50,000	1) 200,000	320,000
Total credits	784,000	453,000	453,000	1,026,000

	Sources	Uses
Sources of working capital		
From operations:		
Net income	1) 200,000	
Plus: Depreciation	2a) 10,000	
Depreciation	2b) 12,000	
Amortization	2c) 1,000	
Less: Gain on sale of equipment		3a) 10,000
Other sources:		
Sale of equipment	3a) 50,000	
Issuance of bonds	4a) 75,000	
Issuance of common stock	7) 100,000	
Uses of working capital		
Purchase of land		4b) 175,000
Purchase of equipment		3b) 70,000
Reclassification of long-term debt		5) 90,000
Declaration of cash dividend		6) 50,000
Increase in working capital		✔ 53,000
Total sources and uses	448,000	448,000

In order to complete this analysis, certain other information is needed. In reality this information would be gathered as the balance sheet and the income statement are prepared. For purposes of this example, the following information pertaining to BMI Computers is collected:

Supplemental Information

1. Net income for the year is $200,000. (See Exhibit 20–2 on page 803.)
2. Depreciation and amortization expense included in selling and general and administrative expenses are:
   a. Depreciation—building = $10,000.
   b. Depreciation—equipment = $12,000.
   c. Amortization—goodwill = $1,000.
3. a. Equipment with a historical cost of $55,000 and accumulated depreciation to date of $15,000 (net book value $40,000) was sold.
   b. Additional equipment was purchased during the year.
4. a. The firm issued $75,000 of bonds at par.
   b. Some of the funds obtained from the issue were later used to purchase another plot of future site land.
5. Long-term notes payable of $90,000 due in 1987 were reclassified to current liabilities.
6. The dividends payable at December 31, 1986 were paid. During 1987 the firm declared dividends totaling $50,000, of which $35,000 was paid.
7. Two thousand shares of $10 par value common stock were issued at $50 per share.

Working Capital from Operations

Because working capital from operations is often a major source of working capital, it is a good place to start our analysis of the noncurrent accounts. A major component of working capital from operations is net income. The net income for the year as shown on the income statement in Exhibit 20–2 is $200,000. Net income for the year is a major reason for the increase in Retained Earnings, and as a result the $200,000 is inserted as a credit to Retained Earnings in column D in the top portion of the worksheet. The offsetting part of the entry is made in the Sources column to Net Income in the bottom portion of the worksheet. This entry, which is shown below, is labeled no. 1 in the worksheet.

1. Sources of Net Working Capital—Net Income   200,000
      Retained Earnings   200,000

After the net income is recorded as a credit to the Retained Earnings account it would appear as follows:

Retained Earnings

	Bal. 170,000
	(1) 200,000
	Bal. 320,000

At this point all the transactions affecting retained earnings are not yet accounted for. The beginning balance of $170,000 plus the net income of $200,000 equals $370,000, yet the ending balance in the account is $320,000. As we will see later, the difference of $50,000 is the result of the declaration of cash dividends.

The next step is to complete the computation of working capital from operations. Item no. 2 under the additional information presents the depreciation and amortization expense included in the operating expenses of BMI Computers. Because these items all reduce net income but do not affect working capital, they must all be added to net income to determine working capital from operations. The worksheet entry, which follows, is a credit to the Accumulated Depreciation accounts and the Goodwill account and a debit to Depreciation and Amortization Expense.

2. Increase in Working Capital—Depreciation	12,000	
Increase in Working Capital—Depreciation	10,000	
Increase in Working Capital—Amortization	1,000	
Accumulated Depreciation—Building		12,000
Accumulated Depreciation—Equipment		10,000
Goodwill		1,000

In this entry the word *increase* rather than *source* is used to emphasize that these items are not really sources of working capital but are necessary adjustments to arrive at working capital from operations.

These items help explain the changes in the Accumulated Depreciation accounts and the Goodwill account. After these items are inserted on the worksheet, the appropriate T accounts would appear as follows:

Accumulated Depreciation—Building

	Bal. 30,000
	(2a) 10,000
	Bal. 40,000
	✔

Accumulated Depreciation—Equipment

	Bal. 24,000
	(2b) 12,000
	Bal. 21,000

Goodwill

Bal. 9,000	(2c) 1,000
Bal. 8,000	
✔	

The accounts with the check mark beneath them indicate that after these items are inserted on the worksheet all entries affecting the account are explained. The Accumulated Depreciation—Equipment account does not yet balance, indicating that there is a reduction in that account that has not been explained.

The Equipment Account

Item no. 3 in the supplemental information listed on page 805 indicates that the net book value of the equipment sold equaled $40,000. The income statement in Exhibit 20–2 shows that the firm recorded a gain of $10,000 on the sale of equipment. As the following formula indicates, there is now enough information to calculate the proceeds from the sale. This figure is important because it represents a source of working capital.

Proceeds from sale	$?
− Net book value	40,000
= Gain or (loss)	$10,000

Proceeds from the sale equal $50,000 ($40,000 + $10,000). You should note that as long as two items of information in the formula are available, the third can be calculated.

Enough information has now been accumulated to make the entries in the bottom portion of the worksheet; more analysis is required to make the entries in the top portion. The gain of $10,000 must be entered in the use column and labeled Gain on Sale of Equipment. Although this $10,000 does not really represent a use of working capital, it is subtracted from net income to reach working capital from operations. The entire $50,000 proceeds are then entered in the source column under Other Sources and called Sale of Equipment. This partial entry is keyed as no. 3a.

The sold equipment's historical cost and its related accumulated depreciation can now be inserted into the proper accounts on the worksheet. The historical cost of $55,000 relating to the sold equipment is credited because the Equipment account is reduced. Similarly, the accumulated depreciation of $15,000 relating to the sold equipment is debited because the Accumulated Depreciation account is also reduced.

After these entries are made, these accounts appear as follows:

Equipment		Accumulated Depreciation—Equipment	
Bal. 120,000	(3a) 55,000	(3a) 15,000	Bal. 24,000
			(2b) 12,000
Bal. 135,000			Bal. 21,000 ✓

Again the check mark indicates that all the transactions affecting the Accumulated Depreciation account have been accounted for. However, the Equipment account still does not balance. A $70,000 debit is still needed ($135,000 − $120,000 + $55,000). Logic and the supplemental information tell us that the cause of this debit is a purchase of additional equipment.

We can also assume that this $70,000 belongs on the statement of changes in financial position as a use of working capital. Although we do not know what the consideration was, we do know that if any working capital account (cash or payable) was involved, working capital would be decreased. If the purchase was made through the issuance of long-term debt or equity, the all financial resources concept would require the purchase to be shown as both a source and a use of working capital. After the $70,000 purchase of equipment is recorded in the worksheet, all items that affected that account have been analyzed. The following T account illustrates this:

Equipment	
Bal. 120,000	(3a) 55,000
(3b) 70,000	
Bal. 135,000 ✓	

It is important to pause at this point in the example and summarize the transactions that affected the Equipment account and the related Accumulated Depreciation account. Our analysis has shown that BMI Computers both sold equipment during the year and purchased additional equipment. The two following journal entries reflect how these transactions were inserted on the worksheet:

<pre>
3a. Source of Net Working Capital—
     Sale of Equipment   50,000
     Accumulated Depreciation—Equipment   15,000
        Gain on Sale of Equipment   10,000
        Equipment   55,000

3b. Equipment   70,000
     Use of Net Working Capital—
        Purchase of Equipment   70,000
</pre>

Note that the actual working capital accounts are not debited or credited because we are only interested in explaining changes in the noncurrent accounts and whether they increased or decreased working capital.

Issuance of Bonds Payable and Purchase of Land

Supplemental item no. 4 indicates that BMI issued additional bonds at par and some of these funds were used to purchase additional site land. Analyzing these two accounts indicates that $75,000 of bonds were issued ($175,000 − $100,000) and that $175,000 of site land was purchased ($375,000 − $200,000). These transactions account for all the changes in these two accounts.

The purchase of land represents a use of working capital while the issuance of bonds payable represents a source of working capital. These two items are now inserted on the worksheet by the following entries, keyed 4a and 4b.

<pre>
4a. Source of Net Working Capital—
     Issuance of Bonds   75,000
        Bonds Payable   75,000

4b. Land   175,000
     Use of Net Working Capital—
        Purchase of Land   175,000
</pre>

Reclassification of Long-term Note Payable

Supplemental item no. 5 indicates that $90,000 of long-term notes payable were reclassified as current. This represents a use of working capital because current liabilities are increased. Thus the $90,000 is inserted on the worksheet as a use of working capital. After this $90,000 is debited to the Notes Payable account on the top part of the worksheet, all transactions in this account are analyzed. The actual entry is:

<pre>
5. Notes Payable   90,000
    Use of Working Capital—
       Reclassification of Long-term Debt   90,000
</pre>

Dividends Payable

Supplemental item no. 6 indicates that the dividends payable at the beginning of the year were paid in cash. Additional cash dividends of $50,000 were declared, of which $35,000 was paid prior to year-end. For our purposes the dividends paid do not affect working capital. Only current accounts, Cash and Dividends Payable, are involved. However, the declaration of dividends decreases Retained Earnings and increases a current liability and thus decreases working capital. Thus, the $50,000 is inserted on the worksheet as a use of working capital. The actual worksheet entry is:

<pre>
6. Retained Earnings   50,000
    Use of Net Working Capital—
       Declaration of Cash Dividend   50,000
</pre>

After the $50,000 debit is posted to retained earnings, this account appears as follows:

Retained Earnings

	Bal.	170,000
(6) 50,000	(1)	200,000
	Bal.	320,000
		✔

All transactions affecting retained earnings have now been accounted for.

Issuance of Common Stock

Supplemental item no. 7 indicates that 2,000 shares of $10 par value common stock were issued at $50 per share. The worksheet entry, keyed as no. 7, is:

7. Source of Net Working Capital—		
Issuance of Common Stock	100,000	
Common Stock		20,000
Paid-in Capital in Excess of Par		80,000

After this entry is made, all items in the Common Stock and Paid-in Capital accounts are accounted for as follows:

Common Stock

	Bal.	80,000
	(7)	20,000
	Bal.	100,000
		✔

Paid-in Capital in Excess of Par

	Bal.	120,000
	(7)	80,000
	Bal.	200,000
		✔

Completing the Worksheet and Preparing the Statement

At this point all the changes in the noncurrent accounts have been accounted for. This can be verified by cross-footing the individual accounts on the top portion of the worksheet. The bottom portion of the worksheet should now be totaled. With the inclusion of the $53,000 increase in working capital, the bottom portion of the worksheet should balance. If it does not, this is an indication that a mistake has been made and you should review your work.

The bottom portion of the worksheet can easily be used to prepare the actual statement of changes in financial position. This statement, which is shown in Exhibit 20–4, illustrates the format for the complete statement. Although this particular format is illustrative of those used in practice, the relevant accounting pronouncements do not prescribe one specific format. Note that under generally accepted disclosure standards a schedule detailing changes in individual working capital accounts is also prepared.

The Worksheet Approach—A Summary

The most efficient way to prepare a statement of changes in financial position is to explain changes in working capital through analyzing all the changes in noncurrent accounts. The use of a worksheet facilitates this approach. The

EXHIBIT 20-4
BMI Computers
Statement of Changes in Financial Position
For the Year Ended December 31, 1987

Sources of working capital		
From operations		
Net income	$200,000	
Plus: Items not requiring use of working capital		
Depreciation	22,000	
Amortization	1,000	
Less: Nonoperating gain on sale of equipment	(10,000)	
Working capital from operations		$213,000
Other sources of working capital		
Proceeds from the sale of equipment		50,000
Issuance of bonds payable		75,000
Issuance of common stock		100,000
Total sources		$438,000
Uses of working capital		
Purchase of noncurrent assets		
Land	$175,000	
Equipment	70,000	$245,000
Retirement of long-term notes payable		90,000
Declaration of dividend		50,000
Total uses		$385,000
Increase in working capital		$ 53,000

EXHIBIT 20-4 (Continued)
Schedule of Changes in Working Capital Accounts

	December 31,		Increase (Decrease) in Working Capital
	1987	1986	
Current assets			
Cash	$ 33,000	$ 20,000	$13,000
Accounts receivable, net	85,000	60,000	25,000
Inventory	150,000	140,000	10,000
Prepaids	4,000	5,000	(1,000)
	$272,000	$225,000	$47,000
Current liabilities			
Current maturities of long-term notes payable	$ 90,000	$ 80,000	($10,000)
Accounts payable	52,000	60,000	8,000
Dividends payable	15,000	20,000	5,000
Other accrued liabilities	7,000	10,000	3,000
	$164,000	$170,000	$ 6,000
Working capital	$108,000	$ 55,000	$53,000

table below summarizes the changes in noncurrent accounts and how these changes affect working capital. Note that credits to noncurrent accounts result in sources of working capital. Because of the double-entry feature, credits represent decreases in noncurrent assets and increases in equity accounts. Both of these types of transactions will cause working capital to increase. On the other hand, debits to noncurrent accounts represent increases in noncurrent assets accounts and decreases in noncurrent equity accounts. These types of transactions require the use of working capital.

STATEMENT OF CHANGES IN FINANCIAL POSITION— WORKING CAPITAL BASIS SUMMARY

Nature of Change	Source or Use	How Recorded in Noncurrent Accounts
Operating		
Net increase from operations	Source	Credit
Net decrease from operations	Use	Debit
Financial		
Decrease in noncurrent assets	Source	Credit
Increase in noncurrent liabilities	Source	Credit
Increase in capital stock	Source	Credit
Increase in noncurrent assets	Use	Debit
Decrease in noncurrent liabilities	Use	Debit
Decrease in capital stock	Use	Debit
Declaration of dividends	Use	Debit

The Statement of Changes in Financial Position— Cash Basis

Although a majority of firms still prepare a working capital-based statement of changes in financial position, the cash-based version has become more important in recent years. Management, investors, and creditors all are interested in the cash flows of the firm. If the FASB issues a statement similar to the exposure draft on cash flows on the subject, the cash flow statement will become mandatory.

Although the amount of working capital tells part of the story, it does not provide all the information needed by investors and creditors. A firm may have a positive working capital position because of a buildup of receivables, inventory, and other nonmonetary current assets but may be facing extreme cash flow problems. Thus, as happened to a commuter airline, these companies may run out of cash and be forced into bankruptcy. A cash flow statement would provide investors and creditors with an indication of these types of problems.

Preparing the Cash Flow Statement

A cash-based statement of financial position is often referred to as a **cash flow statement.** This statement defines financial resources as cash and explains what caused the changes in the cash balance during the year. The form of the cash flow statement is similar to a working capital–based statement of changes in financial position. Sources are divided into cash flows from operations and cash flows from financial activities. Uses are also categorized as net uses of cash from operations, if appropriate, and uses of cash from financial activities.

As we did with the working capital statement, we can use the data provided by two consecutive balance sheets and the income statement for the period to prepare the cash-based statement of changes in financial position. The first step in the preparation of the statement is to determine cash flows from operations.

Determining Cash Flows from Operations

Determining cash flows from operations essentially involves converting the income statement from the accrual to the cash basis. The best way to understand the required procedures is to work through an example.

Exhibit 20–5 presents the December 31, 1986 and 1987 balance sheets and the income statement for the year ended December 31, 1987 for the East-West Company. Because the statements are prepared according to generally accepted accounting principles, they are based on the accrual method. In order to simplify the example the following assumptions are made:

1. All sales are on account.
2. All inventory purchases are made on account. The Accounts Payable account is used solely for this purpose.
3. All other operating expenses are first recorded in the Accrued Liabilities account.
4. Additions to the Prepaids account are made in cash.
5. There have been no sales or additions to Property, Plant, and Equipment.

Cash Basis Sales

On the cash basis, sales represent cash collected from customers on account as well as cash sales during the year. In the example in Exhibit 20–5 there were no cash sales; all sales were made on credit.

From the data in the balance sheet we know the beginning and ending balances in the Accounts Receivable account. Accrual basis sales represent increases in the Accounts Receivable account. Cash collections represent decreases or credits to the Accounts Receivable account. If the firm were on the cash basis, these cash collections would represent the revenues for the period. From this data we can determine that cash basis sales totaled $485,000, or the beginning balance of $20,000 plus credit sales of $500,000 less the ending balance of $35,000 ($20,000 + $500,000 − $35,000).

From an analytical view we see that the beginning balance of the Accounts Receivable account plus the accrual sales of $520,000 represent the maximum cash collections the firm could receive during the year. The fact that the ending balance in the Accounts Receivable account is $35,000 indicates that this is the amount of credit sales that remains uncollected at year-end. Thus, cash collections or cash sales in this case are only $485,000. If the Accounts Receivable balance increases during the year, cash basis sales will be less than accrual basis by the amount of the increase. Similar reasoning indicates that if the Accounts Receivable balance decreases during the year, cash basis sales will exceed accrual basis sales by that amount. To see this you should rework the previous example, only this time assume the December 31, 1987 Accounts Receivable balance is only $15,000. You will see that in this situation cash basis sales are $505,000.

EXHIBIT 20-5

East-West Company
Balance Sheets
December 31,

Assets	1987	1986	Equities	1987	1986
Cash	$ 39,000	$ 10,000	Accounts payable	$ 30,000	$ 35,000
Accounts receivable	35,000	20,000	Accrued liabilities	22,000	20,000
Inventory	60,000	40,000	Stockholders' equity	150,000	90,000
Prepaids	3,000	5,000			
Property, plant, and equipment	65,000	70,000			
Total assets	$202,000	$145,000	Total equities	$202,000	$145,000

EXHIBIT 20-5 (Continued)

East-West Company
Income Statement
For the Year Ended December 31, 1987

Sales		$500,000
Cost of goods sold		340,000
Gross margin on sales		$160,000
Operating expenses		
Depreciation	$ 5,000	
Prepaids used	10,000	
Other operating expenses*	85,000	100,000
Net income		$ 60,000

*Includes general and administrative, selling, interest, etc.

Prepaid Expenses on a Cash Basis

To continue with the example let's now look at the Prepaid account. (We will turn to the Inventory account next.) Using the data in Exhibit 20–5, we know that $10,000 worth of prepaids were used or expired during the year. This is represented by the $10,000 credit to the Prepaids account. Prepaid expenses on the cash basis represent additions to the Prepaids account and in this case amount to $8,000 (the ending balance of $3,000 plus prepaids expired during the period of $10,000 less the beginning balance of $5,000). Remember that we assumed that all additions to the prepaid account are made in cash, and on the cash basis all prepaids are expensed as incurred. As a result, prepaid expenses on an accrual basis are $2,000 less than cash-based prepaid expense. In effect, the $2,000 decrease in the balance of the Prepaids account means that $2,000 more of prepaids expired than were purchased during the year, and thus accrual-based expenses are $2,000 more than cash-based ex-

The Statement of Changes in Financial Position

813

penses. In general, a decrease in the balance of any prepaid account means that accrual basis expense will exceed cash basis expense by that amount, and that an increase in the balance of any prepaid account means that cash basis expense will exceed accrual basis expense by that amount.

Cash Basis Cost of Goods Sold

Accrual-based cost of goods sold is represented by inventory decreases during the year. However, on a cash basis, cost of goods is simply the cash paid for inventory during the year. If all inventory purchases are made on account through Accounts Payable, what must be determined is the decrease or debit to the Accounts Payable account. This represents the amount paid in cash for inventories during the period. Thus the relationship between accrual- and cash-based cost of goods sold involves both the Inventory and Accounts Payable accounts.

The first step is to analyze the Inventory account. From the balance sheet, we know the amount of the beginning and ending inventory, and from the income statement we know the amount of cost of goods sold. Using these data, we can determine that the amount of inventory purchased during the year was $360,000, as follows:

Cost of goods sold	$340,000
Ending inventory	60,000
Cost of goods available for sale	400,000
Less: Beginning inventory	(40,000)
Inventory purchases	$360,000

Because we made the assumption that all inventory purchases are made on credit, the inventory purchases of $360,000 also represent an increase in Accounts Payable. Therefore, the cash purchases for inventory are determined to be $365,000, as follows:

Beginning balance in accounts payable	$ 35,000
Inventory purchases	360,000
	395,000
Less: Beginning balance in accounts payable	(30,000)
Cash payments on account	$365,000

In effect, when the Inventory account increases this indicates we purchased more goods during the year than we sold. In this case our Inventory account increased $20,000, and thus inventory purchases were $20,000 greater than the cost of goods sold. The decrease of $5,000 in the Accounts Payable account indicates that $5,000 more goods were paid for during the year than were purchased. Thus actual cash payments during the year were $365,000. The $365,000 cash basis expense is $25,000 more than cost of goods sold on the accrual basis and is a result of the combination of the $20,000 Inventory increase and the $5,000 Accounts Payable decrease.

Other Operating Expenses

In our example, all other operating expenses were originally recorded in the Accrued Liabilities account. When other operating expenses are accrued,

EXHIBIT 20–6
Conversion of Accrual to Cash

Account	Balance during Year	Effect on Income or Expense Account	Cash Basis Net Income in Relation to Accrual Basis
Accounts Receivable	Decrease	Cash basis sales exceed accrual basis sales.	Higher
Other Receivables (e.g., interest)	Decrease	Cash basis income exceeds accrual basis income.	Higher
Other Nonmonetary Assets (e.g., supplies, prepaids)	Decrease	Accrual basis expense exceeds cash basis expense.	Higher
Payables	Increase	Accrual basis expense exceeds cash basis expense.	Higher
Accounts Receivable	Increase	Accrual basis sales exceed cash basis sales.	Lower
Other Receivables (e.g., interest)	Increase	Accrual basis income exceeds cash basis income.	Lower
Other Nonmonetary Assets (e.g., supplies, prepaids)	Increase	Cash basis expense exceeds accrual basis expense.	Lower
Payables	Decrease	Cash basis expense exceeds accrual basis expense.	Lower

they are recorded as credits in that account. The debit to that account represents cash payments for expenses and in this case is $83,000, or the beginning balance of $20,000 plus accrued expenses during the year of $85,000 less the ending balance of $22,000.

Accrual to Cash-Based Income—A Summary

Exhibit 20–6 summarizes the relationships discussed above. Notice that when the balance in an asset account decreases during the year, cash basis income is higher than accrual basis income. When the balance in these same asset accounts increases, cash basis income is lower than accrual basis income. The opposite occurs when liability accounts are involved: then increases in these liability accounts cause cash basis income to exceed accrual basis income and vice versa.

Exhibit 20–7 shows how the data developed in the previous discussion can now be used to convert East-West Company's income statement from the accrual to the cash basis. Note that on a cash basis there is no depreciation expense because there is no outflow of cash at the time depreciation expense is recorded. In this simple example there were no other changes in noncurrent accounts, so cash basis income equals the net increase in cash during the year. That is, the cash balance increased by $29,000 (from $10,000 to $39,000), which is the amount of cash basis net income for the year.

EXHIBIT 20–7

East-West Corporation
Income Statement—Conversion to Cash Basis
For the Year Ended December 31, 1987

	Accrual Basis	Increase (Decrease)	Cash Basis
Sales	$500,000	($15,000)	$485,000
Cost of goods sold	340,000		
Change in inventory balance		20,000 ⎱	365,000
Change in payables balance		5,000 ⎰	
Gross margin on sales			$120,000
Operating expenses			
Depreciation	5,000	(5,000)	$ 0
Prepaids used	10,000	(2,000)	8,000
Other operating expenses	85,000	(2,000)	83,000
			$ 91,000
Net income—Cash basis			$ 29,000
Beginning cash balance (Exhibit 20–5)			$ 10,000
Net income—Cash basis (above)			29,000
Ending cash balance (Exhibit 20–5)			$ 39,000

A Cash Flow Statement for BMI Computers

In order to illustrate the preparation of a more complex cash-based statement of changes in financial position, we return to the BMI example. During 1986 cash increased from $20,000 to $33,000, which represented a $13,000 increase. (See Exhibit 20–2 on pages 802 and 803.) The cash flow statement explains the reasons for this increase.

Cash Flow from Operations

The first step in the preparation of the cash flow statement is to determine cash flow from operations. Essentially this involves converting the accrual basis net income of $200,000 to cash flow from operations. Using the procedures we outlined earlier, the statement on the top of page 817 illustrates how cash flow from operations of $168,000 is determined:

In determining cash flow from operations, we added to net income decreases in current assets, depreciation, and amortization. Depreciation and amortization must be added back because they reduce net income but do not affect cash flows. In this example there were no increases in payables that relate to operations. However, if there had been, they also would have been added to net income to determine cash flow from operations. Changes in current maturities of notes payable and dividends payable are financial changes and are shown on the next part of the statement.

Increases in current assets and decreases in current payables must be subtracted from net income to determine cash flow from operations. In addition, the $10,000 gain on the sale of land must be subtracted. This is a financial change and, as on the working capital–based statement, the entire proceeds are shown under the caption Other sources.

BMI Computers
Cash Flow from Operations

Net income		$200,000
Add: Decrease in prepaids	$ 1,000	
Depreciation expense	22,000	
Amortization expense	1,000	24,000
Less: Increase in receivables	$25,000	
Increase in inventories	10,000	
Decrease in payables	8,000	
Decrease in accrued liabilities	3,000	
Gain on sale of equipment	10,000	(56,000)
Cash flow from operations		$168,000

Financial Sources and Uses of Cash

The next step is to determine the financial sources and uses of cash. After making two changes relating to dividends and current maturities of notes payable, we can use the data already developed in preparing the working capital–based statement.

Exhibit 20–8, which presents the entire cash-based statement, illustrates the various financial sources and uses of cash. Other sources are the same as on the working capital–based statement and include proceeds from the sale of equipment assets, issuance of long-term debt, and issuance of common stock. We implicitly assumed that all these items resulted in increases in cash. However, because of the all financial resources concept this assumption is not important. For example, if the firm issued capital stock directly for the purchase of land this transaction would be shown as both a source and a use of cash.

The financial uses of cash are the same as in working capital–based statements except for the payment of current maturities of notes payable and dividends. During 1987 two transactions occurred that affected the current maturities of notes payable. The $80,000 1986 balance was paid in 1987 and $90,000 was transferred during 1987 from the long-term to the current category. On a cash-based statement the $80,000 is the relevant transaction because it involves a use of cash. On the working capital–based statement the $90,000 is the relevant event because that is the amount of the decrease in working capital.

Dividends are handled in a similar manner. Cash payments for dividends are the relevant event for a cash-based statement. During 1987 cash dividend payments were $55,000, or the $20,000 beginning dividends payable balance and $35,000 of dividends *declared and paid* during the year. (See the supplemental items on page 805.)

The result of netting the sources and uses of cash is an increase in cash of $13,000. In this example BMI's operations are a significant source of cash for the company. The firm is using this cash as well as cash from the sale of assets and issuance of debt and equity to finance expansion.

EXHIBIT 20–8

BMI Computers
Statement of Changes in Financial Position—Cash Basis
For the Year Ended December 31, 1987

Sources of cash		
Cash flow from operations		
Net income		$200,000
Add: Decrease in prepaids	$ 1,000	
Depreciation expense	22,000	
Amortization expense	1,000	24,000
Less: Increase in receivables	$ 25,000	
Increase in inventories	10,000	
Decrease in payables	8,000	
Decrease in accrued liabilities	3,000	
Gain on sale of equipment	10,000	(56,000)
Cash flow from operations		$168,000
Other sources of cash		
Proceeds from sale of equipment		50,000
Issuance of bonds payable		75,000
Issuance of common stock		100,000
Total sources of cash		$393,000
Uses of cash		
Purchase of noncurrent assets		
Land	$175,000	
Equipment	70,000	$245,000
Repayment of current maturities of notes payable		80,000
Cash dividends paid		55,000
Total uses of cash		$380,000
Increase in cash		$ 13,000

Using a Worksheet to Prepare a Cash-based Statement of Changes

Most of the data necessary to prepare a cash-based statement of changes in financial position for BMI Computers had previously been developed. As a result, we did not need a worksheet to facilitate its preparation. However, if the cash-based statement is going to be prepared before the working capital–based statement is, a worksheet is helpful.

Exhibit 20–9 presents a cash-based worksheet for BMI Computers. Its format is the same as the working capital–based worksheet except that all the accounts are listed on the top portion of the statement, because we are trying to explain the changes in all the noncash accounts. The bottom portion of the worksheet, as before, is the skeletal statement of changes.

Except for the entries that explain the changes in the current assets and liabilities accounts, all entries on this worksheet are the same as those on the working capital–based one. Those entries for the noncurrent accounts are keyed with the same numbers as before. The changes in the current accounts are keyed (a) through (e). The entries for those accounts on the top portion of the worksheet explain the net changes in the current accounts. The entries for

EXHIBIT 20–9

BMI Corporation
Statement of Changes in Financial Position—Cash Basis Worksheet
For the Year Ended December 31, 1987

Description	Account Balances 12/31/86	Analysis of Interim Transactions for 1987 Debit	Credit	Account Balances 12/31/87
Debits				
Cash	20,000	✔ 13,000		33,000
Accounts receivable	60,000	a) 25,000		85,000
Inventory	140,000	b) 10,000		150,000
Prepaids	5,000		c) 1,000	4,000
Land	200,000	4b) 175,000		375,000
Building	400,000			400,000
Equipment	120,000	3b) 70,000	3a) 55,000	135,000
Goodwill	9,000		2c) 1,000	8,000
Total debits	954,000			1,190,000
Credits				
Current maturities—Notes payable	80,000	5) 80,000	5) 90,000	90,000
Accounts payable	60,000	d) 8,000		52,000
Dividends payable	20,000	6) 55,000	6) 50,000	15,000
Other accrued liabilities	10,000	e) 3,000		7,000
Accumulated depreciation—Buildings	30,000		2a) 10,000	40,000
Accumulated depreciation—Equipment	24,000	3a) 15,000	2b) 12,000	21,000
Notes payable—Long-term	260,000	5) 90,000		170,000
Bonds payable	100,000		4a) 75,000	175,000
Common stock—$10 par	80,000		7) 20,000	100,000
Paid-in capital in excess of par	120,000		7) 80,000	200,000
Retained earnings	170,000	6) 50,000	1) 200,000	320,000
Total credits	954,000	594,000	594,000	1,190,000

		Sources	Uses	
Sources of cash				
From operations				
Net income		1) 200,000		
Plus: Decrease in prepaids		c) 1,000		
Depreciation		2b) 12,000		
		2a) 10,000		
Amortization		2c) 1,000		
Less: Increase in receivables			a) 25,000	
Increase in inventories			b) 10,000	
Decrease in payables			d) 8,000	
Decrease in accrued liabilities			e) 3,000	
Gain on sale of equipment			3a) 10,000	
Other sources:				
Sale of equipment		3a) 50,000		
Issuance of bonds		4a) 75,000		
Issuance of common stock		7) 100,000		
Uses of cash				
Purchase of land			4b) 175,000	
Purchase of equipment			3b) 70,000	
Repayment of current maturities of debt			5) 80,000	
Dividends paid			6) 55,000	
Increase in cash			✔ 13,000	
		449,000	449,000	

those accounts on the bottom portion of the statement are adjustments to net income to arrive at cash inflow from operations. For example, the entry for Accounts Receivable, keyed (a), is as follows:

Accounts Receivable	25,000	
Increase in Cash Flow from		
Operations—Accounts Receivable		25,000

Other entries for current assets and liabilities are made in a similar manner. After the worksheet is completed, a cash-based statement of changes in financial position can easily be prepared.

The Statement of Changes in Financial Position— A Summary

Much of this chapter has been involved with discussing the procedures required to prepare a statement of changes in financial position. These procedures are often complex for the beginning accounting student as well as the experienced practitioner. As a result, it is easy to lose sight of the importance of the statement of changes in financial position. This statement, whether prepared on a working capital or a cash basis, provides valuable information to present and potential investors and creditors. By analyzing current and past statements and comparing them with those of similar firms, financial-statement users can answer such questions as the following:

1. What are the sources of the firm's financial resources?
2. What proportion of the firm's financial resources is generated internally or from operations?
3. What financing and investing activities took place during the year?
4. How was cash or working capital generated during the year?

Thus the statement of changes in financial position plays an important role in analyzing and understanding a firm's present activities and future prospects.

Summary of Learning Objectives

1. *The purpose of a statement of changes in financial position.* The statement of changes in financial position is one of the primary required financial statements. The statement describes the changes in the financial resources of a firm. It helps present and potential investors and creditors assess the liquidity of the firm and how the firm is financing present and expected future activities.

2. *Financial resources defined.* In terms of the statement of changes in financial position, financial resources can be defined as either working capital or cash, and thus the statement can be prepared on either basis. Presently most firms prepare the working capital-based statement although the cash-based statement is becoming more popular.

3. *The difference between operating and financial changes.* Changes in financial resources are caused by either operating or financial changes. Operating activities relate to the purchase, production, and sale of the

firm's goods and services. With some exceptions, these are the same items that enter into the determination of the firm's net income. Financial activities are all those activities not considered operating and generally relate to changes in noncurrent assets, noncurrent liabilities, and stockholders' equity accounts.

4. *Preparing a working capital–based statement of changes in financial position.* A working capital–based statement of changes in financial position can be prepared with the use of a worksheet. Changes in working capital are analyzed by describing changes in nonworking capital accounts. Working capital from operations is determined by starting with net income and making the necessary adjustments. The financial sources and uses are inferred from analyzing noncurrent accounts.

5. *Preparing a cash-based statement of changes in financial position.* A cash basis statement of changes in financial position can be prepared using comparative balance sheets and an income statement. The major task is to determine cash flow from operations, which essentially means converting from an accrual-based net income to a cash-based net income.

6. *Overall importance of the statement of changes in financial position.* The statement of changes in financial position provides valuable information to present and potential investors and creditors. By analyzing this statement, financial statement users can answer such questions as "What are the sources and uses of the firm's financial resources?" and "What proportion of these resources is generated internally and externally?" Thus, this statement plays an important role in analyzing and understanding the firm's present activities and future prospects.

Key Terms

All Financial Resources Concept
Cash Flow Statement
Financial Changes

Financial Resources
Operating Changes

Problem for Your Review

The Statement of Changes in Financial Position. The information on the top of page 822 is given to you concerning The Ikelin Corporation.

Additional Information (Keyed to Worksheet Entries):
1. Net income, $250,000 (see income statement on page 822).
2. Included in the depreciation and amortization expense is $4,000 of copyright amortization.
3. Furniture and fixtures with a historical cost of $40,000 were sold for $20,000 cash.
4. Land was purchased for a cash down payment and through the issuance of 10% bonds and the issuance of no-par stock.

Required:

With the aid of a worksheet, prepare a statement of changes in financial position based on:
a. Working capital.
b. Cash.

The Ikelin Corporation
Comparative Balance Sheet
December 31

Assets	1987	1986	Liabilities and Stockholders' Equity	1987	1986
Current assets:			Current liabilities:		
Cash	$ 35,000	$ 45,000	Current maturities of notes payable	$ 100,000	$ 150,000
Accounts receivable, net	140,000	100,000	Accounts payable	240,000	190,000
Inventory	374,000	350,000	Accrued liabilities	10,000	15,000
Prepaids	8,000	10,000	Dividends payable	20,000	10,000
Total current assets	$ 557,000	$ 505,000	Total current liabilities	370,000	365,000
Property, plant, and equipment:			Long-term liabilities:		
Land	$ 300,000	$ 100,000	Notes payable, long-term	350,000	450,000
Building	400,000	400,000	Bonds payable	100,000	0
Less: Accumulated depreciation	(50,000)	(40,000)	Total liabilities	$ 820,000	$ 815,000
Furniture and fixtures	140,000	120,000			
Less: Accumulated depreciation	(41,000)	(48,000)	Stockholders' equity:		
			Common stock, no par	$ 150,000	$ 100,000
Total property, plant, and equipment	$ 749,000	$ 532,000	Retained earnings	380,000	170,000
			Total stockholders' equity	$ 530,000	$ 270,000
Other assets:					
Copyright, net	$ 44,000	$ 48,000	Total liabilities and		
Total assets	$1,350,000	$1,085,000	stockholders' equity	$1,350,000	$1,085,000

The Ikelin Corporation
Income Statement
For the Year Ended December 31, 1987

Revenues		
Sales		$1,600,000
Expenses		
Cost of goods sold	$1,100,000	
Depreciation and amortization	22,000	
Loss on sale of furniture and fixtures	5,000	
Other operating expenses	223,000	1,350,000
Net income		$ 250,000

Solution
a. Working Capital Basis

The Ikelin Corporation
Statement of Changes in Financial Position—Worksheet
For the Year Ended December 31, 1986

Description	Account Balances 12/31/86	Analysis of Interim Transactions for 1987		Account Balances 12/31/87
		Debit	Credit	
Debits				
Working capital	140,000	✔ 47,000		187,000
Land	100,000	4) 200,000		300,000
Buildings	400,000			400,000
Furniture and fixtures	120,000	3b) 60,000	3a) 40,000	140,000
Copyrights, net	48,000		2b) 4,000	44,000
Total debits	808,000			1,071,000

Description	Account Balances 12/31/86	Analysis of Interim Transactions for 1987		Account Balances 12/31/87
		Debit	Credit	
Credits				
Accumulated depreciation—Building	40,000		2a) 10,000	50,000
Accumulated depreciation—Furniture and fixtures	48,000	3a) 15,000	2a) 8,000	41,000
Notes payable—Long-term	450,000	A) 100,000		350,000
Bonds payable	0		4) 100,000	100,000
Common stock, no par	100,000		4) 50,000	150,000
Retained earnings	170,000	B) 40,000	1) 250,000	380,000
Total credits	808,000	462,000	462,000	1,071,000

		Sources	Uses	
Sources of working capital				
From operations				
Net income		1) 250,000		
Plus: Depreciation		2a) 10,000		
Depreciation		2a) 8,000		
Amortization		2b) 4,000		
Loss on sale of furniture and fixtures		3a) 5,000		
Other sources				
Sale of furniture and fixtures		3a) 20,000		
Issuance of bonds		4) 100,000		
Issuance of common stock		4) 50,000		
Uses of working capital				
Purchase of furniture and fixtures			3b) 60,000	
Purchase of land			4) 200,000	
Reclassification of notes payable			A) 100,000	
Declaration of cash dividends			B) 40,000	
Increase in working capital			✔ 47,000	
Totals		447,000	447,000	

Notes Keyed to Worksheet Entries:

2. Since there is no activity in the Building account, we can assume that the increase in the Accumulated Depreciation account represents depreciation expense of $10,000.

3. Determination of book value of furniture and fixtures sold:

Proceeds	$20,000
− Book value ? =	25,000
= (Loss) or gain	($5,000) from income statement
Historical cost	$40,000
− Accumulated depreciation ? =	15,000
= Book value	$25,000 from above

After these transactions are inserted in T accounts, they appear as follows:

Furniture and Fixtures

Bal.	120,000		
Purchase	60,000	40,000	Sale
Bal.	140,000		

Accumulated Depreciation— Furniture and Fixtures

		Bal.	48,000
Sale 15,000			8,000
		Bal.	41,000

The Statement of Changes in Financial Position

As a result, we can infer:

> The purchase of new furniture and fixtures of $60,000
> ($140,000 + $40,000 − $120,000)
>
> Depreciation expense of $8,000
> ($41,000 + $15,000 − $48,000)

4. Land purchase and issuance of bonds and common stock are shown as both a source and a use.

Additional Information Needed (Keyed as A and B on Worksheet):

1. Assume decrease in Notes Payable due to reclassification as current.
2. Dividends of $40,000 needed to balance Retained Earnings account ($170,000 + $250,000 − $380,000).

The Ikelin Corporation
Statement of Changes in Financial Position—
Working Capital Basis
For the Year Ended December 31, 1987

Sources of working capital		
From operations		
Net income	$250,000	
Plus: Items not requiring use of working capital		
Depreciation and amortization	22,000	
Loss on sale of furniture and fixtures	5,000	
Working capital from operations		$277,000
Other sources		
Proceeds from sale of furniture and fixtures		20,000
Issuance of bonds		100,000
Issuance of common stock		50,000
Total sources		$447,000
Uses of working capital		
Purchase of noncurrent assets		
Furniture and fixtures	$ 60,000	
Land	200,000	$260,000
Reclassification of long-term debt to current		100,000
Declaration of dividends		40,000
Total uses		$400,000
Net increase in working capital		$ 47,000

---

b. Cash Basis

Explanation: The cash-based statement on the top of page 825 is prepared from data already developed for the working capital–based statement. However, these additional changes must be made:

1. Cash flow from operations must be determined. See Exhibit 20–6 on page 815 for correct treatment of increases and decreases in current accounts other than cash.
2. All other items except repayment of long-term debt and dividends are the same.
   a. For cash statements we are interested only in repayment of the current portion of long-term notes, or $150,000.
   b. For dividends we are interested in actual dividends paid, or $30,000. (See T account on page 825.)

The Ikelin Corporation
Statement of Changes in Financial Position—Cash Basis
For the Year Ended December 31, 1987

Sources of cash		
Cash flow from operations		
Net income		$250,000
Add: Decrease in prepaids	$ 2,000	
Increase in accounts payable	50,000	
Depreciation and amortization	22,000	
Loss on sale of furniture and fixtures	$ 5,000	79,000
Less: Increase in receivables	$ 40,000	
Increase in inventories	24,000	
Decrease in accrued liabilities	5,000	(69,000)
Cash flow from operations		$260,000
Proceeds from sale of furniture and fixtures		20,000
Issuance of bonds		100,000
Issuance of common stock		50,000
Total sources		$430,000
Uses of cash		
Purchase of noncurrent assets		
Furniture and fixtures	$ 60,000	
Land	200,000	260,000
Repayment of current portion of long-term loan		150,000
Payment of dividends		30,000
Total uses of cash		$440,000
Decrease in cash		$ (10,000)
Cash balance, 11/1/87		45,000
Cash balance, 12/31/87		$ 35,000

Dividends Payable

Dividends paid	30,000	Bal.	10,000
		Dividends declared	40,000
		Bal.	20,000

Questions

1. Describe in your own words the statement of changes in financial position. List some of its important purposes.

2. What are financial resources? List the types of activities that cause changes in financial resources.

3. Why does a firm need to maintain an adequate amount of working capital? What are the primary sources of working capital?

4. Differentiate between operating changes and financial changes and describe how they affect a statement of changes in financial position based on working capital.

5. A great number of transactions that affect net income also affect working capital from operations. List four such transactions. Also list three transactions that affect net income but do not affect working capital from operations.

6. One of your fellow students said that the more depreciation a firm has, the better off it is because depreciation is a source of funds. How would you respond to this statement?

7. What is the all financial resources concept, and how does it affect the statement of changes in financial position? Illustrate your answer using the following example: The firm issued 1,000 shares of no-par common stock for land with a fair market value of $500,000.

8. During the year the King Corp. earned net income of $1 million. Included in this net income figure are depreciation of $80,000 and a gain on sale of a building of $50,000. What is the amount of working capital from operations?

9. During the year the firm declared dividends of $50,000 but paid dividends of only $45,000. How should this transaction be handled on a statement of changes in financial position based on working capital? How would this transaction be handled on a cash-based statement of changes in financial position?

10. The Martin Co. has a mortgage payable that is due in monthly installments. At the beginning of 1987 the balance in the Current Maturities account of long-term debt was $4,500. During the year this balance was paid and $4,200 was transferred from the Long-term Debt account to the Current Maturities account. How should this transaction be handled on a statement of changes in financial position based on working capital? How would this transaction be handled on a cash-based statement of changes in financial position?

11. During the year a firm extinguished debt with a carrying value of $550,000 at a cost of $500,000. Explain how this transaction would be handled on a statement of changes in financial position.

12. Explain the differences between a statement of changes in financial position based on working capital and one based on cash. Which do you think is more important and why?

13. Describe several transactions that increase cash from operations but do not affect working capital.

14. At the beginning of the year the balance in the Accounts Receivable account was $100,000 and the balance at the end of the year was $150,000. Accrual basis sales were $270,000. What are cash basis sales?

15. During the year the balance in a prepaid asset account increased. Is the related cash basis expense more or less than the related accrual basis expense?

16. Explain in your own words how working capital from operations could increase by a substantial amount although the cash balance decreased during the year.

17. List and explain some of the information that you can obtain by reviewing a firm's statement of changes in financial position that cannot be obtained from reviewing the firm's other financial statements.

Exercises

1. Transactions Affecting Working Capital. Explain whether the following transactions would have no effect, would increase, or would decrease working capital and, if appropriate, by how much?

   a. Issued 100,000 shares of $5 par value stock for $20 per share.
   b. The firm obtained a $100,000 bank loan payable in 5 equal installments over the next 5 years.
   c. Sales during the year amounted to $500,000, of which $200,000 was for cash and the remainder was on credit.
   d. The firm sold one of its buildings with a book value of $100,000 for $90,000.
   e. Cash collections on account amounted to $50,000.
   f. Dividends of $20,000 were declared; $18,000 was paid in the current year.

2. Transactions Affecting Working Capital. Complete the following table by placing an X in the appropriate column depending on whether the transaction is a source of working capital, is a use of working capital, or has no effect on working capital.

Transaction	Effect on Working Capital		
	Source	Use	No Effect
1. Amortization of intangible asset			
2. Conversion of bonds payable to common stock			
3. Sales on account			
4. Purchase of inventory on account			
5. Declaration of a dividend			

Transaction	Effect on Working Capital		
	Source	Use	No Effect
6. Payment of current accounts payable			
7. Collection of accounts receivable			
8. Amortization of premium on bonds payable			
9. Sale of building at a loss			

3. Transactions That Affect Working Capital. State which of the following are (a) a source of working capital, (b) a use of working capital, or (c) neither a source nor a use of working capital by placing an X in the appropriate blank space:

Items	Source	Use	Neither
1. Payment of accounts payable			
2. Sale of merchandise on account			
3. Sale of bonds			
4. Receipt of $60,000 from sale of a patent from a discontinued product			
5. Depreciation of $5,000 for the year			
6. Declaration of dividends payable in cash, $30,000			
7. Payment of dividends declared in (6)			
8. Return of merchandise to the supplier for credit of $18,000			

4. Preparation of Statement of Changes in Financial Position from Journal Entries. The condensed balance sheet of the Yam Company at the beginning of 1987 is as follows:

Yam Company
Balance Sheet
January 1, 1987

Assets		Equities	
Current assets		Current liabilities	
Cash	$ 10,000	Accounts payable	$ 22,000
Accounts receivable	14,000	Current maturities	
Inventory	66,000	of long-term debt	18,000
Total current assets	$ 90,000	Total current liabilities	$ 40,000
Noncurrent assets		Long-term debt	$ 60,000
Property, plant, and equipment, net	$100,000	Stockholders' equity	
Other assets	10,000	Common stock	$ 45,000
Total noncurrent assets	$110,000	Retained earnings	55,000
			$100,000
Total assets	$200,000	Total equities	$200,000

During the year the following transactions occurred:
1. Total sales were $200,000, of which $50,000 was for cash.
2. Cost of sales amounted to $130,000.
3. During the year the firm purchased $100,000 of inventory on account, of which $80,000 was paid prior to year-end.

4. Cash collections on accounts receivable totaled $120,000.

5. Land of $100,000 was purchased. A 20% down payment was made and a long-term note payable was taken out for the remainder.

6. During the year the following expenses were incurred on account:

Wages	$10,000
Advertising	5,000
Taxes	4,000
Interest	1,000

7. Depreciation expense for the year amounted to $5,000.

8. Accounts payable paid during the year amounted to $30,000.

9. Current maturities of long-term debt were paid and $15,000 of long-term debt was reclassified as current.

Required:

Prepare a statement of changes in financial position on a working capital basis for the year ended December 31, 1987. Working capital at year-end is $65,000.

5. Determining Working Capital from Operations. During the year the Mancini Corporation earned net income of $100,000. Included in net income were the following items:

Depreciation on plant and equipment	$20,000
Bad debts expense	4,000
Extraordinary gain on early extinguishment of debt	8,000
Loss on sale of land	9,000
Discount amortization on bonds payable	1,000

Required:

Determine working capital provided from operations.

6. Account Analysis and the Statement of Changes in Financial Position. Answer the appropriate questions for each of the following independent situations:

a. At the beginning of the year the balance in the Building account (shown net of accumulated depreciation) was $500,000. By the end of the year the balance was $600,000. The income statement for the year showed that depreciation expense related to the building was $40,000 and that there was a loss of $10,000 on the sale of a building. Your investigation shows that the proceeds from the sale of the building were $80,000. Explain which events would affect the statement of changes in financial position based on working capital and by how much.

b. The beginning balance in the Retained Earnings account was $240,000. At the end of the year the balance was $232,000. During the year the company reported a loss of $5,000. Included in the net loss were a depreciation expense of $8,000 and a gain on the sale of land of $12,000. Determine working capital from operations. What other transaction that the firm entered into affected working capital?

c. At the beginning of the year the Land account had a balance of $150,000 while at the end of the year the balance was $190,000. During the year the company purchased land of $80,000. The income statement reported a gain on sale of $20,000. Explain which events would affect the statement of changes in financial position based on working capital and by how much.

7. Preparing a Statement of Changes in Financial Position. Barney Smith, the accountant for Stock Inc., is new to accounting and is having trouble preparing the statement of changes in financial position. He has prepared the data on the top of page 829 relating to a statement of changes in financial position:

During your analysis you were able to determine the following information:

1. The face value of the bonds issued was $100,000.

2. The book value of the equipment sold was $50,000.

3. Actual dividends declared during the year amounted to $90,000.

4. Working capital at the beginning of the year was $304,000, and it was $491,500 at the end of the year.

Sources from operations				
Net income	$500,000			
Depreciation expense	20,000			
Bad debts expense	15,000			
Discount on bonds payable	500			

Other sources			Uses	
Issue of bonds payable,			Purchase of equipment	$ 85,000
net of discount of $8,000	92,000		Repayment of	
Proceeds from sale			long-term debt	400,000
of equipment	65,000		Payment of dividends	80,000
Issuance of capital stock	100,000			

Required:

Prepare in good form a revised statement of changes in financial position based on working capital for the year ended December 31.

8. Preparation of a Statement of Changes in Financial Position. Comparative balance sheets for the Susuki Plumbing Co. as of December 31, 1987 and 1986 follow:

Susuki Plumbing Co.
Comparative Balance Sheets

	December 31,	
Assets	1987	1986
Current assets	$ 52,000	$ 42,000
Investments	23,000	25,000
Land	90,000	80,000
Building, net	100,000	103,000
Patents	50,000	0
Total assets	$315,000	$250,000
Equities		
Current liabilities	$ 40,000	$ 38,000
Long-term debt	120,000	100,000
Capital stock	60,000	50,000
Retained earnings	95,000	62,000
Total equities	$315,000	$250,000

In addition you obtained the following information:

1. Net income for the year was $38,000.
2. Land with a cost of $10,000 was sold for $12,000.
3. The only change in the Building account was due to depreciation expense.
4. Patents were purchased for cash at the end of 1987. No amortization was taken in 1987.
5. Investments were sold at their book value.
6. All other changes were due to normal transactions.

Required:

Prepare in good form a statement of changes in financial position on a working capital basis for the year ended December 31, 1987.

9. Conversion from Accrual to Cash Basis. The data on the top of page 830 were taken from comparative trial balances of the Alka Pro Swimware Co.

In addition you determined that the firm keeps its books on the accrual basis. Included in operating expenses are depreciation of $2,000 and amortization expense of $1,000.

The Statement of Changes in Financial Position

	December 31,
	1987	1986
Accounts receivable	$190,000	$150,000
Interest receivable	500	700
Inventories	220,000	200,000
Prepaid insurance	1,800	1,000
Accounts payable	230,000	190,000
Other accrued expenses payable| 8,000	10,000
Net sales	800,000	
Interest revenue	1,500	
Cost of goods sold	600,000	
Insurance expense	2,000	
Accrued operating expenses	80,000	

Required:

Determine the following information:
  a. Cash basis sales.
  b. Interest income collected during the year.
  c. Cash paid for insurance during the year.
  d. Cash paid for inventory purchases during the year.
  e. Cash paid for operating expenses during the year.
  f. Cash generated from operations.

10. Preparing a Cash-based Statement of Changes in Financial Position. Following and on the top of page 831 are comparative balance sheets for the High Solar Coal Corporation as well as the income statement for the year ended December 31, 1987:

High Solar Coal Corporation
Comparative Balance Sheet

December 31

Assets	1987	1986
Cash	$ 69,000	$ 40,000
Accounts receivable	55,000	60,000
Inventory	150,000	100,000
Land	250,000	200,000
Plant and equipment, net	390,000	400,000
Total Assets	$914,000	$800,000

Equities	1987	1986
Accounts payable	$ 45,000	$ 30,000
Dividends payable	10,000	0
Accrued liabilities	7,000	8,000
Long-term debt	240,000	200,000
Capital stock	300,000	300,000
Retained earnings	322,000	262,000
Treasury stock	(10,000)	0
Total equities	$914,000	$800,000

Additional Information:
  1. Dividends declared during the year were $40,000.
  2. Land was purchased for $50,000 cash.

830

High Solar Coal Corporation
Income Statement
For the Year Ended December 31, 1987

Sales		$1,000,000
Cost of goods sold		600,000
Gross margin on sales		$ 400,000
Operating expenses		
Depreciation	$ 10,000	
Other operating expenses	290,000	300,000
Net income		$ 100,000

3. The only change in the Plant and Equipment account was due to depreciation.
4. All other balance sheet changes are the result of normal transactions.

Required:

Prepare in good form a statement of changes in financial position on a cash basis. Include a supplemental schedule computing cash from operations.

Problem Set A

20A–1. Identifying Changes in Financial Position. Below are a number of independent transactions. For each transaction, indicate whether it is a source (S) of financial resources, a use (U) of resources, or has no effect (NE) on resources. Mark each item first on a working capital–based financial position and then on a cash-based financial position. Item 1 is done for you as an example.

	Financial Position Defined As	
Item	Working Capital	Cash
1. Payment of accounts payable	NE	U
2. Purchase of merchandise on account		
3. Sales on account		
4. Purchase of land for cash and long-term notes		
5. Declaration of dividends		
6. Collection of trade receivables on account		
7. Reclassification of long-term debt to current liability		
8. Conversion of preferred stock to common stock		
9. Depreciation expense		
10. Sale of long-term investments above cost		
11. Amortization of premium on bonds payable		
12. Purchase of current marketable securities		

20A–2. Effect of Transactions on Working Capital. State which of the following are (a) sources of working capital, (b) uses of working capital, or (c) neither sources nor uses of working capital by placing an X in the appropriate space.

Item	Source	Use	Neither
1. Net income for the year, $3,000			
2. Purchase of a new building through the issuance of a mortgage for the entire amount			
3. Issuance of dividends in the form of capital stock, $20,000			
4. Collection of accounts receivable, $12,000			
5. Purchase of merchandise on credit, $9,000			
6. Declaration of cash dividends, $12,000			
7. Issuance of additional common stock, $300,000			
8. Depreciation for year, $6,000			
9. Purchase of equipment for cash, $12,000			
10. Sale of bonds, $25,000			
11. Sale of merchandise on account, $35,000			
12. Deposit of cash in a savings account, $5,000			

20A-3. Determining Working Capital from Operations. The Alfredo Ice Cream Company reported net income of $500,000 for the year ended June 30, 1985. You have been able to gather the following additional information:

Unrealized loss on writedown of current marketable securities	$ 1,000
Depreciation expense	12,000
Bad debts expense	5,000
Loss on sale of land	20,000
Extraordinary gain on early extinguishment of debt	70,000
Purchase of long-term investment	55,000
Increase in balance of accounts receivable during year	8,000

Required:

Prepare a schedule calculating working capital from operations.

20A-4. Preparation of a Statement of Changes in Financial Position. Comparative financial statements for the Cal Bear Corporation follow:

Cal Bear Corporation
Comparative Balance Sheets

	December 31, 1987	1986
Assets		
Cash	$ 4,000	$ 15,000
Marketable securities	12,000	0
Accounts receivable, net	32,000	25,000
Inventories	86,500	73,000
Supplies	8,000	7,000
Property, plant, and equipment, net	97,500	0
Long-term notes receivable	0	15,000
Total assets	$240,000	$135,000
Equities		
Accounts payable	$ 20,000	$ 18,000
Other accrued payables	10,000	7,000
Long-term note payable	95,000	25,000
Common stock, no par	50,000	50,000
Retained earnings	65,000	35,000
Total equities	$240,000	$135,000

In addition, you have gathered the following data:

1. Net income for the year amounted to $40,000. The other change in retained earnings was due to the declaration and payment of a cash dividend.

2. During the year the company undertook a major expansion. Property, plant, and equipment with a cost of $100,000 were purchased. A 30% down payment was made; the rest was financed by issuing long-term notes that will mature in five years. The building has a 40-year life and no salvage value. Straight-line depreciation is used. There was no other depreciation expense recorded during the year.

3. The long-term note receivable was from a stockholder. Although it was not due until 1988, it was paid in full during 1987.

4. The company decided to invest excess cash in marketable securities.

Required:

a. Prepare a schedule of changes in the components of working capital for the year ended December 31, 1987.

b. Prepare a statement of changes in financial position (working capital basis) for the year ended December 31, 1987.

20A–5. Preparation of a Statement of Changes in Financial Position. The KTLA Corporation's comparative balance sheets for December 31, 1986 and 1987 follow:

The KTLA Corporation
Comparative Balance Sheets

	December 31, 1987	December 31, 1986
Cash	$ 18,000	$ 20,000
Accounts receivable, net	39,600	45,000
Inventory	53,600	80,000
Supplies	5,400	6,000
Land	90,000	80,000
Plant and equipment, net	110,000	100,000
Patents	5,400	6,000
Total assets	$322,000	$337,000
Notes payable	$ 31,000	$ 32,000
Accounts payable	7,000	10,000
Current maturities of mortgages payable	6,200	6,000
Dividends payable	1,000	4,000
Long-term note payable	15,000	0
Mortgages payable, long-term portion	53,800	60,000
Common stock	100,000	100,000
Retained earnings	108,000	125,000
Total equities	$322,000	$337,000

In addition, you have been able to gather the following data:

1. During the year the company incurred a net loss of $15,000. However, the company declared dividends of $2,000 during the year. Dividends paid in cash during the year were $5,000.

2. During the year land was purchased for $10,000 cash.

3. Plant and equipment with a book value of $10,000 were sold for $7,000 cash. Depreciation expense related to plant and equipment was $4,000. This was total depreciation expense during the year.

4. No patents were sold or purchased during the year.

5. All other changes were the result of normal balance sheet transactions.

Required:

Prepare a statement of changes in financial position on a working capital basis for the year ended December 31, 1987.

20A–6. Preparation of a Statement of Changes in Financial Position. The president of The Hardcastle Corporation understands that a statement of changes in financial position is one of the required financial statements. He asks your assistance in preparing the statement. He provides you with the following comparative balance sheets for 1987 and 1986 as well as the income statement for the year ended December 31, 1987 (at the top of page 835).

The Hardcastle Corporation
Comparative Balance Sheets

	December 31, 1987	December 31, 1986
Assets		
Current assets		
Cash	$ 5,200	$ 4,200
Accounts receivable	20,000	28,000
Inventory	47,000	33,000
Prepaid expenses	1,500	1,000
Total current assets	$ 73,700	$ 66,200
Property, plant, and equipment		
Land	$ 3,800	$ 2,800
Machinery and equipment, net	8,700	8,500
Buildings, net	42,000	47,000
Total property, plant, and equipment	$ 54,500	$ 58,300
Other assets		
Patents	$ 1,500	$ 1,700
Total assets	$129,700	$126,200
Equities		
Current liabilities		
Notes payable	$ 4,000	$ 5,800
Current maturities of long-term debt	2,000	1,900
Accounts payable	5,500	6,000
Accrued liabilities	15,000	13,000
Total current liabilities	$ 26,500	$ 26,700
Long-term debt	$ 18,000	$ 30,000
Stockholders' equity		
Common stock, no par	$ 61,000	$ 60,000
Retained earnings	24,200	9,500
Total stockholders' equity	$ 85,200	$ 69,500
Total liabilities and stockholders' equity	$129,700	$126,200

In addition, the president has provided you with the following information:

1. Included in depreciation and amortization expense are:

Building depreciation	$12,000
Machinery and equipment depreciation	800
Patent amortization	200

The Hardcastle Corporation
Statement of Income and Retained Earnings
For the Year Ended December 31, 1987

Revenues		
Sales		$174,000
Expenses		
Cost of goods sold	$112,000	
General and administrative	30,000	
Depreciation and amortization	13,000	
Interest	2,000	
Loss on early retirement of long-term debt	400	
Loss on sale of machinery and equipment	200	157,600
Net income		$ 16,400
Retained earnings, January 1		9,500
Less: Dividends		(1,700)
Retained earnings, December 31		$ 24,200

2. Machinery and equipment with a book value of $300 were sold for cash.
3. Land was acquired in exchange for common stock.
4. Long-term debt with a face value of $10,000 was retired early.
5. Short-term notes payable were issued for the purchase of machinery during 1985.
6. All other changes represent normal balance sheet transactions.

Required:

Prepare a statement of changes in financial position on a working capital basis for the year ended December 31, 1987.

20A–7. Preparation of a Statement of Changes in Financial Position—Cash Flow Basis. Using the data from Problem 20A–6, prepare a statement of changes in financial position on a cash basis.

20A–8. Determining Cash Flow from Operations. The selected data below and on the top of page 836 were taken from the comparative trial balance of The Electric Horse Company:

	December 31,	
	1987	**1986**
Accounts receivable	$360,000	$400,000
Rent receivable	4,200	4,000
Inventories	140,000	100,000
Property, plant, and equipment	600,000	500,000
Accumulated depreciation	105,000	100,000
Supplies	1,000	700
Accounts payable	210,000	200,000
Other accrued liabilities	44,000	42,000
Retained earnings	105,200	75,000

In addition, you learned that property, plant, and equipment with a historical cost of $20,000 were sold during the year for cash. Depreciation related to the assets sold was $5,000.

Required:

a. Prepare a schedule determining cash generated from operations.
b. Determine what caused the changes in the Property, Plant, and Equipment account.

The Electric Horse Company
Income Statement
For the Year Ended December 31, 1987

Revenues		
Sales		$460,000
Rental income		7,200
Gain on sale of property, plant, and equipment		2,000
Total revenues		$469,200
Expenses		
Cost of goods sold	$345,000	
Supplies used	4,000	
Other accrued expenses	77,000	
Depreciation expense	10,000	
Total expenses		436,000
Net income		$ 33,200

Problem Set B

20B-1. Identifying Changes in Financial Position. Below are a number of independent transactions. For each transaction, indicate whether it is a source (S) of financial resources, a use (U) of resources, or has no effect (NE) on resources. Mark each item first on a working capital–based financial position and then on a cash-based financial position. Item 1 is done for you as an example.

	Financial Position Defined As	
Item	Working Capital	Cash
1. Receipt of cash on account	NE	S
2. Payment of dividends payable		
3. Distribution of stock dividend		
4. Purchase of building in exchange for common stock		
5. Declaration of stock dividends		
6. Payment on accounts payable		
7. Purchase of treasury stock		
8. Conversion of convertible debt to common stock		
9. Amortization expense		
10. Increase in deferred tax credit account		
11. Amortization of discount on bonds payable		
12. Sale of current marketable securities at a loss		

20B-2. Effect of Transactions on Working Capital. State which of the following are (a) sources of working capital, (b) uses of working capital, or (c) neither sources nor uses of working capital by placing an X in the appropriate space.

Item	Source	Use	Neither
1. Net loss for the year, $7,500			
2. Sale of treasury stock in excess of its cost			
3. Declaration of cash dividends on preferred stock, $10,000			

Item	Source	Use	Neither
4. Collection of note receivable from shareholder, $1,000			
5. Return of defective merchandise purchased for cash, $500			
6. Payment of preferred dividends in (3)			
7. Conversion of preferred stock into common, $200,000			
8. Amortization for year, $3,000			
9. Purchase of equipment for cash, $22,000 plus issuance of note payable			
10. Issuance of convertible bonds, $50,000			
11. Purchase of inventory on account, $15,000			
12. Establishment of petty cash fund, $200			

20B–3. Determining Working Capital from Operations. The Allison Allite Co. reported a net loss of $100,000 for the year ended December 31, 1987. You have been able to gather the following additional information:

Gain on sale of equipment	$ 8,000
Depletion expense	6,000
Investment income from increase in equity of subsidiary on equity method of accounting	10,000
Purchase of current marketable securities	15,000
Increase in balance of accounts payable during the year	42,000
Decrease in balance of deferred tax account during the year	15,000
Write-off of an account receivable from a customer in bankruptcy proceedings, previously allowed for	2,500

Required:

Prepare a schedule calculating working capital from operations.

20B–4. Preparation of a Statement of Changes in Financial Position. Comparative financial statements for the Oski Corporation follow:

Oski Corporation
Comparative Balance Sheets

	December 31,	
Assets	1987	1986
Cash	$ 11,500	$ 25,000
Marketable securities	0	15,000
Accounts receivable, net	15,000	40,000
Inventories	95,500	80,000
Prepaid insurance	8,000	6,000
Property, plant, and equipment, net	145,000	100,000
Long-term investment	50,000	0
Total assets	$325,000	$266,000

Equities		
Accounts payable	$ 25,000	$ 29,000
Other accrued payables	18,000	12,000
Long-term note payable	52,000	55,000
Common stock, no par	150,000	100,000
Retained earnings	80,000	70,000
Total equities	$325,000	$266,000

The Statement of Changes in Financial Position

In addition, you have gathered the following data:

1. Net income for the year amounted to $15,000. The other change in retained earnings was due to the declaration and payment of a cash dividend.

2. During the year the company sold all of its current marketable securities for a gain of $12,000. The total proceeds plus additional cash of $23,000 were invested in long-term bonds, which management intends to hold to maturity. The investment was made at the face value of the bonds.

3. The company purchased additional plant and equipment of $50,000 by issuing common stock in that amount. The only decrease in this account is due to depreciation expense for the year.

4. The decrease in the long-term payable represents a reclassification from a long-term liability to a current liability. The current portion is included in other accrued payables.

Required:

a. Prepare a schedule of changes in the components of working capital for the year ended December 31, 1987.

b. Prepare a statement of changes in financial position (working capital basis) for the year ended December 31, 1987.

20B–5. Preparation of a Statement of Changes in Financial Position. The McHenry Corporation's comparative balance sheets for December 31, 1986 and 1987 follow:

The McHenry Corporation
Comparative Balance Sheets

	December 31, 1987	1986
Cash	$ 58,000	$ 45,000
Accounts receivable, net	45,000	85,000
Inventory	150,000	120,000
Office supplies	9,000	8,000
Land	148,000	120,000
Plant and equipment, net	220,000	200,000
Long-term note receivable	0	6,000
Total assets	$630,000	$584,000
Accumulated depreciation	$ 45,000	$ 40,000
Accounts payable	17,000	32,000
Current maturities of mortgages payable	8,500	8,000
Dividends payable	4,000	5,000
Long-term note payable	25,000	25,000
Mortgages payable, long-term portion	66,500	75,000
Common stock	220,000	180,000
Retained earnings	244,000	219,000
Total equities	$630,000	$584,000

In addition, you have been able to gather the following data:

1. During the year the company's net income amounted to $30,000. During the year the company paid dividends of $6,000.

2. During the year land with a historical cost of $12,000 was sold for $18,000. Additional land was purchased in exchange for common stock.

3. Plant and equipment were purchased for cash. There were no other changes in the Plant and Equipment account.

4. The long-term note receivable was due late in 1989. However, it was collected in full early in 1987.

5. All other changes were the result of normal balance sheet transactions.

Required:

Prepare a statement of changes in financial position on a working capital basis for the year ended December 31, 1987.

20B–6. Preparation of the Statement of Changes in Financial Position. The president of The King Corporation understands that a statement of changes in financial position is one of the required financial statements. She asks your assistance in preparing the statement. She provides you with the following comparative balance sheets for 1986 and 1987 as well as the income statement for the year ended December 31, 1987 (at the top of page 840).

The King Corporation
Comparative Balance Sheets

Assets	December 31, 1987	December 31, 1986
Current assets		
Cash	$ 9,300	$ 8,500
Marketable securities	2,000	2,000
Accounts receivable, net	20,000	24,000
Inventory	86,000	50,000
Supplies	4,500	2,000
Total current assets	$121,800	$ 86,500
Property, plant, and equipment		
Land	$ 40,500	$ 10,500
Equipment, net	19,500	18,500
Buildings, net	107,000	90,000
Total property, plant, and equipment	$167,000	$119,000
Other assets		
Long-term investments	$ 6,000	$ 5,000
Total assets	$294,800	$210,500

Equities		
Current liabilities		
Notes payable	$ 16,000	$ 15,000
Current maturities of long-term debt	5,000	3,000
Accounts payable	18,500	16,000
Dividends payable	8,500	6,000
Total current liabilities	$ 48,000	$ 40,000
Long-term debt	$ 65,000	$ 50,000
Stockholders' equity		
Common stock, no par	$125,000	$ 75,000
Retained earnings	56,800	45,500
Total stockholders' equity	$181,800	$120,500
Total liabilities and stockholders' equity	$294,800	$210,500

In addition, the president has provided you with the following information:

1. Included in depreciation expense is:

Building depreciation	$13,000
Equipment depreciation	2,000

2. Equipment was sold for cash. Other than the sale and depreciation expense, the only transaction affecting this account was the purchase of additional equipment for $6,000 cash.

The Statement of Changes in Financial Position 839

The King Corporation
Statement of Income and Retained Earnings
For the Year Ended December 31, 1987

Revenues		
Sales	$260,000	
Gain on sale of building	12,000	
Total revenues		$272,000
Expenses		
Cost of goods sold	$169,000	
General and administrative	50,000	
Depreciation	15,000	
Interest	13,000	
Loss on sale of equipment	1,200	248,200
Net income		$ 23,800
Retained earnings, January 1		45,500
Less dividends		(12,500)
Retained earnings, December 31		$ 56,800

3. Land was acquired in exchange for $10,000 cash and a long-term note payable for $20,000. No land was sold. The other change in the long-term note payable was due to the reclassification of the current portion.

4. Buildings with a book value of $20,000 were sold for cash. Other than depreciation expense, the only transaction affecting this account was the purchase of additional buildings in exchange for common stock.

5. There were no sales of long-term investments during the year.

6. All other changes represent normal balance sheet transactions.

Required:

Prepare a statement of changes in financial position on a working capital basis for the year ended December 31, 1987.

20B–7. Preparation of a Statement of Changes in Financial Position—Cash Flow Basis. Using the data from Problem 20B–6, prepare a statement of changes in financial position on a cash basis.

20B–8. Determining Cash Flow from Operations. The selected data below and on the top of page 841 were taken from the comparative trial balance of the Fonda Fondue Company:

	December 31,	
	1987	1986
Accounts receivable	$260,000	$250,000
Interest receivable	3,500	3,000
Inventories	94,000	80,000
Property, plant, and equipment	333,000	350,000
Accumulated depreciation	60,000	70,000
Prepaid rent	1,000	1,200
Accounts payable	120,000	140,000
Other accrued liabilities	23,000	21,000
Retained earnings	105,200	65,000

In addition, you learned that property, plant, and equipment with a historical cost of $37,000 were sold during the year for cash. Accumulated depreciation related to the assets sold was $17,000.

a. Prepare a schedule determining cash generated from operations.

b. Determine what caused the changes in the Property, Plant, and Equipment account.

The Fonda Fondue Company
Income Statement
For the Year Ended December 31, 1987

Revenues		
Sales		$350,000
Interest income		5,000
Total revenues		$355,000
Expenses		
Cost of goods sold	$210,000	
Rent expense	2,000	
Other accrued expenses	56,000	
Depreciation expense	7,000	
Loss on sale of equipment	6,000	
Total expenses		281,000
Net income		$ 74,000

Using the Computer

Using the data in Problem 20A–6, prepare on an electronic spreadsheet a worksheet to facilitate the preparation of a statement of changes in financial position.

Understanding Financial Statements

Braniff Airlines, a major U.S. airline in the late 1970s and 1980s, declared bankruptcy in May 1981. The consolidated statement of changes in financial position for 1979 through 1981 is presented on page 842.

Required:

Assume that you are a financial analyst reviewing Braniff's statements prior to the time it declared bankruptcy. Write a brief memo to your clients indicating the danger signals contained in the statement of changes in financial position.

Financial Decision Case

The president of Denslowe Associates has become very concerned about the performance of his firm in the last couple of years. He understands that by analyzing the firm's statement of changes in financial position, he might get a clue as to the problems the firm has encountered. However, since he is not very familiar with accounting concepts he asks your help. In this regard he provides you with the information on page 843.

Required:

    a. The president of Denslowe Associates has reviewed these statements and has several questions. First, he would like you to explain in your own words what information this statement provides about the present and potential prospects of the company.

    b. He also is concerned that the statement shows that there has been an increase in working capital but that the company is having trouble meeting its current debts. He would like you to help explain the reason for this.

    c. Can you suggest to the president how these statements can be revised to provide the information he needs?

Braniff International Corporation and Subsidiaries
Consolidated Statement of Changes in Financial Position

	Years Ended December 31		
	1981	1980	1979
	(In thousands)		
SOURCES OF FUNDS			
From operations:			
Net loss	$(160,611)	$(131,436)	$ (44,330)
Charges against (credits to) operations not affecting working capital:			
Depreciation and amortization	85,998	91,480	77,884
Gains on property and equipment dispositions	(8,568)	(79,090)	(1,972)
Provisions for losses under aircraft purchase contracts	5,694	—	—
Undeclared preferred dividend requirements	4,112	343	—
Unrecoverable preoperating costs	1,270	20,329	1,086
Deferred federal income tax credit	—	(7,463)	(35,968)
Funds used for operations	(72,105)	(105,837)	(3,300)
Amount received under aircraft sales agreement	32,500	—	—
Proceeds from property and equipment dispositions	32,296	227,016	5,671
Additions to long-term pension liability	19,678	3,269	412
Reductions of equipment purchase deposits	199	22,471	68,652
Additions to long-term obligations	—	93,544	457,747
Proceeds from issuance of redeemable preferred stock	—	35,000	—
Other	6,458	5,805	2,336
Total sources of funds	19,026	281,268	531,518
APPLICATIONS OF FUNDS			
Reductions of long-term obligations, less current maturities	72,072	105,723	190,581
Purchases of property and equipment	3,662	233,859	322,823
Additions to equipment purchase deposits	1,566	5,804	31,688
Common dividends declared	—	1,001	7,207
Other	3,324	12,834	30,484
Total applications of funds	80,624	359,221	582,783
DECREASE IN WORKING CAPITAL	$ (61,598)	$ (77,953)	$ (51,265)
CHANGES IN COMPONENTS OF WORKING CAPITAL			
Increase (decrease) in current assets:			
Cash and cash equivalents	$ 31,375	$ (13,694)	$ 20,328
Accounts receivable	(27,049)	1,425	31,879
Inventory of spare parts, materials and supplies	(2,156)	(2,725)	11,700
Other	277	1,743	5,615
Total	2,447	(13,251)	69,522
Increase (decrease) in current liabilities:			
Notes payable	—	47,078	66
Current maturities of long-term debt	58,526	19,391	9,215
Current liabilities under capital leases	(5,789)	(341)	2,561
Accounts payable	(36,860)	(22,308)	61,815
Air traffic liability	7,537	8,905	18,190
Accrued compensation and retirement benefits	7,733	6,364	4,801
Accrued interest	23,889	2,445	5,512
Other	9,009	3,168	18,627
Total	64,045	64,702	120,787
DECREASE IN WORKING CAPITAL	$ (61,598)	$ (77,953)	$ (51,265)

Denslowe Associates
Statement of Changes in Financial Position
For the Year Ended December 31, 1987

Sources		
Working capital provided from operations:		
Net income	$10,000	
Add: Items not requiring the use		
of working capital	60,000	
		$ 70,000
Other sources		
Sale of land held for future plant expansion		80,000
Increase in long-term note payable		40,000
Total sources		$190,000
Uses		
Repayment of long-term bonds		$ 80,000
Payment of preferred dividends, including		
all those in arrears		70,000
Total uses		$150,000
Net increase in working capital		$ 40,000

Denlowe Associates
Schedule of Working Capital Accounts

	December 31,	
Assets	1987	1986
Cash	$ 10,000	$ 40,000
Accounts receivable	120,000	80,000
Inventories	160,000	120,000
Supplies	5,000	10,000
Total	$295,000	$250,000
Accounts payable	$100,000	$ 90,000
Accrued liabilities	30,000	20,000
Short-term notes payable	15,000	30,000
Total	$145,000	$140,000

Interpreting Financial Statement Data and Accounting for Multinational Enterprises

21

LEARNING OBJECTIVES

After reading this chapter you should be able to:

1. State the purposes of financial statement analysis.
2. Identify the sources of financial information about firms.
3. Discuss the techniques involved in financial statement analysis.
4. Know how to calculate common financial statement ratios.
5. State the limitations of financial statement analysis.
6. Show how foreign currency transactions are accounted for.
7. State the basic procedures involved in translating foreign currency statements to U.S. dollar statements.
8. Discuss efforts to harmonize international accounting standards.

As we have often stated in this book, one of the primary objectives of financial reporting is to provide information to present and potential investors and creditors and other users in making rational investment, credit, and similar decisions. The decisions made by these people require that they look at more than the bottom line or earnings per share. They must interpret the past performance of companies and assess their future prospects. This requires detailed financial and nonfinancial information that can be compared and contrasted among firms in the same and different industries. Once this information is gathered it must be analyzed and interpreted in a meaningful way. The purpose of this chapter is to introduce you to the tools of financial analysis and interpretation with the goal of understanding how to make meaningful decisions based on financial data. In addition, this chapter introduces you to the special accounting problems faced by multinational enterprises, and provides the tools to help you interpret the financial statements of these firms.

The Purposes of Financial Statement Analysis

Financial statement analysis is the set of techniques designed to provide relevant data to decision makers. It is generally based on the firm's published financial statements and other economic information about the firm and the industry the firm is in. Major techniques involved in financial statement analysis include trend, vertical, and ratio analysis. The major users of such analyses are a firm's present and potential investors, its creditors, and its management.

Present and Potential Investors and Creditors

One aspect of relevant accounting information is its ability to help present and potential investors and creditors generate predictions about the outcome of future events. Essentially, an investment or credit decision involves giving up cash today in the expectation of receiving a greater amount of cash in the future. One of the purposes of financial reporting is to help users assess the amounts, timing, and uncertainty of prospective net cash inflows to the enterprise, and ultimately to them. Thus, investors and creditors analyze financial statements and other data in the hope of gaining insights into the future profitability and cash flows of companies.

In many cases the past performance of the company as well as its current financial position is a good indication of the ability of the company to generate future cash flows. For example, if in the last few years the operations of a company have caused continual decreases in working capital, this would be an indication that the company may be facing future cash flow problems. Information concerning backlogs and back orders provides some indication about the future profitability of the company and the cash that will flow to the company. Often trend analysis is employed to use past information for making predictions about the future.

Ratio analysis is an important tool in measuring the past and current performance of a firm. By investigating key ratios such as the current ratio and debt-equity ratio, users are able to assess the current financial position of the firm and how it has changed over the immediate past. In addition, models using various ratios have been developed that help predict bankruptcy and financial distress. Ratio analysis is discussed in great detail later in this chapter.

Forming expectations about the relative risk of a company is another important aspect of financial statement analysis. Investors demand a higher rate of return for riskier investments than they do for less risky investments. Furthermore, in putting together a portfolio of investments, investors often like to combine risky investments with less risky ones in the hope that such diversification will reduce their overall risk. Thus, financial statement analysis can be used by investors and creditors to assess the current and future risk of companies.

Management

A firm's management is both a major supplier and a user of financial statement information. Through its published financial statements, management provides much of the information used in financial statement analysis. Every day management uses various ratios and other analytic tools in the evaluation and control of the firm and its various divisions. Control involves setting benchmarks and evaluating performance against these benchmarks. Many of these benchmarks are expressed as ratios, and performance is measured by determining variances from these ratios. Although we concentrate on present and potential investors and creditors in this chapter, the importance of financial statement analysis to management should not be overlooked.

Sources of Financial Information

Most users of financial statements do not have direct access to a firm's records. They must rely on a variety of sources to gather the information necessary to analyze and interpret a firm's financial statements. For public companies this information is readily available in the form of the firm's annual report, business periodicals, and business and investment advisory services. However, for private companies this information is difficult if not impossible to obtain. As a result, we concentrate here on how to gather information about public companies. The two primary sources are reports published by the firm itself, such as annual reports, and external sources, such as business and investment advisory services.

Published Reports

Public companies are required to publish annual reports to shareholders and to file certain reports with the Securities and Exchange Commission (SEC). Under certain circumstances some of these reports required by the SEC can be combined with the firm's annual report.

SEC Reports

Under current laws publicly held companies are required to file annual and quarterly reports as well as documents notifying the SEC when an important event has impacted the company. These reports are available to shareholders, often free of charge, and to the public at large for a small fee. The annual report filed with the SEC is called **Form 10-K.** Essentially this is an expanded version of the annual report sent to shareholders. However, nonfinancial information such as the president's letter is not included in Form 10-K. Current SEC regulations allow a company to integrate the annual report with Form 10-K and thus, if it chooses, it has to prepare only one combined document. Because Form 10-K generally contains more information than can be found in the annual report alone, it is a valuable source of information for analyzing and interpreting financial statement data.

Public firms are also required to file quarterly reports with the SEC called **Form 10-Q.** These reports provide the SEC with condensed quarterly information about the firm. In addition, all firms are required to file a **Form 8-K** within 10 days after the end of the month of certain major events affecting the firm. Such an event might be the disposal of a major segment or the firing of the firm's auditor. This is an important report as it provides the SEC and other users with up-to-date information concerning the company.

The Annual Report

All public companies produce an annual report which is mailed to shareholders and other interested parties free of charge. Most annual reports contain the following sections (not necessarily in this order):

1. The president's or chairperson's message.
2. Information about the company's activities during the year.
3. Management's discussion and analysis of operations.
4. A five-year summary of activity.
5. The financial statements, including the auditor's report.

The president's message and the section containing information about the activities of the company are descriptive in nature and do not provide a great deal of information that is useful for financial statement analysis. Generally, these sections paint the best possible picture of the company and in some cases can make an unprofitable year sound like a successful one.

Management's discussion and analysis of operations is one of the newest and most informative sections of the annual report. Because of SEC requirements, it is included in both the annual report to shareholders and Form 10-K. The disclosure requirements in this section include discussions of the firm's liquidity, capital resources and results of operations, favorable or unfavorable trends and significant events and uncertainties, causes of material changes in the financial statements, narrative discussion of the effects of changing prices, and projections or other forward-looking information. Thus, data needed for financial statement analysis and interpretation can be found in this section.

The five-year summary also provides useful information for financial analysis. The summary includes five years of data concerning earnings, financial statistics, and other information. For example, in the five-year summary contained in Safeway's annual report such data as sales, gross profit, net income, working capital, the current ratio, number of employees, and the market price range of the common stock are reported for the five most recent years.

From a financial analysis point of view, the financial statements and related footnotes represent the heart of the annual report. Much of this book has centered around discussing the generally accepted accounting principles behind financial statements and how to understand the information contained in them. However, it is worth emphasizing the usefulness of the footnotes in financial statement analysis. Footnotes, such as the one that summarizes the significant accounting policies used by the company and the one that reports certain financial information by segment and geographic area, are valuable in comparing the activities of one company with those of another.

Finally, all public corporations issue quarterly financial reports containing condensed financial statements. These statements are reviewed by the firm's accountants rather than audited as the annual statements are. Quarterly reports are useful in spotting emerging trends and seasonal variations.

External Sources

Financial statement analysis requires that the performance and operations of one company be compared with those of another. In today's sophisticated business world, rule-of-thumb measures, such as "the current ratio should be two to one," are not adequate. Firms and industries have specific characteristics and one rule of thumb cannot be applied to all firms. Thus, understanding industry characteristics and the environment in which the firm operates are important ingredients of financial analysis. External reports such as business periodicals and investment advisory services are very useful in this regard.

Business Periodicals

Business periodicals represent a valuable source of information for financial analysts. General sources include *The Wall Street Journal, Forbes, Barron's, BusinessWeek,* and *Fortune.* These journals are published either daily, weekly, or biweekly and provide valuable information about the economy as a whole, specific industries, and individual firms. Trade journals provide another valuable source of information. These journals, such as *Retail World,* give the reader detailed information about specific industries and firms within those industries.

Investment Advisory Services

There are a number of investment advisory services that publish valuable and timely information about specific industries and companies. Included are such services as *Moody's Investors Services, Standard and Poor's Industrial Surveys,* and *The Value Line Investment Survey.* These services all provide information such as the economic outlook for the industry, condensed financial information concerning specific firms, the outlook for the firm, and opinions as to the future performance of the firm.

Other Sources

There are a variety of other external sources that are commonly used by financial statement analysts. They generally provide data on average industry ratios and norms. For example, Robert Morris Associates, a banking association, publishes the *Annual Statement Studies.* This annual compendium provides industry facts and ratios for 220 companies. Other sources for industry ratios and relationships include Dun and Bradstreet's *Key Business Ratios* and Prentice-Hall's *Almanac of Business and Industrial Financial Ratios.*

The Techniques of Financial Analysis

Financial statement users and analysts have developed a number of techniques to help them analyze and interpret financial statements. The most common of these include horizontal analysis, vertical analysis, and ratio analysis. All of these techniques focus on relationships among items in the financial statements and on the financial statements themselves. However, in making decisions based on the results of your analysis you must remember the limitations inherent in financial statement analysis; these are discussed later in the chapter.

Horizontal and Trend Analysis

In trying to understand the current financial position of the firm and its future outlook, it is important to consider changes from year to year as well as trends over several years. One way to accomplish this is to use comparative financial statements and the five-year summary of data found in the firm's annual report to spot important or emerging trends.

Horizontal Analysis

A technique that is commonly used in this regard is horizontal analysis. **Horizontal analysis** focuses on the dollar and percentage changes that have occurred in certain accounts from year to year. The determination of the percentage change is important because it relates the amount of the change to the actual amounts involved. Thus, percentage changes are better for comparative purposes with other firms than are actual dollar changes. For example, a $1 million increase in General Motors' cash balance is likely to represent a much smaller percentage increase than a corresponding $1 million increase in American Motors' cash balance.

In order to calculate percentage changes, the following formula should be used:

$$\text{Percentage change} = \frac{\text{Dollar amount of change}}{\text{Base year amount}} \times 100$$

The base year is always considered to be the first year in the comparison. For example, Safeway's total current assets were $1,861,389,000 in 1984 and $2,026,481,000 in 1985. This represents a dollar increase of $165,092,000 and a percentage increase of 8.87% calculated as follows:

$$8.87\% = \frac{\$2,026,481,000 - \$1,861,389,000}{\$1,861,389,000} \times 100$$

Horizontal analysis can be used in conjunction with both the balance sheet and the income statement. As an example, Exhibits 21–1 and 21–2 present comparative balance sheets and income statements for Safeway Stores, Inc. showing dollar and percentage changes. Several interesting balance sheet changes are apparent. During 1985 Safeway experienced a large increase in its short-term investments. As noted by Safeway's management, this was principally from cash received on the sale of the operations in West Germany and Toronto, and reinvestment of short-term borrowings at rates in excess of the cost of borrowings. In addition, although total net property increased by only 1.4%, there was a large increase in buildings partially offset by a large decrease in property held under capital leases. There was a corresponding large decrease in the long-term liability, Obligations under Capital Leases.

Horizontal analysis of the income statement also provides some interesting information. Although 1985 sales were essentially even with 1984 sales, cost of goods sold decreased by about 0.9%. This resulted in an increase in gross profits of 3.03%. As noted by Safeway's management, "gross profit as a percentage of sales continued to increase. Changes in product mix, improved purchasing practices and continued distribution cost control measures have increased gross profit as a percentage of sales. . . ."

Trend Analysis

Horizontal analysis can easily be expanded to include more than a single change from one year to the next. This is called **trend analysis.** In many cases it is important to look at changes over a period of time in order to evaluate emerging trends that are likely to have an impact on future years' performance. The five-year summary of selected financial data which is found in all annual reports is particularly useful in this regard.

When more than two years are involved, index numbers are used instead of percentage changes. Essentially, one year is selected as the base year and is set to 100%. All other years are represented as a percentage of the base year. An index number can be calculated by the following formula:

$$\text{Index number} = \frac{\text{Index year dollar amount}}{\text{Base year dollar amount}} \times 100$$

EXHIBIT 21–1
Safeway Stores, Inc.
Consolidated Balance Sheets
(in thousands)

Assets	1985	1984	Increase or (Decrease) Amount	Percentage
Current assets:				
Cash	$ 54,593	$ 49,179	$ 5,414	11.01
Short-term investments	170,021	25,263	144,758	573.00
Receivables	111,870	105,166	6,704	6.37
Merchandise inventories	1,565,566	1,563,244	2,322	0.15
Prepaid expenses and other current assets	124,431	118,537	5,894	4.97
Total current assets	2,026,481	1,861,389	165,092	8.87
Property:				
Land	247,769	236,876	10,893	4.60
Buildings	431,410	345,001	86,409	25.05
Leasehold improvements	600,091	557,504	42,587	7.64
Fixtures and equipment	2,164,072	2,023,914	140,158	6.93
Transport equipment	186,831	186,485	346	0.19
Property under capital lease	1,010,277	1,144,409	(134,132)	(11.72)
	4,640,450	4,494,189	146,261	3.25
Less: Accumulated depreciation and amortization	2,003,752	1,894,333	109,419	5.78
Total property, net	2,636,698	2,599,856	36,842	1.42
Investments in affiliated companies	122,195	27,251	94,944	348.41
Other assets	55,237	48,733	6,504	13.35
Total assets	$4,840,611	$4,537,229	$303,382	6.69

EXHIBIT 21–1 (Continued)

Liabilities and Stockholders' Equity	1985	1984	Increase or (Decrease) Amount	Percentage
Current liabilities:				
Notes payable	$ 80,848	$ 44,913	$ 35,935	80.01
Current obligations under capital leases	43,396	45,427	(2,031)	(4.47)
Current maturities of notes and debentures	52,049	48,274	3,775	7.82
Accounts payable	1,151,426	1,038,268	113,158	10.90
Accrued salaries and wages	167,798	167,739	59	0.04
Other accrued expenses	201,357	170,905	30,452	17.82
Income taxes payable	27,827	20,431	7,396	36.20
Total current liabilities	1,724,701	1,535,957	188,744	12.29
Long-term debt:				
Obligations under capital leases	625,551	746,178	(120,627)	(16.17)
Notes and debentures	689,470	646,532	42,938	6.64
Total long-term debt	1,315,021	1,392,710	(77,689)	(5.58)
Accrued claims and other liabilities	178,275	139,539	38,736	27.76
Total liabilities	3,217,997	3,068,206	149,791	4.88
Stockholders' equity:				
Common stock	101,411	99,756	1,655	1.66
Additional paid-in capital	273,776	246,964	26,812	10.86
Cumulative translation adjustment	(164,035)	(155,994)	(8,041)	5.15
Retained earnings	1,411,462	1,278,297	133,165	10.42
Total stockholders' equity	1,622,614	1,469,023	153,591	10.46
Total liabilities and stockholders' equity	$4,840,611	$4,537,229	$303,382	6.69

Safeway Stores, Inc.
Consolidated Statements of Income
(in thousands)

	1985	1984	Increase or (Decrease)	
			Amount	Percentage
Sales	$19,650,542	$19,642,201	$ 8,341	0.04
Cost of sales	14,872,247	15,004,547	(132,300)	(0.88)
Gross profit	4,778,295	4,637,654	140,641	3.03
Operating and administrative expenses	4,350,635	4,214,443	136,192	3.23
Operating profit	427,660	423,211	4,449	1.05
Interest expense	(172,906)	(151,263)	(21,643)	14.31
Gain on sale of foreign operations	49,046	0	49,046	100.00
Other income, net	49,816	26,874	22,942	85.37
Income before provision for income taxes	353,616	298,822	54,794	18.34
Provision for income taxes	122,316	113,811	8,505	7.47
Net income	$ 231,300	$ 185,011	$ 46,289	25.02
Net income per share	$3.83	$3.12	$0.71	22.76

To illustrate, Safeway's sales in 1981, the base year, were $16,580,318,000. Sales in 1985, the index year, were $19,650,542,000 and the index for 1985 was 118.52, calculated as follows:

$$118.52 = \frac{\$19,650,542,000}{\$16,580,318,000} \times 100$$

This means that Safeway's sales in 1985 were 118.52% or 1.19 times 1981 sales. Another way of representing this is to say that 1985 sales were approximately 19% greater than 1981 sales. Index numbers for other items are calculated in the same manner.

Index numbers are particularly useful in measuring real growth. For example, in the Safeway illustration, sales increased a little less than 19% from 1981 to 1985. Does this represent a real growth of sales, the same unit sales only at higher prices, or a combination of both? One way to answer this question is to compare the index number for sales growth to the rate of inflation for the same period measured by an index such as the Consumer Price Index for All Urban Consumers, or a specific price index for the industry. In the same five-year period, the Consumer Price Index increased about 18%. Thus, in constant dollars there was little real growth in sales.

Vertical Analysis

Vertical analysis is used to evaluate the relationships within single financial statements. Essentially, the appropriate total figure in the financial statement is set to 100% and other items are expressed as a percentage of that figure. For the balance sheet this figure is usually total assets or the total of liabilities plus stockholders' equity. Net sales is usually the total figure used in the income statement. The financial statements that result from using these percentages are often referred to as **common dollar statements.** Exhibits 21–3 and 21–4

852

EXHIBIT 21-3
Safeway Stores, Inc.
Consolidated Balance Sheets
(in thousands)

Assets	1985	1984	Percentages 1985	1984
Current assets:				
Cash	$ 54,593	$ 49,179	1.13	1.08
Short-term investments	170,021	25,263	3.51	.56
Receivables	111,870	105,166	2.31	2.32
Merchandise inventories	1,565,566	1,563,244	32.34	34.45
Prepaid expenses and other current assets	124,431	118,537	2.57	2.61
Total current assets	2,026,481	1,861,389	41.86	41.02
Property:				
Land	247,769	236,876	5.12	5.22
Buildings	431,410	345,001	8.91	7.60
Leasehold improvements	600,091	557,504	12.40	12.29
Fixtures and equipment	2,164,072	2,023,914	44.71	44.61
Transport equipment	186,831	186,485	3.86	4.11
Property under capital lease	1,010,277	1,144,409	20.87	25.22
	4,640,450	4,494,189	95.86	99.05
Less: Accumulated depreciation and amortization	2,003,752	1,894,333	41.39	41.75
Total property, net	2,636,698	2,599,856	54.47	57.30
Investments in affiliated companies	122,195	27,251	2.52	0.60
Other assets	55,237	48,733	1.14	1.07
Total assets	$4,840,611	$4,537,229	100.00	100.00

EXHIBIT 21-3 (Continued)

Liabilities and Stockholders' Equity	1985	1984	Percentages 1985	1984
Current liabilities:				
Notes payable	$ 80,848	$ 44,913	1.67	0.99
Current obligations under capital leases	43,396	45,427	0.90	1.00
Current maturities of notes and debentures	52,049	48,274	1.08	1.06
Accounts payable	1,151,426	1,038,268	23.79	22.88
Accrued salaries and wages	167,798	167,739	3.47	3.70
Other accrued expenses	201,357	170,905	4.16	3.77
Income taxes payable	27,827	20,431	0.57	0.45
Total current liabilities	1,724,701	1,535,957	35.63	33.85
Long-term debt:				
Obligations under capital leases	625,551	746,178	12.92	16.45
Notes and debentures	689,470	646,532	14.24	14.25
Total long-term debt	1,315,021	1,392,710	27.17	30.70
Accrued claims and other liabilities	178,275	139,539	3.68	3.08
Total liabilities	3,217,997	3,068,206	66.48	67.62
Stockholders' equity:				
Common stock	101,411	99,756	2.10	2.20
Additional paid-in capital	273,776	246,964	5.66	5.44
Cumulative translation adjustment	(164,035)	(155,994)	(3.39)	(3.44)
Retained earnings	1,411,462	1,278,297	29.16	28.17
Total stockholders' equity	1,622,614	1,469,023	33.52	32.38
Total liabilities and stockholders' equity	$4,840,611	$4,537,229	100.00	100.00

EXHIBIT 21–4

Safeway Stores, Inc.
Consolidated Statements of Income
(in thousands)

| | 1985 | 1984 | Percentages | |
			1985	1984
Sales	$19,650,542	$19,642,201	100.00	100.00
Cost of sales	14,872,247	15,004,547	75.68	76.39
Gross profit	4,778,295	4,637,654	24.32	23.61
Operating and administrative expenses	4,350,635	4,214,443	22.14	21.46
Operating profit	427,660	423,211	2.18	2.15
Interest expense	(172,906)	(151,263)	(0.88)	(0.77)
Gain on sale of foreign operations	49,046	0	0.25	0
Other income, net	49,816	26,874	0.25	0.14
Income before provision for income taxes	353,616	298,822	1.80	1.52
Provision for income taxes	122,316	113,811	0.62	0.58
Net income	$ 231,300	$ 185,011	1.18	0.94
Net income per share	$3.83	$3.12		

present comparative common dollar balance sheets and income statements for Safeway Stores.

Common dollar statements are very useful in noting important changes in the components of financial statements. For example, one would expect that current assets as a percentage of total assets would remain fairly constant over the years, or that net income as a percentage of sales would not radically change from year to year. When changes, especially radical ones, do occur, they are signals to external users as well as managers that the company has been affected by internal or external forces such as a recession or severe competition.

Examining Exhibits 21–3 and 21–4 indicates that there have not been many significant changes in these percentages for Safeway. Between 1984 and 1985 operating profit and net income as a percentage of sales have increased. Safeway's management explains these results in its discussion and analysis of operations as follows:

> Net income increased 25.0% in 1985 to $231.3 million from $185.0 million in 1984 and $183.3 million in 1983.

> Excluding the gain on the sale of foreign operations, 1985 net income increased 6.2% to $196.5 million, due primarily to improved operations in the U.S.

Common dollar statements are also useful in comparing the financial statements of different companies. For example, it is difficult to compare the dollar financial statements of Safeway with those of a smaller retail grocery chain because of the difference in the magnitude of the numbers. However, when the financial statements are expressed in percentages, the differences in magnitude disappear and it is easier to compare the financial position and performance of two companies that are significantly different in size.

Ratio Analysis

Ratio analysis is a shortcut method of expressing relationships among various items on the financial statements. However, ratios are not substitutes for looking deeper into the financial position of the company. There is a danger that inexperienced financial statement analysts might use what we call rule-of-thumb analysis to make important decisions. That is, one might decide that the current ratio should be two to one and make decisions on that basis. However, there are few rules of thumb that are adequate in today's complex financial world. With that caveat in mind, the following section discusses some of the more common ratios that are used by financial analysts.

Common Financial Ratios

There are a multitude of ratios that can be used in financial statement analysis. Throughout this text we have introduced important ratios in appropriate chapters. Our purpose in this chapter is to summarize and further explore these and other ratios. We concentrate on the most commonly used ratios. Where appropriate, we use the data for Safeway Stores, Inc. found in Exhibits 21–1 and 21–2.

A useful way to discuss ratio analysis is to categorize the ratios by the type of financial statement user who is most likely to use the particular ratio. The three most common user groups in this regard are common and preferred stockholders, short-term creditors, and long-term creditors. However, these groups are not exclusive, and sophisticated users, including management, will use all of these ratios, as well as others, to make their decisions. The categories do, however, serve as a useful way to organize the discussion.

Common and Preferred Stockholders

Common and preferred stockholders provide the permanent equity for the firm. They are interested in a variety of ratios that measure earnings per share to return on total assets. Because common shareholders have the residual equity interest in the firm and outnumber preferred shareholders, the discussion centers around ratios most useful to them. However, in most cases these ratios will also be of interest to the preferred shareholder.

Earnings per Share

As we discussed in Chapter 17, earnings per share (EPS) is one of the most commonly used and possibly abused of all the ratios. Its purpose is to provide the common shareholder with a comparative figure of the earnings of the company on a per-share basis. We noted how complex the actual EPS computation can be; this chapter reviews the calculation of EPS when a simple capital structure exists. Earnings per share is calculated as follows:

$$EPS = \frac{\text{Net income less preferred dividends, if any}}{\text{Weighted average number of common shares outstanding}}$$

Safeway Stores, Inc. has no preferred shares outstanding, and the average number of shares outstanding during 1985 was 60,360,000. As a result EPS in 1985 was $3.83, calculated as follows:

$$\$3.83 = \frac{\$231,300,000}{60,360,000 \text{ shares}}$$

Price-Earnings Ratio

The price-earnings (P-E) ratio measures the relationship of the market price of a firm's common stock to its earnings per share. This ratio is useful to present and potential investors because it provides a comparative measure of how the stock market values the earnings of a company.

The P-E ratio is calculated as follows:

$$\text{P-E ratio} = \frac{\text{Market price per common share}}{\text{Earnings per share}}$$

A firm's P-E ratio fluctuates daily with the change in the price of the firm's stock. At the end of 1985 (when Safeway's closing price was \$36.875) Safeway's P-E ratio was 9.6, calculated as follows:

$$9.6 = \frac{\$36.875}{\$3.83}$$

This means that Safeway's stock was selling at over nine times its earnings.

A P-E ratio of 9.6 is not meaningful by itself. It must be compared with other firms in the same industry and firms in other industries. For example, the P-E ratio for Kroger, a comparable retail grocery chain, was 11. Generally, a higher P-E ratio is an indication that investors feel that the firm's earnings are going to rise at a faster pace than for other companies. Conversely, a lower P-E ratio is often taken as a negative assessment of the future earnings of the company. However, generalizations such as these must be used carefully.

Dividend Yield

Some investors are primarily interested in dividends rather than in the appreciation of the market price of their stock. That is, they purchase the stock in the hope of receiving a steady flow of cash in the form of dividends. To these individuals the dividend yield ratio is very important. The dividend yield ratio is determined by the following formula:

$$\text{Dividend yield ratio} = \frac{\text{Dividends per share}}{\text{Market price per share}} \times 100\text{[1]}$$

Although this ratio can be figured for both common and preferred stock, it generally refers to yield on common stock. The dividend yield on Safeway's common stock at the end of 1985 was 4.4%, calculated as follows:

$$4.4\% = \frac{\$1.625}{\$36.875} \times 100$$

In evaluating this ratio the investor must compare it with alternative investments. At the end of 1985, an investment in Safeway stock provided a P-E ratio of over 9 and a dividend yield of over 4.4%. Although this appears to be a satisfactory return, investors have alternative investments with similar or different risks. The returns provided by Safeway stock must be compared with these alternative investments.

---

[1]Certain ratios are customarily expressed as percentages. Therefore, this ratio as well as certain others is multiplied by 100 in order to express the relationship as a percentage.

Book Value per Share

Chapter 16 contained a complete discussion of the concept behind book value per share and the procedures for computing this statistic. Although we will not repeat that discussion, we again recalculate the book value per share of Safeway's common stock at the end of 1985:

$$\text{Book value per share} = \frac{\text{Total common shareholders' equity}}{\text{Number of common shares outstanding}}$$

$$\$26.67 = \frac{\$1,622,614,000}{60,840,420}$$

Return on Investment

The management of a firm obtains resources from creditors and stockholders and then is charged with maximizing the return on these resources. Two ratios are often calculated to measure management's performance in this regard. They are return on total assets and return on common stockholders' equity.

Return on Total Assets

The return on total assets measures how efficiently the assets of the firm are being employed. It is one of the most important ratios because it answers the basic question, "What rate of return has the firm earned on the assets under its control?" This question is not only important to stockholders as they analyze alternative investments, but is also of utmost importance to the management of the firm itself. Corporate management uses this ratio in evaluating the performance of various divisions and the managers of those divisions.

There are a number of ways to calculate this ratio based on different levels of sophistication. For our purposes we will use this standard formula:

$$\text{Return on total assets} = \frac{\text{Net income} + \text{Interest expense}}{\text{Average total assets}} \times 100$$

There are two important points to note about the way this ratio is calculated. First, interest expense is added back to net income so that the numerator of the formula is net income before interest expense. Interest represents a payment or distribution to creditors for the use of funds that were used to acquire assets. The purpose of the ratio is to determine how well the assets of a business are employed regardless of how the assets were financed. Thus, interest expense is added back to net income.

Second, the denominator is average total assets, rather than assets at the end of the year, because net income accrues over the entire year, and thus it would not be accurate to relate that figure to assets at one point in time. For this reason an average is used in the denominator. The more exact the average the better. However, for most purposes a two-point average calculated as follows is sufficient:

$$\frac{\text{Asset balance at beginning of year} + \text{Asset balance at end of year}}{2}$$

An average such as this should be used whenever an income statement figure is used in the numerator of a ratio and a balance sheet figure is used in the denominator.

The return on total assets for Safeway Stores, Inc. for 1985 and 1984 is calculated as follows:

	(in thousands)	
	1985	1984
Net income	$ 231,300	$ 185,011
Interest expense	172,906	151,263
Income before interest expense	$ 404,206	$ 336,274
Total assets, beginning of year	$4,537,229	$4,174,363
Total assets, end of year	$4,840,611	4,537,229
Average total assets	$4,688,920	$4,355,796
Return on total assets	8.62%	7.72%

Again, in order to properly evaluate these ratios they must be compared with those of other firms in the retail grocery industry. For example, for grocery firms of similar size, the average industry return on total assets is 6.4%.

Components of Return on Total Assets. Return on total assets is a summary ratio. Du Pont developed a system of financial control that broke this ratio down to its various components. As the diagram below illustrates, the two major components are the profit margin percentage and asset turnover ratio. When these two ratios are multiplied together, the result is return on total assets.

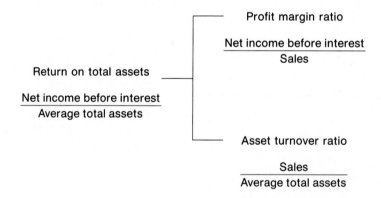

The profit margin percentage and asset turnover ratio for Safeway Stores for 1985 are calculated at the top of the next page.[2]

These ratios indicate that Safeway is a low-profit-margin, high-turnover business. That is, Safeway makes a profit before interest of about 2.06% which is a fairly low figure on an economy-wide basis. Therefore, in order to generate substantial profits Safeway must efficiently utilize its assets to generate billions in sales. Thus, it must have a fairly high asset turnover ratio. Safeway's overall

[2]For purposes of this example, we calculated the profit margin percentage using income before interest. Traditionally, however, net income is used to calculate this percentage, and this is the way in which it is calculated later in this chapter.

858

	(in thousands) 1985
Profit margin percentage (based on income before interest):	
Net income before interest	$ 404,206
Sales	19,650,542
Profit margin percentage	2.06%
Asset turnover ratio:	
Sales	$19,650,542
Average total assets	4,688,920
Asset turnover ratio	4.19%
Return on total assets: 8.63% = 2.06% × 4.19 (.01 difference due to rounding)	

return on total assets can be increased by increasing either or both of these ratios.

Return on Common Stockholders' Equity

A primary concern to common shareholders is the return that is generated to them. The return on common stockholders' equity is a ratio that measures the return generated to common stockholders for each dollar they have invested. Because of interest payments to creditors and dividend payments to preferred shareholders, this ratio is likely to be different from the return on total assets. The return on common stockholders' equity is calculated as follows:

$$\frac{\text{Net income less preferred dividend requirements}}{\text{Average common stockholders' equity}} \times 100$$

Because this ratio measures the return to common stockholders, preferred dividend requirements are subtracted from net income. Since interest expense has already been subtracted from net income, the numerator of this ratio represents a figure that is net of all distributions to creditors and preferred stockholders. Thus, it is the income available to common stockholders. The denominator, common stockholders' equity, is total stockholders' equity less any capital accounts related to preferred stockholders.

Because Safeway has no preferred stock, the calculation of this ratio is straightforward:

	(in thousands)	
	1985	1984
Net income	$ 231,300	$ 185,011
Common stockholders' equity, beginning of year	$1,469,023	$1,390,354
Common stockholders' equity, end of year	1,622,614	1,469,023
Average common stockholders' equity	$1,545,819	$1,429,689
Return on common stockholders' equity	14.96%	12.94%

Leverage

Leverage (often called trading on equity) refers to the amount of resources raised by borrowing or by issuing preferred stock. Highly leveraged companies have a greater proportion of their assets financed through debt and preferred stock than do companies that are less leveraged. The degree of leverage affects the relationship between the return on total assets and the return on common stockholders' equity.

To illustrate the concept of leverage, let's compare the return on total assets and return on common stockholders' equity for Safeway:

	1985	1984
Return on total assets	8.62%	7.72%
Return on common stockholders' equity	14.96%	12.94%

In both cases the return on common stockholders' equity is greater than the return on total assets. This is the result of the effective use of leverage which is caused by the fact that funds raised by borrowings or through the issuance of preferred stock earn a greater return than the required payment to creditors or preferred stockholders. That is, if a firm can borrow funds at 10% and earn a return of 12% on these funds, the common stockholder will benefit; once the creditor is paid the required interest, the differential between the interest rate and the rate of return earned on these funds accrues to the common shareholder.

However, leverage can be dangerous. If the interest rate on borrowed funds or the dividend rate on preferred stock exceeds the rate of return the company can earn on these funds, the return to common stockholders will be below the return on total assets. In the early 1980s this happened often. Many firms had loans tied to the prime rate of interest. When this rate reached 20%, the return on common stockholders' equity began to decline as firms were unable to earn a rate of return on these funds anywhere near 20%.

The Equity Ratio

The equity ratio is a measure of the amount of leverage used by a particular firm. This ratio is calculated as follows:

$$\text{Equity ratio} = \frac{\text{Total stockholders' equity}}{\text{Total assets}} \times 100$$

This ratio measures the proportion of assets supplied by the stockholders versus the proportion supplied by the creditors. The lower this ratio is, the higher is the degree of leverage. Because the total assets of a particular firm must be supplied by the stockholders and creditors, 100% minus the equity ratio produces the debt ratio. This ratio measures the amount of assets supplied by the creditors and can be calculated independently as follows:

$$\text{Debt ratio} = \frac{\text{Total liabilities}}{\text{Total assets}} \times 100$$

The equity and debt ratios for Safeway follow:

	(in thousands)	
	1985	1984
Total liabilities	$3,217,997	$3,068,206
Total stockholders' equity	1,622,614	1,469,023
Total assets	$4,840,611	$4,537,229
Equity ratio	33.52%	32.38%
Debt ratio	66.48%	67.62%

Thus, in Safeway's case about two-thirds of the assets are supplied by creditors and one-third by stockholders.

In summary, the degree of leverage is an important financial decision of the corporate management. The judicious use of leverage can lead to increased returns to common stockholders. However, as we noted, too much debt, especially in a period of rising interest rates, can lead to decreased returns to common stockholders and ultimately to bankruptcy. Because of these factors the relationship between the return on total assets and return on common stockholders' equity is closely watched by financial analysts.

Income Statement Analysis

Stockholders as well as the management of a firm are particularly interested in certain income and expense relationships. These relationships, derived through vertical analysis, were discussed previously. However, the most important of these from the stockholders' perspective is the profit margin percentage. This statistic measures percentage of each sales or revenue dollar that results in net income, and it varies widely among industries. The profit margin percentage, calculated by dividing net income by total revenues, for Safeway is:

	(in thousands)	
	1985	1984
Net income	$ 231,300	$ 185,011
Total sales	$19,650,542	$19,642,201
Profit margin percentage	1.18%	0.94%

As these percentages indicate, each dollar of sales results in a little more than one cent of net income. The low margin is common in the retail grocery industry. For comparison, the profit margin percentage of McDonald's was almost 11% in 1985.

Evaluation of Market Risk

Investors are interested in determining the relative risk of their current and potential investments. They demand a higher rate of return for riskier investments. In addition, information about the riskiness of stocks is useful to investors in forming portfolios. Recently, financial analysts have begun to use a measure of risk that relates the volatility of the price of a specific stock in relation to the volatility of the prices of other stocks. This measure is called **Beta** (β) and is determined through multiple regression analysis. The stock-market as a whole is considered to have a Beta of 1. Thus the price of stocks with a Beta of higher than 1 are more volatile than the market as a whole while those with a Beta of less than 1 are less volatile.

Although we will not attempt to calculate the Beta for Safeway, it is available from the investment advisory services previously discussed. At the end of 1985 the Beta for Safeway was .80.

Summary

The common and preferred stockholders have a long-term equity interest in the firm. As a result, they are interested in practically all aspects of the firm's operations. However, they are keenly interested in ratios that focus on such measures as return on investment, EPS, the P-E ratio, and return on stockholders' equity. Many of these ratios are calculated by the firm and are presented in its annual report.

Long-term Creditors

During their evaluation of a company, present and potential long-term creditors are particularly interested in the risk of the company, its ability to repay interest on its debt, and finally its ability to repay the principal of its debt. Although they are interested in profitability of the company, this is so only to the extent that it affects the ability of the company to make timely interest and principal payments. This is true because very few loan agreements call for the creditor to share in the profits of the firm beyond receiving interest payments.

The Debt Ratio

As we noted previously, the debt ratio measures the relative proportion of assets contributed by the shareholders and the creditors. All else being equal, the higher the debt ratio is, the less likely it is that a creditor would lend additional funds to the company. This is so because a highly leveraged company is riskier to a potential creditor than is a less leveraged firm. Clearly the creditor's margin of protection decreases as the total debt of a firm increases.

The Debt-Equity Ratio

The debt-equity ratio is another ratio that measures the balance of funds being provided by creditors and stockholders. This ratio is calculated by dividing total liabilities by total stockholders' equity. Clearly the higher the debt-equity ratio is, the more debt the company has, and all else being equal the riskier it is. The debt-equity ratio for Safeway is:

	(in thousands)	
	1985	1984
Total liabilities	$3,217,997	$3,068,206
Total stockholders' equity	1,622,614	1,469,023
Debt-equity ratio	1.98	2.09

These ratios appear to be high considering that the industry average for large retail grocery firms is about 1.6.

Times Interest Earned

Creditors like to have an indication of the ability of the company to meet the required interest payments. Times interest earned is the ratio of the income that is available for interest payments to the annual interest expense. The computation of times interest earned is as follows:

$$\text{Times interest earned} = \frac{\text{Income before interest and taxes (operating profit)}}{\text{Annual interest expense}}$$

Safeway's times interest earned ratios for 1985 and 1984 are 2.47 and 2.80, respectively. The calculation of these figures is as follows:

	(in thousands)	
	1985	1984
Operating profit	$427,660	$423,211
Interest expense	$172,906	$151,263
Times interest earned	2.47	2.80

These figures are not particularly high, but they are satisfactory. The decline in this ratio in 1985 was the result of a larger percentage increase in interest expense than in operating profit.

It is important to keep in mind that the times interest earned ratio does not directly measure the cash available to make the required interest payments. Operating profits are not totally equivalent to cash flows from operations. For this reason bankers and other creditors often ask the firm to provide additional cash flow information.

Summary

Long-term creditors provide substantial capital to many businesses. In evaluating the credit decisions, these individuals are primarily concerned with the ability of the firm to meet its interest and principal payments. Thus long-term creditors tend to focus on such ratios as the debt ratio and times interest earned.

Short-term Creditors

Short-term creditors, as well as long-term creditors, are interested in all aspects of the company. However, their interest lies primarily in measuring the ability of the company to meet its short-term commitments. Thus, short-term creditors are interested in such items as liquidity and working capital. The ratios that are most often calculated are the current ratio, the quick ratio, inventory turnover and receivable turnover.

The Current Ratio

The current ratio, which is determined by dividing current assets by current liabilities, is one of the most common measures of liquidity and the ability of the company to meet its short-term debt. The current ratio of Safeway for 1985 and 1984 is:

	(in thousands)	
	1985	1984
Current assets	$2,026,481	$1,861,389
Current liabilities	$1,724,701	$1,535,957
Current ratio	1.17:1	1.21:1

The ratio for these two years is a little lower than the industry average of about 1.4:1.

The current ratio, like all ratios, is significantly affected by the generally accepted accounting principles a firm uses. For example, because Safeway used LIFO to cost a large portion of its inventories, the current ratio was less than if FIFO had been used.

The Quick Ratio

Inventories generally represent a large portion of a firm's current assets. Inventories are not really liquid in that management cannot turn them into cash at its discretion. Thus, the current ratio can overstate the liquidity of the company and its ability to meet its obligations. The quick ratio overcomes this limitation of the current ratio by comparing only cash, marketable securities, and receivables to current liabilities. Marketable securities and receivables are included because management can quickly turn them into cash, if necessary.

For illustrative purposes we calculate these ratios for Safeway as follows:

	(in thousands)	
	1985	1984
Cash	$ 54,593	$ 49,179
Short-term investments	170,021	25,263
Receivables	111,870	105,166
Total	$ 336,484	$ 179,608
Current liabilities	$1,724,701	$1,535,957
Quick ratio	0.20:1	0.12:1

However, these figures are very misleading and illustrate some of the dangers of using ratios that are inappropriate for a particular firm or industry. The retail grocery business is a cash-and-carry business. Inventories are very liquid because of the speed in which they turn over. Thus, in this case, the current ratio is a better measure of liquidity than is the quick ratio. Obviously, there are many cases in which the quick ratio is a good measure of liquidity.

Inventory Turnover

Inventory turnover measures how quickly the inventory moves. This is an important ratio for firms such as Safeway that have significant amounts of inventory. However, the inventory turnover ratio would be meaningless when analyzing an airline. The inventory turnover ratio is calculated as follows:

$$\text{Inventory turnover} = \frac{\text{Cost of goods sold}}{\text{Average inventories}}$$

If possible, average inventories should be figured by dividing the total of inventories at the end of each month by 12, because many firms choose a year-end at a point that their inventories are at a yearly low. Thus a simple two-point average using the inventories at the beginning and end of the year can be misleading. However, inventory levels at the end of each month are often not available, and as a result the simpler two-point average is often used.

The inventory turnover ratio for Safeway is:

	(in thousands)	
	1985	1984
Cost of goods sold	$14,872,247	$15,004,547
Inventories, beginning of year	1,563,244	1,433,254
Inventories, end of year	1,565,566	1,563,244
Average inventories	1,564,405	1,498,249
Inventory turnover	9.51	10.01

As you would expect, the inventory turnover is very high. Merchandise moves very quickly in a retail grocery store. However, you should keep in mind that use of LIFO increases the inventory turnover because cost of goods sold is higher and inventories are lower than if other methods were used.

Another way to express the inventory turnover is to determine the average number of days needed to turn the inventory over. This is easily calculated by dividing the inventory turnover into 365 days. Thus, in 1985 it took Safeway about 38 days to turn over its inventories ($365 \div 9.501 = 38.4$).

Accounts Receivable Turnover

For most companies the accounts receivable turnover ratio is very important. This ratio, calculated in the same manner as the inventory turnover ratio, measures how quickly the firm is converting its accounts receivable into cash. In a cash-tight economy, a primary task of management is to quickly turn its accounts receivable into cash and thus improve its cash from operations.

The accounts receivable turnover ratio is calculated as follows:

$$\text{Accounts receivable turnover} = \frac{\text{Net credit sales}}{\text{Average accounts receivable}}$$

We will not calculate this ratio for Safeway because it would be clearly inappropriate to do so. All of Safeway's sales are for cash and the receivables result from other minor activities and from amounts due from bad checks from customers.

To illustrate how this ratio is calculated, assume the following data from the Steamer Corporation:

	1985	1984
Net credit sales	$1,200,000	$1,500,000
Accounts receivable, beginning of year	140,000	175,000
Accounts receivable, end of year	160,000	140,000
Average accounts receivable	150,000	157,500
Accounts receivable turnover	8.0	9.52

The average age of the receivables can be determined by dividing the turnover into 365 days. For the Steamer Corporation the average ages of the receivables are 45.63 and 38.34 days for 1985 and 1984, respectively. In this example, the length of time needed to collect receivables has increased. This is a dangerous trend because it means the inflow of cash into the company has slowed. Thus, it is important for the firm's management to review its credit and operating policies and to try to reverse this trend.

Summary

Short-term creditors provide cash or services to the firm on a short-term basis. As a result, they are primarily interested in the liquidity of the firm and its ability to meet its short-term obligations. Thus, these individuals focus on such ratios as the current ratio, the quick ratio, and various turnover ratios.

Ratio Analysis—A Summary

Exhibit 21–5 lists and describes the ratios that have been discussed in this chapter. You should keep in mind the limitations of financial statement analysis discussed next.

Limitations of Financial Statement Analysis

Before we end our discussion of the techniques of financial statement analysis, it is important to understand the limitations of such analysis and how these limitations can be partially overcome. Naive financial statements users, who do not fully understand the limitations of financial statement analysis, are likely to make substantive judgment errors. Two problems involved in such analysis are (1) that firms use different accounting principles and methods and (2) that it is often difficult to adequately define what industry a firm is really a part of.

Differences in Generally Accepted Accounting Principles

A firm's management has the right to select among a set of generally accepted accounting principles and methods. As a result, even firms in the same indus-

EXHIBIT 21–5
Summary of Significant Ratios

Ratio	Calculation	Significance
Common and Preferred Stockholders		
Earnings per share	$\dfrac{\text{Net income less preferred dividend}}{\text{Average number of common shares outstanding}}$	Comparative figure of earnings on a per-share basis
Price-earnings	$\dfrac{\text{Market price per common share}}{\text{Earnings per share}}$	Comparative measure of how the market values earnings of firm
Dividend yield	$\dfrac{\text{Dividends per share}}{\text{Market price per share}} \times 100$	Measures dividend return to investors
Book value per share	$\dfrac{\text{Common stockholders' equity}}{\text{Number of common shares outstanding}}$	Investors' share of assets at historical cost
Return on total assets	$\dfrac{\text{Net income} + \text{interest expense}}{\text{Average total assets}} \times 100$	Measures profitability of firm and how efficiently assets are employed
Return on common stockholders' equity	$\dfrac{\text{Net income} - \text{preferred dividend}}{\text{Average common stockholders' equity}} \times 100$	Measures profitability of investment to owners
Equity ratio	$\dfrac{\text{Total stockholders' equity}}{\text{Total assets}} \times 100$	Measures proportion of assets supplied by creditors and owners
Debt ratio	$\dfrac{\text{Total liabilities}}{\text{Total assets}} \times 100$	Same as previous ratio
Profit margin	$\dfrac{\text{Net income}}{\text{Total revenues}} \times 100$	Net income per dollar of revenue
Long-term Creditors		
Debt-equity	$\dfrac{\text{Total liabilities}}{\text{Total stockholders' equity}}$	Another measure of debt versus equity financing
Times interest earned	$\dfrac{\text{Income before interest and taxes}}{\text{Interest expense}}$	Ability of firm to meet interest payments
Short-term Creditors		
Current ratio	$\dfrac{\text{Current assets}}{\text{Current liabilities}}$	Measures short-term liquidity of firm
Quick ratio	$\dfrac{\text{Monetary current assets}}{\text{Current liabilities}}$	Measures ability of firm to meet immediate debt
Inventory turnover	$\dfrac{\text{Cost of goods sold}}{\text{Average inventories}}$	Measures amount of inventory carried and how quickly it moves
Receivables turnover	$\dfrac{\text{Net credit sales}}{\text{Average accounts receivable}}$	Measures amount of accounts receivable relative to sales and how quickly collected

try select different methods to account for the same event. For example, one firm in the steel industry may use LIFO while another may use FIFO. Obviously the financial statements of these two firms, as well as key ratios and relationships based on these statements, will be significantly different. This makes the direct comparison of firms within the same industry difficult.

Careful reading of management's discussion and analysis of opera-

Interpreting Financial Statement Data 867

tions and the footnotes to the financial statements can partially overcome this problem.

For example, as we noted, Safeway primarily uses the LIFO inventory method, but management's discussion and analysis of operations provides the following information about how the inventories would be stated if FIFO were used:

> Had the company valued its inventories using the FIFO method, its current ratio would have been 1.36, 1.42, and 1.35, and working capital would have been $614.5 million, $643.7 million, and $519.9 million at year-ends 1985, 1984, and 1983 respectively.

Thus, financial statement analysts can use this data to compare Safeway's performance with those companies in the retail grocery industry that use FIFO or vice versa.

The footnotes to the financial statements also provide important information concerning the use of accounting principles. Current reporting rules require that a footnote to the financial statement summarize the significant accounting policies used by the company. This is usually the first item in the footnote section (see Footnote A in Safeway's financial statements reproduced in Appendix A for an example) and provides such information about the firm as its basis of consolidation, translation of foreign currencies, and depreciation methods. A sophisticated financial analyst can use this data to make the necessary transformations that allow for meaningful comparisons among firms using different accounting methods.

The Industry a Firm Is In

Using industry norms as a basis for financial statement analysis presupposes being able to define what industry a firm actually is a part of. For some companies such as Safeway or Apple Computer, this is an easy process because they both operate in well-defined industries. However, many U.S. companies are truly conglomerates and operate in a variety of industries. For example, what industry is ITT in, or what industry is U.S. Steel in now that it owns a large oil subsidiary? This question is difficult to answer because both firms are diversified companies that operate in many industries of different natures.

Early in its existence, the Financial Accounting Standards Board recognized this problem and issued Statement 14. This Statement requires that firms disclose certain operating and financial data by industry segments and, where appropriate, by geographical location. Essentially, the Statement requires diversified companies to report revenue, income from operations, and identifiable assets for each operating segment as well as similar information by geographical area. Exhibit 21–6 shows a partial illustration of how Sears, Roebuck and Co. discloses segment information.

Accounting Problems Related to Multinational Corporations

Since World War II there has been an unprecedented growth in the number of U.S. corporations doing business abroad. These foreign operations range from occasional import/export activities to the establishment of worldwide production and sales activities. In fact, many of the largest U.S. corporations can

EXHIBIT 21-6
Sears, Roebuck and Co.
Five-Year Summary of Business Group and Segment Financial Data

Following is a five-year summary of pertinent business group data, which is derived from the accompanying statements and includes a further refinement by industry segments. Corporate operations include revenues and expenses which are of an overall holding company nature including that portion of administrative costs and interest which is not allocated to the groups. Corporate assets are principally intercompany receivables, Sears Tower, cash, and invested cash.

millions

Revenues	1985	1984	1983	1982	1981
Sears Merchandise Group					
Merchandising	$21,549	$21,671	$20,439	$18,779	$18,229
Credit	2,098	1,894	1,404	1,158	1,040
International	2,905	2,943	3,246	730	933
Sears Merchandise Group total	26,552	26,508	25,089	20,667	20,202
Allstate Insurance Group					
Property-liability insurance	8,244	7,551	7,004	6,487	5,970
Life-health insurance	2,089	1,404	1,079	930	737
Non-insurance operations	46	34	41	42	37
Allstate Insurance Group total	10,379	8,989	8,124	7,459	6,744
Dean Witter Financial Services Group					
Securities-related operations	2,031	1,845	1,544	1,110	—
Consumer banking operations	826	651	564	487	451
Dean Witter Financial Services Group total	2,857	2,496	2,108	1,597	451
Coldwell Banker Real Estate Group	949	826	704	470	110
Sears World Trade, Inc.	236	189	79	—	—
Corporate	188	170	117	120	105
Inter-group transactions	(446)	(350)	(338)	(293)	(225)
Total	$40,715	$38,828	$35,883	$30,020	$27,357

be classified as multinational or transnational organizations. For example, in 1985 over 43% of IBM's revenues and over 47% of its net income came from non-U.S. sources.

Multinational corporations face a number of accounting problems that increase the complexity of their financial statements. The two issues that have caused the most controversy are accounting for foreign currency transactions and translating foreign currency statements to U.S. dollar statements. These issues, as well as attempts at the harmonization of international accounting standards, are discussed in this part of the chapter.

Exchange Rates

Accounting for both foreign currency transactions and foreign currency financial statements involves the need to translate the currency of one country into that of another. Because we are dealing with U.S. firms doing business abroad, we are concerned with translating foreign currencies into U.S. dollars. Translation is accomplished by applying an **exchange rate** (the rate at which one currency can be exchanged for another) to the foreign currency that is to be translated into U.S. dollars. For example, assume that an individual has 5,000 British pounds and wishes to exchange them for U.S. dollars. If the current exchange rate is £1.00 = $1.20, the individual would receive $6,000, or £5,000 × 1.20.

Exchange rates change daily depending on the supply and demand for particular currencies. This supply and demand are affected by inflation rates, interest rates, and other factors in individual countries. The following table expresses several foreign currencies in U.S. dollars as of April 5, 1985, and October 2, 1986:

Country	U.S. Dollar Equivalent	
	April 5, 1985	October 2, 1986
British pound	$1.23	$1.45
Canadian dollar	.73	.72
West German mark	.32	.49
Japanese yen	.0040	.0065

As we will see, accounting for foreign currency transactions and foreign currency financial statements is complicated by the fact that currency values continuously change and, as shown above, these changes can be quite significant. In this example, the U.S. dollar declined against the British pound, West German mark, and Japanese yen.

Accounting for Foreign Currency Transactions

When a U.S. firm buys and sells its goods and services abroad, it can do business in either U.S. dollars or a foreign currency. If the transaction is carried out in U.S. dollars (and U.S. dollars are received in payment or made in payment), no accounting problems arise. The entire transaction is recorded in U.S. dollars at the time of sale or purchase. For example, assume that the Kwon International Co. sells 100 computers to Mishka, Ltd., a West German company. Each computer is sold for $1,000 and payment is to be made in U.S. dollars. The journal entries to record the sale and the subsequent cash collection are:

Accounts Receivable, Mishka, Ltd.	100,000	
Sales		100,000
To record sale of 100 computers at $1,000 each, payable in U.S. dollars.		
Cash	100,000	
Accounts Receivable, Mishka, Ltd.		100,000
To record collection from Mishka, Ltd.		

Foreign purchases payable in U.S. dollars are treated in a similar manner. That means the purchase and the payable are recorded at the agreed-on U.S. price and dollars. When the subsequent payment is made in U.S. dollars, Accounts Payable is debited and Cash is credited.

In many cases, however, the transaction is denominated in the foreign currency. That is, a U.S. firm makes a sale to an overseas firm and agrees to accept payment in the foreign currency. Conversely, a purchase is made from an overseas firm and payment must be made in the foreign currency. These are examples of **foreign currency transactions.** In this situation an exchange gain or loss will occur if the exchange rate changes between the time the sale or purchase is made and the receivable or payable is settled in the foreign currency. This gain or loss must be recorded in the financial statements of the U.S. company making the sale or purchase. Further, if the transaction has not been completed at a balance sheet date, the firm must record an unrealized gain or loss on any changes in currency values.

To illustrate, assume that the Imke Company purchases £200,000 of goods on April 2 from its major British supplier. Payment in British pounds is due July 10. The firm prepares quarterly financial statements on June 30. The following exchange rates apply:

	U.S. dollars per British pound	Event
April 2	$1.25	Purchase
June 30	1.22	Financial statements prepared
July 10	1.23	Payment on account

On April 2 the Imke Company records the purchase and the account payable in the U.S. dollar equivalent of $250,000, or £200,000 × $1.25. The following entry is made:

Purchases	250,000	
Accounts Payable		250,000
To record purchase of goods at		
current exchange rate of $1.25.		

On June 30 the firm prepares its quarterly financial statements. Because the transaction is still open, the Imke Company must account for changes in exchange rates since the transaction was first recorded. In this case the British pound decreased in value and is now worth only $1.22. If the Imke Company had to settle the contract on June 30 it would have to pay only $244,000, or £200,000 × $1.22. As a result, the firm must record an exchange gain of $6,000, or £200,000 × ($1.25 − $1.22). To record the exchange gain, the payable is adjusted downward. However, the Purchases account is not adjusted. The credit is recorded in a separate income account, Exchange Gains and Losses. As a result, the following journal entry is made at June 30:

Accounts Payable	6,000	
Exchange Gains and Losses		6,000
To adjust liability account to current		
exchange rate of $1.22.		

Interpreting Financial Statement Data

On July 10 the Imke Company settles its liability by making a payment to its British supplier in British pounds. However, in the interim since June 30 the pound has increased in value. On July 10 the pound is currently worth $1.23, an increase of $.01. In order to satisfy this liability the firm will need $246,000, or £200,000 × $1.23. However, the liability had been reduced to $244,000 or $250,000 less the debit of $6,000 on June 30. As a result, the firm has suffered a $2,000 exchange loss in the period June 30 to July 10. The following journal entry is made to record this loss:

Accounts Payable	244,000	
Exchange Gains and Losses	2,000	
Cash		246,000
To settle liability on July 10 and record exchange loss.		

The result of all these transactions is to record a purchase of $250,000 and a net exchange gain of $4,000, or $6,000 exchange gain less the $2,000 exchange loss. Many firms believe that the unrealized gain on June 30 should not be recorded. They feel that in many cases large currency fluctuations can distort quarterly earnings even though by the end of the year transaction gains and losses may net out to a rather immaterial figure. However, others note that recording these transactions at their current exchange rates better reflects economic reality.

Accounting for sales denominated in a foreign currency follows the same pattern. However, Accounts Receivable and Sales are involved rather than Accounts Payable and Purchases.

Foreign Currency Translation

Financial statements prepared by U.S. multinationals for distribution in the United States must be prepared according to U.S. generally accepted accounting principles and must be denominated in U.S. dollars. U.S. multinational firms conduct their business in many countries, and often the host country's currency is used as a basis for the operations in that country. For example, a French subsidiary of a U.S. firm is likely to keep its books in French francs. When this subsidiary and others in different countries are combined in the preparation of consolidated financial statements, all currencies must be translated to U.S. dollars.

Foreign currency translation means that one currency is restated in terms of another currency. For example, assume that the Land account on the French subsidiary's books is recorded at 1 million French francs. When these statements are consolidated, the Land account must be restated to U.S. dollars. Assuming that the appropriate exchange rate is one French franc equals $.10, the land would be shown at $100,000, or F1,000,000 × $.10.

There has been considerable controversy as to what exchange rates should be used and how the resulting accounting gain or loss from changes in exchange rates should be handled. In 1981 the FASB issued Statement 52, which requires a dual approach. For foreign subsidiaries whose operations are fairly well self-contained in the host country and conduct most of their operations in the foreign currency, the FASB requires that all balance sheet items be translated at the current exchange rate at the date of the financial statements. Income statement items are translated at the average exchange rate for the period. This is referred to as the **current rate method.** Further, any resulting exchange gains and losses from statement translation can be accumulated in a special stockholders' equity account, thus bypassing the income statement. You should note, however, that gains and losses from foreign currency transactions are still shown on the income statement.

Some foreign subsidiaries are really just an extension of the parent company's operations. Most of their operations are conducted in U.S. dollars. For these companies the FASB requires a different translation method. Monetary assets and liabilities are translated at current rates, while nonmonetary assets and liabilities are translated at rates when the particular item was acquired. Income statement items are translated at the average exchange rate for the period. This is called the **temporal method.** In contrast to the translation method previously described, translation gains and losses on translating the subsidiary's statements go directly to the income statement.

Foreign Currency Translation Example

Because the first method is the most prevalent, we provide a brief illustration showing how foreign currency statements are translated when a subsidiary is a self-contained unit operating in the host country and does most of its business in the host country's currency. Thus, the current rate method is used.

The Michele Corporation is a 100% owned French subsidiary of Dumfies, Inc., a U.S. multinational. Exhibit 21–7 (on the following page) presents a worksheet translating Michele Corporation's financial statement from French francs to U.S. dollars. At year-end one French franc equaled $.10, and the average for the year was $.12. When the subsidiary was formed and the stock issued the exchange rate was $.25.

As shown on the worksheet, all balance sheet accounts other than common stock and retained earnings are translated at the exchange rate in effect on December 31. Retained earnings cannot be translated because it represents many items that have been translated in the past at several different rates. We are assuming that the retained earnings at January 1 in U.S. dollars are $36,600. When the income of $8,400 is added to the beginning balance of $36,600, the ending retained balance of $45,000 is obtained. This example assumes that no dividends have been declared.

The cumulative translation adjustment is a debit of $27,500 and is the amount needed to make the liabilities and stockholders' equity equal the total assets. It is a cumulative figure that represents the net translation gains and losses from all previous periods as well as the current period.

Interpreting Cumulative Translation Gains and Losses

Translation gains and losses occur when exchange rates fluctuate. In 1983 and 1984 the dollar appreciated against many currencies, or conversely foreign currency devalued against the dollar. However, in 1985 the dollar began to depreciate against most major currencies. When this occurs firms are likely to incur a translation loss.

For example, in its 1985 annual report IBM reported the following:

IBM

> Non-U.S. subsidiaries which operate in a local currency environment account for approximately 85% of the company's non-U.S. gross income. The remaining 15% of the company's non-U.S. gross income is from subsidiaries and branches which operate in U.S. dollars or whose economic environment is highly inflationary.
>
> The dollar, which had continued to strengthen during 1983 and 1984, began to weaken in 1985. However, for the full year 1985, IBM's gross income was still adversely affected by currency rates.

EXHIBIT 21-7
Worksheet

Dumfies, Inc.

December 31, 1987

Accounts	French Francs	Exchange Rate	U.S. Dollars
Balance Sheet			
Cash	50,000	.10	5,000
Accounts receivable, net	125,000	.10	12,500
Inventory	100,000	.10	10,000
Building, net	200,000	.10	20,000
Land	50,000	.10	5,000
Total assets	525,000		52,500
Accounts payable	35,000	.10	3,500
Notes payable	65,000	.10	6,500
Common stock	100,000	.25	25,000
Retained earnings	325,000		45,000
Cumulative translation adjustment			(27,500)
Total liabilities and stockholders' equity	525,000		52,500
Income Statement			
Sales	700,000	.12	84,000
Cost of goods sold	500,000	.12	60,000
Selling expenses	80,000	.12	9,600
General and administrative expenses	50,000	.12	6,000
Total expenses	630,000		75,600
Net income	70,000		8,400

The magnitude of these cumulative translation adjustments can be great. At December 31, 1985 IBM's cumulative translation adjustment was a debit item in stockholders' equity amounting to over $1.4 billion.

International Accounting Standards

Throughout this book we have noted that accounting concepts in a particular country are related to that country's social, political, and economic systems. As a result, there are significant differences between accounting concepts in the United States and those in other countries. However, present and potential investors and creditors need to compare firms that are based in various countries. Sophisticated individuals often invest in securities of non-U.S. firms. However, differences in accounting practices make it difficult to compare the results of operations and the financial position of a firm that follows U.S. generally accepted accounting principles with one that follows accounting principles of another country.

To overcome these problems the international accounting community has attempted to harmonize accounting standards. Harmonization, however, does not imply standardization. Harmonization allows different accounting information to be communicated to various users, while standardization implies the communication of the same information in the same manner to all users. In a broad sense, harmonization makes it possible to have compatible reporting standards between countries without requiring all countries to adopt the same standards.

Over the last 50 years several international groups have looked at the issue of harmonization of accounting standards. The charge of the **International Accounting Standards Committee (IASC),** created in 1973, is to develop basic accounting standards and to promote the worldwide acceptance and observance of these standards. Following a procedure similar to that of the FASB, the IASC issues international accounting standards. As of mid-1985, the IASC had issued 24 standards.

The IASC has had only an indirect effect on the external reporting practices of U.S. multinationals. The AICPA, for example, has pledged its best efforts to gain acceptance of IASC standards. Yet the FASB, not the AICPA, sets U.S. accounting standards, and this body has done little to harmonize its standards with those of the IASC. U.S. firms are bound by FASB and not IASC standards and are not presently required to disclose whatever differences exist between these two sets of standards. However, it should be noted that there are not many significant differences between the two sets of standards.

In 1976 the **International Federation of Accountants (IFAC)** was formed. Accounting bodies in various countries are eligible for membership in the IFAC. The broad objective of the IFAC is the development and enhancement of a coordinated worldwide accounting profession with harmonized standards. The IFAC is essentially a coordinating body of professional accounting organizations and does not have the responsibility for setting international accounting standards.

The ultimate benefit of accounting harmonization to present and potential investors and multinational firms depends to a large extent on the type of standards that eventually evolve. If these standards are broad in nature and help to improve international disclosures, they can improve the accounting practices of multinational firms. However, if international standards evolve as detailed principles that are in conflict with many national requirements, they will not meet with acceptance. The current efforts appear to be taking the former approach and thus can serve as an integrating force in world business.

Summary of Learning Objectives

1. *Understanding the purposes of financial statement analysis.* Present and potential investors and creditors are the primary external users of financial statement information. Financial statement analysis helps these users as well as others to assess the past performance of a firm and to assess its future prospects.

2. *Sources of financial information.* There are a variety of sources of information about public companies. All public companies publish an annual report to shareholders and in addition prepare several reports to the SEC. The SEC reports include Forms 10-K, 10-Q, and 8-K. There are several external sources of information available to interested indi-

viduals. These include general business periodicals as well as specialized trade journals.

3. *Techniques of financial statement analysis.* The most common types of financial statement analyses include horizontal, trend, vertical, and ratio analysis. Horizontal and trend analyses are useful in understanding changes in the firm's financial position from year to year as well as changes over several years. Vertical analysis is used to evaluate the relationships within single financial statements. An appropriate total figure in the financial statement is set to 100%, and other items are expressed as a percentage of that figure. Finally, ratio analysis is a method of expressing relationships among various items on a set of financial statements.

4. *Common financial ratios.* There are a number of ratios that can be used by financial statement analysts. Groups with particular needs have developed their own ratios. However, there are certain ratios that are used by equity holders, such as common stockholders, long-term debt holders, and short-term debt holders. These ratios are summarized in Exhibit 21–5.

5. *Limitations of financial statement analysis.* Although financial statement analysis is very useful, it does have a number of limitations. Firms use different accounting principles, and as a result it is often difficult to compare the financial position and operations of different firms directly. Generally, the first footnote to the financial statements lists the accounting principles used in preparing the financial statements; thus, this footnote is very important to financial statement users.

Industry norms are often used in financial statement analysis. However, it is often difficult to determine exactly what industry a firm is part of. Again, the segment information contained in the footnotes to the firm's financial statements is helpful in assessing the different parts of the firm's operations.

6. *Accounting for foreign currency transactions.* Foreign currency transactions occur when a firm makes sales or purchases that are denominated in a foreign currency. These transactions are originally recorded in U.S. dollars based on the exchange rate at the date of the transaction. When the transaction is settled, or at a balance sheet date prior to settlement, the firm must recognize a gain or loss due to any changes in the exchange rate. These gains and losses go directly to the income statement.

7. *Accounting for foreign currency translation.* Statements of foreign subsidiaries of U.S. companies must be translated to U.S. dollars when consolidated with the U.S. parent. In most cases the current rate method is used, and thus balance sheet items are translated at the rate in effect at the balance sheet date and income statement items are translated at the average rate for the period. Resulting translation gains and losses do not affect current period's income but are a direct adjustment to stockholders' equity.

8. *The harmonization of accounting standards.* In recent years there has been an attempt by the international accounting profession to harmonize accounting standards. The two most important groups in this regard are

the International Accounting Standards Committee and the International Federation of Accountants.

Key Terms

Beta
Common Dollar Statements
Current Rate Method
Exchange Rate
Financial Statement Analysis
Foreign Currency
  Transactions
Foreign Currency Translation

Form 8-K
Form 10-K
Form 10-Q
Horizontal Analysis
International Accounting
  Standards Committee
  (IASC)
International Federation of

Accountants (IFAC)
Leverage
Ratio Analysis
Temporal Method
Trend Analysis
Vertical Analysis

Problems for Your Review

A. Interpreting Financial Statements. Presented below are the financial statements for the Valda Valdes Corporation:

Valda Valdes Corporation
Balance Sheet
December 31, 1987

Assets	1987	1986
Current assets		
Cash	$ 26,000	$ 13,500
Accounts receivable, net	75,000	53,000
Inventory	86,000	67,000
Total current assets	$187,000	$133,500
Property, plant, and equipment		
Land	$120,000	$120,000
Buildings, net	136,000	141,000
Equipment, net	15,200	14,600
Total property, plant, and equipment	$271,200	$275,600
Other assets	$ 25,800	$ 12,400
Total assets	$484,000	$421,500

Equities	1987	1986
Current liabilities		
Accounts payable	$ 68,000	$ 70,000
Current maturities of long-term debt	3,000	3,000
Wages payable	1,200	1,000
Taxes payable	10,000	8,000
Interest payable	22,800	12,500
Total current liabilities	$105,000	$ 94,500
Long-term liabilities		
Mortgage payable, less current portion above	$150,000	$153,000
Stockholders' equity		
No par common stock, 10,000 shares outstanding	$100,000	$100,000
Retained earnings	129,000	74,000
Total stockholders' equity	$229,000	$174,000
Total equities	$484,000	$421,500

Valda Valdes Corporation
Income Statement
For the Year Ended December 31, 1987

Sales		$1,200,000
Cost of goods sold		768,000
Gross margin on sales		432,000
Operating expenses		
Selling	$200,000	
General and administrative	100,000	300,000
Income before taxes		132,000
Income taxes		57,000
Net income		$ 75,000

Additional Information:

1. Dividends issued during the year amounted to $20,000.
2. Market price per share of common stock at year-end was $34.25.
3. Included in operating expenses is interest expense of $18,000.
4. Credit sales of the year amounted to $720,000.

Required:

Calculate the following ratios for 1987:

  a. Earnings per share.
  b. Price-earnings ratio.
  c. Dividend yield ratio.
  d. Book value per share.
  e. Return on total assets.
  f. Return on common stockholders' equity.
  g. Equity ratio.
  h. Debt ratio.
  i. Gross margin percentage.
  j. Profit margin percentage.
  k. Debt-equity ratio.
  l. Times interest earned.
  m. Current ratio.
  n. Quick ratio.
  o. Inventory turnover.
  p. Accounts receivable turnover.

Solution

a. Earnings per share

$$\text{EPS} = \frac{\text{Net income less preferred dividends, if any}}{\text{Weighted average number of common shares outstanding}}$$

$$\$7.50 = \frac{\$75,000}{10,000}$$

b. Price-earnings ratio

$$\text{P-E ratio} = \frac{\text{Market price per common share}}{\text{Earnings per share}}$$

$$4.57 = \frac{\$34.25}{\$7.50}$$

c. Dividend yield ratio

$$\text{Dividend yield} = \frac{\text{Dividends per share}}{\text{Market price per share}} \times 100$$

$$5.84\% = \frac{\$2.00^*}{\$34.25} \times 100$$

*$20,000 dividends ÷ 10,000 shares.

d. Book value per share

$$\text{Book value per share} = \frac{\text{Total common stockholders' equity}}{\text{Number of common shares outstanding}}$$

$$\$22.90 = \frac{\$229,000}{10,000}$$

e. Return on total assets

$$\text{Return on total assets} = \frac{\text{Net income plus interest expense}}{\text{Average total assets}} \times 100$$

$$20.54\% = \frac{\$75,000 + \$18,000}{(\$484,000 + \$421,500) \div 2} \times 100$$

f. Return on common stockholders' equity

$$\text{Return on common stockholders' equity} = \frac{\text{Net income less preferred dividends}}{\text{Average common stockholders' equity}} \times 100$$

$$37.22\% = \frac{\$75,000}{(\$229,000 + \$174,000) \div 2} \times 100$$

g. Equity ratio

$$\text{Equity ratio} = \frac{\text{Total stockholders' equity}}{\text{Total assets}} \times 100$$

$$47.31\% = \frac{\$229,000}{\$484,000} \times 100$$

h. Debt ratio

$$\text{Debt ratio} = \frac{\text{Total liabilities}}{\text{Total assets}} \times 100$$

$$52.69\% = \frac{\$255,000}{\$484,000} \times 100$$

i. Gross margin percentage

$$\text{Gross margin \%} = \frac{\text{Gross margin}}{\text{Sales}} \times 100$$

$$36\% = \frac{\$432,000}{\$1,200,000} \times 100$$

j. Profit margin percentage

$$\text{Profit margin \%} = \frac{\text{Net income}}{\text{Sales}} \times 100$$

$$6.25\% = \frac{\$75,000}{\$1,200,000} \times 100$$

k. Debt-equity ratio

$$\text{Debt-equity ratio} = \frac{\text{Total liabilities}}{\text{Total stockholders' equity}}$$

$$1.11 = \frac{\$255,000}{\$229,000}$$

l. Times interest earned

$$\text{Times interest earned} = \frac{\text{Income before interest and taxes}}{\text{Annual interest expense}}$$

$$8.33 = \frac{\$75,000 + \$18,000 + \$57,000}{\$18,000}$$

Interpreting Financial Statement Data   **879**

m. Current ratio

$$\text{Current ratio} = \frac{\text{Current assets}}{\text{Current liabilities}}$$

$$1.78 = \frac{\$187,000}{\$105,000}$$

n. Quick ratio

$$\text{Quick ratio} = \frac{\text{Cash} + \text{Marketable securities} + \text{Receivables}}{\text{Current liabilities}}$$

$$.96 = \frac{\$26,000 + 75,000}{\$105,000}$$

o. Inventory turnover

$$\text{Inventory turnover} = \frac{\text{Cost of goods sold}}{\text{Average inventory}}$$

$$10.04 = \frac{\$768,000}{(\$86,000 + \$67,000) \div 2}$$

$$\frac{\text{Average days to}}{\text{turn over inventory}} = \frac{365 \text{ days}}{10.04} = 36.4 \text{ days}$$

p. Accounts receivable turnover

$$\text{Accounts receivable turnover} = \frac{\text{Credit sales}}{\text{Average accounts receivable}}$$

$$11.25 = \frac{\$720,000}{(\$75,000 + \$53,000) \div 2}$$

$$\frac{\text{Average age of}}{\text{accounts receivable}} = \frac{365 \text{ days}}{11.25} = 32.4 \text{ days}$$

B. Foreign Currency Transactions. The All American Company purchased a laser from the Canada Co. for $100,000 Canadian. The purchase was made on September 21 when the exchange rate was $.75 per Canadian dollar. Payment was made on October 15 when the exchange rate was $.70 per Canadian dollar. No interim financial statements were prepared. Make the journal entries to record the purchase and payment of the laser. Record the laser in an equipment account.

Solution _____

September 21	Equipment	75,000	
	Accounts Payable		75,000
	To record purchase of equipment when exchange rate equaled $.75.		
	$100,000 Canadian $\times$ $.75 = $75,000.		
October 15	Accounts Payable	75,000	
	Exchange Gains and Losses		5,000
	Cash		70,000
	To record payment of $70,000 and exchange gain of $5,000.		

Accounts Payable
Cash payment required: $100,000 Canadian $\times$ $.70

Exchange gain: $75,000
                      70,000
                  $ 5,000

Questions

1. Who are the primary users of financial statements? How do they use financial statements, and for what purposes do they use financial statement analysis?

2. How can financial statement users assess the past performance of a firm as well as its future prospects?

3. List and explain the primary reports that are published by publicly held companies.

4. What are the main sections found in most annual reports? Which do you think are most useful?

5. Financial analysts use a number of external sources in evaluating a firm. List and discuss the primary ones.

6. The facts that firms use different generally accepted accounting principles and that it is often difficult to define what industry a firm is part of are often cited as causing limitations in financial statement analysis. Do you agree or not? How can these potential problems be overcome?

7. What does the term *horizontal analysis* refer to? How is it useful in financial statement analysis?

8. Sales for the Olympic Co. during 1986 were $1.5 million. During 1987 sales grew to $1.8 million. What is the percentage change in sales from 1986 to 1987?

9. What does the term *trend analysis* mean? How is it useful in financial statement analysis?

10. Gross margin on sales in 1984 for the Caladonia Corp. was $500,000. In 1986 gross margin on sales was $600,000. If 1984 is the base year with an index of 100, what is the 1986 index?

11. What is *vertical analysis* and how is it useful in financial statement analysis?

12. Sometimes financial statements that are expressed in percentages are referred to as common dollar statements. What does the term *common dollar* mean and why are these statements useful?

13. If you were a common shareholder, what ratios would you find most useful in evaluating the company?

14. How are earnings per share and the price-earnings ratio related?

15. Describe the relationship among return on total assets, return on common shareholders' equity, and leverage.

16. A business person that you know has a very conservative philosophy and feels that all debt is bad. As a result, his firm is primarily financed by stockholders. How do you feel about this financing philosophy?

17. Over the last couple of years a firm's debt-equity ratio has increased. At the same time the times interest ratio has decreased. As a long-term creditor, how do you feel about these trends?

18. Many people consider the current ratio a good measure of a firm's liquidity. Describe this ratio and discuss its strengths and weaknesses as a measure of liquidity.

19. Ratio analysis is the best way to evaluate the strengths and weaknesses of a firm. Do you agree or disagree with this statement? Why?

20. What is a foreign currency transaction? How must firms account for such transactions?

21. On April 15 the Smoothe Company sold some computer chips to an English company and the Smoothe Company agreed to take English pounds in full payment The price was £50,000. At the time of the sale the exchange rate was one pound equals $1.20. When the Smoothe Company received payment from the English company one pound equaled $1.23. Determine the amount of the exchange gain or loss the Smoothe Company should recognize.

22. Why must foreign currency statements of U.S. subsidiaries operating abroad be translated to U.S. dollars?

23. Briefly describe the translation method required for foreign subsidiaries whose operations are well contained in the host country and conduct most of their business in a foreign currency.

24. What does harmonization of accounting standards mean? Do you think it is feasible to do so?

25. Describe the functions of the International Accounting Standards Committee and the International Federation of Accounts.

26. Do you consider accounting to be an asset or liability?

Exercises

1. Horizontal Analysis. At the top of the following page are condensed balance sheets of the Laguna Sea Corporation.

Required:
Determine the dollar and percentage changes in the accounts from 1986 to 1987 and comment on the significance of these changes.

Laguna Sea Corporation
Comparative Balance Sheets
December 31,

Assets	1987	1986
Current assets	$ 34,212	$ 40,250
Property, plant, and equipment, net	150,000	120,000
Total assets	$184,212	$160,250

Liabilities and Stockholders' Equity		
Current liabilities	$ 27,500	$ 25,000
Long-term liabilities	62,500	50,000
Stockholders' equity	94,212	85,250
Total liabilities and stockholders' equity	$184,212	$160,250

2. Horizontal Analysis. Following are comparative income statements of the Sizzler Company.

Sizzler Company
Comparative Income Statements
For the Years Ended December 31

	1987	1986
Sales	$1,365,000	$1,300,000
Cost of goods sold	914,550	845,000
Gross margin on sales	450,450	455,000
Operating expenses	210,000	200,000
Income before taxes	240,450	255,000
Taxes	96,180	102,000
Net income	$ 144,270	$ 153,000

Required:

Determine the dollar and percentage changes in the accounts from 1986 to 1987 and comment on their significance.

3. Trend Analysis. The following data are taken from a five-year summary of consolidated financial data of Sears, Roebuck and Co.

	(in millions)				
	1982	1981	1980	1979	1978
Revenues	$30,020	$27,357	$25,161	$24,528	$24,475
Cost and expenses	27,382	25,375	23,401	22,581	22,381
Operating income	1,011	462	627	1,029	1,353
Net income	861	650	610	830	909

Required:

    a. Assuming that 1978 is the base (index 100), prepare a trend analysis for the Sears, Roebuck and Co. data. (Round off to two decimal points were appropriate.)

    b. Comment on the trends.

4. Vertical Analysis. Following are comparative income statements for the Times Mirror Company (a large publishing company). These statements have been slightly simplified.

Times Mirror Company and Subsidiaries
Comparative Statements of Consolidated Income

For the Years Ended December 31

(in millions)

	1982	1981
Sales	$2,200	$2,131
Cost of goods sold	1,321	1,297
Gross margin	879	834
Operating expenses	614	554
Total operating income	265	280
Other income (expense)		
Interest	(52)	(49)
Other income	35	25
Total other income (expense)	(17)	(24)
Income before taxes	248	256
Taxes	110	106
Net income	$ 138	$ 150

Required:

a. Prepare common dollar statements for both years. (Round off to two decimal points where appropriate.)

b. Comment on the significance of these statements and the percentages therein.

5. Vertical Analysis. Following are comparative balance sheets of the King Smith Company:

King Smith Company
Comparative Balance Sheets

June 30,

Assets	1987	1986
Current assets	$ 50,000	$ 57,000
Property, plant, and equipment, net	200,000	180,000
Total assets	$250,000	$237,000

Liabilities and Stockholders' Equity		
Current liabilities	$ 20,000	$ 25,000
Long-term debt	70,000	60,000
Stockholders' equity	160,000	152,000
Total liabilities and stockholders' equity	$250,000	$237,000

Required:

a. Prepare common dollar balance sheets for both years. (Round off to two decimal points where appropriate.)

b. Comment on the significance of these figures and the changes that occurred.

6. Ratio Analysis—Common and Preferred Shareholders. You have obtained the following data relating to the Summerfeld Corporation for the past two years:

	1987	1986
Earnings per share	$ 2.50	$ 2.40
Market price per share—year-end	20.00	18.00
Dividend per share	1.20	1.00
Net income	37,500	
Interest expense	1,700	
Total assets	500,000	480,000
Stockholders' equity (no preferred stock issued)	300,000	296,000

Required:

Compute the following ratios for 1987 or at the end of 1987:

   a. Price-earnings.

   b. Dividend yield.

   c. Return on total assets.

   d. Return on common stockholders' equity.

   e. Equity ratio.

   f. Debt ratio.

7. Ratio Analysis—Long-term Creditors. You have obtained the following data from the West Corporation:

	1987	1986
Total assets	$600,000	$550,000
Total liabilities	240,000	192,500
Interest expense	10,000	6,000
Taxes	15,000	12,000
Net income	60,000	49,500

Required:

   a. Compute the following ratios for both years:

      1. Equity ratio.

      2. Debt ratio.

      3. Debt-equity ratio.

      4. Times interest earned.

   b. Comment on the changes that have taken place from 1986 to 1987.

8. Ratio Analysis—Short-term Creditors and Liquidity Analysis. Comparative balance sheets (unclassified) for the Peterson Company are at the top of the following page.

Additional Information:

Sales for year, all on credit	$445,000
Cost of goods sold during year	$302,600

Required:

   a. For both years calculate the following ratios:

      1. Current ratio.

      2. Quick ratio.

      3. Receivables turnover and number of days receivables are outstanding (1987 only).

      4. Inventory turnover and number of days to turn inventory over (1987 only).

      5. Book value per share of common stock.

   b. Explain how the current ratio, the quick ratio, and the inventory turnover ratio would change if the firm had used the **LIFO** method of inventory costing and prices were rising during both years.

Peterson Company
Comparative Balance Sheets
December 31,

Assets	1987	1986
Cash	$ 28,000	$ 25,000
Current marketable securities	10,000	8,000
Accounts receivable, net	45,000	47,000
Inventories, FIFO cost	82,000	73,000
Supplies	5,000	2,000
Property, plant, and equipment, net	95,000	93,000
Long-term investments and receivables	10,000	12,000
Total assets	$275,000	$260,000

Liabilities and Stockholders' Equity		
Accounts payable	$ 40,000	$ 45,000
Current maturities of long-term debt	20,000	17,000
Other accrued payables	12,000	15,000
Long-term debt, less current portion	80,000	100,000
Common stock, $5 par value	100,000	80,000
Retained earnings	23,000	3,000
Total liabilities and stockholders' equity	$275,000	$260,000

9. Determining Missing Figures and Analysis. The financial records of the Herbal Tea Company were destroyed in a fire. You were able to gather the following fragmentary data as of year-end:

Cash	$ 50,000
Land	200,000
Plant and equipment, net	300,000
Other accrued liabilities	90,000
Current maturities of long-term debt	16,000
Common stock	300,000
Current ratio	2.5:1
Debt ratio	.48

Net credit sales are $1 million and the receivable turnover ratio is 10. Cost of goods sold for the year is $1,080,000 and the inventory turnover ratio is 4. Turnover ratios are based on year-end data only.

Required:

Prepare a classified balance sheet in good form. You need to determine the balances in the following accounts:

   a. Accounts receivable, net.

   b. Inventories.

   c. Accounts payable.

   d. Long-term debt.

   e. Retained earnings.

10. Company Comparisons and Industry Averages. You have obtained the condensed income statements from the Ace and Beta companies, both in the same industry (shown at the top of the next page). Data for the industry average are also provided.

Required:

   a. Prepare common dollar financial statements for the two companies in columnar form. Add a column for the industry averages. Round to whole percentages.

Interpreting Financial Statement Data   885

	Ace	Beta	Industry Average
Sales	$955,850	$136,550	100%
Cost of goods sold	573,510	71,006	53
Gross margin on sales	382,340	65,544	47
Operating expenses			
Selling	91,762	9,668	6
General and administrative	61,174	6,718	4
Total operating expenses	152,936	16,386	10
Income before tax	229,404	49,158	37
Income taxes	97,094	10,315	9
Net income	$132,310	$ 38,843	28%

b. Compare the performance of Ace and Beta with the industry averages. Comment on any significant differences. What areas need improvement?

11. Differences in Accounting Methods. The Ace Company and the Zeta Company are both retailers of children's toys. Both companies are the same size and similar in their operations. The Ace Company, however, is rather conservative in its accounting policies and thus uses LIFO for inventory costing purposes and sum-of-the-years-digits for depreciation. On the other hand, the Zeta Company uses FIFO and straight-line depreciation. Both companies began business last year, and prices have increased during the year.

Required:

Explain which company will have the higher amount for each of the following ratios. For simplicity, ignore taxes. If you feel that you cannot make a determination, so state.

a. Quick ratio.

b. Working capital ratio.

c. Inventory turnover.

d. Accounts receivable turnover.

e. Return on total assets.

f. Debt to total assets.

g. Return on stockholders' equity.

12. Change in Accounting Method. The following note was taken from the 1983 annual report of Wang Laboratories:

During the year ended June 30, 1983 the Company retroactively adopted a change in accounting treatment for repairable service parts used in the maintenance of customer and internally used equipment. These parts were previously classified as inventories, with usage and provisions for obsolescence recognized as incurred. The new method of accounting results in the classification of service parts as noncurrent assets, with associated costs being depreciated over a period of seven years on a straight line basis. . . . Since the depreciation resulting from the new method is substantially equal to usage and obsolescence recognized under the prior method there is no cumulative effect of the change presented in the statement of consolidated earnings, and the change is not expected to materially affect future results of operations.

Required:

How would each of the following ratios be affected by this change? Explain how you reached your conclusion.

a. Current ratio.

b. Asset turnover ratio.

c. Inventory turnover ratio.

d. Return on total assets.

e. Earnings per share.

13. Foreign Currency Transactions. The Lawrence Radiation Company purchased some specially made equipment from the Liexor Corporation, a Swiss firm. The purchase was made on

November 12 when one Swiss franc equaled $.40. Payment of 500,000 Swiss francs is due on December 15. When payment was made, one Swiss franc equaled $.38.

Required:

Make the journal entries to record the purchase on November 12 and the payment on December 15.

14. Foreign Currency Transactions. On December 18 the Woo Import Company, a U.S. company, purchased goods for resale from its primary Japanese supplier. The total cost, payable in yen, was Y3,000,000. Payment is due January 30. The following exchange rates apply:

Date	$ per Yen
December 18	$.0035
December 31	.0040
January 30	.0038

Required:

   a. Make the required journal entries on the books of the Woo Import Company to record these transactions. The firm closes its books each December 31.
   b. How should the exchange gains and losses be reported on the books of the Woo Import Company?

15. Translating Financial Statements. The Hamilton Company's chief financial officer provided the following data relative to certain account balances of its foreign subsidiary:

Account	Translated at Current Rates	Translated at Historical Rates
Cash	$ 100,000	$ 105,000
Inventory	700,000	750,000
Plant and equipment	900,000	890,000
Sales	3,500,000*	3,600,000
Common stock	500,000	450,000

*Represents average for the year.

Required:

Assuming the subsidiary operations are self-contained and it conducts most of its business in the local currency, state at what amount each of the accounts should be translated.

Problem Set A

21A-1. Trend Analysis. The following information is taken from the annual report of the Kellogg Company:

	(in millions, except per-share data)				
	1982	1981	1980	1979	1978
Net sales	$2,367	$2,321	$2,151	$1,847	$1,691
Pre-tax earnings	411	378	338	282	272
Net earnings	228	205	184	162	144
Per common share:					
Net earnings	$2.98	$2.69	$2.41	$2.11	$1.89
Cash dividends	1.53	1.43	1.34	1.29	1.20

Required:

   a. Prepare a trend analysis for Kellogg assuming that 1978 is the base (index 100).
   b. Comment on the results.

21A–2. Horizontal and Vertical Analysis. The statements below and at the top of the next page were taken from the 1985 annual report of the Kellogg Company. Data are in millions.

Kellogg Company and Subsidiaries
Consolidated Balance Sheet
At December 31,

(millions)	1985	1984
Current assets		
Cash and temporary investments	$ 127.8	$308.9
Accounts receivable, less allowances of $2.2 and $2.3	203.9	182.5
Inventories		
Raw materials and supplies	135.6	119.7
Finished goods and materials in process	110.3	101.4
Prepaid expenses	40.5	39.0
Total current assets	618.1	751.5
Property		
Land	25.6	25.6
Buildings	321.2	277.7
Machinery and equipment	903.2	762.4
Construction in progress	280.4	215.7
Accumulated depreciation	(494.5)	(425.4)
Property, net	1,035.9	856.0
Intangible assets	28.3	30.5
Other assets	43.8	29.1
Total assets	$1,726.1	$1,667.1
Current liabilities		
Current maturities of debt	$ 34.8	$ 340.6
Accounts payable	189.7	127.4
Accrued liabilities		
Income taxes	29.4	51.4
Salaries and wages	41.8	38.7
Promotion	71.3	60.2
Interest	30.9	8.3
Other	46.4	37.5
Total current liabilities	444.3	664.1
Long-term debt	392.6	364.1
Other liabilities	12.3	9.5
Deferred income taxes	193.9	142.2
Shareholders' equity		
Common stock, $.25 par value—shares authorized 165,000,000;		
issued 153,613,602 and 153,432,062	38.4	38.4
Capital in excess of par value	44.5	40.8
Retained earnings	1,288.5	1,118.4
Treasury stock, at cost—30,245,018 and 30,300,000 shares	(576.8)	(577.8)
Currency translation adjustment	(111.6)	(132.6)
Total shareholders' equity	683.0	487.2
Total liabilities and shareholders' equity	$1,726.1	$1,667.1

See notes to financial statements.

Required:

a. Prepare a schedule showing dollar amount and percentage changes from 1984 to 1985 for the income statement and the balance sheet. (Round percentages to one decimal point.)

b. Prepare a common dollar income statement and balance sheet for 1984 and 1985.

c. Comment on the above statements, including any significant changes or apparent trends.

Kellogg Company and Subsidiaries
Consolidated Earnings and Retained Earnings
For the Year Ended December 31,

(millions)	1985	1984	1983
Net sales	$2,930.1	$2,602.4	$2,381.1
Interest revenue	7.2	27.7	18.6
Other revenue (deductions), net	(2.8)	3.9	18.1
	2,934.5	2,634.0	2,417.8
Cost of goods sold	1,605.0	1,488.4	1,412.3
Selling and administrative expense	766.7	650.8	554.4
Interest expense	35.4	18.7	7.1
	2,407.1	2,157.9	1,973.8
Earnings before income taxes	527.4	476.1	444.0
Income taxes	246.3	225.6	201.3
Net earnings—$2.28, $1.68, and $1.59 a share	281.1	250.5	242.7
Retained earnings, beginning of year	1,118.4	991.5	872.8
Dividends paid—$.90, $.85, and $.81 a share	(111.0)	(123.6)	(124.0)
Retained earnings, end of year	$1,288.5	$1,118.4	$ 991.5

See notes to financial statements.

21A-3. Ratio Analysis. This problem asks you to use the data from the Kellogg financial statement shown in Problem 21A-2 to calculate certain ratios.

Required:

a. Calculate for both years the following ratios:
1. Book value per share of common stock.
2. Equity ratio.
3. Debt ratio.
4. Debt-equity ratio.
5. Times interest earned.
6. Current ratio.
7. Quick ratio.

b. For 1985 only, calculate the following ratios:
1. Return on total assets.
2. Return on common stockholders' equity.
3. Inventory turnover.
4. Receivables turnover. (Assume all sales are on credit.)

21A-4. Ratio Analysis and Accounting Principles. The following data were obtained from the records of the Hitch Trailer Company at the end of 1987:

Sales (all on credit)	$1,800,000
Cost of goods sold (FIFO cost)	1,080,000
Average inventory (FIFO cost)	216,000
Average accounts receivable	200,000
Interest expense	25,000
Income taxes (40%)	144,000
Net income	216,000
Average total assets	3,102,500
Average total liabilities	1,500,000

Required:

a. Determine the following ratios of statistics:
1. Gross margin percentage.
2. Profit margin percentage.

Interpreting Financial Statement Data

3. Inventory turnover.
4. Receivables turnover.
5. Return on total assets.
6. Return on total stockholders' equity.

b. Now assume that the company is considering switching to the LIFO method of accounting. The controller tells you that if the company had been on LIFO in 1987, average inventories would have been $162,000 and cost of goods sold for the year would have been $1.2 million. Recompute the above ratios and statistics and comment on the differences.

21A–5. Effect of Transactions on Certain Ratios. The working capital accounts of the Quincy Medical Center at December 31, 1987 are provided below:

Cash	$ 70,000
Marketable securities	150,000
Accounts receivable, net	90,000
Inventory	250,000
Prepaid expenses	40,000
Accounts payable	140,000
Current maturities of long-term debt	80,000
Other accrued liabilities	60,000

During 1988 the company entered into the following transactions:
1. Additional shares of common stock were issued for $100,000 cash.
2. Accounts payable of $180,000 were paid.
3. A cash dividend of $40,000 that was previously declared was paid.
4. Inventory with a cost of $100,000 was sold on account for $150,000.
5. Accounts receivable of $120,000 were collected.
6. Marketable securities with a cost of $60,000 were sold for $50,000.
7. Inventory with a cost of $110,000 was purchased on account.
8. Plant and equipment with a cost of $50,000 was purchased for cash.
9. Land with a cost of $100,000 was purchased through the exchange of the firm's common stock.
10. A 10% stock dividend was declared.

Required:
a. Compute the following items at the beginning of the year:
   1. Working capital.
   2. Current ratio.
   3. Quick ratio.
b. For each of the 1988 transactions, show its effect on working capital, the current ratio, and the quick ratio. Use a table similar to the one below and show whether the effect is an increase, decrease, or none. The first item is done for you as an example.

Transaction	Working Capital	Current Ratio	Quick Ratio
1	Increase	Increase	Increase

21A–6. Comparison of Two Companies. Presented on pages 891 and 892 are the financial statements, simplified for analysis purposes, for Lucky Stores, Inc., a retail grocery chain.

Additional Information:
Dividends per share:
   Common $1.16 a share
   Preferred   Total dividends in both years $1,368,000
Market prices per common share at 1985 and 1984 year-end are $25.00 and $17.50, respectively
Inventory method: LIFO

890

Lucky Stores, Inc.
Consolidated Balance Sheet
At February 2, 1986 and February 3, 1985 (in thousands)

	1985	1984
Current assets		
Cash, including short-term investments of $45,143 in 1984	$ 12,742	$ 119,406
Receivables	70,381	60,743
Inventories	793,193	688,520
Prepaid expenses, and supplies	36,799	29,692
Total current assets	913,115	898,361
Property and equipment at depreciated cost	815,447	660,451
Property under capital leases, less $86,104 and $87,097		
accumulated amortization	112,186	123,904
Property under construction	50,041	76,797
Licenses, receivables and other assets	28,724	28,695
Excess of cost over net assets acquired	12,947	13,551
Total assets	$1,932,460	$1,801,759
Current liabilities		
Accounts payable	$ 443,778	$ 404,822
Current portion of long-term and capital lease obligations	14,789	14,205
Income taxes	14,536	26,203
Other taxes	51,824	54,410
Payroll and employee benefits	104,193	93,575
Other accrued liabilities	113,370	84,143
Total current liabilities	742,490	677,358
Long-term obligations	239,701	231,903
Capital lease obligations	140,066	152,466
Deferred income taxes	52,840	56,639
Other deferred liabilities	101,140	56,551
Commitments—see Long-term leases		
Redeemable preference shares, redemption value $22,914	19,861	17,400
Common shareholders' equity		
Common shares, $1.25 par value; outstanding 51,043 and		
50,851 shares	63,804	63,563
Capital in excess of par value of shares issued	198,017	194,854
Retained earnings	374,541	351,025
Total common shareholders' equity	636,362	609,442
Total liabilities and shareholders' equity	$1,932,460	$1,801,759

*By convention, redeemable preferred shares are shown separately outside of the common shareholders' equity section and are not included in the total of common shareholders' equity. They are, however, part of total stockholders' equity.

In addition, you have been able to gather the following selected industry average data:

Current ratio 1.4:1	Gross margin percentage 22.2%
Quick ratio 0.4:1	Profit margin percentage 1.1%
Inventory turnover 13.5	Times interest earned 2.9

Required:

a. Using data from Lucky Stores, compute the appropriate ratios from Exhibit 21–5 for both years. If an average is required for 1984, use year-end figures only.

b. Compare the performance of Lucky Stores, Inc. with that of Safeway. The Safeway data is in the chapter as well as in Appendix C.

c. If you were to make an investment, which stocks, if either, would you buy?

Lucky Stores, Inc.
Consolidated Earnings
Years ended February 2, 1986, February 3, 1985, and January 29, 1984
(in thousands except per share amounts)

	1985 (52 weeks)	1984 (53 weeks)	1983 (52 weeks)
Sales	$9,382,282	$9,236,529	$8,388,155
Cost of goods sold	7,146,932	7,111,514	6,460,461
Gross margin	2,235,350	2,125,015	1,927,694
Expenses			
Selling, general and administrative	1,951,969	1,836,748	1,634,916
Depreciation and amortization	103,084	87,223	77,861
Interest, net of interest income of $8,230, $13,871, and $18,120	32,236	27,627	21,900
	2,087,289	1,951,598	1,734,677
Earnings before income taxes	148,061	173,417	193,017
Income taxes	61,535	78,786	87,617
Net earnings	$ 86,526	$ 94,631	$ 105,400
Earnings per common share:			
Primary	$ 1.67	$ 1.84	$ 2.05
Fully diluted	$ 1.64	$ 1.81	$ 2.02

Consolidated Retained Earnings
Years ended February 2, 1986, February 3, 1985, and January 29, 1984
(in thousands except per share amounts)

	1985	1984	1983
Beginning of year	$ 351,025	$ 316,708	$ 271,494
Net earnings	86,526	94,631	105,400
Cash dividends			
Preference	(1,368)	(1,370)	(1,372)
Common—$1.16 a share	(59,130)	(58,944)	(58,814)
Amortization of the excess of redemption value over fair value of preference shares	(2,512)	0	0
End of year	$ 374,541	$ 351,025	$ 316,708

21A–7. Foreign Currency Transactions. The First American Company purchased some specialized X-ray equipment from a well-known Canadian manufacturer. The cost of the equipment is $200,000. The following exchange rates applied to the transaction:

Date	Event	Exchange Rate ($U.S. per $Canadian)
August 23	Date of purchase	$.77
September 30	Balance sheet prepared	.80
October 12	Payment made	.75

Required:

   a. Assuming that the purchase is payable in U.S. dollars, make the appropriate entries on the books of the First American Company.

   b. Assuming that the purchase is payable in Canadian dollars, make the appropriate entries on the books of the First American Company.

21A–8. Translating Foreign Currency Statements. The Pomex Company operates in Mexico and is a 100% owned subsidiary of a U.S. company. Its operations are self-contained in Mexico and it carries out its operations in pesos. In the process of preparing consolidated financial statements, the controller in the headquarters office must translate the Mexican subsidiary's balance sheet to U.S. dollars. He provides you with the following information and asks your help:

The Pomex Company
Balance Sheet
December 31, 1987

Accounts	Amounts (in pesos)
Cash	250,000
Accounts receivable, net	425,000
Inventory	800,000
Building, net	1,000,000
Land	500,000
Total assets	2,975,000
Accounts payable	235,000
Notes payable	465,000
Common stock	1,500,000
Retained earnings	775,000
Total equities	2,975,000

Additional Information:

1. Retained earnings at the beginning of the year in U.S. dollars are $25,000.
2. Net income in U.S. dollars is $5,000.
3. Exchange rates are as follows:

Date	Exchange Rate $ per Pesos
December 31, 1987	$.035
Average for 1987	.040
When common stock issued	.050

Required:

Using a worksheet similar to that in the text, translate the Mexican subsidiary's balance sheet to U.S. dollars.

21A–9. Translating Foreign Currency Statements. The Excello Watch Company is a 100% owned Swiss subsidiary of U.S. Watches, Inc. In preparation for consolidation with the U.S. parent, the controller of the Swiss subsidiary prepared the financial statements in Swiss francs (shown at the top of the next page).

Additional Information:

1. Retained earnings in U.S. dollars at the beginning of the year are $320,000.
2. The following exchange rates apply:

	$ per Swiss Franc
December 31, 1987	$.40
Average for 1987	.42
When common stock issued	.30

BALANCE SHEET

Accounts	Swiss Francs
Cash	60,000
Accounts receivable, net	90,000
Inventory	150,000
Building, net	400,000
Land	800,000
Total assets	1,500,000
Accounts payable	70,000
Notes payable	65,000
Common stock	600,000
Retained earnings	765,000
Total equities	1,500,000

INCOME STATEMENT

	Swiss Francs
Sales	1,000,000
Cost of goods sold	650,000
Selling expenses	120,000
General and administrative expenses	50,000
Total expenses	820,000
Net income	180,000

Required:

Using a worksheet similar to that in the text, prepare translated statements to be included in the consolidation with the U.S. parent. Use the current rate method.

Problem Set B

21B-1. Trend Analysis. The following information is taken from the annual report of the Bristol Myers Company (in millions except per-share amounts):

	1982	1981	1980	1979	1978
Net sales	$3,000	$3,497	$3,158	$2,753	$2,450
Pre-tax earnings	606	552	492	423	376
Net earnings	349	306	271	232	203
Per common share:					
Net earnings	$5.18	$4.58	$4.08	$3.50	$3.08
Cash dividends	2.035	1.78	1.56	1.385	1.19

Required:

a. Prepare a trend analysis for the Bristol Myers Company assuming that 1978 is the base year (index 100).

b. Comment on the analysis.

21B-2. Horizontal and Vertical Analysis. The financial data for the Weldon Zipper Company are shown on the following page.

Required:

a. Prepare a schedule showing dollar amount and percentage changes from 1986 to 1987 for the income statement and the balance sheet. (Round percentages to one decimal point.)

b. Prepare comparative common dollar income statements and balances for 1986 and 1987.

c. Comment on the above statements, including any significant changes or apparent trends.

Weldon Zipper Company
Comparative Income Statement
For the Years Ended December 31

	1987	1986
Sales	$700,000	$500,000
Cost of goods sold	500,000	350,000
Gross margin on sales	200,000	150,000
Operating expenses		
Selling	70,000	45,000
General and administrative	30,000	25,000
Total operating expenses	100,000	70,000
Income taxes	40,000	25,000
Net income	$ 60,000	$ 55,000

Weldon Zipper Company
Comparative Balance Sheet
December 31

Assets	1987	1986
Cash	$ 45,000	$ 35,000
Accounts receivable	70,000	60,000
Inventories	100,000	110,000
Property, plant, and equipment, net	150,000	130,000
Total assets	$365,000	$335,000

Equities	1987	1986
Current maturities of long-term debt	$ 10,000	$ 9,000
Accounts payable	60,000	61,000
Other accrued liabilities	20,000	10,000
Long-term liabilities	100,000	120,000
Common stock, $1 par value	25,000	25,000
Retained earnings	150,000	110,000
Total equities	$365,000	$335,000

21B–3. Ratio Analysis. This problem asks you to use the data from the Weldon Zipper Company to calculate certain ratios. In addition to those data, you have the following data:

1. Total dividends issued—$20,000.
2. Market price at end of 1987—$21.60; at end of 1986—$18.40.

Required:

a. Calculate for both years the following ratios:
   1. Book value per share of common stock.
   2. Equity ratio.
   3. Debt-equity ratio.
   4. Earnings per share.
   5. Price-earnings ratio.
   6. Current ratio.
   7. Quick ratio.

b. For 1987 only, calculate the following ratios:
   1. Return on total assets. (Assume that included in operating expenses is interest expense of $5,000.)
   2. Return on common stockholders' equity.
   3. Inventory turnover.
   4. Receivables turnover. (Assume that all sales are on credit.)

21B–4. Ratio Analysis and Accounting Principles. The following data were obtained from the records Congress Supply Store at the end of 1987:

Sales (80% on credit)	$2,000,000
Cost of goods sold (LIFO cost)	1,400,000
Average inventory (LIFO cost)	450,000
Average accounts receivable	400,000
Interest expense	30,000
Income taxes (30%)	102,000
Net income	238,000
Average total assets	1,780,000
Average total stockholders' equity	950,000

Required:
   a. Determine the following ratios or statistics:
      1. Gross margin percentage.
      2. Profit margin percentage.
      3. Inventory turnover.
      4. Debt-equity ratio. (Use average figures.)
      5. Return on total assets.
      6. Return on total stockholders' equity.
   b. Now assume that the company is considering switching to the FIFO method of inventory accounting. The president of the firm tells you that if FIFO had been used, average inventories would have been $600,000 and cost of goods sold would have been $1.2 million. Recompute the above ratios and statistics and comment on the differences.

21B–5. The Effect of Transactions on Certain Ratios. The working capital accounts of the Garner Western Ware Store at December 31, 1987 are shown below:

Cash	$ 50,000
Loans receivable	25,000
Accounts receivable, net	85,000
Inventory	150,000
Supplies	10,000
Notes payable	60,000
Accounts payable	50,000
Other accrued liabilities	10,000

During 1988 the company entered into the following transactions:
   1. Bonds payable, due in 1993, were issued for $50,000 cash.
   2. Additional inventory of $90,000 was purchased on account.
   3. A 10% stock dividend previously declared was distributed.
   4. Sales of $200,000 were made of which 60% was on account and the rest was for cash.
   5. The cost of the sales in Item 4 was $125,000.
   6. Collections on accounts receivable amounted to $150,000.
   7. Payments on account were $100,000.
   8. Land with a cost of $100,000 was sold for $120,000. Twenty thousand dollars was received in cash, and a long-term note receivable was received for the remainder.
   9. Convertible preferred stock was converted into common.
   10. Treasury stock with a cost of $10,000 was purchased.
   11. The cash balances in excess of $25,000 were invested in current marketable securities.

Required:

a. Compute the following items at the beginning of the year:
   1. Working capital.
   2. Current ratio.
   3. Quick ratio.
b. For each of the 1988 transactions, show the effect on working capital, the current ratio, and the quick ratio. Use a table similar to the one below and show whether the effect is an increase, decrease, or none. The first item is done for you.

Transaction	Working Capital	Current Ratio	Quick Ratio
1	Increase	Increase	Increase

21B-6. Completing a Balance Sheet from Incomplete Data. You obtained the following information from the Lost Data Company:

Lost Data Company
Balance Sheet
December 31, 1987

Assets	
Cash	$ 97,500
Accounts receivable	?
Inventory	?
Property, plant, and equipment, net	?
Total assets	$1,400,000

Equities	
Accounts payable	$ 300,000
Current maturities of long-term debt	?
Long-term debt	?
Common stock	300,000
Retained earnings	?

You have obtained the following additional information:
1. The current ratio is 2:1.
2. The debt ratio is 60%.
3. The inventory turnover is 6 and cost of goods sold is $1.2 million. The beginning inventory is $190,000.
4. Sales are $2 million, of which 75% is on credit and the rest is for cash. The receivables turnover is 4. Receivables remained constant throughout the year.

Required:

Using the data above, complete the balance sheet.

21B-7. Foreign Currency Transactions. The Great Import Company sold some pollution control devices to a German company for $50,000. The following exchange rates applied to the transaction:

Date	Event	Exchange Rate (German Mark per U.S. Dollar)
May 10	Date of purchase	$.35
June 30	Balance sheet prepared	.40
July 18	Payment made	.41

Required:

    a. Assuming that the sale is receivable in U.S. dollars, make the appropriate entries on the books of the Great Import Company.

    b. Assuming that the sale is for 143,000 German marks, make the appropriate entries on the books of the Great Import Company.

21B–8. Translating Foreign Currency Statements. The London Company operates in England and is a 100% owned subsidiary of a U.S. company. Its operations are self-contained in England and it carries out its operations in pounds. In the process of preparing consolidated financial statements, the controller in the headquarters office must translate the English subsidiary's balance sheet to U.S. dollars. He provides you with the following information and asks your help:

The London Company
Balance Sheet
December 31, 1987

Account	Amount (in Pounds)
Cash	70,000
Accounts receivable, net	95,000
Inventory	300,000
Building, net	700,000
Land	500,000
Total assets	1,665,000
Accounts payable	85,000
Notes payable	165,000
Common stock	700,000
Retained earnings	715,000
Total equities	1,665,000

Additional Information:

    1. Retained earnings at the beginning of the year in U.S. dollars is $400,000.

    2. Net income in U.S. dollars is $50,000.

    3. Exchange rates are as follows:

Date	Exchange Rate (Pound per Dollar)
December 31, 1987	$1.25
Average for 1987	1.20
When common stock issued	1.50

Required:

Translate the English subsidiary's balance sheet to U.S. dollars.

21B–9. Translating Foreign Currency Statements. The Smithe Co. Ltd. is a 100% owned Canadian subsidiary of U.S. Oils. In preparation for consolidation with the U.S. parent, the controller of the Canadian subsidiary prepared the financial statements (shown at the top of the next page) in Canadian dollars.

Additional Information:

    1. Retained earnings in U.S. dollars at the beginning of the year is $600,000.

    2. The following exchange rates that apply follow the financial statements.

Account	Canadian Dollars
Balance Sheet	
Cash	160,000
Accounts receivable, net	180,000
Inventory	250,000
Building, net	800,000
Land	510,000
Total assets	1,900,000
Accounts payable	170,000
Notes payable	365,000
Common stock	700,000
Retained earnings	665,000
Total liabilities	1,900,000
Income Statement	
Sales	1,400,000
Cost of goods sold	800,000
Selling expenses	320,000
General and administrative expenses	150,000
Total expenses	1,270,000
Net income	130,000

	$U.S. per $Canadian
December 31, 1987	$.75
Average for 1987	.70
When common stock issued	.85

Required:

Prepare translated statements to be included in the consolidation with the U.S. parent.

Using the Computer

The financial statements on pages 900 and 901 were taken from the 1984 annual report of Walt Disney Productions and Subsidiaries. Using an electronic spreadsheet, determine the dollar changes and percentage changes from 1983 to 1984. Also prepare common dollar income statements and balance sheets. Use the format in Exhibits 21–1 through 21–4.

Understanding Financial Statements

The following was excerpted from an article appearing in the January 17, 1984 edition of *The Wall Street Journal* (pg. 10):

> The recovering economy helped push General Electric Co.'s fourth-quarter earnings up 10% despite a slight sales decline. . . .
>
> Full-year profit rose 11% to $2.02 billion or $4.45 a share, from $1.82 or $4.00 a share earned in 1982 despite only a 1% gain in sales, to $26.8 billion.

Required:

a. In your opinion, what factors would cause profit to rise 11% when sales rose only 1%?

b. General Electric common stock closed at 57 1/8 on January 16, 1984. Determine the price-earnings ratio at this date.

Walt Disney Productions and Subsidiaries
Consolidated Statement of Income
(In thousands, except per share data)

Year ended September 30	1984	1983	1982
Revenues			
Entertainment and recreation	$1,097,359	$1,031,202	$ 725,610
Filmed entertainment	244,552	165,458	202,102
Community development	204,384		
Consumer products	109,682	110,697	102,538
	1,655,977	1,307,357	1,030,250
Costs and Expenses			
Entertainment and recreation	904,664	834,324	592,965
Filmed entertainment	242,303	198,843	182,463
Community development	162,158		
Consumer products	55,819	53,815	54,706
	1,364,944	1,086,982	830,134
Income (Loss) Before Corporate Expenses and Unusual Charges			
Entertainment and recreation	192,695	196,878	132,645
Filmed entertainment	2,249	(33,385)	19,639
Community development	42,226		
Consumer products	53,863	56,882	47,832
	291,033	220,375	200,116
Corporate Expenses (Income)			
General and administrative	59,570	35,554	30,957
Design projects abandoned	7,032	7,295	5,147
Interest expense (income)—net	41,738	14,066	(14,781)
	108,340	56,915	21,323
Income Before Unusual Charges, Taxes on Income and Accounting Change	182,693	163,460	178,793
Unusual charges	165,960		
Income Before Taxes on Income and Accounting Change	16,733	163,460	178,793
Taxes on income (benefit)	(5,000)	70,300	78,700
Income Before Accounting Change	21,733	93,160	100,093
Cumulative effect of change in accounting for investment tax credits	76,111		
Net Income	$ 97,844	$ 93,160	$ 100,093
Earnings per Share			
Income before accounting change	$0.61	$2.70	$3.01
Cumulative effect of change in accounting	2.12		
	$2.73	$2.70	$3.01
Average number of common and common equivalent shares outstanding	35,849	34,481	33,225

c. As of January 16, 1984 General Electric had a dividend yield of 3.5%. What is the amount of dividends per share issued by General Electric?

d. Determine General Electric's profit margin ratio in 1983.

e. Determine General Electric's profit margin ratio in 1982.

Financial Decision Case

Professor Holder has contacted several individuals about starting a company to produce and market a super floppy disk that he invented. Professor Holder estimates that it will take about $1 million to finance the new company. One of his associates, an accounting professor, has suggested three ways of raising the needed funds:

Walt Disney Productions and Subsidiaries
Consolidated Balance Sheet
(in thousands)

September 30	1984	1983*
Assets		
Cash ($8,800 restricted in 1984)	$ 35,346	$ 18,055
Accounts and notes receivable, net of allowances	172,762	104,746
Taxes on income refundable	60,000	70,000
Merchandise inventories	83,467	77,945
Film production costs	102,462	127,010
Real estate inventories	229,424	
Entertainment attractions and other property, at cost		
Attractions, buildings and equipment	2,413,985	2,251,297
Less accumulated depreciation	(600,156)	(504,365)
	1,813,829	1,746,932
Construction and design projects in progress	94,710	108,190
Land	28,807	16,687
	1,937,346	1,871,809
Other assets	118,636	111,630
	$2,739,443	$2,381,195
Liabilities and Stockholders Equity		
Accounts payable, payroll and other accrued liabilities	$ 239,992	$ 182,709
Taxes on income payable	24,145	13,982
Borrowings	861,909	352,575
Unearned deposits and advances	178,907	109,556
Deferred taxes on income	279,005	321,845
Commitments and contingencies		
Stockholders equity		
Preferred shares, no par		
Authorized—5,000 shares, none issued		
Common shares, no par		
Authorized—75,000 shares		
Issued and outstanding—33,729 and 34,509 shares	359,988	661,934
Retained earnings	795,497	738,594
	1,155,485	1,400,528
	$2,739,443	$2,381,195

*Restated to conform to nonclassified presentation.

1. All $1 million will be raised through the issuance of common stock to Holder and his associates.
2. Half ($500,000) will be raised through the issuance of common stock to Holder and his associates and the other half will be raised by issuing preferred stock with a stated dividend rate of 12% to a venture capitalist.
3. Half ($500,000) will be raised through the issuance of common stock to Holder and his associates and the other half will be raised by issuing convertible bonds with a stated interest rate of 12%.

Required:

a. Assuming that the company can earn $300,000 before interest and taxes and the tax rate is 40%, determine
   1. The net income accruing to common shareholders, and
   2. The return on common shareholders' equity

   under each of the three methods. Assume all stocks and/or bonds are outstanding all year.
b. Repeat your analysis now assuming that the firm will be able to earn $100,000 before interest and taxes and the tax rate remains at 40%.
c. Make recommendations to Professor Holder.

VI

Accounting Information for Planning, Control, Costing, and Decision Making

Accounting Information for Management and Cost Terms and Concepts

22

LEARNING OBJECTIVES

After reading this chapter you should be able to:

1. Define the nature of management and the three elements of the management process: planning, decision making, and control.
2. Explain the role that the accounting system plays in planning, decision making, and management control, and the characteristics of managerial accounting.
3. Describe responsibility accounting and the four types of responsibility centers: cost centers, revenue centers, profit centers, and investment centers.
4. Calculate return on investment for an investment center.
5. Describe the nature of cost objectives and direct and indirect costs.
6. Compare manufacturing and nonmanufacturing costs.
7. Define the three manufacturing costs: direct materials, direct labor, and factory overhead.
8. Prepare a schedule of cost of goods manufactured and an income statement for a manufacturing firm.
9. Define product costs and period costs.

Throughout this book, we have indicated that accounting is useful in managing businesses and other organizations. We have noted that accounting is an information system that is intended to provide information for management decisions and actions.

This chapter gives an overview of the accounting system as it relates to the management process and introduces a number of terms related to management accounting and accounting for manufacturing companies. We first examine the nature of management and then explain how accounting plays a vital role in the management process.

The Nature of Management

The term *management* has many different meanings. We define **management** as the process of using resources to achieve objectives.

Management has three components: process, resources, and objectives. First, management is viewed as a **process,** or a series of steps (e.g., plans, decisions, actions), designed to operate an organization. In order to achieve objectives, managers use **resources**—things that have expected service potential. Examples of resources are land, machinery, equipment, people, and money. The primary objective of any business is to earn a profit. To earn a profit, a business must develop a certain share of the market for its products; this, too, is an objective of management.

Elements of Management Process

Accounting plays a significant role in three major aspects of the management process: planning, decision making, and control. We will describe these three aspects of management and the role played by accounting in each of them.

The Role of Accounting in Management Planning

There are several types of planning—namely strategic, operational, contingency, and budgetary (budgeting). Planning in general means analyzing information about an organization and its environment, establishing its objectives, and developing action plans to achieve them, as shown in Exhibit 22–1.

The Nature of Management Planning

In the initial stages of the planning process, managers analyze information about an organization and its environment in order to assess such matters as (1) the current trends in the economy and their implications for the organization, (2) the opportunities to provide products or services at a satisfactory profit, (3) present and potential resources and how they can be used in the most profitable way, and (4) whether the organization needs to be changed.

Once the organization has analyzed information about itself and its environment, its next step is to establish objectives regarding the critical areas of organizational performance in order to achieve economic success in such areas as marketing, production, service delivery, personnel, and profitability.

Once objectives have been set, an organization must develop **action plans** that outline the steps that must be performed to achieve each objective. Although action plans need not be employed to achieve all objectives, they are useful for performing complex projects and tasks.

Accounting's Role in Strategic Planning

Accounting plays a role in all aspects of planning. Strategic planning means defining an organization's business, analyzing its customers and their buying

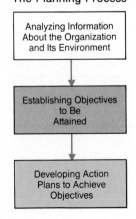

EXHIBIT 22–1
The Planning Process

Analyzing Information About the Organization and Its Environment

Establishing Objectives to Be Attained

Developing Action Plans to Achieve Objectives

habits, and deciding how to produce products or services that customers value at a satisfactory profit.

Accounting plays a major role in the strategic planning process by using techniques to provide information used by management to earn a satisfactory profit. For example, the technique of capital budgeting helps management evaluate whether a firm can earn a satisfactory return on an investment before committing funds to it. Similarly, accounting provides some of the raw data needed to project future profitability.

Accounting's Role in Operational Planning

A strategic plan typically lasts for several years. Once a strategic plan has been developed, an operational plan takes effect and determines the day-to-day operations of a firm. An operational plan is concerned with the level of sales for the coming year, and it designates the product lines that will be promoted above others. An operational plan projects the amount and cost of materials and labor as well as the numbers and types of personnel needed. Other costs, such as rent, utilities, supplies, and insurance, are also planned.

Accounting's Role in Budgetary Planning

Accounting plays an important role in budgetary planning or, more simply, budgeting. Budgeting means translating an organization's (or any of its subunits) operational plans into financial terms, expressed in the form of a budget. Thus, a **budget** is an organization's operational plan expressed in financial terms. There are several different kinds of budgets: sales budgets, expense budgets, and profit budgets (also termed profit plan). A sales budget contains the financial results expected from the planned or anticipated sales of a firm's products or services. An expense budget contains the financial cost of expenditures that will be made in order to operate the business. A profit budget represents the aggregation of sales and expense budgets for an organization. Budgeting and budgetary planning are examined in greater detail in Chapter 26.

Accounting's Role in Contingency Planning

Accounting also plays a role in contingency planning. Planning for contingencies means asking and answering questions such as: "What if sales increase or decrease by 10%?" or "If we increase advertising costs, how much do sales need to increase in order to break even?" Accounting techniques such as flexible budgeting and cost-volume-profit analysis are useful tools in contingency planning and are discussed in later chapters.

The Role of Accounting in Management Decision Making

Managers constantly are faced with the need to (1) define problems, (2) gather relevant information, (3) identify alternative courses of action, (4) evaluate the costs and benefits of each alternative, and (5) make a decision or choose among alternatives. These five steps make up the process of management decision making, as shown in Exhibit 22–2 on the following page.

EXHIBIT 22–2
Steps in
Decision Making

Define
Problems

Gather
Relevant
Information

Identify
Alternative
Courses of
Action

Evaluate Costs
and Benefits
of Each
Alternative

Choose
among
Alternatives

Types of Management Decisions

Managers are confronted with many different types of decisions regarding every aspect of a business or other organization, including areas such as production, marketing, finance, personnel, and capital investment. Following are typical management decisions:

1. The products a firm produces
   a. What emphasis should be placed on each product line
2. The price of products and services
3. The amount to spend on advertising
4. Whether to acquire a new computer system and, if so:
   a. Should it be purchased or leased?
   b. Which vendor should be selected?
   c. Is a maintenance contract necessary?
5. Whether to continue having AT&T provide telephone services or to purchase a new telephone system
6. How much to spend on employee benefits
   a. Which employee benefits should be offered: life insurance, disability insurance, pension plan, etc.?
7. Whether to accept a large order for products at a price below full cost
8. Whether to make a component product required by the manufacturing process or buy it from an outside vendor
9. Whether to keep a product line that is operating at a loss or to discontinue it
10. The action that should be taken if sales revenues are less than had been forecast
    a. Which expenses should be reduced or deferred?

It is useful to think about decisions in different ways. Some decisions are strategic; others are operational. Some decisions are short-term in consequence (one year or less); others have effects for many years. Some decisions are production decisions; others are marketing, personnel, or financial decisions.

Exhibit 22–3 presents a sample of different types of decisions classified by two different perspectives: (1) the type of planning involved (strategic, operational, etc.) and (2) the decision time horizon (short-term versus long-term). Note that some decisions can be classified in more than one way; that is, certain decisions that *appear* to be short-term and operational in fact have long-term strategic consequences. For example, the decision to make or buy a component product, usually thought of as a short-term decision, may affect the long-term development of an organization's in-house technological capabilities.

Accounting's Role in Decision Making

Accounting information plays a major role in management decision making. Accounting helps to identify problems through many different types of reports, and it provides information used to evaluate alternative courses of action.

Accounting and Problem Identification

In the first step of the decision-making process, managers identify problems requiring decisions and action. Managers or their staff analyze financial statements and other accounting reports produced by the organization's accountants in order to determine unfavorable results of operations and to detect potentially unfavorable trends.

EXHIBIT 22–3
Examples of Decisions
Classified by Type of Planning and Decision Time Horizon

Type of Planning	Decision Time Horizon (Decision Consequences)	
	Short-Term	Long-Term
Strategic Decisions	• How much of each product line should we produce? • Should we drop a product line?	• Which products should we produce?
Operational Decisions	• Should we make or buy a component for our product? • Should we accept a special order at less than full cost?	• Should we add plant capacity? • Should we replace or repair plant and equipment?
Budgetary Decisions	• How much should we spend on advertising?	• Should we acquire a new computer system?
Contingency Decisions	• If actual sales are less than forecast, which expenses should we reduce?	• Should we close down our outdated operations if recession continues?

Consider, for example, the operations of a branch of a residential real estate company, that is, a company of brokers who sell single-family residences. The branch manager of the Happy Valley office of the Metropolitan Realty Corporation receives a monthly financial report, including an income statement and a detailed schedule of branch operating expenses, as shown in Exhibit 22–4 on the following page. The branch manager, Harold Walker, reviews this schedule in order to ascertain whether expenses have exceeded the amounts appropriate for the branch. He also tries to determine whether it is feasible to reduce or eliminate any branch expenses.

To help Mr. Walker make his evaluation, the schedule of branch operating expense shows:

1. The actual branch expenses for the current month—August 1987.
2. The actual expenses incurred for the year.
3. The ratio of each expense category (advertising, personnel, etc.) to sales, expressed as a percentage of sales for both the current month and the year to date.

By analyzing this report, Mr. Walker can get some idea about the extent to which expenses are under control, that is, whether particular expenses are in keeping with the branch's level of revenues.

As Exhibit 22–4 shows, most of the expense categories appear to bear the same relation to revenues during the current month as for the year to date with the exception of the other expense category. For the year to date, the ratio for this category is 6.9 percent, whereas for the current month it is 9.3 percent, a difference of 2.4 percent. Based on this information, Mr. Walker must ask:

1. Is the difference significant enough to justify further management analysis?
2. If so, what has caused the expenses in this category to increase?

Accounting Information for Management and Cost Terms and Concepts   909

EXHIBIT 22–4
Schedule of Branch Operating Expenses
Happy Valley Office
Metropolitan Realty Corporation
August 1987

Expense Categories	Current Month*		Year to Date	
	Actual	Percentage of Revenues	Actual	Percentage of Revenues
Advertising	$ 2,325	15.5	$ 19,000	15.7
Personnel	3,500	23.3	28,000	23.1
Office services	600	4.0	4,000	3.3
Telephone	2,200	14.7	14,900	12.3
Facilities	2,500	16.7	20,000	16.5
Sales expense	750	5.0	6,000	4.9
Other expense	1,400	9.3	8,400	6.9
Totals	$13,275	88.5	$100,300	82.7

*Current-month branch revenues were $15,000.

If Mr. Walker decides the difference is significant, he will proceed to obtain additional information about the costs incurred in the other expense category; if he feels the amount is not significant, he will ignore it.

The example of Mr. Walker's analysis of the schedule of branch operating expenses is a simple illustration of how accounting plays a role in the problem-identification phase of the management decision-making process.

Accounting's Role in Obtaining Information for Decision Making

In the second step of the decision-making process, managers obtain information relevant to making management decisions. For example, if Mr. Walker investigated the difference he found in the other expense category he would need detailed information from accounting records on each of the individual expenses involved in order to determine what caused the problem.

Firms also need accounting information when they make nonroutine decisions. For example, suppose that a large manufacturing company has been buying from an outside supplier a component that is used for the production of its own product. The company's managers decide to determine whether it would be less costly for the company to produce the component itself rather than to continue to purchase it from the outside supplier.

To analyze this decision, which is called a *make-or-buy decision*, the manufacturer must obtain the following accounting information: (1) the cost of making the product itself and (2) the cost of buying the product from an outside supplier. An example of a make-or-buy decision at National Computer Corporation is examined in detail in Chapter 24, which deals with short-term decisions.

Accounting's Role in Evaluating Alternatives

Although the process of generating decision-making alternatives is a managerial activity, accounting plays a role in assisting decision makers to evaluate their alternatives. The accounting information provided as inputs to decisions often form the basis for choosing among alternatives.

Suppose, for example, that the administrative manager of a law firm is deciding which new photocopy machines to purchase and wishes to base her choice on the total cost of the machines. Assume that the firm is considering two brands of photocopy machines—Xerox and Savin.

The manager may ask the accountant to obtain information about operating costs such as the cost of supplies, maintenance, and repairs for both brands. She then compares the difference between the operating costs of the two brands as well as the difference, if any, in the initial purchase price of the machines in order to make a sound decision about which brand to buy.

The Role of Accounting in Management Control

The third major aspect of the management process is termed **management control** or, more simply, control. All organizations (businesses, hospitals, universities, governmental units) channel the efforts of people to attain goals. To help influence or control the behavior of people, organizations use a variety of procedures and processes, including personal supervision, job descriptions, performance evaluations, budgets, and accounting reports. Together these procedures and processes form an invisible but very real system: the organizational control system.

The Organizational Control System

The **organizational control system** is defined as a set of processes and techniques that are designed to increase the likelihood that people will behave in ways that lead to the attainment of an organization's objectives. Control systems are not easily seen or perceived by observers because they are composed of a set of independent but related organizational processes, such as the strategic planning process, the budgeting process, and performance evaluation.

Organizations have informal as well as formal control systems. The formal control system is a system designed explicitly to motivate or influence behavior and includes such items as plans, goals, standards, and rewards. The informal control system consists of the norms and values of an organization, or what we may call its culture.

Elements of Formal Control Systems

This book is primarily concerned with the formal control system and the role that accounting plays in it. (See the schematic model of the components or elements of a formal control system, shown in Exhibit 22–5 on the next page.)

As Exhibit 22–5 shows, a formal management control system consists of five basic parts or subsystems:

1. the planning system,
2. the operations system,
3. the measurement system,
4. the feedback system,
5. the evaluation-reward system.

An examination of each of these five parts follows.

EXHIBIT 22–5
Schematic Model of the Control System

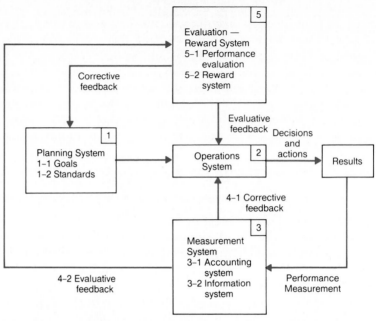

The Planning Component of a Control System

An organization's planning system is put into effect in order to develop objectives and action plans for the important areas of the firm, such as production and marketing. The planning system may be viewed not only as a separate management system per se but as a critical part or component of a larger management control system.

The planning system functions as part of the management control system by providing objectives for critical areas of a business. Objectives, in turn, serve to motivate and guide the behavior of operating personnel. Objectives also serve as performance standards against which actual performance will be compared.

The Operations Component of a Control System

The operations component of a control system is the ongoing system for performing the functions required for day-to-day organizational activities. Operations are the responsibilities and activities specified in organizational job descriptions. Through personal supervision managers try to ensure that day-to-day operations are carried out to meet the objectives set up in the planning process.

The Measurement Component of a Control System

In organizations, measurement is the process of assigning numbers to represent aspects of organizational behavior and performance. The overall measurement system includes the accounting system with its measures of financial performance. It also includes nonfinancial measures of financial performance, including production indexes, scrap rates, and measures of product quality.

The Feedback Component of Control

The fourth component of a control system is feedback. This is the information that is derived from the measurement system, and the evaluation-reward system described next. Feedback serves to link or connect the other major elements of a control system.

There are two major types of feedback—corrective feedback and evaluative feedback. Corrective feedback is information about the performance of the operational system; it is designed to help improve operations in the future through the planning process. Through corrective feedback the organization may change planning assumptions and methods of operations in order to improve performance. Evaluative feedback also is information about how well the operational system is doing, but it is used for the purpose of evaluating performance and administering rewards.

The Evaluation-Reward Component of Control

The evaluation-reward system refers to mechanisms for performance appraisal and the administration of organizational rewards. Rewards may be such things as compensation, promotions, or recognition for good performance.

Accounting's Role in Management Control

The accounting information system plays an important role in the process of management control in two ways:

1. The managerial accounting technique of budgeting provides the mechanism for translating many of an organization's objectives into quantifiable goals.
2. Accounting information offers management many of the measurements required to provide corrective and evaluative feedback.

The role of budgeting in control is examined in Chapter 26. The role of accounting information as corrective and evaluative feedback has already been illustrated in our discussion on accounting's role in problem identification; it is examined in more detail in later chapters. From this overview of the management process and the role of accounting in that process, we turn from financial accounting to managerial accounting.

Characteristics of Managerial Accounting

Managerial accounting is that part of accounting that provides information to managers inside the organization, as opposed to financial accounting, which provides accounting information to users outside of the organization, such as stockholders and creditors. Managerial accounting, as we have seen, helps management in planning, decision making, and control. Because of this orientation, managerial accounting has certain characteristics that are significantly different from financial accounting:

1. *Different users.* The users of managerial accounting information are the managers within the firm as opposed to the external users of financial accounting information.

2. *Not regulated by GAAP.* Because it is used internally, managerial accounting information does not have to be prepared according to GAAP. There are no rules and regulations governing how information or reports must be prepared; the major criterion for the preparation of managerial accounting information is its usefulness to management. For example, if the management

of a firm required information on sales orders, the firm's accountants would provide it, even though for financial accounting purposes sales orders are not considered revenue until title passes.

3. *Future oriented.* Managerial accounting is geared to what will happen in the future. As we have seen, one of the basic functions of management is planning; estimates of future revenues, costs, market share, and economic conditions play a major role in managerial accounting. Conversely, financial accounting information is based on past events and historical cost.

4. *Not required.* Managerial accounting is not required for business firms. Therefore, managerial accounting information differs from firm to firm. Some companies have very sophisticated computerized systems that prepare a variety of reports for many different purposes, and other firms may prepare only some of the estimates needed for budgeting. The needs of the organization and what management is willing to pay for managerial accounting information determine the nature and scope of any given system. Financial accounting, however, is required for all publicly held companies, and even the smallest of firms must prepare financial reports for tax purposes.

Responsibility Accounting

Responsibility accounting is based on the idea that individuals within an organization are accountable for items over which they have control. A responsibility accounting system classifies the costs and revenues of an organization according to the various levels of management that have control over them and holds managers responsible for differences between planned goals and actual results. A *responsibility center,* therefore, is a part of an organization whose manager has control over specified costs and revenues and is held accountable for performance relative to organizational plans. A responsibility center could be as small as one individual or as large as a department, manufacturing plant, and even an entire company. In this type of system, costs and revenues are accumulated and reported by levels of responsibility. There are four basic types of responsibility centers: (1) cost centers, (2) revenue centers, (3) profit centers, and (4) investment centers.

Cost Centers

In a cost center the manager has control over the incurrence of costs but is not expected to generate sales revenue. A machining department in a factory might be a cost center, as well as such service departments as personnel and accounting. The manager of a cost center is expected to incur costs in line with the budget and is held responsible for significant differences between actual costs and what was budgeted. The monthly performance report for the personnel department of Westport Publishing Company is shown at the top of the next page. The costs shown on the report are considered to be controllable by the department manager, and he or she might have to explain why the department spent more than what was budgeted on supplies and recruitment.

Revenue Centers

In a revenue center the manager has control over the revenue but not the full costs against which the revenue will be matched. The manager of a revenue center may control certain costs, but the primary unit of control is revenue.

| PERSONNEL DEPARTMENT | | | |
| Performance Report—June 1988 | | | |
	Budget	Actual	Difference
Salaries	$10,000	$10,000	—
Supplies	2,000	2,400	$(400)
Recruitment	5,000	5,500	(500)
Training	1,000	900	100
Total	$18,000	$18,800	$(800)

For example, a sales department of a manufacturing company might be a revenue center.

The manager of a revenue center is expected to generate revenues in line with the budget and is held accountable for significant differences between actual and budgeted revenues. The monthly performance report for the West Coast branch of Grid Graphics Manufacturing Company follows. The report shows sales revenue by product line as well as the difference between actual and budgeted revenues.

| Grid Graphics Manufacturing Company | | | |
| Performance Report—October 1988 | | | |
	Budget	Actual	Difference
Monitors	$350,000	$420,000	$70,000
Terminals	150,000	140,000	(10,000)
Total	$500,000	$560,000	$60,000

Profit Centers

In a profit center the manager has control over both costs and revenue. A profit center is expected to sell its goods to produce revenue. The manager of a profit center can be evaluated by comparing income statements with the planned objectives for costs and revenue. A department in a department store may be a profit center as may be the branch office of a bank or a company owned by another company. For example, Westport Publishing Company is a profit center within the communications division of IRW, Inc., but its personnel department is a cost center. The performance report for Westport Publishing for the month of June 1988 is shown at the top of the following page. Note that the cost data for the company include the total costs of the personnel department as well as other cost and profit centers.

Investment Centers

An investment center is a responsibility center in which the manager has control over not only costs and revenue but investments in assets as well. We use

Accounting Information for Management and Cost Terms and Concepts   915

Westport Publishing Company
Income Statement
For the Month Ending June 1988

	Budget	Actual	Difference
Sales	$1,200,000	$1,000,000	$(200,000)
Less:			
Production costs	600,000	550,000	50,000
Marketing costs	100,000	98,000	2,000
Personnel costs	18,000	18,800	(800)
Other costs	60,000	65,000	(5,000)
Net income	$ 422,000	$ 268,200	$(153,800)

the term *investment* not just in the context of buying stocks and bonds but to signify control over the funds for such assets as plant and equipment, receivables, and inventory. Therefore, investment center managers have a great deal of power and responsibility, and such centers tend to be divisions in large, decentralized organizations such as General Motors, Johnson & Johnson, and ITT.

To measure the performance of investment centers, one may use income statements to determine profitability and other measures that try to relate profitability to the assets under the control of the investment center manager. The most widely used of these measures is the rate of return on investment, called ROI. This measure compares net income with the investment in assets for a given investment center in order to determine the percentage rate of return on that investment:

$$\frac{\text{Net income}}{\text{Investment in assets}} = \text{Return on investment (ROI)}$$

Westport Publishing Company, as was noted before, is a profit center within the communications division of IRW, Inc., a large, decentralized organization. The communications division is an investment center within IRW, Inc. The performance of the communications division may be measured by examining income statements and by calculating the rate of return on investment. The division has invested a total of $7 million in plant, equipment, inventory, receivables, and other assets. The components of the total net income for the division are shown at the top of the next page and the calculation of the return on investment for June 1988 follows:

$$\text{Return on Investment}$$
$$\frac{\text{Net income}}{\text{Investment in assets}} = \text{ROI} \qquad \frac{\$1,069,000}{\$7,000,000} = 15\%$$

The communications division's ROI is 15%, and this can now be compared with the ROI of other divisions within IRW, Inc., as well as with the budget. Information on the performance of all IRW divisions is evaluated at central corporate headquarters and is used to make decisions regarding such matters

916

IRW, Inc.	
Communications Division	
Net Income—June 1988	
Westport Publishing	$ 268,200
Reston Software	400,000
Grid Graphics	150,800
U-Print Copy Centers	250,000
Total	$1,069,000

as the introduction of new product lines and the allocation of corporate funds for investments in assets.

The use of ROI in performance evaluation may cause problems for firms that rely on it exclusively. A division manager who takes an action designed to increase the division's short-term ROI risks causing long-term problems for the firm. For example, deferring maintenance on plant and equipment will increase net income and ROI in the short term. Similarly, postponing the purchase of a major asset will decrease the investment base and increase ROI. Both actions, however, will have a negative long-term effect on the corporation. Managers who are evaluated only on the ROI of their divisions also may reject investment opportunities that increase the ROI of the company as a whole but do not increase the ROI of their divisions. This too has a negative effect on the corporation as a whole. Some firms that use ROI try to avoid these problems by evaluating managers through other factors such as market share, cost efficiency, new products, and new technology. Responsibility accounting, therefore, is a means of structuring an organization so that management can more fully carry out its roles of planning, decision making, and control. It has become most important in large, decentralized organizations because it offers managers greater responsibility while providing a means of accountability to the organization.

The first part of this chapter has outlined the role of accounting in the management process and has given a brief introduction to responsibility accounting. Next is an introduction to accounting for the manufacturing process, and a method of understanding how managers may use costs for both financial statements and the management process within the firm.

Costs for Different Purposes

The management process is based on planning, decision making, and control. In all of these aspects of the management function, the accounting system provides information to help managers perform their job. The accounting system accumulates data about the costs incurred by the organization for different purposes. Accountants usually define **costs** as the resources sacrificed or given up in order to attain goods or services. Let us look more closely at costs and the ways that we measure them.

Cost Objectives

The term *cost* both in accounting and everyday usage, brings to mind the cost *of* something. One may want to know the cost of a new car or the cost of a vacation, just as the manager in a business wants to know the cost of a piece of equipment or the cost of introducing a new product line. In all of these instances, the item that we attempt to calculate the cost of, such as the new car or the new product line, is a **cost objective.** For example, if management inquires about the cost of running a centralized data processing department in a large corporation, the data processing department becomes a cost objective. Similarly, if a defense contractor calculates the costs incurred on a particular government contract, the contract becomes the cost objective. Managers generally need to know the cost of manufacturing a particular product, and in that case the product is the cost objective. A business organization may have many different cost objectives, but they are generally chosen to help management in the decision-making process.

Direct and Indirect Costs

When we have chosen a particular cost objective, we then must decide whether costs are direct or indirect relative to that objective. For example, if we wanted to know the cost of running a data processing department, we would look for the costs that could be traced easily to that department, such as the salary of the department manager. Those costs that are easily traced to a particular cost objective are considered **direct costs** of that cost objective. Other costs are **indirect costs** because they are incurred for more than one cost objective. For example, the salary of the president of a large corporation is incurred for the overall operations of the firm and so would be an indirect cost of running the data processing department. Indirect costs sometimes are called common costs because they are incurred for more than one part of an organization and must be allocated to cost objectives. Thus, the president's salary could be allocated to the different departments of the firm based on their percentage of the total revenues of the company. A good illustration of the nature of direct and indirect costs can be found in the manufacturing process. Firms need to know the cost of making their product, and so the cost objective is the unit of product. Some manufacturing costs are direct costs of making the product while other manufacturing costs are indirect costs and must be allocated to the product. Let us now examine the nature of the costs incurred in manufacturing a product.

Manufacturing Costs

A manufacturing firm changes raw materials into finished products by using labor and the production facilities of a factory. A manufacturing firm generally is more complex than a merchandising firm because it must both produce and sell a product. Manufacturing firms must keep track of how much it costs to make each product, for management uses that information in pricing and decision making. Therefore, one of the functions of the accounting system is to collect information each period on the use of the three basic **manufacturing costs**—direct materials, direct labor, and factory overhead. Following is an examination of these costs.

Direct Materials

Direct materials are all materials that become an integral part of a finished product and that can be conveniently and economically traced to that product. Examples of direct materials are subassemblies for automobiles, wood for furniture, and chocolate chips for cookies. There are some materials used in manufacturing products that may be difficult and costly to trace. For example, in a furniture factory minor items such as glue or nails are usually considered **indirect materials** and the costs of such items are considered part of factory overhead.

Direct Labor

Direct labor is the labor that can be conveniently and economically traced to the creation of a finished product. Examples of direct labor are assemblers and machine operators in a factory and electricians and carpenters on a construction site. Many labor costs involved in the manufacturing process are difficult to trace directly to the units of product, and these labor costs are considered *indirect*. Examples of **indirect labor** are material handlers, supervisors, janitors, and plant guards. Like the cost of indirect materials, the cost of indirect labor is considered part of factory overhead.

Factory Overhead

Factory overhead includes all manufacturing costs other than direct materials and direct labor, namely, indirect materials and indirect labor. Factory utilities, rent or depreciation on a factory facility, property taxes, and insurance are considered part of overhead too, but only if they relate to the manufacturing process. That is why depreciation on an office building is considered an administrative expense but depreciation on a factory building is included in factory overhead. Note that all of the factory overhead costs are indirect costs of manufacturing a product; they are necessary for the creation of the finished product, but it is difficult and costly to trace them to individual units of product. Consequently, overhead costs are divided among each unit of product by calculating an overhead rate before each period starts. For example, a firm may estimate that the overhead costs for the coming year will be $550,000 and that it will employ 100,000 direct labor hours (DLH). The firm may compute its overhead rate as follows:

$$\frac{\text{Estimated overhead cost (\$550,000)}}{\text{Estimated activity (100,000 DLH)}} = \$5.50 \text{ per DLH}$$

During the period, $5.50 of overhead cost will be added to the cost of the product each time the firm uses one direct labor hour. In Chapter 27 we show how this predetermined overhead rate is calculated and used to determine the cost of a unit of product.

Factory overhead is known by a number of names, including factory burden, factory expense, and manufacturing overhead.

Nonmanufacturing Costs

Nonmanufacturing costs are all the costs a company incurs, other than direct materials, direct labor, and factory overhead. There are two categories of nonmanufacturing costs—selling and administrative. Items such as sales salaries, sales commissions, advertising, and shipping are considered selling costs and as such are separated from the costs incurred in manufacturing products. Administrative costs are nonmanufacturing costs that relate to the overall running of the organization and include such items as the president's salary, costs incurred by the legal department and the public relations department, and secretarial support.

Effect of Manufacturing on Financial Statements

Manufacturing firms are more complex in structure than are other types of firms, and their financial statements reflect a greater diversity of costs. We now examine the differences in the balance sheet and the income statement for a manufacturing firm and a merchandising firm.

Balance Sheet

The greatest difference between the balance sheets of manufacturers and of merchandisers is in the inventory category. A merchandising firm has one inventory account that reflects the goods purchased from suppliers, whereas a manufacturing firm has three types of inventory, each corresponding to a stage in the production process:

1. *Raw materials inventory.* Goods purchased as raw materials waiting to go into the manufacturing process.
2. *Work-in-process inventory.* Units of product undergoing the production process, partially complete.
3. *Finished goods inventory.* Units of product completed but unsold.

Exhibit 22–6 (shown at the top of the next page) compares the current asset sections of the balance sheets of a manufacturing and a merchandising firm, showing three inventory accounts for the manufacturing firm and one inventory account for the merchandising firm. The numbers in the accounts have been assumed for purposes of illustration.

The three manufacturing costs—direct materials, direct labor, and factory overhead—are collected in the work-in-process inventory until the units of product are completed, at which time their cost becomes part of the finished goods inventory. The costs remain there until the units of product are sold, at which time their cost gets transferred to cost of goods sold, as shown below:

Work in Process	Finished Goods	Cost of Goods Sold
Direct material Direct labor Factory overhead →	→ →	→

Income Statement

The income statements of manufacturing and merchandising firms differ in the same way that their balance sheets do, that is, in the inventory category. Exhibit 22–7 depicts the income statements of the Washington Manufacturing Company and Chic Boutique. Note that in computing cost of goods sold, the boutique shows the cost of purchases from outside suppliers, whereas the manufacturing company shows the cost of manufacturing its own goods.

920

```
                        EXHIBIT 22-6
                   Current Assets Sections of
                        Balance Sheets

Manufacturing Firm
Cash                                         $ 25,000
Accounts receivable                            40,000
Inventories:
   Raw materials              $10,000
   Work in process             30,000
   Finished goods              60,000         100,000
Prepaid expenses                               12,000
Total current assets                         $177,000

Merchandising Firm
Cash                                         $ 20,000
Accounts receivable                            45,000
Merchandise inventory                         140,000
Prepaid expenses                               10,000
Total current assets                         $215,000
```

On the income statement, the cost of goods manufactured is derived from a supporting schedule that is called a **schedule of cost of goods manufactured,** as shown in Exhibit 22–8 for the Washington Manufacturing Company. The first part of the schedule shows the method of calculating the cost of the raw materials used in the production process for the period. This calculation is formatted in the same manner as is cost of goods sold, and the same format is used to show any amount transferred from an account in a given period:

```
Beginning balance                     $X,XXX
Add: Increases in the account          X,XXX
Total available                        X,XXX
Less: Ending balance                   X,XXX
Amount transferred out of account     $X,XXX
```

The amount of raw materials used in production in Exhibit 22–8 is $66,000, the cost of the raw materials that Washington Manufacturing Company transferred from the raw materials inventory and used in production during 1987. The cost of raw materials used in the production process is added to direct labor and overhead costs to total the manufacturing costs for the period—$97,000.

The schedule shows the method of calculating cost of goods manufactured in the same way that it shows raw materials used in production, except that in calculating cost of goods manufactured the beginning balance is on the second line rather than the first because the costs of the work-in-process inventory must be added to the total manufacturing costs for the period. Likewise, ending work-in-process inventory must be deducted in order to determine the cost of the goods manufactured. The word *manufactured* means that the units of product were completed and transferred from the work-in-process

Accounting Information for Management and Cost Terms and Concepts

EXHIBIT 22-7
Income Statements—Manufacturing and Merchandising Firms

Washington Manufacturing Company
Income Statement
For the Year Ended December 31, 1987

Sales		$250,000
Cost of goods sold:		
Beginning finished goods inventory, 12/31/86	$ 25,000	
Add: **Cost of goods manufactured**	98,000	
Cost of goods available for sale	123,000	
Less: Ending finished goods inventory, 12/31/87	20,000	
Cost of goods sold		103,000
Gross margin		147,000
Less: Selling and administrative expenses		85,000
Net income		$ 62,000

Chic Boutique
Income Statement
For the Year Ended December 31, 1987

Sales		$450,000
Cost of goods sold:		
Beginning merchandise inventory, 12/31/86	$120,000	
Add: **Purchases**	300,000	
Cost of goods available for sale	420,000	
Less: Ending merchandise inventory, 12/31/87	109,000	
Cost of goods sold		311,000
Gross margin		139,000
Less: Selling and administrative expenses		89,000
Net income		$ 50,000

inventory to the finished goods inventory. After the cost of the goods manufactured is calculated on the schedule, the total is transferred to the income statement and is listed under cost of goods sold.

Product Costs and Period Costs

In addition to classifying costs according to their function as manufacturing and nonmanufacturing, we can classify costs according to when they are matched against revenues on the income statement, as product costs and period costs.

Product Costs

Product costs are those costs identified with goods manufactured for resale or with goods purchased for resale. They become part of the costs in the Inventory account, and for this reason they also are called *inventoriable costs.* Direct materials, direct labor, and factory overhead are product costs as well as manufacturing costs because their costs are included in the cost of the units of product in inventory, where they will remain (as an asset) until the units of product are sold. When the units of product are sold, the cost of manufacturing them is transferred to cost of goods sold and is deducted as an expense. Similarly, when a merchandising company purchases goods for resale, their cost is assigned to inventory and is deducted as an expense on the income statement only when that inventory is sold. Therefore, these product costs can be incurred in one period, but if the units of product are not sold, those costs remain in the Inventory account as assets on the balance sheet at the end of the period; they will become cost of goods sold expenses in the period in which the units are sold. Exhibit 22-9 (on the following page) shows the flow of product costs from the balance sheet to the income statement for a manufacturing firm and a merchandising firm.

Period Costs

A **period cost,** as the name suggests, is associated with the accounting period rather than the units of product. When a period cost is incurred, it is immediately deducted from revenues as an expense of the period. All selling and administrative expenses—the nonmanufacturing costs—are treated as period costs and are deducted from revenues in the period in which they are in-

EXHIBIT 22–9
Product and Period Costs

Manufacturing Company

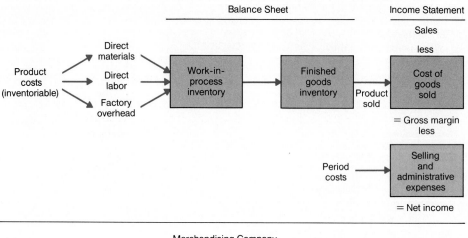

Merchandising Company

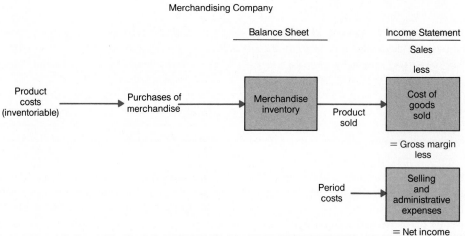

curred. This is another example of the importance of the matching convention in determining net income. Recall that the matching convention states that the expenses incurred in a period to earn the revenues of that period should be offset against those revenues. Selling and administrative expenses are considered to be incurred in order to earn the revenue for a given period and are, therefore, considered costs of that period and are listed as expenses on the income statement.

The accounting system in manufacturing firms must clearly distinguish between period and product costs. For example, assume that a company has depreciation expense of $15,000 for 1988, of which two-thirds applies to operation of the factory and one-third to selling and administrative activities. Of the total depreciation expense, two-thirds (or $10,000) would be a product cost added to work-in-process inventory. As units of product are completed, the cost is transferred to finished goods inventory. The $10,000 remains in an asset account, Work in Process or Finished Goods, and will not become an expense in cost of goods sold until the units of product are sold, which may not be until the following year. In contrast, the $5,000 of depreciation expense that applies to selling and administrative activities is deducted immediately as an expense of 1988. Exhibit 22–9 shows period costs for the merchandising and manufacturing firms. Note that these costs never flow on to the balance sheet; they go directly to the income statement.

Summary of Learning Objectives

1. ***The nature of management and the three elements of the management process.*** Management is the process of using resources to achieve objectives. The three elements of the management process are planning, decision making, and control. The process of planning involves analyzing information about the organization and its environment, establishing objectives to be attained, and developing action plans to achieve those objectives. Management uses four methods of planning: strategic, operational, contingency, and budgetary. Management decision making begins with defining a problem and gathering relevant information. Next, alternative courses of action are identified, the costs and benefits of each alternative are evaluated, and a choice is made among alternatives. An organizational control system is a set of processes and techniques designed to increase the likelihood that people will behave in ways that help an organization attain its objectives. A formal control system consists of five parts: the planning system, the operations system, the measurement system, the feedback system, and the evaluation-reward system.

2. ***The role of accounting in management planning, decision making, and control, and the characteristics of managerial accounting.*** Accounting information plays a major role in the management process. In long-term strategic planning, accounting provides data to evaluate investment alternatives; short-term operational planning is based on the budgeting process, whereby the operational plan is expressed in financial terms in the form of accounting reports such as profit budgets. Accounting reports also provide basic information for the decision-making process; analysis of accounting information leads to the identification of problems, and accounting data also are used to identify and evaluate the costs and benefits of alternative courses of action. In management control, the accounting information in the budgeting process provides a mechanism for translating many of an organization's objectives into quantifiable goals, whereas accounting data are the measurements needed to provide corrective and evaluative feedback to management.

   Managerial accounting has the following basic characteristics: (1) It provides information for internal use by management; (2) it does not have to be prepared according to generally accepted accounting principles; (3) it is future oriented; and (4) it is not required.

3. ***Responsibility accounting and the four types of responsibility centers.*** Responsibility accounting is a system that classifies the costs and revenues of an organization according to the various levels of management that have control over them and holds managers responsible for differences between planned goals and actual results.

A cost center is a responsibility center in which the manager has control over the incurrence of costs, but he or she is not expected to generate sales revenue. The manager of a cost center is expected to incur costs in line with the budget and is held responsible for significant differences between actual results and the budget.

A revenue center is a responsibility center in which the manager is primarily responsible for generating revenue. The manager may have control over the incurrence of some but not all of the costs necessary to produce a product. The manager of a revenue center may be evaluated by comparing actual revenues with budgeted revenues.

A profit center is a responsibility center in which the manager has control over both costs and revenues. The manager of a profit center may be evaluated by reviewing income statements relative to the planned objectives for costs and revenues.

An investment center is a responsibility center in which the manager has control over not only costs and revenues but investments in assets as well. The manager of an investment center may be evaluated by profitability, as shown by income statements and by the rate of return on investment, which measures the relationship between net income and the level of investment in assets.

4. *Calculating the return on investment for an investment center.* The rate of return on investment compares net income with the investment in assets for a given investment center to determine the percentage rate of return on that investment:

$$\frac{\text{Net income}}{\text{Investment in assets}} = \text{Return on investment (ROI)}$$

5. *The nature of cost objectives and direct and indirect costs.* A cost objective is any item or activity that one attempts to determine the cost of. Costs that are easily and economically traced to a particular cost objective are considered direct costs of that cost objective. Costs that are incurred for more than one cost objective are indirect costs, and such costs must be assigned or allocated to cost objectives.

6. *Comparing manufacturing and nonmanufacturing costs.* Manufacturing costs are the costs a company incurs to produce its product. There are three basic manufacturing costs—direct materials, direct labor, and factory overhead. Nonmanufacturing costs are selling costs—such as advertising and sales commissions—and administrative costs, that is, those costs related to the overall running of the organization as a whole.

7. *Defining manufacturing costs.* Direct materials are all materials that become an integral part of the finished product and that can be conveniently and economically traced to the finished product. Direct labor is labor that can be conveniently and economically traced to the creation of the finished product. Factory overhead is made up of all manufacturing costs other than direct materials and direct labor. It is an indirect cost of the finished product.

8. *Preparing the schedule of cost of goods manufactured and the income statement for a manufacturing firm.* The basic format for the schedule of cost of goods manufactured follows:

Any Manufacturing Company
Schedule of Cost of Goods Manufactured
For the Year Ended December 31, 1988

Raw materials:		
Beginning raw materials inventory, 12/31/87	$xxx,xxx	
Add: Purchases of raw materials	xxx,xxx	
Raw materials available for use	xxx,xxx	
Less: Ending raw materials inventory, 12/31/88	xxx,xxx	
Raw materials used in production		$ xxx,xxx
Direct labor		xxx,xxx
Factory overhead:		
Indirect materials	$ xx,xxx	
Indirect labor	xx,xxx	
Utilities, factory	xx,xxx	
Depreciation, factory building	xx,xxx	
Depreciation, factory equipment	xx,xxx	
Total overhead costs		xxx,xxx
Total manufacturing costs, 1988		xxx,xxx
Add: Beginning work in process inventory, 12/31/87		xx,xxx
Total manufacturing costs to account for		x,xxx,xxx
Less: Ending work in process inventory, 12/31/88		xx,xxx
Cost of goods manufactured		$ xxx,xxx

The basic format for the income statement for a manufacturing firm is shown below:

Any Manufacturing Company
Income Statement
For the Year Ended December 31, 1988

Sales		$x,xxx,xxx
Cost of goods sold:		
Beginning finished goods inventory, 12/31/87	$ xxx,xxx	
Add: Cost of goods manufactured	xxx,xxx	
Cost of goods available for sale	x,xxx,xxx	
Less: Ending finished goods inventory, 12/31/88	xxx,xxx	
Cost of goods sold		x,xxx,xxx
Gross margin		x,xxx,xxx
Less selling and administrative expenses		xxx,xxx
Net income		$x,xxx,xxx

9. *Defining product costs and period costs.* Product costs are those costs identified with goods manufactured for resale or with goods purchased for resale. They are included in the costs in the Inventory account, an

asset shown on the balance sheet. When the units of product are sold, those costs are transferred to cost of goods sold on the income statement.

Period costs are associated with the accounting period rather than with units of product, and such costs are immediately deducted from revenues in the period when they are incurred. All selling and administrative expenses are treated as period costs.

Key Terms

Action Plans	Indirect Labor	Period Costs
Budget	Indirect Material	Process
Cost Objective	Management	Product Costs
Costs	Management Control	Resources
Direct Costs	Managerial Accounting	Responsibility Accounting
Direct Labor	Manufacturing Costs	Schedule of Cost of Goods
Direct Materials	Nonmanufacturing Costs	Manufactured
Factory Overhead	Organizational Control	
Indirect Costs	System	

Problem for Your Review

Cost of Goods Manufactured and Income Statement. Rawhide Corporation manufactures wallets, coin purses, key holders, and other small leather accessories. The following information on the firm's costs, sales, and inventories for the first quarter of 1987 is available:

Raw materials purchased	$ 45,000
Direct labor cost	32,600
Supervisory salaries, factory	25,000
Sales commissions	42,000
Maintenance and repairs, factory	12,000
Depreciation, factory machinery	5,000
Rent, factory	15,000
Administrative expenses	38,500
Advertising expenses	14,500
Indirect materials	2,600
Sales salaries	20,000
Sales revenue	450,000
Inventories:	
Raw materials, 1/1/87	15,000
Raw materials, 3/31/87	18,000
Work in process, 1/1/87	57,000
Work in process, 3/31/87	45,900
Finished goods, 1/1/87	139,600
Finished goods, 3/31/87	97,400

Required:

  a. Prepare a schedule of cost of goods manufactured and sold for the first quarter of 1987.

  b. Prepare an income statement showing the computation of cost of goods sold for the period.

  c. List the period costs and the product costs. Classify the product costs as direct (D) or indirect (I).

a.

Rawhide Corporation
Schedule of Cost of Goods Manufactured
For the Quarter Ended March 31, 1987

Raw materials:		
Beginning raw materials inventory, 1/1/87	$15,000	
Add: Purchases of raw materials	45,000	
Raw materials available for use	60,000	
Less: Ending raw materials inventory, 3/31/87	18,000	
Raw materials used in production		$ 42,000
Direct labor		32,600
Factory overhead:		
Supervisory salaries, factory	25,000	
Maintenance and repairs, factory	12,000	
Depreciation, factory machinery	5,000	
Rent, factory	15,000	
Indirect materials	2,600	
Total overhead costs		59,600
Total manufacturing costs, 1/1/87–3/31/87		134,200
Add: Beginning work in process inventory, 1/1/87		57,000
Total manufacturing costs to account for		191,200
Less: Ending work in process inventory, 3/31/87		45,900
Cost of goods manufactured		$145,300

b.

Rawhide Corporation
Income Statement
For the Quarter Ended March 31, 1987

Sales		$450,000
Cost of goods sold:		
Beginning finished goods inventory, 1/1/87	$139,600	
Add: Cost of goods manufactured	145,300	
Cost of goods available for sale	284,900	
Less: Ending finished goods inventory, 3/31/87	97,400	
Cost of goods sold		187,500
Gross margin		262,500[a]
Less: Selling and administrative expenses		115,000
Net income		$147,500

[a]Selling and administrative expenses:	
Sales salaries	$ 20,000
Sales commissions	42,000
Advertising expenses	14,500
Administrative expenses	38,500
	$115,000

c.

Period Costs	Product Costs
Sales commissions	Direct labor cost (D)
Administrative expenses	Supervisory salaries (I)
Advertising expenses	Maintenance and repairs (I)
Sales salaries	Direct materials used (D)
	Depreciation, machinery (I)
	Rent, factory (I)
	Indirect materials (I)

Questions

1. Do you agree that accounting can play a useful role in management planning? Why or why not?

2. What are some of the uses of accounting in the management decision-making process?

3. How does managerial accounting differ from financial accounting?

4. Give some examples of decisions in which accounting information would be useful.

5. What is responsibility accounting?

6. Define a cost center.

7. How does a profit center differ from an investment center?

8. One of your fellow students has stated, "If a division operates at a loss, then it can't be a profit center." Do you agree or disagree? Why?

9. What is the difference between direct and indirect costs?

10. Is the cost of shipping a product to the customer a manufacturing or nonmanufacturing cost?

11. Define factory overhead. Why is it considered to be an indirect cost of the finished product?

12. You overheard a student saying that the cost of goods manufactured for a manufacturing firm is similar to the cost of purchases for a merchandising firm. Do you agree or disagree? Why?

13. Describe the differences between the inventory section on the balance sheet of a manufacturing firm and that of a merchandising firm.

14. Define product costs and period costs.

15. Can a product cost that is incurred in 1987 be expensed in 1988? Explain your answer.

Exercises

1. Accounting and Management Control. Using the following table, indicate whether each of the following aspects of accounting plays a role in a management control system by placing a checkmark in the appropriate box:

Elements of a Control System

Elements of Accounting	Planning System	Operating System	Measurement System	Feedback System	Reward System
Net income					
A budget					
ROI					
Expenses					
Revenue					

2. Accounting and Decision Making. You are vice-president of Geotech, a medium-sized producer of computer components. In which of the following types of management decisions would you find accounting information useful?

    a. Should we keep a product line that is operating at a loss?

    b. Should we make or buy a subcomponent for our product?

    c. Should we hire Bradley or Harris?

    d. Should we accept an order from Hightech Manufacturing Company at a price below our regular price?

    e. Should we change our bank from Wells Fargo to Bank of America?

3. Accounting Information for Capital Decisions. Arrowhead Company is interested in buying a photocopy machine. The accountant has obtained the following information about the operating costs of two brands, X and Y:

	Brand X	Brand Y
Purchase price	$3,000	$5,000
Supplies	300	200
Annual maintenance	600	300

Compute the number of years it will take before the cost savings from operating Brand Y will reimburse the company for the greater initial cost of Brand Y.

4. Responsibility Accounting. Refer to the following organization chart for the Metropolitan Realty Company. The sales department is responsible for selling homes and incurs costs for office space and staff. The property management and leasing departments are responsible for leasing homes and managing them (collecting rents, etc.) for the lessors. The mortgage department borrows money from investors and lends it to home buyers in the form of mortgages. The administration department performs the support services needed to run the company.

METROPOLITAN REALTY COMPANY

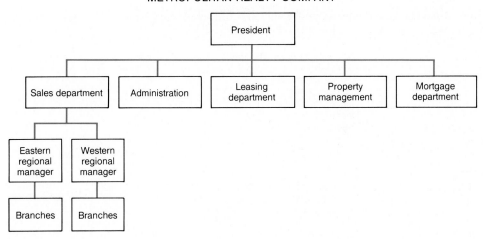

Indicate which of the following are cost centers (C), revenue centers (R), profit centers (P), or investment centers (I):

a. The sales department.

b. The mortgage department.

c. The administration department.

d. The property management department.

e. The leasing department.

f. The company as a whole.

5. ROI. Selected data for three divisions follow:

	X	Y	Z
Sales	$100,000	$80,000	$90,000
Net income	15,000	12,000	14,000
Investment in assets	50,000	60,000	90,000

Required:

a. Calculate the ROI for each division.

b. Each of the divisions has an investment opportunity that would yield a rate of return of 18 percent. Which divisions will accept and which will reject the opportunity? Why?

6. Product and Period Costs. Classify the following costs from a manufacturing company as either product costs (PR) or period costs (PE):

a. Factory supervisors' salaries.

b. Advertising in an industry publication.

c. Depreciation of factory machinery.

d. Rent for central corporate headquarters.

e. Depreciation of cars used by salespeople.

f. Rent for the factory building.

g. Salary of the president's executive secretary.

h. Cost of the factory workers' unemployment insurance.

i. Oil and other lubricants used on machinery.

j. Entertainment expense at the annual sales meeting.

k. Materials used to ship products to customers.

l. Salaries of the factory security guards.

m. Utilities used in central corporate headquarters.

n. Depreciation on corporate jet used by the company executives.

o. Utilities used in the factory.

7. Cost of Goods Manufactured and Sold. The following data have been taken from the accounting records of Wilshire, Inc. for 1989:

Purchases of raw materials	$ 8,000
Direct labor cost	10,000
Indirect labor cost	6,000
Indirect materials	1,000
Depreciation, factory building	1,500
Depreciation, factory equipment	1,000
Depreciation, office equipment	1,200
Maintenance, factory equipment	1,800
Maintenance, office equipment	1,600
Utilities, factory building	900
Beginning raw materials inventory	5,000
Ending raw materials inventory	6,000
Beginning work-in-process inventory	5,000
Ending work-in-process inventory	7,000
Beginning finished goods inventory	18,000
Ending finished goods inventory	13,000

Required:

a. Prepare a schedule of cost of goods manufactured for 1989.

b. Calculate the cost of goods sold for 1989.

8. Classification of Costs. Global, a large aerospace company, earns most of its revenues from defense contracts with the U.S. government. The company therefore keeps track of the revenues and expenses associated with each government contract rather than with the individual units of product. Following is a list of costs Global incurred in making the B-85 bomber. Using the contract for the bomber as the cost objective, classify the costs as either product (PR) or period (PE); then classify the product costs as either direct (D) or indirect (I).

a. Metal used in the production of the plane.

b. Salary of the production supervisor.

c. Utilities used in Global factories for the production of all products.

d. Corporate advertising costs.

e. Labor used in production.

f. Salary of the test pilot.

g. Salary of Global's vice-president of production.

h. Lobbying costs to secure contract.

i. Salaries of the corporate legal department.

j. Depreciation of all Global factory equipment.

9. Responsibility Accounting. The container manufacturing division of General Products Corporation produces tin food cans, bottle caps, and a general line of containers. The largest amount of the firm's products are manufactured in the firm's Midwest plant. The firm has three sales branch offices located in the midwestern and eastern parts of the United States. The manager of the manufacturing plant is responsible for all manufacturing operations and their related costs and he reports to the general manager of the division. Each sales branch is responsible for generating specified amounts of sales according to a plan originated by the general manager of the container division. Indicate whether each of the following is a cost center (C), revenue center (R), or profit center (P):

a. The manufacturing plant.

b. The three sales branches.

c. The office of the general manager of the division.

10. Finding Missing Data. The following data relate to the inventory of Talbot Manufacturing Corporation:

	Inventories	
	Beginning	Ending
Raw materials	$108,000	$115,000
Work in process	84,000	96,000
Finished goods	130,000	115,000

Additional Information:

Factory overhead	$200,000
Raw material used	231,000
Cost of goods available for sale	820,000

Required:

Supply the following data:

a. Raw materials purchases.

b. Direct labor costs incurred.

c. Cost of goods sold.

Problem Set A

22A-1. Cost of Goods Manufactured and Income Statement. The following data were taken from the records of the Portman Company at the end of 1987:

Direct labor payroll	$ 55,000
Raw material used	95,000
Factory utilities	7,000
Machine maintenance	8,000
Factory supervision	18,000
Manufacturing supplies used	4,000
Depreciation of factory machinery	9,000
Factory rent	15,000
Miscellaneous factory costs	4,000
Sales revenue	280,000
Selling and administrative expenses	60,000
Inventories, work in process:	
January 1, 1987	25,000
December 31, 1987	35,000
Inventories, finished goods:	
January 1, 1987	45,000
December 31, 1987	55,000

Required:

a. Prepare the statement of cost of goods manufactured for the year 1987.

b. Prepare an income statement for the year 1987.

22A-2. Analysis of Differences between Budget and Actual. West Coast Marine Repair Corporation is a commercial and naval ship repair firm. The firm is located in a large metropolitan city on the west coast of the United States. The firm specializes in commercial ship repair but also does work for the U.S. Navy. The firm's annual profit budget and related actual income are shown on the following page.

Required:

    a. Evaluate the firm's performance for the year and indicate the areas where problems exist or where potential problems would indicate a need for further investigation.

    b. State your reasons or criteria for deciding whether or not a problem exists.

West Coast Marine Repair
1988 Profit Budget and Income Statement

Classification	Budget	Actual	Difference
Gross sales	$34,000	$32,500	$(1,500)
Sales allowance	3,740	3,250	490
Net sales	$30,260	$29,250	$(1,010)
Cost of sales	20,740	20,475	265
Gross profit	9,520	8,775	(745)
Operating expenses	6,800	7,475	(675)
Net income before taxes	$ 2,720	$ 1,300	$(1,420)

Notes:
1. Brackets ( ) denote unfavorable differences.

22A–3. Cost Identification. The Woodworks Company makes reproductions of antique wood furniture for sale to specialty stores. Classify the following costs of the company as period costs (PE) or product costs (PR) and then indicate if the product costs are direct (D) or indirect (I) relative to the units of product:

    1. Depreciation, office equipment
    2. Indirect materials
    3. Utilities, factory
    4. Direct labor
    5. Advertising brochure
    6. Direct materials
    7. Depreciation, factory building
    8. Office supplies for accounting department
    9. Supervisory salaries, factory
    10. Fees for CPA firm
    11. Insurance, factory building
    12. Sales commissions
    13. Freight charges for shipping furniture
    14. Utilities, office
    15. Factory cafeteria

22A–4. Critical Performance Areas and Management Objectives. Ron Wagner is the general manager of the container manufacturing division of General Products Corporation. The division's products are tin food cans, bottle caps, and a general line of containers. Prior to the beginning of each year, the firm prepares a budgeted income statement based on forecasted sales revenue and expected operating costs. The vice-president of General Products Corporation to whom Ron Wagner reports, Harriet Schwartz, has stated that she believes that customer service, employee safety, and personnel development are very important aspects of any business unit's operations.

Required:

    a. Identify the most important areas of performance for the container manufacturing division.

    b. For each of those areas, state a nonnumerical objective that might be reasonable for the division to achieve.

    c. How would you propose to measure each of those objectives in order to evaluate the division's performance?

22A–5. ROI Calculation and Analysis. Wilshire Industries designs, manufactures, and markets a line of medical instruments used in surgical departments. The firm has two regional divisions. In order to maximize transportation costs and provide accessibility to customers, each division is responsible for manufacturing and selling its own products in different parts of the country. The West Coast division was established 2 years ago, and the East Coast division was established 12 years ago. The factory equipment in the West Coast division was acquired new within the last two years; the factory equipment in the East Coast division was acquired aproximately 11 to 12 years ago. The expected life of the equipment is 12 years. Basic data for both divisions for 1988 follow:

	West Coast	East Coast
Sales	$3,500,000	$3,400,000
Cost of goods sold	1,800,000	1,750,000
Gross margin	1,700,000	1,650,000
Selling and administrative expenses	800,000	875,000
Net income	$ 900,000	$ 775,000
Investment in assets	$6,000,000	$3,100,000

Required:
   a. Calculate the ROI for each division.
   b. Robert Morese, president of Wilshire Industries, has stated, "It's clear that the East Coast division is being run better than the West Coast division, and the bonus for each manager should reflect this." If you were the manager of the West Coast division, how would you respond to Mr. Morese's remark?
   c. Would you expect this situation to remain the same in 1989? Why or why not?
   d. What are some of the problems associated with using a single measure of performance evaluation?

22A–6. Cost of Goods Manufactured and Income Statement. DataStore is a small electronics firm that produces a single product. The following cost, production, and sales data relate to 1987:

Number of units produced	50,000
Production costs:	
Materials purchased	$ 80,000
Direct labor	150,000
Utilities, $5,000 per year + $.20 per unit produced	————
Machinery and equipment depreciation (production accounts for 85% of total corporate depreciation)	100,000
Maintenance, $8,000 per year + $.25 per unit produced	————
Other indirect labor	18,000
Indirect material	5,000
Insurance, factory	1,000
Rent, factory	25,000
Selling and administrative costs	120,000
Inventories:	
Raw material, January 1, 1987	$ 20,000
Raw material, December 31, 1987	25,000
Work in process, January 1, 1987	50,000
Work in process, December 31, 1987	64,500
Finished goods, January 1, 1987	42,350
Finished goods, December 31, 1987	119,350
Sales	$500,000

During 1986, the average cost of production was $7.70 per unit. The units on hand at the end of 1987 were all produced in 1987.

Required:

    a. Prepare a schedule of cost of goods manufactured for 1987.

    b. Prepare an income statement for 1987.

    c. Calculate the cost per unit for 1987 production.

    d. How many units are left in finished goods inventory at the end of 1987?

    e. What is the selling price per unit that DataStore charged in 1987?

22A-7. Reconstruction of Missing Data. NiftyWear, a producer of sporting goods, uses micro-computers to keep track of its manufacturing process and general accounting system. James U. Dolt, an employee in the accounting department, was sipping coffee and chatting with friends while processing the firm's data for 1989. To his horror, he discovered that he had managed to both erase all the data on the computer and spill coffee on the backups. Some information is left on scraps of paper, and Dolt tries to reconstruct the missing data from what was available as follows:

    1. Gross margin was equal to 20% of sales for the year.

    2. Sales for 1989 were $600,000.

    3. Prime costs were $331,000.

    4. Raw material purchased totaled $200,000.

    5. Direct labor cost $210,000.

    6. Cost of goods available for sale was $520,000.

    7. Direct material at January 1, 1989 cost $20,000.

    8. Work in process at January 1, 1989 cost $44,000.

    9. Finished goods at January 1, 1989 cost $35,000.

    10. Factory overhead is equal to 40% of conversion costs.

Required:

Calculate the following:

    a. Raw materials inventory at December 31, 1989.

    b. Work-in-process inventory at December 31, 1989.

    c. Finished goods inventory at December 31, 1989.

Hint: Prime costs = Raw materials used + Direct labor.

        Conversion costs = Direct labor + Factory overhead.

Problem Set B

22B-1. Cost of Goods Manufactured and Income Statement. The following data were taken from the records of the Thomasville Company at the end of 1988:

Direct labor payroll	$ 75,000
Raw material used	115,000
Factory utilities	27,000
Machine maintenance	28,000
Factory supervision	38,000
Manufacturing supplies used	24,000
Depreciation of factory machinery	29,000
Factory rent	35,000
Miscellaneous factory costs	24,000
Sales revenue	493,000
Selling and administrative expenses	80,000
Inventories, work in process:	
January 1, 1988	45,000
December 31, 1988	55,000
Inventories, finished goods:	
January 1, 1988	65,000
December 31, 1988	75,000

Required:

    a. Prepare the statement of cost of goods manufactured for the year 1988.

    b. Prepare an income statement for the year 1988.

22B–2. Decision Analysis and Responsibility Accounting. The Able division of Northwest Lumber Company manufactures paper boxes. It acquires its paper liner board, the raw material for the boxes, from two sources: the Baker division of Northwest Lumber Company and Craft Paper Company, an independent supplier. The Baker division has quoted a price of $650 per thousand units of liner board, whereas Craft has offered to supply the raw material at $595 per thousand. The Baker division's gross margin is 20%. Roger Craig, the manager of the Able division, is concerned that if he buys the liner from the Baker division, his division's performance will not look as good as if he buys the liner from Craft Paper.

Required:

    a. Is Northwest Lumber Company better off if the Able division buys the liner board from the Baker division or from Craft Paper? Explain your answer.

    b. Is the Baker division a revenue center, a cost center, or a profit center? Explain your answer.

22B–3. Cost Identification. Rasputin Manufacturing Company makes knives and precision instruments. Some of the costs Rasputin has incurred are listed below. Classify each cost as product (PR) or period (PE); then classify the period costs as selling (S) or administrative (A), and the product costs as direct (D) or indirect (I).

    1. Depreciation of corporate administration building
    2. Factory rent
    3. Salespeople's samples
    4. Assembly labor
    5. Machine maintenance supplies
    6. Factory utilities
    7. Advertising
    8. Executive development program
    9. Supervisors' salaries in factory
    10. Commissions for salespeople
    11. Freight-out
    12. Fees for audit by CPA firm
    13. Depreciation of factory machinery
    14. President's salary
    15. Salaries of shipping clerks
    16. Janitorial services, factory
    17. Janitorial services, administration building

22B–4. Cost of Goods Manufactured and Income Statement. Trendy, a manufacturer of jeans and exercise gear, has compiled the following data for the fiscal year 1987:

Raw material purchased	$124,000
Direct labor costs	100,000
Factory utilities	7,700
Factory supervisory salaries	15,000
Machine maintenance and repairs	9,000
Depreciation, factory machinery	11,000
Factory rent	18,000
Insurance, factory	2,000
Indirect supplies	1,000
Sales revenue	389,500
Raw materials inventory, 1/1/87	20,000
Raw materials inventory, 12/31/87	34,000
Work-in-process inventory, 1/1/87	27,000
Work-in-process inventory, 12/31/87	38,000
Finished goods inventory, 1/1/87	45,000
Finished goods inventory, 12/31/87	55,000
Selling and administrative expenses	88,000

Required:

    a. Prepare a statement of cost of goods manufactured for the fiscal year 1987.

    b. Prepare an income statement for 1987, including a detailed cost of goods sold section.

    c. What are the product costs for 1987?

    d. What are the period costs for 1987?

22B-5. ROI Calculation and Analysis. Kiddiefun Corporation manufactures and sells a line of children's construction toys to stores all over the country. The firm has found that it is easiest to operate by using two regional divisions, with each division having responsibility for manufacturing and selling its products and deciding on the level of investment in assets. The firm uses ROI to evaluate the performance of divisional managers. The northern division is based in Chicago, and the southern division is based in Houston. The managers of both divisions report to the vice-president of the firm in New York. Until this past year, both divisions were using the same equipment, purchased five years ago, with an estimated life of seven years. This year the manager of the northern division decided to invest in new machinery that would eventually cut down on labor costs. Basic data for both divisions for 1987 follow:

	Northern	Southern
Sales	$4,850,000	$4,750,000
Cost of goods sold	3,000,000	2,900,000
Gross margin	1,850,000	1,850,000
Selling and administrative expenses	750,000	950,000
Net income	$1,100,000	$ 900,000
Investment in assets	$8,000,000	$4,500,000

Required:

a. Calculate the ROI for each division.

b. The above data have been sent to the vice-president in New York, Sheila Clark. She remarks to the president at their next meeting that "the southern division seems to be doing a much better job in meeting performance objectives, and this should be reflected in the bonuses we give out next month." If you were the manager of the northern division, how would you respond to Ms. Clark's remarks?

c. Would you expect the situation to remain the same in 1988?

d. What are some of the problems with using a single measure of performance evaluation?

22B-6. Cost of Goods Manufactured and Income Statement. PerkyPen is a small manufacturing company that produces a single product, a ballpoint pen with a small radio inside. The following cost, production, and sales data relate to 1989:

Number of units produced	60,000
Production costs:	
Materials purchased	$ 96,000
Direct labor	160,000
Utilities, $6,000 per year + $.24 per unit produced	————
Machinery and equipment depreciation (production	
accounts for 80% of total corporate depreciation)	120,000
Maintenance, $9,500 per year + $.30 per unit produced	————
Other indirect labor	22,000
Indirect material	6,000
Insurance, factory	1,200
Rent, factory	30,000
Selling and administrative costs	75,000
Inventories:	
Raw material, January 1, 1989	$ 24,000
Raw material, December 31, 1989	30,000
Work in process, January 1, 1989	60,000
Work in process, December 31, 1989	73,300
Finished goods, January 1, 1989	86,640
Finished goods, December 31, 1989	76,965
Sales	$600,000

During 1988, the average cost of production was $7.22 per unit. All the units on hand at the end of 1989 were produced in 1989.

Required:

a. Prepare a schedule of cost of goods manufactured for 1989.

b. Prepare an income statement for 1989.

c. Calculate the cost per unit for 1989 production.

d. How many units are left in finished goods inventory at the end of 1989?

e. What is the selling price per unit that PerkyPen charged in 1989?

22B-7. Reconstruction of Missing Data. WonderWoolies, a producer of long underwear, recently suffered a fire in its accounting department, destroying the records for the last six months, January 1–June 30, 1988. An employee of only six months, Martha B. Pyro, was in the area at the time. As the senior accountant for WonderWoolies, you must try to reconstruct the missing data based on information found on scraps of paper at the scene:

1. Gross margin was equal to 30% of sales for the period.
2. Sales for the 6-month period totaled $840,000.
3. Prime costs were $540,000.
4. Raw materials purchased totaled $292,000.
5. Direct labor cost $250,000.
6. Cost of goods available for sale was $625,000.
7. Raw materials at January 1, 1988 cost $24,000.
8. Work in process at January 1, 1988 cost $55,000.
9. Finished goods at January 1, 1988 cost $42,000.
10. Factory overhead is equal to 35% of conversion costs.

Required:

Calculate the following:

a. Raw materials inventory at June 30, 1988.

b. Work-in-process inventory at June 30, 1988.

c. Finished goods inventory at June 30, 1988.

Hint: Prime costs = Raw materials used + Direct labor.

Conversion costs = Direct labor + Factory overhead.

Using the Computer

The data below have been taken from the accounting records of Colby, Inc. for the period ending 1987:

Purchases of raw material	$11,000
Direct labor cost	13,000
Indirect labor cost	9,000
Indirect material cost	4,000
Depreciation, factory building	4,500
Depreciation, factory equipment	4,000
Depreciation, office equipment	4,200
Maintenance, office equipment	4,600
Utilities, factory building	3,900
Beginning raw materials inventory	8,000
Ending raw materials inventory	9,000
Beginning work-in-process inventory	8,000
Ending work-in-process inventory	10,000

Required:

a. Using an electronic spreadsheet available at your university, prepare a statement of cost of goods manufactured using the format shown on page 927.

b. The internal auditors have found that an error has been made and that both indirect materials and labor were 10% greater than had been thought, purchases were $900 higher, and direct labor had been understated by $1,800. Prepare a new statement of cost of goods manufactured that incorporates the new data found by the auditors.

Decision Case

The Barker Corporation is a large, highly diversified company that grants its divisional executives a significant amount of authority in operating the divisions. Each division is responsible for its own sales, pricing, production, and costs of operations and for the management of accounts receivable, inventories, accounts payable, and use of existing facilities. Cash is managed by corporate headquarters. All cash in excess of normal operating needs of the divisions is periodically transferred to corporate headquarters for redistribution or investment.

The divisional executives are responsible for presenting requests to corporate management for investment in assets. The proposals are analyzed and documented at corporate headquarters. The final decision to commit funds to acquire equipment, to expand existing facilities, or for other investment purposes rests with corporate management.

The corporation evaluates the performance of division executives by the return-on-investment (ROI) measure. The investment in assets used to calculate ROI is made up of fixed assets employed plus working capital exclusive of cash.

The ROI performance of a divisional executive is the most important appraisal factor for salary changes. In addition, the annual performance bonus is based on the ROI results, with increases in ROI having a significant impact on the amount of the bonus.

The Barker Corporation adopted the ROI performance measure and related compensation procedures about 10 years ago. The corporation did so to increase divisional management's awareness of the importance of the profit-asset relationship and to provide additional incentive to the divisional executives to seek opportunities for investment in assets.

The corporation seems to have benefited from the program. The ROI for the corporation as a whole increased during the first years of the program. Although the ROI has continued to grow in each division, the corporate ROI has declined in recent years. The corporation has accumulated a sizable amount of cash and short-term marketable securities in the past three years. Corporate management is concerned about the increase in the short-term marketable securities. A recent article in a financial publication suggested that the use of ROI was overly emphasized by some companies, with results similar to those experienced by Barker.

Required:

a. What types of actions might division managers have taken to cause ROI to grow in each division but to decline for the corporation?

b. Is there a difference between the goals of the divisional managers and those of the corporation? Explain. Does Barker's overemphasis on the use of ROI relate to the recent decline in the corporation's return on investment and the increase in cash and short-term marketable securities?

c. What other factors could be included in Barker's compensation policy to avoid this problem?

Cost Behavior and Cost-Volume-Profit Analysis

23

After reading this chapter you should be able to:

1. Understand what is meant by cost behavior.
2. Define variable, fixed, and mixed costs.
3. Use the cost-volume-profit formula.
4. Compute the break-even point.
5. Use the cost-volume-profit formula in profit planning.
6. Calculate and use contribution margin and contribution margin ratio.
7. Use cost-volume-profit analysis for multiproduct companies.
8. Use the cost-volume-profit formula for after-tax profit planning.

Management accounting techniques and reports are important to management planning and control. The accounting system supplies essential data and analyses for managerial decisions, and when accounting information is used within an organization, it does not have to conform to all of the rules and regulations established for published financial reports (GAAP). In Chapter 22, costs were characterized as direct or indirect, manufacturing or nonmanufacturing, and product or period costs. In this chapter, we view costs in terms of how they respond to changes in business activity. This chapter examines the major cost behavior patterns and shows how cost behavior can be used for planning and decision making through cost-volume-profit analysis.

941

Cost Behavior

Cost behavior refers to how a cost will respond to changes in the level of business activity or volume. In order to plan intelligently, managers need to know what will happen to various types of costs if business activity goes up or down. Will the cost rise or fall with the level of business activity or will it remain constant? We usually distinguish among three basic types of cost behavior: variable, fixed, and mixed.

Variable Costs

A **variable cost** is one that changes in direct proportion to changes in volume or level of business activity. For example, Bella's Pizza, a company that produces frozen pizza, uses a half pound of cheese for each deluxe pizza it produces at a cost of $1 per pizza. Every time production volume increases and a deluxe pizza is produced, the company incurs a cost of $1 for cheese. If 20 pizzas are produced the company's cheese cost is $20, and if 40 pizzas are produced its cheese cost rises to $40. The total cost of cheese incurred by Bella's Pizza varies in direct proportion to the number of pizzas produced, but on a per-unit basis the cost remains constant. If Bella's produced 3 pizzas or 50, the cost per pizza would remain constant at $1, provided the company continued to use a half pound of cheese for each pizza. The nature of this variable cost can be seen clearly in Exhibit 23–1.

Variable costs are found not only in manufacturing firms, but in retail and service firms as well. Commissions paid to salespeople, for example, are often considered a variable cost in retail firms. In firms that pay 10% of sales

EXHIBIT 23–1
Bella's Pizza
Variable Cost Behavior Pattern

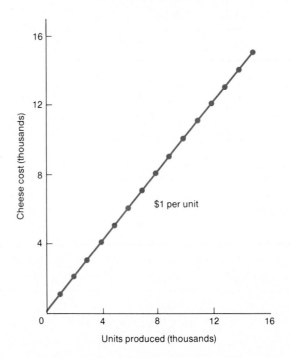

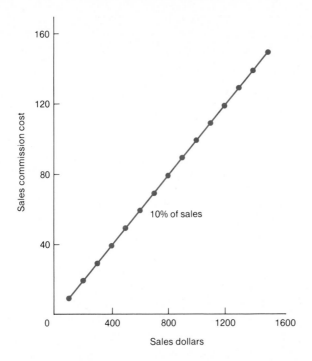

EXHIBIT 23-2
Variable Cost Behavior Pattern

dollars as commission, the total cost of commissions varies in direct proportion to changes in sales dollars, although the amount per unit (or sales dollar) remains constant at 10%. Exhibit 23-2 illustrates variable cost for a firm that pays commissions in this manner. In such a firm, the cost of sales commissions is $20 when sales dollars are $200 and is $40 when sales dollars are $400, changing in direct proportion to the change in business activity as measured in sales dollars.

Examples of other types of variable costs are items such as supplies and freight, the cost of direct labor, and the cost of goods sold of a merchandising firm, which varies directly with the amount of sales dollars.

By constructing graphs like those in Exhibits 23-1 and 23-2, firms can predict at a glance what costs would be at various levels of activity because those costs are represented by a straight line. True variable costs are curvilinear, as shown in Exhibit 23-3 on the following page. Economists believe that this is a more accurate picture of cost behavior because there is not a proportionate change in cost behavior at very high and low levels of volume. Accountants and managers, however, need to be able to use linear relationships, and so they concentrate on the behavior of a cost within a fairly narrow range of activity, called the **relevant range.** Within the relevant range, they plot cost behavior as a straight line because that is the expected range of activity during a given time period, usually one year. Notice in Exhibit 23-3 that the portion of the cost curve within the relevant range is quite close to a straight line, and for accounting purposes, it is treated as such.

Fixed Costs

Fixed costs are those costs that remain unchanged, regardless of changes in the level of business activity. For example, Bella's Pizza pays rent of $50,000

EXHIBIT 23–3
The Relevant Range

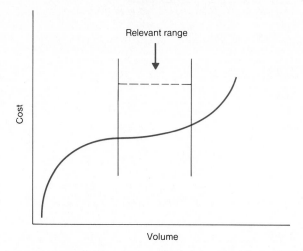

per year for its factory facilities. That amount will not change, as long as the firm only makes use of that facility. Exhibit 23–4 shows how rent cost looks when it is depicted as a straight line. Notice that total rent cost is constant at $50,000, but on a *per-unit* basis it will decrease if Bella's produces more pizzas, and it will increase if Bella's produces fewer pizzas. For example, when production is at 50,000 units, the rent cost per unit is $1. If production is increased to 100,000 units, the rent cost per unit drops to $.50 per unit. The cost per unit goes up to $5 when 10,000 units are produced. The total amount of a fixed cost stays the same, but the cost per unit changes. Other examples of

EXHIBIT 23–4
Fixed Cost Behavior Pattern

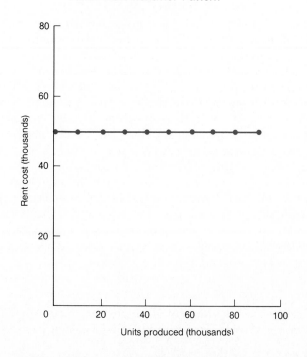

fixed costs are depreciation, insurance, salaries determined on a yearly basis, and some leasing costs.

Fixed costs are planned generally for one year because it is too uncertain to plan costs for a longer period. The idea of a relevant range of activity in which to predict cost behavior is also used for fixed costs. If Bella's Pizza were to become very successful, the owner would, perhaps, have to rent additional factory facilities in order to keep up with demand for the product. Rental cost would increase, and the relevant range of activity would change. Exhibit 23–5 shows that for a relevant range of 10,000–75,000 units, rental cost remains at $50,000, but when the range of activity is increased to 150,000 units, the fixed cost for rent increases to $95,000.

EXHIBIT 23-5
Fixed Costs and the
Relevant Range of Activity

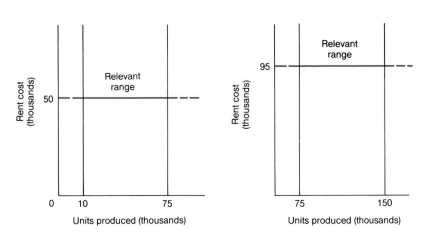

Mixed Costs

A **mixed (semivariable) cost** is a cost that has both fixed and variable components. Generally, the fixed portion of a mixed cost is what the consumer has to pay to have a service available, whereas the variable portion represents the amount paid to use that service. For example, a customer may pay a fixed sum to rent a car for a week, but any additional use is charged at a variable rate per day. Similarly, businesses may lease space from other firms to store supplies and old files; the companies that own the space usually charge a monthly fee for basic storage and a variable amount each time the lessee has materials brought back to the office. Likewise, service contracts for office equipment such as copy machines often stipulate mixed costs by charging a fixed annual rate for basic service plus a variable charge for service when use exceeds a certain number of copies. Exhibit 23–6 (on the following page) illustrates a mixed cost using the cost of a service contract for a copy machine. The fixed portion of the cost is $450 per year, and customers are billed an additional $.008 per copy when use exceeds 50,000 copies per year. Examples of other mixed costs are leases, telephone charges, electricity, heat, repairs, and maintenance. In order to be able to use cost behavior information for planning and control purposes, mixed costs must be divided into their fixed and variable components. For example, if a firm is preparing its budget for the coming fiscal year, it must know which costs will remain constant and which will vary with volume in order to make an accurate projection for that period. Once the company determines that the fixed portion of the copy machine's service cost is $450, it adds that amount to its other fixed costs in the budget. Similarly, the variable portion of the cost, $.008 per copy over 50,000 copies, will be multiplied by the projected use over 50,000 copies and then added to the other projected costs in the budget. After a firm's costs are classified as either fixed or variable, the firm can use that information for many types of planning and decision-making activities such as cost-volume-profit analysis.

EXHIBIT 23–6
Mixed Cost Behavior Pattern

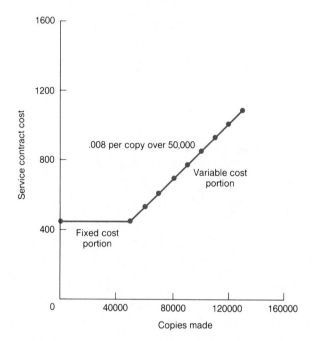

Cost-Volume-Profit Analysis

Cost-volume-profit analysis is a way of looking at changes in volume to see how such changes affect costs and profitability. It is a useful tool for managers in planning and decision making in the short term—a year or less. For example, if hourly wages for certain employees are to increase in the coming year and management wants to maintain or increase profitability, management must decide whether to try to increase volume, decrease other costs, or increase sales price. Cost-volume-profit analysis (C-V-P analysis) allows managers to see the effects of various options in the decision-making process.

Cost-Volume-Profit Formula

The formula for C-V-P analysis is a variation of the familiar income statement format. The income statement deducts various types of expenses to arrive at net income. Following is a translation of an income statement into a formula:

Sales − (Cost of goods sold + Selling and administrative expense) = Net income

946

CHAPTER 23

That same income statement, shown in terms of its cost behavior pattern, looks like this:

$$\text{Sales} - (\text{Variable costs} + \text{Fixed costs}) = \text{Net income}$$

The two formulas differ because both cost of goods sold and selling and administrative expenses consist of fixed and variable components. The following, more common version of the formula emphasizes sales by moving the fixed and variable costs to the other side of the equal sign, thus changing their signs from negative to positive. This version of the **C-V-P formula** is shown below:

$$\text{Sales} = \text{Variable costs} + \text{Fixed costs} + \text{Net income}$$
$$\text{or}$$
$$S = VC + FC + NI$$

The basic C-V-P formula also may be broken down to show all of its component parts as follows:

$$\text{Sales price per unit (volume)} = \text{Variable cost per unit (volume)} +$$
$$\text{Fixed costs} + \text{Net income}$$
$$\text{or}$$
$$SP(\text{volume}) = VC(\text{volume}) + FC + NI$$

Break-even Point

A company's **break-even point** (BE point) occurs when its revenues equal its costs; there is neither profit nor loss, and net income is equal to zero. Although firms want to do more than break even, the concept of the break-even point is useful in planning. Anyone starting a new business needs to know how much revenue must be generated in order to at least cover costs. Bella's Pizza, for example, is trying to decide whether to start a new line of frozen pizza snacks. Based on previous experience and estimates of cost behavior, the firm projects the following cost and revenue structure:

Sales price per box of snack pizzas	$1.80
Variable costs:	
Raw food materials	$ .90
Labor	.25
Packaging materials	.05
Utilities and factory supplies	.05
Freight	.05
Total variable costs	$1.30
Annual fixed costs:	
Rent	$20,000
Annual salaries	24,000
Insurance	1,000
Total fixed costs	$45,000

In deciding whether to start this new product line, Bella's management uses the C-V-P formula to determine how many boxes of snack pizzas must be sold simply to cover the fixed and variable costs. Let X equal the number of boxes that must be sold in order to break even:

$$\text{Sales} = \text{Variable costs} + \text{Fixed costs} + \text{Net income}$$
$$\$1.80X = \$1.30X + \$45,000 + 0$$
$$\$.50X = \$45,000$$
$$X = \frac{\$45,000}{\$.50}$$
$$X = 90,000 \text{ units}$$

To determine the break-even point in sales dollars, we multiply X by the unit sales price:

$$90,000 \text{ units} \times \$1.80 \text{ per unit} = \$162,000$$

The data that Bella's has gathered also may be expressed graphically in a cost-volume-profit graph as shown in Exhibit 23–7, where the vertical axis represents dollars of revenue or cost and the horizontal axis shows units or volume. The line parallel to the volume axis represents total fixed costs at $45,000, whereas the total cost line increases at a variable rate of $1.30 per unit. The revenue line increases at $1.80 per unit and intersects the total cost line at 90,000 units, the break-even point.

Profit Planning

Cost-volume-profit analysis also may be used to determine profitability. Bella's management would like to earn a $10,000 profit before taxes in the first year of operations of the new product line. How many boxes of snack pizzas must be sold in order to achieve this? To answer that question, Bella's again uses the C-V-P formula with X equal to the number of pizzas they must sell:

EXHIBIT 23–7
Cost-Volume-Profit Graph

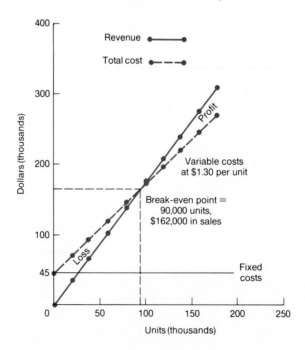

$$S = VC + FC + NI$$
$$\$1.80X = \$1.30X + \$45,000 + \$10,000$$
$$\$.50X = \$55,000$$
$$X = \frac{\$55,000}{\$.50}$$
$$X = 110,000 \text{ units}$$
$$\text{Sales dollars} = 110,000 \text{ units} \times \$1.80 = \$198,000$$

The break-even point is determined to be $198,000. Management may now consider the information generated along with other nonquantitative factors to decide whether it is feasible to go ahead with the new product line.

Contribution Margin

Like the break-even point, the concept of **contribution margin** (CM) also is based on cost behavior patterns. It represents the amount left from sales revenue after all variable costs have been deducted. Thus, contribution margin equals sales price less variable costs as follows:

$$\text{Sales price} - \text{Variable costs} = \text{Contribution margin}$$

Contribution margin shows how much revenue is left to contribute to coverage of fixed costs after variable costs have been covered by revenue; it may be expressed on a per-unit basis or as a total amount. In the case of Bella's frozen snack pizzas, for example, the contribution margin per unit is $1.80 − $1.30 = $.50. Each unit contributes 50 cents toward coverage of fixed costs, so if Bella's sells 90,000 units, the company will just cover its fixed costs and break even.

The idea of contribution margin may be used to develop another method of C-V-P analysis. To find the break-even point, for example, to know that it occurs where variable and fixed costs are just covered by sales revenue, one may multiply the contribution margin per unit by a given number of units to equal fixed costs as follows:

$$\text{Contribution margin per unit} \times \text{volume} = \text{Fixed costs}$$

Bella's Pizza might employ that formula as follows:

$$\$.50 \times 90,000 = \$45,000$$

When a company can determine its fixed costs and contribution margin per unit but not the number of units involved, then it rearranges the equation, dividing both sides by contribution margin per unit, to find volume:

$$\text{CM per unit} \times \text{BE volume} = \text{Fixed costs}$$
$$\text{BE volume} = \frac{\text{Fixed costs}}{\text{CM per unit}}$$

In the pizza snack illustration:

$$\$.50 \times \text{BE volume} = \$45,000$$
$$\text{BE volume} = \frac{\$45,000}{\$.50}$$
$$\text{BE volume} = 90,000 \text{ units}$$

Note that the third line of the equation on page 949 achieves the same results. In accounting, as in other fields, there is often more than one method for determining the same information.

This method also may be used for profit planning because after variable and fixed costs have been covered, anything left represents profit. (Note that in the examples in this chapter thus far, "net income" refers to income before taxes have been deducted.) Therefore, multiplying contribution margin per unit by volume equals fixed costs plus net income, and dividing both sides of the equation by the contribution margin per unit will isolate the volume:

$$\text{CM per unit} \times \text{Volume} = \text{Fixed costs} + \text{Net income}$$

$$\text{Volume} = \frac{\text{Fixed costs} + \text{Net income}}{\text{CM per unit}}$$

Returning to the Bella's Pizza example, management wants to determine how many units must be sold in order to earn a profit of $10,000:

$$\text{Volume} = \frac{\$45,000 + \$10,000}{\$.50}$$
$$= \frac{\$55,000}{\$.50}$$
$$= 110,000 \text{ units}$$

The result again is equal to the third line of the equation on the previous page.

It is a matter of personal preference as to whether to use the full equation or the contribution margin concept when solving problems. This book uses both methods.

Contribution Margin Income Statements

The contribution margin also can be used to create a different type of income statement that emphasizes cost behavior rather than the usual functional expense categories. In this **contribution margin income statement,** variable costs are deducted from sales to arrive at the contribution margin for the firm; fixed costs are deducted from the contribution margin to produce net income. Shown below is the basic format for a contribution margin income statement:

Sales	XXX
Less: Variable costs	XXX
Contribution margin	XXX
Less: Fixed costs	XXX
Net income	XXX

The contribution margin income statement gives management useful information for planning and decision making and thus is used in a variety of situations, as this chapter shows. Note, however, that a contribution margin income statement is not found in published financial reports because published financial reports must be prepared according to generally accepted accounting principles; firms use contribution margin income statements for internal purposes only. Exhibit 23–8 shows how the Bella's Pizza data (at a volume of 110,000 units) would look in a contribution margin income statement as well as a functional-type income statement published in annual reports. Note that the figure for net income is the same in both statements because the dollar amount of costs is the same. The costs are classified differently in the two reports in order to serve two purposes: (1) the needs of managers for planning and decision making and (2) the needs of creditors, stockholders, and other external users of financial reports.

EXHIBIT 23–8
Two Types of Income Statements
Bella's Pizza

Contribution Margin Income Statement for Internal Uses

Sales (110,000 units × $1.80)		$198,000
Less: Variable costs		
Raw materials (110,000 × $.90)	$99,000	
Labor (110,000 × .25)	27,500	
Packaging materials (110,000 × .05)	5,500	
Utilities and factory supplies (110,000 × .05)	5,500	
Freight (110,000 × .05)	5,500	
Total variable costs		143,000
Contribution margin		$ 55,000
Less: Fixed costs		45,000
Net income		$10,000

Functional Income Statement in Published Financial Reports

Sales			$198,000
Less: Cost of goods sold			
Direct materials (110,000 × $.90)		$99,000	
Direct labor (110,000 × $.25)		27,500	
Factory overhead:			
Rent	$20,000		
Utilities and factory supplies	5,500	25,500	152,000
Gross margin			46,000
Less: Selling and administrative expenses			
Packaging materials		5,500	
Freight		5,500	
Salaries		24,000	
Insurance		1,000	$ 36,000
Net income			$ 10,000

Contribution Margin Ratio

The contribution margin may be expressed as a percentage of total sales, and when it is shown in this way we call it the **contribution margin ratio** (CM ratio). The contribution margin ratio for Bella's Pizza, assuming a desired net income of $10,000, is shown at the top of the following page.

To calculate the CM ratio, sales are always shown as 100%. The contribution margin ratio is the percentage of sales dollars left after variable costs have been covered. Bella's contribution margin ratio is 27.778%. The contribution margin ratio can be very useful in calculating how a change in total sales dol-

	Total	Per Unit	Percent
Sales	$198,000	$1.80	100.000
Variable costs	143,000	1.30	72.222
Contribution margin	$ 55,000	$ .50	CM ratio 27.778
Fixed costs	45,000		
Net income	$ 10,000		

lars affects the total amount of contribution margin. For example, if Bella's Pizza increases sales by $10, its contribution margin will increase by $2.78. This general relationship is shown below:

$$\text{Change in total sales dollars} \times \text{CM ratio} = \text{Change in total CM}$$

When there are no changes in fixed costs, the change in the contribution margin would equal the expected change in net income. For example, if Bella's Pizza currently earns $10,000 in net income on its frozen pizza snack line and expects total sales dollars to increase by $36,000, the firm would expect its total contribution margin to increase by $10,000 ($36,000 × CM ratio of 27.778%). Because Bella's projects no change in fixed costs, the increase in the contribution margin will equal the increase in net income. Bella's income statement showing the total sales increase of $36,000 from $198,000 follows:

	Total	Per Unit	Percent
Sales	$234,000	$1.80	100.000
Variable costs	168,948	1.30	72.222
Contribution margin	$ 65,000	$ .50	27.778
Fixed costs	45,000		
Net income	$ 20,000		

Note that net income rose from $10,000 to $20,000, which is what was predicted by multiplying the contribution margin ratio by the increase in total sales dollars.

When a firm has many different product lines, the contribution margin ratio is especially useful because management can make comparisons across product lines using the CM ratios of the various products. For example, if one product line has a significantly higher CM ratio than another, it usually makes sense for management to put a greater selling effort into the line with the higher CM ratio, for the latter will generate more contribution margin and, thus, more profit.

In addition, the CM ratio may be used in cost-volume-profit analysis in the same way as contribution margin per unit. Because the contribution margin ratio is expressed as a percentage of sales dollars, the break-even volume or target profit volume may be found directly in sales dollars by using the CM ratio as follows:

$$\text{Break-even volume in sales dollars} = \frac{\text{Fixed costs}}{\text{CM ratio}}$$

$$\text{Volume in sales dollars} = \frac{\text{Fixed costs} + \text{Net income}}{\text{CM ratio}}$$

This method is most useful for multiproduct companies that calculate desired volumes in sales dollars for the company as a whole.

Changing Variables and Profit Planning

Managers use C-V-P analysis to see the effects of possible changes in costs on the break-even point and profitability. For example, the management of Bella's Pizza predicts that the cost for raw food materials for the snack pizza line will increase by 5 cents per box in the coming year from $1.30 to $1.35. To determine how this increase will affect the break-even point, Bella's uses the basic equation with X equal to volume at the break-even point:

$$\text{Sales} = \text{Variable costs} + \text{Fixed costs} + \text{Net income}$$
$$\$1.80X = \$1.35X + \$45,000 + 0$$
$$\$.45X = \$45,000$$
$$X = 100,000 \text{ units}$$

The break-even point increases from 90,000 to 100,000 units as a result of the change in variable costs. The contribution margin approach looks like this:

$$\text{Break-even point} = \frac{\text{Fixed costs}}{\text{CM per unit}}$$
$$= \frac{\$45,000}{\$.45}$$
$$= 100,000 \text{ units}$$

Bella's management still wants to earn $10,000 in profit, but to do so would require more units; X is equal to the volume needed to earn $10,000 in profit:

$$\text{Sales} = \text{Variable costs} + \text{Fixed costs} + \text{Net income}$$
$$\$1.80X = \$1.45X + \$45,000 + \$10,000$$
$$\$.45X = \$55,000$$
$$X = 122,222 \text{ units}$$

or

$$\text{Sales volume} = \frac{\text{Fixed costs} + \text{Net income}}{\text{CM per unit}}$$
$$= \frac{\$45,000 + \$10,000}{\$.45}$$
$$= \frac{\$55,000}{\$.45}$$
$$= 122,222 \text{ units}$$

Note that the volume necessary to earn the desired profit of $10,000 rose from 110,000 units to 122,222 units, a greater increase than that required to break even. This is so because an increase in variable costs reduces the contribution margin per unit, making it more difficult to generate profit after the break-even point.

Change in Fixed Costs

Bella's management uses the original data to see what would happen if there were a change in fixed costs. They predict that if the snack pizza line is successful, the manager's salary will increase by a total of $3,000 and rent will go up by $1,000. They use the following formula to determine what the new break-even point would be, with X equal to volume at the break-even point:

$$\text{Sales} = \text{Variable costs} + \text{Fixed costs} + \text{Net income}$$
$$\$1.80X = \$1.30X + \$49,000 + 0$$
$$\$.50X = \$49,000$$
$$X = 98,000 \text{ units}$$

or

$$X = \frac{\$49,000}{\$.50}$$
$$= 98,000 \text{ units}$$

The effect of such a change on volume when desired profitability remains at $10,000 may be calculated as follows:

$$\$1.80X = \$1.30X + \$49,000 + \$10,000$$
$$\$.50X = \$59,000$$
$$X = 118,000 \text{ units}$$

or

$$X = \frac{\$49,000 + \$10,000}{\$.50}$$
$$= \frac{\$59,000}{\$.50}$$
$$= 118,000 \text{ units}$$

Unlike variable costs, this change in fixed costs does not affect the contribution margin. Therefore, it does not cause as large an increase in the number of units needed to earn a profit after the break-even point is reached.

Simultaneous Changes

In many situations, managers must examine several changes simultaneously because a change in one area may affect others. American automobile manufacturers, for example, pass cost increases on to consumers by raising sales prices, and this lowers sales volume. In the case of Bella's snack pizzas, management believes that a $.05 increase in variable costs is very likely, and they would like to raise the sales price from $1.80 to $1.89, although they think that raising the price would reduce volume by about 10%. To determine how these changes would affect profitability, Bella's returns to the basic equation:

$$\text{New selling price} = \$1.80 + \$.09 = \$1.89$$
$$\text{New variable costs} = \$1.30 + \$.05 = \$1.35$$
$$\text{New contribution margin} = \$.54$$
$$\text{New volume} = 110,000 - (110,000 \times 10\%) = 99,000$$

$$\$1.89 \,(99,000) = \$1.35 \,(99,000) + \$45,000 + X$$
$$\$187,110 = \$133,650 + \$45,000 + X$$
$$\$187,110 = \$178,650 + X$$
$$\$8,460 = X$$

or

$$99,000 = \frac{\$45,000 + X}{\$.54}$$
$$53,460 = \$45,000 + X$$
$$\$8,460 = X$$

The analysis indicates that Bella's management should not increase the sales price of the frozen snack pizza to $1.89 because such a change would generate profits of $8,460 rather than the desired profit of $10,000.

Bella's management further concludes that because of competition from rival manufacturers, they cannot raise the sales price above $1.84 without causing too large a reduction in volume. If they sell the snack pizzas at $1.84 per box, volume will drop to 108,000. Bella's needs to figure the maximum amount that can be paid in variable costs and still earn a $10,000 profit on this product line. To do so, Bella's lets X equal the amount of variable cost per unit and calculates as follows:

$$\$1.84 \ (108,000) = X \ (108,000) + \$45,000 + \$10,000$$
$$\$198,720 = 108,000X + \$55,000$$
$$\$143,720 = 108,000X$$
$$\$1.33 = X$$

The company can afford to spend $1.33 on variable costs and still earn the desired profit, which is above the current variable cost per unit of $1.30. If, however, raw material costs increase by five cents during the year, the company will have to look for ways of cutting other variable costs by two cents per unit in order to maintain profit levels. Thus, C-V-P analysis allows management to project a variety of possible changes and to see their effect on the overall profitability of the firm. That is why it is an important part of the planning and decision-making process for many firms.

Multiproduct C-V-P Analysis

Many firms have more than one product line but still can use cost-volume-profit analysis for individual products or groups of products, and for all the products of the whole firm. This depends on the **sales mix** remaining the same, which means that the various products of the firm will be sold in the same proportions. Over time, many firms develop a sales mix pattern. If the sales mix is fairly predictable, C-V-P analysis may be used with a weighted average contribution margin in order to assess the current situation or project the effects of possible changes in sales mix. For example, assume that the management of The Record Shop, a chain of stores, wants to determine whether to put greater emphasis on selling tapes as opposed to records. They are aware of the current sales mix and have determined average selling prices and variable costs for tapes and records as follows:

	Tapes	Records
Average sales price	$9.00	$8.00
Variable costs	5.00	3.00
Contribution margin	$4.00	$5.00
Percentage of sales mix	40%	60%

Management would like to determine the break-even point for each store with the current sales mix, knowing that fixed costs are $40,000 per store. We can use the contribution margin method we developed earlier, using a **weighted average contribution margin,** that is, a contribution margin based on the relative proportion of sales for each product line. The weighted average contribution margin is computed by taking the contribution margin per unit for each product, multiplying it by that product's percentage of sales mix, and adding the two resulting numbers together:

$$\text{Break-even point} = \frac{\text{Fixed costs}}{\text{weighted average contribution margin}}$$

$$= \frac{\$40,000}{40\% \ (\$4.00) + 60\% \ (\$5.00)}$$

$$= \frac{\$40,000}{\$1.60 + \$3.00}$$

$$= \frac{\$40,000}{\$4.60}$$

$$= 8,696 \text{ units for the store as a whole}$$

Tapes: $8,696 \times 40\% = 3,478$

Records: $8,696 \times 60\% = 5,218$

This means that in order to break even, each store must sell a total of 8,696 units of product, of which 3,478 would be tapes and 5,218 would be records.

The company would like each store to earn approximately $12,000 in profit. In order to do this, how many tapes and records should they be selling? Using the same weighted average contribution margin, management learns that each store would have to sell approximately 4,522 tapes and 6,782 records:

$$\text{Volume} = \frac{\text{Fixed costs} + \text{Net income}}{\text{Weighted average contribution margin}}$$

$$= \frac{\$40,000 + \$12,000}{\$4.60}$$

$$= \frac{\$52,000}{\$4.60}$$

$$= 11,304 \text{ units for the store as a whole}$$

Tapes: $11,304 \times 40\% = 4,522$

Records: $11,304 \times 60\% = 6,782$

The Record Shop management also wants to decide if greater selling emphasis should be put on tapes so that they would account for 50% of sales rather than 40%. What would be the break-even point for each store if this was done? Again, using the weighted average contribution margin, they calculate as follows:

$$\text{BE volume} = \frac{\$40,000}{50\% \ (\$4.00) + 50\% \ (\$5.00)}$$

$$= \frac{\$40,000}{\$4.50}$$

$$= 8,889 \text{ units for the store as a whole}$$

Tapes: $8,889 \times 50\% = 4,444$

Records: $8,889 \times 50\% = 4,445$

Changing the sales mix in favor of selling more tapes raises the break-even point for each store and makes profitability more difficult. The firm would want to maintain the current sales mix or put even greater emphasis on records because of their higher contribution margin per unit, even though their sales price is lower.

Multiproduct C-V-P analysis thus allows a business to determine the best mix of product lines for the profitability of the firm as a whole. In some cases companies must balance other factors with profitability in deciding on their sales mix. American automobile manufacturers, for example, make the greatest profit on larger cars and the least profit on smaller cars. Government regulations, however, require automobile manufacturers to meet standards of fuel consumption, expressed in miles per gallon of gasoline. In order to satisfy these requirements, automobile manufacturers produce more smaller cars that use less fuel even though they are less profitable. The basic tool of C-V-P analysis, however, is fundamental to the planning process.

C-V-P Analysis and Microcomputers

The increased use of microcomputers has allowed business organizations to use tools for planning and control more frequently and in more sophisticated ways. Cost-volume-profit analysis is one of the tools that readily lend themselves to being used in the spreadsheet programs available for microcomputers. Spreadsheets such as VisiCalc, Lotus 1-2-3, and MultiPlan allow users to set up relationships among variables and, once the basic relationships have been established, to change one or more variables to see what would happen. For example, after setting up the cost-volume-profit formula as the basic relationship on the spreadsheet, one can determine easily profitability at many different levels of sales, use a variety of changes in cost structure and sales to determine what would happen to profitability, or use several possible targeted net income figures to structure costs and volume. Microcomputer spreadsheets make the use of cost-volume-profit analysis both straightforward and accessible. Exhibit 23–9 (on the following page) shows how the data from Bella's Pizza would look on such a spreadsheet. Note that once the relationships are set up, they can be applied to a variety of situations. For example, column B, line 7 (B7) shows sales revenue at a volume of 110,000 units ($198,000). The formula for sales revenue also is shown on that line as B3*B4, or the number of units sold (B3)—found on column B, line 3—times the sales price per unit (B4)—found on column B, line 4. The same formula is then repeated along line 7 for different numbers of units sold. The sales price remains constant throughout the example although that, too, would sometimes vary. The formula for net income is shown in column B, line 11 as B7-B8-B10. It is equal to sales revenue (B7) less variable costs (B8) and fixed costs (B10); it, too, is repeated across the line. The number of columns shown is limited only by the size of the page. The ease with which different "what if" situations can be analyzed makes microcomputers and spreadsheets extremely important in cost-volume-profit analysis.

C-V-P Analysis and Income Taxes

Until this point in the chapter, income has referred to *income before taxes*. Most firms, however, pay a percentage of income to the government in taxes, and so it is important to differentiate between income before and income after taxes.

Assume, for example, that Bella's Pizza has an income tax rate of 25%. The company has already determined that in order to earn a target net income of $10,000, 110,000 units must be sold to earn $198,000 in sales. In order to determine how to earn $10,000 on an after-tax basis, the formula must be changed to reflect the tax. The basic equation used up to this point follows:

Sales = Variable costs + Fixed costs + Income before tax

In order to calculate after-tax income, the relationship between income before tax and income after tax must be examined. Income after tax is basi-

EXHIBIT 23-9
Bella's Pizza
Spreadsheet in Cost-Volume-Profit Analysis

	A	B	C	D	E	F	G	H
1								
2								
3	No. of units sold	110,000	100,000	150,000	90,000	80,000	120,000	130,000
4	Sales price per unit	$1.80	$1.80	$1.80	$1.80	$1.80	$1.80	$1.80
5	Variable cost per unit	$1.30	$1.35	$1.40	$1.30	$1.32	$1.34	$1.29
6								
7	Sales revenue	B3*B4= 198,000	C3*C4= 180,000	D3*D4= 270,000	E3*E4= 162,000	F3*F4= 144,000	G3*G4= 216,000	H3*H4= 234,000
8	Variable costs	B3*B5= 143,000	C3*C5= 135,000	D3*D5= 210,000	E3*E5= 117,000	F3*F5= 105,600	G3*G5= 160,800	H3*H5= 167,700
9	Contribution margin	B7 – B8= 55,000	C7 – C8= 45,000	D7 – D8= 60,000	E7 – E8= 45,000	F7 – F8= 38,400	G7 – G8= 55,200	H7 – H8= 66,300
10	Fixed costs	45,000	45,000	30,000	45,000	40,000	40,000	40,000
11	Net income	B7 – B8 – B10= 10,000	C7 – C8 – C10= 0	D7 – D8 – D10= 30,000	E7 – E8 – E10= 0	F7 – F8 – F10= (1,600)	G7 – G8 – G10= 15,200	H7 – H8 – H10= 26,300

Note: *Denotes multiplication.

cally equal to income before tax less the income tax. Using Bella's 25% tax rate, the relationship can be stated algebraically in the following way:

$$\text{Let } B = \text{Income before taxes}$$
$$A = \text{Income after taxes}$$
$$.25 = \text{Income tax rate}$$

$$A = B - .25B$$
$$A = B(1 - .25)$$
$$\text{Solving for B:} \quad B = \frac{A}{1 - .25}$$

In more general terms:

$$B = \frac{\text{After-tax income}}{1 - \text{Tax rate}}$$
$$\text{Income before taxes} = \frac{\text{After-tax income}}{1 - \text{Tax rate}}$$

To restate the basic C-V-P equation, taking into account the effect of income taxes:

$$\text{Sales} = \text{Variable costs} + \text{Fixed costs} + \frac{\text{After-tax income}}{1 - \text{Tax rate}}$$

Bella's Pizza calculates what it must sell in order to earn after-tax income of $10,000 as follows:

$$\$1.80X = \$1.30X + \$45,000 + \frac{\$10,000}{1 - .25}$$
$$\$1.80X = \$1.30X + \$45,000 + \frac{\$10,000}{.75}$$
$$\$.50X = \$45,000 + \$13,333$$
$$\$.50X = \$58,333$$
$$X = \frac{\$58,333}{.50}$$
$$X = 116,666 \text{ units}$$

Without taking tax into consideration, Bella's had to sell only 110,000 units for an income of $10,000 but, more realistically, they must sell an additional 6,666 units in order to be able to keep $10,000 in profit. The importance of income on an after-tax basis varies with the size of a given firm's tax rate, ranging from a low of 15% to nearly 50%.

Assumptions Underlying C-V-P Analysis

The use of C-V-P analysis implies the following assumptions:

1. Management can accurately divide expenses into variable and fixed cost categories.
2. The behavior of costs is linear within the relevant range, so that total fixed costs are constant over the relevant volume range and total variable costs are proportional to volume.
3. Sales price per unit is unchanged.
4. Either the analysis deals with a single product, or the sales mix is assumed to be constant.
5. Changes in beginning and ending inventory levels are not considered.
6. Efficiency, productivity, and managerial policies do not change.

Change is a constant aspect of business life, so the user of C-V-P analysis must examine assumptions about costs, prices, and sales mix on an ongoing basis. When these items are kept current, cost-volume-profit analysis can be a useful tool for making a variety of important decisions and offering an overall picture of the short-term relationship among profit, costs, and volume.

Summary of Learning Objectives

1. **Defining cost behavior.** Cost behavior means how a cost will respond to changes in business activity. Business activity, in this chapter, means sales volume.

2. **The nature of variable, fixed, and mixed costs.** A variable cost is one that changes in total in direct proportion to changes in volume or level of business activity. The cost of the raw material in a product, for example, is a variable cost. Fixed costs remain constant in total regardless of changes in business activity. The annual salary of a supervisor is a fixed cost. A mixed or semivariable cost has both fixed and variable components, so that a portion of it varies with volume or activity. A utilities expense is an example of a mixed cost. These basic cost behavior patterns are assumed to take place within a relevant range of activity.

3. **The cost-volume-profit formula.** Rearranging the income statement based on cost behavior patterns results in the following statements of the cost-volume-profit formula:

$$\text{Sales} = \text{Variable costs} + \text{Fixed costs} + \text{Net income}$$
or
$$\text{Sales price per unit (volume)} = \text{Variable cost per unit (volume)} + \text{Fixed costs} + \text{Net income}$$
or
$$\text{SP(volume)} = \text{VC(volume)} + \text{FC} + \text{NI}$$

4. **The break-even point.** The break-even point occurs when total revenue equals total cost. It is computed using the C-V-P formula with net income equal to zero:

$$\text{Sales} = \text{Variable costs} + \text{Fixed costs} + \text{Zero}$$
$$\text{SP(volume)} = \text{VC(volume)} + \text{Fixed costs} + \text{Zero}$$

5. **Using the cost-volume-profit formula in profit planning.** The C-V-P formula may be used to determine the sales volume necessary to earn a target amount of net income, which is particularly useful for managerial planning. The basic C-V-P formula is used with volume as the unknown. It is used in other situations to predict the effects of changing variables such as sales price or variable cost per unit on profitability or volume.

6. **Contribution margin and contribution margin ratio.** The contribution margin for a unit of product is sales price less variable cost. Its purpose is to determine how much revenue remains to cover fixed costs and create profit. Contribution margin may be used to calculate the break-even point and the volume necessary to attain a target net income before taxes. (Refer to the top of the following page.) The contribution margin also can be used to structure an income statement based on cost behavior.

$$\text{BE volume} = \frac{\text{Fixed costs}}{\text{Contribution margin per unit}}$$

$$\text{Sales volume} = \frac{\text{Fixed costs} + \text{Target net income}}{\text{Contribution margin per unit}}$$

The contribution margin ratio is the contribution margin expressed as a percentage of sales price. It may be used to quickly calculate the amount of contribution margin to be expected from a change in total dollar sales and to calculate break-even volume or desired sales volume in sales dollars:

Change in total sales dollars $\times$ CM ratio = Change in CM

$$\text{Break-even volume in sales dollars} = \frac{\text{Fixed costs}}{\text{CM ratio}}$$

$$\text{Volume in sales dollars} = \frac{\text{Fixed costs} + \text{Net income}}{\text{CM ratio}}$$

7. *Cost-volume-profit analysis for multiproduct companies.* Many firms have more than one product or product line, but if the sales mix can be predicted, C-V-P analysis can be used as follows:

$$\text{BE volume} = \frac{\text{Fixed costs}}{\text{Weighted average contribution margin}}$$

$$\text{Sales volume} = \frac{\text{Fixed costs} + \text{Net income}}{\text{Weighted average contribution margin}}$$

8. *The cost-volume-profit formula in after-tax profit planning.* The basic cost-volume-profit formula, which assumes income before taxes, can be restated to reflect the relationship between income before taxes and income after taxes:

$$\text{Income before taxes} = \frac{\text{After-tax income}}{1 - \text{Tax rate}}$$

$$\text{Sales} = \text{Variable costs} + \text{Fixed costs} + \frac{\text{After-tax income}}{1 - \text{Tax rate}}$$

Key Terms

Break-even Point	**Contribution Margin Ratio**	**Relevant Range**
C-V-P Formula	**Cost-Volume-Profit Analysis**	**Sales Mix**
Contribution Margin	**Cost Behavior**	**Variable Costs**
Contribution Margin	**Fixed Costs**	**Weighted Average**
Income Statement	**Mixed (Semivariable) Costs**	**Contribution Margin**

Problems for Your Review

A. Basic C-V-P Analysis. The Richard Company manufactures and sells a single product for $20 per unit. The variable costs per unit are $14 and the fixed costs are $12,000 per month.

Required:

1. What is the conribution margin per unit of product?
2. What is the monthly break-even point expressed in units and in sales dollars?
3. How many units would have to be sold each month to earn a target net income of $3,600? Prove your answer by preparing a contribution margin income statement at the target level of sales.

Solution

1. Each unit of product contributes $6, the difference between the selling price of $20 per unit and variable costs of $14 per unit.

2. The break-even point in units is calculated most simply by dividing the fixed costs by the contribution margin per unit:

$$\text{Break-even} = \frac{\$12{,}000}{\$6.00} = 2{,}000 \text{ units}$$

$$= 2{,}000 \text{ units} \times \$20 = \$40{,}000$$

3. In order to calculate the volume that is required to earn a profit of $3,600, add the target profit to the fixed costs and divide by the contribution margin per unit. After fixed and variable costs are covered, all revenue will be profit:

$$\text{Volume} = \frac{\$12{,}000 + \$3{,}600}{\$6.00} = 2{,}600 \text{ units}$$

The contribution margin income statement for sales of 2,600 units is shown below:

Sales (2,600 units @ $20)	$52,000
Less: Variable costs (2,600 units @ $14)	36,400
Contribution margin	15,600
Less: Fixed costs	12,000
Net income	$3,600

B. Multiproduct C-V-P Analysis. The Lawrence Company sells two types of candy bars—Fudge Delight and Peanut Crunch. Sales and variable cost data for a package of 8 candy bars are as follows:

	Fudge Delight	Peanut Crunch
Sales price	$8.00	$7.00
Variable costs	5.00	4.50

The company has two marketing plans for next year. The first plan would sell 60% of Fudge Delight and 40% of Peanut Crunch; fixed costs would be $28,000. The second plan would sell 40% of Fudge Delight and 60% of Peanut Crunch; fixed costs under this plan would be $25,650.

Required:

1. What is the break-even point in units for the company under each plan?

2. The company wants to earn a profit of $15,000. Which plan can more easily achieve this goal?

Solution

1. Plan 1

$$\text{Weighted average contribution margin} = [60\% \times (\$8 - \$5)] + [40\% \times (\$7 - \$4.5)]$$
$$= \$2.80$$

$$\text{Break-even point} = \frac{\text{Fixed costs}}{\text{Weighted average contribution margin}}$$
$$= \frac{\$28{,}000}{\$2.80}$$
$$= 10{,}000 \text{ units}$$

To break even, the company must sell 6,000 units of Fudge Delight (10,000 × 60%) and 4,000 units of Peanut Crunch (10,000 × 40%).

Plan 2

$$\text{Weighted average contribution margin} = [40\% \times (\$8 - \$5)] + [60\% \times (\$7 - \$4.5)]$$
$$= \$2.70$$

$$\text{Break-even point} = \frac{\$25,650}{\$2.70}$$
$$= 9,500 \text{ units}$$

To break even, the company must sell 3,800 units of Fudge Delight (9,500 × 40%) and 5,700 units of Peanut Crunch (9,500 × 60%).

2. Plan 1

$$\text{Volume} = \frac{\text{Fixed costs} + \text{Net income}}{\text{Weighted average contribution margin}}$$
$$= \frac{\$28,000 + \$15,000}{\$2.80}$$
$$= 15,357 \text{ units}$$

Plan 2

$$\text{Volume} = \frac{\text{Fixed costs} + \text{Net income}}{\text{Weighted average contribution margin}}$$
$$= \frac{\$25,650 + \$15,000}{\$2.70}$$
$$= 15,055 \text{ units}$$

The Lawrence Company should use Plan 2 because under this plan the firm can earn $15,000 of net income by selling only 15,055 units. Under Plan 1, more units (15,357) would have to be sold to generate the same amount of income.

Questions

1. Why is the study of cost behavior important to management?

2. How do accountants and managers justify the use of linear cost relationships?

3. Distinguish between variable, fixed, and mixed costs.

4. How would you classify the following costs?
   a. The salary of a factory manager.
   b. Straight-line depreciation for office equipment.
   c. Equipment maintenance costs.
   d. Cost of iron ore used in making steel.

5. In which of the following decisions is cost-volume-profit analysis relevant?
   a. Determining the capacity of equipment to be purchased.
   b. Deciding the selling price of a product.
   c. Preparing an advertising budget.

6. Define the term *contribution margin*. Why is it a useful concept for managers? What is the contribution margin ratio? How would you use it in planning?

7. Give three examples of variable production costs.

8. Define:
   a. Fixed costs per unit.
   b. Variable costs per unit.

9. Give three examples of a mixed cost.

10. A firm invests heavily in new equipment, increasing its fixed costs substantially and increasing its contribution margin per unit from $4 to $5.
    a. What would you expect to happen to the break-even point? Why?
    b. What would be the profit if the firm sold 100,000 units above break-even?
    c. What assumption is management making about future volume?

11. What information is provided in a contribution margin income statement that cannot be obtained from the usual income statement?

12. What are the major assumptions underlying cost-volume-profit analysis?

13. Break-even points for multiproduct firms are likely to be less reliable than those for single-product firms. Do you agree or disagree? Discuss.

14. The profits of major airlines (those with revenues greater than $1 billion) are more sensitive to changes in the economic business cycle than are the profits of smaller airlines. Explain why.

15. An officer of a leading automobile corporation was quoted as saying that the major problem facing the industry in the 1980s was one of high break-even sales. What steps could individual automobile manufacturers have taken to lower their break-even points?

Exercises

1. Cost Behavior.

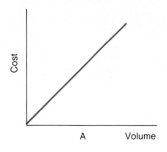

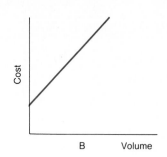

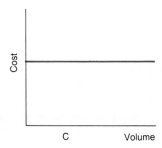

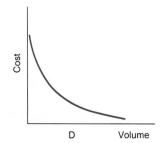

Graphs (A) through (D) show possible variations in the behavior of costs in relation to volume. Which graph or graphs best describe the behavior of the following costs?

    a. Total variable costs.
    b. Variable costs/unit.
    c. Total fixed cost.
    d. Fixed cost/unit.
    e. Total costs.
    f. Total costs/unit.

2. Relationship between Variables. Fill in the blanks in each of the following independent situations:

a.

	Selling Price/Unit	Variable Cost/Unit	Number Sold	Contribution Margin	Fixed Costs	Income
1.	5	3	?	3,000	500	?
2.	8	6	1,000	?	?	600
3.	10	6	?	?	600	3,000

b.

	Sales	Variable Costs	Contribution Margin	Fixed Costs	Income
1.	40,000	?	60%	20,000	?
2.	?	?	40%	60,000	40,000
3.	180,000	126,000	?	?	35,000

3. Contribution Margin Income Statement. Each of the following situations (1 through 4) is independent:

	Selling Price/Unit	Variable Cost/Unit	Fixed Costs	Sales in Units
1.	5	3	10,000	14,000
2.	10	7	35,000	20,000
3.	12	10	80,000	35,000
4.	15	9	66,000	16,000

a. For each case (1 through 4) prepare a contribution margin income statement.

b. For each case (1 through 4) calculate the break-even point in units and dollars.

4. Value of Variables at Break-even. Roll Paper Company has a break-even sales volume of 40,000 units per month. An increase in insurance premiums resulted in an increase in fixed costs from $10,000 to $12,500. The sales price remained the same at $2 per unit, and variable costs were unchanged. Calculate the following:

a. Variable costs per unit.

b. The increase in price that would allow break-even volume to remain at 40,000 units.

c. The contribution margin ratio.

5. Sales Mix. The Kiddie Company manufactures two products: ActionRobot sells for $20 per unit, with variable costs of $15 per unit; CuddleMouse sells for $8 per unit, with variable costs of $5 per unit. The company's fixed costs are $72,000 per month. Calculate the following:

a. The break-even sales volume if ActionRobot represents 30% of total sales.

b. The break-even sales volume if ActionRobot represents 70% of total sales.

6. Break-even Relationship between Variables. Ardon Company produces and distributes a commercial cleaning fluid that sells for $1.60 per gallon. Its variable production costs are $.50 per gallon, and variable selling expenses are $.40 per gallon. Fixed production costs, including factory overhead, are $10,000 per month, and fixed selling costs are $4,000. Calculate the following:

a. The break-even sales volume.

b. The selling price per gallon if a minimum profit of $15,000 is required when the monthly sales volume is 40,000 gallons.

7. Price/Volume Change. Lambert Connectors is reviewing the price of its major product, which currently sells for $20 per unit. The company is considering implementing a 10% price decrease, which would increase sales by 5,000 units. Current sales volume is 20,000 units. Variable costs are $15 per unit, with total fixed costs of $45,000. Calculate the following:

a. The current net income.

b. The net income if the price is decreased by 10%.

c. The current contribution margin ratio and the effect on net income if sales increase by $50,000.

8. Simultaneous Change in Variables. The manager of an appliance store is trying to decide whether to lease an additional store that has become available. Currently his monthly sales volume is $25,000, with total variable costs of $12,000 and monthly profits of $6,000.

a. Calculate the current amount of monthly fixed costs.

b. If both sales volume and variable costs would increase by 10% if the additional space were leased, what is the maximum increase in monthly rent the company can pay and still maintain monthly profits of $6,000?

c. Refer to the changes in Item b. If the company has a 30% tax rate, what is the maximum increase in monthly rent the company can pay and still maintain after-tax monthly profits of $6,000?

9. Analysis of Cost Structure. The Newman Corporation and the Morris Company have the unit prices and variable costs for the same product as shown at the top of the following page.

a. Calculate the break-even point for each firm in units.

b. If sales increase by 1,000 units above the break-even point, calculate the profits of both companies.

c. If sales dropped to 4,000 units, which firm would do better? Why?

d. If additional competition drove the selling price down to $4.25, which firm would be in a better position? Why?

Newman Corporation

Selling price per unit	$5
Variable cost per unit	3
Annual fixed cost	$15,000

Morris Company

Selling price per unit	$5
Variable cost per unit	4
Annual fixed cost	$7,500

10. Profit Planning. Reckless Corporation, a manufacturer of designer jeans for the teen market, is trying to plan for the coming year. The company had the following income statement for 1987:

Sales (120,000 pairs at $45)		$5,400,000
Cost of goods sold		2,700,000
Gross margin		$2,700,000
Selling expenses	$450,000	
Administrative expenses	270,000	720,000
Net income		$1,980,000

The vice-president of the company, Guido Zappa, is in charge of projecting an income statement for 1988. He knows that the sales price of the jeans will remain the same, and he has the following information:

1987

Variable costs:	Cost of goods sold, $3.00 per unit selling costs
Fixed costs:	Administrative expenses

Changes in 1988

Variable costs:	Cost of goods sold increases $1.50 per unit Selling costs increase $.30 per unit
Fixed costs:	Selling costs increase $30,000 Administrative costs increase $45,000

a. Help Mr. Zappa by preparing a contribution margin income statement for 1988, using all the information he has.
b. How many units would the firm have to sell in 1988 in order to earn as much profit as it did in 1987?

Problem Set A

23A–1. C-V-P Graph. The ABC Machine Company manufactures one product. Its annual fixed costs are $50,000 and its variable costs are $15 per unit. The company sells its product for $20 per unit.

Required:
a. Prepare a C-V-P graph showing the revenue line, total cost line, and total fixed costs.
b. Indicate on the graph the profit and loss areas, the break-even point, and the contribution margin when the sales volume is 20,000 units.

23A–2. Basic C-V-P Analysis. The Singer Company sells its product for $10 per unit. Variable costs are $6 per unit and fixed costs are $20,000.

Required:

  a. What is the contribution margin per unit?

  b. What sales volume is required to make a profit of $16,000?

  c. If variable costs increase by one-third, what sales volume would now be required to generate a profit of $16,000?

  d. If fixed costs were to increase by 5% and sales volume and variable costs were to remain the same as in Item c, what would be the new net income?

  e. Based on the original data, what is the contribution margin ratio? What is the volume in sales dollars necessary to produce income of $28,000?

  f. Based on the original data, what would be the expected increase in income if total sales dollars increase by $60,000?

23A–3. Basic C-V-P Analysis and After-Tax Profits. The XYZ Toy Company manufactures electric trains. Variable costs are $25 per unit, fixed costs are $10,000, and the selling price is $30 per unit.

Required:

  a. Calculate break-even sales.

  b. What sales volume is necessary to make a profit of $30,000?

  c. If fixed costs were to increase by 10% and variable costs were to increase by 5%, what sales volume would be needed to keep profits at $30,000?

  d. If volume decreased by 20% for every 5% increase in price, what would be the effect on profits if the price increased to $36? Assume sales volume and costs are the same as in Item b.

  e. Based on the data in Item c, what is the sales volume needed to keep profits at $30,000 on an after-tax basis if the company has a tax rate of 40%?

23A–4. Contribution Margin Statement and C-V-P Analysis. The following is a summary of the Taylor Company's income statement:

Sales (20,000 units)		$160,000
Cost of goods sold:		
Materials	$45,000	
Labor	30,000	
Overhead:		
Variable	8,000	
Fixed	12,000	95,000
Gross profit		65,000
Selling and administrative expenses:		
Variable	10,000	
Fixed	21,000	31,000
Net income		$34,000

Required:

  a. Prepare a contribution margin income statement, assuming all materials and labor costs are variable. Include columns showing sales, variable costs, and contribution margin as a percentage.

  b. Calculate the break-even sales volume in units and in dollars.

  c. Which of the following actions would reduce the break-even point the most:

    1. Increasing selling price by 5%?

    2. Decreasing variable costs per unit by 10%?

    3. Decreasing fixed costs by 10%?

  d. Using the original data, how many units would Taylor have to sell to earn $34,000 on an after-tax basis if the firm had a tax rate of 30%?

23A–5. Multiproduct C-V-P Analysis. The Mannings Petrochemical Company produces three chemicals. Fixed costs are $150,000 per month. Data for the current year's operations are as shown at the top of the following page.

	Chemical X	Chemical Y	Chemical Z
Sales price per gallon	$ 5	$15	$ 8
Variable cost per gallon	3	10	5
Sales mix percentage	30	40	30

Required:

  a. Calculate total break-even sales volume.
  b. What is the total sales volume required in order to earn a profit of $50,000?
  c. If the sales mix changes to 20:40:40 for Chemicals X, Y, and Z, respectively, what is the new break-even sales volume?
  d. What is the weighted average contribution margin of the sales mix that would increase profits to $70,000, for the same total sales volume as in Item b?

23A–6. Sales Mix and Multiproduct C-V-P Analysis. The Range Specialty Company sells two appliances, regular and deluxe ranges. The market for both products is relatively stable. Current data on sales, prices, and costs per unit are as follows:

	Regular	Deluxe
Units sold	6,000	3,000
Sales price	$15	$24
Unit material and labor cost	$8	$10
Variable selling expenses	$2	$4
Fixed overhead expenses = $50,000		

Management is planning an advertising strategy for the next year. Increasing the advertising budget for 1 of the 2 products by $5,000 is being considered. This increase would not produce additional unit sales but would shift sales of 2,000 units from one product to the other, depending on which product is emphasized.

Required:

  a. Calculate net income if the advertising budget increase is applied to the regular range.
  b. Calculate net income if the deluxe range is promoted.
  c. Should the company change its advertising policy?

23A–7. Sales Volume. Rift Technologies is a leading manufacturer of home computers and must decide whether or not to take advantage of a recent technological breakthrough in automated production of computers. The new process, which would reduce production costs by $30 per unit, requires an investment of $500,000, to be depreciated on a straight-line basis over 5 years. Rift sells to its distributors at a price of $400 per unit. Current variable production and selling costs are $250 per unit, with current annual fixed costs of $500,000.

Required:

  a. Calculate the sales volume required for a net income of $100,000:
    1. With current facilities.
    2. With the new production process.
  b. At what level of sales would the net income be the same regardless of the option chosen? *Hint:* Equate the net income of the two options.

Problem Set B

23B–1. C-V-P Graph. The XYZ Company makes a product that sells for $22 per unit. Average monthly sales volume is 2,000 units and the company has the following monthly expenses:

  1. Rent of factory building is $3,000.
  2. Electricity flat rate is $50, plus $15 per KWh (average usage = 500 KWh).
  3. Equipment depreciation is $4,000.
  4. Production manager's salary is $3,000.

5. Administrative staff salary is $4,000.
6. Raw materials are $12,000.
7. Production labor cost is $3,000.
8. Selling expenses (60% variable) are $2,500.

Required:
   a. Prepare a C-V-P graph showing the total revenue line, total cost line, and total fixed costs.
   b. Show on the graph the break-even volume, profit and loss areas, and the contribution margin for average monthly sales of 2,000 units.

23B–2. Basic C-V-P Analysis. Gray Company has an annual fixed cost of $45,000. Sales volume in previous years has varied between 10,000 and 20,000 units (maximum capacity). The company plans to double its capacity to 40,000 units next year and estimates that the total fixed cost will increase to $75,000. Variable costs per unit will remain unchanged at $10, and the selling price per unit will remain unchanged at $15.

Required:
   a. Sketch a graph showing the behavior of total fixed costs for the company at the current capacity of 20,000 units. Sketch a second graph showing total fixed costs if the company doubles its capacity to 40,000 units.
   b. Calculate the break-even volume in each case.
   c. Calculate net income if sales volume after expansion is:
      1. 20,000 units.
      2. 40,000 units.
   d. If sales of 20,000 units are assured, what is the minimum price Gray can charge and still make a profit of $10,000 after expansion?
   e. Refer to the original data and assume that the company doubles its capacity. Compute the contribution margin ratio. If the firm is at the 20,000-unit level and total sales dollars increase by $150,000, what will be the effect on net income?

23B–3. Basic C-V-P Analysis and After-Tax Profits. Thomas Gilders produces a line of roller skates that is currently very popular with teenagers. The company has a reputation for high-quality merchandise and employs a large, skilled work force. Skates sell for $20 per pair, and variable costs are $15 per pair. Fixed costs are $5,000 monthly. The company has been unable to meet the demand for its skates and is considering purchasing machinery that would increase fixed costs by $10,000 monthly and decrease variable costs by $2 per pair.

Required:
   a. What is the current monthly break-even volume? What would be the monthly break-even volume after the equipment is purchased?
   b. How many units does the company currently have to sell to earn net income of:
      1. $15,000?
      2. $60,000?
      3. $100,000?
   c. After the expansion, how many units will the company have to sell to earn net income of:
      1. $15,000?
      2. $60,000?
      3. $100,000?
   d. Why does the difference in units increase as projected profit increases?
   e. Assuming a tax rate of 40%, how many units will the company have to sell after the expansion to earn income on an after-tax basis of:
      1. $15,000?
      2. $60,000?
      3. $100,000?

23B–4. C-V-P Analysis. Grace Manufacturing produces a line of vacuum cleaners. The average selling price is $60 per unit, with variable costs of $40 per unit and annual fixed costs of $250,000. Annual production (sales) volume is 20,000 units. Grace is facing increasing competition that is expected to reduce sales by 5,000 units next year. Three alternative actions, each of which will maintain sales at current levels, are being considered:

1. Increasing the advertising budget, which would increase fixed costs by 5%.
2. Increasing sales commissions by 3% of net sales.
3. Reducing the selling price by 5%.

Required:

    a. Which of these actions would result in the largest net income? Show your calculations.

    b. The company estimates that increasing the advertising budget by 5% while reducing the selling price by 5% would further increase sales by 2,000 units. Should Grace choose this option? Show your calculations.

23B–5. Multiproduct C-V-P Analysis. The Cedar Furniture Company makes patio tables and chairs for department and furniture stores. The estimated cost of each is as follows:

	Chairs	Tables
Material	$5.00	$18.00
Labor	2.00	13.00
Variable factory overhead	1.00	4.00
Variable selling and administrative expenses	1.00	3.50

Total fixed costs are $40,000 annually. Cedar sells sets of six chairs and one table.

Required:

    a. If Cedar's current break-even volume is 6,000 units and the price of a table is $50, what is the selling price per chair? *Hint:* Contribution margin per chair is the unknown variable in the break-even sales formula.

    b. How many tables and chairs have to be sold annually to make a profit of $25,000?

23B–6. C-V-P Analysis. The North Western Junior School has decided to publish a monthly children's magazine to raise funds for its annual summer camp. The publications committee estimates that publication costs will be $1 per magazine. Distribution would be done by volunteers. Fixed costs for the use of the printing press and for professional printing services will be $3,000 per month. The committee estimates that 2,000 copies can be sold by distributing within the school and two other nearby schools. Circulation could be increased by 50% by selling through stores in the area, but this would increase costs by 20% on every magazine sold through the stores. A local company also indicated that it would be willing to pay $1,000 a month for 2 full-page advertisements in the magazine.

Required:

    a. If the school hopes to raise $10,800 annually from the magazine, what price should it charge per unit, assuming that circulation is restricted to schools?

    b. How much should the school charge if sales are also made through stores?

    c. If the committee decides not to have advertisements in the magazine, what would the selling price have to be in order to compensate for the loss of advertising revenue? Assume that sales will be made to schools and through stores.

23B–7. Multiproduct C-V-P Analysis. Mr. Brown operates a small foodstand that sells hamburgers and soft drinks. Generally, he sells one soft drink with each hamburger, and on average, he sells 300 hamburgers per day. A rival stand that sells only soft drinks has recently opened, and Brown has been forced to lower his soft drink price to remain competitive. He estimates that at the new price he is selling at a loss, with a negative contribution margin of $.15 per drink. He is considering eliminating sales of drinks but estimates that this would reduce sales of hamburgers by 20%. The contribution margin per hamburger is $1.25 and the average daily fixed cost is $150.

Required:

    a. If Mr. Brown is concerned mainly with maximizing daily profits, what decision should he make?

    b. If the previous contribution margin for soft drinks was $.10, what increase in the price of hamburgers would be required to keep profits at the same level as before the price decrease? Assume that the daily sales volume would be unchanged.

Using the Computer

Mom's Old-Fashioned Cookie Company has the following financial figures for its business operations, in which the sales unit is a six-ounce bag of cookies.

Number of units sold	100,000
Sales price per unit	$1.80
Variable costs per unit	$1.30
Fixed costs	$45,000

Required:

Use an electronic spreadsheet and C-V-P analysis to compute sales revenue, variable costs, contribution margin, and net income in each of these cases:

a. Use the information just noted.

b. If volume increases by 20% to 120,000 and all other figures are held constant, what are the financial results?

c. Volume increases again to 130,000 but fixed costs rise unexpectedly to $60,000. What are the results? Does Mom's now have a positive net income?

d. Assume sales volume does not increase over the year; however, variable costs go up by 5 cents per unit. Compute the resulting figures for this period.

e. Mom's decides to lower the price for a bag of cookies to $1.75. As a result, sales go up to 160,000 units. Variable costs increase 2 cents per unit to $1.37, and fixed costs increase to $65,000. What are the financial results of these changes?

f. Refer to the price in Item e. Somehow Mom's is able to raise its price 15 cents per unit without losing the volume attained in Item e. However, fixed costs rise to $70,000 and variable costs per unit increase to $1.45. Compute the results.

g. Refer to Item f. Mom's now raises its price an additional 11%. Volume drops slightly by 10%. Variable costs increase very slightly to $1.47 per unit and fixed costs increase by 7%. What happens to net income?

Decision Case

General Products Corporation is a large, diversified company with annual revenues in excess of $1 billion. It operates throughout the United States. In late 1988, General Products acquired Industrial Abrasives, Inc. as a wholly owned subsidiary. Industrial Abrasives now operates as a division of the Industrial Products Group of General Products Corporation.

Industrial Abrasives is a distributor of a full set of abrasive products for industrial firms that use such products in their own manufacturing process. The company has four major product lines:

1. *Loose abrasives,* including such items as sand or grain.
2. *Bonded abrasives,* materials which have been bonded into grinding wheels.
3. *Coated abrasives,* including such products as sandpapers.
4. *Precision abrasives,* including such items as diamond vitrified bonded abrasives.

The Industrial Abrasives division is small but offers considerable growth potential. The division has its headquarters and its major distribution facility in a major metropolitan area. The firm also has one satellite branch office in another major city approximately 500 miles away. The income statement for Industrial Abrasives for 1989 is shown on the following page.

Required:

a. Does the Industrial Abrasives income statement format provide sufficient information for the division's management? Explain.

b. Does the income statement format provide sufficient information for the management of the parent company, General Products Corporation? Explain.

c. Prepare a revised income statement format for Industrial Abrasives using a contribution margin approach. List the accounts involved. You do not have to use actual numbers. In preparing the statement, assume the following: (1) Cost of sales consists only of variable

Industrial Abrasives
General Products Corporation
Income Statement before Income Taxes
For the Year Ended September 30, 1989

Sales	$15,098,070
Cost of goods sold	11,990,034
Gross margin	3,108,036
Operating expenses:	
Advertising	15,458
Bad debt provision	17,913
Car expense	74,235
Commissions	5,765
Contributions	9,265
Data processing services	44,546
Depreciation	77,752
Entertainment	89,651
Freight-out	77,860
Insurance, general	61,102
Insurance, group	58,999
Interest	39,211
Medical and dental	6,716
Office expense	44,276
Postage	14,611
Professional fees	15,427
Profit sharing	75,500
Rent	99,039
Repairs and maintenance	29,159
Salaries, managerial	320,096
Salaries, office	609,756
Salaries, sales	449,634
Salaries, warehouse	282,964
Shipping supplies	14,016
Taxes, payroll	91,876
Taxes and licenses	18,520
Telephone	64,301
Travel	19,394
Utilities	13,524
Total operating expenses	2,740,566
Income before income taxes	$ 367,470

expenses; (2) all of the other expenses listed in the income statement may be classified in three categories:

    Selling expenses
    Warehouse overhead
    Administrative expenses

Each of these three categories has fixed and variable components.

Accounting Information for Short-term Decisions

24

LEARNING OBJECTIVES

After reading this chapter you should be able to:
1. Understand the nature of differential costs and revenues.
2. Define sunk costs.
3. Define opportunity costs.
4. Use the steps involved in decision making.
5. Solve make-or-buy problems.
6. Make decisions about pricing special orders.
7. Decide whether to add or drop product lines or departments.
8. Allocate joint production costs and decide whether products should be sold or processed further.
9. Calculate the most profitable use of scarce resources.

Managers must constantly make decisions that affect the future of a firm. They must decide which products to sell, price orders, decide whether to make a part or buy it elsewhere, and evaluate products and departments. Decision making is difficult because the future is uncertain; there are no guarantees of success in choosing one course of action over another. The decision-making process is a way of dealing with some of these uncertainties by using the best available information in a systematic manner. Managers must be able to distinguish information that is useful in decision making from information that is not.

In short-term decisions managers deal with time periods of a year or less, and they try to make the best possible use of the existing capacity of the firm. This chapter looks at short-term decision making. Chapter 25 looks at long-term decision making, which deals with questions of plant and equipment and changes in the overall capacity of the firm.

In making decisions that are not part of a business's ordinary operating routine, the manager of that business is faced with a bewildering array of data on revenues and costs along with information that cannot be quantified. The manager must be able to decide which data are relevant to the decision at hand and then must organize them so that they are useful in the decision-making process. After a quantitative analysis, the manager will look at the preferred alternative in light of qualitative factors—those factors affecting a decision that are very difficult to measure in monetary terms. For example, deciding whether to buy a part from an outside supplier may depend as much on the reliability of the supplier as on the costs of the part. The first step in the decision-making process, however, is to gather the quantitative data that are relevant to that decision.

Differential Costs and Revenues

Differential costs and revenues are the ones that are relevant to a decision; they are the costs and revenues that will change if one decision is chosen over another. For example, suppose that a small firm is paying $100 per month for gardening services on the grounds of its building. The owners are somewhat dissatisfied with the nature of the service that they are getting and receive a bid from another company for the work. The new firm promises to do more but asks for $145 per month. What is the differential cost of deciding to switch to the new gardeners? If they keep the current gardeners they will continue to pay $100, and if they change gardeners they will pay $145. They will pay at least $100 as long as they use one of the two gardeners. The differential cost, therefore, is $45—or the difference between choosing one alternative over another. In a decision situation managers need to consider the differential costs and revenues.

EXHIBIT 24–1
Differential Costs

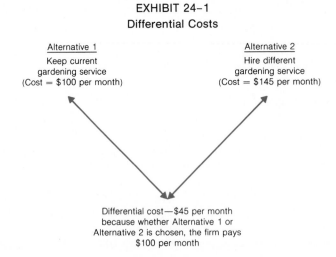

Alternative 1
Keep current
gardening service
(Cost = $100 per month)

Alternative 2
Hire different
gardening service
(Cost = $145 per month)

Differential cost—$45 per month
because whether Alternative 1 or
Alternative 2 is chosen, the firm pays
$100 per month

Sunk Costs

Sunk costs are those costs that already have been incurred. They will not change, because they have happened in the past and can be ignored when making decisions. What a firm has paid for assets in the past is not relevant to a future decision, although past costs may serve as a basis for estimating future costs. The book value of existing assets—original cost less accumulated depreciation—also is considered a sunk cost. Suppose that a firm has purchased some machine tools with a life of 9 months for $750. After the tools have been in use for 2 months, a new version becomes available on the market with the potential for saving $75 per month in labor. The new tools cost $850, however. Which items are relevant to their decision? The original cost of the current machine tools is a sunk cost because it already has been incurred. The cost savings of $75 per month and the cost of the new tools are both differential costs and are relevant to a decision regarding the purchase of new tools.

If the firm purchases the new tools, there will be a savings of $75 per month for 7 months for a total savings of $525, but $850 would have to be spent for the new machine. In other words, $325 more would be spent than would be saved, and therefore, the firm is better off keeping the old machine tools. Any salvage value for the old tools now or for the new ones in seven months, however, is also relevant to the decision.

Opportunity Costs

In certain types of management decisions, a third category of cost sometimes is considered. **Opportunity costs** are the benefits given up when management chooses one alternative over another. For example, suppose you have $1,000 to invest and are considering two alternatives: buying stock or buying shares in a money market fund. If you decide to put your funds into the money market fund because of high interest payments, you will have an opportunity cost because you will have given up the benefits of dividends from the stock in favor of high interest. The opportunity cost is equal to the dollars of dividends given up in choosing the other investment alternative. In practice, opportunity costs are used most frequently in decision making when there are three or more alternatives, where the opportunity cost would be the benefits given up for the alternative that is most profitable after the one chosen.

Opportunity costs, like other estimates of future costs and revenues, are not entered on the books of an organization, but they may have a major impact on a decision if the benefits given up are substantial. For example, a firm's decision to buy a component from an outside supplier as opposed to making it in the firm's own factory may depend on whether there are alternative uses for the space and therefore an opportunity cost if the firm makes the component.

Steps in Problem Solving

Managers often must be able to identify different types of costs when making decisions. The best way to learn to make effective management decisions is to simulate management problems and solve them in the same way a manager would.

When a management decision problem presents a large amount of data, it is useful to have a method of analysis to effectively solve the problem. The following suggested steps may be helpful. They do not have to be used for every decision problem and are intended simply as guidelines to help you develop your own mode of analysis.

1. Read the problem carefully at least two times before you write or calculate anything.

2. Decide what type of decision the problem requires and list the alternatives.
3. Choose one alternative for purposes of analysis. That is, assume you are going to carry out a decision one way or another. It does not matter which alternative you choose. The end result of the analysis will be the same, but the signs of the numbers will be reversed.
4. Look at your data and eliminate any sunk costs.
5. Eliminate future revenues or costs that will not change as a result of this decision.
6. List the differential revenues and costs that are relevant to the decision. Calculate the differential income or loss that would result from the decision.
7. If there are opportunity costs, compare them with the income or loss.
8. Look at the results of your quantitative analysis in light of qualitative factors, if they are known, and see if your decision would remain the same.

To use these guidelines to analyze a typical decision, assume the following:

The General Appliance Corporation makes a variety of kitchen appliances under its own name and also sells some appliances to major department store chains which sell the products, with some modification, under their own names. General Appliance is considering an offer from Slater Stores to produce 15,000 clothes dryers for $300 each. General Appliance incurs a cost of $310 for each machine, of which 40% is fixed. The normal selling price per unit is $375. The Slater Stores order also requires some modifications that would add $30 to the cost of each unit. General Appliance has a total capacity of 80,000 units and is currently operating at 75% of that capacity. In order to be more competitive General Appliance has spent $10,000 to renovate the production lines that would be used for the Slater order. Should General Appliance accept the special offer from Slater Stores?

Apply the steps outlined above:

1. Read the problem carefully.
2. In this problem, General Appliance has to decide whether or not to accept a special order from Slater Stores. The company's two alternatives are (a) to accept the special order or (b) to reject the special order.
3. For purposes of analysis, assume that they decide to accept the special order. Remember you can choose either alternative.
4. The $10,000 that General Appliance has spent already to renovate the production lines is a sunk cost. It has been incurred and will not change whether General Appliance accepts the special order or not. Therefore, it should be eliminated from the analysis.
5. Among the given data are some future revenues and costs that will not change if General Appliance accepts the special order. For example, General Appliance is producing 60,000 units now at a cost of $310 per unit with a sales price of $375 each. The revenue and costs from those units will remain the same whether or not General Appliance accepts the special order and therefore must be disregarded in this analysis. In addition, although each special order unit has a total cost of $310, 40% of that cost is fixed. The fixed cost will be incurred in this period regardless of the decision; therefore, 40% of $310, or $124, must be eliminated from the analysis.
6. List the differential revenues, costs, and profit. All of these items relate to the special order of 15,000 units:

	Per Unit	Total
Differential revenue (15,000 units × $300)	$300	$4,500,000
Differential costs:		
variable manufacturing costs ($310 − $124 = $186)	186	2,790,000
Slater modifications	30	450,000
Total cost	216	3,240,000
Differential income	$ 84	$1,260,000

7. In this problem, there are only two alternatives and opportunity costs are not considered in the analysis.
8. Based on this quantitative analysis, General Appliance should accept the special order from Slater Stores. General Appliance's income and contribution margin will increase by $84 per unit (or $1,260,000) if the order is accepted. In this problem, there are no qualitative factors to consider such as whether General Appliance's regular customers might be negatively affected by this type of order.

Use of Differential Costs and Revenues

In the preceding example, only differential costs and revenues were used to make a decision. However, the decision would have been the same if all the data given in the problem had been used. Exhibit 24–2 shows how all of the cost and revenue data might have been used.

Notice that the conclusion is the same when all the available data are used. General Appliance would be well advised to accept the special order. Currently only 60,000 clothes dryers are sold, at an income of $3,900,000; if the new order is accepted, income would increase to $5,160,000. The difference between those two figures represents the differential income generated by the special order. The differential income of $1,260,000 is responsible for the increase in total income.

Although a wrong answer will not result from using all of the cost and revenue data available, it is generally advisable to focus only on the differential items. It is less time-consuming to use differential costs and revenues when a large amount of information is given, but even in a short problem like the one involving General Appliance, there is more calculation when all costs and revenues are used. In addition, only limited data may be available to solve certain problems, and a decision maker should be able to recognize which costs and revenues are relevant. By focusing on differential costs and rev-

EXHIBIT 24–2
Using All Cost and Revenue Data

	(60,000) Original Units	+	(15,000) Special Order	=	(75,000) Total Units
Revenue	$22,500,000	+	$4,500,000	=	$27,000,000
Cost	18,600,000	+	3,240,000	=	21,840,000
Income	$ 3,900,000	+	$1,260,000	=	$ 5,160,000

enues, the manager sharpens his or her analytical skills and lessens the chance of using unnecessary data in a confusing or incorrect way in the future.

Short-term Decisions

Following are some typical short-term decision-making situations that apply the concepts and guidelines enumerated thus far.

Make-or-Buy Decisions

Many manufactured products are made up of a number of component parts that must be assembled into the finished product. The components of an automobile, for example, include among many other things an engine, the transmission, and seating, all of which are put together on an assembly line. Each manufacturer must decide whether to make a given component or to buy it from an outside supplier; this raises the question of how management wants to use its facilities. A number of qualitative factors must be considered when making this type of decision. For example: Does the supplier make a product that is equal in quality to what the firm could produce in its own plant? Would the supplier be reliable in meeting delivery dates? For how long is the supplier making a commitment to the quoted price? If a firm decides to make a component part that it has previously purchased elsewhere with satisfaction, management should consider whether it is desirable to permanently destroy a good relationship with a supplier.

In addition, there are important quantitative factors to consider in the **make-or-buy decision.** The costs of purchasing a part, as opposed to the costs of manufacturing that can be avoided if the part is purchased, are differential costs. In addition, when the firm's facilities can be used for other functions that generate income, the opportunity cost of making a part must be considered.

Following is an example of the make-or-buy decision for the National Computer Corporation. The firm makes a line of microcomputers and has been buying the disk drives for the computers from an outside supplier. The company has excess capacity, however, that could be used to produce the disk drives. The accounting department has computed the following costs for producing the annual requirement of 100,000 disk drives:

Variable costs:	
Materials	$ 400,000
Labor	500,000
General factory overhead	300,000
Total	1,200,000
Fixed costs:	
Manufacturing	$ 400,000
Share of central corporate costs	200,000
Total	600,000
Total costs	$1,800,000

National Computer has been paying $17 per unit to an outside supplier for the 100,000 disk drives needed each year. The company also spent $3,000 for painting and other renovations of the factory area where the disk drives would be produced. Using the framework for problem solving outlined on pages

978

975–976, and assuming there are no alternative uses for the firm's facilities, the company's make-or-buy decision problem may be solved as follows:

National Computer can either make disk drives in its own plant or continue to buy them from an outside supplier. For purposes of analysis, assume they decide to make the disk drives in National's own plant. Management must look at what will change as a result of that decision. The $3,000 already spent to renovate part of the factory is a sunk cost and will not change under either alternative. Therefore, that amount is not considered in the analysis. There also is a future cost that will not change if the disk drives are made—the $200,000 share of central corporate costs. The corporation will incur those costs whether the disk drives are made in-house or continue to be purchased. Therefore, they are not relevant to this decision. The $400,000 of fixed manufacturing costs would be incurred only if the decision were made to make the disk drives; fixed costs, like all differential costs, are relevant to the make-or-buy decision. The differential costs of making the disk drives are shown in Exhibit 24–3.

EXHIBIT 24–3

National Computer
Make-or-Buy Decision
(Assumption: Make the disk drives)

Differential costs:	
Materials	$ 400,000
Labor	500,000
General factory	300,000
Fixed manufacturing	400,000
Total cost of making drives	1,600,000
Cost of purchasing drives (saved):	
100,000 units × $170	1,700,000
Differential cost savings from making disk drives	$ 100,000

Exhibit 24–3 lists only the figures that would change if the company made the disk drives. The firm would incur the costs of making the part—an outflow of funds—but would save what is currently being paid to an outside supplier. Because the savings exceed the new manufacturing costs by $100,000, the firm would be better off making the parts. Assuming no alternative uses for the facilities, quantitative analysis leads to the decision to make the drives. The firm then would weigh this against important qualitative factors to make the final decision.

Opportunity Cost

In the preceding example it was assumed that there were no alternative uses for the space that would be used to make the disk drives. Therefore, there was no opportunity cost to consider in the decision to make the drives. If, however, those facilities could be used for some other purpose, then the opportunity cost of making the disk drives must be considered in the decision.

Assume now that National Computer could use the disk drive facilities to produce additional units of its larger computers that would generate $250,000 in profit. The opportunity cost of making the disk drives is $250,000 because that is what the company would give up if it chose to make the drives. Does this opportunity cost affect the decision? Exhibit 24–4 shows what the quantitative analysis looks like when the opportunity cost is included.

When the opportunity cost of making the disk drives is considered, it becomes clear that the total cost of making the disk drives exceeds the benefits. The total cost of making the disk drives is $1,850,000, but only $1,700,000 is saved; therefore, the firm would be $150,000 better off if the drives are bought from the outside supplier. Although opportunity costs may not always change a decision, they should be considered when they exist.

Special Orders

Generally, prices are set to cover all of the costs of a product and to generate profit. Sometimes, however, firms sell products below their normal price in order to earn revenue that might otherwise be lost. For example, manufacturers sometimes make products for other companies, particularly retail chains, to sell under their own brand name, as was the case in the General Appliance example. Retail chains usually sell the products for less than do stores selling the same product under the manufacturer's brand name. Similarly, firms may bid for a contract and accept a price that is lower than normal in order to compete, and sometimes firms charge lower prices for damaged or obsolete merchandise.

Companies with unused capacity generally accept **special orders** when their selling price exceeds the differential cost of making the product. When solving special order problems, figure the differential costs of the special order and subtract them from the price charged, which represents differential revenue. If the result is a positive number, the special order would bring a profit. Following is an example of a special order problem.

The Daisy Bicycle Company makes children's bicycles in one of its plants. The firm sells the bicycles for $75 and projects sales of 20,000 bicycles in the coming year. The total cost of manufacturing next year's bicycles is figured as follows:

Material	$ 500,000
Labor	400,000
Variable factory costs	200,000
Fixed factory costs	200,000
Total costs	$1,300,000

The factory can make 35,000 bicycles per year. A buyer from a chain store has approached the sales manager of Daisy and has offered to buy 10,000 bicycles at $60 each. Each bicycle would require a special metal tag with the chain store's name that would cost $1.50 per unit.

The sales manager of Daisy is not sure whether to accept this order because she thinks it might be unprofitable. To determine whether the order should be accepted, the sales manager uses a problem-solving procedure like the one outlined earlier. She decides that the company's two alternatives are (1) to accept the special order from the chain store or (2) to reject the special order. She decides to assume for problem-solving purposes that Daisy accepts the special order in order to see what would happen to costs and revenues. She could have made the opposite assumption and arrived at the same answer with the signs reversed. In this problem there are no sunk costs or opportunity

EXHIBIT 24–4

National Computer
Opportunity Cost Included
(Assumption: Make the disk drives)

Cost of making disk drives (From Exhibit 24–3)	$1,600,000
Opportunity cost—profit forgone from alternative use of facilities	250,000
Total cost	1,850,000
Cost of purchasing drives (saved) (From Exhibit 24–3)	1,700,000
Difference in favor of buying from outside supplier	$ 150,000

costs to consider. There are, however, future costs and revenue that will not change whether or not Daisy accepts the special order. Projected regular sales of 20,000 units are in this category, and the fixed factory costs that are committed to in the short run. The sales manager figures the differential costs and revenue for the special order as shown in Exhibit 24–5 on a per-unit and total-cost basis. (See bottom of this page.) Note that the amount per unit was derived by taking the total cost of $1.3 million and dividing by the 20,000 bicycles on which the calculation was based.

Daisy should accept the special order because $35,000 more profit will be generated. Although the revenue per unit is less than the normal selling price, it is high enough to cover the differential costs of making the special order. Any sales price above $56.50 would generate profit that the company otherwise would not have had. In the short run, the fixed factory cost is not a differential cost, so it does not have to be covered by this particular order. Over a longer period, the firm must cover all costs.

Qualitative factors also can be important in special order decisions. For example, does acceptance of a special order at a lower price ultimately affect

EXHIBIT 24–5

Daisy Bicycle Company
Special Order Decision
(Assumption: Accept the special order)

	Per Unit	Total
Differential revenue 10,000 units × $60	$60.00	$600,000
Differential costs:		
Material	25.00	250,000
Labor	20.00	200,000
Variable factory	10.00	100,000
Special insignia	1.50	15,000
Total costs	$56.50	$565,000

sales to regular customers at regular prices? Will the timing of a special order affect regular production? These and other factors must be considered carefully with the quantitative analysis when making a special order decision.

Adding and Dropping Product Lines and Departments

Managers frequently must evaluate the parts or segments of a business—such as departments, sales territories, and product lines—in order to decide whether to add or drop a particular segment. This is a difficult process of evaluation that depends on careful analysis of accounting data. Here, too, management must evaluate what changes would result if they decide to add or drop a segment of a business. For example, the management of Sloan's Clothing, a large men's clothing store with four major departments—suits, sportswear, shirts and ties, and shoes—is considering dropping its shoe department because last month it lost $2,000, as it has sometimes done in the past. Exhibit 24–6 shows the most recent monthly data for the store.

Would the firm be better off if the shoe department was dropped? Assume that the store has decided to drop the department in order to analyze the changes resulting from that decision. The costs and revenues of the three other departments would stay the same. Therefore, one need only focus on the data given for the shoe department in order to find the differential costs and revenues. If the company drops the shoe department it will lose sales revenue of $20,000 but will not incur the costs of the department. Would all the shoe department costs be eliminated if the company closed the department? The variable costs would become zero when activity in the department ceased. The fixed costs, however, are broken down into two categories—direct and indirect (or joint)—and these require further analysis.

EXHIBIT 24–6

Sloan's Clothing
Department Income Statements
(in thousands)

	Suits	Sports-wear	Shirts and Ties	Shoes	Total
Sales	$100	$65	$35	$20	$220
Variable costs	60	35	15	10	120
Contribution margin	40	30	20	10	100
Fixed costs:					
Direct	12	7	5	6	30
Indirect	8	3	3	6	20
Total fixed costs	20	10	8	12	50
Net income (loss)	$ 20	$20	$12	$ (2)	$ 50

Direct Fixed Costs

Direct costs, as noted in Chapter 22, are those items that can be traced specifically and economically to a particular cost objective. In this case, the cost objective is the shoe department at Sloan's Clothing. For example, the shoe department hired some part-time salespeople for the year, and their salaries represented $1,000 of the direct fixed costs. If the department is dropped, those salaries will no longer be incurred as a cost by the store. The department manager's salary, $3,000 per month, also will be eliminated, as will be $1,000 worth of shoe advertising. The remaining $1,000 is for depreciation on special furnishings and display areas that would not be eliminated if the shoe department is dropped. In many cases, the direct fixed costs for a segment of a business can be eliminated by dropping that segment, but not always. Information on fixed costs must be carefully analyzed.

Indirect (Joint) Fixed Costs

Fixed costs that are incurred by all of the segments of a business are common costs that must be divided up or allocated among the various departments, divisions, sales territories, or product lines. Sloan's rent, for example, and the salary of the store manager are indirect fixed costs. All of the store's departments share a portion of those costs, but when a department is eliminated, the costs still remain. They simply are divided up among the remaining departments. Therefore, indirect (or joint) fixed costs are future costs that *do not* change whether a company drops a department or keeps it. They are not differential costs.

Exhibit 24–7 shows the differential costs and revenues involved in the decision of whether to drop Sloan's shoe department. Although the department was not producing net income, it did have a positive contribution margin that went toward coverage of fixed costs. If the department was dropped, Sloan's would eliminate only $5,000 in fixed costs, whereas the remainder of the shoe department's fixed costs would be divided among the three other departments. The cost savings would be only $15,000, whereas $20,000 in revenue would be lost, resulting in a net drop in profit of $5,000.

Based on the differential analysis, Sloan's should not drop the shoe department. Although the department appears unprofitable when the allocated indirect fixed costs are considered, Sloan's would lose income of $5,000 if the shoe department was eliminated. Exhibit 24–8 shows what the other departmental income statements would look like if the shoe department was dropped and its fixed costs were divided up among the other departments.

EXHIBIT 24–7
Sloan's Clothing
(Assumption: Drop shoe department)
(in thousands)

Differential revenue		
(lost if department was dropped)		$(20)
Differential costs		
(saved if department was dropped)		
Variable costs	$10	
Direct fixed costs	5	
Total cost savings		15
Differential loss in income		$(5)

EXHIBIT 24-8

Sloan's Clothing
Department Income Statements
(in thousands)

	Suits	Sports-wear	Shirts and Ties	Total
Sales	$100	$65	$35	$200
Variable costs	60	35	15	110
Contribution margin	40	30	20	90
Fixed costs:				
Direct[a]	12	8	5	25
Indirect[b]	10	5	5	20
Total fixed costs	22	13	10	45
Net income	$ 18	$17	$10	$ 45

[a]One thousand dollars direct fixed costs from the shoe department are given to sportswear because that department now uses the furnishings.

[b]Six thousand dollars indirect fixed costs from the shoe department are divided equally among the remaining three departments.

If the shoe department was eliminated, the total income for the store last month would have decreased from $50,000 to $45,000, the change being the differential loss of $5,000. The contribution margin for the store would have decreased from $100,000 to $90,000, with fixed costs decreasing by only $5,000. Sloan's would be wise to keep the shoe department unless the space can be used to bring in a larger contribution margin or income. Furthermore, it should be considered whether there would be complementary positive or negative effects on other departments or products if the shoe department was dropped. For example, dropping the shoe department might decrease sales of shirts and ties. A manager must consider every possible effect and weigh every alternative when doing a differential analysis.

Accounting for Joint Product Costs

Many manufacturing processes simultaneously produce two or more separately identifiable products from a common set of inputs, called **joint products.** A distinguishing characteristic of joint products is that no one of the products may be produced without the simultaneous production of one or more other products. Joint products are often produced in basic industries that process natural raw materials; they are not found in all manufacturing processes. For example, a lumber mill uses raw materials, direct labor, and overhead to produce different types and grades of lumber. Similarly, a meat-packing plant cannot slaughter cattle and produce only steak; a variety of cuts of meat, hides, and other items, all joint products, will simultaneously be produced. The point at which joint products become individually identifiable is called the **split-off point.** The manufacturing costs incurred before the split-off point are called **joint product costs.** For example, the material, labor, and

EXHIBIT 24–9
Joint Products

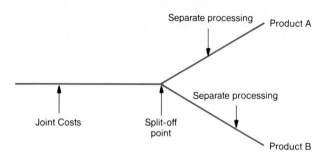

overhead costs incurred to process the carcass of a steer to the point where it can be divided into the different types of dressed meat are joint product costs.

Some joint products can be sold at the split-off point, whereas others require further separate processing before they can be sold. Exhibit 24–9 shows joint costs, the split-off point, and separate processing.

Joint product costs are similar to the joint fixed costs used in the Sloan's Clothing illustration. Both types of costs are incurred for more than one cost objective. In the Sloan's example, the joint fixed costs are incurred for several departments, whereas joint product costs are incurred in order to produce two or more products. Just as Sloan's allocated the indirect fixed costs among the departments, joint production costs are divided up among all joint products. Data from Lennox Chemical Corporation will illustrate how firms allocate joint production costs. Lennox incurs joint costs of $15,000 when it produces two chemicals, Geon and Nexun. The firm's annual output is 20,000 gallons of Geon and 25,000 gallons of Nexun. Geon sells for $3.50 per gallon; Nexun is $1.90 per gallon. There are two widely used methods for allocating joint production costs to products. One is based on physical measures and the other relies on relative sales value.

Physical Measures Method

The **physical measures method** uses physical measures such as gallons, liters, pounds, and grams as a basis for allocating joint product costs. Each product's proportionate share of the total quantity produced is used to allocate a like proportion of the joint product costs to that product. For example, Lennox Chemical produced 20,000 gallons of Geon and 25,000 gallons of Nexun, for a total quantity of 45,000 gallons. The ratio of each product to the total physical quantity is multiplied by the joint cost in order to properly allocate the joint cost to each product.

	Total Gallons	Ratio	×	Joint Cost	=	Joint Cost Allocation
Geon	20,000	$\frac{20,000}{45,000}$ (44%)	×	$15,000	=	$ 6,600
Nexun	25,000	$\frac{25,000}{45,000}$ (56%)	×	$15,000	=	$ 8,400
Total	45,000					$15,000

If Lennox sells its entire inventory of both products, the gross margin for Geon and Nexun is calculated as follows:

	Geon	Nexun
Sales	$70,000	$47,500
Cost of goods sold	6,600	8,400
Gross margin	$63,400 (91%)	$39,100 (82%)

Using physical measures to allocate joint production costs is relatively easy, but sometimes it can seriously distort the income produced by different products, particularly if there is a great difference between the physical measure of the product and its revenue-producing ability. For the Geon and Nexun example, it was reasonable to allocate joint production costs based on physical measures, but such is not the case for two mineral products, Alfite and Borgite, with production of Alfite equal to 800 pounds and production of Borgite equal to 200 pounds. The firm has calculated that its joint production costs for the two products are $10,000, with Alfite selling for $30 per pound and Borgite selling for $50 per pound. The allocation of joint costs to Alfite and Borgite follows:

	Total Pounds	Ratio	×	Joint Cost	=	Joint Cost Allocation
Alfite	800	$\frac{800}{1,000}$ (80%)	×	$10,000	=	$ 8,000
Borgite	200	$\frac{200}{1,000}$ (20%)	×	$10,000	=	$ 2,000
Total	1,000					$10,000

The gross margin for Alfite and Borgite shows that the disproportionate physical quantity of Alfite gives the product a share of the joint costs out of line with its revenue-producing ability:

	Alfite	Borgite
Sales	$24,000	$10,000
Cost of goods sold	8,000	2,000
Gross margin	$16,000 (67%)	$ 8,000 (80%)

Because Alfite is produced in large quantities, its share of the joint production costs is very high; consequently, the gross margin as a percentage of sales is much higher for Borgite. Notice that the difference in gross margin percentages for Alfite and Borgite is much greater than that for Geon and Nexun where there was a relatively small difference in the physical quantities produced between the two products. It would be more reasonable to allocate the joint costs of producing Alfite and Borgite using a method called relative sales value.

Relative Sales Value Method

The **relative sales value method** often is used to allocate joint production costs; this method calculates each product's proportionate share of the total sales value of all the products and then allocates the same proportion of joint product costs to each product. The relative sales value method is based on the idea that costs should be allocated according to the revenue-generating power of the individual products. The sales value is assumed to be what the product could be sold for at the split-off point. Continuing with the Lennox Chemical example, the procedure is similar to what was shown earlier.

	Sales Value at Split-off	Ratio	$\times$	Joint Cost =	Joint Cost Allocation
Geon	20,000 $\times$ $3.50 = $ 70,000	$\dfrac{\$ 70,000}{\$117,500}$		(60%) $\times$ $15,000 =	$ 9,000
Nexun	25,000 $\times$ $1.90 = $ 47,500	$\dfrac{\$ 47,500}{\$117,500}$		(40%) $\times$ $15,000 =	$ 6,000
Total		$117,500			$15,000

The gross margin for the two products can differ dramatically depending on which cost allocation method is used. Using physical measures to allocate joint production costs resulted in gross margin percentages of 91% and 82% for Geon and Nexun. Using the relative sales value method, both products have gross margin percentages of 87%:

	Geon	Nexun
Sales	$70,000	$47,500
Cost of goods sold	9,000	6,000
Gross margin	$61,000 (87%)	$41,500 (87%)

The relative sales value method is considered to be somewhat superior because it allocates costs according to the revenue-generating ability of the products, and gross margin as a percentage of sales is equal for all products when it is calculated at the split-off point.

Using the relative sales value method shows an even greater difference for Alfite and Borgite. The joint cost allocation follows for those products:

	Sales Value at Split-off	Ratio	$\times$	Joint Cost =	Joint Cost Allocation
Alfite	800 $\times$ $30 = $24,000	$\dfrac{\$24,000}{\$34,000}$		(70.6%) $\times$ $10,000 =	$ 7,060
Borgite	200 $\times$ $50 = $10,000	$\dfrac{\$10,000}{\$34,000}$		(29.4%) $\times$ $10,000 =	$ 2,940
Total		$34,000			$10,000

The calculation of gross margin for Alfite and Borgite follows:

	Alfite	Borgite
Sales	$24,000	$10,000
Cost of goods sold	7,060	2,940
Gross margin	$16,940 (71%)	$ 7,060 (71%)

The gross margin percentage for Alfite is only 67% using physical measures to allocate the joint costs because that product was produced in greater quantity and therefore received more of the cost allocation. Using relative sales value to allocate joint costs gives a better indication of the relative profitability of Alfite and Borgite.

Both the physical measures and the relative sales value methods are arbitrary devices used to divide up costs for the purposes of inventory valuation and financial reporting. For management use in planning and decision making, however, joint cost allocation does not need to be considered; more important to management is what will happen after the split-off point.

Sell or Process Further Decision

Manufacturers who produce joint products frequently have to decide whether a product should be sold at the split-off point or processed further, assuming both options are available. For example, the management of a meat-packing plant may need to decide whether to sell the meat when cut or to process it further into luncheon meat. The costs and revenues relevant to the **sell or process further decision** are those that will differ depending on the decision to sell or process further. The joint costs incurred up to the split-off point will not be affected by the decision; they are sunk costs. The decision to process a product further after the split-off point must be made by comparing the differential revenue after the split-off point with the costs of further processing. Manufacturing companies try to achieve the most profitable mix of products; this requires frequent analysis of the options that may be changing rapidly.

To illustrate the decision of whether to sell products at the split-off point or to process them further, again consider the case of Lennox Chemical Corporation which incurs joint costs of $15,000 in order to produce two chemicals, Geon and Nexun. Both products can be sold at the split-off point or processed further for use as industrial cleansers. At the split-off point, Geon can be sold for $3.50 per gallon and Nexun for $1.90 per gallon. The costs for additional processing for both products are as follows:

	Geon	Nexun
Fixed costs	$5,000.00	$3,000.00
Variable cost per unit	$1.10	$.60

After additional processing, Lennox can sell Geon for $5.25 per gallon and Nexun for $2.10 per gallon. The expected annual output is 20,000 gallons of Geon and 25,000 gallons of Nexun.

Lennox Chemical must decide whether to sell the two products at the split-off point or to process them further. Assume that the firm has decided to process the two chemicals further. Find the differential costs and revenues associated with that decision and eliminate irrelevant items. The $15,000 joint cost incurred before the split-off point is considered a sunk cost in the decision, regardless of how it is allocated. Exhibit 24–10 projects the changes in costs and revenues for both products if they are processed further. The revenue they would each bring if sold at the split-off point is shown as an opportunity cost because that is what is sacrificed in the decision to process further.

EXHIBIT 24–10
Lennox Chemical Corporation
(Assumption: Process both products further)

	Geon	Nexun
Revenue		
(20,000 gallons × $5.25)	$105,000	
(25,000 gallons × $2.10)		$ 52,500
Costs:		
Fixed	5,000	3,000
Variable:		
(20,000 gallons × $1.10)	22,000	
(25,000 gallons × $ .60)		15,000
Opportunity costs:		
(20,000 gallons × $3.50)	70,000	
(25,000 gallons × $1.90)		47,500
Total costs	97,000	65,500
Net income (loss)	$ 8,000	$(13,000)

Based on the quantitative analysis in Exhibit 24–10, Lennox Chemical Corporation should process Geon further and sell Nexun at the split-off point. Exhibit 24–11 applies the same data to the manufacturing process as depicted in Exhibit 24–10, using the type of diagram shown earlier.

EXHIBIT 24–11
Lennox Chemical Corporation
(Assumption: Process both products further)

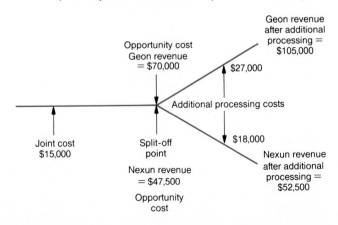

EXHIBIT 24-12

Lennox Chemical Corporation

(Assumption: Process both products further)

	Geon	Nexun
Differential revenue:		
($5.25 − $3.50 × 20,000)	$35,000	
($2.10 − $1.90 × 25,000)		$ 5,000
Differential costs:		
Fixed	5,000	3,000
Variable	22,000	15,000
Total costs	27,000	18,000
Differential profit (loss)	$ 8,000	$(13,000)

Exhibit 24–12 uses the same data but emphasizes differential revenues. In this analysis, the revenue that would be gained by selling each of the products at the split-off point is subtracted from the revenue that would be earned after additional processing resulting in the differential revenue earned from the decision to process further. When the differential revenue exceeds the differential cost, it is more profitable to process the product further.

Analyzing Exhibit 24–12 leads one to the same conclusion as analyzing Exhibit 24–10. Process Geon further and sell Nexun at the split-off point.

Although accountants have devised a variety of ways to divide up joint costs among joint products, these allocation methods do not alter the irrelevance of joint product costs to the decision to process further or sell at the split-off point. Even when allocated joint costs are included on the income statements for product lines, they will not affect a decision regarding what to do after the split-off point. Sometimes joint costs are included in statements because they are required for published financial reports, but they are not relevant for decision-making purposes.

Use of Scarce Resources

Managers frequently have to deal with the question of how to best use scarce resources. For example, a retail store may have a limited amount of floor space. Management must predict which product lines will generate the largest amount of contribution margin in the smallest amount of space. In this example, floor space is the scarce resource. Many high-tech firms do not have enough skilled engineers and programmers; for these companies, engineering and programming labor hours are the scarce resource. They try to maximize contribution margin by concentrating on products that generate the largest contribution margin with the smallest number of skilled labor hours.

When a company has a scarce resource, it must try to concentrate on products or services that provide the greatest possible contribution to profit per unit of the scarce resource, regardless of individual contribution margins. This can be done by calculating the total contribution margin in relation to the scarce resource:

$$\text{Contribution margin per unit of scarce resource} \times \text{Units of scarce resource available} = \text{Total contribution margin}$$

For example, Westronics has two product lines, Alborgs and Wuarks, with the following revenue and cost characteristics:

	Alborgs	Wuarks
Sales price per unit	$100	$150
Variable cost per unit	70	90
Contribution margin	$ 30	$ 60
Contribution margin ratio	30%	40%

Looking only at this information, the Wuark line would appear to be more profitable because it has a higher contribution margin per unit and a higher contribution margin ratio. However, it takes 3 machine-hours to produce 1 Wuark and 1 machine-hour to produce 1 Alborg, and the division manager has only 3,000 machine-hours of capacity available. The machine-hours are, therefore, a scarce resource, and it must be determined which product yields the highest contribution margin in the least number of machine-hours. Following is a calculation of the contribution margin per machine-hour and the total contribution margin for each product for the hours available:

	Alborgs	Wuarks
Contribution margin per unit	$30	$60
Machine-hours needed per unit	1	3
Contribution margin per machine-hour	$30	$20
Total contribution margin:		
Machine-hours available	3,000	3,000
Contribution margin per machine-hour	× $30	× $20
Total contribution margin	$90,000	$60,000

Even though Wuarks have the highest contribution margin per unit, Alborgs provide the highest contribution margin when the scarce or limiting factor, the number of machine-hours available, is taken into account. Management would be wise to focus production on the Alborg line in order to maximize the total contribution margin.

In many situations there are a number of factors that may be in limited supply for a variety of products. For example, there may be limits to floor space, advertising, and certain types of labor, and a firm has to try to find the right combination of products given the constraints under which it operates. In such situations, the quantitative techniques of linear programming are generally used, but this is an area beyond the scope of this text.

Summary of Learning Objectives

1. *The nature of differential costs and revenues.* Differential costs and revenues are the costs and revenues that will change depending on which alternative is chosen in a management decision and are, therefore, relevant to the decision-making process.

2. *Sunk costs.* Sunk costs are costs that already have been incurred and therefore are not affected by or considered relevant to management decisions.

3. *Opportunity costs.* Opportunity costs are the benefits that are sacrificed when one course of action is chosen over another. Although they are not entered in accounting records, when opportunity costs exist they can play a major role in the decision-making process.

4. *The steps involved in decision making.*
   a. Read the problem carefully.
   b. Decide what type of decision is required and what alternatives are feasible.
   c. For purposes of analysis choose one alternative.
   d. Eliminate sunk costs.
   e. Eliminate future revenues and costs that will not be affected by the decision.
   f. List the differential revenues and costs in order to find differential profit or loss. If there is no revenue, find only the differential costs.
   g. If there are opportunity costs, compare them with the income or loss already derived.
   h. See if your decision remains the same after all important qualitative factors are considered.

5. *Solving make-or-buy problems.* When firms decide whether to manufacture a part themselves or to buy it from an outside supplier, they compare the cost of purchasing the part with the cost of manufacturing it themselves. If the cost of purchasing the part is greater than the cost of manufacturing it, the firm should make the part. In addition, when the firm's facilities can be used for more profitable purposes than manufacturing that merchandise, opportunity costs must be considered.

6. *Pricing special orders.* If a firm has unused capacity, it should accept a special order if the differential revenue received for the order is greater than the differential costs of filling the order, even if the price is less than the regular price. Such a decision also must be evaluated in light of its possible impact on a firm's regularly priced products.

7. *Deciding whether to add or drop product lines or departments.* Management must determine the differential costs and revenues of each product or department. Many direct fixed costs that can be traced specifically to a product, department, or other segment of a business will change if a segment is added or dropped. Indirect fixed costs, the common costs that are divided up among business segments, are not affected by management decisions and are not differential costs.

8. *Allocating joint production costs and deciding whether products should be sold or processed further.* Joint production costs are those incurred to produce two or more separate products, and they must be divided among those products. Two methods are generally used to allocate joint product costs: the physical measures method and the relative sales value method. The first method divides joint product costs according to each product's share of the total amount produced (pounds, liters, gallons, etc.). The second method divides joint product costs according to each product's share of the total sales value of the products at the split-off point.

When joint products are produced in a manufacturing process, the decision to process a product further after the split-off point should be made by comparing the revenue at split-off with the differential revenue and cost of processing further. The joint costs incurred up to the split-off point are sunk costs.

9. *Calculating the greatest contribution margin per unit of scarce resources.* When a firm has a scarce resource such as a limited amount of floor space, advertising dollars, or skilled labor time, calculating the simple contribution margin per unit is not the best approach for decision making. The company must concentrate on the products or services that provide the greatest contribution to profit per unit of the scarce resource because that results in the largest total contribution margin:

Contribution margin per unit $\times$ Units of scarce resource
of scarce resource available
= Total contribution margin

Key Terms

Differential Costs and Revenues
Joint Product Costs
Joint Products
Make-or-Buy Decision
Opportunity Costs
Physical Measures Method

Relative Sales Value Method
Sell or Process Further Decisions
Special Orders
Split-off Point
Sunk Costs

Problems for Your Review

A. Special Order. Eggroll Inn makes and sells egg rolls. Based on a weekly volume of 5,000 egg rolls, the production cost is $.60 per unit:

Rent of restaurant	$ 500
Administrative and other fixed overhead costs	1,000
Direct labor (5,000 units @ $.10)	500
Direct materials (5,000 units @ $.20)	1,000
Total costs	$3,000
Number of units	5,000
Cost per unit	$.60

Michael High, the manager of a college dormitory, has offered to purchase 1,000 egg rolls at a price of $.40 per unit. The purchase would have no impact on the firm's other business. Should Eggroll Inn accept the offer?

Solution

The factors that influence the decision are the direct labor and direct material costs. The remaining costs are fixed and would therefore not be affected by the decision to accept or reject the offer. If the offer was accepted, the restaurant would receive additional revenue of $.40 per unit and would incur additional costs of $.30 per unit ($.10 in direct labor and $.20 in direct materials), calculated as follows:

	Per Unit	Total (1,000 Units)
Differential revenue	$.40	$400
Differential costs:		
Direct material	(.20)	(200)
Direct labor	(.10)	(100)
Total costs	(.30)	(300)
Differential income	$.10	$100

It is therefore in the interest of Eggroll Inn to accept the offer. The firm's profitability increases with the sale of the additional 1,000 units, although the special order price is lower than full production cost.

B. Dropping or Keeping a Division. Telecare is the division of TV World that does repairs on the television sets sold by TV World. Telecare has never been profitable; it does, however, support the sales division of TV World, enabling it to provide a full range of services to its customers. The following data are from the 1987 operations of Telecare. This pattern is expected to hold true in the future.

Revenue (500 repairs @ $50)	$25,000
Expenses:	
Variable costs (500 repairs @ $20)	10,000
Salaries	10,000
Rent	10,000
Operating loss	$ (5,000)

J&B TV Repairs has offered its services to TV World for a fee of $40 per repair. TV World would still receive the revenue of $50 per repair from its customers. It would be able to eliminate all of the variable costs and rent, and would reduce salaries by $2,000. Should TV World maintain the Telecare division or acquire repair service from J&B? What qualitative factors might influence the decision?

Solution

In this situation, revenue would not be affected by a choice between the two alternatives. If TV World decides for purposes of analysis to contract for the service with J&B, then they must look for the differential costs that would be saved and compare them with the amount that would be paid to J&B:

Differential costs:	
Cost savings:	
Variable costs (500 @ $20)	$10,000
Rent	10,000
Salaries	2,000
Total cost savings	$22,000
Cost of services from J&B:	
(500 @ $40)	(20,000)
Net difference in favor of accepting offer from J&B	$ 2,000

Based on the above analysis, TV World should accept the offer. Another factor that should be considered in the decision is whether the quality of J&B's repair service is up to the standards expected by TV World customers. In addition, the firm should check on the dependability of J&B and consider whether the $40 price can be maintained for a reasonable period of time. Such factors could influence the decision.

C. Sell or Process Further. Sumner Company produces three products—X, Y, and Z. Each product may be sold at the split-off point or processed further. The following information is available on a per-unit basis:

Product	Units	Cost before Split-off	Sales Price at Split-off
X	5,000	$1.00	$2.00
Y	4,000	$1.20	$3.00
Z	5,000	$0.80	$1.50

If product X is processed beyond the split-off point, Sumner will incur additional fixed costs of $3,000 and additional variable costs of $1.20 per unit and will be able to sell X for $4 per unit. Product Y can be sold after the split-off point for $5 per unit, but there would be additional processing costs of $4,000 fixed and $.50 per unit variable. If product Z is processed after split-off, the company would incur additional fixed costs of $4,500 and additional variable costs of $.70 per unit and would be able to sell Z for $3 per unit.

Should Sumner Company sell the products at the split-off point or process them further? Would the decision be the same if products X and Z had to be sold together either at the split-off point or after further processing?

Solution

In this situation the costs incurred before the split-off point are not relevant to the decision because they become sunk costs by the time the split-off point is reached. Examine the differential revenues and costs for each alternative. For purposes of analysis, assume that the three products will be processed further:

	X	Y	Z
Differential revenue:			
[($400 − $2.00) × 5,000]	$10,000		
[($5.00 − $3.00) × 4,000]		$8,000	
[($3.00 − $1.50) × 5,000]			$7,500
Differential costs:			
Fixed	(3,000)	(4,000)	(4,500)
Variable:			
($1.20 × 5,000)	(6,000)		
($0.50 × 4,000)		(2,000)	
($0.70 × 5,000)			(3,500)
Differential profit (loss)	$ 1,000	$2,000	$ (500)

Based on the above analysis, Sumner Company should process X and Y further and sell Z at the split-off point.

If products X and Z had to be sold together, then Sumner should process all the products beyond the split-off point because products X and Z together have a differential profit of $500 ($1,000 profit from X and $500 loss from Z).

Questions

1. Define the terms *sunk cost* and *opportunity cost*.

2. Variable costs and differential costs are the same. Do you agree? Explain your answer.

3. Why is differential analysis considered superior to comprehensive analysis, an analysis that reflects all revenues and costs?

4. Explain the concept of relevant costs and irrelevant costs in decision making.

5. Are fixed costs always considered sunk costs? Explain your answer.

6. What is the meaning of the term *make or buy?*

7. Is opportunity cost relevant to the make-or-buy decision? Explain your answer.

8. Wellers Manufacturing has to decide whether to accept a special order that would require overtime hours in order to meet the due date. In making the decision, which of the following costs would be considered as a differential cost, opportunity cost, or future cost that will not change:

   a. Cost of overtime labor time required.
   b. The production supervisor's salary.
   c. Income from the production of an alternative order.

9. What qualitative factors influence decisions regarding special orders?

10. DXT Electronics is considering subcontracting the manufacture of one of the components of a major product. What factors should be considered in arriving at the decision?

11. Company X uses the relative sales value method to allocate joint production costs. Product Y has been allocated $80,000 of joint costs, and the firm is trying to decide whether to sell the product at the split-off point or process it further. If differential profit after split-off is $60,000, should the firm sell product Y at the split-off point or process it further? What information is relevant to this decision?

12. A manufacturing firm is considering dropping one of its product lines. Which costs would be relevant? Which costs would be irrelevant?

13. "My division would show a profit if we were not allocated such a large percentage of corporate overhead!" As a staff assistant at corporate headquarters, how would this statement by a division manager be reflected in the report you are preparing that identifies unprofitable divisions to be sold by the parent company?

14. Bradley Department Store has a limited amount of floor space and is trying to decide which departments should get the largest amount of space. What type of calculation should management use in making this decision? Why?

15. What factors should be considered in deciding whether to sell a joint product at split-off or to process it further?

Exercises

1. Relevant Costs. The following costs are associated with product A: allocated joint fixed costs, direct fixed costs, variable production costs, variable selling costs, and book value of product equipment.

Required:

Which of these costs are relevant to the following decisions?
   a. Deciding whether to drop product A.
   b. Deciding whether to accept a special order for product A.
   c. Determining the minimum acceptable price for a special order of product A.

2. Special Order. Ames Electrical has received a special one-time order for 3,000 sockets at $7 per unit. It currently produces 15,000 units (60% capacity) that sell for $12 per unit. Variable costs are $6 per unit and would remain unchanged if the company accepts the order. Fixed costs are currently $3 per unit. To handle the order, the company would have to purchase equipment worth $2,000 that would not be required in its other operations and has no salvage value.

Required:

   a. Should the company accept the order?
   b. How large would the order have to be to make a profit of $2,500 on the order?

3. Make or Buy. It costs Altman Manufacturing $80,000 to make 5,000 units of a component for one of its products. An outside supplier has offered to supply the component for $10 per unit. Forty percent of the total product cost is fixed and will remain unchanged if the company purchases the part.

Required:

   a. What decision should the company make? Support your answer.
   b. What is the maximum price the company should be willing to pay for the component?

4. Make or Buy. Datatron is considering subcontracting the manufacture of one of its intercom products. Currently, the cost of manufacturing 15,000 intercoms is as follows:

Direct labor	$45,000
Material	$30,000
Overhead (60% variable)	$90,000

The minimum price to Datatron from outside suppliers is $10 per unit.

996

Required:

  a. Determine whether Datatron should subcontract assembly of the intercoms.

  b. Would your answer change if Datatron can use current facilities to make an alternative product with an annual contribution margin of $20,000? Why or why not?

5. Special Order. Accupoint is currently operating at 80% capacity producing 12,000 pens that sell for $15 each. Per-unit costs are as follows:

Materials	$3.00
Labor	4.50
Variable overhead	1.10
Fixed overhead	2.30

Accupoint receives a special order for 750 units.

  a. What price should the company charge in order to make a profit of $1,000 on the special order?

  b. If Accupoint would incur an additional variable cost of $.90 per unit to handle the order and it is offered $9 per unit, should the offer be accepted?

6. Special Order. ABC Furniture has monthly production capacity of 220 end tables. Normal production volume is 200 end tables. Each unit sells for $20. Variable costs are $8 per unit, and fixed costs are $6 per unit. Woodstar Inc. offers to buy 60 end tables at $16 apiece. The fixed costs and unit variable costs would be unaffected by the sale. To meet the order ABC Furniture would have to reduce its current operation.

Required:

  a. What is the opportunity cost of accepting the order?

  b. How would net income change if ABC Furniture accepts the order?

  c. What qualitative factors might influence the decision?

7. Eliminating a Division. Tandem Products is considering eliminating one of its divisions which has been operating at a loss for several years. Results of the division's operations last year were as follows:

Sales	$ 60,000
Materials	$ 21,000
Direct labor	15,000
Variable overhead	5,000
Direct fixed costs	12,000
Joint fixed costs	22,000
Total costs	$ 75,000
Net loss	$(15,000)

Assume that the direct fixed costs could be avoided if the division was eliminated.

Required:

  a. Should the company eliminate the division?

  b. If Tandem had the opportunity to lease the building now occupied by the division for $20,000 annually, how would this affect the decision?

8. Allocation of Joint Costs; Sell or Process Further. Helm's Organic produces three chemicals from a single raw material, Zenon. Ten pounds of Zenon yield two pounds of chemical Anton, four pounds of chemical Borite, and four pounds of chemical Corton. Helm's spends $10,000 for raw material Zenon, direct labor, and manufacturing overhead to produce 1,000 pounds of Anton, 2,000 pounds of Borite, and 2,000 pounds of Corton. Each product can be processed further and sold for a higher price. The following data relate to one pound of each chemical:

	Anton	Borite	Corton
Selling price (split-off)	$1.00	$2.00	$3.00
Additional processing cost	.50	1.50	4.00
Selling price after additional processing	4.00	3.50	6.50

Required:

    a. Allocate the joint production costs using the physical measure of number of pounds produced.

    b. Allocate the joint production costs using the relative sales value at split-off point.

    c. Determine which product or products should be sold at split-off.

9. Scarce Resource. Westland Company produces three types of food processors—Astral, Bestchef, and Cookmatic. The selling price, variable costs, and contribution margin for one unit of each food processor are as follows:

	Astral	Bestchef	Cookmatic
Selling price	$90	$135	$120
Less: Variable costs			
Direct materials	$41	$ 21	$ 60
Direct labor	18	48	24
Variable overhead	4	12	6
Total	$63	$ 81	$ 90
Contribution margin	$27	$ 54	$ 30
Contribution margin ratio	30%	40%	25%

Westland's products are in great demand, and the firm is working at full capacity. The company must decide which of the three products to focus on in the next month, as there is a shortage of labor time. There are only 6,000 hours of labor time available at an hourly rate of $12.

Required:

    a. Calculate the amount of contribution margin per hour of labor time spent on each product.

    b. Recommend to management which product line should be concentrated on in the next month. Show your calculations.

10. Adding a Product and Opportunity Cost. Wright Company is considering adding a new flashlight to its product line. The projected sales volume of 10,000 units will cost $10 per flashlight to produce (60% variable cost and 40% direct fixed) and will sell for $12 per unit. Adding the new flashlight would reduce sales of existing products by 10%. The data concerning the current sales volume of 30,000 units are as follows:

Sales	$150,000
Materials and labor	75,000
Direct fixed overhead	25,000
Joint overhead	28,000

Required:

    a. What is the opportunity cost of adding the product?

    b. Should the company add the new product?

Problem Set A

24A-1. Special Orders. Forbes Furniture makes standard writing desks for sale to department stores. They also make desks according to customer specifications. The monthly cost data for Forbes are given at the top of the next page.

    Forbes has received an order from a valued customer to provide 25 custom-built desks at $200 per desk. Because the company is working at capacity, monthly production of standard desks would have to be reduced by 50% in order to fill the order. Assume utilities are fixed.

Required:

    a. Identify all costs relevant to the decision of whether or not to accept the order.

	Custom Desks	Standard Desks
Sales (dollars)	27,000	13,200
Sales volume (units)	125	80
Materials	$ 8,000	$ 4,500
Labor	10,000	4,500
Depreciation	2,000	1,400
Rent	1,500	500
Utilities	800	700

b. Should the order be accepted? Show your analysis.

c. What qualitative factors might influence the decision?

24A–2. Make or Buy. Alpha Stereos has discontinued manufacturing one of its products. It could use the floor space that has become available to manufacture a component for its main product. Fifteen thousand units of the component part are required annually. The current purchase price is $10 per unit. If the company makes the component part, production costs would be as follows:

Materials	$2.70
Direct labor	3.60
Variable overhead	.75
Direct overhead	1.50

As an alternative, the company could manufacture a new product which would have a contribution margin of $70,000 and direct fixed costs of $50,000.

Required:

a. Should the company make or buy the component? Show your analysis.

b. If 10,000 units were required instead of 15,000 units, would the decision be the same? Support your answer.

24A–3. Make or Buy. The Contemporary Toy Company makes models of popular TV characters. Sales have been steadily increasing. With sales of the most popular model at maximum production capacity, the company is considering ways of increasing output. A contribution margin income statement for this model is as follows:

Sales volume (units)	25,000
Sales	$150,000
Less: Variable costs	75,000
Contribution margin	75,000
Less: Fixed costs	
Direct	20,000
Joint	15,000
Net income	$ 40,000

The company has two alternatives for increasing output:

1. An outside supplier has offered to supply models at $3.50 each. Contemporary Toys would have to spend an additional $1 per toy to affix its emblem.

2. The company could expand its own capacity, which should increase direct fixed costs by $15,000.

Required:

a. Assuming that the company could sell an additional 15,000 models annually, determine which option should be taken. Show your analysis.

b. At what purchase price would both options be equally feasible? Show your analysis.

c. What qualitative factors should be considered in making the decision, given the situation described in Item a.

24A–4. Elimination of a Division and Opportunity Cost. Shapely Electronics Corporation has several major divisions. The profit summaries for two of these divisions are as follows:

	Division A	Division B
Sales	$298,000	$425,000
Variable expenses	215,000	304,000
Contribution margin	83,000	121,000
Direct fixed costs	94,000	95,000
Joint fixed costs—allocated	15,000	45,000
Net income	$ (26,000)	$ (19,000)

The following information is available for the two divisions:

1. The building occupied by Division A is leased for $15,000 per year. The lease can be terminated with one month's notice. Division B also leases a building for $15,000 per year. The lease expires in three years and is not cancelable.

2. The production manager for Division A has an annual salary of $50,000. If the division is eliminated, the production manager would be dismissed.

3. Annual depreciation expense for machinery for Division A is $29,000. Nine thousand dollars of this represents depreciation expense for computer equipment that would be reassigned to other divisions. The remainder is depreciation for specialized machinery that would be sold. The proceeds would equal current book value.

4. Division B has a service contract for supply and maintenance of equipment at a cost of $30,000 per year.

5. Advertising expense for Division B is $50,000 per year.

Required:

a. Determine whether it would be profitable to eliminate one or both of these divisions.

b. Assuming the company can use the facilities made available by the elimination of both divisions to manufacture a new product with a contribution margin of 60% on sales of $300,000 and direct fixed costs of $75,000, what should the decision be?

24A–5. Joint Cost Allocation and Sell or Process Further. Cleanrite Corporation produces two industrial cleaners, X-Cel and B-Rite, through a joint process. Joint costs total $12,000 per batch of output. A batch is made up of 20,000 liters—75% X-Cel, and 25% B-Rite. The selling price for X-Cel is $1.50 per liter, and the selling price for B-Rite is $2.00 per liter. Assume all production is sold.

Required:

a. Allocate the joint production costs using the physical measures method. Prepare income statements for each product to the gross margin line, showing gross margin as a percentage of sales.

b. Allocate the joint production costs using the relative sales value method. Prepare income statements for each product to the gross margin line, showing gross margin as a percentage of sales. Which method of cost allocation would the manager of B-Rite prefer?

c. Cleanrite also could process both products further to produce more intense cleaning agents that sell for a higher price. If the firm spent an additional $.15 per liter on materials, $.25 per liter on direct labor, and $.80 per liter on overhead for X-Cel, it could sell the cleaner for $3.05 per liter. B-Rite requires additional direct materials of $.30, direct labor of $.40, and manufacturing overhead of $.90 in order to be salable at $3.50 per liter. Should the firm sell X-Cel and B-Rite at the split-off point or process them further? Show your calculations.

d. Refer to the data in Item c. Company researchers have discovered a new process that changes the intense form of B-Rite into a super cleaning agent called Ultra-Clean. The new product could be sold at a price of $5.00 per liter, but it would require additional costs of $1.65 per liter. Should the firm process B-Rite into Ultra-Clean? Show your calculations.

24A–6. Break-even and Incremental Income. Ace Manufacturing extrudes 15-foot metal beams that are used in the heavy construction industry. The company's monthly production is 45,000 feet, and the selling price is $20 per foot. Production cost data (per foot) are as follows:

Materials	$7
Direct labor	$4
Variable overhead	$2
Fixed overhead	$3

The company is considering using its excess production capacity to make end plates that could then be welded onto the beams. This additional processing would increase material cost by $2.50 per foot and labor by $1.50 per foot and would require additional tooling costs of $20,000 per year.

Required:

a. If the company decides to sell the beams with end plates, what minimum price should be charged in order to break even?

b. If the company decides to charge $26 per foot for beams with end plates, what is the incremental income? Assume all current production would be sold with end plates.

24A-7. Special Order. The Fairfax Home Construction Company makes prefabricated houses. As part of its efforts to integrate the production process, the company set up a subsidiary plant to assemble doors and windows. The manager of the new plant estimates from a review of the production schedule of the main plant that he will be operating at 75% capacity for the next three months. He has recently received a request from a hardware supplier for 4,000 doors at a price of $60 each. Delivery would be required within 60 days. The current monthly production costs for 6,000 doors (75% capacity) are as follows:

Materials	$150,000
Labor	60,000
Overhead (60% fixed)	180,000

The main plant can obtain doors from outside suppliers at $75 per door. Doors manufactured by the subsidiary plant are billed to the main plant at cost.

Required:

a. Calculate the costs the manager of the subsidiary plant should consider in making the decision whether or not to accept the special order.

b. If the manager accepts the special order and during the manufacturing period there is an increase in production in the main plant resulting in the outside purchase of 1,000 doors, what would have been the real gain to the company of accepting the special order?

Problem Set B

24B-1. Special Orders. Able Motor Components manufactures a special gear for automatic transmissions which it sells to an automobile manufacturer. The gear sells for $40, and the company normally produces and sells 800,000 gears annually. The cost per gear based on the 800,000 volume is as follows:

Materials	$10
Labor	$ 6
Manufacturing Overhead (80% fixed)	$10
Selling and administrative (25% fixed)	$ 8

The company has received an offer to sell 30,000 of its gears to a foreign automobile manufacturer. Its domestic sales will be unaffected. Variable costs will increase by $1.25 per unit because of shipping, insurance, and import duties. To process the order, equipment worth $150,000 would have to be purchased. The equipment has a salvage value of $3,000 and no alternative use.

Required:

a. What cost per gear should be considered when quoting the foreign manufacturer a price?

b. If the company wishes to earn a profit of $100,000 per order, what price should it charge per gear?

24B-2. Relevant Costs. Refer to the data in Problem 24B–1. Able Motor Components has 8,000 gears in inventory that are several years old and cannot be sold to regular customers. The gears are carried in inventory at $30 each. The company is considering the following alternatives:

1. Sell the gears as scrap for $5 each.
2. Rework the gears at a cost of $25 each so they are exactly the same as current gears and sell them through normal channels.
3. Melt the gears down at a cost of $6 each and use the material to manufacture new gears.

Required:

a. Which alternative would be most profitable for the company?
b. How does the carrying cost of the gears in inventory affect your analysis? Explain.

24B-3. Joint Cost Allocation and Sell or Process Further. Westways Electric Corporation manufactures products X, Y, and Z from a joint production process. The firm spends $120,000 on direct materials, labor, and manufacturing overhead to produce 9,000 units of X; 4,500 units of Y; and 4,500 units of Z. Westways can sell product X for $10 per unit, product Y for $14 per unit, and product Z for $12 per unit. Assume all production is sold.

Required:

a. Use the physical measures method to allocate the joint production costs to products X, Y, and Z. Prepare income statements to the gross margin figure for each product, and show gross margin as a percentage of sales.
b. Use the relative sales value method to allocate the joint production costs to products X, Y, and Z. Prepare income statements to the gross margin figure for each product, and show gross margin as a percentage of sales. Which method would the manager of product Y prefer?
c. Westways also has the option of spending additional funds on X, Y, and Z after the split-off point and selling them for a higher price. Product X requires additional processing costs of $1.65 per unit in order to be sold for $11.50; product Y would incur processing costs of $2.25 per unit and would sell for $16.50; product Z has additional processing costs of $1.10 per unit and could then be sold for $14.25. Which products should be sold at the split-off point and which should be processed further? Show your calculations.

24B-4. Decision Alternatives and Special Orders. Ames' paper towel division is facing increased competition. A major competitive factor is delivery time. Management estimates that if same-day delivery could be provided for 90% of all orders, sales would increase by 20%. The current annual production data for the division are as follows:

Sales volume	150,000 dozen
Sales	$1,050,000
Materials	350,000
Labor	250,000
Variable overhead	82,500
Fixed overhead	75,000
Selling and administrative	150,000
Allocated overhead	80,000

The company's production capacity is adequate to meet the increased volume. All orders are supplied from inventory. The company can provide same-day service by increasing its fleet of delivery trucks and starting second-shift operations to boost daily production. This would increase variable overhead costs by $.50 per dozen towels and would increase the selling and administrative expenses by 50%. As an alternative way of improving delivery service, the company could rent warehouses in regions of highest customer density. The total rental cost would be $40,000 annually. Both alternatives would have an equal effect on sales.

Required:

a. Is it profitable for the company to improve its delivery service?
b. Which option should it choose?
c. The firm has been requested to fill a special order for 25,000 dozen paper towels at a price of $6 per dozen and has sufficient capacity to produce the order without affecting production of regular orders. Accepting the order, however, would affect the delivery of regular orders, and sales would be expected to improve by only 15% despite action taken to improve the delivery service. Should Ames accept the order? Show your calculations.

1002

d. Refer to Item c. What price should the company charge per dozen towels if it wishes to earn a profit of $5,000 on the order?

24B–5. Adding a Department. Main Street Department Store has the option of leasing additional floor space for $1,000 per month. It is considering two alternatives:

1. Adding a toy department, which would generate sales of $4,000 per month. The contribution margin would be 60%. Additional fixed costs, exclusive of lease expenses, would be $500 per month. Sales throughout the store would be expected to increase by 4% as a result of the increased traffic.

2. Adding a shoe department, which would generate sales of $6,000 per month. Contribution margin would be 40% and additional fixed costs, exclusive of lease expenses, would be $1,000 per month. Sales throughout the store would be expected to increase by 5% as a result of the increased volume of customers.

A typical contribution margin income statement for the store follows:

Sales	$400,000
Variable expenses	200,000
Contribution margin	200,000
Fixed costs	105,000
Net income	$ 95,000

Required:
   a. Assuming that net income is the main criterion, which of the two departments should be added? Show your analysis.
   b. What other factors would you consider important in making this decision?

24B–6. Make or Buy. Among the products of Fox Stationery Supplies is a popular student notebook. The company has just received an offer from an outside supplier to supply these notebooks at $.85 per book. The company is interested in the offer because its own production is nearing capacity. Its current production volume of 90,000 notebooks represents 90% of its total capacity. On the recommendation of its production engineers, plant capacity should be increased in increments of 50,000 units. Fixed costs would be expected to increase by $15,000 for each 50,000-unit capacity increase. The current cost of producing each notebook is as follows:

Materials	$.20
Labor	.15
Overhead	.30

Sixty percent of the overhead cost is unavoidable fixed costs; the remainder is variable.

Required:
   a. If the company expects to sell an additional 30,000 notebooks next year, what decision should it make?
   b. How would this decision change if it could sell all it produced after increasing capacity?

24B–7. Relevant Costs and Make or Buy. A natural food chain of restaurants specializes in dishes with natural ingredients. The owners have several restaurants and are trying to raise capital to expand operations. To do this they are considering selling their poultry farm and the associated processing facilities that provide chickens for the restaurant chain. A wholesale meat outlet has offered to supply the company's annual requirement of 720,000 pounds of chicken at $.25 per pound. Current variable costs of production are $72,000; fixed costs are $57,600. The proceeds from the sale of the farm and associated facilities would be used to establish two new restaurants that would provide an annual net income of $80,000. Total requirements for chicken would be unchanged.

Required:
   a. Identify all costs relevant to the decision of selling the farm and the associated processing facilities.
   b. Based on quantitative factors only, should the company accept the wholesaler's offer?
   c. What qualitative factors are important in making the final decision?

Using the Computer

Caps Cola Company has four variations of cola products: regular (nondiet), diet, regular decaffeinated, and diet decaffeinated. Management is concerned that sales of the diet decaffeinated cola have been proving unprofitable. Over the last year, it was the only product that did not have a positive net income, even though there was a positive contribution margin of $250,000. Caps' income statement figures by product line for last year follow:

Caps Cola Company
Income Statement
(in thousands)

	Regular	Regular Decaffeinated	Diet	Diet Decaffeinated	Total
Sales	$1.00 m*	$500	$700	$400	$2.600 m*
Variable costs	300	150	200	150	800
Contribution margin	700	350	500	250	1.800 m*
Fixed costs:					
Direct	250	170	200	200	820
Indirect	100	80	90	100	370
Total fixed costs	350	250	290	300	$1.190 m*
Net income	$350	$100	$210	$ (50)	$ 610

*m = millions

Required:

a. As a result of negative net income, Caps must decide whether to drop the diet decaffeinated soda product line. Sixty thousand dollars of the direct fixed costs would not be eliminated if the product line is dropped, nor would $90,000 of the indirect fixed costs. Should Caps Cola Company drop the diet decaffeinated formula? Using a spreadsheet, show only the differential items involved in this decision.

b. If Caps decides to drop the diet decaffeinated drink from the product line, the $60,000 of direct fixed costs would be distributed equally among the direct fixed costs for production of the three other types of cola. On the other hand, indirect fixed costs are divided in the following way: The regular cola division absorbs $40,000, the diet cola division absorbs $30,000, and the nondiet decaffeinated cola absorbs the remaining $20,000 in additional indirect costs. Over the next year, regular decaffeinated cola and diet cola sales increase by 20% as a result of drinkers' switching to them. Regular cola sales are unaffected. Does it benefit Caps to drop the diet decaffeinated formula? Which of its products is the most profitable? Using a spreadsheet, prepare income statements for the three remaining product lines.

c. Return to the data in Item b but now assume that the decision to drop the diet decaffeinated drink had a negative effect on Caps' entire market. Diet cola sales fell by 20%, decaffeinated cola sales went down 10%, and regular cola sales also decreased 10%. What is Caps' net income? Which of its products is the most profitable? Use the same spreadsheet you set up in Item b.

Decision Case

Metropolitan Realty, Inc. _____

In November 1987 Harold Walker was appointed manager of the Happy Valley office of Metropolitan Realty, Inc. (MRI). Happy Valley is located in the greater metropolitan area of a major city. MRI has 10 other offices located throughout the greater metropolitan area. These offices range in size from 12 to 30 sales associates. The Happy Valley office currently has 20 sales-persons who are all full-time, licensed independent contractors.

Happy Valley's Current Situation

The office currently has a positive contribution margin but a net operating loss. Also, it is not earning enough to meet its 1988 budgeted profit. (See Exhibits 1 and 2.) Revenues have fallen below budget. A summarized income statement for the past eight months is shown in Exhibit 1. A statement of branch office expenses is shown in Exhibit 2.

EXHIBIT 1
Happy Valley Office
Income Statement
January 1, 1988–August 31, 1988

	Year to Date		
	Actual	Budget	Variance
Revenue			
Gross sales	$327,600	$369,000	$(41,400)
Less: Cancellations	57,960	73,800	15,840
Net sales	269,640	295,200	(25,560)
Less: Sales staff*	148,302	162,360	14,058
Net company share	121,338	132,840	(11,502)
Branch operating expenses excluding corporate overhead	100,280	92,000	(8,280)
Office margin	21,058	40,840	(19,782)
Share of MRI indirect corporate overhead costs**	32,000	32,000	0
Net operating income (loss)	$ (10,942)	$ 8,840	$(19,782)

*55%.
**MRI charges each office $200 per sales desk per month; Happy Valley has 20 sales people at $200 per month for 8 months = $32,000.

EXHIBIT 2
Happy Valley Office
Detail of Branch Operating Expenses

	Year to Date						1987
						Variance %	Last Year
	Actual	%	Budget	%	Variance	of Budget	to Date
Advertising	19,000	19	17,500	19	(1,500)	−9	17,211
Personnel	28,000	28	27,600	30	(400)	−1	25,500
Office Services	4,000	4	3,700	4	(300)	−8	3,400
Telephone	14,900	15	15,600	17	700	+4	14,700
Facilities	20,000	20	20,000	22	-0-	-0-	19,000
Sales Expense	6,000	6	3,700	4	(2,300)	−62	3,250
Other Expenses	8,380	8	3,900	4	(4,480)	−1.15	3,200
Totals	$100,280	100	$92,000	100	$(8,280)	−9	86,261

Walker's Reaction to MRI's Accounting System

About MRI's accounting system, Harold Walker stated:

It's tough enough to be a manager without the accounting system making you look worse. First of all, I think I should be evaluated on office margin and not net operating income. But Van Jensen, my regional manager, says that makes no sense. I don't control those indirect corporate overhead costs. Why should I be charged for them?

Required:

a. Do you agree with Walker that he should be evaluated on office margin or with regional sales manager Jensen, who says that Walker should be evaluated on net operating income? Explain your answer.

b. If Metropolitan Realty, Inc. were considering closing the Happy Valley office, would you use office margin or net operating income as the criterion for your decision? Explain your answer.

c. Evaluate the format of the statement of detail of branch operating expense, shown in Exhibit 2. Is it a good format?

d. What changes, if any, would you recommend in the format of Exhibit 2?

Accounting Information for Long-term Decisions: Capital Budgeting

25

LEARNING OBJECTIVES

After reading this chapter you should be able to:
1. Define capital budgeting.
2. Use present-value concepts in capital budgeting.
3. Define what is meant by discounted cash flow techniques.
4. Define the cost of capital.
5. Use the net-present-value method of problem solving.
6. Define the internal rate of return and use it to solve problems.
7. Rank investment alternatives for decision making.
8. Use and discuss the payback method.
9. Apply the accounting-rate-of-return method in problem solving.

All business organizations plan for the future. Sometimes planning is short-term, that is, a year or less. Chapters 23 and 24 have shown how cost-volume-profit analysis and differential decision methods can help organizations in short-term planning. This chapter concentrates on strategic planning, which is long-term in nature. Strategic planning questions include such basic decisions as what products to produce and what markets to pursue for maximum profitability. The strategic planning process includes decisions about how much to invest in machinery, buildings, equipment, land, and other long-term assets. This chapter examines the methods managers use to make decisions that involve large sums of money and that play a significant role in the long-term profitability of an organization.

What Is Capital Budgeting?

Capital budgeting is the process of planning for long-term investment decisions. It is called *capital* budgeting because the capital (or wealth) of a firm is used to acquire resources that will increase income and profitability in the future. Most firms have a limited supply of capital, and so management must choose carefully the most lucrative investment alternatives.

Capital budgeting is used to measure the rate of return on each investment alternative in order to make the best use of capital. Although the term *investment* may bring to mind the purchase of stocks and bonds, it also can apply to the purchase of other long-term assets. When a firm spends $300,000 on machinery, it is investing its capital just as if it took the $300,000 and bought bonds. When a firm invests in plant and equipment and other long-term operational assets, its management tries to get the best possible rate of return on the firm's investment, in the same way that individuals or organizations try to pick stocks or bonds that will result in the greatest possible rate of return on investment. The capital budgeting methods that are detailed in this chapter are ways for organizations to determine what rate of return they should expect on various investments in long-term operational assets. Companies need this information because they *must* invest in long-term assets in order to survive and grow; stocks and bonds, however, are optional investments.

Capital budgeting is important because it deals with large expenditures of capital that can affect the profitability of a firm for many years. In addition, capital budgeting decisions are not easy to change. The decision to build a new plant, for example, is difficult to terminate if a mistake has been made, whereas stocks or bonds can be resold in the marketplace.

Capital Budgeting Situations

What types of decisions require capital budgeting? When funds are being spent now in order to acquire some benefit a year or more in the future, capital budgeting is useful. Some typical decisions that would require capital budgeting are:

1. Should a firm expand its plant capacity?
2. Should new equipment be purchased that will reduce costs, even though the equipment in use does not need replacement?
3. If a company has decided to buy a new machine, should machine A, B, or C be purchased?
4. Should new plant facilities be leased, purchased, or constructed?
5. When should old equipment be replaced rather than repaired?

These types of decisions generally deal with two basic questions: (1) Should an investment be made? Does it meet the minimum standard of acceptability for a particular firm? This may be called the **screening decision.** For example, a company may have a policy of investing only when the investment will bring a rate of return of 18% before taxes. Any proposed project that promises a return of less than 18% will be rejected. (2) Which alternative is the best when there are several acceptable proposals? This is called the **ranking decision,** for after investment decisions have been screened for acceptability, a decision must be made among the acceptable alternatives. This chapter deals first with the techniques for screening decisions and later shows how they can be used in ranking decisions. First, however, we must review basic concepts of present value and see how they are used in capital budgeting.

How to Use Present Value Concepts in Capital Budgeting

Capital budgeting decisions extend over relatively long periods of time. Money changes its value over time because money received now can be invested and earn interest. Therefore, long-term investments must be analyzed in terms of when cash flows in and out in order to see the true value of a proposed investment.

Return on Investment

If you deposited $5,000 in a savings account, you would expect, after 5 years, to be able to withdraw your original $5,000 plus the interest that had accumulated over that period of time. If the $5,000 accumulated interest at a rate of 6% for 5 years, you would now be able to withdraw $6,690. We can divide that sum into two parts: (1) the return *of* investment, that is, the return of the original principal invested. In this case, $5,000 is the return of the original investment and (2) the return *on* investment, the return to the investor of the earnings on the original money invested. In this case, $1,690 is the return on investment.

Investing in a long-term asset, however, is different from putting money in a bank because long-term assets generally have little value at the end of their useful lives. Like savings, assets must earn enough to return the original investment plus a return on that investment in order to justify the investment. For example, if the $5,000 that you invested in the previous example had been invested in a piece of machinery rather than being placed in a savings and loan association, that machinery would have had to save you more than the original investment in order to provide a return on investment because the machine itself would have little value after five years.

The Time Value of Money

If you were offered $50 now or a year from now, which would you choose? Most people would prefer $50 now rather than at some point in the future because they could immediately invest the money, which would earn interest, and at the end of a year they would have an amount greater than $50. The **time value of money** is simply another way of stating that money on hand now is worth more than money received in the future because money on hand now can be invested and can earn interest. Chapter 18 explained this concept in regard to the pricing and interest rates of long-term bonds. The same basic principles apply for investments in long-term assets. Capital budgeting examines the expenditure of large sums of money in the present in terms of expected cash inflows to see whether a specific investment should be undertaken. The cash inflows derived from a long-term asset, however, are usually future cash inflows. In order to compare the cash inflows and outflows for a given project, their value at one common point in time must be determined. The present is usually chosen as the point of reference because it is easiest to determine the present value of cash flows. The process of **discounting** determines the present value of a future cash flow. Future cash flows are discounted to their present values in order to meaningfully assess the value of a proposed investment.

The Present Value of Cash Flows

Just as most people would choose $50 now rather than a year from now, most firms would choose projects that offer larger cash flows on a present value basis. A proposed investment that offers greater returns early in its life is more attractive than one whose cash flows come later on. For example, a firm has decided to replace its old machine with Machine A or Machine B and estimates that either machine would provide total cost savings of $10,000 over a 3-year period. A and B both cost $8,000. Machine A would save the firm $2,000 in the first 2 years and $6,000 in the third year. Machine B would save the firm $6,000 in the first year and $2,000 in the next 2 years. Exhibit 25–1 on the bottom of this page depicts the timing of the cash flows for the two machines. In order to compare them, the firm must discount the cash flows to their present value. The firm expects to earn at least 10% on its investments and therefore uses that rate to evaluate investment projects.

The present-value tables in Appendix A show that the present value of $1 at 10% for one period is .909. The cash savings for each machine at the end of the first year is multiplied by .909 to determine its present value. Machine A saves the firm $2,000 at the end of the first year, but on a present-value basis $2,000 is worth $1,818. Similarly, Machine B saves the company $6,000 at the end of the first year, and that is worth $5,454 on a present-value basis. Exhibit 25–2 on the top of the next page shows the expected cash flows for both machines.

The present value of the cost savings for Machine A totals $7,976, whereas the present value of the savings for Machine B is $8,608. Although both machines save the company $10,000, Machine B is a better investment because it saves the firm money earlier.

Comparing the present value of the total savings for both machines with the initial cost of $8,000 (a cash outflow) results in a negative number for A and a positive number for B. Therefore, the firm would be unwise to invest in Machine A. Present-value analysis allows a firm to consider all of the various cash flows involved in an investment decision though they take place at different points in time and to see what they are worth at the present moment. For more examples, see Appendix A which describes present-value concepts in detail and presents some problems to work through.

EXHIBIT 25–1
Cash Flows—Investment Alternatives

Machine A

Purchase	Year 1 savings	Year 2 savings	Year 3 savings
$(8,000)	$2,000	$2,000	$6,000

Machine B

Purchase	Year 1 savings	Year 2 savings	Year 3 savings
$(8,000)	$6,000	$2,000	$2,000

EXHIBIT 25-2
Present Value of Cash Savings

Machine A

Cash Savings	×	Present-Value Factor	=	Present Value of Cash Savings
Year 1 $2,000	×	.909	=	$1,818
2 2,000	×	.826	=	1,652
3 6,000	×	.751	=	4,506
				$7,976

Machine B

Cash Savings	×	Present-Value Factor	=	Present Value of Cash Savings
Year 1 $6,000	×	.909	=	$5,454
2 2,000	×	.826	=	1,652
3 2,000	×	.751	=	1,502
				$8,608

Cash Inflows

In capital budgeting, **cash inflows** are any items that are expected to generate revenue or reduce costs, now or in the future. For example, if a firm is considering replacing one piece of machinery with another, management must consider that there may be a scrap value for the older machinery now as well as scrap value for the new machine in the future. Both are cash inflows. If a new machine would reduce costs each year, the amount of that reduction, too, is a cash inflow and should be discounted to its present value. When the same cash inflow is received for two or more years in a row, it may be discounted as an annuity (a series of equal payments evenly spaced in time) instead of having to find the present value of the individual cash flows. For example, Precision, Inc. is considering investing in a new machine that would have a salvage value of $1,500 after 4 years and would save the firm $2,000 per year until it is sold. The machine it is replacing can be sold for $800. The firm uses an interest rate of 10% to evaluate investments because that is the rate of return Precision can expect to earn on investments. An analysis of these cash flows follows:

	Time	Cash Flow	×	Present-Value Factor	=	Present Value of Cash Flows
Salvage value of old machine	Now	$ 800	×	1.000	=	$ 800
Cash savings	Years 1–4	2,000	×	3.170	=	6,340
Salvage value of new machine	Year 4	1,500	×	.683	=	1,025
Total present value of cash inflows						$8,165

Note that the salvage value of the old machine is at its present value because the $800 would be received now, whereas the salvage value of the new machine would bring a cash inflow at the end of the fourth year and so must be discounted to see what $1,500 received in 4 years is worth now. The cash savings of $2,000 is an annuity because it would be the same year after year, and to find its present value use Table 4 in Appendix A. Using the column for 10%, move down to the line for 4 periods and find the present value of an annuity of $1 at 10% for 4 periods, which is 3.170. Multiply 3.170 by $2,000 to get the present value of the series of cash flows. You would get the same answer if you did four separate calculations for years 1 through 4, but using the annuity table saves time.

Cash Outflows

Capital budgeting of **cash outflows** always includes the initial cost of an investment as well as any other future cash outlays undertaken due to that investment. For example, investing in a new product line may involve cash outflows for the product itself, factory production costs, selling, and advertising. Investing in new machinery can result in cash outflows for supplies and labor needed to maintain the machinery in good working order. Although depreciation is deducted as an expense on the income statement, it is a noncash item that is not considered in capital budgeting situations. Remember, depreciation is the allocation of the original cost of an asset over the years of its life. In capital budgeting the entire initial cost of an asset is deducted immediately as a cash outflow. For example, assume that the machine that Precision, Inc. was considering has an original cost of $7,000 and requires $600 per year to be spent for supplies and other maintenance costs. The present value of these cash outflows, assuming the firm uses an interest rate of 10% to evaluate investments, is calculated as follows:

	Time	Cash Flow	×	Present-Value Factor	=	Present Value of Cash Flows
Initial cost	Now	$7,000	×	1.000	=	$7,000
Cash outflow	Years 1–4	600	×	3.170	=	1,902
Total present value of cash outflows						$8,902

To buy the machinery, Precision must spend $7,000 now, which therefore is the present value of the initial cost. The cash outflow for maintenance is the same each year and so is treated as an annuity, by multiplying the present value factor by $600. Sometimes it is possible to calculate the net amount of inflows and outflows. For example, the machine had a cash outflow of $600 per year and a cash inflow of $2,000 per year; this could be treated as a net cash inflow of $1,400 per year, saving some calculation. Thus, the total present value of the cash outflow for this particular piece of machinery is $8,902, which is greater than the present value of the cash inflow of $8,165 found earlier. Therefore, Precision would be unwise to invest in this machine. In making capital budgeting decisions, the net present value of cash inflows is compared with the net present value of cash outflows.

Discounted Cash Flow Methods

Capital budgeting decision methods that fully recognize the time value of money are called **discounted cash flow methods.** These are methods that compare discounted cash inflows and outflows in order to see if an investment is worthwhile. There are two methods that use discounted cash flows—the net-present-value method and the internal-rate-of-return method. Before detailing these two methods, we will explain how firms decide what interest rates to use in discounted cash flow computations.

The Cost of Capital

Firms need to use interest rates to evaluate investments. How is that interest (or discount) rate determined? Generally, an acceptable rate of return on an investment is the company's **cost of capital,** which is the average cost of a firm's debt and equity capital. As you may recall, firms raise capital from creditors and owners in the form of bonds and other debt instruments, common stock, and preferred stock. When raising capital, there is an interest rate that determines how much companies have to pay for needed funds. We have seen how that mechanism operates to determine the price at which a firm's bonds will sell. The actual computation of a firm's cost for debt and equity capital is a complex task and will not be explained here. For the purposes of this book, assume the cost of capital is the weighted average cost, expressed as a percentage, of the company's debt and equity. The cost of capital serves as the acceptable rate of return on an investment. A project that does not yield a rate of return equal to the cost of capital should be rejected. In the examples and problems in this chapter, assume that the cost of capital already has been calculated and simply has to be used to evaluate possible investments.

The Net-Present-Value Method

The **net-present-value method** is a discounted cash flow technique for capital budgeting decisions that compares cash inflows and cash outflows. Add the inflows and outflows; if the net present value is a positive number, the investment is considered acceptable. If the net present value is a negative number, the investment is not acceptable. The discount or interest rate used to find the present value of the cash flows is given in this book.

As in all problem-solving situations, there are some helpful steps that can be followed in order to understand the given data and to set up a framework to see what needs to be done. The following suggestions are useful in capital budgeting problems:

1. Read the problem carefully, at least twice, before writing anything.
2. Write down the alternatives involved in the decision.
3. For purposes of analysis, choose any alternative. Remember, it makes no difference which alternative you choose; only the signs of the numbers will be different, for what is positive using one alternative is negative using the other. For example, when considering purchasing a building as opposed to renting one, the decision to buy the building would result in a cash outflow of the purchase price and a cash inflow of the savings on rent. Conversely, if the decision is made to rent facilities, the rental expense would be a cash outflow and the funds not paid for the building would be a cash inflow.
4. Set up a time line that shows when the various cash flows involved in the problem will take place. In this as in all decision problems, only *future* cash flows are considered.
5. Find the present-value factors for each cash flow based on the interest rate and the number of periods involved. Use the present-value tables in Appendix A, either for single sums or for annuities.
6. Multiply the present-value factors and the relevant cash flows.

7. Find the difference between the cash inflows and outflows in order to get the net present value (NPV).
8. If the NPV is positive (i.e., PV of inflows > PV of outflows), the investment is acceptable for the firm; if the NPV is negative (i.e., PV of outflows > PV of inflows), the investment is unacceptable.
9. Consider the qualitative factors involved in the decision. For example, the philosophy of top management toward capital spending may differ considerably from organization to organization. Some firms favor growth and capital spending, whereas others are more conservative. Decision makers also must consider management's attitude toward risk and whether a particular asset is viewed as so desirable that economic factors play a smaller role. Some firms, for example, purchased costly computer systems before they really were necessary on an economic basis, but top management wanted such systems as part of the image they were trying to project for the company.

Consider the following data that illustrate the net-present-value method in a simple problem situation:

Brown Electronics is considering purchasing a special-purpose machine that will cost $8,160 and will save the company $2,800 per year for the next 4 years. The company uses 12% as its minimum desired rate of interest.

Use the steps outlined above to solve the problem.

1. Read the problem carefully.
2. Brown Electronics has two options: to buy the machine or to continue using the current equipment.
3. For purposes of analysis, assume the company will buy the machine.
4. A time line for cash flows shows the following:

Now	Year 1	Year 2	Year 3	Year 4
purchase	savings	savings	savings	savings
$(8,160)	$2,800	$2,800	$2,800	$2,800

5. The cash outflow to purchase the machine takes place now, and so the $8,160 is at its present value. The savings over four years must be discounted to its present value. The table for annuities may be used because the savings is the same each year. The table shows that the present-value factor for $1 at 12% for 4 periods is 3.037.
6. Multiply the present-value factors and the cash flows.

Cash flow	×	Present-value factor	=	Present value of cash flows
$(8,160)	×	1.000	=	$(8,160)
$2,800	×	3.037	=	$ 8,504

7. Net present value = $ 344

8. The net present value is a positive number here, which means that if the company expects a 12% return on investments, this machine is acceptable for the firm. In the absence of adverse qualitative factors, Brown Electronics would buy the machine.

The net-present-value screening method is straightforward when the cash flows involved in a given investment and the interest rate the company uses in evaluating investment opportunities are known. The same method of analysis may be used to solve more complex problems:

1014

Reston Company has the opportunity to acquire the rights to a new product line from the current owners at a cost of $100,000. The product is being produced in a leased facility which would require lease payments of $12,000 per year for 5 years, payable at the end of each year. At the end of the lease, the machinery and equipment in the facility would have a salvage value of $7,000. Cash operating costs per year are $60,000, and cash income is $85,000 per year. Reston uses a 10% interest rate to evaluate investments.

Follow the standard steps in analysis:

1. Re-read the problem.
2. Reston can acquire the rights to the new product line or turn it down.
3. For purposes of analysis, assume that Reston will acquire the new product line.
4. A time line for the cash flows shows the following:

Now buy $(100,000)	Year 1	Year 2	Year 3	Year 4	Year 5
	Lease $(12,000)	Lease $(12,000)	Lease $(12,000)	Lease $(12,000)	Lease $(12,000) salvage $7,000
	Income − Expenses $25,000	Income − Expenses $25,000	Income − Expenses $25,000	Income − Expenses $25,000	Income − Expenses $25,000

5. The cash outflow of $100,000 to acquire the product line takes place now, so it is at its present value. The lease payments take place over a five-year period and must be discounted to their present value using the annuity table. The present-value factor for $1 at 10% for 5 periods is 3.791. The same present-value factor can be used to discount the yearly cash inflow of $25,000, the net amount from cash income of $85,000 per year, and cash operating costs of $60,000 per year. The salvage value of $7,000 would be a cash inflow at the end of the fifth year. Therefore, it is discounted to its present value using the present-value table for single sums. The present value of $1 at 10% for 5 periods is .621.
6. Multiply the present-value factors by the cash flows:

Cash flow	×	Present-value factor	=	Present value of cash flows
$(100,000)	×	1.000	=	$(100,000)
$(12,000)	×	3.791	=	$(45,492)
Total cash outflows				$(145,492)
$7,000	×	.621	=	$ 4,347
$25,000	×	3.791	=	$ 94,775
Total cash inflows				$ 99,122

7. Net present value   = $ (46,370)

8. The net present value is a negative number, indicating that Reston should reject the opportunity to acquire the new product line. It does not generate enough income to justify the payment of such a large sum for the initial purchase in addition to lease payments.

Another way of thinking about this method is to view net present value as the present value of all future cash flows less the initial outlay. The Reston data are presented below with the present value of the future cash outflows less the present value of the future cash inflows. That sum ($53,360 less the initial outlay of $100,000) is equal to a negative amount of $46,370, the same net present value found earlier:

Cash flow × Present-value = Present value of
       factor   cash flows

Present value of future cash outflows:
$(12,000) × 3.791   = $(45,492)

Present value of future cash inflows:
  $7,000 × .621   = $ 4,347
  $25,000 × 3.791   = $ 94,775
Total cash inflows $ 99,122

Present value of future cash flows $ 53,630
Less initial outlay   (100,000)
Net present value $ (46,370)

Internal-Rate-of-Return Method

The **internal-rate-of-return method** (or time-adjusted rate of return) is a discounted cash flow method that looks for the true return promised by an investment project over its useful life. This method is used when the rate of return offered by an investment is not known; the cash inflows and outflows are used in order to find the present-value factor of the rate of return and from that the interest rate itself can be found. The internal rate of return is compared with the firm's cost of capital to see if an investment is acceptable.

Use the following steps to solve internal-rate-of-return problems:

1. Read the problem carefully, at least two times.
2. Divide the proposed investment by the net amount of annual cash inflows. The resulting number is the present-value factor of the internal rate of return.
3. Find the present-value factor in Table 4 in Appendix A for the specified number of periods and see what interest rate the present-value factor is listed under. That is the internal rate of return of the proposed investment.
4. Compare the internal rate of return with the company's cost of capital. If the internal rate of return is equal to or greater than the company's cost of capital, the investment is acceptable. If the internal rate of return is less than the company's cost of capital, the project should be rejected.
5. If more than one investment option is being considered and capital is limited, accept the one with the highest rate of return.

Now use these steps to analyze the same data that illustrated the net-present-value method. Brown Electronics is considering purchasing a special-purpose machine that would cost $8,160 and would save the company $2,800 per year for 4 years. To find the internal rate of return on this investment:

1. Read the data carefully. Be sure you know what is being asked for.
2.

$$\frac{\text{Investment in project}}{\text{Net cash inflows}} = \frac{\text{Present value factor of}}{\text{internal rate of return}}$$

$$\frac{\$8,160}{\$2,800} = 2.914$$

3. Turn to Table 4 in Appendix A and find the line for four periods. Move along the line until you find 2.914. When you have located the present-value factor, you will see that it is under the column for 14%. This means that the internal rate of return on the special-purpose machine is 14%.
4. Previously it was found that Brown's minimum stated rate of interest is 12%; therefore, the machine is an acceptable investment because its rate of return exceeds the rate that Brown uses as its cost of capital.

Another way of viewing the internal rate of return is as the interest rate that produces a net present value of zero when the cash inflows and outflows of a project are compared. When the Brown Electronics cash inflows and outflows are discounted using a 14% discount rate, the net present value is zero:

Cash flow	×	Present-value factor	=	Present value of cash flows
$(8,160)	×	1.000	=	$(8,160)
$2,800	×	2.914	=	8,160
Net present value			=	$ 0

In the previous example the initial cost of the investment was divided by the cash inflows and the present-value factor was found in Table 4 in Appendix A. In many situations, however, the present-value factor for the internal rate of return of an investment does not appear on the table. We may find numbers that are very close to the present-value factor, and this means that the internal rate of return of the investment falls somewhere between two interest rates listed on the table. It is necessary to use a process called **interpolation,** by which it is possible to find the exact rate of interest promised by an investment.

To illustrate interpolation, consider a firm's trying to find the rate of return of an investment with an initial cost of $15,000, annual cash inflows of $4,000, and a 5-year service life. Divide the initial cost by the cash inflows to find the present-value factor not shown in Table 4:

$$\frac{\$15,000}{\$4,000} = 3.750$$

When you look at Table 4 along the line for five periods, you will not find 3.750. You can find, however, the two present-value factors that are closest to it, 3.605 and 3.791. Those factors are found in the columns for 12% and 10%, and therefore, the true rate of return of the investment is somewhere between those two rates.

Exhibit 25–3 shows how the differences between present-value factors and interest rates can be used to find the rate of return of an investment. Column 1 shows the difference between the high and low present-value factors, .186. Column 2 shows the difference between the high present-value factor (3.791) and the present-value factor for the rate of the investment (3.750). Column 3 shows the difference between the interest rates for the high and low present-value factors, 10% and 12%. Now divide .041 (the difference from column 2) by .186 (the difference from column 1) and multiply that by the difference from column 3 (2%). Add the resulting number to 10% the interest rate of the high present-value factor to obtain the true interest rate of the investment, 10.4%. Interpolation is used to explain how much of the difference between the high factor and the low factor is caused by the difference between the high factor and the factor for the rate of the investment. That difference is fairly

EXHIBIT 25-3
Interpolation—Internal-Rate-of-Return Method

	(1) Present-Value Factors			(2)		(3) Interest Rates
High	3.791		High	3.791		10%
Low	3.605		Investment	3.750		12%
Difference	.186			.041		2%

$$\text{Interest rate of investment} = 10\% + \frac{(.041 \times 2\%)}{.186}$$
$$= 10\% + .004$$
$$= 10.4\%$$

small here because the factor for the rate of the investment is quite close to the high factor, so the internal rate of return is very close to 10%.

Both of these illustrations used cash flows that were the same each year. In some situations, however, there are salvage values at the end of the life of an investment, or an uneven pattern to the cash flows. In such cases, the annuity table cannot be used, and a trial-and-error process must be tried that discounts each cash inflow at an assumed rate until the cash inflows equal the cash outflows. For example, assume that the Westlake Corporation is considering the purchase of a machine with the following characteristics:

Original cost	$15,000
Service life	4 years
Cost savings:	
Year 1	$6,500
Year 2	4,500
Year 3	5,000
Year 4	3,000
Salvage value at	
end of year 4	2,200

In finding the internal rate of return up to this point, the initial investment has been divided by the net cash inflows to find the present-value factor of the internal rate of return. In this case, however, we do not have the same cash inflows each year, and so we must approximate the net cash inflows over the life of the machine. Adding the cash inflows over the life of the investment and dividing by 4, we find the average cash flow to be $5,300.

$$\frac{\$15,000}{\$5,300} = 2.830$$

In Table 4 of Appendix A, look for the present-value factors that are closest to 2.830 on the line for 4 periods. The table shows that the present-value factor for 15% is 2.855 and the present-value factor for 16% is 2.798. Using trial and error, discount the cash flows over the life of the machine at a rate of 15%:

15% Discount Factor				
Year	Cash inflow	× Present-value factor	=	Present value of cash inflows
1	$6,500	× .870	=	$ 5,655
2	4,500	× .756	=	3,402
3	5,000	× .658	=	3,290
4	5,200	× .572	=	2,974
				$15,321

At 15% the total present value of the cash inflows is greater than the initial investment of $15,000, and so the true rate of the investment must be higher. If the net present value is greater than the investment, try a higher rate. If the net present value of the cash flows is less than the initial investment, try a lower rate. When during the trial-and-error process the present value of the cash inflows is equal to the investment, the rate of return of the machine has been found. Now discount the cash inflows at a rate of 16%.

16% Discount Factor				
Year	Cash inflow	× Present-value factor	=	Present value of cash inflows
1	$6,500	× .862	=	$ 5,603
2	4,500	× .743	=	3,344
3	5,000	× .641	=	3,205
4	5,200	× .552	=	2,870
				$15,022

At a discount rate of 16%, the present value of the cash inflows almost exactly equals the initial cost of the machine, $15,000. The present value is so close to the cost that interpolation is not needed, and it is proper to conclude that the rate of return promised by this investment is 16%. Because of the complexities involved in this type of procedure, computer programs and business calculators may be used to perform the necessary calculations to find the internal rate of return for an investment when there are uneven cash flows.

Ranking Decisions

Up to this point, the chapter has been examining screening decisions, that is, using the net-present-value and internal-rate-of-return methods to decide whether an investment is at all acceptable to a firm. After screening decisions are made, however, a company may have several acceptable prospective investments to consider, and because most firms have limited amounts of capital to invest, they must rank the projects in order of priority. Nonquantitative factors also play a role in that decision, as may a consideration of the risks involved and the availability of funds. The ranking decision follows the screening decision and enables a company to invest its limited resources in those projects that promise the greatest rate of return. Both the internal-rate-of-return and the net-present-value methods can be used in ranking decisions.

Ranking and the Internal-Rate-of-Return Method

If the internal-rate-of-return method has been used to determine the rate of return on an investment, the most desirable project will be the one with the highest internal rate of return. For example, assume a company is considering three projects—A, B, and C—with internal rates of return of 14%, 16%, and 13%, respectively. The company's cost of capital is 12%, and so all three projects are acceptable investments. If the firm can fund only one project, project B will be chosen because it has the highest internal rate of return; project A would be ranked second and project C third. Ranking projects in this manner enables the firm to prioritize acceptable investment opportunities so that if additional resources become available, they know that project A is next in line to receive funding. This method of ranking projects is widely used because it is easily understood and requires no additional computations.

Ranking and the Net-Present-Value Method

When the net-present-value method has been used to screen investments, the task of selecting one project over another is less simple than when the internal-rate-of-return method has been used. It is difficult to directly compare the net present value of one project with that of another, unless the investment required by both projects is equal. For example, consider two projects—A and B—that require investments of $15,000 and $25,000, respectively, and promise the same net present value:

	Project A	Project B
Investment required	$(15,000)	$(25,000)
Present value of net cash inflows	20,000	30,000
Net present value	$ 5,000	$ 5,000

The use of a **profitability index** makes it possible to compare these two projects and rank them, for although they have the same net present value, they may not be comparable. The profitability index is computed by dividing the present value of the net cash inflows by the funds required for the investment:

$$\frac{\text{Present value of net cash inflows}}{\text{Required investment}} = \text{Profitability index}$$

The profitability index for projects A and B is shown below:

Project A	Project B
$\dfrac{\$20,000}{\$15,000} = 1.33$	$\dfrac{\$30,000}{\$25,000} = 1.20$

Project A requires a smaller investment to produce the same net present value as B and thus has a higher profitability index than B. When two or more investment projects are being considered, the project with the highest profitability index is ranked first.

The profitability index is a useful method of comparing acceptable investments because it reveals the most profitable alternative, even when projects have unequal lives and different earning patterns.

1020

The discounted cash flow techniques we have just discussed are among the better methods available for use in capital budgeting decisions. There are, however, other methods that have been used which do not take into account the time value of money. The payback method and the accounting-rate-of-return method are relatively simple to use, but their results must be interpreted with care.

The Payback Method

The **payback method** is used to determine how long it will take for an investment to repay its original cost from the cash inflows it generates. Using this method, calculate the payback period, usually expressed in years, as follows:

$$\frac{\text{Required investment}}{\text{Annual net cash inflows}} = \text{Payback period}$$

The shorter the payback period, the more quickly the firm will have recovered its original investment. The advantage of the payback method is that it is simple to use and easy to understand. It can be a useful first step as a screening device in capital budgeting decisions, but when the payback method is the *only* approach used, the results can be misleading.

Consider the following investment alternatives and their payback periods:

$$\frac{\text{Required investment}}{\text{Annual net cash inflows}} = \text{Payback period}$$

$$\text{Machine A:} \quad \frac{\$4,500}{\$1,500} = 3 \text{ years}$$

$$\text{Machine B:} \quad \frac{\$6,500}{\$1,500} = 4.33 \text{ years}$$

Using the payback method as the sole criterion for making an investment, a firm faced with such alternatives would choose Machine A because it has the shorter payback period. The service lives of the two machines have not, however, been considered. If Machine A has a service life of three years and Machine B has a service life of six years, choosing Machine A would be less profitable for the firm. Machine A generates no profit after it has recovered its initial investment, whereas Machine B contributes toward profitability for one and two-thirds years after its payback period. This demonstrates one of the major weaknesses of the payback method as a basis for investment decisions: its focus is on a period of time rather than on profitability.

The payback method also does not take into account the time value of money, so that cash received in the present is viewed in the same way as cash received years in the future. As this chapter has shown, when using discounted cash flow techniques, the timing of cash flows can make a great difference in the value of investment alternatives.

The payback method can be useful as a first step in eliminating investment alternatives, however, when other methods also are used. Payback allows the manager to determine when a project will recover the cash invested, and if a firm expects to need cash by a certain point in time, this is useful information. Discounted cash flow techniques should then be used to determine if an investment that has an acceptable payback period meets the firm's requirements for rates of return on an investment.

Accounting-Rate-of-Return Method

The **accounting-rate-of-return method**, like the internal-rate-of-return method, is used to find the percentage return a project offers. The accounting-rate-of-return method does this by finding the relationship between the expected increases in net income directly resulting from an investment and the initial investment cost:

$$\frac{\text{Expected increase in average annual net income}}{\text{Initial investment}} = \text{Accounting rate of return}$$

It is called the accounting-rate-of-return method because it uses the expected increases in net income as found in the financial statements rather than the cash flows found in the net-present-value and internal-rate-of-return methods. It also is referred to as the "simple-rate-of-return method" and the "unadjusted-rate-of-return method."

To illustrate the accounting-rate-of-return method, assume the following situation:

> Bradford's, a local department store, is considering whether to add a new department that would sell video games and low-cost computers over the next five years. The manager estimates that revenues from the new department would be $90,000 per year, and expenses would be $78,480. The investment required to start the department is $80,000, and the firm normally expects a return of 12.5% on investments. What is the accounting rate of return on the proposed department?

The accounting rate of return is calculated as follows:

$$\frac{\$11,520}{\$80,000} = 14.4\%$$

Notice that the expected increase in net income for the department is the expected revenue of $90,000 less expected expenses of $78,480. Bradford's requires a return of 12.5%, and so the proposed department would be acceptable.

The basic weakness of using the accounting-rate-of-return method as the basis for investment decisions is that it does not consider the time value of money. Unlike the internal-rate-of-return method, the accounting-rate-of-return method assumes that all cash flows are the same regardless of when they take place, and this method uses annual averages. Therefore, although the accounting rate of return is used by firms, caution is needed, and like the payback method, it is best used in conjunction with a discounted cash flow method.

Income taxes often play a role in decision-making situations, and this is also true in capital budgeting. The payment of income taxes is frequently a major cash disbursement, and the tax rates themselves can influence both the timing and the magnitude of cash flows. For example, although depreciation is a noncash item, it is a deductible expense for tax purposes. If a firm with a tax rate of 40% projects depreciation expense of $10,000 on a machine, that amount is deductible for tax purposes and would save the company .40 × $10,000, or $4,000.

The timing of cash flows also can be influenced by the choice of depreciation methods. The role that taxes play in capital budgeting is a complex one, a role that also can change as a result of changes in the tax code. For these reasons, basic accounting courses concentrate on the fundamentals of the different capital budgeting techniques and leave the tax implications for more advanced courses.

The capital budgeting techniques outlined in this chapter are part of the long-term strategic planning process for an organization. Once a strategic plan has been developed, a firm needs to plan for day-to-day operations on a yearly basis. The next chapter shows how that is accomplished through the budgeting process.

Summary of Learning Objectives

1. *Define capital budgeting.* Capital budgeting is the process of planning for long-term investment decisions in operational assets such as plant and equipment through analysis of alternative uses of funds in order to find the greatest rate of return on investment for a firm.

2. *Using present-value methods in capital budgeting.* Money changes its value over time, and therefore the timing of cash inflows and outflows affects the value of a proposed investment. Money on hand now is worth more than money in the future, and all the cash flows resulting from a long-term investment must be analyzed at one point in time—the present. Present-value tables display the present value of $1 for various periods and interest rates; the present value of $1 can then be multiplied by the amount of any cash inflow or outflow in order to determine its value in the present.

3. *Discounted cash flow methods.* Discounted cash flow methods are those capital budgeting methods that discount future cash flows back to the present in order to decide if there is a sufficient rate of return on a proposed investment.

4. *The cost of capital.* Companies raise capital through debt instruments and stocks, and there is usually an interest rate that determines how much firms have to pay for needed funds. The cost of capital is the interest rate that a firm has to pay for its debt and equity, generally computed on a weighted average basis. When doing capital budgeting, the cost of capital serves as an acceptable rate of return on an investment.

5. *The net-present-value method of problem solving.* The net-present-value method is used to find the net present value of a project by comparing the net present values of cash inflows and outflows. The following steps may be used to solve problems:
   a. Read the problem carefully.
   b. Write down the alternatives presented in the decision.
   c. For purposes of analysis, choose one alternative.
   d. Set up a time line to depict the cash flows involved in the problem.
   e. Find the present-value factors for each cash flow based on the interest rate and time involved by using the tables in Appendix A.
   f. Multiply the present-value factors by the relevant cash flows.
   g. Find the difference between cash inflows and outflows in order to calculate the net present value.
   h. If the net present value is positive, the investment is acceptable for the firm; if the net present value is negative, the investment is unacceptable.
   i. Consider the qualitative factors involved in the decision.

6. ***Using the internal-rate-of-return method to solve problems.*** The internal-rate-of-return method is used to find the true rate of return promised by an investment. The following steps may be used in problem solving:

a. Read the problem carefully.
b. Divide the investment in the project by the net amount of the annual cash inflows. The resulting number is the present-value factor of the internal rate of return.
c. Find the present-value factor in Table 4 in Appendix A for the number of periods and see what interest rate the present-value factor represents. If the factor is not found in the table, choose the two factors closest to it and use interpolation to find the actual rate of return. If the cash flows are uneven, a trial-and-error process must be used whereby an estimated internal rate of return is used to discount the cash flows until the rate is found where the net present value of the cash flows is equal to the initial investment (a net present value of zero).
d. Compare the internal rate of return with the company's cost of capital; if the rate is equal to or greater than the cost of capital, the investment is acceptable. If the internal rate of return is less than the cost of capital, the project is unacceptable.
e. If there is more than one investment option being considered and the capital is limited, accept the one with the highest rate of return.

7. ***Ranking investment alternatives.*** When two or more investments are considered acceptable, a firm must rank them in order of priority. If the internal-rate-of-return method has been used to screen projects, the most desirable project will be that with the highest internal rate of return. If the net-present-value method has been used, a profitability index is computed in order to rank investments:

$$\frac{\text{Present value of net cash inflows}}{\text{Required investment}} = \text{Profitability index}$$

The higher the profitability index, the more desirable the investment.

8. ***The payback method to solve problems.*** The payback method is used to determine how long it will take for an investment to repay its original cost from the cash inflows it generates:

$$\frac{\text{Required investment}}{\text{Annual net cash inflows}} = \text{Payback period}$$

The weakness of the payback method is that it does not consider the time value of money or the profitability of projects.

9. ***Using the accounting-rate-of-return method to solve problems.*** The accounting-rate-of-return method is used to find the percentage return a project offers, but it ignores the time value of money in finding that return. It uses the changes in net income due to the investment to find the rate of return:

$$\frac{\text{Expected increases in average annual net income}}{\text{Initial investment}} = \text{Accounting rate of return}$$

Key Terms

Accounting-Rate-of-Return Method	Discounted Cash Flow Methods	Net-Present-Value Method
Capital Budgeting	Discounting	Payback Method
Cash Inflows	Internal-Rate-of-Return	Profitability Index
Cash Outflows	Method	Ranking Decision
Cost of Capital	Interpolation	Screening Decision
		Time Value of Money

Problems for Your Review

A. Net Present Value. Albert Manufacturing Company is considering acquiring a new machine. Two machines are available, machine A and machine B. Both machines have a life of four years. Machine A costs $3,000 and would generate cash savings of $1,000 per year. Machine B costs $3,050; it generates cash savings of $1,400 the first year, $1,100 the second year, $800 the third year, and $700 the last year. The company uses an interest rate of 8% to evaluate investments.

Required:

Which machine should the company acquire?

Solution

Discount the cash inflows and outflows to their present value in order to calculate the net present value offered by each machine as follows:

MACHINE A

	Cash Flow $\times$	Present-Value Factor $=$	Net Present Value
Cash inflows:			
First year	$ 1,000 $\times$	.926 $=$	$ 926
Second year	1,000 $\times$	.857 $=$	857
Third year	1,000 $\times$	.794 $=$	794
Fourth year	1,000 $\times$	.735 $=$	735
Total present value of cash inflows			$ 3,312
Cash outflow:			
Purchase	$(3,000) $\times$	1.000 $=$	$(3,000)
Net present value			$ 312

MACHINE B

	Cash Flow $\times$	Present-Value Factor $=$	Net Present Value
Cash inflows:			
First year	$ 1,400 $\times$	.926 $=$	$ 1,296.40
Second year	1,100 $\times$	.857 $=$	942.70
Third year	800 $\times$	.794 $=$	635.20
Fourth year	700 $\times$	.735 $=$	514.50
Total present value of cash inflows			$ 3,388.80
Cash outflow:			
Purchase	$(3,050) $\times$	1.000 $=$	$(3,050.00)
Net present value			$ 338.80

Both machines are acceptable investments because they both have a positive net present value. Machine B should be acquired, however, because it has a higher net present value.

B. Four Capital Budgeting Techniques. The Blackwood Company is considering buying a machine that costs $25,000. It generates annual cost savings of $5,000 before consideration of taxes and has a 10-year service life.

Required:

a. Compute the net present value, assuming the company's cost of capital is 14%.

b. Calculate the internal rate of return on the investment.

c. Compute the payback period of the investment.

d. Calculate the accounting rate of return on the investment, assuming straight-line depreciation will be used.

Solution

a. The cash inflows of the investment are the same each year, so use a present-value factor from the annuity table to discount the cash inflows and compare them with the cash outflow for the purchase:

	Cash Flow	×	Present-Value Factor	=	Net Present Value
Cash inflows:					
Years 1–10	$ 5,000	×	5.216	=	$ 26,080
Cash outflow:					
Purchase	$(25,000)	×	1.000	=	(25,000)
Net present value					$ 1,080

b. Let X equal the internal rate of return and F equal the present value factor:

$$\$25,000 = \text{Present value of \$5,000 per year at X\% for 10 years}$$
$$= (F) \times \$5,000$$

$$F = \frac{\$25,000}{\$5,000}$$
$$= 5.000$$

It's necessary to interpolate because 5.000 is not found in the table:

Present-Value Factors				Interest Rates
High	5.019	High	5.019	15%
Low	4.833	Investment	5.000	16%
Difference	.186		.019	1%

$$\text{Interest rate of investment} = 15\% + \frac{(.019 \times 1\%)}{.186}$$
$$= 15\% + .001$$
$$= 15.1\%$$

c.
$$\text{Payback period} = \frac{\text{Required investment}}{\text{Annual net cash inflow}}$$
$$= \frac{\$25,000}{\$5,000}$$
$$= 5 \text{ years}$$

d.
$$\text{d. Accounting rate of return} = \frac{\text{Expected increase in average annual net income}}{\text{Initial investment}}$$
$$= \frac{\$5,000 - \$2,500 \text{ (Depreciation)}}{\$25,000}$$
$$= 10\%$$

Questions

1. Why is capital budgeting important to the long-run profitability of the firm?

2. What is the major difference between capital budgeting and short-term decision analysis?

3. Why is a dollar today worth more than a dollar one year from now?

4. Explain the difference between the present value of an annuity of $1 and the present value of $1.

5. What factors need to be considered in capital budgeting decisions?

6. In establishing a minimum rate of return for its investments, what factors should a company consider?

7. State the disadvantages of the payback method of evaluating an investment.

8. Should a project with a zero net present value be rejected? Explain your answer.

9. Depreciation is not considered explicitly in capital budgeting problems. Why is this so?

10. What are the advantages of using discounted cash flow techniques for capital budgeting?

11. A project has a net present value of $50,000 at a discount rate of 12%. Would you expect this to increase or decrease if the discount rate was changed to 15%? Explain your answer.

12. Describe the terms *discounting* and *time value of money*.

13. Can a project have a negative net present value? Explain your answer.

14. If a large company uses the internal-rate-of-return method for evaluating capital projects, how would division managers be affected if the firm had to pay more to raise capital from stocks and bonds?

15. You have been given the choice of getting $8,000 from your endowment plan immediately or waiting 3 years and receiving $11,000. You believe an appropriate discount rate is 10%. What option would you choose? Explain your answer.

Exercises

1. Net-Present-Value Calculations. Calculate the net present value of the following independent cases. Assume the time value of money is 12% and all amounts are received at year-end.

   a. Alice Jones will receive $50,000 2 years from now.
   b. John Lopez is planning an investment of $15,000 now, which will result in $30,000 5 years from now.
   c. Kevin Corcoran is considering investing in a fund that will pay him $5,000 per year for 5 years.
   d. Linda Katz, vice-president of Robertson Corporation, is evaluating an investment of $6,000 in new machinery that would generate cash flows of $1,200 for the first 2 years, $1,000 for the next 3 years, and $3,600 at the end of the sixth year.

2. Four Capital Budgeting Techniques. The XYZ Tool Company is considering purchasing machinery costing $11,000 that will save the company $2,800 a year in cash operating costs for the next 10 years. There is no salvage value after 10 years. The company expects to earn at least 14% on all investments. Find the following:

   a. Net present value.
   b. Internal rate of return.
   c. Payback period.
   d. Accounting rate of return.

3. Cash Flows; Net Present Value. Hi-Fi Electronics is considering purchasing a new computerized inventory system. The new system would cost $25,000 and have a salvage value of $7,500 at the end of 7 years, which is its useful life. The managers estimate that the new system would allow them to reduce the part-time help needed by 3 workers, each earning $2,500 per year. Hi-Fi Electronics likes to earn at least 10% on investments. Should Hi-Fi buy the machine?

Required:

   a. Show the cash inflows and outflows associated with this decision on a time line, as shown in the chapter.
   b. What is the net present value of the proposed investment?

Accounting Information for Long-term Decisions: Capital Budgeting   1027

4. Capital Budgeting Techniques. Roll's Tires is planning to modernize its production facilities at a cost of $250,000. The improvement in production efficiency will increase annual cash flows by $35,000. The equipment purchased has a useful life of 10 years. The expected salvage value is zero.

Required:

Calculate the following:

   a. The accounting rate of return.
   b. The payback period.
   c. The internal rate of return.

5. Cash Flows. Warren Company wishes to replace its existing machine. Relevant cost data are as follows:

Investment required for new machine	$100,000
Salvage value of old machine	10,000
Annual cost savings	28,000

The machine's useful life is six years. The company expects a 14% return on all investments. Derive the cash flow from the present through year 6, which would be used for capital budgeting purposes and calculate the net present value. Should Warren Company invest in the new machine? Ignore the effect of income taxes.

6. Net Present Value. A company can purchase one of two types of equipment. The following costs are associated with each type:

	A	B
Investment	$50,000	$78,000
Annual cost savings	16,000	20,000
Useful life	5 years	6 years

Required:

   a. Ignoring the effect of taxes and assuming a time value of money of 10%, determine which option should be selected using the net-present-value method.
   b. How would this decision be affected if the required rate of return was 7%?

7. Net Present Value; Ranking Decision. Company B requires a 15% return on capital investment. Using this criterion, determine which of the following projects would be selected by the company. Assume the company can finance only one project. Ignore the effect of income taxes.

	Investment, Year 0	Cash Inflows (End of Year)				
		Year 1	Year 2	Year 3	Year 4	Year 5
A	15,000	—	—	10,000	15,000	15,000
B	15,000	10,000	10,000	5,000	—	—

8. Payback Method.

   a. Refer to the data in Exercise 7. If the company uses the payback method to select projects and it wants payback within three years, which project should it select?
   b. Discuss the value of this approach and the reliability of the evaluation.

9. Net Present Value and Internal Rate of Return. A firm has an opportunity to invest in equipment at a cost of $65,667. The net cash inflow from this equipment would be $21,000 per year and would continue for 5 years. The cost of capital for the firm is 12%.

Required:

   a. Compute the net present value of the investment.
   b. What is the internal rate of return for the investment?

10. Comparison of Payback and Net Present Value. Consider two projects, X and Y, each costing $300 and each with the following cash flows:

Year	X	Y
1	$200	$100
2	100	200
3	100	100

Required:
a. Which project is more desirable according to (1) the payback method and (2) the net-present-value method?
b. Explain the differences in the results.

Problem Set A

25A–1. Net Present Value. The operations manager of Bowling Connectors has just heard of a new type of mold production equipment that could decrease annual production costs by $25,000. He believes the equipment he is currently using, which is already fully depreciated, can be sold to a smaller company for $40,000. The new equipment costs $250,000 and has an estimated useful life of 8 years and expected salvage value of $10,000. Bowling's required return on investments of this kind is 15%.

Required:
Calculate the net present value of the planned investment. Assume that the company could continue to use the existing equipment for the next 8 years. Should the firm purchase the new equipment?

25A–2. Net Present Value. Mike's Printing Services is considering purchasing a high-quality photocopying machine that costs $150,000. The machine would be paid for in two equal installments, one at the end of the first year and the other at the end of the second year. The manager estimates that the copier would increase income of the other services of the store by $15,000 per annum. Expected annual revenue from the copier itself is $40,000. Maintenance and other fixed costs, excluding depreciation, would be $20,000. The manager expects to replace the copier after six years, with no salvage value. The cost of capital for the store is 10%.

Required:
a. Calculate the net present value of the investment.
b. How would net present value change if the total payment is made at the beginning of the first year?

25A–3. Cash Flows. Highlife Recreational Products is planning to market a new game. The company expects the game to be a "fad" item, with sales gradually declining to zero after 5 years. The following data were assembled for the product:
1. Expected sales volume the first year is 20,000 units, increasing 25% for 2 successive years and then decreasing 50% for the next 2 years.
2. The initial retail price per game will be $4 for the first year, increasing by 5% every year.
3. Variable costs of production per unit will be $2 the first year. This will increase by 5% each year.
4. Fixed costs excluding depreciation will be $10,000 annually.
5. Promotional and advertising costs will be $15,000 for the first 2 years.

Required:
Calculate the net cash flow for each year of the game's life that Highlife Recreational Products would use in the capital budgeting process.

25A–4. Internal Rate of Return; Uneven Cash Flows. Bayson Electronics is considering two different types of equipment to update the manufacturing process for Snarks, their large memory computer chip. One alternative, A, calls for an initial investment of $100,000 and promises annual net cash inflows of $31,000. The machinery has a five-year service life and has no salvage value. A second alternative, B, requires an initial investment of $90,000, has a service life of 5 years, a salvage value of $15,000, and the following cash inflows: year 1, $40,000; years 2 and 3, $30,000; year 4, $20,000; year 5, $16,000.

Required:

a. What is the internal rate of return promised by alternative A? Use interpolation.

b. What is the internal rate of return promised by alternative B? Use trial and error.

c. Assuming Bayson requires a 16% return on all capital investments, which alternative, if either, would the firm choose?

25A–5. Net Present Value. Tom Ferguson is a college senior considering attending business school who wishes to base his decision on financial criteria. One of his objectives is to be no worse off financially within five years of graduation than he is now. To help his analysis, he has assembled the following data:

	1st Year	2nd Year
Tuition and fees	$5,000	$5,250
Books and supplies	350	370
	$5,350	$5,620
Expected earnings during college	$3,000	$3,000

After graduating from the MBA program Tom expects an income of $2,000 per month, increasing annually by 5%. He currently has a job offer with income of $1,200 per month, increasing 5% annually. To effectively compare alternatives, he assumes his basic annual expenses (room and board plus miscellaneous expenses) are the same for both alternatives and therefore can be eliminated from the analysis.

Required:

If the time value of money is 10%, calculate the net present value of both alternatives, assuming the time involved in both alternatives is 7 years.

25A–6. Payback and Net Present Value. Ryan Company is considering two projects. Each requires an investment of $1,000. The cost of capital for the company is 10%. The net cash inflows from both projects are shown below:

Year	A	B
1	$500	$100
2	400	200
3	300	300
4	100	400
5	10	500
6	10	600

Required:

a. Which project should Ryan choose according to (1) the payback method and (2) the net-present-value method?

b. Explain why the decisions might be different under different methods and recommend which one Ryan should use.

25A–7. Four Capital Budgeting Techniques. You are the accountant for the Lawrence Company. The company is considering replacing a machine with a new one that will increase earnings from $20,000 per year to $40,000 per year. The new machine will cost $100,000 and will have an estimated life of 8 years with no salvage value. The firm's cost of capital is 12%. The old machine can be sold to another company for $600.

Required:

a. Compute the following items for the new machine:
1. Payback period.
2. Accounting rate of return.
3. Internal rate of return.
4. Net present value.

b. Using the net-present-value method, do you recommend replacing the old machine with the new one? What do you recommend if the company requires that all investments earn a minimum return of 10%?

Problem Set B

25B–1. Net Present Value. The operations manager of Range Manufacturing has just heard of a special machine that could decrease annual production costs by $10,000. The existing equipment could be sold for $8,000. The new machine costs $95,000, has an estimated useful life of 6 years, and has an expected scrap value of $2,000. Range's required return on investments of this kind is 10%.

Required:

Calculate the net present value of the planned investment. Assume the company could continue to use the existing equipment for the next 6 years. Should Range invest in the new machinery?

25B–2. Net Present Value. Joe's Bakery is considering purchasing a large oven costing $80,000 to bake English scones. The oven would be paid for in two equal installments, one at the time of purchase and the other one year later. The manager estimates sale of scones will increase revenues of other pastry items by $6,000 per annum. Expected annual revenues from the actual sale of scones is $18,000. Maintenance and other fixed costs (excluding depreciation) associated with the oven will be $8,000 annually. The manager expects to sell the oven in 10 years for $2,000. The cost of capital for the bakery is 12%.

Required:

a. Calculate the net present value of the investment.
b. How would this change if the total payment was made at the beginning of the first year?

25B–3. Cash Flows. Squeezy Toys is planning to market a new toy. The company expects it to be a novelty item, with sales gradually declining to zero after six years. The following data were assembled for the product:

1. Expected sales volume the first year is 50,000 units, increasing 30% for 3 successive years and then decreasing 50% for the next 2 years.
2. The initial retail price per toy will be $6, increasing 5% each year.
3. Initial variable costs of production will be $3 per unit, increasing 5% each year.
4. Fixed costs excluding depreciation will be $8,000 annually.
5. Promotional and advertising costs will be $16,000 per year for the first 3 years.

Required:

Calculate the net cash flow for the 6 years of the proposed new toy's life.

25B–4. Internal Rate of Return; Interpolation; Uneven Cash Flows. Doom and Gloom Hospital is considering the purchase of new equipment for its operating room at a cost of $32,000 with cash savings of $6,000 per year. If the hospital buys the new equipment it can sell its old equipment for $3,000. The estimated life of the new equipment is 10 years.

Required:

a. What is the internal rate of return on the new operating room equipment?
b. The hospital administrator, Mr. Yorick, is concerned that the manufacturer's estimate of the service life may not be accurate. Compute the internal rate of return on the equipment if the estimated service life is (1) 6 years, and (2) 15 years.
c. Mr. Yorick has heard rumors that there could be a new type of equipment, in the development stage now, that could make the proposed equipment obsolete in 5 years. If this happens, the hospital could dispose of the equipment for $4,500 at the end of the fifth year. What is the internal rate of return on the proposed equipment if this happens? If the hospital must earn at least 15% on capital expenditures, should Mr. Yorick buy the equipment?

25B–5. Net Present Value of Decision Alternatives. The owner of a factory building, currently leased, has to decide whether to sell the factory now or keep it for another 3 years. He has assembled the following data for the two alternatives:

1. *Sell now:* The factory can be sold for $360,000. The cost of sale is 3% of the proceeds. The outstanding mortgage balance is $275,000, payable when the factory is sold.

2. *Sell after three years:* Estimated market value of the factory is $385,000 and the outstanding mortgage balance $270,000. The cost of sale is 3% of the proceeds. Expected revenues from leasing is $6,000 per month. The monthly mortgage payments are $4,500. Annual maintenance, taxes, and insurance costs will average $8,000 per annum. Assume that lease revenue and mortgage payments are made at the end of each year.

Required:

If the time value of money is 8%, what decision should the owner make?

25B-6. Net Present Value. Paula Kloner, a biology major considering medical school, wishes to make a decision based on financial criteria. One of her objectives is to be no worse off financially within four years of graduation than she is now. To help with her analysis, she obtained the following estimates for a four-year program at a state university:

	Annual
Tuition and fees	$1,500
Books and supplies	450
	$1,950
Expected earnings during college	$2,500

On graduating from medical school, Paula expects income of $1,500 per month, increasing by 15% annually. She currently has a job offer of income of $1,100 per month, increasing 5% annually. To effectively compare alternatives, she assumes annual expenses (room and board plus miscellaneous expenses) are the same for both alternatives and therefore can be eliminated from the analysis.

Required:

If the time value of money is 12%, calculate the net present value of both alternatives, using 8 years as the period of time for analysis. Discount all incomes on a yearly basis.

25B-7. Three Capital Budgeting Techniques. Robinson Appliance Company is planning to introduce a new product to its line of small home appliances. Annual sales of this new product, code-named Marvel, are estimated to be 10,000 units at a sales price of $40 per unit. Variable production costs are estimated to be $20 per unit; fixed production costs (other than depreciation) are $30,000 annually; and selling and administrative costs related to the Marvel are $40,000 annually.

To manufacture the Marvel, the company must invest $468,000 in equipment with a useful life of five years and no salvage value.

Required:

a. Compute the net cash flows expected from this project for each year.
b. Compute the following items for the Marvel:
   1. Payback period.
   2. Internal rate of return.
   3. Net present value, using a discount rate of 10%.

Using the Computer

A. Kamen's Shoe Factory manufactures several lines of tennis shoes, and management is considering adding the production of casual-wear shoes. In order to incorporate this new merchandise, Kamen's must provide additional space and machinery within its headquarters. The initial construction cost would be $200,000, which includes the price of new machinery. The cash income over a 3-year period is estimated to be $50,000, $80,000, and $100,000, whereas cash operating costs are estimated at $10,000 per year. After a period of 3 years, the added equipment used to manufacture the shoes is assumed to have a salvage value of $20,000. Kamen's bases its net-present-value figures on an interest rate of 10%. Using a spreadsheet, calculate the net present value of this investment alternative. Should Kamen's go ahead with production of casual-wear shoes?

B. Kamen's also is considering an alternative way of entering the casual-wear shoe market. On a recent trip to the Far East, the president of the firm met with a Korean manufacturer who was interested in supplying Kamen's with the sole portion of the new shoe for an estimated annual cost of $20,000. Management would, as in the previous case, base its decision for this option on financial estimates over a 3-year period. Under this alternative, cash operating costs are anticipated to fall to $7,000 per year. Construction and initial outlay costs are estimated to be $115,000, because much less machinery would be needed and the factory would expand less drastically. In addition, the salvage value of equipment is expected to be $15,000 at the end of 3 years. Cash income is assumed to be unaffected by the option to import from overseas. Should Kamen's adopt this alternative for entering the market for casual-wear shoes?

Decision Case

Boring Corporation plans to replace an old piece of equipment that is now obsolete. The equipment is fully depreciated and has no salvage value. The firm is considering two possible pieces of equipment as replacements. Machine A would cost $20,000; it would increase revenues by $12,000 per year and would cost $6,000 per year in maintenance and upkeep. Machine B costs $23,650; it would increase revenue by $15,000 per year and would cost $8,000 in maintenance and upkeep. Both machines have a service life of 5 years, with no salvage value. The company estimates that its cost of capital for investment purposes is 14%.

Required:

a. Calculate for Boring Company the following items for Machines A and B:

   1. Payback period.
   2. Accounting rate of return.
   3. Net present value.
   4. Internal rate of return.
   5. Profitability index rankings.

Assume all operating revenues and expenses occur at the end of the year.

b. Should Boring Company purchase Machine A or B? Explain why.

c. Which of the decision models should Boring Company use in deciding which machine to purchase? Why? What are some nonquantitative factors that could play a role in this type of decision?

Budgeting for Planning and Control

26

LEARNING OBJECTIVES

After reading this chapter you should be able to:
1. Describe the budgeting process and the role of budgeting in organizations.
2. Identify the behavioral implications of the budgeting process and describe the major behavioral concepts relevant to budgeting.
3. Identify the parts of the master budget.
4. Prepare a sales budget.
5. Prepare a production budget.
6. Prepare budgets for direct materials, direct labor, and factory overhead.
7. Prepare budgets for ending inventory, cost of goods sold, and selling and administrative expenses.
8. Prepare a cash budget.
9. Prepare a budgeted income statement and balance sheet.
10. Use and understand flexible budgets.

We have examined the role of accounting as it relates to planning and decision making, both in the short term, as in cost-volume-profit analysis and differential analysis, and in the long term, in dealing with capital budgeting. We now turn to the ways in which accounting information is used in the planning and control process. This chapter focuses on the planning process, as illustrated by the budgetary system. The following two chapters deal with the organizational control system.

Budgeting and the Planning Process

The planning process is one of the basic responsibilities of management in the achievement of organizational objectives and goals. Organizations plan for long-term as well as for short-term operational needs. The basic process of planning involves analyzing information about an organization and its environment, establishing objectives to be attained, and developing plans to achieve these goals and objectives. Exhibit 26–1 depicts the overall process of planning.

Budgeting is the planning process through which the plans for the day-to-day operation of the firm are put into financial form, that is, expressed in dollars and cents. For example, a manufacturing firm may expect a 10% growth in the sales of one of its product lines. This will bring in more dollars in revenue but also will entail additional costs for materials, labor, overhead, shipping, and so forth. The manager of the firm must know what these projected items will be in dollar terms in order to plan the production process. In addition, the manager will want to project cash receipts and expenditures to see if it will be necessary to borrow any money during the period. A **budget**, then, expresses the operating plan of an organization in financial terms for a period. A budget may be prepared for an organization as a whole or for any of the parts or segments of the organization. After a period is over, most managers compare what actually happened in the period with the budgeted plan for the period in order to see how well goals were met. In large organizations, budgeting usually involves many people from various departments. Next we examine the role of budgeting in large organizations and the nature of the budgeting process.

EXHIBIT 26–1
Diagram of the Planning Process

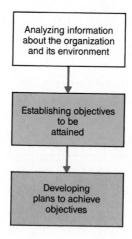

The Role of Budgeting

Although different organizations carry out the process of budgeting in different ways, the budget preparation process serves some basic functions in all organizations. Following are the most important roles the budgeting process performs:

1. A budget forces managers to focus on the future in an organized manner. It formalizes financial planning.
2. After the budget is finished and approved, it provides managers with specific objectives for a period, expressed in quantitative terms. Motivation tends to be higher when objectives are clearly known rather than vaguely hinted at. These objectives can then be used to evaluate performance when a period is over.
3. The process of preparing the budget helps to coordinate the activities of the various parts of an organization. This ensures that the parts of a firm are consistent with the overall goals of the whole organization.
4. Budgeting can improve communications within a firm. Discussing budget requests from the different parts of an organization can help managers learn about the functioning of all of the departments in the organization. At times, discussion and negotiation are necessary in order to finish a budget, and this can be a learning process for the managers involved.

Budgeting can be highly beneficial to a firm if management is clearly committed to the budgeting process and communicates that commitment to the entire organization. The usefulness of a budget, however, is not limited to large organizations. Small organizations and individuals need to prepare budgets as well. Have you ever made estimates of what it would cost to take a vacation? You probably tried to find out the costs of transportation, hotels, food, and entertainment in order to see if you had enough funds. You needed to make budget estimates of those items in order to intelligently plan your vacation. The process is more complicated, but similar, for a business. Planning is essential for business, but the need for coordination and communication is even greater, and the plan can then be used to evaluate performance.

The Budgeting Process

The way in which the budgeting process is carried out varies from organization to organization. In some organizations the budgeting process is very centralized, with senior management making the decisions about budgeted sales and expenditures in each division, department, or other organizational unit. In some companies the process is more decentralized, with the managers who are responsible for specific organizational units having a great deal of authority or influence over the budgeted amounts of revenue and expense.

In a centralized organization, senior management has the final responsibility for deciding the amount of budgeted sales, expenses, and profits. Division and department managers are assigned a budget to which they must adhere. In some companies there may be a budget committee comprising senior managers who represent the different functional areas of the enterprise, such as sales, production, engineering, finance, and purchasing. This committee prepares the budget for the organization. In other companies that operate under a more decentralized style of budgeting, the budget committee serves as a reviewing body; the members review the requests made by the specific functional areas.

The typical role of the accounting department or controller's office in the budgeting process is to (1) prepare the budgetary forms to be used by each department to develop its budgetary requests and (2) compile or aggregate the data from each department or division into a company-wide master budget. The accounting department usually does not make the final budgetary decisions; that is the prerogative of senior management.

The Motivational Aspects of Budgeting

There is a motivational side to budgeting. The budget provides managers with specific objectives for a period, and motivation tends to be higher when objectives are clearly stated. Thus, budgeting has a behavioral impact on people.

Behavioral Concepts Relevant to Budgeting

The field of behavioral science has contributed some concepts and research findings that are relevant to managing the budgeting process. The most important of these are (1) the concept of the level of aspiration, (2) research findings concerning the effects of participation on one's degree of commitment to achieving budgeted goals, (3) research findings concerning the psychology of success and failure, and (4) the concept of reinforcement.

Organizational psychologists define **level of aspiration** as the level of performance on a task that an individual seeks to achieve, and they have found that people form expected levels of aspiration for various tasks. In budgeting, a budgeted amount represents a goal that an organization would like an individual to internalize as his or her level of aspiration.

Behavioral research also suggests that people are more likely to accept a goal as their level of aspiration if they have participated in establishing the goal. This means that the more decentralized styles of budgeting in which people participate to some extent in establishing their budgetary goals are more likely to lead to a greater degree of motivation, and the goals themselves are therefore more likely to be achieved.

Another important behavioral research finding relevant to budgeting is that after a person has been successful in task performance, his or her level of aspiration will increase in future repetitions of that task. After a failure, one's level of aspiration is likely to decrease.

The fourth behavioral idea that is relevant to budgeting involves the concept of **reinforcement.** Motivational research has indicated that when an individual's behavior is followed by a positive response (or "reward"), the behavior tends to be repeated, whereas if behavior is followed by a negative response or no response, it tends not to be repeated. This psychological law, known as Thorndike's Law of Effect, suggests that managers must "reinforce" behavior that they wish to be repeated and extinguish (by not reinforcing) behavior that they do not wish repeated.

Three questions that relate to the motivational or behavioral aspects of budgeting are: (1) At what level of difficulty should a budget be estimated? (2) To what extent should budgeting be centralized or decentralized? and (3) How should management react to situations in which actual performance does not fulfill budgeted objectives?

The following discussion uses behavioral concepts and research findings to suggest answers to these three important budgeting issues.

The Level of Budget Difficulty

A critical decision in budgeting is how difficult budgeted objectives should be. In order to motivate people to meet their optimum level, should a budgeted objective be (1) so low that it is virtually certain to be attained, (2) realistic and attainable but not without significant effort and a chance of failure, or (3) virtually impossible to attain in order to make people work their hardest? The answer to this question is that all three alternatives are correct, but under different conditions.

For most typical organizational situations, the ideal level at which to set budget objectives are where they are realistic and attainable but not without significant effort. Objectives ought to be set at a level where people perceive that they can be achieved with effort, but where people are not totally certain that the objectives will actually be achieved. At this level of difficulty, people are usually motivated to achieve goals. They will be neither frustrated that the objectives are unattainable nor so overconfident that the objectives can be achieved that they do not experience any challenge from their accomplishment.

Under certain conditions, it is appropriate to set easily attainable objectives. For example, if an organization's history has been characterized by low performance, the manager's best strategy is probably one of incremental improvement. This means that the budget objectives ought to be set sufficiently low that there is a very high probability of attainment. Once the unit attains a given objective, the objectives for the next period ought to be increased to a higher level. On the contrary, if an organization has a history of always meeting its objectives, it may be feasible to set an almost unattainable objective as a new challenge or motivator. For example, in a rapidly growing electronics manufacturing company, one division always had met or exceeded its budgeted sales and profit objectives. Management challenged the division to double its annual objectives in return for a substantial bonus. Although the initial reaction of the division's employees was that the objective was "impossible," they accepted the challenge and actually exceeded the budget.

Behavioral research findings on the "psychology of success and failure" indicate that after successfully achieving a budget people tend to raise their levels of aspiration, whereas after not achieving a budget people tend to lower their levels of aspiration.

Centralization or Decentralization of the Budgeting Process

Another important behavioral issue in budgeting is whether the budgeting process ought to be centralized or decentralized. The important behavioral finding that is relevant to this issue is the relation between participation and motivation.

Centralization of budgeting requires less participation by people than does decentralization. Under a decentralized budgeting process, people who will be responsible for achieving budgeted objectives are responsible for preparing the budget, subject to senior management's review. Behavioral research suggests that people who participate in budgetary decisions are more likely to be motivated to achieve budgeted objectives than are people who are merely told what their budgeted goals are.

Participation leads to a greater likelihood that an individual will be com-

Budgeting for Planning and Control   1039

mitted to achieving objectives because those who set the objectives are more likely to perceive them as realistic and attainable.

In brief, behavioral research findings suggest that a decentralized system of budgeting is more likely to result in positive motivation toward the achievement of budgeted objectives.

Behavioral Issues When Budgets Are Not Achieved

When there is a negative difference (or variance) between a budget objective and actual performance, management may take corrective action. There will almost always be some difference between actual and budgeted performance. Management needs an idea of how much of a difference between budget and actual performance is significant. In some companies, anything less than a 10% difference between budget and actual is deemed not to be significant. However, in other companies even small differences of 5% or less can be significant.

To effectively use budgets as a motivational device, it is necessary to reinforce positive behaviors and to extinguish negative behaviors. If actual performance compared with a sales or expense budget is within normal range, management must reinforce performance by providing some rewards to personnel. The rewards can be recognition, praise, or some financial compensation such as a salary increase or bonus. The lack of a reward is equivalent to a form of punishment.

The Master Budget

The **master budget** is the comprehensive budget for the entire firm for a given period. The master budget is prepared after the budgets for individual segments of the organization, such as divisions, departments, and functional areas (i.e., marketing and production). The master budget consolidates all other budgets so that top management has an overall view of what is projected for the entire firm. Most master budgets start with estimates of sales, followed by budgets for production, selling, and administrative activities. Exhibit 26–2 shows a master budget with its network of interrelated budgets that ultimately lead to the budgeted financial statements. Note that long-term strategic planning is necessary for both sales projections and capital budgeting. Although a capital budgeting decision may affect an organization for several years, it can require cash outlays in the immediate period and therefore must be included in the budgeting process.

Because the size of budgets, the managerial style of budget makers, and the process of budgeting for departments or functional areas varies so much from firm to firm, it is difficult to generalize about that part of the budgeting process. The remainder of this chapter focuses on the master budget. From the master budget, it is easier to understand the interrelationships among the different parts of the budget and how budgeting can play a vital role in the planning process. To illustrate how the master budget is prepared, this chapter examines each part of the master budget for a manufacturing firm using the following data:

Selectron Manufacturing Corporation specializes in making a tool called the Fixit that is widely used in home improvement. The company offers two types of Fixits, regular and deluxe. The budgeting process for fiscal year 1987

EXHIBIT 26–2
Master Budget Relationships

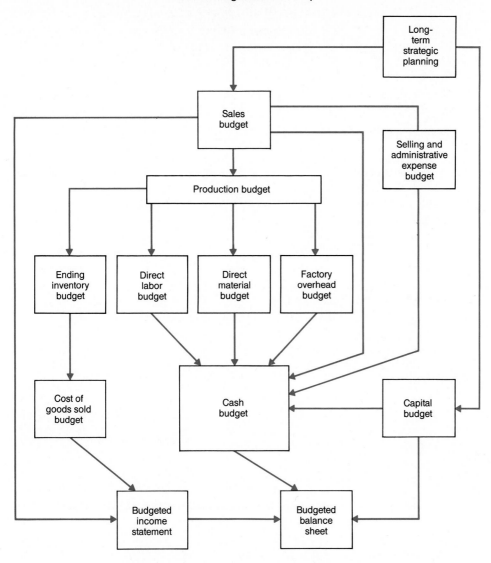

is about to begin. Exhibit 26–3 on the following page shows the balance sheet at December 31, 1986; basic data on costs, inventories, and sales follow.

Basic Data
Units of Product

	Regular	Deluxe
Expected sales	32,000	15,000
Selling price per unit	$10	$20
Beginning inventory 12/31/86	2,500	2,200
Desired ending inventory 12/31/87	4,500	1,200

EXHIBIT 26–3

Selectron Manufacturing Corporation
Balance Sheet
December 31, 1986

Assets

Current assets:		
Cash		$ 35,000
Accounts receivable (net)		28,100
Inventories:		
Raw material	$ 3,750	
Work in process	6,200	
Finished goods	30,575	40,525
Other current assets		3,000
Total current assets		$106,625
Property, plant, and equipment	$185,000	
Less: accumulated depreciation	46,000	139,000
Total assets		$245,625

Liabilities and Stockholders' Equity

Liabilities:		
Accounts payable		$ 37,000
Accrued income taxes payable		2,700
Accrued wages payable		2,000
Total liabilities		$ 41,700
Stockholders' equity:		
Common stock		$120,000
Retained earnings		$ 83,925
Total stockholders' equity		$203,925
Total liabilities and stockholders' equity		$245,625

Work in process does not fluctuate and will remain the same as on the December 31, 1986 balance sheet.

Direct Materials	Price
Material X	$ .50 per pound
Material Y	$1.00 per pound

	Regular	Deluxe
Material X	3 pounds	3 pounds
Material Y	1 pound	2 pounds

Direct Material Cost per Unit

	Regular	Deluxe
Material X		
3 × .50	$1.50	$1.50
Material Y		
1 × 1.00	1.00	
2 × 1.00		2.00
	$2.50	$3.50

Direct Labor

Labor rate per hour = $5.00

Direct Labor Cost per Unit

	Regular	Deluxe
Hours per unit of product	1/4	1/2
× Rate =	$5.00	$5.00
Cost	$1.25	$2.50

Direct Material Inventories in Pounds

	Material X	Material Y
Beginning inventory 12/31/86	4,500	1,500
Desired ending inventory 12/31/87	5,000	2,000

Factory Overhead Cost

Variable	Per Direct Labor Hour
Supplies	$ .60
Indirect labor	.80
Maintenance, variable portion	.26
Utilities, variable portion	.20
Total	$1.86

Fixed	
Depreciation	$10,000
Property taxes and insurance	4,100
Supervision	13,000
Maintenance, fixed portion	4,500
Utilities, fixed portion	1,570
Total	$33,170

Selling and Administrative Expense

Variable: After cost behavior analysis it was determined that these costs fluctuated $.63 for every unit of product sold.

Fixed	
Administrative salaries	$150,000
Sales salaries	40,000
Advertising	9,000
Utilities, fixed portion	690
	$199,690

Miscellaneous Data

1. Accounts receivable at the end of the fiscal year generally were 10% of yearly sales.
2. The levels of accounts payable and accrued wages payable remained the same as on the December 31, 1986 balance sheet.
3. The company has a minimum required cash balance of $35,000.
4. The capital budgeting process calls for the upgrading of the firm's computer system, with total capital expenditures for 1987 of $60,000.
5. Depreciation averages 10% of the original cost of property, plant, and equipment.
6. Other current assets remained at the same level as on the December 31, 1986 balance sheet.

Using this basic data, Selectron Manufacturing Corporation can construct its master budget for the 1987 fiscal year.

Sales Budget

The sales budget is the first step in the budgeting process because it directly or indirectly determines the levels of most of the other parts of the budget. Because the sales budget is so important, many firms use a variety of means to forecast demand for their products. The following factors are considered most frequently in making **sales forecasts:**

1. Historical data on past sales volume.
2. Relationship of sales to economic indicators such as gross national product, prices, employment, and industrial production.
3. Pricing policies.
4. General economic conditions.
5. Industry-wide conditions.
6. Advertising.
7. Competition.
8. Market research studies.
9. Production capacity.

Sometimes elaborate economic models and statistical tools are used in predicting sales data. Sales forecasts, as seen from the preceding list, are broader in nature than the **sales budget**, which projects expected sales for operations for one period. After all the data have been analyzed, the firm can prepare the sales budget, showing the expected sales for the coming fiscal year. Schedule 1 below shows the sales budget for 1987. The expected number of units for each type of Fixit is multiplied by the selling price per unit to get the numbers of total sales.

SCHEDULE 1

Selectron Manufacturing Corporation
Sales Budget
For Budget Year 1987

	Units	Selling Price per Unit	Total Sales
Fixit regular	32,000	$10	$320,000
Fixit deluxe	15,000	$20	300,000
			$620,000

Production Budget

Once the sales budget has been prepared, the number of units needed to be produced for the coming period can be determined. The production cycle, that is, how long it takes to produce a finished unit from raw materials, also determines the **production budget.** Production has to be planned to allow enough time to manufacture the products before the estimated date of sale. Most firms want to make sure there is always enough on hand to meet sales needs, and they therefore plan to have a certain number of finished units in inventory at all times. The basic relationships involved in planning production are shown below:

Units needed for sales	XXXX
Add: Desired ending inventory of finished goods	XXXX
Total units needed	XXXX
Less: Beginning inventory of finished goods	XXXX
Units to be produced	XXXX

Schedule 2 shows the budgeted production for Selectron for 1987. Notice that the first line of the schedule shows the number of units of product necessary in order to meet expected sales demand for the regular and deluxe lines. The second line shows the number of units that the firm plans to have in ending inventory at the end of the fiscal year. Most firms need enough units in inventory to meet demand at any time, while incurring the lowest possible storage costs. Those two items together represent the total number of units needed for the coming fiscal year, which is why they are added together on line 3. However, it is not necessary to produce all of those units if there are already some on hand. That is why the number of units in finished goods inventory at the beginning of the fiscal year is subtracted from the total needed in order to get the number of units that must be produced during the year. Work through the numbers in Schedule 2 to be sure you understand where the final numbers come from.

SCHEDULE 2
Selectron Manufacturing Corporation
Production Budget in Units
For Budget Year 1987

	Regular	Deluxe
Expected sales (Schedule 1)	32,000	15,000
Add: Desired ending inventory of finished goods	4,500	1,200
Total units needed	36,500	16,200
Less: Beginning inventory of finished goods	2,500	2,200
Units to be produced	34,000	14,000

Direct Materials Usage and Purchases Budget

After the number of units to be produced has been determined, the next step in the budgeting process is to compute the amount of direct materials that will be used and purchased. That item is found in the **direct materials budget.** Both the regular and deluxe lines use three pounds of Material X, whereas the regular unit uses one pound of Material Y and the deluxe unit uses two pounds of Material Y. Part A of Schedule 3 shows each of these items multiplied by the number of units to be produced of each model.

The second part of Schedule 3 shows the computation of the number of pounds of each raw material that need to be purchased. The calculation of this is similar to the process followed in Schedule 2 for the units to be produced. In this case, Selectron needs enough of each material for the units to be produced during the period. In addition, there is usually a desired level of direct material ending inventory for the budget period. These two items represent the total number of pounds needed for each direct material. If there is some material in beginning inventory, it is not necessary to buy all of the necessary pounds from suppliers. Therefore, the number of pounds to be purchased is the difference between the total needed and what is already in inventory at the beginning of the period. We multiply the number of pounds to be purchased by the price per pound in order to know how much we will have to spend on direct material purchases for the budget period. A summary of how to calculate the amount of material to be purchased is shown at the top of the next page.

SCHEDULE 3
Selectron Manufacturing Corporation
Direct Materials Usage and Purchases Budget
For Budget Year 1987

A. Usage

Direct Materials	Regular (34,000)	Deluxe (14,000)	Total (Pounds)	Price per Pound	Cost of Direct Materials Used
3×34,000 (X)	102,000				
3×14,000 (X)		42,000	144,000	$ .50	$ 72,000
1×34,000 (Y)	34,000				
2×14,000 (Y)		28,000	62,000	$1.00	62,000
					$134,000

B. Purchases

	Material X	Material Y	Total
Needed for production	144,000	62,000	
Add: Desired ending inventory, direct materials	5,000	2,000	
Total pounds needed	149,000	64,000	
Less: Beginning inventory, direct materials	4,500	1,500	
Pounds to be purchased	144,500	62,500	
× price per pound	$.50	$1.00	
Cost of purchases	$72,250	$62,500	$134,750

Direct material needed for production		XXXX			
Add: Desired ending inventory of direct materials		XXXX			
Total materials needed		XXXX			
Less: Beginning inventory of direct materials		XXXX			
Materials to be purchased		XXXX			

Direct Labor Budget

The **direct labor budget** also depends on the production budget. Once Selectron knows the estimated number of units produced for the budget period, management can estimate the number of labor hours required to meet production needs. This also helps to avoid unnecessary fluctuations in the labor force that result in rapid hiring and firing of employees or costly overtime.

Schedule 4 multiplies the number of units to be produced for each product line by the number of direct labor hours (DLH) required to produce a single unit. The total direct labor hours needed for production are then multiplied by the direct labor rate per hour in order to develop the total labor cost.

SCHEDULE 4

Selectron Manufacturing Corporation
Direct Labor Budget
For Budget Year 1987

	Units Produced	DLH per Unit	Total DLH	× Rate	Total Cost
Regular	34,000	1/4	8,500	$5	$42,500
Deluxe	14,000	1/2	7,000	$5	35,000
Total			15,500		$77,500

Factory Overhead Budget

The **factory overhead budget** provides data about all production costs other than direct materials and direct labor. This information is needed for planning the work of the production departments as well as for determining how much factory overhead should become part of the cost of each unit of product.

Schedule 5 (on the next page) is broken down by cost behavior patterns. Variable costs are assumed to change proportionately with changes in direct labor hours. The rate per direct labor hour for each variable cost is then multiplied by the total estimate of direct labor hours taken from Schedule 4 to obtain the total amount of each variable cost. The fixed costs for the period are added together, and the total overhead cost of $62,000 is divided by the estimated direct labor hours for the period to get a predetermined overhead rate of $4 per direct labor hour. This means that every time a direct labor hour is used in the production process, $4 of overhead cost is added to the cost of the units produced. It will become clear how this works when the cost of finished units of product is determined in Schedule 6.

Budgeting for Planning and Control 1047

Selectron Manufacturing Corporation
Factory Overhead Budget
For Budget Year 1987

Variable Costs	Rate/DLH	Total DLH (Schedule 4)	Total Cost
Supplies	$.60	15,500	$ 9,300
Indirect labor	.80	15,500	12,400
Maintenance	.26	15,500	4,030
Utilities	.20	15,500	3,100
Total variable	$1.86		$28,830

Fixed Costs			
Depreciation			$10,000
Property taxes and insurance			4,100
Supervision			13,000
Maintenance			4,500
Utilities			1,570
Total fixed			$33,170
Total overhead			$62,000

$$\text{Overhead rate:} \quad \frac{\text{Estimated total overhead}}{\text{Estimated direct labor hours}} = \frac{\$62,000}{15,500} = \$4/\text{DLH}$$

Ending Inventory Budget

In order to draw up a budgeted balance sheet for the fiscal period, Selectron must know the dollar amounts to be assigned to ending inventories of direct materials and finished goods. This is done in the **ending inventory budget.** The estimates of the pounds of Materials X and Y expected to be left in inventory at the end of the period is known. These are multiplied by the price per pound in section A of Schedule 6 (on the next page) in order to compute the dollar cost of the direct materials inventory at the end of the fiscal year.

Part B of Schedule 6 follows a similar procedure for the finished units left in inventory at the end of the fiscal year. The expected number of units is multiplied by the cost per unit for each product line to derive the total amount for the ending inventory of finished goods shown on the balance sheet. Note that each unit of product is allocated a share of factory overhead based on the predetermined overhead rate that was derived in Schedule 5.

Cost of Goods Sold Budget

After the costs for the ending inventories of direct materials and finished goods have been computed, the company can use those items in developing the **cost of goods sold budget.** The cost of goods sold is necessary to prepare the budgeted income statement. Schedule 7 (on page 1050) adds the costs of the materials, labor, and overhead used in manufacturing for the projected fiscal period. Beginning work-in-process inventory is added to the period manufacturing costs for the total cost of the units of product in process during the

Selectron Manufacturing Corporation
Ending Inventory Budget
For Budget Year 1987

A. Direct Materials

	Pounds	Price per Pound	Total Cost
X (from basic data)	5,000	$ .50	$2,500
Y	2,000	$1.00	2,000
			$4,500

B. Finished Goods

	Units	Cost per Unit		Total Cost
Regular	4,500*	Direct material*	$2.50	
		Direct labor*	1.25	
		Overhead**	1.00	
			$4.75	$21,375
Deluxe	1,200*	Direct material*	$3.50	
		Direct labor*	2.50	
		Overhead**	2.00	
			$8.00	9,600
				$30,975

Total cost
*From basic data.
**From Schedule 5: Overhead Rate = $4 per direct labor hour.
    Regular: $4 × 1/4 hour = $1 per unit.
    Deluxe: $4 × 1/2 hour = $2 per unit.

period. Ending work-in-process inventory is then deducted to calculate the cost of goods manufactured (i.e., finished for 1987). The beginning finished goods inventory is added to the cost of goods manufactured because these two items represent the total cost of all the goods available for sale during 1987. The units that were not sold—the ending finished goods inventory—is then deducted to arrive at the cost of the units sold.

Selling and Administrative Expense Budget

This item, which often appears on the income statement as one or two broad categories, is a complex mixture of costs relating to everything other than the manufacturing process. Everything ranging from sales commissions to central corporate headquarters may be included. Selectron believes it is valuable to use cost behavior analysis in order to prepare the **selling and administrative expense budget.** On Schedule 8 (on the next page) the variable cost per unit sold is multiplied by the total units expected to be sold for the period to find the total variable selling and administrative cost. Included in variable selling and administrative expenses are such items as freight, part-time clerical help,

Budgeting for Planning and Control

SCHEDULE 7
Selectron Manufacturing Corporation
Budgeted Cost of Goods Sold
For Budget Year 1987

Cost of direct material used (from Schedule 3)	$134,000
Cost of direct labor (from Schedule 4)	77,500
Cost of factory overhead (from Schedule 5)	62,000
Total manufacturing costs incurred	273,500
Add: Beginning work in process inventory (from 12/31/86 balance sheet)	6,200
Cost of goods in process	279,700
Less: Ending work in process inventory (unchanged)	6,200
Cost of goods manufactured	273,500
Add: Beginning finished goods inventory (from 12/31/86 balance sheet)	30,575
Cost of goods available for sale	304,075
Less: Ending finished goods inventory (from Schedule 6)	30,975
Cost of goods sold	$273,100

SCHEDULE 8
Selectron Manufacturing Corporation
Selling and Administrative Expense Budget
For Budget Year 1987

Variable:	
Budgeted sales in units	47,000
Variable selling and administrative expense per unit sold	× .63
Total variable expense	$ 29,610
Fixed:	
Administrative salaries	$150,000
Sales salaries	40,000
Advertising	9,000
Utilities, fixed portion	690
Total fixed expense	$199,690
Total selling and administrative expense	$229,300

and the variable portion of nonmanufacturing utilities. This is then added to the estimated fixed selling and administrative expenses.

Cash Budget

The **cash budget** is essential to the planning process because in accrual accounting, revenues and expenses are not necessarily cash items. There is often a time lag between the recognition of revenue and the receipt of cash, or the recognition of an expense and the disbursement for it. That is why a separate budget including only items affecting cash is prepared. It is then possible to determine whether cash flow is satisfactory, if it is necessary to borrow for the short term, or if there is excess cash to invest temporarily. Cash budgeting makes it possible to plan for cash needs, to avoid surprises, and to bargain for better interest rates. Although Selectron shows a cash budget for the fiscal year, cash budgets also are prepared for smaller periods such as quarters or months depending on the firm's requirements.

The basic items in the cash budget are cash receipts and cash expenditures. The beginning cash balance is added to the cash receipts in a period to determine the total cash available. Collections on sales to customers is usually the largest cash receipt, although other items such as interest or the sale of fixed assets may be found. Based on past exerience, about 10% of Selectron's yearly sales remain uncollected at the end of the fiscal year. Using that information and Schedule 9, Selectron's management determines that they can expect to collect 90% of current-year sales for 1987 in addition to the receivables held at the end of 1986.

Selectron's cash expenditures are varied, including such items as payments for the purchases of materials, selling and administrative expenses, taxes, and dividends—all listed in Schedule 9. Note that although depreciation is an expense that is counted on the income statement, it is a noncash item that is deducted from the overhead total for the cash budget.

The difference between total cash receipts and total cash expenditures on Schedule 9 is the ending balance for cash that will appear on the balance sheet at the end of the period. Note that Selectron's ending cash balance is well above the minimum required balance of $35,000. If the firm had projected a

---

SCHEDULE 9

Selectron Manufacturing Corporation
Budgeted Cash Receipts and Expenditures
For Budget Year 1987

Beginning cash balance (from 12/31/86 balance sheet)		$ 35,000
Add: Receipts		
Accounts receivable 12/31/86	$ 28,100	
Collections*	558,000	
Total receipts		586,100
Total cash available		621,100
Less: Expenditures		
Purchase of direct material (Schedule 3)		134,750
Direct labor cost (Schedule 4)		77,500
Factory overhead** (Schedule 5)		52,000
Selling and administrative expense (Schedule 8)		229,300
Income tax payments (from 12/31/86 balance sheet)		2,700
Fixed assets		60,000
Total expenditures		$556,250
Ending cash balance		$ 64,850

*Total sales less 10% uncollected at end of year.
**$62,000–$10,000 depreciation (a noncash item).

deficiency of cash, it would have had to borrow funds from a bank or other credit source. When a company is regularly in debt, its cash budget has an additional section showing amounts borrowed, payment of interest, and repayment of principal.

Budgeted Income Statement

Data from all of the other schedules are used to develop the income statement for the next fiscal period. The budgeted income statement is a critical item that gives management a profitability goal against which to measure performance for the coming period.

Schedule 10 shows Selectron's budgeted income statement for the 1987 fiscal year.

SCHEDULE 10
Selectron Manufacturing Corporation
Budgeted Income Statement
For Budget Year 1987

Sales (Schedule 1)	$620,000
Less: Cost of goods sold (Schedule 7)	273,100
Gross margin	346,900
Expenses:	
Selling and administrative (Schedule 8)	229,300
Depreciation*	14,500
Total expenses	243,800
Income before taxes	103,100
Estimated income tax (30%)	30,930
Net income	$ 72,170

*10% of new property, plant, and equipment	=	$ 6,000
10% of existing property, plant, and equipment	=	18,500
Subtotal		$24,500
Less: Depreciation in factory overhead included		
in cost of units of product		10,000
Depreciation expense, nonmanufacturing		$14,500

Budgeted Balance Sheet

When the estimated net income for the period is known, the budgeted balance sheet can be prepared. The budgeted balance sheet allows management to see the total effect of planned operations on the assets and equities of the firm. This is particularly important for large publicly held corporations, for ratios such as earnings per share can affect stock prices. Look again at Exhibit 26–3 which showed Selectron's balance sheet as of December 31, 1986. Note which items have changed. Schedule 11 shows Selectron's balance sheet at the end of budget year 1987. Note that retained earnings increased by the amount of net income for the period.

Selectron Manufacturing Corporation
Budgeted Balance Sheet
December 31, 1987

Assets

Current assets:

Cash (Schedule 9)		$ 64,850
Accounts receivable (net)		62,000
(10% of sales)		
Inventories:		
Raw material (Schedule 6)	$ 4,500	
Work in process (unchanged)	6,200	
Finished goods (Schedule 6)	30,975	41,675
Other current assets		3,000
Total current assets		$171,525
Property, plant, and equipment	$245,000	
Less: Accumulated depreciation	70,500	174,500
Total assets		$346,025

Liabilities and Stockholders' Equity

Liabilities:

Accounts payable (unchanged)		$ 37,000
Accrued income taxes payable		30,930
Accrued wages payable (unchanged)		2,000
Total liabilities		69,930
Stockholders' equity:		
Common stock		120,000
Retained earnings 12/31/86	$83,925	
Add: Budgeted net income	72,170	
Retained earnings 12/31/87		156,095
Total stockholders' equity		276,095
Total liabilities and stockholders' equity		$346,025

The preparation of budgeted or pro forma financial statements completes the preparation of the master budget. It now can serve as a plan of operations for the coming period.

Flexible Budgeting

In Selectron's master budget, all of the numbers in the various schedules were derived from projected sales volume for regular and deluxe Fixits. If the firm had projected that a larger number of units would be sold in 1987, revenue would have been greater, as would some of the costs. For example, Selectron's variable selling and administrative expenses increased $.63 for every unit sold. Similarly, variable overhead costs rose by $1.86 for each direct labor hour used. Knowing how variable costs behave in relation to volume makes it possible to prepare budgets at different projected levels of sales. The master budget can be adjusted for changes in volume; the result is a **flexible budget.** A flexible budget allows a firm to construct budgets at any level of activity in the relevant range.

Flexible budgets are a big help to management in the planning process. Preparing sales forecasts and budgets is not a precise science; there is much room for subjectivity and error. Using a flexible budget, management can easily project revenues, costs, and profits at different levels of volume before choosing the level that will set objectives in the operating budget for the coming period.

Flexible budgets are even more useful in the control process because they allow management to evaluate performance based on the actual output of the period. For example, assume that Selectron was not able to sell the 47,000 units projected for 1987; assume that 40,000 units were sold. In Schedule 8, Selectron budgeted a total of $229,300 for selling and administrative expenses for 1987, but assume that during the period only $226,690 was actually spent. The difference between the budget and the actual expenditures (the variance) was $2,610. This appears to be a favorable variance because Selectron spent less than the budget, but is that a proper conclusion to draw? Selectron would be comparing apples and oranges if management compared a budget based on one level of volume with actual operations based on another. Instead, Selectron needs to evaluate what was actually spent in relation to a budget based on actual volume. Selectron's performance report compares actual selling and administrative costs with a budget for those costs based on sales of 40,000 units as follows:

Performance Report
Selectron Selling and Administrative Expense
1987

Budget for 40,000 Units		Actual	Variance
Variable:			
$0.63 × 40,000 =	$ 25,200		
Fixed	199,690		
Total	$224,890	$226,690	$1,800 unfavorable

The performance report shows an unfavorable variance because Selectron spent more than it should have considering only 40,000 Fixits were sold. Using a flexible budget, Selectron can compare budgeted and actual costs at the same activity level—40,000 units sold. Firms use knowledge of cost behavior patterns to prepare flexible budgets for any activity level within the relevant range. This enables management to make valid comparisons between budgeted and actual objectives, a critical part of the planning and control process.

1054

Computers and Budgeting

Computers have greatly aided the process of budgeting, allowing firms to make changes easily before finally agreeing on a budget. In addition, if basic conditions change during the budget year, the computer can be used to alter the original plan. Increasing use of microcomputers allows even the smallest firms to use budgets in the planning process, and once cost behavior patterns are determined, flexible budgets can be used for control.

Summary of Learning Objectives

1. *The budgeting process and the role of budgeting in organizations.* The budget expresses the operational plans of an organization for a specified period in financial terms. The budgeting process usually reflects the nature of a firm; more centralized firms tend to budget from top management down, whereas in more decentralized organizations, managers at different levels participate in the budgeting process.

   The budgeting process has several roles in an organization:
   a. It forces managers to focus on the future in an organized way.
   b. It gives managers specific quantitative objectives.
   c. It helps to coordinate the parts of an organization with the overall goals of the organization.
   d. It facilitates communication within an organization.

2. *The behavioral implications of the budgeting process and the major behavioral concepts relevant to budgeting.* The most important behavioral implications of the budgeting process are questions of how difficult budgetary objectives should be, how much participation there should be in budgeting, and what to do when budgets are not achieved.

   Four major behavioral concepts can be applied to the area of budgeting:
   a. The level of aspiration is the level of performance on a task that an individual seeks to achieve. A budgeted objective is what the organization would like the individual to internalize as his or her level of aspiration.
   b. Research on the psychology of success and failure suggests that success in task performance will increase an individual's level of aspiration, whereas failure will lower it.
   c. Research on the effects of participation on an individual's degree of commitment to achieving budgeted objectives suggests that participation in the budgetary process leads to greater motivation and acceptance of the budgeted objective as the level of aspiration.
   d. Reinforcement refers to the psychological law that rewarded behavior tends to be repeated, whereas behavior followed by negative or no response tends to be extinguished or not repeated.

An employee's success in meeting budgeted objectives should be rewarded, and unsuccessful performance should receive negative or no response so that ineffective behaviors may be extinguished.

3. **The parts of the master budget.** The master budget for a manufacturing firm is made up of the following parts:

  a. Sales budget.
  b. Production budget.
  c. Direct materials usage and purchases budget.
  d. Direct labor budget.
  e. Factory overhead budget.
  f. Ending inventory budget.
  g. Cost of goods sold budget.
  h. Selling and administrative expense budget.
  i. Cash budget.
  j. Budgeted income statement.
  k. Budgeted balance sheet.

4. **Preparing a sales budget.** The sales budget is the critical first step in the budgeting process. It is prepared by multiplying the expected number of units of each product to be sold by the selling price per unit to get total sales dollars.

5. **Preparing a production budget.** The number of units of product needed for sales is added to the desired number of units in ending inventory to find the total number of units needed for the period. Units in beginning inventory are deducted from the total needed to determine the number of units that need to be produced during the budget period as follows:

Units needed for sales	XXXX
Add: Desired ending inventory of finished goods	XXXX
Total units needed	XXXX
Less: Beginning inventory of finished goods	XXXX
Units to be produced	XXXX

6. **Preparing budgets for direct materials, direct labor, and factory overhead.** Direct material usage is determined by multiplying the units to be produced of each product by the number of pounds of material required for each unit and then adding the total number of pounds of each material needed for production to the desired ending inventory in order to calculate the total number of pounds needed. The material in beginning inventory is deducted from the total needed to determine the number of pounds of direct material that need to be purchased from suppliers:

Direct material needed for production	XXXX
Add: Desired ending inventory of direct materials	XXXX
Total materials needed	XXXX
Less: Beginning inventory of direct materials	XXXX
Materials to be purchased	XXXX

  The direct labor budget calculates the total direct labor hours needed for each product by multiplying the units produced by the amount of direct labor required per unit. The total direct labor hours are multiplied by the rate per hour to determine the total labor cost for the budget period.

  The factory overhead budget is divided into variable and fixed cost behavior patterns. The variable cost per direct labor hour, or some other activity base, is multiplied by the direct labor hours for the period to calculate the total variable cost. This is added to the fixed costs to determine total overhead for the budget period. The budget also may show how the overhead rate is developed.

7. *Preparing budgets for ending inventory, cost of goods sold, and selling and administrative expenses.* The ending inventory budget shows the cost of the materials and units of finished product left in ending inventory at the end of the budgeted fiscal period. The cost for direct materials is derived by multiplying the pounds of each material left in ending inventory by the price per pound. The cost for finished goods is calculated by multiplying the number of units of finished product left in inventory by the total production cost per unit.

The cost of goods sold budget adds together the costs of the direct materials, direct labor, and factory overhead used in producing the units of product for a period to calculate the total manufacturing costs incurred. The beginning work-in-process inventory is added to the manufacturing costs to derive the cost of the goods in process. Ending work-in-process inventory is then subtracted from the cost of goods in process to calculate the cost of goods manufactured. Beginning finished goods inventory is added to the cost of goods manufactured to find the cost of the goods available for sale. Ending finished goods inventory is then deducted from the goods available for sale to derive the cost of goods sold.

The selling and administrative expense budget multiplies the variable cost per unit sold by the budgeted number of units sold for the period to calculate the total variable cost. The fixed selling and administrative expenses are added to the variable cost to calculate the total selling and administrative cost.

8. *Preparing a cash budget.* To prepare the cash budget, budgeted cash receipts for a period are added to the beginning cash balance to find the total cash available for the period. Total cash expenditures for the period are then deducted from the cash available to derive the ending cash balance that goes on the balance sheet.

9. *Preparing a budgeted income statement and balance sheet.* The figures for sales, cost of goods sold, and the expenses on the budgeted income statement all are derived from other schedules. Income before taxes is multiplied by the tax rate to determine the income tax expense for the period, which is then deducted to calculate the amount of net income expected for the budget year.

The budgeted balance sheet is based on the same format as the statement for the previous period. The items either come from one of the earlier schedules or are the result of adding the changes expected in the budget period to the amounts shown on the balance sheet for the previous period. Retained earnings must be changed by adding the budgeted net income (loss) for the period to the balance found on the beginning balance sheet.

10. *Using and understanding flexible budgets.* A flexible budget is a budget that can be adjusted for changes in levels of activity because it is based on cost behavior patterns. Flexible budgets can be used in the planning process to project revenues, costs, and profit at different levels of volume. In the control process, flexible budgets allow management to compare budgeted and actual costs at the same activity level.

Key Terms

Budget
Cash Budget
Cost of Goods Sold Budget
Direct Labor Budget
Direct Materials Budget
Ending Inventory Budget
Factory Overhead Budget
Flexible Budget

Level of Aspiration
Master Budget
Production Budget
Reinforcement
Sales Budget
Sales Forecast
Selling and Administrative Expense Budget

Problem for Your Review

Master Budget. The McMaster Company is preparing its master budget for fiscal year 1988. The following information has been prepared:

1. Production data:

	Unit Price	Product A	Product B
Direct material	$2/unit	2 units	2.5 units
Direct Labor	4/hour	5 hours	6 hours

Overhead is applied to the units of product on the basis of direct labor hours.

2. The balance sheet as of December 31, 1987 follows:

Assets		
Current assets:		
Cash	$ 10,000	
Accounts receivable	15,000	
Direct materials	15,000	
Finished goods	20,000	
Total current assets		$ 60,000
Fixed assets:		
Land		$ 30,000
Buildings	360,000	
Less: Accumulated depreciation	60,000	300,000
Total assets		$390,000

Liabilities & Stockholders' Equity		
Current liabilities:		
Accounts payable		$ 9,000
Stockholders' equity:		
Capital stock	$350,000	
Retained earnings	31,000	381,000
Total liabilities and stockholders' equity		$390,00

3.

	Product A	Product B
Expected sales, in units	4,000	5,000
Selling price per unit	$80	$100
Expected ending inventory, in units	200	170
Beginning inventory, in units	100	120

4.

Direct Material	
Expected ending inventory, in units	6,000
Beginning inventory, in units	7,500

Budgeted Factory Overhead	
Supplies, variable	$20,320
Indirect labor	20,000
Maintenance, variable portion	10,160
Depreciation	10,000
Fringe benefits	40,000
Power, variable portion	15,240
Maintenance, fixed portion	26,000
Miscellaneous	10,680

5. Selling and administrative expenses:

Sales commissions, variable	$ .50 per unit
Advertising	$ 5,000
Salaries and wages	25,000
Miscellaneous	15,000

6. Eighty percent of gross sales will be collected in the year of sale, and the other 20% will be collected in the year following the sale. Eighty percent of material purchases will be paid by cash, and the other 20% will be paid in the year following the purchase. The beginning accounts receivable and accounts payable on January 1, 1987 will be collected and paid during 1988.

7. An investment in new equipment with a cost of $230,000 will be incurred at the end of 1988.

8. There is no beginning or ending work in process.

Required:

Prepare a master budget for 1988. Show the following schedules:

  a. Sales budget.
  b. Production budget.
  c. Direct materials purchases and usage budget.
  d. Direct labor budget.
  e. Factory overhead budget.
  f. Ending inventory budget.
  g. Cost of goods sold budget.
  h. Selling and administrative expense budget.
  i. Cash budget.
  j. Budgeted income statement. (Ignore income taxes.)
  k. Budgeted balance sheet.

Solution

a.

SCHEDULE 1
Sales Budget
For Budget Year 1988

	Units	Selling Price per Unit	Total Sales
Product A	4,000	$ 80	$320,000
Product B	5,000	$100	500,000
			$820,000

b. After sales are budgeted, the production budget can be prepared. The total units needed for production are determined as follows:

$$\text{Units to be produced} = \text{Budgeted sales} + \text{Desired ending inventory of finished goods} - \text{Beginning inventory of finished goods}$$

SCHEDULE 2

Production Budget in Units

For Budget Year 1988

	Product A	Product B
Expected sales (Schedule 1)	4,000	5,000
Add: Desired ending inventory of finished goods	200	170
Total needed	4,200	5,170
Less: Beginning inventory of finished goods	100	120
Units to be produced	4,100	5,050

c. After the production budget has been determined, the schedules for direct materials (DM), direct labor, and factory overhead can be constructed.

SCHEDULE 3

Direct Materials Usage and Purchases Budget

For Budget Year 1988

A. Usage	Price per Unit	Cost of DM Used
Product A: 4,100 × 2 = 8,200 units	$2	$16,400
Product B: 5,050 × 2.5 = 12,625 units	$2	25,250
		$41,650

B. Purchases	
Needed for production	20,825
Add: Desired ending inventory (DM)	6,000
Total units needed	26,825
Less: Beginning inventory (DM)	7,500
Units to be purchased	19,325
Times price per unit	$2
Cost of purchases	$38,650

d.

SCHEDULE 4

Direct Labor Budget

For Budget Year 1988

	Units Produced	DLH per Unit	Total DLH	× Rate	Total Cost
Product A	4,100	5	20,500	$4	$ 82,000
Product B	5,050	6	30,300	$4	121,200
Total			50,800		$203,200

e.

Factory Overhead Budget
For Budget Year 1988

Variable Costs	Rate per DLH	Total DLH (Schedule 4)	Total Cost
Supplies	$.40	50,800	$ 20,320
Maintenance	.20	50,800	10,160
Power	.30	50,800	15,240
Total variable	$.90		$ 45,720

Fixed Costs			
Depreciation			$ 10,000
Indirect labor			20,000
Fringe benefits			40,000
Maintenance			26,000
Miscellaneous			10,680
Total fixed			106,680
Total overhead			$152,400

Overhead rate: $\dfrac{\text{Estimated total overhead}}{\text{Estimated direct labor hours}} = \dfrac{\$152,400}{50,800} = \$3/\text{DLH}$

---

f. In order to prepare a budgeted balance sheet, the company must know the dollar amounts to be assigned to the ending inventories of direct materials and finished goods. Schedule 6 shows the calculation of these items.

SCHEDULE 6

Ending Inventory Budget
For Budget Year 1988

A.	Units	Price per Unit	Total Cost
Direct materials	6,000	$2	$12,000

B. Finished Goods

	Units	Cost per Unit		Total Cost
Product A	200*	Direct materials*	$ 4	
		Direct labor*	20	
		Overhead**	15	
			39	$ 7,800
Product B	170*	Direct materials*	5	
		Direct labor*	24	
		Overhead**	18	
			$47	7,990
				$15,790

*From basic data.
**From Schedule 5: Overhead rate = $3 per direct labor hour.
    A: $3 × 5 hours = $15 per unit.
    B: $3 × 6 hours = $18 per unit.

---

g. After the valuation of the ending inventories is established, the budgeted cost of goods sold can be calculated.

SCHEDULE 7
Budgeted Cost of Goods Sold
For Budget Year 1988

Cost of direct materials used (from Schedule 3)	$ 41,650
Cost of direct labor (from Schedule 4)	203,200
Cost of factory overhead (from Schedule 5)	152,400
Total manufacturing costs incurred	397,250
Add: Beginning finished goods inventory	20,000
Cost of goods available for sale	417,250
Less: Ending finished goods inventory	15,790
Cost of goods sold	$401,460

---

h.

SCHEDULE 8
Selling and Administrative Expense Budget
For Budget Year 1988

Variable:	
Commission (.5 × 9,000 units sold)	$ 4,500
Fixed:	
Salaries and wages	25,000
Advertising	5,000
Miscellaneous	15,000
Total fixed expenses	45,000
Total selling and administrative expenses	$49,500

---

i.

SCHEDULE 9
Budgeted Cash Receipts and Expenditures
For Budget Year 1988

Beginning cash balance (from 12/31/86 balance sheet)		$ 10,000
Add: Receipts		
Accounts receivable 12/31/87	$ 15,000	
Collections*	656,000	671,000
Total cash available		681,000
Less: Expenditures		
Purchase of direct materials (Schedule 3)***		30,920
Accounts payable of 12/31/87		9,000
Direct labor cost (Schedule 4)		203,200
Factory overhead** (Schedule 5)		142,400
Selling and administrative expense		49,500
Purchase of fixed asset		230,000
Total expenditures		665,020
Ending cash balance		$ 15,980

*Total sales less 20% uncollected at end of year.

**Depreciation is a noncash item.

***Eighty % of the amount from Schedule 3.

j.

SCHEDULE 10
Budgeted Income Statement
For Budget Year 1988

Sales (Schedule 1)		$820,000
Less: Cost of goods sold (Schedule 7)		401,460
Gross margin		418,540
Expenses:		
Selling and administrative expenses (Schedule 8)		49,500
Net income		$369,040

---

k.

Budgeted Balance Sheet
December 31, 1988

Assets

Current assets:		
Cash (Schedule 9)	$ 15,980	
Accounts receivable	164,000	
Direct materials	12,000	
Finished goods (Schedule 6)	15,790	
Total current assets		$207,770
Fixed assets:		
Land		30,000
Building	590,000	
Less: Accumulated depreciation	70,000	520,000
Total assets		$757,770

Liabilities and Stockholders' Equity

Current liabilities:		
Accounts payable		$ 7,730
Stockholders' equity:		
Capital stock	$350,000	
Retained earnings:		
12/31/87	$ 31,000	
Add: Net income 12/31/88	369,040	
	400,040	
Total stockholders' equity		$750,040
Total liabilities and stockholders' equity		$757,770

Questions

1. Define the term *budgeting*.

2. Discuss the differences in the budgeting process between a centralized and hierarchical organization and a decentralized organization.

3. What are the most important roles the budgeting process plays?

4. Do you agree with the statement that "a budget is useful for large organizations but not for individuals"? Explain your answer.

5. Discuss, from the viewpoint of motivation, what might happen if excessive emphasis is placed on using a budget to evaluate performance.

6. What is a master budget? Briefly describe the interrelationships among its components.

7. Why does the budgetary process always start with the sales budget?

8. Express as an equation the determination of production levels.

9. Do you agree that budgeting can help a firm plan its employment policy? Explain your answer.

10. Why is it necessary to have a cash budget?

11. Why is depreciation handled differently on income statements and cash budgets?

12. What information is needed to prepare a direct material usage and purchases budget and a direct labor budget?

13. Coordination is as essential as planning. Discuss what would happen if a firm set a budget without checking with its production department.

14. Do you agree with the statement that "the budgeting process increases management's ability to shape the organization's future"? Explain your answer.

15. Why is a flexible budget of more help than a static budget in helping management evaluate performance for a given period?

Exercises

1. Sales and Production Budget. A sales forecast shows that 24,000 units of product A and 24,500 units of product B are going to be sold at a price of $21 and $20, respectively. Ending inventory of product A is expected to be 30% higher than its beginning inventory, which is 2,000 units. Beginning inventory of product B is 2,000 units and its ending inventory is expected to be 10% of production.

Required:

Based on this information, prepare a sales budget and a production budget for both product A and product B.

2. Production Budget. Oakwood Company currently has a finished goods inventory of 10,000 units. The firm produces one product. Unit sales estimates for 1988 follow:

Quarter	Unit Sales
1st	60,000
2nd	80,000
3rd	90,000
4th	75,000
1st 1989	100,000

Oakwood wants an ending inventory each quarter equal to 25% of the next quarter's planned sales.

Required:

Prepare a production budget for Oakwood for each quarter of 1988 and for the year as a whole.

3. Material Purchases Budget. ABC Company manufactures three products—X, Y, and Z. These are made of two materials—M1 and M2. The following information is supplied:

		Cost per Unit	Per-Unit Usage		
			X	Y	Z
a.	M1	$.80	1	—	2
	M2	.50	2	4	1

b. There is no beginning or ending inventory. The production budget is 20,000 units for each product.

Required:

Prepare the material purchases budget.

4. Cash Receipts Budget. The following information is from May Sales Company's 1987 sales account and sales budget:

Sales:	August	$105,000
	September	93,000
Expected sales:	October	90,000
	November	110,000
	December	120,000

Cash sales are 25% of total sales for every month. Approximately 70% of the accounts receivable is collected in the month of sale. Another 20% is collected in the month after sale, and 5% is collected in the second month after sale. The remaining 5% is never collected.

Required:
   a. Prepare a cash receipts budget for May Sales Company for each month of the fourth quarter of 1987.
   b. How might the company motivate the sales force to reduce uncollected sales?

5. Direct Labor Budget. The general manager of a manufacturing company is wondering whether to hire two more workers. The production budget shows that 34,000 units of product X and 36,000 units of product Y are expected to be produced next year. Each unit of product X requires one-half hour of direct labor, and each unit of product Y requires three-quarters of an hour of direct labor. The workload now is 40,000 hours, and each worker is expected to work 2,000 regular hours. The additional cost of hiring a new worker is $8,000; overtime pay is one-half higher than regular pay, which is $10 per hour now. The manager is responsible only for the profitability of the company.

Required:
   a. Compute the total labor cost if the company hires two more workers, and compute the cost if overtime is used instead of hiring new workers.
   b. Which is the more profitable choice?

6. Cash Budget.

Required:
Based on the following information, prepare a cash budget for February 1988 for Handmaster Selling, Inc.:
   1. Sales in February are expected to be 10% higher than those in January, which were $300,000.
   2. Purchases were $200,000 for January and are expected to be $215,000 in February.
   3. There are no cash sales. Credit sales are collected 30% in the month sold and 70% in the month following the sale.
   4. Purchases are paid 50% in the month of purchase and 50% in the month following purchase.
   5. Selling and administrative expenses are as follows:

Salaries and commission	$3,200
Advertising	500
Depreciation, office equipment	2,000

   They are paid when incurred.
   6. A capital investment in office equipment of $20,000 will be made.
   7. The cash balance on February 1 is $15,000.
   8. Ignore income taxes.

7. Factory Overhead Budget.

Required:
Fill in the missing amounts in the following overhead budget:

		January	February
Direct labor budget (in labor hours)		35,000	36,000
Cost	Per direct labor hour		
Variable			
Indirect labor	$?	$28,000	?
Utilities	0.75	?	?
Maintenance	?	?	?
Supervision	0.20	?	?
Total	$2.15	$?	$?
Fixed			
Depreciation		8,000	?
Property taxes and insurance		20,000	20,000
Total		$?	$106,400

8. Cost of Goods Sold Budget. Given the following information prepare a cost of goods sold budget.

Cost of factory overhead	$50,000
Cost of direct labor	80,000
Cost of direct material	50,000
Work-in-process inventory, beginning	15,000
Work-in-process inventory, ending	19,000
Finished goods inventory, beginning	30,000
Finished goods inventory, ending	29,000

9. Income Statement Budget. Given the following data, prepare a budgeted income statement for 1988 for Sharpum Company:

a. Accounts receivable, which has a $2 million balance on December 31, 1987, will increase by $560,000.

b. Credit sales are 80% of total sales, and 100% is collected in the year following the sale.

c. Production cost data are as follows:

Factory overhead cost	$100,000
Direct labor cost	750,000
Direct material cost	650,000
Finished goods inventory, December 31, 1987	270,000
Finished goods inventory, December 31, 1988	250,000
Work-in-process inventory, December 31, 1987	150,000
Work-in-process inventory, December 31, 1988	120,000

d. Selling and administrative expenses are $480,000 plus 10% of total sales.

e. Depreciation expense is $100,000 per year.

f. The estimated income tax rate is 30%.

10. Flexible Budget. The Gatwick Company production foreman has prepared the following comparison between the budget for factory overhead in the master budget and the actual costs incurred:

	Master Budget	Actual	Difference
Supplies	$ 4,500	$ 4,100	$ 400
Utilities	2,250	1,950	300
Indirect labor	4,750	4,500	250
Maintenance	3,200	3,100	100
Depreciation	2,000	2,000	
Total	$16,700	$15,650	$1,050

The foreman believes he has done an excellent job by coming in below the budget and having a favorable variance. Is he right? You have the following additional information:

1066

1. Production level in the master budget is 7,500 units or 15,000 DLH.
2. Actual production level is 6,000 units or 12,000 DLH.
3. Cost behavior patterns of overhead costs are as follows:

Supplies	$.30 per DLH
Utilities	.15 per DLH
Indirect labor	$1,000 + .25 per DLH
Maintenance	2,000 + .08 per DLH
Depreciation	fixed

Required:

a. Prepare a flexible budget for factory overhead based on actual production levels and compare it with the actual costs incurred. Your budget should show all overhead costs. How well did the department do?

b. The foreman reports to the plant manager. What can the plant manager do to motivate the foreman in the future?

Problem Set A

26A-1. Sales through Direct Labor Budgets. Following is information from the Eastwood Company:

			Inventory	
Product	Selling Price per Unit	Expected Sales	Beginning (Actual)	Ending (Expected)
Regular	$4,000	$8,000,000	800	720
Deluxe	$5,000	$6,000,000	600	560

Each unit of finished goods requires the following units of direct materials and direct labor:

	Material		Direct Labor Hours
Product	M1 @ $2.50	M2 @ $3	@ $8 per hour
Regular	6 pounds	4 pounds	2 hours
Deluxe	2 pounds	8 pounds	3 hours

Direct materials inventories are as follows:

	Pounds	
Material	Beginning	Ending
M 1	2,000	3,000
M 2	4,000	4,200

Required:

Prepare the following budgets:

a. Sales.
b. Production.
c. Direct materials purchases and usage.
d. Direct labor.

26A-2. Direct Materials Purchases Budget. Nucomation Company is preparing to do its budget for the first quarter of 1988. The following information has been gathered:

1. Production is budgeted at 2,640 units for January, 2,200 units for February, and 2,625 units for March.
2. Each unit of finished goods needs two pounds of raw material. The purchase price of raw material is expected to be $2 per pound.
3. Actual inventory of raw materials on January 1 is 1,500 pounds. Ending raw materials inventory on March 31 is budgeted at 1,570 pounds.
4. In January, Nucomation will purchase 30% of the total purchases for the first quarter. In February the firm will purchase 35% of the first quarter's purchases, and in March the firm will purchase 35% of the first quarter's purchases.

Required:

a. Compute how many pounds of raw materials will be purchased for each month.
b. What is the ending raw materials inventory for January and February?

26A-3. Sales through Cost of Goods Sold Budgets. Davis Siegal & Sons, Inc., provides you with the following data to be used in preparing budgets for the second quarter ending June 30, 1987. The president has told you to assume that:

1. Eighty thousand units of product are expected to be sold at a price of $50 per unit.
2. Finished goods inventory worth $125,000 at April 1 has a cost of $25 per unit. The ending inventory at June 30 is expected to be 20% higher than the beginning inventory.
3. Each unit of finished goods uses four units of direct material A, three units of material B, and two hours of direct labor. Direct labor cost is $6 per hour.
4. Direct materials inventory at April 1 is 30,000 pounds of A and 32,000 of B. Ending inventory for A and B are expected to be 28,000 pounds and 30,000 pounds, respectively. The purchase price for A is 50 cents per pound, and for B it is 60 cents per pound.
5. Variable factory overhead is expected to be 20% of direct labor cost, whereas fixed factory overhead is expected to be $400,000.
6. The sales manager believes that it is unrealistic to assume that 80,000 units of product can be sold.

Required:

a. Prepare a sales budget.
b. Prepare a production budget.
c. Prepare a direct materials purchases and usage budget.
d. Discuss the motivational issues involved in budgeting 80,000 units of product for the quarter ending June 30, 1987.
e. Prepare a direct labor budget.
f. Prepare a cost of goods sold budget.

26A-4. Cash Budgets. In order to forecast next year's operating cash flows, the controller of Laurie's Company made the following cash budget.

Required:

Fill in the missing amounts (in thousands).

	1	2	3	4	Total
Beginning cash balance	$12	$?	$?	$?	$?
Add: Collections	?	?	90	?	345
Total cash available	92	?	?	?	?
Less: Expenditures					
Purchase of direct material	?	28	?	24	?
Direct labor cost	30	29	28	?	115
Factory overhead	15	14	13	?	55
Selling and administrative	10	10	9	?	38
Fixed assets	15	10	5	10	?
Total expenditures					

	1	2	3	4	Total
Excess (deficiency) of cash available over expenditures	(8)	?	15	?	?
Financing:*					
Borrowings	?	6	—	—	?
Repayments	—	—	(?)	(6)	(?)
Total financing	?	?	?	?	?
Ending cash balance	$?	$?	$?	$?	$?

*A minimum cash balance of at least $5,000 is required to start each quarter. Ignore interest expense.

26A–5. Production, Direct Materials Purchases Budgets, Income Statement, Cash Budget.
Your company began negotiating for a short-term loan with National Bank. In considering the loan, the bank requires a budgeted income statement and a cash budget for the month of April. As the controller of the company, you have the following information:

1. The company manufactures and sells only one product. Sales are budgeted at 100,000 units per month in April, May, and June. Actual sales in March are 98,000 units.
2. The selling price is $4 per unit. Past experience indicates that 60% of the customers pay the bill in the month of sale. The remainder pay in the month following the sale, except for bad debts which average 1 percent.
3. The company wants to have finished goods on hand at the end of each month equal to 20% of expected sales for the following month. This was met on April 1.
4. There is no work in process. Beginning materials inventory on April 1 was 22,000 pounds at a cost of $11,000. Ending inventories of material for each month are to be maintained at no less than 40% of production requirements for the following month. Materials are purchased as needed in quantities of 25,000 pounds per shipment. Material purchases are paid for in the month of purchase. Other manufacturing costs incurred in April for direct labor and factory overhead totalled $293,000.
5. All other costs and expenses are paid on the last day of each month. Selling expenses are 10% of gross sales, administrative expenses (excluding depreciation) total $24,000 per month, and depreciation of office equipment is $500 per month.
6. Gross profit is 25% of sales, and depreciation on factory equipment is $2,000 per month.
7. The cash balance on May 1 is expected to be $40,000.
8. Each finished good uses one-half pound of direct material and one-half hour of direct labor.

juired:

a. Prepare a production budget for April.
b. Prepare a direct materials purchases budget for April.
c. Prepare a budgeted income statement for April.
d. Prepare a cash budget for April.

26A–6. Production Budget through Budgeted Income Statement.
Delta Manufacturing Company has asked for your assistance in developing its budget for 1988. You are supplied with the following data:

1. Expected sales for each quarter are 50,000, 60,000, 80,000, and 54,000 units, respectively. In addition, expected sales for the first quarter of 1989 are 52,000 units. The sales price per unit is $50.
2. The ending inventory of finished goods is 50% of next quarter's sales. The beginning inventory for the first quarter of 1988 is 25,000 units, worth $600,000.
3. Work-in-process at the end of 1987 was $24,000. Work-in-process ending inventory for each quarter of 1988 is expected to be $21,000, $27,000, $22,000, and $28,000.
4. Each unit of finished goods uses one direct labor hour and $3 of direct material. The direct labor rate is $8 per hour.

5. Fixed factory overhead for each quarter is $300,000, and the variable overhead rate is $9 per direct labor hour.
6. Variable selling and administrative expenses are 3% of total sales. Fixed selling and administrative expense for each quarter is $200,000.
7. Income tax is 40% of net income.

Required:

Prepare for each quarter of 1988 and for the total year the following:
 a. A production budget.
 b. A direct labor usage budget.
 c. A cost of goods sold budget.
 d. A budgeted income statement.

26A–7. Cash Budget, Income Statement, Balance Sheet. The balance sheet of Beta Company as of December 31, 1986 follows:

Beta Company
Balance Sheet
December 31, 1986

Assets

Cash	$ 17,250
Accounts receivable	15,200
Inventory	22,750
Plant and equipment, net of depreciation	100,000
Total assets	$155,200

Liabilities and Stockholders' Equity

Accounts payable	$ 16,200
Note payable	20,000
Capital stock	110,000
Retained earnings	9,000
Total liabilities and stockholders' equity	$155,200

The following information has been gathered for the preparation of the budget for January 1987:
1. Sales are budgeted at $100,000. All sales are credit sales. Eighty percent of sales will be collected in the month of sale; the remainder will be collected in the month following the sale. All of December 31, 1986 accounts receivable will be collected during January 1987.
2. Purchases of inventory are expected to be $75,000 during January, all on account. Fifty percent of all purchases are paid for in the month of purchase; the remainder is paid the following month. All of December 31, 1986 accounts payable will be paid during January.
3. The ending balance of inventory is budgeted at $28,000.
4. Operating expenses for January are expected to be $24,000, including depreciation of $2,000. All of these expenses will be paid in cash during January.
5. An investment in equipment costing $2,000 will be made on January 25. Cash will be paid on January 27, the day the equipment will be installed.

Required:
 a. Prepare a cash budget for January.
 b. Prepare a budgeted income statement for January.
 c. Prepare a budgeted balance sheet as of January 31, 1987.

1070

Problem Set B

26B–1. Production through Cost of Goods Sold Budgets. One gallon of A and 1 1/2 gallons of B are required to produce each unit of product P, which is expected to have total sales of 120,000 units at $50 per unit. The costs of A and B are $.80 and $.60 per gallon, respectively. Direct labor of one hour is required for each unit, at a direct labor rate is $8 per hour. Variable factory overhead is 60% of direct labor dollars. Fixed factory overhead is $400,000 per year. There is no work in process at any time. Actual and desired inventory of finished goods and materials are as follows:

	Actual, January 1, 1986	Desired, December 31, 1986
Finished goods	20,000 units ($16 per unit)	25,000 units
Direct material A	60,000 gallons	50,000 gallons
Direct material B	40,000 gallons	35,000 gallons

Required:
- a. Prepare a production budget for 1986.
- b. Prepare a direct materials purchases budget for 1986.
- c. Prepare a direct labor usage budget for 1986.
- d. Prepare a cost of goods sold budget for 1986.
- e. Explain whether the company's employees are more likely to be motivated to achieve these budgets if they are perceived as (1) realistic but attainable, (2) very difficult to attain, or (3) easy to attain.

26B–2. Production, Direct Materials, Direct Labor Budgets. Glenn Company provides you with the following data to be used in preparing budgets for 1988:

Product	Expected Sales (Units)	Inventory Levels (Units)	
		Actual, December 31, 1987	Desired, December 31, 1988
A	1,500	80	100
B	25,000	8,000	1,000
C	8,000	300	400

Each product requires the following units of material and labor:

Product	Material (@ $2 per Pound)	Labor (@ $5 per Hour)
A	2	2
B	3	3
C	1	4

Direct material inventory on December 31, 1987 was 1,800 pounds and is expected to be 2,000 pounds on December 31, 1988.

Required:
- a. Prepare a production budget for 1988.
- b. Prepare a direct materials purchases and usage budget for 1988.
- c. Prepare a direct labor budget for 1988.
- d. These budgets are substantially higher than last year's budgets. Is that fact likely to increase or decrease employees' motivation to achieve the budgets?

26B–3. Production, Direct Materials, Direct Labor Budgets. The Barker Company expects to sell 130,000 units of its product in the first quarter of 1987; 100,000 in the second quarter; 240,000 in the third quarter; and 150,000 in the fourth quarter. Expected sales for the first and second quarters of 1988 are 100,000 units. Ending finished goods inventories for each quarter are required to be maintained at 50% of expected sales for the coming quarter. Beginning inventory for the first quarter of 1987 is expected to be 60,000 units. Each unit of finished goods uses 2 units of material A, 1 unit of B, and .80 direct labor hours. Beginning inventories of materials A and B at the start of 1987 are 40,000 units and 30,000 units, at a cost of $32,000 and $30,000, respectively. Ending inventories are required to be maintained at 10% of the next quarter's production. The company has 60 direct labor workers; each is expected to work 50 weeks for 40 hours per week, at a rate of $6 per hour. The overtime rate is $9 per hour.

Required:

a. Prepare a production budget for each quarter of 1987.

b. Prepare a direct materials purchases and usage budget for each quarter.

c. Prepare a direct labor budget for each quarter.

26B–4. Cash Budget. You are asked to assist in preparing a cash budget. The following information is available:

1.

Expected 1987 sales:	January	$400,000	Actual 1986:	November	$480,000
	February	420,000		December	500,000
	March	480,000			

2. Collections are usually 60% during the month of sale, 30% in the first month following the sale, and 10% in the second month following the sale.

3. The cost of goods purchased averages 70% of the selling price. Half of the purchases are paid for during the month of purchase, and the other half are paid for in the month following the purchase. The inventory remains at a constant level.

4. Variable expenses amount to 15% of sales. Fixed expenses are $50,000 per month, of which $25,000 is for depreciation. Payment for expenses is 60% during the month incurred and 40% in the following month.

5. A cash dividend of $10,000 will be paid on January 15.

6. Office equipment of $100,000 will be purchased at the end of March.

7. The cash balance on December 31, 1986 is $120,000.

8. The minimum required cash balance is $100,000.

Required:

Prepare a cash budget for each month of the first quarter of 1987.

26B–5. Cash Budget, Income Statement, Balance Sheet. The following information comes from Mayflower Company as of March 31, 1988:

1.

Cash	$ 12,000
Accounts receivable	20,000
Inventory	30,000
Equipment, net of depreciation	150,000
Accounts payable	32,000
Capital stock	165,000
Retained earnings	15,000

2. Sales for April are budgeted at $100,000. Of these sales, $40,000 will be for cash. Sixty percent of credit sales will be collected in the month of sale, and 40% will be collected in the month following the sale. All of the March 31 accounts receivable will be collected during April.

3. Purchases of inventory are expected to be $60,000 during April, all on account. Forty percent of purchases are paid for in the month of purchase; the remainder is paid for in the month following the purchase. All of the March 31 accounts payable will be paid during April.

4. The April 30 inventory balance is expected to be $28,000.

5. Operating expenses for April are expected to be $25,000 (including depreciation, which is $3,000). All expenses will be paid for in cash in the month incurred.

6. Office equipment valued at $20,000 will be acquired for cash on April 1.

Required:

a. Prepare a cash budget for April 1988.

b. Prepare a budgeted income statement for April 1988.

c. Prepare a budgeted balance sheet as of April 30, 1988.

26B–6. Sales, Production, Direct Materials Budgets. Crocker Company makes and sells a single product. Management has gathered the following information in order to prepare the budget for the first two quarters of 1989:

1.

Sales

	1st Quarter	2nd Quarter
Selling price	$2	$2
Sales (units)	100,000	120,000

2.

Inventory

	1st Quarter	2nd Quarter
Finished goods (units)		
Beginning	30,000	40,000
Ending	40,000	36,000
Materials		
Beginning	$10,000	$12,000
Ending	$12,000	$12,000

3. Gross profit is 40% of sales.

4. Selling and administrative expenses are $.30 per unit sold plus $35,000 per quarter.

5. Each unit of finished goods requires $.50 direct materials.

Required:

a. Prepare sales budgets for the first two quarters of 1989.

b. Prepare production budgets for the first two quarters of 1989.

c. Prepare direct materials purchases and usage budgets for the first two quarters of 1989.

26B–7. Cash Budget, Income Statement, Balance Sheet. Buill Company is preparing its budget for September; the following information is available:

1. Actual sales in August were $20,000. Sales are expected to be $25,000 for September and $32,000 for October.

2. Sales are 40% for cash and 60% on credit. Accounts are collected in the month following the sale.

3. The gross profit rate is 30% of sales.

4. Monthly expenses are as follows: salaries and expenses, 15% of total sales; rent, $1,100 per month; other fixed expenses (excluding depreciation), 5% of sales. Depreciation is $5,000 per month.

5. Ending inventory at the end of each month is required to be 25% of the following month's sales.

6. Half of the purchases are paid for in the month of purchase, and the other half are paid for in the month following the purchase.

7. Major accounts from the balance sheet as of August 30 are as follows:

Cash	$ 3,000
Accounts receivable	12,000
Inventory	13,000
Fixed assets, net	75,000
Accounts payable	8,000
Capital stock	87,000
Retained earnings	8,000

Required:

a. Prepare a budgeted income statement for September.

b. Prepare a cash budget for September.

c. Based on the cash budget, what kind of financing should be arranged to meet the requirement of a minimum ending cash balance of $25,000?

d. Prepare a budgeted balance sheet as of September 30.

26B–8. Master Budget. Assume the operating results in 1987 were exactly the same as budgeted for the Selectron Manufacturing Corporation discussed in this chapter. Now prepare a master budget for Selectron for the fiscal year 1988 based on the following information:

1.

Expected Sales

	Regular	Deluxe
Units of product	40,000	18,000
Selling price per unit	$10	$20
Beginning inventory 12/31/87 (units)	5,000	1,200
Desired ending inventory 12/31/88 (units)	4,000	1,200

2. Work in process will not change and will remain at the same level as on the December 31, 1987 balance sheet.

3. Direct materials cost, direct labor costs, and factory overhead costs, and selling and administration expense will remain the same as the 1987 estimates shown on page 1043.

4. Direct material inventories in pounds:

	Material X	Material Y
Beginning inventory 12/31/87	5,000	2,000
Desired ending inventory 12/31/88	4,800	1,800

5. Accounts receivable at the end of the fiscal year generally were 10% of yearly sales.

6. The levels of accounts payable and accrued wages payable will remain the same as on the December 31, 1987 balance sheet.

7. Office equipment will be installed in 1988 at a cost of $40,000.

8. Depreciation averages 10% of the original cost of property, plant, and equipment.

9. Other current assets remained at the same level as on the December 31, 1987 balance sheet, shown in Schedule 11.

Required:

a. Prepare a sales budget for 1988.

b. Prepare a production budget in units for 1988.

c. Prepare a direct materials purchases and usage budget for 1988.

d. Prepare a direct labor budget for 1988.

e. Prepare a factory overhead budget for 1988.

f. Prepare an ending inventory budget for 1988.

g. Prepare a cost of goods sold budget for 1988.

h. Prepare a selling and administrative expense budget for 1988.

i. Prepare a cash budget for 1988.

j. Prepare a budgeted income statement for 1988.

k. Prepare a budgeted balance sheet as of December 31, 1988.

Using the Computer

A. Using the data from Problem 26B–2, prepare a single spreadsheet that includes a production budget, a direct materials purchases and usage budget, and a direct labor budget for Glenn Company.

B. The market for Glenn Company's products has become more competitive, with a resulting decrease in sales for products A, B, and C of 10%, 20%, and 15%, respectively. Calculate the new budget figures on the spreadsheet. How much did the direct materials purchase cost and direct labor cost change?

C. Glenn Company has decided to upgrade products A and C in order to compete more effectively. The firm believes that the projected changes will increase sales by 20% for each product (from the level in part B). The new version of A requires 3 pounds of direct material, and B needs 2 pounds of direct material. Because more material is being used, the firm now wants an ending materials inventory of 2,700 pounds. In addition, product A now requires an increase of one-half hour of direct labor, while product B requires an increase of one hour of direct labor. Prepare a production budget, a direct materials purchases and usage budget, and a direct labor budget for Glenn Company. How much did the cost of direct materials and direct labor change from the amount you calculated in part B? Do these changes increase or decrease the direct labor cost?

Decision Case

ActionLine, Inc. operates two stores that sell athletic shoes of all types, as well as some lines of shorts, sweatshirts, and pants for men and women. The firm has not done formal budgeting in the past, but the president believes it would be beneficial in the coming year to prepare budgeted income statements. The managers of the two stores have prepared the following budget data:

	Eastside Store	Westside Store
Sales revenue:		
Athletic shoes	$435,000	$250,000
Clothing	100,000	72,000
Total	$535,000	$322,000
Store expenses:		
Rent	$ 22,000	$ 24,050
Supervisory and clerical salaries	32,000	20,050
Sales salaries	16,000	17,000
Utilities	4,600	4,200
Depreciation, furniture and fixtures	5,100	5,900
Total	$ 79,700	$ 71,200

During the next year, the athletic shoes the firm purchases are expected to cost 45% of the selling prices, and the selling prices of the clothing lines are expected to be double their purchase cost. The president has prepared budget data for the coming year for the head office:

Executive salaries	$ 70,000
Clerical salaries	36,000
Rent	19,000
Advertising	30,000
Office supplies	4,500
CPA fees	3,800
Miscellaneous	1,600
Total	$164,900

Required:

   a. Prepare budgeted income statement data for the coming year.

   b. What assumptions did you use in preparing the data?

   c. What problems do you think the president and the store managers faced in preparing their sales and expense data? What were their principal sources of information?

Accounting Information for Control of Cost Centers: Job Order and Process Costing

27

LEARNING OBJECTIVES

After reading this chapter you should be able to:

1. Understand the functions of cost accounting systems.
2. Trace the overall flow of costs in a manufacturing system.
3. Compare the general characteristics of job order and process costing systems.
4. Account for materials and labor in a job order system.
5. Account for actual overhead costs and apply factory overhead using a predetermined overhead rate.
6. Determine the cost of finished units of product and cost of goods sold in a job order system.
7. Understand the basic concepts and steps involved in process costing.
8. Calculate the equivalent units of production.
9. Identify the flow of costs and determine the unit cost and cost of goods sold in a process cost system.
10. Prepare a cost production report for a processing center.

The last four chapters have explained how accounting information is used in planning and decision making. This chapter focuses on the area of control. Recall that Chapter 22 defined the organizational control system as "a set of processes and techniques designed to increase the likelihood that people will behave in ways that lead to the attainment of an organization's objectives." Exhibit 27–1 depicts the model of a control system shown earlier.

This chapter focuses on the measurement aspects of the control system shown in Exhibit 27–1 (on the next page), in particular, the manufacturing departments that are usually viewed as cost centers. Within the framework of responsibility accounting as described in Chapter 22, a cost center is held

EXHIBIT 27–1
Schematic Model of the Control System

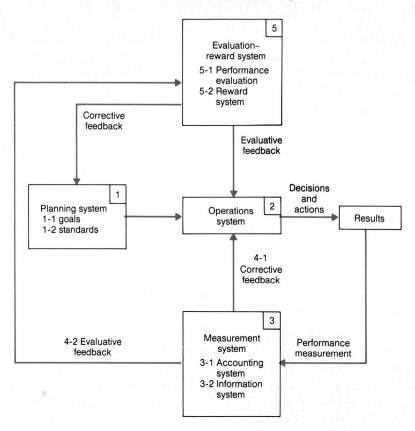

responsible only for incurring costs in the manner set forth in the budget. The accounting system measures how a cost center incurs costs, and that information is then used in the evaluation of performance and subsequent rewards.

The Nature of Cost Accounting Systems

A manufacturing firm must carefully account for the costs involved in the manufacturing process. As shown in Chapter 26, many of the schedules used in the budgeting process are designed to estimate what various manufacturing costs will be for the next period. **Cost accounting systems** are the systems set up as part of the overall accounting system to identify the costs of making a product. These costs are then used to determine the value of inventory and cost of goods sold for financial reports, for pricing, and for certain types of decision making such as cost-volume-profit analysis. As we have seen, in order to make many short-term decisions, the management of manufacturing firms must know the cost of manufacturing a product in different situations.

The cost accounting system simultaneously accumulates information to determine the cost of the units of product and distributes the cost information to the various departments involved in the manufacturing process. Most of these departments or smaller areas, such as groups of machines, are viewed as cost centers. The cost accounting system thus has two objectives in measuring performance for a period: (1) determining the cost of making the units of product for financial reporting and decision-making purposes and (2) accumulating the costs incurred by the cost centers involved in the manufacturing process in order to evaluate their performance relative to budget. The same cost data can be viewed in more than one way, depending on the uses of the information. We will concentrate on the first objective, the cost of making the units of product. Keep in mind, however, that while the accounting system accumulates data on the cost of units of product, it also uses those cost data to evaluate the performance of cost centers.

Flow of Costs in a Manufacturing System

The accounting system shows what happens to a firm's costs in dollar terms when units of product are manufactured. The flow of costs through the accounting system is very similar to what happens in the actual manufacturing process. Exhibit 27–2 shows both the manufacturing process and the flow of costs through the accounts. When a firm buys materials and supplies, they are stored in a warehouse, and the account Raw Materials shows the number of dollars spent on those items. When materials are issued to the production department in a factory, they are combined with labor and overhead in the production process. Similarly, the Work in Process account shows the cost of direct materials, direct labor, and factory overhead used in making units of product. When the product is finished, it leaves the factory and is sent to a finished goods warehouse, and the accounting system transfers the costs of finished units of product to a Finished Goods inventory account. When a product is sold, it is shipped to the buyer, and the accounting system transfers the cost of the units sold to the Cost of Goods Sold account. It is useful to keep the actual manufacturing process in mind because the flow of costs in manufacturing systems parallels what happens in physically making units of product.

EXHIBIT 27–2
Flow of Costs in a Manufacturing Firm

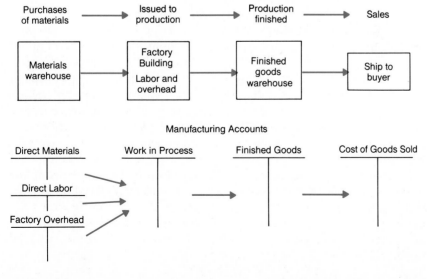

There are two basic types of product costing systems: job order costing and process costing. The nature of the product and the manufacturing process determines which type of system a firm will use.

Job Order Costing

Job order costing is a cost accounting system that accumulates the cost of manufacturing specific products, jobs, or batches of production. It is used in manufacturing situations where each job or batch of products is different from other jobs. In the construction industry, for example, each construction project may require different amounts of materials, labor, and overhead. Similarly, a printing job for wedding invitations differs from a job for business cards. Therefore, the accounting system accumulates the materials, labor, and overhead for each job on a job cost sheet. From the total cost of each job, a firm can figure out the cost of each unit in the job.

Process Costing

Firms use **process costing** when a product is manufactured and all units of the product are identical. The units of product flow through the manufacturing process on a continuous basis, generally in large volumes. In industries such as textiles, lumber, and food processing, it would not be practical or useful to keep track of individual batches of product. Each batch of frozen french fries, for example, is supposed to be just like all the other batches. For this reason, in a process costing system, costs are accumulated for the various processes or departments used to manufacture the product. Total manufacturing costs for a process or department in a given period of time are then divided by the units produced during that time to attain a broad average cost per unit of product.

Job Order Costing

A job order cost system focuses on the individual job or batch of product. The system keeps track of the costs of each job, and a job cost sheet is used for this purpose. Exhibit 27–3 shows a typical job cost sheet for Precision Machine Company. Each **job cost sheet** is divided into three basic sections—materials, labor, and overhead—so that each cost element can be accounted for separately. In addition, there is usually a section that summarizes the costs and determines the cost of each unit of product. A job cost sheet is prepared only when a company has a firm sales order with terms agreed on in writing.

The job cost sheet is, however, only one part of a job order cost system. The example following Exhibit 27–3 on the next page will show how materials, labor, and overhead flow through the entire system in order to determine product costs for financial reporting and decision making. Data for the month of December 1988 for the Precision Machine Company will be used. The company had two jobs in process at the beginning of December: job 20 with $20,000 already spent on the job by December 1, and job 21 with $25,000 of manufacturing costs accumulated by December 1. During December the firm started work on new jobs 22 and 23. The inventory accounts and job cost sheets on December 1 follow:

EXHIBIT 27–3
Job Cost Sheet

Job Cost Sheet								
Customer _____			Job Number _____					
Product _____			Date Promised _____					
Quantity _____			Date Started _____					
			Date Completed _____					

Dates	Direct Materials		Direct Labor			Factory Overhead		
	Requisition Numbers	Amt.	Time Ticket Number	Hours	Amt.	Base	Rate	Amt.
Totals								
Comments:							Total Job Cost	

Raw Materials		Work in Process		Finished Goods	
Balance 5,000		Balance 45,000			

Job 20	
Balance 20,000	

Job 21	
Balance 25,000	

Accounting for Materials

Precision Machine Company uses two kinds of materials directly in the production of its products—materials A and B. During December the firm purchased $25,000 each of direct material A and direct material B. It also bought $10,000 of material C, which is used in many jobs and is considered to be an

EXHIBIT 27–4
Materials Ledger Card

| | Materials Ledger Card | | | | | |

Name _____

Number _____

Supplier _____ Description _____

Invoice Number and Date	Received		Issued		Balance	
	Quantity	Price	Quantity	Price	Quantity	Price

indirect material. Precision must keep track of each material as well as the total purchases of raw materials. This is done by keeping a **materials ledger card** for each material used in the manufacturing process and by recording the total cost of materials purchased in the Raw Materials inventory account. Exhibit 27–4 shows a typical ledger card for materials, with the balance at the start of the month, the quantities purchased and their corresponding costs, the material issued to production, and the balance left. Many firms now keep these types of records on computer files, but although they may no longer be actual cards, materials records must keep track of each material used in production.

The journal entry, labeled (1), to record the total purchases of raw materials for the month of December follows:

(1)

Raw Materials	60,000	
Accounts Payable		60,000

Exhibit 27–5 shows the ledger cards for materials A, B, and C and the Raw Materials inventory account with the total cost of purchases for the month. The Raw Materials inventory account serves as a control account for the individual materials ledger cards. The costs on all of the materials ledger cards should equal the total cost shown in the Raw Materials inventory account.

During December materials were issued to the production department from the storeroom. Some type of materials requisition form usually is necessary to release materials from the storeroom; it specifies the quantities and types of materials and the jobs they are to be used on. Precision Machine

Company's production department requisitioned $24,000 each of direct materials A and B during the month of December, and they requisitioned $6,000 of indirect material C. The cost of direct materials A and B are posted to the Work in Process inventory account and on the individual job cost sheets. Indirect material C, a part of the factory overhead costs for the period, is posted to the Factory Overhead account. Journal entry (2) is made to record the issuance of materials to production for December:

(2)

Work in Process	48,000	
Factory Overhead	6,000	
Raw Materials		54,000

Exhibit 27–6 (on the next page) shows how direct materials A and B are assigned to specific jobs in production. For example, job 20 used $2,000 worth of material A, job 21 used $1,000, and jobs 22 and 23 used $12,000 and $9,000, respectively. Because materials A and B are assigned directly to jobs, they are charged to Work in Process. Note that the Work in Process account summarizes all of the information on the individual job cost sheets so that it, too, functions as a control account. Perform a check now by adding all of the costs shown on all of the job cost sheets in Exhibit 27–6. They should add up to $93,000, the total in Work in Process. The Factory Overhead account accumulates overhead costs for the period, which is why indirect material C is posted to that account.

EXHIBIT 27–5
Purchase of Raw Materials

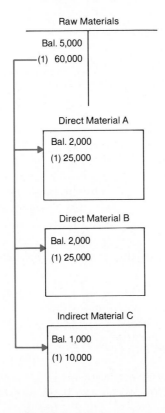

EXHIBIT 27–6

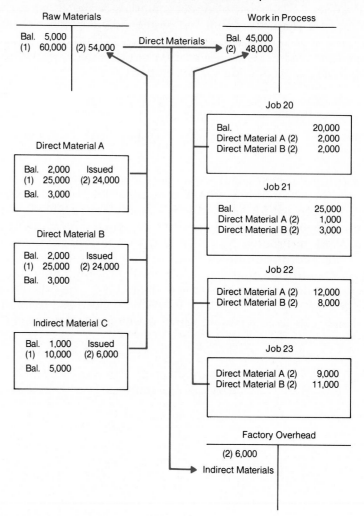

Accounting for Labor

As employees perform their work during a period, they record their hourly activities on time tickets which are then forwarded to the accounting department. There the hours are multiplied by the labor rates to calculate the cost of labor for the month. Direct labor costs are charged to Work in Process and to the individual jobs on which they were incurred. Indirect labor costs, such as maintenance and supervision, are part of factory overhead for the period. Journal entry (3) summarizes the cost of direct labor for Precision for the month of December:

(3)

Work in Process	60,000	
Factory Overhead	10,000	
Wages Payable		70,000

Exhibit 27–7 illustrates how direct labor costs are distributed to each job cost sheet, with the total of $60,000 charged to Work in Process. The job cost sheets

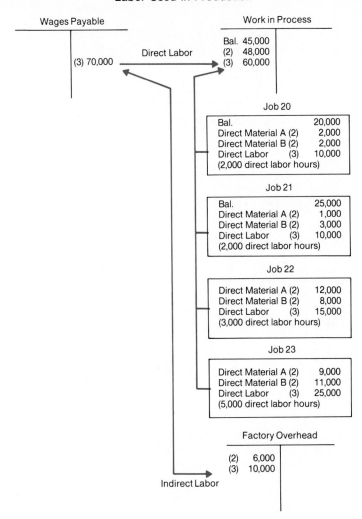

EXHIBIT 27-7
Labor Used in Production

Wages Payable			Work in Process	
	(3) 70,000		Bal.	45,000
			(2)	48,000
			(3)	60,000

Direct Labor

Job 20

Bal.		20,000
Direct Material A	(2)	2,000
Direct Material B	(2)	2,000
Direct Labor	(3)	10,000
(2,000 direct labor hours)		

Job 21

Bal.		25,000
Direct Material A	(2)	1,000
Direct Material B	(2)	3,000
Direct Labor	(3)	10,000
(2,000 direct labor hours)		

Job 22

Direct Material A	(2)	12,000
Direct Material B	(2)	8,000
Direct Labor	(3)	15,000
(3,000 direct labor hours)		

Job 23

Direct Material A	(2)	9,000
Direct Material B	(2)	11,000
Direct Labor	(3)	25,000
(5,000 direct labor hours)		

Factory Overhead

(2)	6,000
(3)	10,000

Indirect Labor

also show how many direct labor hours have been used on each job. The indirect labor of $10,000 is a part of factory overhead, whereas the total labor costs of the period ($70,000) are shown in Wages Payable. The preceding example has ignored payroll withholding taxes in order to focus on manufacturing costs.

Accounting for Actual Factory Overhead

As noted before, the Factory Overhead account includes all manufacturing costs other than direct materials and direct labor. These costs are entered in the Factory Overhead account as they are incurred. Because overhead includes many types of costs, generally there are subsidiary accounts to keep track of individual items. Assume, for example, that Precision Machine Company had the following overhead costs, in addition to the indirect materials and indirect labor already posted to the overhead account:

Depreciation of equipment	$ 5,000
Rent	25,000
Insurance	3,000
Utilities	8,000
Taxes	2,000
Supervisory salaries	27,000
Total	$70,000

Journal entry (4) shows how the preceding items would be recorded. Assume for simplicity that all of the items except deprciation are credited to Accounts Payable:

(4)

Factory Overhead	70,000	
Accumulated Depreciation		5,000
Accounts Payable		65,000

The T accounts for these items follow:

Factory Overhead		**Accumulated Depreciation**	
(2) 6,000			(4) 5,000
(3) 10,000			
(4) 70,000			

Accounts Payable	
	(4) 65,000

Note that recording actual factory overhead costs for the month of December had no effect on Work in Process because the amount of factory overhead that is charged to Work in Process is calculated through an overhead rate that is decided on during the budgeting process.

Applying Factory Overhead Using a Predetermined Rate

Factory overhead is a basic manufacturing cost, but it is made up of a wide variety of costs—both fixed and variable—that are difficult to trace directly to a specific product or job. Overhead includes only costs that are indirect costs of making the unit of product. For example, Precision would find it very diffi-cult to trace the $8,000 of utilities spent in December to specific jobs. Because of this, some other method has to be used to assign overhead to jobs and to work in process. Most firms do this by estimating overhead cost for the coming period and dividing that estimate by an activity base that is common to all of the products the firm manufactures. The most frequently used activity bases are direct labor hours (DLH), direct labor cost, and machine hours. For exam-ple, Precision believes that direct labor hours is the activity that has the great-est effect on the levels of manufacturing costs. As the number of direct labor hours used in the production process increases, the quantity of all manufactur-ing costs increases. Therefore, during the budgeting process Precision esti-mated factory overhead costs for the coming year and estimated the usage of direct labor hours for the year. The overhead cost is divided by the estimated activity level to calculate the overhead rate. The overhead rate is then used to apply overhead costs to jobs as they are finished during the period. The basic relationship for computing the overhead rate follows:

$$\frac{\text{Estimated factory overhead costs}}{\text{Estimated activity base level (i.e., DLH)}} = \frac{\text{Predetermined overhead rate}}{\text{(i.e., per DLH)}}$$

Actual overhead costs are not used to calculate the overhead rate because overhead is not known until the end of the period. A company cannot wait until a period ends before finding out the cost of a job because that information is needed for pricing and to make other decisions throughout the year. In addition, some overhead costs, such as utilities, may fluctuate from season to season, and if those costs were used to allocate overhead to the product, the cost of the product also would fluctuate. Thus, a company is better off using an annual estimate so that product costs also do not fluctuate. As shown in Chapter 26, during the budgeting process estimates of factory overhead and activity levels are made so that an overhead rate can be used throughout the next period for costing units of product.

A **predetermined overhead rate** is used throughout the year to assign overhead cost to individual jobs and to work in process. Precision Machine Company, for example, estimated factory overhead costs for 1988 at $1 million and direct labor hours for the year at 200,000 when the overhead rate was calculated:

$$\frac{\$1,000,000}{200,000 \text{ DLH}} = \$5 \text{ per DLH}$$

During December the company used 12,000 direct labor hours, so the total cost of overhead for the month is $60,000 (12,000 × $5). Journal entry (5) shows how the total cost of overhead is recorded:

(5)		
Work in Process	60,000	
Factory Overhead		60,000

Exhibit 27–8 (on the following page) illustrates how the overhead cost is distributed to individual job cost sheets as well as to Work in Process. Remember that Exhibit 27–7 showed not only the dollar cost of the labor for each job, but the number of direct labor hours as well. For example, job 22 used 3,000 direct labor hours in December, and therefore it receives $15,000 of the overhead cost (3,000 × $5). Again, the total of the job cost sheets should equal the total costs in Work in Process.

Look carefully at the Factory Overhead account and note that the cost calculated through the predetermined overhead rate is removed from the Overhead account and posted to Work in Process. This is called applying overhead to work in process. The actual overhead costs remain in the Overhead account throughout the period. Exhibit 27–9 on the next page illustrates basic acounting for overhead in T accounts, showing actual overhead and **applied overhead.**

Usually there is a difference between actual overhead costs and the portion of overhead applied to Work in Process because the predetermined overhead rate is based on estimates. In Exhibit 27–8, for example, actual overhead was $86,000, whereas only $60,000 was applied to Work in Process. This example illustrates what is called **underapplied overhead,** because less overhead was applied to Work in Process than the actual overhead costs for the period.

EXHIBIT 27–8
Factory Overhead

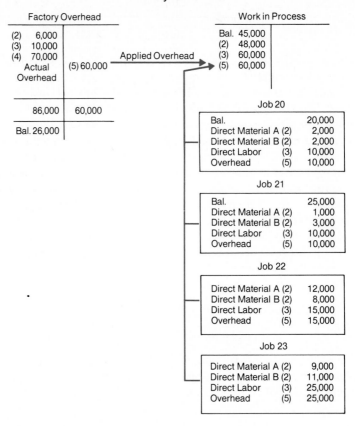

When applied overhead exceeds actual overhead, the result is **overapplied overhead.** The differences that arise from month to month are usually carried forward because the underapplied overhead of one month is offset against the overapplied overhead of another month. At the end of a year, any final difference between actual and applied overhead is either divided up among the inventory accounts and Cost of Goods Sold or just closed into Cost of Goods Sold. Although it is more accurate on a theoretical basis to show that the difference between actual and applied overhead relates to all units of inventory in Work in Process, Finished Goods, and Cost of Goods Sold, it is rarely done in practice because it is much simpler to adjust only Cost of Goods Sold. The adjusting entry to close the Factory Overhead account and transfer the

EXHIBIT 27–9
Accounting for Actual and Estimated Overhead

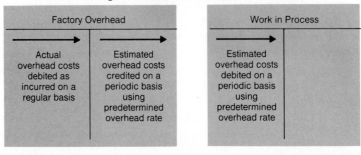

difference to Cost of Goods Sold at the end of the fiscal year follows. Because Precision applied less overhead to Work in Process than the actual overhead costs, the difference of $26,000 is added to Cost of Goods Sold:

(I)

Cost of Goods Sold	26,000	
Factory Overhead		26,000

Cost of Finished Units of Product

When a job is finished, it is transferred from production to the finished goods warehouse. At the same time, the cost accounting system must transfer the cost of the job from Work in Process to Finished Goods Inventory. Precision Machine finished jobs 20 and 21 in December. Each of these jobs had a beginning balance and incurred additional costs of direct materials, direct labor, and factory overhead. Job 20 now has a balance of $44,000 and job 21 has a balance of $49,000. Journal entry (6) shows the transfer of these two jobs to Finished Goods:

(6)

Finished Goods Inventory	93,000	
Work in Process		93,000

The T accounts in Exhibit 27–10 (on the next page) show this process in more detail. The total costs for jobs 20 and 21 are now available, and the firm can compute the cost per unit of finished product. For example, job 20 consisted of 10 machines, at a cost per machine of $4,400. This information helps management in pricing and decisions about future jobs. The exhibit also shows that the firm needs to keep information about each type of finished product as well as the total cost. Therefore, there usually is some type of finished goods subsidiary ledger and the total cost of finished goods is carried in the Finished Goods Inventory account which then functions as a control account. The costs shown for the individual finished items should equal the total in the Finished Goods Inventory account.

Cost of Goods Sold

When units of product are sold, the unit cost is used to transfer the cost of the units sold from Finished Goods to the Cost of Goods Sold account. At the same time, the sales revenue and the asset received—cash or a receivable—also are recognized. To continue the example, Precision Machine sells two units from job 20 for $6,000 each. Journal entries (7) and (8) summarize this transaction:

(7)

Cost of Goods Sold	8,800	
Finished Goods Inventory		8,800

(8)

Accounts Receivable	12,000	
Sales Revenue		12,000

Exhibit 27–11 (on the next page) illustrates the sale of these units in T account form. Note that the subsidiary ledger for finished goods reflects the sale of the units so that management knows the current stock on hand. The

EXHIBIT 27-10
Cost of Finished Units of Product

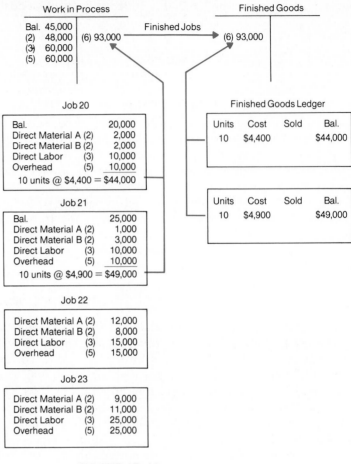

EXHIBIT 27-11
Cost of Goods Sold

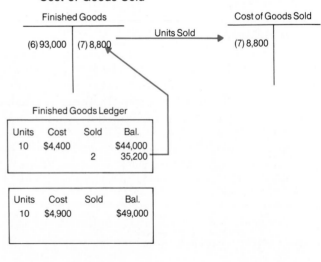

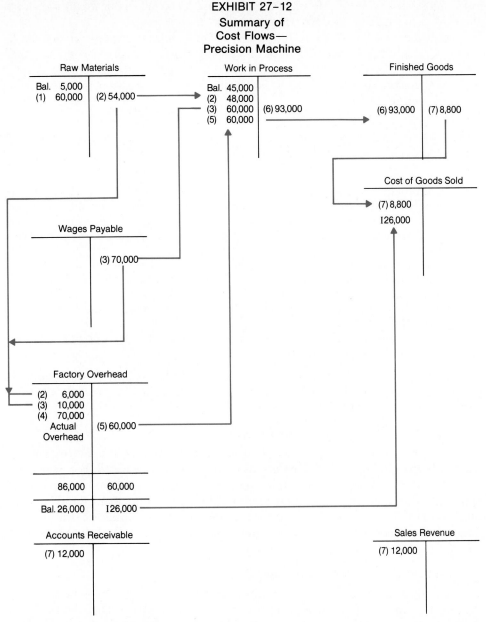

EXHIBIT 27-12
Summary of
Cost Flows—
Precision Machine

Raw Materials	
Bal. 5,000	(2) 54,000
(1) 60,000	

Work in Process	
Bal. 45,000	(6) 93,000
(2) 48,000	
(3) 60,000	
(5) 60,000	

Finished Goods	
(6) 93,000	(7) 8,800

Cost of Goods Sold	
(7) 8,800	
126,000	

Wages Payable	
	(3) 70,000

Factory Overhead	
(2) 6,000	(5) 60,000
(3) 10,000	
(4) 70,000	
Actual	
Overhead	
86,000	60,000
Bal. 26,000	126,000

Accounts Receivable	
(7) 12,000	

Sales Revenue	
	(7) 12,000

cost of the units sold will eventually be found on the income statement, whereas the balance left in the Finished Goods Inventory will be shown with the other inventory accounts on the balance sheet.

Exhibit 27-12 summarizes the entire sequence of transactions for the Precision Machine Company.

Process Costing

As noted earlier, process costing is used to account for manufactured products that are alike. In such industries as lumber, bricks, paint, cement, and food processing, there is a continuous flow of homogeneous products. The flow of

Accounting Information for Control of Cost Centers

costs is essentially the same in process costing as in job order costing except the costs are assigned to departments rather than to jobs.

A process costing system, therefore, divides the manufacturing costs of a process for a period by the output of that period in order to get a broad average cost per unit. The cost of production report summarizes the activity in a system for a period, usually a month. Following are the basic steps involved in a process costing system.

Steps in Process Costing

Five basic steps are generally followed in a process costing system:

1. Identify the process centers involved in manufacturing a given product.
2. Accumulate the three basic manufacturing costs—direct materials, direct labor, and factory overhead—for each processing center for the specified period of time.
3. Calculate how many units of finished product were produced by each processing center.
4. Divide the total costs for each processing center by the number of equivalent finished units of product produced to determine the cost per unit of product for each process. Use the cost per unit of product in a process to calculate the cost of the units finished and transferred out of the process and the cost of the units left unfinished.
5. Add the unit costs of all of the processing centers in order to determine the total cost of each unit produced.

We will examine each of these basic steps in order to explain the concepts of process costing, and then we will turn to a more complex example of how such a system operates.

Identification of Process Centers

The **process centers** are the locations or departments in a factory where work is performed directly on the goods that are being produced. For example, a company producing a soft drink might have mixing and bottling process centers, and a firm making metal containers might have cutting and assembling process centers. In a processing center, all of the units of product go through the process in a uniform manner, and therefore, all of the units that emerge are, for the most part, the same.

Accumulate Manufacturing Costs

The basic procedures for accumulating manufacturing costs in Work in Process is similar for job order and process costing systems. The difference is that, in process costing, the costs are accumulated for a processing center, usually a department, rather than for a job. Materials are requisitioned from the storeroom and debited to departments. Direct materials are posted to the Work in Process account for the department; indirect materials, used by many departments, are posted to Factory Overhead. Similarly, labor used directly by a department is charged to the Work in Process account for that department, and labor costs incurred by many departments go to Factory Overhead. Each department or process has a Work in Process account where manufacturing costs are accumulated. Predetermined overhead rates also can be calculated by department or process, and over- or underapplied overhead is handled in the same way as in job order costing. Exhibit 27–13 illustrates the flow of costs to processing centers in a process costing system.

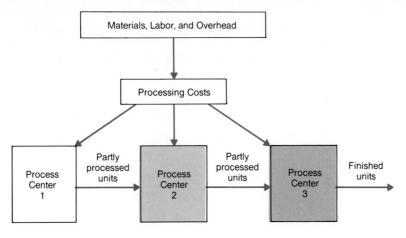

EXHIBIT 27–13
Flow of Costs to Processing Centers

Calculate Units of Finished Product

In order to determine the cost per unit of product for each processing center, a firm needs to know the manufacturing costs for that department and the number of units produced:

$$\frac{\text{Manufacturing costs for process}}{\text{Finished units produced}} = \text{Cost per unit}$$

For example, assume that the mixing department of a soft drink company has accumulated the following costs for the month:

Direct materials	$3,500
Direct labor	1,500
Factory overhead	1,000
Total	$6,000

The department has produced 7,500 liters of product during the month, and the computation of cost per unit is straightforward:

$$\frac{\$6,000}{7,500} = \$.80 \text{ per unit}$$

Most of the time, however, there are some units of product that are not finished at the end of a period, but it is still necessary to account for the work done on those units, even though they are not finished. In order to accurately measure the total productive output of the department, the work done on partially finished units is converted into the equivalent of finished units of product. These are called **equivalent units** of production, defined as the productive output of a process or department for a period expressed in terms of finished units of product. For example, two units of product, each half-finished at the end of a period, are equivalent to one finished unit. Although both units are *not* finished, the work done on them is equivalent or equal to one finished

EXHIBIT 27–14
Concept of Equivalent Units

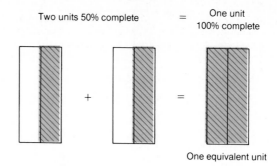

unit. A calculation of the work done during that period would combine the completed units of product and the equivalent units of finished product. Exhibit 27–14 diagrams the concept of equivalent units of production.

Returning to the mixing department example, assume that the firm has incurred the same $6,000 of manufacturing costs. Assume, however, that the department finished 7,000 liters of product during the month and had 500 liters left in process that were 25% complete. To compute the equivalent units of production for the period, add the finished units to the work done on the partially finished units, expressed in terms of finished units of product:

	Work Done	Equivalent Units
Units totally finished at end of period	7,000	100%	7,000
Units in process	500	25%	125
Total			7,125

The computation of cost per unit follows:

$$\frac{\text{Manufacturing costs}}{\text{Equivalent units of finished product}} = \text{Cost per unit } \frac{\$6,000}{7,125} = \$.84 \text{ per unit}$$

The previous illustration assumed that materials, labor, and overhead were all added evenly throughout the manufacturing process. In some manufacturing processes, however, materials, labor, and overhead may be added at different points; when this happens it affects the amount of productive work done for a period for the different manufacturing cost centers. For example, if all of the direct materials are added at the start of the manufacturing process, a unit of product that is unfinished may still contain all of its direct materials. The unit may not require more materials—only more labor and overhead— and so different amounts of equivalent units for materials as opposed to labor and overhead are calculated. Materials often are added at the start of a process, at some specific point during the process, or at the end of a process in the form of packing materials. This situation is not uncommon; as a result, labor and overhead are frequently added together and called **conversion costs.** It is convenient to combine direct labor and factory overhead because they are generally incurred uniformly throughout the manufacturing process. Therefore, equivalent units are calculated separately.

Returning to the previous illustration, assume that the soft drink manufacturer added all of the direct materials at the beginning of the manufacturing process, and incurred labor and overhead costs evenly throughout the manufacturing process. All of the other data are exactly the same, except that the equivalent units for direct materials and for conversion costs, direct labor, and overhead must be calculated as follows:

			Equivalent Units	
		Work Done	Direct Materials	Conversion
Units totally finished at end of period	7,000	100%	7,000	7,000
Units in process				
Direct materials	500	100%	500	
Conversion costs	500	25%		125
Total			7,500	7,125

The computation of cost per unit is shown below:

$$\frac{\text{Direct material costs}}{\text{Equivalent units—direct materials}} = \text{Cost per unit—direct materials}$$

$$\frac{\$3,500}{7,500} = \$.47 \text{ per unit—direct materials}$$

$$\frac{\text{Conversion costs}}{\text{Equivalent units—conversion}} = \text{Cost per unit—conversion}$$

$$\frac{\$2,500}{7,125} = \$.35 \text{ per unit—conversion}$$

$$\text{Total cost per unit} = \$.47 + \$.35 = \$.82$$

Calculate Total Cost of Units Produced

When a product passes through two or more processes, the final total cost of the units produced contains the costs incurred in all of the departments. The output of one department or process is transferred to the next process. For example, in the mixing department 7,000 liters of product were finished for the period, at a cost of $.82 per liter, totaling $5,740. The total was transferred to the bottling department, where additional materials, labor, and overhead were added. The cost per unit in the bottling department is applied to the units finished in that department and then transferred to Finished Goods inventory. The journal entry to show the transfer from mixing to bottling follows:

Work in Process, Bottling	5,740	
Work in Process, Mixing		5,740

The format for the entry to show the transfer of units from bottling to Finished Goods Inventory is as follows, without actual figures:

Finished Goods Inventory	X,XXX	
Work in Process—Bottling		X,XXX

Process Costing with Two Departments

We will illustrate process costing with the Zip Bottling Company, a small soft drink manufacturer that produces a single soft drink product made from natural ingredients. The firm processes the soft drink through a mixing department and a bottling department.

The basic flow of costs in a process costing system is essentially the same as in a job order system. Return to Exhibit 27-2 to review the basic flow of costs. In a process costing system, direct materials, direct labor, and factory overhead are posted to Work in Process and then moved to Finished Goods and Cost of Goods Sold. There are work in process accounts for every department or process involved in production.

Mixing Department

The following example traces the flow of costs and units for the mixing department for the month of April 1987. In the mixing department, the direct materials—a combination of orange and grapefruit juice, sugar, and water—are added at the beginning of the process, whereas labor and overhead (the conversion costs) are added evenly throughout the process.

On April 1 there were 500 liters of Zip soft drink in process, 100% complete as to materials and 25% complete as to labor and overhead. These liters had a total cost of $410, made up of direct materials of $240, direct labor of $100, and overhead of $70. During April direct materials costing $5,000 were placed into production in the mixing department. Based on departmental payroll records, the total cost of direct labor used by the mixing department was $2,200. The firm uses a predetermined overhead rate of 75% of direct labor cost. In April, overhead charged to Work in Process for the department was $1,650 ($2,200 × 75%).

During the month, 10,000 liters were placed into production, and 10,200 liters were completed and transferred out to bottling. On April 30 there were 300 liters in process in the mixing department, 100% complete as to material and 50% complete as to labor and overhead, the conversion costs. A T account for Work in Process (on the top of the next page) shows the costs for the department, and the following journal entries (1), (2), and (3) show the transfer of these costs to the mixing department.

The firm uses the basic steps found on page 1092 to do process costing. The process centers have been identified and the firm has already accumulated the three basic manufacturing costs for the mixing department for the month of April. The third step calls for calculating the units of finished product produced by the mixing department. The firm must calculate the equivalent units of production because the mixing department has partially finished units.

Equivalent Units

In the mixing department, materials are added at the beginning of the process, and labor and overhead costs are incurred uniformly throughout. Therefore, equivalent units for materials and conversion costs need to be calculated separately. In order to clarify the flow of units, most manufacturing firms generally include a summary of the **physical flow of units,** a description of the number of units of product in process at the start of the period, the number of units started during the period, and the number of units remaining in Work in Process at the end of the period. In the mixing department, there

Work in Process, Mixing

Beg. Bal.	410	
Direct Material	5,000	
Direct Labor	2,200	
Overhead	1,650	
	9,260	

(1)

Work in Process, Mixing	5,000	
Materials		5,000

(2)

Work in Process, Mixing	2,200	
Wages Payable		2,200

(3)

Work in Process, Mixing	1,650	
Factory Overhead		1,650

were 500 liters in process at the beginning of the month and 10,000 liters were started; therefore, the department worked on a total of 10,500 liters. Only 10,200 were finished, however, and 300 liters remained in mixing at the end of the month. The summary of the physical flow of units and the calculation of equivalent units of production for April follows:

Physical Flow	
Units in process, April 1	500
Units started during April	10,000
Total units worked on	10,500
Less: Units finished and transferred to bottling	10,200
Units in process, April 30	300

Calculation of Equivalent Units

			Equivalent Units	
	Number	Percentage	Direct Materials	Conversion
Units totally finished at end of period	10,200	100%	10,200	10,200
Units in process:				
Direct materials	300	100%	300	
Conversion costs	300	50%		150
Total			10,500	10,350

Cost per Unit

The firm has calculated the number of units of finished product and must divide that number into the manufacturing costs to determine the cost per unit for the mixing department as follows:

$$\frac{\text{Direct materials costs}}{\text{Equivalent units—direct materials}} = \text{Cost per unit—direct materials}$$

$$\frac{\$240 + \$5,000}{10,500} = \$.4990 \text{ per unit—direct materials}$$

$$\frac{\text{Conversion costs}}{\text{Equivalent units—conversion}} = \text{Cost per unit—conversion}$$

$$\frac{\$100 + \$70 + \$2,200 + \$1,650}{10,350} = \$.3884 \text{ per unit—conversion}$$

$$\text{Total cost per unit} = \$.4990 + \$.3884 = \$.8874$$

Note that the costs of the units in process on April 1 and the costs incurred during April have been added together to derive total costs. In doing this, the firm has used what is called a **weighted average cost flow assumption,** meaning that they have not distinguished between costs incurred in April and those incurred before April. An accountant using the weighted average cost flow assumption treats the material and conversion costs in beginning inventory as if they were added during the current period and simply adds them to current costs when calculating cost per unit. The FIFO cost flow assumption also can be used in process costing, but it is more complex to calculate and is not essential for understanding the basics of process costing.

Calculate Total Cost of Units Produced

The Zip Bottling Company cannot calculate the total cost of units produced in April until the cost per unit of mixing and of bottling is known. In order to be able to figure these costs, the cost of the units finished in the mixing department must be transferred to the bottling department. The mixing department finished 10,200 liters in April at $.8874 per liter, incurring a total cost of $9,051. Journal entry (4) shows the transfer:

(4)

Work in Process, Bottling	9,051	
Work in Process, Mixing		9,051

The T accounts for the two departments after this transfer are:

Work in Process, Mixing				Work in Process, Bottling		
Bal. 4/1	410	Transferred to bottling	9,051	Transferred from mixing	9,051	
Direct materials	5,000					
Direct labor	2,200					
Overhead	1,650					
	9,260					
Bal. 4/30	209					

Cost Production Report

As each processing center finishes units of product, it transfers the units and their costs to the next processing center. The **cost production report** summarizes the work done by a processing center during a specified period. The center must account for the number of units worked on during the period and the costs associated with those units. Exhibit 27–15 illustrates the cost production report for the mixing department for the month of April. Note that the top part of the report summarizes what happened to units of product in the department during the month. This first part of the report is frequently called a

EXHIBIT 27–15
Cost Production Report
Mixing Department—April 1987

Units to Be Accounted For	Number of Units
Units in process, April 1	500
Units started	10,000
Total units to account for	10,500

Units Accounted For	
Units completed and transferred out	10,200
Units in process, April 30	300
Total units accounted for	10,500

Costs to Be Accounted For		Costs
Work in process, beginning:		
Materials	$ 240	
Conversion	170	
Total		$ 410
Costs incurred during month:		
Materials	$5,000	
Conversion	3,850	
Total		8,850
Total cost to be accounted for		$9,260

Equivalent Unit Costs

	Total Cost	÷ Equivalent Units*	= Cost per Equivalent Unit
Materials	$5,240	10,500	$.4990
Conversion	4,020	10,350	.3884
Total	$9,260		$.8874

Costs Accounted For

	Equivalent Units	× Cost per Equivalent Unit	= Total Cost
Transferred to bottling	10,200	$.8874	$9,051**
Work in process, ending:			
Materials	300	.4990	150**
Conversion	150	.3884	59**
			$ 209
Total costs accounted for			$9,260

*Equivalent Unit Computation

	Materials	Conversion
Units transferred out	10,200	10,200
Ending work in process:		
Materials (300 units × 100%)	300	
Conversion (300 units × 50%)		150
Total	10,500	10,350

**Rounded

Accounting Information for Control of Cost Centers

quantity schedule because it reports on the physical quantity of units of product. The second part of the report shows the costs that the department must account for, and the third section summarizes the development of the cost per equivalent unit for materials and conversion costs. The last part of the report shows how the mixing department accounted for costs, detailing the dollars that were transferred to the bottling department and the costs of the units remaining in work in process. The total costs accounted for, in this case $9,260, must equal the costs charged to the department for the month, and they do.

Bottling Department

In the bottling department, the soft drink is put into one- and two-liter plastic bottles. Materials are added at the beginning of the process in the bottling department, and direct labor and factory overhead are incurred evenly throughout. There was no beginning inventory in the bottling department on April 1. As already stated, 10,200 liters were transferred in from the mixing department at a cost of $9,051. During the month, direct materials costing $1,200 were placed into production in the department. Direct labor for April was $2,000, and factory overhead of $1,500 was charged to Work in Process, using a predetermined rate of 75% of direct labor cost.

At the end of the month, 10,000 liters had been completed and transferred to finished goods inventory. On April 30, 200 liters remained in process, complete as to materials and 25% complete as to labor and overhead. A T account for Work in Process shows the costs for the department, and journal entries (5), (6), and (7) show the transfer of costs to the bottling department.

Work in Process, Bottling

Transferred from mixing	9,051	
Direct Materials	1,200	
Direct Labor	2,000	
Overhead	1,500	
	13,751	

(5)

Work in Process, Bottling	1,200	
Materials		1,200

(6)

Work in Process, Bottling	2,000	
Wages Payable		2,000

(7)

Work in Process, Bottling	1,500	
Factory Overhead		1,500

As in the case of the mixing department, the bottling department uses the basic steps involved in process costing. Management has already identified the processing centers and has accumulated the manufacturing costs for the bottling department. Now the equivalent units of finished product must be calculated.

1100

Equivalent Units

As was noted, in the bottling department materials are added at the start of the process and labor and overhead are incurred evenly throughout. Therefore, the firm needs to separately calculate equivalent units for materials and the conversion costs of labor and overhead. There is, in addition, a third cost element in the bottling department—the cost transferred in to the bottling department from the mixing department. Equivalent units for the **transferred-in cost** also must be calculated, although they are always assumed to be 100% complete because they have come from a previous department. The transferred-in cost is treated like other costs that have to be accounted for, as if the bottling department had purchased something from an outside supplier. The summary of the physical flow of units and the calculation of equivalent units of production for the bottling department for April follow:

Physical Flow	
Units in process, April 1	0
Units transferred in	10,200
Total units worked on	10,200
Less: Units completed and transferred to finished goods	10,000
Units in process, April 30	200

Calculation of Equivalent Units				
			Equivalent Units	
	Work Done	Direct Materials	Conversion	Transferred in
Units finished at end of period	10,000	100%	10,000	10,000	10,000
Units in process					
Direct materials	200	100%	200		
Conversion	200	25%		50	
Transferred in	200	100%			200
Total			10,200	10,050	10,200

Cost per Unit

The firm now finds the cost per unit for direct materials, conversion costs, and transferred-in costs as follows:

$$\frac{\text{Direct materials costs}}{\text{Equivalent units—direct materials}} = \text{Cost per unit—direct materials}$$

$$\frac{\$1,200}{10,200} = \$.1176 \text{ per unit—direct materials}$$

$$\frac{\text{Conversion costs}}{\text{Equivalent units—conversion}} = \text{Cost per unit—conversion}$$

$$\frac{\$3,500}{10,050} = \$.3483 \text{ per unit—conversion}$$

$$\frac{\text{Transferred-in costs}}{\text{Equivalent units—transferred in}} = \text{Cost per unit—transferred in}$$

$$\frac{\$9,051}{10,200} = \$.8874 \text{ per unit—transferred in}$$

$$\text{Total cost per unit} = \$.1176 + \$.3483 + \$.8874$$
$$= \$1.3533$$

Calculate Total Cost of Units Produced

The firm uses the cost per unit of $1.3533 to transfer the cost of the 10,000 liters completed at the end of the period. The total amount transferred to Finished Goods Inventory is $13,533 (10,000 × $1.3533). Journal entry (8) shows the transfer:

(8)

Finished Goods Inventory	13,533	
Work in Process, Bottling		13,533

The T accounts for Bottling and Finished Goods are:

Work in Process, Bottling				Finished Goods Inventory		
Transferred from mixing	9,051	Transferred to finished goods	13,533	Transferred from bottling	13,533	
Direct materials	1,200					
Direct labor	2,000					
Overhead	1,500					
	13,751					
Bal. 4/30	218					

Cost Production Report

The bottling department also uses a cost production report to summarize the work done in the department during the month of April. Exhibit 27–16 illustrates the cost production report for the department. The only difference between this report and the one for the mixing department is the inclusion of another cost element—the costs transferred from the mixing department. As noted earlier, these costs are always assumed to be 100% complete and are handled exactly like other manufacturing costs incurred by the department. Examine Exhibit 27–16 on page 1104 to see where all the numbers came from.

Process Costing—Two Materials

In some production processes, materials are added at two different points in the process, or packing materials are added at the end of the process. When that occurs, the firm must separately calculate equivalent units for materials added at different points in the manufacturing process. Consider, for example, the Mighty Mite Toy Company which manufactures in a single process a popular series of action figures made out of plastic. The major raw material used in the production of the action figures is Zylon. It is added at the start of the manufacturing process, whereas finishing and packaging materials (called F & P) are added at the end of the process. Direct labor and factory overhead are incurred evenly throughout. The firm has gathered the following information for August:

Units:	
Work in process, August 1	0
Units started	75,000
Completed and transferred to finished goods	50,000

Costs:
Material—Zylon	$300,000
Material—F & P	105,000
Direct labor	90,000
Factory overhead	103,000

Ending inventory is 40% complete.

The firm has one manufacturing process, and all costs have been accumulated in Work in Process for the month. The T account and journal entries showing cost accumulation for the month of August follow:

Work in Process

Zylon	300,000		
F&P	105,000		
Direct labor	90,000		
Overhead	103,000		
	598,000		

(1)

Work in Process	300,000	
Raw Materials		300,000

(2)

Work in Process	105,000	
Raw Materials		105,000

(3)

Work in Process	90,000	
Wages Payable		90,000

(4)

Work in Process	103,000	
Factory Overhead		103,000

Equivalent Units

Mighty Mite must calculate three types of equivalent units: one for each type of material and one for conversion costs. The summary of the physical flow of units and the calculation of equivalent units of production for work in process for August follow:

Physical Flow

Units in process, August 1	0
Units started	75,000
Total units worked on	75,000
Less: Units completed and transferred to finished goods	50,000
Units in process, August 31	25,000

(Continued on page 1105.)

EXHIBIT 27–16

Cost Production Report
Bottling Department—April 1987

Units to Be Accounted For	Number of Units
Units in process, April 1	0
Units transferred in	10,200
Total units to account for	10,200

Units Accounted For

Units completed and transferred out	10,000
Units in process, April 1	200
Total units accounted for	10,200

Costs to Be Accounted For

Work in process, beginning		0
Costs incured during month:		
Materials	$1,200	
Conversion	3,500	
Transferred in	9,051	
Total		$13,751
Total cost to be accounted for		$13,751

Equivalent Unit Costs

	Total Cost	Equivalent Units*	Cost per Equivalent Unit
Materials	$ 1,200	10,200	$ .1176
Conversion	3,500	10,050	.3483
Transferred in	9,051	10,200	.8874
Total	$13,751		$1.3533

Costs Accounted For

	Equivalent Units	Cost per Equivalent Unit	Total Cost
Transferred to finished goods	10,000	$1.3533	$13,533
Work in process, ending:			
Materials	200	.1176	24**
Conversion	50	.3484	17**
Transferred in	200	.8874	177**
			$ 218
Total costs accounted for			$13,751

***Equivalent Unit Computation**

	Materials	Conversion	Transferred In
Units transferred out	10,000	10,000	10,000
Ending work in process:			
Materials (200 units × 100%)	200		
Conversion (200 units × 25%)		50	
Transferred in (200 units × 100%)			200
Total	10,200	10,050	10,200

**Rounded

Calculation of Equivalent Units	Work Done	Equivalent Units		
		Zylon	F & P	Conversion
Units finished at end of period	50,000 100%	50,000	50,000	50,000
Units in process:				
Zylon	25,000 100%	25,000		
F & P	25,000 0			
Conversion	25,000 40%			10,000
Total		75,000	50,000	60,000

Cost per Unit

The firm can now figure the cost per unit for the two types of materials and the conversion costs:

$$\frac{\text{Zylon costs}}{\text{Equivalent units—Zylon}} = \text{Cost per unit—Zylon}$$

$$\frac{\$300,000}{75,000} = \$4.000 \text{ per unit—Zylon}$$

$$\frac{\text{F \& P costs}}{\text{Equivalent units—F \& P}} = \text{Cost per unit—F \& P}$$

$$\frac{\$105,000}{50,000} = \$2.100 \text{ per unit—F \& P}$$

$$\frac{\text{Conversion costs}}{\text{Equivalent units—conversion}} = \text{Cost per unit—conversion}$$

$$\frac{\$193,000}{60,000} = \$3.216 \text{ per unit—conversion}$$

$$\text{Total cost per unit} = \$4.000 + \$2.100 + \$3.216$$
$$= \$9.316$$

Calculate Total Cost of Units Produced

The firm found the cost per unit to be $9.316, and this unit cost was used to transfer the cost of the 50,000 units completed at the end of the period. The total amount transferred to Finished Goods Inventory was $465,800 (50,000 × $9.316). Journal entry (5) shows this transfer:

(5)		
Finished Goods Inventory	465,800	
Work in Process		465,800

The T accounts for Work in Process and Finished Goods are shown below, with the cost of the units finished during the period and transferred out of Work in Process, and the cost of ending Work in Process inventory:

Work in Process				Finished Goods Inventory		
Zylon	300,000	Transferred		Transferred		
F & P	105,000	to finished		from work		
Direct labor	90,000	goods	465,800	in process	465,800	
Overhead	103,000					
	598,000					
Bal. 8/31	132,200					

Job order and process cost accounting systems both provide manufacturing firms with the cost of a unit of product, an essential piece of information for financial reporting and managerial decision making. As has been noted, the cost per unit allows a firm to calculate the value of ending inventory and the cost of goods sold for financial reporting purposes. That same information also is used in cost-volume-profit analysis, pricing, and other areas of decision making.

Summary of Learning Objectives

1. *The functions of cost accounting systems.* Cost accounting systems have two basic objectives: (a) to determine the cost of making units of product for financial reporting and decision-making purposes and (b) to accumulate the costs incurred by production departments in order to see if they are incurring costs according to the objectives set out in the budget.

2. *The flow of costs in a manufacturing system.* The flow of costs in a manufacturing system parallels the physical manufacturing process, with direct material, direct labor, and factory overhead charged to Work in Process. Finished units of product are transferred to Finished Goods Inventory, where their costs remain until the units are sold and charged to Cost of Goods Sold.

3. *Compare the general characteristics of job order and process costing systems.* A job order costing system assumes that each job or batch of products is different, and therefore the system accumulates manufacturing costs by job on a job cost sheet. A process costing system assumes that the product is uniform, flowing through the manufacturing process in large volume. A process costing system therefore accumulates manufacturing costs by process or department and manufacturing costs are divided by units produced to determine a broad, average cost per unit.

4. *Accounting for materials and labor in a job order system.* Total purchases of raw materials are shown in the control account and a subsidiary ledger is used to keep track of individual materials. When materials are requisitioned for production, the direct materials are charged to Work in Process and indirect materials are charged to Factory Overhead.

   Labor activity is recorded on time tickets, with direct labor charged to Work in Process and indirect labor charged to Factory Overhead.

5. *Accounting for actual overhead costs and applying factory overhead using a predetermined overhead rate.* All actual factory overhead costs are charged to the Factory Overhead account. The amount of factory overhead that is charged to Work in Process is calculated with an overhead rate determined during the budgeting process. The basic formula to calculate the predetermined overhead rate is:

$$\frac{\text{Estimated factory overhead costs}}{\text{Estimated activity base level (i.e., DLH)}} = \frac{\text{Predetermined overhead rate}}{\text{(i.e., per DLH)}}$$

The difference between actual overhead and the overhead applied to Work in Process is carried forward from month to month; at the end of the year, the difference is either divided among the inventory accounts and Cost of Goods Sold or closed to Cost of Goods Sold.

6. *Determining the cost of finished units of product and the cost of goods sold in a job order system.* When a job is completed, direct materials, direct labor, and factory overhead on the job cost sheet are added and divided by the number of units produced in the job (or batch) to determine the cost per unit of the finished product. The total cost of the job is transferred to Finished Goods Inventory, and the unit cost is used to transfer the cost of the units sold from Finished Goods to the Cost of Goods Sold account.

7. *The basic concepts and steps involved in process costing.* In a process costing system, manufacturing costs for a process for a period are divided by the output of that period in order to determine an average cost per unit. The basic steps involved in a process costing system are:
   a. Identify the process centers in manufacturing a product.
   b. Accumulate for each processing center for a specific period the three basic manufacturing costs: direct materials, direct labor, and factory overhead.
   c. Calculate how many units of finished product were produced by each processing center.
   d. Divide the total costs for each processing center by the number of finished units of product produced to determine the cost per unit of product for each process. Use the cost per unit to calculate the cost of the units transferred out of the process and those left unfinished.
   e. Add the unit costs of all of the processing centers in order to determine the total cost of each unit produced.

8. *Calculating equivalent units of production.* In order to account for the work done by a department on partially finished units of product, process costing systems use equivalent units of production. The productive output of a process or department is expressed in terms of finished units of product. The work done on unfinished units is converted into the equivalent of finished units of product by multiplying the percentage of work done by the number of units left in Work in Process. This allows a firm to calculate the output of each processing center in terms of finished units. If materials are added at a different time in the process than the conversion costs, the firm must separately calculate equivalent units.

9. *Identifying the flow of costs and determining the unit cost and cost of goods sold in a process cost system.* In a process system, costs flow in essentially the same way as in a job order system, but in the former system there are work in process accounts for all of the departments or processes involved in production.

   In a process costing system, unit costs are calculated by dividing the manufacturing cost by the equivalent units of production. If the number of equivalent units is different for materials, labor, and overhead, then the cost per unit for each will be different and they must be added together to determine the total cost per unit for each process.

   If two or more processes are used to manufacture a product, the cost transferred out of the first process becomes part of the cost of the next process. The total cost per unit based on all the manufacturing processes is used to transfer the cost of units to Finished Goods and Cost of Goods Sold.

10. ***Preparing a cost production report for a processing center.*** The cost production report summarizes the activity of a process or department for a period. The report shows how physical units are accounted for, the costs charged to the department, the calculation of the cost per unit, and how the cost per unit is used to determine the costs transferred out of the department; the report also shows the costs remaining in ending Work in Process Inventory.

Key Terms

Applied Overhead	Overapplied Overhead
Conversion Costs	Physical Flow of Units
Cost Accounting Systems	Predetermined Overhead Rate
Cost Production Report	Process Centers
Equivalent Units	Process Costing
Job Cost Sheet	Transferred-in Cost
Job Order Costing	Underapplied Overhead
Materials Ledger Card	Weighted Average Cost Flow Assumption

Problems for Your Review

A. Job Order Costing. During May 1987, Northwest Manufacturing Company began working on job 100. The following information pertains to job 100 and the manufacturing process for May:

1. Raw materials costing $100,000 were purchased and received.
2. Production requisitioned direct materials costing $40,000 for job 100.
3. Four thousand direct labor hours were used in job 100. The direct labor rate is $8 per hour.
4. Factory overhead is applied to work in process based on direct labor hours. The estimated factory overhead for May, based on 10,000 estimated direct labor hours, is as follows:

Supervision	$ 60,000
Depreciation	30,000
Maintenance	40,000
Power	20,000
Lubricants	25,000
Miscellaneous	15,000
Total	$190,000

5. The actual bill for factory power came to $18,500; it was paid in cash.
6. During May, job 100, which contained 100 units, was finished.
7. On May 31, 90 units out of the 100 were sold at a price of $1,600 per unit.

Required:
Use journal entries to record the preceding information.

Solution

1.	Raw Materials	100,000	
	Accounts Payable		100,000
	To record the purchase of raw materials.		

2.

Work in Process	40,000	
Raw Materials		40,000

To record requisition of materials for job 100.

3.

Total direct labor cost = $8 \times 4,000 = \$32,000$.

Work in Process	32,000	
Wages Payable		32,000

To record direct labor cost for job 100.

4.

$$\text{Predetermined overhead rate} = \frac{\text{Estimated factory overhead cost}}{\text{Estimated direct labor hours}}$$
$$= \frac{\$190,000}{10,000 \text{ DLH}}$$
$$= \$19/\text{DLH}$$

Factory overhead applied to job 100: $19 \times 4,000$ DLH
$$= \$76,000$$

Work in Process	76,000	
Factory Overhead		76,000

To record applied factory overhead for job 100.

5. The actual factory overhead costs are stored in the factory overhead account:

Factory Overhead	18,500	
Cash		18,500

6. The total cost of job 100 is $148,000 ($40,000 + $32,000 + $76,000), and this is the cost transferred to Finished Goods Inventory:

Finished Goods Inventory	148,000	
Work in Process		148,000

To record the completion of job 100 and its transfer to finished goods inventory.

7.

The cost per unit for job 100 is $\frac{\$148,000}{100} = \$1,480$.

Cost of goods sold = $1,480 \times 90$ units = $133,200.

Cost of Goods Sold	133,200	
Finished Goods Inventory		133,200

To record the cost of the units sold.

The sales revenue for the transaction = $90 \times \$1,600 = \$144,000$.

Accounts Receivable	144,000	
Sales		144,000

To record the revenue for 90 units sold from job 100.

B. Process Costing. Altman Chemical Company uses a process costing system. At the beginning of June 1989, the Work in Process Inventory account contained 5,000 units of semifinished product, 100% complete as to materials and 50% complete as to direct labor and factory overhead. The costs associated with beginning Work in Process Inventory total $50,000, made up of materials costing $10,000, direct labor costing $20,000, and factory overhead costing $20,000. During June, 25,000 units of product were put into production. Materials costing $50,000 were required, and direct labor costs of $124,000 and factory overhead costs of $140,600 were incurred. At the end of June, 28,000 units of product were completed and transferred to the Finished Goods Inventory. The units in ending Work in Process Inventory were 100% complete as to materials, 40% complete as to direct labor, and 60% complete as to factory overhead.

Required:

Prepare a detailed cost production report for June.

Solution _____

Cost Production Report
Altman Chemical Company—June 1989

Units to Be Accounted For	Number of Units
Units in process, June 1	5,000
Units started	25,000
Total units to account for	30,000

Units Accounted For

Units completed and transferred out	28,000
Units in process, June 30	2,000
Total units accounted for:	30,000

Costs to Be Accounted For

Work in process, beginning:		
Materials	$10,000	
Direct labor	20,000	
Factory overhead	20,000	
Total		$ 50,000
Costs incurred during month:		
Materials	$ 50,000	
Direct labor	124,000	
Factory overhead	140,600	
Total		314,600
Total cost to be accounted for		$364,600

Equivalent Unit Costs

	Total Cost	Equivalent Units*	Cost per Equivalent Unit
Materials	$ 60,000	30,000	$ 2.00
Direct labor	144,000	28,800	5.00
Factory overhead	160,600	29,200	5.50
Total	$364,600		$12.50

Costs Accounted For

	Equivalent Units	Cost per Equivalent Unit	Total Cost
Transferred to finished goods	28,000	$12.50	$350,000
Work in process, ending:			
Materials	2,000	2.00	4,000
Direct labor	800	5.00	4,000
Factory overhead	1,200	5.50	6,600
			$ 10,600
Total costs accounted for			$364,600

*Equivalent Unit Computation

	Materials	Direct Labor	Factory Overhead
Units transferred out	28,000	28,000	28,000
Ending work in process:			
Materials (2,000 units × 100%)	2,000		
Direct labor (2,000 units × 40%)		800	
Overhead (2,000 units × 60%)			1,200
Total	30,000	28,800	29,200

Questions

1. In the measurement part of the control process, what are the two objectives of a cost accounting system?

2. Do you agree that the flow of costs through the accounting system is very similar to what happens in the actual manufacturing process? Explain your answer.

3. What are the factors that determine which type of product costing system a firm will use?

4. Give examples of companies that would be well suited to a job order costing system.

5. What is a job cost sheet? What is its purpose in a job order costing system?

6. What is a predetermined overhead rate, and how is it determined?

7. Why do firms use estimated overhead costs rather than actual overhead costs in predetermined overhead rates?

8. What is *underapplied overhead*? What is *overapplied overhead*? What disposition is made of these amounts at the end of the accounting period?

9. What steps generally are involved in a process costing system?

10. Under what conditions would a firm find the process costing system most suitable?

11. Define *equivalent units.*

12. Why is it necessary to determine equivalent units and how are they used?

13. What is a cost production report?

14. You have overheard a fellow student saying, "Cost accumulation is easier under a process costing system than under a job order costing system." Do you agree? Explain your answer.

15. When using a process costing system, why is it necessary to summarize material, labor, and factory overhead by processing centers rather than merely to determine total cost for the finished product?

Exercises

1. Journal entries. The Start Painting Company ordered and received 100 gallons of paint at a cost of $50 per gallon on September 2, 1987. The cost sheet of job 9A shows the following information:

Direct materials used = 20 gallons of paint
Direct labor used = 120 hours, @ $8 per hour
Factory overhead applied = based on 125% of direct labor cost

Required:

Make the necessary journal entries for the purchase and issuance of materials, the use of direct labor, and the application of factory overhead.

2. Journal Entries. Actual factory overhead incurred by the production department of the Beaver Company for the month of September 1988 was as follows:

Depreciation	$250
Rent	300
Insurance	150
Miscellaneous	650
	$1,350

The production department applied factory overhead at a rate of 150% of direct labor cost. In September the overapplied overhead amounted to $150.

Required:
a. Compute the direct labor cost.
b. Make journal entries to record the incurrence and the application of factory overhead.

3. Factory Overhead. Arrowhead Company applies factory overhead using direct labor hours in Department X and on a material cost basis in Department Y. They made the following estimates for 1988:

	Department X	Department Y
Direct labor hours	5,000	1,000
Direct labor costs	$40,000	$8,000
Direct materials	$10,000	$80,000
Machine hours	1,000	2,000
Factory overhead costs	$17,500	$20,000

The cost sheet for job 30 shows the following actual information for the month of September:

	Department X	Department Y
Direct labor hours used	100	80
Material cost incurred	$500	$840
Machine hours used	24	130

Required:

a. Compute the predetermined overhead rate for Department X and Department Y for 1988.
b. How much overhead is to be applied to job 30 for September?
c. What is the total cost of job 30?
d. Assume the company's fiscal year ends on September 30. Actual overhead costs on all jobs for the year totaled $18,600 in Department X and $21,482 in Department Y. Applied overhead in Department X was $17,900 and applied overhead in Department Y came to $20,860. Prepare the adjusting entry to close Arrowhead Company's overhead accounts.

4. Applied Factory Overhead. ABC Company has two departments: assembly and packaging. The company uses a job order costing system and computes a predetermined overhead rate for each department. The assembly department bases its rate on machine hours, and the packaging department bases its rate on direct labor costs. Estimated costs for 1989 are given:

	Assembly	Packaging
Machine hours	50,000	10,000
Direct labor costs	$60,000	$100,000
Overhead costs	$125,000	$ 60,000

Required:

a. Compute the predetermined factory overhead rate for each department.
b. Actual overhead costs amounted to $22,000 with 9,000 machine hours for assembly. Packaging had actual overhead costs of $5,050 and direct labor costs of $8,500. Was overhead over- or underapplied for each department? By how much?

5. Unit Cost. Lee Manufacturing Company uses a job order costing system. Transactions completed during March were as follows:

1. Received purchase of material: $18,000.
2. Materials requisitioned:

> Job 3A, $5,000
> Job 3B, $2,000

3. Direct labor used:

> Job 3A, 500 hours @ 7.50 per hour
> Job 3B, 300 hours @ 7.50 per hour

4. Predetermined overhead rate: $3 per direct labor hour.
5. Actual overhead incurred:

> Job 3A, $1,480
> Job 3B, $1,020

6. Both job 3A (200 units) and job 3B (125 units) were started and completed in March and were transferred to finished goods.

7. Shipment to customers:

from Job 3A, 100 units
from Job 3B, 50 units

(Sales price of $80 per unit for 3A and $125 per unit for 3B.)

Required:
a. Prepare journal entries to record these transactions.
b. What is the ending balance in Finished Goods Inventory?

6. Equivalent Units. Silkwood Company produces only one product. Materials are added at the beginning of production. Conversion costs are incurred evenly throughout the process. Following are the September data:

1. No beginning work in process.
2. Fifty thousand units started.
3. Ten thousand units in ending Work in Process Inventory (75% complete).

Required:
Calculate the equivalent units for both materials and conversion costs for September.

7. Equivalent Units. A company computed that equivalent units for its conversion costs were 7,000 units and ending Work in Process Inventory was made up of 1,200 units, 50% complete. Direct materials are added at the end of the manufacturing process. Conversion costs are incurred evenly throughout the process.

Required:
What is the number of equivalent units for direct materials?

8. Equivalent Units. The Magic Toy Company manufactures various kinds of plastic toys. All materials are added at the beginning of the process in Department A. Departments A and B add labor and factory overhead evenly throughout the manufacturing process. Data for October follow:

	Department A	Department B
Beginning Work in Process	0	0
Units started	20,000	
Units received from preceding department		15,000
Units transferred to next department	15,000	12,000
Ending Work in Process	5,000	3,000
	(80% complete)	(50% complete)
Total units accounted for	20,000	15,000

Required:
a. Determine the equivalent units of production for both materials and conversion costs for Department A.
b. Determine the equivalent units for conversion costs and transferred-in costs for Department B.

9. Accounting for Costs. The following data are available for your use in completing a cost production report:

1. Equivalent units are 1,500 for materials and 1,400 for conversion costs.
2. Beginning inventory: Work in Process 500 units, 25% complete.

Material costs	$100
Conversion costs	$100

3. Current costs:

Material costs	$1,400
Conversion costs	$2,000

4. One thousand three hundred units were transferred to the next department; ending inventory consists of 300 units, two-thirds complete as to materials and one-third complete as to conversion costs.

Required:

Determine the cost of the units transferred out and the cost of the ending Work in Process Inventory.

10. Unit Cost. Below are data concerning Department B, a department in a manufacturing firm that uses a process costing system:

Units started this month	25,000
Beginning work in process	5,000
Units transferred to finished goods	28,000
Ending work in process (all materials; 50% complete as to conversion costs)	2,000
Costs incurred last month:	
Direct materials	$6,000
Direct labor	2,500
Overhead	500
Costs added this month:	
Direct materials	$24,000
Direct labor	41,000
Overhead	14,000

Required:

   a. Determine the cost per unit for materials and conversion costs.
   b. Compute the cost of the units transferred to Finished Goods.
   c. Compute the cost of ending Work in Process Inventory.

Problem Set A

27A–1. Journal Entries. The cost records of the Summit Company's job order costing system show the following selected data for September 1987:

   a. Received a shipment of 800 pieces of direct materials costing $4 per piece.
   b. Direct materials were issued as follows:

Job 901, 200 pieces
Job 902, 350 pieces

   c. Direct labor amounted to $2,000. Job 901 used $1,200 and Job 902 used $800.
   d. Factory overhead costs were applied using a rate of 50% of direct labor cost.
   e. Actual factory overhead costs incurred:

Rent	$2,500
Utilities	2,800
Depreciation	650

   f. Job 901, consisting of 20 units of product, was completed.
   g. Twelve of the units completed on Job 901 were shipped to customers at a price of $185 per unit.

Required:

Assume there was no beginning work in process and prepare journal entries to record the transactions of the Summit Company in September.

1114

27A-2. Overhead Rates and Job Cost. Premier Company uses a predetermined rate in applying factory overhead to production. Overhead is applied in Department A on the basis of direct labor hours and is applied in Department B on the basis of machine hours. The budget estimates for the current year follow:

	Department A	Department B
Direct labor cost	$100,000	$50,000
Factory overhead cost	$250,000	$250,000
Machine hours	10,000	50,000
Direct labor hours	25,000	10,000

Job 305 was started and completed in the month of March. The cost record for this job shows the following information:

Job 305 (1,000 units)

	Department A	Department B
Direct materials	$8,000	$4,000
Direct labor cost	$6,000	$4,000
Direct labor hours	1,200	800
Machine hours	100	500
Factory overhead cost	$12,500	$2,400

Required:

a. Compute the predetermined factory overhead rate for each department.

b. Compute the total cost and unit cost of Job 305.

c. Assume that Job 305 is the only work done in both departments; determine the over- or underapplied factory overhead for each department for March.

d. If the firm's fiscal year ends on March 31, prepare the adjusting entries to close the overhead accounts.

27A-3. Journal Entries, Income Statement. The Davis Brothers Company maintains a job order costing system. They provide you with the following information for the month of June 1989:

a. June 1 beginning inventories:

Raw materials	0
Work in process (41,000 units)	$12,000
Finished goods	0

b. Materials ordered and received; $30,000.

c. The direct labor cost incurred was $30,000.

d. The factory overhead cost incurred, excluding depreciation, was $6,000.

e. The factory depreciation recorded was $4,000.

f. Administrative expenses incurred were $10,000.

g. Direct materials requisitioned totaled $25,000.

h. Miscellaneous factory overhead cost incurred was $5,000.

i. Selling expenses incurred totaled $6,000.

j. Factory overhead is applied on the basis of 50% of direct labor cost.

k. No new units were started in June. All units were completed in June, and 40,000 units were sold at a price of $3 per unit.

Required:

a. Prepare journal entries to record the activities of Davis Brothers in June.

b. Prepare an income statement for June.

27A-4. Missing Data. Fill in the following missing data:

Accounting Information for Control of Cost Centers 1115

Neotec Company
Cost Production Report
June 1988

Units to Be Accounted For	Number of Units
Units in process, June 1	1,000
Units started	?
Total units to account for	8,000

Units Accounted For

Units completed and transferred out	7,100
Units in process, June 30	
(½ materials, ⅓ labor,	
⅔ factory overhead)	?
Total units accounted for	8,000

Costs to Be Accounted For

Work in process, June 1:	
Materials	$9,000
Direct labor	5,500
Factory overhead	800
Total	$?
Cost incurred in June:	
Materials	?
Direct labor	$31,500
Factory overhead	?
Total	$?
Total costs to be accounted for:	
Materials	$67,950
Direct labor	?
Factory overhead	?
Total	$?

Equivalent Unit Costs

	Total Costs	÷	Equivalent Unit Costs	=	Costs Per Unit
Materials			?		$?
Direct labor			?		?
Factory overhead			?		$2
Total					$?

Costs Accounted For

Transferred to finished goods		?
Work in process, June 30		
Materials	$?	
Direct labor	?	
Factory overhead	1,200	
Total costs accounted for		$?

27A-5. Equivalent Units, Unit Costs—Two Departments. A company makes a single product in two processes. Department A mixes and partially processes the basic ingredients, which are then transferred to Department B for further processing and packaging. There is no beginning Work in Process in either department. The flow of product through the departments during September follows:

Department A Work in Process		Department B Work in Process	
Started	To Department B	From Department A	To Finished Goods
40,000 units	36,000 units	36,000 units	30,000 units

Cost data are as follows:

	Department A	Department B
Direct materials	$ 5,700	$21,450
Direct labor	9,500	12,540
Factory overhead	4,750	8,580
	$19,950	$42,570

Ending work in process in each department was 50% complete as to both materials and conversion costs which are added evenly throughout processing.

Required:
a. For Department A, determine the equivalent units of production, unit cost, and the cost of the units transferred to Department B.
b. For Department B, compute the equivalent units of production, unit cost, the cost of the units finished and transferred out, and the cost of ending Work in Process.

27A-6. Cost Production Report—Two Departments. Boston Manufacturing Company uses a process costing system. Units finished in Department 1 are transferred to Department 2. In both departments, materials are issued at the beginning of the process and conversion costs are evenly incurred throughout the process. The following data are available:

	Department 1	Department 2
Beginning work in process	0	0
Units started	20,000	18,000
Units transferred out	18,000	15,000
Ending work in process	2,000	3,000
	(1/2 complete)	(1/3 complete)
Raw materials used	$32,000	$27,000
Direct labor costs	53,200	44,800
Factory overhead cost	42,560	35,840

Required:
a. Prepare a cost production report for Department 1.
b. Prepare a cost production report for Department 2.

27A-7. Correction of Errors in the Cost Production Report. XYZ Company produces a single product in two departments. The following information is related to the cost production report for department A for the month of April:

Beginning work in process (500 units)		
100% complete as to materials		$ 800
50% complete as to conversion costs		800
Costs incurred during April		
Direct materials		4,000
Conversion costs		4,240
Total costs to be accounted for		$9,840
Units completed and transferred to		
finished goods (2,400 units)		$9,840
Ending work in process (600 units;		
100% complete as to materials,		
20% complete as to conversion costs)		0
Total costs accounted for		$9,840

Required:

a. Check for any errors in this report.

b. If there is any error found in item a, prepare a correct and detailed cost production report for April. Support your report with a schedule showing the computation of equivalent units.

Problem Set B

27B–1. Journal Entries. Sleeky Jeans Company, which manufactures jeans to order, uses a job order costing system. The following is a summary of July operations. (There were no beginning inventories on July 1.)

a. Materials purchased at a cost of $40,000 were received.

b. Requisitions for materials totaled $36,000. Materials were used as follows: for job 7A, $10,000; for job 7B, $12,000; and for job 7C, $14,000.

c. Direct labor costs totaled $32,000 as follows: for job 7A, $7,000; for job 7B, $11,000; and for job 7C, $14,000.

d. Factory overhead was applied using a rate of 80% of direct labor cost.

e. Actual factory overhead incurred was $27,000.

f. Jobs 7A and 7B were completed and transferred to finished goods.

g. Job 7B was shipped to a customer and the customer was billed $44,300.

Required:

Prepare journal entries to record all transactions of Sleeky Jeans in July.

Problem 27B–2. Overhead Rates and Job Cost. Dynamo Company uses a job order costing system and a predetermined rate in applying factory overhead to individual jobs. The predetermined rate in Department A is based on machine hours, and the rate in Department B is based on direct labor cost. At the beginning of 1989, the company's management made the following estimates for the year:

	Department A	Department B
Direct labor hours	20,000	40,000
Machine hours	40,000	10,000
Direct labor cost	$100,000	$200,000
Factory overhead	$100,000	$120,000

Job 505 was started in production on May 2 and completed on May 29. The record for this job shows the following cost information:

Job 505 (400 units)

	Department A	Department B
Direct materials cost	$1,000	$500
Direct labor costs	$500	$1,500
Direct labor hours	100	300
Machine hours	400	125
Factory overhead incurred	$985	$980

Required:

a. Compute the predetermined overhead rate for each department.

b. Compute the total factory overhead applied to job 505.

c. What would be the total cost of job 505? Unit cost?

d. Assuming that job 505 was the only job done in May, what was the amount of over- or underapplied overhead in each department in May?

e. Assuming that Dynamo's fiscal year ends on May 31, what adjusting entries would the firm use to close the factory overhead accounts?

27B-3. Missing Data. The following data are selected from ledger accounts of the Oak Company for 1988:

Direct Materials Inventory

1/1 Bal. 20,000	1988 credits
1988 debits	?
50,000	
12/31 Bal. 18,000	

Factory Overhead

| 1988 debits | 1988 credits |
| 65,000 | ? |

Work in Process

1/1 Bal. 30,000	1988 credits
DM 50,000	
DL 64,000	
OH 64,000	
12/31 Bal. ?	

Factory Wages Payable

1988 debits	1/1 Bal. 2,000
68,000	1988 credits
	67,000
	12/31 Bal. 1,000

Finished Goods

1/1 Bal. 50,000	1988 credits
1988 debits	184,000
183,000	
12/31 Bal. ?	

Cost of Goods Sold

| 1988 debits | |
| ? | |

Required:

a. Compute the following:
   1. Factory overhead applied.
   2. Indirect labor cost.
   3. Indirect materials cost.
   4. Ending work in process.
   5. Cost of goods sold for 1988.

b. What was the predetermined factory overhead rate based on direct labor cost for 1988?

c. Determine the over- or underapplied factory overhead for 1988.

d. Close the Factory Overhead account to Cost of Goods Sold.

e. Assume a perpetual inventory system is used in this company. If $7,000 of ending work in process is direct materials cost, how much of it is direct labor cost? Factory overhead cost?

27B–4. Equivalent Units, Unit Costs—Three Departments. The Angeles Manufacturing Company, which makes electrical dolls, started operations on January 3, 1988. Each finished unit goes through three process centers. The company accumulated the following information for 1988:

| | Centers | | |
	1	2	3
Cost added to production			
Direct materials	$20,000	$27,000	$29,160
Conversion costs	$19,000	$16,800	$31,600
Units started in production			
or transferred in during 1988	20,000	?	?
Ending inventory (units)	2,000	1,800	1,600
State of completion	50%	33.3%	75%

The direct materials are added at the beginning of each process. Conversion costs are incurred evenly throughout each process.

Required:

a. Determine the number of units transferred out of each process center during 1988.

b. Determine the equivalent units in terms of materials and conversion costs for each center.

c. Compute the unit cost for a finished unit of product.

27B–5. Equivalent Units, Unit Costs—One Department. Crown Company makes orange juice in two departments, squeezing and bottling. All materials are added at the beginning of the squeezing process, and conversion costs are incurred evenly throughout the process. The finished goods are then transferred to the bottling department, where they are put into bottles and made ready for distribution. Data for May are as follows for the squeezing department:

	Units	Costs
Beginning work in process:		
Materials	40,000 gallons	$5,000
Conversion costs	(50% complete)	1,500
Completed and transferred out	350,000	
Units started in May:		
Materials	? gallons	395,000
Conversion costs		91,000
Ending work in process:		
Materials	50,000 gallons	?
Conversion costs	(40% complete)	?

Required:

a. How many gallons of materials were put into production during the month?

b. Compute the equivalent units in the squeezing process during May in terms of materials and conversion costs.

c. Compute the unit costs of finished goods transferred to the bottling department in May.

d. Compute the cost of ending work in process inventory for squeezing.

27B–6. Cost Production Report—One Department. Production and cost data for March for one department of Rio Company's process costing system follow:

Beginning inventory (500 units; 25% complete as
to materials, 50% complete as to direct labor,
25% complete as to overhead)

Cost from preceding department	$600
Materials	562.50
Direct labor	750
Factory overhead	250

Current costs:

Cost from preceding department (1,300 units)	$1,560
Materials	1,650
Direct labor	3,000
Factory overhead	2,000

Ending work in process (400 units; 50%
complete as to materials, 25% complete as to
direct labor, 25% complete as to overhead)

Units completed during March, 1,760

Required:

Prepare a cost production report for March.

27B–7. Correction of Errors. The Northpole Company started operations one year ago. The general manager asks your opinion of its first year's income statement which was prepared by a clerk who has very little knowledge of accounting. The income statement is as follows:

The Northpole Company
Income Statement
For Year Ending December 31, 1989

Sales (10,000 units @ $4)			$40,000
Cost of sales:			
Materials purchased	$29,000		
Direct labor	9,200		
Factory overhead	4,600	$42,800	
Less:			
Material inventory, December 31	5,000		
Work in process, December 31:			
1,000 units, all materials			
50% labor and overhead)	800		
Finished goods, December 31 (1,000 units)	1,000	6,800	36,000
Gross profit			$ 4,000
Operating expenses			
Selling costs		$ 2,000	
Administrative costs		3,000	5,000
Net loss			($ 1,000)

Required:

What is your opinion? If you think that the income statement is poorly or even falsely prepared, prepare a correct income statement for Northpole Company. Support your statement with a cost production report.

Using the Computer

A. Refer to the cost production report on page 1099 of the chapter. The Zip Bottling Company prepares one of these reports each month for the mixing and bottling departments. Produce a spreadsheet, displaying a cost production report, for the month of May that would follow from the report for April, as shown in the text. Translate the following figures onto the spreadsheet: Units in process on May 1 (that is, those 300 units left in process on April 30) have a cost of $300. It is estimated that 35% of this cost pertains to direct materials and the remaining portion to direct labor and overhead. Eighty-seven hundred units of the soft drink were put into production during the month, and 8,300 units were completed and transferred to the bottling department. On May 31, 700 units were left in the mixing department; they were 100% complete as to direct materials and 75% complete as to direct labor and overhead. Records show that the following costs were incurred during May: Six thousand dollars of direct materials were placed into production; $2,800 was spent on direct labor, and the overhead cost was determined to be $2,100, using the predetermined overhead rate of 75% of direct labor cost.

B. Produce another cost production report for June, assuming the following data for the month:

1. Seven hundred units were in process on June 1 (from Part A).
2. Beginning inventory had a cost of $500, made up of 35% direct materials and 65% direct labor and overhead.
3. Nine thousand units were started in June.
4. Nine thousand three hundred units were completed and transferred to bottling.
5. Four hundred units were left in process on June 30.
6. Ending work in process was 100% complete as to direct materials and 50% complete as to conversion costs.
7. Costs incurred during June were:

Materials	$7,000
Labor	$4,000
Overhead (75% × 4,000)	$3,000

Decision Case

In March the Klassic Clothing Company started working on a special order of fall suits ordered by Winston's, a regional chain of specialty stores in the southeast United States. Winston's agreed to pay $800,000 for the suits. When the order was nearly finished, there was a complete management change in Winston's, and the buyer who had ordered from Klassic was replaced. The new buyer wanted the fall clothes to reflect only her own taste, and she canceled the order from Klassic. The president of Klassic called other firms in an effort to sell the suits and got an offer of $536,000. The sales manager frantically called other companies to try to get a better offer. Redburns, a group of stores in the Northeast, offered $600,000 for the suits if some distinctive buttons and more expensive trim could be added.

In order to decide what to do, the sales manager got the following information about the order from the production manager:

	Costs to Date
Materials	$119,850
Direct labor (24,500 hours @ $5.50)	134,750
Factory overhead @ $11 per hour	265,400
Total	$520,000

The factory overhead rate includes $4.40 variable overhead and $6.60 fixed overhead. The production manager made the following estimates of the costs necessary to finish the order:

	Original Order	Redburns' Offer
Materials	$15,500	$34,600
Direct labor hours	2,600	6,300

Required:

a. What is the full cost of the job if (1) the order is completed according to the original specifications? (2) the order is completed according to Redburns' specifications?

b. Which offer should the president accept? Why?

Accounting Information for Control: Standard Costing

28

LEARNING OBJECTIVES

After reading this chapter you should be able to:

1. Define standard costs and understand how they relate to control systems.
2. Understand different types of standard costs and how they are set.
3. Prepare direct materials variances.
4. Prepare direct labor variances.
5. Analyze factory overhead costs to prepare flexible budgets.
6. Prepare variances for factory overhead.
7. Describe the ways in which variances are investigated.
8. Evaluate the advantages and disadvantages of standard cost systems.

Chapter 27 examined how accounting information is used in cost control when cost accounting systems accumulate the cost of making a product and operating manufacturing departments. An organizational control system facilitates the attainment of an organization's objectives. Standard costing is a more sophisticated and precise method for cost planning, measurement, and evaluation that is used most frequently in manufacturing organizations.

What Are Standard Costs?

In general English usage, a **standard** is something set up as a model or example, a criterion that defines what a thing should be. There are standards for the quantity and types of metal used in coins and for weights and measures. We refer to standard time and aspire to a particular standard of living. In accounting, standards also are frequently used to regulate the costs and quantities of things used to produce goods or to provide services.

Many types of firms use cost standards. Banks, for example, may set a standard for the amount of time it should take to process a check, and fast food chains set standards for the price and quantity of the potatoes in french fries and the meat in hamburgers. Automobile repair shops may set standards for the amount of time it should take to perform the most frequent types of jobs, and accounting departments within firms may set standards for the amount of time it should take to process a transaction. The most complete and widespread use of standard costs, however, is found in manufacturing firms that have developed standards for price and quantity for materials, labor, and overhead. That is why, in accounting, **standard cost** usually refers to the standard cost of a unit of product, what it *should* take to produce a unit of product as opposed to the actual price and quantity.

In a manufacturing firm using standard costing, standards are set for the price that *should* be paid for materials, labor, and overhead. Actual prices are compared with the standards in order to evaluate performance. Similarly, standards are set as to how much material and how many labor hours should be used; later, actual quantities are compared with the standards in order to evaluate performance.

Standard Costs and Control

An organizational control system helps an organization to attain its objectives through planning, measurement, and evaluation. Standard costs give management more precise information in each of these areas. For example, planning the purchase of direct materials in a standard cost system allows management to budget the price that should be paid and the exact number of pounds that should be used for the planned units of production. Measurement of actual production focuses on the price paid and the quantities used for the basic manufacturing costs. Performance evaluation for responsibility centers can then be made based on the differences between actual and standard costs. The difference between actual cost and standard cost is called a **variance.**

A standard cost system also allows managers to determine when corrective action may be necessary. There frequently are variances between actual and standard costs, but many of these are relatively small and can be considered part of normal operations. Company guidelines often establish acceptable levels of variance, and management may take corrective action to reduce only large or significant variances. This is called management by exception, a concept that means managers should not spend time on things that are running smoothly according to plan, but should use their limited time for problems or exceptions. Budgets and standards are plans for what should happen, and variances are the differences between actual performance and those plans. Managers need to know the acceptable levels of variance so that they can focus their efforts on the important variances while allowing small differences from standard as part of normal operations.

Types of Standards

There are different types of standards, based on different expectations about performance, that are used to measure and evaluate performance in organizations. An easy way to understand this idea is to refer to the grading system your instructor uses on your accounting examinations. Suppose that your instructor has decided that an "A" on an accounting examination can be earned only if a student receives 100 out of a possible 100 points. We would call this an **ideal standard** because it is unlikely that most students can attain such a score on a difficult test. Professors who use this type of standard assume that the highest grade should be earned only through perfect mastery of every problem. In business, managers who use ideal standards also require complete efficiency and performance all of the time. Firms that use ideal standards assume that there are no interruptions of work or machine breakdowns. Most employees cannot meet ideal standards, and many managers believe setting ideal standards has discouraging effects on employee motivation and morale. In addition, the variances from such standards are less significant because standards are never attained and there is always some variance.

Sometimes standards are set to make costs **currently attainable.** These are the costs that should be incurred under very efficient operating conditions. In the grading example, this would be equivalent to earning an "A" for scoring at least 90 from a possible 100. A currently attainable standard rewards excellence as opposed to perfection; although difficult, it is possible to achieve. In manufacturing, currently attainable standard costs allow for normal spoilage, machine breakdown, and loss of time. Like receiving an attainable "A," however, such standards are not easy to achieve; attainable manufacturing standards require highly efficient performance on the part of workers. In manufacturing, currently attainable standards are used most often because of their positive motivational effects on employees and the usefulness of the variances obtained.

Setting Standards

Setting standards for manufacturing costs is a complex process involving engineers, accountants, purchasing agents, and managers. Materials, labor, and overhead are calculated separately and added together on a **standard cost card,** which details what the manufacturing cost should be for one unit of product. The standards are flexible budgets for each individual unit of product, stipulating quantities and prices for materials, labor, and overhead. Once standards have been determined, actual performance can be evaluated against a budget for that level of activity.

Materials Standards

Because they design the products and control the production process, industrial engineers generally determine the standards for the quantities of materials that should be used in products. The purchasing agent usually has responsibility for setting standards for the prices paid for raw materials. When a firm has a new product, the standards come from engineers' blueprints and suppliers' quoted prices.

Labor Standards

Standards for labor hours are difficult to establish. Industrial engineers often do time-and-motion studies in which they observe employees at work and then make suggestions for improving worker efficiency. Such studies are generally not popular with labor. Firms also use work measurement to determine standards for labor hours. In work measurement, engineers have established standards for certain types of basic activities such as lifting, grasping, or pulling. A firm then breaks down each job into the basic component activities and adds together the standard times for those activities to determine the standard time for the job. Determining the amount of time necessary to complete a given job is subjective and requires professional judgment.

Companies that have union contracts allow the wage rates in the contracts to determine labor rate standards. Many jobs require the services of many workers, each at different skill levels and wage rates. The standard wage rate, therefore, may be a mixture of many wage rates, assuming a certain mix of employee skills. In nonunion plants, management and personnel departments often set wages.

Overhead Standards

Developing standards often starts with the analysis of cost behavior patterns for the various costs included in overhead. Accountants then use the cost behavior formula for overhead as a whole to understand how overhead costs have behaved in the past; they use that information to predict how the same or similar costs will behave in the future. They then can determine whether overhead has been used efficiently and whether past cost behavior patterns will repeat themselves. The cost behavior formula allows management to predict what overhead will be at any level of production within the relevant range of activity. A predetermined overhead rate can be calculated for any level of production for fixed and variable overhead. Those rates then serve as standards during the production process.

Revision of Standards

Setting standard costs is frequently a trial-and-error process that requires much revision, particularly when the standards are first set. Standards should be reevaluated periodically—at least once a year—so that the variances in the system have some significance. For example, the purchase price of raw material may increase as a result of circumstances beyond the control of the purchasing area. In this situation, the variance from the standard price should not be used to evaluate performance. Standards need to be changed to correspond to current conditions.

Preparation of Direct Materials Variances

In order to understand the preparation of the variances for direct materials, we will use the following data for Weston Manufacturing Company, a small firm that makes one product and uses a standard cost system:

Direct materials standards:	
Price	$.75 per pound
Quantity	3 pounds per unit
Total standard cost per	
unit for materials	3 × $.75 = $2.25
Actual data—June, 1988:	
Price	$.70 per pound
Purchased	3,500 pounds
Used in production	3,300 pounds
Produced	1,000 units

As noted earlier, every standard for a cost element is made up of the quantity to be used and the price to be paid. The **variances** therefore focus on the amount actually paid compared with standard, and the amount actually used compared with standard.

Direct Materials Price Variance

Exhibit 28–1 shows the formula for the **direct materials price variance** measuring the difference between the standard price of a direct material costing $.75 per pound and the actual price paid of $.70 per pound. In the example, the 3,500 pounds that were purchased was the actual quantity used to find the variance, indicating that Weston calculates the materials price variance when direct materials are purchased rather than when they are put into production. The materials inventory is then carried at standard cost in the accounts rather than at actual cost, which simplifies accounting during production. Calculating the variance at the time of purchase also gives management early information about variances.

The variance in Exhibit 28–1 shows that the company spent $175 less than standard on the purchase of the raw materials for which the calculation was made. A firm's purchasing area is generally responsible for materials price variances, and when a variance is significantly higher than expected, management usually requests an explanation, whether the variance is favorable or unfavorable. Sometimes a favorable price variance results from making quantity purchases with discounts; at other times purchasing is not so efficient and has to pay a higher price; and sometimes price changes of materials are out of the company's control. The key idea in variance analysis is investigation if a variance is significant.

The materials price variance calculates the difference in the price paid between actual and standard, and therefore the quantity is held constant. This relationship is emphasized by expressing the calculation of the variance in terms of a formula:

$$AQ = \text{Actual quantity}$$
$$AP = \text{Actual price}$$
$$SP = \text{Standard price}$$

$$AQ(AP - SP) = \text{Materials price variance}$$
$$3{,}500(\$.70 - \$.75) = \$175F$$

The formula is a simplified version of Exhibit 28–1. Both formats are acceptable for calculating variances, and which one is used is a question of individual

EXHIBIT 28–1
Direct Materials Price Variance

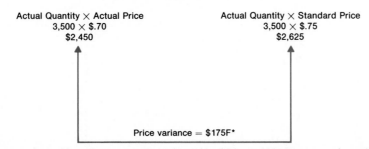

Actual Quantity × Actual Price
3,500 × $.70
$2,450

Actual Quantity × Standard Price
3,500 × $.75
$2,625

Price variance = $175F*

*F indicates a favorable variance, as opposed to a U, which would indicate an unfavorable variance.

preference. Remember to always indicate the nature of the variance with an "F" for favorable or a "U" for unfavorable.

Firms usually prepare a report showing the performance of a given department or area for a period, usually a month. Performance reports communicate variance information to management, who in turn investigate significant variances from company guidelines. The June performance report for Weston's purchasing area follows:

Weston Manufacturing Company
Purchasing Department Performance Report
June 1988

Item	Actual Price	−	Standard Price	=	Difference	×	Actual Quantity	=	Materials Price Variance
Direct materials	$.70		$.75		$.05		3,500		$175F

Direct Materials Quantity Variance

The **direct materials quantity (or usage) variance** calculates the difference between the number of pounds of material actually used in production during a month and the number of pounds of material that should have been used for the units produced. Exhibit 28–2 depicts the calculation of this variance.

Note that the quantity shown in the exhibit under actual quantity is the 3,300 pounds actually used in the production process. Accountants calculate this variance in order to measure how efficiently a production process was carried out during a period. They compare the number of pounds of material actually used in production with the number of pounds of material that *should* have been used in production according to the standard. Weston produced 1,000 units of product during June, and the standard called for 3 pounds of material for each unit. Therefore, the standard quantity in Exhibit 28–2 is 3,000 pounds, the amount of direct material that should have been used to produce 1,000 units. The standard of 3 pounds of material per unit is a flexible budget formula for each unit of product, so management can calculate how much material should be used at any level of production. In this case it was

EXHIBIT 28–2
Direct Materials Quantity Variance

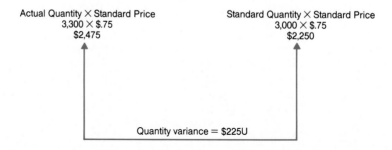

Actual Quantity × Standard Price
3,300 × $.75
$2,475

Standard Quantity × Standard Price
3,000 × $.75
$2,250

Quantity variance = $225U

applied to 1,000 units, the amount actually produced. Because the process used more material than the standard called for, the $225 is unfavorable.

Using the shorter formula to calculate the quantity variance highlights how the price factor is kept constant at standard while looking at the difference in the number of pounds.

$$SP(AQ - SQ) = \text{Materials quantity variance}$$
$$\$.75(3,300 \text{ lbs.} - 3,000 \text{ lbs.}) = \$225U$$

The production area is responsible for any materials quantity variance. If Weston's management considered the $225 significant, they would investigate the variance. Many factors could cause an unfavorable variance, including faulty machinery, poorly trained workers, inferior quality of materials, or poor supervision. Sometimes, the purchasing area causes the unfavorable quantity variance, for example, when buyers select poor quality materials at bargain prices. When this happens, a highly favorable price variance may lead to an unfavorable quantity variance, but in this situation the purchasing area is responsible, not production.

The June performance report for the production area follows:

Weston Manufacturing Company
Production Department Performance Report
June 1988

Item	Actual Quantity	— Standard Quantity	= Difference	× Standard Price	= Materials Quantity Variance
Direct materials	3,300	3,000	300	$.75	$225U

Preparation of Direct Labor Variances

The direct labor standards for Weston and actual data for the month of June are next:

Direct labor standards:
Rate $5.00 per hour
Quantity   2 hours per unit
Total standard cost per unit for labor $2 \times \$5.00 = \$10.00$

Actual data—June 1988:
Rate $5.05 per hour
Quantity   2,300 hours
Produced   1,000 units

Calculating direct labor variances is very similar to calculating variances for direct materials. The major difference is in terminology, for in the direct labor formula, the term *rate*, as opposed to *price*, is used to refer to labor, and the quantity in the formula refers to hours of labor time. Note that the rate of $5 per hour and the quantity of 2 hours per unit are flexible budget formulas for each unit that can be used to determine the prices and quantities that should have been used at actual levels of production.

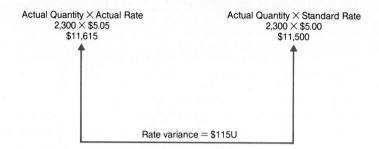

EXHIBIT 28–3
Direct Labor Rate Variance

Direct Labor Rate Variance

The **direct labor rate variance** is the difference between the actual rates paid during production and the standard rates. Exhibit 28–3 shows how to calculate this variance. Note that the format is identical to the one used in computing the materials price variance.

In June, Weston spent $115 more than standard as shown by the fact that the actual wage rates were higher than standard rates. Company guidelines would determine whether the variance should be investigated. When they exist, union contracts set wage rates and these are used as the standard rates. However, when management uses highly paid skilled workers to do less-skilled jobs, the result is an unfavorable rate variance. In nonunion organizations, too, assigning overskilled workers to jobs can create variances that are the responsibility of the assigning supervisors.

The equation for calculating the rate variance shows the difference in rates and keeps the quantity, the hours, constant:

$$AH = \text{Actual hours}$$
$$AR = \text{Actual rate}$$
$$SR = \text{Standard rate}$$

$$AH(AR - SR) = \text{Labor rate variance}$$
$$2{,}300(\$5.05 - \$5.00) = \$115U$$

Direct Labor Efficiency Variance

The **direct labor efficiency variance** compares how much labor time is used to produce the units of product with the amount of labor time that should have been used according to the standard. In calculating the labor efficiency variance, like the materials quantity variance, inputs are used, such as pounds of material or hours of labor. Both variances compare the amount of inputs actually used with the standard amount that should have been used to produce the units of product—the outputs. For example, the standard for labor calls for two hours of labor time to be used, the input, to produce one unit of product, the output. When there is an input-output relationship, efficiency can be measured, producing units of product, the outputs, with the right amount of pounds or hours, the inputs. Given enough time and materials, any number of products can be produced. For example, Weston could produce one unit of product using five labor hours, but that would be an inefficient use of labor time because it can be done in two hours. Efficiency variances measure whether products were produced with the right amount of inputs.

Exhibit 28–4 shows the formula used to calculate the labor efficiency

1132

EXHIBIT 28–4
Direct Labor Efficiency Variance

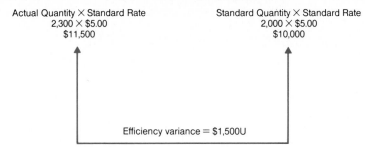

variance. Weston shows an unfavorable efficiency variance of $1,500 because production used more labor hours in June than the standard called for. The firm should have used 2,000 labor hours to produce 1,000 units (1,000 × 2 hours), but it actually used 2,300 hours. The inputs were too high relative to the outputs, and labor was inefficiently used.

The labor efficiency variance is very important because it shows whether workers are productive. An unfavorable efficiency variance may derive from a number of causes, including poor supervision, lack of motivation, inadequate training of workers, faulty machinery, or a poor grade of materials. When a variance exceeds company guidelines, it is investigated, whether it is favorable or unfavorable. Some large firms keep staffs on hand to conduct such investigations, whereas in other firms investigating variances requires additional investments of time and money.

Following is the formula for calculating the efficiency variance where SH is equal to standard hours:

$$SR(AH - SH) \quad = \quad \text{Labor efficiency variance}$$
$$\$5.00(2,300 \text{ hours} - 2,000 \text{ hours}) \quad = \quad \$1,500U$$

Weston's performance report for the production area showing the efficiency variance for June follows:

Weston Manufacturing Company
Production Department Performance Report
June 1988

Item	Actual Quantity	−	Standard Quantity	=	Difference	×	Standard Rate	=	Labor Efficiency Variance
Direct labor	2,300		2,000		300		$5.00		$1,500U

Analyzing Factory Overhead Costs

As already stated, factory overhead is composed of a variety of variable and fixed costs; therefore, it is a complex process to develop standards and variances for overhead costs. Developing overhead standards requires knowledge of a variety of concepts explained in previous chapters, including cost behavior patterns, budgeting, and the flow of costs in cost accounting systems.

Cost Behavior and Flexible Budgets

Chapter 23 showed basic cost behavior patterns and explained how mixed costs could be broken down into their fixed and variable components in order to be used in the planning process. Factory overhead is made up of fixed, variable, and mixed costs. In order to be able to develop standards for overhead, the accountant must analyze the cost behavior patterns of individual overhead items as well as overhead as a whole and see if their increases or decreases are connected to the increases or decreases in some activity base such as direct labor hours. When such a relationship has been determined, total overhead cost behavior can be expressed as a cost behavior formula similar to those described in Chapter 23.

$$\text{Total cost} = \text{Fixed cost} + \text{Variable cost}$$

The cost behavior formula for overhead is another example of a flexible budget that allows one to construct budgets at any level of activity in the relevant range. After a period ends, the firm's accountant prepares budgets based on the firm's actual activity level in order to evaluate performance. The term *flexible budget* rather than *standard cost* tends to be used to refer to overhead costs because overhead comprises a variety of costs.

A flexible budget can be used for all types of costs, provided there are enough data to determine cost behavior patterns. To determine factory overhead variances, cost behavior patterns must be analyzed for individual costs as well as for overhead as a whole. The cost behavior patterns are then used to budget overhead costs at the activity level prescribed in the master budget. At the same time, the predetermined overhead rate, used to apply overhead to work in process throughout the year, is calculated. During the year, as operations are carried out, overhead is applied to work in process using the rate decided on earlier, and overhead variances can be analyzed monthly using flexible budgets. At the end of the year, any remaining differences between actual and applied overhead left in the accounts are either closed to Cost of Goods Sold or prorated to Cost of Goods Sold, Work in Process, and Finished Goods. Exhibit 28–5 depicts the typical sequence of events just described for budgeting and control of overhead costs.

EXHIBIT 28–5
Budgeting and Control of Overhead Costs

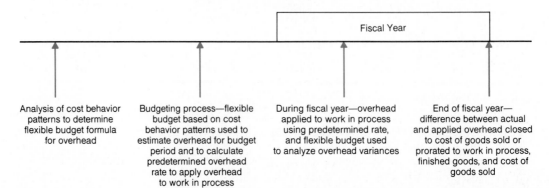

| Analysis of cost behavior patterns to determine flexible budget formula for overhead | Budgeting process—flexible budget based on cost behavior patterns used to estimate overhead for budget period and to calculate predetermined overhead rate to apply overhead to work in process | During fiscal year—overhead applied to work in process using predetermined rate, and flexible budget used to analyze overhead variances | End of fiscal year— difference between actual and applied overhead closed to cost of goods sold or prorated to work in process, finished goods, and cost of goods sold |

Using data from Weston Manufacturing Company, we will follow the sequence shown in Exhibit 28–5. The firm has done an analysis of the behavior patterns of their overhead costs and has found a relationship between changes in overhead and changes in direct labor hours as shown on the following page.

Cost Behavior Information

Variable:

Indirect material	$ .75 per DLH
Indirect labor	1.00 per DLH
Utilities, variable portion	.50 per DLH
Total	$2.25 per DLH

Fixed—annual:

Supervision	$ 75,000
Depreciation	36,000
Utilities, fixed portion	24,000
Total	$135,000

Total overhead cost = $135,000 + $2.25/DLH

According to its 1988 budget, Weston plans to produce 15,000 units of product in 1988 and to use 30,000 direct labor hours. The labor standard allows for two labor hours per unit. Using this activity level and the cost behavior formula shown above, Weston can estimate the total overhead cost for 1988:

$$
\begin{aligned}
\text{Total overhead cost} &= \$135{,}000 + \$2.25/\text{DLH} \\
&= \$135{,}000 + \$2.25(30{,}000\text{DLH}) \\
&= \$135{,}000 + \$67{,}500 \\
&= \$202{,}500
\end{aligned}
$$

After finding the relationship between budgeted overhead and the estimated activity level for the coming budget year, Weston can calculate the predetermined overhead rate that will be used to apply overhead to work in process throughout the coming year:

$$
\frac{\text{Estimated factory overhead costs}}{\text{Estimated direct labor hours}} = \text{Predetermined overhead rate}
$$

$$
\frac{\$202{,}500}{30{,}000\text{DLH}} = \$6.75 \text{ per DLH}
$$

The total overhead rate is $6.75 per DLH, which is easily divided into its fixed and variable parts: Of the $6.75, $2.25 is the cost per DLH for variable overhead; the difference of $4.50, therefore, is fixed overhead. To check the calculation, divide the fixed cost of $135,000 by 30,000 direct labor hours. The result should be $4.50.

All the calculations done thus far have been on an annual basis, but variance analysis for overhead is done most frequently on a monthly basis. We now use Weston's data to calculate variances for the month of June 1988.

Calculating Monthly Overhead Variances

For simplicity, assume that the annual budget estimates for Weston are to take place evenly throughout the year. This means that the budget calls for 15,000 units to be divided by 12 months—or 1,250 units per month—and 2,500 direct labor hours per month (1,250 × 2 DLH per unit). Similarly, the overhead budget for the month, with variable costs constant on a per-unit basis, would be as follows:

Overhead Budget—June 1988

Variable:		
Indirect material	$ .75	per DLH
Indirect labor	1.00	per DLH
Utilities	.50	per DLH
Total	$2.25	per DLH
Fixed:		
Supervision	$ 6,250	
Depreciation	3,000	
Utilities	2,000	
Total	$11,250	

Total overhead cost = $11,250 + $2.25/DLH

During June, Weston accumulated the following actual costs:

Actual Overhead Costs—June 1988

Variable:		
Indirect material		$ 1,775
Indirect labor		2,400
Utilities, variable portion		1,100
Total		5,275
Fixed:		
Supervision		6,500
Depreciation		3,000
Utilities, fixed portion		2,250
Total		11,750
Total overhead		$17,025
Units produced	1,000	
Direct labor hours	2,300	

Weston now has accumulated enough data to calculate three factory overhead variances: the spending variance, the efficiency variance, and the volume variance. The first two are similar to the price and quantity variances already calculated, whereas the volume variance tries to measure whether or not the estimates made during the budgeting process were accurate.

Overhead Spending Variance

The **overhead spending variance** compares actual overhead cost with a flexible budget for overhead at the actual activity level of 2,300 direct labor hours as follows:

Actual overhead	$17,025
Flexible budget at 2,300 DLH:	
Total overhead = $11,250 + $2.25(2,300DLH)	
= $11,250 + $5,175 =	16,425
Spending variance	$ 600U

There is an unfavorable variance for the month because Weston's actual overhead, at an activity level of 2,300 direct labor hours, was greater than the amount that should have been incurred at 2,300 direct labor hours. Exhibit 28–6 also shows the spending variance but breaks it down to provide information about individual overhead items.

Exhibit 28–6 provides more detailed information on overhead costs. Weston spent less than had been expected on the variable portion of utilities but more on indirect materials and labor. Note that the firm spent less than originally planned on two of the fixed overhead items. It is possible to have spending variances for fixed overhead items because budgets are basically estimates. Individual overhead costs need to be controlled and investigated when there is a significant variance.

Exhibit 28–7 on the next page shows how to calculate the spending variance using the same format as for direct materials and direct labor.

EXHIBIT 28–6
Overhead Spending Variance—Individual Items

	Actual	Budget Based on 2,300 Direct Labor Hours	Variance
Variable costs:			
Indirect material	$ 1,775	$ 1,725 (.75 × 2,300)	$ 50U
Indirect labor	2,400	2,300 (1.00 × 2,300)	100U
Utilities, variable	1,100	1,150 (.50 × 2,300)	50F
Total variable	5,275	5,175	100U
Fixed costs:			
Supervision	6,500	6,250	250U
Depreciation	3,000	3,000	0
Utilities, fixed	2,250	2,000	250U
Total fixed	11,750	11,250	500U
Total overhead	$17,025	$16,425	$600U

EXHIBIT 28–7
Overhead Spending Variance

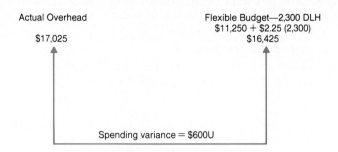

Actual Overhead

$17,025

Flexible Budget—2,300 DLH
$11,250 + $2.25 (2,300)
$16,425

Spending variance = $600U

Overhead Efficiency Variance

The **overhead efficiency variance** is similar in nature to the direct labor efficiency variance and the direct materials quantity variance. All of these variances examine the quantity of inputs used to produce the units of product in a given period, and all compare that quantity to the inputs that should have been used to produce the units of product according to the standard. Therefore, the overhead efficiency variance is computed by comparing a budget at the actual activity level with a budget at the standard activity level as follows for the Weston Manufacturing Company:

Flexible budget at 2,300 DLH:
　Total overhead = $11,250 + $2.25(2,300DLH)
　　　　　　　　 = $11,250 + $5,175　　　= $16,425

Flexible budget at 2,000 DLH:
　Total overhead = $11,250 + $2.25(2,000DLH)
　　　　　　　　 = $11,250 + $4,500　　　= 15,750
Efficiency variance　　　　　　　　　　　$　675U

Weston's overhead efficiency variance for June was unfavorable because the firm used 2,300 direct labor hours, whereas they should have used 2,000 direct labor hours (1,000 units $\times$ 2 DLH per unit). The fixed overhead of $11,250 is the same in both budgets, but the variable costs change as the number of direct labor hours changes. Note that the relationship here is not as direct as in the case of the labor efficiency variance because it is assumed, based on cost behavior analysis, that the inefficient use of direct labor hours also causes the inefficient use of overhead. When Weston used too many direct labor hours to produce 1,000 units in June, it caused direct labor costs to increase and produced an unfavorable efficiency variance. When there is an unfavorable labor efficiency variance, there also is an unfavorable overhead efficiency variance because both are calculated by measuring the difference between actual and standard hours for actual units produced.

　　The overhead efficiency variance for the most part derives from the variable overhead costs because only variable costs change as the activity level increases or decreases. This is shown clearly when the variance is computed with a formula similar to that for the labor efficiency variance. The standard rate is the rate for variable overhead:

SR(AH − SH)　 = Overhead efficiency variance
$2.25(2,300 hours − 2,000 hours) = $675U

EXHIBIT 28-8
Overhead Efficiency Variance

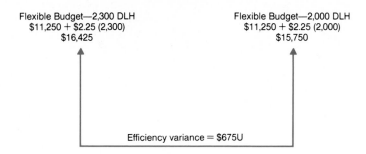

Exhibit 28-8 shows another way to calculate the overhead efficiency variance. To repeat, the way that one chooses to calculate a variance is based on personal preference.

Overhead Volume Variance

The **overhead volume variance** differs from the other variances studied in this chapter because it attempts to measure how well firms have used the capacity planned in the budgeting process. For example, Weston planned to produce 15,000 units of product and to use 30,000 direct labor hours in the 1988 budget, assuming that costs were incurred evenly throughout the year, and so the budget stipulated production of 1,250 units of product in June and 2,500 direct labor hours. Weston calculates the volume variance to measure whether this planned capacity actually has been used. The firm compares the amount of overhead applied to work in process with an overhead budget based on the standard activity level. The overhead applied to work in process is based on the predetermined overhead rate calculated during the budgeting process. Return to Exhibit 28-5 on page 1134 and review the sequence in the planning and control of overhead. Weston used a predetermined overhead rate of $6.75 for 1988 that was applied to work in process based on the standard hours allowed for the actual output:

Flexible budget at 2,000 DLH:
   Total overhead = $11,250 + $2.25(2,000DLH)
                         = $11,250 + $4,500   = $15,750
Applied overhead:
   2,000 standard DLH × $6.75   =   13,500
Volume variance $ 2,250U

Why is this an unfavorable variance? Weston applied overhead based on 2,000 standard direct labor hours called for by production of 1,000 units but had originally budgeted 2,500 direct labor hours (or 1,250 units) for the month of June. The firm has not produced as much as the planned capacity of 1,250 units and, therefore, an unfavorable variance occurred. The volume variance measures how well a firm has used its capacity. Capacity is tied to fixed overhead costs because variable costs change as activity changes. If fewer units than planned are produced, fixed costs are divided among fewer units than planned when the overhead rate originally was calculated during the budgeting process. Therefore, the volume variance relates to fixed overhead costs. The following formula for the variance clearly shows the difference between

Accounting Information for Control: Standard Costing

EXHIBIT 28-9
Overhead Volume Variance

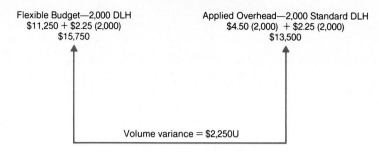

Flexible Budget—2,000 DLH
$11,250 + $2.25 (2,000)
$15,750

Applied Overhead—2,000 Standard DLH
$4.50 (2,000) + $2.25 (2,000)
$13,500

Volume variance = $2,250U

the number of hours in the budget and the standard hours applied and keeps the standard fixed overhead rate constant:

$$\text{SR(Budgeted hours} - \text{Standard hours)} = \text{Volume variance}$$
$$\$4.50(2{,}500 \text{ hours} - 2{,}000 \text{ hours}) = \$2{,}250U$$

Exhibit 28–9 shows another way to calculate the volume variance. Note that the amount of variable overhead is the same in both calculations, but there is a difference in the amount of fixed overhead as a result of producing fewer units of product than called for in the original budget.

The reason there is a volume variance is best seen in Exhibit 28–10, which depicts fixed overhead cost in a graph. This exhibit shows that estimates of fixed overhead for planning and control purposes are regarded as one amount fixed within the relevant range. The line labeled *budget* in Exhibit 28–10 has a fixed cost behavior pattern. In order to include fixed overhead in the cost of units of product, however, that fixed cost must be divided into an amount per unit of product and applied to the units in work in process. When we do this we are forcing the fixed overhead cost to behave as if it were a variable cost. That is why the line showing the amount of fixed overhead ap-

EXHIBIT 28-10
Budgeted and Applied Fixed Overhead

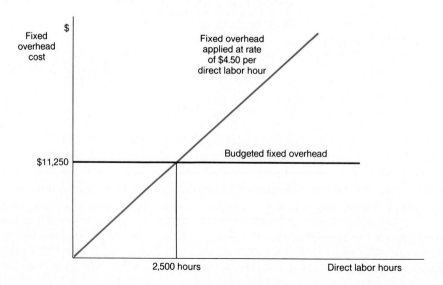

plied to work in process behaves in a variable manner. These two ways of viewing fixed overhead cost derive from two different accounting purposes. In order to calculate the cost of the units of product, accounting authorities, as well as the IRS, require that every unit of product include some portion of fixed overhead costs. The more units produced, the more fixed overhead is applied to work in process. For planning and control purposes, however, fixed overhead is regarded as a lump sum that is fixed within the relevant range. Therefore, the volume variance occurs when there is a difference between the fixed overhead in the budget and the amount of fixed overhead applied to work in process.

Over- and Underapplied Overhead

Chapter 27 explained why there is a difference between the amount of overhead applied to work in process and the actual overhead costs accumulated in the overhead account. When a firm's actual overhead exceeds applied overhead, they are said to be underapplied. If applied overhead exceeds actual overhead, its overhead is overapplied. In effect the over- or underapplied overhead represents the total sum of all of the variances for factory overhead. For Weston Manufacturing Company, actual overhead in June 1988 was $17,025, and applied overhead was $13,500. Weston was underapplied for June by the amount of $3,525. Adding together all of the variances computed thus far for overhead, Weston finds that the total is $3,525:

Spending variance	$ 600U
Efficiency variance	675U
Volume variance	2,250U
Underapplied overhead	$3,525U

It is useful when working problems on overhead variances to know that all of the variances must add up to the amount of over- or underapplied overhead.

Summary of Variances

Exhibit 28–11 on the next page summarizes all of the variances explained in this chapter. Note that there are strong similarities among some variances. For example, the direct materials price variance, the direct labor rate variance, and the overhead spending variance measure the difference between what was paid and what should have been paid according to standard. Similarly, the direct materials quantity variance, the direct labor efficiency variance, and the overhead efficiency variance all measure the actual inputs (pounds or labor hours) for the units produced relative to the standard inputs for the units produced. The volume variance alone measures the use of plant capacity compared with planned capacity in the budget. The difference between total actual overhead and total overhead applied to work in process is the sum of all overhead variances.

Variance Investigation

This chapter has emphasized that some variances fall within an acceptable range according to management guidelines. With management by exception, only the exceptional variances need to be investigated, because **variance in-**

EXHIBIT 28-11
Summary of Variance Analysis

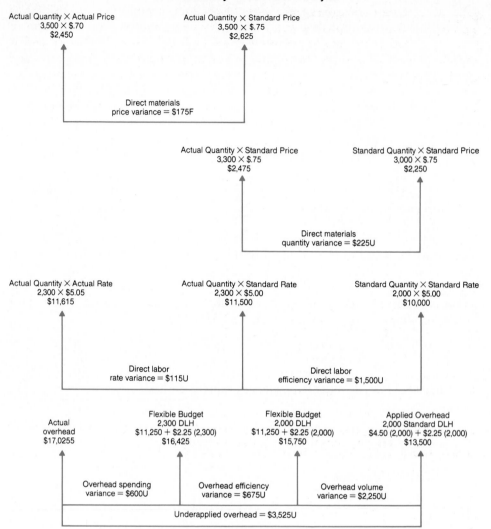

vestigation costs time and money. Therefore, firms typically set guidelines establishing their criteria for investigating variances. Some of the most commonly used criteria are the following:

1. *Materiality.* Management sets either a dollar amount or a percentage of standard cost that is considered to be large enough to investigate. For example, a large aerospace firm investigates variances that are higher or lower than 3% of standard cost. A variance that is significantly lower than standard is just as important as one that is higher. In many cases, firms combine percentage-guideline and absolute-dollar-amount data. A variance might be considered significant if it is greater than 5% of standard cost, or $1,000.

2. *Frequency.* If a variance is consistently above or below standard, it may indicate that a standard is out of date or is not being adhered to by supervisors.

3. *Controllability.* Separating costs into those that are controllable by

managers and those that are not is basic to responsibility accounting. Some variances may be significant in size but out of the control of the responsible manager. Sometimes, for example, when labor wage rates are set by union contract, increases are not under the control of management. Similarly, changes in utility rates, tax rates, and insurance rates are beyond management control.

4. *Importance.* Some costs are more important to the long-run profitability of a firm than others. For example, in many firms maintenance costs often are carefully monitored to ensure that necessary procedures are not postponed. Consistently favorable variances may produce short-run savings but may lead to expensive repairs or breakdowns in the future. The guidelines for maintenance and similar costs are frequently more stringent than for other types of costs.

5. *Statistical techniques.* These techniques, more precisely than the non-statistical criteria, try to isolate the variances that are *not* due to random causes. Firms using statistical methods to set criteria for variance investigation use a range of acceptable variances, rather than one number. If a variance falls within the acceptable range, it is regarded as being due to random causes out of management control. Variances that fall outside the acceptable range are considered exceptions that management should investigate. Exhibit 28–12 shows a simple version of a control chart after the variance data have been statistically sampled and plotted. The dots represent the variances for the period, and the dotted lines show the acceptable range for variances according to the budget. Variances falling within the dotted lines are considered normal fluctuations in the production process. The variances falling outside of the dotted lines would be investigated. The wider the bands within the dotted lines, the fewer variances would be investigated. Management sets the limits based on past experience and the nature of the individual production process.

EXHIBIT 28–12
Statistical Control Chart

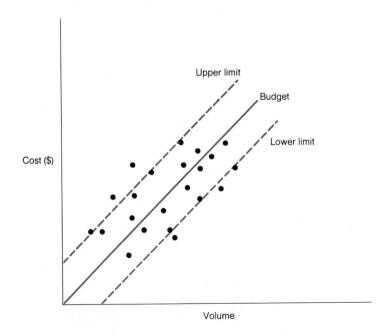

Advantages and Disadvantages of Standard Cost Systems

Standard cost systems are widely used because they offer some advantages to organizations. Some of the most important advantages of standard cost accounting systems as opposed to actual cost accounting systems follow:

1. Standard costs add a much greater degree of precision to the planning and control process. Standards can measure efficiency by calculating whether the right amount of inputs is used to produce the outputs, the units of product. Control systems measure performance and provide feedback; standard costs allow organizations to do this in a precise way.
2. Standard costs help organizations to use management by exception, which allows managment to spend its time on problems rather than on normal operations.
3. A standard cost accounting system simplifies the bookkeeping process. Materials, labor, and overhead accounts are kept at standard rather than actual cost, and the differences are isolated in variance accounts.
4. Standard costs also help in responsibility accounting because variances provide an important means of evaluating the performance of responsibility center managers.
5. Standard costs can be a motivating force for employees when they are set at realistic levels and are periodically revised.

There are sometimes disadvantages to using a standard cost system. The most important follow:

1. The use of variances for performance evaluation may cause employees to focus on only those variables that are consistently measured and to ignore other aspects of their work. Employees also may feel that they are noticed only for items that produce significant variances, and consequently are reprimanded for inadequate performance and are not praised enough.
2. A standard cost system is expensive to develop, and it may require additional funds to update and improve standards over the years.
3. Labor may view the setting of efficiency standards with mistrust, seeing it as a means of forcing employees to work harder.
4. It is sometimes difficult to discover the cause of a particular variance, which may result from the interaction of many factors.

Generally, standard cost systems are beneficial if they are wisely designed and administered. We have focused on the use of standard costs in manufacturing firms because that is where they are most widely used; however, the implementation of standard cost systems has become more and more common in other types of firms because of their usefulness in planning and control.

Summary of Learning Objectives

1. *Standard costs and their relation to control systems.* The standard cost of a unit of product is the amount that it should take to produce the unit of product as opposed to the actual cost. The standard cost is a flexible budget formula for each individual unit of product.

   Standard cost systems give management more precise price and quantity figures than actual cost systems to use in planning, measurement, and performance evaluation.

2. *Understand the different types of standards and how they are set.* Ideal standards are set with the expectation of complete efficiency and performance all of the time—that work will never be interrupted and machines will never break down. Currently attainable standards are those that should be incurred under very efficient operating conditions but that take into account normal spoilage, machine breakdowns, and time loss.

Setting standards for manufacturing costs is a complex process involving industrial engineers, accountants, purchasing agents, and managers. Separate calculations are made for materials, labor, and overhead and are added together on the standard cost card, which shows what one unit of product should cost.

3. *Direct materials variance.* When the materials inventory is carried at standard cost, the materials price variance is calculated when materials are purchased. The actual quantity used in the variance formula is the quantity of material purchased. The formula for computing the direct materials price variance is:

$$AQ(AP - SP) = \text{Materials price variance.}$$

The materials quantity variance is prepared when materials are issued to production, and the actual quantity used in the formula is the number of pounds used in production for a given period. The formula for computing the materials quantity variance is:

$$SP(AQ - SQ) = \text{Materials quantity variance.}$$

4. *Direct labor rate variance.* The direct labor rate variance measures the difference between the actual rate paid for labor and the standard rate, while using the actual labor hours as the quantity. The formula for computing the direct labor rate variance is:

$$AH(AR - SR) = \text{Direct labor rate variance.}$$

The direct labor efficiency variance formula keeps the rate constant at standard while calculating the difference between the actual number of direct labor hours used and the standard number of direct labor hours, the number of hours it should have taken to produce the actual output. The formula for calculating the direct labor efficiency variance is:

$$SR(AH - SH) = \text{Direct labor efficiency variance.}$$

5. *Factory overhead costs expressed as flexible budgets.* Because factory overhead is made up of a variety of fixed, variable, and mixed costs, it is necessary to analyze the cost behavior patterns for overhead in order to develop standards. The cost behavior formula used in the budgeting process is a flexible budget that can be constructed for various levels of activity in the relevant range. The flexible budget formula for overhead is used to calculate the overhead cost for the master budget. The predetermined overhead rate can then be calculated by dividing the budgeted overhead by the estimated activity level for the budget year. A flexible budget also can be used when the period is over to evaluate performance by preparing budgets based on the actual and standard quantities.

6. *Preparing variances for factory overhead.* The overhead spending variance formula measures the difference between actual overhead cost and a flexible budget at the actual activity level. It is often used for evaluating individual overhead costs as well as for overhead as a whole. The formula for calculating the overhead spending variance is:

Actual overhead − Overhead budget at actual activity level =
Overhead spending variance
or (if data are available)
AH (AP − SP) = Overhead spending variance.

The overhead efficiency variance is based on the assumption that the efficient or inefficient use of an activity base such as direct labor hours will cause a similar efficient or inefficient use of overhead. The overhead efficiency variance formula calculates the difference between an overhead budget at the actual activity level and an overhead budget at the standard activity level:

Overhead budget at actual activity level − Overhead budget at standard activity
level = Overhead efficiency variance
or
(variable) SR(AH − SH) = Overhead efficiency variance.

The overhead volume variance formula measures the difference between the overhead applied to work in process and an overhead budget based on the standard hours allowed for the actual units of product produced. The amount of applied overhead is based on the predetermined overhead rate, which is calculated by using a budgeted capacity level. The volume variance measures whether a firm has actually used the capacity planned for in the budgeting process. The formula for finding the volume variance is:

Overhead budget at standard activity level − Applied overhead =
Overhead volume variance
or
(fixed) SR(Budgeted hours − Standard hours) = Volume variance.

7. *The ways in which variances are investigated.* Most firms set guidelines for variance investigation. Some of the most commonly used criteria are (a) materiality—a dollar amount and/or a percentage of standard cost, (b) frequency—consistent occurrence of a variance, (c) controllability—some variances may be significant but may not be under the control of management, (d) importance—costs that are critical to the long-run profitability of a firm may be investigated more readily, and (e) statistical techniques—a range of acceptable variances is established through plotting data on a control chart.

8. *The advantages and disadvantages of standard cost systems.* The major advantages of standard cost systems compared with actual cost systems are:
   a. Standard costs add a greater degree of precision to the planning and control process.
   b. Standard costs aid management by exception.
   c. A standard cost accounting system simplifies the bookkeeping process because when it is used, manufacturing accounts are kept at standard, which makes transfers among manufacturing accounts much faster.

d. Standard costs and variances aid in responsibility accounting by providing a basis for evaluating the manager of a responsibility center.

e. Standard costs systems can motivate employees.

The most important disadvantages of standard cost systems are:

a. Performance evaluation solely by variance analysis may cause employees to ignore non-evaluated tasks.

b. A standard cost system is expensive to develop and maintain.

c. Labor may react negatively to efficiency standards.

d. It is sometimes difficult to discover the cause of a variance because variances are often the result of complex interactions of many factors.

Key Terms

Currently attainable standards	Overhead spending variance
Direct labor efficiency variance	Overhead volume variance
Direct labor rate variance	Standard
Direct materials price variance	Standard cost
Direct materials quantity (or usage) variance	Standard cost card
Ideal standard	Variances
Overhead efficiency variance	Variance investigation

Problem for Your Review

Materials, Labor, and Overhead Variances. The International Chemical Company is a small company that produces one product and uses a standard cost system. The purchasing manager is responsible for the materials price variance, and the production manager is responsible for the materials efficiency and direct labor variances.

The following information is available for the operations of January 1987:

	Standard	Actual
Direct material:		
Price	$2.00/lb.	$1.80/lb.
Quantity used in production	5 lbs./unit	2,400 lbs.
Direct labor:		
Rate	$8.00/hr.	$9.00/hr.
Quantity	3 hrs./unit	1,600 hrs.
Factory overhead (figures derived from annual projections made during budgeting process):		
Fixed cost	$3,000/mo.	
Variable cost	$2.50/DLH	
Total		$7,600

Pounds of direct material purchased = 2,600 pounds
Units of product produced during the month = 400 units
Budgeted production level for January = 600 units

Required:

a. Direct materials price variance.

b. Direct materials quantity variance.

c. Direct labor rate variance.

d. Direct labor efficiency variance.

e. Factory overhead spending variance.

f. Factory overhead efficiency variance.

g. Factory overhead volume variance.

h. As a result of labor trouble, some less-skilled workers were used in January. If you were the general manager, how would you interpret the materials and labor variances?

Solution

We use the formulas here because it is a simpler format.

a. Direct materials price variance:

$$AQ(AP - SP) = \text{Materials price variance}$$
$$2,600(\$1.80 - \$2.00) = \$520F$$

b. Direct materials quantity variance:

$$SP(AQ - SQ) = \text{Materials quantity variance}$$
$$\$2.00(2,400 \text{ lbs.} - 2,000 \text{ lbs.}) = \$800U$$

c. Direct labor rate variance:

$$AH(AR - SR) = \text{Labor rate variance}$$
$$1,600(\$9.00 - \$8.00) = \$1,600U$$

d. Direct labor efficiency variance:

$$SR(AH - SH) = \text{Labor efficiency variance}$$
$$\$8.00(1,600 - 1,200) = \$3,200U$$

e. Factory overhead spending variance: This formula compares actual overhead cost with a flexible budget for overhead at the actual activity level of 1,600 direct labor hours.

Actual overhead		$7,600
Flexible budget at 1,600 DLH:		
Total overhead = $3,000 + $2.50(1,600 DLH)		
= $3,000 + $4,000	=	7,000
Spending variance		$ 600U

f. Factory overhead efficiency variance: This variance is computed by comparing a budget at the actual activity level with a budget at the standard activity level.

Flexible budget at 1,600 DLH:		
Total overhead = $3,000 + $2.50(1,600 DLH)		
= $3,000 + $4,000	=	7,000
Flexible budget at 1,200 DLH:		
Total overhead = $3,000 + $2.50(1,200 DLH)		
= $3,000 + $3,000	=	6,000
Efficiency variance		$1,000U

g. Factory overhead volume variance: This formula compares the budget based on the standard activity level with the amount applied to work in process. We first compute the overhead rate used to apply overhead to work in process; this is based on the budgeted production of 600 units at 3 DLH per unit.

$$\text{Overhead rate} = \frac{\$3,000 + \$2.50(1,800 \text{ DLH})}{1,800 \text{DLH}} = \$4.167/\text{DLH}$$

Flexible budget at 1,200 DLH:		
Total overhead = $3,000 + $2.50(1,200 DLH)		
= $3,000 + $3,000	=	$6,000
Applied overhead:		
1,200 standard DLH × $4.167	=	5,000
Volume variance		$1,000U

h. Less-skilled workers used too much material and labor time, resulting in unfavorable variances for the use of material and labor. Using more material than the standard allowed in producing the units of product led to an unfavorable materials quantity variance. Similarly, less-skilled workers spent more time than the standard allowed in making the units of product, and this led to an unfavorable labor efficiency variance.

1148

Questions

1. Define *standard cost*.

2. How are standard costs used in management control systems?

3. Briefly discuss different types of standards.

4. Discuss some of the problems that might be created by standards that are set too high.

5. What is meant by the term *management by exception?*

6. Describe briefly how standard costs are set for (a) materials, (b) labor, and (c) overhead.

7. Who generally is responsible for the materials price variance?

8. Give reasons to justify the calculation of the materials price variance at time of purchase rather than when materials are put into production.

9. Express in terms of a formula the calculation of (a) materials price variance, (b) materials quantity variance, (c) direct labor rate variance, and (d) direct labor efficiency variance.

10. Briefly describe what each of the following variance formulas attempts to measure: (a) materials price, (b) materials quantity, (c) labor rate, and (d) labor efficiency.

11. Generally, the responsibility for the materials quantity variance lies with the production area. When is production not responsible?

12. Discuss the importance of the labor efficiency variance in the management control function.

13. Describe some of the most commonly used criteria used to set guidelines for variance investigation.

14. Discuss the advantages and disadvantages of standard cost systems.

15. What does the volume variance tell a manager?

Exercises

1. Materials Variance. During the month of October, 2,000 pounds of material M were purchased for the production of product P by Westwood Manufacturing Company.

Direct materials standards:	
Price	$.75 per pound
Quantity	4 pounds per unit of P
Actual data—October 1988	
Price	$.80 per pound
Actual usage	1,700 pounds
P produced	400 units

Required:
Calculate:
   a. The direct materials price variance.
   b. The direct materials quantity variance.

2. Direct Labor Variance. The direct labor standard for the production of one unit of product P is 2 1/2 hours. As in Exercise 1, 400 units of product P were produced during October. The standard hourly direct labor rate is $7.50. During October, 950 actual hours were used at an hourly rate of $7.80.

Required:
Calculate for October:
   a. The total direct labor variance.
   b. The direct labor rate variance.
   c. The direct labor efficiency variance.

3. Overhead Rate. The Jacob Company uses a standard cost system. The overhead budgets for January are given at the top of the next page.

Required:
Calculate:
   a. The total standard monthly overhead cost.
   b. The monthly predetermined overhead rate.

Variable:		
Indirect materials		$.80 per DLH
Indirect labor		.60 per DLH
Utilities, variable portion		.75 per DLH
Fixed, monthly:		
Supervision	$2,000	
Insurance	500	
Depreciation	400	
Utilities, fixed portion	600	
Total	$3,500	

Standard monthly production: in units = 700
in direct labor hours = 1,400

4. Overhead Variance. Assume that the Jacob Company described in Exercise 3 accumulated the following actual data for January 1989:

Actual Overhead Costs Incurred	
Variable:	
Indirect materials	$1,150
Indirect labor	820
Utilities, variable portion	1,250
Fixed, monthly:	
Supervision	1,800
Insurance	500
Depreciation	400
Utilities, fixed portion	750
Total	$6,670

Units produced in January = 650
Direct labor hours used = 1,400

Required:

Calculate:

a. Overhead spending variance.

b. Overhead efficiency variance.

5. Overhead Variance.

Required:

Assume that in the preceding question actual direct labor hours were 1,350. What is the overhead volume variance? What is the volume variance if actual labor hours are 1,500?

6. Direct Materials Variance. The direct materials standards for one unit of product A follow:

	Standard Quantity	Price per Pound	Standard Cost
Direct material x_1	2 pounds	$2	$4
Direct material x_2	3 pounds	3	9

During the first quarter of 1987, the following information is accumulated:

a. Forty thousand pounds of direct material X_1 are purchased at a total cost of $78,000. Fifty thousand pounds of direct material X_2 are purchased at a total cost of $155,000.

b. Twenty-seven thousand pounds of material X_1 and 42,500 pounds of material X_2 are used to produce 14,000 units of product A.

Required:

a. Compute for both X_1 and X_2 the materials price variance.

b. Compute for both X_1 and X_2 the materials quantity variance.

7. Direct Labor Variance. The direct labor standard per unit of product in Allison Company is two hours at the rate of $6 per hour. During 1988 the company worked 8,200 hours to produce 4,000 units of product, and the direct labor cost amounted to $51,250.

Required:

a. What is the standard labor cost for 4,000 units of product? What is the total direct labor variance?

b. Compute the direct labor rate variance and the direct labor efficiency variance.

8. Materials Variance. The Fleetwood Company uses a standard cost system and produces only one product. The standard calls for two pounds of material per unit of product. The following additional information is given:

Materials price variance	
(for 8,000 pounds purchased)	$800F
Materials quantity variance	$800U
Standard price per pound	$4
Standard quantity per unit of product	2 pounds
Actual units produced	3,500 units

Required:

a. Compute the unit price of material and total cost of the material purchased.

b. How many pounds of materials were used?

9. Direct Labor Variance. In December 1988 a total of 3,535 units of product were produced by the Allex Manufacturing Company. The following information is given:

Direct labor standard: Rate	$5.50 per hour
Quantity	4 hours per unit
Actual data—December 31, 1988	
Direct labor rate variance	$4,200U
Direct labor efficiency variance	770F

Required:

Compute the actual labor rate and total labor cost for the month of December.

10. Overhead Variance. The 1989 production budget and overhead cost behavior patterns for the Weston Company are as follows:

Variable overhead	$1.50 per DLH
Fixed overhead—annual	$150,000
Production budget	15,000 units
Standard direct labor hours per unit of product	4 hours

During 1989 the company experienced an unexpected booming market, and actual production, which was 16,000 units, exceeded the original budget. Actual overhead amounted to $251,000, and 66,000 hours of direct labor were used.

Required:

Calculate:

a. The spending variance.

b. The efficiency variance.

c. The volume variance.

Problem Set A

28A-1. Materials and Labor Variances. Studley Shirts, Inc. manufactures men's shirts. The standard costs for a dozen long-sleeved Dulex shirts are:

Direct materials	20 yards @ $1.00	$20.00
Direct labor	4 hours @ $6.50	26.00
Standard cost per dozen		$46.00

During September 1988, 74,000 yards of direct materials were purchased at a price of $.98 per yard. In addition, 20,800 yards of material and 3,920 hours of direct labor were used in manufacturing 1,000 dozen Dulex shirts. The direct labor rate was 5% greater than standard.

Required:
Calculate:

a. The direct materials price and quantity variances.
b. The direct labor rate variance and direct labor efficiency variance.
c. What are some possible reasons for the direct materials price variance? What area is generally responsible for this variance?

28A-2. Materials and Labor Variances. The Davis Company, a small company producing a single product, uses a standard cost system. Standard cost for one unit of product is:

Direct materials	4 pounds	$20.00
Direct labor	4 hours	24.00

During July, 4,000 pounds of direct materials were purchased, and there was an increase of 10% in both materials cost and wages. Three thousand two hundred fifty pounds of direct material and 3,300 hours of direct labor were used in production. There was a $250 unfavorable materials quantity variance.

Required:

a. Calculate July's direct materials price variance.
b. How many units of product were produced in July?
c. What is Davis's direct labor rate and efficiency variance for July?

28A-3. Materials, Labor, and Overhead Variances. The Norman Products Company manufactures one product. Standard costs for one unit of product are as follows:

Materials: 5 pounds @ $2.00	$10.00
Direct labor: 2 hours @ $6.00	12.00
Factory overhead: 2 hours @ $.75	1.50
Total unit cost	$23.50

The factory overhead is based on a yearly volume of 12,000 units, or 1,000 units per month. Budgeted factory overhead totals $18,000 per year, which includes $12,000 fixed costs and $.25 per direct labor hour in variable cost. Production and cost data for the month of April 1988 are as follows:

Units of product manufactured	1,100 units
Direct materials purchased	6,000 pounds
Direct material used	5,500 pounds
Direct labor hours incurred	2,250 hours
Purchase price per pound of direct material	$2.10
Direct labor rate per hour	$5.80
Factory overhead cost incurred	$1,880

Required:

a. Compute the materials price and quantity variances for April.
b. Compute the direct labor rate and efficiency variances for April.

1152

c. Compute the factory overhead spending variance, the factory overhead efficiency variance, and the factory overhead volume variance.

d. What is the total amount of under- or overapplied overhead?

28A-4. Overhead Rates. The following information relates to the 1987 factory overhead budget for the Greenberg Manufacturing Company:

Factory Overhead Cost	
Variable portion:	
Indirect materials	$0.50/DLH
Indirect labor	0.60/DLH
Lubricants	0.40/DLH
Supplies	0.25/DLH
Utilities	0.25/DLH
Total	$2.00/DLH
Fixed portion:	
Utilities	$200,000
Depreciation	30,000
Rent	60,000
Setup time	10,000
Total	$300,000
Total overhead cost =	
$300,000 + $2.00/DLH	

The production budget for 1987 is 150,000 units of product, or 300,000 direct labor hours.

Required:

a. Compute the estimate of total overhead cost for 1987.

b. What is the predetermined overhead rate for 1987?

c. Compute the overhead budget for each month, assuming that factory overhead is incurred evenly throughout 1987.

d. If Greenberg Manufacturing produces 10,000 units in February 1987, what is the overhead volume variance? Explain why it is favorable or unfavorable.

28A-5. Overhead Variances. Assume that the Greenberg Manufacturing Company in Problem 28A-4 gathered the following data for operations in January 1987:

Actual units produced	12,000
Actual direct labor hours worked	25,000
Actual factory overhead cost	
Variable portion:	
Indirect materials	$13,000
Indirect labor	15,500
Lubricants	10,900
Supplies	6,200
Utilities	6,400
Total	52,000
Fixed portion:	
Utilities	16,800
Depreciation	2,500
Rent	5,000
Setup time	900
Total	25,200
Total factory overhead	$77,200

Required:

a. Compute Greenberg's factory overhead spending variance for July 1987.

b. Compute Greenberg's factory overhead efficiency variance for July 1987.

Accounting Information for Control: Standard Costing

c. Compute Greenberg's factory overhead volume variance for July 1987.

d. What is the amount of over- or underapplied overhead in July?

e. If Greenberg produces 13,000 units in August, will the volume variance be favorable or unfavorable? Why?

28A–6. Materials, Labor, and Variable Overhead Variances. The standard cost for one unit of product manufactured by the Lyon Company follows:

Direct materials	4 units at $3	$12
Direct labor	2 hours at $4	8
Variable overhead	2 hours at $3	6
Total standard cost per unit		$26

During January, 1,000 units of product were manufactured, and 4,100 units of direct materials and 2,050 hours of direct labor were used. There was no beginning inventory of materials, and at the end of January, 1,000 units of material purchased during January were still on hand at a cost of $3,100. Direct labor cost and variable overhead cost incurred in January were $8,610 and $5,945, respectively.

Required:

a. Compute Lyon's direct materials price and quantity variances for January.

b. Compute Lyon's direct labor rate and efficiency variances for January.

c. Compute Lyon's spending and efficiency variances for variable overhead in January. The factory overhead rate is based on direct labor hours.

d. If overhead is applied to production on the basis of direct labor hours, is it possible to have a favorable direct labor efficiency variance and an unfavorable variable overhead efficiency variance? Explain.

28A–7. Materials, Labor, and Overhead Variances. Assume that the Weston Manufacturing Company incurred the following actual costs in July 1988:

Direct materials:		
Purchase price	$.72 per pound	
Units purchased	3,600 pounds	
Units used in production	3,500 pounds	
Direct labor:		
Rate	$5.10 per hour	
Hours worked	2,100 hours	
Factory overhead:		
Variable:		
Indirect materials	$ 1,800	
Indirect labor	2,350	
Utilities, variable portion	1,320	
Total	5,470	
Fixed:		
Supervision	6,600	
Depreciation	3,000	
Utilities, fixed portion	2,300	
Total	11,900	
Total overhead	$17,370	

One thousand one hundred units of product were manufactured in July. The standard costs were unchanged from those of June as shown in the chapter.

Required:

a. Compute direct materials price and quantity variances.

b. Compute direct labor rate and efficiency variances.

c. Compute factory overhead spending, efficiency, and volume variances.

d. What is the total amount of over- or underapplied overhead for July?

Problem Set B

28B–1. Standard Materials Cost; Materials and Labor Variances. The Magidget Company manufactures only one kind of gidget. The standard cost of production of one gidget is:

Direct materials	5 lbs. @ ?	?
Direct labor	4 hours @ 7.50	$30.00

During June, the company purchased 22,000 pounds of direct materials at a total cost of $41,800, 95% of its standard price. Production used 21,000 pounds of direct materials to produce 4,000 gidgets. Total direct labor cost amounted to $130,350. Actual direct labor used exceeded the standard by 500 hours.

Required:
   a. What is the standard price per unit of direct materials?
   b. Compute Magidget's direct materials price and quantity variances for June.
   c. Compute the company's direct labor rate and efficiency variances for June.
   d. What are some possible reasons for the direct materials price variance? What area is generally held responsible for this variance?

28B–2. Materials and Labor Variances. The Ming Company uses a standard cost system. The standard for one unit of product X follows:

Direct materials price	$8.00 per pound
Direct materials quantity	2 pounds
Direct labor rate	$7.50 per hour
Direct labor quantity	1 hour

The actual data for February 1989 follow:

Direct materials purchased	1,000 pounds @ 112.5% of standard price
Direct materials used	10 pounds more than the standard quantity allowed
Direct labor rate	125% of the standard rate
Direct labor hours used	20 hours more than the standard hours allowed
Units of product produced	450

Required:
   a. Calculate the company's direct materials price and quantity variances.
   b. Calculate the company's direct labor rate and efficiency variances.

28B–3. Materials, Labor, and Overhead Variances. The Delta Manufacturing Corporation manufactures one product. Standard costs for materials, direct labor, and factory overhead are as follows:

Materials, 10 gallons @ .50	$ 5.00
Direct labor, 1 hour @ $8	8.00
Factory overhead, 1 hour @ 2.50	2.50
Total standard cost per unit	$15.50

The factory overhead is based on a normal yearly volume of 1.2 million direct labor hours. Budgeted overhead costs are estimated to be $3 million per year.
   Production and cost data for October 1987 are as follows:

Units of product manufactured	100,000 units
Direct materials purchased	1,200,000 gallons
Direct materials used	1,050,000 gallons
Direct labor hours incurred	99,500 hours
Purchase price of direct materials per unit	$.52
Labor rate per hour	$7.80
Actual factory overhead incurred	$255,000

Required:

 a. Compute Delta's materials price and quantity variances for October.

 b. Compute the company's direct labor rate and efficiency variances for October.

28B-4. Calculation of Unknowns. The following data are available on the single product produced by the Albert Manufacturing Company:

Standard Cost per Unit	
Materials: Price	$4 per pound
Quantity	?
Direct labor: Rate	$?
Quantity	?
Variable factory overhead	?
Standard cost per unit	?

During February, the company paid $33,550 for 6,100 direct labor hours, all of which were used in the production of 3,000 units of the product; 6,400 pounds of materials were purchased; and 5,900 pounds were used in production. Variable factory overhead is applied to work in process based on direct labor hours. The following variance data are available:

Materials price variance	1,280U
Materials quantity variance	400F
Direct labor rate variance	3,050U
Total direct labor variance	3,550U
Variable factory overhead efficiency variance	500U
Variable factory overhead spending variance	0

Required:

 a. Compute the actual cost paid per pound for direct materials.

 b. Compute the direct labor efficiency variance.

 c. Compute the standard pounds allowed for the direct materials.

 d. Compute the standard direct labor rate per hour.

 e. Compute the standard variable factory overhead rate and total variable factory overhead cost.

28B-5. Materials, Labor, Variable Overhead Variances. The Magic Instrument Co., Inc. is a large producer of musical instruments. The company uses standard costs for all of its products. Following are the standard and actual costs for May 1988 for one of the company's products:

		Standard Cost	Actual Cost
Direct materials:			
Standard	1.5 pounds @ $2.40 per pound	3.60	
Actual	1.6 pounds @ $2.30 per pound		3.68
Direct labor:			
Standard	0.5 hours @ $6.40 per hour	3.20	
Actual	0.6 hours @ $6.20 per hour		3.72
Variable overhead:			
Standard	0.5 hours @ $3 per hours	1.50	
Actual	0.4 hours @ $2.25 per hour		.90
Total per-unit cost		$8.30	$8.30

Actual production for the month was 10,000 units.

Required:

   a. Compute the following variances for May:

      1. Materials price and quantity.
      2. Direct labor rate and efficiency.
      3. Variable overhead spending and efficiency.

   b. Based on the above answers, explain to the manager what might be the reasons for the zero total variance during May.

28B-6. Materials, Labor, and Overhead Variances. The Mitsuyasu Company uses a standard cost system in accounting for its production costs. The standard cost of a unit of product follows:

Direct materials	2 gallons @ $7.50 per gallon
Direct labor	2 hours @ $6.00 per hour
Factory overhead, variable portion	2 hours @ $5.00 per hour

Fixed factory overhead costs are budgeted at $150,000 per month. The actual unit costs for the month of January 1987 were as follows:

Direct materials	2.1 gallons @ 7.50 per gallon
Direct labor	1.9 hours @ $6.30 per hour
Variable factory overhead	2.1 hours @ 5.20 per hour

The production budget for 1987 is 2,000 units per month. In January, 1,050 units of product were manufactured; fixed overhead amounted to $155,000.

Required:

   a. Compute the direct materials quantity variance for January.
   b. Compute the direct labor rate and efficiency variances for January.
   c. Compute factory overhead spending, efficiency, and volume variances for January.
   d. What is the total amount of over- or underapplied overhead for January?
   e. If Mitsuyasu had produced 2,325 units in January, would the volume variance have been favorable or unfavorable? Why?

28B-7. Materials, Labor, and Overhead Variances. Assume that the company discussed in the preceding question incurred the following actual costs in February:

Direct materials (4,150 gallons)	$31,540
Direct labor (4,080 hours)	$26,520
Variable factory overhead (4,080)	$21,216

Two thousand fifty units of product were manufactured in February; fixed overhead amounted to $14,900. Assume total units of purchase for materials equaled total units of usage.

Required:

   a. Compute the direct materials price and quantity variances for February.
   b. Compute the direct labor rate and efficiency variances for February.
   c. Compute the factory overhead spending, efficiency, and volume variance for February.

Using the Computer

Elma's Homestyle Cookies uses standard costs in the budgeting process and in performance evaluation. On a computer spreadsheet, calculate all direct materials, direct labor, and overhead variances for the month of March 1987, using the following information about the company's standards and actual costs. Indicate whether each variance is favorable or unfavorable.

   a. Direct materials standards:

Price:	$0.40 per ounce
Quantity:	2.5 ounces per batch (unit)

Actual data:

Price:	$0.38 per ounce
Quantity purchased:	2,200 ounces
Amount used in production:	2,000 ounces
Amount produced:	750 units

Note: Elma's management calculates the materials price variance at the time of purchase.

b. Direct labor standards:

Wage rate:	$7.00 per hour
Quantity:	1.5 hours per unit produced

Actual data:

Wage rate:	$6.90 per hour
Quantity:	1,200 hours

c. Calculate the predetermined overhead rate from the following:

Variable cost:	$1.75 per DLH
Total fixed cost estimate for year:	$48,000
Direct labor expected for year:	12,400 hours

d. Calculate the overhead spending, overhead efficiency, overhead volume, and total overhead variances from the following:

Overhead budget:

Variable cost:	$1.75 per DLH
Total fixed cost:	$4,000 (from yearly estimate above)

Actual overhead costs:

Total variable cost:	$1,900
Total fixed cost:	$3,775

e. In the month of April, Elma's Homestyle Cookies had the following information about actual costs:

Price of a unit of cookies:	$0.42
Units purchased:	2,000
Units used in production:	1,900
Quantity of labor:	1,150 hours at a rate of $6.90
Amount produced:	698 units
Total variable overhead cost:	$2,500
Total fixed overhead cost:	$3,775

Required:
Prepare all direct materials, direct labor, and overhead variances for the month of April.

Decision Case

Ray Carlson, president of Scientific Equipment Manufacturing Company, wants to introduce standard costing into his company's factory. As a result of his participation in a two-week management development course at a nearby university, Mr. Carlson is convinced that some kind of standard costing system is just what he needs to strengthen his control over factory cost. The factory now has a simple job order costing system, and no one has ever attempted to establish standard costs.

Scientific Equipment makes and sells a line of highly technical equipment for industrial users. The company is located in a small midwestern city with a population of 80,000 people. Quality, or the supplier's ability to meet exacting technical specifications, is a major consideration for most of the company's customers when deciding where to place an order.

Production is organized on a job order basis, and orders are typically manufactured to customer specifications. Most of the orders can be filled by producing items of standard design and specifications, or items that require only minor modifications to the standard designs. Jobs requiring major redesign and the use of nonstandardized production techniques amount to 30% of the total. The cost estimates that Ray uses in developing price bids for this kind of nonstandardized business have been close to the actual costs of filling the orders in most cases, or at least close enough to satisfy him.

Scientific Equipment is a small company with about 75 employees. The 2 largest segments of the work force are 30 machine operators and 20 assemblers. The job of machine operator requires a considerable degree of skill and experience. The job of assembler is fairly routine but requires a good deal of concentration to avoid costly assembly defects. The employees generally lunch together in a nearby cafeteria, and some socialize off the job.

Ray is considering engaging a consulting firm to develop and install a standard costing system. A letter from the managing partner of the consulting firm contained the following key paragraphs:

> In order to motivate people to their maximum productivity, standards must be based on the company's best workers and what they can achieve. If the standard were lower, the high performers could meet it too easily, and it wouldn't offer sufficient motivation for the low performers. I'd set the standard at the level of performance of the top 10 to 15 percent of your employees. This would establish a high aspiration level for your people and, therefore, motivate their best efforts.
>
> I also suggest that superior performance be well rewarded. This means that employees who exceed standard should receive a substantial bonus, and those who do not exceed standard should receive no bonus.

Since Ray does not feel qualified to evaluate this kind of statement, he has contacted the faculty member who conducted the sessions on standard costing at the local university (you), asking what you think of the philosophy underlying the proposed system.

Required:

a. Prepare a reply to Ray. Should he engage the consultant?

b. If you agree with the consultant's basic approach, outline how you would implement it at Scientific Equipment Manufacturing Company. If you disagree with the consultant, state the basic principles underlying an alternative system and outline how you would go about developing a standard costing system for this company.

Appendix: Time Value of Money Concepts

The purpose of this appendix is to elaborate on the time value of money concepts introduced in Chapter 25.

Interest and the Time Value of Money

Perhaps you have heard the advertisements that claim that beginning at age 30, if you invest $2,000 a year in an Individual Retirement Account (IRA), you will accumulate over $500,000 by the time you retire at age 65. As the advertisements claim, you will receive substantially more than the $70,000 ($2,000 × 35 years) you invested because of the interest that you will earn on your investment. This points out the importance of interest and how quickly it accumulates over a period of time. The focus of this appendix is on the time value of money and how this concept is used in personal and business financial decisions.

All investment decisions revolve around giving up a certain amount of money today in the hope of receiving a greater amount at some future time. In order to determine whether you have made a wise investment, you must consider the time value of money. For example, assume that you were given the following investment opportunity: A real estate developer offered to sell you a vacant lot today for $100,000 and guaranteed to repurchase it 10 years later for a minimum of $250,000. Does that sound like a good investment? Although it is tempting to say yes, because you would be making a profit of $150,000, you must also consider the time value of money. The $250,000 you will receive in 10 years is not really comparable to the $100,000 you have to give up today. This is so because money that you will receive in the future will not be as valuable as money you receive today. This is due to the fact that money received today can be invested and, as a result, will increase in amount. In our example, if you did not make the investment but instead put the $100,000 in a savings account that earned 12% interest per year, you would accumulate over $310,000 at the end of 10 years.

The best way to analyze investment opportunities such as this is to determine the rate of return they offer. In this example, if you invested $100,000 today and received $250,000 in 10 years, you would earn a rate of return of about 9.6%. You can compare this rate of return with those of other investments of similar risk and logically decide which one presents the best opportunity. In order to make this and similar analyses, you must understand five concepts:

1. Simple versus compound interest.
2. The future value of a single amount.
3. The present value of a single amount.
4. The future value of an annuity.
5. The present value of an annuity.

Simple versus Compound Interest

Interest is payment for the use of money for a specified period of time. Interest can be calculated on either a simple or a compound basis. The distinction between the two is important because it affects the amount of interest earned or incurred.

Simple Interest

Simple interest means that the interest payment is computed on only the amount of the principal for one or more periods. That is, if the original principal of the note is not changed, the interest payment will remain the same for each period. Most of the examples in this book so far have assumed simple

A2

interest. For example, if you invested $10,000 at 12% interest for 3 years, your yearly interest income would be $1,200 ($10,000 × .12). The total interest earned over the 3 years would be $3,600, and you would eventually receive $13,600 ($10,000 + $3,600).

Compound Interest

Compound interest means that interest is computed on the principal of the note plus any interest that has accrued to date. That is, when compound interest is applied, the accrued interest of that period is added to the amount on which future interest is to be computed. Thus, by compounding, interest is earned or incurred not only on the principal but also on the interest left on deposit.

To demonstrate the concept of compound interest, assume that the interest in the previous example now will be compounded annually rather than on a simple basis. As the following table shows, in this case your total interest income will be $4,049.28 rather than the $3,600 in the simple interest case.

Year	Principal Amount at Beginning of Year	Annual Interest Income, 12%	Accumulated at End of Year
1	$10,000.00	$1,200.00	$11,200.00
2	11,200.00	1,344.00	12,544.00
3	12,544.00	1,505.28	14,049.28

During year 1, interest income is $1,200, or 12% of $10,000. Because the interest is compounded, it is added to the principal to determine the accumulated amount of $11,200 at the end of the year. Interest in year 2 is thus $1,344, or 12% of $11,200, and the accumulated amount at the end of year 2 is now $12,544. The interest and the accumulated amount at the end of year 3 are calculated in the same manner.

Interest Compounded More Often Than Annually

Interest can be compounded as often as the lender desires. The more often interest is compounded, the more quickly it will increase. For example, many savings and loans institutions compound interest daily. This means that interest is calculated on the beginning balance of your account each day. This interest is then added to the accumulated amount to determine the base for the next day's interest calculation. Clearly, this is more advantageous than if interest is compounded yearly.

When calculating interest that is compounded more than annually, it is quite easy to make the necessary adjustments. If interest is compounded more than annually, there is more than one interest period each year. For example, if interest is compounded quarterly, there are four interest periods in each year. In our example of a 3-year investment, there would be 12 interest periods if interest were compounded quarterly. But the interest rate that is stated in annual terms must be reduced accordingly. Thus, instead of using an interest rate of 12% in our example, the interest rate would be 3% each quarter. As a general rule, the annual interest rate is divided by the number of compounding periods to determine the proper interest rate for each period.

If interest is compounded quarterly in the previous $10,000, 12% example, it will equal $4,257.60 and the total amount of the investment will grow to $14,257.60. This is shown in the following table:

Period	Principal Amount at Beginning of Period	Amount of Interest Each Period at 3%	Accumulated Amount at End of Period
1	$10,000.00	$300.00	$10,300.00
2	10,300.00	309.00	10,609.00
3	10,609.00	318.27	10,927.27
4	10,927.27	327.82	11,255.09
5	11,255.09	337.65	11,592.74
6	11,592.74	347.78	11,940.52
7	11,940.52	358.22	12,298.74
8	12,298.74	368.96	12,667.70
9	12,667.70	380.03	13,047.73
10	13,047.73	391.43	13,439.16
11	13,439.16	403.17	13,842.33
12	13,842.33	415.27	14,257.60

Thus, in this straightforward example, the total interest increases by $208.32, from $4,049.28 to $4,257.60, when interest is compounded quarterly instead of annually.

The Future Value of a Single Amount

In the previous example we were really trying to determine what the future amount of $10,000 invested at 12% for 3 years would be, given a certain compounding pattern. This is an example of determining the **future value of a single amount.** Future value means the amount to which the investment will grow at a future date if interest is compounded. The single amount means that a lump sum was invested at the beginning of year 1 and was left intact for all three years. Thus, there were no additional investments or interest withdrawals. These future value or compound interest calculations are important in many personal and business financial decisions. For example, an individual may be interested in determining how much an investment of $50,000 will amount to in 5 years if interest is compounded semiannually versus quarterly, or what rate of return must be earned on a $10,000 investment if $18,000 is needed in 7 years. All of these situations relate to determining the future value of a single amount.

One way to solve problems of this type is to construct tables similar to the one above. However, this method is time-consuming and not very flexible. Mathematical formulas can also be used. For example, the tables used above and on the previous page to determine the accumulated amount of a single amount at different compounded rates are based on the following formula:

$$\text{Accumulated amount} = p(1 + i)^n \quad \text{where}$$
$$p = \text{Principal amount}$$
$$i = \text{Interest rate}$$
$$n = \text{Number of compounding periods}$$

That is, in the example of the $10,000 compounded annually for 3 years at 12%, the $14,049.28 can be determined by the following calculation:

$$\$14,049.28 = \$10,000(1 + .12)^3$$

However, one of the simplest methods is to use prepared tables that give the future value of $1 at different interest rates and for different periods. Essentially these tables interpret the preceding mathematical formula for various interest rates and compounding periods for a principal amount of $1. Once the amount for $1 is known, it is easy to determine the amount for any principal amount by multiplying the future amount for $1 by the required principal amount. Many hand calculators also have function keys that can be used to solve these types of problems.

To illustrate, Exhibit A–1, which is an excerpt from the compound interest and present-value tables at the end of this appendix, shows the future value of $1 for 10 interest periods for interest rates ranging from 2% to 15%. Suppose that we want to determine the future value of $10,000 at the end of 3 years if interest is compounded annually at 12% (the example previously used). In order to solve this, we look down the 12% column in the table until we come to 3 interest periods. The factor from the table is 1.405, which means that $1 invested today at 12% will accumulate to $1.405 at the end of 3 years. Because we are interested in $10,000 rather than $1, we just multiply the factor of 1.405 by $10,000 to determine the future value of the $10,000 principal amount. The amount is $14,050, which, except for a slight rounding error due to using only three decimal points in the table, is the same as we determined from the table on the previous page.

We can generalize the use of the future value table by using the following formula:

Accumulated amount = Factor (from the table) × Principal
$14,050 = 1.405 × $10,000

This formula can be used to solve a variety of related problems. For example, as we noted above, you may be interested in determining what rate of interest must be earned on a $10,000 investment if you want to accumulate $18,000 at the end of 7 years. Or you may want to know the number of years an amount must be invested in order to grow to a certain amount. In all these cases, we have two of the three items in the formula, and we can solve for the third.

EXHIBIT A–1
Future Value of a Single Amount

(n) Periods	2%	4%	6%	8%	10%	12%	15%	(n) Periods
1	1.020	1.040	1.060	1.080	1.100	1.120	1.150	1
2	1.040	1.082	1.124	1.166	1.210	1.254	1.323	2
3	1.061	1.125	1.191	1.260	1.331	1.405	1.521	3
4	1.082	1.170	1.262	1.360	1.464	1.574	1.749	4
5	1.104	1.217	1.338	1.469	1.611	1.762	2.011	5
6	1.126	1.265	1.419	1.587	1.772	1.974	2.313	6
7	1.149	1.316	1.504	1.714	1.949	2.211	2.660	7
8	1.172	1.369	1.594	1.851	2.144	2.476	3.059	8
9	1.195	1.423	1.689	1.999	2.358	2.773	3.518	9
10	1.219	1.480	1.791	2.159	2.594	3.106	4.046	10

Interest Compounded More Often Than Annually

As we stated, interest usually is compounded more often than annually. In these situations we simply adjust the number of interest periods and the interest rate. If we want to know what $10,000 will accumulate to at the end of 3 years if interest is compounded quarterly at an annual rate of 12%, we just look down the 3% column until we reach 12 periods. (See Table 1 on page A19.) The factor is 1.426, and employing our general formula, the accumulated amount is $14,260, determined as follows:

$$\text{Accumulated amount} = \text{Factor} \times \text{Principal}$$
$$\$14,260 = 1.426 \times \$10,000$$

Determining the Number of Periods or the Interest Rate

There are many situations in which the unknown variable is the number of interest periods that the dollars must remain invested or the rate of return (interest rate) that must be earned. For example, assume that you invest $5,000 today in a savings and loan association that will pay interest at 10% compounded annually. You need to accumulate $8,857.80 for a certain project. How many years does the investment have to remain in the savings and loan association? Using the general formula, the answer is six years, determined as follows:

$$\text{Accumulated amount} = \text{Factor} \times \text{Principal}$$
$$\text{Factor} = \frac{\text{Accumulated amount}}{\text{Principal}}$$
$$1.772 = \frac{\$8,857.80}{\$5,000.00}$$

Looking down the 10% column in Exhibit A–1 the factor of 1.772 appears at the sixth-period row. Because the interest is compounded annually, the sixth period is interpreted as six years. This example was constructed so that the factor equals a round number of periods. If it does not, interpolation is necessary. The examples, exercises, and problems in this book will not require interpolation.

We can use the same method to determine the required interest rate. For example, assume that you invest $10,000 for 8 years. What rate of return or interest rate compounded annually must you earn if you want to accumulate $30,590.23? Using the general formula, the answer is 15%, determined as follows:

$$\text{Accumulated amount} = \text{Factor} \times \text{Principal}$$
$$\text{Factor} = \frac{\text{Accumulated amount}}{\text{Principal}}$$
$$3.059 = \frac{\$30,590.23}{\$10,000.00}$$

Looking across the eighth-period row, we find the factor of 3.059 at the 15% column.

The Present Value of a Single Amount

In many business and personal situations, we are interested in determining the value today of receiving a set single amount at some time in the future. For example, assume that you want to know the value today of receiving $15,000 at the end of 5 years if a rate of return of 12% is earned. Another way of asking this question is, What is the amount that would have to be invested today at 12% compounded annually if you wanted to receive $15,000 at the end of 5 years? These are **present-value-of-a-single-amount** problems, because we are interested in knowing the present value, or the value today, of receiving a set sum in the future.

Intuitively, we know that the present value will be less than the future value. For example, if you had the choice of receiving $12,000 today or in 2 years, you would take the $12,000 today. This is so because you can invest the $12,000 so that it will accumulate to more than $12,000 at the end of 2 years. Another way of looking at this is to say that because of the time value of money, you would take an amount less than $12,000 if you could receive it today, instead of $12,000 in 2 years. The amount you would be willing to accept depends on the interest rate or the rate of return you receive.

In present-value situations, the interest rate is often called the discount rate. Because we are discounting a future value back to the present. Some individuals refer to present-value problems as discounted present-value problems.

One way to solve present-value problems is to use the general formula we developed for future-value problems. For example, returning to the previous example, assume that at the end of 5 years you wish to have $15,000. If you can earn 12% compounded annually, how much do you have to invest today? Using the general formula for Table 1, the answer is $8,513.05, determined as follows:

$$\text{Accumulated amount} = \text{Factor} \times \text{Principal}$$
$$\text{Principal} = \frac{\text{Accumulated amount}}{\text{Factor}}$$
$$\$8,513.05 = \frac{\$15,000}{1.762}$$

This is equivalent to saying that at a 12% interest rate compounded annually, it does not matter whether you receive $8,513.05 today or $15,000 at the end of 5 years. Thus, if someone offered you an investment at a cost of $8,000 that would return $15,000 at the end of 5 years, you would take it if the minimum rate of return were 12%. This is so because at 12% the $15,000 is actually worth $8,513.05 today, but you would need to make an outlay of only $8,000.

Using Present-Value Tables

Rather than using future-value tables and making the necessary adjustments to the general formula, we can use present-value tables. As is the case with future-value tables, present-value tables are based on the mathematical formula used to determine present values. Because of the relationship between future and present values, the present-value table is the inverse of the future-value table. Exhibit A–2 presents an excerpt from the present-value tables (Table 2) found on page A20. The table works the same as the future-value table does, except that the general formula is

$$\text{Present value} = \text{Factor} \times \text{Accumulated amount}$$

For example, if we want to use the table to determine the present value of $15,000 to be received at the end of 5 years, compounded annually at 12%, we simply look down the 12% column and multiply that factor by $15,000. Thus the answer is $8,505, determined as follows:

$$\text{Present value} = \text{Factor} \times \text{Accumulated amount}$$
$$\$8,505 = .567 \times \$15,000$$

Time Value of Money Concepts

The difference between $8,505 and $8,513.05 determined previously is again due to rounding.

(n) Periods	2%	4%	6%	8%	10%	12%	15%	(n) Periods
				EXHIBIT A–2				
			Present Value of a Single Amount					
1	.980	.962	.943	.926	.909	.893	.870	1
2	.961	.925	.890	.857	.826	.797	.756	2
3	.942	.889	.840	.794	.751	.712	.658	3
4	.924	.855	.792	.735	.683	.636	.572	4
5	.906	.822	.747	.681	.621	.567	.497	5
6	.888	.790	.705	.630	.564	.507	.432	6
7	.871	.760	.665	.583	.513	.452	.376	7
8	.853	.731	.627	.540	.467	.404	.327	8
9	.837	.703	.592	.500	.424	.361	.284	9
10	.820	.676	.558	.463	.386	.322	.247	10

Other Present-Value Situations

As we did in the future-value case, we can use the general formula to solve other variations, as long as we know two of the three variables. For example, assume that you want to know what interest rate compounded semiannually you must earn if you want to accumulate $10,000 at the end of 3 years, with an investment of $7,050 today. The answer is 6% semiannually or 12% annually, determined as follows:

$$\text{Present value} = \text{Factor} \times \text{Accumulated amount}$$
$$\text{Factor} = \frac{\text{Present value}}{\text{Accumulated amount}}$$
$$.705 = \frac{\$7,050}{\$10,000.00}$$

Looking across the sixth-period row, we come to .705 at the 6% column. Because interest is compounded semiannually, the annual rate is 12%.

Distinguishing between Future Value and Present Value

In beginning to work with time-value-of-money problems, you should be careful to distinguish between present-value and future-value problems. One way to do this is to use time lines to analyze the situation. For example, the time line relating to the example in which we determined the future value of $10,000 compounded at 12% for 3 years is as follows:

```
      0           1           2           3
  $10,000                              $14,050
```

But the time line relating to the present value of $15,000 discounted back at 12% for 5 years is:

0   1   2   3   4   5
$8,505 $15,000

The Future Value of an Annuity

An **annuity** is a series of equal payments made at specified intervals. Interest is compounded on each of these payments. Annuities are often called rents because they are like the payment of monthly rentals. Annuity payments can be made at the beginning or the end of the specified intervals. If they are made at the beginning of the period, the annuity is called an *annuity due,* and if the payment is made at the end of the period, it is called an *ordinary annuity.* The examples in this book use ordinary annuities, and so we will always assume that the payment takes place at the end of the period.

Annuities are commonly encountered in business and accounting situations. For example, a lease payment or a mortgage represents an annuity. Life insurance contracts involving a series of equal payments at equal times are another example of an annuity. In some cases it is appropriate to calculate the future value of the annuity, and in other cases it is appropriate to calculate the present value of the annuity. We first explain how to determine the future value of an annuity.

Determining the Future Value of an Annuity

The **future value of an annuity** is the sum of all the periodic payments plus the interest that has accumulated on them. To demonstrate how to calculate the future value of an annuity, assume that you deposit $1 at the end of each of the next 4 years in a savings account that pays 10% interest compounded annually. The following table shows how these $1 payments will accumulate to $4.641 at the end of the fourth period, or year in this case.

END OF YEAR IN WHICH INVESTMENT IS MADE

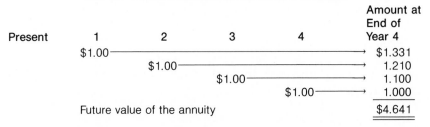

Present	1	2	3	4	Amount at End of Year 4
	$1.00				→ $1.331
		$1.00			→ 1.210
			$1.00		→ 1.100
				$1.00	→ 1.000
Future value of the annuity					$4.641

The future value of each dollar is determined by compounding interest at 10% for the appropriate number of periods. For example, the $1 deposited at the end of the first period earns interest for three periods. It earns interest for only three periods because it was deposited at the end of the first period and earns interest until the end of the fourth. Using the factors from Table 1 at the end of the appendix, the future value of this first $1 single payment is $1.331, determined as follows:

Future value = Factor × Principal
$1.331 = 1.331 × $1.00

The second payment earns interest for 2 periods and accumulates to $1.21, and the third payment earns interest for only 1 period and accumulates to $1.10. The final payment, made at the end of the fourth year, does not earn any interest because we are determining the future value of the annuity at the end of the fourth period. The total of all payments compounded for the appropriate number of interest periods equals $4.641 and represents the future value of this ordinary annuity.

Fortunately, we do not have to construct a table like this one in order to determine the future value of an annuity. We can use tables that present the factors necessary to calculate the future value of an annuity of $1, given different periods and interest rates. Table 3 at the end of this appendix is such a table. This table is constructed by simply summing the appropriate factors from the compound interest table. For example, the factor for the future value of a $1 annuity at the end of 4 years at 10% compounded annually is $4.641, which is the amount we determined when we performed the calculation independently by summing the individual factors.

Problems Involving the Future Value of an Annuity

By using the general formula below, we can solve a variety of problems involving the future value of an annuity:

$$\text{Future value of an annuity} = \text{Factor} \times \text{Annuity payment}$$

As long as we know two of the three variables, we can solve for the third. Thus, we can solve for the future value of the annuity, the annuity payment, the interest rate, or the number of periods.

Determining Future Value. Assume that you deposited in a savings and loan association $4,000 per year at the end of each of the next 8 years. How much will you accumulate if you earn 10% compounded annually? The future value of this annuity is $45,744, determined as follows:

$$\text{Future value of an annuity} = \text{Factor} \times \text{Annuity payment}$$
$$\$45,744 = 11.436 \times \$4,000$$

Determining the Annuity Payment. Assume that at the end of 15 years, you need to accumulate $100,000 to send your daughter to college. If you can earn 12% at your local savings and loan association, how much must you deposit at the end of each of the next 15 years in order to accumulate the $100,000 at the end of the fifteenth year? The annual payment is $2,682.40, as determined in the following:

$$\text{Future value of an annuity} = \text{Factor} \times \text{Annuity payment}$$
$$\text{Annuity payment} = \frac{\text{Future value of an annuity}}{\text{Factor}}$$
$$\$2,682.40 = \frac{\$100,000}{37.280}$$

Determining the Interest Rate. In some cases you may want to determine the interest rate that must be earned on an annuity in order to accumulate a predetermined amount. For example, assume that you invest $500 per quarter for 10 years and want to accumulate $30,201 at the end of the tenth year. What interest rate is required? You need to earn 2% quarterly, or 8% annually, determined as follows:

$$\text{Future value of an annuity} = \text{Factor} \times \text{Annuity payment}$$

$$\text{Factor} = \frac{\text{Future value of an annuity}}{\text{Annuity payment}}$$

$$60.402 = \frac{\$30,201}{\$500}$$

Because the annuity payments are made quarterly, we must look across the fortieth-period (10 years × 4) row until we find the factor. In this case it is at the 2% column. Thus the interest rate is 2% quarterly, or 8% annually.

In some situations the interest rate is known, but the number of periods is missing. These problems can be solved by using the same technique we used to determine the interest rate. When the factor is determined, you must be sure to look down the appropriate interest column to find the factor on the annuity table.

The Present Value of an Annuity

The value today of a series of equal payments or receipts to be made or received on specified future dates is called the **present value of an annuity.** As in the case of a future value of an annuity, the receipts or payments are made in the future. Present value is the value today, and future value relates to accumulated future value. Furthermore, the present value of a series of payments or receipts will be less than the total of the same payment or receipts, because cash received in the future is not as valuable as cash received today. On the other hand, the future value of an annuity will be greater than the sum of the individual payments or receipts, because interest is accumulated on the payments. It is important to distinguish between the future value and the present value of an annuity. Again, time lines are helpful in this respect.

Mortgages and certain notes payable in equal installments are examples of present-value-of-annuity problems. For example, assume that a bank lends you $60,000 today to be repaid in equal monthly installments over 30 years. The bank is interested in knowing what series of monthly payments, when discounted back at the agreed-on interest rate, is equal to the present value today of the amount of the loan, or $60,000.

Determining the Present Value of an Annuity

Assume that you want to determine the value today of receiving $1 at the end of each of the next four years. The appropriate interest or discount rate is 12%. To solve this, we can construct a table that determines the present values of each of the receipts:

END OF YEAR IN WHICH $1.00 IS TO BE RECEIVED

Present Value at Beginning of Year 1	1	2	3	4
$0.636				$1.00
0.712			$1.00	
0.797		$1.00		
0.893	$1.00			
$3.038	Present value of the annuity			

Thus, the present value of receiving the four $1 payments is $3.038 when discounted at 12%. Each of the individual dollars was discounted by using the factors in the present value of a single amount table in Exhibit A–2. For example, the present value of the dollar received at the end of year 4 when discounted back 4 years is $0.636. It must be discounted back four years because the present, or today, is the beginning of year 1. The dollar received at the end of year 3 must be discounted back three periods; the dollar received at the end of year 2 must be discounted back two periods; and so forth.

As with the calculation of the future value of an annuity, we can use prepared tables. Table 4 on page A22 is such a table. It is constructed by summing the individual present values of $1 at set interest rates and periods. Thus, the factor for the present value of four $1 to be received at the end of each of the next 4 years when discounted back at 12% is 3.037, the value we determined independently except for a minor rounding error.

Problems Involving the Present Value of an Annuity

Problems involving the present value of an annuity can be solved by using the following general formula:

Present value of an annuity = Factor $\times$ Amount of the annuity

As long as we know two of the three variables, we can solve for the third. Thus, we can determine the present value of the annuity, the interest rate, the number of periods, or the amount of the annuity.

Determining the Present Value. To demonstrate how to calculate the present value of an annuity, assume that you were offered an investment that paid $2,000 a year at the end of each of the next 10 years. How much would you pay for it if you wanted to earn a rate of return of 8%? This is a present-value problem because you would pay the value today of this stream of payments discounted back at 8%. This amount is $13,420, determined as follows:

Present value of an annuity = Factor $\times$ Amount of the annuity
$13,420 = 6.710 $\times$ $2,000

Another way to interpret this problem is to say that it makes no difference whether you keep $13,420 today or receive $2,000 a year for 10 years, if you want to earn 8%.

Determining the Annuity Payment. A common variation of present-value problems requires computing the annuity payment. In many cases these are loan or mortgage problems. For example, assume that you purchase a house for $100,000 and make a 20% down payment. You will borrow the rest of the money from the bank at 10% interest. To make the problem easier, we will assume that you will make 30 yearly payments at the end of each of the next 30 years. (Most mortgages require monthly payments.) How much will your yearly payments be?

In this case you are going to borrow $80,000 ($100,000 $\times$ 80%). The yearly payment would be $8,486.26, determined as follows:

$$\text{Present value of an annuity} = \text{Factor} \times \text{Amount of the annuity}$$
$$\text{Amount of the annuity} = \frac{\text{Present value of an annuity}}{\text{Factor}}$$
$$\$8,486.26 = \frac{\$80,000}{9.427}$$

Determining the Number of Payments. Assume that the Black Lighting Co. purchased a new printing press for $100,000. The quarterly payments are $4,326.24 and the interest rate is 12% annually, or 3% per quarter. How many payments will be required to pay off the loan? In this case, 40 payments are required, determined as follows:

$$\text{Present value of an annuity} = \text{Factor} \times \text{Amount of the annuity}$$

$$\text{Factor} = \frac{\text{Present value of an annuity}}{\text{Amount of the annuity}}$$

$$23.115 = \frac{\$100,000}{\$4,326.24}$$

Looking down the 3% column in Table 4 (page A22) we find the factor 23.115 at the fortieth-period row. Thus 40 quarterly payments are needed to pay off the loan.

Combination Problems. Many accounting applications related to the time value of money involve both single amounts and annuities. For example, say that you are considering purchasing an apartment house. After much analysis, you determine that you will receive net yearly cash flows of $10,000 from rental revenue, less rental expenses from the apartment. To make the analysis easier, assume that the cash flows are generated at the end of each year. These cash flows will continue for 20 years, at which time you estimate that you can sell the apartment building for $250,000. How much should you pay for the building, assuming that you want to earn a rate of return of 10%?

This problem involves an annuity—the yearly net cash flows of $10,000— and a single amount—the $250,000 to be received once at the end of the twentieth year. As a rational person, the maximum that you would be willing to pay is the value today of these two cash flows discounted at 10%. That value is $122,390, as determined below:

Present value of the annuity of $10,000 a year for 20 years $10,000 × 8.514 (Table 4)	$ 85,140
Present value of the single amount of $250,000 to be received at the end of year 20 $250,000 × .149 (Table 2)	37,250
Total purchase price	$122,390

Accounting Applications of the Time Value of Money

The concepts related to the time value of money, especially present value, have many applications in financial and managerial accounting. For example, from a theoretical perspective, assets and liabilities should be valued at the present value of the future cash inflows expected from the asset or of the cash outflows from the liability. Accountants rarely use this valuation method to value assets because of the difficulty of estimating future cash flows and discount rates. However, present value is often used to value long-term liabilities at their valuation date, because the cash flows for liabilities such as mortgages and bonds are known with certainty.

Using Present Value to Determine Bond Prices

Given the prevailing market interest rate, the stated or coupon interest rate, and the maturity date, bond prices can be calculated using present-value techniques. When bonds are issued, the borrower agrees to make two different types of payments: an annuity made up of the future cash interest payments and a single future amount consistituting the bond's matuity value. Rational investors would not pay any more than the present value of these two future cash flows, discounted at the desired yield rate.

To illustrate the issuance of bonds at a discount, assume that on January 2, 1987 the Valenzuela Corporation issues $100,000, 5-year, 12% term bonds. Interest of 6% is payable semiannually on January 2 and July 1. (See page 707 in Chapter 18.) The bonds were issued when the prevailing market interest rate for such investments was 14%. Thus the bonds were issued at a discount to yield 14%. This rate is also called the effective interest rate. Based on this effective rate, the bonds would be issued at a price of $92,976.

The journal entry to record the Valenzuela bonds is:

Jan. 2, 1987	Cash	92,976	
	Discount on Bonds Payable	7,024	
	Bonds Payable		100,000
	To record issuance of $100,000,		
	5-year, 12% bonds for $92,976.		

The issue price of $92,976 is calculated below. The issue price is composed of the present value of the maturity payment of $100,000 discounted at 7% for 10 periods, and the present value of semiannual cash interest payments of $6,000 ($100,000 × .06) also discounted at 7%. Ten periods are used because the 5-year bonds pay interest semiannually. The discount rate is the semiannual yield, or an effective rate of 7%. You should remember that the $6,000 annuity, which is the cash interest payment, is calculated on the actual semiannual coupon rate of 6%. In this case, the factors from the table are expressed in five decimal points in order to be more exact.

DETERMINATION OF BOND PRICE
($100,000, 5-year, 12% bonds issued to yield 14%)

Present value of $100,000 to be received at end of 10 periods at 7% semiannually $100,000 × .50835	$ 50,835
Present value at 7% of semiannual interest payments of $6,000 ($100,000 × .06) to be received at the end of each of the next 10 interest dates $6,000 × 7.02358	42,141
Total issue price	$ 92,976
Amount of discount	
Face value of bonds	$100,000
Total issue price	92,976
Amount of discount	$ 7,024

To illustrate the calculation for bonds issued at a premium, we will now assume that on January 2, 1987 the Valenzuela Corporation issues $100,000, 5-year, 12% term bonds. Interest is payable semiannually on January 2 and July 1. In this case, however, the bonds are issued when the prevailing market interest rate for such investments is 10%. The bonds therefore are issued at a premium to yield 10% and are sold at a price of 107.7212, or $107,722. The entry to record this bond issue is:

Jan. 2, 1987	Cash	107,722	
	Premium on Bonds Payable		7,722
	Bonds Payable		100,000
	To record issuance of $100,000, 5-year, 12% bonds at 107,722.		

The illustration below shows how the price of the Valenzuela Corporation's 5-year 12% bonds issued to yield 10% can be determined. These calculations are similar to those of the discount example, except that the cash flows are discounted at the semiannual yield rate of 5%. Again, the factors are expressed in five decimal points.

DETERMINATION OF BOND PRICE
($100,000, 5-year, 12% bonds issued to yield 10%)

Present value of $100,000 to be received at the end of 10 periods at 5% semiannually	
$100,000 × .61391	$ 61,391
Present value at 5% of semiannual interest payments of $6,000 ($100,000 × .06) to be received at the end of each of the next 10 interest dates	
$6,000 × 7.72173	46,331
Total issue price	$107,722
Amount of premium	
Total issue price	$107,722
Face value of bonds	100,000
Amount of premium	$ 7,722

Key Terms

Annuity
Compound Interest
Future Value of an Annuity
Future Value of a Single Amount

Present Value of an Annuity
Present Value of a Single Amount
Simple Interest

Problems for Your Review

Solve each of the following time-value-of-money problems:
1. Determine the future value of:

a. A single payment of $15,000 at 8% compounded semiannually for 10 years.

b. Ten annual payments of $2,000 at 12%.

2. Determine the present value of:

a. Six semiannual payments of $1,000 at 10% compounded semiannually.

b. A single payment of $12,000 discounted at 12% annually, received at the end of 5 years.

3. You have decided that you would like to take a 'round-the-world trip at the end of 10 years. You expect that the trip will cost $150,000. If you can earn 10% annually, how much would you have to invest at the end of each of the next 10 years to accumulate the $150,000?

Solutions

1(a). Future value of single amount—$15,000, 8% compounded semiannually for 10 years (4% × 20 periods):

$$\text{Principal} \times \text{Factor} = \text{Accumulated amount}$$
$$\$15,000 \times 2.191 = \$32,865$$

1(b). Future value of an ordinary annuity—10 payments, 12% interest:

$$\text{Annuity payment} \times \text{Factor} = \text{Future value of annuity}$$
$$\$2,000 \times 17.549 = \$35,098$$

2(a). Present value of six semiannual payments discounted at 5% semiannually:

$$\text{Annuity payment} \times \text{Factor} = \text{Present value of annuity}$$
$$\$1,000 \times 5.076 = \$5,076$$

2(b). Present value of single payment of $12,000 discounted at 12% for 5 years:

$$\text{Future value} \times \text{Factor} = \text{Present value}$$
$$\$12,000 \times .567 = \$6,804$$

3. Determine annual payment required to accumulate $150,000 at the end of 10 years at 10% interest (future value of an annuity):

$$\text{Annuity payment} = \frac{\text{Future value of annuity}}{\text{Factor}}$$

$$\$9,412.06 = \frac{\$150,000}{15.937}$$

Questions

1. Explain the difference between simple and compound interest. If all else were equal, would you rather earn simple or compound interest?

2. Describe the differences among the following:

a. The future value of a single amount.
b. The future value of an annuity.
c. The present value of a single amount.
d. The present value of an annuity.

3. You are considering purchasing a car that will be financed through a bank loan. The bank loan will be for $7,000 at 12% for 4 years. Payments are to be made monthly. You are attempting to determine the monthly payments. Describe how you would solve this problem. It is not necessary to make the actual calculations.

4. Assume that you are determining the future value of an annuity. If the interest you can earn falls from 15% to 10%, what will happen to the future value of the annuity?

5. Your firm is considering establishing a fund that will be used in 10 years to retire a large amount of long-term debt. You need to accumulate $5 million. You are contemplating making annual payments in a fund that will earn 7%, and you want to know how much you must contribute to the fund. Describe how you would solve this problem. It is not necessary to make the actual calculations.

6. Assume that you are trying to determine the present value of an annuity. If the discount rate increases from 10% to 12%, what effect will this have on the present value of the annuity?

7. Below are several situations. Which of them, if any, do not involve time-value-of-money concepts? Explain your answer.

a. Determining the monthly mortgage payment on a loan.
b. Determining whether you should make an investment today that will provide you with $1,000 a year for the next 10 years.
c. Deciding whether you should pay cash or take out a five-year loan when purchasing a new car.
d. Deciding whether to purchase a new machine that will increase cash flows by $5,000 a year for 5 years.

A16

Exercises

The following exercises refer to the time value of money. Their descriptions are intentionally not included, because a major part of understanding time-value-of-money concepts is determining the type of problem you are dealing with.

1. Determine the future value of $10,000 deposited in a savings and loan association for 5 years at 12% interest under each of the following compounding assumptions:
   a. Annual compounding.
   b. Semiannual compounding.
   c. Quarterly compounding.

2. Assume that you invested $10,000 today at 10% interest compounded annually. Several years later you accumulated $25,940. For how many years did your investment compound?

3. At the end of 10 years you will receive $25,000. If the interest rate is 10%, what is the present value of this amount, assuming that the interest is compounded:
   a. Annually?
   b. Semiannually?
   c. Quarterly?

4. If you have a $2,000 investment that will accumulate to $3,078 at the end of 5 years, what rate of interest did you earn, compounded annually?

5. You are approached with the following investment opportunity: If you invest $7,000 today, you will receive a guaranteed payment of $13,000 at the end of 6 years. If you desire a 15% rate of return for this type of investment, would you make the investment? Why or why not?

6. Mr. Fumble is considering the following two investment alternatives:
   a. Ten thousand dollars in a savings account earning interest at 10% compounded semiannually for four years.
   b. Ten thousand dollars in a thrift account earning 11% simple interest for four years.
Which one should he make?

7. If $500 is invested at the end of each of the next 7 years at 8% interest compounded annually, what will it accumulate to at the end of the seventh year?

8. At the end of 10 years you are planning to take a 'round-the-world cruise that will cost $81,215. You are planning to save for this cruise by making yearly deposits in a savings and loan association. If you can earn 15% interest compounded annually and the payments are made at year-end, how much must the yearly deposits be?

9. At the end of 10 years you wish to accumulate $226,203 by making $3,000 quarterly deposits in your interest-earning money market account. What interest rate do you have to earn on a quarterly basis? All payments are made at quarter-end.

10. What is the present value of receiving $10,000 at the end of each of the next 12 years at an interest rate of 8% compounded annually?

11. Charlie Kaplan is considering making a $95,075 investment that will provide a guaranteed return of $12,500 at the end of each of the next 15 years. What interest rate, compounded annually, will Charlie earn on this investment?

12. Lisa West is considering whether to borrow $6,000. Under the proposed terms of the loan, she will have to repay the loan in 36 monthly payments, including interest at 2% per month on the unpaid principal. What will the amount of Lisa's monthly payments be?

13. You are deciding whether to undertake the following investment: You must make an initial payment of $2,500 and then an additional $100 per quarter at the end of each of the next 40 quarters. If the investment earns 10% compounded quarterly, how much will it be worth at the end of 10 years?

14. The Walbanger Corporation is planning a major plant expansion in eight years. However, it wants to start accumulating the funds today in a special interest-earning account. The firm estimates that it will need $2.5 million to finance the expansion. The company decides to invest 20% of the funds today and the rest on a quarterly basis for the next 8 years. If the firm can earn

8% compounded quarterly, what will be the amount of its quarterly deposits into the special fund? All payments are made at quarter-end.

15. You have been offered the following investment opportunity: You will receive $100,000 at the end of 15 years. In addition, you will receive semiannual payments of 4% of the $100,000 until the $100,000 is paid. If you want to earn 10% compounded semiannually, what is the maximum that you would pay for this investment?

16. A local used car dealer is advertising interest-free 48-month loans. However, after shopping around for comparable cars, you notice that his prices are higher than those of other dealers. Why do you think this is so?

17. In order to enjoy her retirement, Becky Webb is contemplating the purchase of a small travel agency. She would like you to help her determine the amount she should pay, based solely on the cash flows that will be generated by the agency. Becky expects to operate the agency for 10 years and then sell it at the end of that time for $200,000. During the 10 years she expects to run the agency, she estimates that it will generate the following net cash inflows:

    Years 1–7: $50,000 per year
    Years 8–10: $40,000 per year

If all the yearly cash flows are received at the end of each year and Becky wants to earn a 10% rate of return compounded annually, what is the maximum she should pay for the agency?

TABLE 1
Future Value of a Single Amount

(n) Periods	2%	2½%	3%	4%	5%	6%	7%	8%	9%	10%	12%	15%	(n) Periods
1	1.020	1.025	1.030	1.040	1.050	1.060	1.070	1.080	1.090	1.100	1.120	1.150	1
2	1.040	1.051	1.061	1.082	1.103	1.124	1.145	1.166	1.188	1.210	1.254	1.323	2
3	1.061	1.077	1.093	1.125	1.158	1.191	1.225	1.260	1.295	1.331	1.405	1.521	3
4	1.082	1.104	1.126	1.170	1.216	1.262	1.311	1.360	1.412	1.464	1.574	1.749	4
5	1.104	1.131	1.159	1.217	1.276	1.338	1.403	1.469	1.539	1.611	1.762	2.011	5
6	1.126	1.160	1.194	1.265	1.340	1.419	1.501	1.587	1.677	1.772	1.974	2.313	6
7	1.149	1.189	1.230	1.316	1.407	1.504	1.606	1.714	1.828	1.949	2.211	2.660	7
8	1.172	1.218	1.267	1.369	1.477	1.594	1.718	1.851	1.993	2.144	2.476	3.059	8
9	1.195	1.249	1.305	1.423	1.551	1.689	1.838	1.999	2.172	2.358	2.773	3.518	9
10	1.219	1.280	1.344	1.480	1.629	1.791	1.967	2.159	2.367	2.594	3.106	4.046	10
11	1.243	1.312	1.384	1.539	1.710	1.898	2.105	2.332	2.580	2.853	3.479	4.652	11
12	1.268	1.345	1.426	1.601	1.796	2.012	2.252	2.518	2.813	3.138	3.896	5.350	12
13	1.294	1.379	1.469	1.665	1.886	2.133	2.410	2.720	3.066	3.452	4.363	6.153	13
14	1.319	1.413	1.513	1.732	1.980	2.261	2.579	2.937	3.342	3.798	4.887	7.076	14
15	1.346	1.448	1.558	1.801	2.079	2.397	2.759	3.172	3.642	4.177	5.474	8.137	15
16	1.373	1.485	1.605	1.873	2.183	2.540	2.952	3.426	3.970	4.595	6.130	9.358	16
17	1.400	1.522	1.653	1.948	2.292	2.693	3.159	3.700	4.328	5.054	6.866	10.761	17
18	1.429	1.560	1.702	2.026	2.407	2.854	3.380	3.996	4.717	5.560	7.690	12.375	18
19	1.457	1.599	1.754	2.107	2.527	3.026	3.617	4.316	5.142	6.116	8.613	14.232	19
20	1.486	1.639	1.806	2.191	2.653	3.207	3.870	4.661	5.604	6.728	9.646	16.367	20
21	1.516	1.680	1.860	2.279	2.786	3.400	4.141	5.034	6.109	7.400	10.804	18.822	21
22	1.546	1.722	1.916	2.370	2.925	3.604	4.430	5.437	6.659	8.140	12.100	21.645	22
23	1.577	1.765	1.974	2.465	3.072	3.820	4.741	5.871	7.258	8.954	13.552	24.891	23
24	1.608	1.809	2.033	2.563	3.225	4.049	5.072	6.341	7.911	9.850	15.179	28.625	24
25	1.641	1.854	2.094	2.666	3.386	4.292	5.427	6.848	8.623	10.835	17.000	32.919	25
30	1.811	2.098	2.427	3.243	4.322	5.743	7.612	10.063	13.268	17.449	29.960	66.212	30
32	1.884	2.204	2.575	3.508	4.765	6.453	8.715	11.737	15.763	21.114	37.582	87.565	32
34	1.961	2.315	2.732	3.794	5.253	7.251	9.978	13.690	18.728	25.548	47.143	115.805	34
36	2.040	2.433	2.898	4.104	5.792	8.147	11.424	15.968	22.251	30.913	59.136	153.152	36
40	2.208	2.685	3.262	4.801	7.040	10.236	14.974	21.723	31.409	45.259	93.051	267.864	40

Time Value of Money Concepts　　**A19**

TABLE 2
Present Value of a Single Amount

(n) Periods	2%	2½%	3%	4%	5%	6%	7%	8%	9%	10%	12%	14%	15%	16%	18%	20%	22%	(n) Periods
1	.980	.976	.971	.962	.952	.943	.935	.926	.917	.909	.893	.877	.870	.862	.847	.833	.820	1
2	.961	.952	.943	.925	.907	.890	.873	.857	.842	.826	.797	.769	.756	.743	.718	.694	.672	2
3	.942	.929	.915	.889	.864	.840	.816	.794	.772	.751	.712	.675	.658	.641	.609	.579	.551	3
4	.924	.906	.888	.855	.823	.792	.763	.735	.708	.683	.636	.592	.572	.552	.516	.482	.451	4
5	.906	.884	.863	.822	.784	.747	.713	.681	.650	.621	.567	.519	.497	.476	.437	.402	.370	5
6	.888	.862	.837	.790	.746	.705	.666	.630	.596	.564	.507	.456	.432	.410	.370	.335	.303	6
7	.871	.841	.813	.760	.711	.665	.623	.583	.547	.513	.452	.400	.376	.354	.314	.279	.249	7
8	.853	.821	.789	.731	.677	.627	.582	.540	.502	.467	.404	.351	.327	.305	.266	.233	.204	8
9	.837	.801	.766	.703	.645	.592	.544	.500	.460	.424	.361	.308	.284	.263	.225	.194	.167	9
10	.820	.781	.744	.676	.614	.558	.508	.463	.422	.386	.322	.270	.247	.227	.191	.162	.137	10
11	.804	.762	.722	.650	.585	.527	.475	.429	.388	.350	.287	.237	.215	.195	.162	.135	.112	11
12	.788	.744	.701	.625	.557	.497	.444	.397	.356	.319	.257	.208	.187	.168	.137	.112	.092	12
13	.773	.725	.681	.601	.530	.469	.415	.368	.326	.290	.229	.182	.163	.145	.116	.093	.075	13
14	.758	.708	.661	.577	.505	.442	.388	.340	.299	.263	.205	.160	.141	.125	.099	.078	.062	14
15	.743	.690	.642	.555	.481	.417	.362	.315	.275	.239	.183	.140	.123	.108	.084	.065	.051	15
16	.728	.674	.623	.534	.458	.394	.339	.292	.252	.218	.163	.123	.107	.093	.071	.054	.042	16
17	.714	.657	.605	.513	.436	.371	.317	.270	.231	.198	.146	.108	.093	.080	.060	.045	.034	17
18	.700	.641	.587	.494	.416	.350	.296	.250	.212	.180	.130	.095	.081	.069	.051	.038	.028	18
19	.686	.626	.570	.475	.396	.331	.277	.231	.194	.164	.116	.083	.070	.060	.043	.031	.023	19
20	.673	.610	.554	.456	.377	.312	.258	.215	.178	.149	.104	.073	.061	.051	.037	.026	.019	20
21	.660	.595	.538	.439	.359	.294	.242	.199	.164	.135	.093	.064	.053	.044	.031	.022	.015	21
22	.647	.581	.522	.422	.342	.278	.226	.184	.150	.123	.083	.056	.046	.038	.026	.018	.013	22
23	.634	.567	.507	.406	.326	.262	.211	.170	.138	.112	.074	.049	.040	.033	.022	.015	.010	23
24	.622	.553	.492	.390	.310	.247	.197	.158	.126	.102	.066	.043	.035	.028	.019	.013	.008	24
25	.610	.539	.478	.375	.295	.233	.184	.146	.116	.092	.059	.038	.030	.024	.016	.010	.007	25
30	.552	.477	.412	.308	.231	.174	.131	.099	.075	.057	.033	.020	.015	.012	.007	.004	.003	30
32	.531	.454	.388	.285	.210	.155	.115	.085	.063	.047	.027	.015	.011	.009	.005	.003	.002	32
34	.510	.432	.366	.264	.190	.138	.100	.073	.053	.039	.021	.012	.009	.006	.004	.002	.001	34
36	.490	.411	.345	.244	.173	.123	.088	.063	.045	.032	.017	.009	.007	.005	.003	.001	.001	36
40	.453	.372	.307	.208	.142	.097	.067	.046	.032	.022	.011	.005	.004	.003	.001	.001	.0004	40

TABLE 3
Future Value of an Annuity

(n) Periods	2%	2½%	3%	4%	5%	6%	7%	8%	9%	10%	12%	15%	(n) Periods
1	1.000	1.000	1.000	1.000	1.000	1.000	1.000	1.000	1.000	1.000	1.000	1.000	1
2	2.020	2.025	2.030	2.040	2.050	2.060	2.070	2.080	2.090	2.100	2.120	2.150	2
3	3.060	3.076	3.091	3.122	3.153	3.184	3.215	3.246	3.278	3.310	3.374	3.473	3
4	4.122	4.153	4.184	4.246	4.310	4.375	4.440	4.506	4.573	4.641	4.779	4.993	4
5	5.204	5.256	5.309	5.416	5.526	5.637	5.751	5.867	5.985	6.105	6.353	6.742	5
6	6.308	6.388	6.468	6.633	6.802	6.975	7.153	7.336	7.523	7.716	8.115	8.754	6
7	7.434	7.547	7.662	7.898	8.142	8.394	8.654	8.923	9.200	9.487	10.089	11.067	7
8	8.583	8.736	8.892	9.214	9.549	9.897	10.260	10.637	11.028	11.436	12.300	13.727	8
9	9.755	9.955	10.159	10.583	11.027	11.491	11.978	12.488	13.021	13.579	14.776	16.786	9
10	10.950	11.203	11.463	12.006	12.578	13.181	13.816	14.487	15.193	15.937	17.549	20.304	10
11	12.169	12.483	12.808	13.486	14.207	14.972	15.784	16.645	17.560	18.531	20.655	24.349	11
12	13.412	13.796	14.192	15.026	15.917	16.870	17.888	18.977	20.141	21.384	24.133	29.002	12
13	14.680	15.140	15.618	16.627	17.713	18.882	20.141	21.495	22.953	24.523	28.029	34.352	13
14	15.974	16.519	17.086	18.292	19.599	21.015	22.550	24.215	26.019	27.975	32.393	40.505	14
15	17.293	17.932	18.599	20.024	21.579	23.276	25.129	27.152	29.361	31.772	37.280	47.580	15
16	18.639	19.380	20.157	21.825	23.657	25.673	27.888	30.324	33.003	35.950	42.753	55.717	16
17	20.012	20.865	21.762	23.698	25.840	28.213	30.840	33.750	36.974	40.545	48.884	65.075	17
18	21.412	22.386	23.414	25.645	28.132	30.906	33.999	37.450	41.301	45.599	55.750	75.836	18
19	22.841	23.946	25.117	27.671	30.539	33.760	37.379	41.446	46.018	51.159	63.440	88.212	19
20	24.297	25.545	26.870	29.778	33.066	36.786	40.995	45.762	51.160	57.275	72.052	102.444	20
21	25.783	27.183	28.676	31.969	35.719	39.993	44.865	50.423	56.765	64.003	81.699	118.810	21
22	27.299	28.863	30.537	34.248	38.505	43.392	49.006	55.457	62.873	71.403	92.503	137.632	22
23	28.845	30.584	32.453	36.618	41.430	46.996	53.436	60.893	69.532	79.543	104.603	159.276	23
24	30.422	32.349	34.426	39.083	44.502	50.816	58.177	66.765	76.790	88.497	118.155	184.168	24
25	32.030	34.158	36.459	41.646	47.727	54.865	63.249	73.106	84.701	98.347	133.334	212.793	25
30	40.568	43.903	47.575	56.085	66.439	79.058	94.461	113.283	136.308	164.494	241.333	434.745	30
32	44.227	48.150	52.503	62.701	75.299	90.890	110.218	134.214	164.037	201.138	304.848	577.100	32
34	48.034	52.613	57.730	69.858	85.067	104.184	128.259	158.627	196.982	245.477	384.521	765.365	34
36	51.994	57.301	63.276	77.598	95.836	119.121	148.913	187.102	236.125	299.127	484.463	1014.346	36
40	60.402	67.403	75.401	95.026	120.800	154.762	199.635	259.057	337.882	442.593	767.091	1779.090	40

Time Value of Money Concepts

A21

TABLE 4
Present Value of an Annuity

(n) Periods	2%	2½%	3%	4%	5%	6%	7%	8%	9%	10%	12%	14%	15%	16%	18%	20%	22%	(n) Periods
1	.980	.976	.971	.962	.952	.943	.935	.926	.917	.909	.893	.877	.870	.862	.847	.833	.820	1
2	1.942	1.927	1.913	1.886	1.859	1.833	1.808	1.783	1.759	1.736	1.690	1.647	1.626	1.605	1.566	1.528	1.492	2
3	2.884	2.856	2.829	2.775	2.723	2.673	2.624	2.577	2.531	2.487	2.402	2.322	2.283	2.246	2.174	2.106	2.042	3
4	3.808	3.762	3.717	3.630	3.546	3.465	3.387	3.312	3.240	3.170	3.037	2.914	2.855	2.798	2.690	2.589	2.494	4
5	4.713	4.646	4.580	4.452	4.329	4.212	4.100	3.993	3.890	3.791	3.605	3.433	3.352	3.274	3.127	2.991	2.864	5
6	5.601	5.508	5.417	5.242	5.076	4.917	4.767	4.623	4.486	4.355	4.111	3.889	3.784	3.685	3.498	3.326	3.167	6
7	6.472	6.349	6.230	6.002	5.786	5.582	5.389	5.206	5.033	4.868	4.564	4.288	4.160	4.039	3.812	3.605	3.416	7
8	7.325	7.170	7.020	6.733	6.463	6.210	5.971	5.747	5.535	5.335	4.968	4.639	4.487	4.344	4.078	3.837	3.619	8
9	8.162	7.971	7.786	7.435	7.108	6.802	6.515	6.247	5.995	5.759	5.328	4.946	4.772	4.607	4.303	4.031	3.786	9
10	8.983	8.752	8.530	8.111	7.722	7.360	7.024	6.710	6.418	6.145	5.650	5.216	5.019	4.833	4.494	4.192	3.923	10
11	9.787	9.514	9.253	8.760	8.306	7.887	7.499	7.139	6.805	6.495	5.938	5.453	5.234	5.029	4.656	4.327	4.035	11
12	10.575	10.258	9.954	9.385	8.863	8.384	7.943	7.536	7.161	6.814	6.194	5.660	5.421	5.197	4.793	4.439	4.127	12
13	11.348	10.983	10.635	9.986	9.394	8.853	8.358	7.904	7.487	7.103	6.424	5.842	5.583	5.342	4.910	4.533	4.203	13
14	12.106	11.691	11.296	10.563	9.899	9.295	8.745	8.244	7.786	7.367	6.628	6.002	5.724	5.468	5.008	4.611	4.265	14
15	12.849	12.381	11.938	11.118	10.380	9.712	9.108	8.559	8.061	7.606	6.811	6.142	5.847	5.575	5.092	4.675	4.315	15
16	13.578	13.055	12.561	11.652	10.838	10.106	9.447	8.851	8.313	7.824	6.974	6.265	5.954	5.669	5.162	4.730	4.357	16
17	14.292	13.712	13.166	12.166	11.274	10.477	9.763	9.122	8.544	8.022	7.120	6.373	6.047	5.749	5.222	4.775	4.391	17
18	14.992	14.353	13.754	12.659	11.690	10.828	10.059	9.372	8.756	8.201	7.250	6.467	6.128	5.818	5.273	4.812	4.419	18
19	15.678	14.979	14.324	13.134	12.085	11.158	10.336	9.604	8.950	8.365	7.366	6.550	6.198	5.877	5.316	4.844	4.442	19
20	16.351	15.589	14.877	13.590	12.462	11.470	10.594	9.818	9.129	8.514	7.469	6.623	6.259	5.929	5.353	4.870	4.460	20
21	17.011	16.185	15.415	14.029	12.821	11.764	10.836	10.017	9.292	8.649	7.562	6.687	6.312	5.973	5.384	4.891	4.476	21
22	17.658	16.765	15.937	14.451	13.163	12.042	11.061	10.201	9.442	8.772	7.645	6.743	6.359	6.011	5.410	4.909	4.488	22
23	18.292	17.332	16.444	14.857	13.489	12.303	11.272	10.371	9.580	8.883	7.718	6.792	6.399	6.044	5.432	4.925	4.499	23
24	18.914	17.885	16.936	15.247	13.799	12.550	11.469	10.529	9.707	8.985	7.784	6.835	6.434	6.073	5.451	4.937	4.507	24
25	19.523	18.424	17.413	15.622	14.094	12.783	11.654	10.675	9.823	9.077	7.843	6.873	6.464	6.097	5.467	4.948	4.514	25
30	22.396	20.930	19.600	17.292	15.372	13.765	12.409	11.258	10.274	9.427	8.055	7.003	6.566	6.177	5.517	4.979	4.534	30
32	23.468	21.849	20.389	17.874	15.803	14.084	12.647	11.435	10.406	9.526	8.112	7.035	6.591	6.196	5.528	4.985	4.538	32
34	24.499	22.724	21.132	18.411	16.193	14.368	12.854	11.587	10.518	9.609	8.157	7.060	6.609	6.210	5.536	4.990	4.540	34
36	25.489	23.556	21.832	18.908	16.547	14.621	13.035	11.717	10.612	9.677	8.192	7.079	6.623	6.220	5.541	4.993	4.542	36
40	27.355	25.103	23.115	19.793	17.159	15.046	13.332	11.925	10.757	9.779	8.244	7.105	6.642	6.234	5.548	4.997	4.544	40

Appendix: An Introduction to Income Taxes

Taxes are a fact of life. As a result, an important aspect of financial planning involves minimizing the tax liability owed by individuals and business. This appendix introduces you to the federal income tax system, examining how individuals and corporations are taxed. Special attention is paid to the major changes that have recently taken place with the passage of the Tax Reform Act of 1986.

The New Tax System

In late 1986, Congress voted to drastically overhaul our tax structure. Supporters of the new federal tax system claim that it will lower personal taxes, stimulate productive effort, simplify reporting, and free millions of low-income individuals from paying any income tax at all. Critics, however, are concerned that various provisions will have an extremely negative impact on businesses. Thus, they contend, the United States will become unable to compete in the world marketplace, create new jobs, or achieve economic prosperity.

These changes will take several years to implement, and their effect cannot be predicted. One thing, however, is clear: The new tax system is certain to have a major impact on our economy and standard of living for many years to come.

An Introduction to Individual Taxation

Determining an individual's income tax liability involves several steps including determining gross income, adjustments to gross income, and itemized deductions. The income tax formula detailing these steps is shown in Exhibit B–1. Most changes brought about by the tax reform act are related to the deductibility of items in each category rather than the category itself. However, there were a number of reclassifications of expenses between categories.

EXHIBIT B-1
Individual Income Tax Formula

Gross income	$ xxx
Less: "AGI*" deductions	(xxx)
Adjusted gross income	$ xxx
Less: Itemized deductions or standard deduction	(xxx)
Less: Exemptions	(xxx)
Taxable income	$ xxx

*Adjusted gross income.

Gross Income

The starting point in tax calculations is determining gross income. **Gross income** includes virtually all sources of income, such as salaries, wages, prizes, rents, royalties, dividends, interest, and gains on property sales. Many items are excluded from gross income, however, to promote important social and economic goals. The most common exclusions are interest on state and local bonds, proceeds from life insurance policies, gifts, inheritances, and accident and health benefits and scholarships. These excluded items do not have to be reported as income on an individual's tax return.

Deductions for Adjusted Gross Income

After determining their gross income, individual taxpayers then claim various deductions. These deductions result in an income measure known as adjusted gross income. The most common deductions claimed in arriving at **adjusted gross income** (often called deductions for adjusted gross income) are expenses incurred in a trade or business, employee business expenses, and contributions to retirement funds such as the Individual Retirement Account (IRA). In addition, there are a variety of other deductions allowed in determining adjusted gross income.

Expenses Incurred in a Trade or Business

All income, other than the exclusions discussed above, earned by an individual or sole proprietor in a trade or business is fully taxable. As a result, these individuals are allowed to deduct expenses incurred in earning this income. All ordinary and necessary expenses such as rent, depreciation, dues, and so forth are deductible. The income and related expenses from a trade or business are summarized on Schedule C of the taxpayer's return.

Employee Business Expenses

An individual employee is likely to incur a variety of expenses related to his or her job, such as travel and transportation. If these expenses are reimbursed by the employer, the reimbursements are included in the employee's gross income. Therefore, these reimbursed expenses are deducted, in full, in computing the employee's adjusted gross income. However, as noted later, unreimbursed employee business expenses are deductible as itemized deductions only above certain limits.

Contributions to Retirement Funds

Under current law, individuals are allowed deductions for adjusted gross income for IRAs, health plans, and self-employment retirement plans. Prior to the Tax Reform Act of 1986, all taxpayers with earned income were allowed a $2,000 maximum deduction for amounts placed in an IRA account. The Act made several controversial changes in the deductibility of IRAs. Individuals are still allowed a deduction of up to $2,000 each to IRAs if neither the taxpayer nor the taxpayer's spouse is an active participant in other employer-sponsored retirement plans. If either the taxpayer or the taxpayer's spouse is involved in such an employer's plan, a deduction for the IRA still may be allowed. However, the amount of the deduction is phased out if the taxpayer and spouse's combined adjusted gross incomes are above $40,000. The effect of these changes is to restrict the number of taxpayers allowed to deduct their contributions to IRAs.

Other Deductions Allowed

There are several other items that qualify as deductions for adjusting gross income. Included are deductions for alimony paid and expenses related to rental property.

Itemized Deductions

The second category of allowable deductions is commonly referred to as **itemized deductions.** These deductions generally relate to expenses that are personal in nature and are subtracted from adjusted gross income to further reduce an individual's tax base. Subject to various limitations, individual taxpayers may claim deductions for mortgage interest payments, state and local taxes other than sales taxes, medical expenses, casualty and theft losses, and charitable contributions.

Interest Payments

Prior to the Tax Reform Act of 1986, both consumer interest (interest on automobiles, credit cards, and other consumer purchases) and home mortgage interest were deductible as itemized deductions. However, Congress decided to phase out the deduction for all consumer interest, so by 1990 only interest on home mortgage loans is deductible in this category. Further, the Act limits the deductible amount of mortgage interest to the interest on the loan secured by the taxpayer's principal residence or a second residence. Interest is disallowed on any part of the loan that exceeds the purchase price of the property plus any improvements and amounts borrowed for educational or medical purposes.

State and Local Taxes

In prior years all state and local taxes paid by the taxpayer were deductible as itemized deductions. The Act repeals the itemized deduction for state and local sales taxes. Thus, beginning in 1987 only state and local income taxes and property taxes will be deductible.

Medical Expenses

For many years the Internal Revenue Code (IRC) has always contained a provision for the deductibility of medical expenses incurred above a certain amount. In recent years the limit has been 5% of adjusted gross income. The Tax Reform Act of 1986 increased this limit to 7.5%, so that currently only medical expenses above 7.5% of the taxpayer's adjusted gross income are deductible.

Other Miscellaneous Itemized Deductions

Certain other miscellaneous deductions are deductible, but only to the extent that they exceed 2% of adjusted gross income. For example, unreimbursed employee travel and transportation costs, outside salespeople expenses, union dues, business periodicals, tax preparation fees, uniforms, and job-related education expenses are deductible as itemized deductions to the extent that they exceed 2% of adjusted gross income.

Charitable contributions to qualified charities are deductible without regard to the 2% limitation. However, there are some limits if the total amount of contributions in any one year reaches 20% of adjusted gross income.

The Standard Deduction

For administrative simplicity, all individual taxpayers are allowed a certain base deduction amount, known as the **standard deduction**, even if they do not itemize their expenses. In 1987, the standard deduction is $3,800 for a married couple filing a joint return and $2,570 for unmarried (single) individuals. Starting in 1988, married couples filing a joint return may claim a $5,000 standard deduction and unmarried individuals may claim a $3,000 standard deduction. Also, starting in 1988 standard deduction amounts will automatically increase in subsequent years to keep pace with inflation.

If a married taxpayer is 65 years old or more, is blind, or has a spouse in either of these cases, he or she is entitled to an additional $600 standard deduction for each status. An unmarried taxpayer is allowed an additional $750 for each condition described above.

Taxpayers with few itemized deductions will claim the standard deduction without having to report itemized deductions. For example, an unmarried taxpayer with $1,500 of itemized deductions will not actually report these deductions. Instead, he or she will just take the much larger standard deduction, $3,000 in 1988, automatically granted to him or her.

In contrast, if a person's itemized deductions are greater than the standard deduction, the taxpayer will find it desirable to claim actual itemized deductions instead of the standard deduction.

Exemptions

Taxpayers may deduct a personal **exemption** for themselves, their spouses, and, under most circumstances, may claim an additional exemption for each dependent they support. Generally, in order for a person to qualify as a dependent of the taxpayer, he or she must meet the following requirements:

1. Be a relative of the taxpayer or a member of the taxpayer's household for most of the taxable year.
2. Have over one-half of his or her financial support provided by the taxpayer.
3. Receives income less than the amount of the exemption for the year, unless the person is the taxpayer's child who is under 19 or is a full-time student.
4. Be a U.S. citizen.
5. Not file a joint return with a spouse if married.

Beginning in 1987, an individual whose claim is dependent on another taxpayer's return, cannot claim a personal exemption.

The new tax law provides that the amount of each exemption will be $1,900 in 1987, $1,950 in 1988, $2,000 in 1989, and an increasingly higher amount thereafter to keep pace with inflation. Thus, for example, a married couple who support two children in 1989 will be able to deduct 4 exemptions at $2,000 each, or $8,000. Finally, a taxpayer who can be claimed as a dependent on another taxpayer's return will not be allowed a personal exemption.

Taxable Income

We are now ready to determine the tax liability owed on **taxable income.** The first step is to determine the taxpayer's **filing status** and then use the appropriate tax rate table to determine the actual amount of the tax.

If taxpayers are married, they will generally find it desirable to choose "married filing jointly" status rather than "married filing separately." Alternatively, if a person is unmarried, he or she will likely file as single (using the rate schedule called "unmarried"). A single person who supports a qualifying child, however, will want to file as "head of household" because this filing status is subject to lower tax rates than is single status.

Second, taxpayers must refer to the appropriate tax table to calculate their tentative tax liability. The tax tables for 1987 and 1988 are reproduced as follows.

1987 Rate Tables				
Tax Rate	Married/ Joint	Head of Household	Single	Married/ Separate
11%	First $3,000	First $2,500	First $1,800	First $1,500
15	$ 3,001–28,000	$ 2,501–23,000	$ 1,801–16,800	$ 1,501–14,000
28	28,001–45,000	23,001–38,000	16,801–27,000	14,001–22,500
35	45,001–90,000	38,001–80,000	27,001–54,000	22,501–45,000
38.5	Over 90,000	Over 80,000	Over 54,000	Over 45,000

1988 and Thereafter Rate Tables				
Tax Rate	Married/ Joint	Head of Household	Single	Married/ Separate
15%	First $29,750	First $23,900	First $17,850	First $14,875
28	Over 29,750	Over 23,900	Over 17,850	Over 14,875

The rates in these tables are significantly lower than previous rates. They were lowered by the Tax Reform Act of 1986 in exchange for the disallowance of several popular deductions. Finally, taxpayers in the highest tax bracket may be subject to a limited additional 5% tax surcharge based on the number of exemptions they claim.

To illustrate these tables, assume that an unmarried taxpayer has $27,850 of taxable income in 1988. The taxpayer will have a tax liability of $5,478 as determined on the next page.

An Introduction to Income Taxes

Tax on first $17,850:	
$17,850 × .15 =	$2,678
Tax on remaining $10,000 ($27,850 − $17,850)	
$10,000 × .28 =	2,800
Total tax liability	$5,478

In contrast, a married couple filing a joint return with the same 1988 taxable income of $27,850 would have a tax liability of only $4,178 ($27,850 × .15).

Tax Credits

After the tentative tax liability has been computed, certain credits are allowed to directly *reduce* this tax liability. **Tax credits** therefore are very favorable because they reduce tax liability dollar for dollar. On the other hand, deductions just lower taxable income, effectively reducing tax liability based on an individual's marginal tax rate. To illustrate, if an individual is in the 28% marginal tax bracket, a $100 credit will save $100 in taxes, while a $100 deduction will only save $28 in taxes.

The most significant credits claimed by individuals relate to child care costs, the rehabilitation of certain buildings, low-income earners, and elderly taxpayers. All of these credits were established to stimulate the economy or further certain social aims. A very popular credit, the investment tax credit, which allowed a credit for purchase of certain equipment, was repealed.

Tax Return Filing

Most individual taxpayers account for their income on a calendar-year basis and must file their return by April 15. If unable to file on time, taxpayers are entitled to an automatic extension until August 15. Also, a taxpayer may request an additional extension until October 15.

Tax Payments

If an individual works as an employee, the employer will have withheld throughout the year a substantial portion, if not all, of the tax liability owed on earned wages or salaries. In some cases, excessive withholding of taxes may occur, resulting in a person's later receiving a tax refund.

If an individual earns significant income from self-employment or investments not subject to withholding, however, he or she must make additional quarterly estimated tax payments throughout the year. If these estimated tax payments plus withholdings do not cover substantially all of the tax liability owed, a taxpayer may be subject to penalties and interest.

Introduction to Corporate Taxation

Because corporations are separate taxable entities, they too are subject to federal income taxes. As with individual taxes, the Tax Reform Act of 1986 made several significant changes in corporate taxation. The key items related solely to computing the liability of corporations are discussed next.

Dividends-Received Deduction

When a corporation invests in the stock of another corporation, the dividends it receives are included in its gross income. These dividends, however, are not deductible by the issuing corporation as expenses. Consequently, since these dividends would effectively be taxed twice, Congress has provided corporations with a special **dividends-received deduction.**

Under this provision, corporations must include all dividends received in their gross income, but they may then deduct 80% of the amount of dividends received from another U.S. corporation. Thus, in net effect, a corporation has to include only 20% of received dividends in its taxable income.

Taxable Income

Unlike individuals, corporations cannot claim personal exemptions. Also, corporations cannot claim itemized deductions and do not receive a standard deduction. Accordingly, the taxable income of a corporation simply equals gross income less allowable deductions, without need for the "adjusted gross income" measure.

Calculating Taxes Owed

The Tax Reform Act of 1986 reduced top corporate tax rates from 46% to 34% beginning July 1, 1987. Lower rates are applicable to taxable income below $100,000. Exhibit B–2 presents a comparison of corporate tax rates beginning on July 1, 1987 with prior-years' rates. Thus, a corporation with taxable income of $500,000 in 1988 will have a tax liability of $158,250, calculated as follows:

Tax on first $50,000:	
$50,000 × .15 =	$ 7,500
Tax on next $25,000:	
$25,000 × .25 =	6,250
Tax on remaining $425,000:	
$425,000 × .34	144,500
Total tax liability	$158,250

EXHIBIT B–2
Corporate Tax Rates

Taxable Income	Prior Law Rate	New Law Rate
0–$25,000	15%	15%
$25,000–$50,000	18%	15%
$50,000–$75,000	30%	25%
$75,000–$100,000	40%	34%
Over $100,000	46%	34%

Key Terms

Adjusted Gross Income

Dividends-Received Deduction

Exemption

Filing Status

Gross Income

Itemized Deductions

Standard Deduction

Taxable Income

Tax Credits

Problem for Your Review

Calculating Individual Income Taxes. Jack and Connie Bumpkin have been married twelve years. They are both under 65 and have three children: Mike, age 10; Bill, age 7; and Samantha, age 5. Both Jack and Connie work for employers that have retirement funds and they both participate to the fullest extent possible. In preparing for their meeting with you, their tax adviser, they have gathered the following data:

Jack's salary	$38,500
Connie's salary	41,500
Interest earned:	
From local savings and loan	450
From State of New York bonds	1,200
Proceeds from life insurance policy in which they were beneficiaries	10,000
Dividends from various stocks	350
Mortgage interest	4,600
Interest on consumer loans	1,500
Real estate taxes on home	1,000
Sales tax on auto purchased during year	600
Medical expenses	4,500
Unreimbursed employee business expenses	2,400
Charitable contributions	800
Taxes withheld from paychecks	12,000

Required:

Determine the amount of their taxable income and the amount of taxes due or refund due the Bumpkins for the calendar year ended December 31, 1988.

Solution

Gross Income:		
Jack's salary		$38,500
Connie's salary		41,500
Interest from savings and loan		450
Dividends from various stocks		350
Total		80,800[a]
Deductions for adjusted gross income (AGI)		0
Adjusted Gross Income		80,800
Itemized deductions:		
Mortgage interest	$4,600	
Real estate taxes	1,000	
Medical expenses—do not exceed 7.5% of AGI	0	
Unreimbursed employee business expenses—in excess of 2% of AGI		
$2,400 − ($80,800 × .02)	784	
Charitable contributions	800	
Total itemized deductions		7,184[b]
		73,616
Less: Exemptions ($1,950 × 5)		9,750
Taxable income		$63,866
Tax liability:		
Tax on first $29,750 ($29,750 × .15)		$ 4,463
Tax on remaining $34,116 @ 28% ($63,866 − $29,750)		9,552
Total tax liability		14,015
Tax withheld		12,000
Tax due		$ 2,015

[a]Interest on State of New York bonds and proceeds from insurance policy excluded from gross income.

[b]Consumer interest and sales tax on auto not deductible.

Questions

1. List the major items involved in the tax formula for an individual taxpayer.

2. What are some of the important items included in gross income?

3. What are some of the important items excluded from gross income?

4. What is adjusted gross income?

5. List some of the major items that are considered as deductions in determining adjusted gross income.

6. List and explain the most common itemized deductions.

7. What is the standard deduction, and what is the amount of the deduction for 1987? For 1988?

8. What are exemptions and who may claim them? Can a taxpayer claim more than one exemption?

9. What determines a taxpayer's filing status? Why is a taxpayer's filing status important?

10. What is the difference between tax credits and deductions? From a taxpayer's point of view, which are better?

11. In what major ways does the calculation of corporate taxes differ from the calculation of individual taxes?

12. Describe some of the major changes made by the Tax Reform Act of 1986.

Exercises

1. Determining Gross Income. Bud Terrell received the following amounts during the current year:

Salary	$50,000
Dividends	1,000
Interest on State of California bonds	2,000
California lottery winnings	100
Inheritances from great aunt	5,000

Required:

Determine Bud's gross income.

2. Determining Adjusted Gross Income. Scott Southron received the following amounts and incurred the following expenses during the year:

Salary	$40,000
Royalties from a best-selling accounting text	20,000
Life insurance proceeds	10,000
Gain on sale of stock	1,000
Reimbursement from employer for expenses incurred	2,500
IRA contribution—Scott is not a member of an employee retirement fund	2,000
Employee business expenses	2,500

Required:

Determine the amount of Scott's adjusted gross income.

3. Itemized Deductions. Karen Clausen's adjusted gross income during the year amounted to $30,000. She incurred the following additional expenses:

Interest on consumer loan	$1,500
Interest on home mortgage	9,000
New York City sales taxes	400
Property taxes	1,000
Medical expenses	1,200
Contributions to charitable organizations	800

Required:

    a. State which of the above items qualify as itemized deductions.

    b. Assuming that Karen is single, is under 65, and has no dependents, determine the amount of her taxable income for 1987.

4. Determining Exemptions. Judi Longden and her husband have been married for many years. Judi is 64 and her husband is 66. They have no children, but support an aunt who qualifies as their dependent. Neither individual is blind, but Judi is a little hard of hearing.

Required:

    Determine the number and the total amount of their exemptions for 1988.

5. Determining Tax Liability. Determine the amount of income tax liability for the following independent case:

    a. Gene Ezell is married, files a joint return, and has taxable income in 1987 of $52,000.

    b. Given the same situation as Item a except that the tax year is 1988.

    c. Vicki Bingham is single and has taxable income of $56,000 in 1987.

    d. Given the same situation as Item c except that the tax year is 1988.

6. Determining an Individual's Income Tax. Susan, a college student, received a $4,000 scholarship for tuition, earned $3,250 from a summer job, and inherited jewelry worth $9,600 upon the death of a distant relative. In addition, she had several stock funds that provided her with dividends from corporations of $500 and interest from state and local bonds of $300.

Required:

    a. Determine the amount of Susan's gross income.

    b. Assuming that Susan had no deductions for adjusted gross income or itemized deductions, determine the amount of her taxable income for 1988.

    c. Determine the amount of her tax liability.

7. Determining Taxable Income. Bill, an unmarried 26-year-old office worker, does not belong to his employer's retirement fund. In 1988, he deposited $2,000 of his $30,000 salary into an IRA. Bill also paid $750 in car payments (including interest of $200), paid $3,000 in state income tax, and made a $1,100 cash contribution to charity.

Required:

    a. Determine Bill's adjusted gross income.

    b. Should Bill claim the standard deduction or itemize his deductions?

    c. Determine the amount of Bill's taxable income and his income tax liability.

8. Determining Taxable Income. In 1989, a married couple earns combined salaries of $52,400 and sells for $108,000 land that originally cost $90,000. This couple has one child attending elementary school and has not itemized deductions.

Required:

    Determine the amount of their taxable income.

9. Determining Taxable Income. A married couple filing jointly has taxable income of $49,750. They are entitled to a $420 child care credit and their employers have withheld federal income taxes of $6,000 from their paychecks during the year.

Required:

    Using the tax rates in effect during 1988, how much additional tax must they pay?

10. Corporate Tax Rates. The Big Corporation is on a June 30 fiscal year. Taxable income earned for 1987 and 1988 is as follows:

June 30, 1987	$200,000
June 30, 1988	300,000

Required:

    Determine the amount of the corporation's tax liability for each year.

Appendix: Illustrative Financial Statements

*Excerpts from Safeway Stores, Inc. Annual Report**

Five-year Summary

(dollars in thousands, except per share amounts)

	1985	1984	1983	1982	1981
Operations					
Sales	$19,650,542	$19,642,201	$18,585,217	$17,632,821	$16,580,318
Percentage annual increase	0.04%	5.69%	5.40%	6.35%	9.78%
Cost of sales	14,872,247	15,004,547	14,249,843	13,628,052	12,945,923
Gross profit	4,778,295	4,637,654	4,335,374	4,004,769	3,634,395
Percent of sales	24.3%	23.6%	23.3%	22.7%	21.9%
Operating and administrative expenses	4,350,635	4,214,443	3,920,736	3,653,561	3,363,478
Percent of sales	22.1%	21.5%	21.1%	20.7%	20.3%
Operating profit	427,660	423,211	414,638	351,208	270,917
Interest expense	(172,906)	(151,263)	(134,270)	(129,484)	(120,393)
Gain on sale of foreign operations	49,046				
Other income, net	49,816	26,874	20,565	26,536	15,822
Income taxes	(122,316)	(113,811)	(117,630)	(88,600)	(58,062)
Net income	$ 231,300	$ 185,011	$ 183,303	$ 159,660	$ 108,284
Percent of sales	1.18%	0.94%	0.99%	0.91%	0.65%
Percent of average stockholders' equity	14.96%	12.94%	14.50%	14.43%	10.16%
Per share	$ 3.83	$ 3.12	$ 3.26	$ 3.06	$ 2.07
Cash dividends per share	$ 1.625	$ 1.525	$ 1.425	$ 1.325	$ 1.300
Average shares of common stock outstanding	60,360	59,227	56,163	52,261	52,232
Financial Statistics					
Working capital	$ 301,780	$ 325,432	$ 230,857	$ 218,124	$ 112,919
Current assets per dollar of current liabilities	1.17	1.21	1.15	1.16	1.08
Additions to property	621,758	701,678	541,238	511,917	518,330
Depreciation and amortization	333,398	295,290	264,553	242,371	226,001
Total assets	4,840,611	4,537,229	4,174,363	3,890,633	3,652,315
Long-term debt	1,315,021	1,392,710	1,187,669	1,256,186	1,137,616
Equity of common stockholders	1,622,614	1,469,023	1,390,354	1,137,095	1,075,098
Per share	26.67	24.54	23.66	21.74	20.59
Cash dividends on common stock	98,135	90,371	80,961	69,228	67,900
Other Statistics					
Employees at year-end	164,385	168,590	162,088	156,478	157,411
Stores opened during the year	114	195	145	153	159
Stores closed/sold during the year	320	131	92	176	98
Total stores at year-end	2,365	2,571	2,507	2,454	2,477
Total store area at year-end (thousands sq. ft.)	70,292	73,284	69,818	66,816	65,483
Average annual sales per store	$ 7,687	$ 7,531	$ 7,395	$ 7,184	$ 6,682
Price range, New York Stock Exchange	$ 26⅞-37⅝	$ 21¼-29¼	$ 21¼-30	$ 13⅛-25⅛	$ 12¼-18⅞

Results of Operations

Consolidated sales of $19.65 billion for 1985 were essentially even with 1984 sales of $19.64 billion, which were 5.7% above 1983 sales of $18.59 billion. The sales reflect lower food price inflation, lower foreign exchange rates and the sale of selected foreign operations. During 1985, the company sold its operations in Australia, West Germany and Toronto. These operations accounted for 5.7% of the company's sales in 1984. Sales of ongoing operations increased 1.7% over those in 1984.

Gross profit as a percentage of sales continued to increase. Changes in product mix, improved purchasing practices and continued distribution cost control measures have increased gross profit as a percentage of sales to 24.3% in 1985 from 23.6% in 1984 and 23.3% in 1983. Application of the LIFO method of valuing certain inventories resulted in a pretax credit of $5.6 million in 1985, a $29.3 million charge in 1984 and a credit of $0.4 million in 1983.

Continued increases in occupancy and employee costs were the primary factors contributing to the increase in operating and administrative expenses. As a percentage of sales, operating and administrative expenses increased to 22.1% in 1985 from 21.5% in 1984 and 21.1% in 1983.

Interest expense increased to $172.9 million in 1985 from $151.3 million in 1984 and $134.3 million in 1983. The 14.3% increase from 1984 results primarily from the company's shift from leasing to mortgage financing for the acquisition of new stores.

A pretax gain of $49.0 million, ($34.8 million after-tax or $0.58 per share) was recognized on the sale of foreign operations. On the sale of its Australian operations, the company acquired a 20% interest in Australia's largest food retailer, Woolworths Limited. These actions are part of the company's continuing program to dispose of underperforming operations and to redeploy the assets into areas expected to yield the best long-term returns.

Other income for 1985 was $49.8 million as compared to $26.9 and $20.6 million in 1984 and 1983, respectively. The increase was attributed primarily to gains on the disposal of closed facilities, foreign currency transactions and an in-substance defeasance of debentures.

The provision for income taxes decreased to 34.6% of pretax income from 38.1% in 1984 and 39.1% in 1983.

The decrease in 1985 was mainly due to taxation of the gain on the sale of the foreign operations at capital gains tax rates rather than statutory tax rates.

Net income increased 25.0% in 1985 to $231.3 million from $185.0 million in 1984 and $183.3 million in 1983. Excluding the gain on the sale of foreign operations, 1985 net income increased 6.2% to $196.5 million, due primarily to improved operations in the U.S.

See Note L for further information on the effects of inflation and changing prices on operating results.

Liquidity

Consolidated working capital decreased $23.6 million to $301.8 million in 1985 from $325.4 million in 1984, compared with $230.9 million in 1983. The current ratio also decreased to 1.17 from 1.21 and 1.15 in those years. Had the company valued its inventories using the FIFO method, its current ratio would have been 1.36, 1.42 and 1.35, and working capital would have been $614.5, $643.7 and $519.9 million at year-ends 1985, 1984 and 1983, respectively.

The increase in short-term investments resulted principally from cash received on the sale of the operations in West Germany and Toronto, and reinvestment of short-term borrowings at rates in excess of the cost of borrowings.

Average commercial paper and bank borrowings were $158.5 million in 1985 compared to $159.6 million in 1984 and $164.5 million in 1983. The average interest rates paid on consolidated short-term borrowings were 8.8%, 10.0% and 9.9% in 1985, 1984 and 1983, respectively.

Capital Resources

Capital expenditures were $621.8 million in 1985, compared with $701.7 and $541.2 million in 1984 and 1983. During 1985 the company opened 114 stores and closed 320, the closed stores including 125 from continuing operations. For ongoing operations, retail store area increased by 1.7 million square feet during 1985. The mix and average size of stores at year-end 1985 were as follows:

	Number	Ave. Size Sq. Ft.
Conventional supermarkets	1,515	25,200
Superstores (over 35,000 sq. ft.)	651	41,200
Liquor Barns	103	19,500
Food Barns	63	32,400
Superwarehouse stores	20	74,000
Other specialty stores	13	23,000
Total stores and overall average	2,365	29,700

Capital expenditures in 1986 are projected to be $660 million and 90 store openings are planned. The company obtains most of its capital from operations and mortgage financing. In 1985, 1984 and 1983, cash provided from operations was $704.6, $411.1 and $476.0 million, respectively.

Consolidated Statements of Income
Safeway Stores, Incorporated and Subsidiaries

For the 52 weeks ended December 28, 1985,
December 29, 1984 and December 31, 1983
(in thousands, except per share amounts)

	1985	1984	1983
Sales	$19,650,542	$19,642,201	$18,585,217
Cost of sales	14,872,247	15,004,547	14,249,843
Gross profit	4,778,295	4,637,654	4,335,374
Operating and administrative expenses	4,350,635	4,214,443	3,920,736
Operating profit	427,660	423,211	414,638
Interest expense	(172,906)	(151,263)	(134,270)
Gain on sale of foreign operations	49,046		
Other income, net	49,816	26,874	20,565
Income before provision for income taxes	353,616	298,822	300,933
Provision for income taxes	122,316	113,811	117,630
Net income	$ 231,300	$ 185,011	$ 183,303
Net income per share	$ 3.83	$ 3.12	$ 3.26

Consolidated Statements of Changes in Financial Position
Safeway Stores, Incorporated and Subsidiaries

For the 52 weeks ended December 28, 1985,
December 29, 1984 and December 31, 1983
(in thousands)

	1985	1984	1983
Cash provided from operations:			
Net income	$231,300	$185,011	$183,303
Charges (credits) to income not requiring (providing) cash:			
Depreciation and amortization	333,398	295,290	264,553
Gain on sale of Australian operations	(48,296)		
Equity in earnings of affiliates	(8,100)	(1,890)	(140)
Deferred income taxes	29,830	34,128	20,194
LIFO charge (credit)	(5,566)	29,275	(444)
Accrued claims and other liabilities	8,531	9,608	(11,035)

(Increase) decrease in current assets:			
Receivables	(9,233)	(13,524)	(18,537)
Inventories at FIFO cost	(59,815)	(159,265)	(94,820)
Prepaid expenses and other current assets	(8,978)	12,689	7,349
Increase (decrease) in current liabilities:			
Payables and accruals	230,035	42,424	93,761
Income taxes payable	11,510	(22,650)	31,824
Total cash provided from operations	704,616	411,096	476,008
Investment activities:			
Additions to property	(621,758)	(701,678)	(541,238)
Retirements or sales of property	131,079	113,091	90,296
Proceeds from sale of foreign operations:			
Net working capital	(26,611)		
Other net assets, at fair value	135,220		
Investments in affiliated companies	(104,272)	(2,265)	(2,432)
Exchange rate effects on property and investments	11,051	57,211	27,308
Cumulative translation adjustments	(28,056)	(41,907)	(18,045)
Other	(9,185)	6,806	(9,691)
Net investment activities	(512,532)	(568,742)	(453,802)
Financing activities:			
Additions to long-term debt	167,500	323,625	205,935
Payments on long-term debt	(174,871)	(104,008)	(266,876)
Increase (decrease) in notes payable	39,900	(5,243)	(37,872)
Exchange rate effects on long-term debt	(6,000)	(14,576)	(7,576)
Increase in current maturities of long-term debt	2,582	23,137	11,155
Cash dividends on common stock	(98,135)	(90,371)	(80,961)
Proceeds from issuance of common stock	28,467	25,936	168,962
Other	(1,355)	(1,986)	(3,207)
Net financing activities	(41,912)	156,514	(10,440)
Increase (decrease) in cash and short-term investments	150,172	(1,132)	11,766
Cash and short-term investments:			
Beginning of year	74,442	75,574	63,808
End of year	$224,614	$ 74,442	$ 75,574

Consolidated Balance Sheets
Safeway Stores, Incorporated and Subsidiaries

As of December 28, 1985, December 29, 1984
and December 31, 1983
(in thousands, except per share amounts)

	1985	1984	1983
Assets			
Current assets:			
Cash	$ 54,593	$ 49,179	$ 51,682
Short-term investments	170,021	25,263	23,892
Receivables	111,870	105,166	91,642
Merchandise inventories:			
FIFO cost	1,878,281	1,881,525	1,722,260
Less LIFO reductions	312,715	318,281	289,006
	1,565,566	1,563,244	1,433,254
Prepaid expenses and other current assets	124,431	118,537	128,676
Total current assets	2,026,481	1,861,389	1,729,146
Property:			
Land	247,769	236,876	210,427
Buildings	431,410	345,001	305,006
Leasehold improvements	600,091	557,504	459,711
Fixtures and equipment	2,164,072	2,023,914	1,789,136
Transport equipment	186,831	186,485	173,576
Property under capital leases	1,010,277	1,144,409	1,155,493
	4,640,450	4,494,189	4,093,349
Less accumulated depreciation and amortization	2,003,752	1,894,333	1,731,138
Total property, net	2,636,698	2,599,856	2,362,211
Investments in affiliated companies	122,195	27,251	26,519
Other assets	55,237	48,733	56,487
Total assets	$ 4,840,611	$ 4,537,229	$ 4,174,363

	1985	1984	1983
Liabilities and Stockholders' Equity			
Current liabilities:			
Notes payable	$ 80,848	$ 44,913	$ 50,156
Current obligations under capital leases	43,396	45,427	45,841
Current maturities of notes and debentures	52,049	48,274	24,723
Accounts payable	1,151,426	1,038,268	1,017,094
Accrued salaries and wages	167,798	167,739	163,021
Other accrued expenses	201,357	170,905	154,373
Income taxes payable	27,827	20,431	43,081
Total current liabilities	1,724,701	1,535,957	1,498,289

C6

Long-term debt:			
Obligations under capital leases	625,551	746,178	765,307
Notes and debentures	689,470	646,532	422,362
Total long-term debt	1,315,021	1,392,710	1,187,669
Accrued claims and other liabilities	178,275	139,539	98,051
Total liabilities	3,217,997	3,068,206	2,784,009
Stockholders' equity:			
Common stock - $1.66 ⅔ par value			
Authorized 150,000, 150,000 and 75,000 shares			
Outstanding 60,846, 59,854 and 58,760 shares	101,411	99,756	97,933
Additional paid-in capital	273,776	246,964	222,851
Cumulative translation adjustments	(164,035)	(155,994)	(114,087)
Retained earnings	1,411,462	1,278,297	1,183,657
Total stockholders' equity	1,622,614	1,469,023	1,390,354
Total liabilities and stockholders' equity	$ 4,840,611	$ 4,537,229	$ 4,174,363

Consolidated Statements of Stockholders' Equity

Safeway Stores, Incorporated and Subsidiaries

For the 52 weeks ended December 28, 1985, December 29, 1984 and December 31, 1983 (in thousands, except per share amounts)	Common Stock		Additional Paid-in Capital	Cumulative Translation Adjustments	Retained Earnings
	Shares	Amount			
Balance, January 1, 1983	26,150	$ 43,583	$ 64,573	$ (96,042)	$1,124,981
Net income					183,303
Cash dividends ($1.425 per share)					(80,961)
Translation adjustments				(18,045)	
Stock issued under stock option plans (pre-split)	50	84	1,841		
Stock issued in 2-for-1 split	26,200	43,666			(43,666)
Stock issued under:					
Public offering	5,500	9,167	136,729		
Dividend reinvestment plan	564	940	13,403		
Stock option plans	150	250	2,470		
Tax Reduction Act Stock Ownership Plan	146	243	3,835		
Balance, December 31, 1983	58,760	97,933	222,851	(114,087)	1,183,657
Net income					185,011
Cash dividends ($1.525 per share)					(90,371)
Translation adjustments				(41,907)	
Stock issued under:					
Dividend reinvestment plan	950	1,583	21,734		
Stock option plans	144	240	2,379		
Balance, December 29, 1984	59,854	99,756	246,964	(155,994)	1,278,297

Net income					231,300
Cash dividends ($1.625 per share)					(98,135)
Translation adjustments				(28,056)	
Translation adjustments realized on sale of foreign operations				20,015	
Stock issued under:					
Dividend reinvestment plan	753	1,256	21,899		
Stock option plans	239	399	4,913		
Balance, December 28, 1985	60,846	$101,411	$273,776	$(164,035)	$1,411,462

Notes to the Consolidated Financial Statements

Note A - Summary of Significant Accounting Policies

Fiscal Year:

The fiscal year for Safeway Stores, Incorporated (the company) and its Canadian subsidiary ends on the Saturday nearest December 31. The fiscal year of the company's United Kingdom subsidiary ends on the Saturday nearest September 30, to allow sufficient time to gather information for U.S. reporting purposes.

Basis of Consolidation:

The consolidated financial statements include the accounts of all significant subsidiaries. All intercompany transactions have been eliminated in consolidation. Investments in affiliates which are not majority owned are included in the financial statements at the company's equity therein.

Translation of Foreign Currencies:

Assets and liabilities of the company's foreign subsidiaries are translated into U.S. dollars at fiscal year-end rates of exchange, and income and expenses are translated at average rates during the year.

Translation adjustments are included in "cumulative translation adjustments," a separate component of stockholders' equity. Gains or losses from foreign currency transactions (transactions denominated in a currency other than the entity's local currency) are included in income. In 1985, foreign currency transactions resulted in a gain of $0.9 million compared with losses for 1984 and 1983 of $2.4 and $2.5 million, respectively.

Provision For Income Taxes:

The provision for income taxes recognizes the tax effect of all transactions entering into the determination of income for financial statement reporting purposes irrespective of when such transactions are reportable for income tax purposes. Deferred income taxes are provided to recognize differences in the timing of income and expense for tax and financial reporting purposes. Investment tax credits reduce the provision for income taxes in the year in which the credits arise.

Merchandise Inventories:

Approximately 68 percent of consolidated merchandise inventories are valued on a last-in, first-out (LIFO) basis at December 28, 1985. Inventories not valued on a LIFO basis are valued at the lower of cost on a first-in, first-out (FIFO) basis or replacement market. Inventories on a FIFO basis include meat and produce in the U.S. and all inventories of foreign subsidiaries.

Application of the LIFO method resulted in a $5.6 million credit to cost of sales in 1985, a $29.3 million charge in 1984 and a $0.4 million credit in 1983. In all three years, fourth-quarter adjustments reduced the LIFO charges accumulated through the first 36 weeks of the year to reflect the actual impact of applying the LIFO method for the full year as determined at year-end. The adjustments increased fourth quarter pretax earnings by $29.8 million in 1985, $2.4 million in 1984 and $23.8 million in 1983.

Property and Depreciation:

Property is stated at historical cost. Interest incurred in connection with construction in progress is capitalized. Depreciation is computed for financial reporting purposes under the straight-line method using the following lives:

Stores and other buildings .... 20 - 40 years

Fixtures and equipment .... 3 - 20 years

Transport equipment .... 6 - 14 years

Leasehold improvements include buildings constructed on leased land and improvements to leased buildings.
Buildings and major improvements are amortized under
the straight-line method over the shorter of the remaining period of the lease or the estimated useful lives of the
assets.

Property under capital leases is amortized under the
straight-line method over the terms of the leases. Accumulated amortization of property under capital leases
was $493.9, $515.2 and $502.9 million at year-ends 1985,
1984 and 1983, respectively.

Depreciation and amortization expense for property of
$331.3 million in 1985, $293.7 million in 1984 and
$263.4 million in 1983 included amortization of property
under capital leases of $53.8, $54.9 and $55.2 million,
respectively.

Pre-Opening Costs:
Costs related to opening new stores are expensed as
incurred.

Self-Insurance:
The company is self-insured for workers' compensation,
automobile and general liability costs. The self-insurance
liability is based upon a review by the company and an
independent actuary of claims filed and an estimate of
claims incurred but not yet filed.

The company is also self-insured to provide post-
retirement health care and death benefits to retirees. The
cost of these benefits is recognized as expense as claims
are paid.

Net Income Per Share:
Net income per share is determined by dividing consolidated net income by the average number of common
shares outstanding during the year.

Reclassifications:
Certain amounts for 1984 and 1983 have been reclassified
to conform with 1985 presentation.

Note B - Sale of Foreign Operations

During 1985, the company sold selected foreign operations, recognizing a pretax gain of $49.0 million ($34.8
million after-tax or $0.58 per share). On the sale of the
Australian operations the company acquired a 20%
interest in Woolworths Limited, the largest food retailer
in Australia. The company's investment in Woolworths

is accounted for under the equity method. The company
also sold its operations in West Germany and Toronto.

Note C - Taxes on Income

The components of the provision for income taxes included in the consolidated statements of income were as
follows (in thousands):

	1985	1984	1983
Current:			
Federal	$ 27,999	$ 21,057	$ 23,589
State	9,622	9,161	12,217
Foreign	50,824	49,465	61,630
	88,445	79,683	97,436
Deferred:			
Federal	30,901	30,321	18,644
State	2,222	2,092	562
Foreign	748	1,715	988
	33,871	34,128	20,194
	$122,316	$113,811	$117,630

Non-current deferred tax credits of $82.0 and $47.5
million were included in accrued claims and other liabilities at year-ends 1985 and 1984, respectively. In 1983
a non-current deferred tax charge of $4.8 million was
included in other assets. Current deferred tax charges of
$25.4, $25.0 and $22.5 million were included in prepaid
expenses and other current assets in those years.

The primary components of deferred income tax expense were as follows (in thousands):

	1985	1984	1983
Accelerated depreciation	$ 23,860	$ 27,730	$ 27,151
Tax benefits acquired through tax leases	11,848	12,956	12,282
Gain on sale of Australian operations	6,109		
Accrued claims	(478)	5,179	(2,270)
Capitalized leases	(330)	(3,779)	(4,213)
Compensation plans	(1,254)	(2,302)	(2,328)
Repairs expense	(21)	425	(5,168)
Other, net	(5,863)	(6,081)	(5,260)
	$ 33,871	$ 34,128	$ 20,194

Distributions have been made to the parent company from the current earnings of certain foreign subsidiaries and provision has been made for any income taxes payable on such distributions. No provision has been made for income taxes which might be payable if earnings not yet distributed through year-end 1985 were distributed to the parent company, since it is the intention of management to make no such distributions. The undistributed earnings on which the company has not provided for income taxes were $710.9, $732.5 and $749.4 million at year-ends 1985, 1984 and 1983, respectively.

U.S. and Canadian corporation income tax returns for all years prior to 1980 and 1977, respectively, have been reviewed by taxing jurisdictions. Substantially all deductions which have been or may ultimately be disallowed are timing differences and will be claimed as deductions in future years, thereby having no significant effect on reported earnings.

A reconciliation of the U.S. federal statutory income tax rate to the company's effective income tax rate follows:

	1985	1984	1983
Statutory federal income tax rate	46.0%	46.0%	46.0%
U.S. investment tax credit	(4.6)	(5.6)	(4.7)
Difference between statutory rate and foreign effective rates	(3.3)	(2.0)	(2.2)
Payroll based tax credit employee stock ownership plan	(1.9)	(1.7)	(1.7)
Gain on sale of Australian operations	(1.9)		
State taxes on income, less federal benefit...	1.8	2.0	2.3
Other, net	(1.5)	(0.6)	(0.6)
Effective income tax rate	34.6%	38.1%	39.1%

Income tax expense for financial statement purposes was reduced by investment tax credits of $16.2, $16.6 and $14.0 million in 1985, 1984 and 1983, respectively. These amounts were reduced by $6.8, $6.9 and $5.5 million as a result of related tax basis adjustments and investment tax credit recapture.

Note D - Financing
Short-term
At year-end 1985, the company had lines of credit with a number of major U.S. and foreign banks amounting to $455 million, of which $385 million is maintained to back U.S. commercial paper borrowings. Compensating balances in support of the lines of credit are not significant and there are no legal restrictions on withdrawals. The company pays annual commitment fees of ⅛th percent on the unused portion of credit facilities to support commercial paper issuance.

Commercial paper borrowings at year-end 1985 amounted to $144.3 million of which $30.0 million were expected to be continually refinanced for a period beyond one year and were reclassified as long-term debt. Under interest rate swap agreements an additional $60.0 million of commercial paper borrowings were reclassified as long-term debt. The interest rate swap agreements enabled the company to obtain long-term financing at rates lower than long-term borrowing rates directly available to the company at the time of the agreement.

Long-term
Long-term debt was comprised of the following (in thousands):

	1985	1984	1983
Mortgage notes payable, secured	$416,379	$363,627	$263,250
Commercial paper and bank borrowings ...	90,000	100,000	49,000
Industrial development revenue bonds	68,245	57,680	33,132
7.40% sinking fund debentures, unsecured, due in installments through 1997...	18,209	37,255	37,780
Other notes payable, unsecured	148,686	136,244	63,923
	741,519	694,806	447,085

Less current maturities	52,049	48,274	24,723
Long-term debt	$689,470	$646,532	$422,362

The mortgage notes payable are secured by properties which are included in the balance sheet at their net book value of $319.6 million. Mortgage notes have terms ranging from 1 to 25 years and bear interest at 5 to 16 percent.

In 1985 the company completed an in-substance defeasance on $18.5 million of the 7.40% debentures by placing funds in an irrevocable trust sufficient to cover all future principal and interest payments on the debentures. A gain of $3.2 million was recognized on the defeasance. The remaining debentures require annual sinking fund payments of $1.6 million. Under the agreement covering the debentures, $1.06 billion of the retained earnings as of year-end 1985 was free of restrictions for dividend payments and acquisitions of common stock. Restrictions include a limitation on the creation of additional debt.

At year-end 1984, the company had completed industrial development revenue bond financings of $88.0 million of which $71.9 and $57.9 million had been released to the company at year-ends 1985 and 1984, respectively. The bonds have terms ranging from 10 to 25 years and bear interest at 6 to 14 percent. No new financing of this type was obtained during 1985.

Aggregate annual maturities of long-term debt for the five years beyond 1985 are (in thousands):

1986	$ 52,049
1987	59,772
1988	59,217
1989	102,959
1990	45,040

Subsequent to year-end, the company's United Kingdom subsidiary issued $57.1 million in unsecured debt. The debt has an effective interest rate of 11.25%. Interest is payable on a semi-annual basis with the principal maturing in the year 2011.

Note E - Lease Obligations

The company and its subsidiaries occupy primarily leased premises. Company premises and equipment were covered by 3,414 leases at year-end 1985 including 1,210 which are capitalized for financial reporting purposes.

Most leases have renewal options with terms and conditions similar to the original lease. Of all the leases

1,452 can be cancelled by the company by offer to purchase the properties at original cost less amortization.

The following schedule shows future minimum rental payments required under leases that have noncancellable lease terms in excess of one year as of year-end 1985 (in thousands):

	Capital Leases	Operating Leases
1986	$ 106,574	$ 155,165
1987	102,625	152,357
1988	98,370	144,194
1989	95,456	140,098
1990	95,660	136,997
Later years	916,497	1,563,636
Total minimum lease payments ..	1,415,182	$ 2,292,447
Less executory costs	16,344	
Net minimum lease payments ...	1,398,838	
Less amounts representing interest	729,891	
Present value of net minimum lease payments	668,947	
Less current obligations	43,396	
Long-term obligations	$ 625,551	

In addition to minimum lease payments, contingent rentals may be paid under certain store leases on the basis of the stores' sales in excess of stipulated amounts. Contingent rentals on capital leases amounted to $6.9 million in 1985, $8.9 million in 1984 and $10.4 million in 1983. The following schedule shows the composition of total rental expense for all operating leases (in thousands):

	1985	1984	1983
Property leases:			
Minimum rentals	$180,885	$172,629	$156,247
Contingent rentals	9,653	10,299	10,296
Less rentals from subleases	(18,320)	(15,472)	(11,589)
	172,218	167,456	154,954
Equipment leases	30,141	27,682	26,071
	$202,359	$195,138	$181,025

Note F - Interest Expense

Interest expense consisted of the following (in thousands):

	1985	1984	1983
Notes and debentures	$ 83,598	$ 63,585	$ 48,201
Obligations under capital leases	76,476	75,060	74,031
Commercial paper and bank borrowings	13,882	16,544	16,329
Other	4,542	3,011	3,017
	178,498	158,200	141,578
Less capitalized interest	5,592	6,937	7,308
	$172,906	$151,263	$134,270

	Shares	SAR's	Option Price
Outstanding, year-end 1982	1,389	546	$14.31-15.81
Granted	838	240	24.56-27.56
Exercised	(251)	(235)	14.31-15.81
Cancelled	(263)	(2)	14.31-15.81
Outstanding, year-end 1983	1,713	549	14.31-27.56
Granted	18	17	22.31-27.19
Exercised	(144)	(135)	14.31-15.81
Cancelled	(187)	(17)	14.31-27.56
Outstanding, year-end 1984	1,400	414	14.31-27.56
Granted	548	320	31.50
Exercised	(239)	(150)	14.31-27.56
Cancelled	(173)	(12)	14.31-27.56
Outstanding, year-end 1985	1,536	572	$14.31-31.50

Note G - Profit-Sharing and Stock Option Plans

The company has profit-sharing plans for eligible U.S. and Canadian employees. Contributions charged to income were $16.2 million in 1985, $17.5 million in 1984 and $16.3 million in 1983.

The company also contributes to U.S. employee stock ownership plans and receives a tax credit equal to the amount contributed. The expense under these plans was $11.4, $9.2 and $10.8 million in 1985, 1984 and 1983, respectively.

The company's qualified "incentive" and non-qualified stock option plans authorize the issuance of 3.0 million shares of the company's common stock. At year-end 1985 there were 762,000 unoptioned shares available for future grants. The options are exercisable at the fair market value of the company's common stock on the date of the grant. Options become exercisable at intervals during the first three years after the date of the grant and expire 10 years after the date of the grant. The plans allow for stock appreciation rights (SAR's) to be granted in tandem with certain stock options. Upon exercise of SAR's, the holder surrenders the related options and receives in cash the excess of the then fair market value of the stock over the option price.

The following summarizes stock option activity during each of the last three years (in thousands, except option price):

At year-end 1985 the weighted average option price for outstanding stock options was $26.67. Of the outstanding options at year-end 1985, 771,000 were exercisable at an option price of $14.31-27.56. The company recognized compensation expense of $3.8, $0.5 and $3.5 million in 1985, 1984 and 1983, respectively, relating to stock appreciation rights.

Note H - Employee Pension Benefits

The company and its subsidiaries participate in various pension plans under collective bargaining agreements and maintain pension plans covering other eligible employees.

Contributions charged to income under collective bargaining agreements were $129.1 million in 1985, $125.6 million in 1984 and $122.0 million in 1983. Under U.S. legislation regarding multi-employer pension plans, a company is required to continue funding its proportionate share of a plan's unfunded vested benefits in the event of withdrawal (as defined by the legislation) from a plan or plan termination. The company participates in approximately 80 multi-employer pension plans and the potential obligation as a participant in these plans may be significant. However, the information required to determine the total amount of this contingent obligation, as well as the total amount of accumulated benefits and net assets of such plans, is not readily available.

Other plans consist of contributory, trusteed pension plans for eligible employees not covered by collective bargaining agreements and a supplemental pension plan for senior executives. The aggregate charges to income for all such plans were $5.5 million in 1985, $6.9 million in 1984 and $6.6 million in 1983.

The actuarial present values of accumulated plan benefits for the U.S. pension plan as of December 31, 1984, 1983, and 1982 were $233.0, $205.2 and $179.0 million as to vested benefits and $5.6, $5.2 and $4.7 million as to non-vested benefits, respectively. The net assets available for benefits at those dates amounted to $509.7, $478.5 and $410.8 million, respectively. The assumed rate of return used to determine the actuarial present value of accumulated plan benefits was 8.0 percent. The "pro-rata unit credit" method is used to determine pension obligations for funding and accounting purposes. The company's foreign pension plans and supplemental pension plan for senior executives are not required to report to U.S. government agencies pursuant to the Employee Retirement Income Security Act. Accordingly, the actuarial present values of accumulated plan benefits, as disclosed for the U.S. pension plan, have not been determined for those plans. The net assets of foreign plans are sufficient to fund vested benefits. The company has purchased cost-recovery life insurance to fund its obligations under the supplemental pension plan for senior executives.

Note I - Commitments
The company has commitments under contracts for the purchase of property and equipment and for the construction of buildings. Portions of such contracts not completed at year-end are not reflected in the consolidated financial statements. These unrecorded commitments amounted to approximately $68 million at year-end 1985.

Note J - Contingent Liabilities - Litigation
There are pending against the company, as of March 3, 1986, various claims and lawsuits arising in the normal course of the company's business, some of which seek damages in very large amounts, as well as other relief which, if granted, would require very large expenditures. Included are suits claiming violation of certain civil rights laws, some of which purport to be class actions.

Although the amount of liability at year-end 1985 with respect to all of the above matters cannot be

ascertained, management is of the opinion that any resulting liability will not materially affect the company's consolidated income or financial position.

Note K - Stock Rights
On February 12, 1986 the board of directors declared a dividend of one common share purchase right on each outstanding share of common stock distributable to stockholders of record on February 24, 1986. The rights will become exercisable if and when any person acquires 20% or more of the company's outstanding common stock, or announces an offer which would result in such person acquiring 30% or more of the company's common stock. The rights will expire February 26, 1996, and may be redeemed by the company for $0.05 per right at any time before a person acquires 20% or more of the company's common stock. If, following such acquisition, there is a merger or other business combination involving the company, each right will entitle its holder to buy a number of shares of common stock of the acquiring company (or of the company, if the company is the surviving entity) having a market value of twice the $100 exercise price of each right.

Note L - Supplementary Information on Inflation and Changing Prices (Unaudited)
The company's primary financial statements are stated on the basis of historical costs. The statements reflect the actual transactions expressed in the number of dollars earned or expended without regard to changes in the purchasing power of the dollar. The following supplementary information attempts to measure the effect of changes in specific prices on the results of operations by restating historical costs to amounts which approximate the current costs to the company of producing or replacing inventories and property.

The computed net income for 1985 under current cost accounting includes restatements of merchandise costs, depreciation and amortization expense. The effects of inflation on merchandise costs have already been recognized in the historical financial statements to the extent that the LIFO method of accounting is used for approximately 68 percent of merchandise inventories.

The provision for income taxes has not been restated to a current cost basis because inflation adjustments are not deductible for income tax purposes.

The purchasing power gain results from an excess of net monetary liabilities over monetary assets. In periods of general inflation monetary assets lose purchasing power because such assets will buy fewer goods. Conversely monetary liabilities gain purchasing power since the liabilities will be repaid with dollars of reduced purchasing power.

In 1985, the current costs of merchandise inventories and property increased by $418.7 million, whereas those assets increased by $225.4 million as a result of general inflation. Thus, the year's increase in inventories and property due to current cost exceeded the increase in general inflation by $193.3 million, indicating a greater increase in the company's specific price indices than the rate of general inflation. At year-end 1985, the current cost of merchandise inventories was $1.9 billion and the current cost of net property was $3.8 billion.

Current cost accounting methods involve the use of assumptions, estimates and subjective judgments, and the results should not be viewed as precise measurements of the effects of inflation.

Amounts shown below for 1985 reflect the current cost assumption discussed above. Prior year amounts are adjusted to reflect the relationship between the average CPI-U for each of the years indicated as measured against the average CPI-U for 1985.

Supplementary Financial Data Adjusted for the Effects of Changing Prices

(in millions)

	1985	
	As Reported in the Consolidated Statement of Income (Historical Cost)	Adjusted for Changes in Specific Prices (Current Cost)
Sales	$19,650	$19,650
Cost of sales	14,872	14,903
Other expenses, net	4,425	4,461
Income before provision for income taxes	353	286
Provision for income taxes	122	122
Net income	$ 231	164
Gain from the change in purchasing power of net monetary liabilities		103
Net income including purchasing power gain		$ 267
Depreciation and amortization expense *	$ 333	$ 422

* Allocated between cost of sales and other expenses in the determination of net income.

Five-Year Comparison of Selected Financial Data Adjusted for the Effects of Changing Prices
(in dollars of 1985 average purchasing power)

	1985	1984	1983	1982	1981
Sales	$19,650	$20,343	$20,068	$19,652	$19,611
Net income (loss)	164	57	22	23	(50)
Net income (loss) per share of common stock	2.72	.96	.40	.45	(.96)
Gain from the change in purchasing power of net monetary liabilities	103	100	96	93	216
Net income including gain in purchasing power	267	158	118	116	166
Increase in the current costs of merchandise inventories and property over (under) the increase due to general inflation	193	(140)	83	(161)	(280)
Net assets at year-end	3,034	2,951	3,045	2,762	2,913
Cash dividends per share of common stock	1.625	1.579	1.539	1.477	1.538
Market price per share of common stock at year-end	36.62	28.48	27.80	25.49	15.67
Average Consumer Price Index (CPI-U)	322.2	311.1	298.4	289.1	272.4

Note: Dollars in millions except per share amounts.

Note M - Quarterly Information (Unaudited)
(in thousands, except per share amounts)

	First 12 Weeks	Second 12 Weeks	Third 12 Weeks	Last 16 Weeks*
1985				
Sales	$4,551,963	$4,548,439	$4,564,158	$5,985,982
Gross profit	1,067,986	1,110,271	1,114,769	1,485,269
Operating profit	74,245	115,087	104,714	133,614
Gain on sale of foreign operations			48,295	751
Net income	25,670	49,908	89,130	66,592
Net income per share	.43	.83	1.48	1.09
Cash dividends per share	.40	.40	.40	.425
Price range, New York Stock Exchange	26⅞-34⅜	29⅜-33½	30-34⅞	29⅝-37⅝
1984				
Sales	$4,402,684	$4,525,660	$4,583,644	$6,130,213
Gross profit	1,014,275	1,076,082	1,082,311	1,464,986
Operating profit	64,442	107,548	91,237	159,984
Net income	22,013	47,544	38,736	76,718
Net income per share	.37	.81	.65	1.29
Cash dividends per share	.375	.375	.375	.40
Price range, New York Stock Exchange	24⅛-27¼	21⅜-25½	21¼-29	24⅝-29¼
1983				
Sales	$4,219,229	$4,287,238	$4,300,321	$5,778,429
Gross profit	955,030	991,805	999,390	1,389,149
Operating profit	65,516	89,586	98,955	160,581
Net income	23,883	37,121	47,122	75,177
Net income per share	.46	.68	.82	1.30
Cash dividends per share	.35	.35	.35	.375
Price range, New York Stock Exchange	24¼-27⅞	24½-30	23¾-27⅜	24¼-28⅞

Note: Dividends are for calendar quarters.
* See Note A - Merchandise Inventories.

Note N - Financial Information by Geographic Area
(in thousands)

	1985	1984	1983
United States*			
Sales	$15,389,928	$15,042,760	$14,056,832
Gross profit	3,886,144	3,691,222	3,400,517
Operating and administrative expenses	3,591,382	3,409,980	3,144,434
Operating profit	294,762	281,242	256,083
Income before provision for income taxes	175,618	165,974	154,967
Provision for income taxes	56,914	62,143	58,658
Net income	118,704	103,831	96,309
Net working capital including merchandise inventories at FIFO cost	414,702	501,554	384,897
Less LIFO reductions	312,715	318,281	289,006

Net working capital	101,987	183,273	95,891
Total assets	3,730,899	3,449,840	3,075,432
Net assets	993,417	925,055	845,623
Cumulative translation adjustments	—	3,156	1,339

Canada

Sales	$ 2,464,676	$ 2,641,738	$ 2,682,836
Gross profit	550,604	573,077	590,412
Operating and administrative expenses	472,626	493,355	491,511
Operating profit	77,978	79,722	98,901
Income before provision for income taxes	76,237	78,620	97,707
Provision for income taxes	30,211	30,517	38,949
Net income	46,026	48,103	58,758
Net working capital	233,198	163,286	175,527
Total assets	697,755	653,632	654,494
Net assets	426,252	434,067	426,178
Cumulative translation adjustments	(115,976)	(86,993)	(62,167)

Other Foreign +

Sales	$ 1,795,938	$ 1,957,703	$ 1,845,549
Gross profit	341,547	373,355	344,445
Operating and administrative expenses	286,627	311,108	284,791
Operating profit	54,920	62,247	59,654
Income before provision for income taxes	101,761	54,228	48,259
Provision for income taxes	35,191	21,151	20,023
Net income	66,570	33,077	28,236
Net working capital deficit	(33,405)	(21,127)	(40,561)
Total assets	411,957	433,757	444,437
Net assets	202,945	109,901	118,553
Cumulative translation adjustments	(48,059)	(72,157)	(53,259)

* *Reflects use of the LIFO method of valuing certain inventories.*
+ *See note B - Sale of Foreign Operations.*

Management's Responsibility for Financial Statements

The consolidated financial statements of Safeway Stores, Incorporated and its subsidiaries have been prepared in accordance with generally accepted accounting principles and necessarily include amounts that are based on management's best estimates and judgments. Management is responsible for the integrity and objectivity of the data in these statements. Financial information elsewhere in this annual report is consistent with that in the financial statements.

To fulfill its responsibilities, management has developed and maintains a strong system of internal account-ing controls. There are inherent limitations in any control system in that the cost of maintaining a control should not exceed the benefits to be derived. However, management believes the controls in use are sufficient to provide reasonable assurance that assets are safeguarded from loss or unauthorized use and that the financial records are reliable for preparing the financial statements. The controls are supported by careful selection and training of qualified personnel, by the appropriate division of responsibilities, by communication of written policies and procedures throughout the company, and by an extensive program of internal audits.

Peat, Marwick, Mitchell & Co., independent certified public accountants, whose report follows the consolidated financial statements, are engaged to provide an independent opinion regarding the fair presentation in the financial statements of the company's financial condition and results of operations. They obtain an understanding of the company's systems and procedures sufficient to provide them reasonable assurance that the financial statements are neither misleading nor contain material errors.

The board of directors, through its audit committee which is composed of outside directors, is responsible for assuring that management fulfills its responsibilities in the preparation of the financial statements. The board, on the recommendation of the audit committee and in accordance with stockholder approval, selects and engages the independent accountants. The audit committee meets with the independent accountants to review the scope of the annual audit and any recommendations they have for improvements in the company's internal accounting controls. To assure independence, the independent accountants have free access to the audit committee and may confer with them without management representation present.

Accountants' Report

Peat, Marwick, Mitchell & Co.
To the Board of Directors and Stockholders
Safeway Stores, Incorporated:

We have examined the consolidated balance sheets of Safeway Stores, Incorporated and subsidiaries as of December 28, 1985, December 29, 1984 and December 31, 1983 and the related consolidated statements of income, stockholders' equity and changes in financial position for the years then ended. Our examinations were made in accordance with generally accepted auditing standards and, accordingly, included such tests of the accounting records and such other auditing procedures as we considered necessary in the circumstances.

In our opinion, the aforementioned consolidated financial statements present fairly the financial position of Safeway Stores, Incorporated and subsidiaries at December 28, 1985, December 29, 1984 and December 31, 1983 and the results of their operations and changes in their financial position for the years then ended, in conformity with generally accepted accounting principles applied on a consistent basis.

Peat, Marwick, Mitchell & Co.

Oakland, California
March 3, 1986

Excerpts from The Philips Group
Annual Report

CONSOLIDATED STATEMENTS OF INCOME OF THE PHILIPS GROUP

	1984	1983
Net sales (1)	**53,804**	46,515
Direct costs of sales (2)	**-39,854**	-34,361
Gross income	**13,950**	12,154
Selling expenses (2)	**-10,034**	-8,790
General and administrative expenses (2)	**-791**	-763
Other business income (3)	**348**	182
Income from operations (4)	**3,473**	2,783
Gearing adjustment	**647**	633
Financial income and expenses (5)	**-2,141**	-2,072
Income before taxes	**1,979**	1,344
Income taxes (6)	**-733**	-638
Income after taxes	**1,246**	706
Equity in net income of unconsolidated companies	**49**	101
Group income	**1,295**	807
Minority interests	**-182**	-140
Net income	**1,113**	667

in millions of guilders

CONSOLIDATED BALANCE SHEETS OF THE PHILIPS GROUP

as of December 31

ASSETS	1984		1983	
Fixed assets				
Intangible fixed assets	-		-	
Tangible fixed assets (7)	**18,676**		16,669	
Unconsolidated companies (8)	**2,163**		1,743	
Sundry non-current financial assets (9)	**1,732**	**22,571**	891	19,303
Current assets				
Inventories (10)	**15,547**		13,615	
Accounts receivable (11)	**14,825**		13,448	
Marketable securities (12)	**222**		181	
Liquid assets (13)	**1,370**	**31,964**	1,507	28,751
Total		**54,535**		48,054

in millions of guilders

LIABILITIES AND EQUITY	1984		1983	
Group equity				
Stockholders' equity (14)	**16,964**		15,307	
Minority interests (15)	**2,682**		2,347	
		19,646		17,654
Long-term provisions (16)		**5,409**		5,205
Short-term provisions (16)		**2,101**		1,749
Long-term liabilities (17)		**9,699**		7,477
Current liabilities (18)		**17,680**		15,969
Total		**54,535**		48,054

ACCOUNTING POLICIES

CONSOLIDATED FINANCIAL STATEMENTS OF THE PHILIPS GROUP

The consolidated financial statements of the Philips Group include the accounts of N.V. Philips' Gloeilampenfabrieken ("N.V. Philips") and its subsidiaries, as well as the United States Philips Trust ("the Trust") and its subsidiaries. The financial statements of N.V. Gemeenschappelijk Bezit van Aandeelen Philips' Gloeilampenfabrieken ("N.V. Bezit") are included separately in this report. The structure of the Philips Group is described in detail on pages 48 and 49.

POLICIES OF CONSOLIDATION

The consolidated financial accounts include all of the subsidiaries in which a majority of the issued share capital is held:
- by N.V. Philips or the Trust, directly, or by either one of them jointly with one or more of its subsidiaries, or
- by one subsidiary or by two or more subsidiaries jointly.

These companies are included in full in the consolidation; the minority interests of third parties are disclosed separately.

In the same manner, the consolidated financial statements of the Group include the financial accounts of the companies in which:
- a majority of the voting shares are held directly or indirectly by one or more of the aforementioned companies,
- half of the issued share capital or voting shares are held by one or more of the aforementioned companies, and, in addition, an agreement exists whereby such companies are regarded as subsidiaries.

POLICIES FOLLOWED IN VALUATION AND INCOME CALCULATION

Current value

The valuation of tangible fixed assets and inventories, as well as the depreciation and/or usage of such, is based on current value which, in general, in order to maintain continuity, represents replacement value unless the lower business value or net realizable value of an asset is required.

The replacement value is determined by taking into consideration such factors as the usage and the location of the assets, as well as the influence of technological developments. The replacement value is calculated using current prices for specific assets or, if this is not possible, using price indices for categories of assets which have been subjected to the same price influences.

The net realizable value of an asset is the amount for which that asset can be sold. The current value of a tangible fixed asset is equal to the net realizable value in the event that the net realizable value is lower than the replacement value, and the asset will no longer be of productive use in the near future. Inventories are valued based on net realizable value when the net realizable value is lower than the replacement value.

The business value of a tangible fixed asset is determined based on the expected net income to be derived from the productive employment of that asset during its remaining useful lifetime, plus the net realizable value upon discontinuation of productive employment of that asset. The current value of a tangible fixed asset is equal to the business value in the event that the business value is lower than the replacement value, and the asset will no longer be productively employed in the foreseeable future.

Changes in the replacement value, which have resulted from fluctuations in the local price level of inventories and tangible fixed assets (i.e., revaluation), are credited or debited to the revaluation surplus account. In the event that the stockholders' equity is greater than the total capital invested in inventories and tangible fixed assets, an amount is added to revaluation surplus and charged to the income account in order to preserve a properly leveraged financial structure. To the extent that the revaluation surplus is not necessary for preserving a properly leveraged financial structure, a gearing adjustment is credited to the income account. In compliance with legal regulations, this gearing adjustment is transferred to the income account in proportion to the usage and/or depreciation of the relevant assets. The deferred gearing adjustment is temporarily accounted for within revaluation surplus in the stockholders' equity section.

A provision for deferred income tax arising from a revaluation of assets is temporarily deducted from revaluation surplus. Upon usage and/or depreciation of the revalued assets, the related income tax is charged to the income account and the provision for deferred income tax is then reversed in the revaluation surplus account.

Foreign currencies
All foreign currency amounts in the balance sheet have been translated to guilders at the official exchange rate on the balance date. In general, the median rate has been used to translate the currencies which have a fixed rate of exchange in relation to the guilder or another currency.
Exchange differences due to fluctuations in the foreign currency exchange rate used for reconciling the outstanding balances on either inter-company accounts or third party accounts have been included in the consolidated income account.
Exchange differences due to the translation of the stockholders' equity of foreign subsidiaries to guilders have been accounted for as translation differences in the stockholders' equity account.
In the consolidated statements of income, the amounts stated for the sales, expenses and results of foreign participations have been translated to guilders based upon the rates of exchange for the periods involved. The year-end balances of the related net income accounts have been translated based upon the rates of exchange used in the balance sheet. The resulting difference between the translated year-end results and the consolidated statement of income is accounted for directly in the stockholders' equity account.

Acquisition and divestment of subsidiaries
Goodwill arising from the acquisition of interests in companies, whereby the purchase price differs from the net asset value, is accounted for directly in the stockholders' equity account. In the event that such an interest is subsequently divested, the acquired goodwill is then transferred from the equity to the income account.

Balance sheet

Intangible fixed assets
Intangible fixed assets are not included in the balance sheet, with the exception of the value of payments to third parties for repertoire, publishing rights and film rights. Such intangible fixed assets are valued based upon either the actual amount paid to third parties or the present value of future revenues, whichever is lower. The depreciation of such assets is calculated in proportion to the expected revenues.

Tangible fixed assets
Tangible fixed assets are valued based on the current value. The book value of tangible fixed assets valued on the basis of their replacement value is determined by reducing the new value by the amount of the accumulated depreciation based on fixed percentages which depend on the type of asset and the expected economic lifetime. In certain instances the asset is depreciated at a rate corresponding to the expected future usage. The book value of tangible fixed assets which are not valued on the basis of their replacement value is equal to either the business value or the net realizable value. The valuation of tangible fixed assets which have been manufactured in our own facilities includes an applicable portion of the overhead expenses and interest expense incurred during the period of manufacture.

Unconsolidated companies
The valuation of investments in unconsolidated companies is stated based on net asset value. The valuation of the assets, liabilities, equity and income of unconsolidated com-

panies reflects, as much as possible, the accounting policies established for the consolidated financial statements.

Sundry non-current financial assets
Sundry non-current financial assets are valued based on either the purchase price or the net realizable value.

Inventories
Inventories, including work in process, are valued based on current value less a provision to cover the risk of obsolescence. Any income derived from inter-company transfers of goods and materials has been eliminated.

Accounts receivable
Accounts receivable are stated at nominal value less an allowance for doubtful accounts.

Marketable securities
Marketable securities are valued at either the purchase price or the market value, whichever is (or has been) lower.

Liquid assets
Cash and bank balances are stated at nominal value.

Minority interests
Minority interests in Group companies are valued based on the net asset value according to the policies established with regard to the consolidated financial statements. In some cases the minority interests consist of capital participation certificates or profit-sharing agreements representing specific financial commitments which are included in the financial statements based on the value of the contribution.

Provisions
The provisions are not associated with specific assets, but are created to cover certain business obligations and risks.
The provisions are stated at nominal value, with the exception of provisions for employee pension benefits and severance payments, which are stated at the present value of the future obligations.

The provision for employee pension benefits is based on actuarial calculations and relates to those pension obligations that are not funded by separate pension funds or by third parties. Past service liabilities are, in general, covered to the retirement dates of the relevant employees. The total pension coverage provided by this provision together with the various separate pension funds is equal to at least the present value of existing pension plans based upon the number of prior years of employment with the Company.

The provision for income taxes includes the deferred income taxes as determined for each fiscal entity. The provision for income taxes includes the deferred income tax liability arising from timing differences between book (commercial) and taxable (fiscal) income as well as the deferred income taxes due to revaluation of assets. The deferred income taxes on the revaluation adjustment represent the future income tax liability on the unamortized portion of the revaluation adjustment. An income tax benefit related to a loss carried forward is only recognized if it will be realized beyond any reasonable doubt. In the event that the deferred income tax benefits exceed the deferred income tax liability for a given fiscal entity, the net income tax benefit is shown as a receivable. Deferred income tax is stated according to the nominal value.

Liabilities
Long-term debt as well as the current liabilities are stated at nominal value.

Statement of income

In view of the principle of a going concern, net income is determined on the basis of current value taking into account the following accounting policies.
Net sales represent the revenues derived from products delivered to, and services performed for, third parties.
The usage of raw materials, the depreciation of equipment and the other costs related to the products and services sold, are all calculated on the basis of current value. Also included in the cost of products and services

Illustrative Financial Statements

sold are the write-downs of any inventories or tangible fixed assets to a lower business value or net realizable value.

Provisions to cover the normal risks of doing business are determined based upon the volume of the related business activities.

The expenditures for research, development, patents, licenses and concessions are charged directly to the income account.

The depreciation expense related to payments to third parties for repertoires, publishing rights and film rights is calculated based upon the current portion of the total estimated revenues. Also included in the cost of products and services sold is any write-down of the total estimated revenues.

The equity in the net income of unconsolidated companies has been recognized, as far as possible, in accordance with the policies followed in the preparation of the consolidated financial statements.

POLICIES FOLLOWED IN VALUATION AND INCOME CALCULATION BASED ON HISTORICAL COST

In the valuation and income calculation based on historical cost, the valuation and depreciation of tangible fixed assets and usage of inventories are generally calculated based on purchase prices in local currencies. In highly inflationary countries, however, these calculations are based on purchase prices expressed in guilders; in these countries the guilder is used instead of the local currency for financial statements based on historical cost. In these instances, the translation differences with regard to the monetary assets and liabilities in local currencies versus the guilder are accounted for in the income account. By using this method of valuation in highly inflationary countries, translation differences do not appear in the equity account. The highly inflationary countries are those countries in which the inflation percentage accumulated over a period of three years has been 100% or more and in which relatively significant subsidiaries of Philips are present.

A FIFO (first-in, first-out) method is used for the valuation of inventories and calculation of costs of sales.

A net balance of goodwill arising from acquisitions is amortized over a period of five years.

All other policies are the same as those used for the valuation and income calculation based on current value.

The calculations based on historical cost reflect the aforementioned policies which are also substantially in conformity with generally accepted accounting principles in the United States of America.

Appendix: Glossary of Key Terms

A

Accelerated Cost Recovery System (ACRS): a system for recovering the cost of capital expenditure by which the cost of depreciable property is recovered over either a 3-, 5-, 10-, or 15-year period of time, depending upon the nature of the asset.

Accelerated Depreciation: methods of depreciation that allocate a greater portion of the asset's cost the early years of its useful life, and consequently less to the later years.

Account: a record that summarizes all of the transactions that affect a particular category of asset, liability, or stockholders' equity.

Accounting: a system of providing quantitative information about economic entities, primarily financial in nature, that is intended to be useful in making economic decisions.

Accounting Controls: a plan of organization, and the procedures and records concerned with the safeguarding of assets and the reliability of the financial records.

Accounting Cycle: a set of standardized procedures performed in monthly, quarterly, or yearly sequence, depending on the needs of the business.

Accounting Equation: an algebraic expression of financial position: assets = liability + owners' equity.

Accounting Information System: a system designed to provide financial information about economic entities.

Accounting Rate of Return Method: a capital budgeting method that is used to find the percentage return a project offers by finding the relationship between the expected increases in net income directly resulting from an investment and the initial investment cost. This method does not take into account the time value of money.

Accounting System: the set of methods and procedures that is used to record, classify, and summarize the financial information to be distributed to users.

Accounts Payable: monies owed to the enterprise's suppliers or vendors for the purchase of goods and services.

Accounts Payable Trial Balance (Schedule of Accounts Payable): a list of the balances in all of the subsidiary accounts payable accounts.

Accounts Receivable Trial Balance (Schedule of Accounts Receivable): a list of the balances in all of the subsidiary accounts receivable accounts.

Accrual Basis: the accounting system in which revenues, expenses, and other changes in assets, liabilities, and owners' equity are accounted for in the period in which the economic event takes place, not when the cash inflows and outflows take place.

Accruals: those expenses that are incurred and the revenues that are earned over time, but which are recorded periodically only.

Accrued Expenses: those expenses that have been incurred but have not been recorded, necessitating the adjustment entries and the inclusion of such items as interest expense, salary expense, and tax expense.

Accrued Revenues: the revenues received for services completed or goods delivered that have not been recorded, necessitating the adjustment of entries and the inclusion of such items as interest revenue and rental revenue.

Action Plans: plans to achieve organizational objectives formulated after the organization has analyzed information about itself and the environment, and then established its objectives.

Additional Paid-in Capital: the amount invested in a corporation by its owners, in addition to the par value of any capital stock.

Additions: enlargements, such as the addition of a new wing to an existing plant.

Adjunct Account: an account, the balance of which is added to the corresponding account in the financial statements.

Adjusted Trial Balance: a listing of the general ledger account balances after the adjustments have been posted.

Adjusting Entries: the entries that record accruals and internal transactions that are necessary to the application of the accrual basis of accounting.

Administrative Controls: a plan of organization and procedures, and records regarding the decision processes leading to management's authorization of transactions.

Aging Method: a method of estimating uncollectible accounts expense that attempts to estimate the percentage of the outstanding receivables at year-end that will ultimately remain uncollected.

All Financial Resources: the concept used in the preparation of the statement of changes in financial position when exchange transactions, such as the exchange of land for capital stock, are considered as both a source and a use of net working capital or cash.

Allowance for Uncollectible Accounts: a contra-accounts receivable account in which appears the estimated total of the as-yet-unidentified accounts receivable that will remain uncollected.

Allowance Method: a method of matching the uncollectible account expense for the period with the sales for the period. Requires an estimate of the uncollectible account expense in the period of the sale.

American Accounting Association (AAA): a professional association of accountants, principally academics and practicing accountants, who are concerned with accounting education and research.

American Institute of Certified Public Accountants (AICPA): the professional association of CPAs.

Amortization: the periodic allocation of the cost of an intangible asset over its useful life.

Annuity: a series of equal payments or receipts at regular intervals.

Applied Overhead: the cost calculated through the predetermined overhead rate which is removed from the overhead account and posted to Work in Process.

Appropriation of Retained Earnings: a restriction of retained earnings that occurs when the board of directors transfers a portion of the retained earnings account into a separate appropriated retained earnings account in order to indicate to stockholders, and to others, that the balance in the appropriated retained earnings account is not available for dividends.

Articulation: the relationship in which the income statement, balance sheet, retained earnings statement, and statement of changes in financial position are all linked together. For example, the amount in one statement, such as net income on the income statement, is carried forward to another statement, in this case the retained earnings statement.

Assets: the economic resources owned or controlled by the firm that are expected to have future economic benefits.

Audit: an examination of a firm's financial statements by a CPA firm.

Auditor's Report: a report by an independent CPA that accompanies the financial statements and the accountant's opinion regarding the fairness of presentation of the financial statements.

Average Collection Period: a ratio that measures the average number of days it takes before the receivable is collected.

Average Cost: an inventory costing method by which a weighted average cost, determined by dividing the total cost of goods available for sale by the number of units available for sale, is applied to both the cost of goods sold and the ending inventory.

B

Balance Sheet: a financial statement that shows the financial position of a firm at a particular point in time.

Bank Reconciliation: the process of accounting for the differences between the balance appearing on the bank statement and the balance of cash according to the depositor's records.

Bank Statement: a monthly statement which the bank prepares and mails to the depositor; the statement lists the beginning balance in the account, all deposits received, checks paid, other debits (charges) and credits (receipts), and the ending balance in the account.

Beta: a measure of risk that relates the volatility of the price of a specific stock to the volatility of the prices of the stock market as a whole.

Betterments: improvements to existing assets, such as the installation of a computer-controlled temperature monitoring system in a department store.

Board of Directors: a group of individuals elected by shareholders, charged with establishing broad corporate policies and appointing senior corporate management.

Bond: a written agreement between a borrower and lenders in which the borrower agrees to repay a stated sum on a future date and to make periodic interest payments at specified dates.

Bond Indentures: those written agreements that bondholders often insist upon, including restrictions as to dividends, working capital, and the issuance of additional long-term debt.

Book Value: the equity that the owner of one share of common stock has in the net assets (assets less liabilities) or stockholders' equity of the corporation.

Break-Even Point: the point at which a company's revenues equal its costs; there is neither profit nor loss, and net income is equal to zero.

Budget: an organization's operational plan expressed in financial terms.

Business Entity Assumption: a separate economic unit, the transactions of which are kept separate from that of its owners.

C

Call Premium: the difference between the call price and par value of a callable preferred stock.

Capital Budgeting: the process of planning for long-term investment decisions in operational assets through analysis of alternative uses of funds, in order to find the greatest return on investment.

Capital Expenditures: expenditures which result in other assets that benefit several accounting periods.

Capital Lease: a long-term lease that is, in effect, an installment purchase of assets.

Capital Stock: a component of stockholders' equity that represents the amount invested by the owners of the business. A general term for common stock.

Capitalized Retained Earnings: retained earnings transferred to permanent capital, unavailable for future cash dividends. Usually occurs when a stock dividend is issued.

Cash: any medium of exchange that a bank will accept for deposits, including coins, paper money, money orders, checks, certified and cashier's checks, and money on deposit in a bank.

Cash Basis: the accounting system in which revenues and expenses are not recognized until the cash is received or paid.

Cash Budget: a budget that only includes items affecting cash, and is made up of cash receipts and cash expenditures.

Cash Flow Statement: a cash-based statement of financial position that defines financial resources as cash, and explains what caused the changes in the cash balance during the year.

Cash Inflows: any items that are expected to generate revenue or reduce costs, now or in the future.

Cash Outflows: the initial cost of an investment as well as any other future cash outlays undertaken due to that investment.

Cash Payments Journal: the specialized journal used to record cash disbursements made by check.

Cash Receipts Journal: the specialized journal used to record the receipt of cash.

Certified Public Accountant (CPA): a professional accountant licensed by individual states to practice accounting after having met a number of requirements.

Change in Accounting Method: a change that occurs when a firm switches from one generally accepted accounting principle or method to another generally accepted one.

Chart of Accounts: a listing of all of the accounts used by a particular firm. Each account is assigned a unique number.

Check Register: a simplified cash disbursements journal with only three debit/credit columns: voucher payable, purchase discounts, and cash. Generally used in conjunction with a voucher system.

Classified Financial Statement: the financial statement that is subdivided into categories to allow for meaningful interfirm and interperiod comparison.

Closing Entries: the journal entries made at the end of the period, used to update retained earnings to reflect the results of operations and to eliminate the balances in the revenue and expense accounts, so that they may be used again in a subsequent period.

Common Dollar Statements: the financial statements in which the appropriate total figure is set to 100%, and in which other items are expressed as a percentage of that figure.

Common Stock Equivalent: a dilutive security that, because of the terms or circumstances at the time of its issue, is essentially equivalent to common stock, allowing the holder to become a common stockholder at some future date.

Comparability: the qualitative characteristic of accounting information that presents information in such a way that the users can identify similarities and differences between two sets of economic events. Can be used to evaluate the financial position and performance of one firm over time or to compare such factors with other firms.

Comparative Balance Sheet: a balance sheet in which data for two or more periods are shown in adjacent columnar form.

Compensated Absences: a liability that arises as employees accrue certain fringe benefits that allow them time off with full or partial pay, including such benefits as vacation and sick pay.

Compensation Record: a record serving to accumulate all of the payroll data relating to an individual employee.

Complex Capital Structure: a capital structure in which there are certain types of bonds, preferred stock, or other securities that are convertible into common shares.

Compound Interest: interest computed on the principal, plus any previously accrued interest.

Conceptual Framework Project: a theoretical framework for accounting used to develop objectives and concepts that the Financial Accounting Standards Board (FASB) uses to decide upon the standards of external financial reporting.

Conservatism: the prudence exercised in financial reporting as a result of the uncertainties surrounding business and economic activities. When faced with accounting alternatives, accountants tend to choose those that are least likely to overstate assets or income.

Consistency: an accounting convention requiring that a firm use the same accounting procedures and policies from one period to the next.

Consolidated Financial Statements: the combined financial statements, less certain eliminations, of a parent company and its subsidiaries.

Consolidated Statements: the combined financial statements of a parent company and its subsidiaries.

Constant Dollar Statements: those financial statements that are adjusted for general price level changes.

Contingent Liability: a possible liability that may or may not occur, depending on some future event.

Contra Account: an account, the balance of which is subtracted from the associated account on the financial statements.

Contributed Capital: the legal capital plus any additional capital contributed by the stockholders or others.

Contribution Margin: the margin based on cost behavior patterns; represents the amount left from the sales revenue after all variable costs have been deducted.

Contribution Margin Income Statement: an income statement, used only for the internal purposes of a firm, that emphasizes cost behavior rather than the usual functional expense categories.

Contribution Margin Ratio: the percentage of sales dollars left after the variable costs have been covered. It is the contribution margin expressed as a percentage of sales price.

Controlling Account: the main or primary account that is maintained in the general ledger.

Conversion Costs: the adding together of labor and overhead costs when calculating the cost per unit of a product.

Convertible Bonds: those bonds that can be converted at some future specified date into the firm's common stock.

Convertible Preferred Stock: the preferred stock that enables preferred stockholders to convert their preferred stock, at a stated rate and time, to common stock.

Copyrights: the exclusive right of the creator or his/her heirs to reproduce and/or sell an artistic or published work.

Corporation: a business entity legally viewed as separate and distinct from its owners—the "stockholders."

Cost Accounting Systems: systems set up as part of the overall accounting system to identify the costs of making a product.

Cost Behavior: the way a cost responds to the changes in level of business activity or volume.

Cost Objective: the item one is attempting to calculate the cost of.

Cost of Capital: the interest rate that a firm has to pay for its debt and equity, generally computed on a weighted average basis. Serves as an acceptable rate of return on an investment when doing capital budgeting.

Cost of Goods Sold: the cost allocated to the merchandise sold by a retail or merchandising firm.

Cost of Goods Sold Budget: a budget that shows the cost of the raw materials, direct labor, and factory overhead to be used in production, the projected cost of goods manufactured, and the projected cost of goods sold.

Cost Production Report: summarizes the work done by a processing center during a specified period. Accounts for number of units worked on during the period and the costs associated with those units.

Cost-Volume-Profit Analysis: an analysis that examines changes in volume to see how such changes affect costs and profitability.

Cost-Volume-Profit Formula (C-V-P Formula): a variation of the income statement format. Sales = Variable costs + Fixed costs + Net income. S = VC + FC + NI.

Costs: resources sacrificed or given up to attain goods and services.

Coupon Bonds: those bonds that are not registered in the name of individual holders, but that are negotiable by whoever holds them.

Credit: an entry on the right side of any ledger account representing a decrease in an asset account and an increase in an equity account.

Current Assets: cash—or other assets reasonably expected to be realized in cash or sold within the normal operating cycle of a business, or within one year (if the operating cycle is longer than one year).

Current Cost/Constant Purchasing Power Dollar Statements: those financial statements that are adjusted for both specific and general price level changes.

Current Cost Statements: those financial statements that are adjusted for specific price changes.

Current Liabilities: those liabilities that will either be paid or require the use of current assets within a year (or within the operating cycle, if longer), or that result in the creation of new current liabilities.

Current Maturities of Long-Term Debt: those portions of long-term liabilities that are payable within one year of the balance sheet date, and as a result are classified as current.

Current Maturity of Long-Term Debt: the portion of long-term liabilities that is payable within 12 months from the balance sheet date.

Current Method: a method of foreign currency translation under which all balance sheet items can be translated at the current exchange rate at the date of the financial statements; income statement items are translated at the average exchange rate for the period.

Current Ratio: the total of current assets divided by the total of current liabilities.

Currently Attainable Standards: standards that require that costs be incurred under very efficient but reachable operating conditions.

D

Date of Record: the date the stockholders are entitled to receive the dividend as per issue.

Debenture: an unsecured bond.

Debit: an entry on the left side of any ledger account representing an increase in an asset account and a decrease in an equity account.

Debt-Equity Ratio: the total liabilities divided by total stockholders' equity.

Debt Securities: long-term notes, bonds, and other liabilities.

Debt-to-Total Assets Ratio: the total liabilities divided by total assets.

Declaration Date: the date the board of directors declares the dividend.

Declining Balance Method: an accelerated method of depreciation in which the asset's book value at the beginning of each ledger is multiplied by a constant percentage.

Default: a happening which ocurs when the borrower or maker of the note fails to make the required payment at the note's maturity.

Denomination: the amount on which the required interest payment is always calculated (also called face value, maturity value, or par value).

Depletion: the process in which natural resources lose their benefits as the resources are removed. Follows the same process as units of production depreciation.

Deposit Slip: a list of the cash and checks to be deposited.

Deposits in Transit: deposits made by the depositor but not yet recorded by the bank.

Depreciable Base: an asset's acquisition cost, less its estimated residual value.

Depreciable Cost: the asset's estimated residual value, less its acquisition cost.

Depreciation: the systematic allocation of the cost of noncurrent, nonmonetary tangible assets (except for land) over their estimated useful life.

Differential Costs and Revenues: the costs and revenues that are relevant to a management decision in that they will change depending on which alternative is chosen.

Direct Costs: costs that are easily traced to a particular cost objective.

Direct Labor: labor that can be conveniently and economically traced to the creation of a finished product.

Direct Labor Budget: an estimate of the number of labor hours required to meet production needs. This budget is dependent on the production budget.

Direct Labor Efficiency Variance: the amount of labor time used to produce the units of product as compared to the amount of labor time that should have been used according to the standard.

Direct Labor Rate Variance: the difference between the actual labor rates paid during production and the standard labor rates.

Direct Materials: all materials that become an integral part of a finished product and that can be conveniently and economically traced to that product.

Direct Materials Budget: the amount of direct materials that will be used and purchased.

Direct Materials Price Variance: the difference between the standard price of a direct material and the actual price paid.

Direct Materials Quantity Variance: the difference between the pounds of material actually used in production and the pounds of material that should have been used for the units produced.

Discount: the selling or pledging of a customer's note receivable to the bank at some point prior to the note's maturity date.

Discounted Cash Flow Methods: capital budgeting decision methods that fully recognize the time value of money.

Discounting: a process that determines the present value of a future cash flow in order to meaningfully assess the value of a proposed investment.

Dissolution of Partnership: this is a result of a change in the partners who make up the partnership. Usually, a new partnership is formed and the partnership business continues.

Dividend Payment Date: the date the dividend is actually paid.

Dividends: a return to stockholders of some of the assets of the corporation that have increased as a result of the profits earned.

Dividends in Arrears: the accumulated unpaid dividends on cumulative preferred stock from prior years.

Double Entry Accounting: the system of accounting in which each transaction has equal debit and credit effects, thus ensuring that the accounting equation remains in balance.

Duration of the Note: the length of time that the note is outstanding, or the number of days called for by the note.

E

Early Extinguishment of Debt: the retirement of debt before maturity.

Earnings per Share: the net income divided by the average number of common shares outstanding during the year; also called net income per share.

Effective Interest Method: a method of determining periodic interest in which a constant interest rate (the effective rate at the time of issue) is applied to the carrying value of the note or bond at the beginning of the period.

Effective Interest Rate: the interest rate at which the bond is issued (*see also* Market Interest Rate).

Ending Inventory Budget: the dollar amounts to be assigned to ending inventories of direct materials and finished goods.

Equities: a collective reference of the liabilities and the owners' equity.

Equity Method: a method of accounting for long-term investments by which the investment is first recorded at its acquisition cost. However, the investment account is adjusted to reflect the proportionate increase or decrease in the investee's stockholder's equity that results from the investee's net income or loss for the period, and the declaration of dividends.

Equity Securities: preferred and common stock, or other instruments that represent an ownership interest.

Equivalent Units: the productive output of a process or department for a period expressed in terms of finished units of product.

Exchange Rate: the rate at which one currency can be exchanged for another.

Expenditures: outflows of cash or other assets or increases in liabilities.

Expenses: the dollar amount of the resources used up by the firm during a particular period of time in the process of earning revenues.

External Transactions: the transactions with an outside party, which are recorded in financial statements.

Extraordinary Items: the gains and losses that result from transactions that are both unusual in nature and infrequent in occurrence, depending on the environment in which the firm operates.

Extraordinary Repairs: a major reconditioning or overhaul to existing assets, such as a major overhaul or the installation of a new engine.

F

Factory Overhead: all manufacturing costs other than direct materials and direct labor. It includes indirect materials, indirect labor, and factory utilities, rent or depreciation on a factory facility, property taxes, and insurance, if they relate to the manufacturing process.

Factory Overhead Budget: provides data about all production costs other than direct materials and direct labor. Gives information for planning the work of the production departments, as well as for determining how much factory overhead should become part of the cost of each unit of product.

Federal Unemployment Tax Act (FUTA): unemployment taxes that employers must pay in addition to their share of social security taxes.

FICA (Federal Insurance Contributions Act) Taxes: a combination of Old Age Survivors and Disability Insurance (O.A.S.D.I.) and Medicare Insurance; also called social security taxes.

FIFO (First In, First Out): an inventory costing method that assumes that the costs attached to the first goods purchased are the costs of the first goods sold.

Financial Accounting Standards Board (FASB): a private-sector body that has responsibility for developing and issuing accounting standards.

Financial Changes: changes in net working capital from other than operating transactions, such as the sale or purchase of noncurrent assets.

Financial Resources: either net working capital or cash, in the context of statement of changes in financial position.

Financial Statement Analysis: the set of techniques designed to provide relevant data to decision makers.

Financial Statements: the reports with which financial information about a particular enterprise is communicated to users.

Fiscal Year: a year that ends on the last day of any month other than December.

Fixed Costs: the costs that remain unchanged, regardless of changes in the level of business activity.

Flexible Budget: the adjustment of the master budget to changes in volume. Allows a firm to construct budgets at any level of activity in the relevant range.

FOB Destination: the terms of the sale in which legal title of the goods does not pass until they reach the buyer's receiving point, and as a result, the seller pays the freight charges.

FOB Shipping Point: the terms of the sale in which legal title to the goods transfers from the seller to the buyer when those goods leave the seller's warehouse, and as a result, the buyer pays the freight charges.

Footnotes to Financial Statements: the footnotes accompanying the financial statements; narrative explanations of the important aspects of various items in the statement.

Foreign Currency Transactions: transactions that are denominated in the foreign currency. For example, a U.S. firm makes a sale to an overseas firm and agrees to accept payment in the foreign currency, or a purchase is made from an overseas firm and payment must be made in the foreign currency.

Foreign Currency Translation: an accounting term meaning that one currency is restated in terms of another currency.

Form 8-K: a published report that all firms are required to file with the SEC within 10 days of certain major events affecting the firm.

Form 10-K: the annual report filed with the SEC.

Form 10-Q: the quarterly reports filed with the SEC.

Franchise: a right to use a formula, design, or technique, or the right to conduct business in a certain territory.

Full Cost Method: a method in which all exploration costs are capitalized into the cost of the natural resource asset account.

Full Disclosure Principle: an accounting convention requiring that a firm's financial statements provide users with all relevant information about the various transactions in which a firm has been involved.

Fully Diluted EPS: the net income available to common shareholders as calculated by the weighted average number of common shares outstanding, plus all dilutive securities, whether or not they are considered common stock equivalents.

Future Value of an Annuity: the amount of a series of payments or receipts taken to a future date at a specified interest rate.

Future Value of a Single Amount: the amount of a current single amount taken to a future date at a specified interest rate.

G

Gains: a firm's increase in equity (net assets) during a set period from all activities (except for revenues and investments by owners).

General Partnership: a form of partnership in which the general partners have unlimited liability.

General Price Level Changes: price changes that measure fluctuations in the ability of the dollar to purchase a variety of goods and services.

Generally Accepted Accounting Principles (GAAP): the concepts and standards underlying accounting for financial reporting purposes.

Going-Concern Assumption: the assumption that unless there is evidence to the contrary, a firm will be in existence long enough to use these assets and derive their benefits.

Goods in Transit: goods that have been purchased (and title has passed to the purchaser) but that have not yet been received by the purchaser.

Goods on Consignment: those goods held by a firm for resale, but which title remains with the manufacturer or owner of the product.

Goodwill: the future benefits that accrue to a firm as a result of its ability to earn an excess rate of return on its recorded net assets.

Governmental Accounting: the practice of accounting as it relates to governmental organizations.

Governmental Accounting Standards Board (GASB): created by the Financial Accounting Foundation in 1984 with the purpose of establishing and improving financial accounting standards for state and local government.

Gross Margin Method: a method used to estimate the value of inventory, by which firms estimate their ending inventory without taking an actual count. Based on the firm's gross margin percentage.

Gross Margin on Sales: the sales minus the cost of goods sold.

Gross Margin Percentage: the gross margin divided by the sales.

Gross Method of Recording Purchase Discounts: a method of recording purchase discounts in which the purchase and the payable are recorded at the gross amount, before any discount.

Gross Method of Recording Sales Discounts: a method of recording sales discounts in which the sale and the receivable are recorded at the gross amount, before any discount.

Gross Sales: the total of cash sales plus those sales made on credit during the period.

H

Historical Cost Convention: the convention under which assets and liabilities are initially recorded in the accounting system at their original or historical cost, and are not adjusted for subsequent increases in value.

Horizontal Analysis: a technique of financial analysis that focuses upon the dollar and percentage changes that have occurred in certain accounts from year to year.

I

Ideal Standards: standards that require complete efficiency and performance all of the time.

Income from Continuing Operations: the excess of gross margin from sales over operating expenses.

Income Statement: a financial statement that shows the amount of income earned by a firm over an accounting period.

Income Summary Account: a temporary account used to provide structure and to control the accuracy of the closing process.

Indirect Costs: costs incurred for more than one part of an organization and that must be allocated to cost objectives. Also called common costs.

Indirect Labor: labor costs incurred in the manufacturing process that are difficult to trace directly to the units of product, and that are considered part of factory overhead.

Indirect Materials: materials used in manufacturing products that may be difficult and costly to trace. The cost of these items is considered part of factory overhead.

Intangible Assets: those assets which have no physical substance but have future economic benefits based on rights or benefits accruing to the assets' owner.

Interest: the cost associated with the use of money over a specified period of time.

Interest Rate: the percentage rate of interest, which is usually stated in annual terms and must be prorated for periods shorter than a year.

Interim Statements: the financial statements issued monthly or quarterly.

Internal Control: the organizational plan that includes specific methods and procedures developed by management to ensure the accuracy and reliability of the accounting records and to safeguard the firm's assets.

Internal Rate of Return Method: a discounted cash flow method that looks for the true return promised by an investment project over its useful life. Also called time-adjusted rate of return.

Internal Transactions: the events which affect the firm only, and are usually recorded by adjusting entries.

International Accounting Standards Committee (IASC): the committee, the charge of which is to develop basic accounting standards and to promote the worldwide acceptance and observance of these standards.

International Federation of Accountants (IFAC): the international accounting body that is essentially a coordinating body of professional accounting organizations, and does not have the responsibility for setting international accounting standards; instead, the broad objective is the development and enhancement of a coordinated worldwide accounting profession with harmonized standards.

Interperiod Income Tax Allocation: the allocation of income taxes among different accounting periods.

Interpolation: a process by which it is possible to find the exact rate of interest promised by an investment.

Intraperiod Income Tax Allocation: the allocation of income taxes in such a way that the total income tax expense for the period is related to the proper component that caused the income.

Inventories: those goods that are owned and held for sale in the regular course of business, including goods in transit, if shipped FOB shipping point.

Inventory Profits: the amount by which the cost of replacing merchandise sold on the sale date exceeds the reported cost.

Inventory Turnover: the rate at which a company sells its inventory.

J

Job Cost Sheet: a part of the job order cost system that keeps track of the costs associated with each individual job.

Job Order Costing: a product cost accounting system that accumulates the cost of manufacturing specific products, jobs, or batches of production, where each job or batch of products is different from the other.

Joint Product Costs: the manufacturing costs incurred before the joint products become individually identifiable.

Joint Products: two or more separately identifiable products made from a common set of inputs. No one of the products may be produced without the simultaneous production of one or more other products.

Journal: the record or book where each transaction is recorded originally. Provides a chronological record of each transaction.

L

Lease: a contractual agreement between the lessor (the owner of the property) and the lessee (the user of the property) that gives the lessee the right to use the lessor's property for a specific period of time in exchange for stipulated cash payments.

Leasehold Improvements: improvements made by the lessee, that at the end of the lease term revert to the ownership of the lessor.

Ledger: a book or file which contains a specific account for each item in the chart of accounts.

Legal (Stated) Capital: the minimum amount that can be reported as contributed capital. Usually equal to the par or stated value of all capital stock.

Lessee: the user of the property in the lease contract.

Lessor: the owner of the property in the lease contract.

Level of Aspiration: the level of performance on a task that an individual seeks to achieve.

Leverage: the use of debt financing, such as bonds and mortgages.

Liabilities: the economic obligations of the enterprise. The amount owed to creditors, employees, the government, or others.

LIFO (Last In, First Out): an inventory costing method that assumes that the costs attached to the latest purchases are the costs of the first items sold.

LIFO Liquidation: a financial event that occurs when a firm sells more units in any year than it purchases, and LIFO layers that have been built up in the past are liquidated.

Limited Liability: a term meaning that the owners of the corporation are not, as individuals, legally responsible for the debts incurred by the corporation, in excess of the amount that they have invested in the corporation.

Limited Partnership: a form of partnership usually made up of one or two general partners and several limited partners. In this type of partnership only the general partners have unlimited liability; the liability of the other partners is limited to their investment in the partnership.

Liquidation of a Partnership: the result of a cessation of the firm's business, the selling of assets, the payment of liabilities, and the distribution of the remaining assets, if any, to the partners.

Long-term Investments: those assets that include holdings in securities (stocks and bonds) not classified as current, and in some circumstances, investments in certain subsidiaries that have not been consolidated with the parent firm.

Losses: the decreases in equity (net assets) affecting the firm during a set period from all activities (except for expenses and distribution to owners).

Lower of Cost or Market: a method of inventory pricing by which the inventory is priced at cost or market, whichever is lower. An application of conservatism in accounting.

M

Make-or-Buy Decision: the decision made by a manufacturer as to whether to make a given component or buy it from a supplier.

Maker: the individual or business who signs the note.

Management: the process of using resources to achieve objectives.

Management Accounting: the part of accounting that provides information to managers inside the organization, and helps in planning, decision making, and control. This type of accounting is the opposite of financial accounting, which provides accounting information to users outside of the organization.

Management Control: the channeling of the efforts of the people in the organization to attain organizational goals through various procedures and processes.

Manufacturing Costs: the costs a company incurs to produce its product. The three basic manufacturing costs are direct materials, direct labor, and factory overhead.

Market: the current replacement cost of inventory.

Market Interest Rate: the interest rate that the money market establishes through hundreds of individual transactions; and that depends on such factors as prevailing interest rates in the economy and the perceived risk of the individual company.

Master Budget: the comprehensive budget for the entire firm for a given period.

Matching Convention: the basic rule underlying accrual accounting. Revenues are recognized as earned. All expenses incurred in earning those revenues are reported also in the period in which those revenues are recognized.

Materiality: an accounting convention that refers the relative importance or significance of an item to an informed decision maker.

Materials Ledger Card: a record of each material used in the production of products, as well as in the total purchase of raw materials.

Maturity Date: the date a promissory note is due.

Maturity Value: the total proceeds of a promissory note; includes principal and interest due at the maturity date.

Merchandising Firm: a firm that purchases a finished product for future sale.

Mixed Cost: a cost that has both fixed and variable components, so that a portion of it varies with volume or activity.

Monetary Assets: cash and those items that represent a specific claim to cash.

Mortgage: a promissory note secured by an asset, the title of which is pledged to the lender.

Multistep Income Statement: a form of the income statement that has various categories and arrives at net income in steps.

Mutual Agency: refers to the fact that each partner can make binding agreement for the partnership as long as the individual partner acts within the normal scope of partnership business.

N

Natural Resources: physical substances that when extracted from the ground are converted into inventory, and when sold, produce revenues for the firm.

Net Assets: the term referring to owners' equity—assets minus liabilities.

Net Book Value: the difference between the cost of a depreciable asset and the associated accumulated depreciation.

Net Income: the difference between the total of revenues and gains and the total of expenses and losses.

Net Method of Recording Purchase Discounts: a method of recording purchase discounts in which the purchase and the accounts payable are recorded at net of the allowable discount.

Net Method of Recording Sales Discounts: a method of recording sales discounts in which the receivable and sale are recorded at net of the allowable discount.

Net Present Value Method: a discounted cash flow technique for capital budgeting decisions that compares cash inflows and cash outflows.

No Par Stock: capital stock that has no par or stated value placed on it by the board of directors.

Nominal Interest Rate: a stated interest rate that is specified on the note or bond at the time it is issued, and that does not change over the life of the note or bond.

Nominal (Temporary) Accounts: the separate revenue and expense accounts used only during the period, which have a zero balance at the beginning of each period. These accounts are closed to retained earnings at the end of each period.

Noncurrent Long-term Liabilities: those liabilities that will not be satisfied within one year or within the operating cycle, if longer.

Nonmanufacturing Costs: all the costs a company incurs, other than direct labor and factory overhead. Consists of two categories: selling and administrative.

Nonmonetary Assets: those assets other than cash or rights to receive cash, that can generate future revenues, such as property, plant, and equipment.

Note Payable: a liability that results from purchases of goods and services or loans. Usually a written instrument that includes interest.

Note Receivable: an unconditional promise in writing by an individual or business to pay a definite amount at a definite date or on demand.

O

Objectives of Financial Reporting: the basic and fundamental purposes behind financial statements.

Objectivity: a term used to indicate asset and liability valuations that are factual and can be verified by others.

Obsolescence: the process of becoming out-of-date, outmoded, or inadequate.

Off Balance Sheet Financing: the fact that certain liabilities are not recorded on the balance, for example, leases that are in substance installment purchases, but are not recorded as liabilities.

Operating Changes: transactions that result from the production, purchase, and sale of the firm's goods and services, and that affect net working capital, and ultimately retained earnings (also called income statement transactions).

Operating Cycle: the average time a business takes to purchase merchandise, sell the merchandise, and receive cash.

Operating Lease: a short-term lease under which regular monthly payments are made by the lessee, but the lessor retains control and ownership of the property.

Opinion: a report issued by the auditor after examination of findings regarding the financial statements of a firm. Often called the accountant's or auditor's report.

Opportunity Costs: benefits sacrificed when management chooses one course of action over another.

Organization Costs: those costs that a corporation incurs during the organization process, including such costs as filing and incorporation fees to the state, attorney's fees, promotion fees, printing and engraving fees, and similar items.

Organizational Control System: a set of processes and techniques designed to increase the likelihood that people will behave in ways that lead to the attainment of an organization's objectives. There are both formal and informal organizational control systems.

Outstanding Checks: checks written by the depositor but yet to be paid by the bank.

Overhead Efficiency Variance: the difference between a budget for overhead at the actual activity level and a budget for overhead at the standard activity level.

Overhead Spending Variance: the difference between actual overhead cost and a flexible budget for overhead at the actual activity level.

Overhead Volume Variance: the difference between the overhead applied to Work in Process and an overhead budget based on the standard hours allowed for the actual units of product produced.

Overlapped Overhead: when applied overhead exceeds actual overhead costs for the period.

Owners' Equity: a general term used to specify the owners' residual interest for sole proprietorships, partnerships, and corporations.

P

Par Value: an amount designated in the articles of incorporation or by the board of directors, and printed on the stock certificate.

Parent Company: the corporation that owns the majority of the common stock of another company.

Partnership: an unincorporated business entity owned by two or more individuals.

Patent: an exclusive right to use, manufacture, process, or sell a product that is granted by the U.S. Patent Office.

Payback Method: a capital budgeting method that is used to determine how long it will take for an investment to repay its original cost from the cash inflows it generates. This method does not take into account the time value of money.

Payee: the person to whom the payment for the note is to be made.

Payroll Register: a listing of the firm's payroll that is prepared each payday.

Percentage of Net Sales Method: a method of estimating uncollectible accounts expense under which the amount of uncollectible accounts expense is determined by the analysis of the relationship between net credit sales and the prior year's uncollectible accounts expense.

Period Costs: costs associated with the accounting period rather than the units of product.

Period Expenses: the expenses of a business that cannot be directly related to a product or service and matched against revenues in the period the revenues are earned.

Periodic Inventory System: an inventory system which does not keep continuous track of ending inventories and cost of goods sold; instead, these items are determined periodically, at the end of each quarter, each year, or other accounting period.

Perpetual Inventory System: an inventory system which keeps a running balance of both inventory on hand and the cost of goods sold (in dollars and units).

Petty Cash Fund: a small fund established by a company for miscellaneous expenditures.

Physical Flow of Units: a description of the number of units of product in process at the start of the period, the number of units started during the period, and the number of units remaining in Work in Process at the end of the period.

Physical Measures Method: a method that uses physical measures (such as gallons, liters, pounds, and grams) as a basis for allocating joint product costs.

Pooling-of-Interests-Method: a method of accounting for a business combination in which the combining companies are treated as if their net assets were pooled instead of one company having purchased outright the other. Assets and liabilities are combined at their net book values.

Posting: the process of transferring information from journal entries to the ledger accounts.

Post-Closing Trial Balance: a trial balance prepared from the ledger accounts after the closing entries have been posted. Used to help ensure that these entries have been posted correctly.

Predetermined Overhead Rate: a rate used throughout the year to assign overhead costs to individual jobs and Work in Process.

Preferred Stock: a type of stock that has certain preferences over common stock.

Present Value: the amount that must be invested now, at a given rate of interest, to produce a given future value.

Present Value of a Single Amount: the value of a future promise to pay or receive a single amount at a specified interest rate.

Present Value of an Annuity: the present value of a series of future promises to pay or receive an annuity at a specified interest rate.

Price-Earnings Ratio: a ratio that is the current market price of a stock divided by the earnings per share.

Primary Earnings per Share: the net income available to common stock, divided by the sum of the weighted average common shares and common stock equivalents.

Principal: the original amount of a promissory note on which interest is calculated.

Prior Period Adjustments: the transactions that relate to an earlier accounting period but that were not determinable by management in the earlier period. Specifically limited by an FASB Statement.

Private Accounting: the practice of accounting in a single firm.

Process: a series of steps (i.e., plans, decisions, actions) designed to operate an organization.

Process Centers: the locations or departments in a factory where work is performed directly on the goods that are being produced.

Process Costing: a product costing system used when one product is manufactured and all units of the product are identical.

Product Costs: costs identified with goods manufactured for resale or with goods purchased for resale.

Production Budget: the number of units needed to be produced for the coming period.

Profit Margin Percentage: the net income divided by the sales.

Profitability Index: an index that makes it possible to compare and rank two alternate projects by dividing the present value of the net cash inflows by the funds required for the investment.

Promissory Note: also called Note (*see also* Note Receivable).

Proxy: a legal document signed by the shareholders that gives another individual or individuals, usually existing management, the right to vote the shares in the manner they deem best.

Public Accounting: the field of accounting that, for a fee, provides a variety of accounting services to individuals and firms.

Publicly Held Corporation: a corporation, the stock of which is owned by outside investors, and which stock and/or bonds are listed on national and regional exchanges.

Publicly Owned: a term indicating that a corporation's stock is traded on an organized exchange (such as the New York or American Stock Exchange), easily enabling individuals to buy or sell shares of stock in these corporations.

Purchase Discounts: the allowances given for prompt payment for merchandise purchased for resale.

Purchase Method: a method of preparing consolidated financial statements in which the net assets of the purchased company are revalued to their fair market value.

Purchase Order: a document prepared by the purchaser that indicates to the seller the quantity, type, and estimated price of the items the buyer wishes to purchase.

Purchase Requisition: a document sent to the purchasing department requesting that it purchase a certain quantity and type of item.

Purchase Returns and Allowances: the refunds and other allowances given by suppliers on merchandise originally purchased for resale.

Purchases Journal: the specialized journal used to record merchandise purchases on account.

Purchasing Power Gains or Losses: those gains or losses that result from holding monetary assets (cash and rights to receive cash) and monetary liabilities (all liabilities other than those requiring the performance of a service) during periods of inflation or deflation.

Q

Quality of Earnings: a concept that judges whether accounting principles and methods selected by management lead to conservative estimates of earnings or inflated earnings.

Quantifiability: a characteristic of the accounting system which admits as inputs only those transactions and events which can be represented in numerical (primarily monetary) terms.

Quantity Discounts: the reductions from list price, as a result of quantity purchases.

R

Ranking Decision: a decision that determines which investment alternative is best when there are several acceptable proposals.

Ratio Analysis: a shortcut method of expressing relationships among various items on the financial statements.

Real Accounts: the balance sheet accounts (including retained earnings), the balances of which extend beyond the accounting period.

Realization Principle: the principle accountants follow to determine when revenue should be recognized.

Realized Gains and Losses: the difference between expenses on a current cost basis and on a historical cost basis, sis, which represents the holding gains or losses the firm has realized through sales or use in the current period.

Receipts: the inflows of cash or of other assets.

Receivable Turnover: a ratio determined by dividing credit sales by the average account receivable for the period.

Redeemable Preferred Stock: preferred stock that can be callable, and that can be returned to the issuing corporation by the owner of the stock under certain conditions for a stated price.

Reinforcement: a concept used in motivation research which indicates that when an individual's behavior is followed by a positive response (or "reward"), the behavior tends to be repeated; whereas if behavior is followed by a negative response, or no response, it tends to be avoided.

Relative Sales Value Method: the method used to allocate joint production costs by calculating each product's proportionate share of the total sales value of all the products, and then allocating the same proportion of joint product costs to each product.

Relevance: a qualitative characteristic requiring that accounting information be impactful in a user's decision.

Relevant Range: that narrow range of business activity that has linear properties, and that is used as the expected range of cost behavior during a given time period, usually a year.

Reliability: the term meaning that the accounting information is unbiased, accurate, and verifiable.

Remittance Advice: a document attached to the sales invoice that is mailed to the customer. It is used to identify the source of the check received.

Research and Development Costs: those expenditures incurred in discovering, planning, designing, and implementing a new product or process.

Residual (Salvage) Value: an estimate of an asset's worth at the end of its life.

Resources: things that have expected service potential and that are used in order to achieve objectives.

Responsibility Accounting: an accounting procedure that classifies costs and revenues of an organization according to the various levels of management that have control over them, and that holds managers responsible for differences between planned goals and actual results.

Retail Method: a method of estimating inventory by which the inventory is taken at retail prices and then converted to cost.

Retained Earnings Statement: a financial statement which details the changes in the retained earnings account for a certain period.

Return on Owner's Equity: the ratio calculated by dividing the net income by the average owner's equity.

Return on Total Assets: the ratio determined by dividing the net income by the average total assets.

Revenue Expenditure: expenditures, the benefits of which are used up or consumed in the current period.

Revenues: the price of goods sold or services rendered by a firm to others in exchange for cash or other assets.

Reversing Entries: entries made on the first day of a new accounting period that reverse certain adjusting entries to allow the routine recording of certain entries.

Review and Compilation: accounting services provided by the CPA firms.

S

Sales: the essential activity of the merchandising firm. At the point of sale the firm's earning process is completed, and objective evidence as to the sales price is available. Revenue is recognized under generally accepted accounting principles.

Sales Allowance: a reduction in the actual sales price that occurs when the particular item does not perform to expectations, or when there are other defects in the product.

Sales Budget: the budget that projects expected sales for operations for one period. The first step in the budgeting process.

Sales Discount: a cash reduction offered to customers in an attempt to ensure that they make prompt payment on their trade accounts.

Sales Forecasts: the means used by firms to predict demands for their products.

Sales Journal: the specialized journal used to record sales on account.

Sales Mix: the proportion in which the various products of the firm are sold.

Sales Returns: a reduction in the actual sales which occurs when a customer, for whatever reason, returns the item for a cash refund or a credit to his/her account.

Schedule of Cost of Goods Manufactured: the supporting schedule on the income statement from which the cost of goods manufactured is derived.

Screening Decision: a decision that determines whether an investment meets the minimum standards of acceptibility for a particular firm.

Securities and Exchange Commission (SEC): a federal agency that has the legal power to set and enforce accounting standards for publicly traded firms.

Segment: a component of an entity, the activities of which represent a separate line of business or class of major customer.

Sell or Process Further Decision: a decision made by manufacturers who produce joint products, as to whether a product should be sold at the split-off point or processed further.

Selling and Administrative Expense Budget: a budget that appears on the income statement as one or two broad categories, and that is a complex mixture of costs relating to everything other than the manufacturing process.

Serial Bonds: those bonds, the principal of which is payable on various dates.

Short-term Investments: cash invested in marketable securities such as stocks, government securities, and corporation bonds. Management generally does not intend to hold them longer than one year.

Short-term Monetary Assets: the current assets, such as cash and those items that represent a specific claim to cash.

Single-step Income Statement: a form of income statement that has only four major categories (revenues, expenses, income before taxes, and net income), and that arrives at net income in a single step.

Sinking Fund: a collection of cash or such other assets as marketable securities, that are set apart from the remaining assets of the firm, and are only used for a specified purpose.

Sole Proprietorship: an unincorporated business entity in which one person is the owner.

Special Orders: when a firm sells products below the normal price in order to earn revenue that might otherwise be lost.

Specialized Journal: a journal that is designed to handle certain transactions such as receipts or sales.

Specific Identification Method: an inventory costing method which determines the actual acquisition cost of each item in the ending inventory.

Specific Price Level Changes: those price changes that reflect the fluctuation in the value of specific goods or services vis-à-vis other goods or services.

Specifically Identifiable Intangible Assets: those intangible assets, the costs of which can easily be identified as part of the cost of the asset, and the benefits of which generally have a determinable life.

Split-off Product: the point at which the joint products become individually identifiable.

Spreadsheet: a computer software program containing an empty matrix of rows and columns that can be labeled individually by the user. Examples include Lotus 1-2-3 and Visicalc.

Standard: a criterion used to regulate the costs and quantities of things used to produce goods or to provide services.

Standard Cost: the amount that should be required to produce a unit of product as opposed to the actual price and quantity.

Standard Cost Card: a record that details what the manufacturing cost should be for one unit of product.

Stated Interest Rate: *see* Nominal Interest Rate.

Statement of Changes in Financial Position: the financial statement that describes the changes (inflows and outflows) in the enterprise's resources. Prepared either on a working capital or cash basis.

Statement of Changes in Owner's Equity: a financial statement that summarizes the transactions and events which affect a variety of owner's equity accounts.

Stock Dividend: a distribution to current shareholders on a proportional basis of the corporation's own stock.

Stock Registrar: an individual employed by a corporation in order to maintain an independent record of the number of shares outstanding.

Stock Split: an increase in the number of outstanding shares with a proportionally decreasing par or stated value.

Stock Transfer Agent: an individual employed by a firm, usually a large bank, to handle all the transfer by canceling the old certificates, issuing new ones, and updating the stockholders' ledger.

Stockholders' Equity: the owners' equity of a corporation representing the residual claims of the owners.

Straight-Line Depreciation: a depreciation method that assumes that depreciation is a constant function of time and results in an equal allocation of the asset's cost to each accounting period of its estimated service life.

Subsidiary: a corporation that is wholly or partially owned by another company.

Subsidiary Accounts: the backup accounts for several particular ledger accounts.

Subsidiary Ledger: a ledger which contains backup or more detailed accounts than does the general ledger.

Successful Efforts Method: a method by which only the exploration costs of successful finds are capitalized into the natural resource asset account.

Sum-of-the-Years-Digits: one variation of accelerated depreciation by which the asset's depreciable base is multiplied by a declining rate.

Sunk Costs: the costs that have already been incurred and will not change.

T

T Account: an account that has a T-shaped form and is used to analyze transactions.

Tangible Assets: those assets that have physical substance and capabilities, such as property, plant, equipment, and other similar productive assets acquired by the company.

Temporal Method: a method of foreign currency translation by which monetary assets and liabilities are translated at current rates, while nonmonetary assets and liabilities are translated at rates in effect when the particular item was acquired. Income statement items are translated at the average exchange rate for the period.

Term Bonds: those bonds for which the entire principal is due in one payment.

Time Period Assumption: the division of the enterprise's life span into time periods that can be as short as a month or a quarter, but rarely longer than a year.

Time Value of Money: the concept that money on hand now is worth more than money received in the future, because money on hand now can be invested and can earn interest.

Trade Accounts Payable: *see* Accounts Payable.

Trade Discounts: those discounts offered to a certain class of buyers.

Transactions: the business events, measured in money, and recorded in the financial records of a particular enterprise.

Transferred-in Costs: manufacturing costs that are incurred when the product is transferred from one department of the company to another department in the same company.

Treasury Stock: the corporation's own stock that it repurchased.

Trend Analysis: a type of horizontal analysis that includes more than a single change from one year to the next, and looks at changes over a period of time, in order to evaluate emerging performance.

Trial Balance: a list of the accounts in the general ledger with their respective debit and credit balances.

U

Unadjusted Trial Balance: a listing of the balances of all ledger accounts prior to the recording of adjusting entries.

Uncollectible Accounts: those receivables that the firm is unable to collect the full amount due from the customer.

Underapplied Overhead: less overhead is applied to Work in Process than the actual overhead costs for the period.

Underwriters: brokerage firms, such as Merrill Lynch, or groups of firms that, for a stated price, purchase the entire stock issue, and assume the risks involved in marketing the stock to their clients.

Uniform Partnership Act: this act defines a partnership as "an association of two or more persons to carry on as co-owners of a business for a profit."

Units-of-Production Method: a method of depreciation that assumes that the primary depreciation factor is use rather than the passage of time, and is appropriate for such assets as delivery trucks and equipment, when substantial variations in use occur.

Unsecured Bonds: those bonds that are not secured by collateral or specified assets of the borrower.

V

Variable Costs: costs that change in total in direct proportion to changes in volume or level of business activity.

Variance: the difference between actual cost and standard cost.

Variance Investigation: an investigation into why a variance does not fall within an acceptable range according to management guidelines. Some criteria for this investigation include materiality, frequency, controllability, importance, and statistical techniques.

Verifiability: a qualitative characteristic of an accounting system; meaning that the data pertaining to the transaction or event must be available, and that if two or more qualified persons examined the same data, they would reach essentially the same conclusion about the data's accounting treatment.

Vertical Analysis: a technique of financial analysis that is used to evaluate the relationships within single financial statements, wherein the appropriate total figure in the financial statement is set to 100%, and other items are expressed as a percentage of that figure.

Voucher: a written authorization for each expenditure.

Voucher System: an elaborate, structured system developed to provide maximum internal control over all disbursements. The primary feature of the voucher system is the high degree of separation of duties.

W

Weighted Average Contribution Margin: a contribution margin based on the relative proportion of sales for each product line.

Weighted Average Cost Flow Assumption: a method used in process costing systems in which the units in beginning Work in Process are treated as if they were started and finished in the current period.

Working Capital: the current assets minus the current liabilities. Often referred to as net working capital.

Worksheet: a type of working paper that is used to aid in the preparation of adjusting entries and financial statements.

Y

Yield Rate: the actual rate at which the bond is issued (also called effective rate).

Index

Note: Numbers in boldface refer to pages where term is defined or introduced.

A

Accelerated Cost Recovery System (ACRS), **476**–477, 673–677
Accelerated depreciation, **471**–473
Accountants, types of, 8–10
Accounting, **4**. *See also specific topics*
  basic assumptions about businesses, 526–529
  changes in method of, 649–651
  concepts and standards of. *See* Concepts and standards of accounting
  decision making and, 5
  double entry, 37
  governmental, **10**
  international standards for, 874–875
  management, **8**
  management processes and, 906–913
    control, **911**–913
    decision making, 907–911
    planning, 906–907
  private, **10**
  public. *See* Public accounting
  standards for, 10–12
  trade-ins and, 499
Accounting controls, **264**
Accounting cycle, **35**–36
Accounting cycle completion, 111–148
  adjusting entries, 111–125
    affecting subsequent periods, 112–118
  five final steps in, 126–138
    adjusted trial balance preparation, 131
    closing entries preparation, 133–137
    financial statements preparation, 131–133
    general ledger postings, 126–130
    post-closing trial balance preparation, 137–138
  merchandising firms and, 195
  reversing entries and, 146–148
  worksheets and, 138–145
    preparation of, 138, 144
Accounting equation, **14**
  debit and credit and, 37
  effects of transactions on, 27–31
  income statement transactions and, 79
Accounting income, 673
Accounting information systems, 23–27
  data input into, 25–26
  recognizing transactions in, 26–27
  worksheet techniques for, 192–197

Accounting Principles Board (APB), 11
  definition of current assets, 216
  subsidiary purchase guidelines, 762–763
Accounting-rate-of-return method of capital budgeting, **1022**–1023
Accounting system(s), **4**
  components of, 31–35, 266–278
    general journal, 277–278
    specialized journals, 269–277
    subsidiary ledgers, 266–269
  computers used in, 278–282
  internal control and, 264–266
  recording process in, 35–47
  trial balances, 47–49
Accounts, **27**
  asset, 32–34
  chart of, 32
  ledger. *See* Ledgers
  liability, 34
  noncurrent. *See* Noncurrent accounts
  subsidiary. *See* Subsidiary accounts
  T. *See* T accounts
Accounts payable, **389**
  as liability account, 34
Accounts payable trial balance, **272**
Accounts receivable, 353–354, 364–365
  as asset account, 33
  in balance sheet, 216
  collection of, 310–313
Accounts receivable trial balance, **268**
Accounts receivable turnover ratio, 865–866
Accrual basis, **76**
  and cash basis of accounting compared, 76–77
  income statement transactions and, 76
  sales and, 178
Accruals, **119**–123
Accrued expenses, **122**–123
  reversing entries and, 148
Accrued interest, 120–121
Accrued revenues, 120–122
Accumulated depreciation account, 116–118
Acquisitions
  consolidated financial statements and, 758–764
    acquisition at 100 percent, 758–760
    acquisition at less than 100 percent, 760–761
  costs of, 462–465, 469
    intangible assets, 503–504

  of current marketable securities, 745
  of long-term equity investments, 754
  pooling-of-interests vs. purchase methods of accounting and, 765–768
  of subsidiaries, 760–761
ACRS. *See* Accelerated Cost Recovery System
Action plans, **906**
Additional paid-in capital, **620**
Additions, **494**
Adjunct account, **711**
Adjusted gross income, B2–3
Adjusted trial balance, **131**, 139
  accounting cycle completion and, 131
Adjusting entries, **111**
  accruals and, 119–123
  expenditures affecting subsequent periods, 112–118
    depreciation and, 115–118
    prepaid assets, 114–115
    supplies, 113–114
  expenditures to be made in subsequent periods, 122–123
  receipts affecting subsequent periods, 118–119
  receipts to be received in subsequent periods, 119–122
  reversing entries and, 146–148
Adjustment columns, 139
  merchandising firms and, 192–194
Administrative controls, **264**
Aging method, **360**–363
All financial resources concept, **797**–798
Allowance for doubtful accounts, in balance sheet, 216
Allowance for Uncollectible accounts, **355**
Allowance method, **354**
Allowance to Reduce Marketable Securities to Market Account, 747–750
American Accounting Association (AAA), 11
American Institute of Certified Public Accountants (AICPA), **9**, 11
  auditing guidelines of, 265
American Stock Exchange, 744
Amortization, **218**, **466**
  cash flow statement and, 816
  effective-interest method
    discount bonds and, 714–715
    premium bonds and, 716–717

Amortization, Cont.
of intangible assets, 504–505
straight-line method
discount bonds and, 709–710
premium bonds and, 712–713
Annual reports, 230. *See also* Financial
reporting
auditor's report, 237
consolidated balance sheet, 230–233
consolidated statements of income,
233–234
depreciation of assets and, 475–476
financial statement analysis and,
847–848
footnotes to the financial
statements, 237
inventories and, 435–436
statement of changes in financial
position, 236
statement of stockholders' equity,
234
Annual Statement Studies, 849
Annuities, A9–13
future value of, A9–11
present value of, A11–13
Annuity due
definition of, A9
Applied overhead, **1087**
Appropriation of retained earnings,
666–667
Arbitrary allocations, 224
Articles of incorporation, 612–613
Articulation, **90**
Asset accounts, 32–34
Assets, **14**, **223**
in balance sheet, 14–15, 216–218, 231
cash flow statement and, 816
current, **216**–218
discarded, 495–496
donated, 624–626
intangible, **218**, **460**, **502**–508
acquisition costs of, 503–504
amortization of, 504–505
· disposition of, 505
specifically identifiable,
502,505–506
investments, 218
long term. *See* Capital budgeting
net. *See* Net assets
noncurrent, nonmonetary, 459–461
operating, 34
prepaid, adjusting entries and,
14–115
property, plant and equipment, 218
return on, 229
return on total, 857–859
self-constructed, 465
short-term monetary, 351–372
accounts receivable and, 353–354,
364–365
classification of, 370
notes receivable, **365**–371
short-term investments, **352**–353
uncollectible accounts, 354–365
tangible, **459**
Asset turnover ratio, 858
Auditing and accounting services, 9
Auditor's reports, **237**
going-concern exception in, 529

Audits
American Institute of CPAs (AICPA)
guidelines for, 265
Congress and, 265
definition of, **9**
Average collection period, **365**
Average cost, **424**
ending inventory system and, 427
perpetual inventory system and,
440–441

B

Balance sheets, **13**–16
accumulated depreciation account
and, 116–118
bonds and, 708–713
budgets and, 1052–1053
classified, 215–224
assets and, 216–218
liabilities and, 218–219
limitations of, 223–224
owner's equity and, 219–221
uses of, 221–223
columns in worksheet for, 139, 144
for merchandising firms, 195
concepts and conventions related to,
16
consolidated, 230–233, 759–765
current costs and, 547
current liabilities and, 396
equity securities and, 747–749
financial statement analysis and, 850
income statement transactions and,
89–90
inventories and, 420–424
of manufacturing and
merchandising firms compared,
920–922
natural resources depletion and, 501
in partnerships, 574–584
distribution of profits and losses,
576–582
formation, 574
liquidation, 588–591
subsequent investments and
withdrawals, 574–575
statement of changes in financial
position and, 798
Bank account transactions, 320–328
checking accounts, 320–327
bank reconciliation, **322**–327
bank statements, **321**
checks, **321**
deposit slip, **320**
petty cash, 327–328
Bank credit cards, 182
Bank loans, 389–392
Bank reconciliation, **322**–327
deposits in transit, **324**
outstanding checks, 323–324
preparation of, 324–325
Bank statements, **321**–322
Basket purchases, 464
Beginning inventory. *See* Inventories
BE point. *See* Break-even point
Beta, **862**
Betterments, **494**
Board of directors, 613–615, **614**

Bond indentures, **701**
Bonding of employees, 266
Bonds, **700**–724. *See also* Debt
securities
basic features of, 700–701
conversion to stock, 720–721
convertible, **701**
investor's accounting for, 721–724
acquisitions, 721–722
amortizing the discount or
premium, 722–723
sale prior to maturity, 723–724
issuers' accounting for, 705–721
amortization by effective-interest
method, 713–717
discount bonds, 707–710
interest dates and, 717–718
issue costs, 718
par or face value, 705–707
premium bonds, 710–713
retirement of, 719–721
year-end accruals of interest and,
718
prices and interest rates of, 702–705
risks of, 705
statement of changes in financial
position and, 808
time value of money and, A14–15
types of, 701–702
Book value, **627**
per share, 857
subsidiary purchase and, 762–764
Break-even point (BE point), **947**–948
Budget (budgeting), **907**, 1035–1055,
1036. *See also* Capital budgeting
in centralized and decentralized
systems, 1037–1040
computers and, 1055
flexible, 1053–**1054**, 1134
master, parts of, **1040**–1055
budgeted balance sheets,
1052–1053
budgeted income statements, 1052
cash, **1050**–1052
cost of goods sold, **1048**–1049
direct labor, **1047**
direct materials, **1046**–1047
ending inventory, **1048**
factory overhead, **1047**–1048
production, **1044**–1045
sales, **1044**
selling and administrative
expenses, **1049**–1050
motivational aspects of, 1038–1040
planning process and, 1036
role of, 1036–1037
Budgetary planning, 907
Budgeted balance sheets, 1052–1053
Budgeted income statements, 1052
Business entity, **6**
Business entity assumption, **25**
Business expenses, B2–3
Businesses. *See also* Corporations;
Manufacturing firms;
Merchandising firms;
Partnerships
accounting assumptions about,
526–529
business-entity assumption, 528

going-concern assumption, 528–529
Business periodicals, financial statement analysis and, 849

C

Callable preferred stock, **618**
Call premium, **618**
Capital
  contributed, **620**
    as stockholders' equity, 619–620
  cost of, **1013**
  donated, 624–626
  legal (stated), **619**
  working. See Working capital
Capital balance interest, in partnerships, 581–582
Capital budgeting, 1007–1023, **1008**. See also Property, plant and equipment
  accounting-rate-of-return method of, **1022**–1023
  discounted cash flow method of, **1012**–1019
    internal-rate-of-return method, **1016**–1019
    net-present-value method, **1013**–1016
  payback method of, **1021**
  present value concepts and, 1009–1012
  problem-solving guidelines for, 1013–1014
  ranking decisions and, 1019–1020
  screening decisions and, 1012–1019
Capital expenditures, **461**, 494–495
Capital formation, corporations and, 611
Capitalization of interest, 465
Capitalizing retained earnings, **661**
Capital leases, 726–727
Capital stock, **220**, 615
Cash, **307**
  as asset account, 32
  over-the-counter sales and, 313ty, **327**–328
  transactions in. See Cash transactions
Cash acquisitions, 463
Cash basis, **76**
  and accrual basis of accounting compared, 76–77
  income statement transactions and, 77–78
Cash budget, **1050**–1052
Cash disbursements, 315, 319
Cash dividends, 658–659
Cash flows, present value of, 1010
Cash flow statement, **811**–820
Cash inflows, **1011**–1012
Cash outflows, **1012**
Cash payments journal, **275**, 275–277
Cash receipts, 310–315
Cash receipts journal, **272**, 272–275
Cash transactions, 307–334
  bank accounts and, 320–328
    checking account and, 320–327
    petty cash and, 327–328

cash budget and, **1050**–1052
errors in, 313–315
management control over, 308–319
  cash disbursements, 315, 319
  cash receipts, 310–315
  internal control, 308–310
in partnerships, 574–575
receivables and, 369–371
stock issuance and, 621–624
variance investigation and, **1141**–1143
voucher system for, **328**–334
  check register and, 332–333
  schedule of unpaid vouchers, 333
  voucher register, 329–332
Certified public accountants, **9**, 10
Change in accounting estimate, **649**, 651–652
Change in accounting method, **649**–651
Changing prices, accounting for, 536–549
  constant dollars and, 542–546
  current cost/constant dollar statements and, 548–549
  current cost financial statements and, 546–548
  FASB statements on, 540–542
  financial statements and, 538–540
  purchasing power gains and losses and, 542–546
  types of changes, 537–538
    general price level, 537
    specific price level, 538
Chart of accounts, **32**
Checking accounts, internal control of, 320–327
  bank reconciliation, **322**–327
  bank statements, **321**–322
  checks, **321**
  deposit slip, **320**
Check register, in voucher system, 332
Checks, **321**
Classified balance sheets, 215
  assets and, 216–218
  liabilities and, 218–219
  limitations of, 223–224
  owner's equity and, 219–221
  uses of, 221–223
Classified financial statements, **215**
Classified income statements, 224–229
  limitations of, 229
  multistep statement, 225–227
  single-step statement, 225
  uses of, 227–229
Closing entries, **133**, 133–137
  drawing account, 136–137
  expense accounts, closing of, 133
  income summary account, 136
  merchandise inventory and, 196–197
  revenue accounts, closing of, 133
Collection of accounts receivable, 310–313. See also Uncollectible accounts
Common dollar statements, **852**–854
Common stock, **220**, **615**, 625–628, 662–664. See also Stocks
  weighted average number of, 653–654

Common stock equivalents, **654**
Communications, 282
Comparability, **531**
Comparative balance sheet, **89**
Compensated absences, **393**–394
Completion of production method of revenue recognition, 535
Complex capital structure, **654**
Compound interest, A3–6
Computers
  accounting systems and, 278–282
  budgeting and, 1055
  C-V-P analysis and, 957
  microcomputers, 280–281
Concepts and standards of accounting, 10–12, 525–536
  basic assumptions about businesses, 526–529
    business-entity assumption, 528
    going-concern assumption, 528–529
  conceptual framework project and, 526
  generally accepted conventions, 533–536
    historical cost, 533
    matching, 534
    revenue and expense recognition, 534–536
    time periods, 533
  development of, 525–526
  qualitative characteristics of financial information, 529–533
    comparability and consistency, 531
    conservatism, 531–532
    full disclosure principle, 532–533
    materiality, 532
    quantifiability, 529–530
    relevance and reliability, 530–531
Conceptual framework project, **526**
Conservatism, **531**–532
Consistency, **531**
Consolidated balance sheets, 230–233, 759–765
Consolidated financial statements, **757**–765
Consolidated income statements, 764–765
Consolidations, 757–758
  acquisitions at less than 100 percent, 760–761
  acquisitions at 100 percent, 758–760
  consolidated financial statements, 757–765
  consolidated income statements, 764–765
  pooling-of-interests vs. purchase methods of accounting and, 765–768
  purchase above or below book value, 762–764
Constant dollar accounting, 542–546
Constant dollar statements, **539**
Consumer Price Index, 852
Contingency planning, 907
Contingent liabilities, **369**, **394**–396
Contra account, **117**, **216**
Contra-asset accounts, 747
  uncollectible accounts and, 355

Contra-liability accounts, 708
Contributed capital, **620**
  as stockholders' equity, 619–620
Contribution margin (CM), **949**–951
  scarce resources and, 990–991
Contribution margin income
    statement, **950**
Contribution margin ratio (CM ratio),
    951–953
Controllability, as variance criteria,
    1142–1143
Controlling account, **266**
Control systems, **911**–913. *See also*
    Internal control
  standard costs and, 1126
Conversion costs, **1094**
Convertible bonds, **701**
Convertible preferred stock, **618**
Copyrights, **505**–506
Corporate charter, 613
Corporations, **6–7**, 219, 609–630. *See
    also specific topics*
  accounting assumptions about,
    526–529
    business-entity assumption, 528
    going-concern assumption,
      528–529
  capital donations and, 624–626
  characteristics of, 610–612
  formation of, 612–613
  income statements of, 644–652
    accounting changes and, 649–652
    continuing operations and,
      646–647
    discontinued operations and,
      647–648
    extraordinary items and, **648**–649
  liquidation of preferred stock and,
    617
  multinational, 868–875
    foreign currency transactions and,
      869–872
    foreign currency translation and,
      872–874
    international accounting standards
      and, 874–875
  organization of, 613–615
  partnerships and sole
    proprietorships compared to,
    610–612
  publicly held, 230–238
    auditor's report, 237–238
    consolidated balance sheet,
      230–233
    consolidated statements of
      income, 233–234
    footnotes to the financial
      statements, 237
    statement of changes in financial
      position, 236
    statement of stockholders' equity,
      234
  stock and, 615–618, 621–624, 626–628,
    628–629
    characteristics of, 615–618
    common stock, 615
    dividends, 658–662
    earnings per share, **652**–657
    internal control of, 628–629

investment indicators and,
  626–628
issuance of, 621–624
preferred stock, 616–618
retirement of, 669–670
splits, **662**–664
stockholders' equity and, 220–221
  components of, 618–621
taxes and, 394, 673–677, B6–7
  accounting vs. taxable income
    and, 673–674
  allocation, 674–677
  journal entries for, 676–677
treasury stock transactions, 667–669
Cost(s), **423**, **917**. *See also* Expenses
  average, **424**
    ending inventory system and, 427
    perpetual inventory system and,
      440–441
  of capital, **1013**
  direct and indirect, compared, 918
  of finished units of product, 1089
  of goods sold, 178, 1089–1091
    determination of, 187
    inventories and, 421–422
    summary of, 192
  importance of, as variance criteria,
    1143
  manufacturing, **918**–925, 1092
    basic types of, 919
    financial statements of, 920–922
    nonmanufacturing costs
      compared, 919–920
    product and period costs
      compared, 922–925
  standard. *See* Standard costs
  types of
    differential, **974**, 977–978
    direct, **918**
    direct fixed, 982–983
    fixed, **943**–945, 953–954
    indirect, **918**
    indirect fixed, 983–984
    inventoriable, **923**
    manufacturing, **918**–925
    mixed, **945**–946
    nonmanufacturing, **919**–920
    opportunity, **975**, 979–980
    period, **923**–925
    product, **922**–923
    sunk, **974**–975
    variable, **942**–943
Cost accounting systems, 1077–1106,
    1078
  basic nature of, 1078–1079
  job order costing system, **1080**–1091
    cost of goods sold account and,
      1089–1091
    factory overhead accounts and,
      1085–1089
    finished goods account and, 1089
    labor and, 1084–1085
    materials and, 1081–1083
  manufacturing systems flow of costs
    and, 1079
  process costing system, **1080**,
    1091–1106
    basic manufacturing costs,
      accumulation and, 1092

process centers identification and,
  1092
with two departments, examples
  of, 1096–1102
with two materials, example of,
  1102–1106
units produced, cost of each
  process and, 1093–1095
units produced, total cost of, 1095
types of, 1080
Cost behavior, **942**–946, 1047
  break-even point and, **947**–948
  contribution margin (CM) and,
    949–951
  C-V-P formula, **947**
  fixed, **943**–945
  mixed, **945**–946
  profit planning and, 948–949
  variable, **942**–943
Cost centers, **914**
Cost flow methods, inventories
    and, 424–431
  average cost, 427
  first-in, first-out (FIFO), 425–426,
    429–431
  last-in, first out (LIFO), 426–427,
    430–431
  rising prices and, 429–430
  specific identification, 427–428
Cost objective, **918**
Cost of goods sold budget, **1048**–1049
Cost per unit
  job order accounting system and,
    1080–1091
    cost of goods sold, 1089–1091
    factory overhead accounts and,
      1085–1089
    finished goods account and, 1089
    labor and, 1084–1085
    materials and, 1081–1083
  process costing accounting system
    and, **1080**, 1091–1106
    basic manufacturing costs
      accumulation and, 1092
    process centers identification and,
      1092
    with two departments, examples
      of, 1096–1102
    with two materials, examples of,
      1102–1106
    units produced, cost of each
      process and, 1093–1095
    units produced, total cost of, 1095
Cost production report, **1098**–1100,
    1102
Cost-volume-profit analysis (C-V-P),
    946–960
  basic assumptions about, 959–960
  break-even point and, **947**–948
  computers and, 957
  contribution margin (CM) and,
    949–951
  contribution margin ratio (CM ratio)
    and, **951**–953
  formula for, **947**
  income taxes and, 957–959
  for multiproduct companies, 955–957
  profit planning and, 948–949,
    953–955

Coupon bonds, **701**
Co-ownership, as feature of
partnerships, 573
Credit
policies of, 354
sales on, 352–353
Credit card sales, 182
Creditors
accounting information and, 7
financial statement analysis and, 846
long-term, 862–863
short-term, 863–866
Credits, 144
income statement transactions and,
79
in ledger transactions, 37
Cumulative dividends, 616
Currency transactions, foreign, **869–872**
Currency translation, foreign, **872–874**
Current assets, 216
Current cost/constant purchasing
power dollar statements, **540**,
548–549
Current cost statements, **539**, **546**
Current cost system, inventories and,
430–431
Current liabilities, 218, **388–396**
types of, 389–394
contingent, 394–396
definitely determinable, 389–393
third party collections, 393–394
Currently attainable standards, **1127**
Current marketable securities, 744–753
debt, 750–752
financial statement presentation of,
752–753
Current maturities of long-term
debt, **219**, **392**
Current rate method of foreign
currency translation, **872**–873
Current ratio, **222**
definition of, **863**–864
C-V-P analysis. *See* Cost-volume-profit
analysis

D

Data-processing services, 279–280
Date of record (of dividends), **659**
Debits, 144
income statement transactions and,
79
in ledger transactions, 37
shareholders' equity and, 621
Debt securities, **744**, 750–752. *See also*
Bonds
Debt to equity ratio, **222**, 862–863
Debt to total assets ratio, **223**
Decision making
accounting and, 5, 907–911
differential costs and revenues and,
974, 977–978
long-term, 1007–1023. *See also*
Capital budgeting
opportunity costs and, **975**, 979–980

problem solving guidelines and,
975–977
ranking decisions and, **1008**,
1019–1020
screening decisions and, **1008**,
1012–1019
short-term, 973–991
definition of, **973**
joint products, **984**–990
make-or-buy, **978**–980
product lines and departments,
982–984
scarce resources and, 990–991
sell or process further decision,
988–990
special orders, **980**–982
sunk costs and, **974**–975
types of decisions, 908
Declaration date (of dividends), **659**
Declining-balance method, **471**–472
Deductions
itemized, B3–4
standard, B4
Deferred income tax accounts, 676–677
Deferred payment plans, 464–465
Denomination of bonds, **700**
Depletion, **466**
of natural resources, 500–502
Deposits in transit, **324**
Deposit slip, **320**
Depreciable base, **116**
Depreciable cost, **469**
Depreciation, **115**, 465–479, 495–499
adjusting entries and, 115–118
basic concepts of, 465–467
cash flow statement and, 816
causes of, 467
expenses and, 115–118
methods of computing periodic,
468–477
comparison of methods, 474–477
declining-balance, **471**–472
straight-line, **469**–470
sum-of-the-years-digits, **472**–473
units-of-production, **470**–471
practical problems of, 477–479
inflation, 479
partial years, 477–478
revision of patterns, 478–479
recording periodic expenses of,
467–468
statement of changes in financial
position and, 806–807
taxes and, 673–677
Development costs, 504
Differential costs and revenues, **974**,
977–978
Direct costs, **918**
Direct fixed costs, 982–983
Direct labor, **919**
Direct labor budget, **1047**
Direct labor efficiency variance,
1132–1133
Direct labor rate variance, **1132**
Direct labor variances, 1131–1133
Direct material budget, **1046**–1047
Direct materials, **919**
Direct materials price variance,
1129–1130

Direct materials quantity (or usage)
variance, **1130**–1131
Direct material variances, 1128–1131
Disbursements
cash, 315, 319
from petty cash fund, 327
Discarded assets, 495–496
Discontinued operations, 647–648
Discount(s), 369
purchase, 188–189
quantity, 179–180
sales, **180**–182
Discount bonds, 707–710, 714–715
Discounted cash flow method of
capital budgeting, **1012**–1019
Discounted notes, 369–370
Discounting, **1009**–1010
Discount on bonds payable accounts,
708–710
Dissolution of a partnership, **588**
Dividends, **220**, 616–618, 658–662
appropriated retained earnings and,
666–667
in arrears, **616**
cash, 658–659
cash flow statement and, 816
equity method of accounting and,
756
financial resources and, 794
property, 660
statement of changes in financial
position and, 808–809
stock, 660–662
yield of, 856
Dividends-received deductions, B6–7
Dividend yield ratio, 856
Donated capital, 624–626
Double entry accounting, **37**
Double taxation, as corporation
characteristic, 611
Drawing account, closing of, 136–137
Duration of the note, **366**

E

Early extinguishment of debt, **719**–720
Earnings, retained. *See* Retained
earnings
Earnings per share (EPS), 627,
652–657, **855**
calculation basics, 652–654
calculation for complex structures,
654–656
income statements presentation of,
656–657
stock splits and, 664
uses and limitations of, 657
Ease of formation, as feature of
partnerships, 572
Economic life, 469
Effective-interest method, 713–717, **714**
discount bond amortization and,
714–715
premium bond amortization and,
716–717
Effective interest rate, on discount
bonds, 707

Effective rate, **704**
Efficiency variances, **1132**–1133
8-K form, **847**
Employees. *See also* Labor; Payrolls
 business expenses of, B2–3
 compensation of, 397
 motivation of, 1038–1040
Ending inventories. *See* Inventories
EPS. *See* Earnings per share (EPS)
Equipment. *See* Property, plant and
 equipment
Equipment accounts, 806–808
Equity, owner's. *See* Owner's equity
Equity method of accounting for
 investments, **755**–757
Equity ratio, 860–861
Equity securities, **743**. *See also* Stocks
 current marketable, accounting for,
 745–750, 752–753
 long-term investments, accounting
 for, 753–758
 consolidated financial statements
 and, 757–758
 no significant influence, 754–755
 significant influence, 755–757
Equivalent units, **1093**, 1096–1097,
 1101, 1103
Error corrections, prior period
 adjustment and, 665–666
Estimates, changes in, 649, 651–652
Evaluation-reward systems, 913
Evaluative feedback, 913
Exchange rate, **870**
Exemptions, B4–5
Expenditures, **74**
 adjusting entries and, 112–118,
 122–123
 income statement transactions and,
 74
Expense accounts, closing of, 134
Expenses, **34–35**, **73**–74, 227. *See
 also*Expenditures
 accrual basis of accounting and, 77
 accrued, 122–123
 adjusting entries and, 112–118,
 122–123
 capital, 494–495
 capital and revenue compared,
 461–462
 cash flow statement and, 813–814
 classified income statements and,
 227
 income statement transactions and,
 73–74
 incurred in a trade or business, B2
 matching convention and, 76
 of operating intangible assets, 504
 owner's equity and, 79
 for property, plant, and equipment,
 461–465, 493–495
 recognition of, 536
 revenue, 493–494
 working capital and, 799
Exploration costs, 502
External transactions, **88**
Extraordinary items, **648**–649
Extraordinary repairs, **494**

F

Face value bonds, 705–707
Factory overhead, **919**, 1085–1089
 standard costs and, 1133–1141
 cost behavior and flexible budgets,
 1134
 overhead efficiency variance,
 1138–1139
 overhead spending variance, **1137**
 overhead volume variance,
 1139–1141
Factory overhead budget, **1047**–1048
Fair market value, subsidiary purchase
 and, 763–764
F & P. *See* Finishing and packaging
 materials
FASB. *See* Financial Accounting
 Standards Board
Federal Unemployment Tax Act
 (FUTA), **402**, 404
Feedback systems, 913
FICA taxes, **398**, 402
FIFO. *See* First-in, first-out
Filing status, B5
Financial Accounting Standards Board
 (FASB), **11**
 changing prices statements, 540–542
 concepts statements of, 526
 objectives of financial reporting and,
 214–215
 Statement 12 on marketable equity
 securities, 746, 749–750, 752
 Statement 14 on industry segments,
 868
Financial activities, definition of, 794
Financial analysis software, 281
Financial charges, **796**
Financial position, statement of
 changes in. *See* Statement of
 changes in financial position
Financial reporting. *See also* Annual
 reports
 generally accepted conventions of,
 533–536
 historical cost, 533
 matching, 534
 revenue and expense recognition,
 534–536
 objectives of, **214**–215
 qualitative characteristics of
 information in, 529–533
 comparability and consistency,
 531
 conservatism, 531–532
 full disclosure principle, 532–533
 materiality, 532
 quantifiability, 529–530
 relevance and reliability, 530–531
Financial resources, **793**. *See also*
 Statement of changes in
 financial position
Financial statement analysis, 845–868,
 846
 limitations of, 866–868
 of multinational corporations,
 868–875
 foreign currency transactions and,
 869–872
 foreign currency translation and,
 872–874
 international accounting standards
 and, 874–875
 purposes of, 846–847
 ratios users prefer, 855–866
 long-term creditors, 862–863
 short-term creditors, 863–866
 stockholders, 855–862
 sources of information for, 847–849
 techniques of, 849–855
 horizontal analysis, **849**–850
 ratio analysis, **855**
 trend analysis, **850**–852
 vertical analysis, **852**–854
Financial statements, **4**, 13–16, 213–238.
 See also Balance sheets; Income
 statement; Statement of
 changes in financial position;
 Statement of owner's equity
 accounting cycle completion and,
 131–133
 analysis of. *See* Financial statement
 analysis
 in annual reports, 847–848
 appropriated retained earnings and,
 666–667
 changing prices and, 538–540,
 546–549
 current cost/constant dollar
 statements, 548–549
 current cost statements, 546–548
 consolidated, **757**–765
 acquisition at 100 percent, 758–760
 acquisition at less than 100
 percent, 760–761
 definition of, **13**
 depreciation of assets and, 475–476
 equity securities and, 752–753
 footnotes to, **237**, 868
 income statement transactions and,
 88–90
 inventories and, 435–436
 of manufacturing firms, 920–922
 of merchandising firms, 195
 objectives of, 214–215
 of Philips Group, excerpt from,
 C20–26
 preparation of, 131–133
 prior period adjustments in, 665–666
 of publicly held corporations,
 230–238
 auditor's report, 237, 237–238
 consolidated balance sheet,
 230–233
 consolidated statements of
 income, 233–234
 earnings per share disclosure,
 656–657
 footnotes, 237
 statement of changes in financial
 position, 236
 statement of stockholders' equity,
 234
 of Safeway Stores, Inc., excerpt
 from, C2–17

Financial strength, in balance sheet, 222–223
Finished goods account, 1089
Finished goods inventory, 920
Finishing and packaging materials, 1102
Firms. *See* Businesses; Corporations; Manufacturing firms; Merchandising firms; Partnerships
First-in, first-out (FIFO), **424**
 ending inventory system and, 425–426
 perpetual inventory system and, 438–440
 rising prices and, 429–431
Fiscal year, **76**
Fixed assets, 34
Fixed costs, **943**–945, 953–954, 982–984, 1047
Fixed ratio method of profit-sharing, 578–580
Flexible budgets, 1053–**1054**, 1134
FOB (Free on Board), **190**
Footing, 38
Footnotes to financial statements, **237**, 868
Foreign Corrupt Practices Act, 265
Foreign currency transactions, **869**–872
Foreign currency translation, **872**–874
Formal control systems, 911–913
Franchises, **506**
Frequency, as variance criteria, 1142
Full cost method, **502**
Full disclosure principle, **532**–533
Fully diluted EPS, **654**–655
Future value of an annuity, A9–11
Future value of a single amount, A4–6
Future value of an annuity, A9–11
Future value of a single amount, A4–6

G

GAAP. *See* Generally accepted accounting principles
Gains, **74**
 debt securities and, 751
 from discontinued operations, 647
 from extraordinary items, 648–649
 foreign currency fluctuations and, 873–874
 income statement transactions and, 74–75
 nonoperating changes and, 800
 on sales of intangible assets, 505
 on trade-ins, 497–498
General journal, 277–278
General ledgers, **32**, 266, 267
 cash and, 322–325
 equity securities and, 745
 property, plant, and equipment and, 500
 voucher system and, 332
Generally accepted accounting principles (GAAP), **10**, 525–526, 673

financial statement analysis and, 866–868
 managerial accounting and, **913**–914
General partnership, **573**
General price level changes, **537**–539
Going-concern assumption, **16**
Goods in public warehouses, 191
Goods in transit, **191**
Goods on consignment, **191**
Goodwill, **218**, 506–508, 806
Governmental accounting, **10**
Governmental Accounting Standards Board (GASB), **12**
Governmental agencies, accounting information and, 8
Government regulation of corporations, 611
Gross income, B2
Gross margin
 inventories and, 421–422, 429–430
 on sales, **178**, 225
Gross margin inventory method, **433**–434
Gross margin percentage, **227**
Gross method of recording purchase discounts, **188**
Gross method of recording sales discounts, **181**
Gross sales, **178**
Group purchases, 464
Growth, financial statement analysis and, 852

H

Historical cost, 188, 224
Historical cost convention, **16**, 533
Horizontal analysis of financial position, **849**–850

I

Importance of costs, as variance criteria, 1143
Income
 adjusted gross, B2–3
 from continuing operations, **646**–647
 gross, B2
 net, **75**, 144, 227, 793–794, 799, 805, 950
  cash flow statement and, 816
  income statement transactions and, 75
 new, 34–35
 from operations, 227
 taxable, 673, B5–7
Income accounting, 673
Income statement(s), 71–90
 budgets and, 1052
 cash flow statement and, 812–815
 classified, 224–229
  limitations of, 229
  multistep statement, 225–227
  single-step statement, 225
  uses of, 227–229
 columns in worksheet for, 139, 144

components of, 72–75
 expenses, **73**–74
 gains and losses, **74**–75
 net income, **75**
 revenues, **73**
 withdrawals by the owner, 75
consolidated, 233–234, 764–765
of corporations, 644–657
 accounting changes and, 649–652
 accounting vs. taxable income, 673–674
 continuing operations and, 646–647
 discontinued operations and, 647–648
 earnings per share and, 652–657
 extraordinary items and, 648–649
current cost and, 547
determining income for, 76–78
 accrual basis, 76–77
 cash basis, 77–78
 matching convention, 76
financial statement analysis and, 850, 861
financial statement preparation and, 88–90
inventories and, 420–424
of manufacturing and merchandising firms compared, 920–922
measurement of income for, 71–72
merchandising firms and, 178, 192
of partnerships, 575–582
recording of transactions in, 78–82
 debit and credit rules, 79
 journal entries, 80–87
statement of changes in financial position and, 798
Income statement analysis, 861
 in worksheets for merchandising firms, 194
Income summary account, closing of, 136
Income taxes, B1–7
 corporate. *See* Corporations, taxes and
 individual, 398, B1–6
 interperiod allocation of, **646**, 674–677
 intraperiod allocation of, **646**
Indirect (joint) fixed costs, 983–984. *See also* Joint products
Indirect costs, **918**
Indirect labor, **919**
Indirect materials, **919**
Individual Retirement Accounts (IRAs), B2–3
Individual taxation, 398, B1–6
Inflation. *See also* Changing prices, accounting for
 depreciation and, 479
Installment basis method of revenue recognition, 535
Intangible assets, **218**, **460**, **502**–508
 acquisition costs of, 503–504
 amortization of, 504–505
 in balance sheet, 218
 disposition of, 505
 specifically identifiable, 505–506

Intercompany debt, elimination of, 760
Intercompany stock ownership,
    elimination of, 759–760
Interest, A2–9
  accrued, 120–121
  capitalization of, 465
  compound, A3–6
  future value of a single amount,
      A4–6
  itemized deductions and, B3
  notes payable and, 390–392
  in partnerships, 581–586
  present value of a single amount
      A6–9, A7
  simple, A2–3
  times interest earned ratio and, 863
Interest dates, bonds and, 705–707,
    717–718
Interest rates, 120
  bonds and, 704–705
  nominal, 700
Interim statements, 76
Internal control, 264
  cash and, 308–310, 315
  of checking accounts, 320–327
    bank reconciliation, 322–327
    bank statements, 321–322
    deposit slip, 320
  of corporate stock records, 628–629
  financial statement analysis and,
      846–847
  of petty cash, 327–328
  of property, plant and equipment,
      499–500
  specialized journals and, 278
  voucher system and, 328–334
Internal-rate-of-return method of
    capital budgeting, 1016–1019
  ranking and, 1020
Internal Revenue Code (IRC), 431, 673
Internal transactions, 88
International accounting standards,
    874–875. See also Multinational
    corporations
International Accounting Standards
    Committee (IASC), 875
International Federation of
    Accountants (IFAC), 875
Interperiod income tax allocation, 646,
    674–677
Interpolation, 1017
Intraperiod income tax allocation, 646
Inventoriable costs, 923
Inventories, 184, 419–441
  annual reports and, 435–436
  as asset account, 33
  cash flow statement and, 814
  direct material budget and,
      1046–1047
  ending, 187–188
  ending inventory budget and, 1048
  ending inventory cost flow methods,
      424–431
    average cost, 427
    first-in, first-out (FIFO), 424–426,
        429–431
    last-in, first-out (LIFO),
        424,426–427, 430–431

rising prices and, 429–430
  specific identification, 427–428
ending inventory estimation, 433–435
income determination and, 420–424
lower-of-cost-or-market rule and,
    432–433
of manufacturing and
    merchandising firms compared,
    920–922
perpetual system cost flow methods,
    437–441
quick ratio and, 864
turnover ratio for, 865
Inventory profits, 429
Inventory purchases, accounting for,
    184–192
  freight, 190
  losses, 191
  periodic systems, 186–188
  perpetual system, 184–186
  physical inventory, 190–192
  purchase discounts, 188–189
  purchase returns and allowances,
      189
Inventory turnover, 435–436
Inventory turnover ratio, 865
Investment(s). See also Capital
    budgeting; Time value of money
  analysis of financial position and,
      849–855
    horizontal, 849–850
    ratio, 855
    trend, 850–852
    vertical, 852–854
  in balance sheet, 218
  in bonds, 721–724
    acquisitions, 721–722
    amortizing the discount or
        premium, 722–723
    sale prior to maturity, 723–724
  equity method of accounting and,
      755–757
  long-term, 1007–1023
  long-term equity, 753–758
    consolidated financial statements
        and, 757–758, 757–765
    controlling interest, 757–758
    no significant influence, 754–755
    significant influence, 755–757
  in partnerships, 574–575, 584–586
  return on, 228–229, 857–859, 916–917,
      1009
  risk of, 861–862
  short-term, 352–353. See also Current
      marketable securities
  stock indicators and, 626–627
Investment advisory services, financial
    statement analysis and, 849
Investment centers, 915
  return on investment rate and,
      916–917
Investment in Marketable Securities
    Account, 745
Investors
  accounting information and, 7
  financial statement analysis and, 846
IRAs, B2–3
Itemized deductions, B3–4

J

Job cost sheet, 1080
Job order costing, 1080–1091
Joint fixed costs, 983–984
Joint product costs, 984
Joint products, 984–990. See also
    Indirect (joint) fixed costs
  physical measures method of cost
      allocation, 985–986
  relative sales value method of cost
      allocation, 987–988
  sell or process further decision and,
      988–990
Journal entries
  accounting cycle completion and,
      113, 126
  bonds and, 705–707, 710–713,
      717–724
  for corporate income taxes, 676–677
  depreciation and, 468
  disposal of assets and, 496–499
  for dividends, 659–662
  equity method of accounting and,
      756
  equity securities and, 746–747
  income statement transactions and,
      80–87
  natural resources depletion and, 501
  notes payable and, 390–392
  payroll and, 402
  periodic inventory systems and, 186
  perpetual inventory system and, 185
  stock issuance and, 621–624
  uncollectible accounts and, 355–357
Journals, 31–32
  recording transactions in, 43–47
  specialized, 269–277
    cash payments, 275–277
    cash receipts, 272–275
    internal control and, 278
    purchases, 272
    sales, 270–272

L

Labor. See also Employees; Payroll
  direct and indirect, 919
  direct labor budget and, 1047
  job order costing system and,
      1084–1085
  standard costs of, 1127–1128
  variances and, 1131–1133
Last-in, first-out (LIFO), 424
  ending inventory system and,
      426–427
  perpetual inventory system and, 440
  rising prices and, 430–431
LCM. See Lower of cost or market rule
Leasehold improvements, 506
Leases, 506, 725–727
Ledger(s)
  definition of, 32
  general, 32, 266, 267
    cash and, 322–325
    equity securities and, 745
    property, plant, and equipment
        and, 500
    voucher system and, 332

property, plant, and equipment and, 499–500
recording transactions in, 36–38
subsidiary, **32**, 266–269
equity securities and, 745
property, plant, and equipment and, 499–500
use of, 42
Ledger accounts
accounting cycle completion and, 126–130
merchandising firms and, 195
sales and, 179
Legal (stated) capital, **619**
Lessee, **725**
Lessor, **725**
Level of aspiration, **1038**
Leverage, **860**
Liabilities, **14**, **219**, **387–388**
in balance sheet, 15, 218–219, 231–232
current, **218–219**, **388–396**
contingent liabilities, 394–396
definitely determinable amounts, 389–393
measurement and valuation of, 388–389
third party collections, 393–394
income statement transactions and, 77
long-term, 699–727, 724–725
bonds, 700–724
leases, 727
mortgages, **724**–725
notes payable, 724
Liability accounts, 34
LIFO. *See* Last-in, first-out
Limited liability, **7**
as corporation characteristic, 610–612
Limited life, as feature of partnerships, 572
Limited partnership, **573**
Liquidating dividends, 658
Liquidation of a partnership, **588**–591
Liquidity
in balance sheet, 221–222
current ratio and, 863–864
Local taxes, B3
Long-term creditors, financial statement analysis and, 862–863
Long-term debt, increase and decrease in, 794
Long-term equity investments, 753–758
consolidated financial statements and, 757–765
controlling interest, 757–768
no significant influence, 754–755
pooling-of-interests vs. purchase methods of accounting and, 765–768
significant influence, 755–757
Long-term investments, 218
Long-term liabilities, **219**, **388**, **699–727**
bonds, 700–724. *See also* Bonds
features of, 700–701
investor's accounting for, 721–724
issuers' accounting for, 705–721

prices and interest rates of, 702–705
types of, 701–702
leases, 725–727
mortgages payable, 724–725
notes payable, 724
Long-term measures of financial strength, 222–223
Losses, **74**
debt securities and, 751
from discontinued operations, 647–648
from extraordinary items, 648–649
foreign currency fluctuations and, 873–874
income statement transactions and, 74–75
in inventories, 191
nonoperating changes and, 800
in partnerships, 573, 576–582, 589–591
on sales of intangible assets, 505
on trade ins, 498–499
Lower of cost or market (LCM) rule, 353, **432**–433
debt securities and, 750, 752
equity securities and, 746–747, 750

M

Maintenance expenditure, 494
Make-or-buy decisions, **978**–980
Maker, **365**
Management, 905–917, **906**. *See also specific topics*
accounting information and, 8
accounting's role in, 906–913
control, **911**–913
decision making, 907–911
planning, 906–907
basic nature of, 906
cash control and, 308–319
cash disbursements, 315, 319
cash receipts, 310–315
internal control, 308–310
corporations and, 611
decisions, types of, 908
elements of, 906
and employee motivation, 1038–1040
financial statement analysis and, 846–847
managerial accounting, characteristics of, **913**–914
responsibility accounting and, **914**–917
Management accounting, **8**
Management advisory services, 10
Management by exception, **1126**
Management control, **911**–913. *See also* Internal controls
Managerial accounting, **913**–914
Manual accounting systems, compared to computerized, 278–279
Manufactured, **921**
Manufacturing costs, **918–925**, 1092
basic types of, 919
financial statements of, 920–922

and nonmanufacturing costs compared, 919–920
product and period costs compared, 922–925
Manufacturing firms, 920–922. *See also specific topics*
flow of costs in, 1079
joint products and, **984**–990
physical measures method of cost allocation, **985**–986
relative sales value method of cost allocations, **987**–988
sell or process further decision, **988**–990
make-or-buy decisions and, **978**–980
master budgets of. *See* Master budgets
special orders and, **980**–982
Marketable securities, as asset account, 32
Market interest rate, **700**
Market risk, 861–862
Market value per share, 626–627
Master budget, **1040–1055**
budgeted balance sheets, 1052–1053
budgeted income statements, 1052
cash, **1050**–1052
cost of goods sold, **1048**–1049
direct labor, **1047**
direct materials, **1046**–1047
ending inventory, **1048**
factory overhead, **1047**–1048
production, **1044**–1045
sales, **1044**
selling and administrative expenses, **1049**–1050
Matching convention, **76**, 534
income statement transactions and, 76
Materiality, **532**
as variance criteria, 1142
Materials
direct and indirect, **919**
job order costing system and, 1081–1083
standard costs of, 1127
variances and, 1128–1131
Materials ledger card, **1082**
Maturity date, **120**, 700–701
Maturity value, **120**
Medical expenses, B3
Merchandising firms, **177**, 920–922
income statements and, 178
inventory purchases accounting, 184–192
periodic inventory system, 186–188
perpetual inventory system, 184–186
physical inventory, 190–192
recording purchases, methods and issues, 188–190
product lines and, 982–984
sales accounting and, 178–184
credit card sales, 182–183
sales discounts, 180–182
sales returns and allowances, 183–184

Merchandising firms, Cont.
   trade and quantity discounts,
     179–180
   worksheet techniques for, 192–197
Microcomputers, 280–281
Miscellaneous itemized deductions, B4
Mixed (semivariable) cost, **945**–946
Mortgage bonds, 701
Mortgages, **724**–725
Multinational corporations, 868–875
   foreign currency transactions and,
     869–872
   foreign currency translation and,
     872–874
   international accounting standards
     and, 874–875
Multiproduct companies, cost-volume-
   profit analysis and, 955–957
Multistep income statement, **225**
Mutual agency, **572**–573

N

Natural resources, **460**, **500**–502
Net assets, **15–16**
Net book value, **117**
Net income, **75**, 144, 227, 793–794, 799,
   805, 950
   cash flow statement and, 816
   income statement transactions and,
     75
Net loss, 144, 794
Net method of recording purchase
   discounts, **188–189**
Net method of recording sales
   discounts, **181**
Net-present-value method
   of capital budgeting, **1013**–1016
   ranking and, 1020
New income, **34–35**
New York Stock Exchange, 744
Nominal interest rate, **700**
Nonbank credit cards, 183
Noncash exchanges, 465
Noncumulative dividends, 616
Noncurrent, nonmonetary assets, **112**.
   See also specific types
   adjusting entries and, 112
   allocation of benefits of, 460–461
   characteristics of, 460
   increase and decrease in, 794
   major accounting issues related to,
     461
Noncurrent accounts, changes in,
   803–809
   bonds payable and purchase of land
     and, 808
   common stock issuance and, 809
   dividends and, 808–809
   equipment account and, 806–808
   notes payable and, 808
   working capital from operations
     and, 805–806
Noncurrent or long term liabilities, **219**
Nonmanufacturing costs, **919**–920
Nonoperating gains and losses, 800
Nonparticipating preferred stock, 617
Nonworking capital accounts, 797
No par stock, **620**

No significant influence, equity
   securities and, 754–755
Notes payable, **389**–392, 808
   cash flow statement and, 816
   as liability account, 34
Notes receivable, **365**–371
   accounting for, 367–368
   as asset account, 32
   cash generation and, 369–370
   default and, **369**
   elements of, 366–367

O

Objectives of financial reporting, **214**,
   214–215
Objectivity, 16
Obsolescence, **467**
Off balance sheet financing, **727**
Operating activities
   cash flow statement and, 812–815
   definition of, 793–794
Operating assets, 34
Operating changes, **795**. *See also*
   Income statement transactions
Operating cycle, **216**
Operating expenses, 227
Operating leases, **506**, 726–727
Operational planning, 907
Operations systems, 912
Opinions, **9**. *See also* Audits
Opportunity costs, **975**, 979–980
Ordinary annuity, definition of, A9
Organizational control system,
   911–913. *See also* Management;
   Internal control
   definition of, **1077**
   standard costs and, 1126
Organization costs, **613**
Other liabilities, as liability account, 34
Outstanding checks, **323**
Overages, in cash transactions, 313–315
Overapplied overhead, **1088**
Overhead, **919**, **1047**–1048, 1085–1089
   over- and underapplied, 1141
   standard costs of, 1128
   variances and, 1133–1141
     cost behavior and flexible budgets,
     1134
     efficiency, **1138**–1139
     spending, **1137**
     volume, **1139**–1141
Overhead efficiency variance,
   1138–1139
Overhead volume variance, **1139**–1141
Over-the-counter market, 744
Over-the-counter sales, 313
Owner's Capital account, income
   statement transactions and, 79
Owner's equity, 34. *See also* Statement
   of owner's equity
   in balance sheet, 15–16, 219–221
   expenses and, 79
   income statement transactions and,
     79
   partnerships, 219–220
   in partnerships, 574, 576
   return on, 229

revenues and, 79
   sole proprietorships, 219
   stockholders' equity, 220–221
Ownership transferability, as
   corporation characteristic, 610

P

Pacific Stock Exchange, 744
Parent companies. *See also*
   Consolidations
Partial income statement,
   merchandising firms and, 192
Participating preferred stock, 617
Partnerships, **6**, 219–220, **571**–592
   advantages and disadvantages of,
     573
   dissolution of, 583–588
     partner admission and, 583–586
     partner death, 587–588
     partner withdrawal, 586–587
   features of, 572–573
   liquidation of, 588–591
   operations of, 574–582
     distribution of profits and losses,
     576–582
     formation, 574
     subsequent investments and
     withdrawals, 574–575
   profits and losses in, 573, 576–582
Par value, **619**–620
Par value bonds, 705–707
Patents, **505**
Payback method of capital budgeting,
   1021
Payee, 365
Payment date (of dividends), **659**
Payroll register, **402**
Payrolls, 396–401
   employee compensation and, 397
   employee withholdings and, 398–400
   employer's tax expenses and, 393,
     402–404
   internal control for, 405–406
   payment of, 404–405
   records of, 400–401
Percentage of completion method of
   revenue recognition, 535
Percentage-of-net-sales method,
   358–360
Period cost, **923**–925
Period expenses, **536**
Periodicals, financial statement
   analysis and, 849
Periodic inventory systems, **186**–188
   worksheet techniques for, 192–197
Permanent differences, between
   accounting and taxable income,
    673–674
Perpetual inventory system, **184**–186,
   437–441
Personal computers, 280–281. *See also*
   Computers
Personnel. *See* Employees; Labor
Personnel department, 405
Personnel policies, 266
Petty cash fund, **327**–328

Philips Group, annual report of, C20–26
Physical flow of units, **1096**–1097
Physical inventory, 190–192
Physical measures method, of joint product cost allocation, **985**–986
Planning
  accounting's role in, 906–907
  budgeting and, 1036
Planning systems, 912
Plant. *See* Property, plant and equipment
Point-of-sale devices, 313
Pooling-of-interests method of accounting for consolidations,**758**, 765–768
Postings, 44
  cash receipts journal to ledgers, 275
  from purchases journal, 272
  from sales journal, 270–271
  to subsidiary accounts, 267–269
Predetermined overhead rate, **1087**
Preference on liquidation, 617
Preferred dividends, 616
Preferred stock, **616**–618, 625–626, 628
Premium bonds, 710–713, 716–717
Premium on bonds payable account, 711–713
Prepaid assets, adjusting entries and, 114–115
Prepaid expenses, as asset account, 33
Present value, **388**
  of an annuity, A11–13
  capital budgeting and, 1009–1012
  of cash flows, 1010
  of a single amount, A6–9, **A7**
Price adjustments, 179–180
Price-earnings (P/E) ratio, **627**
Price variances, 1129–1130
Primary earnings per share, **654**
Principal, **120**
  notes payable and, 390–391
Prior period adjustments, **664**–666
Private accounting, **10**
Problem-solving
  capital budgeting and, 1013–1014
  guidelines for, 975–977
Process, **906**
Process centers, **1092**
Process costing, **1080**, 1091–1106
Product costs, **922**–923
Production budget, **1044**–1045
Production costing systems. *See* Cost accounting systems
Product lines, 982, 990
Profit(s)
  cost-volume-profit analysis and, **946**–960
    break-even point and, **947**–948
    contribution margin (CM) and, **949**–951
    contribution margin ratio (CM ratio) and, **951**–953
    C-V-P formula, **947**
    income taxes and, 957–959
    for multiproduct companies, 955–957
    profit planning and, 948–949
  inventory and, 429–430

in partnerships, 573, 575, 576–582, 588–589
Profitability, classified income statements and, 227–228
Profitability indexes, **1020**
Profit centers, **915**
Profit margin percentage, **228**, 858
Profit planning, cost-volume-profit analysis and, 948–949, 953–955
Profit-sharing arrangements, 576–582
Promissory notes, **366**–371, 389–392
  accounting for, 367–368
  cash generation and, 369–370
  default and, **368**
  elements of, 366–367
Property, plant and equipment, 459–480, **460**, 493–500. *See also* Capital budgeting
  acquisition costs of, 462–465
  as asset account, 34
  in balance sheet, 218
  capital vs. revenue expenditures and, 461–462
  depreciation computing and, 468–477
    comparison of methods, 474–477
    declining-balance method, **471**–472
    straight-line method, 469–470
    sum-of-the-years-digits method, **472**–473
    units-of-production method, **470**–471
  depreciation concepts and, 465–468
  depreciation problems, 477–479
    inflation, 479
    partial years, 477–478
    revision of patterns, 478–479
  depreciation records on disposal, 495–499
  disposal of, 495–499
    discarded assets, 495–496
    sales, 496–497
    trade-ins, 497–499
  internal control of, 499–500
  statement of changes in financial position and, 806–808
  subsequent expenditures, types of, 493–495
    capital, 494–495
    revenue, 493–494
Property dividends, 660
Public, accounting information and the, 8
Public accounting, 9–10
  use of computers in, 282
Publicly held corporations, **7**, **744**. *See also* Corporations
Purchase and disbursement cycle, 315, 319
Purchase discounts, **188**
  inventories and, 188–189
Purchase method of accounting for consolidations, **758**, 765–768
Purchase order, **315**
Purchase requisition, **315**
Purchase returns and allowances, **189**
Purchases, inventory, 184–192
  freight, 190
  losses, 191

periodic systems, 186–188
perpetual system, 184–186
physical inventory, 190–192
purchase discounts, 188–189
purchase returns and allowances, 189
Purchases journal, **272**
Purchasing power gains or losses, **539**, 542–546

Q

Qualitative Characteristics of Accounting Information, 526
Quantifiability, 529–530
  definition of, **25**
Quantity schedule, **1098**–1100
Quantity discounts, **179**–180
Quantity variances, 1130–1131
Quick ratio, **864**

R

Ranking decision, **1008**, 1019–1020
Rate of exchange, **870**
Rate of return. *See* Interest
Rate variances, 1132
Ratio analysis of financial position, 846, **850**–866, **850**–866
  debt-equity ratio and, 862–863
  long-term creditor preferred ratios, 862–863
  short-term creditor preferred ratios, 863–866
  stockholder preferred ratios, 855–862
    book value per share ratio, 857–859
    dividend yield, 856
    earnings per share (EPS), **855**
    equity, 860–861
    income statement analysis, 861
    leverage, **860**
    market risk, 861–862
    price-earnings (P-E) ratio, **856**
    return on common stockholders' equity ratio, 859
    return on investment, 857–859
    return on total assets ratio, 857–859
Raw materials. *See* Materials
Raw materials inventory, 920
Readily marketable securities. *See* Current marketable securities
Real accounts, **79**
Realization principle, **534**
Receipts, **74**
  adjusting entries and, 118–122
  cash, 310–315
  and expenditures, relationship to revenues and expenses, 74
  income statement transactions and, 74
Receivable turnover, **365**
Redeemable preferred stock, **618**
Registered bonds, 701
Regulation, of corporations, 611
Reinforcement, concept of, **1038**

Relative sales value method, of joint product cost allocations, **987**–988
Relevance, **530**–531
Relevant range, **943**
Reliability, **530**–531
Remittance advice, **310**
Rent. *See* Annuities
Repairs, extraordinary, 494
Repairs and maintenance expenditures, 494
Reporting. *See* Financial reporting
Research and development costs, **504**
Residual value, **116**, 469
Resources, **905**
  direct material budget and, **1046**–1047
  scarce, 990–991
Responsibility accounting, **914**–917
Responsibility centers, **914**
  cost, 914
  investment, 915–917
  profit, 915
  revenue, 914–915
Retail inventory method, **434**
Retained earnings, 220, 643–670
  appropriations of, **666**–667
  dividends and, 658–662
  earnings per share (EPS), **652**–657
  income statements and, 644–652
    accounting changes and, 649–652
    continuing operations, 646–647
    discontinued operations and, 647–648
    extraordinary items, **648**–649
  prior period adjustments, **664**–666
  and shareholders' equity, 621
  stock splits and, 662–664
  treasury stock transactions and, 667–669
Return on common stockholders' equity ratio, 859
Return on investment (ROI), 857–859, 916–917, 1009
  classified income statements and, 228–229
Return on owner's equity, **229**
Return on total assets, **229**, 857–859
Revenue centers, **914**–915
Revenue expenditures, **461**, 493–494
Revenue recognition, 534–535
Revenues, **34**–35, 73
  accrual basis of accounting and, 77
  accrued, 120–122
  adjusting entries and, 118–122
  differential costs and, 974, 977–978
  and expenses, relationship to receipts and expenditures, 74
  income statement transactions and, 73
  matching convention and, 76
  owner's equity and, 79
  from sales, 178
  unearned, 118–119
Reversing entries, **146**
  adjusting entries and, 146–148
Reviews and compilations, **9**
Risk of investments, 861–862

S

Safeway Stores, Inc., annual report of, excerpt from, C2–17
Salaries, 397
  in partnerships, 580–581
Sales, **178**
  of assets, 496–497
  cash flow statement and, 812, 815
  cost-volume-profit analysis and, **946**–960
    break-even point and, **947**–948
    contribution margin (CM) and, **949**–951
    contribution margin ratio (CM ratio) and, **951**–953
    C-V-P formula, **947**
    income taxes and, 957–959
    for multiproduct companies, 955–957
    profit planning and, 948–949
  financial statement analysis and, 852
  of intangible assets, 505
  merchandising firms and, 178–184
    credit card sales, 182–183
    returns and allowances, 183–184
    sales discounts, 180–182
    trade and quantity discounts, 179–180
  over-the-counter, 313
  relative sales value method of joint product cost allocation, **987**–988
  revenue recognition and, 534–535
  sell or process further decision and, **988**–990
  special orders and, **980**–982
Sales allowances, **183**, 183–184
Sales budget, **1044**
Sales discounts, **180**, 180–182
  gross method of recording, 181
  net method of recording, 181–182
Sales forecasts, **1044**
Sales journal, **270**, 270–272
Sales mix, **955**
Sales returns, **183**, 183–184
Sales taxes, 393
Salvage value, 469
Scarce resources, 990–991
Schedule of accounts payable, **272**
Schedule of accounts receivable, **268**
Schedule of cost of goods manufactured, **921**
Schedule of unpaid vouchers, 333
Screening decision, **1008**, 1012–1019
Secured bonds, 701
Securities, 743–768. *See also* Stocks
  current marketable investments, 744–753
    debt, 750–752
    equity, 745–750
    financial statement presentation of, 752–753
  long-term equity investments, 753–758
    consolidating financial statements and, 757–758
    controlling interest, 757–758
    no significant influence, 754–755
    significant influence, 755–757

Securities and Exchange Commission (SEC), **12**, 744
  reports required by, 847
Segment (of business), **647**
Self-constructed assets, 465
Selling and administrative expense budget, **1049**–1050
Sell or process further decision, **988**–990
Senior management of corporations, 615
Separation of duties, in accounting systems, 266
Serial bonds, **700**–701
Service firms, 177, 192
Shares (shareholders). *See* Stocks; Stockholders' equity
Shortages, in cash transactions, 313–315
Short-term creditors, financial statement analysis and, 863–866
Short-term investments, **352**–353
Short-term monetary assets, 351–372
  accounts receivable, 353–354, 364–365
  cash generation and, 369–371
  classification of, 371
  notes receivable, **365**–371
    accounting for, 367–368
    cash generation and, 369–370
    default and, **369**
    elements of, 366–367
  short-term investments, **352**–353
  uncollectible accounts, 354–365
    aging method estimates of, 360–363
    allowance method recording of, **354**–357
    estimates vs. experience, 363–364
    management control of, 364–365
    percentage-of-net-sales estimates of, 358–360
Significant influence, equity securities and, **755**–757
Simple interest, A2–3
Simple-rate-of-return method. *See* Accounting-rate-of-return method
Single-step income statement, **225**
Sinking funds, 218, **719**
Social security taxes, 398
Software programs, 280–282
Sole proprietorships, **6**, 219
Specialized journals, **269**–277
  cash payments, 275–277
  cash receipts, 272–275
  internal control and, 278
  purchases, 272
  sales, 270–272
Special orders, **980**–982
Specifically identifiable intangible assets, **502**
Specific identification
  ending inventory system and, 427
Specific identification method, **424**
Specific price level changes, **538**–540
Spending variances, 1137
Split-off point, **984**, 988–990

Spreadsheet, **281**
  C-V-P analysis and, 957
Standard cost card, **1127**
Standard costs, 1125–1144, **1126**
  advantages and disadvantages of, 1144
  control systems and, 1126
  currently attainable, **1127**
  direct labor variances and, 1131–1133
  direct material variances and, 1128–1131
  establishment of, 1127–1228
  factory overhead and, 1133–1141
    cost behavior and flexible budgets, 1134
    overhead efficiency variance, **1138**–1139
    overhead spending variance, **1137**
    overhead volume variance, **1139**–1141
  ideal standards, **1127**
  revision of, 1128
Standard deductions, B4
Standards, accounting. *See* Concepts and standards of accounting
Stated interest rate, **700**
Statement of changes in financial position, **229**, 236, 791–820
  cash-based version, 811–820
    cash flows determined from operations, 812–815
    worksheet approach to preparation of, 818–820
  causes of changes in, 793–794
  purpose of, 792–794
  working capital-based version of, 794–810
    all financial resources concept and, **797**–798
    net change in working capital, determining, 801–802
    noncurrent accounts, changes in, 803–809
    transactions affecting working capital and, 795–796
    transactions not affecting working capital and, 796–798
    working capital determined from operations, 799
    worksheet approach to preparation of, 800–811
Statement of owner's equity, **88–89**
Statement of stockholders' equity, **234**, 670
State taxes, B4
Statistical techniques, variances and, 1143
Stock dividends, **660**–662. *See also* Dividends
Stockholders, 6, 614–615
Stockholders' equity, **220**, 618–621, 643–670
  appropriation of retained earnings and, **666**–667
  in balance sheet, 220–221, 232–234
  debt-equity ratio and, 862–863
  dividends and, 658–662
  earnings per share and, 652–657

income statements and, 644–652
  accounting changes and, 649–652
  continuing operations and, 646–647
  discontinued operations and, 647–648
  extraordinary items and, **648**–649
  return on, 859
  statement of, **234**, 670
  statement of changes in financial position and, 798
  stock splits, 662–664
  treasury stock transaction and, 667–669
Stock-page listing, 626–627
Stock registrar, **629**
Stocks. *See also* Securities; Stockholders' equity
  bond conversion to, 720–721
  book value per share, 857
  common, 615, 625–628, 662–664
  conversion of, 625–626
  corporate treasury, 667–668
  dividends of, 616–618, 658–662
  dividend yield ratio and, 856
  earnings per share (EPS) of, 652–657, 855
  equity, 745–750
  increase and decrease in, 794
  investment indicators of, 626–628
  issuance of, 621–624
  leverage and, 860–861
  preferred, 616–618
  price-earnings (P-E) ratio of, 856
  retirement of, 669–670
  return on investment ratios, 857–859
  risk of investments and, 861–862
  statement of changes in financial position and, 809
  stockholders' equity and, 220
  stock page analysis and, 626–627
Stock splits, **662**–664
Stock transfer agent, **629**
Straight-line method of depreciation, **116**, 469–470
  discount bond amortization and, 709–710
  premium bond amortization and, 712–713
Strategic planning, 906–907
Subsidiaries. *See also* Consolidations
Subsidiary accounts, **266**
  postings to, 267–269
Subsidiary ledgers, **32**, 266–269
  equity securities and, 745
  property, plant, and equipment and, 499–500
Successful efforts method, **502**
Sum-of-the-years-digits method, **472**–473
Sunk costs, **974**–975
Supplies, adjusting entries and, 113–114

T

T accounts, **36**, 36–38
  balancing, 38
  bank reconciliation and, 325–327

bonds and, 707, 709, 712, 723, 723
  equity method of accounting and, 756–757
  periodic inventory systems and, 187
  reversing entries and, 146–148
  statement of changes in financial position and, 806–807
Tangible assets, **459**
Taxable income, 673, B**5**–7
Tax credits, B**6**
Taxes, B1–7
  corporate, 394, 611, 673–677, B**6**–7
    accounting vs. taxable income and, 673–674
    allocation, 674–677
    journal entries for, 676–677
  C-V-P analysis and, 957–959
  depreciation of assets and, 476–477
  FICA, **398**, 402
  income. *See* Income taxes
  LIFO conformity rule, 431
  in partnerships, 575
  payment of, 404–405, B**6**
  rate tables for 1987 and 1988, B5–6
  return, filing of, B**6**
  sales, 393
  state and local, B3
  unemployment, 402, 404
Tax preparation and planning, **9**
Tax Reform Act of 1986, B1–7
Temporal method of foreign currency translation, **873**
Temporary accounts, **79** 10-K form, **847** 10-Q form, **847**
Term bonds, **700**–701
Third party collections, 393–394
Thorndike's law of effect, management and, 1038
Time-adjusted rate of return method. *See* Internal-rate-of-return method
Timekeeping, payroll and, 405
Time period assumption, **76**, 533–534
  income statement transactions and, 76
Times interest earned ratio, 863
Time value of money, **1009**–1010, A2–15
  accounting-rate-of-return method and, 1022
    annuities and, A**9**–13
    future value determination, A**9**–11
    present value determination, A**11**–13
  bonds and, A14–15
  interest and, A2–9
    future value of a single amount, A4–6
    present value of a single amount A6–9, A7
    simple and compound compared, A2–4
  payback method and, 1021
Timing differences, between accounting and taxable income, 673–674
Trade accounts payable, **389**
Trade discounts, **179**, 179–180
Trade-ins, 497–499

Trading on equity, **860**
Transactions, **4**
  analysis of, 39–42
  cash. *See* Cash transactions
  classifying and summarizing, 4
  in foreign currency, 869–872
  recording in the journal, 43–47
  recording in the ledger, 36–38
Transferability of ownership, as
  corporation characteristic, 610
Transferred-in cost, **1101**
Translation of foreign currency,
  872–874
Treasury stock, **621**
  and shareholders' equity, 621
Treasury stock transactions, 667–669
Trend analysis of financial position,
  846, **850**–852
Trial balances, **47–49**, **137**, 192
  adjusted. 139
  post-closing, 137–138
  unadjusted, 124–125, 139, 192–194

U

Unadjusted-rate-of-return method. *See*
  Accounting-rate-of-return
  method
Unadjusted trial balance, **124**, 139
  merchandising firms and, 192–194
Uncollectible accounts, **353**, 354–365
  allowance method recording of,
    354–357
  estimates of, 358–364
    and actual experience compared,
      363–364
    aging method, **360**–363
    percentage-of-net-sales method,
      358–360
Underapplied overhead, **1087**
Underwriters, **621**
Unearned revenues, 118–119
  income statement transactions and,
    77
Unemployment taxes, 402, 404

Uniform Partnership Act, **571**–572
Units-of-production method, **470**–471
Unlimited liability, as feature of
  partnerships, 573
Unrealized loss account, 748–749, 755
Unsecured bonds, **701**
Usage variances, 1130–1131
Useful life, 469
Users of accounting information, 7–8

V

Variable costs, **942**–943, 1047
Variance investigation, **1141**–1143
Variances, **1126**, 1128–1143
  in direct labor efficiency, **1132**–1133
  in direct labor rate, **1132**
  in direct materials price, **1129**–1130
  in direct materials quantity (or
    usage), **1130**–1131
  investigations of, **1141**–1143
  over- and underapplied overhead
    and, 1141
  in overhead efficiency, **1138**–1139
  in overhead spending, **1137**
  in overhead volume, **1139**–1141
Venture capitalist, **611**–612
Verifiability, **530**
  definition of, **25**
Vertical analysis of financial position,
  852–854
Volume variances, 1139–1140
Voluntary association, as feature of
  partnerships, 572
Vouchers, **327**
Voucher system, **328**–334
  check register, 332–333
  schedule of unpaid vouchers, 333
  voucher register, 329–332

W

Wages, 397
Weighted average contribution margin,
  955

Weighted average cost flow
  assumption, **1098**
Weighted average number of common
  stock, 653–654
Withdrawals by the owner, income
  statement transactions and, 75
Withdrawals from partnerships, 586
Withholding taxes, 398
Word processing, 282
Working capital, **221**, 221–222
  statement of changes in financial
    position based on, 794–811
    all financial resources concept
      and, **797**–798
    expenses and, 799
    net change in working capital,
      determining, 801–802
    noncurrent accounts, changes in,
      803–809
    transactions affecting working
      capital and, 795–796
    transactions not affecting working
      capital and, 796–798
    working capital from operations,
      799, 805–806
    worksheet approach to
      preparation of, 800–811
Work-in-progress inventory, 920
Worksheets, **138**
  accounting cycle completion and,
    138, 144
  cash flow statement and, 818–820
  merchandising firms and, 192
  statement of changes in financial
    position and, 800–811
    noncurrent accounts, changes in,
      803–809
    working capital net change
      determined, 801–802
Write-offs, 356–357

Y

Yield rate, **704**